Financial Services and Financial Institutions

Value Creation in Theory and Practice

J. Kimball Dietrich
University of Southern California

Prentice-Hall International, Inc.

0-13-393620-1

A Simon & Schuster Company
Upper Saddle River, New Jersey 07458

Printed in the United States of America
10 9 8 7 6 5 4 3 2 1

ISBN 0-13-393620-1

Prentice-Hall International (UK) Limited, *London*
Prentice-Hall of Australia Pty. Limited, *Sydney*
Prentice-Hall Canada, Inc., *Toronto*
Prentice-Hall Hispanoamericana, S.A., *Mexico*
Prentice-Hall of India Private Limited, *New Delhi*
Prentice-Hall of Japan, Inc., *Tokyo*
Simon & Schuster Adia Pte. Ltd., *Singapore*
Editora Prentice-Hall do Brasil, Ltda., *Rio de Janeiro*
Prentice-Hall, Inc., *Upper Saddle River, New Jersey*

Brief Contents

PART I THE FINANCIAL SERVICES INDUSTRY

PART II VALUE PRODUCTION IN FINANCIAL SERVICES

PART III THE ECONOMIC ENVIRONMENT OF FINANCIAL INSTITUTIONS

Contents

PART V FINANCIAL INSTITUTION PLANNING AND STRATEGIC ISSUES

Preface

The changes rumbling through the financial services industry are fundamental and have pervasive effects on our local and world economies. In the face of this revolution, answers to basic questions regarding the determinants of growth and survival must be asked and answered.

- What do financial services do to produce value?
- What are the basic services this industry provides and why are they demanded?
- What factors determine changes and shifts in the need for and satisfaction of financial services?
- What determines the returns and risks to participants in the industry?
- How can managers and regulators quantify and deal with these critical factors?

This book presents an integrated framework within which these questions can be asked and, in some cases, answered. In other cases, answers must be sought, and the analyses contained in this book will guide the reader in looking for the answers. The approach is simple: Break critical questions down into simple, logical components that become the focus of economic and financial analysis. Financial services are classified into six basic types: credit, securities related, transaction processing, insurance, asset management, and information and advisory services. Each of these services requires the performance of six basic activities: pricing, delivery, monitoring, marketing, funding, and risk bearing.

The treatment of financial services here, although comprehensive, focuses on basic principles that unify or differentiate them. As guidance for arraying the critical issues facing the financial services industry now and in the future, current economic and financial thinking is brought to bear. The innovation of industry analysis within the competitive strategy framework, developments in information economics in agency and contract theory, breakthroughs in financial thinking on asset pricing in financial markets—all are focused on the basic services and activities involved in producing financial services. This analytical approach provides a single, unified financial and economic treatment of developments in the financial industry.

WHY IS THIS BOOK SIGNIFICANT?

The financial services industry nationally and internationally is huge, growing, and of critical significance to the health of the global economy as well as that of individual businesses and consumers. Employment in financial services has increased as a percent of the workforce. These developments are cited as part of the "information revolution" and the transformation to a "service economy." Deregulation, globalization, and technological change have shattered the fundamental operating environment within which financial service firms operate. The crisis in the thrift industry at the end of the last decade and the weakness in the early 1990s in commercial banking and insurance threaten the functioning of the U.S., European, and Japanese economies. The collapse of Communism demands the creation of complete private market-based financial systems. Mergers, failures, and spectacular gains and losses in the fortunes of individual firms provide a never-ending source of drama and excitement in the daily business press.

Despite the policy significance and career potential the financial services industry offers, no comprehensive treatment of the economics of the industry has been available as a guide for the exciting and turbulent developments in the industry. Excellent books describe and analyze commercial banking, insurance, and investment banking, but no treatment of the overall industry has examined developments in all its segments simultaneously. Until now, no existing text has described and integrated the many basic similarities in the underlying economics of value production across the range of financial services. No previous text has provided a unified treatment of the determinants of survival and growth in the face of change and challenge.

In offering an integrated treatment of the underlying economics and institutional forces shaping the financial services industry, this book provides a much-needed guide to a terrain that is heavily traveled but to a large extent unchartered. The book provides both an understanding of the financial services industry as it exists and the forces governing its future.

INTENDED AUDIENCE AND USE OF THIS BOOK

This book is intended for university students who have a basic understanding of accounting and finance and others with an interest in financial services. As a single course or as part of a financial services sequence, the text is envisioned as the main reading for a one-semester course in financial institution management at the senior undergraduate or second-year MBA level. The text assumes basic accounting, economics, finance, and statistics as prerequisites. A money and banking or money and capital markets course background might be encouraged, although necessary terms and concepts are covered in this text and such a course could profitably be taken concurrently.

In designing the text, one goal was maximum flexibility for instructors in allowing a variety of sequences of reading the text. The basic outline of the book follows a logical progression, but individual instructors may wish to change the order of presentation or omit some sections in a given semester. The fundamental analytical treatment of financial services is contained in Part II, and other parts, such as those dealing with regulation (Part III) or with financial institution performance (Chapters 4 and 5), could be adopted in any order with no loss in comprehension.

Coverage of topics in the text is comprehensive in that basic materials—such as the determinants of share values in Chapter 4 or the economics of consumer time and risk preferences in Chapter 6—are presented in self-contained discussions. Some of these topics may already have been covered in students' prior coursework so may be omitted or reviewed briefly. The inclusion of basic topics is important for other students who have not previously covered this material or who would benefit from a review of fundamental concepts. The inclusion of basic material means that the level of discussion in the text varies from introduction of basic concepts to advanced applications. The goal is to make advanced applications of economics and finance accessible to students of a wide variety of backgrounds.

Chapter summaries concisely review the major topics covered in each chapter. End-of-chapter problems provide applications of basic concepts to real situations and extend analyses to similar or related problems not discussed explicitly in the text. The basic objective is to provide students with a thorough grounding in the economic, financial, and analytical principles covered in the text together with a firm understanding of how these principles are reflected in the real world.

ARCHITECTURE OF THE BOOK

The text is organized into five parts. Part I describes the book's conceptual framework, provides an overview of the firms and markets in the financial services industry, and delineates the way these institutions currently fit into the international economy. The objective that guides financial service firm management is value production. Here, basic management activities are related to the basic types of financial services. Measuring the performance of financial services firms is introduced in Part I and related to the analytical framework used throughout the text.

Part II is the analytical core of the text. Its chapters examine each of the six basic financial services in terms of how value is produced for those who demand these services. Economic analysis is illustrated by current practice and performance of these basic activities, and further explored by assessing the dynamics of the changes in financial service markets. The importance and role of efficient financial markets in providing a benchmark against which to assess strategic decisions is used throughout.

Part III examines the environment within which financial service firms operate and assesses the determinants of the risk and return opportunities confronting managers. The conceptual framework of this part—macroeconomic and microeconomic sources of risks—envisions interest rate and economic activity risks within a macroeconomic assessment of determinants of interest rate risk and demand risk. Regulatory, tax, and market competitive factors are examined for particular financial service industry segments from the viewpoint of a microeconomic analysis of the sources of business risk.

Part IV introduces methods used to deal with risk in financial strategies. Portfolio management techniques for dealing with economic risk, such as hedging or portfolio composition, are discussed with examples of current and emerging techniques. This part introduces students to "rocket science" and the applications of recent breakthroughs in asset pricing using option theory.

Part V of the book reviews the strategic issues relevant to intermediate and long-term planning and introduces the financial methods used to forecast and project future performance. Thus, the broader conceptual issues of formulating strategies in the financial services industry in the future are raised.

BUILDING AN INNOVATIVE COURSE

The approach in this book is an innovative, perhaps revolutionary, approach to teaching financial institutions management. The instructor's manual available for *Financial Services and Financial Institutions* provides a number of ideas on how the course can be organized. Teaching aids include answers or discussion outlines for end-of-chapter questions guiding classroom application of analytical approaches and techniques. The manual also provides ideas for additional questions, problems, and assignments, and for the use of cases and/or projects as student assignments applying the approach of the book to real-world problems.

The author is eager to work with instructors adopting the book to improve the contents of *Financial Services and Financial Institutions* for future editions and to develop teaching methods and materials making its innovations compelling for students. In this first edition there are surely topics and specific insights into value creation in financial institutions from theory or practice that might benefit from more examples, institutional details, or applications. The author welcomes suggestions from users about strengthening the depth or breadth of specific areas in order to enhance students' understanding.

The author is excited about working with users of *Financial Services and Financial Institutions* to make its innovative and comprehensive approach more useful and exciting for students and their instructors in covering issues associated with the emerging financial services industry of the future. The author wants to open communication with and between instructors using the book to create a force united in an effort to improve understanding and change outdated perceptions of the financial services industry in their courses. The instructor's manual outlines ways of gathering information from users and communicating this information directly to the author and other users on the Internet system. It suggests ways instructors brave enough to embark on a new approach to the study of financial institutions management can work with the author to make their effort as easy, productive, and fun as it can be made to be.

ACKNOWLEDGMENTS

Many have helped along the way. Special acknowledgment belongs to my students, the reviewers of drafts, and the people at Macmillan and Prentice Hall who advised me. Many provided help in too many ways for me to recount all of them here. I would like to single out students who have taken my financial institutions classes at the University of Southern California. They put up with a bulky manuscript and have been liberal with their criticisms and reactions. Special thanks to Fran McCann, who as a banker and teacher, provided a uniquely valuable sounding board. The reviewers, Harry Guenther, Donald Hakala, Chip Haley, James Harriss, Eric Kirzner, James Kolari, Anjan Thakor, Haluk Unal, and Oliver Wood, provided criticisms, guidance, and many detailed suggestions, for which I am very grateful. Finally, at Prentice Hall, Bill Oldsey supported me in this project from beginning to end, Paul Donnelly cheered me over the finish line by overseeing the final design and production, Teresa Cohan has been a source of much-appreciated assistance, and Susan McLaughlin and MaryBeth Sanok contributed their expertise in making the book a reality.

Bonnie Lieberman and Stephen Dietrich and their combined knowledge of books and the book business were important inspirations and resources graciously available to me. Finally, I thank my wife, Judith Blumenthal, who not only endured the tedium of living with someone writing a book, but had enough patience and goodwill to voluntarily urge consideration of her own perspectives on the management issues raised herein.

C H A P T E R

1

Financial Services: An Industry in Transition

Introduction

Evolution and revolution provide opportunities and provoke terror. Evolution accelerated by technological change and revolution in competitive conditions from global integration and deregulation are shaking traditional financial institutions. Fascinating stories dominate news about financial services—stories that raise fundamental questions that management, investors, and regulators of financial institutions must address. A few of these stories and questions open our book, and the following sections introduce the focus, methods, and structure used throughout.

1.1 RECENT DEVELOPMENTS IN FINANCIAL SERVICES

A look at some recent developments in the financial services industry introduces the range of activities and events we will discuss and seek to understand in this text.

Crossing Traditional Boundaries

Commercial banks are expanding beyond their traditional regional operations: New York–based Citicorp operates in California, California-based Bank of America operates in New York. Superregional banks operate across state boundaries, covering whole regions of the Northeastern, Southeastern, Middle Western, and Western United States with branches and representative offices. German banks operate in England and English banks in Europe. Regional boundaries that used to be barriers to business activity are routinely vaulted by banks and other financial institutions.

Regional boundaries are not the only barriers that are falling. Federal regulators such as the Federal Reserve allow commercial banks like Morgan Guaranty to provide investment banking services in the United States despite the continued existence of the Glass–Steagall Act of 1933 that prohibits such activity. Banks sell annuities and other insurance products, while insurance companies offer loans and money market mutual funds that are similar to traditional banking products.

Why are traditional boundaries being broken? What are the underlying economic strategies that lead financial institutions to expand into new areas? Why did barriers exist in the first place and are they likely to be rebuilt? These issues are increasingly being faced by managers of firms providing financial services.

Global Competition: Japanese Banks in the United States

Japanese banks in the mid-1980s, flush with low cost (low interest) deposits raised in regulated and uncompetitive markets at home and serving a booming economy generating floods of foreign exchange, sought new business frontiers. Between 1985 and 1990, Japanese bank assets in the United States rose from $180 to $436 billion, largely competing with U.S. banks in California and New York. Their market share of bank assets in California grew from 16 to 27.5 percent; Japanese banks now own five of the ten largest banks in California. They aggressively entered the construction and real estate loan markets. By 1992, falling property values caused 9.4 percent of the California loans and 15.5 percent of the New York loans to be bad. The Japanese lost vast amounts of money in their investments in U.S. banking.

The story of Japanese banks in the United States is only one example of the globalization of financial services. Expansion of financial institutions outside of their home countries raises interesting questions, especially in view of the eagerness of American, European, and Japanese financial institutions to enter emerging markets in Southeast Asia, Eastern Europe, and Latin America. What can financial firms bring to foreign markets to add value to their customers and investors? What are the lessons to be learned from the problems experienced by the Japanese? What is the best strategy for the Japanese banks now that the Japanese economy has weakened?

New Opportunities: The Rise of Market Economies

The fall of Communist governments and the spread of democracy and market economies in Eastern Europe, the former Soviet Union, and China have opened vast opportunities for rapid transformation and modernization of huge economies and populations. Governments in these countries are writing entire new laws to regulate newly formed financial entities. Outside government officials, executives, and consultants are advising them on how to structure their financial systems.

Reduced government intervention and opening to foreign competition in India, Mexico, and other Latin America and Asian markets have produced more high-return investment opportunities than domestic savings can finance. Financial services promote growth by placing funds from savers around the world into investments with the highest expected returns. Financial institutions and individual investors seeking geographical diversification want to participate in these investment returns and finance this growth.

What determines the demand for financial services in growing economies? How can financial institutions participate in the high returns these economies offer and avoid the problems experienced by Japanese banks in the United States? Should these emerging economies model their laws and regulations on those of developed economies? What can be learned from the experience of advanced economies?

Government Policy in Developed Economies: Deregulation

In developed economies like those in the United States and the United Kingdom, waves of deregulation have altered the boundaries between financial service firms and encouraged new types of competition. Banks sell mutual funds and brokers offer checking accounts. Thrifts make credit card loans and institutional investors invest in credit card receivables packaged by investment bankers. New services and new ways of delivering old services are reducing the costs and increasing the returns to customers of financial institutions.

At the same time, a world-wide recession and deflation have caused massive losses at financial institutions, decimating the U.S. thrift industry and causing massive government intervention in banking markets in Scandinavia. Insurance companies and banks are under pressure around the world. Legislators and regulators have been aggressively revising statutes and rules in an effort to control these gigantic economic developments.

Is regulation useful? What rationale is offered for regulation? How do laws and regulations and changes in them condition the business environment for managers of financial institutions? What is the role in deregulation in recent financial crises?

Corporate Restructuring

American Express bought Fireman's Fund insurance company in 1968 and then sold it off in two stages, completing the sale in 1989. American Express bought the Shearson brokerage firm in 1981 and sold it in 1993, keeping Investors Diversified Services, a financial planning and money management firm. Shearson was bought by Primerica, formerly the American Can Company. Primerica already owned Smith Barney, and the combined Smith Barney–Shearson would be second only to Merrill Lynch in terms of numbers of brokers and offices. Primerica also completed the purchase of Travelers Insurance (it already owned 27 percent) in 1993 and adopted its name. Meanwhile, Mellon Bank bought Dreyfus Corporation and the Boston Company, managers of mutual funds and other assets. Standard Charter, the giant English banking corporation, bought the business banking activities of First Interstate Bancorporation of California in 1992, and the huge French bank, Credit Lyonnais, bought the business of the defunct American insurance company, Executive Life, in 1993.

These are only a few of the transactions that exemplify the recent restructuring of the financial services industry. Strategies in this industry are evolving in response to rapid changes in the global competitive environment. Purchases and sales of financial institutions are so frequent that the publication *Mergers and Acquisitions* found the banking industry to be one of the top three most active merger areas in the United States in each of the last five years.

Restructuring of financial services will continue for decades; it may never end. Many of the changes involve purchases and sales of financial firms, and each transaction raises questions: What determines the value of financial institutions? Where are the sources of value in combinations of firms or in separation of firms? What are the underlying principles defining successful and risky strategies?

Energies stimulated by increased competition between financial service providers across national boundaries and across financial service segments have produced frantic product innovation, new business combinations, and fabulous successes—and failures. As dramatic as all these developments are, they are driven by timeless economic and financial forces operating within markets that can be studied and analyzed rationally. The purpose of this book is to focus on the unchanging laws of economic behavior and market dynamics in order to address the questions raised by developments represented in the stories above. Our goal is to prepare managers to exploit opportunities and avoid disasters. We seek to understand and be able to form strategies within this dynamic environment that are based on the most logical and consistent analysis.

1.2 PEOPLE AND FINANCIAL INSTITUTIONS

Financial service firms hire the best and brightest from colleges and universities around the world, and they need talent of every variety. They hire lawyers, accountants, and engineers. They are the largest market for graduates of business schools, and they are large employers of part-time and night workers.

Careers in financial firms are challenging and rewarding. The accumulating value of training and experience make performance of the same basic job desirable over an entire working career. The gradual broadening of responsibility and scale of operations can provide continuing stimulation in the same essential task. On the other hand, completely nontraditional financial service jobs can evolve from technological or competitive demands. Innovation and creativity are critical elements to success in these jobs. Many careers are characterized by frequent job changes and assignments.

Relatively small management teams make many important financial institutions relatively intimate job environments. Other firms are global in scope with some executives and employees spending the bulk of their careers away from home. Firms in the same industry may be organized very differently: some are partnerships, others are corporations or mutuals. Small firms often compete effectively with the largest to attract the best employees by paying the highest wages.

Financial institutions are among the prominent and well-known economic entities in every country and region. The size of many financial institutions—with assets often totaling in the billions of dollars—guarantees some notoriety. At the end of 1993, there were at least 62 commercial banks and 43 diversified financial service companies in the United States valued at over one billion dollars to their owners. Globally, at least 11 banks and 11 insurance companies had *profits* of over $1 billion (*Fortune,* May 1994, August 1994).

Everyone knows the names of the biggest banks and thrifts in the region. Insurance companies are everywhere and often on our minds as we are concerned about our insurance coverage and premiums. The stock market is in the news every day with commentators from brokerage firms or investment advisors interpreting the events of the day. People are naturally interested and concerned with financial institutions and the services they provide.

An increasing number of people are employed in the financial services industry. In fact, employment in this field has been growing faster than the total labor force in the United States. Table 1.1 provides some statistics. For example, the table shows that employment in finance (including insurance and real estate) grew at an annual rate of 3.61 percent from 1970 to 1990, while the total labor force grew only 2.04 percent over the same period. Employment in financial services and real estate as a percent of total employment grew from 5.01 percent in 1970 to 6.80 percent in 1990. Employment in financial institutions grew faster than in other services industries, although growth slowed in the period 1980 to 1990.

Employees of financial institutions often reflect the power and influence of their employers. Investment banker Felix Rohatyn worked with the City of New York to solve its financial crisis of the 1970s. In the 1980s, Thomas Clausen went from chairman of Bank of America to President of the World Bank and back to chairman of Bank of America. Three Treasury Secretaries in the United States

TABLE 1.1 Employment in the Financial Services Industry

		NONFINANCIAL SERVICES		*FINANCIAL SERVICES*	
	TOTAL U.S. EMPLOYMENT	*NUMBER OF WORKERS (IN THOUSANDS)*	*AS PERCENT OF TOTAL U.S. WORKERS*	*NUMBER OF WORKERS (IN THOUSANDS)*	*AS PERCENT OF TOTAL U.S. WORKERS*
Employment					
1970	78,678	20,385	25.91%	3,945	5.01%
1980	99,303	28,752	28.95%	5,993	6.04%
1990	117,914	39,084	33.15%	8,021	6.80%
Growth Rates					
1970–80	2.36%	3.50%		4.27%	
1980–90	1.73%	3.12%		2.96%	
1970–90	2.04%	3.31%		3.61%	

since 1980 were senior executives of investment banks (Donald Regan, Nicholas Brady, and Robert Rubin).

Some segments of the financial services industry are noteworthy for other reasons. The 1980s saw a major debacle in the savings and loan industry. The government plan to bail out the industry is expected to cost upward of $100 billion (Barth 1991, Table 3.13). The whole financial services industry in Texas and other energy-industry dominated states has undergone wrenching changes and consolidation.

What do financial institutions do that they command such power and influence? How can they get into such trouble? What is their role in our economy and what services do they provide? What kind of jobs have to be done in these institutions? What major managerial problems do these institutions face? These are questions we will consider and attempt to answer in this book.

1.3 METHODS USED IN THE BOOK

The dramatic developments in the financial services industry in the last few decades have been accompanied by major innovations in the organization, regulation, products, and services of firms in the industry. Managers, customers, employees, and other observers of the industry need an integrated approach to understanding the many developments of the past and future that are shaping this industry. That is the purpose of this book: to provide an integrated theoretical and practical framework to analyze the elemental forces that shape current and future developments in the financial services industry.

Financial Economics and Recent Developments in Finance

Our approach is to look at the wide range of issues and problems in the financial services industry using analytical tools and techniques that have revolutionized thinking about corporate finance in the last thirty years. A quick overview here of three of the major developments in financial economics will demonstrate the impact these innovative ideas have had on the way many business problems are formulated and analyzed by corporate decision makers today.

A review of recent theoretical developments in corporate finance could start with the first contributions to an enormous literature discussing application of microeconomic analysis to financial decisions faced by the management of corporations. Franco Modigliani and Merton Miller (1958), in a pathbreaking and widely cited article, examined the dividend payout decision and corporate capital structure decision for corporations. Miller was awarded a Nobel Prize in economics in 1990 for his work. In their analysis, they used the microeconomic analysis of competitive markets.

In the early 1960s, large computerized databases of financial data were developed, especially the University of Chicago's Center for Research in Securities Prices (CRSP) database of stock returns. These computerized databases revolutionized the analysis of corporate financial performance by making possible the use of computers to conduct sophisticated statistical studies. Resulting pathbreaking research on the efficiency of financial markets was summarized and reviewed by Eugene Fama (1970) in another widely cited article.

Growing use of mathematics in finance made possible the solution of complex analytical problems. One problem proving to have wide application was the equilibrium value of a call option on common stock. A major study on pricing options by Fisher Black and Myron Scholes (1973) is an example of a theoretically powerful and practically useful solution to equilibrium pricing of financial assets in efficient capital markets.

From an intellectual viewpoint, developments like these in finance are extremely exciting. Some are fairly sophisticated and difficult to comprehend at first, but efforts to understand how these ideas relate to financial problems have payoffs with important applications in the real world. These innovations have had a dramatic impact on the study of corporate finance, as reflected in best-selling textbooks that introduce students of corporate finance to these modern financial developments. Application of these ideas and insights will be hard to avoid, since corporate treasurers, investment advisors, and financial service firm representatives must be conversant with the most current financial techniques in order to interact effectively in today's financial marketplace.

Despite the value and impact of the developments in modern financial theory on corporate finance in the last few decades, most textbooks in financial institutions have not completely integrated these developments. Books on banking, insurance, or other financial services usually discuss the subject of financial services using a descriptive approach, presenting current managerial practice in one segment of the financial services industry, such as bank management or insurance. Many of these books are excellent guides and introductions and provide a wealth of detail on how things work in the financial services industry. Many fall short, however, of providing a unifying approach to all financial services and firms, based on an integrating analytical structure.

This book begins all analysis with the underlying economics of financial services using a financial economics approach. The treatment here stresses application of modern financial analysis to all financial services, whether offered by banks, insurance companies, or other financial service firms. The discussion seeks to find parallels or common aspects of all the services and to identify problems and solutions shared by firms in all segments of the industry. The goal is to integrate within one conceptual framework all of the developments and problems encountered in the different types of financial service firms we observe in the real world, and will observe in the future.

Financial Economics and This Book

Financial economics is the application of economic theory to problems arising in finance. Much of economic theory begins with the concept of competition and competitive markets. The implications of competitive markets are covered in the first course in microeconomics: you learn there that prices in competitive markets are pulled or pushed into equality with the marginal costs of producing the goods or services traded in the market. If there are no barriers to competition, economic forces erode the excessive profits of those firms able to produce revenues from sales greatly exceeding costs. *Competitive markets* are a conceptual benchmark upon which economic analysis of industries and firms is built and are a touchstone from which to begin to analyze the performance and prospects of an industry.

Markets for products and services are not all competitive. When there are restrictions on the forces of competition, whether from regulations, entry barriers to the market, or cost economies from large scale production, extraordinary profits can be earned by firms. The strategy of finding markets where there is potential for short- or long-term profit opportunities underlies much corporate planning today. The influential works of Michael Porter (1980, 1985) explore how corporate managers can identify situations where they have some competitive advantages in producing high returns. These advantages may stem from departures from perfect competition due to a number of factors, such as specialized resources or regulatory barriers to entry. The important element in developing strategies and understanding the dynamics of industry change is to know what the competitive economic model of markets tells us so we can narrow our focus in looking for profitable departures from competition.

Competitive markets for goods and services are the benchmark from which economic analysis begins. Much of the work in financial economics referenced above has supported the view that financial markets are competitive in the same sense as markets for goods. This work has also supported the view that financial markets are *efficient* in the sense that buyers and sellers in financial markets act as if they are aware of relevant information affecting the values of the assets they transact. *Efficient market theory* provides another analytical paradigm from which to analyze where value is produced by firms and managers.

In efficient markets, assets are priced fairly at underlying intrinsic values. How can excess investment returns, above those compensating investors for risk, be earned in such markets? Under what circumstances might some markets fail to be efficient? Do market participants reward firms providing financial services that they could provide for themselves? These are important questions that must be answered if one is to understand this industry, its products, and their future evolution. The answers focus on the sources of value produced by financial service firms.

Competitive and efficient markets for financial assets and liabilities have implications in predicting future returns of financial assets with different risk characteristics. Rational investors in efficient markets can be assumed to behave in ways that allow analysts to derive intrinsic values for financial assets when financial markets are in equilibrium. These pricing relationships can be derived from models of rational investor behavior in efficient markets, and have yielded *equilibrium asset pricing models*. These models have been important theoretical *and* practical contributions to financial economics.

Equilibrium asset pricing theories explain how risk/return relationships are evaluated by investors in financial service firms and other financial assets. The *Capital Asset Pricing Model* (CAPM) and *Arbitrage Pricing Theory* (APT) are useful beginning points in analyzing the value of securities and the relevant measures and effects of risk on those values. These theories have provided major insights into how risk affects asset values.

This book discusses the industry using these and other important economic and financial concepts. We explain and apply financial economic theories to help us understand in a unifying, synthesizing way the important questions facing financial institutions and markets today.

A coherent theoretical presentation of the underlying economics affecting the financial services industry is a beginning for our analysis. Theories are not enough without supporting evidence. A growing number of tests of many of the theories and models we employ in analyzing financial services are available in the literature. Presenting this evidence is an important augmentation of the financial economics discussion. Whenever possible, it is the approach of this book to review supporting (and conflicting) evidence concerning the theories presented.

Evidence comes in two basic forms. The most reliable form of evidence in any area of study is careful analysis of large numbers of observations on the phenomenon studied. Usually this evidence is presented in academic studies or commissioned analyses in the form of statistical examination of large bodies of data. When possible and available, these statistical studies are discussed.

Sometimes evidence to support theories or explanations is only available in the form of anecdotes. Even when supporting statistical evidence is available, single examples or small samples make results more comprehensible, and we present such examples of theories and techniques whenever possible.

1.4 OVERVIEW OF THE BOOK

This book has five parts. Part I is an introduction and overview. Part II discusses the economics of financial services in depth. Part III presents the sources of macroeconomic and regulatory risk that dominate this industry. Part IV presents a range of analytical techniques relevant to understanding the measurement and management of the balance sheet and off-balance sheet risks and returns of financial institutions. Part V contains a discussion of issues relevant to projecting the future performance and strategies of financial service firms. We expand on the contents of the five parts below.

The remaining chapters of Part I introduce the financial services industry and the criteria used in our analysis of financial services. The current constitution of the financial services industry in the United States and abroad cannot be understood without understanding its historical evolution and the role financial institutions play in the economy. Chapter 2 discusses how value is produced for customers and describes the important activities associated with the six types of financial services offered in the market. Chapter 3 presents sectors of the economy, financial markets, and traditional types of financial institutions. Chapters 4 and 5 present the methods analysts use to determine whether the performance of financial firms has been poor, fair, or excellent. Part I as a whole presents the agenda for the remainder of the book.

Part II forms the core of the analysis in the book. Financial services are introduced using a financial economics framework, stressing the long-term contractual or regulated nature of the interaction of financial service firms and their customers in financial service markets. Each financial service is discussed in detail, emphasizing that basic financial services are offered by many different types of financial firms. Each service is presented in terms of the underlying economics of where value is produced for the customer and the firm. For each service, the roles of human skills, capital resources, and technology in the production of value are stressed.

Part III introduces macroeconomic policy and the taxation and regulation of financial service firms. Macroeconomic policy conditions the economic environment within which all businesses, including financial service firms and their customers, conduct their affairs. Macroeconomic policy affects inflation, interest rates, economic activity, and virtually all the factors producing risk for business men and women and their firms, thus its impact on the key variables for financial service firms is discussed. Taxation and regulation, and changes in them, are reviewed in detail, for they are an extremely important factor in the business environment for financial service firms. Understanding the political and economic forces that circumscribe the business environment for financial institutions is essential for dealing with the risks and assessing future prospects for firms, products, and markets.

Part IV presents models and techniques relevant to all financial service firms and their customers: how to manage portfolios of assets and liabilities to minimize risks and maximize returns. These chapters contain introductions to recent developments in financial markets, including the new products and markets being used to shift and share a variety of financial and other economic risks. The discussion covers some of the most sophisticated techniques being employed to find intrinsic values of financial instruments developed to deal with risks so that they can be priced in the market. These topics are relevant not only for the management of financial institution balance sheets, but also for the development of new financial services in the future.

Part V of the book presents major issues confronting the management of the future financial services industry. In these final chapters of the book, approaches for forecasting future financial service market demands are considered. The measurement of financial service costs and the importance of cost structure to strategy are reviewed. The problems of organizing firms so that the motivation of the employees is in line with the objectives of the firm are discussed. Developing and implementing meaningful strategies in the exciting world ahead demands methods to assess and evaluate assumptions underlying the assessment of strategic options, and we discuss such methods in Part V.

1.5 CONCLUSION

The financial services industry is important and dynamic, and it provides many opportunities for investors, customers, and employees. But the bewildering array of facts and issues, developments and institutions, participants, products, and markets, requires an organizing viewpoint to integrate a study of the industry. This book approaches the financial services industry from the vantage of financial economics. It poses many questions about what is happening and will happen in this industry, and provides a framework within which to find meaningful answers to questions about appropriate actions or strategies in the face of these changes. The book challenges readers to use the methods presented to find answers to critical questions—and thereby build a solid basis for successful careers as customers, employees, investors, or managers of financial institutions in this exciting arena.

REFERENCES

BARTH, JAMES R. 1991. *The Great Savings and Loan Debacle,* Washington, D.C.: The AEI Press.

BLACK, FISCHER and MYRON SCHOLES. 1973. "The Pricing of Options and Corporate Liabilities," *Journal of Political Economy* 81, pp. 637–659.

FAMA, EUGENE F. 1970. "Efficient Capital Markets: A Review of Theory and Empirical Work," *Journal of Finance* 25, pp. 383–417.

Fortune. May 30, 1994. "The Service 500," pp. 196–268.

Fortune. August 22, 1994. "The World's Largest Service Corporations," pp. 180–208.

MODIGLIANI, FRANCO and MERTON MILLER. 1958. "The Cost of Capital, Corporate Finance and the Theory of Investment," *American Economic Review* 48, pp. 261–297.

PORTER, MICHAEL E. 1980. *Competitive Strategy.* New York: The Free Press.

PORTER, MICHAEL E. 1985. *Competitive Advantage.* New York: The Free Press.

CHAPTER

2

Financial Services and Value Production

Introduction

Some venerable financial institutions have endured for hundreds of years. Eager entrepreneurs start up new ones by the thousands each year and some blaze into prominence in a breathtakingly short time. Old established firms and some newer firms go bankrupt annually. Some firms pay investors and employees fabulous returns and salaries. Others limp along unsure of their survival.

- What are the unique characteristics of financial institutions and services driving developments that will affect investors or workers in the future?
- What determines the survival, growth, or failure of individual financial service firms or segments of the industry?
- What are the critical activities determining competitive success or failure for firms in financial services?
- What services are the source of value that financial firms provide to the economy?

We begin the chapter by introducing measures of value produced by all businesses—*value added* and *return on investment*—and contrasting value production in financial institutions with that in other firms. Next we investigate the unique activities performed by financial service firms by applying the *value chain* concept first presented by Michael Porter of Harvard. Finally, we describe the basic services offered by financial service firms. Taken together, these various aspects form a framework for our discussion in the remainder of the book.

2.1 VALUE ADDED IN FINANCIAL SERVICES

Workers and managers are hired by financial institution owners and investors to make money. Successful managers know that to attract investors they must promise—and deliver—high rates of return. Equally important, to attract required human resources they must promise—and deliver—good pay. To meet these obligations, financial institutions must produce value. To focus on value production in financial services, we start with the concept of *value added*. Even though output is hard to measure, value added does measure the value of output, and does so without being overshadowed by the enormous financial revenues and costs and funds flows typical of most financial institutions.

Value added is simply the difference between revenues and total nonlabor costs like interest expense or telephone costs. Value added is what customers are paying for above the costs of inputs when they use financial services firms. Value added consists of profits, wages, and taxes. The concept is simple: Labor works with investors' capital to add value to inputs by turning them into goods or services sold to customers at a profit. Value added is used worldwide as the basis for taxation, specifically *value added taxes* (VATs). The usual application of VATs, in Europe for example, is in manufacturing or retailing industries where nonlabor costs are dominated by raw materials and goods for resale.

In financial services the value added concept is an especially good measure of productivity for financial institutions because other measures of inputs and outputs are overwhelmed by financial costs and revenues. There are very few material inputs into the production of financial services, and output is hard to characterize. Examination of value added focuses on the value to customers of a financial firm's activities.

Value added can be calculated for any firm using the following equation:

$$\text{Value Added} = \text{Wages} + \text{Profits} + \text{Taxes}.$$

For example, Charles Schwab, the discount brokerage firm, reported in 1992 \$306.6 million in compensation and benefits, taxes of \$65 million, and profits of \$81.2 million, meaning that for Schwab value added is

$$\text{Value Added} = \$306.6 + \$81.2 + \$65 = \$452.8$$

in millions. This measures the value provided to customers of Schwab in 1992.

A number useful in comparing firms and industry segments is *value added per employee* (VAPE) calculated simply as follows:

$$\text{VAPE} = \frac{\text{Value Added}}{\text{Number of Employees}}.$$

For example, Charles Schwab had 4,500 employees in 1992, meaning that for VAPE for Schwab was:

$$\text{VAPE} = \frac{\$452.8\text{ million}}{4{,}500} = \$100{,}622.$$

Table 2.1 provides some value added and VAPE calculations for firms in various segments of the financial services industry. The table demonstrates that labor costs are a large element in the value added of financial service firms. For example, the value added over $100,000 per employee for Charles Schwab calculated above can be compared to average compensation paid to workers for the firm, $68,133 ($306.6 million divided by 4,500 employees). To appreciate the importance of labor costs to the value produced for the owners of that firm, compare labor costs to taxes and income. We discuss the importance of labor in financial services below.

Any value added by the firm that is not paid to employees or tax authorities belongs to owners of the firm. Investors and managers of financial service firms must know how to produce value. The way all firms add value is to provide products or services that are worth more to customers than they cost to produce. What are the key inputs in providing financial services? The detailed analysis required by this question occupies the rest of the book. In this section, we suggest some generalizations and provide an overview of what lies ahead.

Until recently, the major source of financial institutions' profitability in the United States and abroad was the difference between financial costs and revenues, primarily the spread between interest income and expense. But in a competitive, deregulated, global financial services industry, relying on the spread between financial costs and returns is not enough to guarantee profitability in the future. Some observers of the financial services industry say "the spread is dead."

TABLE 2.1 Value Added in Financial Services

	LABOR EXPENSE	*PROFITS*	*TAXES*	*TOTAL VALUE ADDED*
Total Economy ($ million)-1990				
U.S. commercial banks	$50,827	$16,175	$7,507	$74,509
German commercial banks	9,826	2,498	2,184	14,508

	LABOR EXPENSE	*PROFITS*	*TAXES*	*TOTAL VALUE ADDED*	*NUMBER OF EMPLOYEES*	*VAPE*
Individual Firms ($1000)-1992						
BankAmerica	3,048,000	1,492,000	1,190,000	5,730,000	83,200	68,870
Fifth Third	137,548	164,092	75,564	377,204	4,579	82,377
Merrill Lynch	4,364,454	893,825	668,984	5,927,263	40,100	147,812
Old Kent Bank	132,467	111,091	52,866	296,424	4,570	64,863
Charles Schwab	306,600	81,200	65,000	452,800	4,500	100,622

*Converted to dollars at 1.61 marks/dollar (1990 average)

SOURCES: Board of Governors of the Federal Reserve System, "Recent Developments Affecting the Profitability and Practice of Commercial Banks," July, 1991, pp. 517, 519; Deutsche Bundesbank *Monthly Report,* "The Profitability of German Banks in 1990," August, 1991, pp. 26, 27; Annual Reports for individual companies.

Excess profits from the spread are no longer a dependable source of value because deregulation and the presence of international firms have eroded barriers to entry, thereby promoting aggressive competition. This has unleashed a movement toward economic efficiency in financial markets. For example, new entrants into traditional markets must offer competitive products. Corporate credit services offered by pension funds and finance companies now compete with commercial banks, which traditionally dominated the market. Market forces drive returns and fees into line with costs. The movement to market efficiency where marginal revenues equal marginal costs is one of the fundamental economic forces discussed in Chapter 1 of this book.

Competition tends to eliminate profit opportunities above competitive levels. When extraordinary profits can be made and there are no barriers to entry, resources move into the business, then competition lowers prices and raises the quality and costs of services. Inexorable market forces tend to move the financial costs of financial firms into line with risks and returns. In equilibrium, there are no *excess* returns.

In order to earn *excess* returns, financial institution managers must find business opportunities where prices exceed costs for products. The search for excess returns places tremendous pressure on managers to innovate with new product designs and applications of new technologies. They must identify services valuable enough to create customer demand and profits high enough to produce attractive returns. To identify opportunities, careful analysis of strengths and weaknesses of firms providing different financial services is required. Managers and students of the industry must understand how value is produced.

Two characteristics of financial services must be emphasized at the outset. One is that financial services involve the creation, dissemination, and use of *information*. This is an information-based industry that has been transformed by the "information revolution." The second common characteristic is that financial services require huge amounts of high quality *labor* to deal with information and communication with the market. We examine each of these characteristics below.

Information is an essential ingredient in the production of financial services. It ranges from relatively straightforward current price and yield information to complex financial statement data. Given that the spread is dead, costs of processing information are increasingly relevant to the profitable production of financial services. Information acquisition and processing as a source of relative efficiency focuses attention on the nonfinancial expenses of financial firms. These costs are concentrated in gathering, analyzing, transmitting, storing, updating, reviewing, and interpreting financial information.

Many of these nonfinancial costs are associated with new electronic transmission and computing technologies. Technological breakthroughs have made practical much of the information processing that was previously impossible. Computers, telephones, printers, facsimile machines, teller machines, satellite transmission, and other modern technology figure into the costs of providing financial services, and efficient use of this technology will be a major source of advantage to some firms in the future.

The new technological environment can, however, be overemphasized, for the predominant nonfinancial costs are people costs in the form of wages and salaries. In the previously regulated and protected financial markets the relative importance of labor costs in the production of financial services was obscured by the financial spread. But the reality is that most value added by financial institutions is paid to workers. The types of labor range from workers performing simple tasks to those undertaking complex analyses and negotiations requiring years of training and experience.

We recall from daily experience tellers, clerks, secretaries, computer operators, and part-time workers. We think of men and women flying around the world making calls to major institutions, negotiating deals, and selling and buying sophisticated financial instruments. We think of insurance agents and securities brokers. The labor intensity of financial services is obvious and making these workers more efficient is a key to adding value.

The importance of labor costs and the role of human inputs in financial service production can be inferred from the salaries paid in this industry. Tables 2.2 shows entry-level salaries for bachelor degreed students in 1993. New hires averaged between $23 and $31 thousand annually, meaning that they soon had to add that much value in the form of financial services to justify their employment.

As an example of how developments in segments of the financial services industry can heat up the demand for human resources, look at the investment banking industry in the early 1980s. An article in *Fortune* described the situation as follows:

> An entire generation of the most sought-after graduates of the top U.S. business schools is getting snookered by a handful of investment banking firms temporarily

TABLE 2.2 Average Yearly Salary Offers from Financial Institutions to Bachelor's Candidates (September 1993)

FUNCTIONAL AREA	*AVERAGE OFFER ($)*
Banking	
Consumer	23,129
Lending	25,515
Insurance	
Underwriting	25,447
Claims	23,556
Investment banking	
Corporate finance	29,374
Mergers and acquisitions	31,100
Investment banking	
Sales and trading	28,396
Brokerage/Portfolio management	24,372

SOURCE: College Placement Council, "Salary Survey," September 1993, p. 4

> overburdened with profit. In unprecedented numbers these young stars are stampeding to Wall Street, lured by jobs that pay, for starters, $80,000 to $110,000 a year in salary and bonus. (Sherman, November 24, 1986, p. 29)

Excess returns being earned in investment banking drove up this demand, temporarily as it turns out. A year later, the stock market crash wiped out those opportunities in investment banking for inexperienced students. Shifts in demand for financial services like stock brokerage, commercial lending, and information processing, cause many sudden shortages or excesses of worker skills accompanied by sharp changes in starting pay.

Table 2.3 shows that for U.S. financial institutions managerial skills command high compensation. Executive compensation in 1992 ranged from $440 thousand to over $15 million, with very few CEOs earning under a million dollars. Good managers and creative individuals can earn fabulous income in finan-

TABLE 2.3 Compensation of Financial Institution Chief Executive Officers, 1992

INDUSTRY/COMPANY	*NAME*	*1992 TOTAL COMPENSATION ($000)*
Banking		
Anchor Bancorp	James M. Large, Jr.	592.1
Banc One	John B. McCoy	2,529.9
Bank of Boston	Ira Stepanian	3,497.4
Bank of New York	J. Carter Bacot	1,755.5
Bank of America	Richard M. Rosenberg	2,447.9
Bankers Trust	Charles S. Sanford, Jr.	6,742.7
Chase Manhattan	Thomas G. Labrecque	1,558.2
Chemical Bank	John F. McGillicuddy	2,250.0
Citicorp	John S. Reed	2,247.2
Continental	John P. Mascotte	675.0
First Bank System	Johsn F. Grundhofer	2,405.5
First Chicago	Richard L. Thomas	1,333.0
First Interstate	Edward M. Carson	1,865.8
First Union	Edward E. Crutchfield, Jr.	3,069.1
Mellon	Frank V. Cahouet	3,298.7
Midlantic	Garry T. Scheuring	1,065.0
J. P. Morgan	Dennis Weatherstone	5,199.4
NationsBank	Hugh L. McColl, Jr.	8,637.5
Norwest	Lloyd P. Johnson	3,921.1
PNC Bank	Thomas H. O'Brien	3,477.1
Republic New York	Walter H. Weiner	953.1
Shawmut	Joel B. Alvord	1,126.3
SunTrust	James B. Williams	4,997.3
U.S. Bancorp	Roger L. Breezley	953.6
Wells Fargo	Carl E. Reichardt	775.0

cial services. Goldman Sachs partners got bonuses of over $5 million each in 1993. Before Michael Milken, the inventor of the revolutionary "junk bond" market, was forced by government legal action to leave Drexel Burnham in 1988, he was paid over $500 million.

Although some of these examples of pay may be extreme (and rare), they do emphasize the importance of human resources and talent in the financial services industry. Our discussion of Table 2.1 introduced value added per employee. A central theme of this book is that the financial services industry is a labor-intensive industry. Value added from providing financial services has to be sufficient to attract the kind of personnel able to thrive in the information revolution and able to satisfy investors by adding more value than they cost in wages.

A variety of skills and attributes are necessary in providing financial services. Data processing activities require employees with technology skills. Customer contact work requires people skills. Creative marketers and product

INDUSTRY/COMPANY	*NAME*	*1992 TOTAL COMPENSATION ($000)*
Thrifts		
Ahmanson	Richard H. Diehl	1,282.2
Dime Savings	Richard D. Parsons	675.0
Glen Fed	Stephen J. Trafton	442.3
Golden West	Herber M. Sandler	4,349.9
	Marion O. Sandler	6,433.5
Great Western	James F. Montgomery	2,402.7
Insurance Companies		
Aetna	Ronald Compton	776.0
AIG	Maurice R. Greenburg	2,247.1
Chubb	Dean R. O'Hare	3,104.7
Cigna	Wilson H. Taylor	2,377.9
General Re	Ronald E. Ferguson	2,060.8
Kemper	David B. Mathis	965.1
St Paul	Douglas W. Leatherdale	928.5
Transamerica	Frank C. Herringer	1,508.0
Travelers	Edward H. Budd	1,026.8
USF&G	Norman P. Blake, Jr.	1,593.5
Securities Firms		
Bear Stearns	Alan C. Greenberg	15,852.0
Merrill Lynch	Daniel P. Tully	6,435.0
Morgan Stanley	Richard B. Fisher	6,239.9
Paine Webber	Donald B. Marron	7,184.1
Schwab	Charles R. Schwab	3,166.2

SOURCE: *Wall Street Journal,* "Executive Pay Survey," April 21, 1993, p. R15.

development talent are essential in this competitive industry, as is the ability to manage large groups of skilled and semiskilled workers. Financial service firms will have to attract, motivate, and retain the human resources they require to survive, grow, and prosper in the future.

2.2 RETURN ON INVESTMENT IN FINANCIAL SERVICES

In order to succeed, managers must make owners and investors of the firms they work for wealthier. The key to success either for investors or for employees is simple: Sell something for more than it costs. The old saying captures this well: "Buy cheap, sell dear." Using this key to unlock the secrets of successful business strategies in financial services is more complex.

Successful strategies are based on a *competitive advantage*. Professor Michael Porter of the Harvard Business School has influenced many business strategists and planners with his analysis. As Porter puts the key to success:

> Competitive advantage grows fundamentally out of value a firm is able to create for its buyers that exceed the firm's cost of creating it. Value is what buyers are willing to pay, and superior values stems from offering lower prices than competitors for equivalent benefits or providing unique benefits that more than offset a higher price. (1985, p. 3)

Porter concentrated his research on tracing the implications of market structure and a firm's position within its markets in the search for a competitive advantage. We will draw on Porter's research and analysis extensively in this chapter and throughout this book.

To survive and prosper, the firms in any industry must attract and maintain resources—the investments of entrepreneurs or savers. The major criterion attracting resources to an industry or industry segment is the *return on investment* (ROI) or the increase in investment value returned to investors expressed as a rate of return. The ROI must be sufficient both to attract resources to a business and to keep them there if the business is to survive and grow. At the same time, salaries and wages paid to employees must be sufficient to attract and keep the talent necessary to the business. Value added must be adequate for both investors and workers.

To focus our attention on producing acceptable returns for investors, we present a simple conceptual formula that is used often in this book. The formula is intended to raise the question, "Where does value come from?" Thinking clearly about answers to this question is critical for managers of financial institutions in the deregulated and competitive financial services industry of the future. Major factors producing returns on investment can be captured by the following:

$$\text{Return on Investment} = \frac{(\text{Price} - \text{Cost}) \times \text{Quantity}}{\text{Investment}}.$$

The formula can be abbreviated:

$$\text{ROI} = \frac{(p - c) \times Q}{I} \tag{2.1}$$

where p and c represent prices and costs for products or services, Q is the quantity or volume of products or services provided, and I denotes necessary investments.

Interpreting the ROI formula is easy but using it analytically can be tough. To illustrate, assume that a financial service can be sold for $1, it costs $.25 to produce, requires an investment of $1 million, and 100,000 units can be sold. The ROI on this $1 million investment is:

$$\text{ROI} = \frac{(\$1 - \$.25) \times 100{,}000}{\$1{,}000{,}000} = \frac{\$.75 \times 100{,}000}{\$1{,}000{,}000} = 7.5\%.$$

From the point of view of managers and employees, the questions posed by this simple formula are profound ones: Is this the highest return we can earn? Why is this service worth $1 to our customers? What does our competitive position tell us about our ability to sell 100,000 units of the service? Can we keep our total costs to twenty-five cents? And so on. Many of these questions are difficult to answer without substantial analysis.

Table 2.4 provides some ROIs for equity investments and illustrates differences in returns among broad aggregates in the financial services industry. These data raise important issues: Why does ROI vary so much from year to year or among industry segments? Where should resources be going? What will affect ROIs in the future? But the ROI formula is intended only to organize thinking; it does not answer questions—it poses them. Successful managers in the future must answer the question, "Which of the factors within this formula are responsible for the value we are producing (or are planning to produce)?"

TABLE 2.4 Percent Return on Equity Investment

	1990	*1991*	*1992*	*1993*
Commercial Banking				
Large Banks	7.7	6.3	11.7	13.7
Midwest Banks	13.0	12.3	11.6	15.7
Canadian Banks	13.4	12.2	5.9	9.4
Insurance				
Diversified	9.2	9.5	5.4	7.1
Life	13.3	12.6	11.1	13.2
Property/Casualty	11.9	11.9	7.7	12.4
Securities Brokerage	7.8	15.7	17.7	20.3
Thrifts	4.1	3.6	3.1	4.2

SOURCE: *The Value Line Investment Survey,* Edition 4, October 7, 1994, pp. 621 and 643, Edition 8, November 4, 1994, pp. 1151, 1185, and 1199, Edition 10, p. 165, and Edition 13, pp. 2001 and 2073.

The ROI formula oversimplifies many issues. It does not account for the timing of sales and investments, which are critical in an accurate accounting of return on investment, nor does it consider the differing risks of investments. The virtue of the simple ROI formula is its focus on the underlying critical management question: How can we produce something at less than it costs in sufficient volume to justify our investment? Each of the four variables in the ROI formula is important: Prices and costs determine the margin of revenues over expenses in providing financial services. Quantity and investments combine with margins to determine the return on investment.

What factors affect each of the elements in the ROI formula? Porter's analysis of competitive strategy uses a simple diagram to show the competitive forces that determine industry profitability. The diagram, reproduced here as Figure 2.1, suggests where we should begin to look for competitive advantages.

Factors that raise prices or lower costs, everything else being equal, will raise ROI. Porter's diagram suggests the kinds of business factors that allow firms to charge higher prices or achieve cost advantages when providing services. Barriers to entry or lack of close substitutes, the top and bottom forces in Figure 2.1, can lead to profitable business strategies, because firms can charge higher prices and maintain volume. Bargaining power over suppliers of inputs, shown at the left side of the figure, can keep costs down. Rivalry provided by other firms

FIGURE 2.1 Five competitive forces

SOURCE: Michael Porter, *Competitive Strategy* (New York: The Free Press, 1980), p.4.

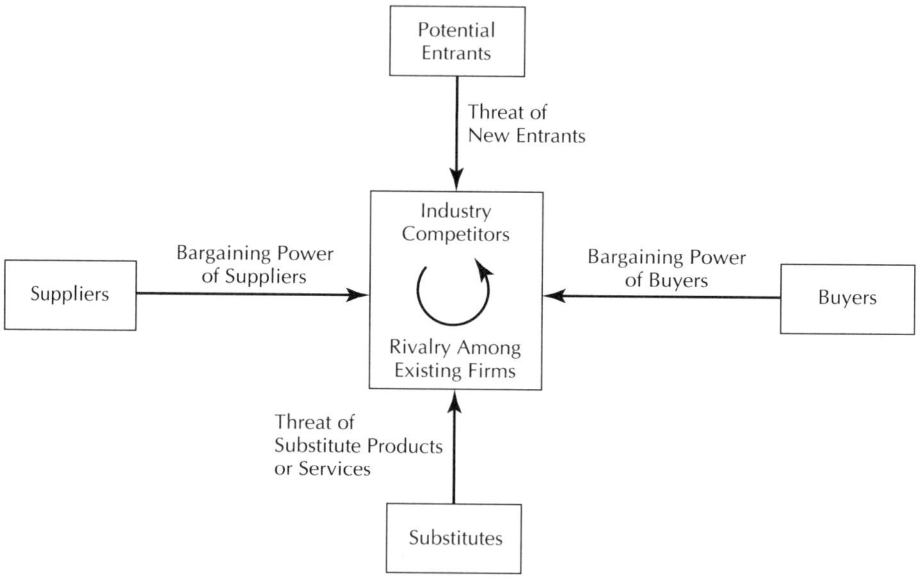

already in the industry can reduce profits (as indicated in the center of the figure) unless superiority in quality or cost performance can be achieved.

Regulatory segmentation (discussed in the next chapter) created barriers to entry and limited supplies of substitute services in the financial services industry. Remote locations and the costs of entering markets, such as location in rural areas far from urban communications infrastructure for agricultural banks or in emerging markets with unfamiliar languages and customs for international banks, may form effective barriers to entry and limit the rivals in a given market. Locating the production of financial services in distant locations where there are few alternative employers may keep labor costs low, exemplified by credit-card processing in South Dakota and insurance claims processing in Ireland. Porter's diagram of competitive forces and the simple ROI formula are an analytical framework for identifying the potential sources of competitive advantage. We use this framework in discussing financial services throughout the book.

It may seem odd to students that scholars debate why financial service firms exist (see Chapter 6). The debate is relevant for managers of financial institutions because it forces them to confront the simple question: What do financial institutions do that people cannot do for themselves? The answer, which will occupy our analysis extensively, is critical because it points the way for financial institutions to create the most value for society. Institutions creating the most value can reward their owners and employees most handsomely. As we discussed in Chapter 1, in efficient markets you cannot make money doing something people can do easily for themselves: To make money, you must add value.

2.3 ELEMENTS IN THE FINANCIAL SERVICES VALUE CHAIN

To understand how some firms add more value than others, thereby earning high returns for investors and good salaries for workers, we must identify the relationship of the various activities performed by the firm. Porter (1985) introduced the concept of a *value chain* as a means of identifying exactly how firms add value and generate high returns.

> Competitive advantage cannot be understood by looking at a firm as a whole. It stems from the many discrete activities a firm performs in designing, producing, marketing, delivering, and supporting its product. Each of these activities can contribute to a firm's relative cost position and create a basis for differentiation. (1985, p. 33)

Most of Porter's examples and applications are for manufacturing firms or retailers or other firms where material inputs, such as raw goods and capital equipment, are important. Porter's value chain for a business consists of five primary activities and associated support activities. He calls the five primary activities: (1) inbound logistics, (2) operations, (3) outbound logistics, (4) marketing and sales, and (5) service.

Inputs to the manufacturing firm are reworked by the combined forces of labor, management, and machines, then are delivered to customers. The value chain represents stages in the process where one firm may have advantages over other firms in its ability to produce goods or services that buyers are willing to pay more for than they cost to produce. The value may be added by the efficiency of the manufacturing process (operations), the distribution system (outbound logistics), and so forth. Different manufactured items have different value chains. A disposable pen company's value may come from marketing and efficient distribution, whereas a machine tool manufacturer's advantage may come in efficient production and service.

The primary activities of financial services firms are different from Porter's analysis in that most inputs and outputs of financial firms are not physical goods. To use the value chain concept effectively, we categorize each of the activities required to produce financial services. After defining the links in the value chain, we can turn in the next section to a description of the six types of services provided by financial firms.

The links in the value chain required to provide financial services and products are listed as the following paired terms:

1. Setting terms and pricing
2. Communicating and marketing
3. Producing and delivering
4. Controlling and monitoring
5. Funding and/or investing
6. Risk bearing and/or risk shifting.

These activities are listed for reference as the rows in Table 2.5.

TABLE 2.5 Financial Services and Value Producing Activities

ACTIVITIES	*CREDIT*	*SECURITIES*	*TRANSACTION PROCESSING*	*INSURANCE*	*ASSET MANAGE-MENT*	*INFORMATION/ ADVISORY*
Setting Terms/ Pricing	Loan rates	Negotiated fees	Fees, balances	Premiums, coverage	Fees, perfor-mance	Offered with other services
Communicating/ Marketing	Calling officers	Calls, reputation	Advertise-ments	Agents, brokers		
Producing/ Delivering			Processing centers			On-Line data
Monitoring/ Controlling	Value collateral		Review funds availability	Review claims	Third party review	
Funding/ Investing	Deposits, asset backed securities					
Risk Bearing/ Shifting	Mortgage insurance					

Each pair consists of closely related activities involved in providing financial services or products. The list is not a sequence—different activities may be performed in a different order. For example, term setting/pricing may be performed before, at the same time, or after communicating and marketing activities. Activity pairs may be required simultaneously or separately depending on circumstances. We describe each activity pair in detail.

Qualitative differences in the activities in the value chain define the primary differences between various financial services. Differences in the requirements to perform these activities provide competitive advantages to some segments of the financial services marketplace. For example, pricing in the insurance business is a very different activity from pricing in the deposit-taking or brokerage businesses. To add value in the insurance business, you have to know how to price insurance products like car insurance or retirement plans. Pricing these products requires special expertise different from other services.

Setting Terms/Pricing

Defining the terms or prices at which financial services are performed is an essential activity in providing financial services and products. Terms and conditions can be announced to the market as part of product design or they can be negotiated with customers. Activities associated with setting the terms of financial arrangements and assigning explicit prices or interest rates to financial products in many cases define the product or service, as with a fixed versus a variable rate loan.

Financial products and services are unique in the complexity of the conditions and terms associated with them. A box of cereal has a single price. In contrast, a typical checking account has a schedule of fees and the charges for services performed will depend on a variety of conditions, such as level of balances. Some financial services, such as insurance policies, are performed over limited time frames; others are performed until one side or the other cancels the arrangement (e.g., a checking account).

When pricing and term setting activities are performed depends on the particular financial service market we are looking at. For mass markets, prices and terms are often set before a given service is offered, perhaps by marketing personnel or product development staffs. The product is provided to all customers who accept the terms. In other markets, usually involving large customers, terms may be negotiated between officials of the financial services firm and the corporation, government, or other users. The terms are part of a "deal."

Communicating/Marketing

If customers are to use products or services offered by firms in the market, they must know about them. Finding out what customers want and telling them that it is available are communicating and marketing activities in financial services. Some services are aggressively marketed through newspaper advertisements and electronic media. Everyone has seen or heard aggressive ad campaigns by local banks, insurance companies, or mutual funds, and brokerage houses vie with brewers for prime advertising time during the playoff games of major professional sports.

Aggressive media advertising is not the only way financial firms send messages to customers. Potential customers learn by referrals from affiliated firms or other customers that a given firm can accommodate financial needs. The most effective information flow between firms and customers must be a two-way street. Financial service firms must determine what their customers want and tell them how they can get it.

Necessary communication links between financial institutions and customers can take many forms. Many customers deal with financial institutions through a local office such as a bank branch and these offices become important communication channels. Other financial firms, such as insurance companies, reach customers using sales agents. Some firms communicate in person by making sales calls, others contact customers by mail or telephone. Marketing and communication activities are a vital link in the value chain.

Producing/Delivering

Activities performed in producing and delivering financial services are sometimes called *operations* or *back-office* activities. Providing financial services usually requires specific actions; for example, money must be provided when a check is cashed. Action is taken and the result is delivered to the user of the financial services. Production of the service is often inseparable from delivery of the service. If you call to inquire about your bank balance, the phone call is the means by which the information you request is delivered. Sometimes production of financial services can be centralized and performed out of sight of the customer, as is the case with sorting checks and posting premium payments.

Production and delivery of financial services are a significant source of costs for many financial institutions, so economies in the costs of labor and capital in the production of services are sought through efficient allocation of resources in space and time. Some production and delivery activities may be most economically performed by third parties.

Controlling/Monitoring

Most financial relationships require performance of specified acts under contracts, such as making timely loan payments or insurance premium payments. The terms and prices accepted or negotiated by customers for financial services must be honored; monitoring activities determine whether or not the terms are met.

If the bank or credit union does not keep track of loan status, customers could delay payments, costing the lender lost profits from investment of the funds. Keeping track of the status of contract terms, such as when payments are made on car loans, is a monitoring activity in the financial services industry.

When terms of an agreement are violated, sanctions or legal remedies must be invoked. For example, if car loan payments are not made, the lender has the right to repossess the car. The threat of sanctions or legal action controls the willingness of parties to stick to their agreements. Calling the auto repossessor is a control activity associated with a car loan.

All financial services require some monitoring and control activities. In most cases, the firm providing the product or service monitors and controls the underlying agreements. In other cases, monitoring and control activities can be done by a third party, such as a collection agency under contract to a lender. On the other hand, nonperformance of a commitment may benefit the financial service firm, like delayed payment of insurance claims. In these cases, monitoring and control activities become the job of the customer or a regulator acting on behalf of customers.

Funding/Investing

Virtually all financial services involve investing or raising money. These activities can be viewed as exchanges of title to financial assets. For example, when cash is deposited in a credit union, the customer exchanges hard-earned cash for a claim on the thrift—the deposit balance. The credit union has obligated itself to paying interest or providing financial services. Paying interest or providing these services requires that the credit union invest the cash to earn additional money to pay interest or cover the costs of providing services. In the case of a car loan, the credit union or bank funds the loan; it advances cash to the car dealer. Thus, the financial institution making the car loan has to acquire cash to pay for the car.

Assets and liabilities of financial service firms reflect their funding and investing activities. Some firms provide both funding and investing activities; for example, banks take deposits and make loans. In this case, funding and investing activities are complementary. In other cases, funding and investing can be substitutes, as when financial firms borrow or invest depending on whether they are short or have excess funds.

Risk Bearing/Risk Shifting

There are risks whenever financial assets, including money, are transferred between parties. There are risks that the terms and prices at which services are provided will not be met. The risks are nonperformance of services, nondelivery of assets, or nonpayment of money. There are risks associated with the losses or gains in the value of the assets from shifts in the general economic environment. None of these risks can be eliminated. They must be borne.

Since all financial services entail risks from nonperformance or valuation risks, one or all of the parties are exposed to risk. Sometimes risks are divided between parties in a carefully planned way that deals with all possible contingencies. Sometimes no one worries about the risks until the unforeseen disasters occur. In most instances, allocation of risks in financial services is an explicit part of the service.

Summary of Value Chain

Each of the six links in the value chain is essential for all financial services. Efficient performance of these different activities requires different talents, resources, and organizational forms. In the following section, we describe six basic financial services. This analysis of financial services provides a six-by-six classification of activities for financial services. This classification forms a framework for financial institution managers to identify competitive advantages by asking the question, "Which of these activities are we good at?" Financial institutions should concentrate resources in those activities where they have a competitive advantage in order to increase their ROI.

2.4 FINANCIAL SERVICES

To organize our discussion and analysis of the financial services industry, we classify the services that financial institutions provide into six basic categories. No classification scheme will satisfy everyone nor will it capture all the subtleties of this industry. The purpose of classification schemes is to provide organizing principles for an otherwise incomprehensible wealth of details.

Financial service firms provide the following basic financial services:

1. Credit
2. Securities
3. Transaction processing
4. Insurance
5. Asset management
6. Information and advice.

These basic financial services are listed as column headings in Table 2.5 thus completing our six-by-six analytical framework for the industry. Recall that the links in the value chain are the rows in the table.

Most financial services are provided in combination, like the credit and loan transaction processing services provided by banks. To assess competitive advantage in financial services, managers must analyze relationships between basic financial services and links in the value chain to decide which services and activities offer the greatest opportunities. Table 2.5 provides a few example of how activities in the value chain can be performed in financial services. For example, calling officers of banks perform the information and marketing activity in business credit. Activities required by a financial service may be performed by several firms instead of a single firm. Some firms may be relatively efficient in an activity like pricing but not in another, like monitoring. Activities may be consolidated and performed by a single provider who is efficient in all or has special access to the market for a financial service.

Innovation in financial services will consist of new combinations of activities and financial services or new separations of activities and services. Value is added by more efficient production or by meeting new customers needs. Fundamental changes in the future of the financial services industry will result from economic forces determining efficient allocation of activities required to provide services having value to consumers. A major objective of this book is to understand the economics underlying these changes.

Credit Services

Credit services are among the greatest sources of social value in financial services. Consumers and investors often require credit to implement consumption plans or take advantage of investment opportunities. The allocation of funds to consumers and investors—both individual and institutional—to implement optimal plans makes the economy more efficient. Economic efficiency is the source of value in credit services and the reason men and women work in the towers of the London, Hong Kong, LaSalle Street, and Wall Street.

Examples of credit services are readily at hand: car loans, credit card loans, student loans, corporate bank loans, and so on. Usually credit services bring to mind the money advanced to an economic unit against promises of future repayment. But funding loans is only one link to the value chain for providing credit services. We consider credit services more analytically in terms of the value chain to identify sources of value and profits in the emerging and dynamic global financial system.

Providers of credit services advertise or otherwise market their willingness to arrange credit to potential users. Referrals from another party in the transaction may be an important link, as when a car dealer suggests possible sources for car loans. Credit services can be part of a package of financial services, like a bank that offers loans and other services. Selling more than one financial service represents cross selling, with credit services offered by "one-stop" financial institutions for both retail and wholesale markets.

Another important link in the value chain for credit services involves setting the terms and pricing the loans. Banks and thrifts often offer all qualified consumers announced interest rates and other loan terms, and they advertise or promote a given loan package. In more complex loans between large corporations and banks or insurance companies, loan terms may be precisely negotiated by corporate officials and financial institution representatives.

Production and delivery of a loan consists of performing borrower analyses, executing necessary documents, and delivering funds to the borrower—all collectively called loan origination. For example, after qualifying for a car loan the borrower gets a cashier's check made out to the dealer. When a large corporate loan deal is closed, the money might be added to the corporation's checking account through a wire transfer. Production and delivery of credit can use an infinite variety of methods.

After acceptance and approval, loan terms have to be monitored. If payments are not made on time, the borrower has to be contacted. If there is collateral, it must be maintained as agreed. If violations of the loan terms occur, control procedures must be invoked. Control procedures may consist of taking possession of collateral or of starting a lawsuit. Monitoring and control activities in credit services provide necessary information and incentives to make the terms of the loan meaningful.

If money is lent, money must be found to lend. In traditional loans—those from banks and thrifts—money for loans comes from deposits and all of the credit-related activities in the value chain are provided by the lender. Our discussion is meant to emphasize that advancing funds is only a part of credit services. In fact, funding credit is increasingly separated from the other activities associated with credit. Many loans are funded by third-party investors like bond funds or limited partnerships.

Traditional banks and thrifts bore the risks associated with the loans they made. Some of these risks were shared or shifted by making specific arrangements with the borrower or third parties, such as with mortgage insurance companies for home loans. If borrowers defaulted in the absence of credit insurance, banks or thrifts lost funds that could not be recovered. If the loan had a fixed interest rate and deposit costs went up in response to a change in economic circumstances, the traditional lender suffered reduced earnings or losses.

More and more in credit markets, credit-related activities in the value chain have been separated or *unbundled*. In mortgage lending, for example, the loan may be marketed by real estate brokers according to terms set by Federal government mortgage lending programs. Some activities associated with loan origination may be done with computers over phone lines by mortgage brokers. Production and delivery of subsequent loan processing and monitoring and controlling may be done by thrifts or mortgage bankers. Funding may be provided by institutional investors investing in mortgage pools. Economic and performance risks may be borne by government agencies, insurance companies, and transactors in futures markets. Other credit markets like credit card loans are similarly becoming unbundled.

The value chain in credit services is experiencing rapid changes in the allocation of activities. In the credit market, you see examples of a single financial firm performing all activities and you see transactions such as loan arrangements where each activity is provided by a different firm. New competitors and new ways of doing business are the rule. Providers and users of credit services, which includes virtually everyone, need to understand the sources of competitive advantage in each link of the value chain providing credit services.

Securities Services

Claims against firms and governments are exchanged on securities markets. The primary market is where new securities or claims are sold by users of funds. For large borrowers, there are many advantages in raising funds in the form of tradable securities as opposed to loans arranged by credit service firms. The market for already issued or "used" financial claims is called the secondary market. Most securities trading occurs in secondary markets.

Designing new securities issues for the market is called *securities origination*. In some instances, financial institutions guarantee the prices of new securities, called *securities underwriting*. After securities are issued, they are traded in financial markets as market conditions and investors' desired portfolio composition change. Trading securities is facilitated by *market makers*—who quote prices

—and brokers—who find buyers for sellers. All of these securities services facilitate the flow of capital into firms and governments by making securities liquid and providing reliable price information at which securities can be issued, bought, or sold.

The same links in the value chain are relevant to securities origination, underwriting, and trading. Terms and prices for services have to be determined. This can be the outcome of heated negotiation, as with large corporate or government underwritings. Terms can be fixed by agreement and regulation, as with brokerage commissions until May 1, 1975, in the United States. After 1975, commissions charged for trading on behalf of institutional investors are lower than prices offered to retail customers. Competitive conditions and costs are important factors in the pricing of securities services.

Marketing and communicating securities origination, underwriting, and trading services vary with the market segment. An example of a complex marketing and communication problem in securities origination service is mortgage-backed securities. Home buyers do not view their mortgage applications as part of a securities origination for a mortgage-backed security but often it is. The mortgage banker, bank, or thrift institution originating the loan has to communicate with the home buyer and the mortgage-backed security has to be marketed to institutional investors. The communication and marketing activities in this instance involve mortgage bankers, thrifts, banks, institutional investors, and government agencies.

Traditional securities origination and underwriting are primarily directed at the institutional market. Marketing and communication with these customers entails explanation and negotiation of complex products and services. Providers must demonstrate responsiveness to changes in the market environment and to the needs of customers. Calling on established customers with a long relationship and referrals through affiliated firms are two traditional communication activities used with this dynamic market, but aggressive firms are reaching out to potential customers in nontraditional ways actively competing for opportunities to do a single deal.

Production and delivery of trading and related activities require intense consultation with customers because of sudden changes in the market or a need for quick decisions. There are required disclosures of information. Document preparation is important in securities origination. Underwriting activities require simultaneous contact with the securities originator and financial market participants like institutional investors and eventually the delivery of funds. Firms performing these activities have many opportunities to innovate in delivery and production using telephones and computers to facilitate close customer contact.

Securities origination, underwriting, and trading all require that customers monitor and control the performance of the service providers. Most of the responsibility for monitoring and controlling these services has fallen to users of the services or regulators under the securities laws. Nonetheless, third parties are available to control certain aspects of these services. For example, institutional investors hire specialists to review transaction prices in the market to assess the performance of their brokers.

Funding underwritings is an important activity of investment bankers. Originators often need to find financing for inventories of assets before they are sold off as securities. Brokers lend customers money on margin to acquire securities. These funding activities are an important activity in financial services and the recent willingness of investment bankers to use their equity capital to provide underwriting services has been an important competitive element in the market.

Risks of changes in securities prices are of course paramount in the financial services associated with securities origination, underwriting, and trading. These risks can be borne or in many cases sold off in whole or in part in the market. Risk bearing is the essence of those aspects of investment banking associated with underwriting new offerings and making markets in securities.

Transaction Processing

Deposits are familiar financial products offered by banks and others. Some deposits can be used in transactions with third parties, i.e., checking accounts; other deposits can be withdrawn with interest at maturity, i.e., time deposits. With all deposits, you can obtain current balance information from the deposit-taking firm. To analyze the activities in the value chain associated with deposit taking and transaction processing, the basic economic role of deposits and transaction processing is reviewed.

Deposit taking at financial institutions developed in ancient times as people left their jewels and gold (checked them) with a reliable businessman or merchant for safekeeping, praying they could get them back later when they needed them. Checking bags at the airport and checking valuables like gold are different. At the airport you want exactly the same bag back. With gold, you cannot tell the difference between one ounce and another. When deposit-taking is limited to valuables that are identical, like gold, money, and similar assets, depositors do not get back exactly the same item left on deposit. They simply expect some prespecified amount returned—perhaps adjusted for interest and fees—when the deposit is claimed. Keeping track of the depositor's claim requires record keeping; each deposit and withdrawal must be recorded.

When a check is used to buy something, the seller puts it in a bank or other deposit-taking institution. The buyer exchanges a claim on a bank or thrift in the form of a deposit balance for whatever was bought. Eugene Fama (1980) calls the deposit-taking system a *transactions system of exchange*. The buyer's account balance decreases and the seller's account balance increases. If buyers and sellers have different banks or thrifts, these institutions will have to settle up: this is the clearing or settlement aspect of transaction processing.

When increases in one person's financial claims are balanced by decreases in someone else's claims to make payments, we have an example of a transaction system of exchange. For example, when a car loan payment is made, the borrower's checking account is reduced and that is balanced by a lowering of the loan balance. Loan payment processing is another example of a transactions processing system. Loan transaction processing is called *loan servicing*.

There are hundreds of examples of transaction processing systems. Credit card processing, mutual fund share processing, changes in stock certificate ownership—the list gets longer as new financial products are developed. Transaction processing is a financial service that is fundamental to a highly developed financial system in which claims or obligations of many financial assets are frequently rearranged among many different parties. Such a society has a highly developed transaction system of exchange.

The terms and pricing for deposit-taking are fixed by law, regulation, and competitive conditions. Other transaction processing services are priced in a more competitive environment with a wide range of arrangements. For example, credit card fees are charged to retailers who accept the cards, and the fees are split between financial institutions like banks, credit card processors, and jointly owned facilities like Visa and Mastercard. We discuss these arrangements in Chapter 10.

Communicating and marketing transaction processes vary with the business segment. Marketing of deposits is typically done by the firm taking the deposits: Local banks and thrifts promote their charge cards and deposit accounts. Other transaction services marketing is performed by a whole range of financial and nonfinancial firms. National advertising campaigns attempt to establish brand identification for credit cards. Loan servicing is marketed to credit institutions rather than borrowers. Bank trust departments call on corporate clients to communicate institutional transaction processing for stock transfer.

Production and delivery of transaction services can be located near the customer, as in a branch office with smaller banks and thrifts, or they can be delivered indirectly through machines with centralized processing, like automatic tellers. Processing can be localized close to paper flows, as in regional check processing centers, or performed in remote locations, like Citicorp's credit card processing center in South Dakota. Manual and computer systems, communication links and customer contacts, access methods and forms of delivery vary from product to product and firm to firm. Some transaction processing services require little customer contact, e.g., keeping track of stock or bond ownership; other services, like credit cards, require close customer relationships and frequent contact, via monthly statements, for example.

Monitoring and controlling transaction processing relationships vary with the customer and the product. If, for example, fees on a checking account depend on balances, the balances have to be monitored. Overdrafts have to be controlled, with payment refused if there is no overdraft protection. Other transaction-based services, like stock clearing or bill paying, require different monitoring and control aspects. As transaction services proliferate, new monitoring and control problems will need to be dealt with in the future.

Transaction processing is a source of funds for deposit-taking firms and the funds have to be invested. Deposit outflows must be covered and may require funding if assets cannot be easily liquidated. Transfers of funds and securities in other transaction services may require funds to be advanced or may produce temporary or longer-term investable funds. Funding and investing are vital links in the value chain for transaction processing.

The risks of transaction processing depend on the particular product or service. There are liquidity risks associated with deposit withdrawals. There are default risks if customers do not deliver in securities transactions. There are operating risks associated with equipment and systems. There are risks associated with interest rates at which fixed-rate deposits can be invested. These risks can be shared or shifted but they must be absorbed or managed to create value from transaction processing.

All of these necessary activities in the value chain for transaction services can be provided by one firm, as with traditional checking accounts, or they can be divided among a variety of providers, separating marketing, production and delivery, funding, and so on. Money market mutual funds often rely on banks for check clearing, for example. Financial institutions offering transaction processing services will have to be alert to the sources of competitive advantage in the value chain as technology and competition increase and complicate the range of transaction processing services demanded in our advanced economy.

Insurance Services

Insurance can protect against a variety of adverse occurrences or events to individuals or firms. In order for a financial service firm to offer insurance against risks, the risks must be well specified and the occurrence of the event insured against has to be verifiable. Insurance risks can be classified into those pertaining to an individual's life and health, those pertaining to the value of property as it would be affected by accident, theft, or fraud, and those involving other economic risks. A life insurance risk would be that a named individual will die within a given time span. A property or casualty risk is that a given piece of property will burn down or be damaged in a storm. An economic risk is that interest rates will rise or fall.

Risk shifting and sharing is the basic activity in insurance products. In the traditional life or casualty insurance business, the insurance company agrees to pay money to beneficiaries or to the insured to cover part or all of the losses due to adverse circumstances. Traditional insurance services are as old as mankind. Ancient tribes or extended families provided primitive "insurance" against the risks of sickness or disability by their commitments to care for the infirm. Communities pooled funds against risks of storms or floods. The risks of modern society have made the industry of providing insurance services much more complex.

Insurance services, like all financial services, include all the links in the value chain in addition to risk shifting and sharing. Prices and other terms of the insurance policy must be determined for different types of insurance customers. Risks insured against have to be defined and the likelihood of the occurrence assessed. Activities associated with determining the risks and pricing them are called the *actuarial* activities in the insurance business. Depending on the type of insurance and the customers in that market, the terms and prices may be offered for general sale, as in home insurance. For special risks or customers, rates and terms may be negotiated, as in space satellite insurance.

The readiness of insurance companies to offer policies is often communicated to the market in traditional ways, through advertising campaigns or sales calls. A number of communication links exist between insurance customers and the insurance firms: direct representational offices, agents, referrals, and so on. Marketing and communicating with potential insurance customers can be separated from the performance of other activities in the value chain of insurance services, as when independent agents are used by insurance carriers.

The actual production and delivery of insurance policies and required services can by performed by one firm integrating all aspects of the business. Allstate uses outlets, many located in its former owner's, Sears', stores, to write and deliver insurance policies. Alternatively, production and delivery can be delegated to independent agents or subcontractors who perform these activities. Insurance also can be delivered through machines, as with air travel insurance.

Premiums must be paid on time for insurance to remain in force. An insurer must pay claims when they occur if policy terms are not violated. Insurance contracts have to be monitored to guarantee that requirements are met and cheating does not occur. Losses, when they occur, must be assessed. These activities are called *insurance adjustment* or *claims adjustment.* As with the other financial services we have discussed, not all of these monitoring and control functions have to be performed by a single company. Independent claims adjustors can work under contract for insurance companies.

The premiums collected for insurance policies have to be invested to produce enough funds to pay claims. Naturally, risks must be borne in the insurance business. However, these risks can be shifted and shared. This can be done by the terms of the insurance with the insured party or can be done by contracts with third parties, such as reinsurers. Not all risks are associated with claims. Economic risks such as those associated with changes in interest rates or other economic magnitudes may be shared or shifted using financial markets.

Future innovation in the life and casualty insurance industry will produce new allocations of the activities in the value chain. Like other financial services, unbundling or combining activities may become economically competitive in some insurance markets as new providers of insurance services enter the market. Other developments in insurance will be associated with the types of risks for which insurance contracts are available. Insurance contracts can be written on any definable risk if demand is sufficient.

Asset Management Services

Virtually all financial service firms manage assets. There are differing ways in which this asset management fits into financial service businesses. For example, financial institutions like trust companies and mutual funds manage assets without owning them; the assets belong to trustees or mutual fund shareholders. For some financial service firms, asset management is connected to other activities of the firm. Deposit-taking firms, for example, use deposit funds to invest in loans and securities. Those firms own assets as part of a leveraged portfolio.

Professional asset managers price and set terms for their services. Portfolios managers must have some understanding or contract with the owners of assets concerning compensation and obligations. Trust departments of banks manage many assets under detailed trust agreements. Some asset management products, such as managing estates in probate court after a death, have terms and prices that are standardized. Other asset management arrangements may be the outcome of competition and negotiation, as with large pension fund management contracts. Mutual funds charge management fees that are determined in a competitive marketplace.

Mutual funds advertise their management expertise aggressively in the pages of the investor press. Trust departments generate business through their reputations, calling on potential accounts, or referrals from other bank departments doing business with major customers. Demand for asset management services changes as customer needs and tastes shift, requiring communication with customers through a number of channels. Appropriate marketing and communication activities with asset management varies with the market and competition, as with all financial services.

Production and delivery of asset management services can be done by a wide range of means. For example, research and asset allocation decisions can be done separately from the actual purchases and safekeeping of assets. Mutual funds managers, like those at Dreyfus Corporation, may choose assets for investment for a given fund and have the transaction processing performed by a specialist in that activity like State Street Boston. A bank trust department, like that of Wells Fargo, may perform all of these activities together.

Trust and asset management services impose on the asset manager many requirements and conditions that must be monitored. When necessary, control procedures or sanctions must be invoked. The range of control and monitoring activities entailed in asset management varies with products and markets. Beneficiaries sometimes hire lawyers to enforce the performance of their asset managers, as when a trust customer sues a bank trust department. Mutual fund owners can exercise control over asset managers to some extent by their ability to withdraw funds at any time.

Investment is the main activity of asset management. There may also be secondary investing or funding activities involved, for example the investment of cash flows from investments before disbursement or the funding redemptions of mutual fund shares before assets can be sold.

The risks associated with asset management include the timing of cash flows or the desirability of the product offered to the market under various interest rate or stock market conditions. For example, mutual fund managers were short of cash to make redemptions when small investors sold mutual fund shares after the stock market crash of 1987. There are risks associated with making fixed commitments on performance of funds under management. There is the risk of not living up to customers' expectations. These risks can be borne by asset managers or are sometimes shared or shifted to third parties directly or through financial markets. A controversial example of such risk shifting is portfolio insurance, which we discuss in Part IV of this book.

Information, and Advising and Advisory Services

There is an enormous amount of information available to potential investors. An investor seeking information can rely on the business press, like *The Wall Street Journal* in its "Heard on the Street" and investor advice columns or the *Investor's Business Daily* with its charts and tables. Investors can read periodicals like *Fortune, Business Week,* or other magazines. They can delve into specialist advisory services, like *Value Line* and *Moodys.* Investors can get information on the latest stock prices over the phone or on personal computer screens, using stock price quotation services.

Information and advice for investors are everywhere and can be offered together or separately. Services can simply provide data or can evaluate assets after extensive research. These services can be thought of as information in three stages: (1) financial information; (2) evaluation; and (3) advice.

Traditional financial service firms offer investment information and advice at various prices and terms. Brokers give stock quotes and tips to their clients free but recover costs through commission income. Banks advice corporate customers about potential merger candidates and charge explicit fees. Thrifts offer free financial planning services as part of promotions or at low prices to gain customers. Investment managers undertake investment research for their clients under negotiated contracts.

The marketing of information and advisory services depends on the types of customers and market conditions. Each day, the business press contains advertisements promoting information services to small investors and institutional investors. Other research and information services sell through office calls on potential customers. Brokers may provide their own firm's research or other companies' assessments or advice as part of their communication with their customers.

The activities of producing and delivering investment information and advice varies with the product. Stock analysis and research can be performed by analysts working with computerized data bases in New York and delivered to clients in the form of research reports provided by brokers. Information on price quotes and transaction prices may be produced electronically and delivered via computer terminals, as with Reuters and Money Market Services information. Advice can be delivered by a phone call or a mailing.

Control and monitoring of information and advisory services is usually informal and up to users of the information. Information services may or may not be responsible for the reliability of their information. Monitoring and control of financial services entailing information and advice varies with the customer and with competitive and regulatory conditions in the market. In the United States the activities of investment advisors are regulated to a certain extent under the Investment Advisors Act.

Investing and funding activities are not a primary activity in providing financial information and advisory services. However, these activities may come into play if there are liabilities associated with the information or advisory service. If assessments or quotes are guaranteed, potential funding may be necessary to ensure performance.

Risks in providing advice and information do not come from direct exposure to investment risks in general, but rather from the level of demand for information and advisory services. For example, the deregulation of brokerage commissions, which took place on so-called May Day, 1975, decimated research departments at brokerage houses because lower revenues could not cover research costs. There are also risks associated with changes in technology, such as changes in efficient means of delivering information and quotations. There are even risks associated with acceptable research methods used in developing assessments or advice: efficient market theories have eroded confidence in advice by chartists and technical analysts.

The demand for good information in a globally integrated economy is insatiable, and the investment information and advisory business is growing dramatically. The business is competitive, technically complicated, and filled with a bewildering array of providers, from individuals writing newsletters in their basements to multinational corporations. Investment advisors are viewed by some customers as charlatans and by others as saints. The business is largely populated with ordinary human beings, like you and me. The potential for innovation and value creation is enormous.

Summary of the Value Chain in Financial Services

We can now see the rows and columns of Table 2.5 as a guide in the search for value provided by financial service firms with different expertise. For example, commercial banks may be good at negotiating terms on short-term loans to businesses and can produce value by their expertise in setting loan rates relative to costs and competitors' quotes. Credit agencies may provide superior service and lower costs to users of credit information by production and delivery of on-line computerized data bases. Credit unions may be efficient in communication with their depositors. Table 2.5 provides a framework to assess where specific firms have particular strengths and potential to create value for customers and investors.

By combining services and value-producing activities, Table 2.5 is an excellent tool for organizing thoughts about business strategies in the financial services industry. Firms can focus narrowly, say on one element such as data processing in transaction processing, and cooperate with other firms to perform other activities. Firms with particular competitive advantages can concentrate on a single link in the value chain for a variety of financial service products. For example, a firm strong in marketing and information gathering could expand horizontally in the table by specializing in marketing and product development in the credit, insurance, and asset management services. Alternatively, some firms can perform all the activities necessary in a set of financial services, say credit and transaction activities—like the traditional banks and thrifts that made loans and took deposits. This strategy moves vertically on the table.

It is extremely unlikely that any management or organization has equal ROI for every element in the value chain services presented in Table 2.5. Good management will determine where their competitive advantage is and will concentrate resources on those activities that maximize ROI and value production. Successful management in the future will understand how the activities in financial services fit together and develop approaches to the market that takes maximum advantage of their expertise.

2.5 SUMMARY

Management creates wealth for owners and investors by creating value in the financial services marketplace for customers. Analysis of value production in financial services suggests the importance of information and labor and human resources in the industry. Financial service firms produce high ROIs the way all firms produce value: They sell products and services for more than they cost to produce. Michael Porter's value chain is adapted to develop a framework analyzing competitive advantage for financial institutions. The value chain consists of six activities required in providing financial services: pricing/term setting, marketing/communicating, producing/delivering, controlling/monitoring, funding/investing, and risk shifting/sharing. They are applied to the six basic financial services: credit, securities, transaction processing, insurance, asset management, and information services. Value production and high ROIs require management to determine their competitive advantage in the value chain for different financial services.

DISCUSSION QUESTIONS AND EXERCISES

1. What examples can you provide of financial service firms that have grown rapidly or that have run into trouble recently? What do you believe is the source of growth or problems for these firms?
2. Using formula 2.1 and the numbers below, assess the performance of two sample firms. Which is better and why? Can you think of real-life examples of this relationship in the financial services industry?

	PRICE	*COST*	*QUANTITY*	*INVESTMENT*
Big firm	\$1.25	\$ .95	1,000,000	\$500,000,000
Small firm	1.50	1.25	100,000	250,000

3. Where have people you know gotten jobs in financial services recently? What do you think is the source of the financial firm's ability to pay them their salaries?
4. List several financial services you currently use and describe how each of the activities involved in the service is provided. For example, the prices and balance requirements for a checking account might be provided on an advertising circular in a branch, etc.
5. Contrast the activities associated with credit services and transaction processing as provided by banks and savings and loans. What similarities and differences in the activities of providing these financial services do you find? What advantages or disadvantages can be found by offering these services in combination?
6. For each activity associated with a consumer checking account, assess what type of expertise and/or techno-

logical requirements are involved, and determine what types of firms *outside* the financial services industry are well-known for efficiency in these activities. Could firms outside the financial services industry perform such activities if they were "unbundled"? Why or why not?

7. Perform the same analysis as in Question 6 for consumer loans.
8. List the types of information associated with a checking account, including prices, yields, balances, etc. How do you think this information is produced? How is it useful? How could it be made more useful? How is it delivered to you? What alternatives are available?
9. Money market mutual funds (MMMFs) are offered by brokers to their customers. MMMFs are pooled investments in short-term securities issued by banks, corporations, and governments who pay market interest rates; these funds usually have check-writing privileges. This product innovation first appeared in the late 1970s when savings account interest rates were regulated and held below market levels. What advantages did these accounts have for customers? What expected benefits did they offer firms like Merrill Lynch which first made them available?
10. Describe to the best of your ability some jobs or positions you are familiar with in financial institutions, and analyze what types of information are important to the performance of each job, what kind of manipulation of that information must be performed, and how the information is obtained, stored, retrieved, and processed.

REFERENCES

BOARD OF GOVERNORS OF THE FEDERAL RESERVE SYSTEM. 1991. "Recent Developments Affecting the Profitability and Practice of Commercial Banks," *Bulletin* (July), pp. 505–527.

DEUTSCHE BUNDESBANK. 1991. "The Profitability of German Banks in 1990," *Monthly Report* (August), pp. 214–231.

FAMA, EUGENE 1980. "Banking in a Theory of Finance," *Journal of Monetary Economics,* pp. 39–57.

Fortune. November 24, 1986. STRATFORD P. SHERMAN "Why the Youngsters' Party May Be Ending," pp. 28–40.

PORTER, MICHAEL E. 1985. *Competitive Advantage*. New York: The Free Press.

PORTER, MICHAEL E. 1980. *Competitive Strategy*. New York: The Free Press.

CHAPTER

3

Financial Services and the Economy

Introduction

Mergers, hostile takeovers, bankruptcies, and international acquisitions occur daily and are revolutionizing the financial services industry. These dramatic changes have implications for us as customers, employees, and students of financial service firms. They are part of a restructuring of the ways the six basic financial services are offered to increase value and efficiency in the global economy.

- What factors were and are important in determining the past and future structure of this industry?
- Where exactly do we and other participants in the economy fit into the financial services market?
- Who are the players in this story and what roles do they play?

We begin by discussing two major factors shaping the industry: segmentation and regulation. The major players and the way they fit into the real and financial markets are introduced next, using the flow-of-funds accounts framework. Traditional financial firms are presented. This background is designed to assist us in identifying trends that are relevant to managers and customers of this industry in the future.

3.1 FINANCIAL SERVICES: SEGMENTATION AND REGULATION

Several aspects of the financial services industry distinguish it from other aspects of the economy. Traditionally, and currently to a large extent, the financial services industry is *segmented*. Firms provide some of the six financial services discussed in

Chapter 2 but do not or cannot provide others. For example, banks do not sell insurance and brokers do not take deposits. This segmentation of the financial services industry is a result of three main factors: (1) *specialization* due to competitive advantage; (2) *regulation* limiting firms to authorized activities; and (3) *taxation*.

The three factors explaining segmentation of financial services are not always separable. Firms specialize in what they do that earns the highest returns. In the United States until 1980, regulation gave commercial banks a monopoly on checking accounts, which allowed them to develop specialized expertise. Banks still dominate the payments system even though nonbanks have been allowed to enter that market.

Regulatory segmentation of financial services results from the accumulated impact of an often capricious history and persists in the face of economic forces working against it. Four basic rationales are advanced for regulation around the world: (1) to promote government policy goals in the allocation of financial resources; (2) to offset the disadvantage to those who are unable to understand financial information; (3) to absorb economy-wide risks too large for individual firms; and (4) to promote competition. Each of these rationales is used to justify legislative and regulatory intervention in financial services in all countries of the world.

The first rationale for government intervention is due to the importance of banks and other financial institutions in the supply and allocation of money. Money can be used for financing wars and colonial adventures—leading naturally to kings' and commissars' historical fascination with banking firms. Presidents and legislators are also fascinated with financial firms. Legislation and regulation to finance public defense justified the National Banking Acts of 1863 and 1864 in the United States. Democratic governments have attempted to promote the reliability of the payments system, for example by establishing the Federal Reserve Bank System in 1913 in the United States. Government laws may attempt to distribute economic power regionally, for example by creating the Bundesbank in Germany after World War II. Many countries, like Japan, subsidize specialized financial institutions for housing or investment.

A second rationale for financial regulation is that markets for financial services can break down or not function because consumers are unable to obtain and process complex information, an outcome called *market failure*. For example, insurance company executives are more sophisticated concerning financial matters than their retail customers. Insurance authorities in most countries regulate insurance contracts for these reasons. The difficulty in understanding or defining some financial products has also led to substantial government interest in the financial sector—for example to prevent speculation as opposed to investment.

The third rationale for regulation, usually used during times of economic stress like the Great Depression, is based on the importance of financial institutions in the functioning of the economy. The argument is that some economic risks are undiversifiable and affect the entire financial system. Governments can use their taxing authority to absorb system-wide risks. The argument continues that if governments do not absorb these undiversifiable risks, firms operating in private markets will offer smaller amounts of financial services (like loans) than is socially optimal. This justification was used for deposit insurance in the United States when it was instituted in 1933.

A fourth rationale used to justify regulation is that regulation can supplement market forces when policy makers believe that competition in an industry is inadequate. Regulation may achieve the benefits of competition when unregulated firms otherwise would extract monopoly or oligopoly profits from customers. Most countries restrict bank mergers, for example. Industry participants sometimes try to use government authority to protect or create market advantages. Banks' recent monopoly on checking accounts to the exclusion of thrifts in the United States and the United Kingdom is one such instance. In the United States and Japan, securities laws have limited banks ability to compete with securities firms. Government intervention can inhibit as well as promote competition.

Taxation of financial service firms is also used to achieve policy goals rationalized as above. For example, in the United States thrifts were given tax breaks for investing in home mortgages, which led to thrifts specializing in mortgage lending to take advantage of the break. The tax environment is critical for financial institutions because changes in tax laws grant or remove profits.

The evolution of financial markets is intertwined with regulation and public policy. Ed Kane, a prominent observer of the industry, calls this evolutionary process the "regulatory dialectic" (Kane, 1977) reminiscent of the historical process described by Karl Marx. The dialectic proceeds as follows: An economic crisis or policy problem confronts legislators and regulators who pass laws and write regulations to "solve" the crisis or problem. Restricted by the new laws and regulations, financial institutions seek to avoid the expenses or lost profits caused by the legislative and regulatory solutions to the "crisis" or "problem." They eventually think of ways around the laws and regulations. When a new crisis or new policy objective emerges, new regulation will be required. The whole process is repeated (and repeated).

The revolution in financial services today is due partly to *desegmentation* stemming from *deregulation*. Financial institutions previously prohibited from offering certain services are now allowed to do so. For example, since 1980 thrift institutions in the United States have been able to offer checking accounts to compete with banks. The nature and pace of such regulatory changes are an important risk for financial service firms because the changes affect their ability to compete and earn profits. Part III of this book is a systematic treatment of regulation and taxation. The regulatory environment and changes in regulation are important determinants of business conditions for financial institution managers and are a major determinant of the industry's current and evolving configuration.

3.2 ECONOMIC SECTORS, FINANCIAL MARKETS, AND FINANCIAL FLOWS

Financial firms are a specialized part of the economic system. They are often called "financial intermediaries" because they *intermediate* the flow of savings into final use in investments. As an example, when someone saves money in a savings bank, the savings bank usually lends that money to a home buyer to finance a home purchase. The savings bank intermediates this flow of savings to the user, the home buyer.

To place financial markets and financial firms into perspective, we introduce a conceptual framework, the "flow-of-funds accounts." These accounts are calculated for many countries. We use these statistics for the United States and Japan to give a sense of the relative size and significance of financial markets and financial and nonfinancial firms. More importantly, the conceptual framework provided by the flow-of-funds accounts allows us to have a bird's eye view of all of the complex financial interrelationships in a developed economy. The flow of funds enable us to think strategically about issues facing financial service firms.

Introduction to the Flow-of-Funds Accounts

To track the flow of funds, government statisticians construct balance sheets, called "Sector Balance Sheets," for each of several broadly defined sectors of the economy. In some cases, only partial balance sheets can be calculated. These are called "Sector Statements of Financial Assets and Liabilities." The *flow of funds* represents changes from period to period in these estimated sectoral balance sheets.

Conceptual sectoral balance sheets and flow-of-funds accounts are given in Table 3.1. A sectoral balance sheet as described in the table is an aggregate *portfolio* as that concept is used in economics and finance. Portfolios consist of several *assets*. Assets can be financed in part by *liabilities* resulting in a *leveraged portfolio*. The value or *net worth* of the portfolio to owners of assets is assets minus liabilities.

Changes in sectoral assets and liabilities constitute the flow of funds between sectors. These changes stem from two basic economic factors: (1) portfolio *growth* through savings that increase net worth; and (2) changes in *portfolio balance*, the shifting of holdings of assets and liabilities without an increase in net worth. Changes in portfolio balance are usually reactions to changes in the relative costs or yields on assets and liabilities.

Primary Sectors

A fundamental distinction is made in flow-of-funds accounts between primary and financial sectors. Primary sectors are the basic decision-making units in an economy. Firms and individuals in the primary sectors make aggregate savings, consumption, and investment decisions that allocate real resources in the economy. The flow of funds defines three primary sectors for an economy: households, businesses, and governments, sometimes subdividing these basic sectors. For example, the flow of funds in the government sector in the United States is separated into state and local governments, the Federal government, and the monetary authority (Federal Reserve). The financial sector intermediates the flow of funds between primary sectors.

The household sector is the "primary primary" sector in market-oriented economies. Households are the largest spenders in the economy and own, either directly or indirectly, all businesses. Voting members of households elect govern-

TABLE 3.1 Flow-of-Funds Accounts (Simplified)

Panel A: Conceptual Sectoral Balance Sheet

ASSETS	*LIABILITIES*
Real Assets	
Buildings	
Equipment	
Land	
Financial Assets	**Financial Liabilities**
Deposits	
Credit-market instruments	Credit market instruments
Equities	Equities

Panel B: Flow of Funds Statement

Change in Real Assets
- Buildings (construction or purchase from other sectors)
- Equipment (production and purchase from other sectors)
- Land (purchase from other sectors)

Changes in Financial Assets (acquired from other sectors)
- Deposits
- Credit-Market Instruments
- Equities

Changes in Financial Liabilities
- Credit Market Instruments (newly issued or retired)
- Equities (newly issued or retired)

ments. Households in democratic societies control all the wealth of the economy, both physical and financial, either personally or indirectly through their agents in business and governments. The household "Sector Balance Sheet" for the United States is given in Panel A of Table 3.2 for the period 1982 to 1992. We will discuss it below.

Businesses are institutions, often corporations, set up to undertake large-scale operations beyond the capacity of individual households. The sectoral balance sheet for nonfinancial corporate business in the United States is provided as Panel A in Table 3.3. The flow of funds also is available for other subcategories of businesses such as noncorporate business, but the largest and most complex business activity in the United States is conducted by corporations.

Governments are institutions performing functions that households cannot provide for themselves, like defense and the judicial system. Government balance sheets are not published but Sector Statements of Assets and Liabilities are available. Panel A in Table 3.4 provides the sector statement for state and local governments and Table 3.5 for the Federal government in the United States. These

TABLE 3.2 Household Sector, 1982–1992*

Panel A: Balance Sheet

		1982	*1983*	*1984*	*1985*	*1986*
1	Total assets	12771.9	13848.1	14875.6	16445.1	17925.6
2	Tangible assets	5378.7	5693.8	6181.3	6625.8	7121.8
3	Reproducible assets	3707.0	3888.7	4124.6	4391.7	4757.8
4	Residential structures	2317.3	2421.6	2552.2	2692.5	2902.5
5	Owner-occupied housing	2265.7	2368.3	2496.8	2634.1	2840.6
6	Nonprofit institutions	51.6	53.3	55.5	58.4	61.9
7	Nonprofit plant & equip.	256.0	273.4	290.9	308.1	327.8
8	Consumer durables	1133.7	1193.8	1281.5	1391.1	1527.5
9	Land	1671.7	1805.0	2056.7	2234.0	2364.1
10	Owner-occupied	1512.9	1636.6	1873.8	2038.5	2159.0
11	Nonprofit insittutions	158.8	168.5	182.8	195.5	205.0
12	Total financial assets	7393.3	8154.3	8694.4	9819.4	10803.8
13	Deposits & cr. mkt. instr.	2562.2	2838.1	3208.8	3525.6	3792.1
14	Checkable deposits & curr.	316.1	342.0	358.4	380.2	475.4
15	Small time & savings dep.	1322.5	1532.6	1685.7	1829.6	1945.7
16	Money market fund shares	189.4	158.4	202.4	211.1	250.7
17	Large times deposits	84.8	56.2	108.5	72.1	49.5
18	Credit market instruments	649.4	748.9	853.8	1032.6	1070.9
19	U.S. govt. securities	272.2	321.0	390.0	427.1	386.4
20	Savings bonds	68.3	71.5	74.5	79.8	93.3
21	Other Treasury issues	170.9	213.6	257.7	260.3	223.0
22	Agency issues	33.0	35.9	57.8	87.0	70.1
23	Tax-exempt securities	153.2	192.1	223.6	302.8	304.2
24	Corporate & fgn. bonds	63.6	53.1	50.7	53.1	103.3
25	Mortgages	126.1	127.1	127.8	127.4	141.2
26	Open-market paper	34.3	55.7	61.6	122.1	135.7
27	Mutual fund shares	66.7	98.0	117.7	206.9	356.9
28	Corporate equities	1128.4	1267.8	1264.5	1611.4	1750.7
29	Life insurance reserves	232.8	240.8	246.0	256.7	274.2
30	Pension fund reserves	1279.3	1520.8	1698.3	1991.9	2314.3
31	Equity in noncorp. bus.	2018.6	2065.4	2033.3	2059.3	2121.8
32	Security credit	17.8	20.6	21.6	35.1	44.0
33	Miscellaneous assets	87.4	102.9	104.2	132.5	149.8
34	Total liabilities	1669.6	1846.6	2073.4	2372.9	2694.1
35	Credit market instruments	1600.3	1766.0	1993.3	2271.0	2584.0
36	Home mortgages	1033.7	1130.1	1265.1	1416.2	1659.6
37	Other mortgages	36.4	38.9	41.4	43.8	49.9
38	Tax-exempt debt	29.6	41.0	51.2	81.3	79.1
39	Installment cons. credit	330.4	374.5	449.5	526.2	581.1
40	Other consumer credit	58.3	63.2	69.8	75.3	78.0
41	Bank loans n.e.c.	38.6	41.8	37.0	43.9	44.9
42	Other loans	73.2	76.5	79.4	84.3	89.4
43	Security credit	25.8	34.2	31.8	50.7	57.4
44	Trade credit	27.9	30.3	33.1	36.0	38.7
45	Deferred and unpaid life Insurance premiums	15.5	16.1	15.1	15.2	13.9
46	Net worth	11102.4	12001.5	12802.2	14072.3	15231.6

1987	*1988*	*1989*	*1990*	*1991*	*1992*
19060.4	20482.7	22535.7	22731.5	24688.9	25695.8
7677.7	8126.4	8731.9	8747.4	9255.0	9515.1
5157.5	5408.7	5773.7	6090.2	6351.2	6631.7
3148.1	3223.4	3440.5	3633.0	3785.5	3974.3
3081.8	3156.5	3370.3	3560.1	3710.9	3898.0
66.3	66.9	70.2	72.9	74.5	76.2
349.9	376.9	403.6	426.6	443.1	466.5
1659.5	1808.4	1929.6	2030.7	2122.7	2191.0
2520.2	2717.6	2958.2	2657.2	2903.8	2883.3
2308.7	2486.6	2711.6	2444.9	2757.0	2799.8
211.4	231.0	246.6	212.2	146.8	83.5
11382.7	12356.3	13803.7	13984.1	15433.8	16180.7
4138.3	4533.5	4959.0	5218.7	5099.4	5142.9
481.4	479.4	493.6	516.0	559.7	672.0
2005.3	2137.2	2225.4	2279.0	2283.1	2215.1
278.8	302.4	388.3	432.5	461.0	461.8
99.1	129.4	141.5	108.9	61.0	2.1
1273.6	1485.1	1710.1	1882.3	1734.7	1791.9
454.2	584.0	680.3	770.9	658.0	650.0
101.1	109.6	117.7	126.2	138.1	157.3
226.4	271.1	274.8	314.6	217.0	186.4
126.7	203.3	287.8	330.1	302.9	306.3
397.3	464.8	527.2	557.5	579.3	599.8
118.4	81.0	116.2	150.9	149.7	130.8
164.9	181.8	213.1	214.8	245.0	302.0
138.8	173.5	173.4	188.2	102.8	109.4
406.3	418.0	491.6	514.5	679.7	897.5
1600.3	1718.9	2004.1	1841.5	2349.1	2535.3
300.3	325.5	354.3	380.0	402.0	434.0
2470.5	2755.0	3210.5	3303.0	4223.4	4585.8
2253.1	2373.1	2524.9	2449.4	2367.8	2263.6
39.1	40.9	53.2	62.4	87.0	79.7
174.9	191.3	206.2	214.6	223.4	242.0
2960.7	3283.6	3618.5	3892.2	4059.7	4281.4
2861.3	3177.3	3508.2	3780.6	3925.5	4160.6
1875.0	2109.4	2360.5	2598.7	2722.6	2913.4
82.2	109.2	122.6	133.5	144.1	153.8
78.2	79.5	81.9	86.0	94.8	101.0
618.5	673.3	728.9	748.5	742.1	741.4
73.5	68.8	62.9	60.7	54.7	57.8
41.6	40.5	52.8	43.3	47.3	46.6
92.4	96.5	98.6	109.8	119.9	126.6
41.8	43.5	42.5	38.8	55.1	56.7
42.5	47.2	51.4	56.3	61.0	64.4
15.1	15.5	16.4	16.5	18.2	19.6
16099.7	17199.1	18917.2	18839.5	20629.1	21414.4

*Data are in billions of dollars.
SOURCE: Flow of Funds,
Board of Governors of the Federal Reserve System,
Washington, D.C. 20551.

TABLE 3.2 (continued)

Panel B: Flows

		1982	*1983*	*1984*	*1985*	*1986*
9	= Gross saving	550.8	571.0	681.2	697.1	742.0
10	Gross investment	547.2	610.2	697.2	700.0	802.1
11	Capital expend. net of sales	344.4	428.5	497.2	537.2	603.8
12	Residential construction	88.8	132.2	156.9	161.4	189.6
13	Consumer durable goods	236.5	275.0	317.9	353.0	389.6
14	Nonprofit plant and equip.	19.2	21.3	22.4	22.9	24.7
15	Net financial investment	202.8	181.7	200.0	162.8	198.2
16	Net acq. of financial assets	295.1	378.7	432.1	469.5	525.8
17	Dep. & cr. mkt. instr.	228.9	271.8	379.1	328.5	280.2
18	Deposits	173.1	176.2	266.0	138.0	232.4
19	Checkable dep. & curr.	21.1	25.8	16.5	21.8	95.1
20	Small time & svgs. dep.	134.3	210.1	153.2	143.9	120.4
21	Large time deposits	–15.1	–28.6	52.2	–36.4	–22.7
22	Money mkt. fund shares	32.8	–31.1	44.0	8.7	39.6
23	Credit mkt. instruments	55.8	95.5	113.1	190.5	47.8
24	U.S. govt. securities	34.1	46.6	77.6	46.6	–35.1
25	Tax-exempt securities	31.8	38.9	31.6	79.2	0.4
26	Corporate & fgn. bonds	–4.0	–9.0	–3.6	0.9	50.2
27	Mortgages	9.7	0.7	1.5	3.4	18.6
28	Open-market paper	–15.9	18.3	6.0	60.5	13.6
29	Mutual fund shares	7.6	26.1	21.9	73.5	141.5
30	Corporate equities	–23.2	–30.1	–71.3	–126.5	–136.3
31	Life insurance reserves	7.2	8.0	5.2	10.7	17.5
32	Pension fund reserves	146.3	172.7	177.8	207.2	231.5
33	Net inv. in noncorp. bus.	–81.9	–87.8	–82.9	–65.8	–34.7
34	Security credit	3.1	2.7	1.0	13.5	9.0
35	Miscellaneous assets	7.1	15.5	1.3	28.3	17.2
36	Net increase in liabilities	92.3	197.0	232.1	306.7	327.6
37	Credit market instruments	85.9	185.7	232.7	284.9	319.4
38	Home mortgages	48.0	116.4	135.6	153.9	245.0
39	Installment cons. credit	14.9	44.1	75.0	76.8	54.9
40	Other consumer credit	1.6	4.8	6.6	5.5	2.7
41	Tax-exempt debt	8.5	11.4	10.2	30.2	–2.2
42	Other mortgages	2.6	2.5	2.5	2.4	6.1
43	Bank loans n.?.c.	2.9	3.2	–.2	6.9	6.3
44	Other loans	7.4	3.3	2.9	9.3	6.6
45	Security credit	2.8	8.4	–2.3	18.9	6.7
46	Trade debt	2.8	2.4	2.8	2.8	2.8
47	Miscellaneous	0.8	0.6	–1.0	0.1	–1.3
48	Discrepancy	3.5	–39.2	–16.0	–2.9	–60.0

1987	*1988*	*1989*	*1990*	*1991*	*1992*
712.0	776.7	817.7	843.5	849.6	915.5
731.7	803.1	917.8	910.3	884.4	960.4
630.4	675.2	699.4	691.5	655.6	710.7
198.3	206.6	205.6	190.7	172.2	191.1
403.7	437.1	459.4	464.3	446.1	480.3
28.4	31.5	34.4	36.5	37.4	39.3
101.3	127.9	218.4	218.8	228.8	249.7
386.4	453.4	528.0	474.3	394.2	471.3
329.6	367.1	380.4	259.9	–4.6	52.0
148.9	168.2	200.9	87.6	20.2	–13.8
4.3	–.8	14.9	22.4	53.3	112.7
66.8	115.3	88.8	53.6	10.0	–68.0
49.6	30.3	11.2	–32.6	–71.7	–59.2
28.1	23.5	85.9	44.2	28.6	0.7
180.7	198.9	179.5	172.3	–24.8	65.8
62.1	123.3	103.5	101.7	–70.4	–8.0
93.1	54.5	62.4	30.3	21.9	20.5
2.5	–35.6	–5.8	6.5	27.8	–10.3
21.0	25.2	19.5	21.3	18.2	57.0
2.0	31.6	–.1	12.4	–22.2	6.7
71.8	2.3	41.9	50.7	129.2	194.3
–103.9	–122.0	–139.1	–27.2	–57.2	–32.9
26.0	25.3	28.8	25.7	24.5	32.0
104.5	193.6	221.4	186.8	267.7	227.3
–60.9	–31.2	–32.5	–39.3	–.8	–10.6
–5.8	1.8	12.3	9.2	24.6	–7.4
25.1	16.4	14.9	8.4	10.8	16.6
285.1	325.5	309.6	255.5	165.4	221.6
296.4	318.6	305.6	254.2	144.9	215.1
227.9	234.8	238.5	212.9	123.9	190.8
37.4	54.8	41.6	19.6	–6.5	–.7
–4.5	–4.7	0.1	–2.1	–6.1	3.1
–1.0	1.3	2.5	4.1	8.8	6.2
32.3	27.0	13.4	10.9	10.6	9.7
–2.7	–1.1	2.5	–2.4	4.1	–.7
6.9	6.5	7.1	11.2	10.1	6.7
–16.3	1.7	–1.0	–3.7	16.3	1.6
3.8	4.7	4.2	4.9	2.5	3.4
1.2	0.4	0.8	0.1	1.7	1.4
–19.7	–26.5	–100.0	–66.8	–34.9	–45.0

*Data are in billions of dollars.
SOURCE: Flow of Funds,
Board of Governors of the Federal Reserve System,
Washington, D.C. 20551.

TABLE 3.3 Nonfinancial Corporate Business Sector, 1982–1992*

Panel A: Balance Sheet

		1982	*1983*	*1984*	*1985*	*1986*	*1987*
1	Total assets	5182.6	5402.6	5722.1	6000.0	6313.1	6663.0
2	Tangible assets (current cost)	3860.4	3979.7	4215.7	4399.3	4547.3	4751.4
3	Reproducible assets	3239.9	3320.3	3513.7	3658.5	3772.8	3938.7
4	Residential structures	33.7	34.5	35.5	36.8	38.4	40.3
5	Nonres. plant & equipment	2526.9	2595.7	2717.7	2853.6	2975.4	3080.6
6	Inventories	679.4	690.0	760.5	768.1	758.9	817.7
7	Land	620.4	659.4	701.9	740.8	774.5	812.7
8	Total financial assets	1322.2	1422.9	1506.5	1600.7	1765.9	1911.6
9	Liquid assets	266.8	301.9	326.0	355.3	416.1	440.8
10	Checkable dep. & currency	53.3	61.9	74.6	94.0	112.8	120.4
11	Time deposits	59.0	70.6	74.4	80.3	87.5	91.6
12	Money market fund shares	19.0	11.2	16.1	14.5	18.1	18.9
13	Security RPs	42.1	48.4	48.8	58.3	70.5	71.3
14	Foreign deposits	22.6	25.7	20.6	18.8	24.8	24.3
15	U.S. government securities	30.5	38.5	42.7	39.0	53.5	57.0
16	Tax-exempt securities	3.5	4.2	4.1	4.9	8.0	10.5
17	Open-market paper	36.7	41.4	44.8	45.3	40.9	46.6
18	Consumer credit	26.3	30.2	32.9	36.7	40.9	47.5
19	Mutual fund shares	3.1	4.5	7.2	10.8	15.7	12.8
20	Trade credit	491.1	542.8	590.3	629.9	655.2	700.9
21	Miscellaneous assets	534.9	543.5	550.1	568.1	638.0	709.7
22	Foreign direct invest. (1)	393.8	382.0	373.9	394.0	419.6	479.1
23	Insurance receivables	50.0	53.5	58.6	62.8	81.6	92.4
24	Equity in spons. agencies	0.7	0.7	0.7	0.8	0.9	1.3
25	Other	90.4	107.3	116.9	110.5	135.8	136.9
26	Total liabilities	1637.1	1766.7	2007.6	2208.1	2466.0	2741.4
27	Credit market debt	1029.0	1111.9	1292.6	1439.8	1650.0	1827.8
28	Tax-exempt debt	74.5	83.9	104.4	127.0	117.1	116.2
29	Corporate bonds	407.0	423.0	469.1	543.2	670.4	749.1
30	Mortgages	93.7	112.8	121.3	109.8	141.6	200.8
31	Home mortgages	11.5	12.0	12.6	13.3	14.0	14.7
32	Multifamily	13.3	13.8	14.4	15.0	15.8	16.5
33	Commercial	69.0	87.1	94.3	81.5	111.9	169.7
34	Bank loans n.e.c.	318.5	340.9	391.1	424.1	473.7	482.4
35	Loans from foreign	15.6	18.3	31.3	32.9	40.8	42.7
36	Commercial paper	37.6	36.8	58.5	72.2	62.9	73.8
37	Acceptance liab. to banks	20.7	27.6	30.4	28.3	28.1	32.6
38	Nonbank finance loans	50.5	58.2	74.8	88.1	100.6	118.8
39	U.S. government loans	10.9	10.4	11.6	14.2	14.8	11.5
40	Taxes payable	35.6	38.6	42.2	39.0	42.8	47.9
41	Trade debt	381.3	418.3	452.0	486.0	499.7	539.6
42	Miscellaneous liabilities	191.3	197.8	220.9	243.3	273.5	326.2
43	Foreign direct inv. in US	153.3	158.3	179.2	195.9	222.8	275.4
44	Pen. fund contr. payable	38.0	39.5	41.7	47.3	50.8	50.8
45	Net worth	3545.4	3635.9	3714.5	3791.9	3847.1	3921.6

1988	*1989*	*1990*	*1991*	*1992*
7130.6	7524.9	7644.5	7423.2	7389.9
5056.6	5335.0	5333.8	5052.7	4858.9
4183.2	4397.6	4581.4	4627.1	4693.2
39.9	41.7	42.0	42.1	41.7
3260.2	3419.9	3577.8	3643.0	3695.7
883.1	936.0	961.6	942.0	955.8
873.3	937.4	752.4	425.5	165.7
2074.0	2189.9	2310.7	2370.5	2531.1
464.7	470.4	487.9	532.3	549.2
137.4	133.6	131.7	139.0	151.7
105.6	103.4	99.3	103.0	95.5
15.6	16.2	26.3	31.5	36.2
79.5	75.5	73.6	69.7	77.4
13.1	17.6	29.5	39.5	33.0
54.3	60.4	64.3	84.8	91.6
12.0	11.4	9.5	11.3	11.5
47.0	52.4	53.8	53.4	52.4
54.0	56.2	59.4	58.4	60.9
10.6	11.7	9.7	15.4	17.7
793.1	837.6	848.9	837.5	889.9
751.6	814.0	904.7	926.9	1013.4
486.9	514.9	576.7	596.3	625.8
102.5	117.2	131.5	145.5	159.2
1.3	1.3	1.3	1.8	1.9
160.8	180.7	195.2	183.3	226.6
3047.1	3296.1	3446.0	3504.3	3590.2
2016.9	2195.3	2273.4	2277.1	2330.6
116.4	115.5	115.2	114.0	112.9
852.2	926.1	973.2	1051.9	1118.3
207.1	228.9	225.3	220.1	209.2
15.4	16.0	16.6	17.0	17.6
17.1	17.8	18.3	18.8	19.4
174.6	195.1	190.4	184.3	172.2
519.3	553.5	555.4	530.5	518.8
53.8	66.6	88.0	71.5	76.8
85.7	107.1	116.9	98.5	108.3
32.6	35.8	29.2	23.3	20.4
139.9	152.2	161.6	159.3	158.1
9.9	9.6	8.8	7.9	7.9
49.6	46.5	45.5	35.5	39.4
598.7	629.3	669.6	680.3	705.2
381.8	425.1	457.6	511.4	515.1
327.7	367.5	399.6	416.4	414.5
54.1	57.6	58.0	94.9	100.5
4083.5	4228.8	4198.5	3918.9	3799.7

*Data are in billions of dollars.
SOURCE: Flow of Funds,
Board of Governors of the Federal Reserve System,
Washington, D.C. 20551.

TABLE 3.3 (*continued*)

Panel B: Flows

		1982	1983	1984	1985	1986
11	Gross investment	263.8	289.5	345.5	344.0	323.2
12	Capital expenditures	285.3	300.1	398.5	374.9	351.9
13	Fixed investment	298.2	282.9	328.3	352.5	335.1
14	Residential construction	1.0	1.3	1.5	1.7	1.8
15	Plant and equipment	297.2	281.6	326.8	350.9	333.3
16	Inventory change - IVA	–20.7	9.4	62.3	18.0	9.6
17	Mineral rts. from U.S. govt.	7.8	7.8	7.9	4.4	7.2
18	Net financial investment	–21.5	–10.6	–53.0	–30.9	–28.8
19	Net acq. of financial assets	47.6	120.4	103.8	83.0	150.4
20	Liquid assets	46.3	35.1	24.1	29.3	60.8
21	Checkable dep. and curr.	5.9	8.7	12.7	19.4	18.8
22	Time deposits	11.3	11.6	3.7	5.9	7.2
23	Money mkt. fund shares	0.6	–7.9	4.9	–1.5	3.6
24	Security RPs	8.7	6.2	0.5	9.5	12.2
25	Foreign deposits	–.4	3.1	–5.1	–1.7	5.9
26	U.S govt. securities	10.3	8.0	4.2	–3.6	14.5
27	Tax-exempt securities	0.1	0.7	–.1	0.8	3.1
28	Commercial paper	9.9	4.7	3.4	0.3	–4.4
29	Consumer credit	0.4	3.9	2.6	3.8	4.2
30	Mutual fund shares	1.1	1.2	2.8	3.7	3.8
31	Trade credit	–15.5	51.7	47.5	39.6	23.4
32	Miscellaneous assets	15.2	28.5	26.7	6.6	56.3
33	Foreign dir. invest.	10.8	8.2	12.0	8.7	12.1
34	Insurance receivables	2.7	3.5	5.1	4.2	18.8
35	Equity in sponsored ags.	0.1	–	–	0.1	0.1
36	Other	1.7	16.9	9.6	–6.4	25.4
37	Net increase in liabilities	69.1	131.0	156.8	113.9	179.2
38	Net funds raised in mkts.	54.0	80.1	98.0	58.5	129.8
39	Net new equity issues	1.9	20.0	–79.0	–84.5	–85.0
40	Debt instruments	52.1	60.1	177.0	143.0	214.8
41	Tax-exempt debt	15.1	9.4	20.5	22.6	–9.9
42	Corporate bonds	18.7	16.0	46.1	74.2	127.1
43	Mortgages	–36.4	–.8	4.9	–10.4	32.3
44	Bank loans n.e.c.	57.2	19.4	50.2	32.0	49.6
45	Commercial paper	–6.1	–.8	21.7	14.6	–9.3
46	Other loans	3.6	16.9	33.6	10.1	24.9
47	Savings&loan assns.	0.1	1.2	4.3	2.8	3.3
48	Finance companies	0.5	6.5	12.2	10.5	9.2
49	U.S. government	1.3	–.5	1.2	–2.6	1.5
50	Accept. liab. to banks	–.8	7.0	2.8	–2.1	–.2
51	Foreign	2.5	2.7	13.0	1.5	11.1
52	SCO issuers	–	–	–	–	–
53	Taxes payable	–4.3	3.1	3.5	–3.2	3.8
54	Trade debt	4.9	37.0	33.7	34.0	13.7
55	Miscellaneous liabilities	14.5	10.9	21.6	24.5	31.9
56	Fgn. dir. invest. in US	9.5	9.5	19.3	18.8	28.5
57	Pen. fund contr. payable	5.0	1.4	2.2	5.7	3.4
58	Discrepancy	–16.3	2.8	–9.2	7.9	13.5

1987	*1988*	*1989*	*1990*	*1991*	*1992*
308.7	369.8	379.9	378.5	394.8	433.9
365.1	394.4	406.0	395.1	363.9	385.3
331.0	365.0	373.4	388.5	370.9	380.3
1.8	1.6	1.6	1.4	1.1	1.5
329.2	363.3	371.7	387.1	369.8	378.8
31.1	26.2	30.3	3.1	–9.8	2.4
2.9	3.3	2.4	3.5	2.8	2.6
–56.4	–24.6	–26.1	–16.6	30.9	48.6
108.6	159.8	106.2	87.3	61.6	164.2
24.7	23.9	5.7	17.6	44.3	17.0
9.6	17.0	–3.8	–1.9	7.3	12.7
4.1	14.0	–2.2	–4.1	3.7	–7.5
0.8	–3.3	0.5	10.2	5.2	4.6
0.8	8.2	–4.1	–1.9	–3.8	7.6
–2.5	–11.2	4.4	12.0	10.0	–6.5
3.6	–2.7	6.0	3.9	20.5	6.8
2.6	1.5	–.6	–2.0	1.8	0.2
5.7	0.4	5.4	1.5	–.4	–1.0
6.6	6.5	2.1	3.2	–1.0	2.4
–2.7	–2.7	–1.6	–1.3	2.7	0.9
45.6	68.3	44.5	11.3	–11.4	52.4
34.1	63.8	55.5	56.5	26.9	91.6
21.9	5.8	21.0	27.7	24.3	34.6
10.7	10.2	14.6	14.3	14.1	13.6
0.4	–	–	–	0.5	–
1.1	47.9	19.9	14.5	–11.9	43.4
164.8	184.4	132.3	103.9	30.8	115.6
67.6	69.3	49.4	23.4	22.0	80.3
–75.5	–129.5	–124.2	–63.0	18.3	26.8
143.1	198.8	173.6	86.4	3.7	53.5
–.9	0.2	–.9	–.3	–1.2	–1.1
78.8	103.1	73.8	47.1	78.8	66.3
30.4	19.5	17.0	4.8	–5.2	–11.0
8.6	36.9	34.2	1.8	–24.9	–11.6
1.6	11.9	21.4	9.7	–18.4	9.8
24.7	27.2	28.0	23.3	–25.5	1.1
–.1	1.3	–1.1	–4.0	–3.5	–4.5
18.3	15.8	13.1	11.6	–.4	2.0
0.1	–1.0	–.4	–.8	–.8	–.1
4.4	–	3.2	–6.6	–5.9	–2.9
1.9	11.1	12.8	21.4	–16.5	5.2
–	–	0.3	1.7	1.7	1.4
5.1	1.7	–3.1	–1.8	–10.0	3.8
39.9	59.1	30.5	40.3	10.7	24.9
52.2	54.2	55.4	41.1	8.0	6.6
52.2	50.9	51.9	40.7	3.6	1.0
?	3.3	3.5	0.4	6.4	5.6
67.3	34.4	20.0	28.0	21.8	19.4

*Data are in billions of dollars.
SOURCE: Flow of Funds,
Board of Governors of the Federal Reserve System,
Washington, D.C. 20551.

TABLE 3.4 State and Local Governments Sector, 1982–1992*

Panel A: Outstanding Levels

		1982	1983	1984	1985	1986	1987	1988	1989	1990	1991	1992
1	Total financial assets	281.6	323.2	365.3	516.0	584.6	651.8	697.3	728.2	768.5	784.6	798.8
2	Checkable dep. and currency	9.4	8.7	13.8	14.8	18.3	19.1	21.2	20.6	19.6	24.7	26.1
3	Time deposits	64.9	58.6	58.9	65.9	61.3	66.6	63.0	62.3	61.2	53.7	48.0
4	Security RPs	15.6	32.4	41.8	50.0	58.0	78.7	103.4	114.3	89.1	74.2	88.5
5	Credit market instruments	172.4	201.3	227.9	358.3	417.1	457.2	475.8	493.7	561.5	595.1	598.8
6	U.S. government securities	118.7	139.2	154.4	276.2	323.6	354.5	367.5	374.6	437.3	466.8	465.2
7	Treasury issues	81.7	104.1	120.4	220.7	251.6	305.5	343.3	359.4	363.1	365.3	361.5
8	Agency issues	37.0	35.1	34.0	55.5	72.0	48.9	24.2	15.2	74.2	101.5	103.4
9	Tax-exempt securities	7.4	8.0	9.0	7.8	7.6	8.0	9.7	11.7	14.2	14.8	11.4
10	Mortgages	46.3	54.2	64.4	74.2	86.0	94.7	98.6	107.4	110.0	113.5	113.4
11	Taxes receivable	19.3	22.1	23.1	27.0	29.8	30.3	33.9	37.4	37.1	37.8	38.2
12	Total liabilities	377.2	412.6	449.3	584.4	645.2	730.2	781.4	847.2	985.1	957.8	1017.4
13	Credit market instruments	357.1	391.7	427.4	561.4	620.6	703.6	752.5	815.7	870.5	932.8	992.2
14	Tax-exempt securities	347.3	380.8	408.8	534.6	593.4	678.7	743.5	806.9	860.9	922.8	982.3
15	Short-term	22.7	21.3	17.6	18.9	23.1	29.3	39.2	38.8	43.6	52.4	56.2
16	Other	324.5	359.6	391.2	515.7	570.3	649.4	704.4	768.1	813.3	870.4	926.1
17	U.S. government loans	9.8	10.9	18.6	26.8	27.3	24.9	9.0	8.8	9.4	10.0	9.9
18	Trade debt	20.1	20.9	21.9	23.0	24.6	26.6	28.8	31.5	34.4	24.9	25.2

*Data are in billions of dollars.

SOURCE: Flow of Funds, Board of Governors of the Federal Reserve System, Washington, D.C. 20551.

Panel B: Flows

		1982	1983	1984	1985	1986	1987	1988	1989	1990	1991	1992
10	= Gross saving	–5.1	1.1	12.4	3.0	–3.3	–14.6	–26.6	–27.3	–35.9	–39.6	–42.9
11	Net financial investment	–3.3	6.2	5.4	15.6	7.7	–17.6	–5.7	–34.9	–43.7	–39.9	–46.5
12	Net acq. of financial assets	28.0	42.1	150.6	68.6	67.3	45.4	31.0	7.7	–1.1	1.9	
13	Checkable dep. and curr.	–1.6	–.7	5.0	1.1	3.5	0.8	2.0	–.6	–1.0	5.1	1.4
14	Time deposits	3.8	–6.3	0.2	7.0	–4.6	1.5	–3.5	–.8	–1.1	–7.5	–3.8
15	Security RPs	2.4	16.9	9.4	8.2	8.0	20.7	24.7	10.9	–16.2	–14.9	14.4
16	Credit market instruments	21.8	28.9	26.5	130.4	58.9	43.9	18.6	17.9	26.2	16.3	–11.5
17	U.S. govt. securities	16.3	20.5	15.2	121.8	47.3	34.7	13.0	7.1	18.3	12.3	–12.6
18	Treasury issues	9.4	22.4	16.3	100.3	30.9	54.0	37.7	16.1	3.7	2.2	–3.8
19	Agency issues	6.9	–1.9	–1.1	21.5	16.5	–19.3	–24.7	–9.0	14.6	10.1	–8.9
20	Tax-exempt securities	0.2	0.6	1.1	–1.2	–.3	0.5	1.6	2.0	2.5	0.5	–3.4
21	Mortgages	5.2	7.9	10.2	9.8	11.8	8.7	4.0	8.8	5.3	3.4	4.5
22	Taxes receivable	1.5	2.8	1.0	4.0	2.7	0.5	3.6	3.5	–.3	–	1.4
23	Net increase in liabilities	31.3	35.4	36.7	135.1	60.8	84.9	51.2	65.9	51.4	38.8	48.4
24	Credit market borrowing	30.4	34.6	35.7	134.0	59.2	83.0	48.9	63.2	48.3	38.5	48.1
25	Tax-exempt securities	29.4	33.5	28.0	125.8	57.8	85.3	52.2	63.4	47.4	38.2	48.2
26	Short-term	6.7	–1.5	–3.7	1.3	4.2	6.2	9.9	–.3	6.7	6.8	3.8
27	Other	22.7	35.0	31.6	124.5	53.6	79.1	42.4	63.7	40.7	31.3	44.4
28	U.S. government loans	1.0	1.1	7.7	8.2	1.4	–2.4	–3.3	–.2	0.9	0.4	–.1
29	Trade debt	0.9	0.8	1.0	1.1	1.6	2.0	2.2	2.7	3.1	0.3	0.3
30	Discrepancy	–1.8	–5.1	6.9	–12.6	–11.0	3.0	–20.8	7.6	7.8	0.3	3.7

(1) Employee retirement funds are included in the insurance sector.

*Data are in billions of dollars.

SOURCE: Flow of Funds, Board of Governors of the Federal Reserve System, Washington, D.C. 20551.

TABLE 3.5 Federal Government Sector, 1982–1992*

Panel A: Outstanding Levels

		1982	1983	1984	1985	1986	1987	1988	1989	1990	1991	1992
1	Total financial assets	281.1	290.7	327.7	371.6	385.4	370.5	360.4	368.3	448.8	498.6	468.4
2	Gold. SDRs & off. fgn. exch.	17.1	19.0	20.3	25.1	28.0	29.1	27.7	31.7	39.7	39.1	38.8
3	Checkable dep. and currency	24.5	16.6	21.8	34.0	32.8	21.4	32.1	26.1	25.4	50.9	31.7
4	Time deposits	1.1	0.7	1.2	1.2	1.4	1.7	1.4	1.3	1.4	1.6	0.9
5	Credit market instruments	203.6	213.2	230.1	248.6	255.2	239.9	213.2	205.1	239.1	247.0	235.1
6	Fed. agency securities	–	–	–	–	–	–	–	–	–	–	–
7	Mortgages	49.4	50.6	51.5	53.3	54.4	49.1	48.0	47.3	82.9	98.3	86.4
8	Other loans	154.2	162.6	178.7	195.3	200.8	190.8	165.2	157.8	156.3	148.7	148.7
9	To foreign	62.3	66.6	70.0	71.3	72.7	70.3	65.2	62.8	59.4	54.0	54.1
10	To others	91.9	96.1	108.7	124.0	128.1	120.5	100.0	95.0	96.8	94.7	94.6
11	Taxes receivable	–	2.1	7.9	11.3	18.4	19.3	24.5	23.8	22.5	16.4	9.9
12	Trade credit	22.4	26.2	31.3	35.0	32.6	41.0	41.1	44.5	42.8	37.8	30.7
13	Miscellaneous	12.4	13.1	15.0	16.4	16.9	18.3	20.4	35.8	69.9	105.9	121.2

Panel A: Outstanding Levels (*continued*)

		1982	1983	1984	1985	1986	1987	1988	1989	1990	1991	1992
14	Total liabilities	1129.5	1332.3	1551.5	1801.4	2049.1	2216.2	2398.8	2581.5	2846.8	3145.1	3472.1
15	Treasury curr. & SDR ctfs.	16.5	16.9	17.5	18.0	18.8	19.2	19.8	23.8	26.3	26.3	24.5
16	Credit market instruments	981.8	1167.0	1364.2	1589.9	1805.9	1949.8	2104.9	2251.2	2498.1	2776.4	3080.3
17	Savings bonds	68.3	71.5	74.5	79.8	93.3	101.1	109.6	117.7	126.2	138.1	157.3
18	Other Treasury issues	909.8	1092.0	1286.3	1506.8	1708.9	1843.5	1972.7	2109.3	2339.6	2619.7	2904.3
19	Budget agency issues	2.2	2.1	2.1	2.0	2.4	4.3	22.6	24.2	32.4	18.6	18.8
20	Loan participations	1.2	1.2	1.2	1.2	1.2	0.9	–	–	–	–	–
21	Residential mortgages	.3	0.2	0.1	0.1	–	–	–	–	52.3	47.5	45.3
22	Trade debt	23.7	26.7	29.9	34.6	44.4	46.8	49.1	58.3	11.8	11.9	11.5
23	Life insurance reserves	9.5	9.7	9.9	10.2	10.5	10.8	11.1	11.5	250.5	276.0	303.5
24	Retirement fund reserves	97.9	112.0	130.0	148.8	169.6	188.4	208.1	228.9	7.7	7.0	6.9
25	Miscellaneous	–	–	–	–	–	1.2	5.8	7.8	25		

*Data are in billions of dollars.
SOURCE: Flow of Funds, Board of Governors of the Federal Reserve System, Washington, D.C. 20551.

Panel B: Flows

		1982	1983	1984	1985	1986	1987	1988	1989	1990	1991	1992
10	Net surplus, NIPA basis	−135.5	−180.1	−166.8	−181.4	−201.1	−151.8	−136.6	−122.3	−166.2	−210.4	−295.2
11	− Insurance credits to HH	11.9	14.2	18.2	19.1	21.1	19.2	20.0	21.2	22.0	25.6	27.0
12	+ Mineral rights sales	7.8	7.8	7.9	4.4	7.2	2.9	3.3	2.4	3.5	2.8	2.6
13	= Gross saving	−139.7	−186.6	−177.1	−196.1	−215.0	−168.1	−153.3	−141.0	−184.7	−233.3	−319.7
14	Net financial investment	−153.4	−191.3	−191.5	−216.8	−243.3	−169.8	−190.4	−186.6	−182.7	−262.4	−361.2
15	Net acq. of financial assets	23.5	13.6	32.6	33.7	7.5	−13.2	−2.9	10.3	65.3	51.0	−31.0
16	Gold. SDRs & fgn. exch.	4.4	2.9	2.6	1.9	−.7	−5.4	1.4	12.7	0.8	−3.0	−4.0
17	Checkable dep. & currency	6.4	−8.3	5.3	13.0	0.4	−8.1	9.0	−14.2	4.8	27.4	−16.3
18	Time deposits	0.5	−.5	0.5	–	0.2	0.2	−.2	−.1	0.1	0.1	−.7
19	Credit market instruments	15.9	9.7	17.1	17.8	9.7	−7.9	−10.6	−3.1	33.7	10.0	−12.4
20	Fed. agency securities	–	–	–	–	–	–	–	–	–	–	–
21	Mortgages	2.4	1.2	0.5	1.8	0.5	−5.3	−1.1	−.8	35.6	15.4	−11.9
22	Other loans	13.6	8.4	16.6	15.9	9.2	−2.6	−9.6	−2.3	−1.9	−5.4	−.5
23	Taxes receivable	−10.2	5.2	0.6	−4.1	−.2	−1.8	−4.7	−3.8	−6.6	−14.6	−6.5
24	Trade credit	4.8	3.8	5.1	3.7	−2.3	8.3	0.2	3.4	−1.8	−5.0	−6.5
25	Miscellaneous	1.6	0.7	1.5	1.4	0.5	1.3	2.1	15.4	34.2	36.1	15.5
26	Net increase in liabilities	177.0	204.9	224.1	250.5	250.8	156.6	187.5	196.9	248.0	313.4	330.2
27	Treasury curr. & SDR ctfs.	1.7	0.5	0.6	0.5	0.8	0.5	0.5	4.1	2.5	–	−1.8
28	Credit market instruments	161.3	185.2	197.2	225.7	216.0	143.9	155.1	146.4	246.9	278.2	304.0
29	Savings bonds	0.2	3.1	3.0	5.3	13.6	7.8	8.5	8.2	8.5	11.9	19.1
30	Other Treasury issues	162.0	182.2	194.3	220.5	202.1	134.6	129.2	136.6	230.3	280.1	284.6
31	Agency issues and mtgs.	−.9	−.1	−.2	−.1	0.4	1.5	17.4	1.6	8.2	−13.8	0.2
32	Life & retirement reserves	11.9	14.2	18.2	19.1	21.1	19.2	20.0	21.2	22.0	25.6	27.0
33	Trade debt	1.9	3.0	3.3	4.6	9.8	2.4	2.3	9.2	−6.3	−4.7	1.1
34	Miscellaneous	0.2	2.0	4.9	0.6	3.2	−9.4	9.6	16.2	−17.1	14.3	−.1
35	Discrepancy	13.8	4.7	14.4	20.7	28.3	1.8	37.1	45.6	−2.0	29.2	41.5

*Data are in billions of dollars.

SOURCE: Flow of Funds, Board of Governors of the Federal Reserve System, Washington, D.C. 20551.

sectoral statements show the borrowing of governments to finance spending not financed by taxes.

Flow-of-funds accounts lump all foreign activity into a "foreign" sector. Conceptually, the primary sectors in every country in the world can be classified into the same four categories: household, business, government, and foreign. There is a German household sector, a Japanese business sector, an Indian government sector, and so forth. Data availability varies from country to country but the conceptual framework of flow-of-funds accounts applies everywhere. The Japanese household sector statement of assets and liabilities is provided in Table 3.6 and Japanese business in Table 3.7.

The foreign sector is particularly important with the globalization of the world economy. Increasing trade and capital movements mean that consumers and investors around the world make their decisions unaffected by international boundaries. They buy goods and assets wherever the prices are most attractive. If savers wish to diversify their portfolios to include foreign assets, as the Japanese have done in the last ten years, they must earn the foreign funds necessary to pay for those assets. Japan's enormous trade surplus with the United States, for example, is simply the other side of the Japanese savers' desire to diversify their savings to include U.S. assets.

Real versus Financial Assets

The flow of funds makes a second fundamental distinction in conceptual balance sheets by distinguishing *real assets* and *financial assets.* Real or tangible assets represent investment goods like cars, refrigerators, houses, factories, machines, and airplanes. Line 2 of the household balance sheet in Panel A of Table 3.2 shows real assets for the U.S. household sector of $9.5 trillion dollars in 1992. Breakdowns of those assets show that $6.8 trillion of the household sector's tangible assets (about two-thirds) are housing related (residential structures of $4 trillion in line 4 and land of $2.8 trillion in line 10). Financial assets represent claims on other sectors. For example, the household sector holds $16.2 trillion in the form of financial assets (line 12). Approximately $2.9 trillion or 18 percent of the household sector's financial assets are deposits (lines 14 and 15).

The Japanese personal sector can be compared to the U.S. household sector by using the sector statements reported by the Bank of Japan (in 100 million yen) in Table 3.6. The personal sector in Japan held 530 trillion yen (approximately $4.2 trillion, using 126.78 yen to the dollar as reported by the Federal Reserve for 1992) in deposits (lines C and D) out of total financial assets of 1,017 trillion yen (line g) (about $8 trillion) in 1992. In Japan deposits account for more than 50 percent of personal financial assets, a higher dollar equivalent and percentage of financial assets than held by U.S. households. If the United States leads other countries in financial market developments as some believe, the Japanese personal sector may hold fewer deposits in the future.

Financial claims on other sectors represent liabilities for the sector receiving the funds. Household assets in the form of municipal bonds issued by state and local governments in 1992 are shown on line 23 of Table 3.2A as "tax-exempt

TABLE 3.6 Sector Statement of Personal Assets and Liabilities for Japanese Households*

		1990		*1991*		*1992*	
		ASSETS	*LIABILITIES*	*ASSETS*	*LIABILITIES*	*ASSETS*	*LIABILITIES*
A	Deposits with Bank of Japan						
B	Cash currency	323,406		330,727		332,672	
C	Demand deposits	558,336		583,366		609,749	
D	Time Deposits	4,098,519		4,468,678		4,691,128	
D	Certificates of deposits	147		89		64	
E	Non-resident yen deposits & foreign currency deposits	3,766		4,060		2,788	
G	Trust	645,488		691,709		754,904	
H	Insurance	1,941,001		2,131,769		2,343,093	
I	Securities	1,675,456		1,598,661		1,438,680	
J	Short-term government securities }	126,420					
K	Government bonds }			110,964		72,638	
L	Local government bonds	11,287		11,398		11,518	
M	Public corporation bonds	30,487		24,627		20,699	
N	Bank debentures	234,865		253,237		264,885	
O	Industrial bonds	53,846		57,409		58,468	
P	Stocks	828,757		795,005		632,148	
Q	Securities investment trusts	389,794		346,021		378,324	
U	Commercial paper						
V	Loans		2,707,792		2,844,547		2,919,690
W	Loans by private fin. instns.		2,199,924		2,294,614		2,327,477
X	Loans by public fin. instns.		507,868		549,933		592,213
Y	Trade credit		570,459		609,222		550,165
e	Others	104,883					
f	Difference		6,072,751		6,355,290		6,703,233
g	Total	9,351,002	9,351,002	9,809,059	9,809,059	10,173,078	10,173,078

*(¥ 100 million)

SOURCE: *Flow of Funds in Japan,* July, 1991, June, 1992, and August, 1993, Bank of Japan.

TABLE 3.7 Sector Statements of Assets and Liabilities for Japanese Corporate Business*

		1990		*1991*		*1992*	
ITEM		*ASSETS*	*LIABILITIES*	*ASSETS*	*LIABILITIES*	*ASSETS*	*LIABILITIES*
A	Deposits with Bank of Japan						
B	Cash currency	35,061		35,736		35,986	
C	Demand deposits	379,151		469,755		498,636	
D	Time deposits	1,318,251		1,169,605		1,126,637	
D	Certificates of deposits	97,137		85,890		82,673	
E	Non-resident yen deposits & foreign currency deposits	107,121		123,651		93,121	
F	Government current deposits						
G	Trust	394,798		414,542		452,797	
H	Insurance						
I	Securities	1372,849	1,348,241	1,378,737	1,452,734	1,076,555	1,482,401
J	Financing bills }						
K	Government bonds }						
L	Local government bonds }	113,564		121,541		117,853	
M	Public corporation bonds }						
N	Bank debentures }						
O	Industrial bonds		392,906		429,236		471,848
P	Stocks	1,209,674	645,723	1,208,471	658,500	907,245	663,185
Q	Securities investment trusts	49,611		48,725		51,457	
R	External bonds		309,612		364,998		347,368
S	Bank of Japan loans						
T	Call money						
U	Bills purchased/sold						
U	Commercial paper	50,915	157,627	41,637	124,004	38,972	121,987
V	Loans		4,908,199		5,211,242		5,435,005
W	Loans by private fin. insts.		4,271,161		4,510,548		4,637,324
X	Loans by public fin. insts.		637,038		700,694		797,681
Y	Trade credit	2,509,665	1,939,206	2,567,719	1,958,497	2,376,201	1,826,036
Z	Deposits with Trust Fund Bureau						
a	Gold & foreign exchange reserves						
b	Foreign trade credits	70,707	16,541	63,855	14,229	57,940	14,132
c	Foreign direct investment	261,370	14,775	271,926	16,601	280,295	20,164
d	Other foreign claims & debts	386,707	290,394	303,209	310,859	284,630	330,721
e	Others		215,296				
f	Financial surplus or deficit (–)		–1,906,547		–2,161,904		–2,826,003
g	Total	6,983,732	6,983,732	6,926,262	6,926,262	6,404,443	6,404,443

*(¥ 100 million)

SOURCE: *Flow of Funds in Japan,* July 1991, June 1992, and August 1993, Bank of Japan.

obligations" of $599.8 billion. Panel A of Table 3.4 shows that state and local government in 1992 had $1 trillion (line 12) in outstanding liabilities. Households own approximately 60 percent of the outstanding debt of state and local government bonds.

Households and businesses in an economy decide how much to invest (acquire real assets) and consume. Additions to real assets by primary sectors add to the accumulated wealth of an economy since real assets do not cancel out like financial assets and liabilities when balance sheets are added up for a whole economy. The wealth of the U.S. economy in 1992, for example, consisted primarily of household holdings of $9.5 trillion in real assets and $4.9 trillion in real assets held by business (Panel A of Table 3.3, line 2). Household's real assets are mostly owner-occupied housing of $3.9 trillion (line 5 of Table 3.2A), land of $2.8 trillion (line 9), and durables of $2.1 trillion (line 8). Acquisition of physical capital represents an increase in society's wealth, whereas financial assets represent transfers of claims on real assets.

Society's wealth includes assets that are not real assets. This wealth includes the productive potential of education (often called human capital) and the value of social institutions which facilitate the productivity of society. These sources of wealth are not accounted for in the flow-of-funds accounts but are important.

The Flow-of-Funds Accounts and Markets

The flow-of-funds accounts both as totals shown on balance sheets or sector statements and as flows showing changes in the levels shown on those accounts can help us appreciate the relative size of financial markets, their relation with the markets for investment goods, and the effects of market activity each period. Primary sectors initiate most real investment decisions, like building housing and factories, and purchasing equipment. Sectoral decisions resulting in either the consumption of goods and services or the acquisition of capital goods are implemented in the markets for goods and real assets but usually require financing affecting financial markets.

The household sector made up of many individual units can be thought of as the *retail* market. Businesses and governments, usually large-scale operations, do business in the *wholesale* or *institutional* market. Transactions between participants in the wholesale and retail market in different countries take place in *international* markets.

Most international transactions are between large institutions. There may be more similarities between two related sectors in different countries than two unrelated sectors in the same country. The German retail market may be more like the American retail market than the German retail market is like the German wholesale market. Businesses can often apply local experience abroad when dealing with related markets.

Classification of markets into retail and wholesale or institutional is used for financial markets as well as good markets. Using the U.S. municipal bond market as an example, the level of accumulated sales (net of redemptions) of tax-exempts to the household sector up to the end of 1992 totaled $599.8 billion. This is an estimate of the total size of the "retail" market for tax-exempt municipal bonds in the United States in 1992. The retail market for deposits totaled $2.9 trillion in the United States as compared to approximately $4.2 trillion in Japan.

Wholesale or institutional markets represent transactions by large-scale entities like corporations and governments. For example, corporate time deposits were $95.5 billion (line 10 of Table 3.3A) in 1992, a fraction of the retail market for time deposits and down from $105.6 billion in 1988. Since transactions in the wholesale market are usually large, a smaller percent profit per transaction can yield bigger dollar gains than many smaller retail transactions. The institutional or wholesale market is marked by fewer but larger transactions than the retail market. Financial institutions clearly must deal with institutional and retail markets in very different ways.

The Flow of Funds and Market Activity

Changes in sectoral balance sheets represent the savings, real investment, and financial investment decisions of market participants. Changes in balance sheets represent portfolio growth and rebalancing as mentioned above. The flow-of-funds accounts calculate changes in the sectoral balance sheets which are reported annually and quarterly for the United States. Panels B of Tables 3.2 and 3.3 show the flow-of-funds accounts for households and business and Panels B of Tables 3.4 and 3.5 show the annual flow of funds accounts for state and local governments and the U.S. government. For example, Panel B of Table 3.2 shows household "gross savings" (including depreciation) of $915.5 billion (line 9) in 1992. The household sector acquired $960.4 billion in assets (line 10) in 1992, with part of the discrepancy, $45 billion, shown as "statistical discrepancy" (line 48). Since these data are estimates, we should not expect much in the way of accuracy.

The flow of funds allows us to track resources and financial flows through the economy. For example, the household sector's $960.4 billion investment in 1992 was used to acquire an estimated $710.7 billion in real assets (Table 3.2B, line 11) and $249.7 (line 15) for net acquisition of financial assets. The "net" represents a $471.3 increase in financial assets (line 16) offset by $221.6 increase in liabilities (line 36). The household sector in the United States in aggregate has a leveraged portfolio since most Americans purchase housing with mortgages and cars with auto loans.

The balance sheet of each sector must balance at each point in time, hence changes in balance sheets shown in the flow of funds must also balance. We can trace changes in sectoral portfolio balance in response to financial market conditions. For example, Table 3.2 shows that in 1992 households in the United States shifted out of time deposits (lines 20 and 21 in Panel B) and into checkable deposits (line 19, Panel B). The impact of major events like the Stock Market Crash of 1987 or federal deficits on financial markets can be followed. Throughout the book we will use the flow-of-funds accounts to illustrate a number of structural and economic environmental changes.

3.3 ORGANIZATION OF THE FINANCIAL SERVICE INDUSTRY

Financial institutions acquire financial claims against primary sectors, like consumer loans from the household sector or corporate bonds from the business sector. They acquire these claims in part by issuing liabilities unique to financial institutions, like deposits or insurance reserves. The role of financial institutions in allocating saving to investment in an economy is called *financial intermediation*. Some financial institution liabilities have characteristics and services that make them attractive forms of saving. As we have seen, households in the United States and Japan hold more of their financial wealth in the form of claims on financial institutions than as direct investments in nonfinancial business.

Historically there are four classes of financial service firms: (1) deposit-taking firms; (2) insurance type firms; (3) investment companies; and (4) securities firms. This classification is based mainly on the kinds of liabilities these firms issue and the regulatory establishment in most developed countries. We warn students that this classification fails to account for hybrids, outliers, and mavericks. Difficult-to-classify firms, like American Express or Travelers, are increasingly important in the evolving financial services industry. The approach of this book is to look at all financial service firms, including hybrids, by function rather than traditional classifications.

Within each of the four basic classes of financial firms, there are a variety of even more specialized types of financial service firms. A brief discussion of each type follows. The specialization of firms within the four classes represents the financial market segmentation discussed at the beginning of the chapter. The global revolution and evolution of the financial services industry in part consists of the formation of hybrid firms, combining functions of two or more specialized types of firms, and creation of whole new products and types of firms. The challenge—and opportunity—facing current and future managers of financial service firms is to identify innovative value-producing financial institutions.

Deposit-Taking Firms

Deposit-taking firms raise funds by issuing deposit liabilities. These liabilities must be redeemed upon demand (demand deposits or checking accounts) or upon maturity (time deposits). Deposit-taking institutions in most countries are segmented, with different institutions concentrating to varying degrees in the wholesale or retail markets. Commercial banks in most countries do both retail and wholesale business. Some deposit-taking institutions, called *thrifts,* concentrate on a retail business although their powers differ in different countries. In some countries, there are deposit-taking firms that specialize in business financing. Segmentation and business concentration in deposit-taking firms have evolved historically and are heavily influenced by regulation and taxation. Each type of firm is organized under specialized laws and its activities typically are restricted to specific financial activities.

History is essential to understanding deposit-taking financial institutions. No current system is based on clear economic reasoning. Even in newly emerging market economies like Poland and China where new financial laws are being written, the laws are written with historical realities in mind. The history and evolution of financial systems have been as heavily influenced by the political environment and changing policy objectives around the world as by economic forces.

Commercial Banks. Commercial banks are ancient institutions. Banking functions are described in the earliest commercial document known to exist, Hammurabai's code. Banking flourished in Roman times and the Middle Ages (see Banking Education Committee 1963 for a history of banking).

The term bank has many meanings around the world and there are many ways of classifying banks. In England and the United States, *commercial banks* take deposits and make loans to businesses and households. In Germany and elsewhere in Continental Europe, some large banks are called *universal banks* to distinguish them from commercial banks because they can take deposits, make business and consumer loans, and are permitted to invest in the equity of non-banking businesses and to underwrite securities. Special purpose banks, such as *trust banks* and *long-term credit banks* in Japan, exist in some form in many countries. Banks are also described by the scope of their geographical operations. In Japan, banks are described as *city banks* and *regional banks,* although this distinction has been dropped in the United States in favor of classification by size into *money center* or *multinational banks, super-regional* and *regional banks,* and *community banks.*

Commercial banks in the United States since 1863 have been chartered by either a state or the Federal government forming a "dual banking" system. This means that commercial banks in the United States are regulated either by state or national authorities as discussed in Chapter 14.

There are approximately 12,000 banks in the United States, of which approximately 3,800 are nationally chartered. The flow of funds provides total financial assets and liabilities for commercial banks in United States as given in Panel A of Table 3.8.

Panel A of Table 3.8 shows commercial bank total financial assets of $2.77 trillion in 1992 (line 1), making banks the largest class of financial intermediaries in the United States. Liabilities of commercial banks consist predominantly of deposits, both time and checking deposits. Banks had total liabilities of $2.9 trillion (line 25) of which $700 billion were checking accounts (line 26) and $1,370 billion were small and saving time deposits (line 30). Remaining liabilities of banks consist mainly of short-term borrowings from other banks and other money market participants.

Commercial banks traditionally lend out deposit dollars. Table 3.8A shows that in 1992 banks had $1.8 trillion (line 14) in loans. In the past, commercial banks concentrated on loans to business, in the flow of funds called "loans not elsewhere classified" (line 17) which amounted to $574.8 billion in 1992, less than half of all bank loans. Loans to business by banks have fallen recently. Mortgage loans and consumer loans are the other large loan concentrations for banks. In 1992, these totaled $842.3 billion for mortgage loans and $362.2 billion for consumer loans (lines 15 and 16). The table shows that in the last few years mortgage lending is up while consumer lending is down. Changes in bank lending represent

TABLE 3.8 Financial Assets and Liabilities for U.S. Chartered Commercial Banks, 1982–1992*

Panel A: Outstanding Levels

		1982	1983	1984	1985	1986	1987	1988	1989	1990	1991	1992
1	Total financial assets	1471.5	1601.8	1798.8	1998.2	2166.0	2257.1	2384.9	2345.3	2644.2	2677.3	2776.1
2	Total bank credit	1364.8	1497.9	1664.1	1847.5	2011.4	2108.4	2237.5	2390.6	2481.4	2531.5	2628.7
3	U.S. government securities	206.8	251.0	252.3	256.9	299.2	324.1	343.9	377.9	432.3	529.0	614.5
4	Treasury	129.2	172.7	175.2	182.6	188.5	185.4	176.0	155.7	157.4	207.8	254.3
5	Agency	77.6	78.3	77.1	74.2	110.7	138.6	167.9	222.1	274.9	321.2	360.1
6	Mortgage pool secur.	–	–	26.4	24.0	49.6	71.9	86.7	123.2	144.7	153.7	155.5
7	Agency-issued CMOs	–	–	–	–	–	–	–	–	54.8	89.4	122.7
8	Other agency secur.	77.6	78.3	50.7	50.3	61.1	66.7	81.2	98.9	75.4	78.1	81.9
9	Tax-exempt securities	157.5	161.3	173.9	231.1	282.8	173.7	150.9	133.2	116.8	102.7	97.0
10	Corporate & foreign bonds	8.1	11.7	15.0	17.2	35.6	56.3	68.6	61.8	65.4	69.7	66.6
11	Private mtg. pool secs.	–	–	0.4	0.4	3.7	3.8	3.1	3.5	3.2	3.5	3.8
12	Privately issued CMOs	–	–	–	–	–	–	–	–	–	28.2	21.6
13	Other bonds	8.1	11.7	14.6	16.9	31.9	52.5	65.5	58.3	62.2	38.0	41.1
14	Total loans	991.6	1073.9	1222.9	1342.3	1473.8	1534.4	1674.0	1810.8	1862.8	1821.9	1842.4
15	Mortgages	294.2	323.5	372.0	421.4	491.7	375.1	644.2	729.7	799.3	822.0	842.3
16	Consumer credit	190.9	213.7	258.8	296.3	321.1	337.6	370.7	382.8	383.7	370.0	362.2
17	Bank loans n.e.c.	469.7	497.1	548.7	577.5	628.8	603.3	621.7	658.2	643.5	592.5	574.8
18	Open market paper	11.7	12.6	11.7	8.5	7.?	9.0	8.3	7.8	8.5	7.5	5.9
19	Security credit	25.1	27.0	31.7	38.5	32.5	29.4	29.8	33.2	27.8	30.0	57.3
20	Mutual fund shares	–	–	–	–	–	–	–	2.2	1.9	3.7	3.4
21	Corporate equities	–	–	–	–	–	–	–	4.7	2.2	4.5	4.9
22	Cust. liabs. on acceptances	47.2	31.8	48.9	37.9	30.6	29.6	26.5	21.3	17.2	12.6	12.6
23	Vault cash & res. at F.R.	44.0	40.1	42.5	48.2	65.5	59.5	60.5	58.7	66.7	59.2	61.1
24	Miscellaneous assets	16.3	12.0	43.2	56.6	58.4	59.6	60.4	74.7	78.9	74.0	73.7
25	Total liabilities	1502.4	1649.4	1811.5	2000.2	2173.7	2274.3	2443.1	2593.0	2696.1	2750.0	2862.7
26	Checkable deposits	363.9	379.4	409.7	461.4	554.6	535.3	551.3	547.8	569.5	607.1	700.1
27	U.S. government	16.9	11.5	15.5	25.8	27.5	21.6	29.0	25.6	30.9	36.4	30.6
28	Foreign	11.6	12.8	15.9	16.0	18.7	17.2	16.7	17.1	16.7	14.5	16.3
29	Private domestic	335.4	355.1	378.2	419.7	508.4	496.7	505.7	505.1	521.8	556.2	653.3
30	Small time & savings dep.	611.4	742.2	816.8	897.2	968.7	996.1	1069.2	1165.7	1287.5	1367.5	1369.6
31	Large time deposits	289.6	250.8	284.7	295.6	289.0	326.7	361.9	385.8	365.4	292.3	216.1
32	Fed. funds & security RPs	138.8	150.1	152.0	178.8	189.6	201.4	217.7	253.3	219.7	192.6	234.2
33	Net interbank liabilities	–102.5	–94.0	–90.2	–82.9	–91.1	–69.6	–65.7	–85.4	–78.6	–68.5	–48.2
34	Federal Reserve float	2.7	1.6	0.9	1.0	1.3	0.8	1.3	1.1	2.6	1.0	3.4
35	Borrowing at F.R. banks	0.7	0.9	3.6	3.1	1.6	3.8	2.2	0.5	0.2	0.2	0.7
36	To domestic banks	–48.1	–46.6	–43.0	–45.5	–49.7	–47.2	–44.5	–56.5	–69.0	–47.9	–32.7
37	To foreign banks	–57.8	–49.9	–51.6	–41.5	–44.2	–27.1	–24.6	–30.4	–12.3	–21.9	–19.6
38	Corporate bonds	6.8	6.6	10.1	14.6	16.8	17.5	17.2	20.0	24.2	25.2	33.5
39	Acceptance liabilities	51.6	54.6	51.1	40.2	31.5	30.5	27.2	22.0	17.6	12.9	12.8
40	Fed. Home Loan Banks loans	–	–	–	–	–	–	–	–	0.4	2.0	6.4
41	Taxes payable	0.4	0.3	0.3	0.4	0.4	0.4	0.6	0.8	0.6	0.5	0.7
42	Miscellaneous liabilities	142.4	159.3	177.0	195.0	214.1	237.9	263.5	282.9	289.9	318.5	337.5
43	Inv. by bank holding cos.	102.1	117.6	136.4	152.1	168.8	172.6	193.8	202.4	207.8	227.2	255.0
44	Other	40.3	41.8	40.5	42.9	45.3	65.3	69.7	80.5	82.1	91.3	82.5

*Data are in billions of dollars.

SOURCE: Flow of Funds, Board of Governors of the Federal Reserve System, Washington, D.C. 20551.

Panel B: Annual Flows

		1982	1983	1984	1985	1986	1987	1988	1989	1990	1991	1992
1	Gross saving	9.3	9.5	10.2	15.5	20.0	21.6	17.7	27.8	34.7	36.2	37.7
2	Fixed nonres. investment	17.1	16.8	19.4	22.5	25.2	27.0	32.1	36.1	34.5	32.1	32.2
3	Net acq. of financial assets	111.1	130.4	165.5	191.6	175.9	91.3	127.9	160.5	99.1	33.3	75.0
4	Total bank credit	104.2	133.9	166.2	183.4	163.8	97.0	129.0	155.2	90.9	50.1	72.9
5	U.S. government securities	26.7	44.2	1.3	4.6	42.4	24.8	19.8	34.0	54.5	96.6	85.5
6	Treasury	19.4	43.5	2.5	7.5	5.9	–3.1	–9.4	–20.3	1.7	50.3	46.6
7	Agency	7.3	0.7	–1.2	–2.9	36.5	27.9	29.3	54.2	52.8	46.3	38.9
8	Mortgage pool secur.	–	–	–4.2	–2.4	23.7	22.3	14.8	36.5	21.5	9.0	1.8
9	Agency-issued CMOs	–	–	–	–	–	–	–	–	23.3	34.6	33.3
10	Other agency secur.	7.3	0.7	3.8	–.4	12.8	5.6	14.4	17.7	8.0	2.7	3.8
11	Tax-exempt securities	4.6	3.8	12.6	57.2	–28.4	–29.1	–22.7	–17.8	–16.4	–14.1	–5.7
12	Corporate-& foreign bonds	1.7	3.6	3.2	2.3	18.4	20.7	12.3	2.4	3.6	4.3	–3.2
13	Private mtg. pool secur.	–	–	–	–	3.3	0.1	–.7	0.4	–.3	0.3	0.3
14	Privately issued CMOs	–	–	–	–	–	–	–	–	–	0.4	–6.6
15	Other bonds	1.7	3.6	3.2	2.3	15.0	20.6	13.0	2.0	3.9	3.6	3.1
16	Total loans	71.2	82.3	149.1	119.3	131.5	80.6	119.6	136.9	51.9	–40.8	–3.8
17	Mortgages	15.1	29.4	44.1	49.4	67.0	80.7	69.1	85.4	62.4	22.7	20.3
18	Consumer credit	6.7	22.7	45.2	37.5	24.8	16.3	33.1	21.2	1.7	–13.7	–7.8
19	Bank loans n.e.c.	47.9	27.3	56.0	28.8	46.6	–14.9	18.5	26.6	–7.6	–51.0	–17.7
20	Open market paper	1.0	0.9	–.9	–3.2	–1.0	1.5	–.7	–.6	0.8	–1.0	–1.6
21	Security credit	0.5	2.0	4.7	6.8	–5.9	–3.2	–.4	4.2	–5.4	2.2	3.1
22	Mutual fund shares	–	–	–	–	–	–	–	–.1	–.3	1.8	–.4
23	Corporate equities	–	–	–	–	–	–	–	–.1	–2.5	2.2	0.4
24	Cust. liab. on acceptances	7.0	4.6	–2.8	–11.1	–7.3	–1.0	–3.1	–5.2	4.1	–4.6	–.1
25	Vault cash & res. at F.R.	1.5	–3.9	2.5	5.7	17.3	–6.0	1.0	–1.8	8.0	–7.5	2.0
26	Miscellaneous assets	–1.6	–4.2	–.3	13.3	2.0	1.3	0.9	12.3	4.4	–4.7	0.1
27	Net increase in liabilities	121.3	146.2	178.5	198.9	178.2	93.6	166.6	149.5	107.9	51.7	93.0
28	Checkable deposits	20.9	15.6	30.2	51.8	93.2	–19.1	15.8	–3.5	21.7	37.6	93.0
29	U.S. government	6.1	–5.3	4.0	10.3	1.7	–5.8	7.3	–3.4	5.3	5.5	–5.9
30	Foreign	–2.2	1.6	3.0	–	2.7	–1.5	–.6	0.1	–.4	–2.2	1.7
31	Private domestic	17.1	19.5	23.2	41.5	88.8	–11.8	9.1	–.2	16.8	34.3	97.1
32	Small time & savings dep.	96.4	130.8	74.6	80.3	71.6	27.4	73.1	96.5	121.9	80.0	2.1
33	Large time deposits	2.3	–38.7	33.9	10.8	–6.6	37.7	35.2	24.0	–20.5	–73.1	–76.2
34	Fed. funds & security RPs, net	9.2	11.3	1.9	26.8	10.8	11.9	16.3	35.6	–33.7	–27.1	17.4
35	Net interbank liabilities	–25.4	6.9	4.8	8.0	–4.8	21.1	1.3	–21.7	9.4	6.9	20.6
36	Federal Reserve float	1.0	–1.2	–.7	0.1	0.3	–.5	0.5	–.2	1.5	–1.5	2.3
37	Borrowing at F.R. banks	–.9	0.2	2.7	–.5	–1.5	2.3	–1.6	–1.7	–.3	–	0.5
38	To domestic banking	–2.0	–.1	4.6	–1.7	–.9	2.2	0.1	–14.0	–9.9	17.9	15.5
39	To foreign banks	–23.5	7.9	–1.8	10.1	–2.7	17.1	2.4	–5.8	18.1	–9.5	2.3
40	Corporate equities	0.6	0.8	1.1	1.4	1.4	1.5	2.5	1.5	2.1	0.9	4.3
41	Corporate bonds	0.6	–.2	3.6	4.5	2.2	0.7	–.3	2.8	4.2	0.9	8.4
42	Acceptance liabilities	9.5	3.0	–3.6	–10.9	–8.7	–1.0	–3.3	–5.3	–4.4	–4.7	–.1
43	Fed. Home Loan Banks loans	–	–	–	–	–	–	–	–	0.4	1.6	4.3
44	Taxes payable	–.1	–.1	–	0.1	–	0.1	0.2	0.2	–.2	–	0.2
45	Miscellaneous liabilities	7.4	16.9	32.0	26.0	19.1	13.6	25.7	19.4	7.0	20.6	19.0
46	Inv. by bank holding cos.	16.2	15.5	18.9	15.6	16.7	10.8	21.3	8.6	5.4	17.4	27.8
47	Other	–8.8	1.4	13.1	10.3	2.4	–6.2	4.4	10.8	1.6	9.2	–8.8
48	Discrepancy	2.4	8.4	3.8	0.3	–2.9	–3.2	24.3	–19.3	9.0	22.5	23.5

*Data are in billions of dollars.
SOURCE: Flow of Funds, Board of Governors of the Federal Reserve System, Washington, D.C. 20551.

portfolio-rebalancing in response to economic conditions and changes in the market for business lending.

Balance sheet numbers do not account for all banking activities. Recently, bank managers and regulators have become as concerned with their "off-balance sheet" activities as those represented on the balance sheet. These fee-generating activities represent a variety of services, like the interest rate swaps discussed in Part IV. Most of these bank activities are an evolutionary extension following from banking's traditional functions of making loans to business.

Saving Institutions. Savings institutions have traditionally been places for small savers. They are also part of the "thrift" industry. The main thrift institutions in the United States are savings banks and credit unions. Savings banks include savings and loans. (In England and Germany, building and loans are very similar to savings and loans.) The crisis in the thrift industry in the 1980s in the United States produced a legislative response blurring the historical distinctions between savings banks and savings and loans—Kane's "regulatory dialectic" at work again. Credit unions, which were imported to the United States from Germany in 1909, continue to be a breed apart.

Savings institutions, like building and loan societies in England and Germany, have roots going back at least as far as banks. They evolved from community self-help organizations with origins in earlier civilizations and still seen in less developed countries. Early thrifts usually work like this: each thrift member periodically contributes a small sum to a savings pool. When enough money has accumulated in the pool, one member of the community—chosen by lot or by a bidding process—borrows the pool for a major purchase like a house. These institutions belong to all members who contribute to the pool. This form of thrift was idealized in the Christmas movie classic, *It's a Wonderful Life,* starring Jimmy Stewart.

As with other deposit-taking institutions in the United States, savings institutions can be state chartered or federally chartered. Financial assets and liabilities for savings institutions in the United States from the flow-of-funds accounts are provided in Panel A of Table 3.9. Until the Deregulation Act of 1980 thrifts concentrated on raising funds in the form of savings accounts. In 1992, small time deposits and savings still accounted for \$703.3 billion (line 21) out of total deposits of \$852.8 billion (line 19)—more than 82 percent of deposits.

Before deregulation in 1980, savings and loans now included in savings institutions concentrated heavily in residential home mortgages. Table 3.9 shows total financial assets in 1992 for savings institutions of \$1,082 billion (line 1) with \$628 billion directly invested in mortgages (line 12), and \$143 billion (line 9) in U.S. Agency issues, primarily mortgaged-backed securities. Mutual savings banks, savings institutions concentrated in the Northeastern United States and included in Table 3.9, can invest in corporate bonds and loans to business, reflected in 1992 totals of \$80 and \$9.1 billion (lines 11 and 14), respectively. After 1980, savings institutions could make a wider range of loans to consumers, such as credit card loans. These increased investment authorities are reflected in the 1992 assets of savings institutions, which had \$43.8 billion in consumer credit (line 13), nearly double 1980 levels. Consumer credit was down from peak levels in the late 1980s.

TABLE 3.9 Financial Assets and Liabilities for Savings Institutions, 1982–1992*

Panel A: Outstanding Levels

		1982	1983	1984	1985	1986	1987	1988	1989	1990	1991	1992
1	Total financial assets	870.3	1011.7	1180.1	1275.3	1377.7	1509.8	1646.9	1520.8	1364.7	1176.4	1082.7
2	Checkable dep. & currency	11.6	12.4	11.2	12.0	12.5	10.2	12.1	11.3	11.0	12.9	13.3
3	Time deposits	14.0	15.1	9.6	11.9	15.9	7.3	7.4	5.3	5.2	5.0	3.7
4	Fed. funds & security RPs	20.8	22.6	26.3	22.1	19.9	19.0	20.2	24.2	21.6	13.1	14.4
5	Corporate equities	3.3	4.3	4.1	5.2	7.0	7.0	8.5	11.0	8.8	10.3	11.2
6	Credit market instruments	756.7	879.5	1018.6	1097.6	1191.0	1310.3	1409.2	1319.4	1158.0	1017.9	940.6
7	U.S. government securities	107.4	158.8	183.4	181.3	231.1	284.2	292.1	235.7	211.5	170.0	177.0
8	Treasury	16.6	31.9	39.7	34.5	38.0	47.5	34.9	26.8	25.9	25.0	34.0
9	Agency	90.8	126.9	143.7	146.8	193.1	236.7	257.2	208.9	185.7	145.0	143.0
10	Tax-exempt securities	3.3	3.1	2.8	3.4	3.1	3.1	2.8	2.6	3.0	2.4	2.1
11	Corporate and fgn. bonds	30.7	42.4	53.7	56.8	64.1	88.2	105.3	91.0	75.6	72.7	80.0
12	Mortgages	576.3	626.9	710.1	765.7	784.8	824.3	888.0	872.5	779.0	705.4	628.0
13	Consumer credit	26.6	31.5	44.2	57.6	62.9	65.3	66.7	65.?	53.7	46.8	43.8
14	Other loans (to business)	5.6	11.7	20.7	29.3	39.8	40.9	49.2	47.0	34.3	19.3	9.1
15	Open market paper	6.9	5.2	3.8	3.5	5.3	4.3	5.1	4.7	0.7	1.3	0.6
16	Reserves at Fed. Reserve	0.4	1.4	2.2	3.9	5.6	4.9	5.3	4.3	3.4	2.9	2.2
17	Miscellaneous assets	63.5	76.4	108.0	122.5	125.8	151.1	184.2	145.1	156.7	112.6	97.4
18	Total liabilities	856.5	999.9	1171.9	1265.5	1361.5	1472.7	1604.8	1484.4	1341.5	1160.3	1067.9
19	Deposits	739.0	856.6	976.9	1033.9	1077.3	1121.4	1193.2	1170.?	1050.4	937.3	852.8
20	Checkable	19.3	28.5	34.9	44.8	61.9	67.2	74.0	72.?	68.0	71.6	80.0
21	Small time and savings	654.5	727.6	792.5	833.9	858.7	889.3	943.4	936.2	862.5	783.8	703.3
22	Large time	65.2	100.5	149.5	155.3	156.7	164.9	175.9	161.7	119.9	82.1	69.6
23	Security RPs	13.5	26.6	43.4	40.4	57.5	85.7	103.9	57.8	42.5	19.6	18.6
24	Credit market instruments	72.5	66.1	89.5	110.2	134.3	162.6	184.3	169.2	139.1	94.6	87.8
25	Corporate bonds	3.7	4.0	5.9	10.5	15.4	19.8	21.7	18.3	12.7	8.6	5.5
26	Bank loans n.e.c.	2.8	3.2	8.9	10.9	10.2	9.7	9.9	9.2	9.7	8.9	8.9
27	Fed. Home Loan Banks loans	66.0	59.0	74.6	88.8	108.6	133.1	152.8	141.8	116.7	77.0	73.4
28	Taxes payable	0.9	1.0	1.0	1.1	1.1	1.2	1.2	1.1	0.9	1.0	1.1
29	Miscellaneous liabilities	30.6	49.6	61.2	79.9	91.2	101.9	122.1	85.6	108.7	107.3	107.6
30	Investment by parent	5.3	5.3	6.5	7.2	7.3	6.5	6.4	6.4	6.0	5.0	4.0
31	Other	25.3	44.3	54.7	72.7	83.9	95.4	115.7	79.2	102.7	102.3	103.6

*Data are in billions of dollars.
SOURCE: Flow of Funds, Board of Governors of the Federal Reserve System, Washington, D.C. 20551.

Panel B: Annual Flows

		1982	1983	1984	1985	1986	1987	1988	1989	1990	1991	1992
1	Gross saving	−18.4	−2.9	−3.0	2.1	3.8	2.6	2.3	−2.3	−.6	−3.3	−2.3
2	Fixed nonres. investment	1.4	1.2	1.2	1.3	1.3	1.2	1.0	0.9	0.9	0.8	0.7
3	Net acq. of financial assets	61.3	140.7	168.5	94.0	105.1	121.1	109.3	−90.3	−163.3	−190.2	−94.6
4	Checkable dep. & currency	2.8	0.8	−1.2	0.8	0.5	−2.3	0.8	−.8	−.3	2.0	0.4
5	Time deposits	7.2	1.2	−5.5	2.3	4.0	−8.5	–	−2.1	−.1	−.3	−1.3
6	Fed. funds & security RPs	4.0	1.7	3.8	−4.2	−4.8	−.9	2.5	3.9	−2.5	−6.6	−.6
7	Corporate equities	−.5	0.3	−.2	−.1	8.9	1.2	0.4	0.3	−1.5	−.4	–
8	Credit market instruments	21.8	123.1	148.6	76.4	94.3	119.1	97.3	−93.8	−163.9	−135.7	−77.3
9	U.S. government securities	34.9	51.5	24.6	−4.7	49.8	33.2	9.7	−56.4	−24.1	−41.5	7.0
10	Treasury	3.4	15.3	7.8	−5.2	3.5	9.6	−10.2	−8.1	−.9	−.9	9.0
11	Agency	31.6	36.2	16.8	0.5	46.3	43.6	19.9	−48.4	−23.2	−40.6	−2.0
12	Tax-exempt securities	−.3	−.2	−.3	0.6	−.3	–	0.2	−.2	0.4	−.6	−.4
13	Corporate and fgn. bonds	5.3	11.7	11.4	3.1	8.2	8.5	13.0	−13.0	−19.3	−2.9	7.3
14	Mortgages	−24.3	50.9	84.7	55.5	19.2	55.0	68.8	−20.8	−96.3	−73.7	−77.4
15	Consumer credit	2.6	4.9	12.7	13.4	5.3	2.4	1.4	−.8	−12.2	−6.9	−3.0
16	Other loans (to business)	1.8	6.0	9.0	8.7	10.5	1.1	3.4	−1.8	−12.7	−10.6	−10.2
17	Open market paper	1.8	−1.7	−1.4	−.2	1.8	−1.0	0.8	−.7	–	0.5	−.7
18	Reserves at Fed. Reserves	0.3	1.0	0.9	1.7	1.7	−.7	0.4	−.8	−1.1	−.5	−.8
19	Miscellaneous assets	25.8	12.5	30.2	17.0	8.4	14.1	7.9	2.9	6.2	−48.7	−15.0
20	Net increase in liabilities	68.5	143.4	172.0	93.6	99.5	116.2	105.6	−80.8	−130.9	−181.5	−92.1
21	Deposits	52.1	117.6	120.2	57.1	47.6	51.3	55.4	−22.4	−120.4	−112.8	−84.7
22	Checkable	6.5	9.2	6.4	9.9	17.1	5.3	6.8	−1.1	−4.8	3.6	8.3
23	Small time and savings	34.1	73.1	64.9	41.4	29.3	37.9	37.6	−4.2	−73.7	−78.7	−80.3
24	Large time	11.4	35.3	48.9	5.8	1.4	8.1	11.0	−15.1	−41.9	−37.8	−12.7
25	Security RPs	−1.8	13.1	16.9	−3.0	17.1	28.1	15.9	−46.2	−15.3	−22.9	−1.0
26	Credit market instruments	1.1	−6.6	20.1	20.7	24.1	28.3	21.7	−15.1	−30.2	−44.5	−6.7
27	Corporate bonds	0.4	0.1	1.9	4.6	4.9	4.4	1.9	−3.6	−5.6	−4.1	−3.2
28	Bank loans n.e.c.	−.1	0.3	2.5	1.9	−.6	−.3	0.1	−.7	0.5	−.7	–
29	Fed. Home Loan Banks loans	0.8	−7.0	15.7	14.2	19.8	24.4	19.7	−11.0	−25.1	−39.7	−3.6
30	Taxes payable	–	–	–	0.1	0.1	0.1	0.1	−.1	−.2	0.2	0.1
31	Miscellaneous liabilities	17.1	19.3	14.9	18.7	10.6	8.4	12.5	3.8	15.2	−1.4	0.3
32	Investment by parent	−.6	–	1.2	0.7	0.2	−.9	–	–	−.4	−1.0	−1.0
33	Other	17.8	19.2	13.7	18.0	10.3	9.3	12.6	3.1	15.6	−.4	1.3
34	Discrepancy	−4.6	−1.5	−.6	0.4	−3.1	−3.5	−2.2	6.3	10.9	4.6	−.3

*Data are in billions of dollars.

SOURCE: Flow of Funds, Board of Governors of the Federal Reserve System, Washington, D.C. 20551.

Most successful savings institutions in the United States today were able to survive the savings and loan crisis by building on their traditional core retail business of the 1980s. They are using their authorities to accept transaction accounts, make consumer loans, and provide trust, brokerage, and insurance services through holding-company affiliates to offer the retail market a much broader range of financial services than commercial banks.

Credit Unions. Credit unions are another type of retail-oriented mutual self-help organization dating from the industrial revolution. The idea for credit unions was imported from Germany in the early twentieth century. The basic concept is that workers from a similar environment with the same employer pool their savings for loans to members for purchases of consumer durables or other desirable consumer expenditures at interest rates more favorable than those of banks. Credit unions can be sponsored by large corporations providing access to workers' cash through payroll deduction. In the United States, credit unions can be state or federally chartered but all are tax-exempt.

Credit union assets and liabilities are given in Panel A of Table 3.10. In 1992 credit unions had total financial liabilities of $247.3 billion (Panel A, line 13), of which $208.1 billion was small time and savings accounts (line 16). However, credit unions, like savings institutions, were authorized in 1980 to offer checking accounts called "share draft" accounts and by 1992 these accounts amounted to a total of $31.5 billion (line 16).

Credit unions have kept close to their traditional charter of making small loans. Of the total of $263.9 billion in assets for credit unions in 1992 (Table 3.10, line 1), $97.6 billion (line 10) represents consumer credit. Most of credit unions' other assets are Treasury and Agency securities.

Although limited to retail deposit and lending activities, credit unions have in some instances become aggressive competitors. Their nonprofit status exempts them from federal taxation and provides a competitive advantage over banks and other thrifts. Credit unions are the fastest growing deposit-taking institution in the United States.

Finance Companies. Many countries like the United States and Germany have specialized credit institutions financed in part by deposits. In the United States there are three types of finance companies: (1) financing affiliates of large manufacturing firms, examples being General Motors Acceptance Corporation (GMAC) or General Electric Credit (GEC); (2) small personal loan companies, partially financed by deposits, examples being Postal Savings and Household Finance Corporation (HFC); and (3) high-risk business lenders, financed in part by deposits, examples being the Foothill Group in Los Angeles and CIT Financial. These finance companies are chartered under state laws and are regulated by states. There is a great deal of disparity in what finance companies can do in these different jurisdictions.

Panel A of Table 3.11 gives the assets and liabilities for finance companies in the flow-of-funds accounts. Their total liabilities of $556.7 billion in 1992 (line 8) consisted of longer-term debt of $195.3 billion (line 10) and short-term borrowings

TABLE 3.10 Financial Assets and Liabilities for Credit Unions, 1982–1992*

		Panel A: Outstanding Levels										
		1982	*1983*	*1984*	*1985*	*1986*	*1987*	*1988*	*1989*	*1990*	*1991*	*1992*
1	Total financial assets	81.0	96.3	110.7	134.5	162.8	178.2	192.3	201.7	217.0	239.5	263.9
2	Checkable dep. and currency	1.8	2.2	2.6	3.3	4.0	4.0	4.2	4.8	4.8	5.4	6.6
3	Time deposits	14.5	16.2	15.0	20.0	27.0	27.4	24.0	21.2	21.7	26.7	27.1
4	Fed. funds & security RPs	3.2	4.3	4.6	8.4	10.9	9.2	9.4	12.5	14.6	13.2	13.5
5	Credit market instruments	57.3	69.4	85.0	98.4	113.9	131.3	148.8	156.0	166.6	179.6	196.8
6	U.S. government securities	5.8	8.9	9.6	13.1	16.7	20.0	21.6	18.4	23.0	33.7	48.6
7	Treasury	1.3	2.7	3.7	6.2	8.0	11.2	14.4	12.1	8.5	14.1	19.9
8	Agency	4.5	6.3	5.9	7.0	8.8	8.8	7.1	6.3	14.4	19.6	28.7
9	Home mortgages	4.2	7.0	9.2	12.4	19.3	29.9	38.1	43.4	48.2	50.4	47.9
10	Consumer credit	47.3	53.5	66.2	72.7	77.1	81.0	88.3	93.1	93.1	92.7	97.6
11	Open market paper	–	–	0.1	0.2	0.7	0.5	0.9	1.1	2.3	2.6	2.7
12	Miscellaneous assets	4.2	4.2	3.5	4.4	7.0	6.2	5.9	7.1	9.3	14.9	19.9
13	Total liabilities	77.1	92.0	105.5	128.3	155.7	169.9	182.7	190.7	204.7	225.8	247.3
14	Shares/deposits	74.8	89.7	102.6	125.5	152.7	166.0	178.4	187.0	200.8	221.3	242.9
15	Checkable	5.7	8.0	9.5	12.6	16.0	17.8	19.4	20.5	22.2	27.3	31.5
16	Small time & savings	68.4	81.0	92.3	111.7	135.2	146.3	156.6	163.5	175.3	190.7	208.1
17	Large time	0.7	0.7	0.8	1.2	1.3	1.9	2.4	3.0	3.3	3.3	3.3
18	Fed. Home Loan Banks loans	–	–	–	–	–	–	–	–	–	–	–
19	Miscellaneous liabilities	2.3	2.3	2.9	2.8	3.0	3.9	4.3	3.7	3.9	4.3	4.4

*Data are in billions of dollars.
SOURCE: Flow of Funds, Board of Governors of the Federal Reserve System, Washington, D.C. 20551.

Panel B: Annual Flows

	1982	1983	1984	1985	1986	1987	1988	1989	1990	1991	1992
1 Gross saving	0.7	0.7	1.4	1.3	0.4	0.7	0.8	0.9	0.9	1.0	1.1
2 Fixed nonres. investment	0.3	0.3	0.3	0.4	0.5	0.6	0.7	0.7	0.7	0.7	0.6
3 Net acq. of financial assets	10.7	15.9	15.6	24.9	28.5	15.8	14.6	9.9	15.7	23.1	25.0
4 Checkable dep. & currency	8.2	0.4	0.4	0.7	0.7	–	0.2	0.6	–	0.6	1.2
5 Time deposits	7.4	1.6	–1.2	5.0	7.1	0.4	–3.5	–2.7	0.4	5.0	0.4
6 Fed. funds & security RPs	0.8	1.1	0.3	3.7	2.5	–1.6	0.1	3.1	2.1	–1.4	0.4
7 Credit market instruments	2.3	12.1	15.3	13.4	15.5	17.5	17.5	7.1	10.6	12.8	17.4
8 U.S. government securities	1.2	3.1	0.4	3.6	3.6	3.2	1.6	–3.2	4.6	10.7	14.9
9 Treasury	0.3	1.4	0.8	2.4	1.8	3.2	3.3	–2.3	–3.6	5.5	5.9
10 Agency	0.4	1.7	–.4	1.1	1.8	–	–1.7	–.9	8.2	5.2	9.1
11 Home mortgages	–.2	2.8	2.2	3.2	6.9	10.5	8.2	5.3	4.9	2.2	–2.6
12 Consumer credit	1.3	6.2	12.7	6.6	4.4	4.0	7.3	4.8	–.1	–.4	5.0
13 Open market paper	–	–	0.1	0.1	0.6	–.3	0.4	0.3	1.2	0.3	0.1
14 Miscellaneous assets	–	0.6	0.8	2.1	2.8	–.4	0.2	1.8	2.6	6.1	5.6
15 Net increase in liabilities	9.3	14.9	13.5	22.8	27.4	14.2	12.8	8.0	14.0	21.1	21.5
16 Shares/deposits	10.2	14.9	12.9	22.9	27.2	13.3	12.4	8.6	13.8	20.5	21.6
17 Checkable	1.8	2.3	1.5	3.1	3.4	1.8	1.3	1.5	1.7	5.1	4.5
18 Small time & savings	8.2	12.6	11.3	19.4	23.5	11.1	10.3	6.4	11.8	15.5	17.1
19 Large time	0.2	–	0.1	0.3	0.3	0.3	0.6	0.7	0.3	–	–
20 Fed. Home Loan Banks loans	–	–	–	–	–	–	–	–	–	–	–
21 Miscellaneous liabilities	–.9	–	0.6	–.1	0.2	0.9	0.4	–.6	0.2	0.6	–.1
22 Discrepancy	–1.0	–.5	–1.1	–1.1	–1.2	–1.5	–1.6	–1.8	–1.6	–1.7	–3.0

*Data are in billions of dollars.
SOURCE: Flow of Funds, Board of Governors of the Federal Reserve System, Washington, D.C. 20551.

TABLE 3.11 Financial Assets and Liabilities for Financial Companies*

Panel A: Outstanding Levels

		1982	1983	1984	1985	1986	1987	1988	1989	1990	1991	1992
1	Total financial assets	242.7	270.4	306.1	365.3	421.3	486.0	534.6	571.2	610.9	633.9	637.2
2	Checkable dep. and currency	4.9	5.1	5.2	5.5	5.9	6.5	7.3	8.3	9.4	10.0	11.9
3	Credit market instruments	212.3	237.6	273.3	319.7	362.4	409.9	448.0	468.6	497.0	484.9	486.6
4	Mortgages	18.7	20.5	23.8	28.6	34.2	42.2	47.3	53.8	65.5	65.8	68.4
5	Consumer credit	93.2	103.7	111.7	132.4	151.0	154.0	155.3	144.6	138.0	126.3	121.7
6	Other loans (to business)	100.4	113.4	137.8	158.7	177.2	213.8	245.3	270.2	293.4	292.9	296.5
7	Miscellaneous assets	25.5	27.8	27.6	40.1	53.1	67.6	79.4	94.3	104.5	138.4	138.7
8	Total liabilities	216.3	241.6	274.7	329.7	382.2	438.9	477.9	503.3	534.5	556.5	556.7
9	Credit market instruments	144.9	159.7	183.6	224.3	275.9	299.1	323.0	350.4	374.4	393.0	389.4
10	Corporate bonds	77.0	81.0	90.5	105.3	131.6	141.2	147.0	162.7	178.2	191.3	195.3
11	Bank loans n.e.c	16.5	18.3	20.0	16.4	20.0	22.9	23.9	27.0	31.0	42.3	37.4
12	Open market paper	51.4	60.5	73.1	102.7	124.3	135.0	152.1	160.7	165.3	159.5	156.4
13	Taxes payable	–	–	–	0.1	0.1	0.2	0.3	0.4	0.6	0.7	0.9
14	Miscellaneous liabilities	71.4	81.8	91.0	105.3	106.2	139.6	154.6	152.5	159.5	162.7	166.5
15	Fgn. dir. invest. in US	0.4	–	1.9	0.4	3.6	–.2	–.5	9.3	4.6	6.2	6.7
16	Investment by parent	23.2	28.1	36.9	52.5	60.0	50.0	36.8	35.2	37.5	34.5	37.8
17	Other	47.8	53.6	52.1	52.4	42.6	89.8	118.4	107.9	117.4	122.1	121.9

*Data are in billions of dollars.

SOURCE: Flow of Funds, Board of Governors of the Federal Reserve System, Washington, D.C. 20551.

Panel B: Annual Flows

		1982	*1983*	*1984*	*1985*	*1986*	*1987*	*1988*	*1989*	*1990*	*1991*	*1992*
1	Gross saving	–.1	1.1	0.5	0.1	0.3	4.4	5.2	5.9	5.2	4.3	4.4
2	Fixed nonres. investment	1.4	2.4	3.8	4.2	5.2	5.2	5.6	6.6	6.2	5.6	6.6
3	Net acq. of financial assets	11.8	27.7	35.7	59.2	56.0	62.7	50.6	36.6	39.7	23.0	3.3
4	Checkable dep. & currency	0.1	0.1	0.2	0.3	0.4	0.6	0.8	1.0	1.1	1.2	1.3
5	Credit market instruments	8.2	25.3	35.7	46.4	42.6	47.6	38.1	32.0	28.4	–12.1	1.7
6	Mortgages	1.9	1.8	3.3	4.8	5.6	8.0	5.1	6.5	11.7	0.3	2.7
7	Consumer credit	5.4	10.4	8.0	20.7	18.6	3.0	1.4	–.7	–6.6	–11.7	–4.6
8	Other loans (to business)	0.9	13.1	24.4	20.9	18.4	36.6	31.6	26.3	23.3	–.6	3.6
9	Miscellaneous assets	3.5	2.3	–.1	12.3	13.0	14.6	11.7	3.6	10.2	33.9	0.3
10	Net increase in liabilities	10.1	25.3	33.1	55.0	52.5	56.7	39.0	25.4	31.2	22.0	0.3
11	Credit market instruments	3.3	14.9	23.9	40.7	51.5	23.2	23.9	27.4	24.0	18.6	–3.6
12	Corporate bonds	8.1	4.0	9.6	14.7	26.3	9.6	5.9	15.6	15.5	13.0	4.0
13	Bank loans n.e.c	1.0	1.8	1.7	–3.6	3.7	2.9	1.0	3.1	4.0	11.3	–4.6
14	Open market paper	–5.8	9.1	12.6	29.6	21.6	10.7	17.1	8.7	4.6	–5.8	–3.1
15	Taxes payable	–	–	–	–	–	0.1	0.1	0.1	0.2	0.2	0.1
16	Miscellaneous	6.8	10.4	9.2	14.3	0.9	33.4	15.0	–2.2	7.0	3.2	3.8
17	Fgn. dir. invest. in US	0.2	–.3	1.9	–1.6	1.2	–.2	–.5	7.2	–3.5	2.7	–.3
18	Investment by parent	6.7	4.9	8.8	15.6	7.5	–10.0	–13.2	–1.5	2.2	–3.0	3.4
19	Other	–.1	5.8	–1.5	0.3	–7.8	43.6	28.8	–7.8	8.3	3.5	0.7
20	Discrepancy	–3.3	–3.7	–5.9	–8.3	–8.5	–6.8	–12.0	–11.8	–9.5	–2.4	–5.2

*Data are in billions of dollars.

SOURCE: Flow of Funds, Board of Governors of the Federal Reserve System, Washington, D.C. 20551.

of \$156.4 billion (line 12), primarily commercial paper. Finance company funds from their manufacturing affiliates are reflected in the "funds from parent companies" of \$37.8 billion (line 16). Deposits are not shown separately on Table 3.11.

Assets of finance companies are concentrated in loans to individuals and businesses. Of total financial assets of \$637.2 billion (line 1), loans to business of \$296.5 billion (line 6), loans to consumers of \$121.7 billion (line 5), and mortgages of \$68.4 billion (line 4), account for most credit activity. Finance companies have been increasing their market share in these credit markets in the United States in recent years.

Insurance-Type Intermediaries

The second major class of financial institutions are "insurance-type" financial intermediaries which includes insurance companies and pension funds. In contrast to deposits, insurance liabilities are contractual commitments to pay money to customers or beneficiaries if certain events occur. In the case of life insurance, the insurance contract requires paying a death benefit. In the case of casualty insurance, payment must be made when a legitimate claim for an insured loss is filed. Pension funds are included in the insurance-type classification of financial institutions because their liabilities are similar to those of life insurance company liabilities. Retirees claim benefits when they retire or their beneficiaries claim death benefits if they die. Insurance-type intermediaries are sometimes called contractual intermediaries because their liabilities are obligations to pay cash under the terms of insurance or pension fund contracts.

Life and Health Insurance Companies. Life insurance companies are among the oldest forms of financial institutions. The first U.S. life insurance company was the Presbyterian Minister's Fund, founded in 1759. The basic formula underlying the life insurance business is simple and is similar to that of thrift institutions. Individuals pool funds by the regular payment of savings into a reserve. In the case of life insurance, the payments are called *premiums,* and the pool of savings becomes *life insurance reserves.* Upon the death of an insured, a payment or *life insurance benefit* is paid to beneficiaries named in the insurance contract.

Balance sheet data for life insurance companies in the United States reflect their operations. Panel A of Table 3.12 shows liabilities of \$1,517.8 billion (line 16) in 1992, of which \$422.6 billion were life insurance reserves (line 17). A recent development in the insurance business is seen in the growth of life insurance companies in providing for retirement benefits. Life insurance pension fund reserves were \$930 billion (line 18) in 1992, more than twice traditional life insurance liabilities.

Life insurance companies' liabilities tend to be long term and this is reflected in the composition of their assets, which are heavily committed to corporate bonds and mortgages. In 1992, bonds owned by life insurance companies accounted for \$653.9 billion (line 11 in Table 3.12A) and mortgages \$246.7 billion (line 12), more than half of the \$1,614.3 billion in total assets (line 1). Other major

TABLE 3.12 Financial Assets and Liabilities for Life Insurance Companies

Panel A: Outstanding Levels

		1982	1983	1984	1985	1986	1987	1988	1989	1990	1991	1992
1	Total financial assets	567.5	632.7	697.2	796.1	905.9	1005.3	1132.9	1260.2	1367.4	1505.3	1614.3
2	Checkable dep. and currency	4.6	4.0	4.6	5.1	5.8	4.9	4.6	5.0	4.9	5.5	5.6
3	Money mkt. fund shares	6.7	4.8	7.0	9.1	10.0	6.9	7.0	6.2	18.1	25.0	27.1
4	Mutual fund shares	2.8	2.7	3.0	3.5	14.5	12.1	18.5	19.1	30.7	46.7	57.8
5	Corporate equities	52.9	62.2	60.3	74.0	76.4	80.5	89.3	106.5	97.9	117.9	134.6
6	Credit market instruments	456.6	509.0	563.1	637.5	724.5	816.2	920.2	1022.0	1116.5	1199.4	1282.0
7	U.S. government securities	35.2	54.5	78.1	101.1	119.0	124.1	134.3	153.8	180.2	241.9	281.8
8	Treasury	16.5	28.6	41.2	51.7	59.0	57.1	58.6	52.9	59.2	77.8	88.8
9	Agency	18.6	25.9	36.9	49.4	60.0	67.0	75.7	100.8	121.0	164.2	193.0
10	Tax-exempt securities	9.0	10.0	8.7	9.7	11.7	10.7	9.1	9.0	12.3	10.2	11.4
11	Corporate & foreign bonds	202.3	219.1	242.8	280.6	321.4	388.3	457.5	511.0	566.9	595.1	653.9
12	Mortgages	142.0	151.0	156.7	171.8	193.8	212.4	232.9	254.2	267.9	265.3	246.7
13	Open market paper	15.1	20.4	22.3	20.0	24.5	27.1	32.2	36.6	27.7	20.8	16.1
14	Policy loans	53.0	54.1	54.5	54.4	54.1	53.6	54.2	57.4	61.6	66.4	72.1
15	Miscellaneous assets	44.0	50.1	59.1	66.8	74.8	84.7	93.4	101.3	99.4	110.7	107.3
16	Total liabilities	540.0	595.7	662.1	750.3	855.4	949.3	1068.2	1185.4	1290.8	1412.7	1517.8
17	Life insurance reserves	223.3	231.1	236.1	246.5	263.7	289.5	314.4	342.8	368.1	393.8	422.6
18	Pension fund reserves	242.9	281.7	328.3	391.7	474.2	536.9	621.9	699.7	784.1	865.2	930.0
19	Fed. Home Loan Banks loans	–	–	–	–	–	–	–	–	–	–	–
20	Taxes payable	0.7	0.6	0.4	0.4	0.4	0.6	0.7	0.8	0.8	0.7	0.8
21	Miscellaneous liabilities	73.1	82.4	97.2	111.6	117.0	122.4	131.2	142.0	137.7	153.0	164.3

*Data are in billions of dollars.

SOURCE: Flow of Funds, Board of Governors of the Federal Reserve System, Washington, D.C. 20551.

Panel B: Annual Flows

		1983	*1984*	*1985*	*1986*	*1987*	*1988*	*1989*	*1990*	*1991*	*1992*
1	Gross savings	3.4	1.8	–.1	–5.7	–9.3	–.8	–2.1	–2.0	–.9	–.3
2	Fixed nonres. investment	2.6	4.0	3.8	4.3	5.1	5.2	5.7	6.1	5.3	5.9
3	Net acq. of financial assets	59.1	66.7	90.6	104.7	101.2	114.7	115.1	111.2	119.9	102.6
4	Checkable dep. & currency	–.6	0.7	0.5	0.7	–.9	–.3	0.5	–.1	0.3	0.1
5	Money mkt. fund shares	–1.9	2.2	2.1	8.9	–3.1	0.1	–.8	11.9	6.9	2.1
6	Mutual fund shares	–.4	0.5	1.1	10.2	–2.2	5.7	–4.1	12.6	8.5	6.5
7	Corporate securities	3.4	0.3	4.8	–2.1	5.7	–3.4	9.7	–5.7	9.5	14.9
8	Credit market instruments	52.5	54.1	74.4	86.9	91.7	104.8	101.8	94.4	83.2	82.4
9	U.S. government securities	19.3	25.6	23.0	17.9	5.1	18.2	19.5	26.4	61.7	39.8
10	Treasury	12.1	12.4	10.5	7.3	–2.0	1.5	–5.6	6.2	18.6	11.0
11	Agency	7.2	11.0	12.5	10.6	7.0	8.7	25.1	20.2	43.1	28.8
12	Tax-exempt securities	0.9	–1.3	1.0	2.0	–1.0	–1.5	–.1	3.3	–2.1	1.1
13	Corporate and fgn. bonds	16.7	23.7	37.8	40.8	66.9	69.2	53.6	55.8	28.2	58.9
14	Mortgages	9.0	5.7	15.1	22.0	18.5	20.5	21.4	13.6	–2.6	–18.6
15	Open market paper	5.3	1.9	–2.3	4.5	2.7	5.1	4.4	–4.9	–6.9	–4.6
16	Policy loans	1.1	0.4	–.1	–.3	–.4	0.6	3.2	4.1	4.8	5.7
17	Miscellaneous assets	6.1	9.1	7.7	8.0	9.9	8.7	8.0	–2.0	11.3	–3.4
18	Net increase in liabilities	55.8	66.3	88.3	105.1	93.9	118.9	117.2	105.4	122.0	105.0
19	Life insurance reserves	7.8	5.0	10.4	17.2	25.7	24.9	28.4	25.3	25.6	28.8
20	Pension fund reserves	38.8	46.7	63.4	82.5	62.7	85.0	77.8	84.4	81.1	64.8
21	Fed. Home Loan Banks loans	–	–	–	–	–	–	–	–	–	–
22	Taxes payable	–.1	–.2	–	–	0.2	0.1	0.1	–	–.1	0.1
23	Miscellaneous liabilities	9.2	14.8	14.4	5.4	5.3	8.8	10.8	–4.3	15.3	11.3
24	Discrepancy	–2.6	–2.6	–6.3	–9.6	–21.6	–1.8	–5.7	–13.9	–4.2	–3.7

*Data are in billions of dollars.
SOURCE: Flow of Funds, Board of Governors of the Federal Reserve System, Washington, D.C. 20551.

investments include U.S. Treasury and Agency securities of $281.8 billion (line 7) and corporate equities of $134.6 billion (line 5).

Health insurance is often offered by affiliates of life insurance companies and it is common to talk of the life and health insurance business. However, the risks of insuring people against the costs of illness are very different from those of life insurance. Health insurance cash flows in the absence of government intervention are similar to those of casualty companies discussed below. The reason for combining life and health insurance is simply that they serve the same market—individuals and families. The flow-of-funds accounts do not report health insurance company reserves for the United States, but they amounted to $30 billion in 1989, up from $10.4 in 1979. Health care is insured by governments in many countries, like Canada and Germany. Health care is at the center of a major policy debate worldwide and will offer financial institution managers many chances to make and lose money in the future as the health insurance environment changes.

Property and Casualty Insurance Companies. Property and casualty insurances also have a long and venerable history. Insurance against accidents goes back to ancient times. The earliest casualty insurance offered by Lloyd's Insurance Exchange in London was against the risk of water transport—maritime risks. The Insurance Company of North America, founded in 1792 and the first American stock insurance company, was formed to write marine insurance.

Property and casualty insurance companies enter contracts promising to compensate insured parties for losses due to accident or theft. There are similarities between life insurance and property and casualty insurance: customers pay premiums to an insurance company that promises to pay cash when a claim is filed. There are two fundamental differences between property and casualty insurance and life insurance: (1) the probabilities of claims and losses are more difficult to estimate than are mortality statistics; and (2) insurance payments are not fixed in dollar amount but vary with the severity of the accident, loss, or theft.

Assets and liabilities of property and casualty insurance companies in the United States are shown in Panel A of Table 3.13. These insurance companies are designated "other insurance companies" in the flow of fund to distinguish them from life insurance. Total financial assets for property and casualty insurance companies in 1992 was $597.1 billion (line 1). In contrast to life insurance companies, assets of property insurers tend to shorter term. Over a quarter of their assets are in Treasury and Agency securities, amounting to $151.4 billion (line 6). Another large asset holding is in tax-exempt municipal bonds, of $134.3 billion (line 9).

Pension Funds. Pension funds are among the fastest growing financial intermediaries. In the dozen years between 1980 and 1992, private pension and local government employee pension funds assets in the United States quadrupled to nearly $2.2 trillion and $955 billion, respectively. The financial asset data for private and local government pension funds are shown separately in Tables 3.14 and 3.15 (line 1). The enormous growth of pension funds led Peter Drucker, the management observer, to describe workers' growing ownership of American business as "pension fund socialism" (Drucker, 1976). By 1992, private and government pension funds owned $982.4 and $448.9 billion in corporate equities, respectively.

TABLE 3.13 Financial Assets and Liabilities for Other Insurance Companies

Panel A: Outstanding Levels

		1982	*1983*	*1984*	*1985*	*1986*	*1987*	*1988*	*1989*	*1990*	*1991*	*1992*
1	Total financial assets	212.3	235.2	250.9	298.6	353.6	405.0	453.9	503.0	533.3	576.8	597.1
2	Checkable dep. and currency	3.0	2.6	3.1	4.3	5.6	5.5	5.4	6.0	6.5	5.3	5.6
3	Security RPs	4.1	13.7	17.9	25.6	23.7	24.6	27.9	27.8	31.0	25.9	32.2
4	Corporate equities	38.5	48.1	44.7	57.0	61.2	65.1	71.4	84.0	79.9	94.1	97.3
5	Credit market instruments	137.0	138.6	150.3	176.5	219.2	258.6	287.9	317.5	344.0	376.3	389.0
6	U.S. government securities	22.6	28.1	37.2	51.0	64.8	73.3	82.6	97.0	111.0	146.2	151.4
7	Treasury	14.1	17.4	23.3	28.8	42.6	51.0	60.0	71.0	79.0	104.0	108.7
8	Agency	8.5	10.7	13.9	22.2	22.3	22.3	22.6	26.0	32.0	42.1	42.6
9	Tax-exempt securities	87.0	86.7	84.7	88.2	101.9	124.8	134.1	134.8	136.9	126.8	134.3
10	Corporate & foreign bonds	25.8	21.6	25.7	33.9	48.0	55.5	65.7	79.3	89.2	97.2	97.9
11	Commercial mortgages	1.6	2.3	2.7	3.3	4.3	5.0	5.6	6.5	6.9	6.2	5.4
12	Trade credit	20.2	22.2	25.0	27.2	32.1	35.7	42.5	45.3	47.2	50.1	49.0
13	Miscellaneous assets	9.5	9.9	9.9	10.0	11.8	15.5	18.9	22.4	24.7	25.1	24.0
14	Total liabilities	130.3	163.2	177.4	214.9	258.5	304.4	335.8	370.1	397.3	415.6	438.9
15	Taxes payable	0.3	0.2	0.2	0.1	0.1	0.1	0.1	0.2	0.4	0.5	0.3
16	Miscellaneous liabilities	150.1	163.0	177.2	214.7	258.4	304.3	335.6	369.9	396.9	415.1	438.7

*Data are in billions of dollars.

SOURCE: Flow of Funds, Board of Governors of the Federal Reserve System, Washington, D.C. 20551.

Panel B: Annual Flows

		1983	1984	1985	1986	1987	1988	1989	1990	1991	1992
1	Gross saving	–.6	–4.2	–6.4	–.8	2.5	3.7	1.2	–.5	–1.2	–8.5
2	Fixed nonres. investment	1.0	1.4	1.4	1.7	2.0	2.1	2.3	2.4	2.1	2.2
3	Net acq. of financial assets	15.7	15.3	33.2	49.4	48.4	45.6	42.6	26.4	14.0	12.2
4	Checkable dep. & currency	–.4	0.5	1.2	1.3	–.1	–.1	0.6	0.5	–1.1	0.2
5	Security RPs	9.6	4.2	5.7	0.1	0.9	3.3	–.1	3.2	–5.1	6.3
6	Corporate equities	2.1	–4.3	–2.0	–.3	2.7	3.6	7.9	–6.9	–15.1	–3.3
7	Credit market instruments	1.7	11.7	26.1	42.7	39.5	29.2	29.7	26.3	32.3	12.7
8	U.S. government securities	5.5	9.1	13.8	13.9	8.5	9.2	14.4	14.0	35.2	5.2
9	Treasury	3.3	5.9	5.5	13.8	8.4	9.0	11.0	8.0	25.0	4.7
10	Agency	2.2	3.2	8.2	0.1	0.1	0.2	3.4	6.0	10.1	0.5
11	Tax-exempt securities	–.3	–1.9	3.5	13.7	22.8	9.3	0.7	2.2	–10.2	7.5
12	Corporate and fgn. bonds	–4.2	4.1	8.2	14.1	7.5	10.1	13.6	9.9	8.0	0.7
13	Commercial mortgages	0.7	0.4	0.7	1.0	0.6	0.6	0.9	0.4	–.7	–.8
14	Trade credit	2.0	2.8	2.2	4.9	3.6	6.8	2.8	2.0	2.9	–1.1
15	Miscellaneous assets	0.7	0.5	–.1	0.7	1.8	2.7	1.6	1.3	0.1	–2.6
16	Net increase in liabilities	14.2	18.5	45.1	49.4	46.4	33.1	36.5	30.0	15.6	26.2
17	Corporate equity issues	1.5	3.9	7.8	6.8	4.0	1.7	2.4	3.4	0.7	3.4
18	Taxes payable	–	–	–.1	–	–	0.1	0.1	0.1	0.1	–.2
19	Miscellaneous liabilities	12.7	14.6	37.3	42.7	42.4	31.3	34.0	26.5	14.9	23.1
20	Discrepancy	–3.1	–2.4	4.1	–2.5	–1.5	–10.9	–7.3	0.8	–1.7	3.4

*Data are in billions of dollars.

SOURCE: Flow of Funds, Board of Governors of the Federal Reserve System, Washington, D.C. 20551.

TABLE 3.14 Financial Assets and Liabilities for Private Pension Funds

		Panel A: Outstanding Levels										
		1982	*1983*	*1984*	*1985*	*1986*	*1987*	*1988*	*1989*	*1990*	*1991*	*1992*
1	Total financial assets	659.4	800.5	861.1	1093.0	1290.8	1367.0	1421.8	1705.6	1629.1	2055.3	2231.7
2	Checkable dep. and currency	2.3	2.7	3.3	4.0	4.3	5.0	4.6	5.8	5.8	4.7	4.7
3	Small time & svgs. deposits	37.9	48.0	54.8	73.5	88.9	103.8	120.0	143.8	134.0	173.7	189.6
4	Large time deposits	11.5	12.9	13.2	16.5	20.5	22.9	31.3	44.2	41.6	55.4	60.6
5	Money mkt. fund shares	4.7	5.9	6.9	9.1	11.0	12.8	14.8	17.8	17.3	18.8	28.1
6	Mutual fund shares	5.8	6.9	7.9	10.8	14.0	29.0	31.2	41.6	45.4	14.4	70.9
7	Corporate equities	282.9	350.3	359.0	464.4	550.9	538.9	609.5	734.7	657.6	888.5	982.4
8	Credit market instruments	227.2	267.8	306.9	378.5	446.2	479.8	509.0	590.2	607.4	692.7	731.5
9	U.S. government securities	107.2	132.2	153.0	189.6	220.7	241.4	250.1	311.2	321.8	362.8	384.1
10	Treasury	59.8	76.1	90.6	115.3	137.6	154.5	164.1	208.9	220.8	253.9	274.0
11	Agency	47.4	56.1	62.4	74.3	83.1	87.0	86.0	102.3	100.9	108.8	110.1
12	Tax-exempt securities	0.6	0.5	0.9	1.5	3.6	1.1	1.1	1.4	1.4	1.6	1.7
13	Corporate & foreign bonds	95.2	107.9	123.4	155.1	178.3	190.1	203.9	226.1	235.5	275.7	293.1
14	Mortgages	9.1	9.9	10.0	12.5	15.5	13.5	17.7	25.1	23.8	31.8	34.5
15	Open market paper	15.2	17.2	19.6	19.9	28.2	33.8	36.3	26.3	24.9	20.8	18.1
16	Miscellaneous assets	87.0	106.0	109.1	136.3	155.1	174.8	101.3	127.6	119.6	157.3	171.9

*Data are in billions of dollars.

SOURCE: Flow of Funds, Board of Governors of the Federal Reserve System, Washington, D.C. 20551.

Panel B: Annual Flows

		1983	1984	1985	1986	1987	1988	1989	1990	1991	1992
1	Gross saving	1.0	1.3	1.7	2.1	2.5	2.8	3.5	3.7	4.3	4.5
2	Fixed nonres. investment	3.4	5.0	5.3	6.1	7.0	6.7	7.9	7.5	7.5	8.4
3	Net acq. of financial assets	80.2	47.3	136.2	114.1	60.0	–28.4	142.4	–11.9	197.5	78.0
4	Checkable dep. and currency	0.5	0.6	0.7	0.3	0.7	–.5	1.2	0.1	–1.1	–
5	Small time & svgs. deposits	10.0	6.9	18.7	15.4	14.9	16.2	23.8	–9.8	39.7	15.8
6	Large time deposits	1.4	0.3	3.3	4.0	2.4	8.5	12.8	–2.6	13.8	5.2
7	Money mkt. fund shares	1.2	1.0	2.1	1.9	1.8	2.0	2.9	–	1.0	1.3
8	Mutual fund shares	0.4	1.1	2.0	2.3	16.5	1.7	6.8	5.7	14.1	4.9
9	Corporate equities	7.1	–4.8	10.6	3.6	–29.6	–12.2	–12.5	–14.4	7.0	–2.7
10	Credit market instruments	40.6	39.1	71.5	67.7	33.6	29.2	81.1	17.2	85.3	38.9
11	U.S. government securities	25.1	20.8	36.6	31.1	20.7	8.7	61.1	10.6	41.0	21.4
12	Treasury	16.3	14.5	24.7	22.3	16.9	9.6	44.8	12.0	33.1	20.1
13	Agency	8.8	6.3	11.9	8.8	3.8	–1.0	16.3	–1.4	7.9	1.3
14	Tax-exempt securities	–	0.4	0.6	2.1	–2.5	–	0.3	–	0.2	0.1
15	Corporate & foreign bonds	12.7	15.5	31.7	23.2	11.8	13.8	22.2	9.3	40.2	17.4
16	Mortgages	0.8	0.1	2.5	3.0	–2.0	4.2	7.4	–1.3	8.0	2.7
17	Open market paper	2.0	2.4	0.2	8.3	5.6	2.5	–9.9	–1.4	–4.1	–2.7
18	Miscellaneous assets	18.9	3.1	27.2	18.8	19.6	–73.4	26.3	–8.0	37.7	14.7
19	Discrepancy	–2.3	–3.6	–3.6	–4.0	–4.5	–3.8	–4.4	–3.8	–3.3	–4.0

*Data are in billions of dollars.

Source: Flow of Funds, Board of Governors of the Federal Reserve System, Washington, D.C. 20551.

TABLE 3.15 Financial Assets and Liabilities for State and Local Government Employee Retirement Funds

Panel A: Outstanding Levels

		1982	1983	1984	1985	1986	1987	1988	1989	1990	1991	1992
1	Total financial assets	260.9	305.4	350.3	398.1	462.3	508.5	596.6	721.9	736.5	859.7	955.0
2	Checkable dep. and currency	1.0	1.4	2.0	2.4	2.0	2.3	2.8	2.4	3.9	4.2	6.7
3	Time deposits	6.0	8.8	12.0	13.3	16.8	14.0	17.4	17.4	14.1	11.6	9.3
4	Corporate equities	60.2	89.6	96.5	120.1	150.2	169.6	219.7	300.1	296.1	386.6	448.9
5	Credit market instruments	190.7	199.8	235.7	257.4	285.2	309.6	346.2	390.9	405.9	439.4	471.6
6	U.S. government securities	71.2	88.2	111.2	123.5	144.2	168.7	184.5	198.2	219.8	242.0	275.5
7	Treasury	36.9	48.9	67.9	82.9	95.0	112.9	128.3	128.1	141.3	155.0	173.3
8	Agency	34.3	39.3	43.3	40.6	49.2	55.9	56.2	70.0	78.5	87.0	102.2
9	Tax-exempt securities	3.1	2.0	1.5	1.1	0.8	0.8	0.5	0.5	0.7	0.8	0.9
10	Corporate & foreign bonds	102.6	95.0	107.7	117.4	124.7	103.0	125.7	158.4	147.1	150.3	151.4
11	Mortgages	13.8	14.7	15.3	15.3	15.6	15.4	15.6	15.3	16.1	16.9	13.6
12	Open market paper	—	–	–	–	–	21.6	19.8	18.6	22.3	29.4	30.2
13	Miscellaneous assets	3.0	5.8	4.2	5.0	8.0	13.0	10.5	11.0	16.5	17.9	18.5

*Data are in billions of dollars.

SOURCE: Flow of Funds, Board of Governors of the Federal Reserve System, Washington, D.C. 20551.

Panel B: Annual Flows

		1983	1984	1985	1986	1987	1988	1989	1990	1991	1992
1	Net acq. of financial assets	35.1	45.3	52.8	57.1	53.3	63.9	68.6	64.0	54.7	58.2
2	Checkable dep. and currency	0.4	0.6	0.4	–.3	0.3	0.5	–.3	1.5	0.3	2.5
3	Time deposits	2.8	3.2	1.4	3.5	1.0	3.4	–	–3.3	–2.5	–2.3
4	Corporate equities	20.0	7.3	28.6	23.1	26.4	25.9	23.7	16.8	22.0	25.1
5	Credit market instruments	9.1	35.8	21.7	27.8	20.6	36.6	44.7	43.5	33.5	32.2
6	U.S. government securities	17.0	23.1	12.3	20.7	24.6	15.8	13.6	21.7	22.2	33.5
7	Treasury	12.0	19.0	15.0	12.1	17.9	15.5	–.2	13.2	13.7	18.3
8	Agency	4.9	4.1	–2.7	8.6	6.7	0.3	13.8	8.5	8.5	15.2
9	Tax-exempt securities	–1.1	–.5	–.4	–.3	–	–.4	–	0.2	0.1	0.1
10	Corporate & foreign bonds	–7.6	12.6	9.8	7.2	–8.9	22.7	32.7	17.3	3.2	1.1
11	Mortgages	0.9	0.6	0.1	0.3	–.2	0.3	–.3	0.8	0.8	–3.3
12	Open market paper	–	–	–	–	5.1	–1.8	–1.2	3.7	7.1	0.8
13	Miscellaneous assets	2.8	–1.6	0.8	3.0	5.0	–2.5	0.5	5.5	1.4	0.6

*Data are in billions of dollars.

SOURCE: Flow of Funds, Board of Governors of the Federal Reserve System, Washington, D.C. 20551.

Pension funds are managed for the benefit of pension fund participants. Most pension funds are managed by professional asset managers. Some large funds, like the largest private pension funds, the Teachers Insurance and Annuity Association (TIAA) and the College Equities Retirement Fund (CREF), have staffs to manage their own assets. Pension funds managed by insurance companies are not included in the assets of private pension funds.

Private pension funds in the United States are the subject of the Employee Retirement Income Security Act of 1974 (ERISA), which covers pension funds set up by companies, unions, or individuals. Qualifying pension funds have substantial tax benefits for participants and sponsors. ERISA has had a major impact on the pension fund industry. In contrast to private pension funds, state and local government pension funds are not regulated by ERISA. These funds are often run by political entities, like city or state governments.

Investment Companies

Pooling savings and investing them is another ancient social and financial activity. The goal of savers is to earn higher returns than those on deposits and to participate in the development of the economy directly by the selection of securities in particular firms. The advantages to pooling savings are lower commissions and fees as well as increased ability to diversify investment holdings. Small saver investment clubs have been around as long as investments could be made.

Increasingly, savers turn their funds over to professionals for management. The major difference between funds invested by investment companies under professional managers and other financial intermediaries discussed previously is that no commitment is made concerning the performance of the funds. Savers have no claim on an investment fund beyond their pro rata share in its performance. No fixed payments, as with deposits, and no claims, as with insurance or pension funds, need be met by the managers of investment funds.

Investment companies in the United States have been regulated by the Securities and Exchange Commission since the 1940 Investment Company Act. This act requires that publicly held investment companies declare a management goal, such as capital gains or income, and make disclosures to purchasers. The tax treatment of investment companies is very important. As long as all income is passed through to the investors, the investment company or fund is not taxed at the Federal level.

Mutual Funds and Real Estate Trusts. Investment companies can be mutual funds or closed-end funds. The most phenomenal growth of investment funds around the world since the Second World War has been in mutual funds. Mutual funds differ from buying shares in closed-end investment companies because fund shares are redeemable at net asset value (NAV). NAV is the market value of the investments of a fund divided by the number of shares held. From inconsequential assets two decades ago, stock and bond mutual fund assets were $1.05 trillion by 1992, as shown in Table 3.16 (Panel A, line 1). Even more remarkable has been the growth of Money Market Mutual Funds shown in Table 3.17. Money market funds are invested in short-term government, corporate, and

TABLE 3.16 Financial Assets and Liabilities for Mutual Funds

Panel A: Outstanding Levels

		1982	1983	1984	1985	1986	1987	1988	1989	1990	1991	1992
1	Total financial assets	76.9	112.1	136.7	240.2	413.3	460.1	478.3	566.2	602.1	813.9	1050.2
2	Checkable dep. and currency	1.2	1.7	2.1	3.8	6.5	6.9	7.2	8.5	8.7	12.3	16.1
3	Corporate equities	49.4	74.4	80.6	113.7	161.2	181.7	187.6	250.5	233.2	351.1	451.2
4	Credit market instruments	26.3	36.0	54.0	122.7	245.8	271.6	283.4	307.2	360.2	450.5	582.8
5	U.S. government securities	5.1	5.7	12.0	64.9	124.2	134.1	114.9	120.0	137.5	191.4	251.8
6	Treasury	5.1	5.7	11.5	52.9	89.3	99.2	81.5	86.8	101.0	143.1	185.3
7	Agency	–	–	0.5	12.0	34.9	34.9	33.4	33.2	36.5	48.3	66.5
8	Tax-exempt securities	8.0	13.4	19.1	33.5	65.3	70.7	78.7	93.6	109.1	137.1	172.9
9	Corporate & foreign bonds	10.2	13.0	16.5	20.1	46.9	54.2	68.4	74.1	87.6	100.5	128.9
10	Open market paper	3.0	4.0	6.4	4.1	9.4	12.6	21.4	19.6	25.9	21.5	29.3
11	Total shares outstanding	76.9	112.1	136.7	240.2	413.5	460.1	478.3	566.2	602.1	813.9	1050.2

*Data are in billions of dollars.

SOURCE: Flow of Funds, Board of Governors of the Federal Reserve System, Washington, D.C. 20551.

Panel B: Annual Flows

		1983	1984	1985	1986	1987	1988	1989	1990	1991	1992
1	Gross saving	-5.3	-3.1	-7.9	-15.0	-17.1	-9.9	-12.3	-12.0	-12.0	-12.0
2	Net acq. of financial assets	24.0	24.2	80.8	145.9	53.2	-3.8	26.3	56.0	138.5	203.4
3	Checkable dep. and currency	0.6	0.4	1.7	2.6	0.5	0.3	1.3	0.2	3.6	3.8
4	Corporate equities	13.7	5.9	10.3	20.2	26.9	-16.0	1.2	14.4	44.6	67.2
5	Credit market instruments	9.8	17.9	68.7	123.1	25.8	11.9	23.8	41.4	90.3	132.3
6	U.S. government securities	0.6	6.4	52.9	59.3	9.9	-19.2	5.1	7.4	53.9	60.4
7	Treasury	0.6	5.8	41.4	36.4	9.9	-17.7	5.3	4.1	42.1	42.2
8	Agency	–	0.3	11.5	22.9	–	-1.5	-.2	3.2	11.8	18.2
9	Tax-exempt securities	5.5	5.6	14.5	31.8	5.4	8.0	14.9	15.6	28.0	35.8
10	Corporate & foreign bonds	2.7	3.6	3.6	26.8	7.3	14.2	5.7	13.6	12.8	28.4
11	Open market paper	1.0	2.4	-2.3	5.3	3.2	8.9	-1.9	4.9	-4.4	7.8
12	Net share issues	29.3	27.3	88.7	160.9	70.2	6.1	38.5	67.9	130.3	215.4
13	Memo: Capital gains dividends	4.4	6.0	4.9	17.5	22.4	6.3	15.0	8.1	14.1	22.2

*Data are in billions of dollars.

SOURCE: Flow of Funds, Board of Governors of the Federal Reserve System, Washington, D.C. 20551.

TABLE 3.17 Financial Assets and Liabilities for Money Market Mutual Funds

Panel A: Outstanding Levels

		1982	*1983*	*1984*	*1985*	*1986*	*1987*	*1988*	*1989*	*1990*	*1991*	*1992*
1	Total financial assets	219.8	179.4	233.6	243.8	292.1	316.1	338.0	428.1	498.4	539.6	543.6
2	Checkable dep. and currency	0.3	–.3	–1.2	0.2	–	–.3	0.7	0.1	11.4	–.2	–2.7
3	Time deposits	40.8	24.0	23.6	16.8	19.1	33.6	32.8	41.2	21.0	33.0	30.9
4	Security RPs	16.2	13.0	22.8	26.1	32.2	39.3	41.7	54.9	59.0	68.2	67.1
5	Foreign deposits	23.8	21.9	21.2	19.0	22.2	21.6	29.7	26.4	27.1	21.6	20.5
6	Credit market instruments	137.0	119.2	164.2	178.1	212.2	214.0	224.7	291.8	372.7	402.7	404.1
7	U.S. government securities	54.6	36.2	42.4	42.7	43.2	41.3	29.9	35.8	82.4	120.9	134.6
8	Treasury	42.6	22.8	25.4	24.6	28.0	14.3	11.6	14.8	45.5	79.6	79.7
9	Agency	12.0	13.4	17.0	18.1	15.1	27.0	18.4	21.0	36.9	41.3	54.8
10	Tax-exempt securities	13.2	16.8	23.8	36.3	63.8	61.4	65.7	69.4	83.6	89.9	94.8
11	Open market paper	69.1	66.2	98.0	99.1	105.3	111.3	129.1	186.6	206.7	191.9	174.7
12	Miscellaneous	1.8	1.5	3.0	3.6	6.5	7.9	8.5	13.7	7.3	14.2	23.7
13	Total shares outstanding	219.8	179.4	233.6	243.8	292.1	316.1	338.0	428.1	498.4	539.6	543.6

*Data are in billions of dollars.

SOURCE: Flow of Funds, Board of Governors of the Federal Reserve System, Washington, D.C. 20551.

Panel B: Annual Flows

		1983	1984	1985	1986	1987	1988	1989	1990	1991	1992
1	Net scq. of financial assets	–40.4	54.2	10.2	48.3	24.0	21.9	90.1	70.3	41.2	3.9
2	Checkable dep. and currency	–.6	–1.0	1.4	–.2	–.3	1.0	–.6	11.3	–11.6	–2.5
3	Time deposits	–16.8	–.4	–4.8	2.3	14.4	–.8	8.3	–20.2	12.0	–2.1
4	Security RPs	–3.2	9.7	3.3	6.1	7.1	2.4	13.2	4.1	9.3	–1.1
5	Foreign deposits	–1.8	–.7	–2.2	3.1	–.6	8.1	–3.3	0.7	–5.4	–1.2
6	Credit market instruments	–17.7	45.0	13.9	34.1	1.8	10.7	67.1	80.9	30.1	1.3
7	U.S. government securities	–18.4	6.2	0.3	0.5	–1.9	–11.4	5.9	46.5	38.6	13.7
8	Treasury	–19.8	2.6	–.8	3.4	–13.7	–2.7	3.2	30.7	34.2	0.1
9	Agency	1.4	3.6	1.1	–3.0	11.9	–8.6	2.7	15.9	4.4	13.5
10	Tax exempt securities	3.6	7.0	12.4	27.5	–2.3	4.2	3.7	14.3	6.2	5.0
11	Open market paper	–3.0	31.8	1.2	6.2	6.0	17.8	57.5	20.1	–14.7	–17.3
12	Miscellaneous	–.4	1.5	0.6	2.7	1.4	0.5	5.2	–6.4	6.9	9.5
13	Net share issues	–40.4	54.2	10.2	48.3	24.0	21.9	90.1	70.3	41.2	3.9

*Data are in billions of dollars.

SOURCE: Flow of Funds, Board of Governors of the Federal Reserve System, Washington, D.C. 20551.

bank securities. Money market funds did not even exist in 1973 yet by 1992 they had $543.6 billion in assets (Panel A, line 1).

Real estate investment trusts (REITs) are investment companies specializing in real-estate related assets. Assets of these professionally managed investment funds have experienced much more variable growth than mutual funds. REITs had more assets in the 1970s (around $17 billion) than they did in 1992 when REIT assets amounted to $13.7 billion, as shown in Table 3.18 (Panel A, line 1). Total assets in these funds reflect changing perceptions of returns in real estate markets.

Professional Asset Management and Institutional Investors

Pension funds and investment companies are managed by professional portfolio managers or asset management firms. Professional asset managers do not own the assets they manage. They are hired under contracts to make decisions concerning the funds they manage in the interest of the beneficiaries of the pension fund or owners of the investment company that hired them. There are many different types of professional asset managers, from individuals operating out of their homes to giants like Bankers' Trust.

The term "institutional investor" is common in describing big investors buying and selling millions of shares as distinguished from retail investors who are small traders of hundreds of shares. Retail savers investing in pension funds or mutual funds are, in fact, turning their savings over to professional asset managers. Professional asset managers are part of what is meant by institutional investors. Institutional investors are asset managers working for bank trust departments, pension funds, insurance companies, and mutual funds. Some discussions of institutional investors leave the impression that institutional investors operate against the interests of small savers. Our discussion should make clear that institutional investors are managing private savers' money. Making markets more efficient for institutional investors benefits all of us.

Securities Firms

Securities are financial claims that can be bought and sold. Examples of securities are familiar to all of us. Nearly all securities are some kind of stock or bond. The fact that securities can be bought and sold differentiates them from many of the financial assets already discussed in this chapter—deposits, insurance policies, pension funds or investment companies—in which ownership of assets cannot be bought or sold.

Securities are issued by corporations and governments to raise funds. Nonfinancial firms and governments are not actively involved in financial market activity and only occasionally do they go to the market for funds. Financial markets evolve rapidly in response to changing economic conditions and occasional participants need guidance when going to the financial market to raise funds by selling securities. Securities firms offer individuals, businesses, and governments assistance in going to securities markets by performing three functions: (1) securities origination; (2) brokerage; and (3) market making.

TABLE 3.18 Financial Assets and Liabilities for Real Estate Investment Trusts

Panel A: Outstanding Levels

		1982	*1983*	*1984*	*1985*	*1986*	*1987*	*1988*	*1989*	*1990*	*1991*	*1992*
1	Total financial assets	3.2	3.5	5.0	7.6	7.5	9.3	10.9	11.6	11.2	11.1	13.7
2	Home mortgages	0.3	0.2	0.2	0.3	0.3	0.3	0.4	0.4	0.4	0.4	0.8
3	Commercial mortgages	1.5	1.5	1.9	3.8	3.9	4.5	5.1	5.4	5.0	4.2	1.8
4	Multifamily mortgages	0.8	0.9	1.3	1.8	1.8	2.1	2.4	2.5	2.3	2.2	4.8
5	Miscellaneous assets	0.6	0.8	1.5	1.7	1.6	2.3	3.0	3.3	3.5	4.3	6.3
6	Total liabilities	3.8	3.8	4.2	5.5	6.4	8.3	10.8	11.5	12.4	14.0	14.3
7	Credit market instruments	3.7	3.5	4.2	4.8	6.4	8.3	10.1	11.4	12.4	14.0	14.1
8	Mortgages	2.0	2.1	2.5	2.5	2.8	3.1	3.5	4.0	4.3	5.1	5.1
9	Corporate bonds	0.7	0.7	0.8	0.9	1.5	2.3	2.5	2.9	3.1	3.0	3.4
10	Bank loans n.e.c.	0.6	0.4	0.4	0.7	1.0	1.5	2.9	3.4	4.0	4.9	4.6
11	Open market paper	0.4	0.4	0.6	0.7	1.1	1.4	1.3	1.1	0.9	1.0	0.9
12	Miscellaneous liabilities	0.1	0.3	–	0.7	–	–	0.7	0.1	–	–	0.3

*Data are in billions of dollars.

SOURCE: Flow of Funds, Board of Governors of the Federal Reserve System, Washington, D.C. 20551.

Panel B: Annual Flows

	1983	1984	1985	1986	1987	1988	1989	1990	1991	1992
1 Gross saving	0.1	–	–.3	0.3	0.1	0.2	0.1	0.1	0.2	0.4
2 Fixed nonres. investment	0.4	0.4	0.5	0.6	0.7	0.6	0.7	0.5	0.5	0.7
3 Multifamily resid. invest.	0.2	0.2	0.2	0.3	0.4	0.3	0.3	0.3	0.2	0.3
4 Net acq. of financial assets	0.3	1.5	2.6	–.1	1.8	1.6	0.8	–.5	–.1	2.6
5 Mortgages	0.1	0.8	2.4	–	1.0	0.9	0.5	–.7	–1.0	0.6
6 Miscellaneous assets	0.2	0.7	0.2	–.1	0.7	0.7	0.2	0.2	0.8	2.0
7 Net increase in liabilities	1.0	2.4	3.9	1.0	3.3	3.0	2.4	1.1	1.4	4.4
8 Corporate equity issues	1.1	2.0	2.6	0.1	1.4	0.5	1.7	0.2	–.2	4.1
9 Credit market instruments	–.3	0.8	0.6	1.6	1.9	1.8	1.3	1.0	1.6	0.1
10 Mortgages	–	0.4	0.1	0.3	0.3	0.3	0.5	0.4	0.8	–
11 Corporate bonds	–	0.1	0.1	0.6	0.8	0.2	0.4	0.2	–.1	0.5
12 Bank loans n.e.c.	–.2	0.1	0.3	0.3	0.5	1.3	0.6	0.6	0.9	–.3
13 Open market paper	–.1	0.2	0.1	0.3	0.4	–.1	–.2	–.2	0.1	–.1
14 Miscellaneous liabilities	0.2	–.3	0.7	–.7	–	0.7	–.6	–.1	–	0.2
15 Discrepancy	0.2	0.3	0.3	0.4	0.5	0.6	0.7	0.9	1.0	1.2

*Data are in billions of dollars.
SOURCE: Flow of Funds, Board of Governors of the Federal Reserve System, Washington, D.C. 20551.

There are many ways to describe securities firms. Using the functional classification above, securities origination is usually performed by *investment banks*. In the United States, investment banking is dominated by big firms like Morgan Stanley and Goldman Sachs whereas in Germany universal banks like Deutsche Bank dominate. Trading and market making functions are provided by small and large *brokerage firms,* like Montgomery Securities in San Francisco and A. G. Edwards in St. Louis. Many large firms, like Nikkei Securities in Japan and Merrill Lynch in the United States, are *full-line brokerage firms,* meaning that they perform all three functions. History has provided additional descriptive terms, such as *wire houses* which receive buy and sell orders from small brokers in the hinterland to transact on the big city exchanges. Regulators describe as *clearing firms* those securities firms that deliver securities for smaller firms, and they further distinguish between *carrying firms,* which hold assets for customers, and *noncarrying firms,* which do not.

Total assets and liabilities of securities firms do not really reflect their level of activity. Brokers for example, do not take title to assets but only find buyers for sellers. The financial assets of securities brokers and dealers in the United States amounted to $372.1 billion in 1992, shown in Panel A, Table 3.19, substantially less than the total for banks, thrifts, or insurance companies. Security credit appears as both a financial asset and a liability for brokers and dealers in Table 3.19, amounting to $53.3 billion as an asset (line 9) and $164.1 billion as a liability (line 13). Other assets and liabilities represent inventories of securities and securities in the process of clearing carried for customers. We discuss the activities of securities firms briefly for investment banks, brokers, and market makers.

Investment Banks. Specialists have evolved to assist corporate and government borrowers requiring funds in going to securities markets; these are investment bankers. Not all fund-raising takes the form of issuing securities; another type of fund-raising assuming major significance in developed economics is private placements. A private placement occurs when a primary sector borrower finds funds from a financial institution or primary sector lender with the assistance of a specialist in placing funds such as an investment bank or commercial bank. In this case the borrower issues a financial liability that may resemble a security in some aspects but usually does not trade in securities markets, at least at first.

The competitive position of investment bankers in arranging for funds in the form of securities issues and private placements has been under major attack by a number of financial institutions who seek to share the large profits of investment bankers. Commercial banks, insurance companies, and finance companies, among others, have been attempting to compete with investment bankers in raising funds for corporations through securities issues or private placements in the United States. Commercial bankers, who already fund corporations with loans, can readily expand into investment banking in countries with universal banking, such as Germany.

Separation of commercial and investment banking was traditional in England and was established by the Glass–Steagall Act in the United States in

TABLE 3.19 Financial Assets and Liabilities for Security Brokers and Dealers

Panel A: Outstanding Levels

		1982	1983	1984	1985	1986	1987	1988	1989	1990	1991	1992
1	Total financial assets	83.3	90.5	118.4	156.0	184.6	137.9	135.9	236.6	262.1	332.5	372.1
2	Checkable dep. and currency	4.5	3.6	3.9	6.3	8.5	7.4	9.4	9.8	10.2	10.2	10.3
3	Corporate equities	4.9	10.0	8.9	14.1	17.7	10.7	12.2	14.1	9.6	14.3	14.8
4	Credit market instruments	38.5	30.7	59.5	65.1	78.3	54.9	46.7	142.9	177.9	226.9	267.1
5	Treasury securities	11.5	4.7	17.5	7.7	25.9	13.1	–4.7	85.2	122.7	162.6	193.3
6	Tax-exempt securities	4.6	6.5	11.0	19.9	16.6	8.3	7.5	7.1	7.9	9.4	11.3
7	Corporate bonds	5.9	7.9	13.7	22.9	23.2	19.4	29.1	32.9	28.9	40.9	50.9
8	Open market paper	16.4	11.6	17.3	14.5	12.6	14.2	14.8	17.8	18.4	14.0	11.4
9	Security credit	25.8	34.2	31.8	50.7	57.4	41.8	43.5	42.5	38.8	55.1	53.3
10	Miscellaneous assets	9.6	11.9	14.3	19.9	22.7	23.1	24.1	27.2	25.6	26.1	26.6
11	Total liabilities	74.9	80.1	108.1	141.3	164.3	114.5	111.5	213.2	239.2	307.4	348.0
12	Security RPs (net)	24.3	8.4	25.5	23.7	35.6	–8.8	–21.9	64.2	81.0	104.7	98.8
13	Security credit	44.1	49.2	56.0	80.5	83.6	73.5	74.8	91.4	98.6	133.8	164.1
14	From banks	26.2	28.7	34.5	45.4	39.6	34.4	33.9	38.2	36.2	46.8	88.0
15	Customer credit balances	17.8	20.6	21.6	35.1	44.0	39.1	40.9	53.2	62.4	87.0	76.1
16	Trade debt	–	1.0	1.5	2.3	3.4	3.2	7.5	13.8	15.3	10.0	21.7
17	Taxes payable	0.6	0.5	0.4	0.8	0.9	0.4	0.5	0.6	0.7	0.9	0.8
18	Miscellaneous liabilities	5.9	20.9	24.6	34.0	40.8	46.2	50.5	43.2	43.6	56.1	62.6
19	Fgn. direct invest. in US	1.8	2.3	3.7	3.8	3.6	3.1	4.8	6.3	3.8	4.5	4.2
20	Due to affiliates	5.7	6.4	6.5	12.9	14.8	29.5	45.9	55.3	45.5	35.2	45.7
21	Other	–1.6	12.3	14.4	17.2	22.3	13.6	–.2	–18.4	–5.6	16.3	12.7

*Data are in billions of dollars.

SOURCE: Flow of Funds, Board of Governors of the Federal Reserve System, Washington, D.C. 20551.

Panel B: Annual Flows

		1983	*1984*	*1985*	*1986*	*1987*	*1988*	*1989*	*1990*	*1991*	*1992*
1	Gross saving	–	−1.2	−.2	−1.3	0.2	−3.0	−1.1	−1.2	−.7	−.3
2	Fixed nonres. investment	1.1	1.2	1.1	1.2	1.2	0.9	0.8	0.6	0.5	0.5
3	Net acq. of financial assets	7.2	27.9	37.6	28.6	−57.2	−2.0	100.7	25.6	70.4	39.6
4	Checkable dep. & currency	−.9	0.3	2.4	2.2	−1.4	1.9	0.4	0.5	−.1	0.2
5	Corporate equities	4.3	−1.0	2.6	1.4	−7.1	0.1	−1.9	−3.3	2.4	−.6
6	Credit market instruments	−7.7	28.8	5.6	13.2	−30.6	−8.2	96.3	34.9	49.0	40.2
7	Treasury securities	−6.8	12.8	−9.8	18.2	−16.4	−17.8	89.9	37.5	39.9	30.7
8	Tax-exempt securities	1.8	4.5	8.9	−3.3	−8.4	−.8	−.4	0.8	1.6	1.9
9	Corporate & foreign bonds	2.0	5.7	9.2	0.3	−4.4	9.8	3.7	−4.0	12.0	10.0
10	Open market paper	−4.8	5.7	−2.8	−2.0	−1.5	0.6	3.0	0.6	−4.4	−2.4
11	Security credit	8.4	−2.3	18.9	6.7	−16.3	1.7	−1.0	−3.7	16.3	−1.8
12	Miscellaneous assets	3.1	2.3	8.2	5.1	−1.8	2.4	6.9	−2.8	2.8	1.7
13	Net increase in liabilities	8.1	30.1	38.5	31.1	−56.1	1.7	102.5	27.1	71.6	40.5
14	Corporate equity issues	1.0	1.1	2.5	2.2	6.3	−1.2	−3.0	3.4	−5.7	−2.3
15	Security RPs (net)	−15.9	17.1	−1.8	11.8	−49.8	−13.1	86.1	16.8	25.7	16.4
16	Security credit	5.2	6.8	24.5	3.2	−11.1	1.3	16.6	7.2	35.2	6.0
17	From banks	2.4	5.8	11.0	−5.8	−5.3	−.5	4.3	−2.0	10.6	16.9
18	Customer credit balances	2.7	1.0	13.5	9.0	−5.8	1.8	12.3	9.2	24.6	−11.0
19	Trade debt	1.0	0.5	0.8	1.1	−.1	4.3	6.3	1.5	−5.3	11.7
20	Taxes payable	−.2	−.1	0.3	0.2	−.6	0.1	0.1	0.1	0.2	–
21	Miscellaneous liabilities	14.9	2.8	8.9	7.6	5.6	3.5	−7.4	3.1	12.4	7.1
22	Fgn direct invest. in US	0.3	0.5	−.3	0.6	2.1	0.9	1.4	0.1	0.7	0.2
23	Due to affiliates	0.7	0.1	6.4	1.9	14.6	16.5	9.4	−9.8	−10.3	10.5
24	Other	13.9	2.1	2.9	5.1	−11.1	−13.8	−18.2	12.8	22.0	−3.6
25	Proprietor net investment	2.1	1.8	3.3	5.1	−6.4	6.8	3.8	−4.9	9.2	1.7
26	Discrepancy	−.2	−.2	−.3	–	0.1	−.1	−.1	−.2	0.1	0.1

*Data are in billions of dollars.

SOURCE: Flow of Funds, Board of Governors of the Federal Reserve System, Washington, D.C. 20551.

1933. The attack on the competitive position of the investment banks is a major characteristic of the increased competition and movement toward desegmentation in the financial services industry. Every year bills are proposed in the U.S. Congress to repeal Glass-Steagall.

Brokers and Dealers. Brokers find buyers for sellers or sellers for buyers. A dealer or market maker offers to buy or sell a security immediately so dealers must hold inventories of securities. Most securities firms are both brokers in many securities and dealers for securities they specialize in. The market for brokerage services is global, with American firms operating in Japan and Europe and vice versa. Brokers and dealers may concentrate in the retail market, like Charles Schwab, the wholesale market, like Jeffreys Securities, or in both, like Merrill Lynch. The market is very competitive.

Mortgage Banks. The mortgage banking business specializes in finding funds for mortgage borrowers from third parties. Mortgage bankers originate mortgages, mainly home mortgages, and sell them to investors. These investors may be financial institutions, like savings banks, or securities firms forming pools of mortgages to be financed by the issuance of mortgage-backed securities as discussed below. Table 3.20 shows the flow-of-funds accounts for mortgage bankers' assets and liabilities. The balance sheet of mortgage bankers represents mainly current inventories of mortgages that will be sold or placed within a few months and do not reflect the level of activity directly.

In the United States and the United Kingdom, increasing amounts of home financing have come from securities backed by claims against pools of home mortgages. Government agencies, like the Federal National Mortgage Association or the General National Mortgage Association in the United States, guarantee home mortgages against default and have fostered the development of markets for securities backed by home mortgages as a matter of public policy. Mortgage bankers have been active in this process, which is called the *securitization* of mortgages.

3.4 ORGANIZATIONAL STRUCTURE OF FINANCIAL FIRMS

Many different forms of business enterprises offer financial services. Corporate organization is dominant in some areas, like banking, while mutual organizations—firms owned by their customers—are common in other financial service areas like the thrift industry and insurance. In other industry segments, partnerships or closed corporation dominate, as in investment banking.

The joint existence and persistence of alternative business organizations within the same line of business, as in insurance, is a puzzle for economists. The usual assumption is that one form of organization will emerge as preferable to another as Fama and Jensen (1983a, p. 327) put it:

> The form of organization that survives in an activity is the one that delivers the product demanded by customers at the lowest price while covering costs. This is the telling dimension on which the economics environment chooses among organizational forms.

TABLE 3.20 Financial Assets and Liabilities for Mortgage Companies

Panel A: Outstanding Levels

		1982	*1983*	*1984*	*1985*	*1986*	*1987*	*1988*	*1989*	*1990*	*1991*	*1992*
1	Total financial assets	18.6	19.5	21.6	24.7	36.6	23.9	16.5	22.6	14.6	25.9	26.1
2	Home mortgages	13.4	14.3	15.7	18.5	29.5	17.7	14.9	20.3	13.1	23.3	22.9
3	Multifamily mortgages	2.2	1.8	1.8	2.0	2.7	1.8	0.8	1.1	0.7	1.3	1.6
4	Commercial mortgages	3.0	3.4	4.1	4.2	4.4	4.4	0.8	1.1	0.7	1.3	1.6
5	Total liabilities	18.6	19.5	21.6	24.7	36.6	23.9	16.5	22.6	14.6	25.9	26.1
6	Bank loans n.e.c.	13.4	14.0	15.5	16.7	25.7	14.5	8.3	11.3	7.3	13.0	13.0
7	Investment by parent	5.2	5.5	6.0	8.1	10.9	9.4	8.3	11.3	7.3	13.0	13.0

*Data are in billions of dollars.

SOURCE: Flow of Funds, Board of Governors of the Federal Reserve System, Washington, D.C. 20551.

Panel B: Annual Flows

		1983	1984	1985	1986	1987	1988	1989	1990	1991	1992
1	Net acq. of financial assets	0.9	2.1	3.2	11.8	−12.7	−7.4	6.1	−8.0	11.4	0.1
2	Home mortgages	0.9	1.4	2.8	11.0	−11.8	−2.8	5.5	−7.2	10.2	−.4
3	Multifamily mortgages	−.4	–	0.2	0.7	−.9	−.9	0.3	−.4	0.6	0.3
4	Commercial mortgages	0.4	0.7	0.1	0.2	0.1	−3.6	0.3	−.4	0.6	0.3
5	Net increase in liabilities	0.9	2.1	3.2	11.8	−12.7	−7.4	6.1	−8.0	11.4	0.1
6	Bank loans n.e.c	0.6	1.5	1.2	9.0	−11.2	−6.2	3.0	−4.0	5.7	0.1
7	Investment by parent	0.2	0.6	2.0	2.8	−1.5	−1.1	3.0	−4.0	5.7	0.1

*Data are in billions of dollars.

SOURCE: Flow of Funds, Board of Governors of the Federal Reserve System, Washington, D.C. 20551.

According to economic theory as presented in Fama and Jensen (1983a, 1983b), the corporate form of organization developed to allow large scale operations to function while spreading the risks of owning specialized assets among many investors. In the corporate form, the owners of the firms own shares of the firm. Share owners may claim any income left over after paying all other parties with claims on the firm, like workers and creditors. Shareholders are called *residual claimants* on the firm's income, because all other parties are paid first.

Fama and Jensen discuss the reasons for the survival of different types of business organizations. They argue that when the assets of the firm are complex and not easily sold and a highly trained management is required to manage those assets, the corporate form of organization most efficiently allocates the risk bearing and asset management function. Corporate shareholders provide capital to acquire the necessary assets and to provide assurances of the firm's performance to parties involved in production of the firm's outputs (e.g., workers and suppliers), and the shareholders hire professional management. The separation of ownership and risk bearing by shareholders and control of the firm's assets by management creates potential conflicts between investors and managers. To resolve this conflict, managers' decisions are monitored by the board of directors elected by the shareholders. Fama and Jensen suggest that commercial banks require a corporate form of organization because banks are complex and invest in risky and illiquid assets like loans to businesses. Bank managers and workers must be highly trained and operate complicated systems that expose the bank to substantial risk, further favoring corporate organization.

In cases where firms do not have a lot of risky assets, alternative organization forms may be more efficient. When the firm's value depends primarily on the value of future professional services provided by the firm's employees, working in teams of highly trained professionals on complicated individual projects, Fama and Jensen argue that professional partnerships are economically efficient. In a partnership, partners share in the total income of the partnership according to sharing rules that are negotiated periodically. Partners commit their personal assets as security for the obligations of the firm. Partnership bonds all partners to the performance of individuals or small teams of firm representatives because all partners share the risks of poor decisions by other partners. Partners will have an interest in monitoring each others' performance and quality of work. The partnership form of organization is most common in investment banking and securities trading where complex professional advice is rendered to customers.

If the scale of the activities and assets grows and the complexity of the organization increases, the partnership form may not be efficient. Many investment banking and securities firms have converted to the corporate form of organization, for example, Merrill Lynch. The reason for these conversions has been the need to raise more capital for investment in risky assets required for expansion and acquired in major financial deals, like corporate takeovers. In cases where firms are making large, risky investments in specialized assets, the Fama and Jensen argument favors corporate organization. The investment bank conversions to stock form fit with their theory.

Mutual organizations are appropriate when assets are not too complex or can be easily liquidated according to Fama and Jensen. The mutual organization eliminates potential conflicts between investors and management by making it possible for customer investors to withdraw their funds when they are unhappy with management decisions. Traditional savings banks and credit unions are fairly simple operations with investments in relatively simple financial assets, like personal loans or mortgages. Mutual funds invest exclusively in marketable securities according to strict guidelines. The mutual organization in these cases may be the most efficient solution to the problems of conflicts between managers and investor-customers.

Another important explanation for organizational form is taxation. Many mutuals are tax exempt or tax advantaged. Credit unions do not pay taxes. Mutual funds do not pay taxes if they pass their income through to owners. Other mutuals are taxed but income usually is taxed only to the extent that it is attributable to owners. The partnership form is also tax advantaged in that partners pay taxes as individuals only once on their share of the partnerships income. In contrast, corporations pay a corporate income tax and then salaries and dividends are taxed again.

3.5 SUMMARY

The financial services industry serves the primary sectors of the economy by intermediating the flow of funds and providing financial services. In large part, financial intermediation places savings of the household sector and foreign sector into business and government sectors to finance investment. There are four basic classes of financial institutions: deposit-taking, insurance, investment companies, and securities firms. Segmentation of the industry into these different classes of firms is explained largely by regulation and legislative history. The future dynamic of the financial services industry will be to find more efficient ways of allocating savings to investors in the world economy. Firms will organize in the economically most efficient way to provide services to savers and investors.

DISCUSSION QUESTIONS AND EXERCISES

1. The last twenty years have been accompanied by large Federal government deficits requiring substantial borrowing by the U.S. Treasury. What are the implications of this for the financial system in terms of market and financial institution activity? What are the possible ramifications of a Federal government surplus on these markets, domestically and internationally?
2. The U.S. population has in general been growing older. What could this mean in terms of the financial needs of the household sector? How would the financial system be impacted if the trend toward aging were reversed, say by increases in reproduction or immigration?
3. Japan does not rely as much as the United States on government-sponsored retirement plans and the

country has a very narrow resource base, for example, it has no sources of oil. What are the implications of Japan's aging population on the flow of funds in Japan and internationally?

4. What are the features of deposits that make them attractive to household savers? What are the disadvantages of deposits as a savings vehicle? Using the household sector balance sheets for the United States, what is happening to the retail deposit market?
5. What types of insurance do you buy, and how do you expect your purchases of insurance to change over your lifetime? What are the implications of changing demographics in the United States and abroad for the sale of different types of insurance?
6. Interest rates in the United States began rising dramatically in 1965, reached a peak in the early 1980s, then fell until October 1993, when they began rising again. Using the flow-of-funds accounts Sectoral Balance Sheets, what basic impact did the changing interest rate environment have on the forms of household savings? What impact on corporate liabilities?
7. Using the flow-of-funds accounts, trace the changes in small time and savings accounts and money market mutual fund shares for the household sector. Interest rates on some small deposits were deregulated in the Garn–St Germain Act of 1982. Is there any obvious impact of these developments in the statistics?
8. Compute the rate of growth of total financial assets for the different types of financial intermediaries. Which have grown the fastest and relatively slowest? Can you give some explanation for the relative growth rates in terms of the inflation and interest rate increases and variability we have experienced in the United States in the last twenty years?
9. Using the Flow of Funds Sectoral Statement of Assets and Liabilities, trace the growth in the mortgage market and the business loan market (loans n.e.c.) What have been the sources of funds financing the growth in mortgages? Have there been major changes in the amounts and sources of funds from year-to-year? What is happening to the share of bank lending to business? Can you relate these changes to general economic conditions and events in the financial markets?
10. Give examples of the various types of business organizations—corporations, partnerships, sole-proprietorships, and mutuals—from outside the financial services industry. What types of assets and labor go into these other businesses? Do the arguments raised for different organizational forms in financial services also work to explain differences in nonfinancial firms?

REFERENCES

BANKING EDUCATION COMMITTEE. 1963. *The Story of American Banking*. New York: The American Bankers Association.

DRUCKER, PETER. 1976. *The Unseen Revolution: How Pension Fund Socialism Came to America*. New York: Harper and Row.

FAMA, EUGENE F. and JENSEN, MICHAEL C. 1983a. "Separation of Ownership and Control," *Journal of Law and Economics* (June), pp. 301–325.

FAMA, EUGENE F. and JENSEN, MICHAEL C. 1983b. "Agency Problems and Residual Claims," *Journal of Law and Economics* (June), pp. 327–349.

KANE, EDWARD J. 1977. "Good Intentions and Unintended Evil: The Case Against Selective Credit Allocation," *Journal of Money, Credit, and Banking* 9 (February), pp. 55–69.

KANE, EDWARD J. 1981. "Accelerating Inflation, Technological Innovation, and the Decreasing Effectiveness of Banking Regulation," *Journal of Finance* XXXVI (May), pp. 355–367.

CHAPTER

4

Assessing Financial Institutions' Stock Performance

Introduction

Financial institution managers must produce value for investors. As the financial services industry restructures, financial firms will be bought and sold. Investors and managers must understand the determinants of the value of financial service firms as they implement investment and business strategies in this dynamic industry.

- Who owns financial institutions?
- What determines good or bad performance by managers?
- What are the determinants of value and how can firms be evaluated?
- How are risks incorporated into valuation?

This chapter uses financial theory to provide answers to these questions. We begin by looking at investors in financial firms and the performance measures they use to assess their investments. The fundamental valuation of corporate financial service firms is introduced and compared to other valuation techniques used by market participants. Recent developments in financial theory in analyzing risk are introduced and applied to assess and price risk for financial institutions.

4.1 OWNERSHIP AND VALUE OF FINANCIAL INSTITUTIONS

Financial institutions are owned by stockholders, partners, individual proprietors, or, in the case of mutual organizations, by their customers. This chapter focuses on the performance of *publicly held* financial corporations from the point of view of investors because this issue is widely relevant and easily illustrated with published data. The valuation principles are equally valid for others forms of ownership.

Shares of corporate financial institutions are owned by individuals and by large institutional investors like mutual funds, pension funds, and bank trust departments. Some firms are owned by other companies: For example, the investment bank Kidder Peabody is owned by brokerage firm Paine Webber after being sold by General Electric subsidiary GE Capital in 1995. First Nationwide Savings, which had been owned by Ford Motor Company, was sold in 1994 to a private group of investors, First Madison. All the shares of the Fireman's Fund, a casualty insurance company, were bought by American Express, the credit card company, in 1968, then some were sold off in 1985. In 1988, American Express sold its remaining shares in Fireman's Fund.

Owners of financial service firms are clearly not a homogeneous group. They are individuals, families, institutions, or other firms. Investors can be as different as the many types of personalities and business firms we encounter in our daily lives. How can managers of firms owned by such a diverse group please all these different people with their different objectives? How can those managers operate when the ownership of the firm can change suddenly?

Modern finance provides a single and simple goal for the managers of corporations with well-informed or well-advised investors who buy and sell stocks in efficient capital markets. The goal: *maximize share values* or maximize owners' wealth. Owners can spend or reallocate profits from their investments as they see fit, making their own consumption and investment decisions in light of their tax situation and risk and return preferences. The only way to please them all is to increase the value of their shares.

A closely held financial institution with a small number of investors may require particular awareness of its investors' cash needs and their tax situations. Sometimes large investors in the firm are also the managers of the firm. For example, the partners of Goldman Sachs, the investment banking firm, own and manage that firm. In these cases, owners' value maximization is still a valid objective for management but share price maximization may not in all instances be the same as value maximization. The two objectives will converge whenever large investors want to sell their ownership interest, as ultimately they or their heirs will want or have to do. Partners in Shearson, Loeb Rhoades, an investment banking firm, did best for themselves when they maximized the value of their firm and sold it to American Express for $915 million in 1981. Managerial objectives departing from share price maximization must be carefully examined and defended. Throughout this chapter, the correct objective for management is assumed to be share price maximization.

Managers of financial service firms do well when their companies do well. They earn raises, promotions, and valuable stock options when their firms excel. Firms that do poorly punish managers in a number of ways. Unhappy shareholders may sell their shares to another company that promises to do better. This is what happened when Marine Midland Bank in England sold the shares it owned in Crocker Bank in California to Wells Fargo in 1986. Following Wells Fargo's purchase of Crocker Bank, many Crocker managers were dismissed. A poorly managed firm may be acquired through a hostile tender offer. Poorly performing firms are often merged into the acquiring firm and the old managers are laid off or given subordinate jobs. An extremely poorly managed firm descends into bankruptcy, resulting in all operations closing down and all employees losing their jobs.

Measuring Corporate Performance

How does the investor in financial institution shares determine how well his managers have done? In general, an investor will compare his or her investment to other investments in order to figure out just how satisfied or dissatisfied he or she is. For example, investors buying shares in Fifth Third Bancorp or Progressive Insurance at the end of 1982 and selling them in 1992, were surely pleased with those firms' managers; they earned an average of 40.07 and 34.08 percent per year, respectively. Investments in those firms were worth over 14 times their 1982 values. Investors in Continental Bank or Paine Webber no doubt were disgruntled because Continental's annual return over the same period averaged *minus* 8.6 percent and Paine Webber averaged only 3.7 percent over the same period.

The future rate of return on an investment determines its future value. The rate of return most important to investors is the market rate of return determined by the price of shares when bought and their value when sold or exchanged in a tender offer plus any other cash flows like dividends. The realized rate of return (ROR) on shares of common stock at the end of the year is calculated as follows:

$$\text{ROR}_t = \frac{D_t + P_t - P_{t-1}}{P_{t-1}}. \quad (4.1)$$

Here, P and D signify market price and dividends paid and subscripts refer to year. The realized rate of return on shares of Fifth Third Bancorp in 1992, for example, is calculated:

$$\text{ROR}_{1992} = \frac{\$.90 + \$54.00 - \$45.33}{\$45.33} = 21.1\%. \quad (4.2)$$

Panel A of Table 4.1 provides annual rates of return over the period 1983 to 1992 for several financial service firms.

The rate of return on stocks is not a fixed obligation of management as it is with bonds or loans. Returns depends on the value of stocks when bought and sold and on dividends received. The value of stock at each point in time is determined by current assessments of the future prospects of the firm—that is, by how well investors expect the firm to perform in the future.

Share prices change both as a firm grows and as assessments of firm's prospects vary with the arrival of new information about its future business prospects. Unforeseen year-to-year variations in stock returns determine a stock's risk to investors. Investors never know exactly when they will want to sell their shares, because they need cash or a better investment opportunity has come along. We concentrate now on factors that determine the current value of shares, and return to discuss risk later.

TABLE 4.1 Market Rates of Return on Selected Financial Institution Stocks

YEAR	*AETNA*	*BANK OF AMERICA*	*FIFTH THIRD BANCORP*	*MERRILL LYNCH*	*PROGRESSIVE INSURANCE*	*S&P500 STOCKS*
			Panel A: Annual Rates of Return			
1983	–11.60%	1.86%	29.45%	85.12%	14.46%	22.27%
1984	6.23%	11.28%	63.08%	118.53%	47.58%	1.07%
1985	8.72%	–5.89%	23.92%	–13.12%	–4.39%	30.35%
1986	52.00%	–7.39%	70.43%	30.28%	101.60%	17.87%
1987	10.31%	–6.40%	9.31%	8.51%	51.09%	4.68%
1988	–14.89%	–52.99%	17.10%	–36.10%	–0.87%	13.92%
1989	30.96%	297.82%	64.78%	11.73%	27.67%	29.82%
1990	–26.09%	2.80%	–8.05%	13.54%	34.36%	–3.61%
1991	19.90%	39.91%	109.61%	129.05%	6.38%	29.76%
1992	11.95%	33.24%	21.10%	2.58%	62.86%	7.06%
Mean	8.75%	31.42%	40.07%	35.01%	34.08%	15.32%
Std. Dev.	21.67%	91.98%	33.79%	53.37%	31.23%	12.02%
			Panel B: Value of $1,000 Invested at the End of 1982			
1982	1,000	1,000	1,000	1,000	1,000	1,000
1983	884	1,019	1,295	1,851	1,145	1,223
1984	939	1,133	2,111	4,045	1,689	1,236
1985	1,021	1,067	2,616	3,514	1,615	1,611
1986	1,552	988	4,458	4,579	3,256	1,899
1987	1,712	925	4,873	4,968	4,920	1,987
1988	1,457	435	5,707	3,175	4,877	2,264
1989	1,908	1,729	9,404	3,547	6,226	2,939
1990	1,410	1,778	8,646	4,028	8,366	2,833
1991	1,691	2,487	18,123	9,225	8,900	3,676
1992	1,893	3,314	21,948	9,463	14,494	3,936
Minimum	884	435	1,000	1,000	1,000	1,000
Maximum	1,908	3,314	21,948	9,463	14,494	3,936

Two features of stock that have value to owners of stock but that are only indirectly related to the future business prospects of a firm are mentioned first. The first feature is that shareholders elect the firm's management. Common shareholders choose the management of a firm by electing members of the board of directors. Holders of voting common stock elect the board of directors on a one-share/one-vote basis; the board of directors, in turn, names the management of the firm. An investor with a large block of shares in a firm can dominate the election of directors. Such a shareholder, whether an individual, family, or firm, can determine the management of the firm. This ability to hire and fire management is a source of the value of common stock called the *value of corporate control*.

A second important attribute of common stock is that investors in common shares cannot lose any more than the amount of their initial investment. This attribute is called *limited liability*. Limited liability has not always been the rule with financial institution stocks. Until the 1930s in the United States, some bank investors could be required to pay in money in addition to their original investments in order to cover losses to depositors. Limited liability protects investors from managers who, in pursuit of higher returns, ignore the possibility of total financial ruin to investors in their companies. Limited liability makes common stock similar to call options, which we discuss in Chapter 21.

Determinants of Share Prices

What determines stock prices of financial service firms? Share prices are the value of the future cash flows to stock owners. Investors discount these future cash flows to present values using *opportunity costs,* the return they expect on investments of similar risk. Shares prices will have higher values when cash flows are anticipated to be larger or opportunity costs lower. Share prices will change when estimates of future cash flows are revised or when the estimated risks or uncertainties associated with those cash flows are changed in the light of new information.

All cash flows received by common stock shareholders can be viewed as dividend payments. Firms paying dividends normally declare their dividends quarterly in amounts voted on by their boards of directors at regularly scheduled meetings. Sometimes boards vote special cash dividends. By dividends we mean cash payments to shareholders—not distributions of paper, called stock dividends, or anything else. This cash payment can be regular dividends, special dividends, liquidating dividends, or any other cash distribution. As Copeland *et al* (1990) put it in their influential book on valuation, "Cash is king." Investors care only about cash.

Fundamental Valuation Equation for Stocks

To understand how the present value of cash dividends or other cash payments to investors relates to rates of return and share prices, look at equation (4.1) from the perspective of investors' expected return from buying stock by rewriting equation (4.1) as:

$$\overline{\text{ROR}}_{t+1} = \frac{\overline{D}_{t+1} + \overline{P}_{t+1} - P_t}{P_t}. \tag{4.3}$$

Expectations of future values are shown with overbars. The dividend and share price at the end of the period, D_{t+1} and P_{t+1}, are *expectations* about dividends and period-ending prices, not the actual data used to calculate realized returns. The expected rate of return is $\overline{\text{ROR}}_{t+1}$.

Solving equation (4.3) for the price at the beginning of the period, P_t, we have:

$$P_t = \frac{\overline{D}_{t+1} + \overline{P}_{t+1}}{\left(1 + \overline{\text{ROR}}_{t+1}\right)}. \tag{4.4}$$

This equation says that the beginning-of-period price is the present value of the expected dividends plus the expected sale price at the end of the period and where the discount rate is the expected return for this stock.

The stock price at the end of the period can be viewed the same way. The end of the period share price, if the expected market rate of return ($\overline{\text{ROR}}$) does not change, is expressed as:

$$\overline{P}_{t+2} = \frac{\overline{D}_{t+1} + \overline{P}_{t+2}}{1+\overline{\text{ROR}}}. \tag{4.5}$$

This equation can be substituted into equation (4.4) to give:

$$P_t = \frac{\overline{D}_{t+1}}{\left(1+\overline{\text{ROR}}\right)} + \frac{\overline{D}_{t+2}}{\left(1+\overline{\text{ROR}}\right)^2} + \frac{\overline{P}_{t+2}}{\left(1+\overline{\text{ROR}}\right)^2}. \tag{4.6}$$

If expected returns are the same in the future, substitutions similar to this can continue, always replacing expected future stock prices with future expected dividends and the next period's expected ending share price. What we get after this is what we said in the beginning: the value of the share price is the present value placed on expected future cash flows or dividends. The *fundamental valuation equation* for common stocks is as follows:

$$P_t = \frac{\overline{D}_{t+1}}{\left(1+\overline{\text{ROR}}\right)} + \frac{\overline{D}_{t+2}}{\left(1+\overline{\text{ROR}}\right)^2} + \frac{\overline{D}_{t+3}}{\left(1+\overline{\text{ROR}}\right)^3} + \ldots. \tag{4.7}$$

The fundamental valuation equation states that share price is the discounted value of cash flow to owners. This valuation approach is called the discounted cash flow (DCF) by some, including Copeland *et al* (1990). The DCF approach is valid for all firms with any conceivable pattern of cash flow.

To illustrate an analysis of a financial firm, assume that cash flows to investors will be \$1 per share for two years and that in two years each share can be sold for \$60. If this kind of investment requires a 12 percent rate of return to satisfy the investor for risk, the firm's shares would be valued as follows:

$$P_t = \frac{\$1.00}{1.12} + \frac{\$1.00}{\$1.12^2} + \frac{\$60.00}{1.12^3} = \$44.40. \tag{4.8}$$

To value stocks, expected cash flows must be projected into the future. Stock analysts' projections of cash flows to investors based on the best information and estimates of future cash flows and expected returns is called *fundamental analysis.*

Evidence Supporting the Fundamental Valuation Equation

Equation (4.7) explains market prices of common stocks if investors discount expected future cash dividends and if they efficiently process the public information available to estimate a firm's ability to pay dividends in the future. Academic research on financial institution common stocks supports the hypothesis that the market is efficient in processing information available to investors.

Several scholarly studies have examined the hypothesis that the market for financial service firm shares is efficient. These academic analyses are based on statistical analyses as pioneered by Fama *et al* (1969) of the effect of widely publicized specific events on stock returns applied to the stock returns of financial institutions. The announcement of publicly available information that promises an unexpected improvement (or deterioration) in the earnings of financial service firms should provide an increase (decrease) in the value of their shares. At the time information is announced, good news should be associated with a one-time stock return significantly above what one could expect given general market conditions for those firms affected by the event. These academic studies are called *event studies*.

Event studies for financial institution share prices show that good news or bad news has the expected impact on affected financial firm stock returns. For example, Larry Dann and Christopher James (1982) looked at stock returns for a sample of savings and loans around three different dates when various deposit interest ceilings were removed. The removal of such ceilings should increase interest expense of these institutions, reducing their cash flows in cases where the ceilings had kept the costs of deposits low. Dann and James's results suggest that the stock prices of savings and loans experienced an accumulated loss in value of 2.4 percent when the 1973 "wild card" accounts with no interest ceilings were authorized. Savings and loan stock prices fell again—this time by an accumulated 6.7 percent—when "Money Market Certificates" with no ceilings were authorized in 1978. On the other hand, when the large deposit (over $100,000) ceiling was eliminated in 1973, there was no significant fall in prices. Savings and loans only raised small amounts of funds in that form at that time.

In another study, James (1983) compared the effects that loosening of controls on maximum interest rates had on wholesale and retail banks. He found that share prices fell 2 percent for retail banks when Money Market Certificate accounts were authorized in 1978, in line with the hypothesis that small account ceilings provided a subsidy to retail banks. Wholesale bank shares *increased* about 3.5 percent in 1970 when large deposit ceilings were removed, in line with James's hypothesis that ceilings on large deposits were a tax on large banks.

Brad Cornell and Alan Shapiro (1986) performed an event study on commercial bank returns during the Latin American debt crisis in 1982 and 1983. Their study is unique in examining the *cumulative* effect on stock returns during the longer time period over which the bad news concerning certain countries' abilities to service their loans became known. After correcting for other factors that could have affected bank stock returns over this period, they found that Latin American credit exposure was associated with a negative return of 9.3 times the exposure in percent of assets over the two years. This result demonstrates that bank stock prices adjusted to the bad news about Latin American countries according to how much Latin American debt they had.

In summary, the evidence from event studies for financial institutions confirms that their stock prices react to public information. The market appears to process this information efficiently. The implication is that share prices of financial institutions, like other stock companies, are determined by rational investors who use the best information they can obtain to make assessments of expected future cash dividends.

4.2 VALUATION OF FINANCIAL SERVICE FIRMS IN PRACTICE

The fundamental valuation equation (4.7) for common stocks is valid for all corporations—financial and nonfinancial. Cash flows to investors in nonfinancial firms are revenues minus costs adjusted for required working capital and long-term investments. The cash flows for equity investors in nonfinancial firms are affected by nonequity financing and taxes. In order to focus on nonfinancial firms' fundamental value as businesses undistorted by financing considerations, Copeland *et al* (1990) suggest evaluating nonfinancial firms as total enterprises rather discounting just equity cash flows.

The cash flows relevant for financial institutions are more complex than for nonfinancial firms as we discuss at length in the next chapter. Financial service firms have no counterpart to sales revenues and their costs are not directly related to any specific output measure. Balance sheet changes such as increases in deposits or insurance reserves, or reductions in loans, all come from providing financial services and result in cash flows that are only indirectly related to the dividends received by equity owners. In contrast to their recommendation for nonfinancial firms, Copeland *et al* advocate concentrating on equity cash flows for financial institutions like banks.

Projection of cash flows for equity owners in financial institutions is the main goal of financial statement analysis of financial institutions, as is discussed in Chapter 5. Our discussion here focuses on several commonly used evaluation methods for financial service firm equity ownership.

A common method of evaluating financial institution shares is to project the next period's earnings or future earnings undistorted by extraordinary events and capitalize them using a price–earnings (P–E) multiple. We start with an analysis of P–E multiples and how use of a P–E multiple relates to the fundamental value equation. We contrast use of P–Es to other standard valuation methods used for financial institutions in the remainder of the section.

Price-Earnings Multiple

Stock analysts say that share prices are simple to determine once you know the *price-earnings (P–E) multiple.* The P–E ratio multiplied by a firm's earnings gives the firm's stock value. For example, if earnings are forecasted to be $5 and the appropriate earnings multiple is ten, the share value is $50. What determines the P–E ratio, and how does that ratio relate to the fundamental equation of value? In order to provide an answer to these questions, we must work through some simple but tedious mathematics.

To translate the fundamental valuation equation (4.7) into the familiar terminology of P–E ratios and earnings multiples, keep in mind that dividends must be paid out of future earnings, $\overline{E}_{t+1}$, $\overline{E}_{t+2}$, etc., where again overbars signify expectations. The dividend each period can be expressed as a proportion of earnings, commonly called the *dividend payout ratio* or $\overline{p}$. Dividends can thus be expressed as the payout ratio times earnings. Assume that the expected payout ratios in periods t+1, t+2, etc., are expected to be $\overline{p}_{t+1}$, $\overline{p}_{t+2}$, etc. Future dividends in equation (4.7) in this case can be expressed as:

$$\overline{D}_{t+1} = \overline{E}_{t+1}\overline{p}_{t+1}$$
$$\overline{D}_{t+2} = \overline{E}_{t+2}\overline{p}_{t+2}$$

and so forth for all future periods. Finally, if each period's future earnings are expressed as an expected growth rate from the previous period's earnings, earnings for t+2 can be expressed as:

$$\overline{E}_{t+2} = \overline{E}_{t+1}(1 + \overline{g}_{t+2}),$$

where $\overline{g}_{t+2}$ is the expected growth rate from period t+1 to the following period, t+2. By a now-familiar process of substitution, we can write any period's future expected earnings as:

$$\overline{E}_{t+k} = \overline{E}_{t+1}(1 + \overline{g}_{t+2})(1 + \overline{g}_{t+3}) \ldots (1 + \overline{g}_{t+k-1})$$

Future dividends are future expected payout ratios times future expected earnings. We can now rewrite equation (4.7) in a new form:

$$P_t = \frac{\overline{E}_{t+1}\overline{p}_{t+1}}{\left(1+\overline{\text{ROR}}\right)} + \frac{\overline{E}_{t+1}\left(1+\overline{g}_{t+2}\right)\overline{p}_{t+2}}{\left(1+\overline{\text{ROR}}\right)^2} + \frac{\overline{E}_{t+1}\left(1+\overline{g}_{t+2}\right)\left(1+\overline{g}_{t+3}\right)\overline{p}_{t+3}}{\left(1+\overline{\text{ROR}}\right)^2} + \ldots \qquad (4.9)$$

Expected earnings, $\overline{E}_{t+1}$, appear in all the terms of the equation, since future earnings are expressed as growth from expected earnings. Factoring out $\overline{E}_{t+1}$ gives:

$$P_t = \overline{E}_{t+1}\left[\frac{\overline{p}_{t+1}}{1+\overline{\text{ROR}}} + \frac{\left(1+\overline{g}_{t+2}\right)\overline{p}_{t+2}}{\left(1+\overline{\text{ROR}}\right)^2} + \frac{\left(1+\overline{g}_{t+2}\right)\left(1+\overline{g}_{t+3}\right)\overline{p}_{t+3}}{\left(1+\overline{\text{ROR}}\right)^3} + \ldots\right] \qquad (4.10)$$

or in the much simpler form:

$$P_t = \overline{E}_{t+1}[P - E] \qquad (4.11)$$

where the P–E in equation (4.11) is a shorthand notation for all the elements in the bracketed expression in equation (4.10).

An earnings multiple includes expectations about a firm's future—the timing and growth of its earnings in the future, the firm's decisions to return cash to investors, as well as the opportunity cost to investors. In other words, the P–E is a way of noting everything affecting the future of the firm. The earnings multiple is a complex, compound statistic on the firm's future prospects.

Some Simple Forms of P–Es

In some cases, the P–E formula in equation (4.10) can be simplified. When the expected return on the stocks and the dividend payout rates are assumed to be constant, and growth rates have some simple pattern, the formula can be made easier to use. The results of making these assumptions are shown in Table 4.2, where values of the P–E are given under different assumptions about future earnings growth from this period's expected earnings. Formula (1) in the table assumes no growth; formula (2) assumes constant growth in earnings for all future time periods; formula (3) assumes constant earnings that last M years without growth; finally, formula (4) assumes earnings growth that continues at a given rate for M years and then growth stops but earnings continue. Although these assumptions are always too simple, evaluating the formula using assumed values for growth and the period of growth can provide benchmarks against which to assess actual P–Es being discussed by an investor or analyst.

Table 4.2 provides examples of using simple formulas for P–E ratios. Assume that a financial service firm is expected to earn a 10 percent return to investors, its earnings are not expected to grow, and it will pay out half its earnings to shareholders. The P–E in this case using formula (1), is .5/.1 or five. If the firm's earnings are projected to be \$2.00, its share value is \$10.00. Using formula (2), we calculate the P–E ratio for a firm that is similar but is projected to grow at five percent

TABLE 4.2 Expressions for Simple P–E Ratios, $P_t/\overline{E}_{t+1}$. (Examples assume ROR = .10 and p_{t+1} = .5)

No Growth in Earnings and Constant Dividend Payout:

Example

Formula (1) $$\frac{\overline{p}}{\overline{\text{ROR}}} \qquad\qquad \frac{.5}{.1} = 5$$

Growth in Earnings in Perpetuity and Constant Dividend Payout:

Example: Growth rate = .05

Formula (2) $$\frac{\overline{p}}{\overline{\text{ROR}} - \overline{g}} \qquad\qquad \frac{.5}{.10 - .05} = 10$$

Earnings for M years (only) and Constant Dividend Payout:

Example: M = 10

Formula (3) $$\frac{\overline{p}}{\overline{\text{ROR}}}\left(1 - \frac{1}{\left(1 + \overline{\text{ROR}}\right)^{M}}\right) \qquad\qquad \frac{.5}{.10}\left(1 - \frac{1}{(1.10)^{10}}\right) = 3.07$$

Growth in Earnings for M Years and Level Thereafter and Constant Dividend Payout:

Formula (4)

Example: M = 10, g = .05

$$\frac{\overline{p}}{\overline{\text{ROR}} - \overline{g}}\left(1 - \frac{\left(1 + \overline{g}\right)^{M}}{\left(1 + \overline{\text{ROR}}\right)^{M}}\right) + \left(\frac{\overline{p}\left(1 + \overline{g}\right)^{M}}{\overline{\text{ROR}}\left(1 + \overline{\text{ROR}}\right)^{M}}\right) \qquad \frac{.5}{.10 - .05}\left(1 - \frac{(1.05)^{10}}{(1.10)^{10}}\right) + \frac{.5(1.05)^{10}}{.10(1.10)^{10}} = 6.86$$

per year. This firm would have a P–E of 10 and consequently would be worth twice as much.

Other examples using simple P–Es from Table 4.2 illustrate earnings growth over limited time frames. Assume that investors require a 10 percent return and that growth is expected to be five percent but only for ten years. Using formula (4) in Table 4.2, the multiple would be 6.86. A firm with ten years of expected growth is worth 69 percent of a firm with growth expected in perpetuity. These examples, and others you can construct from the table with different assumptions, illustrate how important it is to assess the growth prospects and required returns using the fundamentals. A basic understanding of the role of growth and expected returns can be gained by working with a variety of assumptions to estimate P–Es using the formulas in the table.

Use of P–E Ratios in Practice

The earnings multiple used by stock analysts to value stocks is the multiple for forecasted earnings. We capture expectations of future earnings relative to current expected levels with the growth term, g_t. When using P–Es reported in published sources, it is very important to know whether a given multiple applies to current forecasted earnings or reported earnings. For example, the *Wall Street Journal* publishes a P–E ratio using last year's earnings divided into the current price. The *Wall Street Journal* multiple is not the multiple in equation (4.11) because it does not account for this year's expected earnings' growth.

Earnings multiples are widely used by analysts because they provide a point of comparison for firms. Firms similar in growth and expected returns can be valued with similar multiples. Industry average P–Es at different points in time for *comparable firms* can guide analysts towards price estimates based on current earnings forecasts. Table 4.3 gives some average P–E multiples for a variety of financial service firms at different times. The P–Es given in the table are from *Value Line Investment Survey* and are computed by dividing two quarters of reported and two quarters of forecasted earnings into recent prices. In other words, the *Value Line* multiple attempts to measure how the market values average past and future earnings.

Table 4.3 demonstrates that P–E multiples change over time. The average market multiple also changes over the business cycle. Why is this? Earnings multiples change when any of the determinants of their value changes: future growth rates in earnings, risk adjusted discount rates, and future dividend payouts.

Table 4.3 also demonstrates that P–E multiples vary across firms and industries. Most of the differences between firms comes from differences in expected growth. Differences in growth prospects can stem from very different causes. Two firms may be expected to grow rapidly; the outlook for one firm can be incredibly good because of strong demand for its services. Another firm can be staggering out of a dismal period of low earnings. Dividend payouts change with cash needs and internal investment opportunities. Many factors can change expected returns.

Analysis of multiples provides comparative benchmarks to capitalize expected earnings for a firm. However, use of a P–E formula to assess value does not relieve

TABLE 4.3 Selected Price–Earnings Multiples

COMPANY	*1983*	*1987*	*1990*	*1993*
Aetna	9.3	8.6	5.6	10.5
BankAmerica Corporation	7.4	NMF	5.0	9.3
A.G. Edwards	8.4	13.7	6.9	9.6
Fifth Third Bancorp	n/a	11.7	7.4	14.8
Merrill Lynch	7.1	14.3	8.4	8.1
Old Kent Financial Corporation	n/a	n/a	5.9	9.6
Progressive Insurance	n/a	11.4	11.0	11.0

NMF = Not meaningful.

SOURCE: *Value Line,* "Summary and Index–Index to Stocks" October 21, 1983, October 16, 1987, October 5, 1990, December 17, 1993.

the analyst of any responsibility. Analysts must estimate current expected earnings for the firm and decide which multiple represents the growth and risk characteristics associated with that firm. Firms differ in the quality of management, the growth in markets, costs of doing business in major locations, and their risk environment. In other words, choosing a P–E multiple in stock valuation does not provide a shortcut from detailed fundamental analysis. It is a convenient way to communicate a complex set of factors affecting the valuation of a given business.

Available market prices for some shares may not mean as much as for others. Transaction prices for stocks that trade infrequently and in small volume may not be efficient in the sense of reflecting all available information. Evaluation of small financial institutions trading in thin markets or in countries without stock markets will be increasingly important as smaller institutions are bought by larger institutions as part of the restructuring of the global financial industry. A common way to evaluate a small firm is to estimate its earnings and use an earnings multiple for comparable firms that are widely traded. For example, an insurance firm similar to Aetna in 1993 might use a multiple of 10.5 in valuing expected earnings. Forecasting the small firm's earning and using Aetna's multiple could value the stock.

Other Evaluation Techniques

The problem of evaluating a financial institution is often approached from a different angle than looking at future cash flows. Two standard alternatives are *market-to-book* analysis and *liquidation value.* These alternatives can be useful as benchmarks against which to assess other valuation methods based on cash flows. Sometimes these approaches are useful in situations where future cash flows are not relevant, as in the liquidation of a financial institution. On other occasions, several approaches can be combined to value different parts of a firm's business.

Many analysts compare current market values of firms to their accounting values by calculating *market-to-book* ratios. For example, at the end of 1992

BankAmerica Corporation common stock sold for $46.50 per share and the book value (the total book of equity divided by the number of shares outstanding) was reported at $35.88. The ratio of market-to-book for BankAmerica was 1.30 or, equivalently, BankAmerica was selling at a thirty percent *premium* to book value. This premium reflects the value BankAmerica managers have created with shareholders' historical investment dollars. Many firms sell below book value; for example Aetna sold for 72 percent of book value at the end of 1992. Market-to-book ratios from widely traded firms could be used to value other firms. If two firms have similar business activity, the ratio for the widely traded firm could be used to assign a value to another firm's accounting value. For example, if a small bank with a book value of $15 per share was judged to be comparable to BankAmerica in terms of its prospects and assets, analysts might assign it a market value of $19.50 (1.30 times $15.00).

Use of market-to-book ratios from an industry average or a specific firm to value a financial institution must be done carefully. The market-to-book ratio for a given firm could reflect a variety of sources of enhanced or depressed value, such as limited competition, unrealized loan losses, potential liabilities, assets bought at historical prices not reflecting current market values, superior or inferior management skill at creating value, and so forth. If the ratio reflects the value of the firm's geographical market and customer base or other specific and possibly quantifiable factors, analysts may use objective standards to assess the validity of one firm's market-to-book ratio in valuing another. If subjective factors or complex and unique operations make firms very different, use of these ratios across firms is perilous.

A second method of valuation estimates the value of the firm as if everything were sold and all liabilities were retired. This method is called *liquidation value*. Each asset and liability must be assigned a value. Some assets can be readily evaluated, such as publicly traded securities and cash. Other asset values can be estimated with a fair degree of accuracy, such as those for office buildings and computer equipment. Some assets have comparables that trade in markets, like mortgage loans, and can be accurately valued.

Other assets like complex business loans are very difficult to give liquidation values. Also very difficult to assess are the value of market share and customer relationships with the firm. Value of training and experience of personnel are also important. These assets are often specific to a firm's franchise, the result of its history, reputation, and location. If these difficult-to-evaluate assets are a major portion of the value of a firm, the value of the firm's equity will be uncertain. When an acquiring firm pays more than book value for a firm, it is paying for what accountants call *goodwill*.

Liabilities of financial service firms also have to be evaluated to estimate liquidation values. Some liability evaluation problems are easy: For example, large negotiable deposits with short maturities have market values equal to their face values. Checking accounts and small deposit liabilities may be worth less than their face value to an acquiring firm because they represent ongoing relationships with a retail customer base. In 1993, the Resolution Trust Corporation sold branches of Home Fed in California to banks and thrifts for 1.8 to 3.7 percent less than their face value. The values of these deposit liabilities were about two percent less than the face value of the deposits.

As with assets, some liabilities are difficult to evaluate. Potential liabilities associated with lawsuits and casualty insurance claims are two examples of difficult valuation problems. Good analysts make clear to users of evaluations the sources of difficulty and the risks associated with the valuation. They direct attention to assets and liabilities evaluated with particular uncertainty and under questionable assumptions. Difficulty in evaluation cannot impede purchases and sales of financial firms because certainty is never possible.

4.3 INVESTORS EXPECTED RETURNS

The fundamental valuation formula in equation (4.7) discounts future expected cash flows at investors' expected rate of return ($\overline{ROR}$) on the stock. This is the opportunity cost to the investor of tying up his investable funds in this stock rather than in some other investment. What determines investors' expected market return? Investors desire or dream about infinitely high returns. Expected returns are realistically determined by market opportunities—the level of yields on other investments with different risks.

Measuring and explaining the effect of risk on expected returns has been a major focus of financial economics since the publication of Markowitz (1952) more than forty years ago. The standard definition of risk is variability of returns; this notion captures risks to investors of unplanned liquidation of investments. Investors never know when they will need to sell their investments for cash because of emergencies or for better investment opportunities. At the end of 1982, no investor knew what the future would hold for Bank of America or any other security. To illustrate investment risk, assume an investor bought \$1,000 in Bank of America stock at year end in 1982 and had to liquidate the shares for unexpected reasons at the end of 1988. Panel B of Table 4.1 shows that a \$1,000 investment in 1982 would have been worth \$435 at the end of 1988, an annual *loss* of 15.3 percent per year. No investor expects a negative return. Not being able to plan on the future value of stock investments is the most important risk faced by investors who do not like uncertainty.

The measure used in finance of year-to-year variation in the value of stock is the *standard deviation* of the return (or its square, the *variance*). This measure computes the average squared deviation of each period's rate of return from the mean, or average. Most business calculators can compute the standard deviation of a return. The standard deviations for several financial institution's annual stock returns are shown in the last row of Table 4.1, Panel A.

Standard deviations for different stocks vary significantly as can be seen in Table 4.1. For example, the highest risk over the time period shown is for Bank of America and the lowest for Aetna, with annual return deviations of 91.98 and 21.67 percent, respectively. How can we interpret these standard deviations? As is clear, higher standard deviations mean more variability. The investor is much less able to count on the future value of an investment with a large standard deviation than of a small one.

If the stock returns from period to period are characterized by the bell-shaped normal distribution, the standard deviation of returns can be interpreted precisely. In the case of normally distributed stock returns, each year's return is equally likely to be above or below the average expected return. There is a range of possible returns, with those closest to the average having the highest likelihood of occurring. Investors earn a yield within two standard deviations of the mean around 95 percent of the time. Normal distribution for Aetna and Merrill Lynch are shown in Figure 4.1.

Standard deviations of stock returns can be calculated for any time interval: a year, a month, a day, or even an hour. The relevant period to calculate is the minimum time period the investor plans to hold the stock, because risk is the uncertainty of value upon sale. The standard deviation of the return increases with the time period, thus a monthly return is more variable than a daily return. The increase in variability is not proportional to time period. It is often assumed that the standard deviation increases with the square root of the time period. For example, an annual return deviation would be *twice* a quarterly standard deviation since it is four times as long.

Stock Return Variability and the "Price" of Risk

Realized market returns on stocks will be affected by whatever affects the firm's dividends and future share prices. Certain factors that affect all stocks to a greater or lesser degree are called systematic risk factors by financial analysts. Other factors are specific to the firm and are called *un*systematic risk factors.

The stock market in general is affected by systematic risks from changes in general business conditions or macroeconomic factors. Changing expectations for unemployment, inflation, real product demand, supply shifts, and so forth, determine expectations of future stock market performance. Business prospects are influenced significantly by government monetary and fiscal policies. The stock market crash of 1929, the boom of 1983, and the stock market crash of 1987 are examples of systematic unexpected stock risks.

FIGURE 4.1 Distribution of returns for Aetna and Merrill Lynch

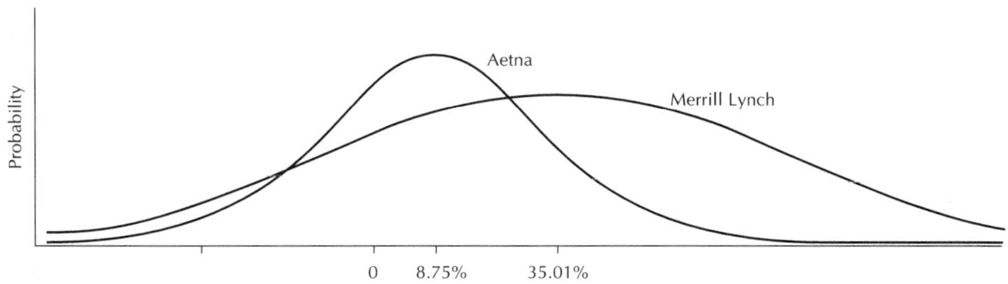

Stock price run ups, due to good news about a company such as unexpected high earnings, are an example of unsystematic risks. Sharp stock market losses associated with the discovery of fraudulent or illegal behavior are another example of unsystematic risk. For example, press reports of $1.22 billion in illegal cash transactions by the Bank of Boston resulted in a drop in its share price from $47 to $43.75 in the week of February 8 to 15, 1985. Since there will always be good news about some companies and bad news about others, the effects of unsystematic risk can be reduced by holding several stocks.

Theories underlying the compensation of investors for bearing risks are simple and should be seen that way. You have to pay investors for bearing risk because risk is bad. Risk that is everywhere is hard to avoid and investors are willing to pay for protection against these risks by accepting lower returns. What can be avoided does not matter so much. The key concept underlying modern financial theory about risk is diversification (as we discuss in Chapter 19). The basic idea is "Don't put all your eggs in one basket." In finance, not putting all your eggs in one basket means not buying just one stock or investment. Diversification of investments means that *un*systematic risks from individual stocks are reduced to an inconsequential level because individual stocks' unsystematic sources of risk are not related to each other. A diversified portfolio of stocks will be influenced mainly by general market movements, that is, by systematic risk.

How many stocks does it take to have enough diversification? Wagner and Lau (1971) show that with sixteen stocks in different industries virtually all unsystematic risk from individual stocks is diversified away. For investors with at least sixteen stocks, the only important source of return variability is systematic risk.

We can see the effect of diversification from the stocks in Table 4.1. If we had invested only in Bank of America from 1982 to 1992, for example, our portfolio would have had a minimum return of minus 52.99 percent and a maximum return of 297.82 percent. If we had invested in a portfolio as diversified as the S&P 500 index, our minimum and maximum returns would have been minus 3.61 percent and 30.35 percent. The standard deviation of the S&P 500 portfolio return was 12.02 percent compared to the undiversified investment in Bank of America of 91.98 percent.

Investors do not like risk but they like high returns. This means that investors can be induced to bear higher risk (that is, higher systematic risk) if they expect returns to compensate them for those risks. In order to see how much they need to be compensated, we must measure the expected returns on risky investments against low risk or riskless alternatives. Certain investments, such as U.S. Treasury securities, have very low risk because there is no default risk (the Federal Reserve can always print money to redeem U.S. government debt). A short-term government security is virtually riskless. There is some risk to the investor in terms of the purchasing power of the investment at the end of the term but that risk is pretty small. Short-term Treasury bills are usually taken as the premier example of a riskless security or investment.

Treasury bills have an expected return over one-month or longer time horizons. Table 4.4 gives three-month and longer Treasury security rates for several years. For example, in May 1993, the one-year Treasury bill rate was 3.23 percent.

TABLE 4.4 U.S. Treasury Security Yields

	11/79	*6/85*	*3/87*	*5/93*
Treasury Securities				
3-month Treasury bill	12.07	6.97	5.45	2.96
6-month Treasury bill	12.14	7.16	5.43	3.07
1-year Treasury bill	11.65	7.37	5.57	3.23
Long-term Treasury bond	10.26	10.60	7.50	6.04
Corporate Bonds				
AAA Long-term bond	10.73	11.09	8.36	7.43
BAA Long-term bond	11.98	12.56	9.64	8.21

SOURCE: Federal Reserve *Bulletin*.

That is, the one-year riskless rate was 3.23 percent. Any investment that is risky must be expected to earn more than the riskless rate.

The Capital Asset Pricing Model (CAPM)

The extra return investors expect over the riskless rate is called the *price of risk* by financial analysts. In the United States, over the years 1926 to 1991, the widely used Standard and Poor's 500 stock return index earned on average about 8.5 percent more than riskless U.S. government bills, as reported by Ibbotson and Sinquefield in *Stocks, Bonds, Bills and Inflation: 1992 Yearbook*. Most American financial analysts identify the risk premium on the stock market as reported in Ibbotson and Sinquefield as the price of systematic risk. A stock of average risk must be expected to earn 8.5 percent above the riskless rate in order to compensate the investor for the risk.

The Capital Asset Pricing Model (CAPM) is an approach to pricing risks of individual stocks. The CAPM was advanced by several financial economists around the same time, namely by William Sharpe (1964), John Lintner (1965), and Jack Treynor (never published.) According to the CAPM, risky assets are priced by investors according to how much systematic risk they have. Systematic risk according to the CAPM is how much a stock return varies with general market movements. To compare stock returns with the general market, regression analysis is used to statistically estimate the average relation between stock returns and market index. The resulting statistical measure, called the *beta* coefficient, is widely used by financial analysts to measure the systematic risk of individual stocks.

Beta coefficients represent the tendency of a given stock to move with the market. Betas do not count that portion of the stock return uncorrelated to the market, the *unsystematic* part of the return. An "average" stock moves with the market point-for-point not counting unsystematic returns so that its average beta coefficient is one. "High beta" stocks are greater than one because they move up and down more than the market. "Low beta" stocks are less than one because they move less than the market and hence are less risky.

Table 4.5 provides some betas estimated by *Value Line* for several financial service firms in selected years. Beta coefficients in 1993 for these firms ranged from certain low beta stocks, like Old Kent Financial with a beta of .90 to high beta stocks like Merrill Lynch with a betas of 1.8. According to the CAPM, the beta coefficient determines the expected rate of return on a stock. For example, using 8.5 percent as the risk premium, the expected rate of return for BankAmerica in 1993 was 12.75 percent (its beta of 1.50 times 8.5 percent) above the riskless rate. Thus, according to the CAPM, investors in BankAmerica had a total expected return (ROR) of 15.98 percent after adding the risk premium of 12.75 to the one-year riskless rate of 3.23 percent for May 1993. Fifth Third Bancorp's expected return was 11.4 percent (its beta of .95 times 8.5 percent, plus the 3.23 riskless rate). The rates used to discount future cash flows from these two firms would be very different. The higher discount rate on BankAmerica because of its higher systematic risk is clearly one of the factors producing its lower earnings multiple relative to Fifth Third.

In principle, there is no reason to restrict estimation of systematic risk to just the stock market return. Some researchers of financial institutions have estimated the risk sensitivity of financial institution stock returns to two risk sensitivity measures or betas: stock market risk and interest rate risks Flannery and James (1984a) and Dietrich (1986). These are called "two-index" models because they measure risk with respect to a stock market index and to an index of interest rate risks. Two-index models have not, however, achieved the general level of acceptance and wide use in financial analysis of the single-index CAPM model.

Beyond the CAPM: Arbitrage Pricing Theory

In the last few years, a number of financial theorists have been troubled by the many assumptions that the CAPM uses to derive the beta coefficient as the only important measure of risk of common stocks (or any risky assets). One concern is the assumption of a single source of risk: general stock market movements. The

TABLE 4.5 Selected Beta Coefficients

COMPANY	*1983*	*1987*	*1990*	*1993*
Aetna	1.05	1.05	.95	1.25
BankAmerica Corporation	.95	1.10	1.05	1.50
A. G. Edwards	1.55	1.60	1.40	1.70
Fifth Third Bancorp	n/a	.65	.75	.95
Merrill Lynch	1.70	1.55	1.20	1.80
Old Kent Financial Corporation	n/a	n/a	.85	.90
Progressive	n/a	.85	1.00	1.10

NMF = Not meaningful (expected average losses).

SOURCE: *Value Line*, "Summary and Index–Index to Stocks" October 21, 1983, October 16, 1987, October 5, 1990, December 17, 1993.

CAPM assumes that investors all invest in the same set of risky investments and in the proportions that these risky investments exist in the total market for risky assets. All investors are assumed to be the same. Many analysts feel the CAPM needs too many assumptions.

Stephen Ross (1976) began a train of thought that has become extremely influential in current financial thinking and that forms an alternative to the CAPM estimates of the price of risk. His theory makes fewer assumptions and is called arbitrage pricing theory (APT). Ross' theory relies on investors managing relatively small portfolios. If investors are rational and informed, and markets are efficient, each investor will balance portfolio risks and returns. In so doing, investors will supply and demand investments in such a way as to drive asset prices and their expected returns into line with any underlying systematic risk factors they are exposed to. There can be several unsystematic risk factors of concern to investors but unsystematic risk still does not matter.

To appreciate the elegance and advantages of Ross's approach, we must understand the concept of a hedge portfolio (discussed in detail in Chapter 19). A hedge portfolio is a set of investments that eliminates exposure to systematic risks by exploiting the differences in the risk sensitivities or betas of the various assets and liabilities. Through careful composition of a portfolio of assets and liabilities of different risk sensitivities (i.e., betas) to risk factors, systematic risks can be eliminated. If investors in efficient capital markets can form hedge portfolios that have no exposure to systematic risks, these hedge portfolios should earn the riskless rate of interest.

According to APT, in market equilibrium the prices and expected returns of risky securities reflect securities' exposures to systematic risks. If some security prices did not reflect their risk exposures correctly, investors could make higher than riskless returns on riskless positions in securities. Investors could do this by buying the high-return, undervalued securities, and form hedge portfolios with other assets and liabilities. In so doing, these investors would earn above riskless rates at no risk.

The process of buying undervalued, high-return securities and selling or issuing correctly valued or overvalued liabilities is called *arbitrage*. Arbitrage means buying something in one place or point in time that is cheap and selling the same thing at a higher price at another place or point in time. Arbitrage by investors buying low-priced, excess-return securities will drive their prices up. APT is built on the arbitrage process which ensures that asset prices reflect the correct risk-adjusted returns. If excess returns exist, buying or selling pressure from arbitrageurs will put pressure on asset prices until the market prices come close enough to equilibrium to reduce the attraction of arbitrage profits or excess risk-adjusted returns.

APT opens the way to go beyond the single risk factor used in the CAPM. The APT can include several economic factors causing general stock market changes. Currently, financial and economic theorists are debating what those factors should be. Nai-fu Chen, Richard Roll, and Steven Ross (1986) (CRR) have suggested five major risk factors determining the market performance of stocks: (1) changes in the level of real economic activity; (2) changes in expected inflation; (3) unexpected inflation; (4) changes in the term premium of interest rates; and (5) changes in the risk premium in expected returns or investor confidence.

The CRR risk factors seem to be a reasonable list of risk factors given financial institutions' businesses. For example, the problems facing many banks and savings institutions are associated with inflation or disinflation, which reduces the value of assets like commodities, farm land, energy, and commercial real estate. In fact, the large loan losses reported by banks and savings and loans in the 1980s were mainly due to a fall in the values of real estate, primary commodities exported by less-developed countries, farm land, and energy.

Customers of financial institutions are particularly affected by the economy as reflected in industrial production. Differences between long- and short-term investment interest rates are a critical source of cash flow risk to investors in financial service firms. The CRR factors appear to capture many, if not most, of the systematic risk factors likely to affect share price performance of financial firms.

Richard Roll (1987) investigated the risk sensitivity of savings and loans shares to the CRR risk factors and found that savings and loans have substantially more exposure to inflation, term structure, and default risks than the average New York Stock Exchange stock. Roll's estimated savings and loan sensitivity measures are provided in Figure 4.2. These graphs show risk sensitivities of savings and loan stocks relative to an average share with a beta of unity. Except for

FIGURE 4.2 Savings and loan Chen–Roll–Ross betas

SOURCE: Richard Roll, "Managing Risk in Thrift Institutions: Beyond the Duration Gap," UCLA Discussion Paper 13-88, October 1987, pp. 21–23.

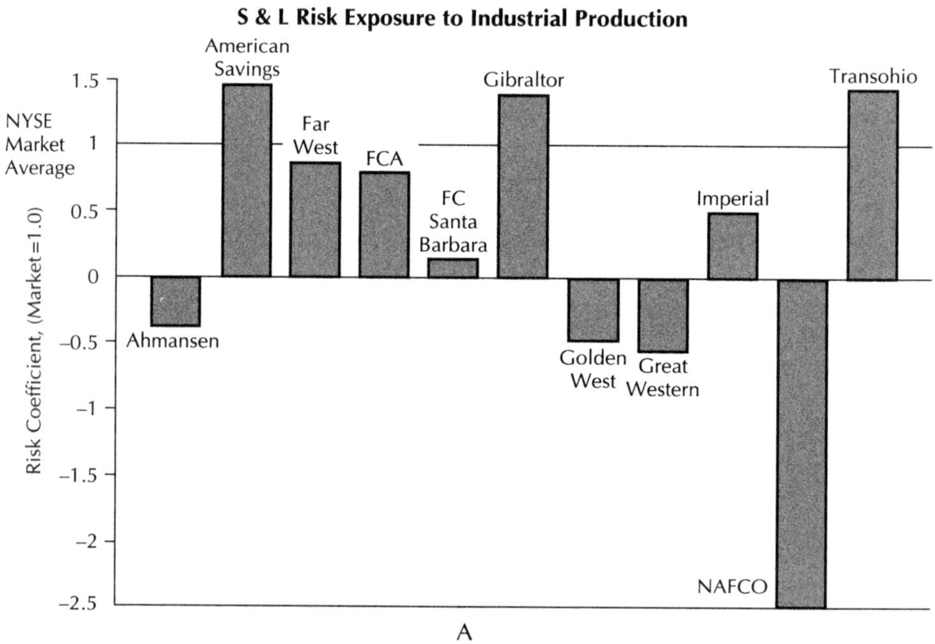

S & L Risk Exposure to Expected Inflation

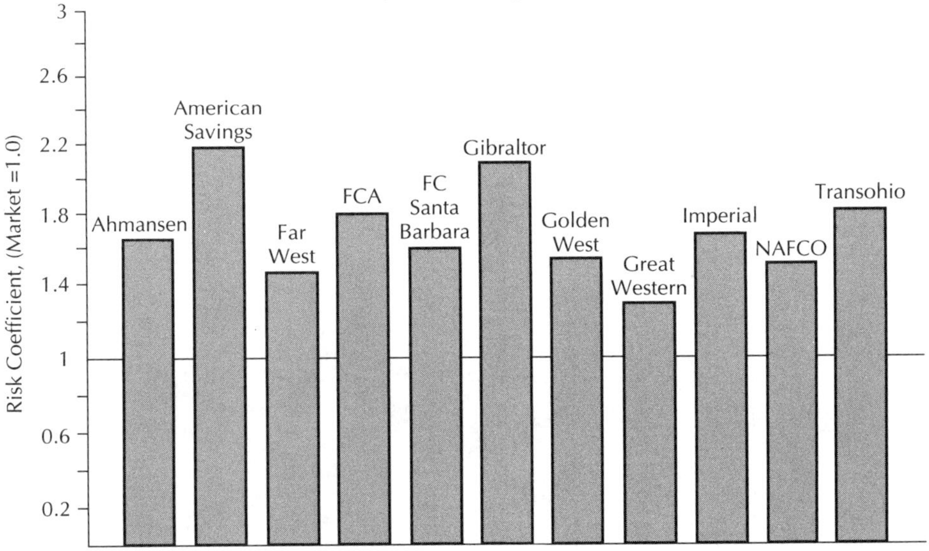

B

S & L Risk Exposure to Unexpected Inflation

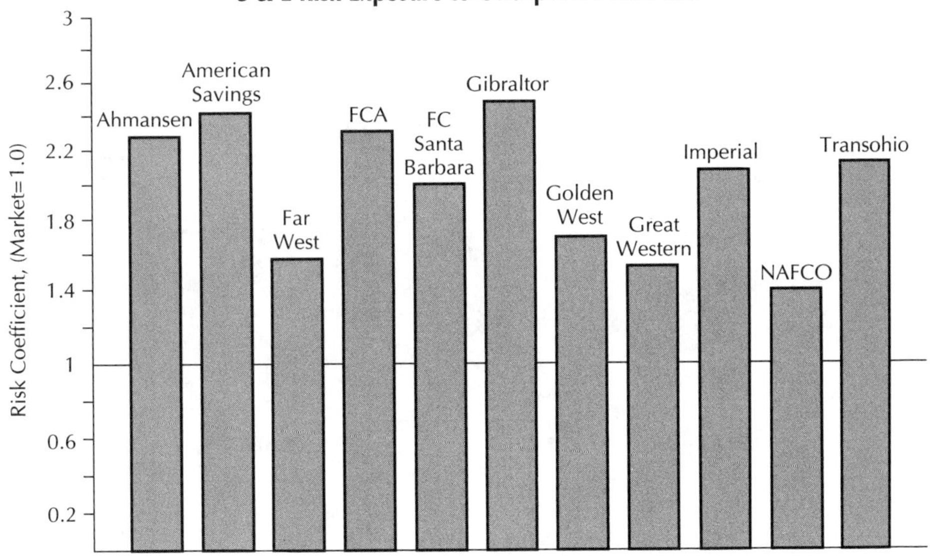

C

industrial production, savings and loans shares demonstrate substantially more than average risk. Dietrich and Weinstein (1989) examined a number of financial service firms and found term and risk premiums to be the most important risks for all financial service firms.

FIGURE 4.2 *(continued)*

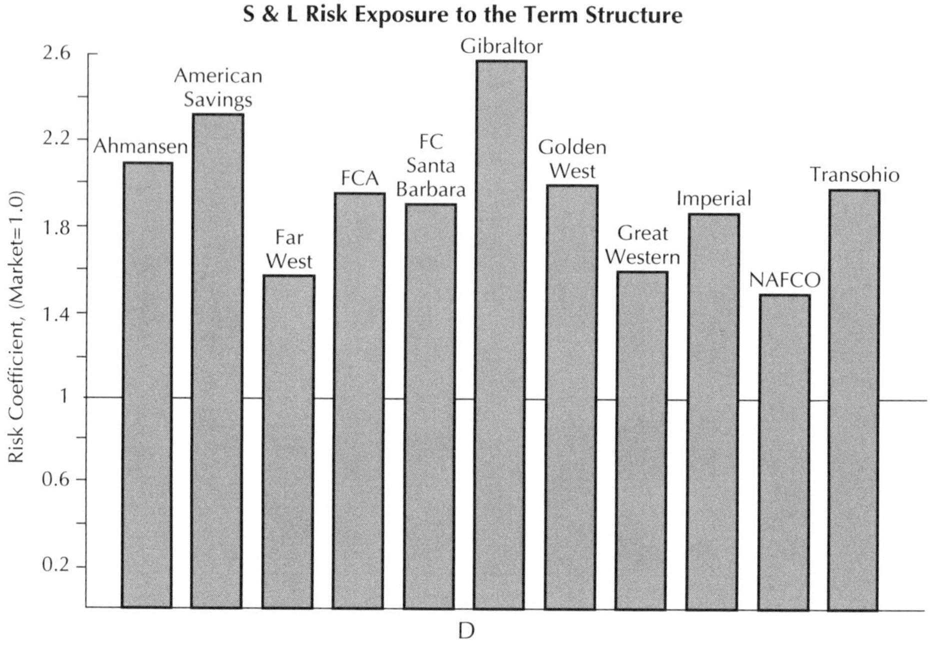

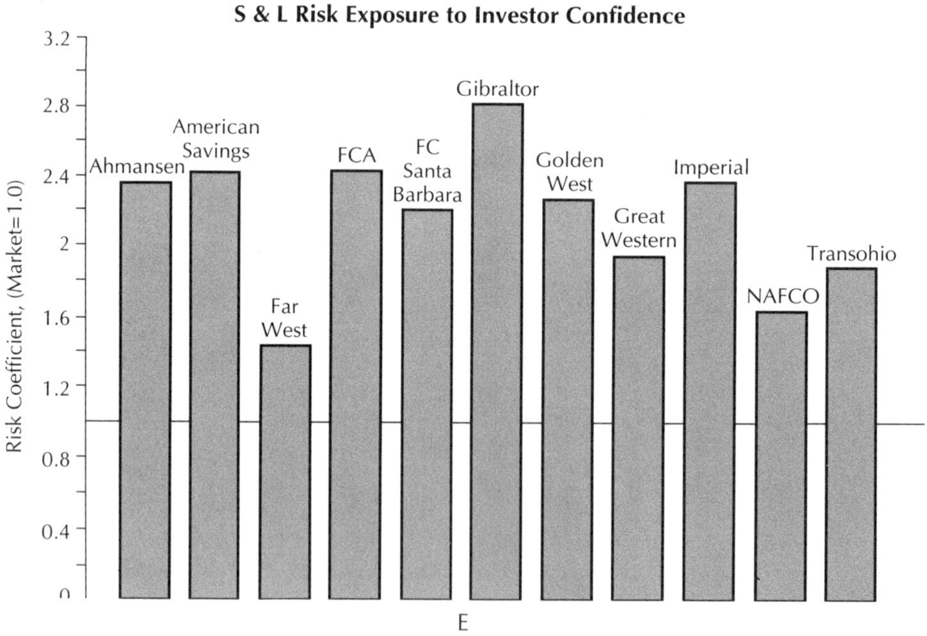

Financial Institution Risk Sensitivity

What causes the differences in the sensitivity of various industries' and firms' stocks to stock market risk in the CAPM or the CRR risk factors used in APT? These differences are due to the economic determinants of cash flows in various businesses, specifically differences in the revenues and cost structures, and the relation of costs and revenues to systematic risks reflected in the stock market or CRR factors.

There are two types of revenues and costs that are important to the cash flows of all business firms: operating cash flows and financing cash flows. If a firm's revenues move with the general economy but it has fixed operating costs, the firm is described as having high operating leverage. For a manufacturing firm this will raise the sensitivity of stock returns to market movements reflecting general economic conditions because stockholders benefit or suffer the residual benefits of variations in operating profits. High fixed financing costs have a similar effect on the stockholders' cash flows. Both high operating leverage and high financial leverage tend to increase betas for manufacturing firms.

Many financial institution CAPM betas are around one. This can be observed by looking at the examples of beta coefficients for financial institutions given in Table 4.5. For these firms the net effect on their systematic risk from operating leverage and financial leverage is about equal to the average firm in the market, including industrial and other service firms. Some observers may find it surprising that financial service firms' betas are not terribly different from those of nonfinancial firms since many financial firms' cash flows are from their financing operations and many raise their funds in the form of deposits or long-term commitments like insurance contracts. Because of the relatively small amounts of equity capital financing their assets, financial service firms are almost always described as "highly leveraged."

The apparently fixed financing costs for financial firms do not contribute to as high a degree of financial leverage as might be thought. Many financial institution asset and liability cash flows are responsive to the same economic events, providing offsetting effects unlike the effect of financial leverage in nonfinancial firms. Many assets of financial firms are low risk, also reducing their stock betas.

Several academic studies have assessed the impact on risk sensitivity of financial institution shares prices from their balance sheets. Flannery and James (1984a) used a two-index model (discussed previously) to demonstrate that the interest rate sensitivity of bank and savings and loan share prices is reduced if they have more short-term assets. They show this in a statistical study of the relationship between bank and thrift interest rate sensitivity measures (betas) and asset composition. In a related study, Flannery and James (1984b) investigated interest rate risk and holdings of noninterest bearing liabilities and assets and found that these liabilities and assets tend to reduce the interest sensitivity of banks. Flannery and James conclude that banks with more short-term assets have lower interest rate sensitivity.

The author (Dietrich, 1986) investigated the simultaneous effect of balance sheet composition on both the stock market beta and interest rate beta of commercial banks. This study found that stock market risk is affected by the amount of loans and deposits as a percent of assets. This study also found that interest rate risk as measured by the interest rate beta is substantially reduced for those banks issuing long-term debt. One implication of this research is that changes in balance sheet composition will change the risk sensitivity of bank stocks.

Haluk Unal (1989) investigated the effect of the removal of large-deposit interest rate ceilings in 1970 on the systematic and unsystematic risk of bank holding company stocks. Unal's study reexamined results reported in a study by Michael Smirlock (1984) using sophisticated statistical techniques. Unal demonstrated that bank systematic risk, as measured by the beta coefficient, went down after deposit ceilings were removed on large deposits. However, Unal does point out that other events occurred in 1970, for example the legislative deliberation of amendments to the Bank Holding Company Act. These other events could confound the interpretation that risk changed due to removal of deposit ceilings.

Studies investigating the relation between risk measures and balance sheet composition suggest that managers of financial institutions can affect the systematic risk sensitivity of the shares of their firms by balance sheet management. This is not to suggest that managing the balance sheet to reduce risk will produce value for investors in the form of excess (more that risk-adjusted) returns, however. We emphasize in Part IV of this book that the focus of management should be on the assessment and management of risk, but not on the elimination of risk. Riskless assets earn the riskless (lowest) rate of return.

4.4 SUMMARY

In this chapter we examine how share prices are determined in the fundamental valuation equation. Value represents the present value of cash flows to investors. We relate price–earning multiples to this present value and discuss practical financial institution valuation techniques. Investors' expected market rate of return on stocks was discussed in terms of the risk adjustment necessary to compensate investors for assuming risk, the so-called market price of risk. To estimate investor's required risk adjustment, we discuss the CAPM betas and explored how APT risk factor sensitivities may be used to refine our understanding of the price of risk. We discussed the relation of financial institution betas to their businesses via their balance sheets.

DISCUSSION QUESTIONS AND EXERCISES

1. Determine the insider and institutional share ownership for A.G. Edwards and Old Kent Bank using data in *Value Line Investment Survey,* Moody's *Bank and Finance Manual,* Standard and Poor's *Stock Guide* and *Stock Record,* and other library sources available to you. Discuss how widely held the shares are and how much of a factor institutional and insider ownership would be for these firms.

2. Using the following closing share price and dividend information for A.G. Edwards (brokers) and Old Kent Bank:

	A.G. EDWARDS		*OLD KENT BANK*	
	CLOSE PRICE	*DIVI-DEND*	*CLOSE PRICE*	*DIVI-DEND*
1982	$2.52	$0.08	$4.30	$0.30
1983	$2.51	$0.08	$6.81	$0.32
1984	$2.52	$0.08	$10.00	$0.36

	A.G. EDWARDS		*OLD KENT BANK*	
	CLOSE PRICE	*DIVI-DEND*	*CLOSE PRICE*	*DIVI-DEND*
1985	\$3.62	\$0.08	\$15.33	\$0.46
1986	\$6.05	\$0.14	\$14.50	\$0.50
1987	\$3.64	\$0.20	\$13.00	\$0.54
1988	\$4.50	\$0.12	\$15.50	\$0.58
1989	\$6.47	\$0.18	\$18.58	\$0.64
1990	\$5.80	\$0.19	\$15.42	\$0.72
1991	\$24.24	\$0.34	\$23.08	\$0.79
1992	\$23.63	\$0.52	\$33.88	\$0.90

Calculate the realized rate of return (ROR) each year for these shares and the standard deviation of the ROR. Compare the market performance of these two stocks to those shown in Table 4.1. (Note: A.G. Edwards closing prices are as of fiscal year end in February.)

3. Determine the P–Es for A.G. Edwards and Old Kent Bank from the sources given in question 1 and discuss the differences between these P–Es and those in Table 4.3 in terms of the discussion in the text.
4. Find the CAPM beta coefficients for A.G. Edwards and Old Kent Bank in the sources given in question 1 and discuss why they are different and relate them to the betas given in Table 4.5.
5. What is the required return using the CAPM for A.G. Edwards and Old Kent Financial as of April, 1995? Can you explain the difference in them in terms of systematic risk?
6. Define "undervalued" in terms of the common stock price of a financial institution, and discuss where the discrepancies between market and value to an acquirer could come from.
7. Many thrift institutions have been declared bankrupt since 1980, yet other thrifts, banks, and other investors have been induced to buy the assets of these institutions by regulators. Why might bankrupt thrifts have value to an acquiring firm? Give some reasons in terms of expected future cash flows.
8. Everything else equal, what are the effects of risk, growth, limited competition, and favorable tax treatment on P–E ratios?
9. Which Chen–Roll–Ross risk factors appear to affect savings and loans the most? Give reasons to justify your choices.
10. Which exchanges do A.G. Edwards and Old Kent Bank trade on? What is their current total market value?

REFERENCES

CHEN, NAI-FU, RICHARD ROLL, and STEVEN ROSS. 1986. "Economic Factors and the Stock Market," *Journal of Business* 59, pp. 383–393.

COPELAND, TOM, TIM KOLLER, and JACK MURRIN. 1990. *Valuation: Measuring and Managing the Value of Companies.* New York: John Wiley and Sons.

CORNELL, BRADFORD, and ALAN SHAPIRO. 1986. "The Reaction of Bank Stock Prices to the International Debt Crisis," *Journal of Banking and Finance* 10, pp. 55–73.

DANN, LARRY Y. and CHRISTOPHER M. JAMES. 1982. "An Analysis of the Impact of Deposit Rate Ceilings on the Market Values of Thrift Institutions," *Journal of Finance* 37, pp. 1259–1275.

DIETRICH, J. KIMBALL. 1986. "Bank Stock Return Sensitivity to Market and Term Structure Risk," working paper, University of Southern California.

DIETRICH, J. KIMBALL and MARK I. WEINSTEIN. 1989. "Risk Characteristics of Financial Institution Share Prices," working paper, University of Southern California.

FAMA, EUGENE F., LAWRENCE FISHER, MICHAEL C. JENSEN, and RICHARD ROLL. 1969. "The Adjustment of Stock Prices to New Information," *International Economic Review* 10, pp. 1–21.

FLANNERY, MARK J. and CHRISTOPHER JAMES. 1984a. "The Effect of Interest Rate Changes on Common Stock Returns," *Journal of Finance* 39, pp. 1141–1152.

FLANNERY, MARK J. and CHRISTOPHER JAMES. 1984b. "Market Evidence on the Effective Maturity of Bank Assets and Liabilities," *Journal of Money, Banking and Credit* 15, pp. 435–445.

JAMES, CHRISTOPHER M. 1983. "An Analysis of Inter-Industry Differences in the Effect of Regulation: The Case of Deposit Rate Ceilings," *Journal of Monetary Economics* 12, pp. 417–432.

IBBOTSON, ROGER G. and REX A. SINQUEFIELD. 1992. *Stocks, Bonds, Bills and Inflation: The Past and the Future.* Charlottesville, VA: Financial Analysts Foundation.

LINTNER, JOHN. 1965. "The Valuation of Risk Assets and the Selection of Risky Investments in Stock Portfolios and Capital Budgets," *Review of Economics and Statistics* 47, pp. 13–37.

MARKOWITZ, HARRY. 1952. "Portfolio Selection," *Journal of Finance* 7, pp. 77–91.

ROLL, RICHARD. 1987. "Managing Risk in Thrift Institutions: Beyond the Duration Gap," University of California, Los Angeles, John E. Anderson Graduate School of Management, Discussion Paper 13–88.

ROSS, STEPHEN A. 1976. "Arbitrage Theory of Capital Asset Pricing," *Journal of Economic Theory* 13, pp. 341–360.

SHARPE, WILLIAM E. 1964. "Capital Asset Prices: A Theory of Market Equilibrium under Conditions of Risk," *Journal of Finance* 19, pp. 425–442.

SMIRLOCK, MICHAEL. 1984. "An Analysis of Bank Risk and Deposit Rate Ceilings," *Journal of Monetary Economics,* 13, pp. 195–210.

UNAL, HALUK. 1989. "Impact of Deposit-Rate Ceiling Changes on Bank Stock Returns," *Journal of Money, Credit and Banking* 21 (May), pp. 206–221.

WAGNER, W. H. and S. C. LAU. 1971. "The Effect of Diversification on Risk," *Financial Analysts Journal* 26, pp. 7–13.

CHAPTER

5

Analysis of Performance Using Accounting Data

Introduction

The goal for managers of financial institutions is to maximize value for owners or investors. Financial analysis of past performance may provide clues to a firm's future performance and value. Careful analysis of financial statements is central to understanding several important issues discussed in this chapter.

- What is the relation between financial data and the market values of financial firms?
- How do we find clues to future performance from financial analysis of firms?
- What is the same and what is different in the financial analyses of different types of financial institutions?

This chapter is a guide to financial statement analysis. We outline financial statements of different types of financial firms and introduce ratio analysis, proceeding in stages to detailed analysis of historical earnings and earning variations for the different types of financial services. We begin with a discussion of the uses of financial statement analysis and the relation between market values and financial data.

5.1 FINANCIAL ANALYSIS AND FINANCIAL STATEMENTS

Finance is a language and like any language it can be used artfully or poorly. The difference comes from knowing the rules and from practice. Any language, including finance, can be used for scientific analysis or poetry or fiction; although poetry may be stretching it, fiction is commonplace. This chapter is intended to be a primer for learning financial analysis of financial service firms. Proficiency will come only with practice and experience.

Finance is used to formulate persuasive arguments to convince customers, managers, boards of directors, buyers, or investors. The intention is to get some decision makers to adopt a recommended course of action: Invest in or buy this firm. Close down this operation. Give me a raise because of my superior management performance.

Financial arguments must be persuasive to be effective. To get a sense for persuasiveness of different arguments, compare these two efforts to convince you to buy a firm: (1) The firm is a good buy; (2) The firm earned more money in four of the last five years than its ten top competitors and is priced low relative to the others and therefore is a good buy. The second argument is more persuasive than the first because it contains financial analysis. Financial analysis ultimately is useful only if it can make a persuasive argument, something that could be called "forensic finance."

In financial debates and discussions, there is no single correct answer. This aspect of finance differentiates it from accounting, because in accounting practice there is a best answer. But financial analysis is only relevant to the future and no one knows what will happen in the future. If decision makers knew the future, they would be operating in a riskless environment. In the real world, the economy, legislation, regulation, or any of a thousand other factors, may change tomorrow.

Good or great financial analysis provides the best guess about what the future can mean for a firm and includes an assessment of the risks. The risks of future outcomes are most often affected by a few major variables. Good financial analysis can consist of simply identifying the major variables affecting future performance, without being able to predict them. Good analysis consists of identifying important numbers among all the numbers available to us. Identifying the largest or most significant numbers in financial analysis poses questions leading to a good understanding of the problem at hand.

In financial analysis, one cannot be shy. Analysts inevitably encounter things they cannot understand or never heard of. In many management meetings, a financial analyst's reputation was made when he or she asked what appeared to be a simple question, the answer to which pointed out a critical variable or assumption for the future. Never be afraid to ask a simple question when performing financial analysis—it may make your career.

A financial analysis is good or great depending on how thoroughly it utilizes available information to delineate the range of likely outcomes and how clearly and persuasively it makes assessments about the future. There is not and never shall be a correct financial analysis. After the fact, all financial analyses will be seen to have contained errors, mistakes, and bad assumptions.

Focus of Financial Analysis

The focus of financial analysis for the management of financial institutions should be always on the performance of the firm measured from the viewpoint of its investors. The realized and expected rates of return (ROR) discussed in the previous chapter are the important concerns of equity investors. Share prices determine actual returns, and current share prices are based on expectations about a firm's future cash flows. A best guess about future performance can be made by analyzing historical performance as detailed in the firm's financial statements.

Financial statements report the operations of the firm as calculated and reported by accountants. We can compute a return to investment using these data. For stock companies, the performance measure corresponding to the ROR is the book rate of return on common equity (BROR). The book value of equity (BVE) per share, corresponds to the share price.

The BROR is calculated by dividing earnings available to common shareholders (EAC) by BVE or their per share equivalents, as shown in the following formula:

$$\text{BROR}_t = \frac{\text{Earnings Available to Common Shareholders}}{\text{Book Value of Equity}} = \frac{\text{EAC}}{\text{BVE}} \tag{5.1}$$

Earnings available for common and book value of equity are the same as net income and common equity in the absence of preferred stock.

We focus now on the relation between a firm's ROR and its BROR. Table 5.1 contains historical RORs and BRORs for several financial service firms for comparison, and it illustrates two key points. First, BRORs for the firms are less variable than the RORs. The smaller variability in book versus realized returns is reflected in the standard deviations of ROR versus BROR for all firms. For example, the standard deviation of Aetna's annual BROR is 3.67 percent versus 21.67 percent for its ROR, and the comparison is even more dramatic for the other firms

TABLE 5.1 Comparison of Market Rates of Return and Book Rates of Return

	AETNA		*BANK OF AMERICA*		*FIFTH THIRD BANCORP*		*PROGRESSIVE INSURANCE*	
	ROR	*BROR*	*ROR*	*BROR*	*ROR*	*BROR*	*ROR*	*BROR*
1983	–11.60%	7.89%	1.86%	8.82%	29.45%	16.30%	14.46%	25.84%
1984	6.23%	4.71%	11.28%	7.84%	63.08%	15.60%	47.58%	24.24%
1985	8.72%	9.39%	–5.89%	–8.79%	23.92%	17.03%	–4.39%	21.50%
1986	52.00%	12.99%	–7.39%	–15.56%	70.43%	15.98%	101.60%	17.76%
1987	10.31%	14.26%	–6.40%	–38.63%	9.31%	14.94%	51.09%	23.12%
1988	–14.89%	10.24%	–52.99%	16.00%	17.10%	16.55%	–0.87%	25.91%%
1989	30.96%	9.22%	297.82%	16.72%	64.78%	15.49%	27.67%	17.92%%
1990	–26.09%	8.68%	2.80%	15.11%	–8.05%	15.38%	34.36%	22.86%%
1991	19.90%	6.84%	39.91%	16.68%	109.61%	15.71%	6.38%	8.91%%
1992	11.95%	0.77%	33.24%	11.93%	21.10%	16.32%	62.86%	26.21%%
Mean	8.75%	8.50%	31.42%	3.01%	40.07%	15.93%	34.08%	21.43%%
Std Dev	21.67%	3.67%	91.98%	17.45%	33.79%	0.59%	31.23%	5.08%

listed. Notice also that ROR and BROR are very different from year to year for all firms on the table.

Relation Between Book and Market Measures of Performance

Given the differences between book and realized return measures, why do we analyze financial statements to assess prospects for investors? We have no choice. Financial statements are the only detailed information available on the firm's business activities and the only basis for analyzing management's potential to generate cash flows in the future. The market value of the firm is an instantaneous assessment of the firm's future prospects. For example, the outlook for Aetna's cash flows for investors improved in 1992 relative to the general market as seen in Aetna's 11.95 percent ROR relative to the market's 7.06 percent return (the latter is shown in Chapter 4, Table 4.1). Why this relative improvement in Aetna's prospects? The only way to answer that question is to know something of the insurance business and Aetna's ability to perform. A detailed assessment of Aetna or any other firm must be based on details of its operations that can only be derived from analysis of detailed financial statements.

Two differences between accounting numbers reflected in financial statements and market values must be kept always in mind. The first difference is that prices or market values are *forward looking* whereas accounting data are *backward looking*. The second difference is that income statements reflect *accrual accounting* methods, not *cash flows*, and balance sheets show assets and liabilities at *historical cost*, not *cash* or *market values*. We discuss both of these differences in turn.

Market Values Are Forward Looking. Market values are assessments of future business conditions and firms' specific prospects for cash flows to investors. Historical performance can be the basis for assessments of the firms' future performances, as Figure 5.1 illustrates. The only reason for financial analysis is to make estimates of *future* performance. If nothing can be learned about the future of the firm from the past, little is to be gained from financial statement analysis.

The disparity between market and book returns can be explained easily when the difference between historical and future orientation of market values is kept in mind. For example, in the second quarter of 1987, Citicorp increased allowances for loan losses on loans to Brazil and other Latin American countries,

FIGURE 5.1 Market rate of return versus book rate of return

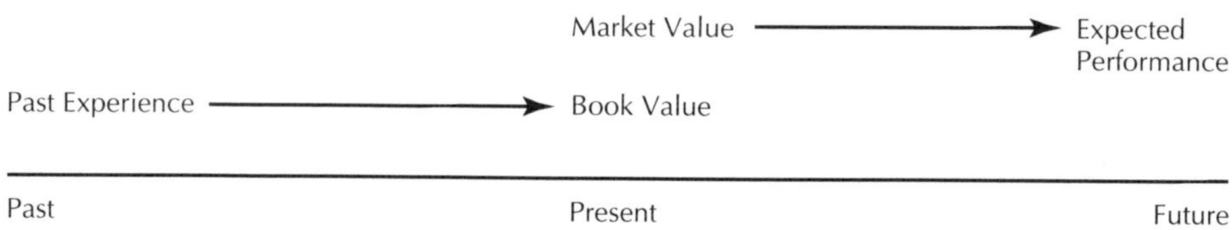

greatly increasing its expenses. Citicorp reported a *minus* 130 percent BROR on an annualized basis, but had a *positive* 67 percent ROR for that quarter. The market felt that the future cash flow prospects for Citicorp had improved despite the accounting loss, presumably due to a tougher future policy on lending to Latin American countries.

Accounting Data versus Cash Flows and Economic Values. The second source of differences between RORs and BRORs comes from differences between cash flows and accounting reports of income and accounting for assets and liabilities on the balance sheet. Income is reported on an *accrual* basis rather than on a cash basis. For example, the loan losses reported by Citicorp in the second quarter of 1987 did not produce any immediate effect on cash flows. Citicorp had already lent the money and was not collecting any interest. There are many examples of more routine differences in reported income and cash flows. For example, prepaid premiums of $1,190.4 million for Aetna in 1992 represent investable cash for that firm. These premiums do not show up as income until later when "earned."

Another important difference between cash values and accounting numbers comes from representation of assets and liabilities on financial statements. Many items on financial institution balance sheets are accounted for in terms of their historical cost, not their value if sold. The cash-generating potential of these investments or sources of funds may not be reflected well or at all in financial statements.

Some assessment of the adjustments to net income necessary to compare it to cash flows may come from studying a firms' statement of cash flows. Cash flow statements explain year-to-year changes in cash balances in terms of operations and financing. Although we focus on income in the following discussion, cash flow is the important number for investors.

Many Sources of Information Available

Users of financial statements are often baffled by the multiplicity of financial reports financial firms generate. All firms keep several sets of accounts. They report to investors, to one or more tax authorities such as the Internal Revenue Service, and to regulators. These reports may differ in the accounting for some items. Common sense about which of the reported measures is most relevant to the task at hand may provide guidance about which numbers to use. For example, in the 1980s well-known problems in the thrift industry led regulators to tolerate generous accounting of capital, called Regulatory Accounting Procedures (RAP), which did not deceive alert analysts about the thrifts' capital shortage. Analysts can often use reasonable assumptions to reinterpret distorted data in order to proceed with analysis, reserving concerns until better data are available from an insider or future events.

Most analysts rely on public financial data such as annual reports. Current accounting standards in the United States require that firms report an income statement, a balance sheet, and a cash flow statement. In our discussion that follows, we will assume that these reports are available. In other circumstances, analysts will have more or less information to work with.

To summarize, financial statements are the only source of detailed information on a firm's operations. Financial analysis is used to project future performance in terms of cash flows for the investor. Historical financial statements use accrual accounting and historical cost analysis and can distort performance, which must be accounted for when assessing future cash flows.

5.2 GUIDE TO FINANCIAL ANALYSIS OF FINANCIAL INSTITUTIONS

Financial analysis of any financial institution starts from the same point—obtaining financial data—and moves through a logical sequence of steps. Table 5.2 provides an outline of the procedure. The analyst focuses on answering the most interesting questions raised in the previous step. We describe each step and give guidance on how to proceed through the analysis in what follows. The analyst's problem is something like walking into a forest. There are a lot of trees and it is easy to become disoriented. In this problem, the compass is the analyst's concern with understanding what determines the return on equity.

Obtain Financial Data (Step 1)

The first step is to obtain financial data. Financial analysts rarely have precisely the data they want. The data are either not detailed enough or too detailed and voluminous to comprehend. Numbers will rarely reflect just those aspects of the problem the analyst would most like to explore. Good financial analysis consists of making the best use of the financial information available, usually identifying critical variables and relationships. Expertise at financial analysis comes from solving many problems over time—that is, through practice. Financial analysis can only be as good as available financial data allow. The analyst must know what data are available—most often these are publicly reported balance sheets and income statements. We use these financial statements in the examples in this chapter because they are the most readily available and widely used, but we discuss other data sources below.

TABLE 5.2 Steps in Analysis of Return on Equity of Financial Institutions

(1) Obtain financial data and determine source, time period, and operating units covered.
(2) Simplify financial statement items into a small set of items.
(3) Calculate and interpret basic ratios and identify important questions to be investigated in the next step.
(4) Analyze segments of operations that are major determinants of performance and performance variation.
(5) Obtain industry, other firm, and historical benchmarks to assess results.
(6) Determine important factors distinguishing firm's performance and identify determinants of performance where unanswered questions are raised or unusual results are obtained.

Once the analyst has financial data to work with, two questions must be asked: First, what business entity or entities are represented by the financial reports? Second, are the financial data the best available?

Most financial institutions today are a part of complex corporate structures. Most banks, insurance companies, thrift institutions, and other financial firms, are only parts of organizations reporting *consolidated* financial statements. These statements reflect all business entities of the corporate parent and are consolidated according to accounting rules. The first task of the analyst is to determine which corporate entity is being analyzed. For example, in 1992, BankAmerica Corporation reported results consolidating the Bank of America NT&SA (National Trust and Savings Association), Seafirst Corporation, a bank holding company whose major subsidiary is Seattle–First National Bank, as well as separately chartered Banks of America in seven Western states. It makes sense to analyze BankAmerica Corporation as a bank, given that nine bank subsidiaries dominate results. A good analyst always knows what the numbers represent before beginning an analysis.

Diversified financial corporation reports can be difficult to interpret because consolidated data may represent several types of financial service firms. In some cases the focus is on a subsidiary of a holding company that is of interest, perhaps because it is to be sold as was the case in 1993 when American Express, a diversified company, sold Shearson Lehman Brothers, an investment bank and brokerage firm. In cases where consolidated statements cannot provide answers to important questions, the analyst must either search for financial data that can be used to assess the performance of given unit or units of a holding company, or be willing to make bold assumptions. The choice depends on the problem and on the time and resources available for the job.

The second question the analyst must answer is: What is the source of these financial data and are they the best available? In most cases, analysts use audited public information. Sometimes unaudited data are available from the firm, which might provide details on operations hidden in the consolidated reports. Often, trade associations or industry groups gather information on specific aspects of operations that can be used to assess a firm's activity in a given area.

There are many public sources of data for financial service firms. Publicly traded corporations must file reports with the Securities and Exchange Commission (SEC), such as the annual Form 10-K. These reports often contain details of operations of various important operating units. Details on revenues, costs, or profits may appear in a description of the firms' operations or in footnotes to the reports. A serious analyst always becomes very familiar with all the pages of reports used in analyzing a firm.

Most financial service firms are regulated. Regulated institutions like banks, thrifts, insurance companies, and brokerages, file periodic financial reports with their regulators. For example, Seattle–First National Bank, although a subsidiary of BankAmerica Corporation, must file reports with the Office of the Comptroller of the Currency (OCC) because it is a national bank. Such reports are publicly available, and their data may be a source of detailed financial information on units of financial holding companies that are of special interest apart from the consolidated operations of the entire firm.

Most analysts today work with computerized financial databases, which eliminates the need to type information into spreadsheets and which make extensive analysis possible within a limited time period. The availability of computer-based data is changing rapidly and an analyst within a specific environment, such as a student, may have different computer resources available than an analyst operating in another environment, such as an investment bank. These differences do not necessarily affect the quality of the analysis, as all these financial data come from the same basic sources.

Analysts using data in computer files should be completely familiar with the sources used by the supplier of the information. It is always preferable to have copies of the original data sources in addition to the computer files. The original data source, like the annual reports, 10-Ks, and regulatory filings, often contain useful information in footnotes or special schedules that are difficult to put into standardized computer files made available by information suppliers. Table 5.3 summarizes important data sources used by many financial analysts. The table is classified by financial services segment.

TABLE 5.3 Standard Sources of Data for Financial Institutions

- All Publicly Traded Financial Service Firms or Holding Companies
  - SEC Form 10-K (annual)
  - SEC Form 10-Q (quarterly)
  - Annual Report to Shareholders
  - Moody's *Bank and Finance Manual*
- Commercial Banks
  - Commercial Banks Regulatory Filings
    - Quarterly Report of Condition (Call Report)
  - Published Financial Statements (semiannual)
  - Computer Databases (and source)
    - Quarterly Reports of Condition (National Technical Information Service, Washington, D.C.)
    - Reports of Condition (variety of sources, e.g. Sheshunoff, Dallas, Texas)
  - Quarterly and Annual Reports of Condition, market price, and other data (Compustat Computer Services, Denver, Colorado)
- Thrifts
  - Savings and Loan Subsidiaries Regulatory Filings
  - Quarterly Financial Statement (currently quarterly)
  - Published Financial Statements (semiannual)
  - Computer Databases (and source)
    - Quarterly Financial Statements (NTIS)
  - Quarterly Financial Statements (variety of sources, e.g. Sheshunoff, Dallas, Texas)
- Insurance Companies
  - Insurance Company Subsidiary Regulatory Filings
    - Annual Convention Blank (State Regulatory Authorities)
    - Best's *Insurance Reports*
    - Computer Databases
      - National Association of Insurance Commissioners (NAIC)
- Investment Banking and Brokerage Firms
  - Broker Dealer Subsidiary Regulatory Filings Focus Report (SEC)

Simplify Financial Statements (Step 2)

Analyzing financial institutions is a different problem from analyzing manufacturing firms. In the case of a manufacturing firm, analysts judge management's policies by whether they can sell the product at a price sufficiently above cost to make money. Most management decisions in manufacturing firms over short time horizons are pricing and production decisions. Price times quantity is sales revenue and subtracting costs produces the accountant's estimate of operating profit. For manufacturing firm in the first instance, management policies are reflected in the so-called "bottom line" of the income statement. Decisions to expand a plant or change capital structure usually evolve slowly over time and change the balance sheet gradually.

Financial institutions contrast sharply with manufacturing firms. Results of many if not most decisions of managers of financial institutions appear simultaneously in the income statement and the balance sheet. Some of the most important financial institution marketing and pricing decisions are reflected instantly in the balance sheet. As an example, if a thrift management implements an aggressive strategy to build market share by lowering its home mortgage rate below its competition and the strategy works, the savings bank will make more mortgage loans. The loans appear as assets on the balance sheet as soon as they are made and funding for them will show up as liabilities. The interest revenues produced by the loans will show up on the income statement in the future.

In much of what follows, the critical analytical task is to link balance sheet items, such as loans, to income statement items, such as loan revenues or interest on loans. Accountants use many terms to describe the income and activities associated with making loans, like revenues, fees, interest, etc. Analysis of performance of a financial institution requires relating the income statement to balance sheet items when possible and relevant. The relation can be made with a few broad categories or many narrow categories of activity.

The number of data categories used by analysts depends on the problem and data at hand. The analyst seeks to identify critical numbers; the only reason to disaggregate data is to focus on questions that can only be answered by disaggregating data. For example, does the analyst wish to determine whether a firm's total loans on average earn less interest revenue than comparable firms or is the analyst concerned exclusively with credit card loans? The question determines the analysis and often comes out of more general results. Key questions emerge from analysis when answers to those questions may explain critical factors affecting performance of a firm.

Financial institutions offer the financial services discussed in Chapter 2, namely:

Credit (lending)
Securities origination, trading, and brokerage
Deposit-taking and transaction processing
Insurance
Asset management
Information and advice.

Specific financial institutions historically have specialized in certain services because of regulatory restrictions or comparative advantage. Financial statements for specific classes of financial institutions, such as insurance companies or thrifts, often reflect their continuing concentration in particular financial services. Thus, the terms used on financial statements in each industry segment tend to be somewhat specialized. Table 5.4 lists balance sheet and income categories often observed in traditional financial institution financial statements.

A useful way to begin analysis of a financial institution is to find income statement revenue items that represent interest or interest-like payments associated with assets and liabilities on the balance sheet. Assets that earn explicit interest or interest-like payments are called *earning assets*. Earning assets such as U.S. Treasury securities would be reflected as interest on securities on the income statement and appear as investments in U.S. Treasuries on the balance sheet. An earning asset with interest-like revenues would be leasing income on the income statement, associated with leases on the balance sheet. Similarly, interest or interest-like expenses on the income statement can be related to funds raised by issuing liabilities shown on the balance sheet. For example, interest expense for deposits can be linked to interest-bearing deposits on the balance sheets for deposit-taking institutions. Total interest expense is often compared to total interest-bearing liabilities shown on the balance sheet.

The classification of income statement and balance sheet items is an important first step. This step is often complicated by the many different terms and conventions used by various firm and industry segments. Table 5.4 provides some standard terms used and the table can be used to correlate income statement and balance sheet categories. No table can solve problems faced by analysts in all situations. The analyst must make a judgment on an item and move on to complete the job, keeping reservations and concerns about each step in mind in interpreting the results.

Simplifying classifications is essential in order to make the comparisons over time, between firms, and to industry averages. Since the overriding objective is to identify major sources of performance, for earning assets and liabilities, computing the return on assets and costs of funds by classifying balance sheets and income statements is needed to find major factors affecting performance.

Many financial product revenues and expenses are not connected to assets and liabilities on the balance sheet. For example, fees for management of those assets not carried by the firm's books are not reflected on the firm's balance sheet. Personnel and occupancy expenses are not explicitly related to balance sheet items. These items will vary in their relative importance for different financial service firms. For deposit-taking and insurance institutions in the past, non–interest-expense items were small relative to financial revenues and expenses, whereas for investment management firms and brokers, they are relatively large. As fee income increases in importance, analysts will increasingly need to look for off-balance sheet activity measures, like assets under management.

At the end of the second step of financial analysis, the analyst will have identified total interest revenues, interest expenses, noninterest revenues, and

TABLE 5.4 Relation between Balance Sheet and Income Statement for Selected Financial Institution Reported Items

BALANCE SHEET	*INCOME STATEMENT*
Credit (Lending)	
Loans	Interest on loans Loan fees Loan revenues
Leases	Leasing revenues Lease fees
Mortgage loans Mortgage receivable Mortgage-backed securities	Interest on loans Interest on loans receivable
Securities Origination, Brokerage, and Market Making	
Trading inventories Securities inventories Trading account securities	Principal transactions Interest and dividends Securities gains/losses
Repurchase/resale agreements	Interest expense/income
Receivable from customers	Margin interest
Payable/receivable to/from brokers and dealers	Usually no income statement item
Transaction Processing and Deposit-Taking	
Cash and due from banks	No income statement item
Interest-bearing deposits	Interest revenues
NOW accounts/interest-bearing checking	Interest and fees Service charges
Demand deposits	Account fees
Insurance	
Insurance reserves Life and annuity reserves Unearned premiums Unpaid claims/claims payable	Premium revenues Benefits paid Claims paid Policy acquisition expenses Claims expenses
Asset Management/Investment Activities	
Investments Securities	Interest/dividends Investment income/revenue
Real estate	Rent Property income and fees

noninterest expenses, all together accounting for income before tax and income after tax. The balance sheet should be classified into earning assets and interest-bearing liabilities. Given the relative importance of different categories of the interest or noninterest items, a subdivision of the revenues and expenses may be undertaken on the income statement and on the balance sheet in subsequent analysis.

Examples of Step 2. Step 2 of financial analysis is illustrated for financial statements of a bank, Fifth Third Bancorp, and an insurance company, Aetna, in Panels A of Tables 5.5 and 5.6. Statements of broker/dealer A.G. Edwards are shown in Table 5.7, Panel A, but analysis of them is left to readers. Those firms' financial statements are followed in Panels B by the simplified statements suggested in Table 5.2. We discuss the process of classification here using the bank and insurance company. We caution students that understanding examples is no substitute for hands-on practice. Practice should begin with the examples not discussed and continue with the end of chapter problems.

Example of Steps 1 and 2: Fifth Third Bancorp. Fifth Third Bancorp's financial statements are contained in Table 5.5. These data are from the 1992 Annual Report and represent Fifth Third Bank in Cincinnati, Ohio, and nine affiliated banks. The discussion in the annual report describes the Midwest Payments System subsidiary, an electronic payments provider, and emphasizes Fifth Third's asset management services. We interpret Fifth Third as primarily a bank but are alert to the importance of fees on its results.

Fifth Third's financial statements are straightforward to simplify for analysis. In fact, subtotals on its 1992 income statement correspond neatly to the categories of interest revenue (IR), interest expense (IE), noninterest revenue (NIR), provision for loan losses (PLL), and noninterest expense (NIE). The balance sheet similarly presents few problems in classifying items as earning assets (EA) and nonearning assets. The resulting scheme is shown in Panel B of Table 5.5.

Example of Steps 1 and 2: Aetna. We illustrate financial analysis of an insurance company with Aetna Life and Casualty Company. Aetna's 1992 consolidated financial statements combine accounting information for its many insurance operations and subsidiaries. The discussion in the annual report makes clear that 1992 was a rough year for Aetna, which was undergoing a substantial reorganization and restructuring. Analysis of Aetna's reported operating results must consider both Aetna's complexity and the financial impact of one-time changes in its operations.

Financial statements for Aetna Insurance in 1992 are presented in Panel A of Table 5.6 and our simplified statements in Panel B of that table. Classification of income statement entries into items related to the balance sheet items for Aetna is more difficult than in our previous example because of the complexity of Aetna's insurance business and its restructuring problems mentioned above. The Aetna example illustrates both simplification of insurance company financial statements and reasonable ways of dealing with operations complicated by special circumstances.

Most insurance company revenues are from two sources: insurance premiums and investment income. Both are easy to identify for Aetna: The company reports premiums (PR) and net investment income and net realized gains, which we combine into investment revenue (IR). We include realized gains and losses as part of investment revenue as these are part of Aetna's asset management performance. Net investment revenues are related to total investments on Aetna's balance sheet which in turn correspond to earning assets (EA).

TABLE 5.5 Financial Statements for Fifth Third Bancorp

Panel A: Consolidated Statements of Income

FOR THE YEARS ENDED DECEMBER 31 ($000s)	***1992***	*1991*	*1990*
Interest Income			
Interest and Fees on Loans and Leases	**$556,423**	558,557	564,842
Interest on Securities			
Taxable	**123,633**	127,026	87,955
Exempt from Income Taxes	**10,789**	12,521	10,674
Total Interest on Securities	**134,422**	139,547	98,629
Interest on Federal Funds Loaned	**2,324**	13,114	22,612
Interest on Deposits in Banks	**1,291**	2,283	3,464
Total Interest Income	**694,460**	713,501	689,547
Interest Expense			
Interest on Deposits			
Interest Checking	**26,145**	31,275	31,217
Savings	**13,673**	15,460	17,732
Money Market	**43,056**	60,837	71,762
Other Time	**147,924**	171,441	167,855
Certificates-$100,000 and Over	**23,456**	57,021	75,921
Foreign Office	**1,714**	756	187
Total Interest on Deposits	**255,968**	336,790	364,674
Interest on Funds Borrowed	**40,696**	42,870	36,542
Interest on Long-Term Debt and Notes	**3,602**	1,620	1,710
Total Interest Expense	**300,266**	381,280	402,926
Net Interest Income	**394,194**	332,221	286,621
Provision for Credit Losses	**65,315**	55,744	39,879
Net Interest Income After Provision for Credit Losses	**328,879**	276,477	246,742
Other Operating Income			
Trust Income	**48,433**	40,263	34,428
Service Charges on Deposits	**49,856**	41,673	35,013
Data Processing Income	**45,842**	40,601	34,830
Other Service Charges and Fees	**54,451**	45,221	40,646
Securities Gains (Losses)	**1,471**	4,153	(52)
Total Other Operating Income	**200,053**	171,911	144,865
Operating Expenses			
Salaries and Wages	**107,816**	95,718	88,981
Employee Benefits	**29,732**	25,652	23,223
Equipment Expenses	**13,354**	12,256	12,608
Net Occupancy Expenses	**20,833**	18,729	15,341
Other Operating Expenses	**117,541**	97,437	83,171
Total Operating Expenses	**289,276**	249,792	223,324
Income Before Income Taxes	**239,656**	198,596	168,283
Applicable Income Taxes	**75,564**	60,446	47,872
Net Income	**$164,092**	138,150	120,411
Net Income Per Share (a)	**$2.75**	2.33	2.05
Average Shares Outstanding (000s) (a)	**59,632**	59,200	58,847
Cash Dividends Declared Per Share (a)	**$.90**	.78	.68

(a) Per share amounts and average shares outstanding reflect the three-for-two stock split effected in the form of a stock dividend paid April 15, 1992. See Notes to Consolidated Financial Statement on pages 19–25.

SOURCE: Fifth Third Bancorp

TABLE 5.5 (*continued*)

Panel A: Consolidated Balance Sheets

DECEMBER 31 ($000s)	***1992***	*1991*
Assets		
Cash and Due from Banks	**$565,948**	501,188
Interest Bearing Deposits in Banks	**790**	22,211
Securities (Market Value 1992-**$1,960,300** and 1991-$2,121,356)	**1,933,008**	2,063,766
Federal Funds Loaned	—	170,000
Loans and Leases		
Commercial Loans	**2,485,310**	2,206,176
Construction Loans	**308,781**	281,021
Commercial Mortgage Loans	**495,818**	435,006
Residential Mortgage Loans	**1,935,254**	1,071,218
Consumer Loans	**1,631,496**	1,440,219
Commercial Lease Financing	**282,579**	248,167
Consumer Lease Financing	**454,607**	229,958
Unearned Income	**(118,986)**	(105,153)
Reserve for Credit Losses	**(114,751)**	(90,324)
Total Loans and Leases	**7,360,108**	5,716,288
Bank Premises and Equipment	**120,650**	111,811
Accrued Income Receivable	**76,000**	76,135
Other Assets	**156,816**	164,731
Total Assets	**$10,213,320**	8,826,130
Liabilities		
Deposits		
Demand	**$1,306,766**	1,151,364
Interest Checking	**1,185,660**	895,437
Savings	**491,764**	358,778
Money Market	**1,405,469**	1,269,883
Other Time	**2,672,344**	2,447,247
Certificates-$100,000 and Over	**399,210**	549,427
Foreign Office	**70,733**	15,126
Total Deposits	**7,531,946**	6,687,262
Funds Borrowed	**1,229,791**	1,042,566
Accrued Taxes, Interest and Expenses	**106,728**	118,209
Other Liabilities	**85,629**	85,795
Long-Term Debt	**111,768**	12,848
Convertible Subordinated Notes	**142,293**	—
Total Liabilities	**9,208,155**	7,946,680
Stockholders' Equity		
Common Stock	**132,859**	87,897
Capital Surplus	**201,887**	187,237
Retained Earnings	**670,823**	604,720
Treasury Stock	**(404)**	(404)
Total Stockholders' Equity	**1,005,165**	879,450
Total Liabilities and Stockholders' Equity	**$10,213,320**	8,826,130

Panel A: Consolidated Statements of Cash Flows

FOR THE YEARS ENDED DECEMBER 31 ($000s)	*1992*	*1991*	*1990*
Operating Activities			
Net Income	**$164,092**	138,150	120,411
Adjustments to Reconcile Net Income to Net Cash			
Provided by Operating Activities			
Provision for Credit Losses	**65,315**	55,744	39,879
Provision for Depreciation and Amortization	**33,087**	15,116	9,869
Provision for Deferred Income Taxes	**4,783**	(3,341)	(2,047)
Realized Securities Gains	**(1,687)**	(4,352)	(1,198)
Realized Securities Losses	**216**	199	1,250
Proceeds from Sales of Residential Mortgage Loans Held for Resale	**155,487**	76,779	8,992
Gains from Sales of Residential Mortgage Loans Held for Resale	**(2,932)**	(2,873)	(372)
Net Increase in Residential Mortgage Loans Held for Resale	**(177,427)**	(91,623)	(24,080)
Decrease (Increase) in Accrued Income Receivable	**135**	8,453	(4,587)
Decrease (Increase) in Other Assets	**26,802**	(63,143)	(6,540)
Increase (Decrease) in Accrued Taxes, Interest and Expenses	**(29,835)**	(3,637)	6,372
Increase (Decrease) in Other Liabilities	**(531)**	44,522	(7,336)
Net Cash Provided by Operating Activities	**237,505**	169,994	140,613
Investing Activities			
Net Decrease (Increase) in Interest Bearing Deposits in Banks	**21,421**	54,835	(48,036)
Proceeds from Sales of Securities	**249,565**	270,165	46,676
Proceeds from Calls and Paydowns of Securities	**650,271**	185,596	76,397
Proceeds from Maturities of Securities	**452,334**	423,883	462,435
Purchases of Securities	**(994,850)**	(1,584,498)	(878,878)
Net Decrease (Increase) in Federal Funds Loaned	**202,374**	90,480	(14,213)
Net Increase in Loans and Leases	**(1,646,561)**	(322,254)	(352,500)
Purchases of Bank Premises and Equipment	**(17,353)**	(13,491)	(18,091)
Proceeds from Disposals of Bank Premises and Equipment	**4,088**	1,626	2,014
Net Cash Acquired in Purchases of Subsidiaries	**13,536**	10,604	—
Net Cash Used in Investing Activities	**(1,065,175)**	(883,054)	(724,196)
Financing Activities			
Net Increase in Deposits	**234,147**	31,945	601,694
Purchase of Deposits	**277,717**	224,425	—
Net Increase in Funds Borrowed	**187,225**	435,019	127,828
Proceeds from Issuance of Long-Term Debt	**98,987**	—	1,636
Repayment of Long-Term Debt	**(221)**	(669)	(726)
Proceeds from Issuance of Convertible Subordinated Notes	**142,207**	—	—
Payment of Cash Dividends	**(51,273)**	(44,979)	(38,911)
Shares Acquired for Treasury	**(491)**	(2,426)	(637)
Fractional Shares Purchased in Stock Split	**(106)**	—	—
Proceeds from Stock Options Exercised	**4,182**	6,219	3,580
Tax Benefit Related to Exercise of Non-Qualified Stock Options	**56**	467	—
Net Cash Provided by Financing Activities	**892,430**	650,001	694,464
Increase (Decrease) in Cash and Due from Banks	**64,760**	(63,059)	110,881
Cash and Due from Banks at Beginning of Year	**501,188**	564,247	453,366
Cash and Due from Banks at End of Year	**$565,948**	501,188	564,247

TABLE 5.5 (*continued*)

Panel B: Simplified Financial Statements

AS REPORTED	*SIMPLIFIED STATEMENT*	*1992 AMOUNT*
Income Statement Items		
Total interest income Interest and fees on loans and leases Interest on securities Interest on Federal funds loaned Interest on deposit in banks	Interest revenues (IR)	$694,460
Total interest expense Interest on deposits Interest on funds borrowed Interest on long-term debt and notes	Interest expense (IE)	300,266
Provision for credit losses	Provision for loan losses (PLL)	65,315
Total other operating income	Noninterest revenue (NIR)	200,053
Total operating expenses	Noninterest expense (NIE)	289,276
Income before income taxes	Earnings before tax (EBT)	239,656
Net income	Earnings available to common shareholder (EAC)	164,092
Balance Sheet Items		
Cash and due from	Cash and reserves (R)	$565,948
Interest-bearing deposits Securities Federal funds loaned Loans and leases	Earning assets (EA)	Note (1)
Bank premises and equipment Accrued income receivable Other assets	Fixed and other assets (FA)	353,466
Total Assets	Total assets (TA)	$10,213,320
Deposits Funds borrowed Accrued taxes, interest and expenses Other liabilities Long-term debt Convertible subordinated notes	Liabilities (L)	Note (2)
Total Stockholders' Equity	Book value of equity (BVE)	1,005,165

Note (1) Computed as a residual using EA = TA – R – FA.

Note (2) Computed as a residual using L = TA – BVE.

TABLE 5.6 Financial Statements for Aetna Insurance

Panel A: Consolidated Statements of Income

FOR THE YEARS ENDED DECEMBER 31, (MILLIONS, EXCEPT SHARE DATA)	*1992*	*1991*	*1990*
Revenue:			
Premiums	**$10,793.9**	$11,444.6	$11,923.1
Net investment income	**5,069.0**	5,514.5	5,608.1
Fees and other income	**1,519.4**	1,365.5	1,290.5
Net realized capital gains (losses)	**114.9**	(282.1)	(122.5)
Total revenue	**17,497.2**	18,042.5	18,699.2
Benefits and Expenses:			
Current and future benefits	**12,931.1**	13,429.8	13,752.0
Operating expenses	**3,742.3**	3,341.1	3,307.9
Amortization of deferred policy acquisition costs	**800.2**	1,028.1	1,089.7
Reorganization charge	**145.0**	—	90.0
Total benefits and expenses	**17,618.6**	17,799.0	18,239.6
Income (Loss) from continuing operations before income taxes and cumulative effect adjustments	**(121.4)**	243.5	459.6
Federal and foreign income tax benefits	**(116.1)**	(122.9)	(21.0)
Income (Loss) from continuing operations before cumulative effect adjustments	**(5.3)**	366.4	480.6
Discontinued operations, net of tax:			
Income from operations	**86.8**	138.8	133.5
Gain on sale	**38.1**	—	—
Cumulative effect adjustments	**48.9**	—	—
Income before cumulative effect adjustments for continuing operations	**168.5**	505.2	614.1
Cumulative effect adjustments for continuing operations:			
Change in accounting for income taxes	**272.5**	—	—
Change in accounting for postretirement benefits other than pensions	**(385.0)**	—	—
Net income	**$56.0**	$505.2	$614.1
Results Per Common Share:			
Income (Loss) from continuing operations before cumulative effect adjustments	**$(.05)**	$3.33	$4.32
Discontinued operations, net of tax:			
Income from operations	**.79**	1.26	1.20
Gain on sale	**.35**	—	—
Cumulative effect adjustments	**.44**	—	—
Income before cumulative effect adjustments for continuing operations	**1.53**	4.59	5.52
Cumulative effect adjustments for continuing operations:			
Change in accounting for income taxes	**2.48**	—	—
Change in accounting for postretirement benefits other than pensions	**(3.50)**	—	—
Net income	**$.51**	$4.59	$5.52
Weighted average common shares outstanding	**110,101,861**	110,056,005	111,277,408

TABLE 5.6 (*continued*)

Panel A: Consolidated Balance Sheets

AS OF DECEMBER 31, (MILLIONS, EXCEPT SHARE DATA)	*1992*	*1991*
Assets:		
Investments:		
Fixed maturities, principally at amortized cost (market $36,510.6 and 35,670.0)	**$34,836.0**	$33,276.1
Equity securities, at market (cost $1,168.9 and $920.5)	**1,495.5**	1,119.6
Short-term investments	**1,510.8**	620.0
Mortgage loans	**18,051.9**	20,703.0
Real estate	**1,596.3**	1,449.2
Policy loans	**463.5**	434.4
Other	**842.5**	854.6
Total investments	**58,796.5**	58,456.9
Cash and cash equivalents	**2,415.0**	2,919.5
Accrued investment income	**767.4**	820.6
Premiums due and other receivables	**2,070.5**	2,452.9
Federal and foreign income taxes:		
Current	**68.7**	89.7
Deferred	**973.1**	326.0
Deferred policy acquisition costs	**1,706.0**	1,523.1
Other assets	**1,409.3**	1,283.7
Discontinued operations assets	—	3,926.6
Separate Accounts assets	**21,721.7**	20,188.6
Total assets	**$89,928.2**	$91,987.6
Liabilities:		
Future policy benefits	**$15,893.8**	$15,350.6
Unpaid claims and claim expenses	**12,925.2**	12,650.1
Unearned premiums	**1,190.4**	1,194.6
Policyholders' funds left with the company	**27,270.2**	29,574.4
Total insurance reserve liabilities	**57,279.6**	58,769.7
Dividends payable to shareholders	**76.1**	76.0
Short-term debt	**24.6**	6.1
Long-term debt	**955.6**	1,019.6
Other liabilities	**2,580.7**	1,676.9
Minority and participating policyholders' interests	**176.1**	175.3
Discontinued operations liabilities	—	2,816.5
Separate Accounts liabilities	**21,597.2**	20,063.0
Total liabilities	**82,689.9**	84,603.
Commitments and Contingent Liabilities		
Shareholders' Equity: Common stock (No par value; 250,000,000 shares authorized; 114,939,275 issued, and 110,270,482 and 110,064,634 outstanding)	**1,417.7**	1,420.1
Net unrealized capital gains	**259.6**	165.9
Retained earnings	**5,777.9**	6,026.0
Treasury stock, at cost (4,668,793 and 4,874,641 shares)	**(216.9)**	(227.5)
Total shareholders' equity	**7,238.3**	7,384.5
Total liabilities and shareholders' equity	**$89,928.2**	$91,987.6
Shareholders' equity per common share	**$65.64**	$67.09

Panel A: Consolidated Statements of Cash Flows

FOR THE YEARS ENDED DECEMBER 31, (MILLIONS)	*1992*	*1991*	*1990*
Cash Flows from Operating Activities:			
Net income	$56.0	$505.2	$614.1
Cumulative effect adjustments	112.5	—	—
Discontinued operations	(86.8)	(72.7)	(71.6)
Cumulative effect of discontinued operations	(48.9)	—	—
Decrease in accrued investment income	51.4	60.7	15.1
Decrease (increase) in premiums due and other receivables	439.7	(158.5)	(101.0)
Increase in deferred policy acquisition costs	(71.4)	(40.5)	(65.8)
Depreciation and amortization	205.6	150.5	138.6
Decrease in federal and foreign income taxes	(128.0)	(310.4)	(234.1)
Net increase (decrease) in other assets and other liabilities	41.1	(63.1)	59.4
Increase in insurance reserve liabilities	280.1	121.2	920.4
Net purchases of fixed maturity trading securities	(1,222.6)	(681.0)	(161.7)
Decrease (increase) in minority interest	6.0	12.7	(4.2)
Gain on sales of subsidiaries	(38.1)	(54.1)	—
Net realized capital (gains) losses	(114.9)	282.1	122.5
Amortization of net investment discounts	(150.1)	(136.1)	(177.8)
Other, net	90.3	(20.3)	(18.6)
Net cash (used for) provided by operating activities	(578.1)	(404.3)	1,035.3
Cash Flows from Investing Activities:			
Proceeds from sales of:			
Fixed maturities	3,862.1	4,751.9	4,824.2
Equity securities	836.7	688.2	925.8
Mortgage loans	82.6	419.7	115.9
Real estate	244.5	298.6	206.2
Investment repayments of:			
Fixed maturities	6,089.9	4,219.9	3,339.5
Mortgage loans	1,893.6	1,345.8	1,318.0
Cost of investments in:			
Fixed maturities	(9,637.3)	(8,872.4)	(8,891.9)
Equity securities	(879.8)	(751.9)	(545.1)
Mortgage loans	(417.3)	(323.5)	(1,918.4)
Real estate	(103.5)	(145.6)	(46.1)
Proceeds from disposal of subsidiaries	1,325.5	100.0	—
(Increase) decrease in short-term investments	(693.0)	1,141.7	(1,438.1)
Increase in property and equipment	(198.9)	(231.0)	(219.2)
Decrease (increase) in Separate Accounts	1.2	(125.7)	1
Other, net	(203.3)	124.0	46.8
Net cash provided by (used for) investing activities	2,203.0	2,639.7	(2,282.3)
Cash Flows from Financing Activities:			
Deposits and interest credited for investment contracts	4,134.6	5,953.6	7,276.3
Withdrawals of investment contracts	(5,903.9)	(6,765.2)	(6,289.6)
Issuance of long-term debt	8.2	13.7	47.4
Repayment of long-term debt	(73.2)	(5.2)	(93.4)
Stock issued under benefit plans	8.2	.7	2.2
Net increase in short-term debt	19.7	4.0	—
Dividends paid to shareholders	(304.1)	(303.7)	(308.0)
Treasury stock acquired	—	(6.3)	(81.1)
Net cash (used for) provided by financing activities	(2,110.5)	(1,108.4)	553.8
Effect of exchange rate changes on cash and cash equivalents	(18.9)	1.7	21.3
Net (decrease) increase in cash and cash equivalents	(504.5)	1,128.7	(671.9)
Cash and cash equivalents, beginning of year	2,919.5	1,790.8	2,462.7
Cash and cash equivalents, end of year	$2,415.0	$2,919.5	$1,790.8

TABLE 5.6 (*continued*)

Panel B: Simplified Financial Statements

AS REPORTED	*SIMPLIFIED STATEMENT*	*1992 AMOUNT*
Income Statement		
Premiums	Premium revenue (PR)	$10,794
Net investment income Net realized gains (Losses)	Investment revenue (IR)	5,184
Current and future benefits Amortization of deferred policy acquisition costs	Losses and reserves (L&R)	13,731
Fees and other income	Noninterest revenue (NIR)	1,519
Operating expenses Reorganization charge	Noninterest expense (NIE)	3,887
Income (Loss) from continuing operations before income taxes and cumulative effect adjustments	Earnings before tax (EBT)	(121)
Federal and foreign income tax benefits Discontinued operations (net of tax) Income from operations Gain on sale Cumulative Effect Adjustments	Taxes and Non operating charges (Credits) (T)	Note (1)
Net income	Earnings available for common (EAC)	56
Balance Sheet Items		
Cash and cash equivalents	Cash and reserves (R)	2,415
Total investments	Earning assets (EA)	58,797
Accrued investment income Premiums due and other receivables Federal and foreign income taxes Deferred policy acquisition costs Other assets Discontinued operations assets Separate account assets	Fixed and other assets (FA)	Note 2
Total assets	Total assets (TA)	89,928
Total insurance reserve liabilities	Insurance liabilities and reserves (RES)	57,280
Total shareholders' equity	Book value of equity (BVE)	7,238

Note (1) Calculated as EAC = EBT – T
Note (2) Calculated as FA = TA – R – EA

TABLE 5.7 Financial Statements for A.G. Edwards

Panel A: Statements of Income

(IN THOUSANDS, EXCEPT PER SHARE AMOUNTS)	*FEBRUARY 28, 1993*	*YEAR ENDED FEBRUARY 29, 1992*	*FEBRUARY 28, 1991*
Revenues:			
Commissions	**$601,484**	$522,736	$344,690
Principal transactions	**215,306**	188,441	156,654
Investment banking	**108,312**	90,853	55,328
Interest	**64,729**	63,941	66,234
Other	**84,557**	72,688	52,001
	1,074,388	938,659	674,907
Expenses:			
Compensation and benefits	**692,127**	594,404	422,524
Communications	**66,899**	62,468	58,323
Occupancy and equipment	**61,701**	56,035	49,783
Floor brokerage and clearance	**15,016**	13,741	11,461
Interest	**1,886**	1,186	4,229
Other operating expenses	**46,774**	42,793	36,925
	884,403	770,627	583,245
Earnings Before Income Taxes	**189,985**	168,032	91,662
Income Taxes	**70,560**	62,500	32,500
Net Earnings	**$119,425**	$105,532	$59,162
Earnings Per Share	**$2.58**	$2.35	$1.37

TABLE 5.7 (*continued*)

Panel A: Balance Sheet

(IN THOUSANDS, EXCEPT SHARE AMOUNTS)	***FEBRUARY 28, 1993***	*FEBRUARY 29, 1992*
Assets		
Cash and cash equivalents	**$27,963**	$41,534
Cash and government securities, at market, segregated under federal and other regulations	**286,239**	213,001
Receivable from brokers and dealers	**475,468**	209,640
Receivable from customers, less allowance for doubtful accounts of $3,250 and $3,100	**950,937**	755,872
Securities inventory, at market:		
State and municipal	**87,418**	92,480
Government and agencies	**34,827**	35,704
Corporate	**27,503**	32,481
Property and equipment, at cost, net of accumulated depreciation and amortization of $106,760 and $92,846	**140,790**	130,876
Other assets	**80,047**	65,555
	$2,111,192	$1,577,143
Liabilities and Stockholders' Equity		
Checks payable	**$113,665**	$102,383
Payable to brokers and dealers	**503,379**	244,223
Payable to customers	**575,283**	484,264
Securities sold but not yet purchased, at market	**10,576**	25,161
Employee compensation and related taxes	**244,226**	192,106
Income taxes	**18,242**	13,354
Other liabilities	**30,581**	23,642
Total Liabilities	**1,495,952**	1,085,133
Stockholders' Equity:		
Preferred stock, $25 par value:		
Authorized, 4,000,000 shares, none issued		
Common stock, $1 par value:		
Authorized, 250,000,000 and 60,000,000 shares; Issued, 46,158,664 and 44,466,285 shares	**46,159**	44,466
Additional paid-in capital	**125,328**	95,033
Retained earnings	**452,045**	357,244
	623,532	496,743
Less—Unamortized expense of restricted stock awards	**8,292**	4,733
Total Stockholders' Equity	**615,240**	492,010
	$2,111,192	$1,577,143

See Notes to Consolidated Financial Statements.

Panel A: Cash Flows

(IN THOUSANDS)	***FEBRUARY 28, 1993***	*FEBRUARY 29, 1992*	*FEBRUARY 28, 1991*
Cash Flows From Operating Activities:			
Net earnings	**$119,425**	$105,532	$59,162
Noncash items included in earnings:			
Depreciation and amortization	**22,056**	18,884	16,811
Amortization of restricted stock awards	**6,477**	3,683	2,490
Deferred items	**(5,896)**	(2,939)	(4,820)
(Increase) decrease in operating assets:			
Segregated cash and government securities	**(73,238)**	(59,422)	(122,028)
Receivable from brokers and dealers	**(265,828)**	160,913	(135,834)
Receivable from customers	**(195,065)**	(218,973)	(20)
Securities inventory	**10,917**	(21,976)	4,957
Other assets	**(10,098)**	(6,489)	(2,159)
Increase (decrease) in operating liabilities:			
Checks payable	**11,282**	24,673	9,890
Payable to brokers and dealers	**259,156**	(105,498)	67,484
Payable to customers	**91,019**	55,923	169,935
Securities sold but not yet purchased	**(14,585)**	11,028	(18)
Employee compensation and related taxes	**52,120**	73,716	15,592
Income taxes	**4,888**	7,047	2,669
Other liabilities	**6,939**	1,486	2,583
Net cash provided by operating activities	**19,569**	47,588	86,694
Cash Flows From Investing Activities:			
Purchase of property and equipment	**(31,970)**	(24,977)	(33,277)
Long-term investments included in other assets	**1,547**	67	(382)
Net cash used in investing activities	**(30,423)**	(24,910)	(33,659)
Cash Flows From Financing Activities:			
Net payments on bank loans			(32,025)
Employee stock transactions	**21,928**	17,521	10,525
Purchase of treasury stock	**(21)**	(7)	(14,387)
Cash dividends paid	**(24,624)**	(20,622)	(15,480)
Net cash used in financing activities	**(2,717)**	(3,108)	(51,367)
Net (Decrease) Increase in Cash and Cash Equivalents	(13,571)	19,570	1,668
Cash and Cash Equivalents, at Beginning of Year	41,534	21,964	20,296
Cash and Cash Equivalents, at End of Year	$27,963	$41,534	$21,964

See Notes to Consolidated Financial Statements.
Income tax payments totaled $68,638 in 1993, $56,695 in 1992 and $34,256 in 1991.
Interest payments totaled $1,862 in 1993, $1,192 in 1992 and $4,302 in 1991.
Supplemental disclosures of noncash financing activities: Restricted stock awards, net of forfeitures, totaled $10,036 in 1993, $5,008 in 1992 and $4,313 in 1991.

TABLE 5.7 (*continued*)

Panel B: Simplified Financial Statements

AS REPORTED	*SIMPLIFIED STATEMENT*	*1993 AMOUNT*
Income Statement		
Commissions Investment banking Other revenue	Noninterest revenue (NIR)	$794,353
Principal transactions	Trading profits (P)	215,306
Interest revenue Interest expense	Net interest (I)	62,843
Compensation and benefits Communications Occupancy and equipment Floor brokerage and clearance Other operating expense	Noninterest expense (NIE)	882,517
Earnings before tax	Earnings before tax (EBT)	189,985
Net earnings	Earnings available for common (EAC)	119,425
Balance Sheet		
Cash and equivalents	Cash (R)	27,963
Securities inventory —Securities sold but not yet purchased	Net trading account securities (S)	139,172
Receivable from customers —Payable to customers	Net earning assets (NEA)	375,654
Cash and government securities, segregated under regulation —Checks payable —Employee compensation Receivable from brokers —Payable to brokers Property and equipment Other assets	Net fixed and other assets (FA)	Note (1)
Total assets	Total assets (TA)	2,111,192
Stockholders' equity	Book value of equity	615,240

Note (1) Computed as a residual.

Complexities associated with Aetna's full line of insurance are found in the classification of insurance-related expenses. We include amortization of policy acquisition costs and several other items in the income statement into insurance expenses, losses and reserves (L&R). The related balance sheet item, policy reserves (RES), is identified on the liability side of Aetna's balance sheet (second page of Panel A) as "Total insurance reserve liabilities." Because insurance policy funds are about two-thirds of Aetna's total assets, the net cost of these funds is an important determinant of the company's performance.

Other income statement and balance sheet items for Aetna are treated as residuals. As an asset manager, Aetna carries nearly offsetting "Separate Account" asset and liability items. We classify these assets as nonearning assets because income from these investments belongs to beneficiaries, although they may generate fee income. The most difficult problems in Aetna's financial reporting are the many income statement items associated with discontinued operations and tax treatment. We treat all these items as nonoperating credits, which reconciles operating income (EBT) with earnings available for common shareholders (EAC). As we discuss below, these simplifications focus on shareholders' prospects for future returns from ongoing insurance operations.

Basic Ratio Analysis: Step 3

All stockholder-owned financial institutions' BROR can be analyzed in terms of a few basic but useful ratios. This step of financial analysis is based on the venerable *Dupont analysis*. Dupont analysis was developed by analysts in that chemical company to assess manufacturing firms' customers. The analysis can be adapted for analyzing financial service firms and is the "first stage" of analysis.

Basic ratio analysis applied to stock-owned financial institutions breaks BROR into three basic ratios, each easily calculated from the simplified financial statements discussed at above. The three ratios are: *pullthrough* (U), the *leverage ratio* (LEV), and the *return on total asset ratio* (ROTA). We define and discuss the calculation of each of these ratios. The resulting ratios for Fifth Third Bancorp and Aetna for 1991 and 1992 are contained in Tables 5.8 and 5.9. These tables also present the percent change in each ratio between the two years. Percent changes standardize changes in ratios from year to year and allow analysts to focus on relatively big changes.

Pullthrough (U) calculates the percent of income shareholders have after taxes and nonoperating expense deductions from operating income. It is defined and illustrated with Fifth Third Bancorp's 1992 results:

$$U = \frac{\text{Earnings Available to Common Shareholders}}{\text{Earnings Before Tax}} = \frac{\text{EAC}}{\text{BVE}} = \frac{\$164{,}092}{\$239{,}656} = 68.47\%.$$

As can be seen in Table 5.8, U for Fifth Third is completely determined by income taxes and is close to 68 percent both years. Most of the time, U can be interpreted as one minus the average corporate income tax rate. This interpretation implies a reasonable average income tax rate close to 32 percent in 1991 and 1992 for Fifth Third.

TABLE 5.8 Analysis of Fifth Third Bancorporation

	Basic Financial Data		
Income Statement	*1991*	*1992*	*% CHANGE*
Interest revenue (IR)	713,501	694,460	–2.67%
Interest expense (IE)	381,280	300,266	–21.25%
Provision for loan losses (PLL)	55,744	65,315	17.17%
Noninterest revenue (NIR)	171,911	200,053	16.37%
Noninterest expense (NIE)	249,792	289,276	15.81%
Earnings before tax	198,596	239,656	20.68%
Earnings available for common (EAC)	138,150	164,092	18.78%
Number of common shares outstanding	59,200	59,632	
Earnings per share	$2.33	$2.75	
Balance Sheet (Partial)			
Cash and reserves (R)	501,188	565,948	12.92%
Fixed and other assets (FA)	352,677	353,466	0.22%
Total assets (TA)	8,826,130	10,213,320	15.72%
Book value of equity (BVE)	879,450	1,005,165	14.29%
Ratio Analysis			
Book rate of return (BROR)	15.71%	16.32%	3.92%
Pullthrough (U) ×	69.56%	68.47%	–1.57%
Leverage (LEV) ×	10.04	10.16	1.24%
Return on total assets (ROTA)	2.25%	2.35%	4.28%
EBT/TA			
Net interest margin ((IR-IE)/E	4.17%	4.24%	1.78%
– Loan Losses – (PLL/EA)) ×	0.70%	0.70%	0.51%
Earning asset ratio (EA/TA)	90.33%	91.00%	0.74%
+ Burden + ((NIR-NIE)/TA	–0.88%	–0.87%	–1.00%
(IR-IE)/EA:			
Return on earning assets IR/EA –	8.95%	7.47%	–16.51%
Cost of liabilities (IE/L) ×	4.80%	3.26%	–32.04%
Liabilities to earning Assets (L/EA)	0.9968	0.9908	–0.60%

Extreme caution must be used in interpreting pullthrough in unusual cases like Aetna in 1991 and 1992. Pullthrough for Aetna as shown on Table 5.9 reflects the company's recent losses and restructuring. Aetna's simplified financial statements include adjustments to EBT from tax credits and discontinued operations, which results in EAC being *larger* than EBT both years. For Aetna, U measures the effects of nonoperating adjustments and tax credits on shareholders' returns, doubling its operating income in 1991 and reversing the loss on operations in 1992. Analysts will note that tax credits and extraordinary income are not dependable sources of cash flows for investors in Aetna in the future.

TABLE 5.9 Analysis of Aetna Insurance Corporation

	Basic Financial Data		
Income Statement	*1991*	*1992*	*% CHANGE*
Premium revenue (PR)	11,445	10,794	–5.69%
Investment revenue (IR)	5,232	5,184	–0.93%
Losses and reserves (L&R)	13,430	13,731	2.25%
Noninterest revenue (NIR)	1,366	1,519	11.27%
Noninterest expense (NIE)	4,369	3,887	–11.03%
Earnings before tax (EBT)	244	(121)	–149.86%
Taxes & non-op'g charges (Credits)	(262)	(177)	–32.21%
Earnings available for common (EAC)	505	56	–88.92%
Number of common shares outstanding	110.1	110.3	
Earnings per share	$4.59	$0.51	
Balance Sheet (Partial)			
Cash and reserves (R)	2,920	2,415	–17.28%
Fixed and other assets (FA)	30,611	28,717	–6.19%
Total assets (TA)	91,988	89,928	–2.24%
Ins. liabilities & reserves (RES)	58,770	57,280	–2.54%
Book value of equity (BVE)	7,385	7,238	–1.98%
Ratio Analysis			
Book rate of return (BROR)	6.84%	0.77%	–88.69%
Composed of:			
Pullthrough (U) ×	207.47%	–46.13%	–122.23%
Leverage (LEV) ×	12.46	12.42	–0.26%
Return on total assets (ROTA)	0.26%	–0.13%	–151.00%
EBT/TA composed of:			
Net return on investment (IR/EA) ×	8.95%	8.82%	–1.50%
Earning asset ratio (EA/TA)	63.55%	65.38%	2.88%
– Cost of ins. funds (PR-L&R)/RES) ×	–3.38%	–5.13%	51.81%
Insurance liability ratio (RES/TA)	63.89%	63.69%	–0.30%
+ Burden + ((NIR-NIE)/TA	–3.27%	–2.63%	–19.36%

The leverage ratio measures how many dollars of assets the firm has per dollar of equity. This ratio is often described as a firm's *gearing*. The ratio is defined and calculated for Fifth Third Bancorp in 1992 in the following equation:

$$LEV = \frac{\text{Total Assets}}{\text{Book Value of Equity}} = \frac{TA}{BVE} = \frac{\$10,213,320}{\$1,005,165} = 10.16.$$

These results are also shown in Table 5.8 for Fifth Third and Table 5.9 for Aetna for two years, 1991 and 1992. For both years, Fifth Third had a little more than ten dollars of assets for each dollar of equity. In other words, total assets were "geared up" from Fifth Third's capital base in a ten-to-one ratio. Aetna was more highly leveraged both years.

The return on total asset (ROTA) is calculated using income before taxes and it captures management's ability to generate operating income from the firm's assets. The ratio is defined and calculated for Fifth Third in 1992 as follows:

$$\text{ROTA} = \frac{\text{Earnings Before Tax}}{\text{Total Assets}} = \frac{\text{EBT}}{\text{TA}} = \frac{\$239{,}656}{\$10{,}213{,}320} = 2.35\%.$$

ROTA is one of the most discussed ratios among analysts. It captures the ability of management to generate income after all financial and nonfinancial costs and expenses. This ratio is usually small, in the case Fifth Third a little more than two percent. Typically this ratio is low for financial service firms.

We measure ROTA before tax. Many analysts use net income instead of EBT, often calling the result return on assets or ROA. But ratio analysis is not standardized. Users of ratios must be certain that calculations are truly comparable when comparing two ratios. We prefer the operating income before tax in the calculation because EBT allows comparisons of ROTA with financial firms having different tax treatments. For example, credit unions are tax exempt and mutual life insurance companies are taxed differently than stock-owned companies.

ROTA is the critical variable for most financial institutions in most time periods. For example, ROTA for Aetna fell from .26 percent in 1991 to –.13 percent in 1992. These small numbers may appear to represent a small change, but in fact the change is a negative 151 percent. This change drove the decline in Aetna's BROR for these two years and illustrates the advantage of using percent changes to focus on large changes in variables of small magnitude. For Fifth Third also, the biggest change from 1991 to 1992 was an improvement in ROTA of 4.28 percent. Changes in ROTA are usually the cause of major changes in a financial institution's performance. The other basic ratios, U and LEV, usually change less from year to year since typically they reflect tax treatment and capitalization. In the "first stage," all financial service firms are analyzed the same way; we concentrate on detailed analysis of sources of changes in ROTA for different segments of the industry in the following section.

5.3 ANALYSIS OF ROTA: SEGMENT ANALYSIS

Return on assets (ROTA) is the key determinant of earnings and earnings variability for most financial service firms including mutuals, partnerships, and corporations. Identifying major sources of change in ROTA is the greatest challenge facing financial analysts—a challenge because there is no *one* way to approach the problem. In contrast to steps 1 to 3 discussed in the previous section, to complete steps 3 to 6 on Table 5.2, we must use different analytical methods depending on which segment of the financial services industry we all concerned with. Good analysts are alert, creative, and persistent.

The analytical approach chosen generally depends on the line of business analyzed. Deposit-taking, insurance, securities, and other financial firms produce earnings differently. Accounting conventions, regulatory review, and management focus each emphasize differences in reporting activity for different types of financial institutions. Experienced analysts are alert to *differences* and *similarities* in financial firms' operations. Analysts must be creative in applying analytical techniques in different contexts. This section illustrates how an analysis of return on assets can be conducted using the firms presented in the previous section as examples, but it cannot provide a universal program to follow. It will accomplish its purpose if readers are ready to practice financial analysis of financial firms. Creative ways of analyzing will be necessary with the many innovations in the future of financial services.

Virtually all financial service firms invest in interest- or dividend-earning assets and nearly all earn fees and other compensation for performing their services, reported as noninterest revenues. All financial service firms incur major expenses from employee compensation—a theme of this book is that financial services are a labor-intensive business. Other expenses are also incurred by most financial firms: costs for computers, telephones, electricity, occupancy, etc. Together these expenses make up noninterest expense. Analysis of return on earning assets and noninterest revenue and expense is similar for all financial institutions.

The "second stage" of financial analysis identifies major changes in ROTA and the causes of consistently low or high returns in business segments. For example, from 1991 to 1992, Fifth Third Bancorp's BROR increased 4 percent caused by a 4 percent increase in ROTA, while Aetna's BROR fell close to zero as its ROTA became negative. What caused these changes in the bank and insurance company ROTAs? To answer these questions we must look at the similar and different determinants of ROTA in these two financial services businesses.

Segment Analysis of a Bank (Step 4): Fifth Third Bancorp

The increase in Fifth Third Bancorp's ROTA from 2.25 to 2.35 was the major source of the improvement in Fifth Third's BROR from 1991 to 1992, as reflected in the percent changes shown in Table 5.8. To investigate changes in deposit-taking institution performance, decomposition of ROTA using simplified financial statements can be useful to pinpoint important factors. ROTA can be written as follows:

$$\text{ROTA} = \frac{(\text{IR} - \text{IE} - \text{PLL} + \text{NIR} - \text{NIE})}{\text{TA}}$$

which can be decomposed as follows:

$$\text{ROTA} = \left(\frac{(\text{IR} - \text{IE})}{\text{EA}} - \frac{\text{PLL}}{\text{EA}} \right) \frac{\text{EA}}{\text{TA}} + \frac{\text{NIR} - \text{NIE}}{\text{TA}}.$$

where IR and IE are interest revenue and expense, PLL is provision for loan loss, and NIR and NIE are noninterest revenue and expense, and EA and TA are earning assets and total assets. This formulation considers changes in ROTA from four basic elements, *net interest margin,* the *loan loss ratio,* the *earning asset ratio,* and *burden,* each discussed in detail in the following. These terms are often used by bank and thrift analysts in discussing performance of deposit-taking financial institutions.

Net interest margin (NIM) focuses on the net earnings from investing with borrowed funds. This factor reflects the *interest rate spread* between assets and liabilities for deposit-taking institutions, traditionally a major source of profitability for banks and thrifts in regulated markets. For Fifth Third, NIM in 1992 is calculated:

$$\text{NIM} = \frac{\text{IR} - \text{IE}}{\text{EA}} = \frac{\$694{,}460 - \$300{,}266}{\$9{,}293{,}906} = 4.24\%.$$

Using results in Table 5.8 to compare 1991, we can see that Fifth Third's NIM improved by seven basis points (.07 percent) by 1992, an improvement of 1.78 percent over the 1991 level. As we discuss below, this small change was a major source of Fifth Third's improved performance in 1992.

Loan losses have recently reached historic highs in the United States, Europe, and Japan. To assess effects on profitability from credit losses, the loss ratio adjusts NIM to account for loan losses. Using Fifth Third's experience in 1992 as an example, the loss ratio is computed:

$$\text{Loss Ratio} = \frac{\text{PLL}}{\text{EA}} = \frac{\$65{,}315}{\$9{,}293{,}906} = .70\%.$$

Comparison with Fifth Third's loss ratio in 1991 indicates only a tiny deterioration (.51 percent increase). This experience contrasts to recent experience of many deposit-taking institutions around the world, where variations in loss ratios have been a major determinant of variation in ROTA.

Net interest margin and the loss ratio are both related to earning assets. The earning asset ratio accounts for balance sheet differences among deposit-taking institutions. It is calculated as follows for Fifth Third in 1992:

$$\text{Earning Asset Ratio} = \frac{\text{EA}}{\text{TA}} = \frac{\$9{,}293{,}906}{\$10{,}213{,}320} = 91.0\%.$$

Although earning asset ratios differ for deposit-taking institutions, is it usually not an important source of year-to-year variability in ROTA. This is the case for Fifth Third from 1991 to 1992, when the earning asset ratio increased from 90.33 to 91 percent, a small .74 percent increase in this ratio.

The final factor determining ROTA for deposit-taking institutions is called *burden* by analysts and compares NIR and NIE to total assets of the institution. Burden for nearly all deposit-taking institutions is negative, meaning that fees and other revenue do not cover labor and other costs. For Fifth Third, burden in 1992 is calculated as:

$$\text{Burden} = \frac{\text{NIR} - \text{NIE}}{\text{TA}} = \frac{\$200{,}053 - \$289{,}276}{\$10{,}213{,}320} = -.87\%.$$

As seen in Table 5.8, burden is negative in both 1991 and 1992 for Fifth Third, but it is less negative in 1992, a 1 percent improvement. Fifth Third Bancorporation has been aggressively increasing fee income and holding down costs. Comparison with other firms would show that Fifth Third's burden is small and our results demonstrate that between 1991 and 1992, it is improving.

Using Benchmarks and Identifying Input Factors (Steps 5 and 6): Fifth Third

The last steps of analysis given on Table 5.2 are the most important for understanding performance. Here we provide simple examples of the use of recent historical benchmarks and identification of key factors from the above discussion. In our analysis of the four factors affecting ROTA for deposit-taking institutions, and Fifth Third, we find that NIM and burden are typically the most important factors periodic variations. Recent experience around the world has focused attention on a cyclical increase in loss ratios. Changes in any of these four factors can affect ROTA. Between 1991 and 1992 for Fifth Third, the most important factors were improvements in both margin and burden.

Given the importance of NIM to most deposit-taking institutions' performances, many analysts explore sources of change in that variable. One way to explore NIM is to look at the return on earning assets and the cost of liabilities, calculated as follows for Fifth Third in 1992:

$$\text{Yield on Earning Assets} = \frac{\text{IR}}{\text{EA}} = \frac{\$694{,}460}{\$9{,}293{,}906} = 7.47\%.$$

Interest costs must be related to the liabilities used to fund earning assets. The liability ratio compares liabilities to earning assets and is calculated for Fifth Third in 1992 as follows:

$$\text{Cost of Liabilities} = \frac{\text{IE}}{\text{L}} = \frac{\$300{,}266}{\$9{,}208{,}155} = 3.26\%.$$

These results can be compared to the 1991 results for Fifth Third in Table 5.8.

Two observations on Fifth Third Bancorporation's experience in 1991 and 1992 illustrate important aspects of NIM. First, both return on assets and cost of liabilities fell from 1991 to 1992, illustrating the important point that the level of yields is not as important as the spread. Competition will pressure spreads with deregulation of deposit interest rates around the world. This had led some to say that the spread is dead, as we noted in an earlier chapter. Second, the improvement in NIM for Fifth Third came from a bigger drop in the cost of funds than in the return on assets. Deposit-taking institution performance can be affected by changes in the spread. This is the source of *interest rate risk* to earnings. The macroeconomic sources of interest rate risk are discussed in Part III and management of interest risk is discussed in Part IV of this book.

Segment Analysis of an Insurance Company (Step 4): Aetna

Aetna's ROTA went from a small positive number, .26, in 1991 to a negative .13 in 1992. In order to investigate factors producing changes in insurance companies, different ratios focusing on the insurance segment of financial services can be used. We can decompose an insurance company's ROTA using the following:

$$\text{ROTA} = \frac{\left(\text{IR} + \text{PR} - (\text{L \& R}) + \text{NIR} - \text{NIE}\right)}{\text{TA}}.$$

This expression can be decomposed into five factors as follows:

$$\text{ROTA} = \frac{\text{IR}}{\text{EA}} \times \frac{\text{EA}}{\text{TA}} + \frac{\text{PR} - \text{L \& R}}{\text{RES}} \times \frac{\text{RES}}{\text{TA}} + \frac{\text{NIR} - \text{NIE}}{\text{TA}}.$$

This formulation analyzes an insurance firm's ROTA in terms of five ratios, three of which are similar to ratios used for deposit-taking institutions. Those are *net return on earning assets,* the *earning asset ratio,* the first two terms, and *burden,* the last term. The two intermediate ratios measure insurance business performance and insurance liabilities as a source of funds. These two ratios are specific to the insurance business segment and are discussed below.

The first pair of ratios in the decomposition above focuses on management's investment performance. They are the net return on earning assets and the earning asset ratio, calculated for Aetna in 1992 as follows:

$$\text{Net Return on Earning Assets} = \frac{\text{IR}}{\text{EA}} = \frac{\$5{,}184}{\$58{,}797} = 8.82\%.$$

$$\text{Earning Asset Ratio} = \frac{\text{EA}}{\text{TA}} = \frac{\$58{,}797}{\$89{,}928} = 65.38\%.$$

The first measure is a *net* return because interest expense is not provided by Aetna in its financial statements. (Aetna's 1992 balance sheet shows total debt under $1 billion, less than 2 percent of earning assets.) Analysts with more data or concern might focus on investment revenue and expense separately instead of net investment revenue. Comparing the results from 1991 and 1992, shown in Table 5.9 for Aetna, net investment return fell slightly and the earning asset ratio increased in 1992, nearly offsetting the effect of lower returns. Investment revenue was little changed for Aetna over the two years.

Burden measures management's control of operating expenses not directly associated with its insurance business. Burden is calculated the same as for deposit-taking institutions. For Aetna, burden improved in 1992, falling by 19.36 percent. The importance of a reduction in burden can be seen by comparing this reduction of close to $500 million (.64 percent reduction in burden times total assets of over $57 billion) to EBT. Expense control for financial service firms is critical as spreads on traditional businesses are squeezed by competition. The improvement in burden for Aetna was not enough, however, to offset the deterioration in its insurance performance.

Insurance performance ratios measure the net cost of funds derived from the insurance business that are used to fund investments. Aetna is a diversified life and casualty company so we use a hybrid ratio, cost of insurance funds, calculated as follows:

$$\text{Cost of Insurance Funds} = \frac{(\text{PR} - \text{L \& R})}{\text{TA}} = \frac{\$10{,}794 - 13{,}731}{\$57{,}280} = -5.13\%.$$

This insurance performance measure is adjusted using an insurance liability ratio to measure the scale of insurance in total assets:

$$\text{Insurance Liability Ratio} = \frac{\text{RES}}{\text{TA}} = \frac{\$57{,}280}{\$89{,}928} = 63.70\%.$$

Table 5.9 demonstrates that the cost of insurance funds increased by 51.81 percent between 1991 and 1992, although insurance funds stayed relatively constant. The performance of Aetna's insurance business was the major source of the deterioration in Aetna's ROTA in 1992. The analysis focuses the analyst's attention on the question of what caused this change. These changes are due to changes in premium revenue, down 5.69 percent, and insurance expenses, up 2.25 percent.

Using Benchmarks and Important Factors (Steps 5 and 6): Aetna

The major changes in recent historical performance for Aetna are identified above as coming from increase in cost of insurance funds and a reduction in burden. The historical benchmarks could be augmented with industry experience to address reasons for changes in performance.

Insurance performance can be investigated by examining in more detail performance in specific lines of the insurance business, which we discuss in Chapter 11. As a full-line company, Aetna offers life and property and casualty insurance. Life insurance companies earn premium revenues and deduct allowances for reserves and benefits. To assess the profitability of the business, life insurance premium revenues and insurance expenses can be expressed as a ratio to funds raised in the form of life insurance reserves. This ratio will differ depending on the growth rate of the company and the demographics of its customer population. Depending on premiums exceeding or falling short of benefits paid over time, an insurance company has *underwriting profits or losses*. Life insurance performance tends to change slowly over time. The net cost of offering life insurance must be exceeded by investment income with enough left over to cover overhead expenses and provide a return to investors.

Property and casualty insurance company performance is determined by revenues provided by premiums minus total costs of claims including claims payments and adjustment expenses. Total claims and expenses as a percent of earned premiums is called the *combined ratio* by industry analysts. The cost of insurance funds will be higher whenever the combined ratio increases. Property and casualty companies experience substantial year-to-year variability in their performance measures. Aetna's management blames asbestiosis settlements ($308 million) and two major storms (Andrew and Beth for $118 million) for a deterioration of its insurance performance in 1992. Most casualty companies lose money on their insurance business but cover these underwriting losses and provide a return to investors with investment income derived by investing premiums.

Summary of Financial Analysis

Our two examples, Fifth Third Bancorp and Aetna Insurance, make clear that anyone can perform financial analysis and identify the critical variables. For both examples, we found that burden was important. We identified other variables that are important over the time period we examined. With Fifth Third, we saw the importance of NIM; with Aetna, we raised concerns about its insurance operations. In later chapters, we will go behind these critical numbers through further decomposition. We are always looking for the *relatively big, important* determinants of variations in performance.

Financial analysis is concerned with future performance prospects. We can project a BROR using recent values for ratios or averages based on historical or other firms' experience. We can make assumptions based on our assessments of future conditions. As an example, assume that in 1993 Fifth Third will have a burden of .87 percent, a NIM of 4.25 percent, an earning asset ratio of 91 percent, with loan losses of .7 percent. With these assumptions, we project a ROTA of 2.36 percent ((4.25–.70) × .91–.87)). Assuming leverage or gearing of 10 and pullthrough of 70 percent, we project that Fifth Third's BROR in 1993 will be 16.52 percent (2.36 × 10 × .70). This is a simple example of financial projections, discussed in detail in Chapter 22. This book is intended to make us more perceptive in our use of past financial data and more sophisticated in our projections of the future. Our simple example displays the essence of the analyst's task.

5.4 ANALYSIS OF FINANCIAL INSTITUTIONS: IMPORTANT ISSUES

In interpreting financial statements, the analyst must be aware of the particular implications of accounting practices applied to financial service firms, and of the significance of normal accounting practice on the interpretation of activity measures of these firms. This section outlines briefly some of the major factors affecting financial service firm accounting that the analyst should keep in mind when using financial statements.

GAAP Accounting

Accounting rules used to calculate the numbers reported in financial statements differ from country to country and at different times. Financial accounting standards for the accounting profession in the United States are set by the Financial Accounting Standards Board (FASB). The Securities and Exchange Commission in the United States has delegated to FASB establishment of standards applied to financial information. The annual reports and 10-Ks we discuss in this chapter reflect FASB accounting standards. Accounting principles determine "generally accepted accounting principles" or GAAP accounting.

FASB accounting standards can have a major impact on the reported profitability of all firms including financial institutions. As examples of the impact of changes in accounting standards, in 1988 the FASB considered changing accounting of deferred income taxes and future tax benefits from allowances for credit or insurance losses. John Reed, CEO of Citicorp, estimated the change would cause Citicorp a loss reducing its equity by $880 million or 10 percent (*Fortune*, 12/19/88, p. 106). The casualty insurance industry avoided a major hit to earnings only by Congressional action in a technical-corrections bill to the 1986 Tax Reform Act.

Another example of the impact of GAAP standards is in the treatment of foreign exchange rate variations. FASB has provided rules for valuing foreign assets and liabilities at current exchange rates, which of course vary substantially from period to period. This means that even without any realized gains or losses, income can be impacted by changes in exchange rates whenever there are differences in the amount of assets and liabilities denominated in different currencies. International banks' earnings have recently demonstrated substantial variation in reported income from this accounting treatment.

Accounting standards affect the income statement and balance sheet items shown for financial institutions. The analyst is concerned with future cash flows, not accounting income. Accounting standards allow the analyst to know how numbers in financial reports are calculated. The real economic impact of accounting numbers on cash flows is limited to two effects: (1) impact on the tax liability of the firm; and (2) impact on contracts (especially debt contracts) and regulatory review. If a financial firm is shown to be insolvent by accounting numbers, it may be sued by creditors or closed by regulators even if it has positive cash flows. Closure obviously affects future cash flows.

GAAP versus RAP Accounting

Deposit-taking and insurance firms file reports with regulators. These reports are prepared according to "regulatory accounting practice" or RAP accounting. An exhaustive treatment of these differences is not possible in this text but a few examples will demonstrate the significance of these differences in particular instances. The most egregious differences in RAP and GAAP accounting occurred in the 1980s with the savings and loan crisis. Because thrift regulators in the 1980s could not afford to close savings and loans that were insolvent by GAAP standards (negative or zero net worth), the regulator of the time, the Federal Home Loan Bank Board, authorized reporting practices inflating the net worth of savings institution. Savings and loans were allowed to write up the value of their offices and land, producing a nontaxable gain and increasing equity. To inflate income and add to equity, they were allowed to amortize the "goodwill" arising from purchases for more than book value of other troubled thrifts at a slower rate than the value of mortgages appreciated relative to their acquisition cost. They were allowed to count pieces of paper issued by regulators as assets. RAP accounting papered over serious operating difficulties and negative cash flows in thrifts.

Banks also benefit from RAP accounting. Banking regulators count loan loss reserves as "primary capital" in capital determining "capital adequacy." Nonredeemable preferred stock and subordinated debentures count as "total capital" for regulators. Insurance companies regulators also use unique accounting rules. Analysts using regulatory reports must be aware of the different RAP standards.

Regulators in the United States are committed to financial institution use of GAAP accounting standards. In other countries, like Japan, government regulation on accounting for financial institutions distorts their financial positions. Analysts must be aware of differences currently in force between RAP and GAAP in the reports being used.

Averages versus Year-End Figures

Management decision can impact balance sheets of financial institutions instantly. The balance sheet as of a given date may not be typical of the firm's operations over a longer time period. For example, we determined previously that Fifth Third Bancorp's yield on earning assets was 7.47 percent in 1992. A more representative number might be based on *average* assets in 1991 and 1992, producing a yield of 8.04 percent. The average earning asset number used previously is only one of many possible averages (quarterly, monthly, etc.). Financial institutions recognize the importance in variations in asset and liability accounts throughout the year. Additional tables in nearly all financial reports include averages of balance sheet items, often *daily* averages. We chose year-ending data in our examples because those data are always available and, in general, results derived from year-ending data are similar to averages. Analysts must be sure that the data used are representative of the firm's operations.

Off-Balance-Sheet Activities

Financial statements recently began to account for *potential* liabilities of firms that could affect cash flows in the future. For example, bank loan commitments that obligate the bank to lend money in the future do not show up on its balance sheet until the loan is made. These obligations are exercised by bank customers only under certain circumstances and are called "contingent liabilities." Contingent liabilities and similar "off-balance-sheet" items have grown in importance for all financial institutions in recent years. Regulators and FASB now require notes in the financial reports documenting the extent of these items.

The list of off-balance-sheet items changes as the financial services industry changes. Potential sources of cash inflows or outflows not reflected in the balance sheet fall into five categories:

1. Loan commitments
2. Credit guarantees
3. Swap contracts
4. Foreign exchange forward contracts
5. Options and futures contracts.

Each of these represents a commitment by a financial institution to pay cash under contracts in some circumstances. Analysts must be careful to look for contractual obligations affecting cash flows in the text or footnotes of financial statements.

Asset and Liabilities Exchanges

On occasion, some financial institutions simply exchange similar assets or liabilities to show a gain on their financial statements. For example, Bank of America sold its headquarters building to show a gain but promptly leased the building back. In economic terms, no value is produced unless the increased income protected the bank from regulatory insolvency, which it did in this case. Profits derived from asset exchanges should be examined carefully by analysts since they cannot be a long-term source of earnings.

5.5 SUMMARY

Accounting data are the only source of detailed performance information. Historical data are the basis of most of our assumptions about the future performance of firms. In order to analyze performance, we must first simplify financial data by aggregating similar categories and relating income statement items to balance sheet items. Ratio analysis can then proceed in careful steps to look at past performance. For stock companies, the focus is the return on equity linked to the return on total assets by leverage and pull-through ratios. For both mutuals and stocks, the key performance measure is ROTA, which must be analyzed differently for firms in different segments of the financial services industry. In any analysis, we must keep in mind that our main concern is with cash flows and not reported income, and we must be wary of distortions occurring in accounting numbers.

DISCUSSION QUESTIONS AND EXERCISES

1. Discuss carefully why analysis of accounting data matters, even though value represents anticipated future performance.
2. Discuss and contrast the goals of financial analysis for stock and mutual organizations. What are analysts trying to explain?
3. Why are audited financial statements desirable? What are the potential problems with unaudited financial data?
4. Why is consolidation of financial statements a problem in analysing the detailed performance of a firm? What types of reports would you like to see? Why? Use a real company as an example in answering this question.
5. In Chapter 4, evidence was presented that retail deposit-taking financial institution share prices went down when deposit ceilings were removed. Which numbers in the financial statements would have changed with the removal of deposit-rate ceilings?
6. What does "good" performance consist of? How would you construct an argument that a firm performed well or poorly? Use an example with a real company.
7. Describe in detail the similarities and differences between financial performance data for commercial banks and insurance companies.
8. Discuss carefully the difference between cash flows and the accounting of "earned" and "unearned" insurance premiums or loan interest.
9. What differences would you expect in the performance ratios for banks or thrifts with substantial market power in the loan and deposit markets relative to institutions under competitive pressure?
10. Analyze the performance of A.G. Edwards using the data provided in Table 5.7. What are the major determinants of ROTA using your analysis? How does analysis of a brokerage firm differ from that of a deposit-taking institution and from that of an insurance company? What different aspects of the brokerage business can be analyzed using the data in the table?

CHAPTER

6

Financial Services: Economic Overview

Introduction

Economic behavior and market forces reflect fundamental determinants of behavior. Understanding basic principles is key to understanding value production in financial services.

- In what ways do customers benefit from financial services?
- How do providers of financial services create value for the economy?
- Why do risk and uncertainty offer special opportunities for financial services?
- What role does information play in providing financial services?

The financial economic approach to answering these questions is an essential background to the analysis of value production in financial services presented in the next six chapters.

This chapter introduces the fundamental building blocks of analysis we need to understand the source of value in financial services. A goal is to use economic analysis to identify how value is created. We use these analytical devices to demonstrate exactly what different economic needs can be satisfied with financial services. In making this presentation, we emphasize key characteristics that are the same or similar for all financial services.

In the following sections, we begin by discussing the differences in tastes, preferences, and opportunities among financial market participants that determine the sources of value in financial intermediation. The role of information in financial services is reviewed. The special nature of the relation between financial service firms and their customers, often bound by negotiated contracts or strict sets of rules, is then presented. This analysis provides the economic rationale for the existence of financial institutions, which is reviewed against the background of the preceding.

6.1 CHARACTERISTICS OF USERS OF FINANCIAL SERVICES

Researchers of the financial services industry ask the basic question, "Why do financial firms exist?" In answering that question, these analysts have had to determine what specialized financial institutions do that individuals and businesses cannot do on their own more cheaply. In the process of this ongoing study, researchers have provided students of the financial services industry with an analytically sound basis for understanding the critical issues facing providers and users of financial services now and into the future. We will review this discussion in this chapter.

Financial services involve at least two people or firms, the service provider and the user. Often financial relationships will involve many parties, as with securities offerings. We will soon see that it is *differences* in these parties that make financial services valuable. The first issue to be addressed is what the parties in these financial relationships want and how their wants or needs differ. Only then can we see how the interaction of users and suppliers of financial services can produce value. The objective of this section is to make precise the differences in the tastes and needs of parties in financial relationships.

Financial institutions intermediate the flow of funds between different economic decision-making units, primarily households and businesses. The following discussion specifies differences between these units in terms of *time preferences, investment opportunities,* and *risk preferences*. Financial institutions raise the value of the allocation of resources to the economy by improving the welfare of market participants in terms of their preferences.

Time Preference

Individuals have different preferences concerning the timing of their consumption. Economists term the relation between the *timing* of consumption and the *utility* of consumption *time preference*.[1] The concept is illustrated in Figure 6.1, where Panel A shows how much utility is associated with the same amount of consumption (for example, a $20,000 bundle of consumption goods in real terms) in each of the next three years for three individuals, identified as Z, N, and P. The graph depicts the utility these individuals now assign to the current and future consumption of the consumption bundles.

Individual Z derives the same utility from the constant amount consumption bundle whenever it is consumed, now or in the future. Individual Z is said to have *zero time preference* because he or she does not care when consumption takes place. The individual does not *discount* or *attach a premium* to consumption in the future relative to current consumption. People like individual Z might

[1]Irving Fisher's classic 1930 book and Hirschleifer's (1970) extension of those concepts are considered the major sources of this analysis.

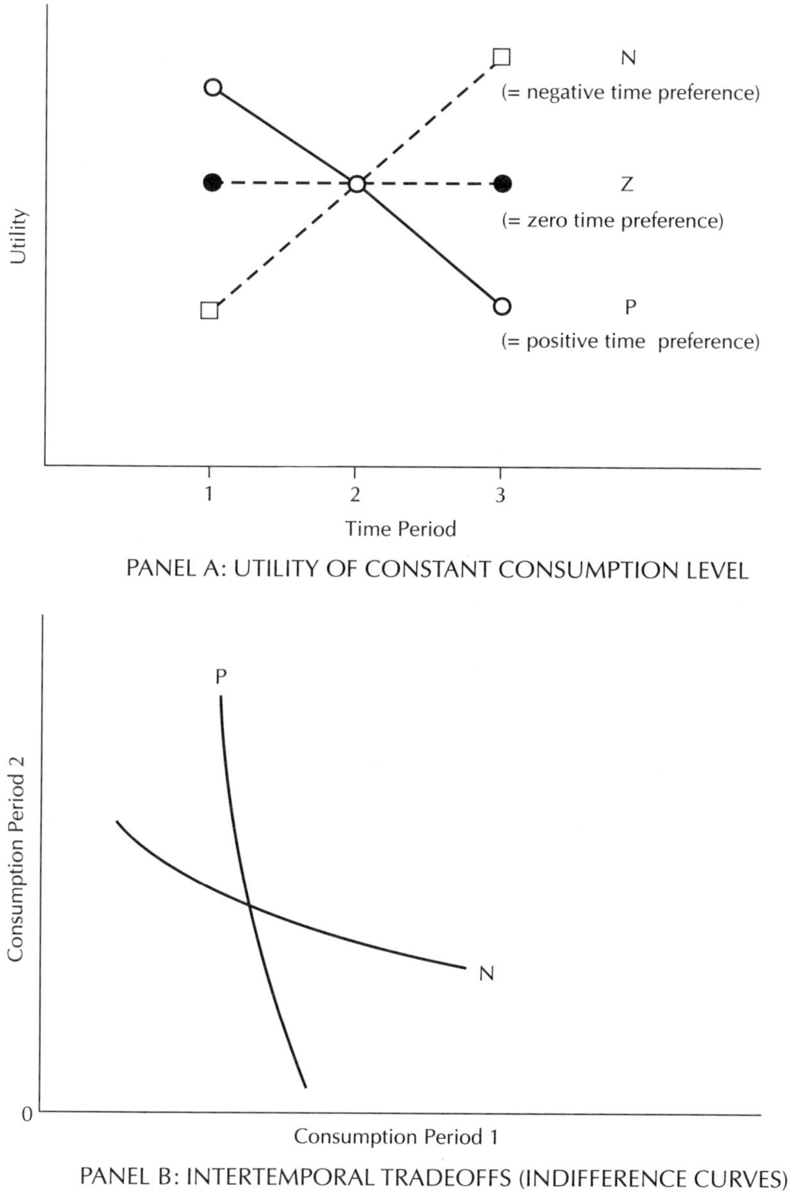

FIGURE 6.1 Time preference

be good to borrow money from because *when* they get the money back does not matter.

Individual P derives more utility from current consumption than future consumption. P does not like to wait and *discounts* the value of future consumption relative to current consumption. P would prefer to consume sooner rather than later. Individual P is said to have *positive time preference.* Individual N would, everything else equal, rather wait because he or she derives more utility from consumption in later time periods. Individuals like N, who attach a premium to future consumption, are said to have *negative time preference.*

The concept of time preference seems a reasonable way to characterize different ways of valuing consumption at different points in time. People are generally assumed to have positive time preference. Do you, for example, wish that the pleasures that await you on the weekend were three days away rather than tomorrow? If you wish the weekend started tomorrow, you have positive time preference.

On the other hand, income earners planning on future education expenses or retirement may have negative time preference. Time preferences for individuals do not need to be as simple as shown in Panel A of Figure 6.1. Time preference over shorter or longer periods of time may represent many factors of concern to individuals and families, like future vacations and retirement.

Time preference is likely related to the age of the individual, with younger individuals tending to have stronger positive time preference, and older individuals with more assets and responsibilities and longer planning horizons tending to have less positive or even negative time preference. Economists and marketing experts alike believe that an individual's position in his or her *life-cycle* is important in determining consumption behavior. According to this view, demographic (population age and growth statistics) factors are important considerations in thinking of aggregate time preference in an economy.

If we confine our analysis to two periods and consider preferences for current consumption and consumption next period, we can portray individuals' time preferences using indifference curves on a two-dimensional graph. Such curves are drawn in Panel B of Figure 6.1. As with any economic indifference curve, it is assumed that for each individual more consumption increases utility and that individuals can substitute some amount of consumption in one period for consumption in another period and remain at the same utility level. Given these assumptions, *intertemporal consumption indifference curves* representing the same level of utility for different combinations of consumption in period 1 and period 2 can be drawn for different individuals.

Panel B of Figure 6.1 shows intertemporal indifference curves for two individuals, N and P. The indifference curves for P are steeper than those for N at the points p and n on the graph. In order to keep P at the same level of indifference, more period 2 has to be offered to offset reduced period 1 consumption than is the case for individual N. P has *positive* time preference relative to N, who needs only a tiny amount of increased consumption in period 2 to compensate him or her for the reduced period 1 consumption. The rate at which P and N substitute period 1 and period 2 consumption at a constant utility level is shown by the slope of the lines tangent to their indifference curves at p and n. This slope is referred to as the *marginal rate of time preference* for P and N at consumption points p and n.

The indifference curves in Panel B of Figure 6.1 are for only two periods. Conceptually, indifference curves can be thought of as existing for many periods, in fact, over an individual's planning horizon or lifetime. It is not possible to draw multidimensional indifference curves, but the basic notion of time preference is shown in these simpler graphs. It is important to remember that individual time preferences are defined over long time periods and vary among individuals in many ways.

Differences in time preferences provide opportunities for financial institutions to create value for their customers. A simple example can be seen in Figure 6.2, where two individuals A and B have income in the form of available consumption represented by points a and b. A has positive time preference at his or her income level relative to B at b. B earns more income in period 1 (B has more consumption in period 1 and less in 2, the opposite from the earnings for A). A reduction in period 1 consumption means less in terms of period 2 consumption to B than to A. The differences in A and B at their respective income points, a and b, are differences in their marginal rate of time preference.

Given their differing marginal rates of time preferences, A and B would be better off switching their patterns of income, with B giving A some of his or her period 1 income in exchange for some of A's period 2 income. Simply switching their consumption points a and b could move A and B to indifference curves marked A″ and B″ in the figure. This is the best they could do, but given the real complexity of our economy, simple exchanges of consumption patterns between consumers with different time preferences do not happen.

Consumers do not often exchange their income patterns in time with each other because they may not be able to find out about each other and their

FIGURE 6.2 Value creation through consumption timing financial services

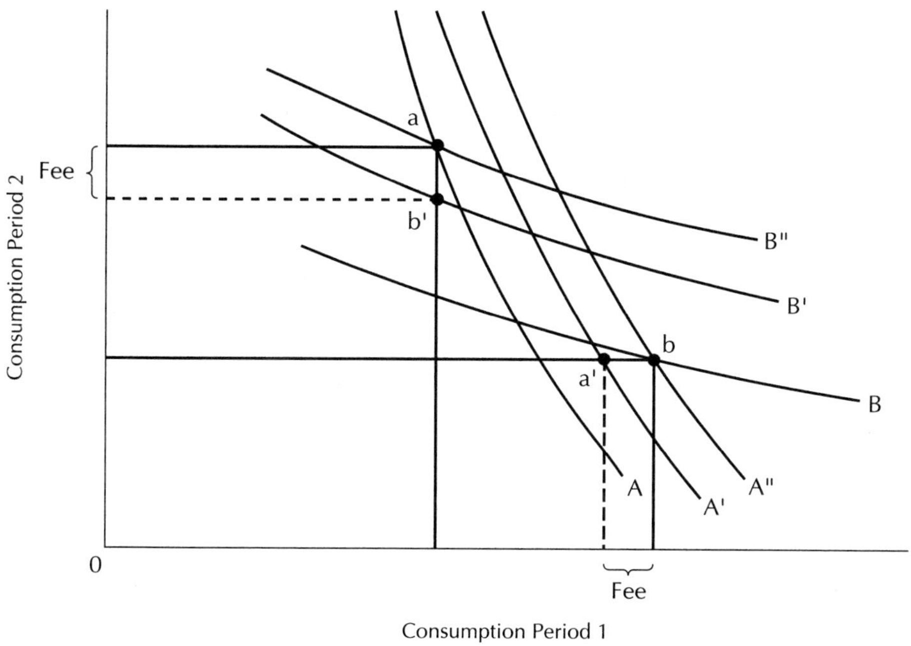

differing preferences. They may not be willing to reveal their preference or needs to each other. They may be reluctant to deal with each other directly, either because they do not know each other or because they are hesitant to enter into promises to exchange resources over time with each other because such promises would be cumbersome to set up and make work.

Financial institutions help rearrange the timing of consumption and income for individuals. A financial intermediary known and trusted by both A and B could take resources from B in period 1, keep a fee for itself, and lend the rest to A, moving A to a higher indifference curve. Next period the financial institution could collect resources from A, keep a fee for itself, and give the rest to B. The financial institution has created value for both A and B by moving them to higher indifference curves, and has made some profit or created value for itself in the form of fees.

With a little imagination, we can see how value can be created by the financial institution in terms of our simple formula from Chapter 2:

$$\text{ROI} = \frac{(p - c) * Q}{I}.$$

In our example, a financial institution produces increases in utility for both A and B by arranging for some of B's income to be provided to A in period 1 in exchange for A giving up some period 2 income, bringing A to a point like a´. B would be moved to a point like b´. Both A and B are better off (at higher indifference curves) even if the financial institution keeps some period 1 and/or period 2 consumption for itself. If fees the financial institution earns, represented by the (p – c) term in the formula, are enough to provide a competitive return given the investment (I) necessary to provide these services and given that the level of activity (Q) is sufficient, the financial institution is producing value for its investors and for the economy consisting of individuals like A and B who are better off in terms of their expected utility levels.

Financial institutions allocating resources between savers and consumers with different time preferences in many periods are performing the function of *maturity intermediation*. Small savers not needing all their funds immediately may finance large purchases like college educations for borrowers now. Financial institutions pooling savings and making large resource advances available to a few borrowers is a function called *denomination intermediation*. When financial institutions perform maturity and denomination intermediation they add value by increasing expected utility through the reallocation of resources through time.

Investment Opportunities

Each individual consumer or business person has an expected future income stream from his or her job or future prospects. Each also has some investment opportunities. These investments could be purchases of consumer durables, which produce future consumption benefits directly in terms of consumption services, like transportation from a car. The investment could be a business opportunity, which produces consumption indirectly through future cash earnings. We consider investment opportunities to be ways to convert current consumable income into future consumption.

Real Investment Opportunities

The investments we consider in this section are real investments, like consumers' automobiles and refrigerators, that produce a stream of valuable services into the future, and plant and equipment investments in a business that produce future profits. These investments will be reflected in household and small business balance sheets as the *real assets* we discussed with the flow of funds in Chapter 3. We focus on the analysis of real investment opportunities in order to highlight the value added by financial markets and financial intermediaries.

Investment opportunities can be ranked by how much a unit of current consumption not spent but invested will yield in future benefits. In finance and economics, there are three equivalent ways to look at investment opportunities: a ranking of projects by *rates of return*, a *marginal efficiency of investment* schedule, and a *transformation curve*. Figure 6.3 illustrates each of the three methods in Panels A, B, and C.

FIGURE 6.3 Ranking of investment projects

Project	Investment	Rate of Return
A	$100	24%
B	$100	20%
C	$100	16%
D	$100	12%
E	$100	8%

PANEL A: RANKING BY RATE OF RETURN

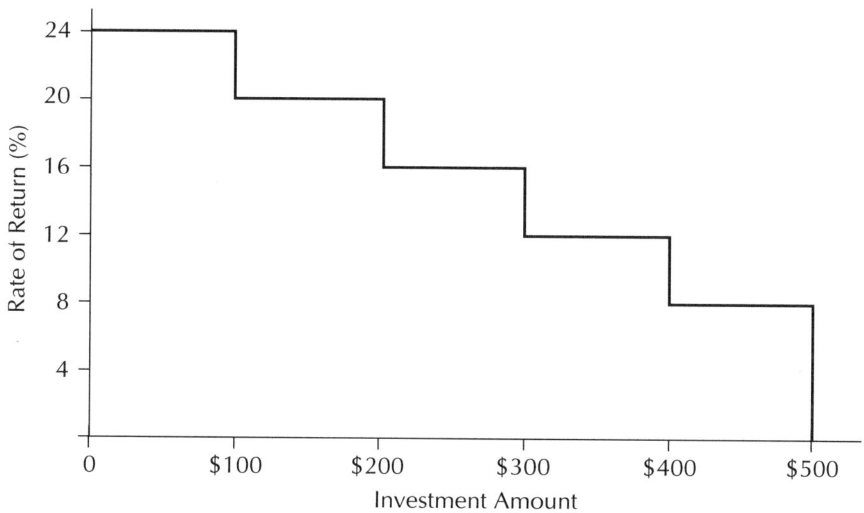

PANEL B: MARGINAL EFFICIENCY OF INVESTMENT SCHEDULE

FIGURE 6.3 (*continued*)

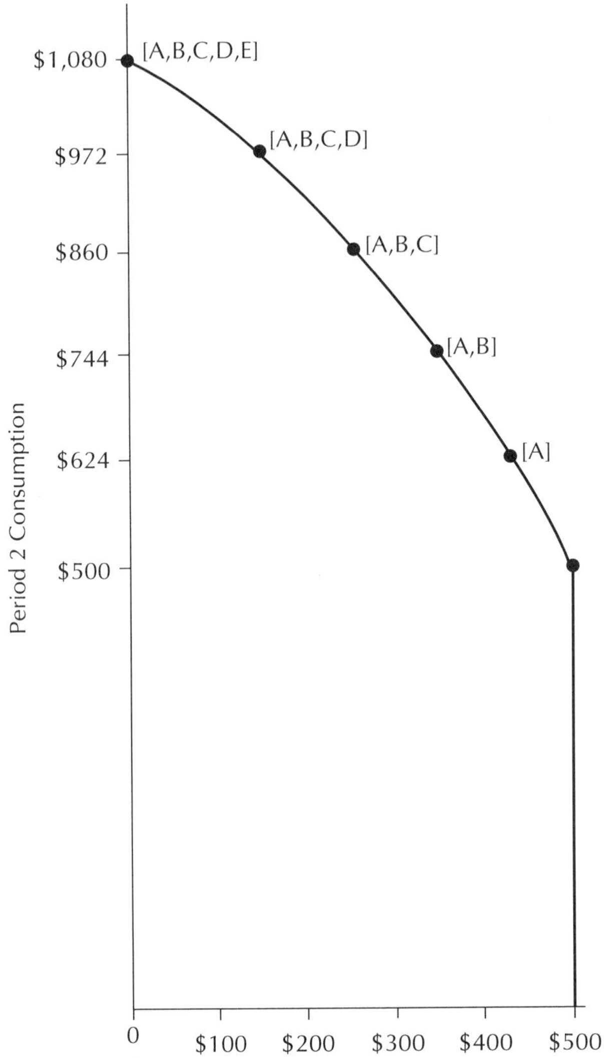

PANEL C: TRANSFORMATION CURVE

Panel A of Figure 6.3 shows five projects with rates of return ranging from 24 to 8 percent, and those returns are available on each of the projects up to a maximum investment of $100. Clearly the best project is A with a return of 24 percent and the least attractive is E with an 8 percent return. By giving up $100 in consumption in period 1 and investing in A, an investor would have $124 dollars in additional consumption in period 2 versus only $108 with project E.

How would an individual choose how much to invest in which projects? In terms of Panel A, a standard decision criterion is to reject projects that have returns below the cutoff rate of return for the investor, representing his or her alternative uses for the investment funds. This approach begs the issue of what determines the cutoff rate of return.

An alternative ranking of investment projects is a marginal efficiency of investment curve as in Panel B of the figure. This curve may seem familiar from macroeconomics where the marginal efficiency of investment curve is used as the demand for savings. A supply schedule for savings available to finance projects determines which investments should be undertaken. Although this is a valid approach for an economy, we are concentrating on the individual decision to forego consumption and make real investments. The supply of savings for an economy represents the aggregate of all individuals' willingness to forego current consumption.

A more complete analysis of the trade-offs facing individual consumer–investors is possible using the investment transformation curve in Panel C of Figure 6.3, which represents another way of showing the consumption/investment trade-offs through time. This approach explicitly relates investment to consumption. Assume an individual has income of \$500 in period 1 and in period 2. If the individual undertakes the maximum investment in project A, the best project, period 1 consumption is reduced by \$100 to \$400 and period 2 consumption is increased by \$124 (a 24% return) to \$624. That is shown by point [A] in the graph. If the maximum investment in both projects A and B is undertaken, period 1 consumption is reduced to \$300 and period 2 consumption is increased to \$744 (\$500 income and \$124 plus \$120), shown as point [A,B] in the graph. The locus of all consumption and investment opportunities is the *investment transformation curve.*

The different rates of return on the investment opportunities can be seen on the investment transformation curve (Panel C). If we look at the slope of the curve at points representing a given level of investment (reduced consumption) and next period consumption, say on the segment of the transformation curve between point [A] and zero investment (consume all \$500), we have a line that has the slope:

$$\text{Slope} = \frac{\text{Units of Rise}}{\text{Units of Run}} = \frac{\$124}{-\$100} = -1.24 = -\left(1 + 24\%\right).$$

The slope of the investment transformation curve at any point will be minus one plus the *marginal return on investment.* On the curve between [A,B,C] and [A,B], the slope will be:

$$\text{Slope} = \frac{\text{Units of Rise}}{\text{Units of Run}} = \frac{\$116}{-\$100} = -1.16 = -\left(1 + 16\%\right).$$

This is the rate of return on project C, in this case of investing \$300 (consuming only \$200) on the last or marginal investment. The slope at each point reflects return on the last project taken.

By connecting any two points with the zero investment strategy (\$500 in current and future consumption) on the investment transformation curve, we obtain a chord inside the transformation curve reflecting the *average rate of return* on all the investments taken to that point. Using point [A,B,C] as an example, we get:

$$\text{Slope} = \frac{\text{Units of Rise}}{\text{Units of Run}} = \frac{\$360}{-\$300} = -1.20 = -(1+20\%)$$

The average of return on projects A, B, and C is 20 percent.

If there are a large number of relatively small projects, the investment transformation curve will appear to be smooth. Such a curve is shown in Figure 6.4. Again, the slope of the curve represents the marginal return on investment, whereas the chord connecting any point on the curve with the zero investment point has the slope of one plus the average rate of return.

FIGURE 6.4 Optimal consumption and investment with no borrowing and lending

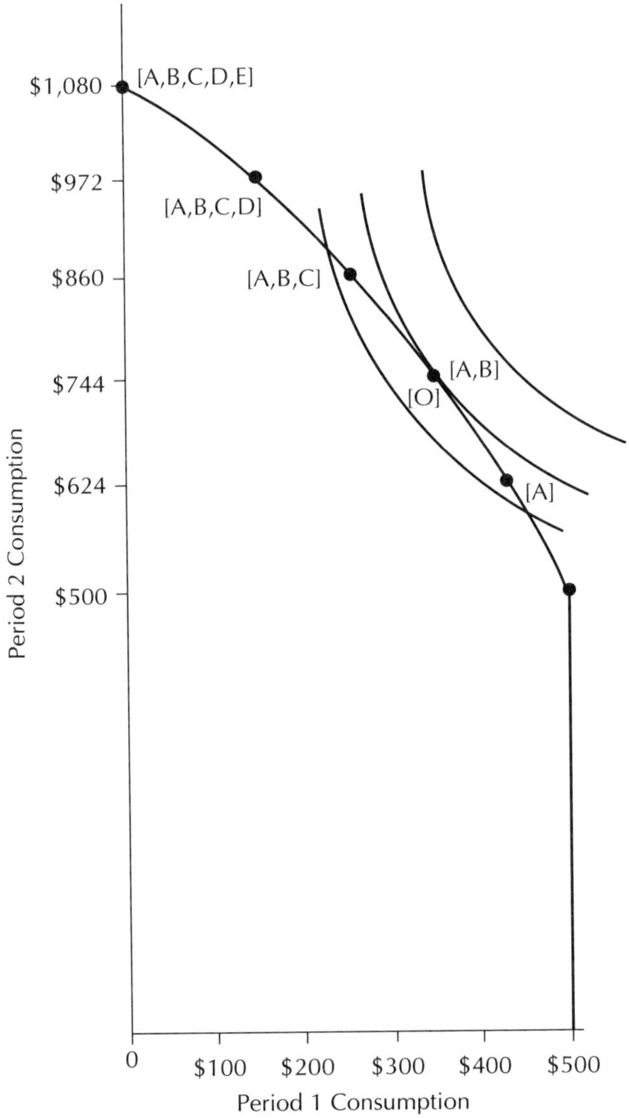

Individuals maximize utility by getting to the highest intertemporal indifference curve. Several of those for a representative individual with given investment opportunities are also shown on Figure 6.4. Individuals achieve the highest level of utility when they invest in all projects up to the point the investment transformation curve is tangent to their indifference curves. In view of our discussion of the slopes of these curves, at the optimum point, marked O on our graph, individuals' marginal rates of time substitution must be equal to the *marginal* rate of return on their investments, not the average return represented by the chord. The decision of how much to invest is made on the basis of the *marginal* returns because only in this way can the individuals reach their highest utility given investors' opportunities and preferences.

Financial Assets and Liabilities. We now consider the effect of financial markets on trade-offs between current and future consumption. We begin by looking at financial assets where an individual can invest in financial assets or borrow by issuing financial liabilities. With financial markets, the investor faces a number of feasible patterns of consumption through time. Assume an individual can borrow (issue financial liabilities) or invest (buy financial assets) at an interest rate of 14 percent. Assume the individual has period 1 income of $500 and period 2 income of $500 as shown in Figure 6.5. If he or she can invest at 14 percent and all $500 of period 1 resources were invested in financial assets, $1,070 in consumption would be possible in period 2 ($500 + $570). Any combination of period 1 and period 2 consumption connecting those two points is feasible. If the individual can *borrow* at 14 percent, he or she could pledge the income from period 2 against loans, and borrow up to $439 for period 1 consumption ($439 borrowed in period 1 at 14% yields $500 in period 2).

The individual with annual $500 income and the ability to invest or borrow at 14 percent could consume any combination between zero in period 1 and $1,070 in period 2 to $939 in period 1 and zero in period 2. These combinations of possible consumption as shown on Figure 6.5 are called the intertemporal *borrowing/investment budget line*. Financial investment opportunities can be shown on the graphs as straight lines with (negative) slopes of one plus the interest rate through the point representing the two periods' incomes: in Figure 6.5, a line with a slope of –1.14 through the period 1 and 2 income point of $500.

Real and Financial Investments and Borrowing. When confronted with both real investment opportunities and financial markets, the individual is best off making all real investments yielding more than the financial rate of return. In our graph, the individual would undertake all real investments yielding more than the financial market rate of 14 percent and then borrow or invest in financial markets to achieve the highest level of utility. This point is shown as point [OO] in Figure 6.5. At the point where the individual reaches the highest possible level of utility, the marginal rate of return on real investments is equal to the rate available in financial markets. The individual invests or borrows to reach the optimum consumption combination where the intertemporal rate of substitution is equal to the rate of financial market rate of interest *and* the marginal return on investment.

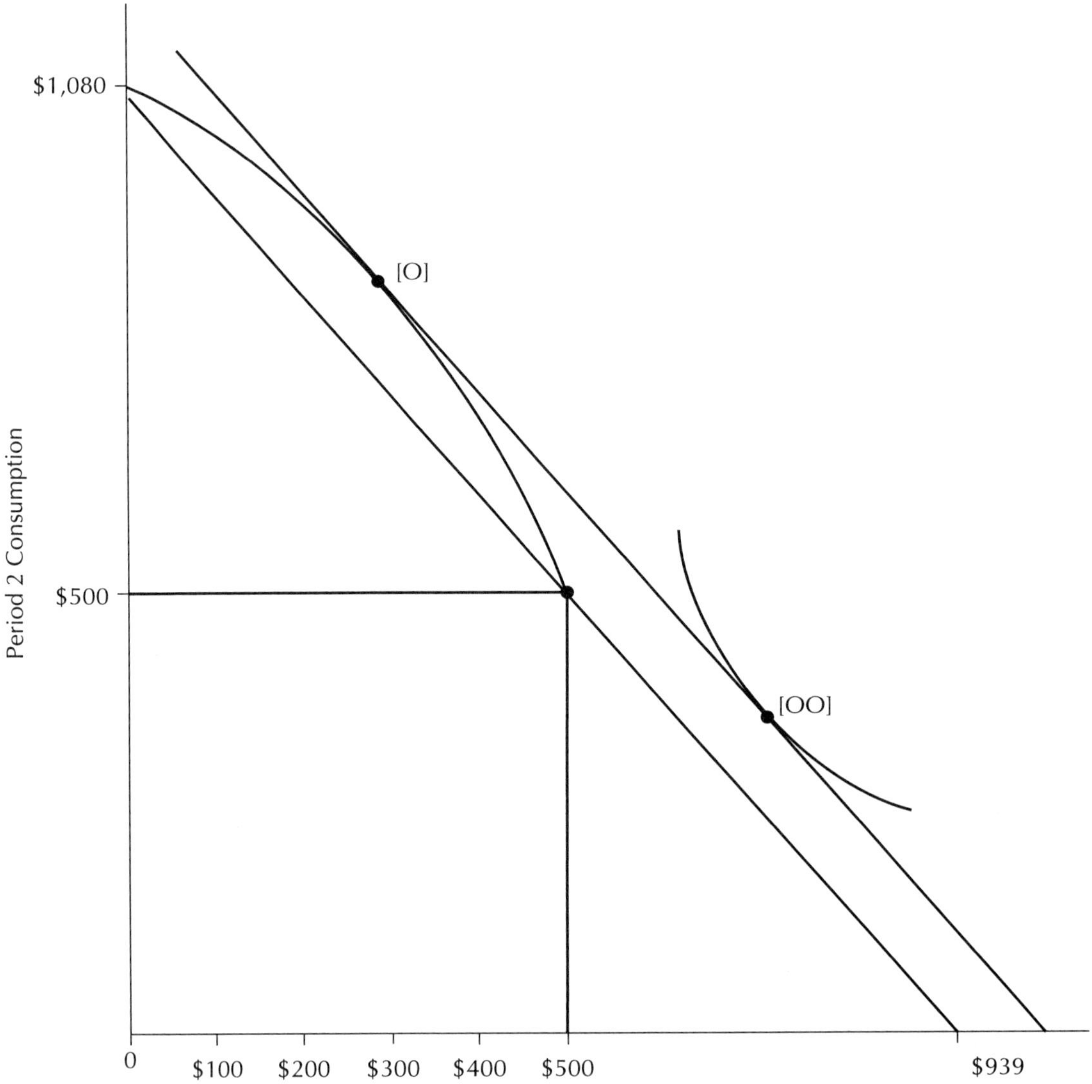

FIGURE 6.5 Optimal consumption and investment with borrowing and lending

Depending on the individual's real investment opportunities, time preferences, and the availability of financial assets or borrowing, individuals can maximize utility by different combinations of real investment, financial investment, and borrowing. Individual decision-making units (households and businesses) are characterized by different time preferences and face different investment opportunities. It is these differences between decision-making units that provide financial institutions with opportunities to add value.

There are two ways financial institutions can produce value: The first is to allocate resources to the highest return investments and the second is to reallocate consumption through time according to differing time preferences. Both of these sources of value are shown in Figure 6.6, where two representative individuals, P and N, have relatively positive and negative time preference and have identical real investment opportunities. In the absence of financial intermediation, P would not take advantage of the high return projects not available. With financial intermediation, P and N can borrow and lend investment and consumption resources so both achieve a higher level of utility. Financial institutions can take some fees or resources for themselves and still produce value for financial

FIGURE 6.6 Optimal consumption and investment and borrowing and lending

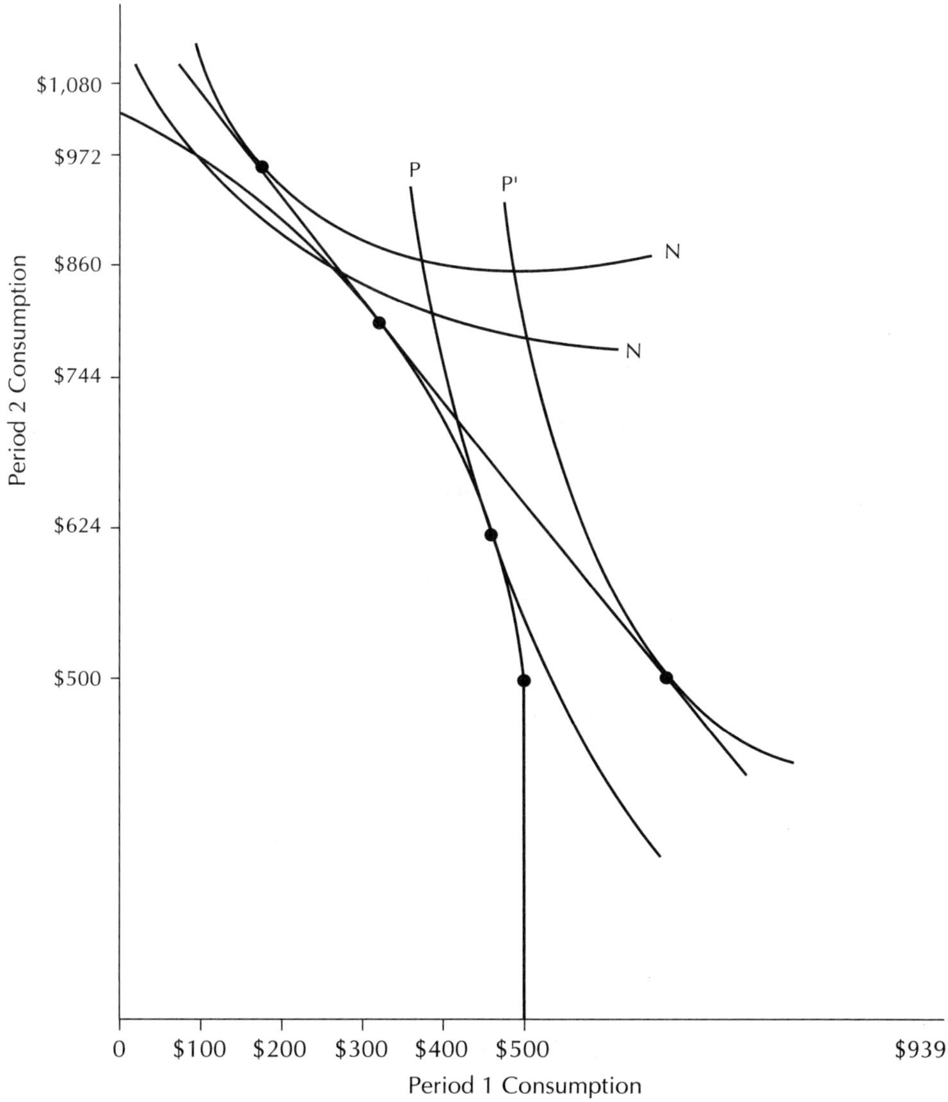

market participants by arranging for them to undertake the best investments and consume according to their time preferences.

Recall the discussion of household balance sheets in the flow-of-funds analysis presented in Chapter 3. Aggregate consumption and investment decisions of individual units in the household sector are reflected in household balance sheets. The balance sheets and changes in them represent the allocation of savings (net worth) to real and net financial investments. These aggregate balance sheets and the changes in them reflect time preferences and investment opportunities of the aggregate household sector at various points in time. Anticipating changes in household balance sheets can be the basis for strategies in providing financial services in the retail market.

Risk Preferences. A significant difference between users and suppliers of financial services is their attitudes toward risk or their ability to diversify risks. In financial economics, we assume most individuals are *risk-averse*. Risk aversion comes from the assumption of diminishing marginal utility of wealth.[2] It is assumed that more wealth in the future makes most consumers better off because additional wealth increases their ability to consume goods. Diminishing marginal utility means that the utility increase associated with an increase in wealth is less than the decrease in utility associated with an equal decrease in wealth making consumers poorer.

The relation between future wealth and utility is shown in Panel A of Figure 6.7 for an individual assumed to be risk averse. Because of the shape of the utility curve, lower future wealth, stemming from lower than expected returns on investment for example, implies a greater loss in utility than an equal increase in wealth would increase expected utility. In technical terms, the utility of wealth curve is concave from below.

Since returns on risky assets are *always* variable in real purchasing power terms, risky assets must have higher expected returns to bring investors to the same level of expected utility as riskless assets. This can be illustrated using Figure 6.7, Panel A, where the expected utility of two equally likely returns on a risky investment of wealth are contrasted to a certain return with the same expected value. The *expected* utility of the uncertain outcome, representing the weighted average of the two possible wealth and utility levels, must be lower than the certain utility from the riskless investment. This comes simply from the curvature of the utility of wealth, namely, the diminishing marginal utility of wealth.

In order for a risky return to produce the same expected utility as a riskless or lower risk return, it must have a higher expected return. Again, we can see this on the graph: increasing the expected return on the risky asset moves the outcomes up the utility curve, increasing the expected utility of future wealth. This compensation for bearing risk in the form of a higher expected return is related to the *price of risk* discussed in Chapter 4.

[2]James Tobin (1958) and Harry Markowitz (1952) wrote the pathbreaking papers incorporating risk in the form of standard deviations of return into economic analysis.

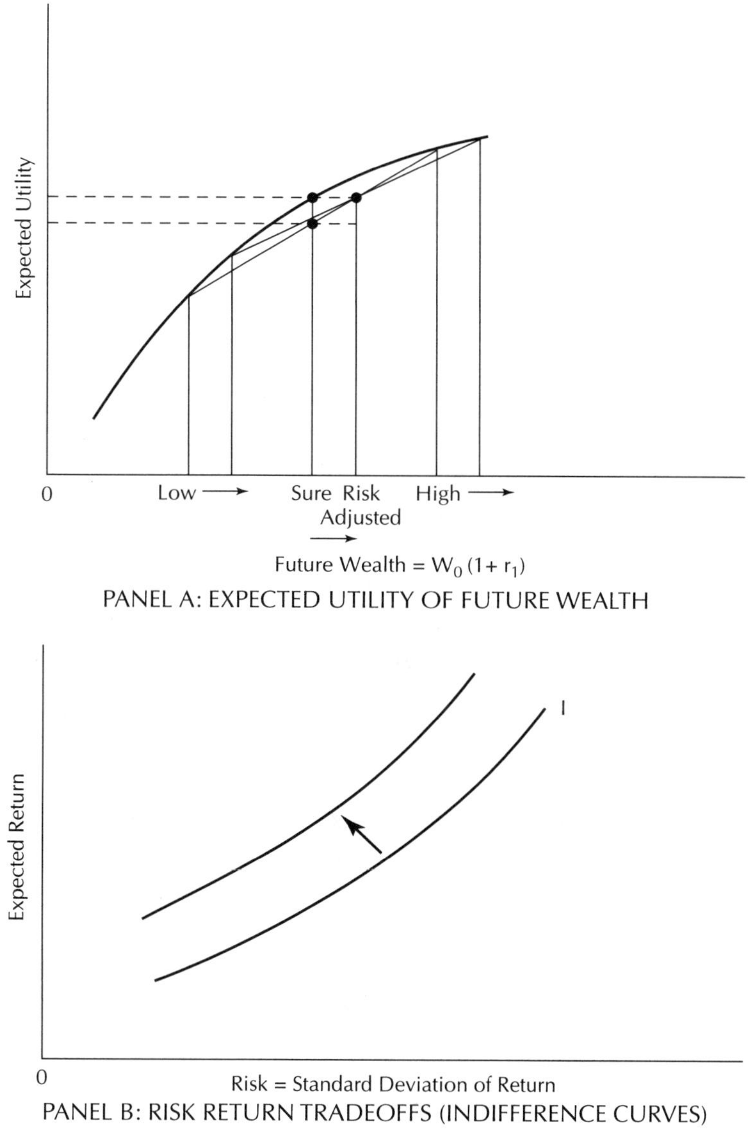

FIGURE 6.7 Risk, expected utility, and returns

For any given individual, we can draw risk/return *indifference curves* as in Panel B of Figure 6.7. Like all indifference curves, each curve represents combinations of economic quantities that make an individual have the same level of utility. Individuals have different degrees of risk tolerance. Flatter indifference curves portray individuals with more *risk tolerance.* In the extreme, individuals with no risk aversion are called *risk neutral* and their indifference curves are horizontal lines; they care only about returns.

The difference between the indifference curves shown in the figure and those encountered elsewhere in economics are that these curves represent combinations of risk and return that provide the same *expected* utility from *future wealth* (not current consumption). Risk is *bad,* so that the indifference curves slope upward (to the northeast), rather than down (to the southeast), for risk averse individuals. Like the usual indifference curves, individuals seek to get to the highest level of expected utility, meaning they wish to move up and to the left (northwest) in the diagram.

Financial service firms can produce value by exploiting the differences in risk preferences between individuals. The differences can be between financial institution owners and their customers and/or between different customers. Financial institutions produce value for their customers by moving them to higher expected utility of wealth. They can do this by reducing risk for the same return or increasing returns for a given level of risk. The financial institutions can keep some of the increased returns for themselves in the form of fees or higher interest rates and still make customers better off.

Look at Figure 6.8 to see the value produced by exploiting differences in risk preferences. An individual faced with investment alternative A, representing a riskless investment (zero standard deviation), and alternative B, representing a risky investment opportunity, has maximum expected utility on indifference curve I. Increasing the individual's expected utility would add value.

Financial institutions can diversify the risks of alternatives like B if it has many customers with similar projects. There are two ways the gains from this diversification can be made. The financial institution can pool the investments, issuing investors claims on a portfolio of B risks, reducing the standard deviation of returns on those investments through diversification and sharing the value of

FIGURE 6.8 Value creation through risk changing financial services

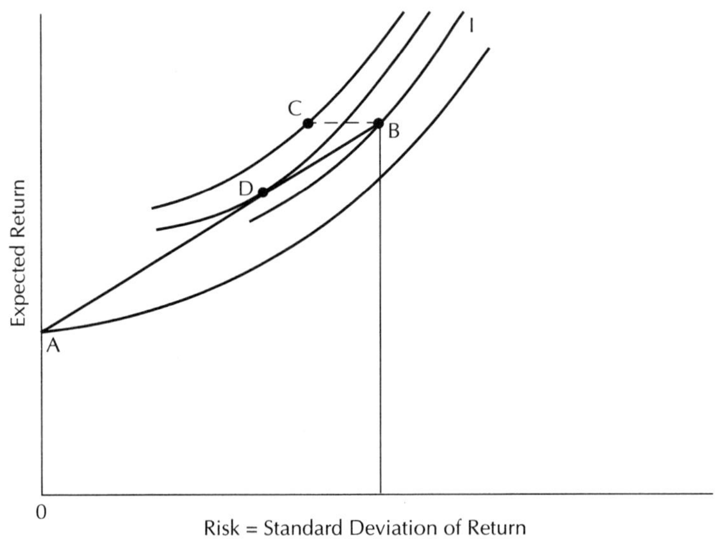

the risk reduction to investors directly, moving from B to C on the figure. Alternatively, a financial institution could lend the investor part of the funds to undertake the business opportunity represented by B, charging a lower interest rate on loans to these borrowers than the expected return on the investment because it can diversify. If the investor undertakes the project with partially borrowed funds, some resources can be invested in the riskless asset, increasing the range of opportunities to include point D.

When a financial services firm permits customers to move to higher indifference curves, as at points C or D in Figure 6.8, and thereby earn a higher return than at the riskless rate represented by A, the customers can share some of their higher returns from the risk of project B with the financial institution in terms of fees and still be better off. Value has been created for both the financial institution and the customer through this exchange, represented by the higher indifference curve for the customer and the higher-than-riskless rate earned by the financial institution.

One important difference between financial service firms and their customers is in the firms' ability to diversify exposure to risks. Individuals or small firms may not be able to diversify their investments economically. For that reason, they may be faced with *unsystematic* risk discussed in Chapter 4. Financial institutions with many customers can provide sufficient diversification to reduce unsystematic risk to levels where it does not affect returns, leaving financial institutions with only *systematic* risk. The financial institution can bear the systematic risk itself or find investors in securities to share the risk in financial markets, as discussed in Part IV of this book.

Financial institutions and their customers differ in their attitudes toward and exposure to risk, both systematic and unsystematic. Large, well-diversified financial institutions may in fact be viewed as nearly risk neutral to unsystematic risk in that they can bear whatever amount of unsystematic risk their smaller customers would like to share with them. Value is produced by redistributing risk between financial institutions and their customers.

6.2 INFORMATION AND FINANCIAL INSTITUTIONS IN THE ECONOMY

The preceding section outlined major opportunities for value creation by financial institutions through their ability to intermediate differences in time preferences, investment opportunities, and risk preferences among different individuals or decision-making units in the economy. Why is it necessary for specialized financial institutions to exist in order to reallocate resources among individuals and through time in order to take advantage of these opportunities for value creation coming from differences among individuals? Why don't consumers and investors get together on their own and reallocate resources? This is the question asked by students of financial institutions and markets: Why do financial institutions exist?

The specific answers to these questions are to be found in the specialized financial services we discuss in the rest of Part II. The general answer is that financial institutions have to be relatively good at bringing individuals and decision-making units with different needs together. This intermediating function requires obtaining and using *information* concerning the differences in individuals. Both the development and use of information are essential economic functions of financial institutions.

There are three basic types of information requiring different technologies and expertise to process in order to exploit value-creating differences in the economy. Use of information will differ in providing the various services financial institutions perform. In this section of the chapter, we discuss the types of information concerning individuals or businesses and governments that financial institutions process, and we consider briefly the problems encountered in gathering these types of information. In the following sections, we describe the use to which this information is put in producing value.

Types of Information

The development and use of information is crucial to understanding how financial service firms produce value. Pinning down just what information has value is hard. Information can consist of facts, like telephone numbers, or it can consist of a synthesis or combination of facts, like combining telephone numbers with demographic characteristics of telephone subscribers to provide marketing information for a telemarketing campaign. We describe information by progressing from the gathering and dissemination of basic information bits to more highly synthesized types of information. In this progression, we discuss (1) *technical,* (2) *market,* and (3) *customer specific* types of information.

Technical Information. Technical information is defined as data concerning transactions (purchases or sales) of financial assets, commodities, or other items of economic importance. Technical information consists of prices, rates of returns, volumes of transactions, and historical data on all those items at different locations or on different markets.

The economic significance of technical information is obvious. If an identical item is trading at two or more locations at different prices, arbitrage profits can be made by buying at the lower price and selling at the higher. If tracking transactions can be used to forecast or anticipate profitable trading opportunities, profits may also be made through access to technical information.

Technical information can be expensive to gather. Financial market data may be recorded by human observers in the marketplace or it may be captured electronically by computer systems as part of trading or accounting systems. In either case, labor and capital are required to get the information into the information network and to transmit it to where the information can be useful.

Technology has always had a role in how information is collected and transmitted to where the data, like prices for the same commodity at two locations, can be used for economic decision making. Usually the latest technology means faster transmission and processing of information. The first person with valuable information gets to make the most profit out of price differentials or other opportunities. History is filled with profits made with the initial uses of such varying technologies as carrier pigeons, pony express, steamships, telegraph, and telephones. It is foolish to believe that current electronic technology represents an advance to end all advances in terms of speed or that it is qualitatively different from past advances.

Market Information. Market information is information concerning buyers and sellers of real and financial items. This information consists of where and who buyers and sellers are, what the extent of their needs are, factors that will shift or change their needs in the near or distant future, and related information. Market information is clearly synthesized information. Relevant data items come from a variety of sources like past sales, economic statistics, and demographic data. Marketing information is not as well defined as technical information because the relationships between important factors affecting supply and demand are not always observable.

The economic value of market information is obvious. A seller cannot sell unless he or she can find a buyer. A borrower cannot borrow unless he or she can find someone willing to lend. Since the seller wishes to sell, it must be that his or her utility will be higher if the transaction in completed. We know from our above analysis that investors, borrowers, and lenders can gain utility from transactions.

If the item to be sold is unusual, or the loan large or complex, or if sellers or borrowers do not go frequently to the market, it may be hard for one side of a situation to find an appropriate counterpart. Financial institutions specialize in gathering marketing information and/or bringing sellers and buyers together more cheaply than buyer or sellers can do it on their own. Value creation comes from bringing buyers and sellers together to increase their expected utilities cost effectively.

Market information consists not only of information concerning the demand and supply of observable commodities or financial instruments, it also concerns the level and distribution of risk and risk preferences. The value in market information may come from being able to package and redistribute risk due to economic and financial sources, from insurance risks to default risks, to those willing to bear risk. One of the most successful and profitable financial market developments in the 1980s was Michael Milken's correct assessment of the market for high-default-risk corporate debt and his ability to turn this marketing information into profits for himself and his employer, investment bankers Drexel, Burnham and Lambert.

Customer-Specific Information. The most difficult information to develop and use effectively is information concerning the specifics of individual customers and firms. Customer-specific information concerns time preferences, investment opportunities, and risk preferences of individual economic decision-making units. Customer-specific information is the essential factor determining market needs and profit opportunities. In practice, specific information is difficult to obtain and communicate as well as hard to describe and measure. Typical consumers do not really plan their lifetime expenditures and make savings and investment decisions in accordance with these plans. Investment opportunities for businesses can be extremely complicated. Expected payoffs and risks may be estimated only with substantial uncertainty.

Developing information on the complex nature of decisions by economic agents in the market is hard enough. The problem facing financial institutions is made even more difficult because economic agents may seek advantage for themselves by not revealing everything. Potential customers of financial service firms may know things about themselves or the actions they might take that financial institutions cannot readily see. Differences in access to information are called *information asymmetries*.

There are two types of information asymmetries that have been analyzed in *information economics*. The first type of information concerns a situation or attributes of an economic agent that the agent knows but that cannot be observed by outsiders. This type of information is called *hidden information*. The second type of information is when actions taken by economic agents cannot be measured or observed by others, called *hidden actions*.

Examples of hidden information are everywhere in our daily experience. The classic analysis of the economic importance of hidden information was by Akerlof (1970). His analysis concerns automobile owners who are trying to sell their cars. Each seller knows whether or not the car is a "lemon." The seller of a lemon will not want to reveal this fact about the car and it cannot be determined from the appearance of the car. The fact that a particular car is a lemon is hidden information. Buyers never know whether a given car is a lemon and are not willing to pay more than the average value of a lemon and a good car. Since good cars are worth more than the average, owners of good cars do not sell, leaving only lemons for sale—and no one wants lemons. The market for used cars, in Akerlof's analysis, breaks down and no one buys or sells used cars.

There are many other examples of hidden information. Job applicants can overstate their experience. Life insurance customers can omit relevant items from their medical history or lie about personal habits, like smoking. In business situations, a firm may not disclose how collectible its accounts are or the possible future litigation associated with its products. This information can be hidden from outsiders like financial firms in order to improve the chances for favorable decisions on applications. Customers may hope to lower prices and terms for financial services like bank loans and insurance policies.

Hidden actions are also commonplace. Analyses of problems with hidden actions in economics began with the labor market. The problem addressed was shirking on the part of workers working for fixed wages. In financial services, an example of hidden actions are the efforts that firms' managers make to ensure the success of investment projects financed with borrowed funds. An example of hidden action from the retail market would be using a car for commuting when the auto insurance only covers pleasure driving.

Hidden information and hidden actions come into play in the form of *adverse selection* and *moral hazard* problems in economics and finance. Adverse selection occurs when individuals or firms take advantage of terms or prices that are favorable for them and hide information that is bad from the point of view of the other party in the relationship. Adverse selection occurs *before* the beginning of a customer relationship. Moral hazard is used to describe the risk of actions that clients, customers, or providers of goods or services can take *after* a relationship is established. The hazard is the damage an individual or firm can cause to other parties while pursuing its own interests.

There are many examples of adverse selection in the financial services industry. Adverse selection occurs when individuals can misrepresent themselves so that firms offering services attract the worst kind of customers for themselves. For example, bad drivers want the most complete car insurance because they expect to have more accidents. Bad drivers will buy low-deductible insurance if it is cheap. Poor health risks buy supplemental health insurance. Presented with given prices and terms, customers select products or services that are the best deals for themselves. These customers may be the worst (or most adverse) for the firm offering the products or services.

Moral hazard is also common in financial services. A boiler insurance customer may not undertake adequate maintenance if damages from boiler explosions are completely covered by inexpensive insurance. A borrower may take the money from a loan and buy a yacht rather than a piece of productive equipment if not monitored.

Financial institutions present problems of moral hazard for their customers. For example, if it were not illegal to do so, a bank trust department could invest trust account money in companies when loans from the bank are going sour. A broker might not try hard to find the best price for a customer. Financial institution customers' concerns about the moral hazard they face must be addressed for them to do business with financial firms.

Customer-specific information plays a key role in the ability of firms and individuals to conduct business in the modern marketplace. Problems of adverse selection and moral hazard are unavoidable in conducting business and making decisions. Information-related problems can cause markets to break down, as in the used car market case, unless the problems can be resolved. In some cases markets may function only inefficiently. Good customers may have to pay more to cover the costs resulting from adverse selection or moral hazard of bad customers.

Market breakdowns are costly because no one can improve expected utility level through voluntary exchanges of resources. Market inefficiencies result in good customers paying too much. If customers have to pay for potential costs of adverse selection and moral hazard, they may not be able to optimize investment and consumption decisions. Reducing these costs of information asymmetries produces value. Some analysts believe that the most important reason for the existence of financial institutions is their ability to find solutions to problems from information asymmetries—that is problems from adverse selection and moral hazard.

Information Costs and Informational Efficiency

Information can be costly to gather. Grossman and Stiglitz (1980) analyzed the effects of costly information and information asymmetries on financial markets and concluded that prices cannot be informationally efficient in the sense that they reflect all available information. According to their analysis, asset prices observed in the market depart from the assets' intrinsic values by enough to compensate for the costs of gathering information and expected losses from information asymmetries. According to Grossman and Stiglitz, market prices can be misleading and hence are inefficient.

Many economists go beyond the Grossman and Stiglitz's argument that prices are not unbiased estimates of underlying values of financial assets. Some market observers believe that information asymmetry problems, such as those stemming from insider information in the presence of uninformed and naive traders, mean that the information value of prices is severely limited. These observers have used complex arguments to demonstrate that stock market prices are "too" volatile, because variations in income of the firms issuing securities is not enough to explain the gyrations we observe in stock and bond markets (Schiller, 1981). Many economists believe that these "problems" with financial markets demand closer supervision and regulation. Calls for stronger regulation of financial markets after the stock market crash of 1987 were based on this type of argument.

Arguments concerning efficiency, inefficiency, or degree of efficiency of markets can never be resolved definitely. The main arguments favoring market efficiency, such as those discussed in Chapter 1, state that analysis of asset price behavior in financial markets *does not rule out* market efficiency. No study purports to prove that the markets are efficient. In order to prove that a market is efficient, one would have to be a god and know what everyone knows and why everyone does everything everyone does.

There are three arguments favoring reliance on the informational efficiency of financial markets upon which most of modern financial analysis and the discussion in this book are based. First, arbitrage, buying undervalued securities and selling overvalued ones, is a powerful force. Arbitrage can overcome major obstacles in driving prices toward consensus intrinsic values. Buyers of undervalued assets with inside information must ultimately—in order to make any money—convince others that the assets are undervalued. The buyer of the undervalued asset must release the information to the market in order to profit by driving prices to (higher) equilibrium values—the inside information must become public information.

Second, market efficiency propositions that prices tend to reflect available information do not mean that we always or ever observe equilibrium prices. Equilibrium arguments only mean that prices are headed somewhere and that somewhere is related to intrinsic value. Tranquil equilibrium arguments are valid guides to understanding turbulent realities since they suggest the direction of change. They do not say whether the ride to equilibrium will be bumpy.

Third, a world where prices are never informationally efficient is atheoretical. In such a world prices reflect the interaction of uninformed and unpredictably mad or impulsive traders. In such a world, there can be no systematic analysis of markets. Uninformed and impulsive behavior is random and not subject to analysis. You cannot study finance under these circumstances. This argument in defense of efficiency is partly a defense of theory.

The often heated assertion that markets are not efficient is usually used to support more regulation and government control. The objection to arguments for more government control of markets is that there is no evidence that regulation is better than market forces at guaranteeing efficiency. Prices in regulated markets reflect regulation as well as information costs and disequilibrium. In some instances, for example in the mandatory disclosure of information to potential investors, regulation may have improved market efficiency. But in other instances of regulation, regulation has reduced the information value of prices, for instance in the regulation of maximum interest rates on deposits. Interest rate ceilings hold interest rates below levels reflecting inflation and investment opportunities and result in misallocation of resources.

To argue that financial market regulation is justified across the board because of the costs of information and information asymmetries is unjustified. Regulation impairs market forces (or it would not be regulation). Prices are also distorted by the costs of regulation. Regulation costs may be worse than information costs in slightly "inefficient" markets. Each case for regulation must be examined carefully, very carefully.

6.3 PRINCIPALS, AGENTS, AND THE THEORY OF AGENCY AND CONTRACTS

Problems caused by asymmetric information and differences in preferences and opportunities resulting in adverse selection and moral hazard can sometimes be resolved, allowing markets to work pretty well even if not as well as if there were no problems. Economists have studied a number of situations to understand how these problems can be solved by the participants. The analysis of these problems is called *agency theory*.

Agency theory is a simplified analysis of the relation between economic decision makers. Agency theory considers two classes of decision makers called *principals* and *agents*. These are the conventional terms used in this analysis and one must be careful to keep straight what characterizes the economic problem from the point of view of a principal and what is the situation of the agent. An economic solution in agency theory induces the agent to make decisions favorable (or not as harmful) to the principal.

A principal is the economic decision-maker (firm or individual) who gains or loses from the hidden action or information of the agent. In nearly all of these problems, the principal entrusts economic resources or transfers resources to an agent under some circumstances in the future. The agent may have an incentive to exploit the relationship to advantage by using hidden information or taking (or not taking) actions that would be in the interest of the principal.

In many cases the terms and conditions governing the relationship between principal and agent can reduce or eliminate danger to the principal from the information asymmetry. These terms and conditions are called a *contract*. The analysis of optimal contract terms solving agency problems is *contract theory*.

A few examples will clarify the concepts of principal and agent: Begin with auto insurance. An auto insurance company is the principal because it has committed itself to indemnifying the driver if there is an accident by paying damages. The driver is the agent in the economic analysis of this case because the driver's ability and recklessness are hidden information and the driver's actions on the road are a moral hazard affecting the principal's payment obligations. The insurance policy is the contract.

A second example is a loan. In this case, the lender is the principal because the lender transfers resources to the borrower. The borrower is the agent in this case because the borrower's understanding of the risks of the investments or actual use of the money can be hidden from the lender. Actions of the borrower once the resources are in hand are not always observable or controllable.

A third example illustrates how a financial institution can be an agent and its customer a principal. A saver turning resources over to an asset manager for investment is a principal. The asset manager in this case possesses information and can take actions not easily observable by the saver. The asset management firm in this case is the agent.

Contract theory provides an analytical approach to solving problems between principals and agents caused by information asymmetries, adverse selection and moral hazard. Subsequent chapters provide many examples of principal–agent problems arising in financial services. In this section, we want to introduce the basic logical structure and common terminology used in these analyses.

First we need to understand the sequence of events occurring in the relationship between principals and agents. Figure 6.9 provides a time line relating the activities in the value chain for financial services performed by the principal and agent. Although these activities may be performed in a different order, we start with the setting of terms and prices, which can be the announcement of a schedule of prices and terms by the principal or negotiation between the parties. Marketing and information gathering activities will typically be performed before the contract is signed. During this period, the principal is exposed to problems of adverse selection. Following the acceptance of the contract, the principal is exposed to the actions (or inaction) of the agent while performing the other activities required of financial services.

Solving Problems of Adverse Selection

In most economic relationships "good" agents do not wish to be confused with risky or inferior agents. Good agents want to avoid the higher prices they have to pay if they are pooled with poor agents in dealing with principals. If they can convince principals that they are good agents and qualify for lower costs or higher benefits, they will *signal* this to the agents. The classic economic analysis of signalling by Spence (1974) dealt with workers who signalled their higher quality and productivity by investments in education. Educational qualifications in his analysis were a signal of quality, even when education does not directly contribute to productivity.

In announcing or negotiating terms in a financial relationship, a principal may be able to reduce problems of adverse selection. For example, several alternative contracts with different prices and other contract terms can be offered to potential customers. If contract terms are carefully chosen by the principal, agent–customers may reveal aspects of themselves by the contract they choose. When contract terms offered to customers induce them to reveal hidden information about themselves, the contract is said to induce *self-revelation*.

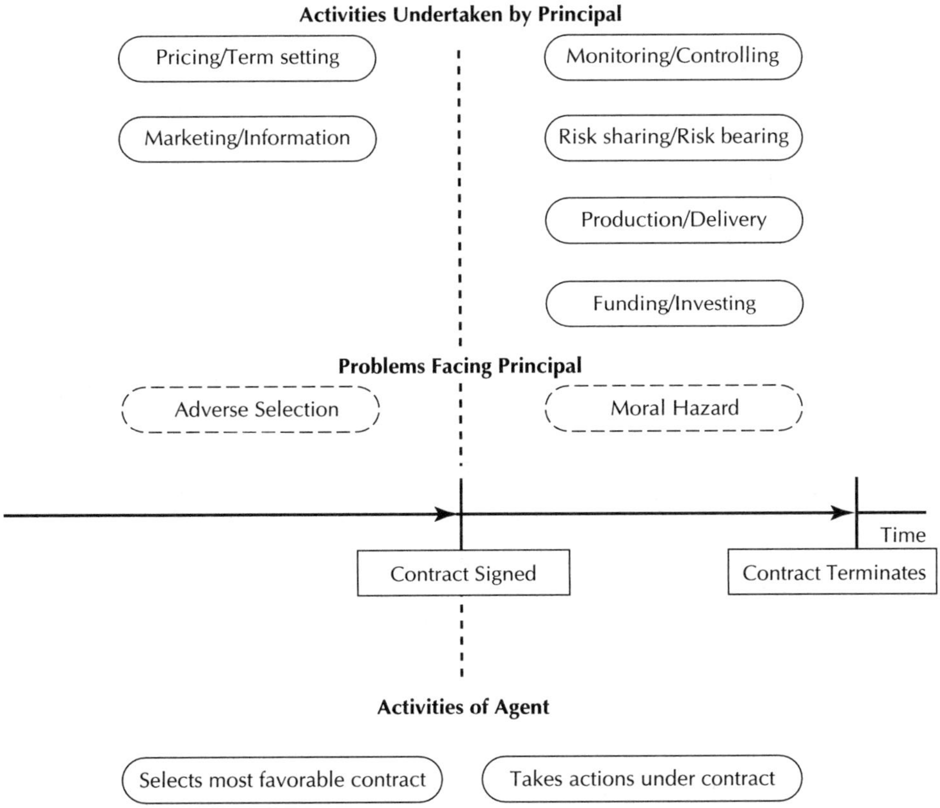

FIGURE 6.9 Activities of principles and agents

A common example illustrates how contract terms induce self-revelation of hidden information. In auto insurance, the insurance company may offer different combinations of premiums and deductible amounts on the different coverages offered in insurance contracts. A high deductible would be associated with lower premiums and low deductibles with higher premiums. Low-risk drivers believe accidents are less probable and choose the high deductibles and lower premiums thereby signalling their lower risk. High-risk drivers want low deductible insurance because they think the likelihood of their having an accident is high. High-risk drivers choose low deductibles and higher premiums, thereby signalling their low quality. The terms of the insurance contract have induced customers to signal hidden information concerning their risk type to the insurance company.

In cases where prices and terms of contracts offered by principals to agents in a financial marketplace induce self-revelation of the agents' hidden information and prices are sustainable in the market, the contract may be said to provide a *separating equilibrium*. Customers with relatively good and bad hidden information about themselves are separated in their natural pursuit of self interest by selecting different contract terms.

If contracts leading to separating equilibrium are not feasible or efficient one possibility is that the market breaks down (the service is not offered). Alternatively, the service may be offered, but only one contract type is offered with average terms reflecting both good and bad risks. In such a case, the market is said to produce a *pooling equilibrium*. Pooling equilibria may be the only outcomes possible in some situations, for example employee health insurance. In these cases the economic value from correctly identifying types of agents, as in separating equilibriums, is insufficient to separate customer types. The market may be less efficient in the allocation of resources because good customers pay more than they should and bad customers pay less then their risk characteristics deserve or it may not matter.

Contract Solutions in the Presence of Moral Hazard

Once a contract is signed, the agent may take actions that harm the principal or the agent may not work as hard as possible to benefit the principal: this is moral hazard. There are two kinds of solutions to moral hazard in agency problems. Contract terms may be written so that incentives of agents are aligned with those of the principal. In such cases the agent's rational course of action in maximizing utility or welfare will benefit the principal. A contract solution of this kind is said to be an *incentive compatible* contract.

A second solution to the problem of moral hazard is that the principal *monitors* the actions of the agent. If agreed-upon actions of the agent under various circumstances are not undertaken, the principal invokes *controls* foreseen by the contract. The difference between these two solutions is that in the first instance the agent freely chooses an optimum course of action from the point of view of the principal. In the second, the agent is forced by threat of coercion to act in the interests of the principal.

The concept of an incentive compatible contract is readily observable in everyday business life. For example, many corporate managers are given options to buy stock in their company at a fixed price below the current value of the stock as part of their compensation. Managers with stock options benefit if the stock price goes up above the fixed price, and hence their incentives are aligned with their owner–employer shareholders who want their wealth maximized.

Examples from financial services are also common. For example, health insurance often guarantees only partial coverage of claims so that an insured party bears some of the costs of medical and hospital costs associated with an illness. Since malingering thus becomes costly to the insured, vacations in hospital rooms at the insurance company's expense are not in the insured's interest. We will explore many incentive compatible contracts covering financial services in subsequent chapters.

Coercion to enforce contract terms is another but usually more costly solution to agency problems. One set of costs of enforcing contact terms is the *monitoring costs*. If the agent cannot be relied on to act in the principal's interest, the agent must be observed. This requires that actions be observed, sometimes measured, documented if proof of contract violations occur, and reported to the principal. Sometimes the information to be monitored is of a financial or technically sophisticated type and monitors have to be highly specialized. Information must be timely to be effective. Constant monitoring of agents' actions by expensive specialists, like credit officials evaluating financial statements, is costly to perform.

The fact that monitoring is costly means that specializing in certain kinds of monitoring activities may produce cost efficiencies. These efficiencies can be the source of competitive advantage in doing business with some agents. Principals may write contracts requiring monitoring activities and share their lower costs of monitoring under the terms of contracts, thus providing services at lower prices. Cost differentials in monitoring activities are considered to be an important advantage of financial institutions in certain lines of business, like bankers who specialize in monitoring the terms of credit contracts for special purpose loans.

The second set of costs required to coerce contract terms are *costs of control.* The most common costs of control are legal costs. In order to force performance on a contract or to invoke sanctions or relief covered in the contract, someone has to call a lawyer and sometimes the sheriff. Lawyers do not work for nothing. Even in cases where dispute settlement clauses in contracts do not involve the courts and lawyers, management time and attention are required in order to coerce or enforce terms of the contracts.

Examples of monitoring and control procedures are common in financial services. A good example is a loan contract or bond indenture. In this case, a trustee, usually a bank trust department, is delegated the responsibility of looking out for the interest of the bond holders, who are the principals in this case. The corporate borrower is the agent. The trustee is responsible for the enforcement of the bond indenture terms or covenants. These covenants may consist of restrictions on the corporation's ability to pay dividends or make investments or borrow more money. If the trustee discovers through monitoring activity that the indenture agreement is violated, the corporation is sued. A dramatic example of this occurred in 1989 when bondholders of RJR Nabisco represented by their trustee, Manufacturers National Bank Trust Department, sued management to enjoin them from accepting the terms of a leverage buyout.

Solution to Agency Problems and Financial Services

The relation between solutions to agency problems and the value chain introduced in Chapter 2 is very important in financial services. Information gathering activities may both reveal potential for value production in reallocation of resources among different economic agents and assess the extent of potential costs due to hidden information. Pricing and term setting in financial contracts can induce self-revelation in some cases and contract specifications may make monitoring and controlling of performance under the contract less costly in other cases. Understanding the risks of moral hazard and adverse selection can make risk bearing and sharing activities more effective. We elaborate on all these points in the rest of Part II of this book.

6.4 RULES AND REGULATIONS AND AGENCY PROBLEMS

Not all financial relationships are between two firms or individuals. In the case of routine transactions, the financial service users may be dealing with a relatively anonymous "market" or "financial system." Negotiating terms of bilateral contracts with each party to a transaction is too costly and time consuming. A main advantage of a highly developed financial system is to make complex transactions routine instead of exceptional and special. To reduce the costs of common, ordinary, and frequent activities in financial markets, alternative systems of obligations and rules often govern the activities of parties to transactions, that is, principals and agents.

One standard solution to the problem of doing routine business with unknown parties is to establish common rules or regulations to which all parties are bound. These rules are similar to clauses in contracts, and principals can monitor performance of agents in terms of the rules. Enforcement or control procedures are available by recourse to the courts or regulatory bodies.

Examples illustrate a system of rules versus contracts as a means of dealing with agency problems. When you deposit a check, you are a principal who depends on your deposit-taking institution as an agent to present the check for payment. What prevents the deposit-taking institution from taking the cost-minimizing method and amount of time to clear the check? Rules of the payments system in the *Commercial Code,* rules of clearinghouses, regulations of the Federal Reserve System, and Federal laws require presentation and payment within a certain time frame in the United States. There is no need to negotiate a contract with your bank to clear the check within a certain time period. Checking account contracts with banks obligate them to observe laws and rules governing the payments system. Failure to perform is grounds for a lawsuit. There are many lawsuits over payment and clearing items that are not routine.

Systems of rules are a means of reducing agency costs to the point where routine transactions can be performed reliably and routinely enough to be a source of value to the economy. The check clearing system, which we analyze in detail in Chapter 10, is a system that works very well, dominating alternative payment systems, like cash. There are many examples of systems of rules replacing detailed contracts in governing the relations between financial service firms and their customers. Obvious examples are to be found in the securities business, where rules about the performance of brokers make buying and selling securities routine.

Agency problems have a range of solutions, from detailed bilateral contracts to the most completely developed systems of rules and procedures. Some financial services have evolved from one end of the system to the other. An example would be stock option trading, which began as a bilateral contract business and evolved into an organized exchange with a system of rules. Stock option trading evolved from a specialized and rare business to a routine activity.

Reducing agency costs can be a source of value. We discuss many agency problems and their solutions in the chapters to follow. The point to keep in mind is that the value of controlling agency costs is derived from being able to exploit the value from differences between economic agents we discussed in the first sections of this chapter. Individuals and firms in the market have different time and risk preferences and investment opportunities. In order to exploit these differences, financial market participants must resolve the agency problems stemming from asymmetric information and moral hazard. Value can be produced by reducing agency costs and providing financial services at the lowest possible cost.

6.5 SUMMARY

The fundamental building blocks of value production in financial services are consumer preferences. Value is produced by increasing the expected utility or welfare of participants in financial markets. Because of differences in time and risk preferences and investment opportunities among financial market participants, value can be produced by financial service firms who identify and implement more efficient allocations of resources. In many cases, agency problems of adverse selection and moral hazard are caused by information asymmetries between parties to financial transactions. Relationships between parties in many financial transactions can be analyzed in terms of principal–agent analysis from economic theory. Agency problems can often be solved by contracts or by systems of rules and regulations. Solutions to agency problems involve activities in the value chain introduced in Chapter 2, like price and term setting and monitoring, and are an important source of value production for financial institutions.

DISCUSSION QUESTIONS AND EXERCISES

1. Draw curves representing the indifference curves of individuals with strongly positive and strongly negative time preference above an initial point of the same marginal rate of substitution. What would be their respective reactions to increases in interest rates? What types of consumers would you expect to display such responsiveness to interest rate changes?
2. What do you think the pattern of desired expenditure for a typical household is over the life cycle of the heads of the household, assuming they raise children and plan for retirement? What does this say about the aggregate time preference for a country with a young population? With a middle-aged or stable distribution of population? With an aging population? Can you think of countries that fit these characteristics? What is their saving/consumption behavior? Is it in line with your life-cycle expectations?
3. Draw the investment transformation curve for two individuals with \$1000 and four investment opportunities of \$250 each, yielding 10, 15, 20, and 25 percent respectively. Which projects would an individual with strongly positive time preference undertake? Strongly negative time preference? What are the economic costs of these two individuals investing in projects with different returns?
4. Draw the investment transformation curve from question 3 and allow for financial borrowing or investing at a rate of 18 percent. Where do the two individuals invest and consume now? Show where economic value has been created.

5. Who is the principal and who is the agent in the following list of financial services?
   Transaction Processing
   Insurance Services
   Credit Services
   Securities Origination, Dealing, and Brokerage
   Investment Advisory and Asset Management Services.
6. Classify the following types of information as technical, marketing, or customer specific:
   Exchange rates in London and New York
   Uses of copper in automobiles
   Demographic information on retirees in Florida
   Interest rates in Korea and Taiwan
   Details of a company's investment strategy
   An individual's plans to get married.
7. Describe the information asymmetries in the following financial services:
   Transaction Processing
   Insurance Services
   Credit Services
   Securities Origination, Dealing, and Brokerage
   Investment Advisory and Asset Management Services.
8. Discuss a financial service with which you are familiar as a contracting problem. Who is the principal and who is the agent? What types of terms and conditions are there and what purpose do they serve in solving agency problems?
9. Give examples of agency problems that have been solved by contracts and of problems that have been solved by systems of rules and regulations. What are the basic differences between these two types of problems? Is there any possibility that the example you gave of a contracting problem could evolve into a system governed by rules and regulations? Why or why not?
10. Discuss in detail the types of information about consumers that the information gathering and marketing activity in the value chain requires for financial services like checking accounts and insurance policies.

REFERENCES

AKERLOF, GEORGE. 1970. "The Market for 'Lemons'; Quality, Uncertainty and the Market Mechanism," *Quarterly Journal of Economics,* pp. 488–500.

FISHER, IRVING. 1930. *The Theory of Interest.* New York: Macmillan.

GROSSMAN, SANFORD J. and JOSEPH E. STIGLITZ. 1980. "On the Impossibility of Informationally Efficient Markets," *American Economic Review* (June), pp. 393–408.

HART, OLIVER and BENGT HOLMSTROM. 1986. "The Theory of Contracts," paper presented at the World Congress of Econometric Society, Cambridge, Massachusetts, 1985.

HIRSCHLEIFER, JACK. 1970. *Investment, Interest and Capital.* Englewood Cliffs, NJ: Prentice Hall.

MARKOWITZ, HARRY. 1952. "Portfolio Selection," *Journal of Finance* 7, pp. 77–91.

SCHILLER, ROBERT J. 1981. "The Use of Volatility Measures in Assessing Market Efficiency," *Journal of Finance* (May), pp. 291–304.

SPENCE, MICHAEL. 1974. "Job Market Signalling," *Quarterly Journal of Economics,* pp. 355–374.

TOBIN, JAMES. 1958. "Liquidity Preference as Behavior Towards Risk," *Journal of Economic Studies* 25, pp. 65–86.

CHAPTER

7

Overview of Financial Service Markets and Instruments: Credit

Introduction

Financial services are offered in increasingly competitive and dynamic global markets. Managers of financial institutions must understand the economics of financial service markets to identify value producing opportunities. In this chapter we use the credit services market as an example to answer questions important to financial institution managers in all financial service markets:

- What factors determine demand for financial services?
- How large are financial service markets?
- What determines cyclical and long-term trends in financial markets?
- What financial institutions and firms perform the activities necessary to provide financial services in these markets?
- What will determine future developments in the provision of financial services in different markets?

Credit services are a primary means of reallocating resources among decision-making units in an economy to exploit differences between time and risk preferences and investment opportunities. Credit services are uniquely important to economic development and improvement in social welfare. We examine the credit services market in detail as an example of financial services markets because of its importance to the economy and the size of the market for these services.

We begin by comparing the credit market to markets for goods and services in terms of demand and supply schedules. Next we describe the size of the United States demand for credit services and note important recent trends. The following section looks at changes in the supply of funds to credit markets. Useful credit market terminology is presented next. We conclude by looking at the how the six activities in the value chain required by credit services are performed in this dynamic and important market.

7.1 MARKETS FOR FINANCIAL SERVICES: THE CREDIT MARKET

A starting point to consider markets for financial services is to analyze them like product markets studied in microeconomics. We begin our analysis of the interaction of supply and demand in a financial service market by reviewing basic concepts using the credit market as an example. Panel A of Figure 7.1 presents a demand curve for loans, D_{loans}. The demand curve is a schedule of how much borrowers would borrow at different interest rates for loans. The interest rate is only one element in the prices and terms for credit but we concentrate on it here. Assume that the demand curve in Figure 7.1A is for loans offered by an individual firm, a small bank, or a thrift institution. The diagram shows that at 14 percent, borrowers would desire $700 (thousand or million) in loans. We discuss the determinants of loan demand in the following sections of this chapter.

If the firm offers lower interest rates on loans, borrowers want more funds and more borrowers want to borrow. How much revenue does a firm gain from additional lending at lower rates? A concept from microeconomics that answers the question is *marginal revenue*. The marginal revenue from expanded credit granted in this example, or additional revenues associated with lowering the prices on any financial service, is a key concept in the management and regulation of financial institutions. Marginal revenue in the loan example can be derived as follows: at an interest rate of 14 percent, loan demand is $700 so *total interest revenue* earned would be $98 (.14 times $700). At a lower rate, say 13 percent, according to the demand schedule the demand for loans would increase to $800, and *total interest revenue* would increase to $104. Marginal revenue is the increase in total revenue due to lower interest rates and increased loan volume. In this case marginal revenue is $104 – $98, or $6.

Marginal revenue in financial markets can also be described as a *marginal return* by dividing the marginal revenue over the increased or *marginal investment* in loans. In the example, the marginal return from lowering the rate on loans from 14 to 13 percent is 6 percent ($6 over the $100 marginal increase in loans.) The *marginal return schedule* is also shown in Panel A of Figure 7.1. Marginal return schedules always lie below the demand curve with downward sloping demand.

The shape and location of demand and marginal return schedules facing financial institutions are critical determinants of their profitability. If a firm can control the demand for its financial services by its pricing strategy, in this example by changing interest rates, marginal returns from those services will vary with the price and quantity of the service provided. If the firm estimates its demand curve and marginal revenue schedule and knows its *marginal costs* of funds, it can maximize its profits by its pricing strategy. Profit-maximizing pricing policy corresponds to the microeconomic strategy of setting *marginal cost* equal to *marginal revenue*.

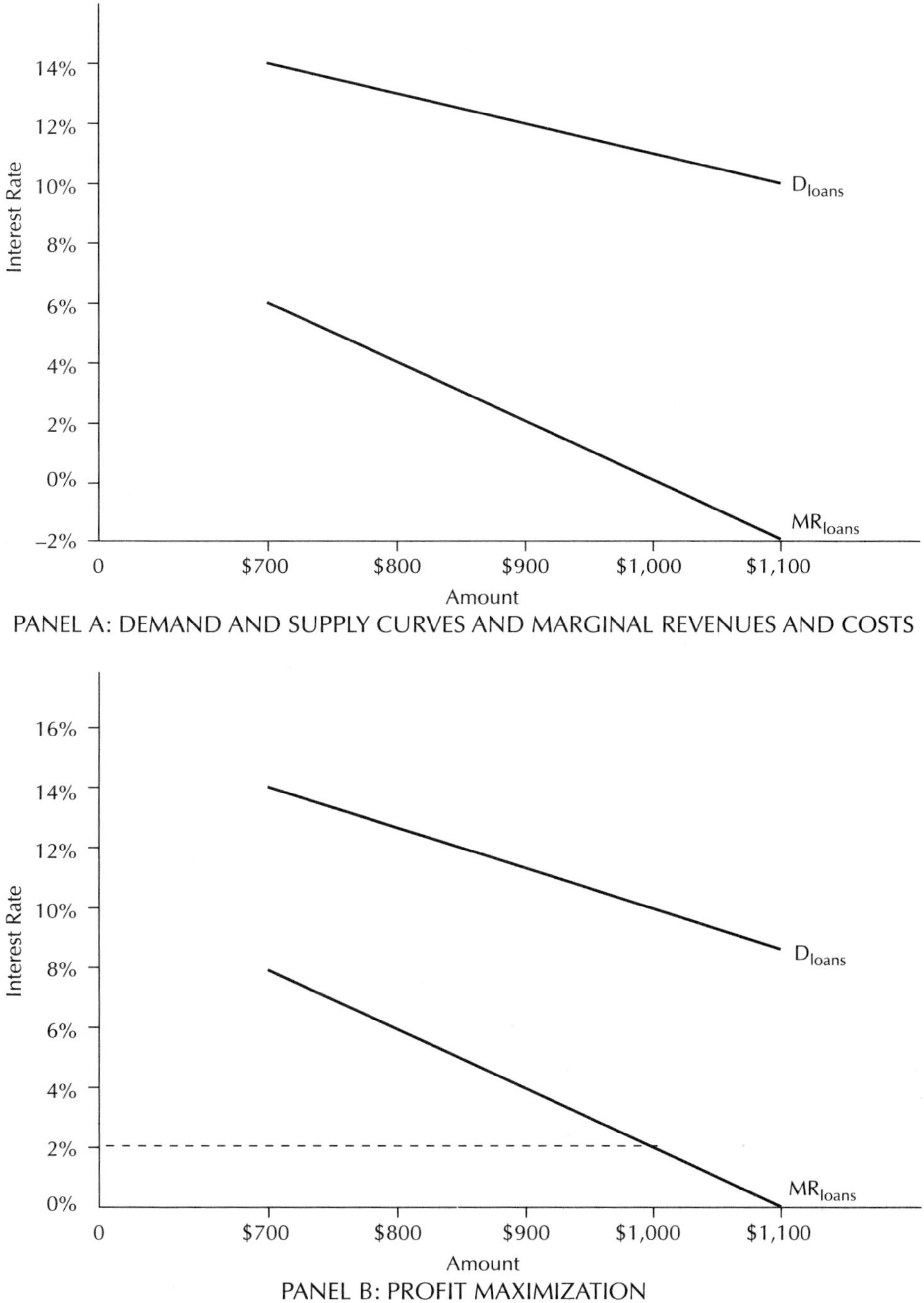

FIGURE 7.1 Demand and supply of credit funds

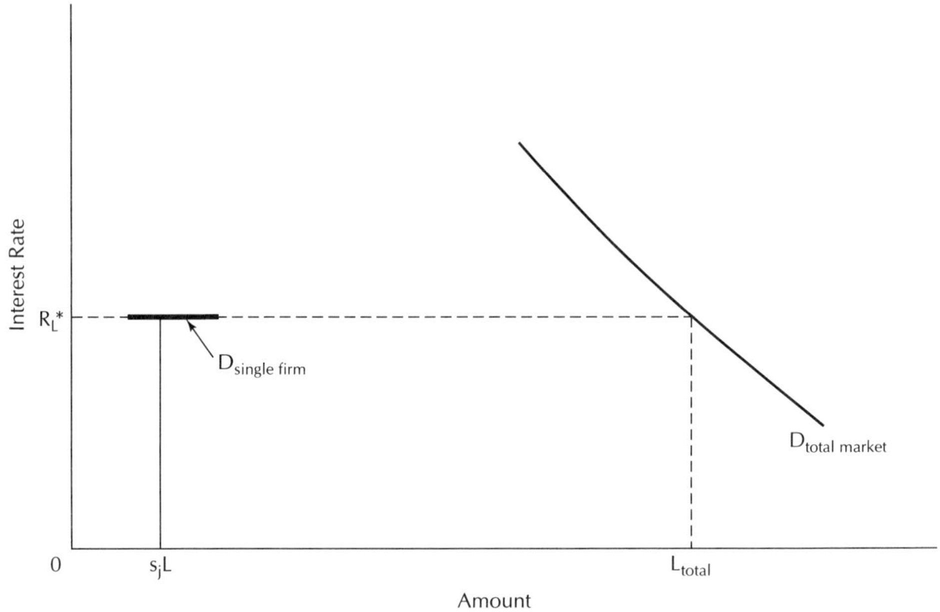

PANEL C: COMPETITIVE MARKET AND FIRM WITH NO MARKET POWER

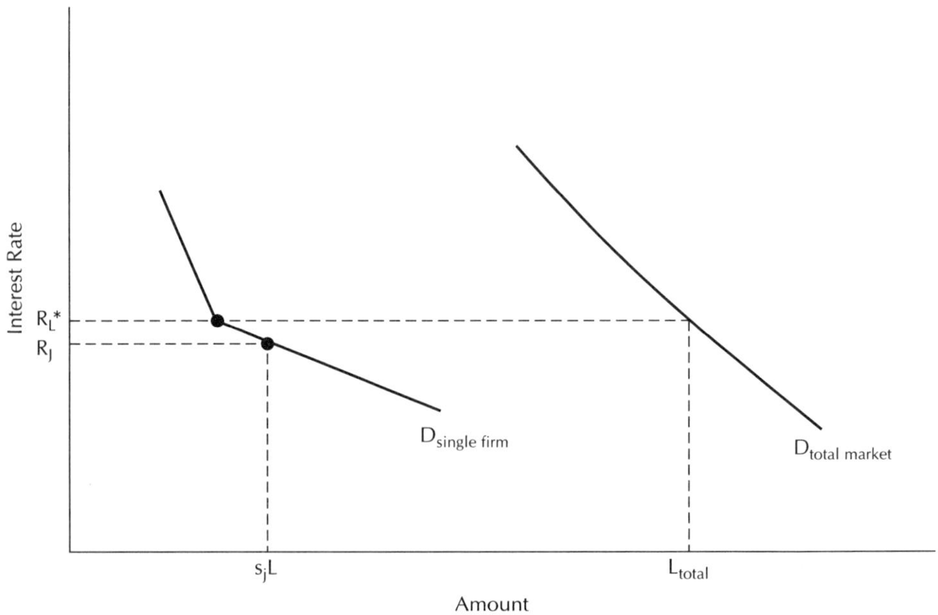

PANEL D: TOTAL MARKET AND FIRM WITH MARKET POWER

FIGURE 7.1 *(continued)*

Changing loan rates from 14 to 13 percent has a *marginal return* on the additional $100 investment in loans of 6 percent in our above example. If funds for the additional loan volume are less expensive than 6 percent, a pricing strategy lowering rates from 14 to 13 percent is profitable. In Figure 7.1, Panel B, we have shown the profit-maximizing loan pricing strategy assuming funds can be raised at a constant cost of 2 percent (the marginal *yield cost* of funds is 2 percent). The firm maximizes profits if it sets its average loan rates at 12 percent, where the marginal return on loans equals the marginal yield cost of funds. This strategy is equivalent to marginal cost equalling marginal revenue in the product markets studied in microeconomics.

The steepness of the demand curve facing a firm determines the responsiveness of a market to changes in its pricing strategy and the ability of the firm to extract profits from the market. The benchmark for a firm is a completely *competitive market.* A competitive market for loans facing a firm is shown in Panel C of Figure 7.1. The total or aggregate loan market is downward sloping and the market equilibrium rate of interest is shown on the diagram as R_L^*. The equilibrium rate is where aggregate loan demand and the supply of funds are equal. Total demand for loans would be increased if interest rates were lower in the market because of increased supply of funds.

A small individual firm faces demand conditions depending on how many competitors there are in the market. In a competitive market, there are so many competitors that tiny increases in rates the firm charges means the firm has no customers. Tiny decreases in rates mean loan demand is too much for the firm to satisfy. The firm in this case faces a *perfectly competitive* demand curve, which is horizontal. Such a demand curve is said to be *infinitely elastic* because small changes in prices produce enormous percent changes in volumes. In competitive markets, aggregate market conditions determine returns and prices but a firm cannot meaningfully use its pricing strategy to affect market share.

A widely used example of a perfectly competitive market is the market for U.S. Treasury securities. No financial institution can influence the interest rates or marginal returns from investment in Treasury securities because the market is too big and too many investors are competing. The demand curve for funds invested in Treasuries at any given point in time is horizontal for a single firm investing in Treasuries, although it is downward sloping for the market as a whole.

Departures from perfectly competitive conditions are what good managers look for. If managers of financial firms can influence the volume of demand for services by their pricing strategy, as in our example by pricing loans according to marginal returns, they have less than infinitely elastic demand or *market power.* Panel D of Figure 7.1 shows a firm with market power. This firm is able to increase its share of the market, s_j, by charging less (R_j) than the market average (R_L^*) because of market power from its downward sloping demand curve. This firm can adjust its market share by its pricing strategy and can choose a maximum profit strategy by setting loan rates such that marginal returns equal the marginal cost of funds.

Market power, if it exists, is extremely important to financial service firms. What produces market power? Our discussion of Michael Porter's analysis in Chapter 2 provided guidance in looking for answers, even though finding them is not easy. Financial firms may have limited competition because of advantages in location or government restrictions on competition. Financial service firms may offer services that are unique or differentiated, perhaps by better service or unique delivery systems. Firms may have innovative products that the competition does not yet offer.

The basic determinant of market power is the absence of substitutes for services. Erosion of market power comes from the arrival of substitutes in the market. For example, alternative sources of credit influence how much borrowers are willing to pay for loans. In deciding whether their firms have market power, managers of financial institutions must be careful to determine the availability of substitutes. Competitive advantage derives from supplying services for which there are no good substitutes, either because of convenience, offering products not available from other providers, or some other reason. Identifying potential sources of competitive advantage is the focus of this book.

The demand curve we have studied relates interest rates to credit demand, but prices, or interest rates in our discussion, are only one dimension affecting the level of demand in a market. The position of the demand curve will be affected by other factors, most importantly *income* or *activity level* factors. In a loan market, for example, an increase in the level of production or sales could shift the demand curve for credit outward at the same interest rate. The demand curve facing a firm or industry segment at any time will be a function of economic activity measures, the availability of substitutes, and other economic and noneconomic factors, like tastes or the costs of switching to substitutes.

7.2 DEMAND FOR CREDIT SERVICES

Markets for credit services have been changing radically in advanced economies in the last few decades. These changes have come more in the funding of credit services than in demand. The demand for credit is derived from evaluation of assets by borrowers, and structural shifts in the demand for credit are related to changes in the underlying asset evaluations. Holdings of real assets by the primary sectors are stable relative to shifts in the sources of supply of credit discussed in the next section. Nonetheless, in the inflationary 1980s the demand for credit backed by real estate expanded with the appreciation of real estate asset values in both the wholesale and retail markets. In this section, we assess the relative and total size of credit demand in the United States.

Wholesale or institutional markets are characterized by large institutional customers; retail markets are comprised of individuals and households. For an overall idea of the total size of these markets, businesses and governments in the United States had financial liabilities (loans and securities) outstanding of close to \$9.8 trillion in 1992, and households had liabilities of close to \$4.1 trillion. In Japan, institutional liabilities (loans and securities) were approximately \$7 trillion and personal liabilities around \$2.3 trillion. Institutional markets are relatively larger in most other countries because their retail markets are not as developed as in the United States.

Classification between wholesale and retail markets breaks down when individuals have large credit needs or complex investment situations, making them like large companies. Corporations or institutions can be very small, making their needs resemble those of sole proprietorships or individuals. No classification scheme will work without exception in a field as complicated as credit services.

Both the wholesale and retail markets for credit services entail arranging the use of borrowed resources or funds. The funds are used to acquire goods and services now and the funds are to be paid back later out of future income or investment returns. We use the classification scheme of wholesale and retail credit markets when discussing the markets for credit. At this point, we wish to stress some basic similarities between the underlying economic determinants of the demand for credit in all credit markets.

The demand for credit comes from investment opportunities for both wholesale and retail credit market customers. Some credit market observers differentiate three reasons to borrow money: *investment* in real assets; *liquidity* to make required payments; and *financial restructuring*. A little thought reveals that all three reasons for credit are variants of the same theme. They all relate to borrowers' evaluations of investment opportunities and current holdings of assets, whether the borrowers are firms or individuals.

Borrowing for real investment—as in plants and equipment or consumer durables—occurs when the investment will earn more in the value of goods and services produced than the cost of the borrowing. At a lower costs of funds, more productive investments are attractive and more credit will be demanded. The demand for loans is downward sloping with respect to interest rates, as discussed in Chapter 6 and as we drew it in Figure 7.1. Market participants' evaluation of investment opportunities are an obvious determinant of the demand for credit services.

The demand for liquidity means borrowing in order to pay bills while avoiding liquidation of assets held. In other words, owners of assets currently value holding those assets more than the option of selling the assets to pay bills. Financial restructuring means buying assets and issuing new debt or selling assets and retiring outstanding debt. Restructuring thus also represents differing valuations of assets or investments. Like the demand for real investment, liquidity and restructuring demands for credit are downward sloping in interest cost of loans.

Although demand for credit for investment, liquidity, and restructuring are similar in being based on the valuation of assets, they differ in the length of time the credit is desired. Borrowing for real investment or restructuring usually is for the longer time periods needed for assets to realize their long-run value. Borrowing for liquidity is typically for shorter time periods. The length of time for credit and purpose of the credit are not strictly linked together. Credit market observers often tell of New England knitting mills renewing their one-year loans annually for fifty years or more.

Markets for credit (or any financial service) are not always sharply separated by purpose or even by the collateral used for loans. Homeowners use the value of homes as collateral to borrow in the mortgage market for the initial purchase.

Homeowners with older mortgages often refinance their homes rather than liquidate other assets to raise cash to consume. An alternative way for homeowners to raise cash is to use equity in houses (value minus current loan balance) as collateral for *home equity loans* (Board of Governors, 1989a, 1988). In the United States, the tax advantage for home financing leads borrowers to use housing assets as collateral to finance other investments. Credit services related to housing assets cannot be separated from credit demand to acquire autos or finance education, or even from vacations charged on credit cards. The same comments apply to wholesale credit. The demand for credit cannot be related strictly to collateral: money is fungible.

Differences in the Retail and Wholesale Demand for Credit

Differences between the retail and wholesale markets for credit stem from the differences in the assets to be acquired in real investment decisions or which assets form the basis of credit for liquidity or restructuring. Wholesale customers are business firms and governments investing in plants and equipment, large public works, or stocks of inventories or customer credit (accounts receivable). Wholesale customers often operate on an enormous scale. Retail markets consist of individuals and households acquiring comparatively inexpensive assets like houses and cars but in large aggregate quantities.

Demand for Wholesale Credit Services

Of the approximately $9.8 trillion in total financial liabilities in the U.S. wholesale market in 1992, approximately one-third was credit and two-thirds were funds raised in securities markets—although the division is not exact. Some business and local government credit is called bonds but these bonds do not trade in securities markets, as we discuss in the following. We use the flow-of-funds accounts introduced in Chapter 3 to assess the size of the institutional market for credit services.

Credit is often described by its intended use. Credit for the development of large-scale investments, like mines or harbors, is called *project financing* or *construction financing*. Permanent financing of projects, arranged before or after completion of the project, often uses the productive asset as collateral, becoming *secured financing*. Secured financing takes the form of *commercial mortgages, revenue bonds, equipment certificates,* or other types of loans, notes, and bonds.

Financing for liquidity purposes is often called *working capital financing*. Working capital financing can be unsecured, with no explicit collateral, or it can be secured by working capital assets like *inventory financing, accounts receivable financing,* or in general in *asset-based financing*. *Trade credit* or *accounts payable* represents financing provided by firms to their customers.

Demands for credit services arising out of corporate restructuring have produced a variety of imaginative financial terms, such as are *junk bonds* or *high-yield bonds,* non–investment-grade bonds sold to acquire assets, and *bridge loans,* the temporary loans used to acquire corporate assets until permanent financing is obtained or sales of assets can retire the debt. *Leveraged buy-outs*

(LBOs) describes the use of debt by a firm's management or a takeover specialist to buy a firm's assets from all the other owners.

Despite the suggestive names of financing, the data available from the flow of funds do not break out the financing by purpose. A corporate bond, for example, could be used for project financing, liquidity, or restructuring. Bank loans can be term loans, for project financing, or short-term loans for liquidity purposes. The data analyzed below are intended only to provide an idea of the size of the credit services markets we are talking about.

Table 7.1 provides data giving the total amounts of different types of liabilities in the United States for the ten years 1983 to 1992 for all nonfinancial business (Panel A) and subtotals for corporate business (Panel B) and noncorporate business (Panel C) in greater detail.

Total 1992 commercial mortgages (line 15, Panel A) accounted for $1,098 billion. Flow-of-funds data indicate that most business mortgages, $832.4 billion (line 15, Panel C) are obligations of noncorporate businesses, namely partnerships. These funds are associated with real estate investment or real estate development. Likewise, the tax-exempt bonds of $114 (line 13, Panel A) are local-government-sponsored real estate development projects financed by tax-exempt debt. Based on the data in Table 7.1, it appears that in 1992 approximately $1.2 trillion of corporate credit is connected to investment in real estate projects. Table 7.1 shows that demands for credit to finance real estate stopped growing in 1989.

The connection between use of funds and type of funds is not so direct for other business credit categories, as with mortgage and tax-exempt borrowing. Corporate bonds accounting for $1,154 billion in 1992 tend to be associated with investment in business plants and equipment, as mentioned previously, but these funds could be used to retire short-term working capital financing or to restructure. The growth in this market, up $200 billion since 1989, reflects in part reduced bank lending discussed in the following.

The amount of business credit for working capital or liquidity is about $1.9 trillion in corporate credit for short-term working capital purposes from the following sources. Bank loans not elsewhere classified (n.e.c.) of $661 billion (line 16, Panel A) in 1992 are primarily short-term working capital financing.[1] Corporate issuances of bankers' acceptances, $20 billion (line 37, Panel B) in 1992 and commercial paper issuances of $107 billion (line 17, Panel A) are short-term borrowings totalling over $125 billion for liquidity or working capital financing. Trade credit, representing interfirm financing of inventories and goods in transit and a major source of business credit for working capital purposes, amounted to $797 billion (line 19, Panel A) in 1992. Another $152.8 billion in 1992 represented nonbank loans to corporate business (lines 34 and 35, Panel B) and $137.1 foreign loans to business (line 38, Panel B).

The preceding summary of credit market data for business in the United States suggests that over $1.2 trillion in corporate credit are related to real estate

[1]According to the "Terms of Bank Lending at Commercial Banks" survey of commercial and industrial loans reported in November, 1993, 89.2 percent of loans in August 1993, are short term (Board of Governors, 1989b).

TABLE 7.1 Market for Business Credit

		Panel A: All Nonfinancial Business									
		1983	*1984*	*1985*	*1986*	*1987*	*1988*	*1989*	*1990*	*1991*	*1992*
11	Total liabilities	2784.6	3182.0	3537.1	3915.3	4273.0	4672.4	5023.3	5211.8	5201.2	5290.0
12	Credit market instruments	1989.5	2303.6	2587.3	2899.8	3135.7	3374.9	3615.7	3728.5	3688.7	3693.3
13	Tax-exempt debt	83.9	104.4	127.0	117.1	116.2	116.4	115.5	115.2	114.0	114.0
14	Corporate bonds	447.0	495.1	578.2	705.4	784.1	887.2	961.1	1008.2	1086.9	1154.2
15	Mortgages	694.8	790.2	887.2	989.0	1082.8	1109.6	1164.4	1162.4	1156.1	1098.2
16	Bank loans n.e.c.	455.3	523.4	558.1	615.4	628.0	670.1	707.9	714.7	677.2	660.8
17	Commercial paper	36.8	58.5	72.2	62.9	73.8	85.7	107.1	116.9	98.5	107.1
18	Other loans	271.8	332.0	364.6	409.9	450.8	505.9	559.7	611.2	556.0	559.3
19	Trade debt	482.2	520.0	557.3	570.7	617.5	686.3	720.6	750.6	753.4	796.9
20	Taxes payable	55.7	60.3	60.6	66.1	71.7	76.4	77.9	73.5	64.6	72.0
21	Miscellaneous liabilities	257.2	298.1	331.7	378.7	448.0	334.8	609.2	659.1	694.5	727.3

*Data are in billions of dollars.

SOURCE: Flow of Funds, Board of Governors of the Federal Reserve System, Washington, D.C. 20551.

Panel B: Nonfinancial Corporate Business

		1983	1984	1985	1986	1987	1988	1989	1990	1991	1992
25	Total liabilities	1805.6	2055.1	2276.3	2561.2	2844.1	3170.4	3453.1	3610.9	3620.7	3730.7
24	Credit market instruments	1149.0	1340.2	1505.2	1729.0	1900.6	2090.6	2281.7	2374.6	2361.6	2405.3
25	Tax-exempt debt	83.9	104.4	127.0	117.1	116.2	116.4	115.5	115.2	114.0	114.0
26	Corporate bonds	447.0	495.1	578.2	705.4	784.1	887.2	961.1	1008.2	1086.9	1154.2
27	Mortgages	115.0	123.5	114.3	147.1	197.5	195.9	219.0	208.6	209.2	186.0
28	Home mortgages	12.0	12.6	13.3	14.0	14.7	15.4	16.0	16.6	17.0	17.6
29	Multifamily	13.8	14.4	15.0	15.8	16.5	17.1	17.8	18.3	18.8	19.4
30	Commercial	89.2	96.5	86.0	117.3	166.4	163.4	185.2	173.7	173.4	149.0
31	Bank loans n.e.c.	340.9	391.1	424.1	473.7	482.4	519.3	553.5	555.4	530.5	518.5
32	Commercial paper	36.8	58.5	72.2	62.9	73.8	85.7	107.1	116.9	98.5	107.1
33	Other loans	125.5	167.6	189.4	222.8	246.6	286.1	325.5	370.5	322.6	325.5
34	Savings institutions	5.8	10.3	14.7	19.9	20.6	24.6	23.5	17.2	9.7	4.5
35	Finance companies	56.7	68.9	79.4	88.6	106.9	122.7	135.1	146.8	146.3	148.3
36	U.S. government	10.4	11.6	14.2	14.8	11.5	9.9	9.6	8.8	7.9	7.9
37	Acceptance liab. to banks	27.6	30.4	28.3	28.1	32.6	32.6	35.8	29.2	23.3	20.4
38	Foreign	24.9	46.3	52.8	71.4	75.2	96.3	120.3	165.9	130.8	137.1
39	ABS issuers	–	–	–	–	–	–	1.0	2.7	4.4	7.3
40	Taxes payable	38.6	42.2	39.0	42.8	47.9	49.6	46.5	41.5	32.1	38.9
41	Trade debt	418.3	452.0	486.0	499.7	539.6	598.7	629.3	658.6	663.3	698.5
42	Miscellaneous liabilities	199.7	220.7	246.0	289.8	356.1	431.5	495.7	536.2	563.7	588.0
43	Fgn. direct invest. in US	158.3	179.2	195.9	235.2	299.3	370.1	423.3	468.4	475.1	491.2
44	Pen. fund contr. payable	41.3	41.5	50.1	54.6	56.8	61.4	72.4	67.7	88.7	96.8

*Data are in billions of dollars.

SOURCE: Flow of Funds, Board of Governors of the Federal Reserve System, Washington, D.C. 20551.

TABLE 7.1 (*continued*)

Panel C: All Nonfinancial Business

		1983	*1984*	*1985*	*1986*	*1987*	*1988*	*1989*	*1990*	*1991*	*1992*
12	Total liabilities	772.5	922.5	1072.8	1188.1	1275.1	1353.3	1424.4	1455.9	1433.5	1410.5
13	Credit market instruments	652.1	775.5	908.7	1014.8	1090.8	1150.4	1199.6	1219.0	1192.3	1152.9
14	Mortgages	466.1	554.3	667.0	746.8	797.5	830.6	865.0	875.5	867.8	832.4
15	Home mortgages	94.6	102.2	112.5	119.4	126.1	132.5	138.7	144.7	149.3	156.5
16	Multifamily	146.2	170.4	199.6	235.1	258.6	273.9	286.5	287.2	284.2	272.5
17	Commercial	225.2	281.7	354.9	392.3	412.9	424.2	439.8	443.6	434.3	403.4
18	Bank loans n.e.c.	75.5	92.4	98.5	110.5	116.6	121.0	123.6	126.5	112.2	107.6
19	Other loans	110.6	128.8	143.2	157.6	176.7	198.8	211.1	217.1	212.4	212.9
20	Taxes payable	17.1	18.2	21.6	23.3	23.9	26.8	31.4	32.0	32.5	33.1
21	Trade debt	45.8	51.5	56.9	61.1	68.6	72.8	79.8	81.9	77.9	85.0
22	Miscellaneous liabilities	57.5	77.4	85.7	88.9	91.9	103.3	113.6	123.0	130.8	139.6

*Data are in billions of dollars.

SOURCE: Flow of Funds, Board of Governors of the Federal Reserve System, Washington, D.C. 20551.

investment, about $1.9 trillion to working capital financing not counting trade credit, and some part of the $1.1 trillion dollars in corporate bonds is related to long-term investment projects. A large portion of corporate bonds held by institutional investors like insurance companies is more like credit than securities financing as we discuss in the following.

Governments represent another set of wholesale customers. Governments borrow to finance real investments like roads and schools. They also borrow to pay workers like teachers and hospital employees in expectation of future tax collections. Government liquidity needs represent the absence of a ready market for the true assets of value for the government: future tax receipts. Table 7.2 provides flow-of-funds data on the aggregate borrowing of state and local governments in the United States, indicating total liabilities of $1 trillion in 1992, of which $926 billion are tax-exempt credit market instruments that are not short-term. The remainder of state and local government credit is short-term borrowing of about $56 billion.

In interpreting the measures of the wholesale credit market activity discussed above, three things should be kept in mind. First, institutional investment activity in the aggregate could be financed with internally generated funds from profits and depreciation for businesses and tax receipts for state and local governments. In 1987, for example, the flow of funds estimated business internal funds at $353 billion while business investment was $322 billion, and state and local governments ran budget surpluses. Wholesale credit market activity reflects differences in investment activities and preferences among firms and government units and a reallocation of investable funds. Second, money is fungible, which means that borrowing for investment looks just like borrowing for liquidity or restructuring in terms of the data. Third, credit totals outstanding do not necessary reflect financial service firms' activity at any point in time. Levels may reflect past activities and may not produce transactions in a given time period. Flow data may reflect activity better but flows are net of repayments and can understate or overstate activity.

Retail Market Demand for Credit Services

Retail customers consist of households or families and individuals. Retail customers demand credit services to implement consumption or investment plans that cannot be financed out of their current income or sales of assets. Most retail investment consists of housing or consumer durables. Table 7.3 provides information on the accumulated borrowing of the household sector, again from the flow-of-funds accounts for the United States.

Retail borrowing can be divided into two basic classes. The first class of borrowing is directed at investment in major consumer investment goods, specifically housing, automobiles, and other consumer durables. These credit needs are met by loans secured by the purchased asset, like a home mortgage. Table 7.3 demonstrates that the household sector's most important asset is housing—with $2,748.5 billion (line 28) in home mortgages outstanding in 1992. The second largest item, other installment credit of $756.9 billion (line 29), represents purchases of consumer

TABLE 7.2 Market for Government Credit

		1983	*1984*	*1985*	*1986*	*1987*	*1988*	*1989*	*1990*	*1991*	*1992*
12	Total Liabilities	412.6	449.3	584.4	645.2	730.2	781.4	847.6	905.1	957.8	1017.4
13	Credit market instruments	391.7	427.4	561.4	620.4	703.6	752.5	816.1	870.5	932.8	992.2
14	Tax-exempt securities	380.8	408.8	534.6	593.4	678.7	743.5	807.3	860.9	922.8	982.3
15	Short-term	21.3	17.6	18.9	23.1	29.3	39.2	38.8	45.6	52.4	56.2
16	Other	359.6	391.2	515.7	570.3	649.4	704.4	768.5	815.3	870.4	926.1
17	U.S. government loans	10.9	18.4	26.8	27.3	24.9	9.0	8.8	9.6	10.0	9.9
18	Trade debt	20.9	21.9	23.0	24.6	26.6	28.8	31.5	34.6	24.9	25.2

*Data are in billions of dollars.
SOURCE: Flow of Funds, Board of Governors of the Federal Reserve System, Washington, D.C. 20551.

TABLE 7.3 Market for Consumer Credit

	1983	*1984*	*1985*	*1986*	*1987*	*1988*	*1989*	*1990*	*1991*	*1992*
26 Total Liabilities	1803.0	2015.5	2325.6	2593.5	2871.2	3175.4	3481.7	3706.2	3896.6	4114.0
27 Credit market instruments	1722.4	1935.4	2223.7	2483.5	2771.8	3069.4	3371.4	3594.8	3762.7	3976.0
28 Home mortgages	1042.8	1220.2	1378.8	1573.7	1795.3	2007.8	2225.8	2419.4	2580.2	2748.5
29 Installment cons. credit	374.5	449.5	526.2	581.1	618.5	673.3	736.3	752.9	749.1	756.9
30 Other consumer credit	63.2	69.8	75.3	78.0	73.5	68.8	63.2	60.1	50.9	52.3
31 Tax-exempt debt	41.0	51.2	81.3	79.1	78.2	79.5	81.9	86.0	94.8	101.0
32 Other mortgages	38.9	41.4	43.8	49.9	82.2	109.2	122.6	133.5	144.1	153.8
33 Bank loans n.e.c.	35.6	23.9	34.0	32.2	31.7	34.3	42.9	33.1	23.7	35.5
34 Other loans	76.5	79.4	84.3	89.4	92.4	96.5	98.6	109.8	119.9	127.9
35 Security credit	34.2	31.8	50.7	57.4	41.8	43.5	42.5	38.8	55.1	53.3
36 Trade credit	30.3	33.1	36.0	38.7	42.5	47.2	51.4	56.2	60.7	65.1
37 Deferred and unsold life insurance premiums	16.1	15.1	15.2	13.9	15.1	15.5	16.4	16.5	18.2	19.6

*Data are in billions of dollars.
SOURCE: Flow of Funds, Board of Governors of the Federal Reserve System, Washington, D.C. 20551.

durables, primarily automobiles. Home mortgages increased slightly, from 61 to 67 percent of household liabilities, and durable financing fell from 21 to 18 percent between 1983 and 1992.

Other forms of consumer borrowing are not directly linked to purchases of investment goods. Total consumer credit not in the form of installment loans amounted to $216 billion in 1992 (lines 30, 33 and 34). This represents credit card loans, checking account overdraft loans, and other types of loans to consumers. We can associate these loans with liquidity demand for credit. Although consumer credit demands are seen to be largely associated with investment demand for housing and consumer durables, the same considerations of fungibility associated with consumer borrowings must be noted as with corporations. Since the Tax Reform Act of 1986, mortgage borrowing is tax advantaged relative to other consumer credit (Board of Governors, 1989a).

Demands for retail credit services for major consumer investments tend to follow patterns in the demand for those investment goods. For example, housing demand fluctuates a great deal over the business cycle and so does the demand for home loans or mortgages. Other factors influence credit market activity. The decline in interest rates unleashed massive mortgage refinancing activity with little construction in 1993. These developments may be traced in the flow of funds but activity can be understated in net flow data.

7.3 SUPPLY OF CREDIT SERVICES

The funding activity in credit services consists of advancing resources to borrowers. Funding in credit services has traditionally been tied to risk bearing as well. Lenders bear two types of risk: *interest rate risk* and *performance risk* (often called *credit* or *default risk*). Changes in interest rates cause risk to profitability in terms of the spread on the credit arrangement over the cost of funds or in terms of the value of the debt instruments. Performance risks in credit relationships come from risk of default or delayed (or accelerated) payments, all of which affect the ultimate yield on the credit advanced.

Credit services have traditionally been supplied by firms falling into neat categories. For example, commercial banks specialized in meeting liquidity or working-capital financing needs of business firms. In traditional credit service firms like commercial banks, arranging the credit and funding the loans were linked. Commercial banks financed the working capital needs of businesses using deposits as the main source of funds. In this traditional credit channel, savings in the form of deposits flowed into investment in working capital financing by banks. This credit flow is associated with the typical bank balance sheet we discussed in Chapter 3.

Financial firms that originate and hold credit instruments are called *portfolio investors*. Banks hold commercial loans in their portfolios and are called *portfolio lenders* in commercial loans. As portfolio lenders, banks perform funding activity for loans and bear interest rate and credit risks associated with the loan. Traditionally, banks making fixed rate loans to borrowers for portfolio purposes did not shift interest rate and credit risks. Similarly, insurance companies were traditional portfolio lenders to corporations in the form of privately placed long-term bonds.

In the retail market, savings institutions have been the traditional portfolio lenders in residential home mortgages. Savings institutions raise substantial funds in the form of savings deposits, and make portfolio investments in home loans. Traditionally, savings and loans funded mortgages and bore interest and credit risks.

Government policy in the United States concerning mortgage markets fostered the development of secondary markets allowing easy sales and purchases of outstanding debt instruments through the development of mortgage-backed securities. Easier sale of mortgages, together with deregulation, has made traditional savings institution portfolio lending in mortgages only a small part of a much larger and more dynamic picture. The mortgage market has been a path-breaking market in separating the funding, risk-bearing, and other activities associated with credit services, as we will discuss below.

The process of separate provision of the activities in credit services is called *unbundling* of credit services. It is an important development in the financial services industry and has led, increasingly, to specialization of activities in credit markets. We discuss the implications of this unbundling of the various activities in the value chain extensively in the sections to follow.

Funding and Risk-Bearing in the Wholesale Credit Market

Corporate and government borrowers historically obtained short-term financing from commercial banks or trade credit and long-term financing from the corporate bond market and private placements with insurance companies. Table 7.4 provides data on sources of financing to corporate and non-corporate business over the last decade. Trade debt and bank loans in 1992 still represent close to $1.3 trillion in financing for business. These items grew rapidly between 1983 and 1988 to levels of $671 and $641 billion, respectively, but bank loans leveled off during the economic slowdown to 1992.

Nontraditional sources of funds for business credit are seeing much more rapid growth than bank and trade financing. Extraordinary growth is seen in nonfinancial businesses' reliance on short-term open market borrowings in the form of commercial paper, growing from $36.8 in 1983 to $107.1 billion in 1992. Before the economic slowdown in 1990, tax-exempt bonds increased from $83.9 in 1983 to $115.5 billion in 1989. Finance company loans more than doubled from a level of $56.7 billion in 1983 to $135.1 billion in 1989 with continued growth to 1992 to $148.3 billion. Foreign credit to business in the United States went from $24.9 billion in 1983 to $137.1 billion in 1992. Nontraditional sources of funds account for business credit of nearly $500 billion in 1992 institutional credit, more than quadruple 1983 levels.

Other sources of institutional credit also grew rapidly over the period. Table 7.4 shows that corporate bonds, largely nonrated or junk bonds, grew from $447 billion in 1983 to $1,154.2 billion in 1992. Table 7.4 shows that major purchasers of corporate bonds were pension funds holding $444.5 billion in 1992, mutual

TABLE 7.4 Supply of Funds to Institutional Borrowers: Business

	1983	*1984*	*1985*	*1986*	*1987*	*1988*	*1989*	*1990*	*1991*	*1992*
Bank loans n.e.c.										
Nonfarm noncorporate business	75.5	92.4	98.5	110.5	116.6	121.0	123.6	126.5	112.2	107.6
Corporate business	340.9	391.1	424.1	473.7	482.4	519.3	553.5	555.4	530.5	518.5
Trade credit										
Nonfarm noncorporate business	45.8	51.5	56.9	61.1	68.6	72.8	79.8	81.9	77.9	85.0
Corporate business	418.3	452.0	486.0	499.7	539.6	598.7	629.3	658.6	663.3	698.5
Commercial paper										
Nonfinancial business	36.8	58.5	72.2	62.9	73.8	85.7	107.1	116.9	98.5	107.1
Funding corporations	25.7	26.1	35.6	54.1	72.5	111.6	125.4	137.9	124.3	135.7
Finance companies	60.5	73.1	102.7	124.3	135.0	152.1	160.7	165.3	159.5	156.4
Tax-exempt Bonds and Loans	83.9	104.4	127.0	117.1	116.2	116.4	115.5	115.2	114.0	114.0
Other loans										
Savings institutions loans										
Noncorporate business	5.8	10.3	14.7	19.9	20.4	24.6	23.5	17.2	9.7	4.5
Corporate business	5.8	10.3	14.7	19.9	20.4	24.6	23.5	17.2	9.7	4.5
Finance company loans										
Noncorporate business	56.7	68.9	79.4	88.6	106.9	122.7	135.1	146.8	146.5	148.3
Corporate business	56.7	68.9	79.4	88.6	106.9	122.7	135.1	146.8	146.5	148.3
Foreign loans to non-financial business	24.9	46.3	52.8	71.4	73.2	96.3	120.5	165.9	130.8	137.1
Corporate bonds	447.0	495.1	578.2	705.4	784.1	887.2	961.1	1008.2	1096.9	1154.2
Commercial mortgages										
Nonfarm noncorporate business	225.2	281.7	354.9	392.3	412.9	424.2	439.8	443.6	434.3	403.4
Corporate business	89.2	96.5	86.0	117.3	166.4	163.4	185.2	173.7	173.4	149.0
Purchasers of Corporate Bonds										
Life insurance companies	219.1	242.8	280.6	321.4	388.3	457.5	511.0	566.9	595.1	653.9
Other insurance companies	21.6	25.7	33.9	48.0	55.5	65.7	79.3	89.2	97.2	97.9
Private pension funds	107.9	123.4	155.1	178.3	190.1	203.9	226.1	235.5	275.7	293.1
State and local government pension funds	95.0	107.7	117.4	124.7	103.0	125.7	158.4	147.1	150.3	151.4
Mutual funds	13.0	16.5	20.1	46.9	54.2	68.4	74.1	87.6	100.5	128.9
Closed-end funds	2.6	2.2	2.5	3.9	6.1	15.4	16.3	14.6	12.7	14.6
Purchases of Open Market Paper (Commercial Paper and Bankers' Acceptance)										
Life insurance companies	20.4	22.3	20.8	24.5	27.1	32.2	36.6	27.7	20.8	16.1
Private pension funds	17.2	19.6	19.9	28.2	33.8	36.3	26.3	24.9	20.8	18.1
State and local government pension funds	–	–	–	–	21.6	19.8	18.6	22.3	29.4	30.2
Mutual funds	4.0	6.4	4.1	9.4	12.6	21.4	19.6	25.9	21.5	29.3
Money market mutual funds	66.2	98.0	99.1	105.3	111.3	1298.1	186.6	206.7	191.9	174.7

SOURCE: Flow of Funds, Board of Governors of the Federal Reserve, September 17, 1993.

funds holding $128.9 billion, and insurance companies, holding $653.9 billion. All these holdings represent rapid growth in total amounts in the share of funding for business credit.

One example illustrates the shift in funding for business credit in the last decade. Money market mutual funds' purchases of open market paper, namely bankers' acceptances and commercial paper, totaled $66.2 billion in 1983. By 1992, holding of open market paper totaled $174.7 billion. This reflects an important shift in household savings as consumers have invested in money market funds rather than banks. Much of the growth in finance company lending to institutional customers is also financed with commercial paper. Commercial paper held by mutual funds and issued by finance companies is eroding traditional lenders' share of the business credit market such as bank portfolio lending.

These shifts in the financing of credit to business have changed the role of traditional participants in the business credit market and created new roles for entrants. An important role in making credit available to business now is finding nontraditional investors willing to fund the loan as a portfolio investment. This activity is called *placing* the loan. For example, in 1989 Chase Manhattan Bank ran an advertisement in the *Wall Street Journal* stating, "One bank believes no possibility of finding investors for private placements is too remote. That's why we have placement power in every corner of the world" (November 15, 1989, pp. A13–A15).

Traditional portfolio lenders now often seek other investors, often nontraditional investors, to fund and share the risks of credit to business. Other lenders provide some of the funds in *loan participations*. In other cases, loans are sold individually in *loan sales* or loans of a similar type are combined into *loan pools*. Pools diversify credit risks, and claims on pools of loans can be sold to a number of investors. Loan placements, participations, sales, and pools are now routine parts of the provision of credit services to business.

The role of traditional portfolio lending by deposit-taking institutions and insurance companies is being redefined by the institutionalization of savings, globalization, and deregulation of the financial services industry. Participants in business credit markets need acute vision to perceive emerging trends in credit demands and sources of investable funds in order to keep on top of developments in these dynamic markets. Trends and developments in advanced economies like the United States can foreshadow developments in other countries and be useful in formulating strategies in those markets.

Funding Retail Credit Market

Revolutionary changes in the sources of residential mortgage funding have occurred in advanced economies like the United States and the United Kingdom in the last three decades. In the United States, total home mortgages increased from $1.2 trillion in 1983 to $2.9 trillion in 1992, as shown in Table 7.5. Table 7.5 demonstrates that nearly $1 trillion of that growth came in the form of government-related mortgage pools. Purchasers of mortgage pools, largely institutional investors, represent nontraditional sources of funds to this market. There were

TABLE 7.5 Suppliers of Funds for Retail Borrowers

		1983	*1984*	*1985*	*1986*	*1987*	*1988*	*1989*	*1990*	*1991*	*1992*
5	Total Home Mortgages	1199.4	1335.0	1504.6	1707.1	1936.1	2155.6	2380.5	2580.6	2746.6	2922.5
6	Households	74.6	68.5	80.7	67.6	107.7	124.2	144.7	114.4	100.6	109.0
7	Nonfarm noncorp. business	10.0	13.3	13.9	16.1	15.0	17.1	17.1	16.9	16.6	16.3
8	State and local governments	33.7	39.2	45.0	49.0	50.1	52.6	57.3	60.9	62.9	62.3
9	U.S. government	22.9	23.5	24.4	24.1	20.8	21.0	21.3	37.9	37.1	35.1
10	Govt. spons. enterprises	83.7	94.4	106.6	101.4	98.9	104.7	110.0	115.3	126.2	156.7
11	Fed. related mortgage pools	239.5	283.0	361.5	519.7	654.0	723.6	842.3	990.4	1126.7	1241.9
12	Commercial banking	182.5	196.2	213.4	235.8	276.3	314.3	368.6	458.0	488.2	513.7
13	Thrift institutions	490.4	540.4	574.1	587.4	603.1	679.7	674.4	625.8	588.8	537.5
14	Savings institutions	483.4	531.1	561.7	568.3	573.2	641.6	631.0	577.6	538.4	489.6
15	Credit Unions	7.0	9.2	12.4	19.3	29.9	38.1	43.4	48.2	50.4	47.9
16	Insurance	22.0	21.6	20.0	21.3	19.0	17.6	21.2	24.7	22.4	22.4
17	Life insurance companies	15.3	14.1	12.4	12.8	13.2	11.2	12.2	13.2	11.5	11.4
18	Private pension funds	2.8	3.7	3.9	5.3	2.3	3.0	5.6	8.2	7.1	7.5
19	St. Elec. govt. rtr. funds	3.9	3.8	3.7	3.2	3.5	3.4	3.4	3.5	3.7	3.4
20	Finance companies	20.5	23.8	28.6	34.2	42.2	47.3	53.8	65.5	65.8	68.4
21	Mortgage companies	14.3	15.7	18.5	29.5	17.7	14.9	20.3	13.1	23.3	22.9
22	REITs	0.2	0.2	0.3	0.3	0.3	0.4	0.4	0.4	0.4	0.8
23	ABS issuers	–	11.0	13.0	16.6	27.8	34.9	43.3	53.3	84.0	132.0
24	Bank personal trusts	4.9	4.4	4.5	4.0	3.4	3.4	3.8	3.9	3.7	3.6

*Data are in billions of dollars.

SOURCE: Flow of Funds, Board of Governors of the Federal Reserve System, Washington, D.C. 20551.

		1983	1984	1985	1986	1987	1988	1989	1990	1991	1992
4	Total Consumer Credit	437.6	519.3	601.6	659.1	692.3	742.1	799.5	813.0	799.9	809.2
5	Installment credit	374.5	449.5	526.2	581.1	618.5	673.3	736.3	752.9	749.1	756.9
6	Nonfarm noncorp. business	2.3	2.5	2.7	2.7	2.9	3.0	2.7	2.7	2.5	2.6
7	Nonfin. corporate business	19.0	20.9	23.9	26.9	32.7	38.5	39.6	40.9	37.4	39.3
8	Commercial banking	172.0	211.6	245.1	266.8	287.2	324.8	342.8	347.1	340.7	331.9
9	Savings institutions	24.0	36.6	49.5	56.6	60.8	63.4	63.3	52.2	46.0	43.5
10	Credit unions	53.5	66.2	72.7	77.1	81.0	88.3	93.1	93.1	92.7	97.6
11	Finance companies	103.7	111.7	132.4	151.0	154.0	155.3	144.6	138.0	126.3	121.7
12	ABS issuers	–	–	–	–	–	–	50.2	79.0	103.6	120.4
13	Noninstallment credit	63.2	69.8	75.3	78.0	73.5	68.8	63.2	60.1	50.9	52.3
14	Nonfarm noncorp. business	2.8	3.0	3.2	3.5	3.7	3.9	4.3	4.4	4.1	4.3
15	Nonfin. corporate business	11.2	11.9	12.8	13.9	14.8	15.6	17.1	17.5	16.6	17.3
16	Commercial banking	41.7	47.2	51.3	54.3	50.5	46.0	39.2	36.6	29.3	30.3
17	Savings institutions	7.5	7.6	8.1	6.3	4.5	3.3	2.6	1.6	0.9	0.4

*Data are in billions of dollars.

SOURCE: Flow of Funds, Board of Governors of the Federal Reserve System, Washington, D.C. 20551.

shifts in traditional portfolio investors: commercial banks' investments in home mortgages increased over $500 billion and their market share went from 18 percent to more than 22 percent. This $1.8 trillion dollar growth in ten years has provided a lot of profit opportunities for participants in the mortgage market.

Growth of mortgage pools has been accompanied by the unbundling of mortgage loan origination from mortgage funding. Mortgage investors acquire mortgages from loan originators like savings institutions, banks, and mortgage bankers, or participate in pools established by investment bankers or government agencies. The mortgage market is the pathbreaking credit market in the United States. Innovations in the origination and servicing of loans separate from funding of loans first seen in the mortgage market are now seen in other credit markets, specifically in installment credit and credit card lending.

Commercial bank investments in installment credit has been flat in the United States since 1989, as shown in Table 7.5. Bank credit for retail consumer durable purchases still represents the largest market share with $331.9 billion, as finance company investments have fallen from a peak of $155.3 billion in 1988 to $121.7 billion in 1992. The largest growth in installment credit comes from asset-backed securities, similar to mortgage pools, whose market share went from 0 to 14.8 percent from 1983 to 1992, reaching a total of $120.4 billion in 1992. The market share of thrift institutions, including savings institutions, authorized to make consumer durable loans in 1980 with the Deregulation Act, went from $77.5 to $141.1 billion over the same period.

Consumer installment credit from finance companies is funded with commercial paper. Since commercial paper is a major investment of money market mutual funds, mutual funds channel savings into installment lending, short-circuiting traditional portfolio lenders like banks raising funds in the form of deposits. Understanding the economics of new credit channels is essential to participants in the credit markets. Tomorrow's short-circuits are tomorrow's opportunities.

7.4 ORGANIZING ACTIVITIES TO PROVIDE CREDIT SERVICES

In this section we present an overview of how the six value-producing activities associated with credit services introduced in Chapter 2 are performed by financial institutions and financial market participants. Those activities are:

1. setting terms and pricing
2. communicating and marketing
3. producing and delivering
4. controlling and monitoring
5. funding and/or investing
6. risk bearing and/or risk sharing.

We build the discussion around examples of traditional and innovative ways of organizing credit services. The revolution in financial services can be interpreted as a reorganization of these activities. As we have mentioned, the activities can be unbundled to achieve greater economic efficiency. First we introduce some terminology and then move to detailed examples.

Terminology Used in Credit Services

Most credit services are described in legal documents covering the credit arrangement. Loans are typically covered in a *loan agreement,* a form of contract, bonds in an *indenture,* and mortgages in a *mortgage contract.* Even in cases where there is no written contract, industry practice and the local Commercial Code will define obligations and responsibilities, as with trade credit. The purpose of this section is to introduce useful terminology that describes credit relationships. We discuss the usage in the institutional and retail markets in general terms and give specific examples below.

Retail and wholesale credit arrangements have five basic types of prices or terms:

1. interest rate
2. time period or maturity
3. type of collateral
4. fees
5. covenants or conditions.

In establishing prices and terms in credit arrangements, competitive conditions will set limits within which offers or negotiating takes place, but within those limits there are no barriers to the terms that credit service firms can offer potential customers. In Chapter 8 we discuss how pricing and term setting in credit contracts can produce value in credit negotiations. Our detailed discussion of examples below illustrates the range of prices and terms typical in credit arrangements.

Institutional Credit Service Activities

Financial contracts issued by firms or governments to raise funds are usually called loans, notes, bonds, or debentures. The distinction between loans and other debt instruments has never been clear and is becoming less clear. Loans are usually a credit arrangement involving two parties, whereas bonds and debentures are debt instruments that can be more easily assumed by third parties. Bond contracts often designate third party trustees to monitor and control terms of the debt instruments where these activities are the responsibility of the lender in the case of loans. More and more often loans are sold outright or on a participation basis, thereby becoming more like bonds.

Unsecured credit does not require collateral and is the most prestigious source of funding for borrowers. Firms raising funds without collateral on the basis of their names or credit standing are the most creditworthy borrowers. Most firms and many governments must provide security for the funds raised. Collateral entails costly documentation, reporting, monitoring, and control activities. Secured credit is less desirable for borrowers than unsecured credit.

An outline of institutional credit arrangements is presented in Table 7.6. The table is divided into *short-term* (under one year) and *long-term* arrangements and *unsecured* credit (no collateral) and *secured* credit. Table 7.7 classifies fees charged to institutional borrowers under terms contained in credit agreements. Table 7.7 can be used in conjunction with Table 7.6 to gain an idea of fees that can be negotiated or paid in a credit arrangement. For example, if a firm raised funds in the form of bankers' acceptances, Table 7.6 indicates that fees for letters of credit and selling expenses are collected and those fees are defined briefly on Table 7.7. Tables 7.6 and 7.7 are a background to the discussion in the next section.

We illustrate the richness of credit market arrangements by discussing examples of a revolving credit agreement, commercial paper, and corporate bonds. They are selected because they are widely used business credit arrangements and because it is impossible to describe all types of credit arrangements—product developments occur daily in financial markets.

Commercial bank business lending is a model of traditional credit relationships between credit service firms and institutional credit customers. The main contact by banks with the institutional credit service user is the *calling officer* who performs the communication and marketing activities. Calling officers inform customers of the whole range of services banks provide and assess customer needs, thus communicating and marketing to customers. Although lending is usually a calling officer's main focus, he or she is often *cross-selling* other bank services, like transaction processing or pension fund management services.

The bank representative in a credit relationship is usually an official of the bank corporation, meaning that he or she has been designated by the board of directors of the bank to negotiate and sign contracts. Banks and other financial institutions have expanded the reach of calling officers by locating branches or affiliates of holding companies such as mortgage banking units or leasing and finance companies in many locations. The purpose of all these local and regional offices is to place calling officers in close contact with their institutional clients. Calling officers not only perform activities of communication and marketing, but also negotiate prices and terms of credit services, and perform initial production and delivery of the credit services. Calling officers also often monitor and control the customer in terms of current credit arrangements.

Most businesses and institutional credit arrangements are coordinated by calling officers, but other representatives are working behind the scenes. Table 7.8 shows the organization of activities in the value chain as provided in a traditional bank in revolving credit and the other credit arrangements we discuss below. Banks in the United States are required by regulators to review credit applications and monitor loan performance. These monitoring and control functions are performed according to guidelines set by "Credit Committees" or "Use of Funds Committees." Officers' activities are reviewed by credit personnel. Calling officers often become advocates of customers vis-à-vis the bank internal credit staff. Routine work involved with monitoring and controlling, and producing and delivering credit services may be handled using computer networks and clerical personnel called *operations* or "back-office" staff.

TABLE 7.6 Types of Institutional Credit Arrangements

DESCRIPTION/SECURITY	*TIME PERIOD*	*INTEREST RATE*	*FEES*	*RESTRICTIONS/ CONDITIONS*
Short-Term Unsecured Credit Arrangements				
OPEN MARKET PAPER				
Directly Placed Commercial Paper				
Largest issuers, like GMAC	< 270 days[1]	Market discount	None	Uniform Commercial Code[2]
Dealer Placed Commercial Paper				
No-name firms, backed by letter of credit	< 270 days[1]	Market discount	Selling, letter of credit	Uniform Commercial Code[2]
Bankers' Acceptances				
Letter of credit, shipping documents	< 6 months[3]	Market discount	Letter of credit, documentation, selling	Uniform Commercial Code,[2] Federal Reserve[4]
Letter of credit, shipping documents	>6 months[3]	Market discount	Letter of credit, documentation selling	Uniform Commercial Code,[2] Federal Reserve[4]
SHORT-TERM LOANS				
Revolving Credit				
Unsecured or secured, formal contract	Negotiable	Negotiable	Negotiable; see Table 7.9 for possible fees	Covenants
Line of Credit				
Informal agreement	Negotiable	Negotiable	None	Conditions in letter

TABLE 7.6 (*continued*)

DESCRIPTION/SECURITY	*TIME PERIOD*	*INTEREST RATE*	*FEES*	*RESTRICTIONS/ CONDITIONS*
SHORT-TERM ASSET-BASED CREDIT ARRANGEMENTS				
Collateralized Loans				
Inventory or accounts receivable pledged as security in bilateral contract	Negotiable	Negotiable	See Table 7.9 for possible	Covenants, recourse on bad accounts, liens on assets, etc.
Warehouse Receipts				
Inventory placed with third party warehouse and receipts used as collateral	Negotiable	Negotiable	Negotiable; see Table 7.9 for possible fees	Covenants, recourse on bad accounts, liens on assets, etc.
Factoring				
Sale of accounts receivable to factor, with or without recourse	Negotiable	Negotiable	Negotiable; see Table 7.9 for possible fees	Recourse possible on bad accounts receivable
Other Collateral				
Securities, personal assets of firm officials	Negotiable	Negotiable	Negotiable; see Table 7.9 for possible fees	

DESCRIPTION/SECURITY	*TIME PERIOD*	*INTEREST RATE*	*FEES*	*RESTRICTIONS/ CONDITIONS*
Long-Term Unsecured Credit Arrangements				
Term Loans				
Bilateral contract between borrower and lender or lenders, can be revolving credits or self-amortizing loans	Negotiable	Negotiable	Negotiable; see Table 7.9 for possible fees	Covenants
Debentures				
Privately placed or publicly offered debt instrument with formal indenture contract	Negotiable	Negotiable	Negotiable; see Table 7.9 for possible fees	Covenants

TABLE 7.6 (*continued*)

DESCRIPTION/SECURITY	*TIME PERIOD*	*INTEREST RATE*	*FEES*	*RESTRICTIONS/ CONDITIONS*
Long-Term Secured Credit Arrangements				
Bonds				
Secured by collateral like equipment, property, securities, or third party guarantees	Negotiable	Negotiable	Negotiable able; see table 7.9 for possible fees	Contained in indenture, often enforced by trustee
Term Loans				
Bilateral contracts between borrower and lender or lenders	Negotiable	Negotiable	Negotiable; see Table 7.9 for possible fees	Contained in loan agreement
Financial Leases				
Equipment user in contract with lessor	Negotiable	Negotiable	See Table 7.9	Internal Revenue Service restrictions on contract designs

[1]Maturities under 270 days not subject to SEC registration.

[2]Uniform Commercial Code spells out legal recourse and conditions.

[3]Under six months not subject to reserve requirements when banks discount in the open market.

[4]Federal Reserve regulates amount of acceptances as percent of accepting bank's capital.

TABLE 7.7 Types of Fees Collected in Institutional Credit Arrangements

TYPE OF FEE	*FUNCTIONS PERFORMED*	*HOW CHARGED*
Origination Fees		
Credit analysis fees	Obtain credit checks, financial data, analyze data	Points, explicit fees paid by borrower or other credit participants
Documentation fees	Write, file and distribute contracts, record liens	Points, explicit fees paid by borrower or other credit participants
Appraisal fees	Assess value of collateral	Explicit fees paid by borrower for other credit participants, continuing compensation in terms of interest rate spread
Servicing Fees		
Collection and processing of payments	Record payments, keep track of payment due and timeliness of payments, provide necessary reports of balances and due amounts	Continuing compensation usually in terms of interest rate spread
Contract enforcement fees	Account for value of collateral and contract requirements, assure conformance with agreed-upon ratios and other covenants	Interest rate spread, fees paid by other credit participants in terms of reduced interest paid
Selling Fees		
Commissions for sale of paper	Find buyers and make market	Usually percent of proceeds or bid/ask spread
Commitment Fees/Compensating Balances		
Compensation for readiness to advance credit without notice	Advance funds against line of credit when borrower requests	Either a fee based on unused portion of line or a minimum collected balance
Guarantees/Letters of Credit		
Guarantee ability of borrower to repay credit upon maturity	Assures investors in less well-known borrowers that investment will be returned	Usually specific fees, perhaps as percent of amount of guarantee
Prepayment/Cancellation Fees		
Compensation for prematurity repayment of credit	Compensate investor for loss of investment at agreed-upon rate	Usually percent of loan amount outstanding at time of prepayment or cancellation
Assumption Fees		
Charge for transfer of credit agreement to new borrower before maturity	Provide lender for compensation and notice of who is obliged to make payments	Usually fixed fee or percent of outstanding loan balance

TABLE 7.8 Organization of Activities in Providing Credit

ACTIVITY IN VALUE CHAIN	*INSTITUTIONAL MARKET RE-VOLVING CREDIT*	*RETAIL MARKET COMMERCIAL PAPER*	*PRIVATELY PLACED BOND*	*MORTGAGE*	*CREDIT CARD*
Pricing/ Term Setting	Lending officer, bank committees	Money market, commercial paper dealer (possibly a bank)	Investment bank, insurance company officer	Government agencies, mortgage bankers, and other pool originators	Issuing bank or savings institution, national credit card company
Communicating/ Marketing	Lending officer	Calling officer, reputation	Investment banker, commercial banker	Real estate brokers, branches of savings mortgage	Issuing bank or savings institution, national credit (e.g. Visa)
Producing/ Delivering	Lending officer, bank operations	Bank and commercial paper dealer	Investment banker, insurance company	Escrow companies, savings institution, mortgage bankers	Issuing bank or savings institution, national credit card company
Monitoring/ Control	Lending officer, bank credit review	Bank issuer of letter of credit	Investor with indenture, possibly third party	Mortgage bankers and savings institutions	Issuing bank or savings institution
Funding/ Investing	Bank deposits, participations	Commercial paper buyer (money market mutual fund, etc.)	Portfolio investor (insurance company, pension fund, bond fund)	Mortgage pool investors, savings institutions, banks	Bank or savings institution deposits, asset-backed security investors
Risk Bearing/ Sharing	Bank, participations	Bank issuing letter of credit	Buyer, financial markets	Private insurance companies, financial markets, investors	Bank and savings institutions

Example of Traditional Credit Service: Revolving Credit. A *revolving line of credit* (or "revolver") is a tightly negotiated bilateral agreement between lenders and institutional customers and is a common business credit arrangement. These credit agreements provide loans up to the *credit limit* (maximum amount) over some time period (typically a year). Revolving credit agreements can be unsecured but when they require collateral as shown on Table 7.6 they are called asset-based lending. The business customer who satisfies conditions of a revolving credit agreement can borrow funds at any time, described as *taking down* some or all of a line of credit. Customers borrow needed cash and avoid interest costs on unused portions of the credit line. Customers can *pay down* loan balances if cash is available and take down more later as their cash needs fluctuate. This flexibility is valuable to the customer.

Credit limits, amount taken down, and payments are shown in Figure 7.2 for a hypothetical $10 million revolving credit. In the figure, the customer has a one-year line of credit. The customer does not need funds in the first 45 days then takes down $1 million until the end of three months, when the balance is raised to $3 million. At the end of six months, the balance is paid down to $2 million, after 6 months and 45 days $4 million is taken down, running the balance to $6 million. After 10 months, another $3.5 million is taken down, so that the loan is close to the credit limit. Forty five days before the end of the year, the balance is paid down to $500 thousand. Finally, just before the end of the year the balance is paid to zero or the line *cleaned up*.

In credit arrangements like revolving credits, all terms are subject to negotiation between the parties, starting from the time period covered in the agreement and the circumstances under which it will be extended. Interest rates can be *fixed* at a given level or they can be *variable* over the period of the loan. Many loan agreements relate or *peg* the interest rate to a reference interest rate, traditionally the bank's *prime rate*. Rates more closely linked to market movements, like the London Interbank Offered Rate (LIBOR), or other widely observed interest rates, such as rates on bank certificates of deposit, are also used as reference rates. The interval between variable rate changes can be daily, monthly, or quarterly.

Typical interest rate terms for a fixed-rate loan agreement might call for borrowed funds to be charged at 300 basis points (3 percent) over prime current at the time the agreement is signed. A variable rate loan agreement may call for

FIGURE 7.2 Business line of credit use

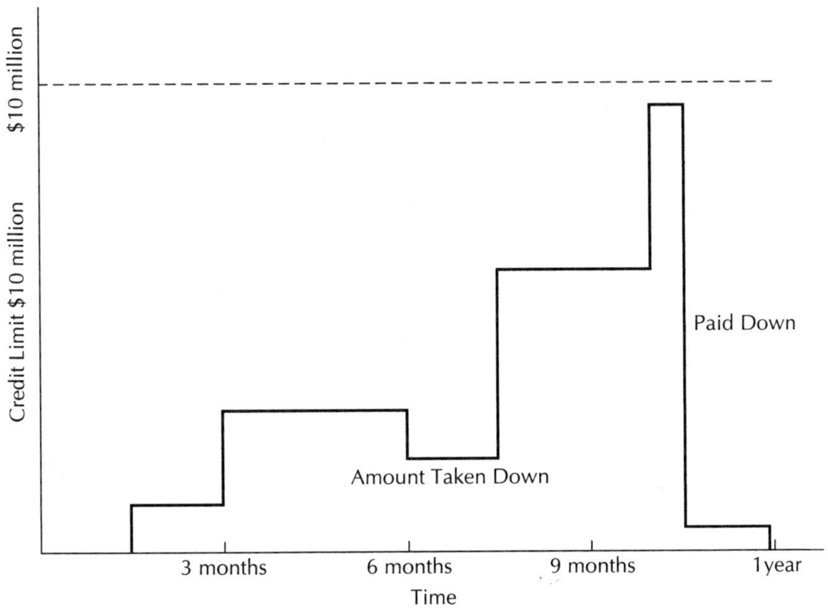

interest to be calculated at 350 basis points over LIBOR, adjusted monthly, and paid quarterly. In recent periods of high and variable interest rates, banks and other lenders have met some customers' concerns about the uncertainty of future interest rates on variable rate loan agreements by agreeing to place *caps* or maximum interest rate charges on loans. Some bank borrowers are willing to promise a *floor* interest rate to a bank in exchange for a cap; these arrangements are called interest rate *collars*. Caps and collars are examples of interest rate options and are discussed in Chapters 8 and 21.

Revolving credit agreements can involve many different kinds of fees as shown in Table 7.6. Several firms may participate in funding the agreement. The financial institution that negotiates and produces documents for the agreement may collect loan origination fees and loan servicing fees. In revolving credit agreements the customer is often charged for the privilege of borrowing against the line without advance notice. The *commitment fee* is essentially a charge for reserving the funds the lender has committed to advance, and it can be shared with other lenders.

Commitment fees are usually quoted as fractions of a percent of the portion of the line not taken down. For example, if a commitment fee of 25 basis points on the unused portion of a line is charged, an unused line of $10 million would pay $25,000, or $6,250 per quarter for the unused line. If $5,000,000 were taken down one quarter, the commitment fee would be reduced to $3,125 for that quarter but interest at the contracted-for rate would be paid on the loan amount.

Some deposit-taking institutions negotiate with the borrower to make no or low interest rate deposits called *compensating balances*. These deposits compensate the deposit-taking firm by providing a low cost source of financing for interest-earning assets or by reducing the net loan balance advanced to the credit customer if the loan is taken down. A compensating balance arrangement, for example, might require an average minimum balance of $1,000,000 of collected funds (see Chapter 10) or 15 percent of the amount taken down on a revolving credit of $10,000,000 maximum loan balance. The borrower would have to leave an average of $1,000,000 on deposit if the line was not used. If more than $6,666,667 were taken down, the minimum balance would be computed as 15 percent of the loan. For example, if the customer took down $8,000,000 and had a compensating balance arrangement as discussed, the required balance would jump from $1 million to $1.2 million as long as the $8 million loan balance was outstanding.

Revolving credit agreements contain *conditions* or *loan covenants* governing the availability of the credit. The covenants of the loan agreement typically obligate the firm to maintain certain balance sheet ratios and levels of working capital. Violation of these terms of the loan agreement can result in cancellation of the agreement at the discretion of the lender, with outstanding loan balances immediately due and payable. Examples of typical loan conditions and covenants are shown in Table 7.9. These conditions provide banks and other financial service firms control over their credit risks and may provide customers desirable flexibility.

TABLE 7.9 Types of Conditions and Restrictions in Credit Agreements

CONDITION	*PURPOSE*	*EFFECT*
Prepayable or Callable		
Credit agreement can be terminated by borrower with notice	Flexibility to borrower	Grant borrower an option to control costs of financing
Due on Sale/Assumable		
Debt payable if collateral sold or obligation is assumed, unless agreement is that obligation is assumable, in which case conditions can be imposed	Provides borrower with flexibility in disposition of assets	Option that can be valuable to borrower or buyer of assets used as collateral
Restrictions on Production and Investment Activity		
Restrict borrower's ability to change business activities, substitute assets for original collateral	Control risks to lender affecting the value of credit arrangement	Requires monitoring of borrower's activities
Restrictions on Payment of Dividends or Cash		
Restricts ability of borrower to take cash and use for purposes not anticipated by credit	Controls risks to lender	Requires monitoring of activities of borrower
Restrictions on Future Borrowing		
Limits ability of borrower to issue further debt instruments	Prevents impairment of value of credit arrangement by dilution of claim	Requires monitoring of borrower
Sinking Funds		
Mandatory payments of principal according to schedule	Provide market for debt instruments, reduce risk of default upon maturity	Requires monitoring of borrower
Reporting Requirements		
Mandatory reports on borrower's financial condition	Provide ability to monitor and control financial performance of borrower	Requires monitoring of borrower

Data based on Smith and Warner (1979).

Examples of Institutional Credit Arrangements: Commercial Paper. Growth in commercial paper issuances in the open market by nonfinancial corporations has been a major development in credit markets. Finance companies have always relied on open market borrowing in the form of commercial paper because their names, like General Motors Acceptance Corporation (GMAC), were synonymous with creditworthiness. Large borrowers like GMAC simply take orders from short-term investors wanting to invest cash in low-risk short-term instruments. The big name issuers' commercial paper is called *directly placed commercial paper* since these firms place their paper directly with investors.

The recent growth in commercial paper issuances has come from smaller firms, so-called "no-name" firms, who borrow in the open market by selling their paper to commercial paper dealers. This *dealer-placed commercial paper* is usually backed by the *credit guarantee* of a bank or other credit service provider that has contracted to lend money to the issuer when the commercial paper is due. If the borrower does not have the cash to repay commercial paper, the credit guarantee assures purchasers of commercial paper that the company will be able to pay off its borrowing at the maturity date. The credit firm usually issues guarantees in the form of a *letter of credit* and charges the customer a fee. The dealer, which may or may not be a bank, charges the issuer selling fees.[2]

Interest rates on commercial paper and bankers' acceptances are quoted on a *bankers' discount* or simply *discount* basis. The rates are set in the very competitive markets for these money market instruments.[3] The interest rate is determined by the market rates for dealer-placed commercial paper and the quality of the credit guarantees, and the maturity is a function of the issuers' needs and market conditions. Interest rate risks are borne by the issuer and the investor in commercial paper.

Negotiations for the use of commercial paper as a source of credit concern fees for the credit guarantees and the dealer for selling the commercial paper and other servicing fees associated with registering and redeeming the commercial paper. The competition for dealing in commercial paper has become so fierce that some major dealers, like Goldman Sachs, dropped out of the market after years of activity.

Open market issues of commercial paper replace bank borrowing but do not eliminate banks or other financial service firms from the credit arrangement. In issuing a firm a letter of credit, the bank or other financial firm must perform the same types of analysis as would be the case for bank portfolio lending. The financial institution issuing the letter of credit bears the credit risk of the firm selling commercial paper, since it must loan the firm money to pay off its debt at maturity. The writer of the letter of credit collects fees for writing the credit guarantee, the seller of commercial paper collects sales commissions, and other processing fees are collected by the provider. The growth of the commercial paper market illustrates the efficiency of unbundling of funding, risk bearing, information and marketing, monitoring and controlling activities in credit services for larger firms.

Institutional Credit Arrangements: Corporate Bonds. Long-term institutional credit is often arranged in the form of a bond. Bonds can be sold in the open market in the form of a public securities offering, as discussed in Chapter 9, or they can be privately placed. A portfolio lender in bonds, like an insurance company,

[2]The maturity of commercial paper is typically less than 270 days at the time of issue, avoiding the requirement of registering open market paper with the Securities and Exchange Commission (SEC) as is required with longer-term paper.

[3]A bankers' discount rate of 12 percent means that only 88 percent of the face value of the note is advanced to borrower, or alternatively that the investor pays only 88 percent of face value of the note, for 360 days. True interest cost is therefore $(1/.88)^{1.013889} - 1 = 1.138383 - 1$ or 13.8383 percent, where 1.010389 is 365/360.

often negotiates directly with the borrower or with investment bankers or other intermediaries as agents for institutional customers assisting in private placements.[4]

The terms and prices of both publicly sold and privately placed bonds may appear very similar but the term setting and pricing process are very different. A publicly sold bond is priced to be attractive to financial markets and must be easily sold. Credit arranged in the form of private placement of a bond with long-term portfolio lenders like insurance companies and pension funds involves detailed negotiations between the borrower and the lender, similar to negotiations associated with bank loans. All the terms of the credit arrangement are negotiated in a private placement.

Bonds may be secured or unsecured. Unsecured debt is typically known as *debentures.* Secured bonds are often identified by collateral, as in *equipment trust certificates,* backed by equipment like railroad cars or airplanes, or *collateral trust certificates* backed by securities. The terms and prices associated with a credit arranged in the form of a bond are contained in a legal contract called an *indenture.* The indenture contains the result of the negotiations between the borrower and the lender.

Bond indentures and loan agreements nearly always contain a variety of conditions that the customer must satisfy in order to conform to the agreements. These conditions are called *covenants.* An example of a loan covenant is a restriction on dividend payments by a corporate borrower if net worth or a variety of balance sheet ratios are not met. Loan covenants are often standard paragraphs with blanks to be filled in or copied from standardized models. Covenants can be carefully negotiated in setting the terms of a particular bond or loan deal or they can be mere "boiler plate." The purpose of covenants is to impose restrictions on borrower behavior that reduce or eliminate problems of moral hazard. Violations of loan covenants can be the basis for cancellation of a loan agreement, and often give the creditor the legal right to demand repayment or invoke legal procedures to liquidate assets held as collateral.

There really is no limit on the restrictions that are possible in a credit agreement. A thorough study of bond covenants by Clifford Smith and Jerold Warner (1979) makes clear that covenants have serious implications for borrowers and lenders. Their analysis is the basis for the summary in Table 7.9 of restrictions contained in loan agreements. Covenants impose real economic costs on the borrower, leading Smith and Warner to conclude that covenants are used to resolve principal–agent problems of the type discussed in Chapter 6 between borrowers and lenders.

Summary of Institutional Credit Arrangements

The above discussion illustrates credit arrangements with examples of a closely negotiated revolving credit agreement, open-market commercial paper, and a privately placed bond. These specific arrangements are intended to illustrate the

[4]Private placements satisfying certain restrictions on the number of investors do not need to be registered with the Securities and Exchange Commission, as discussed in Chapter 15.

provision of activities in the value chain. They also demonstrate the range of terms that can be negotiated or offered in credit arrangements. We have shown the organization of activities in these credit arrangements in Table 7.8. In the following chapter, we will assess how activities in the value chain in credit arrangements can produce value for arrangers of credit.

Retail Credit Arrangements

Consumer loans, like institutional loans, are either unsecured or secured. Most unsecured retail lending is short-term. Unsecured loans are quantitatively less important than secured loans like mortgages and car loans but the market for unsecured lending is growing. The major consumer markets, as we have discussed, are for secured loans in the form of home mortgages and car loans.

The problems of pricing and setting terms for the retail market are different from those in the institutional market. There are many retail customers, and volume is the major challenge. Pricing and designing terms on consumer credit agreements are directed both at controlling adverse selection and moral hazard and at innovative marketing to create competitive advantage. In most circumstances, new retail credit products, like charge cards or home equity loans, evolve out of new credit contract designs exploiting technology and changes in regulations and tax codes. The products are designed for mass appeal with standardized terms.

An overview of the main consumer credit arrangements is provided in Table 7.10. As with institutional credit arrangements, the main elements are time period, interest rate, collateral, fees, and conditions. To illustrate the six activities in the value chain for price and term setting providing consumer credit, we examine credit card loans and mortgages in detail in the next section.

Retail Market Credit Service Activities. Retail credit services tend to be the same or similar for many customers. The challenge facing financial firms offering credit services in the retail market is reaching the market cost effectively. There are three main ways financial service firms provide activities required by credit services in the retail market: branch offices, mail, and point-of-sale systems.

For deposit-taking firms, branch systems have been an important way to perform many activities. Branches offer current and potential customers convenient locations and an effective communication and marketing channel. Deposit-taking institutions can consolidate activities associated with a number of financial services, like checking accounts and other credit services, in branches as sales and promotion centers. Branch managers are the key coordinators of credit related services and some back-office operations (verification of applications and documentation). Some activities may be consolidated in regional centers.

Branches are capital intensive and require large staffs. Alternative delivery mechanisms for retail financial service can be cost effective relative to branches. Delivery systems can be built around mail and telephone or point-of-sale delivery systems. Technological advances in communications and information processing are revolutionizing how credit services are delivered to the retail market.

TABLE 7.10 Types of Consumer Credit Arrangements

DESCRIPTION/SECURITY	*TIME PERIOD*	*INTEREST RATE*	*FEES*	*RESTRICTIONS/CONDITIONS*
UNSECURED SHORT-TERM CREDIT ARRANGEMENTS				
Credit Card Financing				
Charges up to some preestablished maximum secured by creditworthiness of individual fees	Monthly payments	Monthly rate	Annual fees	Conditions laid out in contract
Personal Line of Credit				
Checks up to preestablished maximum	Usually monthly payments	Rate fixed or variable	Origination and servicing fees	Contract defines terms and conditions
Overdraft Facility				
Deposit-taking institutions honors checks without funds	Usually due on per item basis	Negotiable rate	Processing fees	Federal Reserve restricts lending through overdrafts
SECURED CONSUMER FINANCING				
Residential Mortgage Loan				
Loan secured by lien or trust deed, contract terms often standardized according to government regulations	Up to 30 years	Fixed or variable	Origination, Servicing, Guarantees	Loan agreement contains conditions
Consumer Durable/Auto Financing				
Loan secured by lien on auto or appliance	Up to 5 years	Fixed, often discounted by manufacturer	Origination	Loan contract contains conditions
Margin Account Lending				
Borrow on common stock or bond collateral	Renewable upon posting of sufficient cash	Adjusts with market rates	Annual account fees or negotiable	Contained in customer agreement, regulated by Federal Reserve and Exchanges

Credit card system like American Express and Visa are examples of delivery systems based on mail and telephone. All contact with retail customers is through these means. Labor intensive processing is concentrated in regional centers like the American Express location in Phoenix, Arizona, and contacts with retail outlets accepting the cards are conducted by regional calling organizations.

Point-of-sale credit services are loans generated at the time a sale is made. One example of point-of-sale credit services is auto financing where large finance companies like GMAC or Ford Credit use car dealership personnel to gather customer specific information, which is transmitted by telephones and computers to the financial firms providing credit. The use of point-of-sale delivery of credit services is spreading to the home mortgage market, where real estate brokers use computer screens giving offered terms to bring borrowers into contact with credit firms.

Example of Consumer-Secured Lending: Mortgages. The terms of mortgage lending affecting the borrower are the amount of loan advanced, both the total and as a percent of the value of the home used as collateral (called the *loan-to-value* ratio), charges made at the time the loan is made or *loan origination fees* and (called *points*), the interest rate, and the length of the contract. Additional loan terms may deal with mortgage default insurance, prepayment options and penalties, and due-on-sale provisions.

Mortgage bankers, mortgage brokers, savings institutions, and banks take loan applications, often referred by real estate brokers. The borrower's creditworthiness must be established in a process called loan *qualification*. Standards in credit, called *loan underwriting* standards, can be established by government agencies, such as the Federal Housing Administration (FHA) in the United States, because they guarantee payment of principal and interest on some loans. Conventional mortgages are not government guaranteed. Deposit-institution regulations set underwriting standards for portfolio investments of regulated firms. Some mortgages are insured against default, which shifts the credit risk from lenders to insurers like the FHA and VA or to a private mortgage insurer.

Credit-Card Lending as an Example of Unsecured Retail Lending. The economic value created by the use of credit cards comes from use of a single card at many establishments. Credit cards are a means of payment. Bookkeeping and credit departments in small stores are eliminated without eliminating retail customer credit. Credit cards have consolidated transaction processing and loan servicing for retail credit in card issuers and specialized firms, like Visa International and Master Card.

Credit cards are issued by retailers and financial institutions. Retailers like Shell Oil or J. C. Penney issue credit cards. Financial firms issuing credit cards are deposit-taking financial institutions, like banks and thrifts, or credit-card companies, such as American Express or Diners Club.

General purpose credit card arrangements entail at least four parties: the cardholder, the issuing financial institution or other issuer, the participating merchants and service providers, and the clearing agencies. The retail customer is only actively involved with two of those, namely the issuing firm and merchants.

The credit card agreement between the issuer and the cardholder is a loan contract. The terms include but are not limited to annual fees and interest charges on credit balances, which usually have a maximum upper limit. Annual fees run from nothing to $100. Interest rates are usually charged on credit balances not paid by a given day of the month (the monthly closing date) and are usually computed on a daily basis. Interest on cash advances is usually charged beginning from the date of the advance. Credit card interest rates are usually high, with 18 percent (1.5 percent per month) common, and higher rates not unknown. There may be other fees associated with transactions, like charges for each advance or automatic payments to cover checking account overdrafts.

Credit card terms often include a variety of other services or terms. Some cards provide automatic cash discounts on purchases. For example, the Sears Discover card offers a 1 percent discount on all purchases. Other cards offer frequent flyer mileage if issued in conjunction with an airline promotion. Some cards automatically include casualty insurance for travelers and travel assistance. All of these services and terms are meant to make cards more attractive for users with specific marketing profiles.

Merchants accepting the cards have a contractual relation with a financial institution that will accept charge slips as a deposit. Merchants fees are typically based on a discount from the face value of a charge slip, with small merchants often paying more than larger firms with many outlets. Typical fees for a small merchant might be a 3 percent discount, and large retailers like a department store chain paying perhaps 1 percent. From the point of view of the merchant, credit card slips are like checks, deposited in his or her account, but discounted. Merchant fees cover the clearing of the charge slips, discussed in Chapter 10, and the credit checks and authorizations.

Many financial institutions now incorporate automatic loan advances from credit card accounts to transfer funds into checking accounts to avoid overdrafts. These overdraft facilities are not really any different than credit-card lending. They require integration of checking and credit-card-loan computer and accounting systems. Use of a credit card is similar to a checking account with a negative balance.

7.5 SUMMARY

The huge and dynamic markets for institutional and retail credit services are increasingly characterized by unbundling of the six activities in the value chain for credit services. We have reviewed the funding and risk bearing activities, noting the growth in nontraditional lenders in both markets, reflecting the institutionalization of savings and globalization of markets. Pricing and term-setting activities are increasingly separated from the production and delivery of credit services in alternative delivery systems like point-of-sale lending. New financial instruments and new organization forms for delivery of financial services are limited only by the imaginations of the participants in the credit markets.

DISCUSSION QUESTIONS AND EXERCISES

1. Using the flow of funds data provided in Table 7.1, determine changes in the share of business credit in the form of bank loans versus bonds since 1983.
2. Using the flow of funds data provided in Table 7.3, assess the changes in the demand for housing and installment credit by households and relate these to changes in residential construction and consumer durables purchases. Would you say the demand for mortgage and installment credit is linked to the demand for household investment?
3. In the *Wall Street Journal* or the annual report of some firm, find a description of a bank credit arrangement and discuss it in terms of the concepts presented in this chapter. Be sure to describe the credit limits, covenants, interest rates, and fees associated with the arrangement.
4. Check the "Money Rates" section of the *Wall Street Journal* and compare the interest rates on commercial paper, bankers' acceptances, and the prime rate relative to short-term U.S. Treasury bills. Compare these interest rates on business loans to the cost of funds to banks reflected in the LIBOR, certificate of deposit rate, and the Federal Funds rate, also given in the "Money Rates" table.
5. Obtain an application for a credit card and discuss the types of information requested in terms of assessing the creditworthiness of an applicant. What kinds of verification would be involved in approving this application? What kind of people with what kind of training would be needed?
6. Obtain the advertisements from some local savings and loans, banks, and real estate brokers on types of mortgages available for the current purchase of residences. Discuss the terms and fees, and compare the loan terms. What trade-offs do mortgage borrowers face in choosing a mortgage in this market?
7. The newly emerging market economics in the former Soviet Union and Eastern Europe undoubtedly offer the credit services industry many opportunities. What are these opportunities? How might financial firms exploit them?
8. How do you know about the credit services provided by various financial and nonfinancial firms? What means have been used to inform you of the conditions and terms on various sources of credit? Which do you feel are effective and which not? Do you have any ideas on how credit services could be better communicated to people like you?
9. According to the *Wall Street Journal* (January 5, 1990), there are over 1.5 million households with net worths over $1 million. What kind of credit services would this market need compared to average households? How would you recommend communicating with and marketing to this market?
10. Japanese banks have been large writers of letters of credit for governments borrowing short term in the municipal bond market. How could they make profits from this service? What economic function is being performed?

REFERENCES

BOARD OF GOVERNORS OF THE FEDERAL RESERVE SYSTEM. 1989a. "Home Equity Lending," *Bulletin* (May), pp. 333–344.

BOARD OF GOVERNORS OF THE FEDERAL RESERVE SYSTEM. 1989b. "Terms of Bank Lending at Commercial Banks: Survey of loans made," *Bulletin* (November), pp. A73–A77.

BOARD OF GOVERNORS OF THE FEDERAL RESERVE SYSTEM. 1988. "Personal Bankruptcies," *Bulletin* (September), pp. 591–603.

BOARD OF GOVERNORS OF THE FEDERAL RESERVE SYSTEM. 1984. "Survey of Consumer Finances, 1983: A Second Report," *Bulletin* (December), pp. 857–868.

SMITH, CLIFFORD W., JR. and JEROLD B. WARNER. 1979. "On financial contracting: An Analysis of bond covenants," *Journal of Financial Economics* 7, pp. 117–161.

CHAPTER

8

Value Production in Credit Services

Introduction

Each of the links in the value chain has the potential to produce value for financial institutions providing credit services. These activities can be carefully analyzed to appreciate sources of competitive advantage. Some relevant issues are:

- How can pricing and terms of credit agreements be used to induce customers of different risk characteristics to reveal themselves to arrangers of credit?
- Why are credit customer relationships important to providers of credit services?
- What are the sources of value in credit origination and how can funding be separated from originating credit arrangements to increase value produced?
- Where does "financial engineering" as a value-producing activity fit into credit?

More efficient allocation of value-producing activities is the economic basis of growth and survival in the dynamic credit markets of today.

This chapter examines how value is produced in performing the activities in the value chain associated with credit services. In analyzing the preceding questions, recent insights provided by agency theory and financial economics are brought to bear. Financial institution managers must always be addressing the issue, "What are we good at?" A detailed look at the elements involved in providing credit activities provides clues as to where to look for maximum competitive advantage.

We begin with an overview of value creation and then look at the complex pricing and term setting that take place in credit arrangements as a way of inducing customers to reveal hidden risk characteristics. Next, the role of information in customer relationships and monitoring and controlling is explored. A discussion of the sources of competitive advantage in originating credit precedes an analysis of alternative ways of unbundling funding from other activities in the value chain for credit services. Finally, risk shifting and sharing using financial engineering are reviewed.

8.1 LOAN CONTRACT DESIGN AND VALUE PRODUCTION

Credit services consist of arranging funds for borrowers who are expected to pay them back to the lender with interest. Business funds are advanced as *loans, notes, bonds,* or other legal contracts as part of a credit relationship. Funds raised through credit services are distinguished from funds raised in the form of equity which is not a fixed claim and includes a voice in the management of the firm. Individuals must raise funds in the form of credit since they cannot sell equity. Firms, however, have a choice of ways to raise funds.

The question why firms raise funds by issuing credit or debt instruments as opposed to issuing additional ownership claims in the form of stock is a complex one and has been the source of much analysis (see, for example, Myers 1984). Funds raised in the form of credit are tax advantaged to firms in countries where interest is a tax deductible expense. Since credit instruments are fixed commitments, equity investors keep all residual earnings and can leverage a firm's earning power with credit. On the other hand, failure to make credit payments can cause bankruptcy and reorganization or liquidation of the firm and loss of credit for individuals.

Funds raised in the form of credit for both individuals and firms have advantages and disadvantages to both the borrower and the lender who have different interests and concerns. These differences must be resolved in order for credit to be advanced. No relationship can avoid bad outcomes for all parties under all circumstances but credit markets have evolved standard ways to deal with many problems encountered in raising funds in the form of credit.

Most retail and wholesale credit arrangements are covered by a contract. As pointed out in previous chapters, contracts can be explicit written documents signed by corporate officials and recorded or they can be implicit in a system of laws (like the Uniform Commercial Code), regulations (like banking regulations), and conventions, as in trade credit. Chapter 6 introduced "contract theory," an analysis of ways of resolving the different interests of lenders and borrowers as principals and agents in financial relationships which cause problems of adverse selection and moral hazard. Carefully fashioned lending agreements or standardized credit products in the retail market may solve or mitigate problems of asymmetric information and moral hazard by eliminating or reducing them. Higher earnings can be made by lenders who arrange loans under contract terms that reduce problems relative to other lenders, who either make less profitable deals or stay out of the market altogether. The value produced by those financial service firms able to solve agency and information asymmetry problems can be used to build market share by reducing rates and fees without incurring greater losses, in which case the borrowers benefit.

Alternatively, the value produced may be increased by concentration in a unique market niche producing excess returns. As discussed in Chapter 7, the ultimate source of value in credit comes from differences in the value or ability to exploit the value of assets to economic decision-makers. If contracts can be replicated by competitors, imitators will eventually erode excess returns from innovations in contract design in credit markets. In all cases, value is created in the economy by allowing credit customers better portfolio composition than would be possible if agency problems in credit services could not be reduced.

Portfolio Lending and Private Placements

The usual procedure of arranging credit for retail customers starts with a visit to a bank or thrift institution to get a loan. In a corporate setting we imagine bank officers and corporate officials hammering out a deal. Banks and thrift institutions are major portfolio lenders. They raise money in deposit markets and invest directly in loans, as discussed in Chapter 7. In many traditional credit arrangements, originating lenders market, price, deliver, and monitor loans funded with deposits, bearing any risks associated with the deal. In this environment, providers of credit services perform all of the activities in the value chain for credit service.

Much less well-known is the role of insurance and finance companies and other nontraditional firms providing credit services. One reason for this is that many insurance company loans are not called loans but are called corporate bonds. Many insurance company bonds are not publicly traded securities such as we discuss in the next chapter, but instead are *private placements* that result from credit relationships. Private placements are purchases of credit instruments by a small number of investors, often only one insurance company or pension fund. The resulting bond or note does not have to be registered with the Securities and Exchange Commission as a security, as we discuss in Chapter 15. Private placements are very much like loans.

In a typical private placement, for example, representatives of the investment function of an insurance company will bargain extensively with the borrowers. Borrowers from insurance companies and pensions funds are usually longer term borrowers like real estate investors or developers of large projects. Terms and conditions for the bond, loan, or note are negotiated in long sessions with lawyers, accountants, and financial analysts from both sides. When the deal is done, the loan contract or bond is added to the portfolio of investments of the lender and funds are advanced to the borrower out of sources available to the lender, like insurance reserves.

The point is that there is no essential difference in credit services provided by traditional bankers and other well-known sources of traditional portfolio lending or emerging portfolio lending from nontraditional lenders, like finance companies and pension funds. Value is created in the deals in the same way, by resolving agency problems and funding positive net present value projects. In all of these cases, the portfolio lenders also hire and pay the lending officers who negotiate the deal.

Portfolio lending by deposit-taking institutions and insurance companies is losing market share in developed economies. Investment bankers, commercial banks, fund managers, and others now establish relationships with institutional and retail borrowers but do not provide funding or even all of the activities in the value chain for credit services. Credit may be arranged by coordinating the activities of many financial service firms. Marketing and communication with borrowers and pricing and term setting may be provided by one firm or institution and other activities may be provided by others, as when pension funds provide financing and bank trust departments provide production and delivery. Unbundling credit services means distribution of activities in the value chain among several service providers. Unbundling allows the most efficient allocation of activities and is proceeding rapidly in the most advanced credit markets.

8.2 PRICING AND TERM-SETTING IN CREDIT SERVICES

When announcing or negotiating terms on credit arrangements, lenders are exposed to adverse selection as borrowers choose the terms most advantageous to themselves. After obtaining credit, borrowers may take actions that are not in the lender's interest, exposing the lender to moral hazard. In this section we show how careful pricing and setting of terms of credit arrangements may reduce or eliminate problems of adverse selection and moral hazard.

Borrowers may be induced to reveal their intentions or attributes by their choice of a particular contract from among several offers. That choice may in some instances reveal their hidden attributes and allow credit service firms to control their exposure to risks and to fine-tune expected returns from different classes of borrowers. Contract terms may induce borrowers to act in lenders' interest and provide a contractual basis for control of moral hazard due to actions by lenders.

Commitment Fees versus Compensating Balances

Adverse selection occurs when a firm offering credit services under contract terms cannot tell "good" customers from "bad" customers on the basis of observation and required information disclosures. It may be possible to offer different contract terms such that potential borrowers will reveal the type of customer they are by their choice of contract, called self-revelation (see Chapter 6). James (1981) analyzed the terms of bank revolving credit agreements to show how terms of credit arrangements can be fixed such that borrowers voluntarily choose contracts that are in the best interest of the financial firm offering the loan terms.

In James's analysis, "good" loan customers know that their creditworthiness is not likely to change over the period of the revolving credit agreement. "Bad" customers know there is a chance that their credit rating will deteriorate, perhaps because a large order on their books will be canceled. But from the point of the view of the lender, customers look the same.

James shows how the lender can induce customers to reveal their type by offering a choice of commitment fees or compensating balances in the revolving credit commitment. The choice must be finely tuned to induce the self-revelation and produce a separating equilibrium so that good and bad customers voluntarily choose the contract designed for them. Successful self-revelation reduces the cost to the lender of the possible deterioration in some of its customers' credit ratings.

The basic idea of James's analysis can be illustrated with an example. The example assumes that bad firms have a 50 percent probability of a bad event such as an order cancellation and will need more credit than is included in their line of credit. Since their credit quality will have deteriorated with the bad event, they will have to pay high interest rates to borrow above their credit line; let us assume a 20 percent interest rate. Compare the expected costs of a credit lines offering a 10 percent compensating balance versus a quarter point (.25 percent) commitment fee. A 10 percent compensating balance has an expected cost of 1 percent of the line (.5 probability times 10 percent times 20 percent) against a commitment fee of .25 percent. Bad firms would prefer commitment fees to compensating balances because a quarter percent is less than one percent. Higher compensating balances would increase expected costs to the bad firm even more.

Good firms have a lower probability of borrowing more than their line at higher rates. Assume good firms have only a 10 percent chance of needing the extra credit. In this case, the .25 percent commitment fee has an expected cost that is more than the expected cost of a 10 percent compensating balance at 20 percent, namely .2 percent of the line (.1 times .1 times .20). Good firms prefer compensating balances to the commitment fee of .25 percent.

Figure 8.1 is adapted from James's analysis and shows expected costs of different levels of compensating balances as a percent of the line for good (C_g) and

FIGURE 8.1 Commitment fees and compensating balances

SOURCE: Adapted from Christopher James, "Self-Selection and the Pricing of Bank Services: An Analysis of the Market for Loan Commitments and the Role of Compensating Balance Requirements," *Journal of Financial and Quantitative Analysis,* Vol. XVI, No. 5, December 1981, p. 733.

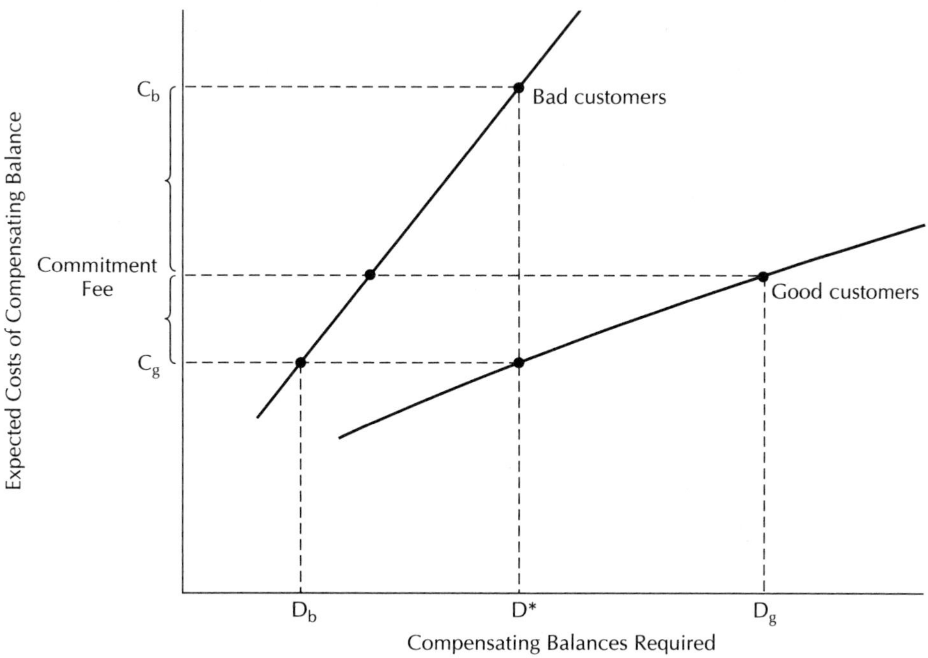

bad (C_b) firms on the vertical axis. Commitment fees are fixed as a percent of the line of credit. The diagram shows that there is a range of compensating balance requirements (like D*) where the expected costs of balances to good firms is less than commitment fees while compensating balances have higher expected costs to bad firms than commitment fees. Terms can be defined so that in choosing the lowest expected cost terms, firms reveal themselves by type in a separating equilibrium.

James's analysis illustrates how pricing of lines of credit can induce credit customers to reveal their risk type. If good customers choose compensating balances and bad customers choose commitment fees, credit service firms identify types of firms. The terminology bad and good does not mean that bad firms are not profitable. In fact, fine-tuning the pricing of the line of credit can make the credit service firm and bad firms both better off in terms of expected profits and costs of funds.

There is a limit to such fine tuning of the terms on loans: the lending firm must not charge too much in either fees or balances because all customers would choose one or the other contract, eliminating the benefits of identifying customer types in the separating equilibrium. Competitive conditions may rule out a separating equilibrium as well. The key concept here is that term setting and pricing strategy can be means of inducing self-revelation by credit customers and such a strategy may be profitable for credit service firms.

Collateral

Chan and Thakor (1987) analyze the role collateral can play in credit given the existence of hidden information and moral hazard with potential borrowers. In their analysis, potential borrowers have identified projects with positive expected returns that they want to finance completely with debt. Projects have different risks that borrowers are aware of, and the borrowers' actions in terms of how much effort they devote to project success are not observable. Since lenders cannot tell the difference between high and low risk investment opportunities on the basis of lender disclosures, there is a hidden information problem. In the absence of well-designed loan contracts, borrowers might take loan funds and not put in full effort to make the investment work, hence there is a moral hazard problem. In the Chan and Thakor analysis, economic value comes from making possible credit financing of risky projects that have positive expected returns on average in the face of these problems.

Financial intermediaries or loan originators can finance the projects with funds from deposits or other sources. These funds may be raised in competitive markets in unlimited amounts at the competitive rate. The funds may come from markets characterized by limited supplies, meaning that higher returns must be offered by financial institutions to raise a larger supply of lendable funds. The amount of funds invested and returns to depositors and interest rates and other terms imposed on credit arrangements represent the interaction of supply and demand conditions in the market for funds. This interaction is important in the Chan and Thakor analysis.

Requiring collateral changes the payoffs to borrowers investing in risky projects. Chan and Thakor point out that these changes can be used to influence the demand for credit. The gross return (one plus the net return) on a project is R. Once the project return is known, the borrower either pays the loan balance plus the interest rate charged by the lender (i) or surrenders the collateral posted, C. The payoffs to the lender and borrower depend on the total project return, as illustrated with an example in Panel A of Table 8.1. For the example, assume that a low risk project has gross returns of either 110 or 120 percent and collateral is $101 for a $100 loan at one percent. The borrower pays off the loan and keeps the collateral and the project return is above the loan interest rate.

In the example in Table 8.1, Panel B, low risk projects have equally likely returns of 10 or 20 percent and high risk project returns are either –15 or +35 percent. Borrowers know how risky the projects are and can take actions that affect the outcome to raise returns one percent, but these actions are costly or unpleasant. This is a realistic characterization of many business situations. The success of a business (or a project) is directly related to the borrowers' effort but the effort is hard work and may not be observed easily by a lender.

A *loan contract* in Chan and Thakor's analysis consists of an offer of loan terms in the form of loan interest and collateral (or i,C) pairs. For example, 13 percent and $113 collateral for a $100 loan or 14 percent and $20 collateral are two possible contracts. These terms correspond to case C in Panel B of Table 8.1. Borrowers weigh expected returns from projects against loan terms and effort required to undertake the investment.

The effect on loan terms in credit markets with different supplies of funds is illustrated by the examples in Panels A and B of Table 8.1. Case A in the table is when enough funds are available at low rates to finance all available low and high risk projects. In this case, all loans are fully collateralized and all borrowers, both high and low risk, have the same easy credit terms—in the example, 1 percent interest and $101 collateral on a $100 loan. There is no risk to lenders. All the benefits of effort are kept by borrowers so they put maximum effort into projects.

TABLE 8.1 Table of Payoffs and Actions with Collateral

Panel A: Payoffs

EXAMPLE	*OUTCOME*	*LENDER*	*BORROWER*	*TOTAL*
	If R > i – C	i	R – i	R
Example (from Case (A) in Panel B) of low risk borrower bad outcome:				
	$110 > $101 – $101 = 0 (as in all cases where C = i)			
		$101	$9	$110.00
	R < i – C	R + C	–C	R
Example from Case (C) in Panel B for high risk borrowers bad outcome:				
	$85 < $114.75 – $20 = 94.75			
		$105	–$20	$85.00

TABLE 8.1 (*continued*)

Panel B: Examples

	LOW RISK PROJECT		*HIGH RISK PROJECT*	
LOAN TERMS	*+10%*	*+20%*	*−15%*	*+35%*
(A) Deposit Funds Sufficient To Finance All Projects. Terms: 1%, $101				
Lender's Return	+1%	+1%	+1%	+1%
Borrower's Net	+9%	+19%	−16%	+34%
Borrower's Expected Return	+14%		=9%	
Lender's Return with +1% Effort	0	0	0	0
Borrower's Return with +1% Effort	+10%	+20%	−15%	+35%
(B) Funds Available To Fund Some Low Risk Projects. Terms: 12%, $112				
Lender's Return	+12%	+12%	+12%	+12%
Borrower's Net	−2%	+8%	−27%	+23%
Borrower's Expected Return	+3%		−2%	
Lender's Return with +1% Effort	+12%	+12%	+12%	+12%
Borrower's Return with +1% Effort	−1%	+9%	−26%	+24%
(C) Funds To Fund All Low and Some High Risk Projects. Terms: 13%, $113 or 14%, $20				
Lender's Return	+13%	+13%	+5%	+14%
Borrower's Net	−3%	+7%	−20%	+21%
Borrower's Expected Return	+2%		+.5%	
Lender's Return with +1% Effort	+13%	+13%	+6%	+14%
Borrower's Return with +1% Effort	−2%	+8%	−20%	+22%

Notes to explain example:

(1) The only case when both collateral and the project are surrendered is in case (C) when the high risk borrower has the bad outcome, that is, when the collateral + payoff = $20 + $85 = $110 < $114.75; in other cases the lender gets collateral or payment of loan in full.

(2) The shaded boxes are the *only* areas of the table where the lender does not earn the full interest on the contract: in case (B), the shaded area means the loan is not made because the borrower has a negative expected return. As noted above, case (C) is the *only* case where the lender makes less than the contract amount in the low outcome case.

(3) Note that the returns to *lenders* go up as the demand for project financing increases relative to the supply of deposits. Depositors must earn higher returns in order to supply more funds, whereas when plenty of funds are available, borrowers earn most of the returns from their projects as in case (A).

(4) The moral hazard problem is only an issue in case (C), when high risk borrowers do not gain full expected value of their effort (lenders gain the result of effort with the bad outcome).

Case B is a situation where there are not enough funds to finance all the low risk projects. The terms, 12 percent and collateral of $112 for a $100 loan, discourage high risk investors who will not apply. The shading in case B indicates that high risk investors have negative expected returns with those terms. There are more low risk investors applying for loans than funds available, so loans will be rationed arbitrarily. Low risk investors reveal themselves by applying for loans, but since in the analysis they are all the same, some low risk applicants simply do not receive funding. When some qualified credit applicants do not receive loans it is called *credit rationing*.

The last case analyzed by Chan and Thakor, case C, illustrates how collateral can induce self-revelation by project risk type. This is the case when there are more than enough funds to finance loans to all low risk projects. Low risk investors are willing to pledge more collateral in order to receive a lower interest rate, namely 13 percent with collateral of $113 for a $100 loan. In our example, high risk project borrowers accept terms of 14 percent and $20 collateral, terms that have a positive expected return for them. In this case, the higher amount of funding means that all low risk and some high risk projects are financed with loans, but some high risk projects are not funded. High risk credit is rationed and high risk borrowers have a reduced expected return from extra effort.

Loan terms consisting of an interest rate and collateral are widespread in both retail and wholesale markets. As discussed in Chapter 7, secured lending is typical in retail lending, as in the case of home and auto financing. In these cases, the amount of collateral is stated in terms of the down payment. If a down payment of 20 percent on a car is associated with, say, a 12 percent loan rate, this means that the loan has 125 percent (1/.8) collateral. In terms of the Chan and Thakor analysis, the borrower is offered a (12%, 125%) rate/collateral contract. A 10 percent down payment loan might then be associated with a 14 percent interest rate (collateral equal to 111 percent), or (14%, 111%). As noted in Chapter 7, collateral is extremely important in business lending, in areas as different as working capital financing and real estate development.

Several major points concerning value production in credit services can be derived from our review of the Chan and Thakor analysis. First, clever bargaining using collateral terms on loans can reduce the costs to lenders of moral hazard and hidden information. Second, the supply of funds materially affects who keeps the economic value that results from making the investment projects. In competitive markets for funds, the borrower and the financial institution arranging the credits keep the economic value. In cases of limited supplies of funds, savers providing funds get to keep some or all of the economic value. Third, the use of separating contracts—that is contract terms that induce self-revelation of borrower type, or pooling contracts, in which they are not distinguished—is a result of the supply of lendable funds. It only pays to separate the types of borrowers in cases where funds are limited in supply such that high rates of return to investors will raise only enough funds to lend to low risk customers or low risk customers and a small percentage of high risk customers. If market conditions are such that the weighted average return required for funds is low enough such that both high and low risk customers can be funded, a pooling contract will be economically optimal.

Additional Terms In Credit Relationship

Credit arrangements between lenders and a firm involve at least three parties: lenders, the owners or equity investors of the firm, and the management of the firm. A range of conflicts of interest arise in the complex of principle–agent problems among these parties. The most obvious example of these problems is the moral hazard faced by lenders. Black (1976) points out that:

> There is no easier way for a company to escape the burden of a debt than to pay out all of its assets in the form of a dividend, and leave the creditors holding an empty shell.

In the presence of such incompatible incentives and information asymmetries, issuing debt with acceptable risk to investors is not easy.

The conflicts between the various parties in debt contracts are not always obvious. For example, management may simply not undertake positive net present value projects when the benefits of the higher earnings and lower risks of the firm due to the projects simply improve the quality of existing debt claims. New loans may be taken at terms that affect the riskiness of old loans. A dramatic case is the financing of RJR Nabisco, where the increased leverage and changed nature of the firm caused bondholders to suffer losses on the value of their bonds.

Loan contracts may be written that reduce or eliminate some of the conflicts between lenders, managers, and owners of firms. Smith and Warner (1979) analyzed contract provisions or *covenants* in loan contracts that can mitigate conflicts of interest. Economic value is created in credit contracts if they result in credit being advanced for positive net present value projects that otherwise would not be undertaken. The value created is available for distribution to lenders, borrowers, and managers depending on their bargaining power, as in the Chan and Thakor analysis.

Smith and Warner classify the types of actions managers and owners may take against bondholders' interests into four major categories: (1) dividend payments; (2) claim dilution; (3) asset substitution; and (4) underinvestment. We have introduced the dividend conflict above. This conflict can be less obvious than simple emptying of the firm. Dividends that reduce future investment also reduce the value of the earning assets securing any debt.

Lenders are concerned that the value and safety of their credit will be diluted by additional borrowing, perhaps promising a higher claim on the assets of the firm. Asset substitution can reduce the value of debt by increasing its risk and may benefit stockholders whose shares increase with the possibility of much higher returns. Possible lower returns do not offset the effect of positive aspect of risk for shareholders because of limited liability.[1] Finally, underinvestment may result from a reluctance by shareholders to undertake investments that have positive net present values at the required return on debt but do not have positive value at risk-adjusted discount rates relevant for shareholders.

In order to control or reduce the problems caused by the conflicts discussed above, sophisticated creditors or their agents insist on terms that include detailed requirements or obligations of borrowers in loan contracts or bond indentures. Failure to observe these covenants causes default on loans. Legal action in extreme cases leads to seizure of the assets of the firm. Table 8.2 provides a classification of a wide variety of commonly used contract provisions according to the four categories provided by Smith and Warner.

Smith and Warner analyzed the economic consequences of restrictions in loan and debt agreements and concluded that restrictions in loan contracts, such

[1]Common stock is often compared to a call option, which we discuss in Chapter 21. Increasing the variance of the return of a stock will increase the value of the option on the stock. If common stock is compared to an option, with the exercise price equal to the face value of debt, increasing asset variance through investment policy can increase the value of the stock. (See Black and Scholes 1973.)

TABLE 8.2 Types of Loan Covenants

Restrictions on the Firm's Production/Investment Policy

Restrictions on Investment

Restrictions on investments in order to prevent asset substitution, that is to prevent changing the risk level of the assets of the firm through the acquisition of financial claims on other firms.

Restrictions on Dispositions of Assets

Prevents piecemeal sale of assets and prevents asset substitution.

Secured Debt

Limits asset substitution.

Restrictions on Mergers

Limits ability to raise risk to bondholders from combining assets of firms to the benefit of shareholders in both firms.

Requirement for Maintenance of Asset Investments

Required maintenance on fixed capital or required levels of working capital (cash, inventory, and accounts receivable) may provide signals to lenders of impending difficulties.

Indirect Restrictions on Production/Investment

Requires extensive and expensive monitoring activities.

Restrictions on the Payment of Dividends

Restrict the ability to liquidate assets or issue debt to pay dividends to shareholders thus changing the risk to lenders. Usually payment of dividends or other distributions to shareholders are restricted to be paid from an "inventory" of accumulated earnings.

Restrictions on Subsequent Financing

Limitations on amounts and priority of debt

Prevent the issuance of debt claims that will reduce the value of the bond by increasing its risk.

Limitations on Rentals, Leases, and Sale-Leasebacks

Leases and rent contracts are like debt and have superior claim on earnings, consequently they can reduce the value of existing debt by increasing its risk.

Restrictions on the Pattern of Payoffs to Bondholders

Sinking Funds

Required repayments of principal allow reduction in the book value of the firm and may loosen the dividend restriction and investment requirements over time, which may be desirable in firms with declining asset values.

Convertibility provisions

Call feature can align interests of bondholders with stockholders since they can convert to stockholders. This may reduce the incentive of stockholders to increase variance of asset returns at expense of bondholders by changing investment policy, since bondholders can share in the increased stock value by exercising their conversion feature.

Callability

Limits the gain bondholder can extract from stockholders upon recapitalization of the firm, when otherwise bargaining between these parties represents a bilateral monopoly.

Requirements for Specific Bonding Activities

Reporting

Cheaper for management to provide audited data required for monitoring covenants than for bondholders.

Required Accounting Techniques

Required use of standard accounting techniques can reduce management's ability to loosen effects of bond covenants.

Official Certificates of Compliance

Cheaper to have officers of the firm certify that the covenants have been met than to determine externally, and engages their personal liability.

Purchase of Insurance

Insurance firms may have comparative advantage in monitoring management activities, such as accident prevention, and may reduce risks to bondholders.

SOURCE: Clifford Smith and Jerold Warner, "On Financial Contracting: An Analysis of Bond Covenants," *Journal of Financial Economics* 7 (1979), pp. 117–161.

as those in Table 8.2, can resolve conflicts between the parties in a loan. They also found that these restrictions have economic costs in terms of reduced flexibility. Since the restrictions are costly, Smith and Warner conclude that contract provisions provide benefits to contracting parties or they would not exist. These *contracting costs* are valuable because they resolve the bondholder/shareholder conflicts.

Resolution of these conflicts in actual situations requires ability and experience to assess risks and choose appropriate clauses to include in contract provisions. Negotiating these contracts is a value-producing service provided by financial institution personnel. Value produced in negotiating terms of credit arrangements is derived from making investments in positive net present value projects possible when there are conflicts of interest. Skills necessary to negotiate these deals are not easy to come by. Training credit officers who gain necessary experience to craft the best possible loan agreement without discouraging the borrower and safeguarding the lender's interests is expensive. When credit personnel are trained, they must be paid well so they will stay and the financial institution can reap the benefits of their skills.

8.3 VALUE CREATION IN INFORMATION AND MONITORING: RELATIONSHIPS

Slovin, Sushka, and Polonchek (1993) estimated the value to corporate borrowers of credit relationships, based on an analysis of the stock price performance of 53 customers of Continental Bank in Chicago. The authors document an average fall in stock prices of the bank customers of about 9 percent when the bank collapsed in 1984. The reduced value in the share prices of these bank customers is an estimate of the value of the relationship they had with their bank and is evidence of the value of banking relationships to business borrowers. What are the economic bases for this value to credit customers? We explore several explanations below.

One explanation of why investments by financial institutions are valuable to their customers is that information concerning the true value of a firm is costly to produce. Campbell and Kracaw (1980) analyzed a market where firms are either better or worse than average and if there is no way to tell the difference, good firms will be undervalued and bad firms overvalued by the market. They show that if there is competition in information production, managers of undervalued firms will be willing to pay financial institutions enough to cover the costs of producing information identifying them as good firms. In their analysis, financial institutions guarantee the quality of their information and transmit their findings concerning which are good firms to financial markets by investing their own funds in undervalued firms. Campbell and Kracaw's analysis therefore makes information production on firm quality an economic function of financial intermediaries.

Credit service firms may be able to develop customer specific information over time that can be used to create value. Long-term credit *relationships,* where borrowers and lenders continue renewable credit relationships although competitors are available, are a widely observed phenomenon in credit markets.

Commercial banks and other financial institutions consider their longtime retail and wholesale customers as special assets. Studies by Sharpe (1990) and Rajan (1992) provide detailed analyses of the economic basis for value in long-term relationships between borrowers and lenders.

Sharpe considers a case where borrowers have risky investment projects when intermediate and long-term (first and second period) results on project success are available. Intermediate results can be observed more accurately by current creditors than outsiders who might compete for credit business at the beginning of the second period. Information on projects' intermediate results increase or decrease the likelihood of success over the long run. Examples of projects might be new products or technologies where initial results signal whether the products or methods have more or less risk of success in the future.

Sharpe shows that initial period lenders—like commercial banks who can learn inexpensively and more accurately than nonlenders about intermediate results—can offer competitive terms on the initial short-term funds. The initial period lender's relatively low cost, high quality information on intermediate results can come from special reports or analysis of internal documents produced under loan agreements. In Sharpe's analysis, loans are renewable after intermediate results are reported at rates depending on the results. The rates can be lower for both successful and riskier borrowers than long-term loans (over both intermediate and long run investments) because intermediate results allow fine-tuning of risks of loans. They can be lower than those offered by competitors who cannot observe intermediate results as accurately as the first period lender.

Sharpe analyzed many cases of competitive conditions in credit markets and different costs of information gathering in his theoretical analysis. The value created by the intermediate information may be appropriated by the lender under market conditions granting monopoly power on the part of the lender over the borrower. Sharpe shows how a lender's reputation for fairness may control its ability to exploit its monopoly power in competitive credit markets. This is another instance of competitive conditions determining the allocation of value produced in credit services between borrowers and credit service providers.

Rajan examined two dimensions of relationships between borrowers and arrangers of credit. First, Rajan's analysis examines the ability of short-term lenders to examine intermediate results of the project when those results show that the optimal policy is to liquidate the project at a loss, even if long-term prospects include a small probability of positive returns. Managers not forced to liquidate continue unsuccessful projects with long-term lenders' funds since they have an expected gain even with high risk projects financed entirely with borrowed money. In Rajan's model, short-term credit providers enhance economic efficiency by forcing liquidation of projects that prove to be too risky based on intermediate information. Long-term investors, without access or ability to act on intermediate information, must charge rates on credit that compensate for the cost of financing continuation of projects that short-term lenders would cancel.

Rajan's second focus is on project managers' efforts. Since short-term lenders can liquidate loans after intermediate results, their ability to deny or renew loans for projects successful in the intermediate period gives the short-term lender with intermediate information power over borrowers in the second period. The lender may insist on sharing the rewards of successful projects over the long term, reducing incentives for maximum effort on the part of project managers. Overall project results may be reduced below optimal levels if lenders reduce managers' incentives by demanding higher loan rates or profit participations in the second period.

Rajan's analysis demonstrates that there is value in credit relationships in terms of economic efficiencies from acting on intermediate information and terminating high-risk projects. This value is offset by reduced borrower incentives to produce in the long run. Rajan's analysis illustrates a contrast between relationship borrowing, where information is shared by borrower and lender, and open-market financing, where long-term contracts induce maximum effort but continue high risk projects that lower average returns. The allocation of the value of intermediate information will be determined by the bargaining power of borrowers and creditors and the competition from long-term borrowers.

Value Creation through Confidential Credit Relationships

Firms and businesses borrow funds to undertake investments at a scale they either cannot finance internally or are unwilling to undertake without diversification. In some cases, the value of a project may come from the fact that no other market participant knows any details about the project. To illustrate the value of confidentiality, take the case of a publicly owned company considering an investment to produce a new product that competes with an existing product manufactured by another firm. Knowledge that a new competitor plans to enter the business would allow the current producer to take defensive actions, such as price reductions or product improvements. The plan's profitability to the new competitor depends on keeping details secret.

Disclosing information about a planned project on a confidential basis to a lender might enable a firm to borrow funds for the project. The danger is that the lender would buy stock or other securities from current owners at current prices that do not reflect the value of the plan because those plans have not been made public. When the plan is announced, the lender who used the confidential information would realize a gain on the securities purchased from uninformed original owners. That gain would have been the former security holders' gain if the lender had not used inside information. How can management raise funds to undertake the project and still retain the benefits of its plan for the current owners of the firm's securities, especially its shareholders, in attempting to maximize their wealth?

Campbell (1979) analyzed the problem of raising funds and preserving gains from implementation of projects for current shareholders when confidentiality is critical for project success. Recipients of private information who arrange funding cannot be allowed to buy stock or other securities in the company before news of the project is public. There must be enough competition among lenders using confidential information that the firm does not have to bargain away all of the gains due to the project in the form of higher borrowing costs. Lenders who arrange credit and commit to not buying common stock or other securities sensitive to future business plans on the basis of confidential information in the form of debt instruments can create value for the current owners of the firm's securities.

Under current United States laws, commercial banks cannot buy common stock (see Chapter 14 for a discussion of the regulations). Banks also have the technical expertise to analyze complex business plans disclosed on a confidential basis. The prohibition on bank stock ownership means that banks can make loans on the basis of confidential or customer-specific information and not participate in the gains to shareholders from the implementation and announcement of the company's previously confidential business strategies.

Other financial institutions, like insurance companies investing in privately placed debt, are in a similar position to create value for borrowers simply by keeping information confidential. The conditions to produce value in credit are that the lender or arranger of credit neither discloses the information to others nor buys other classes of securities that will increase in value from the ultimate disclosure of the information on the project. The credit service firm may do this either through an enforceable agreement or by submitting to regulations (like bank regulations) preventing ownership of different classes of securities in the same firm.

The Value Produced by Monitoring

The preceding discussion introduced a number of credit contract provisions that can remove or mitigate the conflict between creditors and owners of firms concerning the use of borrowed funds and the proceeds of investments. These provisions would have no importance to borrowers if they were not enforced. It is necessary to monitor the actions of the borrower of funds to ensure that the loan terms are observed.

The expertise required to monitor borrowers, especially in complex business situations where financial and technical business operating data require skilled interpretation, means that there may be economies in monitoring the activities of borrowers. Diamond has argued (1984) that the ability of financial institutions like commercial banks to monitor borrowers' activities is an important source of value to the economy and hence to investors in financial institutions and a reason for their existence.

In Diamond's analysis there are two sources of credit to borrowers who are entrepreneurs with risky but positive net present value projects that need funds. One source is individual investors or nonfinancial firms, which he calls lenders. The other source of funds is financial intermediaries who raise funds from individual investors. Individual lenders have the option of lending directly to entrepreneur/borrowers or turning funds over to a financial institution to invest on their behalf. Funds turned over to intermediaries can be in the form of deposits or other financial instruments.

In terms of principal–agent analysis, lenders are principals who can be harmed or helped by the actions and information of users of funds. The entrepreneur is an agent who in the absence of monitoring alone knows how investments turn out and how much money is available to pay off lenders. When lenders turn funds over to financial intermediaries, the financial intermediary becomes the agent making decisions concerning the use of the lenders' funds affecting their welfare. The financial intermediary takes lenders' funds and makes loans to entrepreneurs.

In the second part of this intermediated transaction, the financial intermediary is the principal and the borrower the agent. Figure 8.2 illustrates the relationships between borrowers, lenders, and financial institutions, showing how financial institutions add another layer to the relationship between users and suppliers of funds.

Diamond's analysis focuses on monitoring costs associated with entrepreneurs' use of funds. Diamond assumes that information needed by any individual investor or firm, for example information on the actual performance of investments or observance of loan covenants, is costly to gather and cannot be observed by others. This is a reasonable characterization of monitoring activities of banks, insurance companies, and other financial intermediaries who track the use of loan funds and follow business performance of borrowers.

If borrowers violate loan agreements and are caught by monitors, Diamond assumes that monitors can impose large costs on borrowers. These costs are important in the analysis. Threat of these economic costs or sanctions mean that expected losses from violations of the loan agreement are greater than loan balances. These sanctions can be thought of as bankruptcy costs or lost future business opportunities. Diamond demonstrates under these assumptions that the optimal arrangement is for the borrower to issue a fixed debt contract to lenders. The fixed obligation ensures that borrowers make maximum effort to pay off the debt to avoid bankruptcy costs.

In Diamond's study lenders are risk neutral (as described in Chapter 6) and have an alternative investment opportunity, meaning they will not accept a rate of return below a certain opportunity cost. Lenders maximize expected returns above the opportunity rate without regard for risk, indifferent between investing

FIGURE 8.2 Financial institutions and delegated monitoring

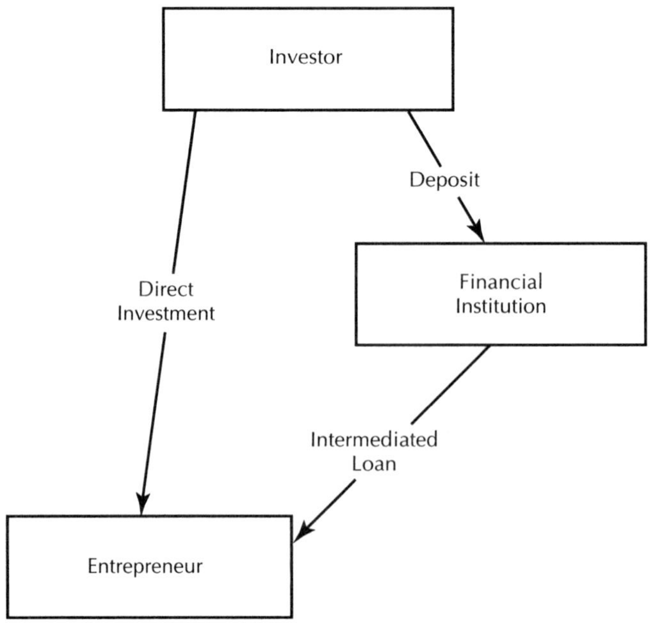

in entrepreneurs' projects and turning funds over to professional investor/monitors (financial institutions) as long as the expected returns are the same.

When entrusted with lenders' funds, financial institutions are agents in principal–agent analysis. Since the investment returns of entrepreneurs will only be observed by financial institutions, they must have an incentive to pay out those returns to lenders. If they are faced with economic sanctions or bankruptcy costs for nonperformance in the same way as entrepreneurs, Diamond shows that the optimal arrangement is for them to issue fixed rate instruments like deposits to lenders. To avoid bankruptcy costs, financial institutions undertake costs of monitoring and pay off depositors out of the proceeds of the entrepreneurs' projects if they possibly can.

Diamond's analysis demonstrates the economic contribution of monitoring activities delegated to financial institutions. The value produced by financial intermediaries comes from two sources: (1) diversification from funding many entrepreneurs' projects; and (2) reduction in costs of monitoring from duplication of monitoring effort by investors and economies of scale in monitoring effort. Diversification of loans to many entrepreneurs by the financial intermediary with economies in monitoring loan contracts justifies economically an extra layer of institutions, financial intermediaries, who can earn enough for their investors to pay lender/depositors at least the same expected rate of return as they would earn on making individual loans with less expected costs of monitoring.

Diamond's analysis is a persuasive and influential argument concerning the sources of economic value produced by financial institutions like banks. Financial institutions produce value by reducing risks for a given return by diversification of investments. They reduce the costs of monitoring and make it possible for entrepreneurs to raise funds from investors in the form of debt instruments. Positive net present value projects are undertaken that might not be otherwise. The costs of monitoring incurred by an additional layer of financial intermediaries are covered while investors continue to earn their reservation yields on investments.

8.4 FUNDING CREDIT AND RISK MANAGEMENT

Funding of credit by traditional lenders like commercial banks and insurance companies as portfolio investments continues to be an important source of credit in financial markets as we saw in the Chapter 7. Traditional lenders often rely on third parties, usually similar financial institutions, to provide part of the funds for large or risky credits to borrowers. The sharing of credit funding by similar institutions is called *participations,* where loan or debt instrument risks and returns are shared on a pro rata basis by the parties funding the credit.

Recent financial market developments have seen nontraditional channels for the funding of credit activities achieve real importance in credit markets. In these flows of funds, nontraditional credit providers, like pension funds, mutual funds, and private investors, fund loans originated by traditional lenders, like commercial banks or investment banks. In some cases, nontraditional lenders, like finance companies, may arrange for funding of loans from nontraditional sources of funds or even traditional portfolio lenders.

We examine in this section the economic issues associated with alternative ways to fund loans originated by traditional portfolio lenders or new entrants to the credit services market. In particular, we scrutinize issues associated with the separation of the funding of credits from the value production in credit services derived from pricing and monitoring analyzed in the previous sections.

There are several ways a lender may raise part or all of the funds for a loan originated by the institution. These funding sources represent a continuum starting with traditional portfolio lending, moving to *loan participations* with similar institutions, proceeding to *loan sales* to third parties or *credit guarantees* arranged by borrowers for direct borrowing in the open market, and extending to *loan securitization*. We show this continuum and critical characteristics of each funding arrangement in Table 8.3.

TABLE 8.3 Funding Arrangements for Loans

Portfolio Lending

Direct lending by a financial institution financed by its own liabilities, such as deposits or insurance reserves. This lending may be restricted by regulation to a percent of assets, to certain types of risks, to a limited amount in certain classifications of loans, or to single borrowers (see Chapters 14 and 16 on regulation.)

Participations

Lending originated by one or more portfolio lenders who share the funding and proceeds of the loan. Participations can be managed by a *lead* institution or a *managing* institution. Participations can be on a *recourse* basis, where the participation must be reversed by the lead or managing institution, or a *nonrecourse* basis, where no reversal is guaranteed. Cash flows from the loan interest and principal may be divided up in any way. Large participations are organized as *syndicates,* with many institutions participating on some pre-agreed basis. Since loan participations are bilateral contracts, they are not readily marketable.

Loan Sale

Loan sales are similar to participations except that they are usually to nonfinancial institutions or different types of institutions; for example, an insurance company may buy part of a bank loan. These loan sales may be on a recourse or nonrecourse basis. Purchased loans are not readily sellable in the open market, since they are bilateral contracts.

Credit Guarantee

Financial institutions may guarantee availability of funds, usually in the form of a *letter of credit,* using their better-known name and credit reputation to back borrowing in the open market, typically in the form of short-term instruments like commercial paper. While the credit guarantee between the borrower and financial institution is not transferable, the open market paper may be readily marketable.

Securitized Loan Sales

Typically, several credit instruments, for example mortgages, are pooled and used as security for a credit market instrument, such as a bond or mortgage pass-through, where all or part of the cash flows from the underlying credit instruments is paid according to predetermined schedules to the buyers of the credit instruments. The credit market instrument is typically marketable in the open market.

Loan participations, loan sales, and loan guarantees can be equivalent or very different depending on the terms between the loan originator and the loan investor. If the loan is participated or sold on a *recourse basis,* meaning that the loan buyer can demand reversal of the sale by returning the loan to the seller, there is no difference between a loan sale and a loan guarantee. A loan guarantor agrees to repay the loan if the borrower cannot repay or refinance it. On the other hand, a *nonrecourse* loan participation or sale is very different from the investment in a loan backed by a credit guarantee because buyers may lose their investment.

Cash flows from loan funding arrangements display a wide variation. Cash flows from a loan sale or participation can be *pro rata* sharing of repayments of principal and interest among loan buyers or participants. Alternatively, cash flows from the loan sale or participation can be divided according to prespecified sharing rules. For example, some participants may have a prior claim on cash flows from payments of principal, but interest may be divided among other participants or buyers.

In all the alternatives to portfolio lending by credit service providers, there is an unbundling of the credit-related activities in the value chain. Funding and risk bearing are separated from the term setting, marketing, delivery, and monitoring activities associated with loan origination and servicing. These activities can in turn be divided among participants or purchasers in different ways. Fees associated with various activities in the loan origination and servicing can be split up or concentrated according to the terms of the loan sale.

There are three sources of economic value from the separation of funding and risk bearing from the other activities in credit services: (1) competitive advantage in loan origination or monitoring; (2) economic advantages from diversification or the ability to make investments restricted by regulators but possible when funding and credit origination are separated; and (3) differences in costs of funds stemming from regulatory or tax treatment or comparative advantage of financial institutions. We discuss each of these sources of comparative advantage briefly below.

Competitive Advantage in Loan Origination

Competitive advantages in loan origination and monitoring come from a variety of sources. The easiest to grasp is local area knowledge possessed by a financial institution, say a bank or the regional office of an insurance company. Calling officers are familiar with the local economy, speak the language, and know the business environment and major players in the various industries represented in the region or country. Local credit officials are likely to be more aware of and understand better the impact of national and regional trends and competitive developments on credit demand and risks in their regional borrowers market.

Regional knowledge translates into a competitive advantage relative to institutions without a local presence in marketing, pricing, delivering, and monitoring of credit to borrowers located in the region. Locally based calling officers or branches may be able to market better to local borrowers and effectively price and deliver to credit service demanders. Local expertise and close observation can improve the effectiveness of loan monitoring and enforcement of contract terms. All of these factors can give the local credit service provider a competitive advantage relative to lenders without a strong local presence.

The competitive advantages associated with particular area knowledge becomes especially strong in international lending. Language problems, differences in legal systems and business practices, and so on, increase the costs for outsiders to acquire knowledge necessary to compete on an even basis with local credit service providers. National boundaries provide real if surmountable barriers to competition among credit service providers, even without regulatory protection of domestic financial institutions.

The competitive advantage based on information for credit service firms is not limited to regional expertise. Lending institutions can specialize in certain industries or classes of borrowers, thereby gaining special expertise in marketing, pricing, delivering, and monitoring these types of credits. For example, some equipment lessors specialize in certain types of equipment use, like International Lease Finance Corporation's specialization in airplanes. Credit service firms may develop competitive advantages in originating certain types of loans or financing.

Regional developments and demands for credit in particular industries may represent opportunities to outside investors who are able to offer credit services that are favorable in terms of lower risks or higher yields relative to their alternatives. Local or specialized credit institutions may not have adequate resources to fund good local projects. To take advantage of these differing investment opportunities, outside financial institutions have the option of establishing a local or special industry presence, which may be costly or prohibited by regulation, or they may fund credits by working with local or specialized financial institutions that originate deals. More value may be created for both local or specialized credit service originators and outside investors by exploiting the competitive advantage of the originating institution instead of direct entry into the market by outsiders.

Loan sales and participations with local credit institutions may be efficient in sharing higher returns and lower risks from local opportunities to outside investors. Loans may be funded for productive investments that otherwise would not be made, making possible fees and commissions earned by financial institutions through loan sales and participations. Local-information-based sources of value can make loan participations and sales more efficient than direct attempts to serve remote markets with branches or representative officers. They allow interregional credit flows to local or specialized financial institutions without an actual presence.

Diversification of Loan Portfolios

Regional and industrial variation in economic activity means substantial reduction in credit risk can be gained from diversification in these two dimensions. The value to be gained by management of risks through diversification, including those from industrial and regional variations, are discussed at length in Part IV of this book. The high cost of establishing representation in many locations or calling on many economic sectors may mean that diversification is gained most efficiently by participations or purchases of loans from other financial institutions.

Diversification of loan portfolios spreads regional and industrial risks. Local institutions should not concentrate in loans specific to their region or industrial concentration. Out-of-region financial institutions want to invest in credits outside their local markets to diversify their investments regionally or by industrial sectors. Regional and industry diversification explains much of the investment flows we observe among commercial bank correspondent banking networks and loan participations. International loan syndications also provide diversification.

Differences in the Cost of Funds

A third source of competitive advantage exploited by loan sales and participations comes from differences in the costs of funds among financial institutions. In the commercial banking business, for example, some small banks have funds from relatively cheap transaction accounts but cannot identify enough local lending opportunities at reasonable cost to use the funds advantageously. Loans made by banks or other financial institutions with larger markets to serve may offer higher returns. Smaller banks in local markets often invest in correspondent banks' loans to share in the higher returns and/or lower risks available to them. Differences in the cost of funds represent one of many sources of differing competitive advantages that can be exploited by financial institutions in maximizing returns and value.

The competitive advantage from lower costs of funds may be especially high when we compare bank to nonbank costs of funds. As pointed out by Pennacchi (1988), banks' costs of funds are increased by reserve requirements on deposits, deposit insurance premiums, and by minimum capital requirements. Nonbank investors, such as mutual funds, pension funds, or nonbank financial institutions like insurance and finance companies, may be able to realize a larger spread over the loan rates than banks can realize when funding credits with deposits. Loan sales can produce value for banks from loan origination fees and capture of their comparative advantage in making loans. Value for loan purchasers comes from favorable spreads over their cost of funds.

James (1988) has made a subtle argument concerning the source of value from loan sales and participations. James argues that banks and other financial institutions may wish to use their low risk loans as collateral for lending funded by other investors with lower average costs. In this way, financial institutions like banks can arrange credits that otherwise would not be in their interest because lower risks of the loans would only benefit current liability holders (like depositors) whose risks would be reduced if banks invested in high quality loans. Since selling loans or issuing credit guarantees for loans funded in the money market allows a lower cost of funding than funding loans with new deposits, more loans will be made.

Loan Sales and Participations and Agency Problems

Loan sales and participations reduce the originating credit service provider's stake in the loan outcome. This reduced stake in the performance of the loan can cause problems that we can analyze in the context of principal–agent analysis. The agent in this case is the originating financial service firm, whose activities in monitoring and controlling the borrower under the terms of the loan contract can affect the performance of the loan. The benefits of the loan go to the buyer or participant, the principal in the arrangement.

Firms originating loans have more information about the loan quality than buyers of loans, another information asymmetry problem. Loan sellers may be tempted to keep good loans and sell poorer quality loans, an adverse selection problem. In loan sales or participations involving complex arrangements or long distances, loan purchasers or participants may not be able to check on how the credit originator is performing its monitoring and controlling functions. This is a moral hazard problem due to the possible underperformance of critical activities because the agent's commitment is lessened due to its reduced stake.

Value can be created by reducing or solving agency problems in the context of loan sales and participations. The underlying economic efficiency comes from the competitive advantage or cost differentials discussed above. Given the extent and growth of loan sales and participations among banks, correspondent banks, international syndications, and nonbank financial institutions, it is clear that these problems can be overcome. Pennacchi (1988) analyzed the economics of loan sales and participations in the context of a principal–agent analysis which we present here.

In structuring loan sales or participations several alternatives are commonly observed. The first and most important is whether the sale or loan is on a *recourse* or *nonrecourse* basis, as we discussed above. If the loan is sold on a recourse basis, the loan purchaser can reverse the sale whenever it is advantageous to do so, most likely when the loan fails to perform or becomes riskier because of changes in economic conditions or market events. Loan sales and participations on a recourse basis reduce the principal–agent problem substantially, since the loan purchaser need only worry about the ability of the loan seller to rebuy the loan if the buyer no longer wishes to hold it.

Regulators (like bank regulators) consider loans sold on a recourse basis to still be on the balance sheet of the financial institution selling the loan or loan participation. In fact, in the United States, loans sold on a recourse basis are treated like deposits and the proceeds of loan sales are subject to reserve requirements. Loans sold on a recourse basis do not really diversify the originator's credit risks. For these reasons, alternatives to selling or participating loans on a recourse basis have been developed.

Pennacchi worked out the economics of loan sales on a nonrecourse basis. He demonstrates that loan sales or participations in which the selling financial institution retains the higher risk portion of the loan can solve the adverse selection and moral hazard problems that concern loan purchasers. By retaining a high risk position, the originating institution's exposure to the bad effects of inadequate monitoring and control activities is increased. As Pennacchi describes an optimal contract sharing loan returns on a nonrecourse basis:

> [The sharing rule] looks very similar to the loan buyer having a debt position and the bank [loan seller] having an equity position in the loan. The contract is characterized by penalizing the bank if low loan outcomes occur and rewarding the bank if high loan outcomes (no default) occur. Giving the bank disproportionate share of the risk

> allows the bank to reap a disproportionate share of the gains from monitoring, enabling a greater amount of the loan to be sold while maintaining monitoring–incentive efficiency. (p. 387)

Loan participations and sales, like loans themselves, require detailed contract negotiation and bargaining.

Value can be produced by financial service firms not only in solving principal–agent problems in the original credit arrangement, discussed earlier, but also in structuring the contracts required to finance the credit. Credit deals require sophisticated assessments of the various investors' and financial institutions' interests and concerns. Negotiation and bargaining related to loan funding are like other aspects of credit services, information intensive and complex. The talents of sophisticated and experienced personnel are required.

Open Market Sales of Loans: Loan Securitization

Credit funding is also possible using loans as collateral for security issues. Larger corporate borrowers routinely use financial institution guarantees as backing to borrow funds in the open market. These guarantees, usually bank or insurance company letters of credit, are used to borrow in the commercial paper market, which has grown enormously, as pointed out in Chapter 7. These corporate or government agency credit arrangements are functionally similar to loan sales on a recourse basis.

We distinguish the guarantees and loan sales and participations discussed above from loans used as collateral for securities issues. The economics of loans used as collateral for securities issues are different from guarantees or recourse sales of loans. Risk return characteristics of individual credit instruments used for loan-backed securities must be understandable and acceptable to the market in order to be marketable. Investors in these securities have a passive involvement in the negotiation of the terms of their participation since they buy widely traded standardized financial instruments. To be understandable and acceptable to the market, standardization of the underlying individual credit arrangements is necessary. Some credit transactions, like home mortgages, have become so routine that claims on diversified pools of mortgages are readily tradable in securities markets. The challenge in loan-backed securities is to design standardized loans acceptable to borrowers and buyers of asset-backed securities. In addition to mortgages, car loans and credit card receivables have been used in loan-backed securities.

8.5 RISK BEARING AND SHARING: FINANCIAL ENGINEERING PRODUCTS

Value production in credit services comes partly from differences in risk exposure or risk preferences. Unprecedented interest rate and exchange rate variability experienced in industrialized countries in the last twenty years (discussed in Chapter 13) have dramatically increased borrowing customers' exposure to financial risks stemming from these factors. Borrower concerns with interest rate and exchange rate variabilities have spawned a vast number of new financial products and services, collectively called "financial engineering" (see Finnerty, 1988).

Financial engineering means design and implementation of solutions to financial problems or concerns using carefully designed financial contracts. An example of a wildly successful type of these contracts is an *interest rate swap,* which is an exchange between two borrowers of their interest rate payment obligations. In a typical exchange, fixed and floating interest rate payments are swapped between two borrowers. Smith, Smithson, and Wakeman (1988) describe the market for interest rate swaps and estimate market size in terms of the principal amounts used to calculate the interest obligations (called the "notional principal") in the United States at $542 billion in 1987.

An interest rate swap is an arrangement between two borrowers. Financial institutions create value by arranging the swap transactions and keeping track of records. Financial firms make the payments of the net differences in the interest payments between the two parties. The financial institution, usually a commercial or investment bank, becomes a so-called "counterparty" to each participant in the deal. In being a counterparty to many swap transactions, a financial institution can manage its exposure to default and timing risks of cash flows, using the hedging techniques discussed Part IV of this book.

Financial engineering has become an important source of value added in credit services. Value production for financial institutions active in the markets for financial engineering products comes from three sources: (1) structuring credit deals to reduce or eliminate specific problems or risks faced by the customer due to specifics of its cash flow needs; (2) arbitraging differences in the term structure or risk structure of financial asset prices for different classes of borrowers; and (3) efficiency in managing the risks associated with portfolios of risks.

Table 8.4 illustrates an interest rate swap. Assume a real estate developer can borrow cheaply in the short-term market where rates fluctuate a lot even though cash flows from long-term lease payments are fixed in amount: the table shows the developer borrowing $1 million at the variable rate shown in the second to last column. Since variable cash commitments from short-term borrowing increase default risk as analyzed by Anthony Santomero (1983), the developer would prefer a fixed rate. If another borrower, like a deposit institution, is reluctant to make a long-term fixed rate commitment because assets are short-term, the two borrowers may both be better off by arranging an interest rate swap. Assume the deposit firm borrows $1 million at the fixed rate of 7.00 percent shown in the table. The swap counterparty takes the difference between the fixed and variable rates ($10,000 when the variable rate is 6.00 percent) plus a fee ($100 in the example) from the developer when variable rates are less than the fixed rate and pays the difference to the deposit firm minus the fee. When the fixed rate is below the variable rate, the swap counterparty collects from the deposit firm and passes the difference through to the developer. The improvement in the developer's and deposit firm's situations provides the value earning

TABLE 8.4 Cash Flows in Interest Rate Swap

INTEREST ON LOAN		*PAYMENT TO COUNTERPARTY AND NET COST*				
DEVELOPER	*DEPOSIT FIRM*	*DEVELOPER PAYMENT*	*DEVELOPER NET COST*	*DEPOSIT FIRM NET*	*VARIABLE RATE*	*FIXED RATE*
60,000	70,000	10,100	70,100	60,000	6.00%	7.00%
62,500	70,000	7,600	70,100	62,500	6.25%	7.00%
75,000	70,000	(4,900)	70,100	75,000	7.50%	7.00%
77,500	70,000	(7,400)	70,100	77,500	7.75%	7.00%
80,000	70,000	(9,900)	70,100	80,000	8.00%	7.00%
70,000	70,000	100	70,100	70,000	7.00%	7.00%

opportunity for the financial institution arranging the swap. The swap arranger is the counterparty to the two borrowers.

A financial institution possessing superior technical information may arrange interest rate swaps lowering net costs of credit for borrowers. For example, if risk premiums for short-term loans are lower than for long-term loans in the market, a risky long-term borrower could benefit by swapping his interest obligations on short-term loans with a low-risk short-term borrower who borrows long-term. The low-risk borrower borrowing in the long-term market swaps those interest payment obligations to the riskier short-term borrower, producing value for both parties. Financial institutions understanding this technical information can price and arrange an exchange of interest obligations in the swap and extract some of the value as fees.

Other financial engineering products developed and sold by financial institutions are too numerous to discuss at length. Finnerty (1988) provides an exhaustive table of products. New risk management and problem-solving products emerge daily, often flourishing and disappearing with changing market conditions. Many products, like *interest rate caps* or *interest rate collars* that restrict interest rate charges on variable rate loans or investments, have option components and are discussed in Part IV. Value produced by financial institutions comes from understanding and creating attractive risk reducing or risk sharing products and being able to price them.

8.6 SUMMARY

Credit services produce value for financial institutions by producing value for their customers. Allowing productive investments to be undertaken requires that the risks stemming from information asymmetry and moral hazard be reduced to tolerable levels. In this chapter, we explored how pricing and other term setting involved in contract design can control borrower actions. We have discussed relationships and monitoring based on information and their roles in resolving conflicts of interest between borrowers and lenders. We explored economic issues associated with funding loans with third party funds in the form of participations, loan sales, or credit guarantees. Finally, value enhancing features in the form of financial engineering can be offered separately or incorporated in credit instruments to provide further profitable opportunities for financial institutions. As with all financial services, one inevitable observation is the high degree of skill necessary to process complex credit arrangements involving technical information. Financial services are a labor-intensive business.

DISCUSSION QUESTIONS AND EXERCISES

1. As a financier secretly accumulating stock in a firm you wish eventually to take over, what are you concerned with in borrowing some of the funds to finance the stock purchases? How could your concerns be removed?
2. Have you ever borrowed money or thought of borrowing money from a financial institution? Carefully think of the different loan terms that could be offered you, why you might find them attractive or unattractive relative to alternatives, and what you may have revealed about yourself in choosing a particular type of loan.
3. Self-revelation of risk type can improve the terms at which financial institutions offer credit to various types of borrowers. Can you think of ways to get retail customers to reveal their riskiness by the credit terms they choose?
4. Provide some examples of collateral and other terms used for personal loans and indicate how the existence of collateral affects the attitude toward accepting a given loan and then servicing the loan as agreed. What types of penalties and/or sanctions are there for not paying as agreed? Relate these to the analysis of collateral in the chapter.
5. Provide examples of the types of monitoring of loan agreement terms that are necessary in order to preserve the risk reducing aspects of the loan in the case of personal loans like auto loans.
6. From your experience in other courses in corporate finance, what types of information would be necessary to assess the risks of lending to a corporation? What financial disclosures and other information would you request? How could you use this information to assess the risks and what skills are necessary in order to use the information as you suggest?
7. Trace the exact cash flow implications of buying a pro-rata share of a loan that fails to perform on a recourse basis versus a nonrecourse basis. What might induce you to invest in a loan on a nonrecourse basis, given the discussion in the text?
8. The demise of Communism in Eastern Europe has opened up vast investment opportunities in the region for investors. What ways of making investments in the form of credit instruments could be considered by individual investors? By financial institutions? Where would the value be produced?
9. Provide some examples from your reading of financial engineering products (bank advertisements in the *Wall Street Journal* are a good source). Where is the value to the customer in these products? How does the finan-

cial institution produce value by providing these products?

10. Many credit unions sell some of their consumer loans to other investors. What issues are those investors concerned with in buying those loans and how can the terms of the sale account for those concerns?

REFERENCES

BLACK, FISCHER. 1976. "The Dividend Puzzle," *The Journal of Portfolio Management* 2, pp. 5–8.

BLACK, FISCHER and MYRON SCHOLES. 1973. "The Pricing of Options and Corporate Liabilities," *Journal of Political Economy,* 81 (3), (May/June), pp. 637–654.

BREALEY, RICHARD A. and STEWART C. MYERS. 1988. *Principles of Corporate Finance* (Third Edition). New York: McGraw-Hill Book Company.

CAMPBELL, TIM S. 1979. "Optimal Investment Financing Decisions and the Value of Confidentiality," *Journal of Financial and Quantitative Analysis* XIV (5), pp. 913–924.

CAMPBELL, TIM S. and WILLIAM A. KRACAW. 1980. "Information Production, Market Signalling, and the Theory of Financial Intermediation," *Journal of Finance* XXXV (4), pp. 863–882.

CHAN, YUK-SHEE and ANJAN V. THAKOR. 1987. "Collateral and Competitive Equilibria with Moral Hazard and Private Information," *Journal of Finance* XLII (2), pp. 345–363.

DIAMOND, DOUGLAS W. 1984. "Financial Intermediation and Delegated Monitoring," *Review of Economic Studies* LI, pp. 393–414.

FINNERTY, JOHN D. 1988. "Financial Engineering in Corporate Finance: An Overview," *Financial Management* 17 (Winter), pp. 14–33.

GORTON, GARY and GEORGE PENNACCHI. 1989. "Are Loan Sales Really Off-Balance Sheet," *Journal of Accounting, Auditing and Finance,* 4 (2), pp. 125–145.

JAMES, CHRISTOPHER. 1981. "Self-Selection and the Pricing of Bank Services: An Analysis of the Market for Loan Commitments and the Role of Compensating Balance Requirements," *Journal of Financial and Quantitative Analysis* XVI (5), pp. 725–746.

JAMES, CHRISTOPHER. 1988. "The Use of Loan Sales and Standby Letters of Credit by Commercial Banks," *Journal of Monetary Economics* 22, pp. 395–422.

LELAND, HAYNE E. and DAVID H. PYLE. 1977. "Informational Asymmetries, Financial Structure, and Financial Intermediation," *Journal of Finance* XXXII (May), pp. 371–387.

MYERS, STEWART C. 1984. "The Capital Structure Puzzle," *Journal of Finance* XXXIX (July), pp. 575–592.

PAVEL, CHRISTINE and DAVID PHILLIS. 1987. "Why Commercial Banks Sell Loans: An Empirical Analysis," *Economic Perspectives,* Federal Reserve Bank of Chicago (May/June), pp. 3–14.

PENNACCHI, GEORGE G. 1988. "Loan Sales and the Cost of Bank Capital," *Journal of Finance* XVIII (June), pp. 375–396.

RAJAN, RAGURAM G. 1992. "Insiders and Outsiders: The Choice between Informed and Arm's Length Debt," *Journal of Finance* 47 (4), pp. 1367–1400.

SANTOMERO, ANTHONY M. 1983. "Fixed Versus Variable Rate Loans," *Journal of Finance* XXXVIII (December), pp. 1363–1380.

SHARPE, STEVEN A. 1990. "Asymmetric Information, Bank Lending, and Implicit Contracts: A Stylized Model of Customer Relationships," *Journal of Finance* 45 (4), pp. 1069–1087.

SLOVIN, MYRON B., MARIE E. SUSHKA, and JOHN A. POLONCHEK. 1993. "The Value of Bank Durability: Borrowers as Bank Stakeholders," *Journal of Finance* 48 (1), pp. 247–266.

SMITH, CLIFFORD, JR., CHARLES W. SMITHSON, and LEE MACDONALD WAKEMAN. 1988. "The Market for Interest Rate Swaps," *Financial Management* 17 (Winter), pp. 34–44.

SMITH, CLIFFORD and JEROLD WARNER. 1979. "On Financial Contracting: An Analysis of Bond Covenants," *Journal of Financial Economics* 7 (June), pp. 117–161.

CHAPTER

9

Securities Trading, Dealing, and Origination

Introduction

Securities investment and trading are among the most publicized and exciting activities in the financial services industry. In line with our earlier discussion of the financial system, securities are only a means of transferring savings to investors.

- How do securities differ in this role from the extensions of credit we discussed in the previous two chapters?
- What are the sources of value from financial firms that trade securities on financial markets to providers and users of funds?
- Why are traders in securities willing to pay to transact sooner rather than later and what specialized firms have emerged to service this demand for immediacy?
- What skills and resources are required in order to bring securities to the market?

Answers to these and related questions are essential to understanding the dynamics governing the transition in this financial industry segment from traditional forms to new and emerging delivery and production systems.

This chapter reviews the basic economics of the value added by securities trading, market making, and securities origination. The emphasis is on economic analysis of these basic financial services to isolate sources of value in the value chain we have used in previous chapters. Securities markets grow in importance as economies grow in extent and sophistication in terms of technology and institutional complexity. Securities markets represent a development beyond raising funds in the form of credit as discussed in the previous chapter. Securities markets can be expected to grow ever more important around the world in the future.

9.1 OVERVIEW OF SECURITIES MARKETS AND INSTRUMENTS

This chapter explores value production in those financial services traditionally associated with brokers and investment bankers. In order to set the stage for the dynamic changes taking place in this sector of the financial services industry, the position of traditional and nontraditional firms in the securities markets and the economic role of securities markets are reviewed in the following sections. The purpose here is to provide perspective on the creation of value in the major services provided by firms active in securities markets.

Firms Active in Securities Markets

The traditional concept of a securities firm is represented by a brokerage firm, like Merrill Lynch, or an investment banking firm, like Salomon Brothers. These and other firms involved in securities markets perform the established functions of buying and selling securities (brokerage) and advising clients on how to originate new securities (investment banker) to raise money. Traditional firms can be providers of the full range of securities markets services or can be more specialized. "Full line" firms like Merrill Lynch offer retail brokerage services and corporate securities advice, and narrowly focused firms like Jefferies Securities concentrate on trading for institutional clients.

In recent years, nonfinancial firms tried providing securities market services: Sears Roebuck, the retail giant and owner of Allstate Insurance, acquired the full-line broker Dean Witter, and then spun it off in 1993. General Electric, maker of refrigerators and jet engines, bought the investment banking concern Kidder-Peabody, and sold it to Paine Webber in 1995. A development of even broader potential significance has been the entrance of nonsecurities-related financial service firms, such as commercial banks and thrift institutions, into securities businesses through expansion of their authorized powers. Other financial service firms have entered the securities business through acquisitions, for example Travelers Insurance (then known as Primerica) bought Smith-Barney and Prudential Insurance acquired Bache.

There are four key factors influencing the future of the industry: (1) possible synergies realized by nonsecurities financial service firms from offering securities markets services; (2) synergies gained by nonfinancial firms from offering securities markets services; (3) technological change; and (4) structural changes in the flow of savings into investment.

Nonsecurities financial firms, principally commercial banks, have a number of synergistic connections to securities market services. Banks are portfolio lenders to nonfinancial firms and are involved in open-market, short-term financing in the form of letters of credit backing commercial paper. As discussed in Chapter 8, banks increasingly arrange credit for their customers. Banks already trade and make markets in a variety of money market and government securities, a natural basis for expansion into the corporate securities markets. Bank branch networks also offer ready marketing outlets for both retail and small corporate securities market services. It seems a natural extension of bank functions to arrange funding in the form of public securities issues. Finally, banks in Germany and Japan already have these authorities.

Nonbanks like large manufacturing corporations have already entered the financial services industry through their finance company subsidiaries, for example General Electric with its subsidiary GE Capital. They offer the securities business one important advantage: a lower cost of funds. Their enormous size, equity capital, and top credit ratings mean that they can commit large amounts of capital to their securities business. Their reputations can be of enormous value in competition for securities market services. Furthermore, nonbanks are not hampered by the regulations limiting traditional securities and deposit-taking financial institutions.

Technology offers vastly cheaper ways of communicating all the types of information required by providers of securities market services. Information on prices and communication with market participants are available at costs below the levels observed even a short time ago. Processing information, applying complex analytical tools, and plugging into related financial service functions, such as clearing networks and information providers, mean smaller firms and new entrants can quickly enter securities markets. These firms can compete on a relatively even footing with established firms for securities business.

Finally, the institutional changes in the flow of funds dramatically alter the markets within which securities markets service firms operate. Globalization integrates world capital markets. American securities firms are active around the world but must compete in the United States with securities firms from Europe and Japan, as well as Singapore and Hong Kong. Political and demographic trends foster emergence of locally important securities markets, like California and the Southeast in the United States, and China, the former Soviet Union, and Latin America abroad. Investment opportunities in these markets attract investors' funds from around the world. The continuing accumulation of savings in institutional investors such as pension funds and money management firms means that the market for trading securities and target markets for new securities issues is more sophisticated than in the past.

To appreciate developments in securities-related financial services, industry observers must understand the role of securities markets and the economic functions performed by financial service firms active in them. After a review of the basic attractiveness of tradable financial instruments and the economic determinants of the demand for each of these services, the underlying economics of the business is examined to identify sources of value in the securities business.

Demand and Supply for Securities

Securities are standardized financial claims that can be readily transferred between parties and therefore traded on securities markets. Typical individuals acquire or dispose of securities in the retail markets for securities services. Large firms and investors operate in the market for institutional securities market services. There are many reasons why individual and institutional investors prefer securities to portfolio investments.

Securities have desirable attributes relative to portfolio investments. They are liquid, meaning they can be exchanged for cash easily because there are markets where the securities are traded (although not always at a prices pleasing to sellers). Securities markets produce technical information (as defined in Chapter 6) including prices for the same or similar investments, unlike portfolio investments which are often difficult to price. Trading volume reflects the depth of the market for securities and investors' ability to convert investments into cash at predictable transaction prices. Publicly traded securities of large corporations in many countries are accompanied by a wealth of information in the form of disclosures. The investment community provides ongoing analysis of securities when they are issued or as they subsequently trade. Finally, securities market services are offered by established firms and institutions with reputations. Rules and regulations govern securities issuance and trading, which can be a source of confidence or a basis for litigation for investors in securities.

Issuing securities in order to raise funds has advantages for users of funds. Issuers may prefer to raise funds through issuance of securities rather than credit or direct placements described in the previous chapter because the liquidity of securities means that costs of funds are cheaper. Technical information reflected in the prices of similar or identical securities provided by securities markets clearly establishes the costs of funds for issuers. Prices and returns associated with alternative or substitute investments traded in securities markets provide issuing firms feedback on opportunity costs of making investments or returning funds to investors.

Development of securities markets expands funds available for investment in an economy by mobilizing savings more efficiently than bilateral credit arrangements. Some of the principal–agent problems between investors and users of funds discussed in the previous chapter may be mitigated when firms with publicly traded issues are willing to disclose information required of them. Firms issuing publicly traded securities can take advantage of competition in securities markets to reduce issue costs relative to costs implicit in negotiated deals with portfolio investors. In the case of some large firms, like Exxon, open market auctions of securities issues may eliminate altogether the need for financial intermediaries and their fees. These considerations also lead firms to prefer securities issues to private deals.

Buyers and sellers of securities, trading either new issues or seasoned issues, are motivated by two basic reasons. The first reason to trade securities for cash or cash for securities is because of normal variations in consumption or business needs for cash. Traders making portfolio adjustments requiring offsetting changes in cash and securities in response to factors unrelated to events in the securities markets are called *liquidity traders*. An individual selling stock to finance a child's education and an insurance company buying bonds to finance future payment of claims are both liquidity traders motivated by their specific portfolio considerations.

A second type of trader knows something that the rest of the participants in the market do not know. This information may be that a lawsuit has been filed or that a takeover attempt is imminent. Traders placing buy or sell orders based on private knowledge are called *information traders*. Information traders expect to profit because they buy securities at prices that are low relative to their true values or sell them at prices that are high relative to what they will sell for when the information the trader possesses becomes available to the market.

Functions of Securities Firms and Security Types

A *broker* finds a buyer for a seller. Because most traders are not continuously buying and selling securities, they turn to professional brokerage firms to complete their trades. Often, a buyer or seller wants to trade sooner than would be possible by waiting for a counterpart seller or buyer to show up in the market. Financial institutions that facilitate quick trades by buying or selling securities on their own accounts are called *market makers* or *dealers* in securities. When offering new securities to investors, firms raising funds require guidance in designing and pricing newly issued securities in order to make them attractive to investors. This guidance is one of the functions performed by financial service firms assisting borrowing entities with *securities origination.*

Brokers and dealers of securities buy and sell a wide range of financial instruments to offer flexibility for investors or issuers in their portfolio or balance sheet composition. The variety of securities makes it possible to fine-tune investments or fund raising to particular investor or borrower needs. Most of us are familiar with securities in the form of common stocks and various types of bonds. Stocks and bonds represent ownership or debt claims against the earnings and underlying income-producing assets of firms. These traditional securities are a significant part of the trading volume in today's markets.

Stocks and bonds are important but relatively simple securities. To achieve an optimal combination of risks and returns against a variety of future economic scenarios, issuers and investors often look for more innovative securities designs. If these securities achieve a better risk and return combination in terms of investors' and issuers' preferences than existing securities, they will be more marketable. Classic examples are convertible bonds, preferred stock, and warrants. Newer examples are collateralized mortgage obligations and index options.

There are an unlimited number of possible risks investors or borrowers may be concerned about. For example, a financial instrument that pays higher returns with higher inflation offers protection against inflation risks. A security that pays off more if automobile demand drops might be useful to some particular investors. Conceptually there are an infinite number of possible future outcomes of concern to individual investors and borrowers.

Creating financial instruments that pay future cash flows under economic conditions offering new protection to market participants is a move toward *completing the market.* A complete securities market offers securities that pay returns under every conceivable circumstance, for example one that pays $1 if Mongolia attacks India next year and zero otherwise.

It is not possible to define much less trade the infinite number of securities that would be necessary to complete financial markets. Practically speaking, financial markets will never be complete. With inventive and aggressive people active in the securities industry, however, there are always opportunities for inventing and trading new securities for which sufficient demand exists because customers desire security payoffs under circumstances important enough to worry about.

Recent developments in futures and options markets, allowing the hedging behavior discussed in Chapters 20 and 21, are described as developments making markets more complete. A 1990 example of a successful innovative security that made the market more complete is the Nikkei put option, which pays off for investors if the Japanese stock market falls, whereas issuers keep the sale price and pay nothing if the Nikkei index rises. Innovating new securities can create value for issuers and investors as well as financial service firms.

Securities can be classified by type of issuer: foreign or domestic corporations, governments, or issues based on consumer borrowing. They also can be classified by the nature of the claim on borrowers. Debt provides investors a fixed claim on the income and assets of issuers. Equity represent a residual claim against income and assets firms after other claims are met. Securities can be convertible into other securities, callable or redeemable for cash, and so forth. Securities can pay in any currency or in amounts indexed to commodities. The list of features is endless and growing with innovations in securities markets. Table 9.1 provides an overview of the basic types of securities that are of major significance in financial markets.

The market for securities issues is large. Table 9.2 provides figures giving the total size of the securities markets in the United States. Panel A of the table provides the value of the entire stock of securities listed on exchanges, with subtotals of issues by class. Some markets, like the market for common stocks, are subdivided by where these issues are traded, such as on the New York Stock Exchange (NYSE) or the so-called over-the-counter (OTC) market. Panel B provides data on trading volume on the exchanges and Panel C provides amounts of new issues of securities for recent years. The tables demonstrate both large growth, as in new issues in Panel C, and substantial variation, as in trading volume in Panel B, in securities markets activities.

TABLE 9.1 Types of Securities

- **Debt (Bonds, Notes, etc)**
  - Unsecured
    - Subordinated
    - Senior
  - Secured
    - Financial Asset
    - Real Property
    - Equipment
  - Guaranteed
- **Derivatives**
  - Futures/Forward Contracts
  - Options
    - Put
    - Call
  - Index Options
- **Claims on Pools**
- **Equity**
  - Common Stock
    - Voting
    - Nonvoting Warrant
  - Limited Partnership Shares
- **Preferred Stock**
  - Convertible
  - Redeemable
  - Auction Rate

TABLE 9.2 United States Securities Markets

Panel A: Market Value of Securities on Registered Exchanges[a] ($ in Thousands)

	TOTAL MARKET VALUE	*STOCKS[B]*	*WARRANTS*	*RIGHTS*	*EQUITY OPTIONS TRADED*	*EQUITY OPTIONS EXERCISED*	*NON-EQUITY OPTIONS[C]*
All Registered Exchanges for Past Six Calendar Years							
1986	$1,867,887,058	$1,705,123,953	$1,633,395	$359,764	$40,054,282	$72,827,859	$47,887,805
1987	2,491,720,836	2,284,165,520	2,713,954	23,314	53,123,325	85,946,102	65,748,621
1988	1,702,047,768	1,587,011,727	884,269	54,773	27,163,915	51,477,127	35,455,956
1989	2,004,034,088	1,844,768,135	2,970,784	28,052	40,423,407	49,492,403	36,351,306
1990	1,746,868,559	1,611,667,363	4,930,237	200,476	27,218,738	51,058,035	51,793,712
1991	1,903,508,966	1,776,275,338	1,849,922	272,762	27,104,021	48,994,517	49,012,406
Breakdown of 1991 Data by Registered Exchanges[d]							
AMEX	$69,106,051	$40,199,890	$639,863	$180,136	$9,267,929	$14,060,670	$4,757,564
BSE	30,651,017	30,651,017	0	0	0	0	0
CSE	14,672,004	14,671,487	447	69	0	0	0
MSE	77,172,024	77,172,024	0	0	0	0	0
NYSE	1,534,334,118	1,531,813,487	1,117,590	75,212	400,462	882,186	45,181
PSE	63,583,012	54,175,044	75,623	17,345	3,530,681	5,725,474	58,846
PHLX	39,284,222	27,347,116	16,399	0	2,441,860	4,580,915	4,897,933
SSE[e]	1,325	1,325	0	0	0	0	0
CBOE	74,461,244	0	0	0	11,463,090	23,745,272	39,252,882
WUNS[f]	243,948	243,948	0	0	0	0	0

Figures may not sum due to rounding.

[a]Data on the value and volume of equity security sales is reported in connection with fees paid under Section 31 of the Securities Exchange Act of 1934 as amended by the Securities Acts Amendments of 1975. It covers odd-lot as well as round-lot transactions.

[b]Includes voting trust certificates, certificate of deposit for stocks, and American Depository Receipts for stocks but excludes rights and warrants.

[c]Includes all exchange trades of call and put options in stock indices, interest rates, and foreign currencies.

[d]Total market value for individual exchanges does not include data for equity options exercised.

[e]The Spokane Stock Exchange terminated trading May 24, 1991.

[f]Wunsch Auction Systems, Inc. commenced trading in April 1991.

TABLE 9.2 (*continued*)

Panel B: Trading Activity on Exchanges[a] (in Thousands)

	STOCKS[B] (SHARES)	*WARRANTS (UNITS)*	*RIGHTS (UNITS)*	*EQUITY OPTIONS* *TRADED (CONTRACTS)*	*EQUITY OPTIONS* *EXERCISED (CONTRACTS)*	*NON-EQUITY OPTIONS[C] (CONTRACTS)*
All Registered Exchanges for Past Six Calendar Years						
1986	48,337,694	195,501	47,329	141,931	14,545	147,234
1987	63,770,625	238,357	74,014	164,432	17,020	140,698
1988	52,533,283	118,662	13,709	114,928	11,395	80,999
1989	54,238,571	166,233	11,986	141,840	14,586	85,161
1990	53,337,731	384,985	23,371	111,426	11,150	98,470
1991	58,031,077	200,028	65,179	104,851	10,783	93,923
Breakdown of 1991 Data by All Registered Exchanges[d,e]						
AMEX*	3,102,872	82,252	30,563	32,829	3,111	5,976
BSE*	1,030,957	0	0	0	0	0
CSE*	501,502	4	0	0	0	0
MIDW	2,715,281	0	0	0	0	0
NYSE*	47,673,705	97,355	31,966	1,901	257	159
PSE	2,068,122	19,186	2,550	13,781	1,518	72
PHLX*	929,997	1,231	0	11,084	1,328	11,281
SSE[f]	2,998	0	0	0	0	0
CBOE*	0	0	0	45,255	4,571	76,435
WUNS*[g]	5,643	0	0	0	0	0

Figures may not sum due to rounding.

[a]Data on the value and volume of equity security sales is reported in connection with fees paid under Section 31 of the Securities Exchange Act of 1934 as amended by the Securities Acts Amendments of 1975. It covers odd-lot as well as round-lot transactions.

[b]Includes voting trust certificates, certificate of deposit for stocks, and American Depository Receipts for stocks but excludes rights and warrants.

[c]Includes all exchange trades of call and put options in stock indices, interest rates, and foreign currencies.

[d]Data of those exchanges marked with asterisk covers transactions cleared during the calendar month; clearance usually occurs within five days of the execution of a trade. Data of other exchanges covers transactions effected on trade dates failing within the reporting month.

[e]Total market value for individual exchanges does not include data for equity options exercised.

[f]The Spokane Stock Exchange terminated trading May 24, 1991.

[g]Wunsch Auction Systems, Inc. commenced trading in April 1991.

Panel C: New Issues Various Years ($ in Millions)

TYPE OF ISSUE OR ISSUER, OR USE	*1990*	*1991*	*1992*
Tax-Exempt State and Local Governments			
1 All issues, new and refunding[a]	120,339	154,402	215,191
By type of issue			
2 General obligation	39,610	55,100	78,611
3 Revenue	81,295	99,302	136,580
By type of issuer			
4 State	15,149	24,939	25,295
5 Special district or statutory authority[b]			
6 Municipality, county, or township	32,510	48,849	60,210
7 Issues for new capital	103,235	116,953	120,272
By use of proceeds			
8 Education	17,042	21,121	22,071
9 Transportation	11,650	13,395	17,334
10 Utilities and conservation	11,739	21,039	20,058
11 Social welfare	23,099	25,648	21,796
12 Industrial aid	6,117	8,376	5,424
13 Other purposes	34,607	30,275	33,589

[a]Par amounts of long-term issues based on date of sale.

[b]Includes school districts.

TYPE OF ISSUE, OFFERING, OR ISSUER	*1990*	*1991*	*1992*
U.S. Corporations			
1 All issues[a]	340,049	465,243	559,729
2 Bonds[b]	299,884	389,822	471,404
By type of offering			
3 Public, domestic	188,848	286,930	377,960
4 Private placement, domestic[c]	86,982	74,930	65,853
5 Sold abroad	23,054	27,962	27,591
By industry group			
6 Manufacturing	51,779	86,628	81,998
7 Commercial and miscellaneous	40,733	36,666	42,869
8 Transportation	12,776	13,598	9,979
9 Public utility	17,621	23,945	48,055
10 Communication	6,687	9,431	15,394
11 Real estate and financial	170,288	219,750	272,830
12 Stocks[b]	40,175	75,424	88,324
By type of offering			
13 Public preferred	3,998	17,085	21,339
14 Common	19,442	48,230	57,199
15 Private placement[c]	16,736	10,109	9,867
By industry group			
16 Manufacturing	5,649	24,111	22,723
17 Commercial and miscellaneous	10,171	19,418	20,231
18 Transportation	369	2,439	2,595
19 Public utility	416	3,474	6,532
20 Communication	3,822	475	2,365
21 Real estate and financial	19,738	25,507	33,879

[a]Figures represent gross proceeds of issues maturing is more than one year; they are the principal amount of number of units calculated by multiplying by the offering price. Figures exclude secondary offerings, employee stock plans, investment companies other than closed-end, intracorporate transactions, equities sold abroad, and Yankee bonds. Stock data include ownership securities issued by limited partnerships.

[b]Monthly data cover only public offerings.

[c]Monthly data are not available.

SOURCE: Securities and Exchange Commission 1992 *Annual Report*. Board of Governors Federal Reserve System *Bulletin*.

9.2 VALUE IN TRADING SECURITIES: ECONOMICS OF MARKET STRUCTURE

Identifying willing buyers for sellers and vice versa is an information problem. Solving this problem is as old as civilized man. Early solutions to the problem of finding partners in trade were market day in the country or annual horse auctions. Markets are a means to reduce the costs of identifying people who want to buy and sell given commodities at different prices.

The microeconomics of securities market organization and price-setting rules has become a major focus of study in financial economics, the economics of *market microstructure*. This line of analysis examines the role market organization, for example auctions or continuous trading, plays in influencing a market's efficiency in absorbing and disseminating new information.

Costs of physically delivering items bought and sold, which are pieces of paper or computer file entries, are very low in securities markets. Trades can be fast and information can change rapidly. The effect of information flow on prices and trading volume and the market's ability to handle variations in the volume of trading under different market organization and structures is an important issue. This is apparent from the Stock Market Crash of October 1987, when different securities market organizations in Chicago, New York, and around the world reacted very differently to the dramatic stresses of that period.

Brokers take buy and sell orders to the market and execute them for their customers. In organizing trading activity, brokers need to produce value for their clients and themselves. Brokers' participation in markets is costly. It takes time to plan, organize, and conduct a market. Physical facilities or electronic counterparts must be arranged. A convenient location is essential to attract other traders: high-rent space in large cities may be necessary. Traders need offices and places to keep records. Communications links must reflect advanced technology.

The fixed and variable costs of participating in markets can be large. Identifiable markets emerge when interest in exchanging claims on financial assets or contracts reaches a point where the investments necessary to develop the infrastructure and train people are justified by the expected future trading income of market participants.

Markets in the United States and around the world take surprisingly wide and varied forms. There are two dimensions to describing market structure. The first is the physical/institutional organization of the market, determining whether trading occurs in one place and is exclusive or is open to all who wish to trade. The second dimension concerns the rules by which the prices at which trades occurs are established. In discussing these different dimensions of market organization, keep in mind that hybrids and combinations are possible. Economic forces may produce an evolution from one form to another.

The physical and institutional aspect of markets concerns whether trading locations or systems are exclusive or open. One structure is for trading to take place in a single location where access is limited to members, called an *organized exchange* or *market*. The most famous example is the New York Stock Exchange (NYSE). A second market structure is that traders are connected by communication links like telephones and wire systems, often augmented with computer screens or other display devices, and that the system is open to all. These markets are called *over-the-counter markets,* since anyone can buy or sell securities who is authorized and is willing to plug into the information network.

When trading is exclusive, only those paying dues can trade. For example, trading on the New York Stock Exchange is limited to members called *seat holders.* Members own the exchange and buy their seats. These seats have value because of the trading privilege on the exclusive floor. Recent seat prices are shown in Table 9.3.

Over-the-counter markets can be open to all traders who have telephones, like the United States Treasury securities or foreign exchange markets. Access to over-the-counter markets can be somewhat restricted, as in the case of the National Association of Securities Dealers Automatic Quotation (NASDAQ) system, which is open only to members subscribing to communication systems.

The second dimension of securities markets concern rules covering trading activity. The most important rules govern how prices for traded securities are established.[1] Brokers and other market participants trading in markets with frequent activity agree on rules in order to prevent chaotic trading and disagreements. Rules are intended to ensure that buyers and sellers obtain the best prices possible and that disputes about transactions are minimized. The economic need for rules will become clear from our discussion below.

Trading rules establishing prices can be described in terms of a two-dimensional table as in Figure 9.1. Members of organized markets agree on rules covering members. Rules in over-the-counter markets can be conventions, regulations, or laws. Figure 9.1 arrays different basic methods of arriving at transaction prices and indicates examples of financial markets that use one or the other of the rules. The two attributes of trading rules described in the array concern the frequency of trading and nature of the traders.

A call auction securities market is a market where orders given to brokers, called *public orders* since brokers represent investors buying or selling securities, are collected at one time. An auction is held on a scheduled basis. Many markets started out as call auction markets, as did the NYSE and the Paris Bourse, meeting

TABLE 9.3 Seat Prices on Organized Exchanges, 1992

New York Stock Exchange	\$475,000–\$600,000
American Stock Exchange	\$ 78,000–\$ 95,000
Midwest Stock Exchange	\$ 35,000
Pacific Stock Exchange	\$ 20,000
Philadelphia Stock Exchange	\$ 20,000

SOURCE: *Wall Street Journal,* February 6, 1992, p. C1.

[1]For an excellent discussion, see Stoll (1990). For a more complete discussion, see Cohen *et al* (1986), Chapter 2.

	Call Market	Continuous Market
Auction	London gold fixing	Contracts traded on Chicago Board of Trade
Dealer	Monday auction of U.S. Treasury bills	U.S. Government bond market

FIGURE 9.1 Trading rules

to conduct auctions at fixed intervals. The first trade prices of the day on most organized exchanges are set by a call auction procedure that clears the buy and sell orders accumulated since the market closed.

When buy and sell orders are constantly being filled with representatives of buyers and sellers negotiating and trading all the time, the market is described as a *continuous* auction. Following the opening on the NYSE and other exchanges, trading is continuous as brokers arrive with buy and sell orders. On the NYSE, the specialist in given securities is charged by exchange rules with assuring an orderly price setting process for the security throughout the day.

The second dimension of price-setting rules concerns the way trades are conducted, specifically, how traders get their price information and close transactions. In an auction market, traders or their broker representatives find out what prices are being offered and conclude transactions with any other traders or brokers currently in the market. In dealer markets, brokers or traders contact securities market participants who specialize or who are designated to quote prices for immediate purchase or sale of the securities. Some markets, such as the NYSE, allow both types of trades.

The price-setting rules on organized exchanges like the NYSE are intended to increase the likelihood that buyers and sellers receive the best prices available. One way to concentrate information on prices for securities to traders is to limit trading to one market where all orders must be filled. Exchange rules often require that members trade only on one exchange and only while that exchange is open. These rules prevent deals at favorable prices from occurring after hours or on other exchanges to the detriment of other traders on the exchange.

Benefits and Costs of Market Concentration

Traders in securities may benefit from the concentration of trading in securities at one trading and information center. Price information is available to all brokers in the market. Organized markets or exchanges display the latest prices on traded securities prominently for all market participants to see. Concentration of buy and sell orders of members of organized exchanges may mean that buyers and sellers obtain the best prices available anywhere. The greater the flow of transactions in a given market, the less likely it is that better buy or sell prices can be found elsewhere. Concentration of trading is said to produce economies of scale. Some exchanges like the NYSE historically achieved a near monopoly in the trading of listed securities.

Restrictions against member brokers trading off the floor are essential to maintaining an exchange's market power. These rules benefit members because they can charge commissions that are higher than costs as long as buyers and sellers believe the best prices will be found on the most active exchange, thereby reducing their total costs of trading including securities prices and commissions. For brokers on exchanges achieving monopolies on trading, abuses in terms of exorbitant commissions relative to transactions costs may be possible.

In contrast to organized exchanges, over-the-counter markets are typically dealer markets. Diffuse information networks of individuals and firms buying and selling particular financial assets are funneled through a smaller number of dealers. The largest market of this type is the United States Treasury securities market, where investors and brokers contact dealers who are linked by telephone and computer networks. Information on prices offered by dealers and technical market information is communicated by a variety of specialized communication and reporting systems. Some of these communication systems are provided by third-party suppliers, like Money Market Services or Reuters, as described in Chapter 12. Other communication systems are owned by dealers, like the NASDAQ system discussed above.

The flow of trading activities on some organized exchanges has been shifting off the floor of the exchange. The costs of transacting on monopoly exchanges or on exchanges where trading activity is cluttered with small orders was higher for some well-informed and active traders than finding alternatives trading partners off the exchange. Large institutional traders sometime trade large blocks of securities "upstairs" at the NYSE, where trades are arranged by member brokers specializing in large block transactions at heavily discounted commissions. This trading activity is called the *second market*. By exchange rules, second market trades and prices are included in the market information flow coming from NYSE and reported immediately on the transaction tape.

Additional competition with the exchanges has come from some firms setting up alternative markets, like Jefferies Securities, that handle large and even some smaller trades totally outside the exchange in the growing *third market*. Increasingly, institutional investors and other large traders avoid trading on exchanges and deal directly with each other, in the so-called *fourth market*. Fourth market transactors do not pay commissions and thus bear only the costs of finding counterparts to trade with.

To summarize, brokers find buyers for sellers through their membership and participation in organized exchanges or their access to the communication linkages typical of over-the-counter markets. Concentration of trading in one location with rules on price setting is one solution to minimizing the costs of finding counterparties to trades. Modern technology and competition increasingly favor more dispersed communication networks typical of over-the-counter dealer markets. The communication advantage in bringing buyers and sellers together in a single place is being replaced by modern technology and alternative price-setting mechanisms.

Pricing and Term Setting in Brokerage

Brokers price their services to cover costs and earn a reasonable risk-adjusted return on their investment. Costs of trading consist of the operating costs and the costs of locating buyers or sellers in the market.

Brokers typically price their services on a per transaction basis. Price setting for brokers in the United States on the NYSE was immeasurably easier and more profitable for member brokers prior to May 1, 1975. Until that date, commission rates on stock transactions were fixed by exchange rules. On May 1, 1975, or "Mayday" as the industry refers to the date, the Securities and Exchange Commission prohibited such price fixing by members.

The U.S. Congress and the Securities and Exchange Commission have required that all transactions of NYSE-listed securities on all exchanges, like the Midwest and Pacific Stock Exchanges, be reported on a Consolidated Transaction Tape so that information on all trade prices is available from one source. The objective is to provide regional market traders information on prices in New York and elsewhere around the country to develop a "National Market System" (NMS). A true NMS would erode the informational advantage the NYSE has due to its larger volume and concentration of information and permit competition from brokers on regional exchanges.

Today, commissions on stock transactions in the United States and some other countries are competitive, described by observers as "negotiated." Commission rates on different stock trades are all over the map. There are different rates for retail customers and institutional traders. There are different commission rates for *odd lots,* small transactions, and for *round lots* or *blocks* (multiples of 100 shares or $5,000 face value of bonds). Commissions on *large blocks* of stocks (hundreds of blocks) are arrived at differently, usually by negotiation or bidding.

Different commission rates charged on different transactions are due in part to costs of executing different trades. Odd-lot trades involve more effort and paperwork per share than large blocks. The costs of finding buyers or sellers for small or large amounts of stock are different given different markets for these transactions. Odd-lot buyers and sellers are primarily small retail investors. Odd-lot brokers must break blocks in order to fill demand, requiring additional activity. Large block traders may be matched in so-called "upstairs" trades with very low per share costs.

The two key aspects affecting brokerage commission rates is the level of competition and other services associated with the trading activity. Since Mayday, most trading activity in the United States has been priced competitively in active and open markets. Pure brokerage charges seem to be closely tied to the costs of providing the trading services. The analysis of brokerage fees is confounded by the fact that most commissions include compensation for other financial services.

Most of the services offered by brokers in addition to finding buyers for sellers are economically different financial services: (1) information services in the form of securities research and/or advising; (2) market making services, which we discuss in the following section; and (3) safekeeping and clearing services, discussed in the next chapter. The point here is that pricing in the brokerage business is bundled with prices for other services.

Many brokerage firms, like Merrill Lynch and Smith Barney, have research departments that make "buy," "sell," and "hold" recommendations on securities they follow. This stock and bond research constitutes the information and advisory services discussed in Chapter 12. Brokerage firms offering trading services and advice are called *full-line* brokers. Brennan and Chordia (1993) analyzed economics of bundling the sale of advice with trading services and priced jointly in the form of higher brokerage commissions. Their analysis demonstrates that careful pricing of full-line brokerage services can produce value for the broker and trader using the advice.

Brennan and Chordia examined the total expected revenues from providing advice under three pricing schemes: (1) fixed charges before advice is rendered so that revenue is fixed, as charged by advisors for newsletters; (2) brokerage commissions charged as a percent of the value of trades (purchases or sales), so that revenue is related to the buy, sell, or hold advice provided; and (3) management fees for information provided indirectly through management of mutual funds. These last two forms of providing information are discussed in Chapter 12 dealing with information and asset management services.

Brennan and Chordia found that when investors have different risk preferences, expected revenues from providing information and trading services with transaction-based fees like trading commissions produce maximum expected revenue for the broker/advisor firm when the broker/advisors' information is relatively precise. Expected revenue is higher than with fixed fees for information or management fees for fund managers.

Traders' expected utilities are maximized even though higher expected brokerage commissions raise the cost of securities traded. The seller of advice shares the risk of variations in trading activity with the trader. When research suggests not trading securities, as when "hold" advice is rendered, low commission volume results. Strong buy or sell advice generates more commission revenue but improves traders' welfare. In contrast, indirect compensation for information, like management fees for mutual funds, produce maximum expected revenue for investment advice when information is imprecise.

The implication of Brennan and Chordia's analysis is that value can be produced for securities traders by providing them with information and charging them for the information through brokerage commissions. This pricing means traders share the revenue/cost risk stemming from implications of the information with brokers. The value is that risk averse traders will pay more for information when they trade securities after receiving the advice. The analysis does not address the dissipation of information's value when it is made public nor the reliability of information providers over time. The analysis does demonstrate that value can be produced by careful pricing of brokerage service when combining advisory services.

Brokers also routinely make money by making markets in securities, as discussed in the next section. Full-line brokers like Merrill Lynch often buy and sell securities directly from traders, profiting from their market-making activities as well as charging commissions. Exchange rules require disclosure of the fact that the broker participated in a trade as a principal. Some discount brokers, like

Charles Schwab, also profit from market-making activities of affiliated firms, like Schwab's Mayer and Schweitzer subsidiary, without revealing that trades are made from their own portfolio (Torres 1993). Brokerage commissions may be priced below cost or competitive rates and be value producing if market-making profits are high enough.

The main example of providing "unbundled" trading services in the retail market for brokerage services is from the so-called "discount" brokers. In the retail market, Fidelity Brokers and Charles Schwab are the best known, although there are many other discount brokers. Pure discount brokers simply take orders and execute them with no frills. A call to a discount broker will confirm that their representatives do not want to chat, they want to earn their commissions as quickly as possible from getting your order and executing it.

Among institutional customers, a strange pricing phenomenon has emerged in terms of "soft-dollar" commissions. In these arrangements, full-service brokers charge higher commissions but give their institutional customers credit toward other services. These services are sometimes research reports or access to computer systems provided by third parties. Brokers using soft dollar commissions compete by nonprice means with discount brokers. A puzzle is why cumbersome nonprice competition with bundled nontrading services is competitive with unbundled services priced at costs with a profit margin.

Marketing and Information Broker Services

Marketing trading services are different in the wholesale or institutional market and the retail market. Large institutions are less likely to want bundled services and will be less subject to habit and familiarity in choosing brokers. On the other hand, wholesale customers will be concerned about reputation and previous experience in assessing the reliability of a broker in providing good execution (i.e., good prices at low commissions) in trades. Posh branch offices and attentive account executives are less effective marketing tools in the institutional than the retail market.

Retail brokers must advertise their services and reach out to their customers. Often brokers must overcome unfamiliarity and fear retail customers have with respect to securities markets. A branch system like that of Merrill Lynch can house trained retail brokers, now called *account representatives,* to identify customers and inform them of the advantages of securities trading. Sears Roebuck thought it saw an ideal synergy between its stores and retail brokerage services and placed some of its Dean-Witter offices in shopping centers on a trial basis. Banks and thrifts also make branch space available to brokers.

Discount brokerage firms and other firms, like the asset management firms offering brokerage services (such as Fidelity) have developed alternative means of dealing with retail customers. Most of these systems are based on media advertising and telephone order-taking systems. These marketing and information dissemination systems are very low cost but are not a particularly flexible way of selling complex and/or new retail financial services based on complicated bundles of products or services, such as advice and transaction processing services.

Monitoring and Controlling Brokers

Securities trading contains a number of principal–agent problems. One problem is the moral hazard problem affecting the trading customer: brokers may not try hard enough to find the best price for a securities trader. Reputations of brokers are an important factor in establishing and maintaining business relationships, and poor executions or self-dealing (making the best trades from their point of view) by brokers, even if not illegal, costs them future business and loses clients if found out.

Maintenance of reputation and fears of retaliation may not be sufficient inducements to control broker activity, especially in the retail market. The solution has been to establish rules and to enforce the rules by self-regulating organizations of brokers, such as the NYSE or NASD. Trading rules mandate that the best possible prices be reasonably assured by brokers. Violations of the rules are punishable by sanctions including expulsion from the exchange or broker organization. Customers can seek relief through arbitration or law suits. The rules themselves are reviewed by the Securities and Exchange Commission. Securities market regulation is discussed at length in Chapter 15.

Another set of problems with brokers comes from the combination of trading services with other financial services, such as advising or portfolio management. Since brokers make their money by trading, they are tempted to advise frequent sales and purchases for their clients, called *churning*. If authorized to manage assets for clients, brokers may churn portfolios with excess trading. There are rules and regulations relating to such churning. The problem comes not intrinsically from trading activities but from the combination of trading activities with other financial services.

Funding/Investing and Risk Bearing and Sharing

Brokers as brokers do not take title to securities but only bring buyers and sellers together. Funding and risk bearing activities are not central to value production in trading or brokerage services. A look at a broker's balance sheet and income statement reveals that brokers borrow substantial funds and that they have huge amounts of securities receivable. Both of these items come from activities not directly related to brokerage but from related financial services. These services include: extension of credit to customers who buy securities on margin, clearing of securities transactions, holding or safe-keeping securities, and market-making activities. The last of these is discussed in the following section. Credit services were discussed in Chapters 7 and 8 and clearing and safe-keeping services are discussed in Chapter 10.

9.3 VALUE PRODUCTION IN MARKET MAKING OR DEALING IN SECURITIES

Traders in securities markets want the quickest and cheapest execution of their orders to buy and sell. The economic reason behind the demand for *immediacy* (a term introduced in Demsetz' 1968 analysis of this problem) is that traders need cash right away, or want to invest cash quickly to earn income. Liquidity traders make their decisions to trade based on their cash needs and are willing to transact at prices close to the most recent traded prices. They fear what will happen to prices as new information on securities arrives over time. Liquidity traders want to transact before security prices change. The demand for immediacy means traders will pay slightly more or accept slightly less in quick transactions.

The demand for immediacy can be shown in Figure 9.2, adopted from Demsetz' (1968) analysis. The horizontal axis in the figure depicts the amount of the security to be transacted, and the vertical axis shows different prices for the security. Assume a liquidity buyer wishes to transact immediately and is willing to pay a slightly higher price than a trader with more time to find sellers. The liquidity trader's demand schedule is shown as D, the supply curve corresponding to the seller providing immediacy is shown as S_i. Correspondingly, the liquidity seller's supply schedule is shown as S and the demand schedule for the buyer providing immediacy is shown as D_i. Because it is costly and will take time to find the ultimate buyers and sellers, the immediate buyer's demand curve is below and the supply curve above those of regular traders.

Market makers or *dealers* in securities stand ready to buy or sell to traders demanding immediacy at quoted prices. On the diagram, immediate demanders buying from a dealer pay the dealer's ask price, P_{ask}, for the security. The ask price is determined by the intersection of the D curve with the dealer's immediate supply curve, S_i. Similarly, an immediate seller with supply schedule S sells to a

FIGURE 9.2 Demand and supply of securities

SOURCE: Harold Demsetz, "The Cost of Transacting," *Quarterly Journal of Economics,* Vol. LXXXII, No. 1 (February), 1968, p.36.

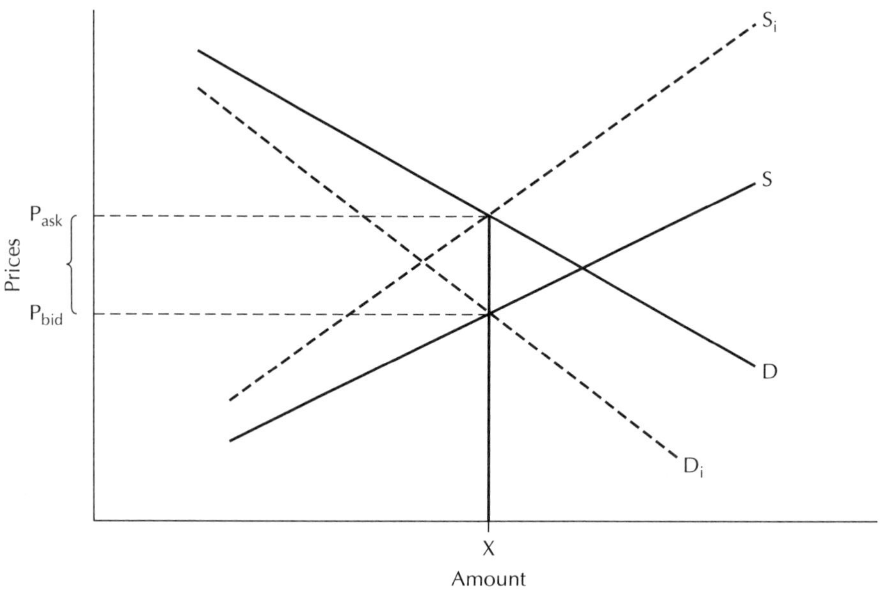

dealer at the dealer's bid price, P_{bid}, determined by the intersection with the dealer's immediate demand schedule, D_i.

The diagram illustrates the simplest case of how dealers cover their costs and make profits. If equal numbers of buy and sell transactions take place with a dealer and for simplicity demand and supply schedules do not move over time, the dealer buys from immediate sellers at P_{bid} and sells to immediate buyers at P_{ask}. The difference between the higher P_{ask} and the lower P_{bid} is the *bid–ask spread* or the *dealer's spread*. The dealer's inventory of securities will fluctuate around a constant level as buy and sell orders arrive. The dealer's spread compensates the dealer for providing immediacy to traders and covers his or her costs.

Pricing and Term Setting by Dealers

Dealers or market makers facilitate the functioning of securities markets through their willingness to buy or sell securities at posted prices with no delay. Traders can always sell some of their position instantly. Market making is defined as quoting prices for immediate sale or purchase by brokers or traders. Value is produced by market makers when the prices they quote to market participants are at levels that cover costs and make profits.

Market makers incur three costs, two of which we discuss now, and the third of which—costs from risk—we discuss later in this section. Most obviously, market makers require communications gear, computer capability, trained staff, and other costs classified as *operating costs.* A second set of costs is tied to being able to quote a price for securities for immediate delivery. To quote an ask price, inventories of securities must be held. To quote a bid price, securities are purchased from traders with no offsetting buyer in sight, and are placed into securities inventories. Dealers' *inventory holding* costs are largely costs of financing inventories, although record-keeping and safeguarding securities in inventory have costs.

A simplified set of financial statements presented in Table 9.4 gives the essence of operating and inventory holding costs facing a market maker in a security when the equilibrium price of a security averages \$15.00. Assume the volume is 10,000 trades per year. Example A shows that at a bid price of \$14.75 and ask price of \$15.25, or a bid–ask spread of \$.50, \$5,000 is generated by market-making activities. These revenues cover operating costs of \$2,500 and the interest costs of \$1,500 from financing \$10,000 in average securities inventory and other assets (like office equipment) of \$10,000 with \$15,000 of debt at interest of 10 percent. The dealer's operations produce a \$1,000 profit on equity of \$5,000, or a 20 percent rate of return on equity in the example.

In competitive financial markets, dealers compete for volume until the lowest ask prices and highest bid prices produce enough revenue to cover costs and return a fair, risk-adjusted return on invested equity to dealers. If dealer activities earn excess returns and there are no barriers to entry, new dealers will enter the market. Some market makers, like NYSE specialists, are protected from competition. In a competitive market, the value from immediacy to traders will be equal to the bid–ask spread. Market makers earn enough to cover costs and compensate them for resources dedicated to providing liquidity.

TABLE 9.4 Simplified Financial Statements for Securities Dealer

	EXAMPLE A	*EXAMPLE B*
Quotation Sheet		
Ask Price	$15.25	$15.35
Bid Price	$14.75	$14.65
Trading Volume	10,000 unit	10,000 units
Income Statement		
Sale of Securities	$152,500	$153,500
Purchase of Securities	147,500	146,500
Loss on Inventories[a]		2,000
Gain on Sale	5,000	7,000
Operating Costs	2,500	2,500
Interest	1,500	1,500
Profit	$1,000	$1,000
Balance Sheet		
Assets		
Securities Inventories	$10,000	$10,000
Plant and Equipment	10,000	10,000
Total Assets	$20,000	$20,000
Liabilities and Equity		
Debt	$15,000	$15,000
Equity	5,000	5,000
Total Debt and Equity	$15,000	$15,000

[a]$2.00 times .1 times 10,000 trades.

In very efficient markets, bid–ask spreads can become very narrow. For example, in the market for U.S. Treasury securities, the bid–ask spread is routinely around one half a basis point (.005 percent) or $50 on a $1,000,000 Treasury bill transaction. Competition in the government dealer market is strong in the face of the enormous growth in the Treasury debt market. Competition has been so intense that some bank primary Treasury dealers, such as First Interstate, dropped out of the market due to low profitability.

A major issue in the economics of market microstructure is the value and allocation of benefits from economies of scale and the risks of concentration in market-making activities in regulated securities markets. Economies of scale are certainly possible in dealer markets. When trading is concentrated on one market, for example listed stocks on the New York Stock Exchange, transaction volume will be increased. If dealers' fixed costs are covered by a larger volume of transactions, spreads can be narrowed and still produce enough profit to pay costs and required returns on investment. Inventory theory suggests that increases in volume also reduce necessary investments since required inventories should increase less than proportionately to trading volume. Lower average fixed costs and inventory costs contribute to economies of scale in market making.

To illustrate economies of scale using the example in Table 9.4, if trading volume were increased to 25,000 at a dealer spread of $.20 by concentrating trading at one location, the same revenue would be produced as at the lower volume and higher spreads. The dealer's bid price could rise in our example to $14.90 and ask price could fall to $15.10. If the higher trading volume can be accomplished with only slightly higher levels of inventories, then the revenues at this much narrower spread offer much better prices for traders and are enough to compensate the dealer for his costs of doing business.

Economies of scale in the market-making function are used to rationalize the NYSE rules limiting trading in listed securities to the trading floor and the informal reality of monopoly of specialists on the NYSE. The question is whether absence of competition is abused by dealers who widen spreads to more than cover costs and provide fair returns. In the above analysis, suppose the market maker only narrowed the spread to $.40 at the higher 25,000 volume, returning revenues of $10,000 and a profit of $6,000, a return of 120 percent on equity. In this case, most of the value from economies of scale is kept by market makers and not shared with traders.

Narrower spreads of exclusive dealers (as in the above example) make it difficult for smaller dealers on other exchanges at lower volumes to compete for business. Smaller dealers' spreads cannot be as narrow and generate reasonable returns. Evidence suggest that specialists on the NYSE earn very high rates of return due to their monopoly positions. Limited competition in market-making can cause other problems: in the 1987 stock market crash, several NYSE specialists went bankrupt. Some argue that small specialist firm monopolies contributed to the NYSE market breakdown in 1987 because these firms did not have enough equity to absorb inventory losses and therefore did not trade many stocks over long time periods during days when the market moved the most. The role of specialists on the NYSE is the focus of a great deal of analysis and regulatory debate.

Bid–ask spreads may also be increased by collusive behavior of several dealers on markets like the NASDAQ. Unpublished academic research by Christie and Schultz reported in 1994 (and subsequently published) documenting high bid–ask spreads on stocks traded on the NASDAQ led the U.S. Justice Department to launch an investigation into whether there was illegal price fixing. Some observers argue that government regulation of trading inadvertedly created barriers to entry in trading small stocks and led market-makers on the NASDAQ to try to preserve benefits from trading concentrated on a few market-makers in that trading system (Madden and Welker 1995).

Inventory Risk and Information Costs

The third important type of dealer costs are costs from risk. Costs due to inventory price risks resulting in trading losses can justify high returns to market makers. Variations in the value of a dealer's inventory must be covered with sufficient capital. These costs are called *capital risk costs.* Market conditions produce constant fluctuations in the value of inventory. Drops in inventory value, as mentioned above with the Stock Market Crash of October 1987 when stock values fell

20 percent overnight and wiped out several specialists' equity, are significant risks. Some market price risk is managed and hedged by dealers as discussed in Part III.

Perhaps more important than market risk to market makers are risks of dealing with information traders. Buyers and sellers who have unique information about individual securities know more than the market maker. The information may based on expensive securities research or inside information. Losses due to use of this information in trades with securities dealers are called *information costs*. If the posted bid and ask prices of a dealer are favorable to information traders given their information, they trade, an example of adverse selection. Information traders look like liquidity traders but they know something that the market in general does not know.

Market makers can produce value in the face of information costs from adverse selection with their price setting. The market microstructure problem facing dealers from adverse selection by information traders has been analyzed in several studies, including influential analyses by Copeland and Galai (1983) and Glosten and Milgrom (1985). The example in Table 9.4 can be modified to illustrate the pricing problem for market makers who know that each buy or sell order may come from an information trader.

Most buyers and sellers are liquidity traders changing portfolio balance due to cash requirements. Assume the dealer expects that 90 percent of the time orders come from liquidity traders and 10 percent of the time orders come from information traders knowing a security should sell for $2.00 above or below the midpoint of his spread. This means that 10 percent of the time, the dealer will sell or buy securities that will change in value two dollars when the information trader's knowledge becomes public. On average, the dealer will lose $.20 (.10 times $2.00) on trades with both liquidity and information traders.

The dealer can resolve this problem of adverse selection by the terms on the bid–ask spread. If the spread is widened by $.20, the dealer's profits will cover the losses incurred in the 10 percent of the trades involving information traders. Example B in Table 9.4, updates the example to include losses on securities inventories. When a security is purchased for $2.00 more or sold for $2.00 less than actual value as in our example, losses occur on securities added to or sold from inventories. The increased spread covers these losses.

The adverse selection problem can in some cases be solved by a pricing strategy as in the above example. The implication is that the more information traders there are and the more reliable their information, the wider will be the spread required by dealers to stay in business. Liquidity traders pay higher transaction costs in terms of the dealer's bid–ask spread. The existence of information traders may require such a wide spread that the market ceases to exist. The collapse of securities markets imposes large costs on liquidity traders who cannot adjust portfolios cheaply. When market makers create immediacy in the face of informed traders, they are creating value for the financial system.

Brokers earn their income from commissions and do not care whether their customers are liquidity or information traders. Brokers are used by information traders to hide their identity from traders on the other side of the transaction, such as market makers, so they cannot guess that trading is based on nonpublic information. For example, a corporate raider might use a broker to acquire shares fearing that word of the attack on the firm would raise its share prices in anticipation of a bidding war for the control of the target corporation. Brokers can create value in terms of anonymity of order origination.

Production and Delivery of Market-Making Services

Market making is a service that can be delivered in a number of ways. The most familiar delivery and production of market-making services are done on the floor of an exchange, as with the New York Stock Exchange. On the NYSE, dealers in securities are assigned a fixed location called the *specialist's post.* Dealer-specialists on the NYSE have computer screens posting bid and ask prices in the stocks they make markets in. The orders flow from traders on the floor or from electronic links to member broker firms. They store limit orders, orders to transact only at preset prices, in the *specialist's book.* This gives specialists exclusive knowledge of latent demand and supply at prices away from the current market price range. On other organized exchanges, such as the Chicago Board of Trade, any member trader can be a market maker who can make money on the spread by providing immediacy in trades to liquidity traders. These arrangements are less formal than the NYSE specialist system.

On over-the-counter markets dealers quote prices and execute trades over computer and telephone systems or use paper-based quotations like the NASD "pink sheets." In the Treasury market, competitive dealers offer quotes on computer screens. To obtain price information of the competing dealers' bid and ask quotes, a broker must subscribe to the dealer communication network. Some brokers make markets in selected securities, as for example in some stocks traded over-the-counter, like Montgomery securities in smaller bank stocks.

Monitoring and Control in Market Making

Dealers in competitive markets rely on their carefully cultivated reputations in order to assure transactors that their quotes are good and delivery will be made. Some dealers, for example U.S. Treasury dealers, become authorized to do business with the Federal Reserve, becoming *primary dealers.* Primary dealership adds substance to a dealer's reputation in exchange for reporting and trading commitments to the government.

Most dealers are members of self-regulatory organizations. Principal–agent problems associated with dealers in self-regulatory organizations are solved by a system of rules known to all active traders. These rules offer complaint and relief procedures resulting from alleged abuses. Under the rules, delivery times and conditions are set and abuses of trading and information advantages are made punishable by fines and sanctions.

The most notorious violation of rules by market makers in the recent past was Salomon Brothers infringement of U.S. Treasury rules in bidding for Treasury securities in 1992. The rules that were broken limited the amount of securities that could be bought for dealers' own accounts. Many commentators at the time felt that the rules were not useful even in terms of lowering the U.S. Treasury's cost of funds. The violation of rules resulted in the resignation of the chairman of Salomon and hefty sanctions and fines. Customer vigilance to ensure enforcement of rules governing market makers is a cost of trading.

Funding/Investing and Risk Bearing and Sharing

Market makers must have inventories in order to quote bid and ask prices for immediate transactions. Financing of inventories is a major cost to dealers and a number of solutions have been developed to deal with this problem. We mention a few of these financing solutions to illustrate the range of possible solutions.

In the U.S. Treasury securities market, many dealers finance inventories with repurchase agreements. Repurchase agreements, or *repos,* are overnight sales of inventories of securities. Since the securities are U.S. Treasury and agency securities and the loans are collateralized, repos have very low risk and low interest rates. The overnight market for dealer financing in the form of repos has grown to enormous size with the growth of the Treasury debt market. Dealers in stocks rely on partly overnight bank loans, called *call loans,* to finance their inventories. They may also lend part of their securities inventories to short sellers who post the requisite margin in order to borrow securities.

Market makers trading on the commodity and futures exchanges often are financed by major brokerage houses who clear their trades for them, so-called *clearing brokers.* These market makers borrow funds for their positions, which seldom last overnight, from the brokers, who in turn borrow the funds from banks or from other money market sources.

Hedging inventory risk is accomplished by a number of hedging instruments and portfolio management strategies discussed in Part IV. Stock and bond market makers currently have a variety of option and futures markets alternatives available to them to reduce inventory price risk.

9.4 VALUE PRODUCTION IN SECURITIES ORIGINATION

Non-financial firms raise funds in the form of securities infrequently. A firm raises funds in a public offering for the first time in an *initial public offering* or IPO. Whether the funds raised are an IPO or subsequent public financing, management of firms raising funds usually concentrate their attention on real resource decisions like adjusting to changes in technology or market developments. Management of these firms know how funds raised will be used and have detailed insider operating information on their firms and its product markets, but they are not usually experts in securities markets.

Securities origination requires detailed knowledge of securities laws, regulations, and market preferences. Firms specializing in securities origination assist with necessary information disclosures, recommend specific features of securities that best serve issuer's needs, and assess demand conditions in financial markets. Securities firms can price and market securities when issued. Investment bankers and other securities originators can buy securities from the issuer at a fixed price to remove uncertainty about proceeds of the securities issue, called *underwriting* the issue.

Investors buying securities in IPOs often know little or nothing about the businesses attempting to raise funds. These investors, especially large institutional investors, know the investment bankers and other securities originators they buy the securities from. Securities originators have long-term relations with their investor clients. Investors depend on investment bankers or other securities originators to find good investment opportunities for them in the new issue market.

These relations between securities issuers, securities originators, and investors in new issues can be placed in the principal–agent framework. The various relationships are depicted in Figure 9.3. Depending on which aspect of securities issuance we focus on, the principal or the agent in the problem may change.

There are large information asymmetries between the securities issuer, the financial service firm, and the investor. Issuers know more about planned uses of funds and their business and intentions. Originators know more about supply and demand conditions in financial markets and the amount of time and effort it will take them to bring a securities issue to market. Investors know little or nothing about firms issuing securities but know the reputation of the financial firms originating the securities.

Securities originating firms perform three functions affecting the parties discussed above: (1) advising; (2) underwriting; and (3) distributing the securities (see Baron 1982 for a discussion). These functions can be performed separately but often they are bundled. Each function requires special expertise and can be a source of value creation.

Advising consists of designing the securities issued and assessing the market demand for the securities, an interdependent process since securities design should enhance marketability of the issue. Issuers seek advice on the relative costs of funds raised in the form of different types of securities. Advisors provide assistance in completing necessary disclosures with regulators (as discussed in Chapter 15.)

Underwriting occurs when securities originators buy securities from issuers at fixed prices. Underwriting guarantees the amount of funds from the issue.

FIGURE 9.3 Securities originations: Relation between participants

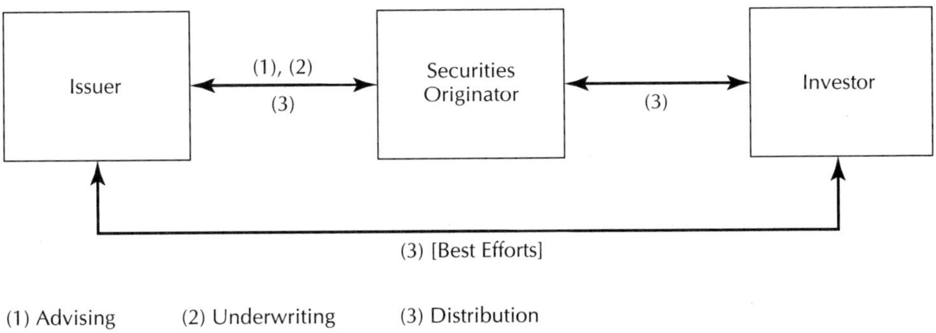

Underwriters also maintain orderly markets in securities after they are issued and assume risks associated with the distribution of the securities.

Distribution of securities consists of lining up commitments to buy securities when they are issued. New issues can be underwritten and resold through distribution channels of the securities originator. Distribution can be performed on a *best efforts* basis, meaning that the securities originator does not guarantee an amount for the issue but attempts to get the most sales possible from its distribution network. Underwriting and distribution functions are often performed in syndicates of investment bankers to spread the risks of committing funds at a fixed price and provide a broader range of contacts among investors to distribute securities issues.

Value Created by Securities Originator for Issuer

Securities originators create value by advising clients on pricing of securities when brought to market and distributing the securities. This source of value concentrates on the relation between the securities originator and the security issuer, as shown in Figure 9.3. In typical arrangements, the issuing firm either sets the price or delegates price setting to the securities firm, who in turn distributes the issue. The issuer receives the sales proceeds of the issue net of the financial firm's fees.

In the pricing and distribution aspects of securities origination, there is a potential conflict of interest that has been cast in the principal–agent framework by Baron (1982). Issuing firms do not possess the securities market expertise of the securities originator—an information asymmetry. If the securities originator sets new issue prices, it is tempted to set prices lower than would be necessary if maximum sales effort were made in distribution. The securities originator prefers less effort in distribution, a moral hazard problem. Baron analyzed contracts between securities originators and issuers that can solve the moral hazard problem.

Baron delineates three ways in which the issuer can contract with securities origination firm: (1) the issuer delegates pricing and distribution to the securities originator, utilizing both advising and distribution services; (2) the issuer sets the issue price based on its limited market information, not using the securities originating firm's advising services but relying on the firm to distribute the issue; or (3) the issuer sells directly to the market, not using either the advising or distribution services of the financial service firm.

A simplified adaptation of Baron's discussion of the price delegation contract with an advisor assumes that the issuer believes a security would sell for a price between \$10 and \$20, as shown in Figure 9.4. At some prices for the security, say \$13, it is cheaper for the issuer to use other sources or not go ahead with the financing. If the securities originator has superior information about the market, the right compensation contract makes alternative (1) above—delegating price setting to the securities originator—the best solution to the issuer's problem.

To show that alternative (1) is best in our example, superior information on the market for the issuer's security is assumed to be a tighter band of prices, which the advisor knows are possible for the issue. In Figure 9.4, in a good market the advisor is assumed to know that the issue would sell out for some price between \$15 and \$18. In other words, the advisor knows that the likely selling

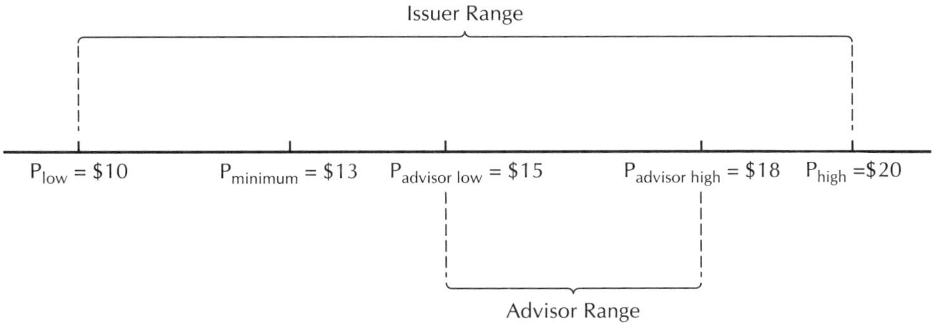

FIGURE 9.4 Information on securities market prices

price makes the security issuer worthwhile for the issue since it will likely sell for more than \$13. The problem for the issuer is that if the pricing of the security is delegated to the advisor, the advisor is tempted to set the price lower than necessary to make it easy to sell the security.

Baron shows that the terms of the contract between the issuer and the advisor can resolve this moral hazard and asymmetric information problem. Baron looks at possible compensation, R, for the advisor to determined by an equation of the following form (simplified from Baron's discussion):

$$R = S\,(P_{high} - P_{advisor\ low}) + T(P_a{}^*N) \tag{9.1}$$

where S times the price information is part of a fee to the securities originator made by the issuer who depends on information the advisor gives the issuer about the market. T represents a percent of the total securities offering retained by the advisor as part of its fee. In the first part of the formula, the advisor's information is the difference between the issuer's assessment of the highest possible price for the issue, P_{high}, and the lowest sales price the advisor feels is necessary for the issue, $P_{advisor\ low}$. Bad news about the market means a high value for the difference. The total proceeds of the offering are the product of the actual price the advisor sets, P_a, times the number of securities sold, N, and the issuer keeps the total proceeds minus the fee to the securities originating firm.

The contract terms presented in equation (9.1) contain two limiting versions observed in real-world investment banking compensation arrangements. When T in the equation is equal to zero, the securities firm is paid a fixed payment unrelated to the issue price. In other words, the advisor is paid on a best-efforts basis. When T is unity, the securities originator keeps the entire amount of the securities sale, and the securities issuer receives a fixed payment from the originator, namely $S(P_{high} - P_{advisor\ low})$. The second alternative corresponds to a fixed price underwritten issue.

Table 9.5 provides an example using Baron's formula with the prices discussed above to demonstrate how choice of a contract could reveal the investment banker's assessment of market demand to the issuer. In the example provided in the table, if information concerning the market is good, the investment

TABLE 9.5 Investment Banking Fee Schedule Example
100,000 Share Issue (= N)

Formula: $R = S\,(P_{high} - P_{advisor\ low}) + T^*\,(P_{average}{}^*\,N)$	
Formula A – S = \$5,000, T = .02	
Formula B – S = \$1,000, T = .05	
Case 1: Good Market	
Price Range	
P-low	\$10
P-advisor low	15
P-advisor high	18
P-high	20
Advisor Expected Issue Price = \$16.50	
R_A = \$25,000 + \$33,000 = \$58,000	
R_B = 5,000 + 82,500 = 87,500	
Case 2: Poor Market	
Price Range	
P-low	10
P-advisor low	10
P-advisor high	13
P-high	20
Advisor Expected Issue Price = \$11.50	
R_A = \$50,000 + \$23,000 = \$73,000	
R_B = 10,000 + 57,500 = 67,500	

banker prefers a fee for pricing and distribution based on a high percent of issue sales price (underlined in the table.) If the market is poor, the investment banker prefers a (mostly) fixed fee for pricing and distribution services, basically a distribution on a best efforts basis. The issuer in this case pays the securities firm its fee and does not issue the security because the expected price is below \$13: the advisor's fee is less than the loss from issuing the security at \$11.50. The issuer has increased value from the offering by minimizing moral hazard in the investment banker's distribution efforts and by knowing whether the banker's expert assessment of market conditions is good or poor.

Baron's careful analysis also provides insights into other aspects of the price-setting function of securities originators for issuers. The more uncertain the issuer is of the range of possible sale prices, the lower is the acceptable price to the issuer. This result is related to the tendency of new issues to be underpriced relative to subsequent market prices.[2] Baron also shows that the value of the advisor's information increases to the issuer with greater uncertainty, increasing the advantage of a delegated pricing contract with the securities originator.

[2]For a review of the analysis of pricing of new issues, see Smith (1986.) For an alternative explanation of underpricing, see the discussion of Rock (1986) in the following section.

Securities originators also produce value for buyers of new issues who are not familiar with issuing firms for pricing strategy. This source of value concentrates on the relation between the securities originator and different types of investors shown in Figure 9.3. Some investors have more information concerning firms issuing new securities while other investors are relatively uninformed. In such a world, uninformed investors would fear buying new securities issues. If informed investors did not buy the new issue, uninformed investors would pay too much. The market for new issues would ultimately fail to function.

Rock (1986) analyzed how the information asymmetry problem between informed and uninformed investors can be resolved. The answer is for new issue prices to be set low enough to compensate uninformed investors for their risks of buying issues not subscribed for by informed investors. Such a pricing strategy explains the tendency for new issues to be underpriced and for some issues to be oversubscribed, requiring rationing of sales.

Beatty and Ritter (1986) explain how investment bankers or securities originators add value by providing a means of preventing "cheating" by firms issuing securities only once. If issuing firms only issued securities once, issuing firms would lead their investment bankers to set higher prices than are justified. These prices would be too high to compensate uninformed investors for their losses from issues not purchased by informed investors as in the above analysis. Beatty and Ritter show that securities originators like investment banks provide value to the securities market by staking their reputations on the prices attached to new securities issues. Uninformed investors, knowing that securities-originating investment banks will be hurt by the loss of future business if their customers are misled into buying overpriced new issues, rely on the reputation of the investment banks. The capital of securities originators is a form of bond to the reliability of the prices of new securities.

Value Creation through Innovation

Securities originators create value by designing securities that produce higher sales proceeds than conventional securities. An example of innovation in securities design that produced dazzling profits in the early 1980s for the innovator, First Boston Corporation, was Collateralized Mortgage Obligations (CMO). These securities allowed issuers like thrift institutions who needed cash to sell securities to investors' who wished to hedge interest rate risk in the extremely volatile interest rate environment of those times. CMOs offered long- or short-term investors securities whose cash flows more nearly matched those of their liabilities. CMOs tended to complete the market.

CMOs repackage cash flows from mortgages into so-called *tranches,* representing a claim on a particular subset of cash flows from the underlying assets like thirty-year mortgages. For example, all the principal payments on the first mortgages in the pool to prepay might be paid to the "A" tranche until the A-tranche's principal was retired. Other tranches might receive only the interest on their principal until the "A" tranche principal was paid. Repackaging cash flows, usually into three or more tranches, produces cash flow patterns that vary from those of the underlying assets. The "A" tranche in the above example would have a much shorter maturity time period than other tranches. The last tranche might well be expected to produce cash flows for up to thirty years.

Securities design produces value for the securities originators by enabling them to market securities for which market participants are willing to pay a premium. Innovative securities design produces value due to the heightened demand for the cash flows when separated into patterns appealing to different market segments of investors. The value comes from completing the securities market in a way that increases investors' expected utility in a cost-efficient way.

Marketing and Information Activities in Securities Origination

Clients of securities originators are public firms or firms that are ready to go public. The marketing and information gathering function of securities originators traditionally was based on close relationships between investment bankers and their corporate clients. Often investment bankers sat on the board of directors of client firms, carefully cultivating a network of clients and potential clients. Eccles and Crane (1988) describe the breakup of the traditional system in *Doing Deals*. In contrast to relationship-based securities origination, large issuing firms now routinely use a variety of investment bankers and turn more and more to nontraditional providers of securities services. Eccles and Crane attribute these developments to the expanded scope and increased competition in these services.

Services provided by securities originators are complex. The analyses and diagnoses of customers and markets that are needed require close communication with financial service firms providing these services. Close communication with current and potential clients via telephone and personal visits are likely to be an unchanging aspect of providing services in this industry despite changes in the competitive environment.

Funding, Investing, and Risk Bearing and Shifting

Securities originators underwriting new issues must finance their purchases. Some large investment banks engage substantial amounts of their own capital, in line with the Beatty and Ritter argument discussed above. Other sources of borrowing, such as special purpose syndicates and credit from other financial service firms, are an important source of funds for the short-term needs associated with bringing new issues to market.

Managing the risks associated with underwriting issues is handled in two ways. First, securities originators usually operate in syndicates with risk sharing rules for large issues. Second, technical risk management techniques such as those discussed in Part IV are employed routinely to limit exposure to the risks of large underwriting.

9.5 SUMMARY

Securities markets represent the highest development of sophisticated and advanced economies. Their economic role is to provide a benchmark for managers of the opportunity costs of funds raised for investment. There are three essential functions associated with interrelating with securities markets: trading securities, making markets in securities, and originating new securities. These functions, like all those we examine in this book, are being dramatically transformed by competition and technological changes.

DISCUSSION QUESTIONS AND EXERCISES

1. Review recent announcements of new securities offerings (tombstone ads) in the *Wall Street Journal* or other financial paper and describe the securities in terms of their special features. What differentiates the offerings and what problems of fund raising by the issuer or demands of investors can these differentiating features be intended to solve?
2. Obtain commission schedules from full-line and discount brokers in your area. What are the differences in the costs of using these brokers for trades of different sizes? What is the difference in the services and commitments to performance advertised by these different types of brokers? What would be the impact on their costs of providing their services?
3. Obtain recent information of activity and estimate commission rates or bid/ask spreads on several financial markets (stock, bond, or derivative) in a financial newspaper. Classify by type of market (organized or over the counter) and estimate using volume statistics the total commissions earned using assumed commission rates or bid–ask spreads. What are the economic costs and invested capital these revenues must cover? What are the annualized revenues implied by your estimates?
4. Corporate executives in the United States must file public reports when they buy and sell securities of firms they work for. What would determine whether these trades are based on information or liquidity needs? What problems would regulators have in trying to demonstrate illegal use of inside information?
5. Locate a list of new securities filed with regulators or announced to the press (for example as listed daily in the *Wall Street Journal* "Financing Business" tables) and determine what you can about terms of the issues and their relation with securities originators.
6. Obtain a *Prospectus* on a new bond issue from a broker and review the disclosures and terms of the issue. What information is contained in the disclosure? How could a securities firm help a nonfinancial issuer in preparation of these disclosures? What terms are intended to appeal to what investors? Examine the relation between the securities firm and the issuer: is the issue underwritten or a best efforts distribution?
7. Put together a fifteen- or twenty-year series on initial public offerings as provided in Table 9.2, Panel C. What trends do you see in the types of securities issued in different economic environments? Can you explain variations in new issue activity in terms of economic conditions?
8. Pick some market other than New York, Chicago, California, or a capital city of a foreign country. Determine if there is a local exchange and local investment banking firms. Given the possibility of economies in concentrating trading, what economic reasons

are there for localized securities markets? Can you determine how active the local markets you choose are?

9. If a bid–ask spread of $1 causes a market breakdown, what information costs cause a breakdown in the market provided in Table 9.4. Answer this question by assuming different probabilities that a given trader is an information trader and different price consequences of information traders' information.

10. The NASDAQ system has successfully been exported to other countries. What does it mean to export a market? What would be attractive and what would be a problem in foreign use of a trading system?

REFERENCES

BARON, DAVID P. 1982. "A Model of the Demand for Investment Banking and Advising and Distribution Services for New Issues," *Journal of Finance* 37 (September), pp. 955–976.

BEATTY, RANDOLPH P. and JAY R. RITTER. 1986. "Investment Banking, Reputation, and the Underpricing of Initial Public Offerings," *Journal of Financial Economics* 15, pp. 213–232.

BRENNAN, MICHAEL J. and TARUN CHORDIA. 1993. "Brokerage Commission Schedules," *Journal of Finance,* 48 (4), pp. 1379–1402.

CHRISTIE, WILLIAM G. and PAUL H. SCHULTZ. 1994. "Why do NASDAQ Market Makers avoid Odd-Eighth Quotes," *Journal of Finance,* Vol. 49, no. 5, pp. 1813–1840.

COHEN, KALMAN J., STEVEN F. MAIER, ROBERT A. SCHWARTZ, DAVID K. WHITCOMB. 1986. *The Microstructure of Securities Markets.* Englewood Cliffs, NJ: Prentice Hall.

COPELAND, THOMAS E. and DAN GALAI. 1983. "Information Effects on the Bid–Ask Spread," *Journal of Finance* 38 (December), pp. 1457–1469.

ECCLES, ROBERT G. and DWIGHT B. CRANE. 1988. *Doing Deals.* Boston, Massachusetts: Harvard Business School Press.

DEMSETZ, HAROLD. 1968. "The Cost of Transacting," *Quarterly Journal of Economics* LXXXII (1), pp. 33–53.

GLOSTEN, LAWRENCE R. and MILGROM, PAUL R. 1985. "Bid, Ask and Transaction Prices in a Specialist Market with Heterogeneously Informed Traders," *Journal of Financial Economics* 14, pp. 71–100.

MADDEN, BARTLEY J. and EARNEST P. WELKER. 1995. "Give Small Investors an Alternative to Nasdaq," *Wall Street Journal,* January 16, p. A12.

ROCK, KEVIN. 1986. "Why are New Issues Underpriced?," *Journal of Financial Economics* 15, pp. 187–212.

SMITH, CLIFFORD W., JR. 1986. "Investment Banking and the Capital Acquisition Process," *Journal of Financial Economics* 15, pp. 3–29.

STOLL, HANS R. 1990. "Principles of Trading Market Structure," Working Paper 90-31, Vanderbilt University, Financial Markets Research Center.

TORRES, CRAIG. 1993. "How Street Turns Your Stock Trades to Gold," *Wall Street Journal,* February 16, p. C1.

CHAPTER

10

Transaction Processing Services

Introduction

The payment system is at the heart of advanced economies. However, payments are only one example of transaction processing which includes functions like loan servicing and bond registration.

- What is the payments system and how does it relate to the traditional organization of financial services industry?
- How are payments processed and what kind of resources are required?
- How does the payments system resemble other transaction processing systems?
- What are the underlying economics of providing transaction processing financial services?
- Who can perform and profit from the activities involved in transaction processing?

Understanding the answers to these questions is central to surviving and winning the competitive battles in this most technologically oriented of the financial services we analyze in this book.

This chapter begins with a detailed examination of the payments system with particular emphasis on check processing. The check processing system is used as a model of transaction processing systems in general emphasizing their economic similarities. The basic elements of all transaction processing and their economic and financial implications are discussed prior to an analysis of how value is produced in this dynamic and changing area of financial services.

10.1 THE PAYMENTS SYSTEM: EXAMPLE OF TRANSACTION PROCESSING

A checking account represents a claim on the assets of a bank or other deposit-taking institution. When you pay with a check, you are exchanging your claim on the deposit-taking institution's assets for the good or service you buy. In the normal course of things, the payer's bank will honor the check and settle up with the payee's bank or other deposit-taking institution. This process is called *check clearing*.

Fama (1980) has called the modern deposit-based payments system an *accounting system of exchange*. In describing banks' role in this system, Fama says:

> We take the main function of banks in the transactions industry to be the maintenance of a system of accounts in which transfers of wealth are carried out with bookkeeping entries. Banks also provide the service of exchanging deposits and other forms of wealth for currency, but in modern banking this is less important than the accounting system of exchange. (p. 39)

Payments with checks represent asset exchanges for purchases, effected through bookkeeping entries in deposit-taking accounts and settling up between banks. In other words, a modern payments system requires keeping track of who owns what claims on banks' and other deposit-taking institutions' assets.

Payments can be made by exchanging claims on other than deposit-taking institution assets. Cash, for example, represents claims on central bank assets. In principle, there is no limit to which assets can be used to back up a means of payment. The economically efficient or best payment devices are those that make the process of exchanging assets easiest and cheapest. This means that parties to payment transactions are sure of the value of the assets exchanged and that the resource costs of making exchanges are minimized. Government regulation limiting competition and subsidizing bank transaction processing has made paper money, checks, and wire transfers between deposit accounts transactions the most widespread mediums of exchange in modern developed economies.

There are three basic modes of completing transactions, illustrated in Figure 10.1: (1) simple exchange of cash for goods and services; (2) written orders to pay cash or credit deposit balances; and (3) direct electronic instructions to transfer deposit balances. The easiest and cheapest is a simple and final exchange between transacting parties, illustrated in the figure by a payment in cash. Transactors communicate directly, usually in person. Other examples of direct exchange can be

FIGURE 10.1 Relation between deposit-taking institutions and customers

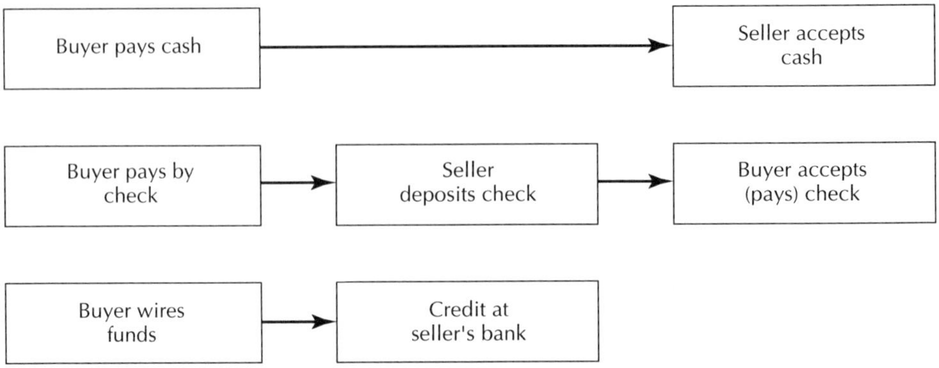

imagined, such as paying for a long cab ride with stock certificates, but they are not common because the values exchanged are less sure.

Table 10.1 contains data on the means of payment used in the United States in 1983 as reported in a study by Humphrey (1984). The table shows that the method of payment used most frequently is cash, but checks and wire transfers between bank accounts comprise the vast majority of the total monetary value of exchanges. Checks and transfers between bank accounts represent exchanges of financial assets for purchases or payments.

A simple exchange is possible between any combination of firms and individuals. Simple exchange is the cheapest but in some ways the least safe means of exchanging assets. Simple exchanges demand a level of trust or a desire to do business confidentially between the transacting parties since no record is generated by the transaction. There is no guarantee of being able to contact the transacting party in case of problems uncovered after the transaction is completed.

Most personal and business transactions rely on written orders to provide a record and avoid the danger of valuable cash being stolen or lost. As is indicated in Table 10.1, the largest dollar amount of payments is made by direct electronic transfers, and the second largest by checks. All of us are very familiar with checks.

We begin our discussion of transaction processing services with a detailed analysis of the check-clearing system. Our objective is to describe the procedures and resources required to operate the transaction processing system for deposits and to generalize on the economic functions associated with an asset-exchange system. In later sections of the chapter we discuss other transaction processing systems and use the deposit processing system as a benchmark for comparison.

Checking Deposits and the Check Clearing System

Checking accounts are contractual relationships individuals or firms have with deposit-taking institutions. When a checking account is opened, a signature card is signed and a deposit of assets such as cash or checks made. The contractual relationship between the deposit-taking institution and the depositor lasts until the account is closed.

In an accounting system of exchange, transactors have a relationship with the financial institution providing them with transaction services. With a checking account, the deposit-taking institution is a debtor and the depositor a creditor. The obligations of both parties are determined by the explicit terms of its deposit contract and the provisions of the prevailing *commercial code*. Fees, minimum balances, penalties, and interest rates for checking accounts are negotiated or offered to customers opening accounts as part of the contract between the deposit-taking institution and the depositor. Services beyond transaction processing, such as information on transaction activity and balances, are provided as part of their relationship.

Legal obligations and rules governing checking accounts are contained in a state or country's commercial code, a set of laws governing commercial practices like sales agreements, debt instruments, and means of payment. In most of the United States, the commercial code is modeled on the Uniform Commercial Code, developed in 1942 by The American Law Institute and the National Conference of

TABLE 10.1 Means of Payment in the United States

	VOLUME (MILLIONS)	*TOTAL VALUE ($ TRILLIONS)*	*ANNUAL GROWTH (1981–1983)*	*VALUE PER TRANSACTION ($)*
Cash[a]	112,000 (very approximate)	$2.8	9%	$25
Check[b]	40,000	36	6%	910
ACH[c]	400	.7	27%	1,800
Wire Transfer[d]	57	142	11%	2,500,000

[a]*Cash*. Cash transactions are not directly reported. An educated guess by a national commission put cash transactions at two-thirds of all types of transactions (National Commission on Electronic Fund Transfers, 1977, p. 333). For retail sales transactions, however, excluding food and drinking establishments, cash transactions are only 30% of total transactions (Curtin, 1983, p. 27). But this likely understates the true percentage as food stores and coin operated machines are not included. The estimate of the total value of cash transactions used in the table relies upon a new survey of currency and transaction amount usage (Survey Research Center, 1984) which indicated that the average family spends $192 per month in coin and currency transactions compared to $2,444 a month on check transactions (excluding checks used to obtain cash). Thus for every $12.73 spent via check, $1 is spent using cash ($192.00/$2,444 = $1/$12.73). Dividing the $36 trillion value for check expenditures in the table by $12.73 gives $2.8 trillion as an estimate of the total value of cash transactions. This, of course, assumes that the ratio in the survey ($192.00 in cash transactions to $2,444 in check transactions) holds for the nation as a whole. The average value per cash transaction in the retail store survey (Curtin, 1983) was $25, with $37 for checks. This check figure compares well with the median value of a check written in 1979 of $36 (Federal Reserve Bank of Atlanta, 1979, p. 178). Dividing the $2.8 trillion estimate of the total value of cash transactions by the $25 average value per transaction gives 112,000 million as an approximate estimate of the total number of cash transactions. This volume figure represents 73% of the total of all types of transactions shown in the table. The annual growth of cash transactions shown reflects the actual growth in coin and currency in circulation, assumed to equal the growth in transaction value.

[b]*Check*. The number of (private) checks written in 1979 was 32.8 billion and the growth rate between 1974–79 was estimated to be 5.6% annually (Federal Reserve Bank of Atlanta, 1979, p. 1). These data suggest that 40 billion checks would have been written in 1983. The average value per check transaction in the Atlanta study was $757 in 1979 (p. 73) and was increased to $910 for 1983 using the 20% inflation rate experienced between 1980 and 1983. The value per check transaction is skewed upwards due to a small number of exceptionally large dollar value checks which are written.

[c]*ACH*. Automatic Clearing House transaction volumes and growth are from the Federal Reserve's cost accounting publication (*Planning and Control System Expense Report*) called PACS, adjusted downward slightly to correct for transfers counted twice when handled by two Federal Reserve offices. The data includes private sector processing volume, which is almost entirely from the New York Clearinghouse. The value per commercial ACH transaction averaged $3,800. This number is strongly influenced by the ACH transfers which occur on the night cycle, which is primarily used for concentrating corporate cash balances from receiving banks to disbursing banks. The average ACH night cycle transfer was $21,000, while day cycle ACH debits (credits) averaged $350 ($700) per transfer. The average government ACH transaction was $500. As government (commercial) ACH volume was 61% (39%) of total volume, the weighted average value per ACH transaction is $1,800 (i.e., .39 ($3,800) + .61 ($500) = $1,787). Multiplying $1,800 by 400 million transactions gives $.7 trillion as an estimate for total ACH value transacted.

[d]*Wire Transfer*. Wire transfer volumes are for FedWire and CHIPS only, as volume on other U.S. networks is small. Volume growth data are from FedWire (all FedWire data are found in PACS, adjusted downward to correct for transfers counted twice when handled by two Federal Reserve offices). Value per transaction reflects FedWire and CHIPS average values (CHIPS data are from unpublished sources). FedWire had 38 million transfers worth $85 trillion (or $335 billion per day over 255 business days). CHIPS had 19 million transfers worth $57 trillion (or $225 billion per day over 255 days). The average value per transaction was $2.2 million for FedWire and $3.0 million for CHIPS.

SOURCE: David Burras Humphrey, *The U.S. Payments System: Costs, Pricing, Competition and Risk*, Monograph Series in Finance and Economics, Solomon Brothers Center for the Study of Financial Institutions, New York University, 1984, p. 6.

Commissioners on Uniform State Laws. Some states, like California, have their own commercial code. The Uniform Code has been revised several times (last in 1987) to account for changes in business practice.

The contract covering the deposit relationship is between the depositor and a deposit-taking institution. The depositor/creditor gives the institution/debtor assets and now has a claim on the deposit-taking institution. The depositor intends to use this claim as a means of payment. Figure 10.2 presents a schematic of the relationships between deposit-taking institutions and their deposit customers. The relationship includes a number of information and reporting flows.

To pay for something, a buyer generates an order to pay funds to a seller using a check on a deposit at the buyer's deposit-taking institution. The seller deposits the payment order with his or her transaction processing financial service firm, to be credited to his or her account. The value of the check is deducted from or *drawn on* the buyer's account and added to the seller's account. For this to occur according to the code governing check clearing, the check must be presented to the buyer's bank for payment and must conform to the rules governing the execution of valid checks.

The Check Collection Process

The physical presentation of checks payable drawn on different deposit-taking financial institutions is called *clearing*. How does this physical payment process work? Sellers deposit checks in their accounts by endorsing checks, thereby

FIGURE 10.2 Customer relation with transaction processing service firm

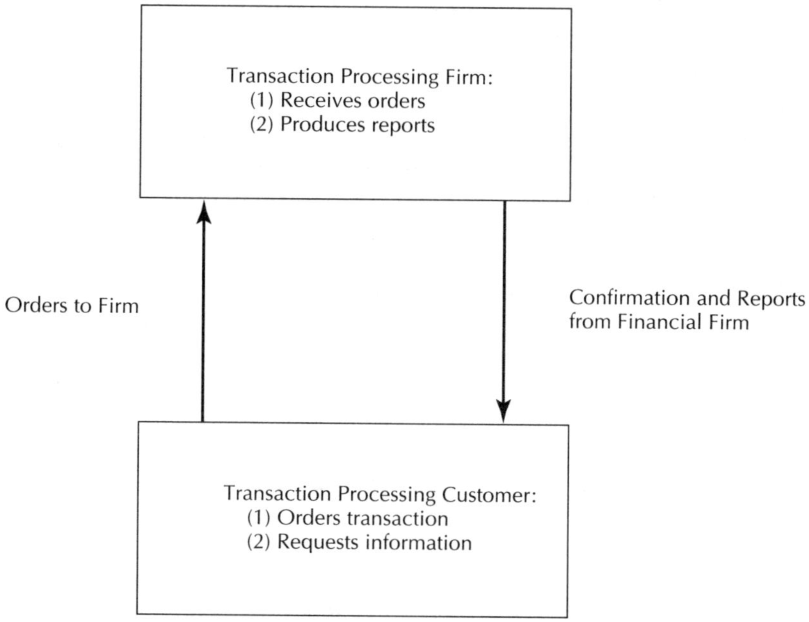

assigning them to their banks as collecting agents, filling out deposit slips including other checks to be collected, and taking or sending deposit slips and checks to their deposit-taking institution. The procedure whereby check depositors receive credit in the form of increased claims on their deposit-taking institution's assets is the check-clearing process. Check clearing is one of the most highly developed examples of Fama's accounting system of exchange.

All the checks or written orders to pay must be physically presented to whatever financial institutions they are drawn on, subtracted from payers' accounts, and credited to customers making deposits. If some checks are not good, because check writers did not have claims on their banks as large as their check amount, called *insufficient funds,* or the check is falsified or illegally executed, they must be identified as bad checks within strict time limits set by the commercial code and laws. Bad checks must be returned, unpaid, to the depositor.

This stream of checks coming into thousands of banks, savings institutions, and credit unions is an enormous transaction processing problem. The problem consists of sorting these pieces of paper into stacks such that all checks drawn on each deposit-taking institution are presented for payment. Given that there are approximately 25,000 deposit-taking institutions in the United States alone, the sorting problem is immense and it has to be done every business day.

Checks have computer account and bank information preprinted on them, but when checks are deposited, the handwritten amount of the check cannot be read by a machine. The first step in processing the stream of checks is to check totals of deposit slips and encode the amounts of each check. Today, this procedure is done by the first large bank maintaining what are called *proof operations.* A proof machine is a machine that can type the dollar amount on a check in computer readable form and keep running totals of deposits and groups of deposits. The check after this stage can be read by scanning machines.

Operating a proof machine is a very labor intensive operation. Proof machine operators are skilled workers who achieve maximum efficiency after months on the job, but the work is numbingly boring and there is very high turnover in these jobs. Given a paper-based checking system, little promise is offered of a large increase in the efficiency of the current operations short of a technological revolution in optical character recognition (OCR). Replacing current methods, if feasible, will require expensive programming and systems talent to implement and make practical.

Amounts on paper checks are machine readable after proofing. Computerized check sorting machines then can begin the process of check sorting. Check sorting machines are computer driven but operate at mechanical speeds. Sorting-machine operators feed boxes of checks into input bins and each check's code is read by the machine while checks are directed into one of the machine's sorting pockets. The maximum number of pockets on the most widely used check sorting machines today is 48. Significantly, one of the pockets is the reject pocket for unreadable checks.

A major activity of deposit-institution operations researchers is to design the most efficient way to sort checks. A critical consideration is meeting the mandatory deadline for presentation of checks to clearing agencies for payment. Financial institutions want to maximize the amount of checks presented for payment to be able to invest as much of this money as soon as possible.

The amount of money in the clearing system in the time between when checks are written and ultimately paid by institutions drawn on is *clearing time float.* Until institutions are presented with checks for payment, they have use of funds represented by the amount of the check. Deposit institutions want use of these funds as long as possible. Deposit-taking institutions, corporations, and individuals all attempt to maximize available funds through the management of float.

Sorting the stream of checks for presentation consists of a number of passes through sorting machines to identify checks drawn on different sets of deposit-taking institutions. The sorting problem is schematized in Figure 10.3. There are four sets of paying institutions: The first is the same institution as the check is drawn on, which banks call *on-us* items. The second set is local institutions, called *city* or *clearinghouse* checks in large cities. The third set is distant banks, called *country* or *transit* items, usually cleared through the Federal Reserve System in the United States. Finally, some checks, especially very large ones, are sent directly to the paying institution. These checks are called *direct sends.*

On-us items are the easiest for deposit-institutions to clear. The account balance of the customer writing the check is checked to see if there are sufficient funds. If there are, the depositor's balance is increased and the payor's balance decreased. There is no effect of the float on the deposit-taking institution, the check writer's float is minimized because of the short time the check is in the clearing system, and the payment recipient's float is reduced, since he or she obtains next-day credit.

City or clearinghouse items must be delivered to the physical location where checks are exchanged. Usually clearinghouses have one or two sessions a day at strict time deadlines. For example, the Chicago Clearing House has two exchanges of checks in Downtown Chicago at 3:00 A.M. and 10:30 A.M. each weekday morning. The checks must be ready for presentation by a deadline for the clearinghouse member to get credit the next day. Clearinghouse members exchange checks drawn on each other and on affiliated banks and present *cash*

FIGURE 10.3 Check sorting

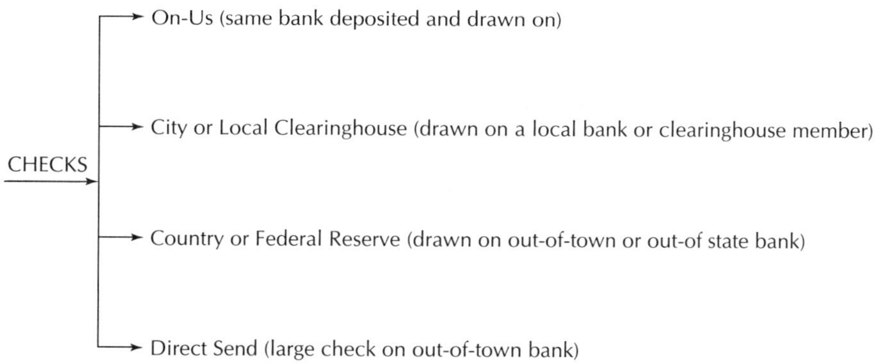

letters representing the total amount owed to depositors of each bank. For example, the Chicago Clearing House has nine members, mainly large downtown banks, and 150 Chicago area banks are affiliated. Member banks calculate net differences in amounts of funds deposited to and drawn on each other in the cash letters. Members of the clearinghouse settle in the form of Federal Reserve Bank deposits or clearinghouse funds. We will discuss the economic role of the clearinghouse in more detail in the next section.

The check-clearing operation of the Federal Reserve system is a national clearinghouse in the United States. Transit items are cleared through the Federal Reserve System (Fed) or central bank. Deposit-taking firms with accounts at the Fed deliver transit items to their local Federal Reserve Bank or Branch. There are 12 Federal Reserve Banks and 24 branches around the United States. Like local clearinghouses, there are strict deadlines as to when batches of checks with their cash letters must be presented for payment. In the case of checks presented to the Federal Reserve, however, credit to banks' balances is made a set number of days after the check is presented. The number of days until credit is received depends on which Federal Reserve District and which part of the district checks are drawn on. Banks get credit for checks presented to the Federal Reserve in one to three days according to a fixed clearing time schedule established by the Fed. The resources used by the Federal Reserve in check clearing are enormous.

Direct sends are checks sent directly to the bank or a correspondent in the same city of the bank drawn on. Float on multimillion dollar checks represent large interest costs or returns to deposit-taking institutions and their customers. For example, the daily interest earned on a million dollars at six percent per year is $164.38. Two or three days' delay in clearing a multimillion dollar check can cost substantial interest; for example, a two-day delay on a $10 million check costs $3,293 at six percent. To speed up the clearing process, banks send checks directly to major cities for more immediate payment and collection.

Figure 10.4 illustrates the relations between customers and their deposit-taking institutions, between those institutions and members of the clearing system, and between clearing system members. These relations are all important to the functioning of a transaction processing system. Customers are primarily aware of their relationship with their deposit-taking institutions. What goes on in the system is of little direct relevance to them unless it affects clearing times. This set of relationships is general in all transaction processing systems and we will discuss it in more general form below.

The Federal Reserve and the Check-Clearing System

The importance of the Federal Reserve in the United States payments system cannot be overstated. The Federal Reserve was set up in 1913 to be a national clearinghouse. The economic functions of a clearinghouse, which we discuss in the next section, were felt by the authors of the Federal Reserve Act to be a proper function of government. Some economists, including two Nobel Prize winners in economics, Milton Friedman and Friedrich von Hayek, do not believe that it is essential to have a government agency run the clearinghouse. They argue that the

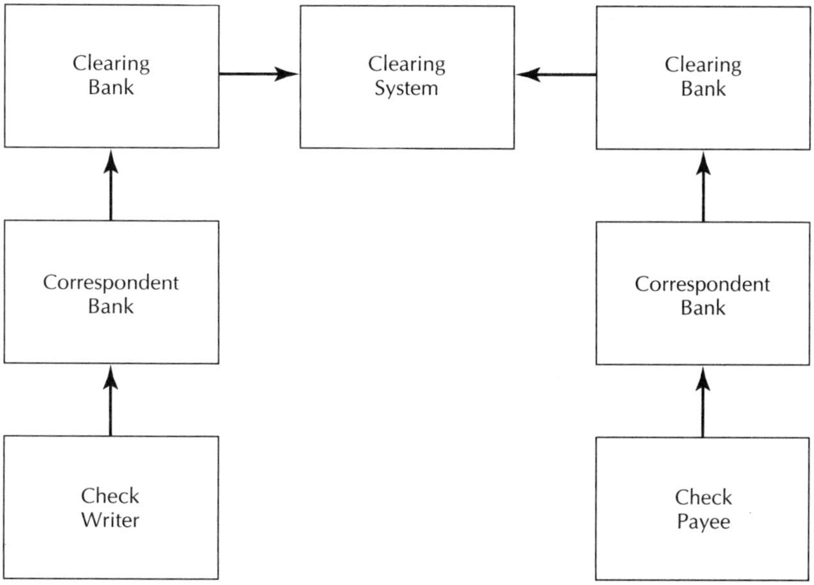

FIGURE 10.4 Relation between check clearing system and customers

national clearinghouse function of the Federal Reserve is separable from its presumed responsibility for controlling the money supply, which we discuss in Chapter 14.

The national clearinghouse function of the Federal Reserve was dramatically altered by the Deregulation Act of 1980. Prior to 1980, to have access to the Federal Reserve clearing system a commercial bank had to become "member" of the Federal Reserve System by buying stock in its local district Federal Reserve Bank and submitting to Fed rules. Member banks had to keep reserve balances against demand (checking) and time deposits in the form of zero-interest bearing deposits at the Federal Reserve Bank. Nonmember state-chartered banks in most states could keep required reserves in the form of interest-bearing securities like Treasury Bills. Fed membership was very costly in times of high interest rates in terms of lost interest on reserve balances.

Before 1980, the Fed compensated member banks for the costs of membership (beyond token dividends on Federal Reserve stock) in a variety of ways. Members received free check clearing services, had use of funds in the clearing process not yet collected (Federal Reserve float) and free use of the Federal Reserve wire system to transfer funds between banks, the so-called Fed-Wire. The Fed also counted currency and coin and delivered them to banks for no charge. The Fed kept track of and stored member banks' U.S. Treasury securities (safekeeping) at no charge. All of these free services and subsidies compensated member banks for the lost interest on their reserve balances at the Federal Reserve.

Title II or "The Monetary Control Act" of the Deregulation Act of 1980 was written to foster more competition in the development of the payments system.

The competitive advantage enjoyed by the Federal Reserve in being able to give away resource costly services, like check clearing services, was removed. The Act mandated that the Federal Reserve charge fees for all services including float—fees to be set at levels a private competitor would have to charge to stay in business, including an allowance for a return to private capital.

Private clearing systems do compete with the Fed. The bank-owned Clearing House Interbank Payments System (CHIPS) competes in clearing international transactions. Private clearing systems, such as the Midwest Payments System run by Fifth Third Bancorp, also compete with the Fed. Banks have their own wire system and check delivery systems.

10.2 ECONOMICS OF CLEARING TRANSACTIONS

Check processing is an example of the clearing process in an accounting system of exchange. The clearing process consists of the presentation of an order to change ownership of assets (*clearing*) and the execution of that order by an exchange of assets (*settlement*). In the case of checks, assets exchanged are claims on depositing-taking firms. Other financial assets, like stocks, bonds, options, short-term loans, and so on, also have highly developed clearing systems.

All clearing systems have the same underlying economic structure. First, an order to execute a change of ownership enters the system. In the case of a check, this occurs when the check written to pay a bill is deposited. In the case of a common stock, it occurs when a trader calls his broker with a sell order and the broker sells the stock. The ownership of both assets must be changed and payment made. We examine the supply and demand for transaction clearing and then discuss the two basic elements required by any clearing system: communication networks and methods of settlement.

Demand and Supply for Transaction Processing

The demand for transaction processing services is unique in that both parties to an exchange must be considered simultaneously: The buyer and seller must both agree to use the same clearing system. Baxter (1983) analyzed the economics of transaction processing systems. He notes that aggregate demand for transaction services must add buyers' and sellers' demands for transaction services *vertically* since their demands are not independent: They must both demand the same transaction system for the system to be useful to complete purchases and sales. Furthermore, buyers and sellers each have their own relationships with financial institutions that provide access to the clearing system, as shown in Figures 10.2 and 10.4. These institutions must provide clearing services in the same system, meaning that the supply curves for the services they provide are derived from the *vertical* sum of marginal cost curves for financial institutions for both buyers and sellers. These supply and demand relations are shown in Figure 10.5.

The costs of a clearing system incurred by financial institutions serving buyers and sellers must be covered by fees and discounts paid by buyers and sellers in a sustainable or equilibrium level of transaction processing. An important

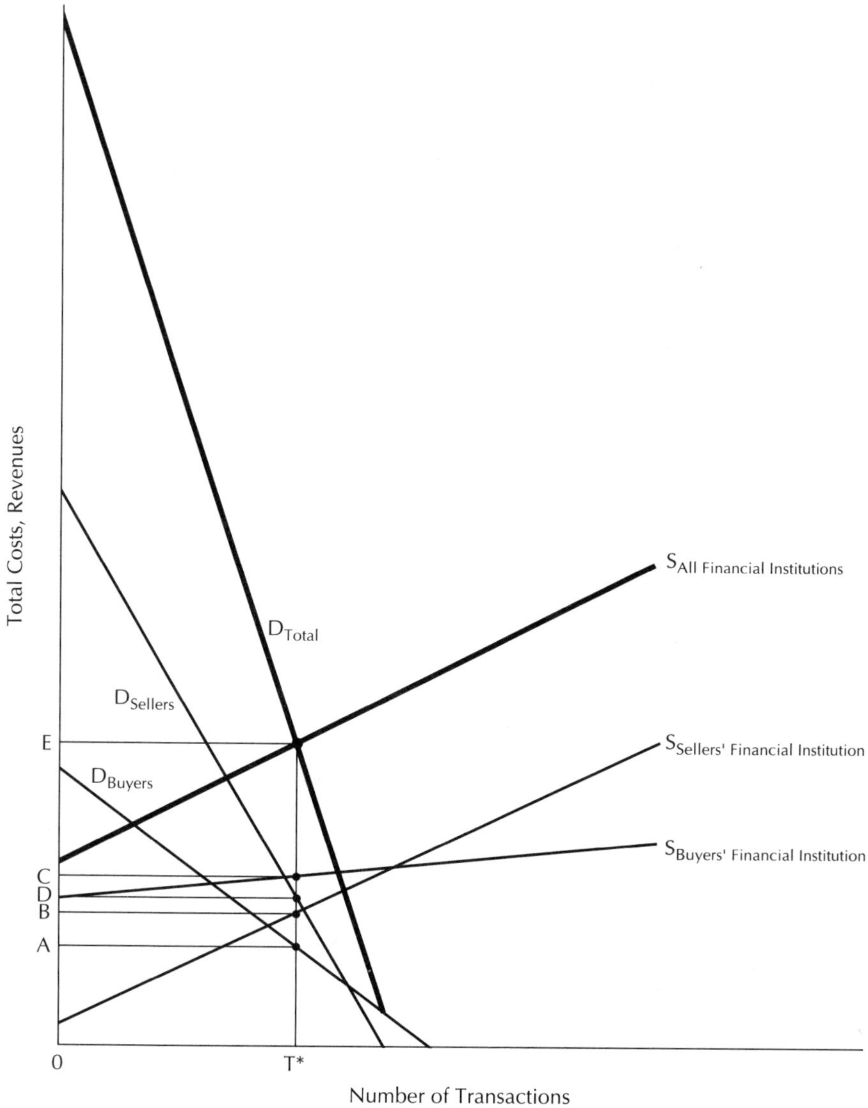

OE = total cost = total fees
OA = value to buyers
OD = value to sellers
OC = cost to buyer's financial institutions
OB = cost to seller's financial institutions

FIGURE 10.5 Supply and demand of transaction processing

implication of Baxter's analysis is that the value of transactions services to buyers (the distance 0A in Figure 10.5) will not in general equal the costs of transaction processing to buyers' financial institutions (shown by 0C). Similarly, the value to sellers (0D) will not in general equal costs to sellers' financial institutions (0B). To achieve an efficient market-clearing level of transactions volume, where aggregate value of demanders of transaction services matches aggregate costs of transaction system suppliers, indirect or side payments may be required between financial institutions to achieve the economic level of transactions. For example, in Figure 10.5, sellers' financial institutions receive 0D and their costs are less than that value, namely 0B. The sellers' institutions must subsidize buyers' institutions costs in order to achieve the optimum level of transactions because buyers value the clearing services less than their financial institutions' costs.

Baxter argues that the system of discounts, premiums, and fees associated with financial transactions in clearing systems are means to achieve optimal transaction volumes. They are used to allocate revenues to cover higher costs for some financial institutions whose customers assign lower values to transaction processing services than their costs. This observation explains why some financial instruments are discounted from par in some clearing systems and why fees and discounts may not be received in direct proportion to value of services. The analysis points out how pricing and allocation of revenues in providing transactions services are an important component of producing value through achievement of optimal volume of clearing activity. We return to this point below.

Communication Networks

Written orders to effect changes in asset ownership are common with registered securities or other financial assets where claims are maintained by book entry. Transactors turn over payments or exchange instructions to a financial institution with access to a clearing system that has direct or indirect access to all other clearing financial institutions.

The check-clearing communication system is flexible because the transaction document—check, draft, or negotiable order of withdrawal—can have any amount, date, source, and destination for the funds. This means that any order to pay in the United States drawn on any of the hundreds of millions of accounts held by individuals and firms in more than 25,000 deposit-taking firms can be handled by a paper-based system. This flexibility is the major advantage to paper-based systems and may assure their survival into the next century, a point expanded on below.[1]

Electronic systems utilize electronic communication and computers to effect the presentation of messages authorizing exchanges of assets. The Fed wire system is a good example of such a system. Electronic means are fastest for a message to be sent from a sender to a particular addressee. The incremental cost of an electronic message is low.

All senders and receivers must be connected and be able to receive and transmit messages on an electronic system. Messages must be completely standardized in order to be interpreted and processed by electronic equipment. Limitations on access to enter or receive messages, the inflexibility inherent in

[1]See Paul B. Henderson, "Modern Money," pp. 17–37 in Solomon (1987) for discussion of different transaction processing systems.

standardized messages encoded for electronic transmission, and large fixed investments are disadvantages of electronic systems.

Transmission of messages in paper-based or electronic systems involves delivery of claims or confirmations, information processing systems, electronic communication, and computer equipment and programming. There is no reason to believe that the skills and expertise necessary to augment, improve, or develop alternatives to current transactions systems are concentrated in traditional financial institutions.

Familiarity with equipment and technological developments in the transaction process are more likely found in telecommunications firms, computer manufacturers, or software houses, than in financial institutions. Alliances between financial service firms and technology companies is becoming common: For example, MCI and Citicorp as well as Electronic Data Systems and First Fidelity have announced cooperative arrangements in the last five years. Nationsbank and BankAmerica announced their purchase of Meca, a bank software firm, in 1995. Financial service firms developing new transaction processing services should examine carefully the basis for presumed competitive advantages of in-house development of transaction processing systems.

Methods of Settlement

Messages entering paper-based and electronic clearing systems authorize exchanges of assets. Different settlement systems determine under what conditions, when, and where the assets will be exchanged. There are two dimensions to the settlement process: (1) times messages are sent and received; and (2) when assets are exchanged. In terms of the timing of exchange messages, transaction systems can have immediate or batched transmission (see Flannery, 1987). Messages either arrive continuously or orders are presented at specified times, as in the Chicago Clearing House example above.

Conditions on delivery of exchanged assets or *settlement procedures* are very important. Settlement can occur on a transaction-by-transaction basis where each delivered asset is immediately offset by an exchange of another asset or cash. Assets or funds may be delivered continuously with settlement at an agreed-upon time later, as at the end of the day. The second system is characteristic of the Fed wire system for cash transfers. A third settlement system is when participants accumulate claims throughout a period of time like a business day and settle *net* differences at the end of that period or after a delay. Net exchange of assets minimizes actual deliveries of assets or funds. Settlement occurs after all transactions are approved. Example of the third system are the CHIPs bank wire system, settling at the end of day, and the Options Clearing Corporation, settling the next morning.

Differences between continuous delivery and settlement, periodic exchange and settlement (the first and third systems described above), and continuous deliveries with delayed settlement as in the Fed wire system are important. If assets are delivered and no offsetting delivery of cash or other assets occurs until later, as in the Fed wire system, a loan or credit has occurred. Other systems eliminate credit risk because both parties approve each settlement.

In Fed wire settlement procedures, the Fed credits reserve balances of the designated financial institution recipient without deducting reserves from the sending bank until the end of day. When advances are larger than a sending institution's balance during a business day, a *daylight overdraft* occurs. Since the Fed advances funds without checking the sending institution's balances and transfers are irrevocable, called *payment finality,* this advance is a loan. The loan may or may not be covered by subsequent transfers into the bank sending the original message. The Fed is exposed to default risk. Current Fed policy is directed at reducing daylight overdrafts by monitoring balances.

Economic Functions of Clearing Systems

Clearing systems perform several economic functions that make them a source of value. First, they establish and enforce rules on delivery and settlement between members, which make transaction processing routine and reliable. Second, they are a way of sharing risks from both operational breakdowns and failures to deliver (credit risk.) Third, restricted membership in clearing organizations limits access to the clearing system and possibly allows exploitation of economies of scale. Members can capitalize on customers' reluctance to turn to competing clearing channels due to adjustment costs.

The clearinghouse function of sharing risks can play a larger or smaller role in particular clearing systems. The Federal Reserve clearing system absorbs all credit risk by the Fed's willingness to advance funds to banks. If a given bank fails to cover its funds outflow, the Fed's payment finality absorbs all risk to other institutions from the failed bank's wire transfers and check clearing.

Failure to deliver funds or securities can be due to difficulties caused by snowstorms or computer failures—examples of operating breakdowns. Nondelivery because a party does not have assets or funds to deliver is a credit failure. Many economists feel that the Fed distorts the economics of the clearing system in the United States by providing credit insurance to participants with payment finality without charging for it.

Private clearinghouses and systems traditionally and currently use alternative ways of dealing with operating and credit risks associated with delivery and settlement of valuable financial assets. They can control risks by the choice of rules for settlement. They can share the risks with mutual guarantees. For example, failures can be covered by pro rata contributions of clearinghouse members. Securities clearing firms, for example, require clearing firm owners to pledge resources to cover shortfalls stemming from failure of a participant to deliver. Finally, clearinghouses can devise temporary solutions to emergencies, such as using clearinghouse receipts or notes promising future funds delivery or arranging loan pools, covering unexpected variations in presentations of demands for payment.

Access to clearing systems is critical for financial institutions wishing to provide transaction services to their customers. Financial institutions gain access to the clearing system directly by being members of the clearinghouse or system. Recently, the Continental European banks Credit-Lyonnais and Deutsche Bank were accepted into the Clearing House Automated Payment System (CHAPS) in the United Kingdom, bringing total membership to sixteen. These banks wished to expand their ability to make payments in British pounds to institutions and large investors quickly (Bray 1993). Member institutions or their sponsoring regulators often attempt to restrict direct access to the clearing system to privileged financial institutions. In Poland, for example, only the nine banks created out of the former central bank were allowed direct access to the Polish clearing system initially.

Financial institutions gain indirect access to the clearing system through correspondent relations with members. In exchange for balances and fees, members clear transactions for their correspondents. Business relations between financial institutions based on clearing can be an important source of profits. Changes in clearing systems due to technological evolution or regulatory change can upset these relations: the 1980 Deregulation Act in the United States and the 1985 creation of the Association of Payments Clearing Systems in the United Kingdom allowed nonmembers, primarily thrift institutions, direct access to national clearing systems and increased competition for transaction accounts and clearing services in those countries.

10.3 TRANSACTION PROCESSING SERVICES

The check-clearing process is a single example of a transaction processing system. All of the elements of that system are applicable to dozens of other transaction processing systems that evolve in a developed economy. Each system consists of four key elements: (1) customer–financial institution relationships, often involving contractual commitments and a range of services; (2) financial institution relationships connecting participating financial institutions either directly or indirectly into the clearing system; (3) the clearing system organization and rules;

FIGURE 10.6 Relation of customers to transaction processing system

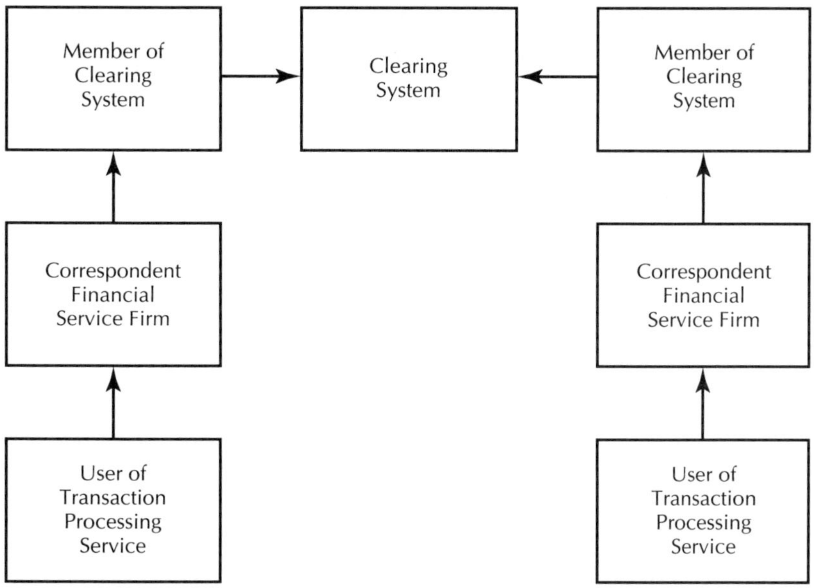

and (4) settlement procedures. These relationships are shown for all clearing systems in Figure 10.6. This section reviews the major transaction processing systems currently important to financial service firms, listed for reference in Table 10.2. The discussion stresses the basic similarities in these systems.

Cash Machines or Automatic Teller Machines

Cash transactions are growing despite forecasts of a noncash economy. The ease of cash purchases and falling costs of obtaining cash due to the widespread installation of cash machines make cash attractive. Most consumers today obtain cash in batches from machines and make small purchases in cash. The first cash machines were tied to individual deposit-taking institutions records: Each withdrawal generated a message to an internal accounting system. Predictably, cash machine networks developed, allowing withdrawals from financial institutions in different states, countries, or parts of the city. Networks require a clearing system. Several networks, like Plus or Cirrus, make cash machines available to depositors of even the smallest financial institutions. Some cash clearing systems are affiliated with credit card clearing agencies.

Cash machines represent a typical transaction processing system. Cash, the asset, is delivered in exchange for an electronic message generated at the machine for a transfer to the financial institution operating the machine. The cash user may pay a transaction fee that is split among the participants in the clearing system.

Credit Cards

Credit cards are a transaction processing system combined with a credit granting services. Use of a credit card at a store or restaurant authorizes payment with a loan by the user's card issuing financial institution. Use of a credit card causes an increase in user's credit card balances rather than a reduction in checking account balances, thus paying with a liability. Checks and credit cards systems are extremely similar in their functioning. Earlier recognition of the similarities in the two systems could no doubt have dramatically reduced the development costs of the credit card system that has evolved.

TABLE 10.2 Clearing Systems

TYPE OF FINANCIAL CLAIM	*CLEARING SYSTEM*	*MAJOR CLEARING CHANNELS*
Deposits	Checks	Local clearinghouses Federal Reserve System
Stocks	Certificates, Book entry	Deposit Trust Corp.
Credit cards	Charge slips	Visa, Master Charge
U.S. Treasury securities	Book entry	Federal Reserve System
Stock options	Book entry	Chicago Option Clearing Corp.
Foreign exchange	Deposits	SWIFT
Futures and options	Contracts	Clearing corporations

Similarities between checks and credit cards consist of account relationships between a firm and a card customer governed by a contract, the credit card agreement. Payment messages occur through the creation of a written order to pay, the charge slip similar to a check, although print-of-sale (POS) technology increasingly replaces paper charge slips with electronic messages. Merchants deposit charge slips just like checks. Charge slips are cleared through clearing organizations.

There are differences between credit card charge slips and checks. First, large charges must be pre-authorized by a control system requiring instantaneous communication: Telephone inquiries match a desired charge against a given charge card customer's authorized credit limit. Authorization requires current updates of total charges against pre-authorized dollar limits. Since a large number of transactions require authorization, a much more efficient balance inquiry and communication system is required than is usually provided for checking account customers. Individual card-issuing financial institutions must update a central communication facility run by the clearing system.

A second difference between check and credit card transaction processing is the absence of the Federal Reserve in the clearing process. Credit card issuing firms have gradually developed two privately owned clearing facilities in the United States, namely Master Charge and Visa. These two clearing systems are owned by participating card-issuing firms, mainly banks and thrifts. Cards bearing the clearing firm logos are typically called "bank cards." In addition to credit card charge clearing, these organizations develop new services, improve technology of clearing, and market the use of the cards. There are clear economies of centralization of these functions.

A third difference between charge slips and checks is the cost to merchants and others who accept the cards. Unlike checks, merchants pay for charge slip processing, usually a percentage of the transaction. Merchant processing charges have become a major arena for competition in the credit card business. Bank cards and other competitors, like American Express, compete for the broadest possible acceptance of their cards by reducing merchant processing fees to the lowest levels while covering costs.

Rapid growth of credit cards in the last thirty years is an example of the dynamics of developments in the financial services industry. Thirty years ago small businesses either did not sell on credit or they maintained their own credit departments or store credit cards. Credit cards began in earnest in the 1960s with Bank of America's "BankAmericard." Credit cards were a way for banks to finance retail receivables directly rather than through the intermediate step of bank loans secured by individual stores' account receivables. Banks economized by central credit evaluation and realized economies of scale in transaction processing. Since credit cards can be used at many stores, they are more valuable to shoppers than cards used at only one store. Credit cards have become an important part of the payment system.

Credit card receivables now dominate retail credit. Few small stores bother with credit accounts. Retail credit card receivables have achieved a volume and level of standardization such that they can be used as collateral for financing through credit card receivable-backed securities. The transaction processing element of this transformation of retail credit is at the heart of this development.

International Payments and Foreign Exchange

Expansion of trade and integration of global capital markets have greatly increased international transactions. These developments have been accompanied by active trading in dollar denominated assets (like Eurobonds) outside the United States and other currency denominated securities outside domestic markets. This has greatly increased the demand for settlement of international payments. Foreign branches of domestic banks and correspondent banks perform many clearing functions for financial institutions abroad.

These developments have induced creation of countless specialized clearing systems. In 1973, a privately owned international communications network was established by hundreds of international banks called the Society for Worldwide Interbank Financial Telecommunications (SWIFT). This network transmits messages that are ultimately settled in clearinghouses like CHIPS in the United States.

Other examples of specialized international clearing systems are to be found in specific securities markets. For example, Euro-Clear is a specialized clearing system developed by Morgan Guaranty Bank for Eurobonds and purchased by about 125 banks in 1972. Cedel, a cooperative clearing system headquartered in Luxembourg and owned by 100 shareholders in 16 countries, also clears Eurobonds. These clearing systems must be linked to each other to clear transactions in the same securities, demonstrating that competing clearing systems can exist.

Stock Transfer and Clearing

Common stocks represent claims on the assets and future earnings of corporations. Stocks are intrinsically no different than checking account claims on the assets of a deposit-taking institution. Historically and to some extent currently, stock claims are certificates, negotiable instruments that can be endorsed over to new owners. Most stocks today represent book entries on computer systems.

Financial institutions keeping track of the ownership of publicly held corporations are called transfer agents. Many transfer agents are bank trust departments. Transfer agents keep a current list of all shareholders and the numbers of shares they hold. The shareholder list is changed whenever stocks are bought and sold. Because stocks normally are delivered after a delay, currently three business days in the United States (after June, 1995), ownership of a corporation is as of a given day and the shareholders are described as shareholders *of record* on that day.

When stocks are bought and sold by brokers and their customers, delivery is accomplished through a clearinghouse owned by the exchanges. The New York Stock Exchange and others own the quaintly titled New York Depository Trust. By agreement, stocks bought and sold are reported to the clearinghouse, which then notifies the transfer agent to update its lists accordingly. The clearinghouse must balance buy and sell orders for each individual security and assure net settlement to the clearing brokers in terms of other securities or cash.

Most active stock traders do not take delivery of stocks in the sense that transfer agent records their own names on the shareholders list. In many cases, stock ownership remains in brokerage house name, commonly referred to as *street name*. The broker keeps account of which stocks are held by which customer in its own accounting system. This means that brokerage firms can borrow securities to lend to others in *short sales,* earning fees and other revenues from those transactions. Stocks held in street name are like deposits in that they can be loaned to others. Although these securities are not called deposits because they cannot be used directly for buying things and their value fluctuates, like deposits they are financial assets.

Stock ownership, transfer, and clearing can be compared to check clearing. Stocks held in street name at brokerage firms are analogous to deposits. Orders to buy and sell, which can be taken over the phone but are documented with written confirmations to the buyer or seller, require brokers to deliver securities transacted to the clearing agency.

Stock transfer services are associated with a number of other financial services. Stocks pay dividends to shareholders of record and the transfer agent is paid fees to issue and mail the checks. The shareholder list is of importance whenever communication with the shareholders is required, as with the periodic disclosures of performance required by the exchanges or as in proxy contests for control of corporations.

Bond Registration

Corporate and government bonds, like common stocks, are hardly ever held as paper certificates today. Most bonds are held in book entry form, meaning that each owner has an account, either directly or indirectly through a financial institution, that lists claims the owner has on issuers. There are several significant differences between processing bond and stock transactions. Some are obvious: bonds mandate periodic payment of interest to owners in contrast to stock dividends that may or not be paid. Payment transactions for bonds are routine except in cases of delinquency and default on the part of the issuer.

The Federal Reserve acts as agent for the U.S. Treasury in transaction processing associated with Treasury and Agency securities. Ownership of U.S. Treasury securities is represented by entries in books on computer systems kept by the Federal Reserve of New York. An individual owner of a U.S. Treasury security has an account with a financial institution, which in turn has an account with the Federal Reserve, either directly or through another institution. There can be several layers in the book entries for claims on U.S. Treasury securities. The U.S. Treasury registration system has grown in sophistication and complexity with the phenomenal growth in the Treasury market. Since Treasury securities are delivered and cleared through the Federal Reserve, payments and deliveries for securities in the form of changes in book entries are extremely quick and efficient.

Computerization of Treasury securities through the Federal Reserve book entry system means that new ways of trading Treasury securities can be accomplished cheaply. For example, principal and interest payments for each future date are bought and sold separately in the Treasury market. Individually traded Treasury commitments to pay coupon or principal amounts in the future are called *stripped* Treasuries. Single future payments backed by stripped Treasury principal or interest are sold at discounts and are equivalent to *zero coupon* bonds.

Entry of the Federal Reserve into clearing of stripped Treasuries illustrates two points. First, availability directly from the Treasury of stripped interest and principal displaced a private market providing single future payments by the Federal government. Investment products developed by investment banking firms like Merrill Lynch placed government securities in trusts and sold individual payments separately, giving them names like CATS (Collaterized Assets Treasury Securities). Sales of these profitable products were preempted by the entry of the government itself into the market for single future payments, illustrating the risk of basing transaction processing or securities origination services on government liabilities.

A second lesson from direct Treasury sales of stripped principal and interest is the example of unexpected ways where arbitrage profits can be earned. When CATs were first offered, investment bankers bought Treasuries and sold their individual stripped payments, thereby making arbitrage profits. Recently, market conditions made it possible to reconstitute Treasury securities from individual zeros at a profit, so investment bankers are buying up stripped Treasuries. It is difficult to imagine products like this being traded without sophisticated computer systems being available for transaction processing.

State and local government and corporate bond registration or transaction processing is dominated by bank trust departments. One reason for this is that many bond indentures name bank trust departments as trustees for the securities. Bond trustees are responsible for monitoring the performance of the indenture contract as discussed in Chapter 7. Bond registration and indenture monitoring are frequently bundled financial services. Processing and updating of bond registers is clearly possible by nonbanks on a contract basis. The dependence on computer and communications systems and the labor intensive nature of aspects of the business noted with other transaction processing systems is true for bond registration.

Loan Servicing

A loan balance is similar to a negative deposit balance, even when the loan is not with a deposit-taking institution. Payments to loan accounts are like deposits to a checking account except that they reduce a negative balance. Since most loan payments are made by checks or transfers from other accounts, the payment clearing in loan processing may be identical with the check clearing system.

Loan customers, like checking account customers, want to know current balances. Loan balances must be reported together with activity, such as payments and interest added, for tax purposes. Information on loan activity is also of interest to the lender, who must report to regulators and investors on balances, delinquencies, and defaults. Loan information such as borrowers' timeliness in making payments may be useful in making future credit decisions.

Accounting for loan activity and balances and processing transactions is called *loan servicing*. Servicing standard credit contracts, such as home and auto loans, has become a competitive financial service market in recent years. Loan originating financial institutions like banks, thrifts, and mortgage bankers often do loan servicing. With the rapid development of the secondary market for asset-backed securities, servicing has become unbundled from credit activities like funding and risk bearing. Servicing rights to packages of loans are being acquired by nonbanks, as when General Motors Acceptance Corporation purchased loan servicing from Norwest Bankcorporation.

Many loans, like home mortgages, have nonloan-related payments, such as to escrow accounts for tax and insurance payments. These activities make accounting and payment requirements more complicated for the mortgage servicer. They also open up additional profit opportunities as escrow balances are a source of funds that often earn low rates of interest.

Mortgage servicing conveys a number of benefits to the servicers, who are compensated for the costs of transaction processing by explicit interest spreads or servicing fees. For example, a servicer processing payments to a pool of 10 percent mortgages might remit only 9.75 percent of the interest to investors, keeping a 25 basis point *servicing spread*. Loan information like balances, age of loan, and payment history are useful for credit evaluations and contain marketing information that can be used in selling other credit and savings financial products. Loan servicing may have asynchronous cash inflows and payments to investors that create earnings opportunities with float.

Large costs of loan servicing come from developing and adapting computer and communication systems to changing regulatory requirements and market conditions. There are often large costs associated with handling exceptions such as partial payments, bad checks, and specific legal problems with individual loans, to name only a few examples. These costs are all labor intensive, requiring highly paid programmers and managers of large loan servicing staffs. Many of the managerial and technical skills to reduce and control these costs require sophisticated and expensive talent. Loan servicing is a more labor intensive business than might be imagined. Economies of scale in loan servicing may be overestimated by financial institutions forming large loan servicing portfolios as part of a business strategy.

Mutual and Pension Fund Processing

Mutual funds and pension funds represent claims on pools of assets. Investors in mutual funds buy and redeem shares in the funds in response to portfolio rebalancing and liquidity needs. Transaction processing of mutual funds must keep track of mutual fund share purchases and redemptions. The assets held are bought and sold in response to mutual fund inflows and outflows which in turn are in response to mutual fund managers' instructions based on changing market conditions. Reports must be generated on the resulting asset holdings and values.

Corporations or workers make contributions to pensions periodically to finance future retirement benefits. Like mutual funds, assets are bought and sold and periodic valuations are necessary. Upon retirement or death, benefits are paid to pension fund beneficiaries. Mutual fund and pension fund inflows and outflows from purchases or contributions and redemption or benefit payments all require transaction processing services and are growing with the institutionalization of savings discussed in Chapter 3.

Bank trust departments have traditionally been active in administering personal trusts and corporate pension funds. Trust accounting, although not growing as dramatically as pension and mutual funds, is a closely related activity requiring detailed transaction and tax record keeping for beneficiaries. Some trust departments, such as State Street Boston, have evolved into specialists in mutual and pension fund transaction processing. Many bank trust departments are active in the business.

Pension and mutual fund processing is computer and communication system intensive. The human resource dimension is also very important. Pension and mutual fund systems require constant adaption to new reporting requirements and new products. The rapid growth of the demand for these services has meant that systems and procedures have had to adopt quickly to take advantage of technological breakthroughs in order to handle changes in volume. New services, such as telephone inquiry of balances and entry of orders to buy and sell mutual fund shares, require constant development or improvement of systems.

Managing changing computer and communication systems means managing programmers, operators, system analysts, and marketing people in complex, coordinated efforts with many ramifications. For example, systems must provide the marketing staff with constant customer contact to anticipate needs and design system changes or enhancements to gain and keep a competitive edge for the fund processing business. Changes in relationships achieved through competition require integration of new accounts into established or newly developed systems, meaning a trained staff is needed to process exceptions and nonroutine changes. Transaction processing requirements for mutual and pension funds are very labor intensive, despite the heavy use of computers and capital intensive communications equipment.

Insurance Transactions Processing

Insurance premiums must be paid in order for a policy to be effective. Premium payments must be billed and collected, examples of transactions processing. If the insured-against events occur, claims must be filed and adjusted, as discussed in Chapter 11. Once the claims are reviewed and documentation of the legitimacy of the claims assured, payment of benefits is authorized and must be processed. Premium collection and benefit payments are parts of a transaction processing system similar to the others we have discussed: status of accounts, balances, and payments must be recorded and processed.

Transaction processing systems for insurance are typically tied to other elements of insurance services since insurance contracts are not valid if premium payments are not made. Reports from insurance transaction processing systems go to insurance customers, who must be billed and advised of payment obligations, and to insurance carriers, whose liabilities are determined by the status of a particular account. Claims payments may involve providers of services, like doctors for medical insurance or auto body shops for auto insurance.

Claims are also of greater concern to insurance carriers than other orders to pay or deliveries we have discussed previously. Claims must be processed for the information they provide to actuaries on pricing risks in basic insurance contracts, as we discuss in Chapter 11. Claims payment management has an important impact on the investable funds of the insurance company. Insurance companies carefully manage claims payments in order to maximize investment income, often to the annoyance of their customers. Insurance companies use drafts payable upon approval instead of checks payable on demand, because the former are paid more slowly when presented through the clearing system.

Recent developments in the insurance industry, such as self-insurance of corporate risks and new health insurance plans managed by companies, have seen the emergence of insurance companies processing premiums and claims on a purely contractual basis without underwriting risks or managing funds. Some insurance companies have moved their transaction processing systems offshore, for example, Prudential has opened processing operations in Ireland to take advantage of lower labor costs there. Third parties, like banks or computer service bureaus, could easily enter the market for insurance transaction processing if relative cost efficiency justified entry into competition for these financial services.

10.4 VALUE CHAIN IN TRANSACTION PROCESSING

Transaction processing appears in many financial services as part of a bundle of financial services. As an example, pension fund accounting by a bank trust department is often integrated into a complete system of portfolio management. Transaction processing can be unbundled from financial services where it has traditionally been offered as part of a service. Unbundling is already common in the case of loan servicing, and unbundling of transaction processing from other services, like insurance processing, is likely to expand in the future with specialization of expertise in these systems.

Pricing and Term Setting in Transaction Processing

Value can be created through the pricing of transactions services. Pricing and term setting has one or more of the following potential sources of value: (1) achievement of optimal levels of transaction processing; (2) encouragement of the use of cost efficient transactions; (3) exploitation of market strengths or customer insensitivity to competitive options; (4) effective cross-selling of synergistic financial services; and (5) inducement of customer self-revelation. We discuss each in turn.

The economics of the demand and supply for transaction services analyzed above revealed that users (buyers and sellers in our discussion) may value services received from their financial institutions above or below the costs incurred by their institutions, even when total value is equal to total costs at the optimum level of transaction volume. As discussed above, revenues derived from prices of transaction services to customers valuing services less than than costs may have to be augmented by subsidies from financial institutions whose customers value services more than costs. Pricing and term setting in transaction processing and clearing systems may require such side payments or subsidies to produce the maximum value of transactions services for all parties in the system. Prices and fees that simply cover each institution's marginal costs could produce lower levels of transactions services than are socially optimal.

Encouraging customers to use the most cost effective and profitable transaction methods when options are available is a second and enormously profitable use of pricing. For example, encouraging use of teller machines economizes on expensive labor. Customer sensitivities are also important when implementing pricing schemes intended to increase efficiency. For example, Citibank attempted to discourage use of tellers by charging fees for use of teller windows. Customer reaction was explosive, with newspapers and politicians joyfully joining in the uproar. Citibank backed down from this pricing practice. Despite this experience, in 1995 First National Bank of Chicago announced a $3 charge for use of teller services.

Most transaction pricing reflects an effort to encourage efficient use of technology. There are many examples: Merchant discounts on credit card sales are lower if they use electronic point-of-sale charge systems, eliminating costly manual encoding of charge slips and reducing collection and float time. Checking account customers pay lower fees if they do not request their cancelled checks back, saving delivery costs. Explicit fee reductions for efficient preprocessing of deposits or other transactions are offered to businesses.

A third source of value in transaction processing comes from exploiting market imperfections in segments of the transaction processing business, perhaps due to customer avoidance of change. Customers may be unwilling or too lazy to change account relationships. Marginal costs may be below prices because the complexity of transactions services obscures the relationship. Pricing may reflect not only direct costs but indirect costs or profits, for example from float, risks of losses from operational breakdowns, fraud, and changes in regulations.

Value may be produced by subsidizing other financial services with unprofitable transaction processing. Merrill Lynch's Cash Management Account with check-writing privileges is a loss leader for profitable securities trading services. Brokerage firms believe customer relationships based on transaction accounts stimulate more trading activity and the possibility of selling asset management services. As another example of bundled services, banks price high balance accounts below costs to take advantage of the investment returns earned on credit or investment management services.

A final source of value uses pricing and term setting to ensure self-revelation of customer types. Pricing schedules for checking accounts are attempts to distinguish high-balance, low-volume accounts customers from low-balance, high-volume customers. The first type of account represents a cheaper source of funds with fewer direct processing costs whereas the second type requires a great deal of service and provides few funds. A common pricing strategy to achieve self-revelation in checking is to offer free checking in exchange for minimum balances over a certain amount or alternatively levy per item charges for low balance accounts.

All transaction processing services entail substantial costs. Pricing to recover these costs and remain competitive is a dynamic and creative area for management of financial institutions. There are several ways to price these services:

1. Fees per transaction, for example $.20 per check written
2. Fixed charges per unit time, for example a $50 annual credit card fee
3. Interest paid on balances, for example 4.25% on a NOW account average balance
4. Quantity-dependent pricing schedules, for example a 3% discount on the first $10,000 credit card charges deposited per month to participating merchant, and 1.5% above that amount
5. Implicit fees or fees based on other services used, for example credit on annual brokerage account for trading activity.

Some fee structures may be prohibited or limited by regulation. Other fee structures may be imposed by membership in a clearing organization. Creative price and term setting is an important source of value in providing all transaction processing services.

Communicating and Marketing to Customers

Transaction processing must be sold to the customer. Once a customer relationship is established, transaction processing systems require communication between the financial service firm and the customer: periodic reports, balances and current status of transactions inquiry, and confirmations and approvals. Substantial information flows on the customers' activities mean that the financial service firm providing transaction processing services can have an intimate understanding of aspects of customer-specific information. These information flows can provide marketing and other opportunities. They can also cause problems with maintaining appropriate security and confidentiality.

The marketing challenges facing transaction processors are twofold: (1) the appearance of homogeneity of products due to regulation and lack of competition, obscuring the variations in service possible, for example in access to information; and (2) customer inertia due to costs of changing account relationships. Both present major challenges to providers of transaction processing services in the future. The appearance that all transaction products are the same is exemplified by checking accounts. A checking account appears to be a checking account because of its historical evolution in a regulated oligopoly and the requirements of standardization in a high volume business. But in fact checking accounts can vary in many ways, such as preauthorized payments, special reports for business accounting, or relation to other accounts.

Opportunities for evolution of transaction processing service are found in the information flows between customers and financial service firms once the relationship has been established. These information flows can be very useful to sophisticated retail and business customers. Transaction information of all types makes it possible to manage cash or investments better with more timely and complete information on the current status of accounts and individual transactions. The further application of modern personal computer and telecommunications technology for transaction-oriented financial services is clearly a major thrust for the financial services industry of the future.

The use of customer information created as a by-product of transaction processing is a developing and controversial area. Transaction processing can be a very productive source of user-specific information. As an example, consider mortgage loan servicing. Loan servicers know the age of the mortgage, the current balance, and the payment history—information that can be used to estimate the borrower's equity in the home, a first step in marketing other services. Combined with loan application data on age and dependents, mortgage information could be used as a tool to develop marketing plans for other financial products, such as credit services for homeowners likely to be financing durables as part of household formation, children's education for more established households, or investment products for homeowners in a later phase of their life cycle. Transaction records and associated files can clearly be an important source of financial product and other product marketing information.

Transaction processing associated with asset holdings, loan and deposit balances, and deposit and credit related transaction activity and history can be useful in assessing customer creditworthiness as well for marketing. This information has value to both the customer and the financial service provider. The value in this information to customers is its relevance to acquisition of credit and the desire to be protected from product solicitations. The value to the transaction service provider is that it may have unique access to information. Unique access to information means a competitive advantage in marketing and credit evaluation. These differing uses of transaction information cause potential conflicts between customer and service provider.

Issues of confidentiality and the use or sale of customer-specific information is a dynamic area. Opportunities are not limited to loan and deposit transaction processing systems. Shareholder and bondholder lists are useful for takeover attempts, for example. The development of control over transaction-based information sources will be determined by the evolution of technology, legislation, regulation, and litigation. Development of financial service strategies based on this information source will depend on changing rights and conflicts associated with use of this information.

Production and Delivery of Transaction Processing Services

Transactions must be initiated, recorded, confirmed, executed, cleared, and settled. Efficient production and delivery of these services are driven by technology and related areas, like software and staff organization. Analysis of trends in technology is beyond the scope of this book. Rather than attempt to anticipate technical developments, we look at some important economic trade-offs to keep in mind when assessing future technology. Several pieces of old but valuable advice are reviewed here.

First, transaction processing service providers should experiment with new methods and services. The largest profits are earned by innovators and early entrants into new markets or price cutters for services in established product markets. Early entrants into markets benefit from the relative lack of competition when new, improved, or cheaper services first become available. Unless there are barriers to entry, early profits will inevitably erode and then disappear as prices are driven to marginal costs. For example, Continental Bank held a temporary competitive edge in the stock transfer business in the 1960s because it developed the first computerized stock transfer operation under government contract for the newly chartered Comsat Corporation. Now that business is competitive.

Second, management should not overcommit to new technologies. New methods have start-up costs and high risks of costs due to blunders, false starts, and mistakes. Technology changes rapidly. Financial service firms should make wide use of test marketing, customer surveys, and shakedown trials with new methods or products. Financial firms should diversify product development efforts, for new breakthroughs often pay off in ways not expected by the inventors. Firms cannot ignore simple and inexpensive ways of processing transactions. Low volume systems may not require mainframe computers. For example, one small bank offered car insurance premium loans with transaction processing performed on personal computers. Cost savings may come less from automation than from making current systems more efficient, for example by avoiding duplicate mailing or reducing the size and complexity of reports to reduce transmission costs.

Finally, in developing strategies for transaction processing services, managers should learn from the past. Transaction processing systems have many common elements as we have noted. These common elements mean that many recent innovations, such as checks, credit cards, and cash machines, followed similar developments. Recognition of common patterns could have avoided some false starts and duplicative efforts in the development of these systems. Managers alert to parallels in similar systems or older versions will be better able to anticipate future developments and capitalize on them.

Monitoring and Controlling Transactions Systems

Value production from careful monitoring and invocation of controls in transaction processing comes from reduction of losses due to foregone interest, credit losses, and fraud. The computerized nature of most transaction processing systems implies that economically effective monitoring and controlling require not only systems that identify items requiring attention but systems, often labor intensive, that can implement appropriate control procedures. As an example of the importance of careful monitoring and controls in transaction processing, many banks suffered losses from negative collected balances on corporate demand deposit accounts until effective reporting systems were developed in the 1970s.

Monitoring and control procedures are an important part of most transaction processing services. Loan servicing requires that delinquent loans be identified and borrowers notified, collection procedures implemented and borrowers warned of consequences. Timeliness in these activities clearly produces value through interest earned on collections and reduced fraud and credit losses. Loan defaults require implementation of legal measures attaching wages or foreclosing on collateral in the case of consumer loans. More complex actions requiring the filing of legal liens on collateral or the formation of creditor committees are required in the case of institutional credits. Monitoring and control activities need to be performed in a timely and flexible way to control costs of fraud and credit failures.

Securities transaction processing entails careful monitoring and control of many phases of these services. Confirmations of trades and resolution of disputes must be handled early to avoid costly delays and disputes. Contractual commitments made by purchasers, such as maintenance of prescribed levels of margins, must be monitored so that early detection of violations allows maximum time to take corrective control actions. Margin calls, for example, must be made and honored quickly to control for potential credit losses.

Funding and Investing

Transaction processing can be unbundled from funding or investing activities. Production and delivery of these financial services are mainly computer and communication driven. Production and delivery activities can readily be provided by third-party vendors such as computer service bureaus, telephone companies, financial information companies, or computer manufacturing firms, requiring that other activities in the value chain be performed by other firms.

If transaction processors take delivery and hold or deliver funds or securities as part of their bundled activities, funding and investing can be important. For example, loan servicing firms develop substantial value from the asynchronous receipt of loan payments and remittances to investors. In other words, they earn interest on float. Securities firms receive securities not required immediately for settlement, and can earn interest on them or earn fees by lending them, for example, to short sellers. Funding and investing activities can be important in transaction processing and obviously require effective control and understanding of the systems producing these financing opportunities.

Risk Shifting and Risk Bearing

Providers of transaction processing services are exposed to two specific risks. First are operating risks, namely unexpected costs from failure of systems. These risks range from the costs associated with a computer or communications failure, perhaps consisting of temporary manual efforts to process transactions and the costs of making temporary or permanent changes to systems and records. An extreme risk is total collapse of the firm due to a failure to perform legal responsibilities such as delivery of securities or from loss of customers concerned about reliable performance of transaction processing.

A second source of risks are associated with nonperformance of customers on transactions. These are primarily credit risks. An example of these risks are the losses faced by First Options of Chicago, a clearing member of the Chicago

Options Clearing Corporation, when it could not recover $90 million in losses generated by an affiliated floor trader writing options during the Stock Market Crash of 1987.

Risk management techniques may or may not be available for operating and credit risks facing transaction processing providers. Some of these risks can be shared or shifted through insurance contracts and/or futures and options markets. Risks can be managed and shared through the contracts relating the principal parties in transaction processing. The major means to do this with clearing systems is with the rules of the clearing organization. For example, operating failures or massive delivery failure risks can be shared among clearing organization members if specified by the rules. Risks such as cash delivery risks may be absorbed by one party, as does the Federal Reserve in providing payment finality in wire transfers over the Fed wire system.

Risks associated with transaction processing may be priced in the market if regulation or competition do not interfere. For example, bad check fees compensate check-clearing firms for the expense of sending checks backward through the check-clearing system. Credit exposures stemming from the clearing process could be priced through short-term interest rates that compensate providers of funds or securities with income to cover expected losses. Most observers believe that an intra-day interest rate on fund transfer systems does not exist solely because of the Federal Reserve's preempting the market by offering payment finality.

Value Added in Transaction Processing

Each of the activities in the value chain for transaction processing is a potential source of value. In developing business strategies including transaction processing for the future, one economic principle should be kept in mind. Competition drives marginal revenues into line with marginal costs when there are no barriers to entry or switching costs. Deregulation and competition have eroded barriers that formerly prevented nontraditional providers from competing for transaction processing business.

The history of check processing is illuminating. The market for check processing services was protected for banks until 1980 and costs were distorted by Federal Reserve subsidies. Service prices were further distorted by controls, like zero interest on demand deposits. Because of limits on competition, cost distortions, and price controls, check processing was bundled with credit services of banks. Deposit processing and lending, as well as other services such as cash management, were offered by the same supplier as the provider of transaction processing. This bundling was not necessarily cost efficient.

Unbundling of the activities in transaction processing has begun and will continue. For example, a financial services firm like Merrill Lynch offers check processing that is cleared by BancOne of Ohio. The most value for investors will be earned by the firms able to identify true competitive advantages. In an area of such reliance on technology, it is unlikely that all financial service firms, including traditional commercial banks, can be relatively expert at all activities involved in the value chain for transaction processing. Value-maximizing firms may turn to outside vendors to perform activities that can be done more cheaply by others, so-called *outsourcing*. Many aspects of financial services associated with transaction processing are built on information derived from transaction processing systems. Use of this information can be separated from the production and delivery of the information from transaction systems.

10.5 SUMMARY

Check processing is an example of a transaction processing financial service and its economic attributes illustrate clearing and settlement systems. Other examples of transaction processing systems offered by financial and nonfinancial institutions are reviewed, and the six activities in the production of value in financial services are analyzed as sources of value from transaction processing. Transaction processing is unique among financial services because of the central role played by technology and communications. The importance of objectivity in identifying an individual financial firm's competitive advantage is emphasized in view of the distortions to competition in the past for services like check processing.

DISCUSSION QUESTIONS AND EXERCISES

1. Examine carefully a check and see if you can get a bank or thrift employee to explain the significance of each of the pre-encoded numbers to the clearing process.
2. Carefully list all the types of information (balances, transactions, history) generated by checking account activity and discuss how each could be useful in running a household or business.
3. Determine whether your deposit-taking institution is a member of a local clearing organization and/or a member of the Federal Reserve System. Does the firm use correspondent banks or is it a correspondent bank for others? Try to lay out a local network along the lines of Figure 10.2 to understand how the clearing process fits in with interbank relations.
4. List and relate to check clearing the other transaction processing systems with which you are familiar. Which firms perform which value-producing activities? What is your assessment of where each firm's comparative advantage is?
5. Calculate the lost float due to clearing times of different lengths at a variety of interest rates of a $10 million check. What are the current opportunity costs of uncollected funds versus one, two, and five years ago? What does this mean in terms of economic incentives to various participants in the clearing system?
6. Clearing brokers have three days to deliver sold securities and often lend them overnight to short-sellers. Discuss the benefits and costs (risks) of this activity.
7. In what ways does a brokerage account differ from a checking account? Detail the differences in terms of the transaction processing requirements, the value of informa-

tion on activity to the customer, and the role of value-producing activities in each.

8. Stock transfer and bond registration represent similar transaction processing functions. Detail the differences in the relationship of these two activities to the various parties in this economic function.
9. Cash usage has increased in recent years, defying notions of a "cashless" society. Explain this development in terms of competition and technology as well as the economics of payment.
10. Detail carefully the advantages and disadvantages of paper-based versus electronic transaction processing systems.

REFERENCES

BAXTER, WILLIAM F. 1983. "Bank Interchange of Transactional Paper: Legal and Economic Perspectives," *The Journal of Law and Economics* XXVI (October), pp. 541–588.

BRAY, NICHOLAS. 1993. "Credit Lyonnais Mulls its Entry in the U.K. Market," *Wall Street Journal,* November 12, p. A9B.

FAMA, EUGENE F. 1980. "Banking in the Theory of Finance," *Journal of Monetary Economics* 6, pp. 39–57.

FLANNERY, MARK J. 1987. "Payments System Risk and Public Policy," prepared for the American Enterprise Institute's Financial Services Project.

GORTON, GARY. 1985. "Clearinghouses and the Origin of Central Banking in the United States," *Journal of Economic History* XLV (1), pp. 277–284.

HUMPHREY, DAVID BURRAS. 1984. *The U.S. Payments System: Costs, Pricing, Competition and Risk,* Monograph Series in Finance and Economics, Salomon Brothers Center for the Study of Financial Institutions, New York University.

SOLOMON, ELINOR HARRIS, ed. 1987. *Electronic Funds Transfers and Payments: The Public Policy Issues.* Boston: Kluwer-Nijhoff Publishing.

TIMBERLAKE, RICHARD H. JR. 1984. "The Central Banking Role of Clearinghouse Associations," *Journal of Money, Credit, and Banking* 16 (1), pp. 1–15.

C H A P T E R

11

Insurance Services

Introduction

Insurance companies pay cash to firms and individuals experiencing hardships or bereavement. Insurance services are critical to the welfare of individuals and the economy.

- How can services based on assistance to troubled economic agents add value to the economy and provide returns to investors in insurance activities?
- What are the risks that insurance companies face?
- What economic forces determine the nature of the insurance business today and what forces can be expected to shape it in the future?
- How is it that insurance company managers have trillions of dollars in funds to invest?

The insurance industry is one of the oldest financial services industries. Understanding the basic economics of the insurance industry is essential to answering the questions posed above and to developing strategies for the management of financial services firms in the future.

11.1 ECONOMICS OF INSURANCE

Insurance services represent contracts or promises issued by insurance firms to pay cash to businesses and individuals if certain events occur. This promise is made for a fee, usually paid in advance, called a *premium*. The cash payment, if made, is called a *benefit* or *claims compensation*. Insurance contracts pay insurance benefits or compensation in the event of adverse outcomes, like deaths, accidents, or losses from other causes. Insurance contracts are an example of a *contingent claim,* which pays a sum of cash only if certain events occur.

Contingent claims are common in finance and economics. To name a few, loan commitments represent a promise by a credit service firm to advance cash to a borrower as needed if the covenants in the loan agreement are satisfied. Securities underwriting represents a commitment by a securities firm to pay a fixed price for a security sale even if the security does not sell in the open market. Deposits represent a commitment to pay cash if the depositor wants cash at any time.

The unique characteristic of insurance contracts is that contingencies determining when cash is advanced are external risks beyond the control of the insurance firm or the insured. In the examples above, users of financial services have discretion concerning the cash flow: A borrower may decide not use a loan commitment, a security issuer may not go ahead with a securities offering, or the depositor may not withdraw cash. Each of these events is partially under the control of the financial service user. Contingencies in insurance contracts are theoretically beyond the control of the service user or provider.

Insurance contracts covering any conceivable contingency can be written in principle. The event insured against can be a common risk like death, fire, or accident, or a more complex risk like loss of business, new technology performance, or hazardous waste spills. Specialists who analyze statistics in an effort to assess risks in terms of assigning a probability of events occurring are called *actuaries*. Although many insurance risks can be analyzed by actuaries, it may not be necessary to know the probabilities of events precisely in order to issue insurance. The only requirement for existence of an insurance contract is that the event or risk insured against be observable or verifiable and that the parties can agree on a premium.[1]

The source of value from insurance comes from risk aversion in consumers. In Chapter 6 we noted that reduced variance at the same expected level of future consumption or income increases expected utility. A reduction in future income from payment of an insurance premium is balanced by the insurance benefit or payoff if a bad event covered by insurance does occur. Insurance guarantees a lower variance in future income or consumption. If the premium and benefit levels are appropriately set, the insurance contract increases expected utility by reducing variance (see Chapter 6 and Figure 6.7.)

Reduction in income or consumption variance in the future comes from risk sharing through the intermediation of the insurance firm. Premiums from those who do not suffer the loss are used to pay benefits to those who do. The insurance firm is contractually obligated to make the benefit payments. If premium revenues are not sufficient to cover losses, the firm must make up the difference out of capital. Risk bearing and risk shifting are the basis for the value insurance firms provided to an economy.

Segments of the insurance business are defined by the types of risks insured against. Some insurance provides protection against contingencies hinging on the mortality of individuals. *Life insurance* and products like *annuities* are purchased

[1]Borch (1990) argues that the standard requirement that the risks be assessable in terms of a probability distribution that the event will occur is too restrictive if agreement can be reached between the parties.

primarily by individuals. Employers provide employee retirement programs in the form of *defined benefit pension plans* and firms sometimes insure the lives of key executives. We discuss these types of insurance services in the next section of the chapter.

Property and casualty insurance products cover losses to property or business from theft, loss, or natural disasters. Property insurance protects insured parties against damage or loss to property and casualty insurance protects them from liabilities to third parties, like accident victims, caused by their property or behavior. These insurance services are bought both by households and businesses. Insurance of primary interest to households covers risks like losses due to automobile accidents or damage to homes and personal property. Businesses buy insurance against risks running the gamut from losses due to accidents, product liability, and malpractice to business interruption. We discuss these types of insurance in Section 11.3 of this chapter.

Health insurance and *workman's compensation insurance* are hybrid types of insurance. They have life insurance components because they both involve risks to human beings and both are often sold or administered by life insurance companies. On the other hand, occurrence of medical problems or disabling industrial accidents are more similar actuarially to risks faced by property and casualty insurers than to life insurance risks. The risks associated with contractual relationship of the insurance provider to the insured have some of the same adverse selection and moral hazard problems as those associated with property and casualty insurance. For these reasons we include our discussion of health and workman's compensation with property and casualty insurance.

Insurance firms produce value through performance of some or all of the six basic activities in the value chain for financial services. The following two sections present and contrast the economics and risks in the basic contracts observed in the life and property and casualty insurance businesses. In the final section of the chapter we examine how value can be produced in performing each of the six activities necessary to provide insurance services.

11.2 ECONOMICS OF LIFE INSURANCE AND RELATED SERVICES

Life insurance and related insurance products provide protection against risks associated with the length of life of individuals. Standard life insurance policies provide benefits to *named beneficiaries* in the event of the death of the insured individual. Probabilities of individuals dying at a certain age can be estimated with precision given the *mortality* or death statistics available. The basic tool of life insurance risk assessment is *mortality tables* which we discuss at length below. Living can also be considered a risk in the case of retirement plans where payments continue as long as the beneficiary is alive. Fixed annual (or more frequent) payments made until a given date or an individual's death is an *annuity*. Risks associated with these promises to pay are also based on mortality statistics.

Vital statistics, data on births and deaths, are collected by government agencies around the world. Estimates of the probability of death and life expectancies for groups of similar individuals are very reliable. Outside of suicide and murder, which are illegal, individuals cannot influence probabilities of life and death much. Individuals generally are reluctant to reduce life expectancy by hazardous life styles, so moral hazard in life insurance from individuals taking actions harming insurance firms is not a great problem.

Actions individuals take that affect life and death probabilities are actions concerning health and accident risks. There are reliable statistics on the effects of unhealthy habits or dangerous jobs on the probabilities of life and death. For example, the effects of smoking on life expectancy are well documented. Smokers are routinely assigned different risk factors in life insurance than nonsmokers.

Although moral hazard is not a big problem in most life insurance or related services, adverse selection is an important problem. Individuals selecting life insurance policies or retirement plans know information about themselves that the life insurance firm does not know. There is asymmetric information concerning individual risks. An applicant feeling terrible or having risky personal habits can keep this information secret. People choose life insurance policies that are relatively attractive to them based on confidential information available only to the insurance policy holder. We discuss the implications of adverse selection in life insurance below.

Mortality statistics do change with developments in medicine and science and some of these changes pose interesting problems for pricing life insurance. For example, new developments in gene mapping can now be used to diagnose some diseases, like Alzheimer's disease or heart problems, before symptoms appear. This information can be used to refine the mortality tables applicable to individuals. Some observers argue that this type of information poses a moral issue because it results in price discrimination based on genetic traits.

The issue of price discrimination due to genetic differences has already been raised. Women the same age as men have a lower risk of dying and a higher probability of living a longer time, but some states in the United States, starting with Colorado, have demanded that insurance firms charge the same rates for women and men.

Use of Mortality Tables

The basic tool of the *life or pension actuary* in assessing risks associated with length of life are *mortality tables*. Table 11.1 gives mortality statistics used in the United States for life insurance purposes. In the table, four columns of statistics are shown for each age from birth (age zero) to age 115. The four columns show "Deaths per 1000" and "Expectation of Life" for males and females. Each age group, for example twenty-five-year olds, is called a *cohort*. For the twenty-five-year-old example cohort, according to the table, .62 males and .35 females per 1000 died over the period the table was calculated. If the future is like the sample in the table, 62 males and 35 females out of 10,000 males and females aged 25 will die in a given year. The average twenty-five-year-old male can be expected to live 54.66 more years, and females the same age are expected to live 59.64 more years.

TABLE 11.1 Mortality Tables

	COMMISSIONERS 1980 STANDARD ORDINARY (1970–1975)				*1983 INDIVIDUAL ANNUITY TABLE (1971–1976)[a]*				*UNITED STATES POPULATION*	
	MALE		*FEMALE*		*MALE*		*FEMALE*		*(1979–1981)*	
AGE	*DEATHS PER 1,000*	*EXPECTATION OF LIFE (YEARS)*	*DEATHS PER 1,000*	*EXPECTATION OF LIFE (YEARS)*	*DEATHS PER 1,000*	*EXPECTATION OF LIFE (YEARS)*	*DEATHS PER 1,000*	*EXPECTATION OF LIFE (YEARS)*	*DEATHS PER 1,000*	*EXPECTATION OF LIFE (YEARS)*
0	4.18	70.83	2.89	75.83	—	—	—	—	12.60	73.88
1	1.07	70.13	.87	75.04	—	—	—	—	.93	73.82
2	.99	69.20	.81	74.11	—	—	—	—	.65	72.89
3	.98	68.27	.79	73.17	—	—	—	—	.50	71.93
4	.95	67.34	.77	72.23	—	—	—	—	.40	70.97
5	.90	66.40	.76	71.28	.38	74.10	.19	79.36	.37	70.00
6	.86	65.46	.73	70.34	.35	73.12	.16	78.37	.33	69.02
7	.80	64.52	.72	69.39	.33	72.15	.13	77.39	.30	68.05
8	.76	63.57	.70	68.44	.35	71.17	.13	76.40	.27	67.07
9	.74	62.62	.69	67.48	.37	70.20	.14	75.41	.23	66.08
10	.73	61.66	.68	66.53	.38	69.22	.14	74.42	.20	65.10
11	.77	60.71	.69	65.58	.39	68.25	.15	73.43	.19	64.11
12	.85	59.75	.72	64.62	.41	67.28	.16	72.44	.25	63.12
13	.99	58.80	.75	63.67	.42	66.30	.17	71.45	.37	62.14
14	1.15	57.86	.80	62.71	.43	65.33	.18	70.46	.53	61.16
15	1.33	56.93	.85	61.76	.44	64.36	.19	69.47	.69	60.19
16	1.51	56.00	.90	60.82	.45	63.39	.20	68.49	.83	59.24
17	1.67	55.09	.95	59.87	.46	62.42	.21	67.50	.95	58.28
18	1.78	54.18	.98	58.93	.47	61.44	.23	66.51	1.05	57.34
19	1.86	53.27	1.02	57.98	.49	60.47	.24	65.53	1.12	56.40
20	1.90	52.37	1.05	57.04	.51	59.50	.26	64.55	1.20	55.46
21	1.91	51.47	1.07	56.10	.53	58.53	.28	63.56	1.27	54.53
22	1.89	50.57	1.09	55.16	.55	57.56	.29	62.58	1.32	53.60
23	1.86	49.66	1.11	54.22	.57	56.59	.31	61.60	1.34	52.67
24	1.82	48.75	1.14	53.28	.60	55.63	.33	60.62	1.33	51.74
25	1.77	47.84	1.16	52.34	.62	54.66	.35	59.64	1.32	50.81
26	1.73	46.93	1.19	51.40	.65	53.69	.37	58.66	1.31	49.87
27	1.71	46.01	1.22	50.46	.68	52.73	.39	57.68	1.30	48.94
28	1.70	45.09	1.26	49.52	.70	51.76	.41	56.70	1.30	48.00
29	1.71	44.16	1.30	48.59	.73	50.80	.42	55.72	1.31	47.06
30	1.73	43.24	1.35	47.65	.76	49.83	.44	54.75	1.33	46.12
31	1.78	42.31	1.40	46.71	.79	48.87	.46	53.77	1.34	45.18
32	1.83	41.38	1.45	45.78	.81	47.91	.48	52.80	1.37	44.24
33	1.91	40.46	1.50	44.84	.84	46.95	.50	51.82	1.42	43.30
34	2.00	39.54	1.58	43.91	.88	45.99	.52	50.85	1.50	42.36
35	2.11	38.61	1.65	42.98	.92	45.03	.55	49.87	1.59	41.43
36	2.24	37.69	1.76	42.05	.97	44.07	.57	48.90	1.70	40.49
37	2.40	36.78	1.89	41.12	1.03	43.11	.61	47.93	1.83	39.56
38	2.58	35.87	2.04	40.20	1.11	42.15	.65	46.96	1.97	38.63
39	2.79	34.96	2.22	39.28	1.22	41.20	.69	45.99	2.13	37.71
40	3.02	34.05	2.42	38.36	1.34	40.25	.74	45.02	2.32	36.79
41	3.29	33.16	2.64	37.46	1.49	39.30	.80	44.05	2.54	35.87

TABLE 11.1 (continued)

	COMMISSIONERS 1980 STANDARD ORDINARY (1970–1975)				*1983 INDIVIDUAL ANNUITY TABLE (1971–1976)[a]*				*UNITED STATES POPULATION*	
	MALE		*FEMALE*		*MALE*		*FEMALE*		*(1979–1981)*	
AGE	*DEATHS PER 1,000*	*EXPECTATION OF LIFE (YEARS)*	*DEATHS PER 1,000*	*EXPECTATION OF LIFE (YEARS)*	*DEATHS PER 1,000*	*EXPECTATION OF LIFE (YEARS)*	*DEATHS PER 1,000*	*EXPECTATION OF LIFE (YEARS)*	*DEATHS PER 1,000*	*EXPECTATION OF LIFE (YEARS)*
42	3.56	32.26	2.87	36.55	1.67	38.36	.87	43.09	2.79	34.96
43	3.87	31.38	3.09	35.66	1.89	37.43	.94	42.12	3.06	34.06
44	4.19	30.50	3.32	34.77	2.13	36.50	1.03	41.16	3.35	33.16
45	4.55	29.62	3.56	33.88	2.40	35.57	1.12	40.20	3.66	32.27
46	4.92	28.76	3.80	33.00	2.69	34.66	1.23	39.25	4.01	31.39
47	5.32	27.90	4.05	32.12	3.01	33.75	1.36	38.30	4.42	30.51
48	5.74	27.04	4.33	31.25	3.34	32.85	1.50	37.35	4.88	29.65
49	6.21	26.20	4.63	30.39	3.69	31.96	1.66	36.40	5.38	28.79
50	6.71	25.36	4.96	29.53	4.06	31.07	1.83	35.46	5.89	27.94
51	7.30	24.52	5.31	28.67	4.43	30.20	2.02	34.53	6.42	27.10
52	7.96	23.70	5.70	27.82	4.81	29.33	2.22	33.59	6.99	26.28
53	8.71	22.89	6.15	26.98	5.20	28.47	2.43	32.67	7.61	25.46
54	9.56	22.08	6.61	26.14	5.59	27.62	2.65	31.75	8.30	24.65
55	10.47	21.29	7.09	25.31	5.99	26.77	2.89	30.83	9.02	23.85
56	11.46	20.51	7.57	24.49	6.41	25.93	3.15	29.92	9.78	23.06
57	12.49	19.74	8.03	23.67	6.84	25.09	3.43	29.01	10.59	22.29
58	13.59	18.99	8.47	22.86	7.29	24.26	3.74	28.11	11.51	21.52
59	14.77	18.24	8.94	22.05	7.78	23.44	4.08	27.21	12.54	20.76
60	16.08	17.51	9.47	21.25	8.34	22.62	4.47	26.32	13.68	20.02
61	17.54	16.79	10.13	20.44	8.98	21.80	4.91	25.44	14.93	19.29
62	19.19	16.08	10.96	19.65	9.74	20.99	5.41	24.56	16.28	18.58
63	21.06	15.38	12.02	18.86	10.63	20.20	5.99	23.69	17.67	17.88
64	23.14	14.70	13.25	18.08	11.66	19.41	6.63	22.83	19.11	17.19
65	25.42	14.04	14.59	17.32	12.85	18.63	7.34	21.98	20.59	16.51
66	27.85	13.39	16.00	16.57	14.20	17.87	8.09	21.14	22.16	15.85
67	30.44	12.76	17.43	15.83	15.72	17.12	8.89	20.31	23.89	15.20
68	33.19	12.14	18.84	15.10	17.41	16.38	9.73	19.49	25.85	14.56
69	36.17	11.54	20.36	14.38	19.30	15.66	10.65	18.67	28.06	13.93
70	39.51	10.96	22.11	13.67	21.37	14.96	11.70	17.87	30.52	13.32
71	43.30	10.39	24.23	12.97	23.65	14.28	12.91	17.07	33.15	12.72
72	47.65	9.84	26.87	12.28	26.13	13.61	14.32	16.29	35.93	12.14
73	52.64	9.30	30.11	11.60	28.84	12.96	15.98	15.52	38.82	11.58
74	58.19	8.79	33.93	10.95	31.79	12.33	17.91	14.76	41.84	11.02
75	64.19	8.31	38.24	10.32	35.05	11.72	20.13	14.02	45.07	10.48
76	70.53	7.84	42.97	9.71	38.63	11.13	22.65	13.30	48.67	9.95
77	77.12	7.40	48.04	9.12	42.59	10.56	25.51	12.60	52.74	9.44
78	83.90	6.97	53.45	8.55	46.95	10.00	28.72	11.91	57.42	8.93
79	91.05	6.57	59.35	8.01	51.76	9.47	32.33	11.25	62.77	8.45
80	98.84	6.18	65.99	7.48	57.03	8.96	36.40	10.61	68.82	7.98
81	107.48	5.80	73.60	6.98	62.79	8.47	40.98	9.99	75.52	7.53
82	117.25	5.44	82.40	6.49	69.08	8.01	46.12	9.40	82.78	7.11

	COMMISSIONERS 1980 STANDARD ORDINARY (1970–1975)				1983 INDIVIDUAL ANNUITY TABLE (1971–1976)[a]				UNITED STATES POPULATION	
	MALE		FEMALE		MALE		FEMALE		(1979–1981)	
AGE	DEATHS PER 1,000	EXPECTATION OF LIFE (YEARS)	DEATHS PER 1,000	EXPECTATION OF LIFE (YEARS)	DEATHS PER 1,000	EXPECTATION OF LIFE (YEARS)	DEATHS PER 1,000	EXPECTATION OF LIFE (YEARS)	DEATHS PER 1,000	EXPECTATION OF LIFE (YEARS)
83	128.26	5.09	92.53	6.03	75.91	7.57	51.89	8.83	90.41	6.70
84	140.25	4.77	103.81	5.59	83.23	7.15	58.34	8.28	98.42	6.32
85	152.95	4.46	116.10	5.18	90.99	6.75	65.52	7.77	107.25	5.96
86	166.09	4.18	129.29	4.80	99.12	6.37	73.49	7.28	117.12	5.61
87	179.55	3.91	143.32	4.43	107.58	6.02	82.32	6.81	127.17	5.29
88	193.27	3.66	158.18	4.09	116.32	5.69	92.02	6.38	137.08	4.99
89	207.29	3.41	173.94	3.77	125.39	5.37	102.49	5.98	147.28	4.70
90	221.77	3.18	190.75	3.45	134.89	5.07	113.61	5.60	158.68	4.43
91	236.98	2.94	208.87	3.15	144.87	4.78	125.23	5.26	171.69	4.17
92	253.45	2.70	228.81	2.85	155.43	4.50	137.22	4.94	185.70	3.93
93	272.11	2.44	251.51	2.55	166.63	4.24	149.46	4.64	200.23	3.71
94	295.90	2.17	279.31	2.24	178.54	3.99	161.83	4.37	214.95	3.51
95	329.96	1.87	317.32	1.91	191.21	3.75	174.23	4.12	229.76	3.34
96	384.55	1.54	375.74	1.56	204.72	3.51	186.54	3.88	243.38	3.19
97	480.20	1.20	474.97	1.21	219.12	3.29	198.65	3.65	256.37	3.05
98	657.98	.84	655.85	.84	234.74	3.07	211.10	3.44	268.68	2.93
99	1,000.00	.50	1,000.00	.50	251.89	2.86	224.45	3.22	280.30	2.82
100					270.91	2.66	239.22	3.01	291.20	2.73
101					292.11	2.46	255.95	2.80	301.99	2.64
102					315.83	2.26	275.20	2.59	310.89	2.57
103					342.38	2.08	297.50	2.38	319.70	2.50
104					372.09	1.90	323.39	2.18	327.86	2.44
105					405.28	1.73	353.41	1.98	335.39	2.38
106					442.28	1.57	388.11	1.79	342.33	2.33
107					483.41	1.41	428.02	1.60	348.70	2.29
108					528.99	1.27	473.69	1.43	354.53	2.24
109					579.35	1.13	525.66	1.26	359.88	2.20
110					634.81	1.01	584.46	1.11		
111					695.70	.89	650.65	.97		
112					762.34	.78	724.75	.83		
113					835.06	.70	807.32	.71		
114					914.17	.67	898.89	.60		
115					1,000.00	.50	1,000.00	.50		

Note: Mortality rates contained in the 1980 Commissioners Standard Ordinary Table were obtained from experience of 1970–1975, but contain an added element designed to generate life insurance reserves of a conservative nature in keeping with the long-term guarantees inherent in life insurance contracts. Premiums for life insurance policies, on the other hand, are based on assumptions that include expected mortality experience. Mortality rates for the 1983 Individual Annuity Tables are, again, conservative as related to the actual and projected experience upon which they are based.

[a]Projected to 1983.

SOURCE: *1992 Life Insurance Fact Book* American Council of Life Insurance. Washington, D.C. pp. 126–127.

All this talk of life and death may be grim, but there is heartening news in the mortality tables. Note that while a twenty-five-year-old male is expected to live 54.66 more years, a male who survives to age twenty six can expect to live another 53.69 years. Living one more whole year only "costs" the twenty-five-year-old .97 years in life expectancy. This bonus for survival continues throughout life, so that a 114-year-old male is expected to live only .67 years according to the table, but if he hangs on until his 115th year his life expectancy is *another six months* (see Table 11.1).

The life expectancy and deaths per 1000 are related statistics. The life expectancy of an individual is simply the probability-weighted chance of surviving to each future year. Mathematically, life expectancy at age A, L_A, is related to all future expected deaths per 1000 in each cohort, D_i, by the equation:

$$L_A = \sum_{t=A}^{t=115} \prod_{1=A}^{i=t} \left(1 - \frac{D_i}{1000}\right) + .5 . \tag{11.1}$$

The formula assumes that death is equally likely at any time in the year in adding .5 years. Life expectancy represents the sum of probabilities that you will not have died each year. The probability you will not have died is the cumulative probability of living to the end of each year, captured in the product term.

Despite changing mortality experience, statistics on life and death in all modern economies are very reliable, especially compared to other risks. They are based on millions of data points, and changes in these statistics evolve slowly. At any given time, life insurance actuaries can predict with extreme accuracy the mortality experience of large groups of individuals identified by sex, age, and other characteristics such as smoking or nonsmoking. Life insurance actuaries often use older mortality tables to be conservative because increasing life expectancies means old statistics overstate death rates.

As an example, a life insurance company expects that .62 of 1000 (62 of 100,000) male twenty-five-year olds will die within one year. A life insurance policy that pays a beneficiary if an insured dies over a specific time period is called *term life insurance*. If the company sells 100,000 one-year term life policies paying $10,000 to beneficiaries of twenty-five-year-old males, the company expects to pay 62 times $10,000 or $620,000 in benefits over the next year. In order to break even on the risk, the company would have to charge each of the 100,000 twenty-five-year-old insureds $620,000/100,000 or $6.20 for the $10,000. The *premium* on this insurance, the $6.20 per $10,000 (or 62 cents per thousand dollars), is determined primarily by expected mortality.

The premium calculated in the example does not take into consideration important costs. Specifically, sales, marketing, and normal business operating expenses are not included. No specific profit requirements for investors are included in the calculation.

The above premium calculation does not consider investment income. The insurance company knows its loss experience will not depart much from recent mortality tables and it knows that deaths occur throughout the year. If premiums are paid in advance, the company can invest premium revenues and earn investment income until benefits are paid. Assuming the company invests half the premiums of $620,000 on average during the year at 10 percent, it will earn approximately $31,000 (10 percent times half $620,000).

The example is representative of the basic economics of all insurance companies. Premium revenue is collected, exposing insurance companies to risks of paying benefits. Premiums are called *unearned premiums* at the beginning of the period and are earned over the term covered. The company earns investment income on premiums, and it can also earn investment income on benefits payable until payments to beneficiaries are made, although our example assumes benefits are paid immediately. These relations are portrayed in simplified financial statements in Table 11.2.

The difference between premiums earned and benefits paid are called *underwriting profits* or *underwriting gain*. In our example company there is no underwriting profit, and, in fact, many insurance companies consistently have underwriting losses. Insurance companies can lose money on insurance risks, in other words have underwriting losses, and still make money if investment income is high enough.

The basic economics of life insurance are the same with more complex policies and more complicated customer age distributions. To solidify our understanding, let us find a premium for a five-year term insurance policy for twenty-five-year olds assuming a 10 percent investment return, Table 11.3 gives the death benefits each year from insuring 100,000 twenty-five-year olds for $10,000 each. The number of deaths and benefits paid each year must account for previous years' deaths in the cohort. For example, in year three of the policy, fewer than 68 individuals die because the cohort had been reduced by the previous two

TABLE 11.2 Financial Statements for Insurance Company Writing One-Year Term Insurance for Twenty-Five-Year-Old Males

Income Statement			
Earned premiums	$620,000		
Benefits paid	620,000		
Underwriting profit	0		
Investment income	31,000		
Earnings	$31,000		
Balance Sheet at Beginning of Year			
Assets		**Liabilities**	
Investments	$620,000	Unearned premiums	$620,000
		Benefits payable	0
		Retained earnings	0
Balance Sheet at End of Year			
Assets		**Liabilities**	
Investments	$31,000	Unearned premiums	$0
		Benefits payable	0
		Retained earnings	31,000

TABLE 11.3 Calculation of Premium for Five-Year Term Life Policy for Twenty-Five-Year-Old Males at 10 and 15 Percent

YEAR	*DEATHS PER 10000*	*BENEFITS ($)*
1	62	620,000
2	65	649,597
3	68	679,137
4	70	698,636
5	73	728,067

years' deaths. Mortality tables give deaths per 1,000 individuals alive at the beginning of the year.

Life insurance premiums setting is fairly easy. To break even, the present value (PV) at the return on investments of premium revenues must equal the present value of benefits paid:

$$\text{Present Value (Benefits)} = \text{Present Value (Premiums)}. \qquad (11.2)$$

In making calculations, account must be taken that policyholders who die no longer pay premiums. The policy premium in our case is found by calculating:

$$\text{Premium} = \frac{\text{PV(Benefits@10\%)}}{\text{PV(Number of Insureds@10\%)}}. \qquad (11.3)$$

The answer is $6.71 per year for the policy.

In our simple example, reserves are accumulated and invested in the early years to finance benefit payments in later years of the policy. If actuarial and investment experience is as assumed in pricing the policy, reserves will be exhausted at the end of the term. If the premiums are high relative to loss experience or investment income is better than assumed in the discount rate, reserves will be left at the end of the period. Favorable underwriting or investment experience can produce positive present values (or equivalently positive future values) in formula (11.3). Value from favorable underwriting or investment experience can be kept by the insurance service provider or shared with the insured according to the life insurance contract. We discuss allocation of excess reserves below.

Types of Life Insurance Policies

Life insurance and defined benefit pension plans are variants of the calculations for term insurance. Calculating expected benefits can get more complicated with life policies or retirement plans, but the basic idea is the same.

Life insurance policies can be classified and described by two different characteristics: (1) time and nature of coverage, called the *life insurance plan;* and (2) how the policy is sold. Table 11.4 presents data on life insurance in the

TABLE 11.4 Life Insurance in Force in the United States

	1985			1989		
PLAN OF INSURANCE	NUMBER OF POLICIES[a] (000 OMITTED)	AMOUNT (000.000 OMITTED)	% OF AMOUNT	NUMBER OF POLICIES[a] (000 OMITTED)	AMOUNT (000.000 OMITTED)	% OF AMOUNT
ORDINARY						
Whole Life						
Continuous Payment	73,100	$1,745,200	53.7	79,200	$2,064,100	41.8
Limited Payment Life, Premium Paying	18,900	166,700	5.1	14,600	258,400	5.2
Paid-up	20,700	84,000	2.6	20,600	182,600	3.7
Endowment and Retirement Income with Insurance	6,700	49,500	1.6	4,100	43,900	0.9
Term						
Extended	8,200	43,700	1.4	7,300	61,200	1.2
Regular						
Decreasing	4,800	126,400	3.9	3,800	170,000	3.4
Other	10,100	780,700	24.0	14,000	1,648,200	33.4
Other						
Decreasing	—	55,300	1.7	—	77,400	1.6
Other	—	195,800	6.0	—	434,200	8.8
Total Ordinary	142,500	$3,247,300	100.0	143,600	$4,940,000	100.0
GROUP						
Term						
Decreasing	2,200	$58,100	2.3	3,000	$78,800	2.3
Other	126,600	2,494,600	97.4	137,100	3,360,500	96.8
Whole Life						
Premium Paying	500	6,400	0.2	800	27,100	0.8
Other	600	2,000	0.1	600	2,500	0.1
Endowment and Retirement Income with Insurance	b	500	c	100	600	b
Total Group	129,900	$2,561,600	100.0	141,600	$3,469,500	100.0
INDUSTRIAL						
Whole Life						
Continuous Payment	5,200	$3,500	12.4	3,200	$1,600	6.6
Limited Payment Life, Premium Paying	6,600	4,900	17.4	3,800	2,400	9.8
Paid-up	25,200	15,300	54.2	24,700	17,400	71.3
Endowment	2,500	1,300	4.6	1,400	700	2.9
Term						
Extended	4,500	3,000	10.6	3,500	2,200	9.0
Other	b	200	0.8	b	100	0.4
Total Industrial	44,000	$28,200	100.0	36,600	$24,400	100.0
CREDIT (TERM)	69,800	$216,000	100.0	72,200	$260,100	100.0
TOTAL LIFE INSURANCE IN FORCE	386,200	$6,053,100	100.0	394,000	$8,694,000	100.0

Note: "Ordinary" and "Group" include credit life insurance on loans of more than 10 years' duration. "Credit" is limited to life insurance on loans of 10 years' or less duration. In 1989, there were 3,300,000 ordinary policies in force under reduced paid-up options which totaled $9,800,000,000. For reporting purposes, the basic portion of combination plans is listed under the appropriate plan while the additional term portion, by rider or otherwise, is listed under term plans.

[a]Includes group certificates.

[b]Less than 50,000.

[c]Less than .05%.

SOURCE: American Council of Life Insurance.

United States classified by each characteristic. We discuss the details on life insurance plans first and discuss the organization of sales efforts next.

Term life insurance coverage lasts for a fixed time period, one year and five years in our two examples. Coverage ceases at the end of the period unless renewed. Some term policies offer automatic renewal without medical examinations or other qualifications for coverage. Risks associated with renewable term can be calculated and included as a surcharge over straight term premium. *Decreasing term* policies are designed to pay lower death benefits in later years of the policy as assets are accumulated by term insurance customers who save regularly.

Whole life policies pay a death benefit as long as premiums are paid. These policies are called continuous payment whole life. If acquired when the insured is young, the premiums on whole life can be low throughout the individual's life. These policies may be attractive for individuals desiring benefits for beneficiaries to cover expenditures like final illnesses and burial or to leave endowments to surviving family members.

Figure 11.1 portrays cash flows associated with premiums and benefits of various life insurance plans for a cohort of insured. All pure life insurance plans present the same basic pricing problem: the present value of benefits must be less than or equal to the present value of premiums for actuarially sound policies. Panel A illustrates the *level payment* life plan where premiums are constant until the insured dies. With level payment plans, expected premium revenues decline as members of the cohort die and benefits are paid. Expected benefits reach their maximum annual amount at the average life expectancy of the cohort. Panel B illustrates a *limited payment* life policy where the insured pays premiums over a limited time span, for example until the retirement age of 65, but life insurance coverage continues until benefits are paid.

Some life insurance policies contain a savings elements as well as death coverage. There are two ways for life insurance to offer more than the commitment to pay a benefit in case of death. The first is a *participating* life insurance contract, meaning that the insured participates in favorable investment performance (higher returns) or better mortality experience (lower benefit payments) than was assumed in pricing the premiums. The insurance firm offers the insured participation in the favorable investment or underwriting experience by accumulating savings or paying cash called policy dividends.

The second method for insurance to be combined with savings is when premiums are calculated above levels necessary to fund future benefit payments and funds are accumulated according to a plan. Policies with planned savings features are called *endowment* policies. Usually endowment policies are associated with retirement-age payments to insureds or their beneficiaries, financed with the planned accumulation of assets.

The bottom half of Figure 11.1 illustrates life policies with endowment properties. Two types of endowment policies are shown. Panel C illustrates policies paying a one-time benefit to insureds who do not die before retirement age. Panel D shows policies paying lifetime income to insureds who survive to retirement.

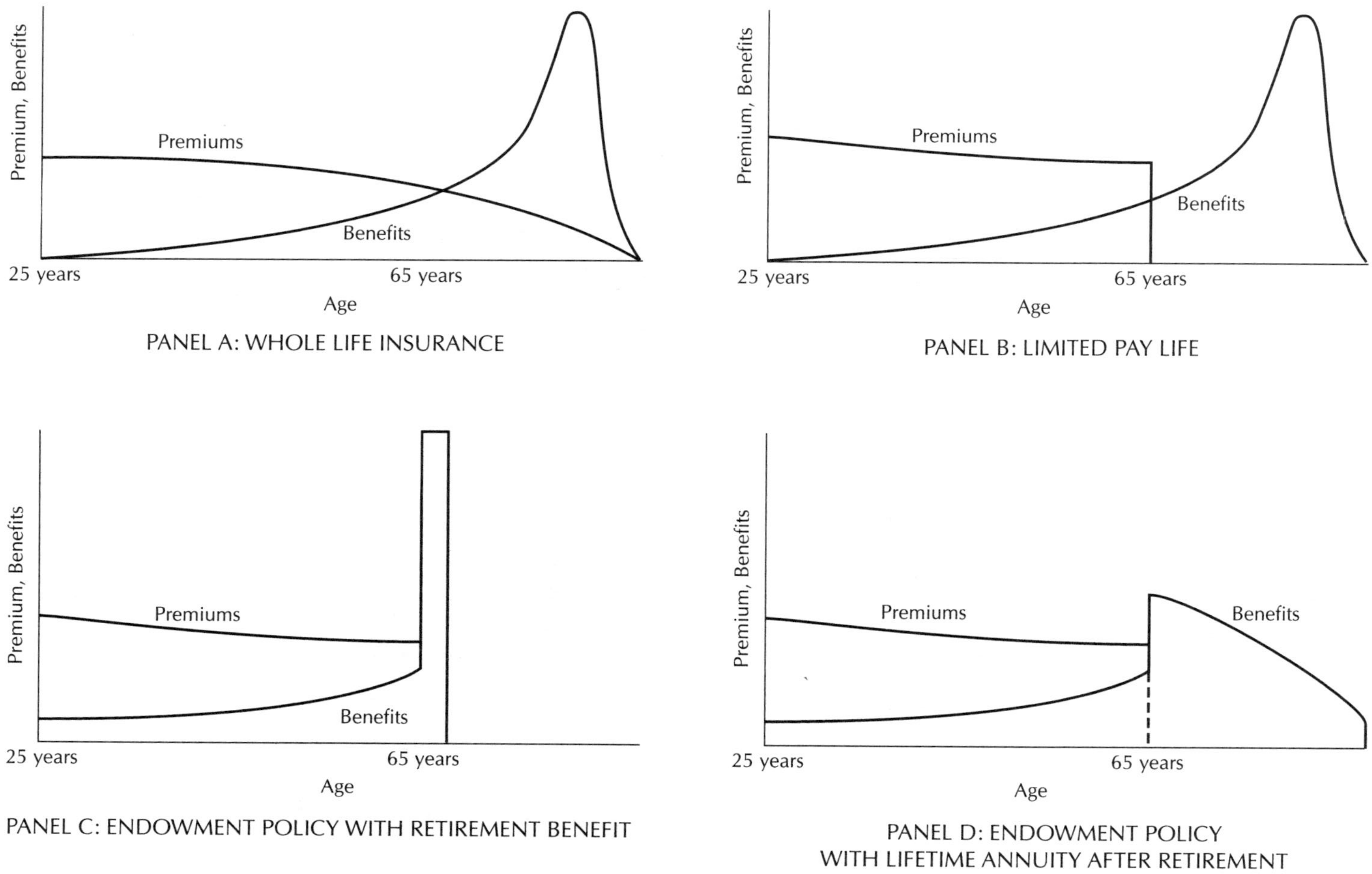

FIGURE 11.1 Patterns in premiums and benefits for various life policies

Insurance customers' claims on accumulations from favorable mortality or investment experience on their insurance policies is called *cash value*. Cash value can be used for one-time cash payments at the end of limited payment life insurance policies or paid upon cancellation of a policy. Cash value can be used as collateral for low interest loans from insurance providers to customers, called *policy loans*. Interest charged on policy loans are often fixed at low rates, making policy loans an attractive source of funds when interest rates are high.

The economic advantage of combining savings with life insurance comes mainly from tax considerations. Income earned on life insurance reserves and accumulated cash value is tax exempt in the United States. This tax exemption is called the tax sheltering of *inside buildup*. Insurance companies have exploited this tax treatment in developing new life insurance products as discussed below.

Life insurance policies often have other features. Many policies pay increased benefits in the case of accidental death, which occurs more unexpectedly than death from illness or old age. Some policies pay double benefits for accidental death, called *double indemnity*. Other features include payments in case of injuries called *disability* benefits. Disability benefits can be one-time payments or lifetime annuities. With statistics available on accidents and life expectancies, features like these can be priced accurately by life insurance actuaries.

With whole life and other long-term life insurance policies, premium revenue is often invested to fund benefit payments a very long time into the future. Figure 11.1 shows that early premiums from young insured with whole life policies may be invested as long as seventy years, the period from the first premium until the last death benefit. Life insurance companies typically have relatively long-term investments in their portfolios for this reason.

Life insurance providers have some short-term liquidity problems. These problems come from policy *cancellations, lapses,* and *policy loans*. Policy cancellations and lapses interrupt planned cash inflows from premium payments. Unexpected cash outflows may occur with participating policies that pay accumulated cash value when policies are cancelled. Policy loans advance cash to insureds borrowing against the cash value of policies, often when interest rates are high relative to fixed policy loan rates.

Selling Life Insurance

A second way to classify life insurance policies is by how policies are sold. Table 11.4 shows four life insurance sales and delivery mechanisms: (1) *ordinary,* (2) *group,* (3) *industrial,* and (4) *credit* life insurance. The first two categories dominate the total life insurance in force in the United States and in most countries. (The United States is the largest life insurance market, but Japan has nearly the same amount of life insurance in force with half the population.)

Ordinary life insurance is sold in the most traditional way. Insurance agents negotiate and sell specific life insurance contracts with various features to individual clients. The insured buys the policy from an insurance agent whose sales effort consists of personal calls, often in homes. The agent can be an employee of the insurance company but most agents are *independent agents*. Independent agents sell life insurance contracts for commissions, often as much as the first year's premium. The independent agent system is an important attribute of life insurance in the United States, as discussed below.

Group insurance is sold to collections of individuals, typically employees of a firm or members of a professional organization. Individuals in the group often pay the same premiums. Most group life policies are term insurance or retirement plans. One advantage of group insurance is that sales costs are minimized because sales are to large numbers of individuals. Individuals sometimes benefit from the pooled risks of a group. Groups with better life expectancies can receive favorable pricing relative to other sources of insurance.

Industrial life insurance is sold door-to-door. Fifty years ago, insurance premiums were collected during monthly visits by agents who noted payments in account books. Industrial insurance is declining in amount and insureds are concentrated in lower income classes. More effective sales methods and collection technology make industrial insurance comparatively expensive as a method of selling and serving life insurance customers.

Credit life insurance is a life policy that pays loan balances or make future payments on consumer loans if a borrower dies. These policies are nonparticipating and represent one of the few areas where noninsurance financial firms like banks have been allowed to sell life insurance. Since mortgage loans can have large balances, mortgage credit insurance policies can form an important part of an individual's contingency planning and have been growing in importance.

Life Insurance Contract Design

Inflation starting in the 1960s reduced the purchasing power of benefits from established whole life policies. Many life policies were cancelled in the 1970s and 1980s. Inflation reduced the value of savings through participating and endowment policies. Risk to the real value of insurance benefits and low investment returns used to price policies made life insurance an increasingly unattractive savings vehicle relative to other investments like housing and mutual funds over time. Many insurance consumers switched to term insurance.

Some life insurance companies responded to inflation by developing new life insurance products that took advantage of the favorable tax treatment of inside build-up. One successful life insurance product is *universal life insurance.* With universal life insurance, the insured deposits funds in the form of a large premium with the insurance provider. The insurance firm deducts expenses including premiums for death benefits under the policy from the initial premium and invests the rest at current interest rates or a combination of minimum rates and current rates. Income is credited on a monthly basis. Investment income is tax-exempt interest as part of the policy's inside build-up. As the policy accumulates cash value from premium deposits and investment income, the insured can increase the insurance death benefit, accumulate cash value, or withdraw funds as tax-free policy loans.

Life insurance firms can be harmed by adverse selection of policy buyers, but many such problems can be managed by requiring proof of age, medical examinations, and affidavits on personal habits like smoking. Problems of adverse selection are more difficult when selling to groups. Individuals in the group will select group insurance when rates are more favorable than those available on ordinary policies.

The economics of life insurance are determined primarily by mortality experience and investment returns. Mortality is unrelated to general economic events or market risk: Mortality risks are *unsystematic*. Investment risks are a function of the investment of reserves. Liquidity and cash flow risks from cancellations, lapses, and policy loans are important and may be systematic but are secondary risks to life insurance returns. Investors in life insurance, owners of life insurance firms, and participants in life insurance policies expect to earn a risk premium based primarily on the risks of the investment portfolio, not on the cash flows from life insurance. Contrast this with the discussion of a "fair rate of return" for casualty companies below.

11.3 ECONOMICS OF CASUALTY INSURANCE

Casualty insurance is similar to life insurance in some ways and different in others. The similarities are: (1) premiums are set and collected to completely or partly cover claims filed by insureds; (2) premiums are collected before earned and can be invested. These similarities mean that profitable casualty insurance income statements and balance sheets are similar to those of a life insurance company. Like a life company, the income statement of a profitable casualty insurance carrier's shows a total of earned premiums and investment income that is larger than claims and other expenses. Like a life insurance company, the balance sheet of a casualty company has unearned premiums, reserves, and claims payable as liabilities.

The differences between life and casualty insurances are easily understood. Two of the most important differences are: (1) the probabilities associated with claims are much harder to estimate and (2) claims are not fixed in dollar amount but vary with the extent of damage experienced by insureds. A third difference results from the previous two: property and casualty insurance contracts tend to be shorter term and subject to frequent repricing. One-year or half-year policies are common. Frequent premium adjustments are necessary as loss and claims experiences change with economic and demographic developments affecting investment returns, claims amounts, and assessment of risks.

Another difference between life and liability insurance is that claims may be filed years after a casualty insurance policy was in effect. For example, health damage claims related to working with asbestos were filed decades after exposure to the toxic substance. These claims are being paid by insurance companies years after policy coverage ended when the damage to health and legal liability of employers was established. Claims filed years after coverage ends illustrate what are called *long-tailed* liabilities of insurance companies.

An important difference between life and property and casualty insurance is the relation of the economy to claims. Losses due to property and casualty insurance claims change with economic conditions. The relation between claims and economic conditions means that efficient pricing of casualty insurance is related to economic risks as well as claims risk, as we discuss below.

A final and important difference between life and property and casualty insurance are risks associated with actions of the insured, namely moral hazard. For example, evidence suggests that property losses due to fires tend to be countercyclical due to moral hazard. Businesses are less careful or even deliberately negligent with unsold inventory or underemployed property during recessions. In contrast, life insurance claims are not affected in an important way by moral hazard. Moral hazard can be minimized by the terms of the insurance contracts, as we discuss below.

Economics of Property and Casualty Premiums and Returns

The returns to investing in the property and casualty insurance services are determined in important part by premium and loss levels. Losses depend on the expected *frequency,* or number of claims, and on the dollar amount of losses or *severity* of claims. As with life insurance, property and casualty insurance policies are actuarially profitable when the present value of expected premiums equals the present value of expected claims. The first consideration in pricing premiums for policies is the expected probability and severity of losses under the policy and expected returns on investment. Moral hazard and adverse selection can be dealt with in prices or contractual terms of policies, such as mandatory inspections or partial loss coverage. We deal with these issues later in the chapter.

Profits, π, from writing property and casualty insurance can be expressed in a simple formulation that highlights the economics of the business (see D'Arcy and Doherty 1988, especially Chapters 2 and 4, for a treatment):

$$\pi = [P - L - X] + [E + k(P - X)]\,r_i. \tag{11.4}$$

Profits are determined by premium revenue net of sales expenses, P, losses from claims including claims processing costs, L, and all other costs of being in the insurance business, X, included in the first term in the equation. L is determined by frequency and severity of claims. Investment income in the second term is determined by invested equity, E, and premiums net of business expenses, rate of return on investments, r_i, and the length of time premiums are held before paid as claims, k. If claims are processed quickly, as for example in auto insurance, k is small. If claims are delayed or liabilities have long tails, k is large, much larger than one if the time is several years.

Several authors have examined insurance company returns to explore equilibrium pricing of insurance in competitive markets, importantly Kraus and Ross (1982), whose work is summarized in D'Arcy and Doherty (1988). Equilibrium pricing in insurance markets produces a "fair" return to investors, a return in line with investments of similar risk. In relating fair returns to insurance profits, D'Arcy and Doherty express claims losses as a percent of premiums (L/P or l). L/P is called the *combined ratio* (combining loss, claims, and selling costs) in the insurance industry. Other operating costs of the insurance business are expressed as a ratio of premiums (X/P or x).

The expected return to an investor in a property and casualty insurance company can be written:

$$E(\text{ROR}) = \frac{\pi}{E} = \left[1 + k\frac{P}{E}(1 - x)\right] r_i + \frac{P}{E}(1 - x - l). \tag{11.5}$$

Applying the Capital Asset Pricing Model (CAPM) discussed in Chapter 4, the beta coefficient of a casualty company can be decomposed into two betas: an asset return beta depending on the risks from investing premium dollars, and an underwriting beta measuring sensitivity of underwriting profits to movements in the market. The underwriting beta is defined as:

$$\beta_u = \frac{\text{Cov}\big((1 - x - l), r_m\big)}{\sigma_m^2}$$

or

$$\beta_u = \frac{\text{Cov}(r_u, r_m)}{\sigma_m^2} \tag{11.6}$$

where (1 – x – 1) or r_u defines the company's underwriting profits as a fraction of premium revenues. A casualty insurance company's total beta and the corresponding expected return on underwriting activity is:[2]

$$\beta = \left[1 + k\frac{P}{E}(1 - x)\right]\beta_i + \frac{P}{E}\beta_u \tag{11.7}$$

and

$$E(r_u) = -k(1 - x)\, r_f + \beta_u\left[E(r_m) - r_f\right] \tag{11.8}$$

where $(E(R_m) - r_f)$ is the market risk premium.

The derivation highlights the importance of the correlation or *beta* of casualty companies' underwriting experience with general economic activity reflected in the market return. The derivation of fair premiums for an insurance company suggests that if the underwriting beta is low, say zero, insurance firms in competitive markets will have underwriting losses at a rate equal to the first term in equation (11.8). The larger is k or the time available to invest premiums net of operating expenses, the larger can be the underwriting losses and still produce a fair return to investors. For example, if the underwriting beta is zero and premiums can be invested one year (k = 1) and operating costs are half premium revenues, underwriting losses as a percent of equity could be a negative return equal to half the riskless rate.

Most casualty insurance companies do experience underwriting losses. Table 11.5, Panel A, provides data on property and casualty insurance companies' operating results in the United States for 1988 to 1990, and Panel B provides a

[2]Derived assuming the company's total beta produces the total expected return and similarly for invested assets in CAPM equilibrium, then solving for the necessary expected return to obtain the company overall expected return. See D'Arcy and Doherty (1988), p. 36.

longer time series of major income statement items for all such companies. As shown in the table, the last year casualty insurance companies had a positive underwriting margin was in 1978. As suggested by the market return analysis, the 1980s with high riskless rates were times of large underwriting losses.

A fair return to investors with negative underwriting returns depends on the underwriting beta, that is the covariance of losses and expenses with the market return. If the underwriting beta is positive, as would be the case with procyclical losses on casualty insurance, expected fair returns for insurance companies would require compensation for systematic risk. Fair insurance premiums could easily be high enough to assure positive expected underwriting experience. For example, if the underwriting beta were 1.5 and the risk premium on the market 8.3 percent, with the assumption of k = 1 and x = .5 in the earlier example, expected underwriting profits would have to be positive for any riskless investment rate below 6.22 percent to ensure a fair expected return.

The key points made by the analysis of fair returns in insurance are that factors affecting expected rates of return in casualty insurance include investment

TABLE 11.5 Operating Results, Property/Casualty Insurers, 1988–1990

Panel A: Operating Data from Property and Casualty Insurance Companies

	1990 ($1,000)	*1989 ($1,000)*	*1988 ($1,000)*	*% CHANGE 1989–90*	*% CHANGE 1988–89*
Assets	$556,313,935	$526,985,299	$476,929,318	5.6	+10.5
Net premiums written	217,824,840	208,387,953	202,014,698	4.5	+3.2
Premiums earned	215,952,506	206,669,462	199,978,326	4.5	+3.3
Losses and adjustment expenses incurred	177,755,908	169,372,469	156,696,193	4.9	+8.1
Loss and loss adjustment ratio	82.31%	81.95%	78.35%	0.4	+4.6
Underwriting expenses incurred	56,916,970	54,248,850	51,942,721	4.9	+4.4
Underwriting expense ratio	26.13%	25.98%	25.71%	0.6	+1.1
Combined ratio (before dividends to policyholders)	108.44%	107.93%	104.06%	0.5	+3.7
Combined ratio (after dividends to policyholders)	109.66%	109.23%	105.45%	0.4	+3.6
Statutory underwriting gain (loss)	(18,218,513)	(16,489,129)	(8,391,819)	–10.5	–96.5
Dividends to policyholders	2,639,756	2,713,420	2,775,958	–2.7	–2.3
Net underwriting gain (loss)	(20,858,269)	(19,202,549)	(11,167,777)	–8.6	–71.9
Net investment income	32,901,121	31,207,257	27,723,269	5.4	+12.6
Operating earnings after taxes	8,983,856	9,060,470	12,888,726	–0.8	–29.7
Policyholders' surplus	138,401,471	133,972,436	118,194,802	3.3	+13.3
Premium to surplus ratio	1.57 to 1	1.56 to 1	1.71 to 1		
Dividends to stockholders	5,660,066	5,523,131	4,852,941	2.5	+13.8

TABLE 11.5 (*continued*)

Panel B: Past Operating Data for Property and Casualty Insurance Companies

	UNDERWRITING RESULTS				
YEAR	*STATUTORY UNDERWRITING GAIN/LOSS*	*POLICYHOLDER DIVIDENDS*	*NET UNDERWRITING GAIN/LOSS*	*INVESTMENT INCOME**	*COMBINED NET INCOME***
1966	$386,927	$406,802	$–19,875	$1,217,980	$1,198,105
1967	233,619	488,577	–254,958	1,351,764	1,096,806
1968	–148,224	420,525	–568,749	1,511,509	942,760
1969	–529,899	518,055	–1,047,954	1,711,806	663,852
1970	77,776	503,558	–425,781	2,005,081	1,579,299
1971	1,381,800	555,629	826,172	2,421,495	3,247,667
1972	1,797,934	736,283	1,061,651	2,799,737	3,861,388
1973	791,761	785,698	6,063	3,325,344	3,331,408
1974	–1,878,371	766,527	–2,644,898	3,832,669	1,187,771
1975	–3,593,959	632,838	–4,226,798	4,150,204	–76,594
1976	–1,558,551	630,100	–2,188,652	4,805,939	2,617,287
1977	1,926,315	814,513	1,111,803	5,815,788	6,927,591
1978	2,548,143	1,251,811	1,296,332	7,289,554	8,585,886
1979	23,606	1,324,377	–1,300,772	9,279,235	7,978,463
1980	–1,712,423	1,621,545	–3,333,968	11,063,492	7,729,524
1981	–4,463,888	1,823,748	–6,287,636	13,248,495	6,960,859
1982	–8,303,039	1,986,827	–10,289,866	14,906,655	4,616,789
1983	–11,087,953	2,234,117	–13,322,070	15,973,234	2,651,164
1984	–19,378,885	2,098,062	–21,476,947	17,659,729	–3,817,218
1985	–22,597,292	2,196,247	–24,793,539	19,507,869	–5,285,670
1986	–13,747,925	2,164,969	–15,912,894	21,924,445	6,011,551
1987	–7,078,243	2,546,258	–9,624,501	23,959,981	14,335,480
1988	–8,391,819	2,775,958	–11,167,777	27,723,269	16,555,492
1989	–16,489,129	2,713,420	–19,202,549	31,207,257	12,004,708
1990	–18,218,513	2,639,756	–20,858,269	32,901,121	12,042,852

*Industrywide investment income, less investment expenses, before taxes. Figures for years prior to 1977 are aggregates and include some duplications because of interownerships within company groups. Totals from 1977 through 1990 have been consolidated to eliminate such duplications.

**Before taxes. Combined net income includes both underwriting gains or losses and investment income.

SOURCE: A. M. Best Company, Inc., *Best's Aggregates & Averages.*

The I.I.I. Insurance Information Institute *1992 Fact Book*

horizons and investment risk, and that underwriting profits need not be positive to earn fair returns in some interest rate environments. Casualty insurance is qualitatively different from life insurance in containing an underwriting risk factor in the determination of expected rates of return.

Lines of Insurance

Property and casualty insurance coverage is classified into *insurance lines* defining classes of risk. Insurance companies have to be *admitted* or allowed to underwrite the specific lines of insurance in most countries and states, as discussed in Chapter 16. Insurance is regulated by state insurance regulators in the United States and by national authorities in Europe, Japan, and elsewhere.

Major lines of insurance are *marine insurance, property insurance, casualty* or *liability insurance, multiple line insurance,* and *fidelity and surety bonds.* Marine insurance, the oldest line of commercial insurance, provides insurance against losses from operations of ships and boats. Property insurance covers losses to the insured from natural hazards, like fires and floods, and accidents, like car accidents or lost baggage. Casualty or liability insurance covers losses caused to other people or property from accidents due to automobiles or slippery sidewalks. Multiple line insurance covers both property and casualty losses. Fidelity and surety bonds provide insurance protection against losses due to nonperformance of firms or individuals on contracts or other legal obligations (like appearance in court) or on financial commitments.

The largest single source of insurance premium revenue in the United States is automobile insurance, amounting to over $95 billion in 1990 and accounting for between one-third and one-half of all property and casualty insurance premiums of about $218 billion that year. Next largest is workmen's compensation, with premiums of approximately $31 billion. Homeowners multiple peril insurance and commercial multiple peril follow as the next largest categories, both at about $18 billion. All other lines are less than $8 billion per year in total premiums.

Reinsurance and Insurance Treaties

Insurance carriers can sell some of their claims risk to other insurance companies. This risk shifting is called *reinsurance.* Selling insurance risks is called *ceding* insurance to the reinsurer. Reinsurance is a means whereby insurance companies control their exposure to catastrophic claims, diversify regional risks, or write policies when capital or reserve levels limit their ability sell more insurance. Reinsurance issued by reinsurance companies like General Re Corporation is protection against excessive losses from particular types of insurance exposure for insurance underwriters. Insurance companies can also cede insurance risks with other companies in *insurance treaties* without reinsurance. With insurance treaties, companies share risks in specific ways.

Insurance risks can also be sold to private investors in insurance markets or exchanges. Investors pledge resources to pay claims in exchange for a share of premiums. The most famous insurance market is Lloyds of London. Recent losses by investors in Lloyds resulted in a restructuring of that market which now allows corporate investors in addition to the traditional (mainly wealthy) individuals or *names.* Competition to Lloyds comes from other insurance markets like the New York Insurance Exchange.

Figure 11.2A shows the way losses on claims are shared by reinsurance and Figure 11-2B shows a hypothetical insurance treaty. In the reinsurance example

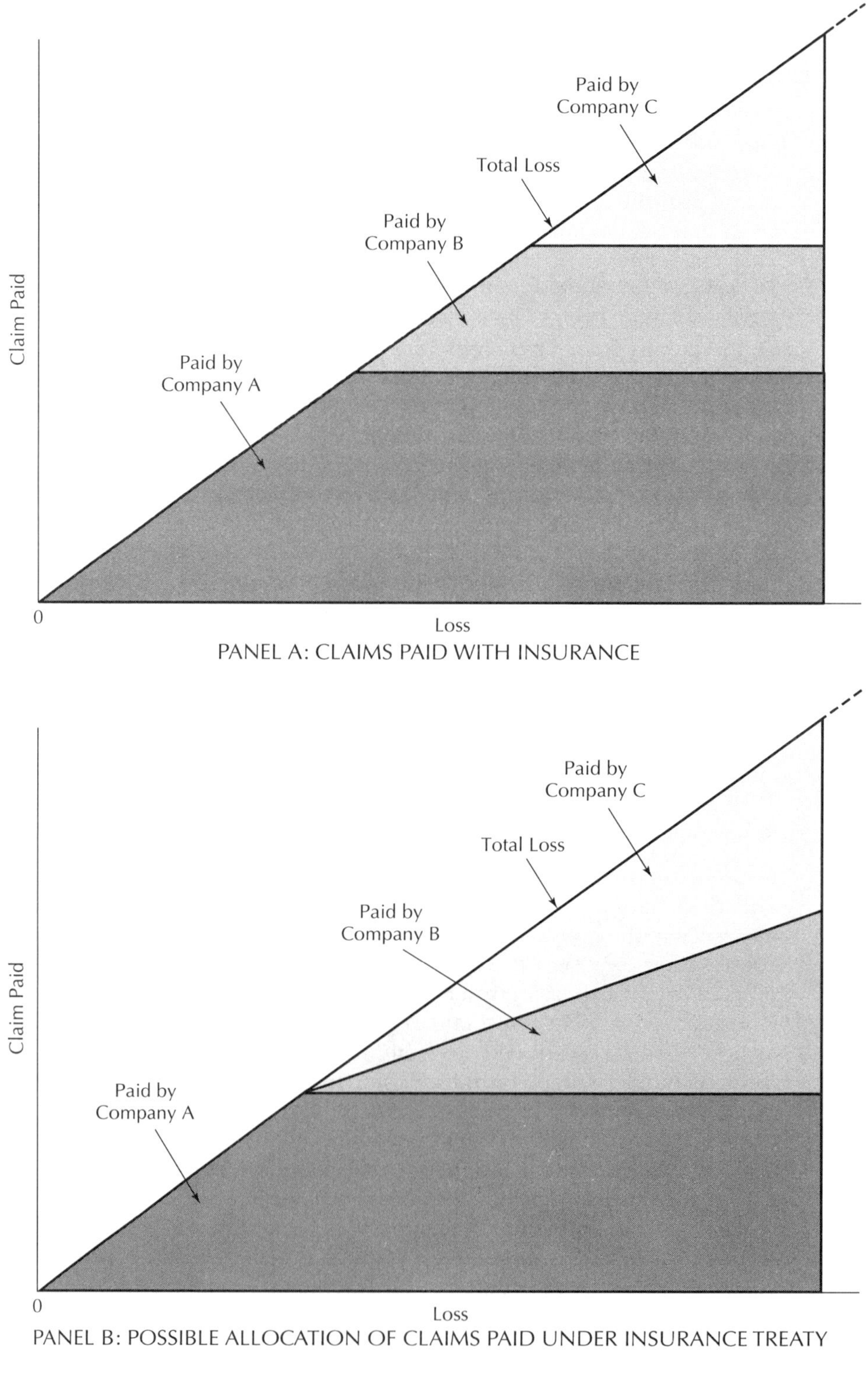

FIGURE 11.2 Claims paid with reinsurance and risk sharing

shown in Panel A, Company A has reinsured losses above a certain point to reinsurance companies B and C. After A, reinsurance company B has the greatest exposure since it must pay claims on lower amounts than reinsurance company C. In most cases, lowest losses have the highest probability of occurrence. Premium income from the insured will be split among insurance companies A and reinsurance companies B and C in accordance with their perception of actuarial risks and their bargaining power.

Panel B illustrates an insurance treaty in which insurance company A assumes risks of claims up to a point. Two other companies have agreed to share risks of claims equally above that point. There is no limit to the ways insurance risks can be reinsured or shared by treaty among insurance companies.

Health and Workman's Compensation Insurance

Health insurance is at the center of a national debate in the United States. Paying for health care is a global issue. Health insurance provided by private insurance carriers is one solution to insuring risks from medical bills. In 1989, private insurance paid about one-third of the costs of health care in the United States (Insurance Information Institute, 1992, p. 52). With many health insurance policies, like *major medical insurance* covering medical bills above a large deductible, health insurance claims are similar to insurance claims in other insurance lines.

The largest growth in health care demand in recent decades is from government programs in developed countries. In the United States, government accounted for over 40 percent of the cost of health care in 1989. Federal government health insurance programs like Medicare for the retired or state and federal health insurance like Medicaid for the poor use taxes to finance health benefit payments. These programs are not true insurance at all. They are government transfer programs.

Frequency and severity of claims under a private health insurance could be estimated and premiums priced as in other types of insurance. Claims are not fixed in nominal terms and there are risks associated with adverse selection and moral hazard. Just as with automobile insurance, probabilities of claims and estimated severity of claim costs can be estimated by examining statistics on health care. Contract provisions, such as tests or affidavits and shared costs of claims, can reduce adverse selection and moral hazard problems.

The major problem in relying on a private health insurance system is the interaction of private and political forces. The atmosphere within which these issues are discussed is emotional. Distortions in the economics of private health insurance can be due to government involvement, like costs from adverse selection forced by nondiscrimination policies. Claims for health care using expensive new cures and procedures, like heart transplants, must be paid—even though not anticipated when policies were written—because of publicity, regulations, and court decisions. The provision of health insurance does not occur in a competitive market environment.

Workman's compensation is similar to health insurance. This insurance covers accidents and disabilities arising in jobs, as well as lost compensation. Like health insurance, the insurance risks are manageable in themselves but the economics of this segment of the business has been distorted by government intervention. Workman's compensation insurance is mandatory in most countries and states. Risks are often not actuarially priced because of state laws or regulations. Private insurers must accept assigned risks of insuring workers who would not be covered at the maximum allowable rates.

Large losses result from this workmen's compensation insurance. In the United States in 1990, this line accounted for 14 percent of premiums but 26 percent of losses (Insurance Information Institute, 1992, p. 10). In addition to changes in mandatory coverage made by governments, courts have often awarded damage claims to workers that are very large relative to apparent costs. Risks from claims are hard to estimate because of long-tails and erratic rewards given by sympathetic juries in trials involving workers.

The political dimension and dynamic nature of both workmen's compensation and health insurance make them unique lines of insurance. Well-known insurance solutions to problems of moral hazard, such as coinsurance and deductibles as discussed below, could be used in providing efficient and profitable private workman's compensation and health insurance. But insurance benefits negotiated between individuals, groups, insurance carriers, and governments are not set in competitive markets. Government policy, unions, subsidized competition, and assigned risks distort the economics of the business. Profits and value added in this line of insurance are clearly possible but many of the innovations and considerations leading to value added in these lines are outside the scope of this book and in the realm of politics.

Selling Property and Casualty Insurance

Most insurance lines are sold directly to individuals by insurance agents, either independent agents or company representatives like Allstate Insurance agents selling policies in retail stores. Insurance brokers are important in retail insurance lines, but they are more important in selling commercial lines. Brokers and independent agents often represent several insurance companies.

Sales expenses of insurance policies in the retail market, most importantly home and automobile insurance, are a major cost component in providing these services. Short contract periods and changing premiums typical in property and casualty insurance mean that these costs are a recurring part of insurance coverage. Most agents and brokers receive large commissions for the first contract period and renewal commissions for policies that are continued in force. Property and casualty selling costs are higher than costs of selling individuals longer-term life insurance.

Insurance is sold to the institutional market by insurance company representatives, independent agents, and brokers like Marsh and McClellan. Marketing inefficiencies in the wholesale insurance business are not as obvious as in retail insurance sales. Business coverage by its nature will differ greatly from firm to firm and there are few economies to be realized from standardization of policies and mass marketing in selling insurance coverage to businesses.

Claims Processing

The costs of claims processing consists of paper processing costs and the costs of assessing damage or loss. Indirect costs come from moral hazard problems in property and casualty insurance. Moral hazard occurs in claims processing at two levels. First, the insured has an incentive to inflate claims under property insurance coverage. Many examples of inflated claims can be presented, such as falsely claiming that valuable items have been lost when filing a claim under lost baggage insurance or homeowners insurance. Second, claims processors making repairs or replacing lost items may inflate losses to improve their own sales or revenues. For example, an auto body shop may throw in a paint job as part of an accident claim, inflating the damage claim to the shopowner's and insured's advantage and to the detriment of the insurance carrier.

Claims processing under property and casualty insurance is necessary to validate the casualty or loss and assess the value of the claim under the policy. If the claim is valid, the claims payment must be processed or repairs made. Claims processing can be performed directly by the insurance carrier, by contractors performing claims processing exclusively, or by authorized suppliers of repair services or replacements for specific types of losses. The principal–agent problem with the use of contractors or authorized suppliers increasing claim costs must be solved to maximize underwriting profits or minimize underwriting losses. Good solutions to these problems are value-producing opportunities for insurance firms.

11.4 VALUE PRODUCTION IN INSURANCE

Value is created in the insurance business by investing premiums and underwriting insurance risks. Value produced by investing premiums comes from credit and asset management services discussed in Chapters 8 and 12. In this chapter, we focus on creating value in the six activities in the value chain for underwriting insurance risks. Value production opportunities in these activities appear to be enormous. Industry observers and potential competitors believe that protection from competition resulting from regulation (discussed in Chapter 16) has created inefficiencies in virtually every facet of insurance. We discuss each activity in the value chain for insurance in the following.

Term Setting and Pricing in Life Insurance

Terms and pricing can be used to resolve problems associated with adverse selection in life insurance. For example, expanded coverage in case of accidental death for a higher premium might be used to induce self-revelation of individuals in risky jobs or with risky life styles. Terms requiring complete physical examinations or limiting benefits under certain circumstances like war may deter critically ill individuals or individuals with certain careers from applying for insurance.

Some insurance providers, like the defunct Executive Life Insurance Company, were successful in developing new products that took advantage of concerns about the economic environment, specifically concerns about inflation and taxes. "Universal life insurance" discussed previously combined conservative mortality assumptions and participating insurance into a savings vehicle that took advantage of the tax treatment of inside build-up and offered some protection against inflation. Protection against inflation, a major concern of the 1970s and 1980s, was provided by paying market rates of interest and allowing changing nominal coverage and flexibility in the real value of life insurance benefits.

Creating value in terms of market share or improving margins through pricing and terms are limited in life insurance related products. The limits come from the mortality tables. Marginal departures from average experience in the tables present few possibilities for creativity in life insurance product design. Some innovation in policy design in the future may be based on demographics like the maturing of "baby boomers." For example, death benefits and savings may appeal to baby boomers concerned with educating children and providing for retirement at the same time in the next few decades. Nonetheless, the reality of mortality tables limits creativity in contract design and life insurance pricing and terms.

Term Setting and Pricing in Casualty Insurance

Pricing and terms to minimize and control adverse selection and moral hazard are basic to value production in property and casualty insurance. Defining insurance contracts that are marketable and manageable from a risk/return standpoint is the challenge of the business. The challenge must be met differently in the retail market and the complex wholesale market of firms and governments.

Adroit use of statistical data can be useful in fine-tuning assessment of risks and utilizing actuarial information to market new retail products. For example, motorcyclists are among the riskiest insurance risks. They are involved in many accidents and injuries are serious. Progressive Insurance Company found a lucrative business by examining statistics and determining that motorcyclists over 40 years old are lower than average risks. By marketing exclusively to this class of risks, Progressive is able to make profits and charge lower premiums than other suppliers.

Business insurance risks are in some cases routine and others completely unique. Risks of fire or industrial accidents can be estimated by examining records kept by government agencies, industry associations, and insurance company data cooperatives. These risks can be estimated with a fair amount of precision and premiums and contracts designed accordingly. Unusual or new risks, like the loss of communication satellites or tanker insurance in the Persian Gulf in wartime, can only be estimated by hunch and application of experience from possibly strained parallel situations.

In both retail and wholesale casualty insurance, pricing and term setting can be used to mitigate or eliminate problems arising from adverse selection and moral hazard. Adverse selection occurs because insurance buyers try to find policies that are cheap for the risks they expect to face. For example, with average-cost auto insurance pricing, low-risk drivers subsidize drivers having higher accident rates. Insurance customers can be distinguished by observable characteristics that affect accident risk, such as sex, age, years of driving experience, and previous driving record, to some extent. Alternative means to minimize adverse selection must be sought for hidden information on risk class.

One alternative is to use deductibles, where claims above a certain amount are paid by the insurance company. For example, a $100 deductible policy might have an annual premium of $1,000, whereas a $500 deductible policy might have a premium of $750. An example of a deductible policy is shown in Figure 11-3A. With deductibles, the insured bears the loss up to a specified limit and the insurance companies only pays claims over that amount up to the policy limit. Drivers who are safer and more cautious choose higher deductibles. Secret auto racers elect lower deductibles because they know they are more likely to have claims. Calibration of deductibles and premiums can induce drivers to reveal themselves as high or low risk by their choice of contract terms. Value is created by managing claims costs and targeting specific classes of risks.

Moral hazard occurs when the insured takes actions increasing the risk of loss to the insurance company. For example, the owner of an insured boiler may not perform required maintenance, increasing the risk of an explosion. Coinsurance is one way to control problems of moral hazard, for losses are shared by the insured and the insurance firm, as shown in Figure 11-3B. The lines and shaded areas show that the insured and the insurance company share the loss according to the terms of the policy up to the policy limit. The terms of an insurance policy may cover only 75 percent of losses, and the insured must pay 25 percent of the losses. Insureds are less likely to risk avoidable losses if they must pay part of damages out of their own funds.

Nonprice terms of insurance contracts can control both adverse selection and moral hazard. For example, documented maintenance expenses on equipment or periodic inspection of buildings or equipment may be required by the insurance contract. Changes in operating procedures or functions may have to be reported to the insurance company to assure coverage. For example, auto insurance premiums and coverage depend on miles driven. Changes in driving needs may have to be reported.

Definition of terms and prices on insurance contracts are limited only by three factors: acceptance by customers in the insurance market, practicality in implementing control and monitoring procedures implied by the terms, and regulatory approval. The last requirement is covered in Chapter 16.

Value Production from Marketing Insurance Products

Nearly all observers of the insurance industry believe that the marketing of life insurance products is inefficient. Most ordinary life insurance is sold by company or independent agents. Sales costs paid to agents often amount to one year's premium. The growth of group and credit life insurance market share can be interpreted as a response to the high cost of sales via agents making direct sales calls. Independent and company agent sales of ordinary insurance still dominate the market in the United States as shown in Table 11.4.

Dominance of the relatively inefficient system of agents is based on several factors. First is the tremendous political influence of independent agents who can

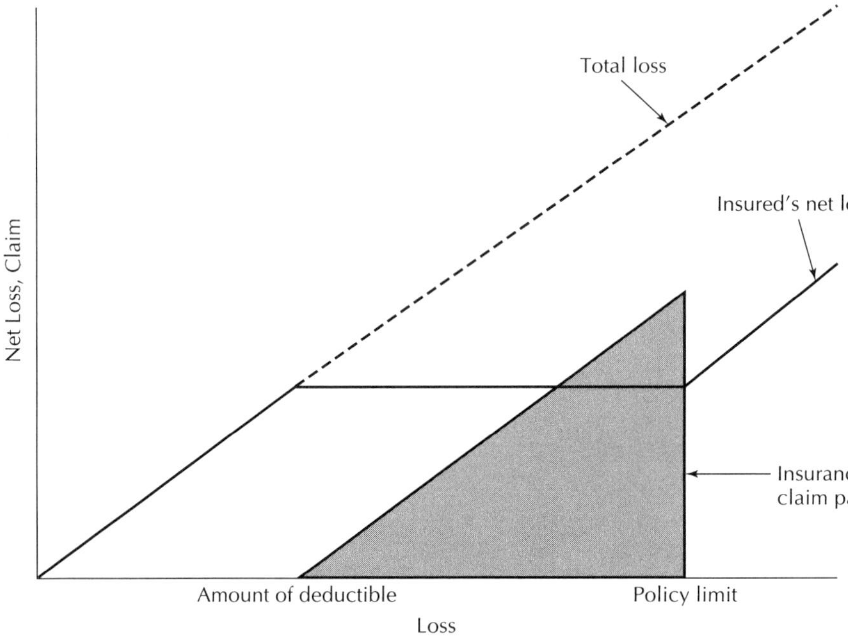

PANEL A: TOTAL LOSS, CLAIM PAID, AND NET LOSS WITH DEDUCTIBLES

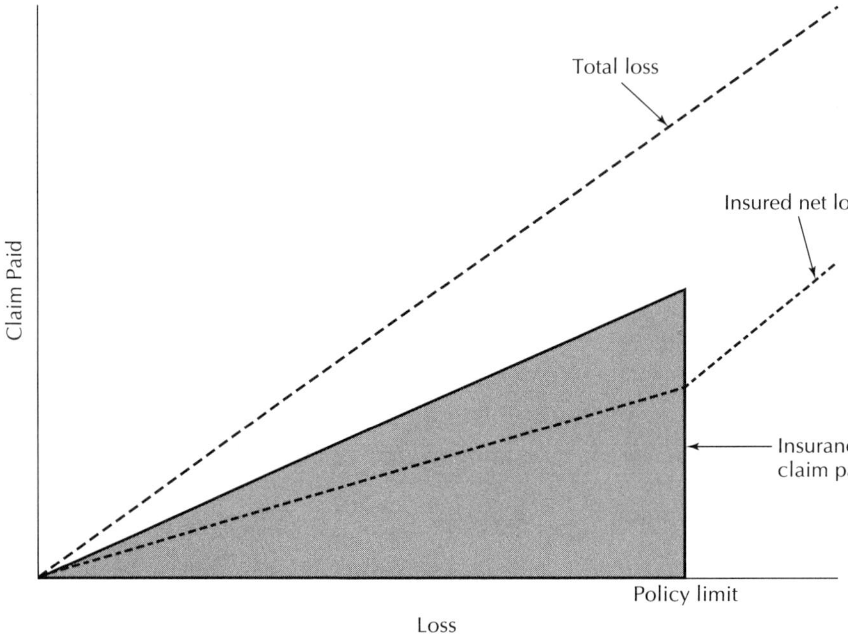

PANEL B: NET LOSS AND CLAIMS PAID WITH COINSURANCE

FIGURE 11.3 Claims paid and net losses under deductibles and co-insurance

fill the halls of Congress with lobbyists and constituents on one day's notice, as they did in 1995 to stop legislation allowing banks to sell insurance. Second, the complexity of the product and individual financial information that must be communicated and explained makes a labor-intensive marketing effort difficult to avoid. A third reason is the complacence of major life insurance underwriters who share the benefits of the imperfectly competitive market with the agents selling their life insurance services.

A number of recent experiments and shifts in position of insurance companies are related to insurance marketing. For example, Merrill Lynch acquired a life insurance company and attempted to sell insurance products through its brokerage offices. Shearson Lehman bought First Capital Life and brokers sold annuities issued by the insurance firm to their clients. Prudential Insurance bought a brokerage firm, Bache.

In Europe, restructuring of insurance through cross-border insurance company alliances and commercial bank merging with insurance is possible with the European Economic Community's "single market" policy for financial services (discussed in Part III). Protected regional insurance service markets in Europe allowed marketing inefficiencies resulting in large price differentials, for example with Spain expensive and England cheap. In one apparently successful attempt to market insurance efficiently, Internationale Nederlande Group (ING) was formed by merging the Netherland's largest insurance company and third largest bank to utilize bank branches for selling insurance products (Bray 1994).

Many experiments to innovate in life insurance product marketing have failed. Merrill Lynch abandoned its insurance venture. Differences in training, compensation, and sales techniques between brokers and insurance salesmen meant they could not work in the same offices effectively. Brokers did not like to sell insurance and insurance salesmen resented the higher pay of brokers. Shearson had to provide guarantees to customers when its insurance subsidiary ran into financial difficulties causing losses to buyers of its insurance products (*Wall Street Journal* 1992). These failures do not rule out innovative low-cost solutions to life insurance marketing in the future but do urge focusing on true efficiencies in marketing insurance products.

Marketing property and casualty insurance is performed by a combination of company agents, independent insurance agents, and insurance brokers. Value production from more economical marketing of insurance products seems more likely in the retail market, in marketing standardized contracts such as auto and home insurance to large numbers of individuals, than in the marketing of commercial lines. In retail casualty insurance, the strength of the independent agents in lobbying efforts to prevent entry into the market by competitors, such as banks, has also limited the channels through which insurance can be offered to individuals.

A number of firms have economized on costs of selling property and casualty insurance to the retail market by short-circuiting the agent system. Notable among them is Twentieth Century Insurance Company, which sells auto insurance only over the phone to the lowest risk customers. The customer's only contact with the firm is through phone and mail. Other firms have attempted to economize on insurance selling costs by using distribution networks already established for other purposes, such as using shopping centers or grocery store stalls for selling insurance. Some deposit-taking financial institutions cross sell insurance in branches directly or with cooperating firms where that is permitted. Group sales of auto and home insurance have increased and are another way of reducing sales and marketing costs while reducing premium payment costs by use of payroll deductions.

The current marketing system for insurance is dominated by independent agents. The agent system has both advantages and disadvantages to insurance companies. An obvious advantage to the insurance companies is that independent agents are compensated (in most cases) by receiving a fraction of premium dollars generated by new and renewed policies. Agents' interests align with those of the insurance carrier as long as increasing the volume of business produces profits.

The disadvantage to insurance underwriters of the agent system is that the labor-intensive sales may not be the most cost-effective method of determining and meeting insurance needs. Higher prices to cover higher costs reduce demand. Marketing of property and casualty insurance products to the retail market is an area where substantial value can be produced by reduction of sales costs and expansion of the market.

The heterogenous nature of business and institutional insurance needs means labor-intensive sales are largely unavoidable. Innovative methods of direct sales versus reliance on an agency system does not seem to have as great a value-creating potential in wholesale market for complex business or public casualty insurance as in retail lines. Standardization of coverage and policies enabling sales to broader institutional markets could be a source of some reduced marketing costs lowering premiums to add value to business and governments.

Monitoring and Controlling as Sources of Value in Insurance

Monitoring and controlling life insurance contracts and related products are routine because of the general absence of moral hazard problems. Most routine monitoring of life insurance contracts is concerned with timely payment of premiums. Payments made under pension funds or annuities by insurance firms may contain conditions requiring monitoring. For example, benefit levels may change depending on survival of both spouses, or claims may be made for disability benefits. Moral hazard problems associated with annuity and pension plans are readily controllable, but monitoring and controlling activities must be performed or costly problems can occur. Given the widely publicized inefficiencies of some life insurance companies, cost savings from better use of human and capital resources in monitoring and controlling activities are possible. Potential payoffs from innovations in the controlling and monitoring activities required for life insurance contracts are hard to estimate but could be large.

Moral hazards in casualty insurance can be classified readily into two types: (1) actions taken before a claim that increase the likelihood of a claim;

and (2) actions that occur after a claim affecting the amount of the claim. Monitoring terms of insurance contracts to reduce the risk of these hazards and implementing control procedures when terms are violated are important value-producing activities for casualty insurance companies. Monitoring these terms can be an expensive capital and labor-intensive business. For example, required on-site inspections of factories or warehouses for compliance with contract commitments may require technical expertise. Assessment of claims may require technical appraisal or even engineering and other expertise to assess. Violations of insurance terms may require expensive legal action.

Some insurance companies develop expertise in certain areas of risk. For example, Hartford Steam Boiler Inspection and Insurance Company provides loss prevention and engineering services to policy holders that keep its underwriting profits, according to one analyst, "the envy of the industry" (*Value Line* 1991). Developing internal expertise in certain areas of insurance risk is the basis for competitive advantage for some casualty insurance companies, who develop and use technical expertise efficiently.

Insurance companies may improve quality or reduce costs of monitoring by using third-party experts. Third-party inspectors can monitor provisions in contracts where the insured is required to take risk-reducing actions. Third-party experts can be used to control costs of claims. Many auto insurance companies, for example, designate certain auto body shops as agents for the determination of the value of damage claimed from auto insurance. As discussed above, the use of third parties in monitoring and controlling insurance claims introduces a principal–agent problem when the third party benefits from the amount of claims.

An alternative to the insurance firm performing its own monitoring and control procedures or using third parties to perform these activities is to use firms offering claims adjustments to the insurance industry. These organizations or firms can be cooperatives of insurance companies or independent companies that depend on the insurance industry for their profitability. Both types of organizations are less likely to take actions adverse to insurance companies from settlement of claims.

Production and Delivery of Insurance Services

Insurance contracts and retirement plans are legal documents and must be produced and delivered, maintained and updated. Execution of these documents is typically part of the sales function. For ordinary life insurance, agents visit insureds in their homes or offices, bringing contracts and obtaining necessary signatures. Insurance agents perform these functions with casualty insurance. With group insurance, employee benefits personnel or company representatives obtain the necessary legal agreements to group policies.

Premiums must be collected and renewals processed. Changes in beneficiaries, coverage, and other contract provisions must be reflected in centralized records. Pension and annuity plans require periodic payments of benefits and continuing contact with beneficiaries. Casualty insurance requires payment of claims.

Making benefits payments presents insurance firms opportunities for cost savings in transaction processing by reducing the costs of holding transaction balances.

Premium collection payments, document control, and updating are typically done in centralized insurance company offices with large clerical staffs and computer systems. These accounting, data storage, updating, and retrieval systems require labor and computer intensive processing. They can be very expensive.

Claims processing function can be produced in a variety of ways. Paying claims is an example of transaction processing as we discussed in Chapter 10. Regional offices or agents can perform these functions or they can be consolidated. Some insurance companies have reduced their labor costs by setting up off-shore operations in countries like Ireland to process paperwork. Computing and communication technology and the evolution of "artificial intelligence" or "expert systems" may allow new efficiencies in claims processing by reducing and relocating labor costs. Some insurance companies are so good at claims processing that they offer services to other insurance providers. For example, Prudential Insurance offers claims processing for medical insurance claims for a variety of insurance providers.

Value in Investment and Risk Management in Insurance

Bearing and shifting actuarial risks is the main source of value produced by the insurance business. We have already discussed the economics of life and property and casualty insurance risks. We have also shown how funding and investing for insurance companies are critical to insurance profitability. Value produced by investing insurance and pension fund premiums and reserves in assets like loans, private placements, or securities is no different from value-producing financial services like credit or portfolio management discussed elsewhere in this book.

11.5 SUMMARY

Life insurance and related products are governed by statistics reflected in the mortality tables. Opportunities to produce value in life insurance services can be found in innovative life insurance and related product designs, although little value can be expected by changing risks of life and death. The greatest opportunities for value creation in life insurance products appear to be in eliminating inefficiencies in marketing, producing, and delivering these products. Property and casualty insurance risks are more susceptible to innovation based on new products that alter and shift risks for consumers and increase their expected welfare. Exploitation of information on risks and preferences related to property and casualty insurance can identify unmet market demands. As with life insurance, many opportunities exist for improved efficiency in the performance of other activities required to provide property and casualty insurance services. The opportunities appear largest in innovations in contract pricing and term setting, marketing insurance, monitoring and controlling claims, and producing and delivering casualty insurance services.

DISCUSSION QUESTIONS AND EXERCISES

1. Calculate the premium necessary to cover benefits paid on a one-year term insurance for thirty-year-old males and females assuming no interest income and no expenses except benefits. Do the same for a five-year term insurance policy. What premium is possible when prepaid premiums can be invested at 10 percent?
2. How much would a male and a female each twenty-five-years old need to contribute to a retirement plan to fund a $1 annuity over their respective expected life spans assuming an investment income of 10 percent? 5 percent?
3. Discuss the advantages and disadvantages of term and endowment policies with changes in inflation and tax rates. What evidence can you find of the effects of these factors on the demand for various life insurance products in Table 11.3?
4. What kinds of property and casualty insurance do you currently have? What are the risks your insurance company faces in terms of likelihood of claims and amount of claims under your policies? How would you go about estimating the risks in order to price these premiums?
5. What kinds of behavior influence the risks discussed in Question 4 or other types of property insurance you can think of? Describe and classify these behavior patterns in terms of asymmetric information, adverse selection, and moral hazard. Can you think of ways not being used by insurance companies to improve on claims cost control?
6. What would be the fair rate of return for a property and casualty insurer if the riskless rate was 5 percent, the risk premium on the market 10 percent, the underwriting beta zero, the expense ratio .2, and the average length of time premiums are invested is one year? What if the beta is 1.2 or .8? What if the expense ratio is .5 or .8? What if the length of time is .5 or 2 years?
7. Contact an independent agent and determine which companies and lines of insurance are handled by the firm. Are there synergies from offering these lines of insurance? What alternative delivery system can you imagine for these insurance products?
8. What kind of information would you use to assess the risks of automobile insurance? What sources can you imagine could be used to find this information?
9. What moral hazard problems are caused by paying insurance sales personnel a salary? A flat commission? A portion of the first year's premium?
10. In what ways are insurance cash flows similar and dissimilar to those associated with deposits?

REFERENCES

American Council of Life Insurance. *1990 Life Insurance Fact Book.* 1001 Pennsylvania Avenue N.W., Washington, D.C. 20004-2599.

Borch, K. 1990. *The Economics of Insurance.* 1990. New York: North-Holland.

Bray, Nicholas. 1994. "Bank-Insurer Merger Is Working Well," *Wall Street Journal,* February 29, p. A9B.

D'Arcy, Stephen P. and Neil A. Doherty. 1988. *The Financial Theory of Pricing Property-Liability Insurance Contracts,* Monograph Number 15, S. S. Huebner

Foundation, distributed by Richard D. Irwin, Inc., Homewood, Illinois.

INSURANCE INFORMATION INSTITUTE. 1992. "The Fact Book: 1992 Property/Casualty Insurance Facts." 110 William Street, New York, N.Y. 10038.

KRAUS, A. and STEVEN A. ROSS. 1982. "The Determination of Fair Profits for the Property-Liability Insurance Firm," *Journal of Finance* 37, (4) (September), pp. 1015-1028.

1992. *Wall Street Journal,* January 28, p. A4.

1991. Value Line Investment Survey, April 12, p. 634.

CHAPTER

12

Asset Management and Information and Advisory Services

Introduction

This chapter completes our review of the six basic financial services by examining the economics of asset management services and information and advisory services. Here we address questions that investment management and financial information firms must consider if they are to prosper in the dynamic environment affecting demand for asset management and information services today.

- What is responsible for the massive growth in the demand for professional fund managers in recent years?
- What do these developments mean for the profitability of asset managers?
- What opportunities are there for value creation in efficient financial asset markets from portfolio management?
- How are the changes in telecommunications and computers influencing the economic role of information and the market for financial information?
- What are the economic determinants of survival for information and investment analysts and appraisers in the "information age"?

This chapter focuses on the relationship between the service providers and their clients. The techniques of providing these services—the state of the art in strategies and techniques used in modern portfolio management—are discussed in Chapters 18 through 21. These techniques are common to all managers of portfolios of financial claims, including managed assets discussed in this chapter and the portfolios of banks, thrifts, and insurance companies.

The technology of information and advisory services is outside the framework of this book. Information gathering, formatting, distribution, and delivery are traditionally problems associated with computers, communications equipment, and traditional journalism.

Of interest to us in this chapter is how providers of asset management and financial information and advisory services produce value for their customers and how they perform activities in the value chains in these financial services.

12.1 TYPES OF INVESTOR/ASSET MANAGER RELATIONSHIPS

Wealth in market economies is owned by individuals or families, as discussed in Chapter 3. Individuals invest their wealth in real assets, like housing and consumer durables, or invest in financial assets, like deposits and corporate securities. Investment management services are provided when savers delegate placement of savings in assets to investment managers. In this discussion, we focus on managers of investments in financial assets. Investment management, asset management, and portfolio management are all terms that refer to the same economic activities.

Investment management consists of five separate functions: (1) determination of risk/return preferences relevant to funds being managed; (2) choice of assets; (3) asset acquisition and safekeeping; (4) monitoring asset and economy performance; and (5) revision of asset holdings as new information and opportunities arise or changes occur in portfolio objectives (see Maginn and Tuttle 1990, Chap. 1, for a description).

Each step in portfolio management can be performed separately. For example, investment advisers can recommend a choice of assets, leaving implementation to the saver or a third party such as a bank trust department. All of the steps can be performed by a single entity, such as a pension or mutual fund manager.

Investment management services, like other financial services, are sold in retail and wholesale or institutional markets. Retail and wholesale markets for asset management are distinguished by whether individuals or corporate or government officials use professional investment managers and make allocations of funds among asset managers.

Retail Market for Asset Management Services

Some lucky individuals have funds from inheritances or gifts. Terms of wills or gifts often name responsible parties, like bank trust departments, as asset managers to manage individual trust funds. Estates of wealthy individuals are often turned over to asset managers until they are settled by probate courts. These two sources of assets form the traditional "trusts and estates" service offered by bank trust departments and trust companies. Since the Deregulation Act of 1980, thrift institutions can also provide trust activities. In 1993, the flow of funds accounts reported personal trusts totaling $619.1 billion in the United States managed by trusts companies and trust departments.

Other well-off individuals do not have the time or training to manage personal accumulations of wealth. Rich people fall into the top of the *retail* market for asset management services. In the United States, middle-class workers save for retirement in the form of Individual Retirement Accounts (IRAs), Keogh plans, and tax deductible retirement savings called 401(k) plans (after the tax regulation covering them). Accumulations of savings in IRAs, Keoghs, and 401(k) plans have grown to substantial sums in the last ten years.[1] Many of these funds find their way to professional asset managers at mutual funds, insurance companies, and other financial institutions providing asset management services.

Individual savers accumulating for future spending such as college educations for children also demand asset management services. Savers with relatively modest accumulations of funds turn them over to professional asset managers by investing in mutual funds and investment companies. As discussed in Chapter 3, assets of mutual funds and money market mutual funds have grown enormously, reaching $1,594 billion by the end of 1992.

Mutual funds are a convenient investment for many savers. Most mutual fund shares can be redeemed in cash (bought back by the mutual fund) for their net asset value (NAV). For example, on January 24, 1995, the NAV for the Fidelity Magellan Fund was $67.79, calculated as the total value of all the investments in the Magellan fund divided by the number of Magellan fund shares outstanding (as discussed in Chapter 3.) NAVs are calculated daily and reported widely in the business press. Mutual fund managers are required to declare an investment objective for each fund they manage: The Magellan fund has a growth objective. Other funds may have dividend income, capital preservation, specific industry or country investments, or other goals.

Institutional Demand for Asset Management

The institutional market for investment management services consists of corporations, governments, universities, and foundations that have funds requiring management for specific purposes. Firms and institutions often lack investment expertise or do not want to manage these funds themselves. Public and private universities, like Harvard and the University of California, hire multiple managers to invest university endowments to pay current bills and finance development in the future. State and local governments, like the California Public Employees Retirement System (CALPERS) and the New York Teachers Retirement Fund, hire many asset managers to invest funds to pay for employee pensions in the future.

The largest and fastest growing accumulation of institutional funds in the United States is corporate and state and local government pension funds. Flow of funds data presented in Chapter 3 show that total financial assets of private pension funds grew from $659.4 billion in 1982 to $2.232 trillion at the end of 1992. State and local government employee retirement funds grew from $260.9 to

[1]401(k) plans alone have $1 trillion in assets in 1993 and will achieve over $5.7 trillion by 2004, overtaking employer-sponsored plans, according to Rose Darby "Trends in 401(k)," in an advertising insert in May 31, 1993 *Fortune*.

$955.0 billion over the same period. Japan, the United Kingdom, Germany, and France reflect similar experiences. The large ownership of corporate stock by pension funds has provoked many broad questions, such as the role of pension funds in controlling corporations.

Some pension funds are managed by corporate or government officials who work directly for the sponsor, full or part time, managing pension fund investments, with a title like "Vice President–Pension Fund Assets." Most governments and corporations with substantial assets in their pension funds choose to delegate management of the funds to one or more professional asset managers. Competition for management of these funds among bank trust departments, insurance companies, and asset-management firms is tough because accumulations of pension funds have potential for large fee income.

Types of Pension Funds and Issues in Fund Management

Pension funds are of two types depending on the pension plan commitments to workers. The first type of pension plan is a *defined contribution* pension plan, where the employer's obligation to workers consists of making specific payments or contributions to workers' retirement accounts. Examples of defined contribution plans are the retirement contributions made by colleges and universities for professors to the Teachers Insurance and Annuity Association (TIAA) and the College Retirement Equities Fund (CREF), two of the largest private pension funds.

Under defined contribution retirement plans, employers make no commitments concerning future benefits. Their obligations are met when the promised contributions have been made. Employers may offer a menu of professionally managed funds to their employees. Because workers are responsible for allocation of plan assets, these plans called *self-directed* retirement plans. With a defined contribution plan, retirees' benefits are determined by the total accumulation of assets workers have in their accounts at the time they convert asset accumulations to retirement income.

The other type of pension plan is a *defined benefit* plan. In these plans, employers guarantee retired workers specific levels of retirement benefits. Defined benefit plans are the predominant way companies or governments and workers negotiate retirement packages in the United States and abroad.[2] Under defined benefit plans, retirement benefits are often tied to years of service and final wage or salary levels. The asset management problems, and risks to sponsors and workers, are very different for defined benefit plans compared to defined contribution plans. In the United States, they are subject to different regulations.

With defined benefit plans, the employer is liable for the future benefits paid. In the United States, employers are required to "fund" these pension liabilities. Conflicts between workers and employers occur when there are disagree-

[2]See Chapter 4 in Maginn and Tuttle (1990) for a discussion of relative growth in defined contribution plans in the United States and see "Tomorrow's Pensions" in the *Economist* (1992) for a survey of funding practices in large industrial countries. Note, for example, that Germany and Japan do not require funding, as do the United States and the United Kingdom.

ments about adequacy of funding levels for future benefits or conflicts in the choice of assets used to fund the plan. Many corporations and governments invest defined benefit plan assets in their own securities or take other actions that may not be in the interests of workers. We discuss some of these principal–agent issues in asset management in following sections.

Efficient Markets and Portfolio Management

Financial economic theory in the last few decades has been influenced by evidence that financial markets are efficient. The objective of asset managers should be to provide maximum returns to their investors for a given level of risk. This goal must be pursued in the face of substantial evidence that has accumulated suggesting it is next to impossible to "beat the market."[3] Efficient market theories and the evidence supporting them do not rule out the possibility that individual asset managers can earn superior returns for their clients. Such claims are heard routinely from asset managers touting the benefits of their services.

It is difficult to measure portfolio performance. Any sports fan or card player understands it is impossible to distinguish a string of good luck from reliable skill. The same is true for an asset manager's performance over finite investment horizons. Despite efficient market theories and evidence, and problems in performance measurement, many corporate and government executives responsible for asset management believe that some managers are better than others.

The most direct impact of efficient market theory on the market for asset management services has been to create a demand for cheaply managed funds that make no effort to beat the market, only to match market performance. So-called *index funds,* as offered for example by Wells Fargo, provide diversified portfolios chosen exclusively to match overall market performance as measured by a market index like the Standard and Poors 500 Industrial Stocks. Asset selection for these portfolios require minimal research, and asset acquisition can be completely or nearly automatic. Index funds usually have the lowest asset management fees.

Index funds offer a *benchmark* against which active asset managers' costs and performance can be measured. Providing benchmark asset returns to measure portfolio performance is an important financial information service discussed later in the chapter. Beating benchmarks or matching them cost effectively is an important goal of asset managers in the face of efficient market theory.

Principal–Agent Problems in Asset Management

Delegating responsibility for managing assets means the beneficiary and the asset manager have divergent interests, creating principal–agent problems as introduced in Chapter 6. In performing each function of asset management, such as

[3]See Sharpe (1981) for a discussion of efficient markets and asset management and any good introductory finance textbook for surveys of the evidence of financial market efficiency (e.g., Ross, Westerfield, and Jaffe 1993).

asset choice or implementation, asset managers (as agents) may exploit their relationship to beneficiaries (principals) to advantage. A simple example of the principal–agent problem is that the asset manager can take a saver's funds and run. The most important problem results from asset managers' incentive to reduce costs or provide low effort service. Other problems are that managers direct funds to investments for other than economic grounds or cheat on reported performance of the asset portfolio.

Asset management functions supplied to individual users of these financial services present several principal–agent problems. Individuals are likely to be more naive or less able to demand a high standard of service. Retail customers may not understand that they are being exploited.

One solution to principal–agent problems in asset management services is government and industry regulation of investment companies, trusts, and investment advisors. Regulation can attempt to prohibit bad behavior by managers. We discuss regulation in Chapter 15. Litigation is also a check against fraudulent behavior or misleading claims and is common; and lawsuits based on the fiduciary or other responsibilities of asset managers are frequent occurrences.

Another limitation to asset managers' willingness to exploit naive clients is fear of losing future business. Reputation is important to the success of asset managers like the Capital Group or Fidelity Funds, and the funds they manage. Loss of reputation is an important threat to an established asset manager's ability to attract customers' funds. Reputation is based in part on reported performance of assets managed by service providers. Funds demonstrating good performance, like Fidelity Magellan fund under the management of Peter Lynch, attract enormous flows of funds, producing large fees for asset management firms.

Given the importance of claims concerning fund performance to current and future customers of asset management services, government regulations cover performance reporting. Disclosures on performance are required in the United States for retail purchasers of investment management services. Firms like Morningside assess performance and provide comparisons of managed assets like mutual funds.

Growth in the retail market for asset management services demonstrates that principal–agent problems can be overcome with regulation, reputation, and penalties imposed by the courts. Nonetheless, clever solutions to problems caused by differing incentives and goals of asset managers and their customers provide continuing opportunities for value production by reducing the expected risks and costs associated with fraud or inefficient performance to users of portfolio management services.

Principal–agent problems in the institutional market are similar to those encountered in the individual market for asset management services. Risk of theft of assets or misrepresentation of management abilities exist in the institutional market. Remedies of regulation, litigation, and loss of reputation are important controls on the ability of asset managers to exploit clients.

The institutional market provides a unique set of principal–agent problems in the case of defined benefit pension plans. Ownership of such a plan's assets is not clear from an economic point of view (see Chapter 4 of Maggin and Tuttle

1990). The plan's sponsors administer the assets but pension obligations are a liability of the sponsor to the workers. For example, if performance of the portfolio backing the pension benefit obligations is above expectations, the pension plan is "overfunded." Who gains from this performance, the sponsor or the workers?

Historic legislation passed in the United States in 1974, the Employee Retirement Income Security Act (1974), called ERISA (discussed in Chapter 16), requires that pension funds be managed "solely in the interest of plan participants." ERISA not only provides ground rules for management of defined benefit plans, it has stimulated demand for professional asset managers. Firms wish to demonstrate responsibility in managing pension plans solely in the interest of the beneficiaries by hiring third-party fund managers.

Laws and courts are concerned with a number of potential conflicts between plan sponsors and beneficiaries. Funds sponsors may manipulate reported income in the way they calculate expenses each year required for contributions to retirement plans. ERISA allows corporate sponsors to take "holidays" from making contributions to "overfunded" plans. Government pension fund plans are not subject to ERISA but governments' pension plans also exposed to principal agent problems. Governments may use tax revenues needed to fund future pension benefits for other uses. Both private and government plan sponsors have an incentive to distort plan performance and understate liabilities implied by promised pension payments.

According to ERISA, company sponsors with defined benefit plans with "excess" funding can remove assets from pension funds and use them in other areas of the business. "Excess" assets can be used to pay cash to owners of the firm sponsoring the plan when the plan is dissolved, as may result from a corporate takeover. ERISA provisions attempt to control principal–agent problems between plan sponsors and workers in defined benefit plans where legal ownership of fund assets are not clear.

Accountants view defined benefit pension plan obligations as an "off-balance" sheet liability of the firm that is offset by plan assets. Disclosure of the extent of under- or overfunding according to the Financial Accounting Standard Board's draft rule No. 87 will standardize reporting of pension liabilities. Standardized accounting rules increase the ability of investors and other stakeholders in the firm to assess the management of the pension plan assets over time.

The economic view of the defined benefit pension plan representing an "off-balance" liability item has implications for the financial management of a firm with a pension fund. Black and Dewhurst (1981) argue that off-balance sheet pension plan financing should consider the tax exemption of returns on pension fund assets. In their view, the firm's high-return taxable assets, mainly fixed-income securities, should be carried as tax-exempt pension plan assets. Assets producing tax-advantaged capital gains should be carried on the firm's own balance sheet. The firm should borrow to fund its pension liabilities to take advantage of tax deductibility of interest at the corporate level. In other words, the firm should use the pension plan as the basis for a tax arbitrage to reduce the cost of labor by paying workers in the form of future pension benefits rather than wages.

12.2 VALUE PRODUCTION IN ASSET MANAGEMENT SERVICES

The six value-adding activities introduced in Chapter 2 are a framework for discussing value production in asset management activities. Rapid growth in demand for asset management services requires a clear definition of both financial service firms' competitive advantage in the asset management marketplace and analytical ability to anticipate and create opportunities out of changing market conditions. In this discussion, differences between the retail and institutional markets must be kept in mind. Equally important is that each function of asset management—portfolio advisement, implementation, and tracking—and each of the six activities can be provided as a package or unbundled. The best business strategy will exploit competitive advantages as discussed in terms of the simple ROI formula introduced in Chapter 2.

Value Production through Pricing and Term Setting

Typical charges for asset management are assessed on the basis of the value of the assets managed. For example, a bank trust department may charge one percent to manage trust assets in portfolios from $200 thousand to $1 million, .75% for $1 to $10 million, and .5% or a negotiated amount over that level. Fees for institutional clients are negotiated and covered by management contracts.

Table 12.1 illustrates various means of calculating management fees. The percent of assets fee structure is illustrated in column (a) using a fixed fee of 40 basis points. The market and portfolio returns for an example asset manager under different future economic conditions as well as the mean and standard deviations of those returns are shown in the first two columns of Table 12.1. With the simple fee structure, the fee is computed as a percent of assets and does not change with portfolio performance.

Management fees must cover all portfolio management functions. Some managers do not report an allocation of management fees and some fund managers separate fees for charged-for functions like advisement, implementation, and record keeping. Fees for performance of all functions depend on the complexity of the assets managed and the amount of funds under management. Complicated assets requiring extensive research, like foreign stocks in emerging economies, or small funds with complicated trust agreements, may be more expensive to manage. Management fees range from more than 1 percent for complex equity funds to a few basis points for large money market funds placed largely in U.S. Treasury securities.

Without proper incentives, portfolio managers may not expend sufficient effort to achieve highest possible performance—a moral hazard problem. One way to shift the risk of underperformance to portfolio managers is to demand that managers guarantee levels of performance above some minimum level, for example two percent above long-term U.S. Treasuries. These commitments shield investors from the risk of low performance and induce asset managers to work harder. Portfolio management techniques discussed in Part III make it possible for asset managers to hedge the risks assumed in guaranteeing minimum performance

TABLE 12.1 Fee Structures for $1 Million Portfolio

		MANAGEMENT FEE				
BENCHMARK RETURN	*MANAGER'S RETURN*	*PERCENT OF ASSETS (a)*	*PERFORMANCE FEE (b)*	*ANALYTICAL FEE CASE (1)*	*ANALYTICAL FEE CASE (2)*	*ANALYTICAL FEE CASE (3)*
–5.00%	0.50%	$4,000	9,100	4,311	3,467	720
0.00%	4.50%	4,000	7,600	4,349	3,493	727
5.00%	8.50%	4,000	6,100	4,375	3,508	732
10.00%	12.50%	4,000	4,600	4,387	3,513	734
15.00%	16.50%	4,000	3,100	4,387	3,508	734
20.00%	20.50%	4,000	1,600	4,375	3,493	732
25.00%	24.50%	4,000	1,000	4,349	3,467	728
30.00%	28.50%	4,000	1,000	4,311	3,432	722
Average Return or Fee:						
12.50%	14.50%	$4,000	$4,263	$4,355	$3,485	$729
Standard Deviation of Return or Fee:						
11.46%	9.17%	$0	$2,910	$29	$26	$5

Fee schedules: (a) simple fee is .4% of assets managed; (b) minimum of .1% of assets managed plus bonus of 15% over benchmark portfolio. Fees related to manager's disclosure of mean and variance claimed for performance: case (1) manager tells truth about performance; case (2) manager claims performance equal to market; case (3): manager claims higher return and lower risk than possible. The formula used is:

Fee = Assets*(1.1*Factor 1 – Factor 1*Factor 2)

Factor 1 = 1.1*log(1 + .04*(Abs(Disclosed/ActualStd.Dev.–1))

Factor 2 = (Portfolio-MarketReturn)^2.

without expending maximum effort, so additional inducements may be required in the management contract. We discuss some of these contract terms below.

Efficient market theory tells us that it is difficult if not impossible for asset managers to earn excess returns above the market-determined risk-adjusted level. In efficient markets, competition pushes management fees to the level of the costs of management plus a normal compensation for invested resources. Departures from fee structures based on costs of asset management plus fair return on invested capital would represent market inefficiencies. If market inefficiencies occur, as is likely given the high fees paid to some managers with mediocre performance, the inefficiencies are probably due to the rapid growth in the market and the time required for beneficiaries to interpret complex information on portfolio performance.

Asset management fees calculated as a percent of assets under management is simple. If markets are efficient and the management contract allows asset withdrawals, this simple fee structure can be a solution to the principal–agent problem due to incentives for managers to reduce cost or reduce effort, or both. Investors withdraw funds from managers who do not perform competitively.

Management fees for open-end mutual funds are competitive for this reason. Investors can withdraw funds at net asset value (NAV) on short notice. NAV is computed as the number of fund shares divided into the market value of assets and is available for most funds daily in the newspaper. Alert investors avoid problems from poor managers by switching funds.

A limitation of management fees computed as a percent of assets is that the incentive for talented or hard-working asset managers to exceed average performance levels is reduced. Some analysts suggest alternative asset-management contracts when portfolio managers have particular talents for identifying undervalued assets and can produce superior portfolio returns if motivated properly. The basic suggestion is to have *performance fees* for asset managers, consisting of a *base fee* (minimum fee) and a *bonus fee* related to the managers' return on the portfolio compared to a benchmark portfolio return (see Davanzo and Nesbitt (1987) for a practical discussion of how performance fees contrast to fixed percent fees under different scenarios). An example of a performance fee structure is shown in Table 12.1, column (b). The manager in the example is paid a minimum fee plus a bonus for beating the market. In the example, the manager beats the market in market loss situations more than in market high situations.

Heckerman (1979) and Bhattacharya and Pfleiderer (1985) examined the implications of alternative compensation contracts for asset managers who know more about market opportunities than savers or other asset managers. A principal–agent problem comes from asymmetric information about investment opportunities. Superior performance measured by returns and variability of returns can be produced by asset managers who have better information on the means and variances of asset returns as the result of research or training and experience. Value creation is possible when superior managers reveal themselves to demanders of management services through pricing of management fees.

Bhattacharya and Pfleiderer (1985) suggest a portfolio manager compensation scheme consisting of payment determined by the portfolio manager's claimed forecast (a precision factor) and reduced by a fraction of the squared difference between the actual portfolio return and the forecasted mean return (a difference factor). Table 12.1 provides examples of such management fee structures. The table shows how asset managers are benefited by revealing their abilities to perform, measured by mean and standard deviations of their returns. The table illustrates how much asset managers under a fee structure following Bhattacharya and Pfleiderer's suggestion would receive under different economic outcomes. When the manager accurately assesses risk/return abilities in case (1) average fees are maximized and are higher than with a base-plus-performance bonus. Case (2) illustrates management fees when the manager claims to match the market, i.e. understating abilities, and case (3) the fees earned when the manager claims a higher return and lower risk. Cases (2) and (3) produce lower fees. The manager has the incentive to reveal true abilities.

Fee structures illustrated in cases (1) to (3) of Table 12.1 induce managers to disclose honestly the variability of returns they can produce. A problem is that standard deviations of returns can only be learned over time. Asset management contracts like those illustrated in the table require careful measurement and monitoring of the manager's performance in order to avoid under- or overpaying for asset management services.

Identifying superior asset managers who accept compensation contracts based on analysis of disclosures and actual performance leads to contract designs more complicated than the simple base and bonus performance contracts described above. Contracts suggested by economic analysis appear to be practical bases for value-producing pricing strategies in asset management services.

A discussion of management contracts is not complete without mention of "soft dollars" discussed in Chapter 9. Many portfolio managers pay brokers commissions above normal rates in order to acquire portfolio advisement or research from the broker or even third parties. There are two possible explanations of this indirect method of compensation for portfolio management services: One is that trading commissions are not scrutinized by beneficiaries of managed funds. Some fund managers may demonstrate superior performance based on third-party research without explicitly reporting costs associated with those services. A second explanation is that including advising with trading commissions may be a superior sharing of risks, as discussed in Chapter 9. In any case, soft dollars are common.

Marketing Asset Management Services

Rapid growth in consumer savings in managed portfolios like mutual funds and self-directed retirement plans in the last few decades means demand for portfolio management has been out of equilibrium with the supply of asset managers. There appear to be inefficiencies in marketing asset management services to the retail market. For example, some mutual funds are marketed directly to purchasers with no sales charge over NAV (so-called *no-load funds*) whereas other similar funds are sold through securities brokers with substantial sales charges (*loads*). The simultaneous existence of load and no-load funds with very similar characteristics suggests marketing inefficiencies.

Mutual funds offer many different risk and return characteristics. They may be managed for long-term growth or current income, for example, by investing in different classes of assets such as bonds, large stocks, or foreign securities. The risk–return properties of these funds must be communicated to retail customers. Ideally, investors' preferences and performance characteristics of funds would match. Description of these characteristics is technical and is an important communication and marketing challenge to the future growth of the retail market for asset management services.

Cross-selling asset management in the form of mutual funds is commonplace in brokerage firms and insurance companies. Some financial institutions, like banks, delayed selling mutual funds to retail customers for regulatory reasons and to protect demand for existing savings instruments, like deposits and insurance. In the United States and Europe, banks are now permitted to sell mutual funds and asset management services in competition or collaboration with established mutual fund managers. Mellon Bank in Pittsburgh bought the asset management firm Dreyfus Corporation for $1.7 billion to expand into managed assets. Increased competition will bring increased efficiency in marketing asset management.

Rapid growth in private and government pensions funds and the requirement that private defined benefit plans be managed solely in the interest of plan participants under ERISA contributed to increases in the demand for professional portfolio managers in the institutional market. Large pension funds are divided among many fund managers for diversification in different markets. Like mutual fund managers, pension fund managers often specialize in categories of assets, like small companies, foreign companies, or fixed-income securities. Sponsors of a $10 billion pension fund could demand as many as 20 or 30 separate fund managers. There is as excess demand for good fund managers.

Marketing institutional asset management services may be as inefficient as the individual market because changing economic conditions can quickly change the demand to portfolio managers specializing in a different class of assets, for example bonds or mortgages. The institutional asset management business has many competitors, but surges in demand for particular expertise produce transitory profits and shortages of managers. Growing and shifting demands for asset management expertise result in a wide range of asset management service providers with very different access to the market, from individuals to large trust departments. Asset managers who improve information on institutional needs and market flexibility in asset management services could create enormous value for providers and users of these services.

Monitoring and Controlling

The burden of monitoring and controlling performance of asset management services falls on plan sponsors or beneficiaries of funds or on the regulatory establishment discussed in Chapter 16. Monitoring and controlling asset managers require performance evaluation, review of portfolio activity, compliance with contractual agreements, and safekeeping and record keeping of portfolio assets. Each of the monitoring and control functions can be performed by separate financial service providers or combined into a single service provider.

Performance measurement is a highly technical area that has spawned the development of a number of firms offering this service for institutional pension plan sponsors, such as Wilshire Associates and SEI. Evaluating returns of a short-term riskless Treasury securities portfolio or a broad market index is not difficult. It is much more difficult to assess performance of more complex portfolios. Allocating returns on risky portfolios above or below the riskless rate to the risk in the portfolio, the skill in asset choices, and the luck of portfolio managers is much harder. In efficient markets, returns above the riskless rate are expected only from risk bearing. Departures of returns from benchmark portfolios due to skill must be determined over time because short-term performance reflects idiosyncratic risks and luck. Complicated mathematical techniques are employed to analyze portfolio managers' performance by specialists.

A source of confusion for naive portfolio beneficiaries is good short-term fund performance from assuming more risk than is desirable. An example is a little old lady or orphan whose assets should be in low-risk bonds but whose manager invests in commodity options. If the manager is lucky, short-term gains may disguise or obscure the risk facing the asset owner. Effective performance monitoring distinguishes superior asset selection from risk bearing and luck.

Trading costs associated with fund management must also be monitored. Churning assets or poor execution of trades can raise trading expenses. Both can result from inefficient fund management or relationships between fund managers and securities traders that disadvantage the portfolio beneficiaries. A number of firms monitor execution prices of trades by different brokers, for example Plexus Group in California. Measured execution costs for trades include commissions and suboptimal prices on securities trades.

Safekeeping and record keeping or *custody* of assets under management are necessary to prevent theft and generate reports necessary for monitoring managers. Separation of portfolio managers from custody of assets is required for mutual funds to control moral hazard in the United States, as discussed in Chapter 16. Trust departments of banks and others perform these activities for fees. Trust departments are responsible as fiduciaries in the legal sense for assets in custody. State Street Boston has made large profits in recent years by keeping and accounting for mutual fund and pension fund assets.

Production and Delivery

Figure 12.1 shows relationships between a fund beneficiary, an asset manager, and a firm providing custody of assets. A custodian that purchases and sells assets following the portfolio managers' instructions is said to have an *agency* relationship with a beneficiary. A financial firm holding assets, making portfolio decisions, and trading securities on behalf of a beneficiary has a *trust* relationship with the beneficiary. Functions associated with producing asset management services can be provided by three separate entities: manager, custodian, and trader.

FIGURE 12.1 Relation between asset owner, manager, and agency

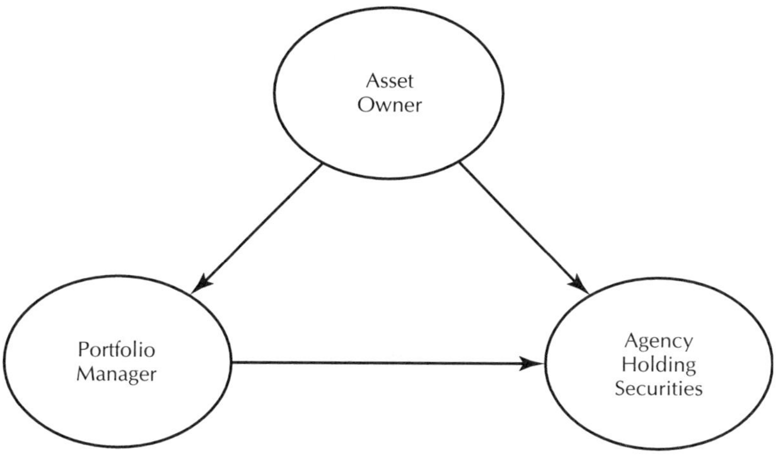

Research and other information-based services could be provided by still other firms. Asset management services can be completely unbundled.

One way of producing and delivering asset management services is to integrate all functions within one firm, as with traditional bank trust departments and insurance companies. It is unlikely that integrated firms can produce and deliver all aspects of asset management equally efficiently. The return-on-investment formula of Chapter 2 ought to guide decision makers in asset management firms in their choice of which services to produce and deliver to the market.

Brokers and trust departments traditionally provide retail customers personal or telephone contact in producing and delivering information, legal documents, reports, and disclosures for managed assets sold or held in accounts with them. Recent developments in the retail market for mutual funds provide clues to the future in the production and delivery of asset management services. Direct mail and electronic communication can be used to establish contact and deliver asset management services. For example, Fidelity Funds is well-known for its use of technology in dealing with its clients.

Departments that produce and deliver research guiding choice of assets can operate in a variety of modes. One low-cost approach is to match market indices without attempting to beat the market, minimizing individual asset research. Researchers working for asset managers use computers to screen databases for assets satisfying predetermined characteristics, such as low price–earnings ratios or high dividend payouts. Asset selection can be virtually automatic given computerized data and standardized software. This approach to producing asset selection decisions is capital intensive rather than labor intensive.

Production of traditional asset choices for portfolios, like that pursued by the Capital Research, depends on sophisticated and highly trained individuals analyzing individual financial assets. Researchers in this environment invest funds or parts of funds directly or work closely with asset managers. These researchers examine data and reports on the industry and on firms they specialize in. They visit firms, go to management presentations, and talk to customers in the market. They write reports and frequently update recommendations. The labor intensiveness and the extensive training and experience necessary mean that production and delivery of asset selections in traditional securities research is expensive.

Rapid growth of managed assets, regulation, technology, changing theories of asset values, and innovations in portfolio management have all contributed to an environment in which the demand for asset management has increased rapidly. Production and delivery of the various functions in asset management services can be fully integrated or completely unbundled. In the long run, efficient producers will dominate the industry, but in the meantime this financial service market appears to be a long way from equilibrium in terms of efficient production and delivery of services.

Funding and Investing and Risk Bearing and Sharing

Asset managers do not take title to assets so funding in general is not a problem for them. One problem facing mutual fund firms is financing obligatory share redemptions at previously recorded NAV when there are market-wide declines leading customers to switch into other investments or cash. Asset managers of redeemable funds face potentially severe liquidity problems if reported NAVs are substantially above the current market value of underlying assets. The funding decision for asset managers is whether to hold precautionary cash or liquid assets at the managed fund level for liquidity needs, thereby reducing fund performance, or holding liquidity at the asset management firm level. The second option requires owners of the asset management firm to assume market risk of assets held by mutual fund customers. Some mutual funds have restrictions on share withdrawals in order to deal with the liquidity problem and the potential funding problem share redemptions on short notice can require. Risk bearing and sharing are portfolio risk management questions that are addressed in Part IV of the book.

12.3 INFORMATION AND ADVISORY SERVICES

Good information identifies assets that are worth more than they cost. Recognition of undervalued assets is the essence of value creation not only in financial services but in the entire economy. Through electronic transmission, information is available faster and in greater quantity than ever before. It can be processed and analyzed quickly with the use of computers. Decisions can be transmitted to relevant markets and actions taken via modern technology and trading systems. The information revolution is a technological revolution in the transmission and analysis of information, but not necessarily in the economics of using good information to identify assets worth more than they cost.

Nearly all financial institutions produce, analyze, and disseminate information. Bank lending officers, for example, acquire confidential disclosures from their customers and use that information to prepare better credit analyses. Relationships between lending officers and other financial service firm professionals, like investment bankers and insurance agents, prevent the disclosure of the information they develop to the public at large. In contrast, the information-based financial services discussed in this section deal with firms and individuals who specialize in obtaining information for sale.

The Technical Information Business

Investors and traders must know prices not only in the market where they trade but in other markets where trading occurs. In order to buy at the cheapest and sell at the highest price, traders need to know what prices other traders in relevant markets are asking or offering. To form expectations about future price movements, investors and traders need to know historical information on prices, trading volumes, and the identity of traders at different locations. All of this is technical information.

One of the most ancient and established methods of disseminating technical information is through periodic newspapers or quote sheets. Well-known examples are the daily tables in the *Wall Street Journal, Investor's Business Daily,* and *Financial Times*. Less well-known services are equally important to financial markets, such as daily *Pink Sheets* published by Commerce Clearing House,

Incorporated. Pink Sheets contain price quotations for roughly 11,000 over-the-counter stocks not traded on the electronic National Association of Security Dealers Automatic Quotation (NASDAQ) system of computer-based electronic quotes for more actively traded issues.

Electronic communication and computers have an enormous impact on sellers of the types of technical information described above. Traditional sources, such as newspapers, are too slow to feed the information needs of traders and investors who are trading electronically 24 hours a day. The NASDAQ system is an example of an electronic system to distribute technical information. In this case, the National Association of Securities Dealers owns and distributes information provided by its members.

Some financial service firms specialize exclusively in selling technical information. For example, Dow Jones and Company, publisher of *The Wall Street Journal,* which foresees declining profits and sales from its newspaper printed with financial tables, has been able to offset declining business with its electronic services: Information Services and Telerate (67 percent owned by Dow Jones). These electronic services deliver technical and other information to computer terminals at traders' and investors' desk (Taylor 1989).

Walk into any trading room and observe the computer screens. Most of the electronic glow comes from bid and ask prices and other trading information sold by a number of technical information services. Telerate specializes in government securities, Information Services provides historical market information. Other well-known services include Blomberg, concentrating in bonds, Reuters Holding from England, specializing in foreign exchange, Quotron, (bought and then sold by Citicorp as part of its foray into information services) with exchange-listed stock quotations, and Knight-Ridder, another newspaper holding company. These firms are among the many vendors of technical information to the financial markets around the world.

The business of providing technical information consists of obtaining and distributing the information. Some information services collect the information from traders and dealers. An example of this is Reuters, which obtains information from traders using Reuters not only for information but for trading purposes. Other services, like the SHARK system, obtain price and trading information from stock exchanges for a fee and distribute the information over telephone lines to computers. Some information vendors provide proprietary software that formats technical information in ways useful to traders and investors. Value added from technical information can come from making data available or by providing a useful presentation of readily available data.

Market Information

Market information is about determinants of the supply and demand of financial services and financial instruments. Market information can consist of information concerning orders or intentions or can consist of detailed surveys and economic analysis. Market information is much harder to define than technical information and comes in many different packages. Some market information is not sold directly to the public but is made available bundled with other financial services. For example, investment bankers develop market information on demand for specific security issuances but make that information available only to customers utilizing their underwriting or securities distribution services.

Some firms specialize in making market information public for a price. For example, the *Bond Buyers Weekly* is a newspaper that specializes in keeping track of offerings of fixed-income securities based on filings with the Securities and Exchange Commission and a reportorial staff that gathers information on forthcoming bond issues. A number of firms specialize in selling information on market conditions implicit in Securities and Exchange Commission filings of intentions to raise funds. One example is *Compact Disclosure,* which publishes summaries of recent filings at the SEC and distributes compact disks containing all the information in those filings.

Market information can be developed by trade organization or specialized analytical firms. For example, the Mortgage Bankers Association keeps track of a number of factors reflecting conditions in the mortgage market by region based on information provided by members. This information is useful in assessing the demand for mortgage originations and performance of mortgage loans. A number of firms, such as A. M. Best and Company, continuously survey a specific financial market to develop an assessment of demand and competition for financial services, in Best's case life and property and casualty insurance. Narrowly focused market analyses are available, like the *Nilson Report* of Santa Monica, California, a weekly newsletter on recent developments in the credit card market.

Market information can be developed for clients by consulting firms. For example, Sheshunoff Data Services provides information on banking markets for clients. The basic information is provided in quarterly call reports for banks. Sheshunov combines this information to make assessments of market competition. Clients of Sheshunov services can obtain general reports sold to many banks or request (and pay for) special reports focused on specific markets or products.

Customer Specific Information

Use of customer specific information is at the heart of value creation in credit services, securities trading, and portfolio management. This information deals with attributes of individual economic entities. Since developing and acting on information having only limited availability enables financial service providers to earn excess returns, this information is often jealously guarded. It is kept confidential until it is in the interest of the possessor of the information to make it public. In some financial services, the value of customer-specific information comes from control of the information, not from selling the information to others.

There may be economies from processing and reporting some customer information, such as financial data for small firms, which make shared customer-specific information valuable. Interpretation of large amounts of data requires sophisticated calculations or economic analysis to reveal the significance to potential users of the information. Data processing, theoretical and analytical skills, and distribution of such information may be efficiently concentrated in specialized firms. Value to users of shared customer-specific information is possible because not all profit opportunities in the information can be realized by a single user.

Retail Customer-Specific Information

Detailed customer specific information is contained in many financial service firms' records. For example, mortgage servicing files, customer applications, and other loan and account records contain information on customers' assets, including housing and autos, other investments, income, nonmortgage debt, and payment history when used in combination. Financial service firms can use this information to market credit, insurance, and investment-related financial services. However, separate and nonintegrated data processing and credit systems have retarded financial service firms from exploitation of their customer-specific information.

A good example of developments in information services related to retail customer specific information is credit histories. In the United States, this information is provided by three firms dominating the market, namely Equifax, Transunion, and TRW. These firms grew out of information sharing by retail stores, banks, and others in local credit bureaus. The growth of national credit cards and the activities of captive finance companies meant that credit histories based on local sources were not complete and required integration of information from a number of sources.

Starting in the 1960s, mass computer storage systems made rapid retrieval and analysis of large amounts of credit data possible. Oddly enough, in the United States retail customer-specific information systems were developed by nonfinancial firms. TRW was an auto parts manufacturer in Cleveland, Ohio. CSC Information Services in Houston acquired other companies to become Equifax Corporation. Transunion started by tracking rail shipments and is owned by the Pritzker real estate developers in Chicago. Credit information is provided directly or through 500 local credit bureaus that have been automated, representing 90 percent of consumers in the United States.

Credit histories come from banks, finance companies, and stores. Computer technology allows using the data to produce individual credit reports in a variety of formats quickly. Computerized databases can prepare lists of consumers satisfying precise criteria. For example, consumers holding three credit cards and paying on time might be used to market a new credit product to low credit risk customers. Revenues for credit information providers come from fees for credit inquiries, production of special lists, and charges from consumers to check their own credit history.

Credit information is not the only customer specific information relevant to identifying potential customers of financial services at the retail level. Insurance applications, major consumer durable purchases, investment activity, and many other consumer financial services produce information useful in assessing the needs and capacities of retail customers.

Mass storage of individual information, errors in that information, and technological feasibility of joining masses of information into refined investigations of individual spending patterns, has made the retail customer-specific information industry a focus of scrutiny and legal disputes in developed economies. Privacy issues concerning gathering and use of customer-specific information will influence the development of financial services based on retail customer-specific information. Modern technology and communications are almost certainly going to continue to generate change and opportunities in this area.

Business and Government Customer-Specific Information

Developing specific information on businesses and governments is much of what reporters uncover and write in articles published in the general, financial, and trade press. Followers of specific industries or public sector activities subscribe to these traditional sources of customer-specific information. The business sections of the national and local press follow the activities of large corporations and important government units. Newspapers and magazines sell because their articles have significance for the future financial prospects or needs of important economic institutions in the community.

Company- and government-specific information services assemble data from a wide variety of sources, including public disclosures like Form 10-Ks filed with the Securities and Exchange Commission, special filings such as 8-Ks announcing special corporate events, annual reports, financial market results, press reports and press releases, and forecasts published by a variety of analysts. Most services provide frequent updates with more recent public announcements and disclosures and financial market data.

Company- and government customer-specific information services have been transformed by computer and communications technology. In the United States, SEC disclosure data are available in computerized form in a variety of formats. The data are available on computer tapes from providers like Standard and Poor's unit, Compustat. On-line time-sharing data information services sell access to the SEC filings through Disclosure, Incorporated, which has the contract with the SEC to store the data on computers. Compact diskettes are available with filings or Compustat data. For example Lotus Corporation makes available a variety of corporate data and information series in spreadsheet formats.

Competition for data and the ability to sell it is intense. Bechtel Corporation, an engineering firm, won a contract with the SEC by bidding against incumbent Disclosure, Incorporated, for renewal of a contract with the SEC to computerize and distribute filings. Bechtel sold the business back to Disclosure who wanted to continue in the business.

A number of financial service firms in developed countries undertake sustained data collections and analysis of companies and governments and evaluate their financial performance. These firms specialize in developing and analyzing customer-specific information and use publicly disclosed financial data on traded firms, like those for financial service firms mentioned in Chapter 4, and large state and local governments. Creation of customer-specific data bases in emerging market economies may offer special information service opportunities in the future. This information is scrutinized by investment advisory services, financial research operations in brokers, and other financial firms like rating agencies.

Traditional investment advisory services provide periodic collections of financial information for large corporations. An example is Dun and Bradstreet Corporation's Moody's Investors Services. Moody's produces *Moody's Industrial Manual* and *Moody's Bank and Finance Manual* in competition with McGraw Hill Publishing Company's subsidiary, Standard and Poors, which publishes *Stock Guide* and *Bond Guide*. Value Line Publishing Company's weekly service, *Value Line Investment Survey*, is another well-known advisory service in the United States.

Specific information on smaller firms and privately held companies is also the object of extensive data collection and analysis. For example, Dun and Bradstreet collects basic financial data on 9.5 million small businesses (Roberts 1989). Gathering this massive amount of information is not dissimilar to the task in the retail market. Indeed, TRW, the consumer credit information firm, is a competitor of Dun and Bradstreet. Financial records and credit histories of small companies vary in quality and availability. Small businesses have many account relations that are less concentrated than consumer credit provided by financial institutions and retailers. Dun and Bradstreet relies on credit reporters to gather information from a variety of sources. This information is available in a wide variety of formats, such as periodicals summarizing ratios, company specific credit reports, and lists satisfying certain criteria.

The wealth of information on publicly traded corporations and governments available through traditional means such as newspapers and periodicals and new technologies such as on-line computerized databases and diskettes for use on computers is familiar to most business students. As we have seen, some of the entrants into the business providing raw information, like TRW and Bechtel, have not been traditional financial service firms but are technology-oriented companies. Our discussion concentrates on information consisting basically of text and numbers. Value added in information-based financial services may come from cost advantages in entering, storing, and retrieving a variety of information types in computers and in communicating that information to users.

Information versus Advice

There is a fine line between obtaining and distributing data and advising clients on the significance of that information. A credit report from TRW or Dun and Bradstreet that shows a lot of delinquent debt is pure information. The conclusion that the individual or firm has a low credit rating contains advice: do not extend credit. The line between information and advice is crossed when the analysis accompanying the data goes beyond reformatting raw information and contains a recommendation.

Like most financial services, information and advice can be provided separately or in combination. For example, *Value Line* provides raw information on 1700 publicly traded companies and combines that information with a recommendation in the form of a ranking of firms from 1 (best) to 5 (worst). Dun and Bradstreet provides credit rankings of the firms in their service and its ratings are one major reason customers use the service (and a major reason firms reported on and customers have complained about the quality of Dun and Bradstreet (Roberts 1989).)

Information and advice or analysis are often unbundled. Rating agencies, most prominently Standard and Poors and Moodys, provide rankings of the quality of securities issued by firms based on their analyses of data. A large quantity of publicly traded corporate and state and local government debt is rated by one or both of these two agencies. Credit ratings assigned to each individual bond issue, such as AAA for low risk and C for risky, are used by investors and regulators in assessing risk of debt instruments.

Bonds with rankings below a certain level, such as Baa, are not considered as "investment grade" by some regulators and cannot be purchased by regulated firms like insurance companies. Below-grade or nonrated bonds are "junk bonds." Firms pay to have a credit rating because high ratings reduce debt costs and some investors will only invest in rated securities. Review and downgrading of a bond issue by ratings agencies lower its value (Herman 1989).

An important source of investment advice unbundled from raw information is brokerage firms. Brokerage houses like Merrill Lynch, Morgan Stanley, and Goldman, Sachs and Company, maintain large research units devoted to analyzing information distilled into "buy", "hold", or "sell" recommendations. Brokerage firms provide the results of their research in the form of reports or buy and sell suggestions to customers in exchange for their securities trading business. They recover their research costs through the profits gained from brokerage trading commissions stimulated by their research recommendations as discussed in Chapter 9. Investor advisory services provided by this research is bundled with trading services.

The market for investment research has become much more competitive, especially since the deregulation of brokerage commissions on Mayday, 1975. For example, in 1989 the Allstate Insurance Company demanded that the major brokerage houses it used price the research they provided explicitly. Allstate indicated that it intended to reduce the amount of research it paid for by monitoring costs and performance of the research it used (Torres 1989). Large institutional investors increasingly want explicit charges for research rather than bundled research and trading.

Investment advice or recommendations are also available on a wide variety of investments from individuals or small research firms. Investment newsletters abound. There are newsletters with recommendations about over-the-counter stocks, penny stocks, and special situations. Recommendations are based on fundamental stock analysis or patterns in stock prices. The list of advisory services is endless. Supply is limited only by the imagination of analysts.

A continuum of investor services extends from raw information to complete management of an investor's portfolio. There is no distinct line separating asset management from financial information services. The border is crossed at the point where the investment manager has control over the assets managed and the financial service firm is compensated by measures directly related to the investor's portfolio performance which is completely under the control of the manager. Advisory services giving persuasive advice to investors are not managing assets. Although the line is not distinct, there is clearly an economic distinction between the types of value added and the activities required to provide information and manage assets.

Value Production in Information Services

As our description of the market for financial information reveals, communications and computer technology revolutionized the demand and supply of different types of information. Value production in the information industry is based on producing a product for less than it costs in sufficient volume to earn satisfactory returns on investment. What differentiates information services from other financial services is the ephemeral nature of the relationship between the supplier and the user of the service.

The short-term nature of the relationship between information supplier and user is based on two elements: (1) information by its very nature must be updated to be worth something, old information loses its value rapidly; and (2) technology is changing rapidly and new types of data and new data production and delivery mechanisms occur with amazing frequency. Long-term relationships simply are not the practice. Financial newspaper and magazine subscriptions always are short term. Even established relationships, like that between Quotron and stock brokerage firms, are severed when contracts come up if the level of service is not competitive, as happened in June 1992, when Quotron lost several established client relationships to an affiliate of Reuters.

Value production from pricing, marketing, monitoring, and producing information are not different from nonfinancial firms. Efficient and timely production and distribution of financial information to meet changing needs are critical to the production of value in information services.

12.4 SUMMARY

Asset management and information-based financial services have grown enormously in the recent past. Markets for these services may be further from equilibrium than the markets for other financial services discussed in this book, meaning that opportunities for profits and losses are greater. Movement toward equilibrium relationships between service providers and demanders requires managers to focus on sources of value they can offer to the market. Innovations in product technology beyond the scope of this book will drive many market adjustments. Managers must focus on where their firms have a competitive advantage. In asset management services, pricing and term setting, marketing and information, production and delivery, and monitoring and control all offer possible advantages and innovations producing value for customers and service providers. In information services, these factors appear to be less important than quick recognition of changes in demand for information or information technology. Short-run profits from innovation in the marketplace is the main value from information-based services.

DISCUSSION QUESTIONS AND EXERCISES

1. Trace the growth in assets under management in the United States using the flow of funds tables in Chapter 3. Has the pace of growth and the share of the market for management of different types of portfolios changed or stayed roughly constant?
2. Examine business publications like the *Wall Street Journal, Fortune,* etc., to determine (1) advertisements and (2) news stories concerning asset management services relating to pension funds or mutual funds. Characterize these stories in terms of the issues raised in this chapter concerning principal–agent problems and value production in asset management.
3. Obtain a period financial statement from a mutual fund and determine the portfolio management fees and other costs to owners from fund management as a percent of assets.
4. Find advertisements, promotional materials, or stories in the financial press concerning mutual funds and compare their performance as measured by return on assets. Discuss the reasons for the differences in returns and relate these differences to the three determinants of portfolio performance discussed in this chapter.
5. What kind of risk/return tradeoffs would be appropriate for savings for retirement by a 25 year old? A 50 year old? A 65 year old? What determines the differences in your assessments? What kinds of savings vehicles are appropriate and how would you market to these different groups?
6. Contact a deposit-taking institution, a broker, and an asset management firm or insurance company concerning products available for IRAs, Keoghs, and 401(k) plans. Contrast the marketing strategies and comparative advantage of these different savings vehicles for smaller retirement funds.
7. Find a recent copy of *Nelson's Directory of Investment Managers* and pick five investment managers at random. Discuss their different size in terms of employees, assets under management, and organization. Can you pick any patterns in the types of managers and the types of funds managed?
8. Read carefully the tables in the *Wall Street Journal* containing price and volume information on trading in securities or other financial instruments. What are the sources of their quotes? Why would current information be of value to traders? Who would pay for current trading information and how could it be delivered or is it being delivered to users?
9. What kind of information could be used to predict the demand for financing for children's college education costs? Where could such information be found in the records of financial institutions? How could it be made available to lenders in education loans?
10. Cellular phone and beeper technology have been exploited for securities market traders in terms of instantaneous

availability of quotes and orders for trades. Could such technology be used in the market for retail credit? Why or why not?

REFERENCES

BHATTTACHARYA, SUDIPTO and PAUL PFLEIDERER. 1985. "Delegated Portfolio Management," *Journal of Economic Theory* 36, pp. 1–25.

BLACK, FISCHER and MORAY DEWHURST. 1981. "A New Investment Strategy for Pension Funds," *Journal of Portfolio Management,* 7 (Summer), pp. 26–34.

DAVANZO, LAWRENCE E. and STEPHEN L. NESBITT. 1987. "Performance Fees for Investment Management," *Financial Analysts Journal,* January/February, pp. 14–20.

Economist. 1992. "Tomorrow's Pensions," June 20, pp. 19–21.

HECKERMAN, DONALD G. 1979. "Motivating Managers to Make Investment Decisions," *Journal of Financial Economics* 2, pp. 272–292.

HERMAN, TOM. 1989. "Downgrading the Credit-Rating Services," *Wall Street Journal,* June 23, p. C1.

MAGINN, JOHN L. and DONALD L. TUTTLE, eds. 1990. *Managing Investment Portfolios: A Dynamic Process,* Second Edition, sponsored by The Institute for Chartered Financial Analysts, Warren, Gorham and Lamont, Boston.

ROBERTS, JOHNNIE L. 1989. "Dun's Credit Reports, Vital Tool of Business, Can Be Off the Mark, *Wall Street Journal,* October 5, p. A1.

ROSS, STEPHEN A., RANDOLPH W. WESTERFIELD, and JEFFREY F. JAFFE. 1993. *Corporate Finance, 3rd ed.* Homewood: Irwin.

SHARPE, WILLIAM F. 1981. "Decentralized Investment Management," *Journal of Finance,* XXXVI (2), pp. 217–234.

TAYLOR, ALEX III. 1989. "A Tale Dow Jones Won't Tell," *Fortune,* July 3, p. 100.

TORRES, CRAIG. 1989. "Challenge to Wall Street: What's Research Worth?" *Wall Street Journal,* December 4, p. C1.

CHAPTER

13

The Economic Environment

Introduction

Wild swings in interest rates, regulation, and international flows of funds in the last few decades have been daily concerns of financial institution managers and their customers.

- What would the economy and the demand for financial services be like if economic growth and changes were smooth and predictable?
- What are the sources of the economic risks we spend so much of our time managing?
- What are the implications of government policy on the risks to financial institution managers?

The importance of these questions cannot be overstated in the current environment for financial services and in view of the recent past.

This chapter places financial institutions in the context of the macroeconomy. The discussion is intended to provide perspective on recent events and form the foundation of an analytical assessment of important economic factors in the future. The chapter begins with a conceptual discussion of long-run economic equilibrium and then relates this concept to the risk environment we actually observe. This framework is used to explore and assess the sources of risk and economic change facing managers of financial institutions from changes in the real economy, macroeconomic policy, and regulation.

13.1 ECONOMIC ENVIRONMENT AND FINANCIAL INSTITUTIONS

Value produced by financial service firms comes from their ability to intermediate differences in the time preferences, investment opportunities, and risk preferences of businesses and households in the economy. Financial institutions and decision-making units in the economy have different degrees of technical, market, and customer-specific information available to them, sometimes causing information asymmetries and principal–agent problems. Services provided and activities performed by financial institutions create value by resolving the problems that prevent efficient allocation of resources between decision-making units as described in the chapters of Part II.

This and the following chapters are aimed at an assessment of the economic environment as it impinges on the ability of financial service firms to produce value. The approach followed is to review the macro and microeconomics elements useful to financial institution managers for assessing the risks and opportunities facing them. The objective is to focus attention on factors in the economy that affect the profitability and risk of providing financial services in the future and to clarify which elements of the environment are manageable and which are beyond management control but must be dealt with. This treatment does not present economic theories but uses current economic and financial thinking to focus attention on key issues for managers of financial institutions.

Equilibrium

Most economic thinking begins with the concept of equilibrium. Equilibrium is an idealized state of an economy where all economic forces resulting from tastes and endowments of economic agents are in balance. Supply equals demand in all markets. Economists distinguish short-run and long-run equilibria. In the short run, temporary departures from ultimate market clearing levels of economic values occur in response to temporary or transitory economic events. In this section, we are thinking in terms of the long-run equilibrium that would occur if all important economic variables were constant or growing at constant rates and no disturbances interfered with achievement and maintenance of equilibrium.

In economic analyses of equilibrium, households and businesses act independently. In making their decisions, they formulate plans and implement them using all information available to them. To the extent that future levels of economic variables can be anticipated accurately, decision makers incorporate *expectations* into their plans. If decision makers know the way the economy works, they use their expectations to construct *rational* plans for consumption and investing in the sense that plans are consistent with their understanding of the economy and expectations are consistent with available information. This characterization of the economy and the long-run steady state of the economy is called *rational expectations* equilibrium. Rational expectations are simply the macroeconomic counterpart to efficient markets used to analyze financial markets.

In a *steady state* long-run equilibrium, levels of economic activity, prices, and interest rates persist or grow at constant rates. Supply and demand are the same each period or grow at a predictable rate. Prices are unchanging or change in predictable ways. There are no unexpected opportunities to improve utility or economic efficiency by arbitraging across time or geography. Actions of economic agents next period and their actions of last period are related in predictable ways.

Predictable and reliable demands and supplies of economic quantities from all decision makers must be observed in *all* markets to achieve such a tranquil economic environment. Factors affecting supply and demand must be changing in a predictable fashion. For individuals and households, *tastes* and *preferences* vary according to predictable patterns, for example as people age and move through their life cycles. Levels of *wealth* and *productivity* change predictably, with predictable increases in skills and productivity producing anticipated accumulations of *human* and *physical capital. Technology* evolves in conformity with these predictable changes. *Demographic* shifts affecting the age of various cohorts of the population are stabilized and predictable.

In our equilibrium economy, growth in total sectoral balance sheets or portfolios introduced in Chapter 3 takes place. There is no need for sudden changes in portfolio balance requiring securities trading and liquidity. Allocation of savings between real and financial assets remains constant or changes predictably because rates of return are unchanging or changing at anticipated equilibrium rates. Financial services required by savings and portfolio management also change at predictable rates.

To trace the implications of an equilibrium economy on economic magnitudes of particular interest to financial institution managers, assume a constant distribution of age groups in an equilibrium economy. Gross domestic product (GDP) and other macroeconomic variables grow at the rate of population growth and the rate of productivity improvement suggested by technological change. In the United States for example, these growth rates would be in the range of 1.3 percent for population and .8 percent for technological change.[1] In contrast, the average real growth rate in the U.S. economy has averaged 3.1 percent from 1950 to 1990.[2]

An equilibrium economy requires predictability of government policy. The economic equilibrium we are envisaging requires that government expenditures and taxes, that is *fiscal policy,* and the growth rate of money, *monetary policy,* change predictably. Monetary and fiscal policies can *grow* in our placid economy but they must grow predictably, meaning unchanging and perfectly forecastable government policies. For example, in one conceivable equilibrium economy, the level of government expenditures as a percent of GDP does not change and government budgets are always balanced. The impact of government policy does not change through time. If monetary growth is equal to long-term equilibrium growth in production, for example using our illustrative 2.1 percent annually, there would be no inflation.

[1]Rate of technological change is that estimated by Solow (1957) and cited and reestimated by Plosser (1989.) In order for the equilibrium economy to grow at the rate implied by the sum of these two number, 2.1 percent per year, each age group must grow at the same rate, meaning immigration and birth rates to produce this unlikely outcome.

[2]The difference between the actual and implied growth rates comes from many factors, including increased labor participation by women and increased immigration disproportionately in working-age demographic groups. Neither of these changes is an equilibrium phenomenon.

A long-run equilibrium economy may have risks. Risk of default on loans or failure of investment projects is possible in such an equilibrium if the economy is sufficiently complex for these risks to be diversified and distributed among savers and financial institutions at bearable levels. Risks are measurable with great precision and prices for financial services and interest rates on risky assets adjust to account for expected losses. Risk premiums are constant or grow at predictable rates. In an equilibrium economy with risk, some savers liquidate savings for planned or unplanned cash requirements, but an offsetting supply of cash is available from other savers at different points in their life cycles or experiencing unexpected windfalls.

Long-Run Equilibrium and Financial Service Firms

Financial institutions have a role in an equilibrium economy. Savers demand financial intermediation and the financial services discussed at length earlier in the book. The flow of savings from consumers is channeled to investors through deposit-taking and insurance intermediaries that provide credit, transaction processing, and insurance services. Savers acquire direct claims on firms and entrust assets to asset managers. Governments and firms raise funds from securities markets, requiring services of securities firms and information services. Because economic factors that affect households and firms, such as wage rates and prices, change predictably, savings flows into financial firms are predictable. Business demand for funds for investment is likewise predictable because interest rates and economic activity are changing in predictable ways.

The equilibrium path of any economy is determined by the following: (1) demographics (age, regional distribution, and population growth); (2) tastes and preferences of economic decision makers; (3) wealth (mainly physical capital and human capital); and (4) the rate of change of technology. These fundamental determinants of an equilibrium economy are determined by culture, the level of development of social institutions, including institutions devoted to the study of science and technology, and history and geography.

Fundamental determinants of the equilibrium path of the economy do change. They change gradually, according to a clock better measured by decades than seconds. Financial institution managers must understand forces driving an economy toward equilibrium to anticipate demand for certain services. For example, fundamental determinants of a growing economy imply the growth rate of wealth. Services associated with gathering and investing savings increase with growth in the economy. Demand for securities trading is a predictable by-product of the liquidity needs of savers as they move through the life cycle and random liquidity needs arise among individual saving units.

Our analysis of the demand for financial services in an equilibrium economy can identify those financial services for which demand would be reduced. Trading in financial assets would be reduced since there are no arbitrage opportunities. Risk management associated with fluctuations in economic activity and price and interest rates is no longer needed. Entire markets and institutions for trading and originating some financial instruments, such as financial futures, options, interest rate and currency swaps, are not necessary. Demand for advice, assistance in portfolio diversification, and technical and market information would certainly decline since most change is predictable. Methods for saving and investing in the face of economic uncertainty are unnecessary. Many services provided by financial firms are unneeded in the idealized equilibrium world.

The Real World

Disturbances driving an economy away from its long-run equilibrium path cause risks for economic decision makers. Short-run adaptions and risks due to unexpected disturbances in the economy are major elements affecting the demand and supply of financial services. With unpredictable economic disturbances, decision makers must still make plans, but now plans must account for unforeseen events.

Unforecastable disturbances make life harder but planners still integrate information and knowledge of the economic system to formulate plans based on *rational expectations*. Information available to decision makers in the real world includes not only levels and expected growth rates of key economic variables but also expected variability. Variability measures represent risk assessments of economic magnitudes.

Figures 13.1 to 13.3 display representative economic variables measuring the state of the U.S. economy. Panel A of Figure 13.1 shows inflation-adjusted Gross National Product (GNP), aggregate hours worked and industrial production, since 1900. GNP and the now more widely used Gross Domestic Product (GDP) both measure output but GDP measures all output produced in the United States whereas GNP measures output produced by American owned firms. Panel B shows GNP divided into its components—consumption, government expenditures, and investment—since 1950, again adjusted to remove the effect of inflation and real GNP growth rates.

A look at these figures makes clear that these economic series are anything but smooth and predictable. Understanding the causes of random movements in economic variables is essential to managers of financial institutions for formulating short-run and long-run strategies. Some broad characterizations of these real economic data can be noted. First, the Great Depression (1929–1939) was unique in the extent of decline in the economy. Second, substantial variation is observable in all the variables, although consumption varies less than the others. Finally, recent decades conclude an unusually long sustained growth period in GNP. Overall, with the exception of the Great Depression, the mean and variability of these series do not seem to be changing all that much, despite the greater understanding of economics of businessmen and policy makers.

Panel A of Figure 13.2 shows the rate of inflation measured by the consumer price index in the United States since 1950 and Panel B the level of short-term interest rates from 1930. Figure 13.2 demonstrates a shift in the economic series. Except for a brief flare-up in inflation after the Korean War in the 1950s, inflation and interest rates became much higher and have had more year-to-year variability starting in late 1960s. Relative to most U.S. experience, the period from the late 1960s to the late 1980s can be characterized as the Great American Inflation.

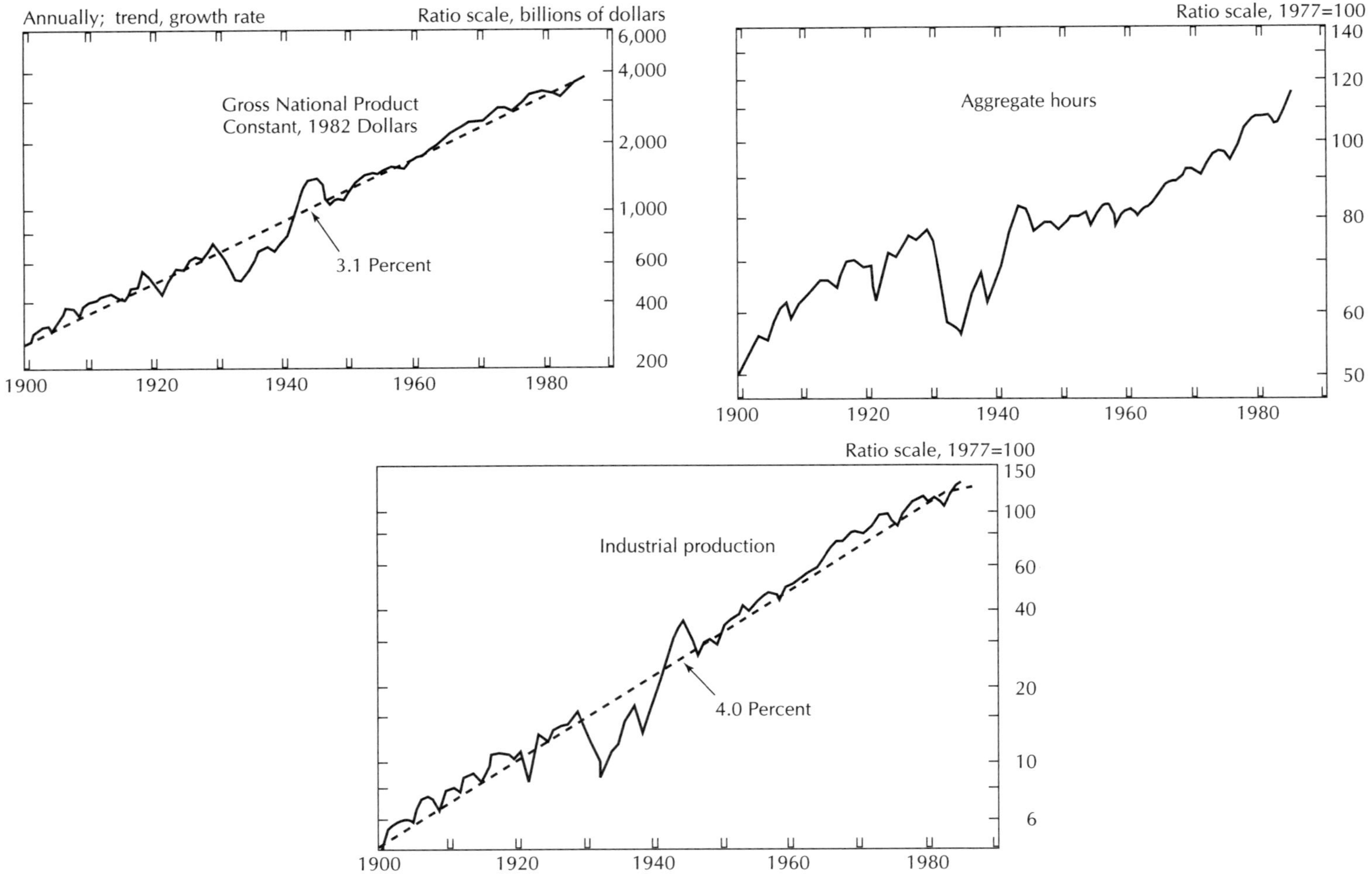

PANEL A: REAL GNP, INDUSTRIAL PRODUCTION, AND AGGREGATE HOURS WORKED

FIGURE 13.1 Measures of real economic activity in the United States

SOURCE: Board of Governors of the Federal Reserve System, *1988 Historical Chart Book*, p. 10.

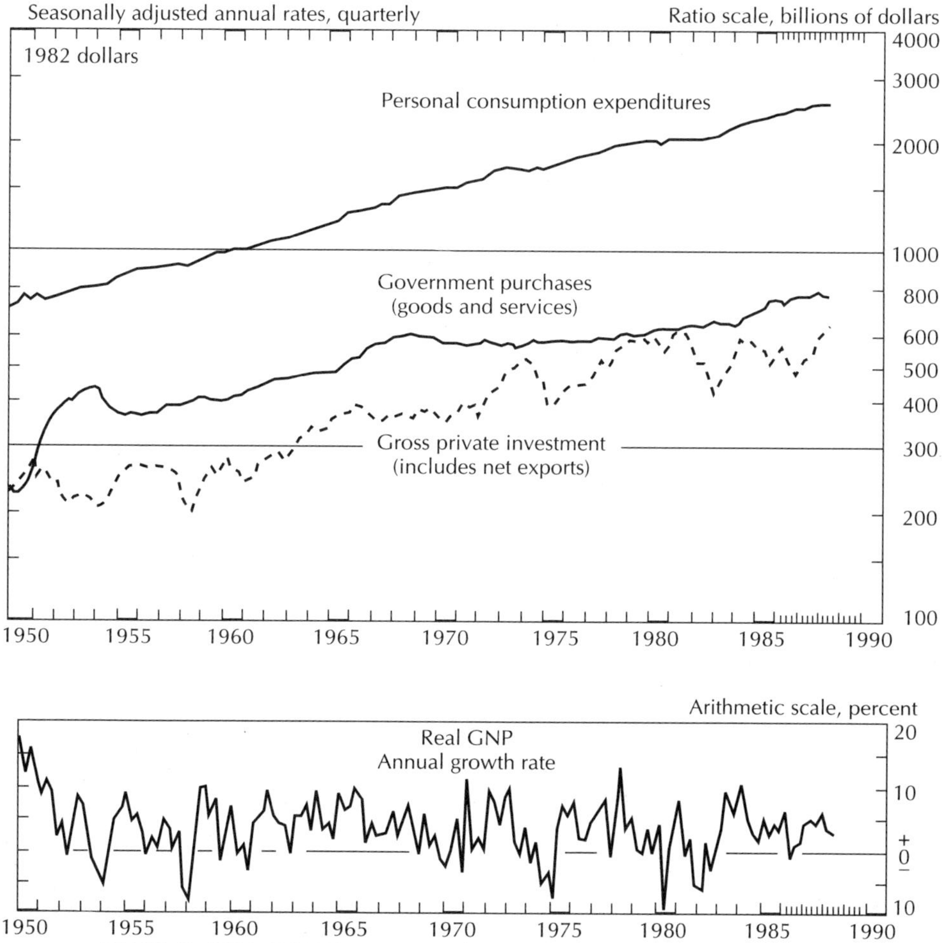

PANEL B: REAL CONSUMPTION, INVESTMENT, AND GOVERNMENT EXPENDITURES AND REAL GNP GROWTH RATES

SOURCE: Board of Governors of the Federal Reserve System, *1988 Historical Chart Book,* pp. 12,13.

Panel A of Figure 13.3 shows current account balances (mainly exports minus imports) since 1950, and Panel B depicts the U.S. dollar exchange rates against a variety of foreign currencies since 1980. The current account balances hovered above zero with no apparent trend until 1971 when they began to go sharply negative, reaching a bottom in 1987. The increase in the level and variability of inflation combined with growing trade deficits starting in 1965 created the necessity of shifting from fixed exchange rates to flexible exchange rates in 1973. The result is the variability in exchange rates seen in Panel B of Figure 13.3.

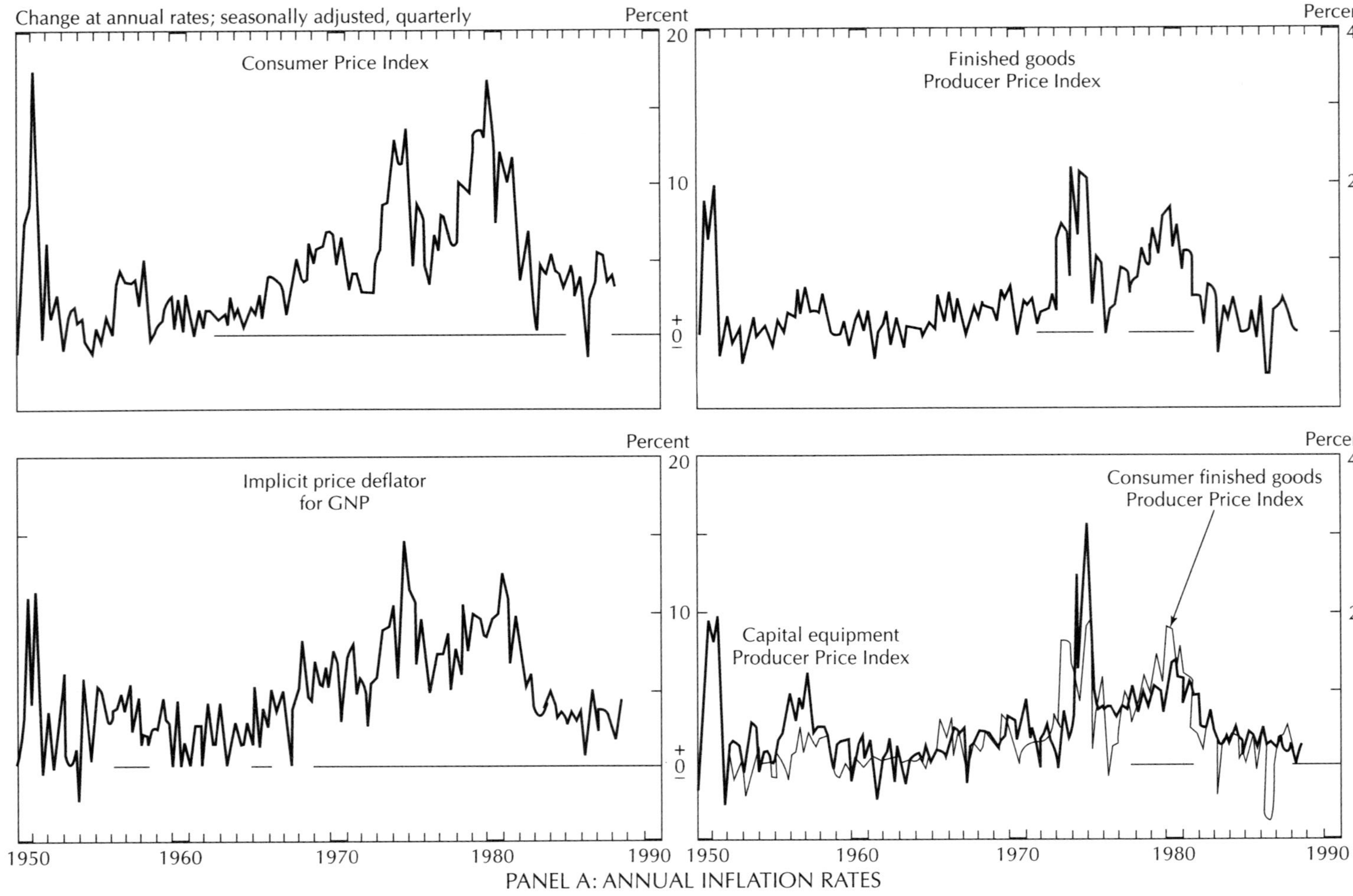

FIGURE 13.2 Interest rates and inflation rates

SOURCE: Board of Governors of the Federal Reserve System, *1988 Historical Chart Book*, p. 37.

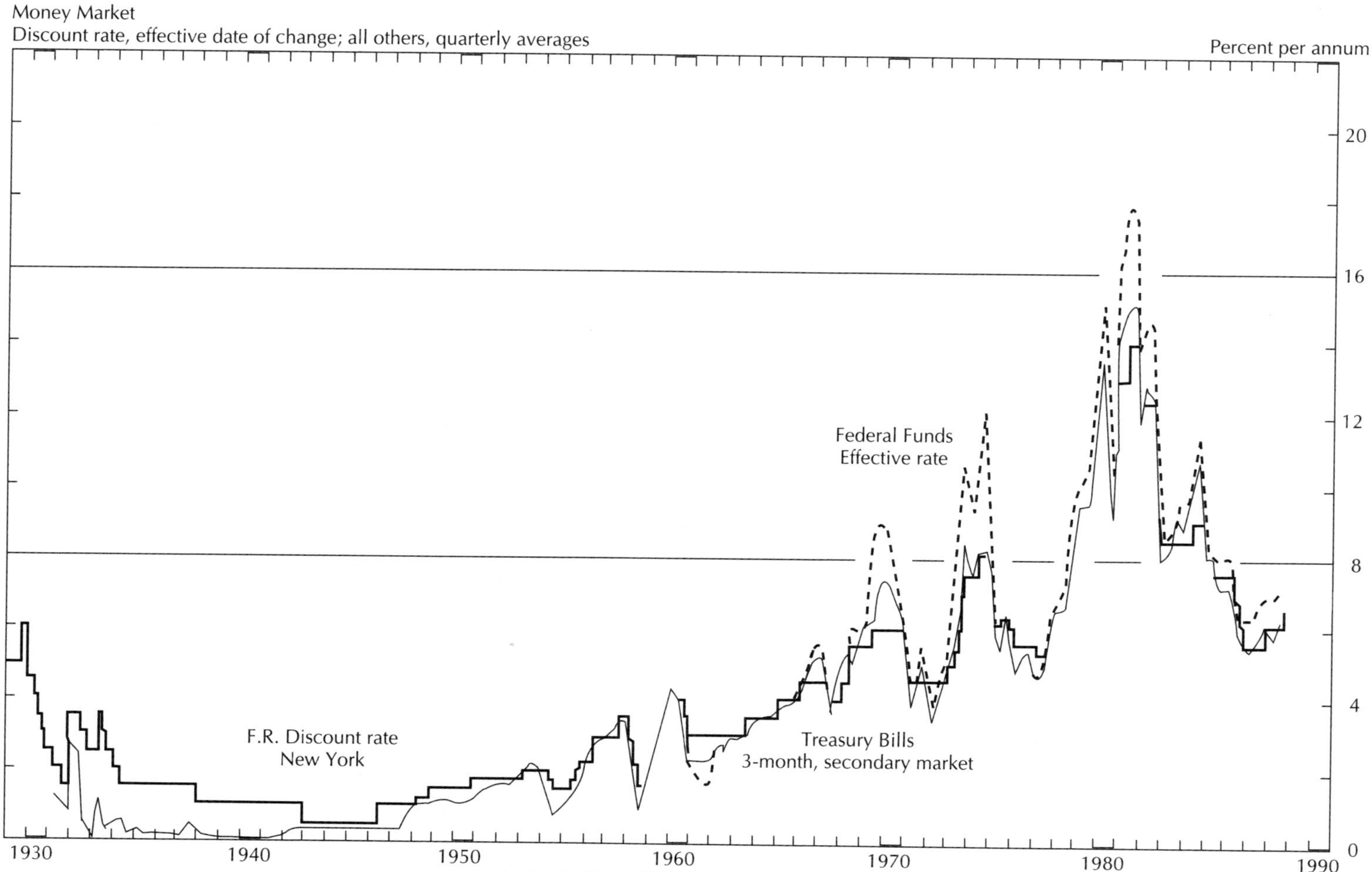

PANEL B: SHORT-TERM INTEREST RATES

SOURCE: Board of Governors of the Federal Reserve System, *1988 Historical Chart Book*, p. 98.

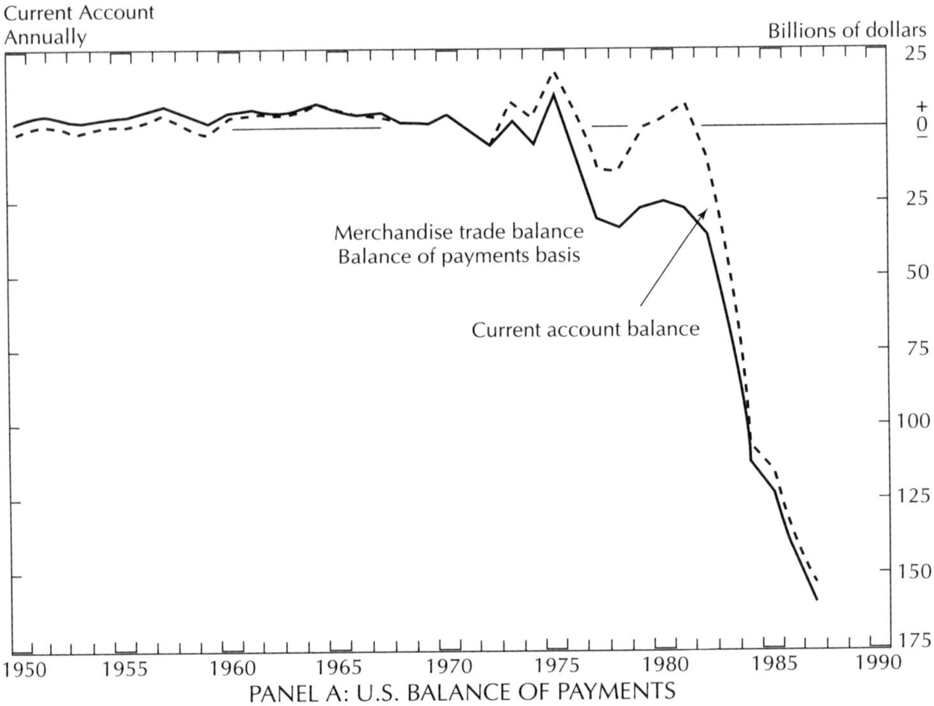

FIGURE 13.3 U.S. balance of payments and dollar exchange rates

SOURCE: Board of Governors of the Federal Reserve System, *1988 Historical Chart Book,* p. 100.

Sources of Variation and Noise in the Economy

Variation in economic time series is the subject of a great deal of economic analysis. One strain of economic thought concerned with economic fluctuations is *real business cycle* analysis, which analyzes the economy assuming the effectiveness of markets in balancing supply and demand in the real and financial markets. This brand of economics is influential in economic policy analysis and focuses on sources of unexpected variations in economic activity. Unexpected variations result in risks to economic decision makers. Sources of variations must be understood in order to assess the impact of changes in the environment on the supply and demand for financial services.

Real business cycle economists think in terms of *shocks,* defined as unexpected and unpredictable changes in economic variables and their effects on the macroeconomic system. Shocks come from unexpected events, like variations in weather, unanticipated technological breakthroughs, wars, and so forth. Economists classify shocks into *real* shocks and *monetary* or *financial market* shocks. We define these terms and examine the sources of these shocks below.

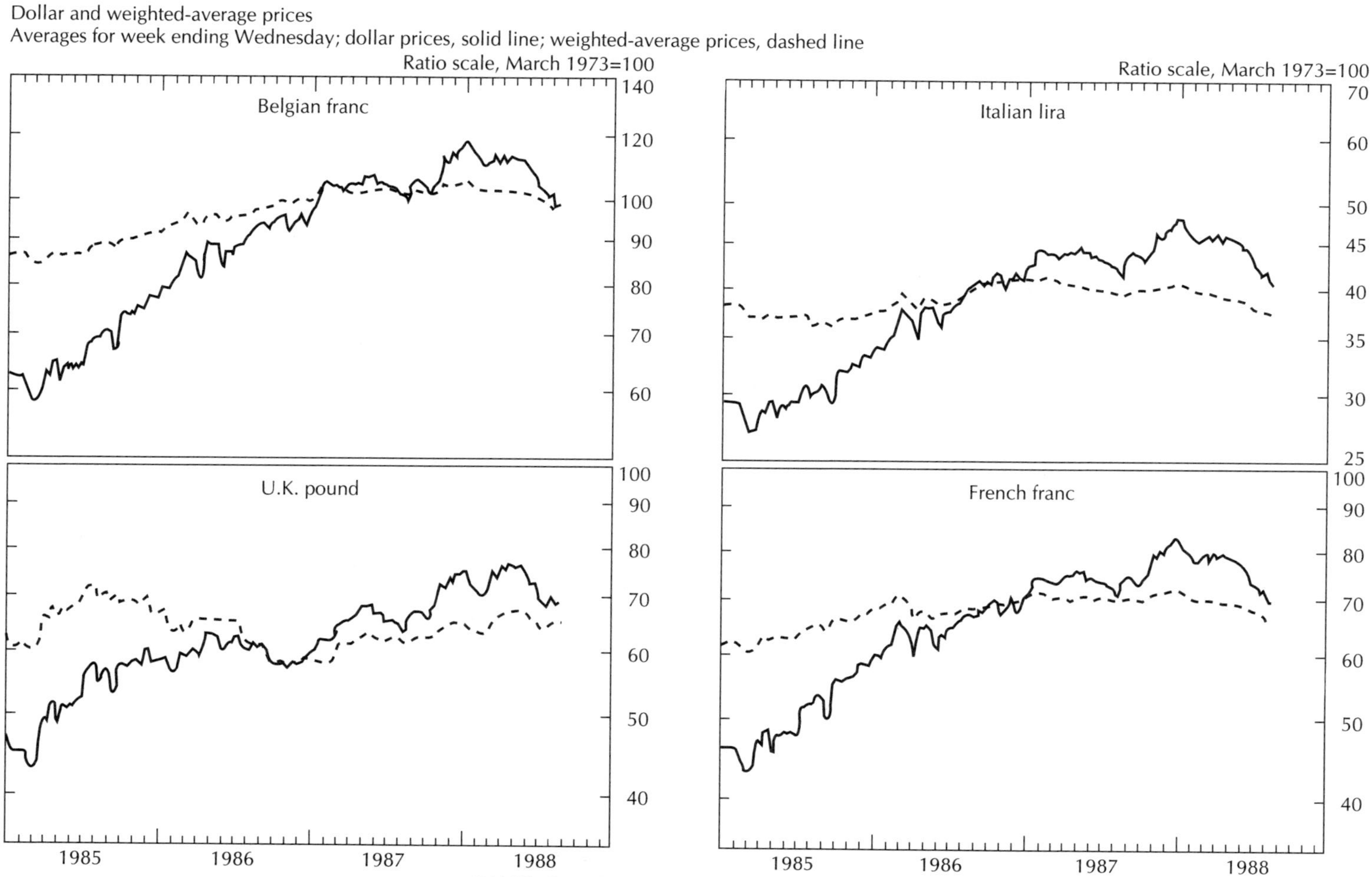

PANEL B: U.S. DOLLAR EXCHANGE RATES

SOURCE: Board of Governors of the Federal Reserve System, *1988 Historical Chart Book*, p. 108–109.

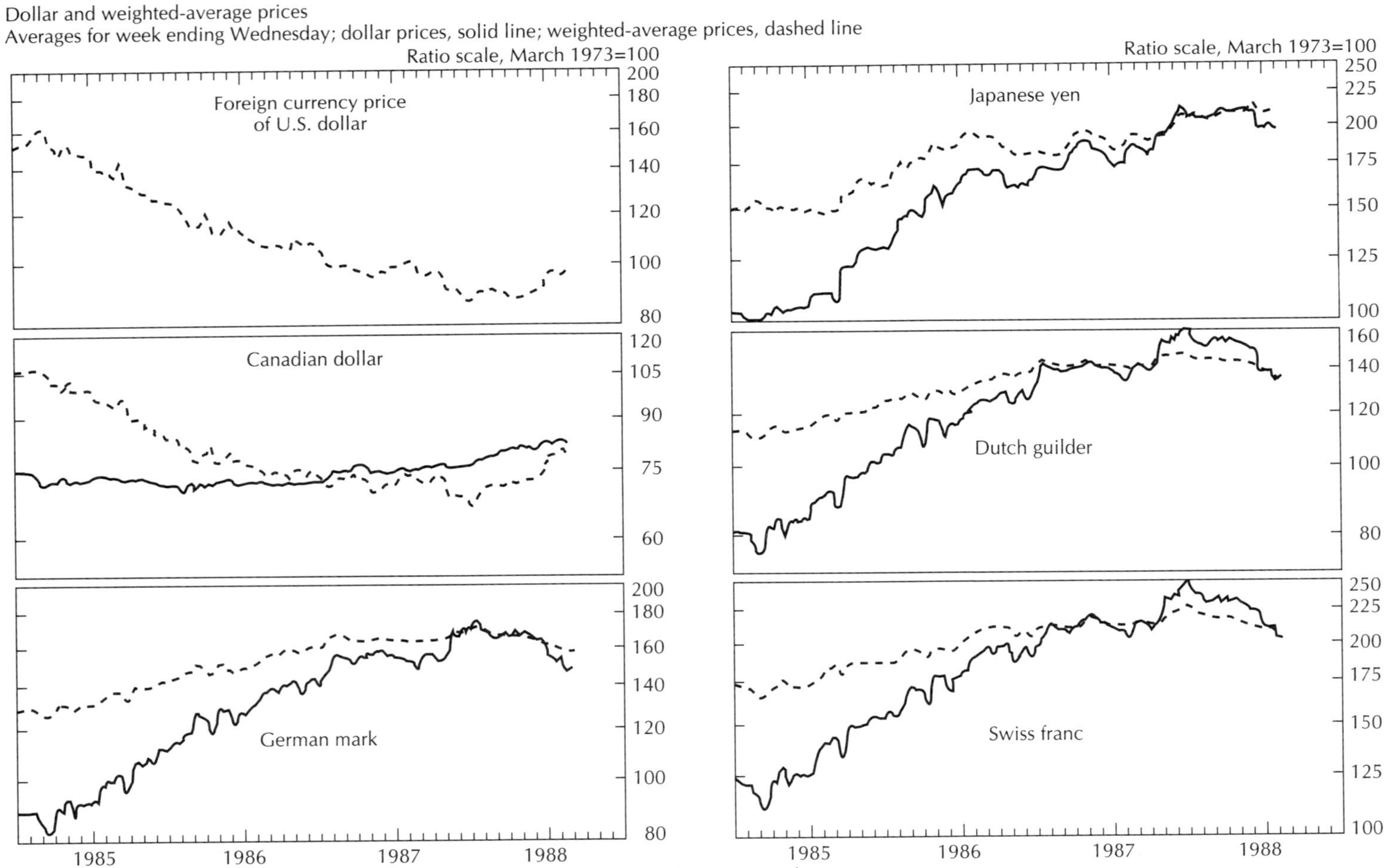

PANEL B: (*continued*)

Real Shocks

Real shocks affect the demand and supply conditions for goods and services. Demand and supply in turn are classified as *private,* coming from the household and business sector, and *public,* associated with governments. Private demand shocks are caused by unexpected changes in tastes, preferences, endowments, or wealth of consumers. Fundamental determinants of demand, like tastes, demographic factors, and wealth, evolve gradually over time, as discussed above. Real demand shocks occur with natural disasters and wars that quickly change the wealth of consumers. Sudden changes in demographic composition can happen because of pestilence or famine.

The "baby boom" following the Second World War in the United States is an example of a demographic disturbance—one that is still working its way through the economy. This disturbance was due to the Great Depression followed by World War II and it altered the course of development of the U.S. economy. A disproportionate number of babies in the 1940s and 1950s was followed by a disproportionate number of teenagers in the 1960s, university students in the 1970s, and yuppies in the 1980s. This demographic shock was important but was relatively gradual and its economic effects mainly predictable. In advanced economies, private demand shocks such as demographic disturbances seem to cause gradual variations in economic activity around equilibrium steady state values.

Private demand shocks affect private investment more than consumption. This is clear from Panel B of Figure 13.1, which shows consumption and gross private investment in the United States since 1950. Investment includes inventory adjustments that occur whenever manufacturers' output is not demanded. Inventory investment is not always desired and in fact may result from demand shocks elsewhere in the economy. Variation in investment in part represents changes in the demand for long-term investment goods and in part demand shocks originating in the business sector, as for example in the 1981 recession.

Public demand shocks are another story. Examination of Figure 13.4 shows that government expenditures and tax receipts in the United States as well as the difference in them, government deficits, have fluctuated over a wide margin in the last half of the 20th century. Beginning with the Vietnam War and the Great Society in the 1960s, expansion in federal government expenditures produced rising deficits. Some economists, like Robert Barro and Robert Lucas, believe government demand shocks in the form of unexpected policy changes are an important source of variation in economic activity.

Supply shocks are more important than private demand shocks. Unexpected changes in the productivity or relative prices of the factors of production—labor, raw materials, and productive capital—occur frequently. Real business cycle theorists examine effects of unexpected changes in the productivity of capital and changes in the relative prices of goods and services. Substantial variations in all sectors of the economy can be explained by such events. For example, Plosser (1989) shows that productivity shocks induce variation in economic models of production, investment, and consumption that closely resemble actual U.S. experience.

Shocks are only shocks if they are unanticipated. For example, the oil price changes in 1973 and 1979 were shocks, often called the "oil price shocks." Shocks

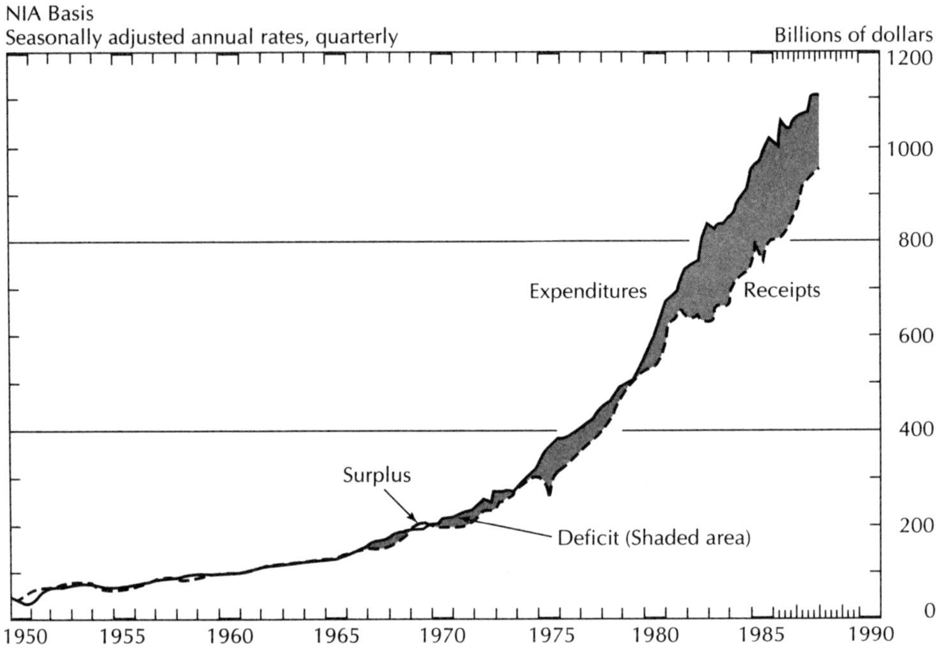

FIGURE 13.4 Federal government receipts and expenditures
SOURCE: Board of Governors of the Federal Reserve System, *1988 Historical Chart Book,* p. 51.

such as wars, unexpected changes in government expenditure policies, and relative price and technology shocks, cannot be forecasted. These shocks provoke real economic adjustments on economic participants, causing changes in real returns as savings, investment, and consumption adjust to accommodate the shocks. Shocks are a source of risk.

Economic decision makers do not like risk. Financial institutions assess risk and develop solutions to problems caused by risk to savers and investors. Many of the services offered by financial institutions are related to real shocks affecting economic activity.

Monetary and Financial Shocks

Real business cycle theorists do not concentrate on the effects of money and financial markets on economic activity. If saving and consumption grow at equilibrium levels and monetary growth is steady, interest rates in real terms would be equal to the marginal return on real capital and nominal interest rates would reflect the expected level of inflation and risk premiums. Even with the possibility of shocks in the form of individual defaults or changes in liquidity needs, interest rates would be unchanging. Inflation and risk premiums at the aggregate would not depart from equilibrium levels.

Figure 13.2 demonstrates how far reality departs from the idealized equilibrium path for inflation and interest rates. What is the source of variability in inflation and interest rates since the 1960s? Some of these financial and inflation variations can be attributed to the transmission of real shocks from savings and investment or government deficits to the financial markets. The remarkable increase in the level and variability of interest rates cannot be so explained.

The increase in inflation and interest rates and their variability since 1965 is attributed by most economists to the increased variability of monetary policy and global financial market integration in the presence of fluctuating exchange rates after 1973. All of these events result from government monetary and financial market policies.

The "Great American Inflation" began in 1965 with the Vietnam War and continued with the end of the gold standard with Richard Nixon's 1972 "New Economic Policy." These events mark the loosening of effective restrictions on the growth rate of the money supply in the United States. Figure 13.5 shows the quarter-to-quarter growth rates in the monetary base and the aggregate money supply since 1950. The figure provides evidence that in the late 1960s a period of substantial variation in financial markets due to variability in monetary policy began. Variation in United States and world monetary policy is reflected in increased variability in inflation, exchange rates, and interest rates of all types as shown in Figures 13.2 and 13.3.

FIGURE 13.5 Growth rates in the U.S. money supply

SOURCE: Board of Governors of the Federal Reserve System, *1988 Historical Chart Book,* p. 6.

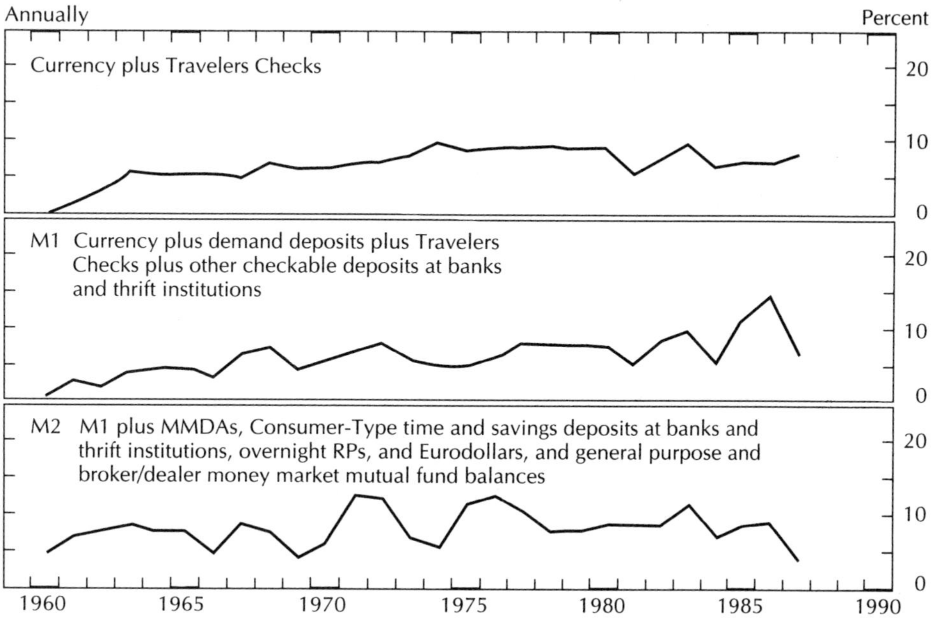

The effects on financial institutions of increased variation from money supply and financial shocks are pervasive. Money supply changes determine changes in the rate of inflation. Interest rates reflect expected inflation. Interest rate and inflation risk are the root causes of the economic problems observed in recent decades, including the savings and loan debacle. Thrift institutions were undone by rapidly increasing and varying short-term interest rates.

Portfolio adjustments required by changing and variable returns on financial assets caused shifts in the demand for savings vehicles and types of financing. Insurance companies lost market share relative to deposit-making institutions and pension funds and mutual funds gained relative to both in the last two decades. Purchasing power risk is substantially greater now than prior to 1965. Variable rate loans are now common. Fine tuning portfolios in response to changing economic conditions increased the demand for trading securities and made risk management contracts like options attractive. Demand for risk management drove much of the innovation and marketing activity in the financial services industry in the 1970s and 1980s, which saw new markets and firms start up and old institutions lose ground.

13.2 ASSESSING THE IMPACT OF MACROECONOMIC FACTORS

All value in finance comes from the present value of cash flows for consumption. To introduce our discussion of the economic environment, we start with the value of any asset as the present value of future cash flows:

$$PV_0 = \sum_{t=0}^{t=\infty} \frac{CF_t}{\left(1 + r_t\right)^t} \tag{13.1}$$

where CF_t is the cash flow each period t, and r_t is the discount rate applied to the cash flows each period. (This discussion follows Chen, Roll, and Ross (1986) as elaborated below.) The economic environment affects economic values according to how they impact cash flows and discount rates associated with any asset, line of business, or financial plan. Risk from the economic environment comes from changes in elements of the fundamental valuation equation.

Risk to Cash Flows

Cash flows from assets result from contractual commitments, like mortgage payments or bond coupons, or equity investments having a residual claim on revenues minus costs in a line of business or provision of a service. All cash flows are affected by the level of economic activity. A growing economy means demand is strong, producing large cash flows for businesses selling products people want when they have money. Economic activity also affects defaults and/or missed payments on mortgages and bonds. The level of economic activity is determined by fundamental factors affecting aggregate supply and demand determining GDP and its private and governmental components.

Industrial production, calculated and reported in the United States by the Federal Reserve Board, represents the level of operation of factories. A time series of industrial production for the United States is shown in Panel A of Figure 13.1. Changes in industrial production result from the net effects of real shocks in the economy. For this reason, Chen, Roll, and Ross (CRR) (1986) use industrial production to represent one of the fundamental risk factors in their implementation of the Arbitrage Pricing Model (APT) discussed in Chapter 4. Other economists use other measures of the effects of real supply and demand shocks; for example, Burmeister and Wall (1986) use retail sales. Sales of consumer goods are shown in Figure 13.6.

Government policy has two effects on cash flows of assets. Governments directly influence the demand for goods and services, for example road construction, as part of their expenditure policies. Changes in local and national priorities occur suddenly and can dramatically change prospects for regional economies, like recent reduced aerospace spending in California, or sectoral activity, like the demand for health care under a new national health system. When changes in government demand are not anticipated, government policy is a source of risk to the economy.

FIGURE 13.6 Consumer purchases

SOURCE: Board of Governors of the Federal Reserve System, *1988 Historical Chart Book*, p. 18.

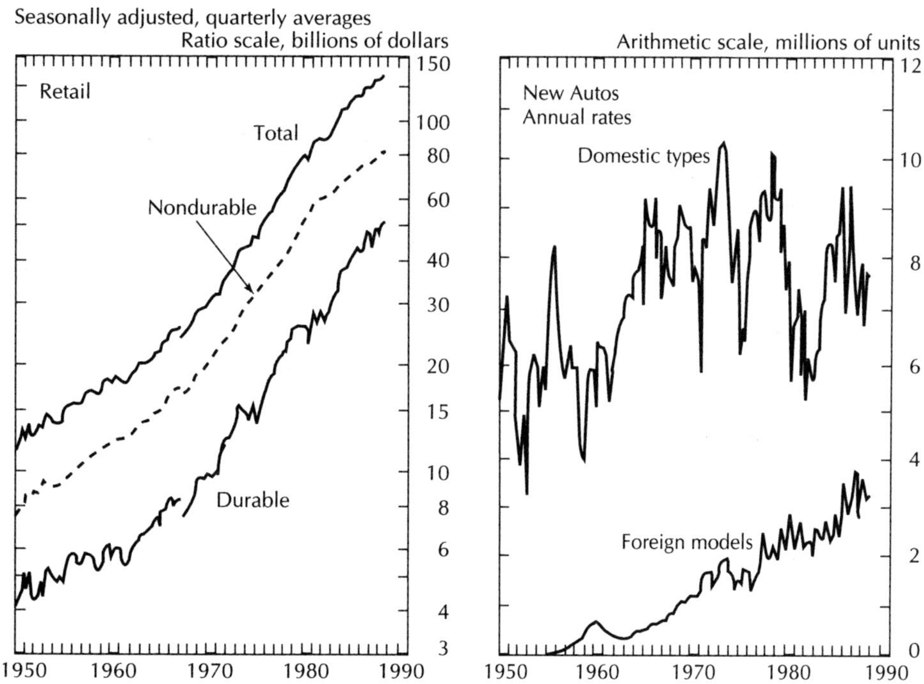

The second influence of government policy is taxation. Changes in tax policy directly change after-tax cash flows. Changes in taxes can be sudden and unexpected. In the United States, for example, the Tax Reform Act (TRA) of 1986 eliminated many tax advantages. Businesses and financial services developed to exploit previous tax laws were hard hit. Changes in real estate income taxation wiped out the business of syndicating real estate partnerships. Removal of the investment tax credit (ITC) eliminated a basic reason for the leasing business. Those changes also resulted in a fall in real estate values, contributing to the savings and loan crisis.

Tax treatment can change cash flows to investors and savers in the economy and change the environment of financial service firms offering services to households and businesses. Tax policy comes from the political process. An excellent history of the TRA by Birnbaum and Murray (1987) demonstrates the capricious nature of tax legislation. For example, the book credits two pitchers of beer at an Irish bar in Washington with a major role in the ultimate success of the tax reform.

A major source of real shocks to the world economy is unpredictable government policy. Recent events in the United States, like the TRA and cutbacks in defense spending, may be tame relative to zigs and zags observed in government policy in other countries. The point is that government fiscal policy is a major source of risk for financial institution managers.

Risk and the Discount Rate

It is useful to think of the discount rate for individual assets as built up of different components. This is shown in Figure 13.7, where interest rates are divided into four components: (1) riskless short-term interest rates; (2) expected inflation premium; (3) term-premium on long-term default-free bonds; and finally, (4) risk premiums for risky assets. Risk premiums are for performance or default risk for bonds and for residual claims like stock that include other risk factors. Figure 13.7 shows two different levels of risk premiums, for low risk bonds (AAA rated) and higher risk (BAA) bonds.

Determinants of short-term riskless rates are analyzed in influential studies by Cox, Ingersoll, and Ross (1985a, 1985b), called the CIR model of interest rates. In their model of the economy, the short-term rate and all other asset prices are functions of risk and time preferences and the *state* of the economy. The state of the economy is measured by key factors determining the productivity of capital.

The productivity of capital changes randomly through time in the CIR analysis. Real shocks are the source of variability. Variability of changes expected in the current and future state of the economy are reflected in the short-term riskless rate and this rate is reflected in other asset prices as a component of the discount rate. Short-term riskless interest rate changes are due to unanticipated changes in factors affecting the state of technology in the CIR analysis. Figure 13.8 shows estimated short-term riskless rates for the United States from 1964 to 1984.[3]

[3]The riskless rate cannot be observed directly, since default risk rates for instruments like Treasury bills include an inflation premium. We have shown estimates as provided by Burmeister, Wall, and Hamilton (1986) in Figure 13.8.

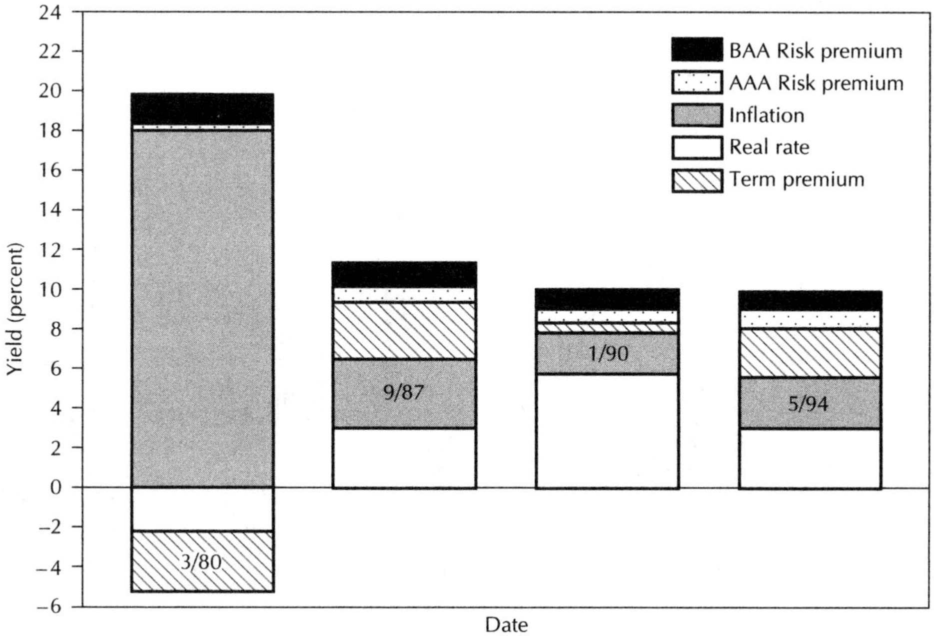

FIGURE 13.7 Components of U.S. interest rates for various time periods
SOURCE: Interest rate data from various issues of the Federal Reserve *Bulletin*.

Short-term interest rates actually observed in newspapers or on trading screens reflect expected inflation (see Fama 1975 for an analysis). The relation between observed or *nominal* interest rates, real short-term rates, and expected inflation is called the *Fisher relation* after Irving Fisher and is written:

$$i_t = r_t + E\left(p_t\right) \tag{13.2}$$

where i_t is the nominal rate quoted at period t, r_t is the real rate, and E(p) is expected inflation. The notion that short-term interest rates reflect expected inflation has been extensively analyzed by economists (especially since Fama 1975). Economists in general believe that a major source of change in short-term interest rates is changes in expected inflation.

Expected inflation is not a number quoted in the newspaper. Allocation of nominal rates between expected real rates and expected inflation must be estimated. Figure 13.8 presents estimates of expected inflation from 1964 to 1984. The graph clearly slows that short-term rates are much more variable after 1965 and especially 1979 than historically. Variability in short-term rates in the 1970s is attributable mainly to changes in inflation expectations. In the 1980s, the variation is due equally to changes in real rates and expected inflation.

CRR distinguish two sources of short-term interest rate risk from inflation. The first risk is that actual inflation, P_t, is different from expected inflation, that is, $P_t - E(p_t)$ is not zero. Unexpected inflation means realized yields in purchasing power terms vary from expected levels. A second source of risk is revision in expected future inflation given availability of new information concerning the economy.

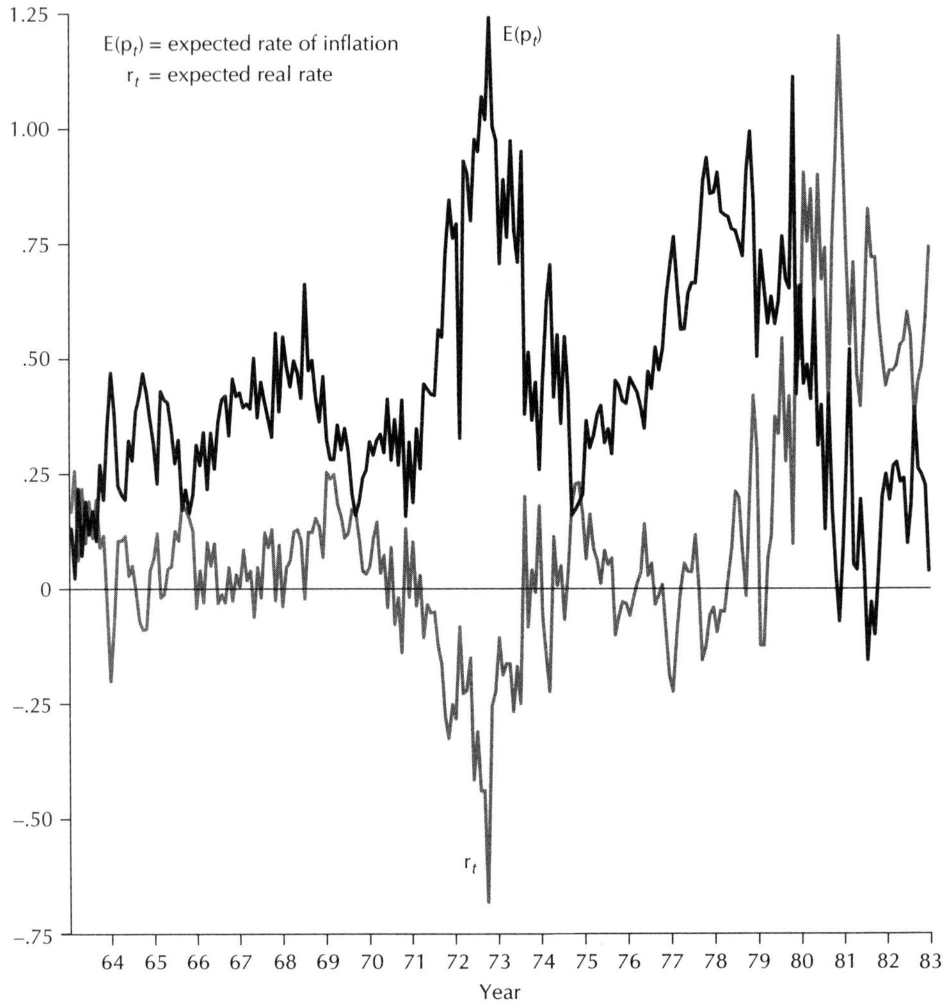

FIGURE 13.8 Expected real short-term interest rates and expected inflation in the United States, 1964–1984

SOURCE: Edwin Burmeister, Kent D. Wall, and James D. Hamilton "Estimation of Unobserved Expected Monthly Inflation Using Kalman Filtering," *Journal of Business & Economic Statistics,"* Vol. 4, No. 2 (1986), pp. 152–153.

Recent History

On October 6, 1979, the recently appointed chairman of the Federal Reserve Board of Governors, Paul Volcker, oversaw implementation of new operating procedures at the Fed, a major event. The new procedures focused Federal Reserve attention on monetary aggregates rather than on short-term interest rates. Instead of keeping short-term rates, especially the Fed funds rate, within a tight band of approximately 25 basis points, the Federal Reserve would tolerate movements in rates up to 400 basis points. Figure 13.2, Panel B, demonstrates much more interest rate variability after October 1979.

Swings in interest rates observed in the early 1980s, as much as a thousand basis points in a few months, are unprecedented in history. The turmoil and adjustment these variations caused world financial markets are nearly impossible to grasp. The unprecedented environment of interest rate risk is due to monetary policy variation and abrupt changes around the world. Recent interest rate variability is unusual and may or may not characterize markets of the future. Interest rate variation was lower between 1985 and 1993, but recent variations are still large relative to historical standards.

Fed Watching

Recent events have made central bank policy changes a major risk factor in the macroeconomic environment of all countries. To assess possible future interest rate and financial market policies, nearly all financial institutions track the Federal Reserve, producing a new specialty, "Fed watching." Most Fed watchers pursue three strategies: (1) determine what the Fed *says* it is doing; (2) measure what the Fed *is* doing; and (3) assess financial market responses to Fed actions. Fed watching is briefly described here to emphasize the role Central Bank policy plays in the risk environment. Sophisticated talent is required to assess and manage those risks.

Fed watchers begin with reports the Federal Reserve presents annually in February and August, "Monetary Reports to the Congress", to determine what the Fed says it is doing. The Federal Reserve policy committee, called the Federal Open Market Committee (FOMC), releases stylized minutes of deliberations following its next meeting. These minutes of the FOMC meetings are available as a press release and are printed in the Federal Reserve *Bulletin*. Federal Reserve officials make frequent speeches and presentations to committees of Congress. Fed watchers review public utterances for hints of change in Fed policy. Finally, the press dogs the tracks of Federal Reserve governors and bank presidents in order to glean tidbits hinting at shifts in Fed policy from stray comments or answers to questions at business meetings.

Many statistical releases are available to determine what the Fed is actually doing. For example, on Thursdays the Fed releases statistical results on the aggregate money supply ten days earlier, the Federal Reserve's balance sheet for the previous Wednesday, and large bank statistics for the previous week. These and other releases show monetary or reserve changes that may be interpreted as shifts in announced Fed policy. The Fed and other central banks are often not doing what they say or think they are doing. In the 1970s, "base drift," changing the base from which growth in money supply is measured, disguised monetary growth substantially larger than policy goals announced by the Fed.

Fed watchers also watch key market indicators for shifts in Federal reserve policy. The immediate focus is the overnight Federal funds rate, the rate the Fed focuses on in open market operations sales and purchases of government securities from primary dealers. Fed watchers also are alert to rumors and gossip in Fed activity with primary dealers. Information services like Money Market Services offer electronic access to the latest rumors on Fed activity.

The Fed and other central banks are important because they are big, having concentrated financial power with billions of dollars or other currencies to invest. They all make policy in a secretive and unpredictable fashion. Many economists call for more openness and predictability in monetary policy. In 1994, the Federal Reserve publicly announced policies to increase interest rates, a change in their policy of secrecy. Secrecy and lack of information concerning monetary policy around the world are major uncertainties or risks to the macroeconomy.

Milton Friedman and his followers argue that central bank "discretionary" control over monetary policy ought to be replaced with invariant rules. Rules would remove central banks as a source of risks and eliminate the need for wasteful activities like Fed watching. Central bankers the world over have a powerful constituency. Benefits to them from commanding complex institutions with all the attention and perquisites means that central bankers are unlikely to give up their power and go away.

Term Premiums

Another building block in discount rates determining values in financial markets is the term premium, the difference in default risk-free long-term versus short-term bonds. Market observers think of the term premium in terms of the *yield curve* or *term structure* of interest rates depicting the array of yields to maturity for default risk-free bonds of different maturities. Figure 13.9 Panel A shows the term structure of U.S. Treasury securities at several points in the last few years; Panel B shows corporate short-term and long-term borrowing rates through time. Panel A demonstrates that the term structure changes, and Panel B, interpreted as the end points of the term structure through time, demonstrates that the yield curve changes all the time. Changes in the term structure are another source of risk to financial asset values.

Term structure shapes are given names by economists. Figure 13.10 provides prototypes of the different curves observed. Panel A represents a yield curve that is described by financial market participants as *upward sloping, ascending,* or *normal.* The last term is used because usually the term structure is upward sloping. Panel B depicts a *downward sloping, descending,* or *inverted* term structure. Panel C shows a *flat* or *horizontal* term structure, and Panel D displays a *humped* term structure.

What determines the term structure at any given time? Changes in the term structure change asset values and are a risk to financial market participants. Economists generally have three approaches or *hypotheses* concerning the determination of the term structure: (1) the *unbiased expectations* hypothesis; (2) the *market segmentation* hypothesis; and (3) the *preferred habitat* hypothesis. We explain each briefly in turn but refer students to economics textbooks for lengthier explanations.

To appreciate the different hypotheses, we introduce the notion of the forward rate. We need some terminology: The *spot* rate is the current, observable

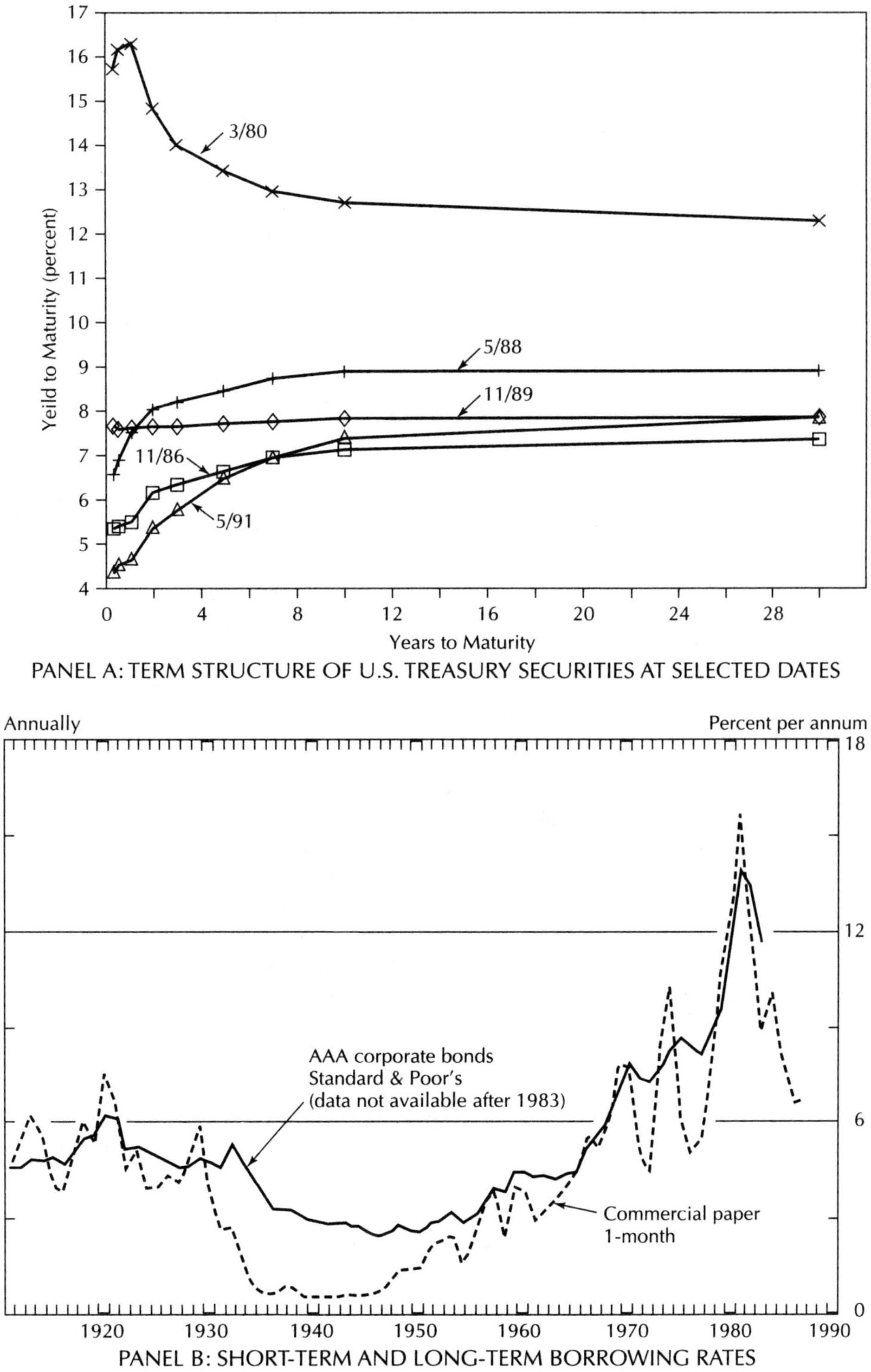

FIGURE 13.9 U.S. interest rates

SOURCE: Board of Governors of the Federal Reserve System, *1988 Historical Chart Book*, p. 96.

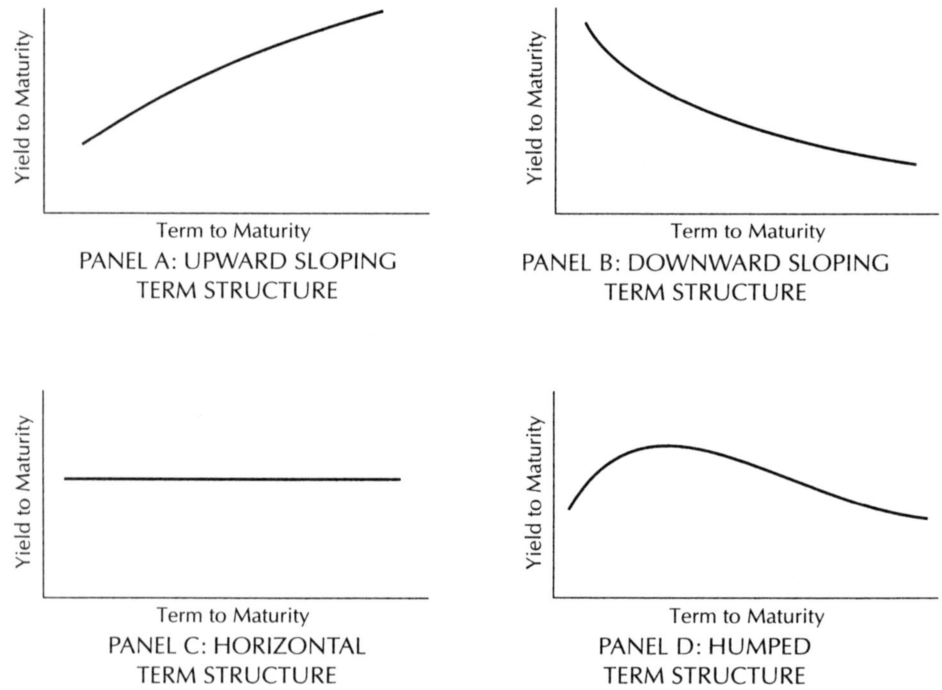

FIGURE 13.10 Term structure shapes

yield on a bond available for immediate delivery. Interest rates we observe in the *Wall Street Journal* are spot rates. The *forward* rate is a conceptual interest rate for an investment or loan at some point in the future, for example one year from now. Using an explicit example, the forward rate for a one-year Treasury bill in one year would be the rate quoted now for delivery in one year of a Treasury bill with one-year maturity at that time. The forward rate is a conceptual rate because forward markets do not exist for all possible future time periods. Conceptually, forward rates exist for all future periods.

The investment return earned on a long maturity discount bond will be equal to that of two shorter maturity bonds if the spot rate on the short bond plus the expected future yield on a bond having a maturity to fill out the investment to the longer bond maturity have a specific relationship. Precisely stated, the forward rate is the interest rate that equates the yields from the two strategies over the longer time horizon, as follows:

$$\left(1 + {}_tR_L\right)^L = \left(1 + {}_tR_S\right)^S \times \left(1 + {}_{S+1}r_{L-S}\right)^{L-S} \tag{13.3}$$

where R represents observable spot rates on discount bonds, with subscript t meaning observed at t for a long maturity bond maturing at L, and a short maturity bond maturing at S. The conceptual forward rate, r, at time period beginning S + 1 periods and ending at the the longer investment time horizon, L, is the forward rate on a discount bond which would equalize returns from buying the long bond or the short bond and reinvesting at the forward rate at the end of the shorter time period. Equation (13.3) defines the forward rate. The forward rate thus defined always exists for the end of the shorter period for similar securities with quoted spot rates for two maturities whether or not there is a forward market.

An example illustrates how to calculate forward rates given two spot rates of different maturity discount bonds, such as U.S. Treasury zero coupon bonds. If L is equal to eight years and S is equal to five years and the respective spot yields are 10 and 8 percent, the forward rate solves the equation:

$$(1.10)^8 = (1.08)^5 \times (1 +_6 r_3)^3 \tag{13.4}$$

$$+_6 r_2 = \sqrt[3]{\frac{(1.10)^8}{(1.08)^5}} - 1 \tag{13.5}$$

$$+_6 r_3 = 13.4\%. \tag{13.6}$$

Since forward rates can be informative, readers should practice with other examples. Term structure hypotheses are discussed in terms of differing interpretations of forward rates implicit in the term structure of spot rates at a point in time.

Unbiased Expectations Hypothesis

The *unbiased expectations hypothesis* states that forward rates represent unbiased expectations of future spot rates. This hypothesis assumes investors are risk neutral and are indifferent between two investment strategies that have the same expected return. In this case, arbitrage forces spot rates into the relation (13.3) above. Forward rates are equal to the expected future spot rate:

$$+_{S+1} r_{L-S} = E\left({}_{S+1}R_{L-S}\right). \tag{13.7}$$

The unbiased expectations hypothesis interprets changes in the term premium as due exclusively to changes in expectations concerning future spot interest rates.

Under the unbiased expectations hypothesis, long-term rates can be interpreted as an average of future expected short-term rates. The following relations are implicit in the unbiased expectations hypothesis:

$$\left(1 + {}_tR_L\right)^L = \left(1 + {}_tR_1\right) \times \left(1 + E\left({}_{t+1}R_1\right)\right) \times \left(1 + E\left({}_{t+2}R_1\right)\right) \times \cdots \times \left(1 + E\left({}_{t+L-1}R_1\right)\right). \tag{13.8}$$

The long-term rate can be solved as:

$$+_t R_L = \sqrt[L]{\left(1 + {}_tR_1\right) \times \left(1 + E\left({}_{t+1}R_1\right)\right) \times \left(1 + E\left({}_{t+2}R_1\right)\right) \times \cdots \times \left(1 + \left({}_{t+L-1}R_1\right)\right)} - 1. \tag{13.9}$$

The expressing under the radical is the *geometric* average of future expected spot rates after period t.

If the yield curve is upward sloping and we accept the unbiased expectations hypothesis, short-term rates are expected to rise. If the term-structure is flat, rates are not expected to change. If it is downward sloping, short-term rates are expected to fall.

Market Segmentation and Preferred Habitat Hypotheses

The *market segmentation hypothesis* assumes that financial market participants are risk averse and only want to issue liabilities or acquire assets with specific maturities. For example, a life insurance company or pension fund wants to match its expected benefit payouts and might want to acquire only long-term assets. A bank raising funds with short-term deposits only wants to acquire short-term assets.

Under this hypothesis of the term structure, interest rates in maturity segments of financial markets are determined by interaction of transactors with particular investment term needs. Bond markets of different maturities are *segmented*. Long-term rates are determined by long-term borrowers and investors independently of events in the short-term market. Borrowers and investors are too risk averse to abandon their market maturity segment no matter what their expectations concerning future interest rates.

Forward rates have no meaning according to the market segmentation hypothesis. Most economists reject the simplistic determination of the term structure of interest rates under this hypothesis. Economists argue that investors can be induced to leave their natural maturity habitats if the expected gains, given their expectations, are sufficient. This leads to the third hypothesis, the *preferred habitat hypothesis*.

The preferred habitat hypothesis is an integration of the extremes of the unbiased expectations and market segmentation hypotheses. It assumes that investors and borrowers are risk averse but not totally risk averse. Investors and borrowers do have preferred maturities where for risk management reasons they prefer to operate. Expectations of higher returns can induce them to leave their preferred maturity habitats.

The major point of the preferred habitat hypothesis is that investors must earn an excess return, called the *liquidity premium*, to leave their preferred habitat. Liquidity premiums compensate investors for bearing risk. Excess returns must be enough to lure investors or borrowers from their natural maturity abode. In the preferred habitat hypothesis, the forward rate contains a premium, noted as follows:

$$+_t r_{L-S} = E\left({}_{S+1}R_{L-S}\right) +_t L_L \qquad (13.10)$$

where L_L is the liquidity premium for a bond with a long maturity. According to the preferred habitat hypothesis, a gently upward sloping term structure can be interpreted as expectation of unchanging future spot rates but higher liquidity premiums for longer maturities.

The explanatory power of the various hypotheses is mixed. A widely cited study by Fama (1976) demonstrates that liquidity premiums do exist on U.S. Treasuries, but that these premiums are small (statistically undetectable) after maturities of longer than nine months. The liquidity premiums estimated by Fama appear to be related to the degree of interest rate and inflation variability in the different time periods he studied. Fama's analysis in general appears to support the unbiased expectations hypothesis for longer term securities.

Expectations are rarely right. It is not required of the expectations hypothesis or market efficiency that expectations be correct every period. The only requirement of market efficiency is that errors in expectations be unbiased. This was the case in Fama's study.

Summarizing, changes in term premiums are a major source of interest rate and macroeconomic risk. These changes appear to come from a mixture of changes in expectations concerning future interest rates and changes in liquidity premiums. Ibbotson and Sinquefield (1993) report that the difference in holding period returns of one-month Treasury bills and long-term bonds average 1.2 percent per year. The range of observed long and short yield differentials observed in the last 20 years in the United States is –2 to +4.5 percent. With these ranges and variation, there is clearly a great deal of risk to financial institution managers from changes in term premiums.

Risk Premiums

With the exception of government securities, all financial assets have risks associated with payment of cash, usually called *default risk*. Even default is rarely a 100 percent loss. Bad bank loans, corporate bonds, municipal borrowing and so on usually return some cash to investors. Default often means only delayed payment. A more precise term is cash flow uncertainty risk. The longer term incorporates risks associated with cash flows for common stocks that cannot default.

Risk premiums are difficult to observe because they differ for each risky asset. For securities without contractual cash flows, like common stocks, they are not defined at all. Discussion of risk premiums is usually conducted in terms of bonds of different risk classes, like the AAA and BAA bonds above, where yields to maturity can be calculated and compared. Panel A of Figure 13.11 provides a graph of yield differentials between short-term riskless Treasuries and risky commercial paper and Panel B provides yield differentials between 10-year U.S. Treasuries and corporate bonds rated AAA (highest quality, lowest default risk) and BAA (lowest quality series available) by Standard and Poors. Risk premiums shown in Figure 13.11 change over time. This component of the discount rate for cash flows is another major source of risk.

There are two determinants of the risk premium. The first is the default premium necessary to bring contractual commitments into line with actual expected yields. The calculated yield to maturity of a bond is the highest possible yield that the investment will provide. It assumes all payments of principal and interest are made in a timely fashion. Yields to maturity reflect a premium to account for the expected defaults on bonds of a given degree of performance risk. A simple example illustrates the increase in contract rates necessary to provide a given expected return. If a loan repaying principal and interest at the contractual rate of i_t at the end of the year has a d_t percent chance of defaulting completely, the expected yield $E(r_t)$ on the loans is given by:

$$E(r_t) = (d_t \times 0 + (1 - d_t) \times (1 + i_t)) - 1. \tag{13.11}$$

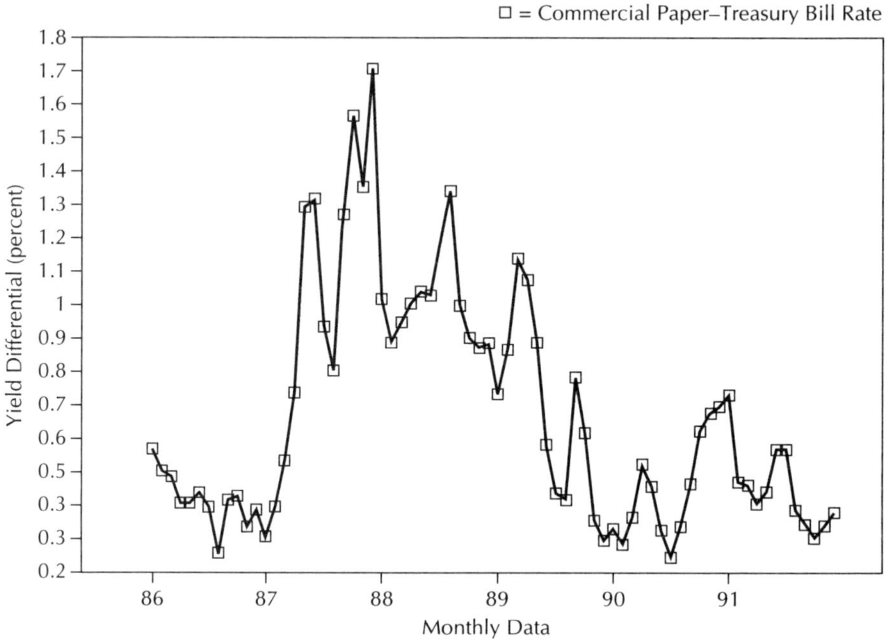

PANEL A: SHORT-TERM RISK PREMIA IN THE UNITED STATES, 1986–1991

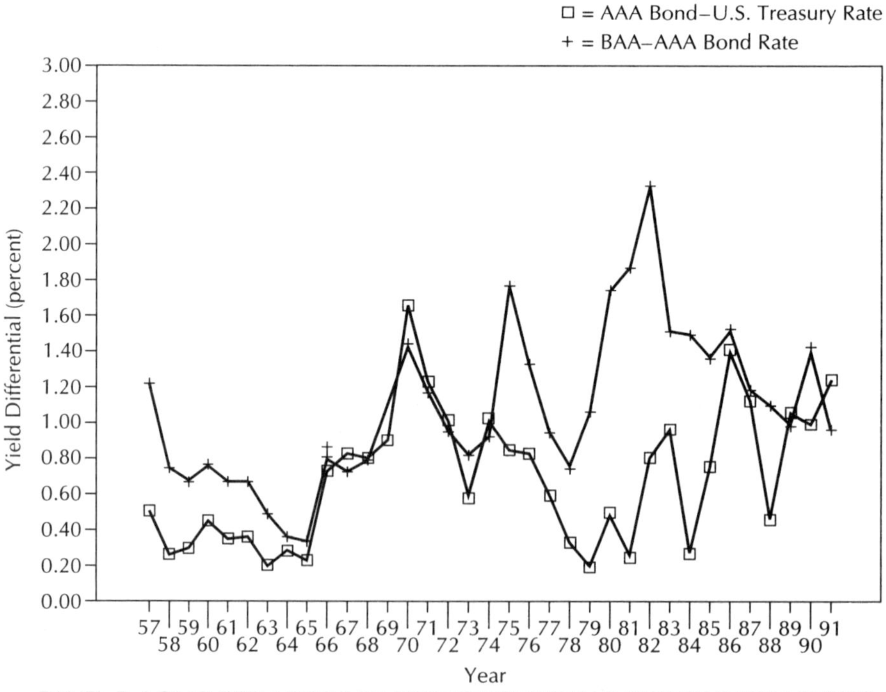

PANEL B: LONG-TERM DEFAULT RISK DIFFERENTIALS IN THE UNITED STATES (AAA OVER BAA AND AAA OVER U.S. TREASURY)

FIGURE 13.11 Risk premia in U.S. interest rates

If the contract rate is 12 percent and the default probability is 2 percent, the expected yield on a portfolio of such loans is:

$$E(r_t) = (.02 \times 0 + .98 \times 1.12) - 1 = 9.76\% \tag{13.12}$$

where the 0 in the first term means a total default. Although the calculated yield to maturity on this loan is 12 percent, the expected yield is below 10 percent. If default probabilities were higher, the contractual rate has to be higher to provide the same expected return.

The difference in the bond yields shown in Figure 13.11 reflects higher probabilities of defaults on lower quality bonds. These risk premiums change through time. There is no doubt that default risk changes with the macroeconomic environment. For example, uncertainty in prices and interest rates will increase variability of all firms' performances.

The second determinant of default risk premiums in discount rates is the expected yield premium investors require in order to bear the risk of changes in asset values from variations in cash flow performance risk. This is a market-wide price of cash performance risk. This risk premium is related to the risk premium for stocks and it varies over time. For example, this risk premium increased during the Stock Market Crash of 1987 as stocks and low quality bonds lost value while Treasury securities increased in value.

Summary of Discount Rate Risk

Macroeconomic risk comes from changes in production due to changes in supply and demand and changes in government monetary and fiscal policies. The macroeconomic environment observed in the United States and other industrialized countries since the 1960s demonstrates much greater variation in all the factors affecting discount rates than earlier. It is unlikely that real shocks from the private sector are larger or more pervasive in the last half of the twentieth century than in prior years. The conclusion of most observers is that government policy is the largest source of increases in risk.

Managers and planners for financial institutions should keep in mind that extreme interest and exchange rate variability observed in the last thirty years is a recent phenomenon. The macroeconomic system could revert to patterns of earlier days, like the 1950s, when inflation was 1 percent and interest rates varied a total of 200 basis points over the decade. Managers should contemplate requirements of producing value in that environment and think through implications of an equilibrium economy with reduced real and monetary shocks on value production strategies.

13.3 MICROECONOMIC RISK FACTORS

Unexpected variation in economic activity often has a local or industry-specific origin specific to narrowly defined markets, the focus of microeconomic analysis. Regional risk, like the collapse of the Texas economy in the last half of the 1980s or recent slowdowns in Europe and Japan, is a significant consideration for financial institutions. There are three basic kinds of regional or industry-specific shocks. The first is local sensitivity to macroeconomic risks: Some regional or industrial markets are particularly sensitive to the macroeconomic environment. For example, the auto industry and Michigan economy or defense and California. The second kind of specific market shocks comes from changes in technology or supply conditions usually associated with a change in relative prices. History is strewn with examples of local economic declines, for example coal mining in England or textiles in New England, or rapid development, like the Middle East with oil. The final source of local economic shocks is changes in government policy. This source deserves extended treatment, which it receives below.

Regional and industry-specific risk is an important cause of financial institution difficulties. The best way of dealing with such risks is to diversify or hedge them, as we discuss in Chapters 18 to 21. Diversification has not been effective in the recent experience of some financial institutions because they were not allowed by regulators to diversify regionally, either in the United States or Europe. Until 1980, in the United States, thrifts could not make loans more than 100 miles from their main office. European banking markets were protected and segmented. Deregulation may allow more effective diversification in the future.

Financial institution managers must try to understand the connection between local or industry-specific microeconomic risks and macroeconomic forces. For example, recent difficulties in real estate loans, less-developed-country loans, and agricultural and energy related lending, were all related to two causes: deregulation of oil prices and reduced inflation expectations. Demand for agricultural land fell with reduced inflation expectations, putting pressure on farmers using land as collateral. Oil-producing regions and less-developed countries dependent on oil both suffered from reduced inflation expectations for commodities and were less able to service debt. The regional impact of these macroeconomic shocks was greater in some areas than others, like Texas, obscuring the common source of these risks.

Regulatory Risk

Changes in the regulatory environment are a source of both risk and value-producing opportunities for financial institution managers. Imagine a business where the government gives a small number of firms an exclusive local franchise to provide a service that everyone needs. Costs of providing the service are subsidized by government agencies and price competition is illegal. A business strategy could be built on the franchise. This was precisely the case with commercial banks and checking accounts in the United States until the Deregulation Act of 1980.

Changes in the regulatory environment that alter or eliminate exclusive franchises or that alter the competitive environment are risks financial institution managers must face. For example, in the United States the Deregulation Act and the Garn–St Germain Acts radically altered the competitive environment for deposit-taking institutions by deregulating interest rates on deposits and authorizing new activities. The European Community's single-market initiative has shaken traditional market boundaries for financial services. Proposed legislation may soon change competitive barriers among deposit-taking institutions and insurance-type intermediaries and securities firms. Changes in regulatory policy produce risks that are of substantial concern to financial institution managers.

Legislative and regulatory changes do not occur in a vacuum. Draft regulations of bank and insurance regulators are typically circulated for comment prior to implementation. Legislation at local and national levels is a public process of deliberation in a democracy. Parties most directly benefiting or harmed by a new policy initiative try to influence the process. Banks, thrifts, insurance brokers and underwriters, securities firms, and other financial institutions are among the largest contributors to political campaigns and have some of the most potent and effective lobbying organizations.

A good example of the balance of forces that must be achieved to change the financial system is the 1980 Deregulation Act in the United States. Major provisions of the act had been advocated persuasively and aggressively by disinterested industry observers and academics for decades. The Hunt Commission in 1968 made recommendations contained in the Deregulation Act, building on work of the Commission on Money and Credit in the 1950s. The Committee on Financial Institutions and the National Economy in Congress made many of the same recommendations in 1973. The explanation for delay in implementing these long-standing recommendations is that strong political forces were balanced so action in Congress was impossible. A nearly miraculous convergence of forces forced the Federal Reserve, banks, thrifts, and the elderly to form a grand, if fleeting, coalition that led to common support for passage of the law in 1980.

The coalition of the Federal Reserve, banks, thrifts, and old people formed because it was in each of their interests to agree. The Federal Reserve was concerned about banks leaving the Federal Reserve system. Banks were concerned about the competition from money market mutual funds as the interest rates banks paid fell below rates on money market instruments. Thrifts wanted expanded powers, including the ability to take consumer checking accounts. Retired people wanted higher interest rates to offset inflation. The convergence of these interest groups favoring a single piece of legislation was historic.

The Deregulation Act illustrates that key legislation affecting the business environment of financial service firms is passed in an atmosphere of aggressive pursuit of narrow interests by dedicated firms and individuals. Each law or regulatory change reflects a complex political–economic process. Laws and regulatory changes result either from delicate bargaining between interest groups and aggressive lobbying or from disasters that demand action.

The business environment facing financial institutions is influenced by political activity from industry groups and individual actions. When the change occurs, it may occur unpredictably after a delay storing up large economic forces. Change is often cataclysmic, as the Deregulation Act and following legislation proved to be. Managers must learn to assess the political risks associated with the regulation of their industry and incorporate those risks into the strategy and tactics.

Value Production and Economic Risks

How can financial institutions produce value given the macroeconomic and microeconomic risks we have discussed. There are three sources of value: (1) value from early identification of trends; (2) value from enlightened defense of self-interest through the political process; and (3) value from assisting customers and clients in dealing with these risks.

The trends underlying economic events have potential for assisting management define business strategies. Two examples may help make this concrete. Demographics suggest that the large cohort of baby boomers who delayed having children until their thirties will be simultaneously putting children through college and saving for retirement. These trends can be exploited by financial service managers assessing the demand for credit and savings instruments among this age group in the future. A second example of a major trend with strategic implications for financial institutions is the formation of a North American Free Trade Area. Trade financing and investment services in this region will undoubtedly grow. Identification of basic economic developments like demographic changes or changes in international economic trade and investment flows can be used by financial institution managers to develop long-run plans to gain a competitive edge over other firms not so forward looking.

The second source of value creation is obvious. Keep track of what is happening in city hall, regional, and national capitals. Many financial firms develop contacts for information and influence in the regulatory and legislative environments and are active in trade associations. All of these channels are exploited to protect existing and gain new competitive advantages.

The final source of value is to develop services and products that assist customers and clients in dealing with these risks. For purposes of this book, this is the most important implication of risks from the macroeconomic and microeconomic environment. Most of the book deals with ways to measure and manage the risks stemming from the economic environment.

13.4 SUMMARY

This chapter reviews sources of macroeconomic and microeconomic risks facing financial institution managers and their customers. The benchmark from which to assess risk is an economy in a conceptual long-run equilibrium. From this analysis it emerges that risks are most likely the result of short-run shocks to the economy, many of which are induced by government monetary and fiscal policy. The impact of risks on asset values comes from their effects on cash flows and discount rates. We trace the impact of shocks on the determinants of cash flows and the elements of discount rates. Microeconomic risks are analyzed as regional and industrial risks and risks due to regulation. Regulatory risk is of particular significance and concern to managers and investors in financial service firms.

DISCUSSION QUESTIONS AND EXERCISES

1. What has happened recently to the major economic time series like GDP growth, industrial production, inflation, and so on? Is the current time period a boom, bust, recovery, or recession? Why?
2. What has happened recently to stock prices and interest rates? What explanations are commentators making for these recent events? How do they compare to what was happening one year and five years ago?
3. What is happening to financial service firms? Are various segments doing well or poorly? Why? Be specific. Relate their current situation and prospects to the macroeconomic risk environment.
4. What demographic trends do you feel are important in your region? What effect will they have on the demand for financial services in the future?
5. Milton Friedman advocates the use of a monetary base growth rule. Do you think that use of such a rule by the Federal Reserve would increase or decrease risk? Why?
6. What is the status of the current debate concerning the regulation of financial services (that is, what changes in legislation and regulation are being discussed)? What impact could the discussed changes have on the business environment of financial service firm managers?
7. What has been the recent level of the various components' long-term risky interest rates? How have they changed in the last six months and year? What elements have changed? Can you relate these changes to macroeconomic risk?
8. Home equity loans have been a very successful product for banks, savings and loans, brokerage firms, and insurance companies. What makes this product attractive to consumers? What are the risks in this product?
9. What are the major sources of the following insurance market risks: change in amounts of required auto insurance coverage, costs of auto repairs, increase in speed limit and number of accidents, awards to victims of auto accidents, increase in local taxes?
10. Can financial firms influence risk stemming from government policy actions? Would such influence produce value? Do financial firms attempt such influence? At what governmental levels?

REFERENCES

BIRNBAUM, JEFFREY and ALAN MURRAY. 1987. *Showdown at Gucci Gulch*. New York: Random House.

BLACK, FISHER. 1987. *Business Cycles and Equilibrium*. New York: Basil Blackwell.

BURMEISTER, EDWIN and KENT D. WALL. 1986. "The Arbitrage Pricing Theory and Macroeconomic Factor Measures," *Financial Review* 21 (1), pp. 1–20.

BURMEISTER, EDWIN, KENT D. WALL, and JAMES D. HAMILTON. 1986. "Estimation of Unobserved Expected Monthly Inflation using Kalman Filtering," *Journal of Business and Economic Statistics* 4 (2), pp. 147–160.

Chen, Nai-Fu, Richard Roll, and Steven Ross. 1986. "Economic Factors and the Stock Market," *Journal of Business* 59, pp. 383–393.

Cox, John C., Jonathan E. Ingersoll, Jr., and Stephen A. Ross. 1985a. "An Intertemporal General Equilibrium Model of Asset Prices," *Econometrica* 53 (2), pp. 363–384.

Cox, John C., Jonathan E. Ingersoll, Jr., and Stephen A. Ross. 1985b. "A Theory of the Term Structure of Interest Rates," *Econometrica* 53 (2), pp. 385–407.

Fama, Eugene. 1975. "Short Term Interest Rates as Predictors of Inflation," *American Economic Review,* 65 (June), pp. 269–282.

Fama, Eugene. 1976. "Forward Rates as Predictors of Future Spot Rates," *Journal of Financial Economics* 3, pp. 361–377.

Ibbotson Roger G. and Rox A. Sinquefield. 1993. *Stocks, Bonds, Bills and Inflation: 1992 Yearbook* Chicago: Ibbotson Associates.

Plosser, Charles I. (1989) "Understanding Real Business Cycles," *Economic Perspectives* 3 (3), pp. 51–77.

Solow, Robert. 1957. "Technical Change and the Aggregate Production Function," *Review of Economic Studies* 39 (August), pp. 312–320.

CHAPTER

14

Regulation of Deposit-Taking Financial Institutions

Introduction

This chapter presents the economics of deposit-taking institution regulation and describes current and emerging regulatory and political environments in the United States and around the world. In the rapidly changing competitive environment for financial service institutions, several questions require not only answers but an analytical framework that can be used to interpret events as they occur.

- What does it mean to be a deposit-taking firm?
- What are the economic advantages to being a deposit-taking institution?
- Why are depository institutions so heavily regulated?
- What types of regulation are there and what is the economic impact?

Advantages of being a deposit-taking institution are shifting and changing. The regulatory environment presents ongoing business risks to financial institution managers. A conceptual framework is essential to formulate value-maximizing strategies and evaluate business trade-offs in the future.

14.1 CHARTERS, FRANCHISES, AND VALUE

To do business as a deposit-taking institution, a financial institution applies for or assumes a charter issued by a regulatory authority. The only reason to be a deposit-taking institution is because deposit-taking authority has value to the owners of the institution. A charter granting the right to do business in a market with limited competition is called a franchise. Limited competition can be a source of value in any business. In most regulatory environments, issuance of deposit-taking charters is restricted and can create franchise value to firms holding charters.

What is the source of the value of the deposit-taking charter and franchise? Deposit liabilities are often assumed by purchasers of bank and thrift branch offices. In efficient and competitive markets, economic theory tells us deposit liabilities should be valued at 100 percent of their face value plus the value of any physical assets like branch buildings. In fact, in the United States, retail deposits are often valued at only 95 to 97 percent of face value. Banks with retail branches are often valued at many times book value in acquisitions. The premium associated with retail deposits must have to do with relationships between customers and the deposit-taking institutions which can be exploited to create value. Retail deposits must be cheaper than other available funds to cause these liabilities to be assumed at a discount from their face value.

Several perhaps complementary attributes of retail deposits explain why they are a cheap source of funds. In the United States, deposit liabilities of officially chartered deposit-taking institutions are insured by agencies of the Federal government. In other countries, particularly European countries, deposit insurance or guarantees vary and may be less publicized than in the United States (Baltensperger and Dermine 1993). Deposit insurance means depositors view deposits as virtually risk free and are satisfied receiving interest close to the risk free rate. Deposit insurance may reduce the cost of funds to deposit-taking institutions.

Deposits have other economic attributes explaining a lower cost or higher value to issuers than alternative sources of funds. One cost advantage is customer inertia in shopping for deposits. It costs consumers time and effort to switch the location of deposits. Because of these costs, customers may accept lower interest or a lower equivalent value in deposit-based services rather than seek alternatives uses of their funds.

Deposit-taking institutions may have a geographical or technological competitive advantage with their current depositors. Competition for deposits geographically may be limited because of regulatory restrictions on new branches. Necessary investments in computer equipment, software, communications, and transportation systems may mean that there are barriers to entry into the deposit-taking business. Regulation may limit access to some government-subsidized activities, such as the clearing system, to authorized franchise holders. Although competition for consumer deposits is increasing around the world, deposits may be cheap due to reduced competition from geographical advantages and barriers to entry.

A final cost advantage may come from experience and information about deposit customers. Knowing customers well may make it easier to do other business with them. Information on deposit activity provides cash flow information to deposit-taking institutions providing credit services. Deposit-taking services may be synergistic with other products offered by the deposit-taking firm, such as credit cards or other loans. Deposit relationships may have value as sales contacts for cross-selling other financial services and products.

In the deregulated and competitive financial services markets of the future, deposit-taking franchises may not be necessary to obtain value from synergies and cross-selling deposit services. For example, brokerage firms offer retail customers check writing privileges by forming relationships with banks, as Merrill Lynch has done with Banc One in Ohio. Deposit-taking services are not provided by Merrill Lynch directly but the value added by combining checking and brokerage services is retained.

To summarize, the reasons to choose a deposit-taking institution charter are that deposit funds may be cheaper than nondeposit sources of funds and financial firms may be able to exploit synergies and cross-selling with other services. Some firms may have relative expertise in the activities associated with processing and marketing deposits since there are unique costs associated with being an authorized deposit-taking institution. Among these costs are extensive regulation.

Supply of Deposit-Taking Charters

In all advanced economies, government or official authority is required to raise funds through deposits. Deposit-taking charters are granted to financial service firms, typically banks, in exchange for restrictions on activities and other requirements, like reporting and examinations. In the United States and in Europe since 1992, deposit-taking institutions have a veritable menu of choices for a chartering authority.

In the United States, the options are to be chartered as a commercial bank, a savings bank, a credit union, or a finance company. State and federal governments both issue charters. In Europe, a charter granted by any member country is valid throughout the Common Market.

Choice of charter represents a choice of regulators, legislative and regulatory authorities, restrictions placed on activities, and on tax treatment. This decision is critical. We emphasize the importance of charter choice in terms of the potential for value production and business environmental risk. The charter decision must be made with the financial institution's business strategy in mind. Authorized activities and risk of regulatory review and changes are specific to the charter obtained.

The Regulatory Establishment in the United States

Which regulator reviews and approves the management decisions of deposit-taking institutions depends on the charter of the firm. Assignment of regulatory responsibility for individual firms is the result of a capricious legislative and regulatory history and a source of business risk. For example, a revolutionary reorganization in these responsibilities occurred in the United States with the Financial Institutions Reform, Recovery and Enforcement Act of 1989 (FIRREA) resulting in the regulatory establishment for banks and thrifts outlined in Table 14.1.

Assignment of deposit-taking institutions to regulatory authorities in the United States depends on whether the institution is chartered under state or federal law. Some deposit-taking institutions, like thrift and loans, are chartered only by state governments. If deposits issued by a deposit-taking institutions are not

TABLE 14.1 Federal Deposit-Taking Institution Regulators

Special Offices of the United States Treasury Department:

Office of the Comptroller of the Currency (OCC)

Established by the National Currency Act (1863) and National Bank Act (1864) to charter and supervise national banks.

Office of Thrift Supervision (OTS)

Established by the Financial Institution Reform, Recovery and Enforcement Act (FIRREA) (1989) to replace the Federal Home Loan Bank Board, an independent agency established by the Home Owners Loan Act (1933) and abolished by FIRREA.

Board of Governors of the Federal Reserve System (FRS)

Established by the Federal Reserve Act (1913) to coordinate activities of 12 Federal Reserve Banks, authorized by Bank Holding Company Act (1956, amended 1970) to regulate acquisitions of bank holding companies.

12 Federal Reserve Banks (FRBs)

Regional, privately owned by members of the Federal Reserve Bank System established by the FRA. Regulates local member banks, operates local discount window, holds local deposit reserves, performs local clearing functions through system of local branches, 36 in all.

Federal Deposit Insurance Corporation (FDIC)

Established by the Banking Act of 1933 to act as receiver of failed banks and to insure qualifying state and national bank deposits. Supervises non–Federal Reserve member state chartered insured banks.

Bank Insurance Fund (BIF)

Bank insurance fund kept separate from savings fund, described below.

Savings Institution Insurance Fund (SAIF)

Savings institution insurance fund established by FIRREA to replace Federal Savings and Loan Insurance Fund (FSLIC) established in the Home Owners Loan Act.

Federal Housing Finance Board

Established by FIRREA to replace Federal Home Loan Bank Board (FHLBB) which was established to oversee the 12 regional Federal Home Loan Banks in the Home Owners Loan Act. The FHFB lost the supervisory powers of the FHLBB, which were assigned by FIRREA to the OTS.

12 Federal Home Loan Banks (FHLBBs)

Regional banks owned by members of the FHLB System, which loans money to members borrowed in bond markets. Membership in FHLB System opened by FIRREA to nonthrift institutions and stripped of regulatory authority.

National Credit Union Administration (NCUA)

Charters and regulates federal credit unions, established by the Federal Credit Union Act (1934) as amended by the Federal Credit Union Administration Act (1970) which also established the National Credit Union Share Insurance Fund (NCUSIF).

---

covered by insurance, no federal agency regulates the institutions. Failure of uninsured state-chartered institutions in Maryland and Ohio in the 1980s caused most states to require federal deposit insurance for all deposit-taking institutions so that virtually all deposit-taking institutions are regulated by one federal agency. Table 14.2 shows the primary regulator depending on whether the chartering statute is state or federal.

TABLE 14.2 Deposit-Taking Institution Charters and Associated Primary Regulator

CHARTER TYPE/LOCATION	*NATIONAL/FEDERAL*	*STATE*
Commercial bank		
	Office of Comptroller of the Currency (OCC)	Federal Reserve Board (Member)
		Federal Deposit Insurance System (FDIC) (Non-Member)
Savings and loan	Office of Thrift Supervision (OTS)	State Agency, FDIC
Savings bank	OTS	State Agency, FDIC
Credit union	National Credit Union Administration (NCUA)	State Agency
Thrift and loan	N/A	State Agency, FDIC (if insured)
Finance company	N/A	State Agency, FDIC (if insured)

Deposit-taking institutions in other countries may be chartered at the national or regional level. For example, in Germany some savings institutions are locally chartered. For the twelve countries within the European Community (EC), at least twelve national chartering authorities are available. The Single European Act of 1986 called for a coordinated effort to integrate European markets. Laws passed in each of the twelve countries were coordinated under the First and Second Banking Directives of the European Commission as part of the single market initiative. Under these laws, deposit-taking institutions are regulated by country of charter and domicile and are allowed to compete within all European markets against local institutions.

Corporations owning deposit-taking institutions are also regulated. Holding companies of commercial banks in the United States are regulated by the Federal Reserve Board. Holding companies of thrifts are regulated by the OTS. FIRREA allowed bank holding companies to acquire thrifts, and the resulting holding company, owning both commercial banks and thrifts, is regulated by the Federal Reserve Board.

In this brief review of regulatory authorities, we stress that the regulatory system determines financial institution business opportunities and risks. The system changes and can dramatically alter competitive conditions. For example, the State of California substantially revised the thrift sections of its financial code in 1983, responding to widespread defections from state to federal charters because of harsh state regulatory treatment. The revision in California law was intended to make the California savings and loan charter attractive again. State legislators substantially deregulated activities of California chartered thrifts, making California charters among the most attractive in the United States. Many of these authorities were revoked by FIRREA in 1989, requiring divestitures and changed business plans of thrifts in California.

Choice of charters and the range of authorized powers and tax benefits associated with different types of charters induces comparative "shopping" for charters by institutions desiring to accept deposits. Kane (1983) calls the search for the best regulatory abode *regulatee avoidance*. Many financial service firms obtain more than one charter through holding companies or subsidiaries. For example, Bank of America owns both federally and state chartered banks. Citicorp owns both bank and thrift institution charters. The ability to have many different deposit-taking charters was authorized in the Garn–St Germain Act (1982) and was expanded in FIRREA (1989) due to the continuing thrift crisis. Managers of financial institutions must keep up-to-date on changing charter characteristics.

Changes in taxation and laws and regulations governing issuance of charters and their associated powers are a source of risks to deposit-taking institution managers. Few other businesses are subject to such sudden shifts in their competitive environment as deposit-taking institutions. In the United States, new competitors, new rules, and new price competition all sprang forth overnight as a result of the miraculous passage of the Deregulation Act of 1980 described in the previous chapter. In Europe, protected national markets were opened to competition from other European Community financial firms. Constant changes in allowable activities, rules, and procedures are an irritating and costly risk to deposit-taking institutions.

14.2 REASONS FOR DEPOSIT-TAKING INSTITUTION REGULATION

Why are deposit-taking institutions regulated? Answers to the question can and should be gauged against the position taken by some economists that there is no reason for these institutions to be as heavily regulated as they are. Economists arguing against regulation point out first that government is not needed to ensure provision of deposit services. In efficient markets with no barriers to entry, deposit-taking institutions would perform the transaction processing and financial intermediation functions we have described. Furthermore, these functions would be provided without the loss of efficiency stemming from the rigidities and privileges associated with the regulatory superstructure. Finally, some reasons advanced for regulation are not justified by economic theory.

What is it that regulation is supposed to provide that unfettered competition would not? Chapter 3 provided a broad framework for arguments in support of financial institution regulation which we repeat here:

1. To promote government policy goals in the allocation of financial resources
2. To offset the disadvantage to those who are unable to understand financial information
3. To accommodate economy-wide risks that cannot be absorbed by individual firms
4. To promote competition.

We discuss the relevance of each of these regulatory objectives to deposit-taking institutions in this and following sections.

Deposit-Taking Regulation To Promote Government Policy Goals

Transaction accounts like demand and other checking accounts are believed by most economists and government officials to play a special role in an economy since they can be used to pay for things: They are money. These deposit accounts are included in many statistical estimates of the "money supply," such as M_1, which is calculated as currency plus demand deposits, or M_2, which is M_1 plus smaller savings deposits in most countries. The first reason usually advanced for regulating deposit-taking institutions is to control the supply of money to influence the efficiency and growth of the economy.

Government influence over the money supply in most countries comes from the government's control of currency and coin. Controlling the amount of government liabilities in the form of currency, coin, and central bank deposits (called *base money* by economists) is an ancient source of government power.

Governments routinely require deposit-taking institutions to hold a fraction of their deposit liabilities in the form of currency and coin or as zero-interest central bank deposits called *reserves*. Deposit-taking institutions are usually required by the terms of their charters or by regulation to hold reserves in order to participate in the central-bank-sponsored clearing system. Required reserves are a means of influencing the money supply and of taxing deposit-taking institutions, which are forced to invest in government liabilities (reserves) earning no interest.

Fractional reserves, typical of nearly all countries, are reserves held against a percent of transaction-oriented deposits and possibly time deposits. Since the fraction is less than 100 percent, deposit liabilities used as a medium of exchange can be much larger than the reserve base. In the United States reserves are 10 percent of transaction accounts.

Governments influence economic activity and inflation and real interest rates through control of the level and growth rate of reserves and currency and their linkage to the supply of money through the fractional reserves. We have discussed the importance of monetary policy to all financial institutions, including deposit-taking institutions, as a source of risk in Chapter 13.

Some economists dispute the special role of deposit liabilities in affecting the level of economic activity. Black (1987) among others argues that the money supply in an economy is endogenous, determined in equilibrium by the supply and demand of financial market participants. According to Black, the government does not determine the money supply, the market does. Reserve requirements and other regulations are inconveniences and hindrances that can be avoided. Fama (1980) argues that base money is used as a means of settlement only because it is easy but deposits are not the only conceivable medium of exchange in advanced economies. If government regulation is too burdensome, many economists argue, it can be avoided.

An even larger number of economists believe that using deposit reserves to manipulate or fine tune the supply of money causes more risks to the financial system than it cures. They argue that government cannot predict the future any better than participants in efficient capital markets. Efforts to "fine tune" the economy through unanticipated changes in the growth rate in reserves is a source of uncertainty and risk to market participants.

Application of Reserve Requirements

In the United States, all transaction accounts, including savings accounts with transaction features, are subject to a 10 percent reserve requirement. Corporate time deposits and personal time deposits are also subject to reserve requirements in many countries but not the United States. Individual savings deposits have been exempted from reserve requirements since 1983 in the United States and for all time deposits, including corporate time deposits, since December 1990. The reserve requirement in the United States was lowered from 12 to 10 percent in April 1992. Changes in reserve requirements are a source of risk to deposit-taking institutions since reserve requirements affect the net cost of deposit funds.

The definition of transaction and time deposits in the United States matters to deposit-taking institutions, since transaction accounts yield only 90 percent (netting out the 10 percent reserve requirement) of their face value in investable funds, whereas time deposits yield 100 percent. The importance of regulatory language and the possibility of skirting limitations and producing value through cost savings can perhaps best be illustrated by the Federal Reserve's current definition of a transaction account in the United States:

> [Transaction accounts] includes all deposits against which the account holder is permitted to make withdrawals by negotiable or transferable instruments, payment orders of withdrawal, and telephone and preauthorized transfers for the purpose of making payments to third persons or others, other than money market deposit accounts (MMDAs) and similar accounts that permit no more than six preauthorized, automatic, or other transfers per month, of which no more than three can be checks (accounts subject to such limits are considered savings deposits). (1995, p. 49, Table 1.15n)

Readers can imagine the energy that managers of deposit-taking institutions devote to thinking of ways to reduce reserve costs by exploiting the complexity and ambiguity of this language as it applies to deposit accounts. They also seek changes in the language through pressure on legislators and regulators.

Calculation of Reserves. In the United States, reserve requirements are calculated according to a *contemporaneous reserve accounting system* (CRAS) as opposed to the *lagged reserve accounting system* (LRAS) used from 1968 to 1984.

The differences between these two reserve calculations have more than historical significance. Industry pressure or legislative caprice may restore LRAS in the future—another risk. Reserve calculation methods can best be illustrated by an example of reserve calculation. Table 14.3 illustrates the calculation of reserves under CRAS.

Required reserves in the United States are computed on the basis of a two-week average of reservable deposit balances. Three main points should be observed concerning reserve requirements: (1) reserve requirements are calculated as a daily average over a time period determined by the reserve computation system; (2) required average reserves must be made available within a limited *reserve settlement* period (under CRAS, two days after the reserve computation period), otherwise a penalty is imposed; and finally, (3) reserve requirements can be met with cash in the vault or deposits at the Federal Reserve. In the example, the deposit-taking institution must make up 200 dollars of reserves from the reserve calculation period on the Wednesday settlement day.

There is a penalty for reserve shortfalls and excess reserves earn no interest. Deposit-taking institutions manage their reserves to avoid either reserve shortfalls or excess reserves. Typically, the *money desk* of a financial institution manages the reserve position. Money desk managers can borrow reserve balances from other deposit-taking institutions in the Federal Funds market if they are short, as in the example. Unneeded balances can be sold to other deposit-taking institutions in the same market. For some banks, Federal funds are a semipermanent source of funds and for others a semipermanent investment, even though most Fed funds are overnight transactions.

TABLE 14.3 Calculation of Reserve Requirements (Contemporaneous Reserve Accounting System (CRAS))

DAY	*DEPOSITS*	*RESERVE REQUIREMENT COMPUTATION*	*RESERVE BALANCE*	*CUMULATIVE RESERVE REQUIREMENT*
Tuesday	1000	100		
Wednesday	1500	150		
Thursday	2000	200	100	0
Friday	2500	250	120	30
Monday	1000	100	150	80
Tuesday	1500	150	200	130
Wednesday	2000	200	180	50
Thursday	1000	100	200	0
Friday	1500	150	150	50
Monday	1000	100	200	150
Tuesday			200	100
Wednesday			To be Settled	200

Reserve management is complicated by several factors. Under CRAS, a deposit-taking institution knows its required reserves only two days before the settlement period. Problems from not knowing required reserves in advance was the rationale behind the now-abandoned LRAS, which used a reserve accounting period two weeks earlier for calculating required reserves. The return to CRAS after a twenty-year experiment with LRAS is an attempt to tighten the Fed's short-term control over the money supply. With CRAS, open-market operations affect the availability of bank reserves to meet banks' required reserves nearly immediately.

Management of the money desk is complicated by daily fluctuations in reserves balances from clearing and wire transfers. Check clearing means changes in reserve balances are not accurately predictable. Even less predictable is the effect of use of the Fed wire system to transfer funds between banks and Federal Reserve districts by customers. Wire transfers immediately decrease or increase reserves. Wire transfers are a larger source of daily reserve account activity than check clearing for larger banks.

Uncertainty concerning the required reserve amount and unpredictable changes in reserve balances force deposit-institution money desk managers to adopt a number of strategies to meet reserves requirements. They can hold excess balances early in the reserve maintenance period to hedge the possibility of reserve outflows or large increases in reserve requirements later in the reserve calculation period. This strategy risks excess holdings of zero-interest bearing reserves. An alternative strategy is to borrow required reserves in the Fed funds market toward the end of the reserve maintenance period, risking high borrowing costs later in the reserve maintenance period. It can be easily verified by daily observation of the Feds funds rate that biweekly Wednesday settlement days exhibit the widest variation. On that day, deposit-taking institutions desperate to make required reserves may pay high rates, or a glut of excess reserves leads to negligible rates on Fed funds sold.

14.3 DEPOSIT INSURANCE AND ABSORPTION OF ECONOMY-WIDE RISKS

Government intervention in deposit markets is argued to be necessary to deal with economy-wide risks that individual firms cannot absorb. Policy makers argue that deposit-taking is essential to an efficient economy but cannot be offered with economy-wide risks from panic and runs on deposit-taking firms without government intervention. Deposit insurance in the United States was first provided with the Banking Act of 1933, in response to the banking crisis in the Depression. Many other countries implemented formal or informal deposit insurance systems in the same period.

Analysts are divided on the importance of deposit insurance. Many proponents of deposit insurance rely on a closely reasoned argument developed by Diamond and Dybvig (1983). Their influential study argues that deposit-taking institutions require government intervention to be able to invest in illiquid assets like loans using funds raised in the form of claims consumers want to hold, like liquid deposits. This economic function of banks is termed the *transmutation* of illiquid assets into liquid liabilities. Understanding the Diamond and Dybvig analysis of the role of deposits is important given the heated debate about the special nature of deposits in the economy.

The Diamond and Dybvig analysis assumes savers may need cash for unexpected consumption before productive project returns are realized. Deposits are liquid since they can be turned into cash on demand. Diamond and Dybvig provide an exact demonstration of the economic benefits of transmutation and how these benefits are lost without government intervention. In their analysis, consumers make decisions in period 0 concerning use of their investible funds. Consumers can invest in projects that pay 1 + R percent of investment in period 2. Consumers may unexpectedly need cash before project returns are realized, called period 1. Projects that are not completed can be liquidated at cost in period 1. If consumers can wait until Period 2 to consume, they realize the full payoff of projects.

If there were no banking system, consumers would all own their own projects. In this benchmark case in Diamond and Dybvig's analysis, each consumer needing cash in period 1 liquidates projects and consumes in period 1. Others wait until projects are completed and consume 1 + R times assets of consumption in period 2. An example without deposits is presented in Part A of Table 14.4 where consumers can consume 100 percent of their savings of $50 in period 1 or 300 percent or $150 in period 2. R equals 200 percent in the example. If 75 percent of consumers will need to consume in period 1, the expected utility is 6.99.

In the Diamond and Dybvig analysis, consumers do not know whether they will need to consume in period 1 or period 2. Risk-averse consumers can be made better off by sharing the risk that they will need to liquidate assets to consume in period 1. If the fraction of consumers needing cash in period 1 is known even though their identity is not, and if consumers actually needing the cash can be observed, the risk of needing cash in period 1 can be covered by insurance. The arithmetic example in Part B of Table 14.4 illustrates how expected utility is higher when the liquidity risk is shared with insurance policies relative to individuals acting independently.

With insurance, all consumers pay a premium, p, in period 0. Period 1 consumers get a payoff of P, the insurance benefit, plus their remaining savings. Period 2 consumers will get 1 + R times their investment net of the insurance premium, p. In the example in Table 14.4B, the premium is 15 out of 50 units of period 0 resources, or 30 percent of the savings, and the benefit is 20 units of period 1 consumption, increasing period 1 consumption by a net of 5 units or 10 percent. Period 2 consumers will lose their premiums but will have the benefit of higher returns including the payoff, of 105 in our example, or a 200 percent return on period 0 resources after the premium.[1]

[1]Strictly speaking, we compare period 1 consumption with discounted period 2 consumption because of positive time preference assumed by Diamond and Dybvig. The rate of return, R, is more than the discount rate. The increased expected utility comes from risk aversion as discussed in Chapter 6.

TABLE 14.4 Examples of Benefits of Sharing Liquidity Risk

	PERIOD 0	*PERIOD 1*	*PERIOD 2*
A. Individuals Acting Independently			
Resources available	50.00	50.00	150.00
Probability of consumption in period		.75	.25
Utility[a]		6.00	9.95
Expected utility[b]		6.99	
B. Insurance with Individual Type Observable			
Resources available	50.00	35.00	105.00
Premium paid	–15.00		
Insurance benefit		20.00	
Probability of consumption in period		.75	.25
Utility[a]		7.27	9.79
Expected utility[b]		7.90	
C. Deposits with Known Probability of Period 1 Consumers			
Resources available	50.00	50.00	105.00
Interest at 10%		5.00	
Probability of consumption in period		.75	.25
Utility[a]		7.27	9.79
Expected utility[b]		7.90	
D. Possible Outcome with Deposits and Unknown Probability			
Resources available	50.00	50.00	15.00
Interest at 10%		5.00	
Realized percent of consumers in period		.90	.10
Utility[a]		7.27	–483.83
Weighted utility[c]		(41.84)	
E. Possible Outcome with Deposits, Unknown Probability of Liquidity Need, Deposit Insurance, and Taxes			
Resources available[d]	50.00	50.00	69.00
Interest		5.00	
Tax on interest		–2.00	
Realized percent of consumers in period		.90	.10
Utility[a]		6.83	8.90
Weighted utility[c]		7.04	

[a]Utility is computed as 10 + 100,000,000*(C^{-4}/–4), where –4 is a parameter in the range often used for utility functions of this kind and other numbers are used to scale utility to positive numbers.

[b]Utility levels as described above weighted by probability of occurrence.

[c]Utility weighted by previously unknown actual percent of outcomes.

[d]A tax of 2 on period 1 deposit withdrawals (4 percent of the original deposit of 50 or 40 percent of interest paid in period 1 of 5) is determined by the government to be used to invest and increase period 2 consumption for period 2 consumers.

A problem arises in the Diamond and Dybvig analysis when consumers cannot identify who needs consumption in period 1 and who can wait. When consumption needs are not verifiable, they cannot be insured. An alternative solution is necessary when consumers' cash needs are not observable or verifiable. In the case when a known fraction will be period 1 consumers but they cannot be identified, an alternative solution is for banks to take deposits and pay fixed interest over one or two periods, as shown in Part C of Table 14.4. Banks hold illiquid assets and announce that they will stop deposit withdrawals in period 1 as soon as the known fraction of period 1 consumption funds has been withdrawn. Expected utility is increased because period 1 consumers receive some interest.

Diamond and Dybvig describe the case where deposit-taking firms stop withdrawals as "suspension of convertibility," a term from pre–Federal Reserve banking when banks would stop honoring requests for deposit withdrawals. With suspension of convertibility, no period 2 consumers withdraw in period 1 because they know their funds with higher interest will be available at the bank in period 2. The improvement in expected utility with a known fraction of period 1 consumers and suspension of convertibility is an economic justification for the existence of deposit-taking firms investing in illiquid assets.

The general case is when the demand for liquidity in period 1 (the fraction of period 1 consumers) is uncertain. In the Diamond and Dybvig model, this uncertainty can cause a run on deposits and banking panics. Runs are the reason for recommending government deposit insurance. The total need for liquidity in period 1 is not known with certainty and only becomes clear during period 1. Since consumers of the two types cannot be told apart, and promised interest of $1 + r_1$ to period 1 consumers means that withdrawals of deposits by consumers demanding liquidity produces returns less than $1 + R$, in fact these returns can be negative, as shown in Part D of Table 14.4. To avoid losses, all depositors panic and try to liquidate in period 1, producing a run on deposits.

The value added by risk sharing between those needing liquidity in period 1 and those who can wait until period 2 is lost when there is an unknown fraction of period 1 consumers unless a solution to the problem of bank panics can be found. With possible runs on deposits, all consumers own their own projects as in the first case and the economic benefits of banking intermediation in the form of higher expected utility of all consumers are lost. Avoiding this real economic efficiency loss is the way Diamond and Dybvig characterize the economic contribution of deposit-taking institutions to the economy.

Diamond and Dybvig advocate tax-financed government deposit insurance to guarantee deposit funds to consumers who can wait until period 2. They point out that a "lender of last resort," like the Federal Reserve, serves the same purpose as a deposit insurer. An important rationale for the deposit insurance system is that the government can use taxes to guarantee deposits. With deposit guarantees and taxes on period 1 deposit interest, only period 1 consumers withdraw in period 1. Period 2 consumers wait because the security of their funds is guaranteed. Projects financed by period 2 consumers' deposits reach their full productivity, as shown in Part E of Table 14.4.

Taxing authority of the government is essential. Only governments can tax period 1 consumers if they need period 1 consumption. Expected withdrawals in both period 1 and period 2 net of tax must provide an expected utility higher than with no banking. Transferring some resources to period 2 consumers will accomplish an expected utility increase. The improvement in expected utility may mean expected reduced period 2 consumption if the fraction of period 1 consumers is large enough. Taxes on deposit withdrawals in period 1 reduce the advantage of panic withdrawals if a consumer is a period 2 consumer. Deposit guarantees induce period 2 consumers to wait.

Critics of deposit insurance attack Diamond and Dybvig's analysis on two levels: (1) that their model is not appropriate; and (2) that assumptions in their model do not match reality and changes in their assumptions change the conclusion that deposit insurance is necessary. Some argue that Diamond and Dybvig's deposit-taking system is really only one big bank. With many banks, runs reassign claims on assets and underlying assets are not destroyed. Bank runs mean a reallocation of claims on productive assets, not destruction of wealth. If bank runs are due to geographical shortages of liquid assets, temporary reallocation mechanisms for liquidity can eliminate the most dangerous aspect of bank runs.

Criticism of the Diamond and Dybvig model has produced alternative solutions to the liquidity problem that do not rely on deposit insurance. For example, Wallace (1988) demonstrates that if timing of withdrawals of period 1 consumers matters, so the first period 1 consumers withdrawing funds receive slightly more than consumers withdrawing later, period 2 consumers are induced to wait rather than panic. They do not fear receiving the benefits of the greater productivity of assets in terms of higher interest on their deposits due to their waiting to withdraw funds.

Historical evidence from the nineteenth century is used to argue that bank runs can be overcome with suspension of convertibility or temporary mechanisms. The disastrous bank runs of the 1930s are characterized as the result of inept policy by the newly created Federal Reserve System and other central banks in a famous study by Milton Friedman and Anna Schwartz (1963). Many argue that lack of deposit insurance did not cause the panic of 1933.

Many discussions of the importance of deposit insurance have focused on the economic costs of the banking collapse in the Great Depression in the United States and the world in the 1930s. The real economic effects of the 1933 banking crisis are analyzed by Bernanke (1983), whose statistical analysis of the decline in real output during the Great Depression assigns a major role to bank failures. Bernanke argues that the loss of valuable credit-related services like the loan analysis and monitoring provided by banks is important in explaining the Great Depression. The loss of bank services reinforced the negative impact of monetary contraction emphasized by Friedman and Schwartz.

Many economists, for example Benston *et al* (1986), argue that the bank runs in the Great Depression were unusual and that bank runs are not so bad. This argument is usually joined with a discussion of distortions in bank management behavior induced by the existence of insured deposits. In these discussions, any benefits of providing deposit insurance is weighed against the negative effects on efficiency and safety of banks coming from the ability of banks to raise funds at a cheap government-insured interest rate. The Diamond and Dybvig analysis does not consider the riskiness of productive assets and bank management's objectives in financing business activity.

The arguments in support of deposit insurance can be summarized as follows: (1) bank runs are bad because they force premature liquidation of productive assets; (2) deposit insurance reduces depositors' inclination to panic and withdraw funds earlier than they are needed; (3) total demand for liquidity may shift such that private market solutions to the illiquidity problem, such as suspension of convertibility or temporary liquidity pools like those organized in the nineteenth century, are not feasible. Critics argue against the first two points using historical evidence that arguments favoring deposit insurance overstate the costs, that lack of deposit insurance was not the problem in previous bank runs, and alternative mechanisms can deal with temporary problems. Many argue that deposit insurance should be evaluated in terms of the distortions it induces in both the costs and uses of government-insured funds raised by deposit-taking institutions.

14.4 REGULATION OF COMPETITION AND PRICES

Regulation of deposit-taking institutions since the 1930s has been bedeviled by two conflicting goals. The first goal is to assure consumers that deposit-taking services are provided in a competitive environment producing efficiency and minimum cost. The second has been to prevent deposit-taking institutions from self-destructing from "cutthroat competition." Policies to advance both goals have been clouded by the active intervention in policy deliberations of financial service firms who gain from protected markets or access to new markets.

Competition is regulated along four dimensions: (1) review of new financial institution charters and applications for branches; (2) review of mergers and acquisitions of deposit-taking institutions and authorization of new competitors; (3) restrictions on ownership of deposit-taking institutions; and finally, (4) price controls and limitations on access to government subsidies. We discuss each in turn.

Chartering and Branching

Deposit-taking institutions require a special charter, as discussed previously. Review of charter applications is a way to control the level of competition in specific markets. Until 1994 in the United States, state laws determined deposit-taking markets. The McFadden Act (1927) limited the branching authority of nationally chartered banks to that allowed state banks in the state where they are headquartered. The Bank Holding Company Act (as amended in 1970) restricted out-of-state purchases of banks unless allowed by state law. These rules were altered by the Riegle–Neal Interstate Banking and Branching Efficiency Act of 1994, which allowed mergers and acquisitions of banks across state lines and interstate branching. In Europe prior to 1992, each country in the Common Market controlled access to local deposit markets. The Single European Act now means that banks can do business across national boundaries.

Restrictions on Mergers, Acquisitions, and New Competitors

Competitive conditions can be altered by new combinations of existing firms in markets and firms moving into new markets. Regulators are concerned with both aspects of competition in deposit-taking markets. In the United States since the 1960 and 1966 Bank Merger Acts, regulators review combinations of commercial banks to assess the impact on competition in the markets where the merged banks operated. Bank mergers and acquisitions must receive the approval of regulators who are required to prove that no reduction in competition will result.

Regulators permitted a wave of bank mergers and acquisitions in both the United States and in the European Common Market in 1980s and 1990s. These combinations are across state or national boundaries as states allowed regional banking in the United States and the Common Market countries implemented the Single Market initiative. Examples are Banc One of Ohio's acquisitions of banks in many states including the largest bank in Arizona, and Nationsbank of North Carolina making major acquisitions in Texas, and Deutsche Bank buying the Bank of America subsidiary in Italy. Some large bank combinations have been within geographical regions, as in the largest bank merger to date, Bank of America and Security Pacific in California. According to *Mergers and Acquisitions* magazine, there have been more mergers and acquisitions in banking than in any other industry in the United States in the last few years.

The wave of bank mergers in the United States has been accompanied by new entrants into deposit-taking markets. Thrift institutions and credit unions were authorized by the Deregulation Act of 1980 to take checkable deposits and were given access to the Federal Reserve check clearing system. Other authorized powers of commercial banks, such as trust powers and credit card lending, were also extended to nonbank charters. Competition in deposit-taking markets has been increased through expanded authorities of other deposit-taking institution charters.

Restrictions on Ownership of Deposit-Taking Institutions

In the United States, limitations on ownership of deposit-taking institutions are contained in the Bank Holding Company Act of 1956 and amendments (mainly in 1970) and the Savings and Loan Holding Company Act. These acts govern holding company structure, restricting who can own deposit-taking firms. Whenever a corporation owns a bank, either by acquisition or by conversion from a stock-owned bank to a bank holding company, the corporation is under law a bank holding company. Parallel provisions apply to savings and loans.

Bank holding companies in the United States are registered with the Federal Reserve. Acquisitions by bank holding companies must be approved by the Federal Reserve Board. The Bank Holding Company Act restricts bank holding companies to ownership of firms in businesses "closely related to banking." Interpretation of the law is left up to the Federal Reserve Board except that insurance and real estate development are explicitly forbidden. The list of acceptable activities shifts with changes in the Federal Reserves attitudes and market developments. It was considered revolutionary when the Federal Reserve approved acquisition by Bank America Corporation of Charles Schwab, a discount brokerage, in 1983 (subsequently sold).

The holding company organizational form is used in the United States to acquire nonbanking activities and to extend deposit-taking activities to other states. For a period before the 1970 amendments to the Bank Holding Company Act, one-bank holding companies were not regulated. Many large banks formed holding companies in order to diversify into "nonbanking" activities. Until changed in the 1980s, commercial banking was narrowly defined to accepting deposits and making commercial loans. Some securities firms and credit card companies acquired "nonbanks" by only doing one of those two activities and thereby avoided Federal Reserve oversight. These loopholes illustrate managerial incentives to get around laws and regulations in order to move into profitable markets.

Savings and loan holding companies were less restricted. Restrictions on their activities mainly differentiated between unitary savings and loan holding companies and multiple savings and loan holding companies. Restrictions on multiple savings and loan holding companies restricted this organizational form being used to circumvent regulatory and tax regulations on allowable activities. Unitary savings and loan holding companies were virtually unlimited until FIRREA.

Pricing

Interest rates and other terms and prices of deposit-taking institutions are or were regulated around the world. In the United States, interest on demand deposits (corporate checking) was prohibited by the Banking Act of 1933 and remains prohibited today. Savings account interest rates at banks were regulated after 1935 and at thrifts after 1968. With the Deregulation Act of 1980 a phase-out of ceilings on savings account and consumer checking account rates began. In Japan, interest rates on deposits were regulated from the end of World War II until 1979, when a gradual phase-out on rate limitations on time deposits began. Many European countries have partially or totally deregulated interest rates in recent years. Other countries, like Korea, move slowly to allow deposit rates to respond to market forces.

Government regulation of interest rates and other prices, such as loan rates, is rationalized in two ways. Rate regulation in the Great Depression was intended to control "cutthroat" competition of banks. Presumably, if left unregulated, banks would compete themselves into bankruptcy. The second rationalization is to "stabilize" financial markets and prevent banks from cheating unwary customers. Using both rationales, interest rate regulation around the world has proven to be a government-sponsored way to fix prices.

The comfortable protection of deposit-taking institutions from market competition broke down in the 1980s for a number of reasons. First, inflation pushed market rates to levels that made consumers and corporations seek alternatives to deposits, such as Treasury bills. Second, active competition for funds by nonbanks, for example open-market issues of commercial paper, developed as deposit-taking institution funds dried up in high-interest rate environments.

Finally, other intermediaries like securities firms moved in to compete for savers' funds in the form of money market mutual funds.

Control over interest rates and other prices of deposit-taking institutions rarely serves consumers' interests. In the long run, protection from competition usually harms deposit-taking firms by allowing them to postpone costly but necessary portfolio adjustments. Thrift institutions were devastated by the sudden deregulation of rates on savings in the United States after 1980. The progress of deregulation of interest rates around the world is nonetheless retarded by bureaucrats reluctant to surrender power and by deposit-taking institutions enjoying market protection and wishing to postpone costly adjustments.

Many services offered by deposit-taking institutions require specific disclosures indicating "true" costs or yields to customers. The most extensive regulation in the United States concerns disclosures on the true yield cost of credit mandated in the Truth in Lending Act. Provisions of this legislation are implemented by the Federal Reserve through Regulation Z. Truth in lending requires retail lenders to disclose the actual interest cost of credit services, including service charges and loan origination fees. Other rules provide retail borrowers with "cooling off" periods within which they can decide not to accept the terms of a loan. These regulations are intended to even up the bargaining between possibly naive retail customers and sophisticated lenders at deposit institutions.

14.5 ASSET AND ACTIVITY REGULATION

Funds above required reserves are used by value-maximizing deposit-taking institution managers to acquire earning assets. Since investments in plant and equipment are trivial for deposit-taking institutions, most assets are financial assets. In an unregulated environment, the safety of deposit-taking institution investments would be determined solely by the assets acquired with deposits and other funds. Concern for depositors or the deposit insurer's safety provides the basic rationale for regulation of deposit-taking institutions' assets.

If deposit markets are inefficient either due to lack of sophistication or lack of information, regulation of asset quality may be necessary to protect naive depositors from exploitation. With deposit insurance, even sophisticated investors do not concern themselves with asset quality. Lack of *market discipline* because of uninformed investors or insured and indifferent investors puts responsibility for asset review of deposit-taking institutions on regulators who must protect the interests of the deposit-insuring agencies and the public funds backing them.

Deposit-taking institution managers may view deposit insurance as a put option (as discussed in Chapter 21) on the assets of the firm given to the equity owners by the deposit-insuring agency. Equity in any firm can be viewed as a call option on the assets of the firm. The value of a deposit-taking firm's equity can therefore be interpreted as the sum of two options, a put and a call on the assets of the firm. The value of the equity in an insured deposit-taking firm is increased when the value of these options increases.

Determinants of option values are discussed at length in Chapter 21 and include the riskiness of underlying assets. Greater risk means a greater chance of high or low values for the assets. Since risks are one-sided for options, risk increases the values of both put and call options. This means that rational value-maximizing deposit-taking institution managers will attempt to maximize the risk of the assets acquired with deposit funds unless hindered by regulatory action.

The crisis in deposit-taking institutions in the United States in the 1980s and 1990s came from a number of sources. Some are the result of macroeconomic risks discussed in the previous chapter. The rest are due to distortions in deposit-taking institution managers' incentives resulting from four policies concerning deposit-taking institutions: (1) making it easy to raise money in insured deposits by increasing maximum deposit insurance to $100,000 and allowing brokered deposits (Deregulation Act of 1980); (2) deregulation of interest rates putting pressure on earnings of thrifts holding low interest fixed rate assets (mortgages) (Deregulation Act and Garn–St Germain Act of 1982); (3) authorization of new powers to thrifts enabling a value-maximizing strategy of increasing the riskiness and expected returns on assets (Deregulation Act and Garn–St Germain Act and revisions in state laws); and (4) liberalization of restrictions on chartering and acquisitions of deposit-taking institutions (Garn–St Germain Act and revision in states laws and regulatory guidelines).

Regulatory restrictions on assets and review of asset quality are policies intended to avoid crises like the thrift and banking crisis of recent decades. The value of regulation can be measured by comparison of intentions and outcomes. Most analysts emphasize the lack of market discipline and distortions in managerial incentives from deposit insurance as causes of these crises. Entrenched industry and regulatory interests are unlikely to favor basic revisions in the deposit insurance system. Asset regulation of deposit-taking institutions will likely continue.

Types of Asset and Activity Regulation

There are three types of asset regulation: (1) prohibition of certain types of assets and activities; (2) regulation of the amount and quality of assets that can be acquired; and (3) examination of assets. Although these are dynamic and changing areas, we review them quickly below. The intention is to convey a flavor of regulation and the decision-making environment within which managers of deposit-taking institutions deploy funds raised in the form of deposits.

Prohibited Investments

Commercial banks in the United States are prohibited from ownership and control in corporate business not closely related to banking. Ownership of equity shares in corporations is prohibited, the only exceptions being investments in so-called *service corporations,* discussed below, and temporary ownership of equity collateral from loans that have gone bad. The prohibition on bank equity participation extends to other classes of investments, such as convertible corporate bonds and preferred stock. Equity can be owned only under circumstances typically related to troubled borrowers, and holdings are subject to time limits. Prohibition of stock ownership by U.S. banks is in marked contrast to countries like Germany and Japan, where banks can and do take large ownership positions and active management roles in manufacturing and other nonfinancial corporations.

State-chartered thrift institutions often have more authority to invest in nonfinancial firms, but the authorities vary with state legislation and regulation. In some states, thrifts were allowed to sell fast food and generate electricity through investments in service corporations. On the other hand, the FDIC imposes limits on nonfinancial activities and qualification for deposit insurance. The tax code, discussed in Chapter 17, provides other economic restrictions on acceptable activities for thrifts.

Nationally chartered commercial banks can invest only in highest rated corporate bonds and are prohibited from speculative investments in land. Most states also impose restrictions on the quality of debt instruments banks may acquire. In contrast, savings and loans were allowed by the Deregulation Act of 1980 to invest in corporate debt without regard to quality up to a percent of asset total (40 percent, which some thrifts exploited to acquire high yield or junk bonds). This authority was revoked by FIRREA in 1989. Thrift sales of junk bonds caused havoc in the junk bond market as thrifts dumped bond holdings within a short adjustment period.

Prohibitions and allowable investment authorities change, often unexpectedly, for deposit-taking institutions. The experience with junk bonds is a case in point. Investment decisions are subject to risk of changes that will alter optimal allowable risk–return portfolio composition for deposit-taking institutions. Changes may provoke expensive portfolio adjustments and can cause turmoil in specific asset markets.

Prohibited Activities: Securities Underwriting

One of the major activity restrictions facing deposit-taking institutions, in the United States and Japan, is underwriting corporate debt and equity securities and state and local government revenue bonds. In the United States, these prohibitions were enacted in the sections of the Banking Act of 1933 known as the Glass–Steagall Act. Similar provisions are in Section 65 of the Japanese financial code and in English banking law. These restrictions are totally absent in "universal banking" countries such as Germany. The Glass–Steagall Act and similar restrictions elsewhere have inhibited commercial banks from expanding into an area that appears to have natural synergies with its commercial lending activities, arranging permanent financing for corporate customers.

Three rationales are used to justify prohibition of commercial banks from investment banking activities. One is to prevent deposit-taking institutions from using deposit funds to buy underwritten issues that cannot be sold and to protect banks from variability in earnings in the securities business. A second rationale is to prevent banks from acting with their trust departments to bail out failing borrowers by having them place debt in trust funds. A third possible rationale is to prevent banks from using investment banking and underwriting activities to control nonbanking firms, expanding their influence into business not closely related to banking.

Prohibition of investment banking activities by banks is another way of dealing with concerns about the quality of assets acquired with deposit funds and concerns about the use of deposit and trust funds to gain control of nonbanking activities. Prohibition of investment banking activities for banks assigns more weight to avoiding problems of asset quality and control of nonbanks than to realizing possible economic efficiencies in expanding competition in investment banking services. Banks are a natural competitor in the market for those services.

Congressional review of the Glass–Steagall Act is a dynamic area and provides perennial debate in the United States. Securities lobbies and big bank lobbies are active in presenting their arguments for and against repeal of Glass–Steagall to legislators in the United States. Federal bank regulators have loosened the prohibition by a more liberal reading of the language contained in the Glass–Steagall Act. The Federal Reserve has authorized banks to conduct investment banking activities as long as revenues from securities units do not exceed a threshold making those revenues "substantial" in the language of the act.

Restrictions on Allowable Investments

Deposit-taking institutions are limited by a variety of often-changing rules on how much or what kind of investments they can make. For example, banks in the United States cannot invest more than 15 percent of their primary capital in any unsecured loan to one borrower or a combined 25 percent secured and unsecured. Restrictions exist on loans to directors, officers, and to correspondent bank officials.

Thrifts are restricted in both the types and terms of mortgage loans they can make to consumers, with restrictions on loans to one borrower also in place. Loans must not have longer than allowable maturities or less than a certain amount of equity. Often, conditions are made on types of lending, for example requiring private mortgage default insurance on mortgages with less than some threshold level of down payment.

Securities investments of deposit-taking institutions are also restricted. For example, no more than 10 percent of a commercial bank's capital may be invested in the securities of a single issuer. Investments in affiliated service corporations or other allowable equity investments are often limited by regulations to certain levels of total assets or equity capital. In other words, even authorized activities are curtailed and restricted by regulation and supervision.

Examination and Reporting

Deposit-taking institutions report extensively on their activities to regulators. Banks and thrift institutions file quarterly financial reports, discussed in Chapter 5. Special reports, covering activities like community investment or international lending, are also required. Reserve accounting requires daily record keeping. Deposit-taking institutions must have sophisticated accounting and reporting systems to meet all their reporting requirements.

Deposit-taking firms are subject to on-site examination. Examinations of deposit-taking institutions are sometimes routine and can even be less thorough when regulators' resources are strained and crises in other segments are draining away examination resources. At other times, examiners look in every drawer and examine detailed procedures and records. These examinations can be a very expensive and costly intrusion into both management time and flexibility.

Loan examination is one of the most critical areas for deposit-taking institutions. Examiners review both credit procedures and individual loans. Violations or perceived departures from regulatory standards can unleash regulatory responses that range from more frequent and intense examinations to legal procedures restricting management from continuation of unacceptable practices.

Review of an institution's loan portfolio can have dramatic impact on managers. Examiners identify loans with excessive risks and questionable collectibility and require that they be reported. In the United States, these loans are categorized into four classifications:

1. *Substandard:* more than "normal" risk
2. *Doubtful:* a probable loss
3. *Loss:* uncollectible
4. *Special mention:* possible future problems.

Classified loans are important because they determine the regulators' assessment of asset quality and capital adequacy, discussed in the next section. These classifications, which are often disputed by managers, may affect the market's assessment of an institution's risk.

Regulatory examination and reporting are expensive and time consuming for deposit-taking institution managers. This review and the reaction of regulators can impair the implementation of a business strategy. For example, in the late 1980s regulators became concerned with bank lending to finance leveraged buyouts. Their concern resulted in definition of *highly leveraged transactions* (HLTs) which required special reports and regulatory review. Banks with significant activity in this competitive credit market were subjected to special scrutiny and attention.

The underlying reason for examination and review is to limit the risk of the deposit-taking institution in order to protect depositors or the deposit-insuring agency. The market, in principle, could enforce similar discipline if creditors worried about the risk of deposit-taking assets. The economic desirability of monitoring and control by regulators must be assessed by weighing the costs from distortions in the deposit market and deposit-institution managers' incentives that result from deposit insurance plus the costs of regulation and regulatory review against the potential losses to uninformed and powerless participants in unregulated, unmeasured markets.

14.6 CAPITAL REQUIREMENTS

Deposit-taking institutions around the world are subject to review and regulation of equity capital. The aim is to ensure a level of *adequate capital*. The standards set for capital are discussed in terms of *capital adequacy*. Definition and enforcement of capital adequacy of deposit-taking institutions has an erratic policy history. The current and future evolution of capital adequacy review are important conditions in deposit-taking institution strategy and risk environment.

In most states and countries, a minimum capital contribution is required to apply for a charter for a deposit-taking institution. Then, following its establishment, authorities require capital of various types (e.g., debt or equity capital). Adequate capital has been set at levels and measured in ways that have changed significantly overtime. For example, when many savings and loans could not meet required capital of 6 percent of assets in the United States in 1981, requirements were reduced to 3 percent. Shortfalls in capital have been met with dramatically varying enforcement methods.

The rationale for capital regulation is simple. The more capital, the more deposit liabilities are protected from a fall in the value of assets. Capital is a buffer protecting depositors or the deposit-insuring agency. A review of balance sheet identities in levels and first-differences yields:

$$E = A - L$$

$$\Delta E = \Delta A - \Delta L$$

where E is equity and A and L are assets and liabilities, respectively. As is clear from the equation, when deposit withdrawals ($\Delta L > 0$) cannot be met by asset reductions ($\Delta A < 0$) the difference can be absorbed by equity. The more equity, the more ability for asset values to fall in the face of withdrawals and protect depositors' ability to withdraw funds without insolvency.

Problems in deposit-taking institutions come from distortions in management incentives which lead value-maximizing managers of deposit-taking institutions to maximize leverage and increase the expected return and risks on assets. With deposit-insurance or a "too big too fail" doctrine (see our following discussion of failure policies), large depositors have no incentive to enforce market discipline. Review of asset risk and regulation of capital adequacy must be undertaken by regulators to protect the taxpayers' interests.

It is difficult to define and measure adequate capital. The last three decades in the United States saw three different approaches to capital adequacy measurement. The Adequate Bank Capital (ABC) approach was succeeded by the Capital-Asset-Management-Earnings-Liquidity (CAMEL) rating scheme and a simple capital to asset ratio. Currently, leverage ratios and risk-adjusted assets are used to measure adequate capital.

International concern with capital standards and fear that banks avoid capital regulation through international operations led to an international regulatory effort to coordinate deposit-taking institution capital standards. The effort began with joint Bank of England–Federal Reserve negotiations leading to multilateral discussions under the leadership of the Bank for International Settlements (BIS) in Basel, Switzerland. The so-called BIS capital standards have been accepted by major industrial nation regulators and were implemented in 1992.

BIS standards use a weighted asset system similar to a system used by the Federal Reserve in the 1950s and 1960s, then called the Adequate Bank Capital (ABC) system. Assets are weighted by assigned risk factors and adequate capital is determined by a ratio of capital to risk-adjusted assets. Table 14.5 provides the asset weights used in the final 1992 standard. One important innovation in the BIS capital standards is the inclusion of off-balance activities in the assessment of risk. For example, a deposit-taking institution with mortgages of $100, commercial loans of $200, and $100 in credit guarantees, has risk weighted assets of $50, $200, and $100, respectively, for total risk adjusted assets of $350.

There are reasons to doubt the effectiveness of deposit-taking institution capital review. A study by Dietrich and James (1983) found that market conditions affecting the pricing on uninsured deposits may be as important as capital review in explaining bank capital decisions. A more direct example is the savings and loan industry. As discussed above, when savings and loans began to fall short of the mandatory capital of 6 percent of assets in 1981, the requirement was reduced to 3 percent. As savings and loans continued to have difficulty meeting the reduced capital level, accounting standards were relaxed, allowing assets to be valued more than by GAAP standards. Regulatory actions were authorized by the Garn–St Germain Act which had the appearance of creating capital through paper transactions. The ultimate outcome of lax capital enforcement standards due to political pressure on regulators and regulatory tolerance are an important cause of the savings and loan crisis.

Deposit-Institution Failure Policies

Capital regulation must be enforced to be effective. Sanctions for failure to meet capital standards begin with regulatory review and letters to management or management agreements. Deposit institution managers may be required to file plans to

TABLE 14.5 Risk-Based Capital Asset Ratio Weights

ASSET	*RISK WEIGHT (%)*
Balance Sheet Amounts	
Cash and government securities	0
Short-term, guaranteed claims (e.g., bank deposits)	20
Residential mortgages	50
All other assets (e.g., loans)	100
Off Balance Sheet Items	
Credit guarantees, letters of credit	100
Loan commitments > one year	50
Loan commitments < one year	0
Net exposure to interest rate and currency swaps	0 to 5

repair capital deficiencies. More extreme regulatory intervention results in issuance of *cease and desist* orders addressed to management obtained by regulators from courts which require specific courses of action, like halting particular lending or asset acquisition programs. The ultimate sanction is closure of the institution.

Closure of a deposit-taking institution due to violation of regulations or capital standards must be at the request of the chartering authority, the state or federal agency issuing the charter. The usual procedure in the United States is for the chartering authority to request the deposit-insurer to act as receiver or conservator of assets of the institution.

A deposit-taking institution regulatory control system can be simple in theory. When a deposit-taking institution is in danger of having inadequate capital or is violating regulated practice, it is warned. When capital actually becomes inadequate or the firm is insolvent, the institution is closed. In practice, the system works less well.

Market values of assets cannot be observed and accounting rules can be applied differently. Insolvency (assets less than liabilities) is a matter of judgment. Regulators' judgment may be influenced by practical realities. If deposit insurance fund reserves are low, as the Federal Savings and Loan Insurance Corporation's (FSLIC) reserves were in 1980s, regulators may hesitate to close marginal violators because of inadequate funds to pay off depositors.

Regulators have different objectives. While they wish to minimize losses to deposit insurance funds, they also wish to minimize risk from fears about the soundness of the financial system. Regulators wish to create confidence in the financial system. In the United States, regulators announced a policy of *too big too fail* (TBTF) in the 1980s, meaning large deposit-taking institutions would not be allowed to fail. TBTF was the reason used to save Continental Bank in Illinois in 1983 and Republic National Bank in Texas in 1989. TBTF meant that uninsured creditors, such as Eurodollar deposit holders or buyers of bank holding company commercial paper, preserved their claims on failing institutions, thereby raising the cost of failures to the deposit-insuring agencies.

TBTF was an expensive doctrine. Congress lost confidence in regulators and passed the Federal Deposit Insurance Corporation Improvement Act (FDICIA) of 1991, changing the rules on deposit-institution closure in the United States. Regulatory discretion was narrowed. TBTF was revoked and deposit-taking institutions with less than 2 percent equity are now closed automatically. The rigidity of FDICIA rules may not survive a large crisis.

14.7 SUMMARY

Deposit-taking institutions are among the most heavily regulated businesses on earth. Their deposit liabilities are the subject of government control and regulation through reserve requirements. Deposit insurance, implemented to protect small uninformed depositors and the viability of the financial system, distorts the incentives of managers and dulls depositor vigilance, requiring extensive regulation of deposit-taking firm activities. Deposit-taking firms are limited to authorized activities and allowable investments are subject to restrictions. Deposit-taking firms must report extensively and are subject to examination. Capital standards are imposed as protection for deposit-insuring agencies and depositors. Difficulties in measurement and implementation mean that capital regulation policies are not always clear. The ultimate sanction of regulators, closure of deposit-taking institutions, for practical and political reasons has not been a simple enforcement function. In any case, regulations and changes in regulations and legislation are part of a risky business environment for deposit-institution managers and can influence value-producing opportunities in this segment of the financial services industry.

DISCUSSION QUESTIONS AND EXERCISES

1. Examine carefully the annual report for a deposit-taking institution and determine the deposit-taking charter or charters it has and determine its main regulatory authorities.
2. Assess the increased earnings from a decrease in reserve requirements from 16.25 percent to 12 percent at 8 percent interest rate on deposits of $100,000,000. Discuss exactly what it meant by the reserve tax.
3. Consult the "Reserve Requirements of Depository Institutions" table and footnotes in the Federal Reserve *Bulletin* for a recent month concerning the actual calculation of required reserves. What are the actual reserve requirements for an institution with $25,000,000 in deposits? $50,000,000? $200,000,000?
4. What are the current interest rates paid on NOW accounts in your part of the country. Contact local deposit institutions and local papers. Are these rates above or below Treasury bill rates? What services, penalties, and options could explain these yield differentials?
5. Consult recent Federal Reserve *Bulletins*' "Legal Development" section. Summarize Federal Reserve Board actions with the intention of discovering the thrust of the Board's regulatory review. Were institutions denied their intended approvals? Why? What reasoning did the Board employ to justify its actions?
6. Characterize current monetary policy as "easy," "tight," or "normal" relying on (1) newspaper commentary; (2) latest Monetary Report to Congress; and (3) other official and professional commentary. What are the implications for deposit-taking institutions in your local market?
7. Determine the total deposits in your state and the market share held by banks, savings institutions, and other deposit-taking institutions, like thrift and loans, over some reasonable and practical time interval. You will need to rely on local Federal Reserve Bank and Home Loan Bank publications, and state regulatory agency publications. Determine the market share of various charter types, average branch size, etc. What changes, if any, are discernable in your data?
8. What is the current status of regulation at the state and federal level affecting the authorized activities, investments, and expansion of deposit-taking institutions? What arguments are being raised and what positions are being taken by various politicians, lobbying groups, and regulators?
9. Relying on primary sources such as central bank bulletins, Bank for International Settlement publications, and secondary sources, contrast the

deposit institution insurance, reserve, and authorized activities in another OECD country.

10. Trace the share of demand deposits of total deposit liabilities using the flow of funds accounts in Chapter 3. What explains the historical patterns? What are the profit implications of these developments for banks?

REFERENCES

BALTENSPERGER, ERNST and JEAN DERMINE. 1993. European Banking: Prudential and Regulatory Issues. In Jean Dermine, ed. *European Banking in the 1990s* (2nd Ed.). Oxford: Blackwell Business Publishing.

BENSTON, GEORGE, ROBERT A. EISENBEIS, PAUL M. HORVITZ, EDWARD J. KANE, and GEORGE G. KAUFMAN. 1986. *Perspectives on Safe and Sound Banking: Past, Present, and Future.* Cambridge, Mass.: American Bankers Association in cooperation with the MIT Press.

BERNANKE, BEN S. 1983. "Nonmonetary Effects of the Financial Crisis in the Propagation of the Great Depression," *American Economic Review* (June), pp. 257–276.

BLACK, FISCHER. 1987. *Business Cycles and Equilibrium.* New York and Oxford: Basil Blackwell.

DIAMOND, DOUGLAS W. and PHILIP H. DYBVIG. 1983. "Bank Runs, Deposit Insurance, and Liquidity," *Journal of Political Economy,* 91, pp. 401–419.

DIETRICH, J. KIMBALL and CHRISTOPHER JAMES. 1983. "Regulation and the Determination of Bank Capital Changes: A Note," *Journal of Finance* VIII (5) (December), pp. 1651–1658.

FAMA, EUGENE F. 1980. "Banking in the Theory of Finance," *Journal of Monetary Economics* 6, pp. 39–57.

Federal Reserve Bulletin. 1995. "Reserve Requirements of Depository Institutions."

FRIEDMAN, MILTON and ANNA SCHWARTZ. 1963. *A Monetary History of the United States 1867–1960.* Princeton, N.J.: Princeton University Press.

KANE, EDWARD J. 1981. "Accelerating Inflation, Technological Innovation, and the Decreasing Effectiveness of Banking Regulation," *Journal of Finance* XXXVI (May), pp. 355–367.

WALLACE, NEIL. 1988. "Another Attempt to Explain an Illiquid Banking System: The Diamond and Dybvig Model with Sequential Service Taken Seriously," Federal Reserve Bank of Minneapolis *Quarterly Review,* Fall, pp. 3–16.

C H A P T E R

15

Regulation of Securities Markets

Introduction

Securities and derivatives markets are a special focus of policy makers in governments around the world.

- Which relationships between securities market participants are regulated?
- Who regulates the activities of securities firms?
- What is the purpose of securities market regulation?
- How do regulations affect the securities firms' business?
- What are the major issues of concern to managers of securities firms and their regulators today?

These questions are important to firms and individuals wishing to earn profits by providing securities-related financial services to investors and to firms raising funds in securities markets.

This chapter begins by introducing the relations between firms and individuals active in securities markets, defined in this chapter to include financial derivatives such as options and futures. The discussion describes how laws and regulations fit into these relations. The emphasis in this chapter as everywhere in this book is on the effect of regulation on the ability of financial service firms to produce value.

15.1 OVERVIEW OF SECURITIES MARKETS: PARTICIPANTS AND ACTIVITIES

Securities regulation in the United States and elsewhere is directed not only at financial service firms but also at investors and securities issuers—businesses and governments raising funds in the form of securities. Most regulatory attention is directed at nongovernmental securities issuers, private corporations, and other private business issuers (like limited partnerships). Regulation directed at securities issuers does not affect securities firms directly but securities firms like investment bankers help issuers comply with regulation. A second object of securities market regulation is behavior of investors, particularly large investors and investors with access to private information. Services provided to investors in completing purchases and sales of securities also involve securities firms in the regulation of investor activities.

Securities firms are regulated on how they conduct business and these regulations are discussed extensively in the following sections. However, regulation of securities firms is only one source of controls on their activities. Lawsuits brought by customers and clients of financial service firms is another and growing source of concern. Pervasive litigation in securities markets results from alleged violations of securities laws. Lawsuits often seek damages for harms alleged to have been inflicted by the actions or inactions of securities firms. Lawsuits and the threat of lawsuits are major factors in doing business in securities markets.

This section outlines the relation of the various participants and institutions in securities market in order to place the effect of regulation and litigation on securities firms into context. We begin by describing participants and their relationships in securities markets. We then review securities regulation against the four basic purposes of regulation discussed in Chapter 2.

There are three classes of participants active in securities markets: investors, issuers, and financial service firms. Interactions between these participants can cause many problems due to differences in objectives and information. In other words, there are many principal–agent problems like those we have discussed in previous chapters. There are also incentives for securities firms, firms issuing securities, and investors to use unfair competitive practices to make money. The government regulatory establishment oversees the many relationships between securities market participants.

The most important regulator of securities markets activities in United States is the Securities and Exchange Commission (SEC). Securities laws (discussed below) passed in 1933 and 1934, following the Stock Market Crash of 1929 and during the Great Depression, established the SEC as the main regulator of securities markets and with an active role in some derivatives markets, like options. The SEC has been a model for many countries. Many foreign country policy debates about securities regulation consist of how many of the SEC functions to emulate in designing local securities market regulation (see Huang and Stoll 1991 for a description of other major stock markets).

Another major regulator of importance to financial markets in the United States is the Commodity Futures Trading Commission (CFTC), established in 1974 to replace a predecessor agency housed in the Agriculture Department. The CFTC has regulatory authority over commodity and financial futures markets. Most futures market trading was related to agricultural products like wheat or soybeans prior to the unprecedented variability of interest rates and other securities values starting in the 1960s. Today the most actively traded financial instruments are financial futures like long-term U.S. Treasury Bond futures traded on the Chicago Board of Trade (CBOT).

Other federal agencies are also active in areas of securities markets trading. The Federal Reserve Board and the Treasury Department have responsibility for regulating aspects of U.S. Treasury securities markets. The Federal Reserve System is involved in several securities market activities, including regulating loans used by investors to acquire securities (*margin* loans). The Comptroller of the Currency and the Federal Deposit Insurance Corporation regulate some bank activities relating to securities and derivatives.

In the United States, individual state securities laws are also important to securities market participants. State laws affect securities activities that are limited in terms of size, number of investors, or geographical distribution so are not covered by federal laws. To a major extent, state laws apply regulation similar to federal regulation to these restricted securities activities.

Federal regulation can interfere with state regulations. For example, in 1992, the SEC proposed relaxation of small firm registration requirements making issuing securities under SEC rules easier than raising funds under state securities laws. State securities officials felt that the SEC changes would weaken controls over issues in their states because firms would register with the SEC instead of state authorities. Although state regulators are not discussed in detail in this chapter, we warn readers that they are important. They can affect practices and profitability of financial firms in different regions.

Other countries locate national securities market regulation in a variety of agencies. In most foreign countries, national agencies, like the Ministry of Finance in Japan, have exclusive responsibility for securities market regulation, with local laws having little significance. Some countries, like Thailand, have an SEC. Others, like China, rely on their central banks. In nearly all countries, securities regulation uses United States regulation as a benchmark.

Purposes of Securities Market Regulation

Stated purposes and rationales used in implementing regulation provide an outline of the arguments used to justify changes in the regulatory environment surrounding securities and derivatives activities. Changes often reduce profits or create profitable opportunities. This is not to say that regulatory intervention is always rational, directed at a rational objective, or beneficial. Legislators and regulators invariably invoke benign objectives when changing the conditions under which financial services firms operate even if the consequences of their actions prove disruptive to securities markets.

The basic reasons for regulation of financial service firms as discussed in Chapter 3 are:

1. To promote government policy goals in the allocation of financial resources
2. To offset disadvantages to some market participants from the asymmetric ability to generate or process financial information
3. To accommodate economy-wide risks that cannot be absorbed by individual firms
4. To promote competition.

To analyze these regulatory objectives in securities and other financial instrument activities, we need to review the relations between the different participants in markets more closely. Our goal is to examine how regulations can resolve problems of information asymmetry, moral hazard, and anticompetitive behavior in financial markets.

15.2 REGULATION OF PARTICIPANTS AND RELATIONSHIPS IN SECURITIES MARKETS

A detailed examination of financial markets displays many possible interrelationships between the various classes of participants. We recall all the participants in securities markets introduced in previous chapters and give them brief designations (italicized below):

1. Individual savers or *investors*
2. Businesses and governments raising funds, or *securities issuers*
3. Financial service firms active in securities and derivatives discussed in Chapter 9 that perform a number of functions separately or together, namely *brokers, market makers,* and *securities originators*
4. Institutions created by brokers, investment bankers, and market makers, to facilitate their businesses, primarily organized *markets* and other *organizations* like trading and clearing systems
5. Asset managers as discussed in Chapter 12, including *investment companies* and *other institutional investors,* like bank trust departments, pension funds, and insurance companies
6. Investment advisors and information providers, also discussed in Chapter 12, or *advisors*.

Figure 15.1 provides a schematic of relationships between securities markets participants.

Regulation governs relations between the participants shown in Figure 15.1 in many ways. Each of the important relationships is identified with an arrow and letter, for example the relationship between securities issuers and investors is arrow (A). The figure portrays nearly all of the relationships that can be a source of problems and that have or could invoke regulation. We discuss these relationships in turn, describing regulatory interventions in the United States where relevant.

Relation between Issuers and Investors

Corporations issuing securities in public securities markets are typically large, complex economic organizations. Investors' ability to acquire information necessary to make informed judgments on risks and returns from these securities is limited by time and expense. Investors relying on poor information make mistakes or are deceived. The information flow between securities issuers and investors, shown as arrow (A) in Figure 15.1, has been a major focus of securities regulation in the United States. Countries around the world have followed this lead.

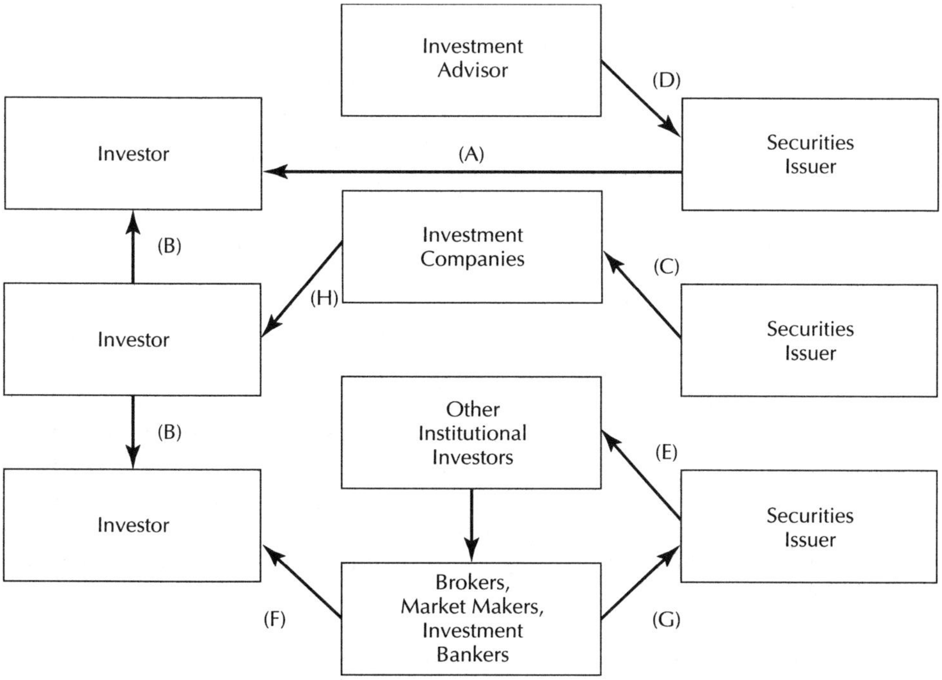

FIGURE 15.1 Relation between participants in securities markets

Regulations on the disclosure of information by firms issuing securities are directed at efficient allocation of resources and balancing the information asymmetries between firms issuing securities and uninformed investors, the second rationale for regulation listed above. Efficient allocation of resources requires that risks and returns of securities be accurately assessed and match investor's needs or goals as much as possible. Good information cannot eliminate risk, but better information can provide better assessments of risks.

Two important federal laws in the United States, the Securities Act (SA) of 1933 and the Securities Exchange Act (SEA) of 1934, are the basis of federal regulation of securities markets. The SA of 1933 requires that all newly issued securities sold to the public be *registered* with the SEC.[1] Basic information on the issuer and the security must be made available to all potential investors at the time the securities are issued in public markets. The information is made available in the form of a *prospectus* which describes the security, the firm, its business, and other information.

[1]Securities that have a small number of investors or do not trade across state boundaries may be exempted from SEC registration requirements but may be subject to state securities laws and regulations as discussed previously.

Regulators are concerned that sophisticated corporations may deceive or confuse consumers into making wrong assessments of securities' risks, an information asymmetry problem as introduced in Chapter 6. Laws against disclosing fraudulent information to investors when issuing securities provide criminal and civil legal sanctions, a hallmark of relations between issuers and investors in United States securities markets. United States disclosure laws are often copied around the world.

The SEA of 1934 covers already issued securities trading in secondary markets like the NYSE or the over-the-counter (OTC) market. Companies that have issued publicly traded securities must make periodic disclosures of operating information contained in *filings* with the SEC, such as the quarterly 8-K and annual 10-K filings. The SEA established the SEC to oversee the requirements of both securities law.

The emphasis in all of these laws and regulations is on producing a flow of information between new or established securities issuers and investors. The information is intended to enable investors to make assessments of a security's risks and returns. Repeating an important point, required information disclosures cannot and should not be expected to eliminate risk or guarantee investment performance.

The impact of financial disclosure on businesses is covered in some detail in any introductory textbook on corporate finance. A hotly argued debate centers on the economic value of required disclosures.[2] Publicly traded corporations voluntarily published periodic performance reports before the 1933 and 1934 acts. Corporate reporting was required by major exchanges like the NYSE prior to the SEA. Many economists question whether the disclosure laws and regulations and their frequent expansion are necessary to obtain meaningful public reporting of corporate activity.

SEC regulation of information disclosure is a dynamic area. New requirements, such as replacement cost accounting of capital equipment or detailed line of business reporting, were examined in academic studies to see whether additional information is valuable to investors. See, for example, Beaver (1982) for effects of the 1933 and 1934 laws and Collins (1976) for the value of expanded reporting. The results suggest that increased reporting is not particularly useful to investors for assessing securities. It costs corporations a lot of money to comply with disclosure requirements, leading some to believe SEC reporting requirements are too burdensome.

Firms raising funds in public markets incur substantial costs in making required information disclosures for newly publicly issued securities. Information disclosures are part of complex *registration statements* that the SEC requires for publicly issued securities. Investment banks advise issuers on how to complete the regulatory requirements. Part of the service of investment bankers is to assist corporations in fulfilling the requirements of registering new issues or help them avoid registration altogether.

[2]See Skousen (1983) for a more detailed discussion of disclosure requirements and Simon (1989) for a discussion of the effect of the information disclosures on security pricing.

Costs of meeting reporting requirements for publicly traded corporations make some corporations want to avoid SEC-mandated reporting requirements. Some corporations have decided to *go private*, meaning management groups or buyout syndicates buy up publicly traded securities. In the 1980s, notorious *leveraged buyouts* by investor groups borrowing most of the money to acquire stock and other securities were hugely profitable while generating highly leveraged firms. Investment banking firms actively assist corporations going private and arranging financing for leveraged buyouts. The profitability of investment banking services based fees earned from firms going private are clear indications of the costs of regulatory compliance. Changes in laws or regulations could alter the demand for these investment banking services, an example of regulatory risk to securities firms from changes in regulations.

Securities laws and regulations on corporate disclosure have indirect effects on firms providing securities services. First, investment bankers and others assist firms in making their mandatory disclosures in regulatory filings as part of the securities issuance process. These firms have responsibilities as advisors, as discussed below. Second, the flow of required information establishes a level of information efficiency and tradition of disclosure influencing all aspects of securities markets activities. Third, the expenses and the exposure associated with public offerings of securities make private offerings attractive to issuers. Securities firms find ways to assist firms in raising funds through private placements or by going private. Finally, disclosure requirements and limitations on investor activities in the United States are more restrictive than in many other countries. This can make foreign activities attractive and affects the choice of location for a lot of securities business.

Regulation of Investor Speculation: Margin Limits

Conventional wisdom and some economists believe that financial market activity can be fueled by frenzied buying or selling. Many observers believe that the Stock Market Crash of 1929 was caused by aggressive purchases by speculators who used borrowed money and pushed securities prices above intrinsic values. These events are called *speculative bubbles*.

Drafters of the Depression era securities laws invoked the rationale of protection against economy-wide risks to control investor behavior causing speculative bubbles. One control was to limit the use of funds borrowed by investors, usually from their brokers, to acquire securities, thereby regulating relationships shown by arrow (F) in Figure 15.1. The Federal Reserve is empowered to establish *margin requirements* and assure that brokers enforce these requirements. Margin requirements limit how much debt can be used to buy securities.

Limits on the amount of borrowed funds used to buy securities are called initial margins and are regulated by Federal Reserve Regulations T, U, and V. For example, Regulation T currently requires stocks traded on exchanges to be purchased with a minimum of 50 percent cash. The remainder can be financed with a loan arranged by the broker or some other lender. Regulations U and V regulate purchases of bonds and convertible bonds, respectively.

Buyers and sellers in derivative markets must also pledge cash to enter financial contracts but cash in this case is not used to acquire assets. Cash in futures and options margins provides assurance that a trader entering into a contract will be able to perform on the contract when required. Margin requirements do not represent a loan from a creditor in futures and options markets but is more like a performance bond.

After the initial purchase of securities or after establishing a derivatives market contract position, customers must meet regular *maintenance margins* defined as minimum margin requirements based on current market values of securities or contract commitments. Maintenance margins are set by exchanges and clearinghouses. Margin requirements are a major focal point of discussions of financial market regulation. Policing initial and maintenance margins is an important and costly function of brokers and dealers.

Recent financial market events have spawned an active debate concerning the economic role of margin requirements and the appropriate level of margin requirements on different financial markets. For example, initial stock margins are 50 percent on stock purchases but stock index futures margins are only a small percent of total contract value. The debate concerning margins has two dimensions. First, not all margin requirements are created equal: Margin requirements used to acquire assets with debt, for example buying stocks on margin, are qualitatively different from the margin used to guarantee performance on a financial derivative such as a futures contract. Both types of margin are used to protect parties in the transactions, but cash behind a margin account loan protects the lender, usually the broker-dealer, while options or futures margin protects the exchange (or the clearinghouse) from using its own funds to satisfy commitments to counterparties on contracts.

Stock exchanges and some regulators argue for higher margins on futures contracts to "harmonize" requirements in trading in cash and futures, especially since the Stock Market Crash of 1987. However, there is no leverage with futures margin requirements. As mentioned above, these margins are like performance bonds. New York Stock Exchange (NYSE) members who demand higher futures margin requirements appear to want to increase costs of futures trading on Chicago futures exchanges relative to cash trading on the NYSE for competitive reasons. The conflict between futures and cash markets, or Chicago versus New York as it is often characterized, is discussed again below.

The second dimension of the debate on margin requirements is whether they serve the regulatory objective of controlling speculation. The notion of speculative bubbles is counter to notions of efficient markets. In the Great Crash of 1929 some observers believed cheap credit resulted in demand for securities unsupported by underlying values. One way to control speculative activity is to limit credit. The existence of speculative bubbles and the effectiveness of margins are debated by economists who feel that sudden changes in margin requirements are more disruptive to markets than excessive borrowing in securities purchases. Changes in margin regulation can be costly to providers of securities services by affecting their customers' cost of trading and by imposing additional operating costs to enforce rule changes. Margin regulation forms a regulatory risk for securities firms.

Regulation of Relations Between Investors

Investors may learn information concerning a firm's prospects which gives them an advantage over less informed investors. Information asymmetries that could benefit some investors to the disadvantage of others affect relations between investors shown as arrow (B) in Figure 15.1 and illustrate Section 10 of the SEA regulations relations between investors as follows:

> It shall be unlawful for any person, directly or indirectly, by the use of any means or instrumentality of interstate commerce or of the mails, or any facility of any national securities exchange—
>
> (a) To effect a short sale, or to use or employ any stop-loss order in connection with the purchase or sale, of any security registered on a national securities exchange, in contravention of such rules and regulations as the Commission may prescribe as necessary or appropriate in the public interest or for the protection of investors.
>
> (b) To use or employ, in connection with the purchase or sale of any security registered on a national securities exchange or any security not so registered, any manipulative or deceptive device or contrivance in contravention of such rules and regulations as the commission may prescribe as necessary or appropriate in the public interest or for the protection of investors.

Rules promulgated by the SEC to enforce these provisions, especially SEC rule 10-b(5), have a large impact on the conduct of securities transactions.

Section 10 of the SEA is used to regulate unfair trading on information known to managers of firms but not available to investors, so-called *inside information*. For example, in 1992 the SEC accused executives of Motel 6 L.P. of profiting from information concerning a takeover by Accor, a French firm, in 1990 (Moses 1992). The suit charged executives of Motel 6, and even their friends and acquaintances up to five steps removed, with profiting illegally from use of the information—a violation of SEC Rule 10-b(5).

Another way to profit unfairly from securities trading is to *manipulate* reported prices and transactions when investors act collectively and trade among themselves. Nonmarket transactions get reported in the price reporting systems of the exchanges. False transaction prices can move security values from fair market values in ways that are favorable to the group, for example by enabling buyers at low prices to sell above true underlying values as uninformed traders believe a price swing is underway.

Another unfair way to make money is to buy securities below the value they would have if it were known that a group of investors plans to gain control of a firm. Investors who have information about a takeover strategy that will change a securities' value when the strategy is made public buy undervalued securities. Investors selling securities below values the securities will have when information concerning new management becomes public are suffering from an information asymmetry.

Securities laws and regulations impose strict limitations on the use of inside information, use of coordinated trading activity to manipulate prices, and use of knowledge of takeover attempts to the disadvantage of uniformed investors. For example, Ivan Boesky and Michael Milken were accused and convicted of taking unfair advantage of information concerning trading strategies and of hiding ownership of securities to avoid disclosure of large accumulations of securities as part of takeover plans.

Regulations concerning investors' use of information are largely directed at the second and fourth goals of regulation, that is to offset unfair information asymmetries from harming uninformed investors and to prevent interference in establishment of fair prices in competitive securities markets. Rules affecting groups of investors on the use of inside information and price manipulation schemes are important in securities and derivative markets and are a major focus of the SEC and CFTC prosecutions.

Prosecution of lawsuits based on the use of inside information and attempts to manipulate markets is difficult. There are gray areas between what information is "inside" information as opposed to the possession of important information representing good research or luck. For example, if a newspaper columnist is going to write an article recommending a stock, is release of the contents of this story to friends and relatives "inside information"? If a group of investors intend to buy blocks of stock, is their own familiarity with their investment strategy "inside information"? Unanswered questions similar to these plague both the definition of abuses and prosecution of violations.

Another issue concerns the economically efficient way to transmit important information known to insiders to markets. Currently the SEC allows exchanges to halt trading in securities when important information, like a minerals discovery or a takeover offer, is forthcoming. To prevent transactions by uninformed investors, trading ceases, the announcement is made, and trading then resumes. This means two things: (1) for a period there is no market in the security at any price; and (2) price changes can be large and abrupt.

Some economists believe that the definition of inside information is too subtle to be the basis for regulation and prosecution. These economists believe that continuous trading and liquidity and gradual price adjustments are better than the alternative of trading halts in securities affected by information announcements. When trading in a security stops, a precipitous change in value can occur between the time that trading ceases, announcements are made, and trading resumes. Trading halts mean that some investors lose because they bought high and could not sell or could not buy low and sell when prices rose.

Regulatory attempts to prevent security price manipulation and unfair use of information are important to financial service firms. These firms may intentionally or unwittingly be involved in implementing strategies viewed as abusive by regulators. Disclosure requirements and restrictions on investor activities do not directly affect securities firms. Indirectly these regulations place a burden of responsibility on employees of securities firms executing trades or providing information to investors. Regulations concerning issuers and investors are a source of risk to securities firms.

15.3 REGULATION OF SECURITIES FIRMS

Policy makers pursue all four regulatory goals mentioned above in regulating securities firms and the institutions, like markets, they establish. Four methods of regulating of securities firms are used to protect investors, primarily consumers, from exploitative actions taken by financial service firms. These methods are: (1) *registration* of securities firms; (2) subjecting those firms to *rules;* (3) imposition of *financial requirements* through regulation of their financial position; and (4) *securities insurance.* To highlight relations between different types of securities firms, issuers, and investors, Figure 15.2 expands Figure 15.1 to show securities firms in more detail. The relation between investors and securities firms is shown by arrow F in both figures.

Protection of Investors: Registration of Securities Firms

Firms trading securities and derivatives must register with the appropriate regulatory agency in order to conduct their business in the United States. Broker-dealers in traded securities register with the SEC. Futures traders register with the CFTC. Registration is open to all qualified firms or individuals. Qualifying proce-

FIGURE 15.2 Relation between securities firms, investors, and issuers

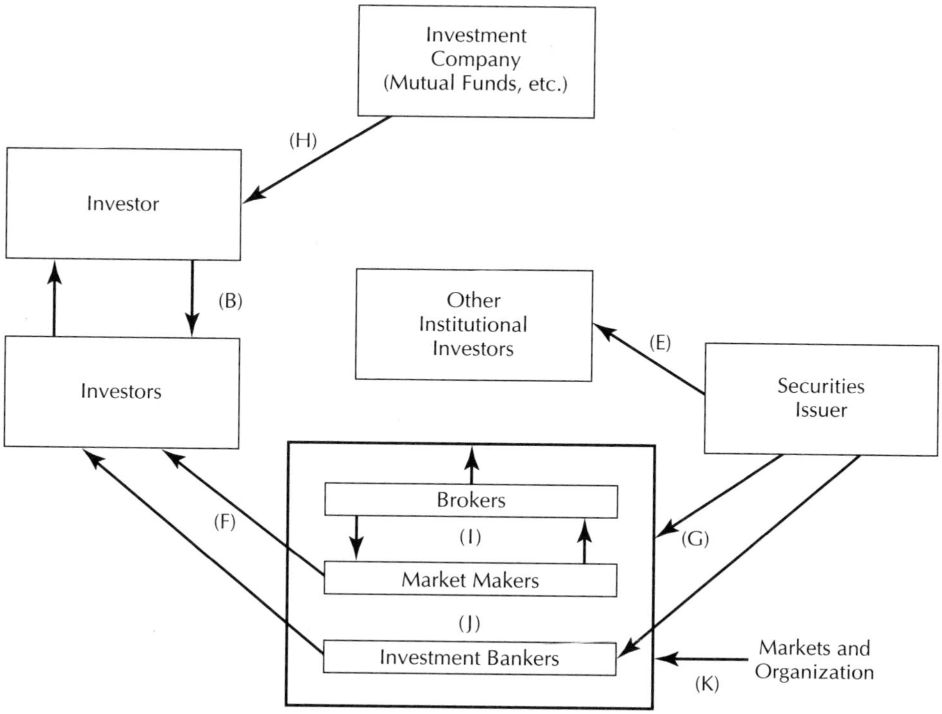

dures are usually administered by a trade association: NASD administers examinations required to register as a broker-dealer, for example. Capital and other financial requirements may also be imposed.

Registration is not used to restrict entry into the securities and derivatives business. Tests necessary to register or to work for registered firms ensure a minimum level of competence of participants in these markets. Firms or individuals meeting minimum requirements can enter the business if not prevented by other regulations, such as banking regulations. The purpose of registration is to bring firms into the rule-making and dispute settlement framework. Registration may also impose periodic reporting requirements for firms in certain business lines, for example registered brokers and futures merchants who carry customer balances.

Rules Governing Securities Firms

Registration and reporting are relatively minor costs for firms active in securities and financial markets. Rules limiting behavior and sanctions for infraction of rules are the real economic factors affecting value production in securities and derivative business. There are two important sets of rules: those covering members in associations of different specialities and those covering markets set up by firms and individuals. Depending on a firm's activities, its activities may be regulated by an association like NASD or a market like the NYSE. Both sets of rules may restrict the activities of firms.

Associations of securities firms like the National Association of Securities Dealers (NASD) or the National Futures Association (NFA) for individuals and firms trading futures contracts and derivatives are relied on by the SEC and the CFTC and other regulators to regulate their members. In the United States and the United Kingdom, definition and enforcement of rules governing behavior relies on these organizations, called *self-regulatory organizations* (SROs). Rules governing firms are determined by the SROs for the activities they register for. For example, broker-dealers are covered by NASD rules.

Rules of SROs establish standards of conduct that regulate the relations between financial service firms and their customers. Regulators review rules of the SROs but in general rely on them to enforce rules and propose rule changes. For example, in 1991 the American Bar Association reported that a record 1,041 disciplinary cases were brought by the four major self-regulatory organization, the NASD, NYSE, American Stock Exchange (ASE), and the CBOT (Siconolfi 1992).

Relying on industry professionals to monitor and regulate industry conduct has the advantage that regulation is cheap and responds flexibly to changes in the economic environment facing industry practitioners. Reliance on SROs can be a disadvantage in that these associations and institutions can exploit economic self-advantage, for example by trying to restrict trading in order to create monopolies for a type of securities business. The associations that securities firms and individual employees belong to are active lobbying groups and attempt to convince lawmakers to write laws protecting their interests. For example, the NYSE actively lobbies to increase regulation of competing futures markets.

The rules governing securities firm conduct with unsophisticated investors are contained in Article III of the NASD "Rules of Fair Practice," (September 1987). They read as follows:

> Section 1. A member, in the conduct of his business, shall observe high standards of commercial honor and just and equitable principles of trade.
>
> Section 2. In recommending to a customer the purchase, sale or exchange of any security, a member shall have reasonable grounds for believing that the recommendation is suitable for such customer upon the basis of the facts, if any, disclosed by such customer as to his other security holdings and as to his financial situation and needs.

Further sections specify specific requirements of securities dealers concerning settlement, charges, publication of quotes, confirmations, etc.

These rules are aimed at protecting investors from differences in sophistication or access to market information and securities firms. Brokers are obligated to recommend only "suitable" investments for savers. This rule is intended to prevent widows and orphans or other unsophisticated investors from being put into complicated investments like derivatives by their brokers. Violations of the suitability criterion often produce lawsuits.

Securities prices to customers cannot be marked up on purchase (or down for sales) beyond amounts necessary to complete transactions. Unlawful pricing practices could occur if securities firms make markets in financial assets and sell them at prices above market value, unknown to investors without access to prices in relevant markets. This practice is called *scalping*.

Another possible abuse of investors by securities firms is brokers undertaking unnecessary purchases and sales of financial instruments to generate commission income called *churning*. Churning and similar practices may be detected by surveillance units of SROs or by complaints and may result in sanctions. Overzealous brokers have wiped out clients' investments with excessive trading activity, opening themselves to litigation.

Financial Requirements for Securities Firms

Regulation of securities firms holding assets or money for customers is different than for firms only completing transactions or providing advice. Many brokerage firms hold securities for customers in so-called "street name" and keep cash balances for trading customers who sell assets or may buy assets in the future. Investors' cash or assets are at risk when held for them by securities firms.

Registered securities and futures firms carrying customer balances are required in the United States to report monthly on assets, liabilities, and capital. Firms regulated by the SEC file the so-called FOCUS (for Financial and Operational Combined Uniform Single) report with their SRO and the SEC. Futures commission merchants registered with the CFTC file reports with their SRO, the NFA. These reports and reporting procedures are subject to audit and review by the SEC and CFTC.

Regulators and SROs use several methods to assure investors that securities firms can make delivery of cash, securities, or other value due them. The first method imposes net capital rules. Net capital is defined as adjusted assets minus liabilities. Asset adjustments are spelled out in regulations, but in general mean that assets of different risk characteristics are reduced in value when calculating total assets. This value reduction is called a *haircut*. The operations of firms carrying or clearing customer transactions can be materially affected when regulations change the haircuts affecting the calculation of net capital.

Current regulations require that a registered broker-dealer maintain minimum net capital of $25,000, and aggregate indebtedness must not exceed 15 times net capital. An alternative net capital rule requires net capital of the larger of $100,000 or 2 percent of debit balances to customers. In cases of capital shortfalls, firms must make up deficiencies or face sanctions like ceasing operations or liquidation.

When a substantial market revaluation occurs, as in the Stock Market Crash of 1987, securities firms carrying customer balances may find themselves short of capital. Furthermore, large market movements may stimulate increased scrutiny and changes in rules by regulators. These regulatory risks must be considered by managers of financial service firms carrying customer accounts.

The second method to assure investors with assets held by securities firms is segregation of customer assets on balance sheets. Regulations require that assets owned outright (not bought on margin) be segregated from other holdings of securities firms carrying customer accounts. When securities purchasers buy securities on margin (discussed previously), brokers arrange for credit from banks in the form of *call money* or other open market borrowings. Segregation of fully paid-for assets creates oversight problems because it is difficult to ascertain whether assets on the asset side of the balance sheet are used as collateral for short-term borrowings. Regulators impose daily reporting requirements and special accounting procedures to ensure that assets not bought on margin held as a convenience for customers are available for delivery.

The situation is different when securities are bought on margin, that is, with borrowed funds. Margin account agreements with customers allow broker-dealers to use assets bought on margin as collateral and to lend the securities to other investors. Securities held in street name and financed with margin account loans is the major source of stock lent to short sellers, who sell borrowed stock. Maintenance margins for securities are enforced by the firms holding stocks. Required margins for short sellers are imposed by brokers selling securities on behalf of short sellers.

Insurance

Government insurance is provided to protect investors from securities firms holding assets in the United States, in pursuit of the third regulatory objective: protection from economy-wide risks of failure in the financial system. The availability of customer assets held by securities firms is guaranteed up to a limit by insurance offered by Securities Investors Protection Corporation (SIPC) established by the Securities Investors Protection Act of 1970. This legislation followed the collapse of several brokerage firms in 1969. All registered broker-dealers must belong to SIPC, which levies annual assessments equal to one-half percent of members' gross revenues. Individual investors are covered to $500,000 in the event of a failure of a firm that cannot cover its obligations to customers out of its assets.

SIPC insurance is radically different from the deposit insurance discussed in Chapter 14. Customers are only guaranteed return of the assets held for them by the broker-dealer up to the insurance limits, not the purchase price of those assets. If assets held by a broker for an investor lose value due to market movements, these market losses are not protected by SIPC insurance. In the case of liquidation of a broker, the customer could receive low value assets or their monetary value, not the original investment. The fixed liability of deposit insurance makes it unique from an economic viewpoint.

15.4 MARKET REGULATION: TRADING PRACTICES AND RULES

Rules of the institutions and associations established by securities firms govern conduct of their businesses when regulation relies on SROs, as in the United States and United Kingdom. These rules govern relations shown by arrows (I), (J), and (K) in Figure 15.2. As discussed in Chapter 9, trading activities sometimes can be more efficient by concentrating the flow of orders. One way to capitalize on these efficiencies is to establish a central market, like the NYSE. Nearly all firms engaged in the trading or underwriting of securities or other financial instruments belong to organizations like organized markets or electronic trading systems in order to realize these efficiencies.

Regulation of securities firms in the United States has focused not just on individuals and firms but on also on institutions and organizations set up by securities firms and individuals created to realize efficiencies from concentration of trading activity. *Exchange* is prominent in the name of the SEC.

The NYSE and the CBOT, for example, are both the instruments and the objects of regulation. These institutions have rules governing conduct of their members. These rules are reviewed by regulators. Exchange rules have several economic functions. First, rules regularize transactions and make large volumes of trading routine by establishing delivery, payment, and exception procedures to be followed by members. Second, they establish rules of conduct to protect members from each other and to protect the public from unfair practices of members. These rules are a major focus of regulation since they protect consumers from fraud or manipulation. Finally, members attempt to protect the value of the exchange by rules governing the actions of members.

We use examples of NYSE rules to illustrate how exchange rules work to achieve each of the three objectives. NYSE stock exchange rules define delivery of stocks in exchange for cash within three business days: Settlement procedures are precisely defined with courses of actions spelled out for exceptional cases, such as failure to deliver.

To protect public investors and exchange members from each other, many rules govern the conduct of brokers and dealers. For example, market makers on the NYSE are called specialists and are effectively monopolists on dealing in listed securities. The NYSE rules place an obligation on specialists to smooth price changes and provide liquidity to the market. Some rules have doubtful or ambiguous effect on investors, like the so-called "uptick" rule preventing short sales of securities whose prices have moved down: Short-selling can only occur on a positive price movement, or uptick.

To protect the value of exchange membership, NYSE rules prevent members from trading exchange-listed securities off the floor of the exchange while the NYSE is open. This rule serves to concentrate trading activity on the exchange, making membership valuable due to the monopoly on trading in listed securities at minimum buy–sell spreads. However, this same rule has made it profitable for some securities firms, like Jefferies Securities, to avoid trading restrictions and other rules governing members of the exchange. The NYSE rule fixing commissions until 1975 was another rule creating economic advantages for members by reducing competition among members.

Exchanges in the United States are responsible for enforcement of rules. Exchanges form an important class of SROs in the U.S. regulatory environment because most major securities firms are members of exchanges. Rules governing exchange members and any rule changes must be reviewed by the appropriate regulator, the SEC or the CFTC. The SEC in 1975 ruled that fixing commissions was not acceptable after May 1975. Methods of enforcement and success of disciplinary actions are also subject to review by the SEC.

An important activity for exchanges in the dynamic and competitive environment of today is to develop new products. On the futures exchanges a new product would be a new futures contract, for example stock index futures. Federal regulators in the United States retain the right to review new products. Competing exchanges will often fight for the right to offer new securities or trading vehicles. Competition among exchanges, as between New York cash markets in stocks and Chicago markets in derivatives like futures and options, leads to battles between federal regulators as the SEC and the CFTC jockey for the right to approve new instruments and to regulate trading.

15.5 REGULATION OF INVESTMENT COMPANIES, ADVISORS, AND INDENTURES

Investment companies, primarily mutual funds, are either open-ended or closed. Both represent assets managed by professional fund managers. Open-ended funds, like the famous Fidelity Magellan Fund, allow shares to be redeemed at net asset value at any time. Closed funds, like Tri-Continental, have a fixed number of shares that trade on exchanges, in this example on the NYSE. We discussed the phenomenal growth in open-ended mutual funds in Chapter 3. In the United States, mutual funds are covered by a federal statute, The Investment Company Act of 1940 (ICA). ICA was passed after a study requested by Congress in 1935 documented abuse in the investment company industry.

Regulation of Investment Companies under the ICA

To protect investors in the United States, the ICA requires investment companies to register with the SEC. The ICA defines three types of investment companies: *face amount certificate companies, unit investment trusts,* and *management companies*. The latter includes mutual funds and is the subject of the discussion here. Registrations provides control over relations shown by arrow (H) in Figure 15.2. A mutual fund registers by filing a registration statement of its investment policy and other disclosures similar to those required in the SA. An investment company registers as either a diversified or undiversified investment company. Only diversified investment companies qualify for the favorable tax treatment discussed in Chapter 17, so nearly all mutual funds are diversified investment companies. Diversified companies hold no more than 5 percent of assets in any one security issue and no more than 10 percent of any single issuer's stock. Registered investment companies must describe their investment strategies or techniques and must file annual reports with the SEC. They are subject to restrictions on activities and marketing discussed below.

Some companies managing financial assets are exempted from registration under ICA. Direct claims issued by commercial banks, savings and loans, and insurance companies, such as deposits and life insurance policies, are exempt from registration and reporting requirements of the ICA. Groups of fewer than 100 investors can combine to invest in financial assets without registration, allowing them to pursue investment strategies not allowed registered investment companies as long as public sales of shares are not attempted.

Mutual fund managers fighting competition from banks and insurance companies has led to litigation and court decisions that some investment products offered by banks and insurance companies must register with the SEC. For example, insurance company variable annuities with separate asset accounts and bank-offered common trust funds have been required by courts to register. Amendments to the ICA in 1970 refined some of these requirements. Future legislation and litigation will be extremely important to managers of firms wishing to compete with mutual funds without registering investment vehicles as investment companies. Mutual fund managers concerned with their competitive environment must be alert to regulatory changes.

Investment company activities are restricted by a number of laws and regulations. To avoid problems of potential theft of assets by managers, mutual fund assets must be held in custody by a third party: State Street Boston has made a specialty of serving mutual funds as custodian and record keeper. Open-ended mutual funds cannot issue debt other than bank debt. There are limitations on the amount of allowable issuance of preference shares and debt issued by closed-end funds. Dividend payments are limited to earnings. As discussed in Chapter 17, tax laws require passing through most dividends to gain favorable tax treatment. Finally, short sales or margin account borrowing are prohibited to registered investment companies. Sophisticated investors pursuing prohibited investment strategies must form pools exempt from registration.

The SEC carefully reviews sales practices of mutual funds. Advertising claims based on investment performance of funds are under constant review with precise calculation of funds' returns subject to scrutiny. Sales commissions on mutual funds sold through brokers, so-called *load* funds, are subject to maximums and there are limitations on allowable payment schedules over time. These regulations are intended to provide clear information on costs and returns in mutual funds to investors.

ICA also restricts relations between investment managers and other securities firms. For example, a brokerage firm can advise mutual funds and also buy and sell securities, but commissions must be "usual and customary." Management fees, usually expressed as a percent of assets, must be "reasonable," and there are limitations on how fees can be calculated for registered investment companies. ICA requires that at least 40 percent of the directors of a registered investment company be unaffiliated with the advisor.

Investment company registration and regulation is costly and restrictive. Litigation by disgruntled investors or the SEC is a constant concern of investment company managers. The investment management business faces a large amount of regulatory risk. These risks have not prevented the recent large growth of this industry, reflected in a 21 percent increase in the number of registered investment companies funds from 1986 to a total of 3,535 in 1990, accompanied by a 75 percent growth in the total value of assets over the same time period to $1.3 trillion in 1990, according to the SEC's *1990 Annual Report,* (p. 47).

Regulation of Investment Advisors

Investment advisors in the United States are regulated under the Investment Advisors Act of 1940 (IAA). The act defines an investment advisor as "any person who engages in the business of advising others, either directly or through publication or writings, as to the value of securities or as to the advisability of investing in, purchasing, or selling securities, or who, for compensation and as part of a regular business, issues or promulgates analyses or reports concerning securities" (Sec. 202 of the IAA). (This section also excludes advisers concentrating exclusively on U.S. Treasury securities or securities guaranteed by the U.S. Treasury.) The act excludes bankers, lawyers, accountants, engineers, teachers, and financial publishers from the definition of an investment advisor. All other investment advisors making their living by providing investment advice must register with the SEC according to the act. This legal language means that friends exchanging stock tips, or professors outlining investment ideas, are not professional investment advisors under the IAA.

Registration is the most direct requirement of securities advisors. Part I of the SEC registration form requires complete disclosure of any past violations of securities laws or regulations. Part II consists of disclosures on fees, educational backgrounds and experience of advisors, target clientele, and types of securities analyzed. Part II also requires a description of the methods of analysis and sources of data used, as well as disclosure of other financial institution affiliations.

The information in Part II of the advisor's registration form must be made available to potential clients. This can be done by providing a copy of the registration form or by preparing a special brochure. These requirements of the IAA are directed at providing investors with information they can use to judge fees, methods, and experience of advisors to assess their appropriateness in providing advice.

As with other securities laws, registration requirements provide a basis for legal actions against advisors who lie about their backgrounds, their methods, or their areas of expertise. The law can provide some restrictions on actions advisors can take, but it cannot restrict the kind of advice given. Advisors are not held to any standard of securities' performance based on their recommendations, nor could they be in risky financial markets. It is not possible for regulation to prevent bad advice. The law does try to prevent bad people from giving advice.

Further Securities Activities Regulation

Three further areas of regulation are mentioned here because of their importance to financial institutions, primarily to bank trust departments. First, the Trust Indenture Act of 1939 (TIA) requires most publicly traded debt instruments to have a designated trustee to look out for the interests of the bondholders and enforce the covenants in the bond indenture (or other debt contract.) Under the TIA, the trustee must receive audited financial statements and other financial and operating disclosures. The trustee must review disclosures to assess their impact on the debt holders and look for violations of covenants or actions detrimental to the bondholders. Trustee financial institutions are subject to litigation if firms issuing debt hurt investors because of inaction or inappropriate actions under their obligations as trustee for the bondholders. For example, in the RJR Nabisco merger, Manufacturers National Bank was sued because some bondholders alleged their claim was worsened by the merger and the bank, as trustee, did not fight the merger.

The Public Utility Holding Company Act of 1935 (PUHCA) requires registration of electric and gas holding companies with the SEC. The registration disclosure is similar to the registration of other public securities. PUHCA further restricts and controls transactions financing utility company operations and transactions between holding company entities. The law requires periodic reporting of company operations of about a dozen public utility holding companies registered with the SEC.

Finally, transfer agents like bank trust departments, which keep track of ownership of securities as discussed in Chapter 10, must be registered with the SEC under the SA. Transfer agents are further required to report annually on their activities.

15.6 REGULATORY RISK FACING SECURITIES FIRMS

Regulation around the world reflects developments in the United States securities markets because of the size and sophistication of those markets. Three of these developments are used to illustrate a discussion of factors influencing regulation and the regulatory responses. The first development was a major restructuring of the securities market called for by Congress with a call to form a National Market System (NMS), initiated in the Securities Acts Amendments of 1975. The second development concerns market and policy makers' reactions to the Stock Market Crash of October 1987. Finally, developments in response to the growing global market in securities are discussed.

National Market System

In the 1975 amendments to the SA, Congress called upon the SEC to work with the securities industry to form a "National Market System" (NMS) for stocks. An NMS would benefit investors by integrating many different regional markets for securities, thereby loosening the dominance of the NYSE. NMS as a policy goal means trading so that buyers and sellers have a chance of finding the best price for a security offered in any market. For example, in an effective NMS a buyer or seller can find the best price for a stock like Bank of America, listed on both the NYSE and the Pacific Stock Exchange. Market fragmentation has allowed the NYSE to use its dominance in trading volume to extract profits well in excess of costs from securities trades. Brokers on the NYSE have been able to charge a little more or offer a little less for securities traded on the NYSE because of concentration of trading on the NYSE floor (see Chapter 9 for a discussion of the economies of scale in order flow.) Better prices than those on the floor of the NYSE might be found on other exchanges if buyers and sellers could only find out about them.

Some progress has been made to develop an NMS and break the near monopoly of the NYSE on trading and integrate flows of information on the NYSE and regional exchanges (see Cohen *et al* 1986, Chapter 8). First, modest technological advances in broadcasting trading information across regional exchanges has occurred. The Intermarket Trading System (ITS) displays bid and ask prices for securities traded on several exchanges and enables orders to be transmitted from the floor of one exchange to another. The results of trades of NYSE-listed securities on all exchanges are reported on the Consolidated Quotation System (the "Consolidated Tape"), the moving row of prices seen in brokerages houses and on financial television.

Progress on breaking the NYSE monopoly on listed securities has occurred on other fronts. NYSE rule 390 forbidding member trading of listed securities off the floor was weakened when the SEC forced the NYSE to amend 390 to exempt securities listed after April 26, 1979. Another attack on the monopoly comes from nonmember firms, like Jeffries Securities, which make electronic markets for large bloc traders in listed stocks.

Nonetheless, the NYSE still dominates trading in listed securities. Recent events, including stock market variability causing large losses by member firms, have fostered consolidation of specialist market making on the NYSE. For example, in 1992, Speer Leeds, one of 41 specialist firms on the NYSE, acquired a unit from Paine Webber Group for $10 million, making it exclusive market maker in 175 NYSE listed stocks with a resulting share of volume exceeding 11 percent (Power 1992).

The NMS remains a policy goal. Much has happened to improve the efficiency of the securities markets since the goal was adopted in 1975, although most of these developments can be attributed to technology, competition, and the growth of institutional investors rather than policy. NMS policies would reduce the profitability of individual securities firms and perhaps cause failure of other firms unable to compete under the changing regulatory environment. Regulatory initiatives like NMS affect the business environment for securities firms. Cultivation of relationships with regulators and legislators can lead to payoffs to firms with friends in high places.

Regulatory intervention in market evolution has been abrupt in other countries. A primary example is the "Big Bang" in the London securities markets unleashed by the Financial Services Act in October 1986. Sudden changes in rules and institutions are business risks facing securities firms in all countries.

Stock Market Crash of 1987

Examples of regulatory risk are found in the policy response to the Stock Market Crash of October 1987. A 20 percent drop in average stock values in the United States, and more in some countries abroad, took place over two days: Friday and Monday, October 16 and October 19, 1987. The crash provoked a serious look at regulation of securities markets in the United States and abroad. In the United States, the "Brady Commission" (properly, the *Presidential Commission on the Stock Market Break of 1987*) was appointed under the leadership of Nicholas Brady, executive head of Blythe, Eastman, Dillon investment banking firm and afterward Secretary of the Treasury. In addition to the "Report of the Presidential Task Force on Market Mechanisms," major studies were also produced by the SEC, the CFTC, and other research institutions, private firms, and interest groups like the NYSE and the Chicago Mercantile Exchange.

The response to the stock crash illustrates several key issues of interest to managers of securities firms. The first observation is increased regulatory risk in the face of rapid price changes, even if the price adjustment is caused by underlying economic conditions and losses are not too damaging. Despite the attention focused on October 1987 events, few failures resulted, the most widely reported at the time being a broker in Grand Rapids, Michigan, and a put writer on the CBOT who defaulted on loans from the First Options Corporation, a subsidiary of Continental Bank in Chicago. United States securities markets worked pretty well.

Legislatures are not in the business of deciding that systems under their review work well. Lengthy hearings to decide what to do to "fix" the securities trading system took place. These hearings under the then leadership of visible and vocal congressional committee chairmen, like John Dingell (Michigan), chairman of the House Energy and Commerce Committee, Henry Gonzalez (Texas) of the House Banking Committee, and Edward Markey (Massachusetts) of the House Telecommunications and Finance Subcommittee, called many witnesses. All the exchanges felt obligated to make rule changes to appease Congress, whether or not rule changes were needed.

The Crash made the economic integration of the securities and derivative markets apparent, a theme underlined by the "single market" focus of the Brady Commission report. The Crash highlighted the need for technology able to respond to rushes in order volume as arbitrage across stock and futures exchanges reduced price differentials. Volume of trades reached an unprecedented maximum during the Crash, 608 million shares on the NYSE on October 19, 1987, straining order entry computer systems and jamming printers. The NYSE was unable to open more than 100 stocks on October 19, 1987. Customers were not able to telephone their brokers on the NASDAQ.

What regulatory response was required to observed technological inadequacies? Exchanges were in the process of expanding capacity since it is in their interest to handle the higher trading volumes. Some of the market failures, like failure to open, may have had to do with rules of the exchanges more than capacity problems. Many of the problems identified during the Crash were self-correcting.

The Brady Commission recommended the legal requirement for "circuit breakers," defined as mandatory trading halts when price changes were "too large." Circuit breakers would allow exchanges in the single market to catch up with one another. Criticisms of circuit breakers are that trading halts reduces liquidity for traders and the exchanges themselves are best able to define rules to accomplish goals of no insolvencies and maximum completed trades.

The Crash demonstrated the integration of world financial markets. Mandatory trading halts create opportunities for those exchanges that do not close. The Hong Kong Stock Market ceased operations in the middle of the crash, driving trading activity in its listed securities to other markets. Investors lost confidence in their ability to buy and sell shares at all times in the Hong Kong market. Costs of trading halts include chasing trading to competing foreign exchanges that are not forced to close.

The complex regulatory structure in the United States produced different responses to the Crash by different parties. The NYSE, regulated by the SEC, accused the Chicago futures markets, regulated by the CFTC, of exacerbating the crash by differences in cash margins, market organization, and trading rules. The NYSE sought to maintain its dominance in the face of its higher trading costs relative to the Chicago exchanges by using the Crash as the basis for limiting trading in instruments substitutable for NYSE stocks, like stock index futures. The Crash was used as an excuse to open disputes over jurisdictional boundaries governing market regulation. Regulatory turf battles between domestic regulators and foreign and domestic regulators are a feature of modern securities markets and affect regulatory risk for securities firms.

Global Securities Market Regulation

Another set of issues is illustrated by the emergence of sophisticated securities markets around the world as discussed in Huang and Stoll (1991). U.S. securities regulation traditionally led the world and was a model for regulation in other countries. The Financial Services Act of 1976 (FSA) in the United Kingdom followed the United States practice in several ways. FSA focuses on protection of the individual investor and relies on self-regulatory organizations. The Securities and Investment Board (SIB) established by the FRA has some functions of the SEC.

Persons or firms conducting a securities business in the United Kingdom must be authorized by the SIB, a process similar to registration in the United States.

Government regulatory responses in other countries to international competition change the competitive environment for securities firms. Many countries rely on government agencies to regulate financial markets. Germany and Japan concentrate many powers to regulate securities activities in their Ministries of Finance. Rules and sanctions replace self-regulation. Government officials are subject to different pressures and goals in policy and rule making than are diverse industry organizations. Government officials' authority can be pervasive in their jurisdictions.

Other countries follow certain aspects of U.S. laws producing hybrid systems of securities regulation. Thailand, for example, has a Securities and Exchange Commission. Despite a global movement towards securities regulation similar to those in the United States, there are vast differences in the laws, regulations, or objectives of self-regulatory organizations in other countries.

The significance of all these different regulatory regimes, from loose to tight, from government-controlled to industry-controlled, is that securities firms can compete for international trading and related activities by seeking the best regulatory environment. Many corporate bonds and other financial instruments are now issued outside their home countries to avoid local securities regulation. For example, Eurobonds, dollar-denominated bonds issued by the United States or other corporations in Europe, escape registration requirements of the SEC. Foreign firms do not list their securities on U.S. exchanges to avoid disclosure requirements.

Global financial market integration means many financial instruments, such as currency contracts, are traded virtually around the clock. Some U.S. exchanges have formed joint ventures with foreign exchanges, such as the CBOT and the Singapore GLOBEX system, to improve the flow of information and ease transactions 24 hours a day. The expansions of trading opportunities are good for participants in securities markets but open the possibility of jurisdictional disputes and competition between countries for trading business.

The future of regulation of securities markets has important profit potential for securities firms and investors. The regulatory environment must be assessed globally. Securities firms naturally seek to conduct business with minimum interference and at lowest costs. With telecommunication breakthroughs and cheap computing, the physical location of trading activities ceases to be of central significance. The objective of securities firms will be to serve customers at minimum cost. Local and international regulation will condition the business environment, and sudden changes in regulatory practice will continue to be a pervasive risk to securities firms.

15.7 SUMMARY

Securities market participants, investors, issuers, and securities firms relate to each other in many ways. Regulations governing relations between issuers and investors, among investors, and between securities firms and investors are reviewed in this chapter. The regulatory environment becomes more uncertain when economic events produce large adjustments like the Crash of 1987, even if the system handles the adjustments well. Jurisdictional battles between domestic and foreign regulators mean rules can change adversely or beneficially due to political, not economic, considerations. Securities activities are increasingly conducted globally. Foreign government policy is a definite source of regulatory risk for securities firms even if their business is exclusively domestic.

DISCUSSION QUESTIONS AND EXERCISES

1. A focus of U.S. securities market regulation is the disclosure of information. Why did exchanges require information disclosure before the SEC was established and would firms voluntarily issue information if not required? Would firms be willing to have their financials audited by independent accountants if not required? Why or why not?
2. Assume a broker carrying customer balances has assets of $170 million and liabilities of $150 million. If the brokers assets require $10 million in "haircuts," what is the broker's net-capital-to-liability ratio? If changes in regulation of asset quality increase haircuts to $15 million, how much capital in dollars and percent increase in equity must the broker raise to meet the 15:1 net-capital-to-liabilities ratio? What is the economic purpose of "haircuts" and what should regulators consider in setting "haircuts"?
3. What is "inside information?" What are the issues associated with making this information public? Who will gain and who will lose with "good" information on earnings prospects? Who should gain and who should lose with this information? Is it possible for no one to lose when information is announced?
4. With an initial 50 percent margin requirement on a stock priced at $50 per share, how much cash would an investor have to put up to buy 100 shares? If the broker maintains a 25 percent maintenance margin, how far could the stock price fall before the investor would have to put up more cash?
5. If the initial margin in the above example were raised to 60 percent, how much stock could the investor purchase with the same amount of cash? How would this affect the demand for stock in general? What is the basis for a "speculative demand" for stock? What effects, direct and indirect, would an increase in margin have on the speculative demand for stock?
6. Obtain a prospectus from a broker for a new issue of stock or debt. Classify the types of information contained in the prospectus (e.g., historical financial, description of the business, etc.). How useful is this information? How many people do you expect review the information thoroughly? What expenses would be incurred in producing this information?
7. The *Wall Street Journal* reports periodically on disciplinary actions taken by the NASD or the exchanges. Locate such a report in a recent edition. Classify the reasons for action taken and the penalties or sanctions imposed and relate them to the regu-

lation of securities brokers discussed in this chapter.

8. The "uptick rule" of the NYSE states that stock may not be sold short following a downward movement in a stock price but only following a minimal move upward (uptick) in the price. What could be the reason for such a rule? What enforcement problems are imposed on the exchange? How could a short-seller seek to get around these rules?
9. In the financial section of a newspaper find recent seat prices on organized exchanges. How does regulation increase and decrease these prices? Given the other determinants of seat prices, what does the recent price change reflect: regulation or general market conditions? What would you expect changes affecting minimum commissions to have been on NYSE seat prices? On the effect of SEC initiative to build a National Market System?
10. What international considerations are relevant in regulation of trading of securities? How does the existence of foreign trading in domestic securities help/hurt domestic investors?

REFERENCES

BEAVER, WILLIAM H. 1982. "Incremental Information Content of Replacement Cost Earnings," *Journal of Accounting and Economics,* 4, pp. 15–39.

COHEN, KALMAN J., STEVEN F. MAIER, ROBERT A. SCHWARTZ, and DAVID K. WITHCOMB. 1986. *The Microstructure of Securities Markets*. Englewood Cliffs, NJ: Prentice Hall.

COLLINS, D. W. 1976. "Predicting Earnings with Sub-Entity Data: Some Further Evidence," *Journal of Accounting Research,* 64, pp. 173–177.

HUANG, ROGER D. AND HANS R. STOLL. 1991. *Major World Equity Markets: Current Structure and Prospects for Change,* Monograph Series in Finance and Economics, New York University Salomon Center.

MOSES, JONATHAN M. 1992. "SEC Names 18 People in Suit over Insider Trading in Motel 6," *Wall Street Journal,* September 25, p. C1.

National Association of Securities Dealers. 1987. *Reprint of the Manual.* September. Washington, D.C.

POWER, WILLIAM. 1992. "Spear Leeds Breaks a Big Board 'Barrier'," *Wall Street Journal,* October 2, p. C1.

ALMEN, KEVIN G. 1992. "State Regulators Criticize SEC Proposals," *Wall Street Journal,* July 28, p. B2.

Siconolfi, Michael. 1992. "Wall Street Self-Regulation Toughened in 1991," *Wall Street Journal,* August 7, p. A7A.

SIMON, CAROL J. 1989. "The Effect of the 1933 Securities Act on Investor Information and the Performance of New Issues," *American Economic Review,* June, pp. 295–318.

Report of the Presidential Task Force on Market Mechanisms. 1988. Washington, D.C.: U.S. Government Printing Office.

SKOUSEN, K. FRED. 1983. *An Introduction to the SEC.* Third Ed. Cincinnati, Ohio: South-Western Publishing Company.

U.S. Commodity Futures Trading Commission. 1991. *Annual Report.* Washington, D.C.

U.S. Securities and Exchange Commission. 1990. *Annual Report.* Washington, D.C.

CHAPTER

16

Regulation of Insurance Activities and Markets

Introduction

Insurance services pervade our daily lives: We buy auto, renters', homeowners', and other insurances to protect against a variety of hazards we face routinely. We incorporate insurance in our contemplation of death.

- What role does government play in the provision of these pervasive financial services?
- How does insurance regulation compare to the regulation of other financial services?
- How does insurance regulation affect the profitability and costs of businesses offering insurance services?

The answers to these questions are of critical significance to managers of firms that are or would like to be part of the delivery of insurance services to the retail and wholesale financial services markets.

This chapter reviews the rationale for insurance regulation and describes the legal context within which insurance regulation takes place. The regulatory process, including the unique role of state regulatory authorities in the United States, is described, followed by a description of the major types of regulatory intervention in the insurance business. Finally, a review of the major issues concerning government policy in the insurance business is presented.

16.1 OVERVIEW OF GOVERNMENT INSURANCE REGULATION

Insurance, one of the most ancient of financial services, is also one of the most heavily regulated around the world. Before beginning our review of insurance regulation, we repeat here the four main reasons advanced for regulation from Chapter 2:

1. To promote government policy goals in the allocation of financial resources
2. To offset disadvantages to some market participants from the asymmetric ability to generate or process financial information
3. To accommodate economy-wide risks that cannot be absorbed by individual firms
4. To promote competition.

Most regulation of insurance is directed at the second purpose of protecting consumers from fraud or mistakes caused by the legal complexity of insurance contracts. The bulk of this chapter describes the regulations that protect consumers from confusion due to insurance contracts' technical language, often in "small print," and from insurance con artists. These purposes are advanced by regulation of policy language and sales practices, as discussed below. The competency and health of insurance underwriters are likewise regulated, purportedly to assure that consumers receive the insurance services they pay for.

Two forms of government intervention in insurance markets are rationalized by the third reason listed above, that some risks are too large to be absorbed by private markets. First, government regulation is often intended to avoid insurance company insolvencies or to take over insurance companies in financial difficulties. Some argue that without the commitment of government backing when insurance companies fail, fear of losses or unplanned transfers of wealth due to liquidation of insurance companies could cause panic cancellations of life or annuity insurance policies similar to bank runs. Panic liquidation of insurance destroys economic value through forced liquidations of long-term assets in a short period. If government did not have a role in insurance markets reducing danger of panics, some argue, insurance markets would fail to exist. Loss of insurance markets would increase risks so much that some economic activity would be impossible, for example shipment of goods exposed to risks of fire or accident.

Another example using the third rationale for regulation, to cover economy-wide risks not insurable in private markets, is used to justify government insurance programs aimed at providing insurance directly, as with deposit insurance discussed in Chapter 14, and flood insurance in the United States. These programs cover economy-wide risks too large for the private market to absorb at reasonable costs but which must be absorbed if the economy is to function effectively. Before the recent cessation of hostilities by Irish nationalists in England, the British government announced that it would reinsure risks from bombings by the Irish Republican Army when private insurers threatened to cease coverage of bombing damage. The British government feared an unbearable cost to the London economy from businesses moving or refusing to open there (*Wall Street Journal* 1992).

Critics argue that many government insurance programs, like those mentioned in the preceding paragraph, subsidize bearing risks that the private economy could absorb or insure without government interference. Others argue that government insurance programs distort economic incentives and lead to inefficient economic activities, for example subsidizing developments in areas likely to experience floods. Finally, it is often argued that alternatives to government involvement, such as industry-wide pooling of risks, work well enough although costs to insureds are higher.

Lip service is paid to promotion of competition in regulating insurance companies, the fourth reason advanced for government regulation. Critics wonder whether the effect of regulation has in fact been to limit competition. A major policy issue in the United States, as discussed below, is whether current regulation has produced enough competition in various areas of insurance coverage. As discussed in Chapter 11, there is evidence of inefficiencies in the marketing and distribution of insurance services around the world which can be related to lack of effective competition in marketing insurance services.

In line with this discussion of rationales for intervening in insurance markets, insurance service providers in other countries are heavily regulated. In Japan and Germany, the central government regulates insurance through agencies housed in their Ministries of Finance, a typical regulatory structure in many European countries. In the United Kingdom, supervision of insurance is provided by the Insurance Companies Division of the Department of Trade and Industry. Insurance bureaucracies regulating insurance by national governments are the rule in all countries except in the largest insurance market of them all, the United States.

Individual states regulate insurance in the United States, in most cases through a state commissioner of insurance or an insurance commission. Until a court case in 1944, insurance contracts were not considered "commerce" and therefore were not subject to regulation of interstate commerce as assigned to the federal government by the U.S. Constitution. State regulation of insurance was the rule from the beginnings of the republic. State authority was confirmed in a famous 1868 Supreme Court decision, *Paul v. Virginia,* which found that an insurance contract was not an instrument of commerce. During the following decades, states regulated insurance without federal government intervention.

The Supreme Court reversed its decision concerning insurance as interstate commerce in 1944 by ruling in *U.S. v. South-Eastern Underwriters Association* case that insurance was commerce after all and subject to federal regulation. The insurance industry and the state regulatory establishment responded to this ruling energetically in order to continue the existing structure of insurance regulation in the United States. The result of efforts to influence Congress was the McCarron–Ferguson Act of 1945, the hallmark federal law governing insurance regulation in the United States today.

The McCarron–Ferguson Act exempted insurance companies from federal regulation as long as they are regulated by state law. Among the more important exemptions of federal regulation of the insurance industry are federal laws covering antitrust and business practices. Provisions of the Sherman Act (1890) making coordinated efforts by businesses to restrain trade or competition illegal, the Clayton Act (1914) making price fixing illegal, and the Federal Trade Commission Act (1914) regulating unfair methods of competition, do not apply to insurance firms if they are regulated by a state agency.

Repeal or amendment of the McCarron–Ferguson Act is at the center of policy debate about insurance regulation in the United States today. Arguments concern the relative merits of the established regulatory system within which many state regulators monitor and control local activities of insurance companies, most of which operate in many states or nationally, versus a national uniform system of federal regulation. The flexibility and responsiveness of a state-based regulation of local insurance company operations are a distinct advantage in the vast and diverse U.S. economy. This advantage must be weighed against the costs of multiple regulatory establishments and their often duplicative requirements for companies operating in many states, rules varying across jurisdictions, and state legislators' susceptibility to industry pressure.[1]

Some insurance industry observers propose a combination of federal and state regulation. In April 1992, Representative John Dingell, then chairman of the Energy and Commerce Committee, introduced a 234-page bill which among other provisions would establish a Federal Insurance Solvency Commission to play a role analogous to the Securities and Exchange Commission in establishing financial requirements for the insurance industry (Thomas 1992). Another provision would establish a National Insurance Protection Corporation to play a role similar to the Federal Deposit Insurance Corporation. This legislation was given little immediate chance of passage, in part due to resistance from the states and the insurance industry.

Chartering Insurance Companies and Insurance Regulation

Governments typically regulate insurance underwriting by insurance companies that are committed to payment of cash benefits if certain events occur. In order to underwrite insurance, a corporate entity must be formed in some jurisdiction. The corporation can be a stock company or a mutual or cooperative organization. Insurance corporations are typically formed under company laws relevant to its headquarters jurisdiction. For example, Aetna Insurance is a Connecticut corporation. Many insurance companies are incorporated in Connecticut because of historically favorable chartering laws in that jurisdiction. Prudential Insurance, a mutual, is incorporated in New Jersey. As discussed below, many insurance companies form several corporate entities within a holding company structure in order to have corporate charters in several jurisdictions.

The insurance business is typically governed by a specific body of law that covers insurance companies and individual insurance professional activities. For example, the State of California has an *Insurance Code,* two thick volumes of laws, which establishes the legal basis for the insurance business and regulation in that state. In the United Kingdom insurance activities are covered by the Insurance Companies Act (1982).

Foreign, national, or state insurance laws typically require a license for an insurance company to underwrite insurance. The statutory requirement for a license and setting the standards for obtaining licenses is the legal basis for insurance regulation. In addition to underwriting insurance, the business of selling

[1]See Black and Skipper 1994, pp. 983–985, or Dobbyn 1989, pp. 291–295, for more extended discussion of the advantages and disadvantages of repeal of McCarran–Ferguson.

insurance services through agents or brokers, which can be companies or individuals, must also be licensed in most jurisdictions.

Since offering insurance services must be licensed under insurance laws in nearly all regions, license applications must be processed and approved or denied. In most states of the United States, the office issuing licenses is the Insurance Commissioner or Commission. In the United Kingdom, the Department of Trade and Industry issues licenses to perform insurance services. In other countries, the Ministry of Finance or some other office processes applications.

An application to offer insurance services typically sets standards to be met by firms or individuals to be licensed. In order for insurance agents and brokers to be licensed, typically they must satisfy some personal requirements, such as no criminal convictions within a specific time period. Qualifications to offer insurance services by individuals are often established by passing examinations administered by the state or a state authorized board.

Companies wishing to underwrite insurance must apply to the regulator for a new license or the approval to transfer an existing license. In the United States, an insurance company is classified by regulators as a *domestic* company, meaning headquartered in the state, a *foreign* company or carrier, meaning headquartered out of state, or an *alien* carrier, meaning chartered and headquartered in another country. Analogous classifications of license applicants are used to distinguish companies seeking authority to conduct an insurance business across other national boundaries. The status of a license applicant may influence the requirements for the granting of an insurance license.

Requirements set by insurance laws and imposed by insurance regulators for a license to underwrite insurance usually consist of: (1) minimum capital or a minimum financial commitment to offer the insurance services in the region applied for; (2) demonstration of ability to offer services applied for competently; (3) acceptable background of principal officers and investors; (4) a business plan in terms of insurance lines to be offered; and (5) deposits of assets to secure locally generated insurance business.

Licensing need not be restrictive and may not restrain competition in the offering of insurance services. For example, Arizona requires only $100,000 in capital and half again as much in free surplus to obtain an insurance license to reinsure life and disability insurance, or $400,000 to write life insurance. On the other hand, insurance regulators can use the license application or license transfer process to limit access to local markets. For example, when British American Tobacco (BAT) applied to acquire Farmers Insurance Group in 1988, the Insurance Commissioners of California and other states raised objections due to presumed inappropriateness of a tobacco company offering insurance services. Objections had to be met in legal proceedings that substantially raised the cost to BAT of entering the insurance business in some states (Hildes 1988).

Licenses to conduct an insurance business are usually defined by statute in terms of types of insurance a company is allowed to offer. The broadest general breakdown of insurance allowed by a particular license is between longer-term insurance contracts, namely life and annuity policies, versus the short-term contracts typical of property and casualty polices. Among the property and casualty policies insurance laws distinguish a number of insurance "lines," such as fire or auto insurance. For example, a firm might apply for a license to offer broken glass insurance in Texas.

Most jurisdictions in the United States issue licenses that restrict an insurance company to offering either life and health or specific lines of insurance. Insurance companies wishing to offer both life and property insurance may form a number of companies within a holding company framework in order to offer a several lines of insurance coverage. The regulatory requirements imposed by licensing and restrictions on insurance lines among companies presumably go a long way toward explaining the complex organizational structure of insurance companies.

16.2 THE REGULATORY PROCESS

Insurance regulators set rules to be followed by insurance companies within their jurisdictions in order to implement requirements of insurance laws. In the United States, with its many insurance commissioners, many different state regulations affecting multistate insurance companies could be confusing and costly to insurance company management. On the other hand, "foreign" or "alien" insurance companies often seek to offer insurance under the most lenient regulations available in other jurisdictions, undermining the effectiveness of local insurance regulation. Promoting fair competition across jurisdictional boundaries and avoiding problems of regulatory confusion is the purpose served for over a hundred years in the United States by the National Association of Insurance Commissioners (NAIC), formed in 1871.

The NAIC's *Tradition of Consumer Protection* (1992) states that the NAIC "provides a forum for the development of uniform public policy when uniformity is appropriate." The NAIC, with headquarters in Kansas City and offices in New York and Washington, D.C., performs a unique role in insurance regulation in the United States. The following paragraphs discuss functions of this complex organization.

NAIC Organization and Tasks

The NAIC has official meetings twice each year, drawing one to two thousand attendees. Meetings are attended by state insurance commissioners, who are accompanied by their staffs, and other government representatives. Interested parties like consumer groups, industry representatives, and academicians, also attend meetings. The NAIC is structured to pursue a number of objectives at biannual meetings, in working committees meeting throughout the year, and by its full-time staff in Kansas City. The main function of NAIC meetings is to discuss and adopt association policy proposed by working committees or NAIC staff.

One way the NAIC adopts policy is to recommend carefully drafted model laws to state legislatures. These model laws are intended as guides to legislation promoting uniform and efficient regulation of the insurance industry in the United States. NAIC policies are formulated during the year by committees organized by type of insurance and region and adopted at annual meetings. The overriding purpose of the NAIC is to standardize insurance regulation across the United States. In drafting model laws and other policy statements, NAIC committees are assisted by a full-time legal staff that also monitors legal developments nationally.

The NAIC supports state insurance commissioners in their regulation of insurance activities. It has focused resources on insurance company financial reporting. Its Financial Services Division produces the *NAIC Financial Condition Examiners Handbook* to standardize insurance company review, and it supports financial review in its Financial Analysis Division located in Washington, where NAIC financial analysts oversee the NAIC Insurance Regulatory Information System (IRIS). IRIS provides financial data on insurance companies. NAIC staff have developed computer-based tools to assist regulators in identifying potential problems from review of insurance company operations.

Another important NAIC function is performed by its Securities Valuation Office (SVO) in New York. SVO has provided values for securities held by insurance companies since 1908. Currently, the NAIC assigns risk grades to corporate and municipal securities, such as NAIC-1 (equivalent to a Standard and Poors A rating) through NAIC-6 (corresponding to Standard and Poors D) and assessments of bond and stock values. The SVO database contains approximately 190,000 securities issued by 30,000 issuers and issues an annual publication, *Valuations of Securities Manual,* which lists the portfolio values of all regulated insurers in the United States.

An example of initiatives undertaken by the NAIC is the adoption of risk-based capital adequacy requirements for life insurance companies similar to those for banks (described in Chapter 14). The proposal was first made at an NAIC meeting in June 1991, adopted in 1992, and implemented starting in March 1994. Life insurance companies are graded on the amount of capital relative to risk-adjusted assets, and companies falling 50 percent below NAIC guidelines are subject to seizure by state regulators (Pullam 1991, Steinmetz 1992, 1994).

New York Commissioner and Recent Events at State Level

The New York Superintendent of Insurance, as the commissioner there is called, has historically exercised a disproportionate influence on life insurance regulation in the United States because a large number of the biggest insurance companies are headquartered in New York. Another reason for New York's importance is the dominance of New York financial markets where insurance companies invest their funds. The New York legislature and insurance commission often take the lead in authorizing new investment powers to insurance companies, such as allowing investments in common stock in addition to bonds. Some states write legislation or rules holding companies to "the New York Superintendent's standard." Recently, the influential role of New York has diminished as other states, like California, increased in size and other state commissioners became active in specific areas of insurance due to popular pressure, like auto insurance. Furthermore, the New York Superintendent of Insurance has recently been criticized as having been too lax in enforcement of insurance regulation (Pullam 1992).

Europe 1992 and Insurance

In Europe, insurance companies are regulated by their home country regulators, often restricting foreign firm entry into local markets unless they satisfy local market licensing requirements. A major thrust of the European Economic Community (EEC) "Single Market 1992" initiative was reciprocal treatment of insurance companies in the twelve EEC countries. With such treatment, any insurance company regulated in one of the twelve countries can also do business in the other eleven. EEC Directives, orders to participating governments, opened EEC borders to insurance competition from other EEC firms and mandated legislative changes in all twelve jurisdictions to harmonize insurance regulation in EEC countries. Opening of insurance markets across EEC borders allows foreign firms to compete in the twelve domestic markets and seeks to reduce incentives for insurance companies to avoid regulation by locating in least restrictive countries.

16.3 REGULATION OF INSURANCE COMPANY ACTIVITIES

A primary purpose of insurance regulation is to protect insurance customers from fraud and from insurance company failure. Regulation of licensed insurance service providers is targeted at two areas: (1) the financial ability of insurance companies underwriting insurance to meet their obligations to insurance customers and; (2) regulation of marketing of insurance products. To achieve these objectives, a variety of regulatory tools are used by insurance regulators in nearly all jurisdictions. It is important to recognize that changes in regulation for either purpose can create or destroy profitable opportunities for individual insurance companies or for the insurance market.

Financial Regulation of Insurance Companies

We discuss the laws and regulations directed at the financial health of insurance companies first. Four tools are used by insurance regulators to protect customers from failure of insurance companies: (1) restrictions on who can own insurance companies and minimum financial requirements in order to be licensed to offer insurance services; (2) requirements for accounting and reporting business activity and status; (3) restrictions on the composition of insurance company assets; (4) and requirements for reserves and capital.

Basic ownership requirements are intended to ensure that owners of insurance companies can provide competent insurance company management. Since insurance companies form subsidiaries to conduct their business in other jurisdictions, ownership of an insurance company with successful operations in other geographical areas by a holding company usually demonstrates competence to manage an insurance company to an insurance commission. Owners or management with criminal backgrounds or with an experience of financial disaster is enough to alert regulators to potential problems. Companies with a bad history must provide evidence that previous problems are no longer of significance. Regulators deal with gray areas with respect to competence of a company to conduct an insurance business. We mentioned previously concerns about BAT's qualifications to own insurance operations.

Most jurisdictions require a minimum capital for stock insurance companies headquartered within a jurisdiction (state or country) to do business. Foreign or alien companies often must deposit assets of some minimum amount in the area where they wish to do business. For example, California law requires minimum capital of $2.6 million for a domestic property and casualty insurance company or a substantial deposit of assets by foreign or alien companies doing business in California. These minimum financial commitments are intended to deter frivolous efforts to undertake an insurance business in a region and to bond management to successful performance of the business.

Insurance Company Financial Reporting

Insurance companies report extensively to authorities in regions where they do business. In the United States, as discussed above, the NAIC has standardized reporting requirements in different states in order to make review of insurance company performance easier. Standardized financial reports are filed annually to commissioners in all jurisdictions where a company is licensed to do business. Since 1871, these reports have been filed on blank forms adopted at conventions of NAIC commissioners. For this reason, financial reports to regulators by insurance companies are called "convention blanks." These reports, predating the computer age, are large format books that can be reviewed by the public at branch offices of insurance regulators' offices.

The NAIC has moved into the computer age. Standardized financial reports are stored in its IRIS database which allows state regulators to review companies operating in their jurisdictions and to perform comparative analysis of insurance company performance and financial strength. NAIC has developed a number of analytical tools for regulators to use in assessing the financial strength of insurance companies.

Insurance authorities have their own statutory accounting practices (referred to as SAP). In the United States, SAP accounting usually follows the NAIC rules used by state commissioners for regulatory purposes. Stock insurance companies or companies with publicly traded security issues also report financial activity to the SEC. Financial reports filed with the SEC and those provided to customers and investors use Generally Accepted Accounting Principles (GAAP). These two methods of accounting can produce very different financial reports.

There are basic differences between SAP and GAAP accounting which result in differences between regulatory filings and other financial statements. A detailed treatment of accounting differences is not possible here but users of insurance company financial results should be aware of at least these several differences: (1) SAP uses only "admitted assets"; (2) SAP and GAAP use different insurance reserve calculations; (3) miscellaneous asset valuation and accrual accounting issues result in other differences. We discuss each difference briefly below. For a more complete discussion, see Black and Skipper 1994, Chapter 32.

SAP calculations of assets of insurance companies include only so-called "admitted assets." These are assets that regulators agree are sound in meeting insurance claims and benefit payment obligations. Nonadmitted assets, not included on SAP reports like the convention blank, include real assets like furniture and equipment, money owed to insurance companies by agents, and overdue interest.

A second difference between SAP and GAAP is in their treatment of liabilities arising from obligations to pay future insurance benefits, shown on financial statements as insurance reserves. Differences between SAP and GAAP accounting rules are especially important with long-term contracts like life insurance and annuities. SAP reserve calculations represent present values of future benefits using interest rates and mortality tables determined by statutes or regulation. GAAP calculation of reserves attempts more realistic calculations of future benefits using market interest rates appropriate as policies are written. GAAP also encourages use of more realistic mortality and policy lapse assumptions based on company experience. For example, high interest rates relative to statutory rates reduce GAAP reserve calculations relative to SAP because investments produce higher income necessary to fund future benefits.

Other differences exist between SAP and GAAP. One difference affecting the value of an insurance company's assets is the SAP requirement for mandatory special valuation reserves. Reserves are netted against the stated value of assets to reflect risk; these reserves are not necessarily related to market conditions. Income accruals may be distorted by the SAP requirement that commissions and policy expenses be charged against income as they occur rather than being amortized over the life of policies. Other differences between SAP and GAAP accounting can be important in individual cases.

Restrictions on Investment Activities of Insurance Companies

Insurance company investments are regulated by law. The regulations take two forms. First, insurance companies are allowed to make only certain investments, like corporate bonds of a certain rating. Second, within categories there may be limitations on the total amount of assets or on asset quality. An example would be a limitation of investment in real estate to 5 percent of total assets. Changes in allowable investments or in allowable amounts alter the ability of insurance companies to produce profits. Investment regulation is an important regulatory risk facing insurance company managers. For example, California law was revised in 1991 in response to the failure of several insurance companies and forced insurance companies doing business in that state to realign their portfolios.

Allowable investments in some states are different for the portion of total assets corresponding to required capital and surplus or policy reserves. In many jurisdictions funds representing capital and surplus are limited to the most secure investments: cash, government securities, and mortgages. Allowable investment activities for insurance company reserves have evolved slowly over time. In the

United States, NAIC in some cases has coordinated a change in allowable investment activities in several or all states. New York commissioners first allowed investment in common stock from life insurance reserves in 1951. As mentioned above, many states adopt the New York commissioners standard for assets.

Sometimes regulatory authorities allow firms in their jurisdiction entirely new investment powers. California allowed insurance companies to invest in real estate development after the Second World War to expand the tight supply of housing. Before that time, insurance companies in the United States were not allowed to invest directly in real estate except for their office buildings. Over time real estate investment authorities of insurance companies in all states have greatly expanded.

Within investment categories, insurance company regulations may restrict the quality of investments, especially those for life insurance companies. For life insurance reserves, for example, law or regulation may limit assets to "investment grade" securities, such as NAIC-1 to NAIC-2 graded instruments. Limitation of insurance investments protects the value of the policyholders' reserves. Restrictions of investments to low risk securities limits the rates of return insurance company portfolio managers can earn on reserves. Participating policies may be exempted from asset quality limitations if policyholders are informed of the risks of higher returns on cash values, as occurs with "universal life" policies.

Strict regulation of life insurance investments in the United States meant that life insurance companies could not compete with other asset managers for pension fund management until restrictions were loosened. Many states began permitting insurance companies to carry "separate account assets" during the 1960s. Special account assets are shown separately on insurance company books and are matched by liabilities representing pension fund claims on these funds. Limitations applying to investments on insurance reserves do not apply to separate account assets.

Besides pension fund assets, funds payable to winners of lawsuits with benefits paid over a number of years (so-called "structured settlements") or private foundation endowments can also be managed by insurance companies through their special account assets. Although many restrictions on life insurance general funds do not apply to special account assets, funds invested in this manner must be raised in competition with other asset managers like brokerage firms and mutual funds.

Quality restrictions on institutional investors like insurance companies segments the markets for securities into markets open to institutional investors trading so-called investment-grade securities, and markets trading securities that are nonrated or below-investment-grade. Changes in regulations allowing life insurance company "separate assets accounts" and broader investment authority for participating policies were partly responsible for growth in the market for nonrated or below-investment-grade bonds commonly known an "junk bonds." Growth in the demand for nonrated or below investment grade debt was essential for development of the junk bond market. Developments in the market for junk bonds, which some blame for failure of insurance companies like Executive Life in California, often resulted from changes or loopholes in regulatory treatment of financial institutions like thrifts and insurance companies. Regulatory changes can have an enormous impact on securities markets.

Casualty companies' investments are not as closely regulated as life insurance companies except for capital and surplus accounts. Insurance laws in some states require investment in low-risk government (federal and local) bonds or mortgages equal to minimum capital requirements. Some states require some portion, for example half, of unearned premiums to be invested in high grade securities. In most cases, property and casualty insurance company assets must be marketable in order to raise funds quickly to pay unexpected claims. Many jurisdictions prohibit casualty insurance companies from investing in real estate.

Requirements for Reserves and Capital

Property and casualty insurance companies are required to maintain a buffer between the value of their assets and their liabilities or potential claims. In the insurance industry, this buffer is called *policyholder's surplus,* although it corresponds conceptually to any other corporation's equity capital. Many regulators limit a property and casualty insurance company's ability to write insurance policies producing premiums to a multiple of surplus value. According to a widely invoked industry standard called the "Kenney rule" (after its author), an insurance company might be limited to writing insurance producing premium revenues to two times capital. For example, a property and casualty insurance company having $100 million in capital and surplus would be limited to generating $200 million per year in policy premiums.

Historically, capital (or surplus) was considered less important for life insurance companies because of the conservative assumptions used in statutory reserve calculations. However, the failure of several major life insurers, including First Capital and Executive Life in 1991, raised concerns about life insurance companies' buffers against declines in asset values. As discussed previously, in 1994, the NAIC implemented requirements for capital based on risk adjusted assets, similar to the banking capital standards discussed in Chapter 14.

Liquidation of Insurance Companies

Insurance regulators attempt to protect policyholders' interests through special procedures if an insurance company becomes insolvent. Several basic differences distinguish insurance firm bankruptcy from ordinary bankruptcy procedures: (1) bankruptcy proceedings are in state courts with the insurance commissioner as receiver; (2) industry-wide guaranty funds, as discussed in the following, are sometimes available to absorb losses suffered by policyholders; and (3) special powers are granted to insurance commissioners to orchestrate the purchase, rehabilitation (reorganization), or liquidation of failed insurance companies to minimize losses to policyholders, if not other creditors, of insurance companies.

When Executive Life failed in California in 1991, the state insurance commissioner, John Garamendi, assumed control of the company's assets and business. He orchestrated the quick sale of some of the company's assets, mainly junk bonds, to Altus Corporation at substantial losses and the remainder of the assets and insurance liabilities to a newly formed insurance company, Aurora Life, capitalized by Credit Lyonnais and other French investors. The reduction in reserves caused by the below-cost sale of the junk bonds was to be replenished by future contributions from state-sponsored life insurance guaranty funds, funded by insurance companies. These contributions amounted to about 25 percent of policyholder claims against the company. Garamendi's solution to the Executive Life failure was very controversial and was widely litigated. Executive Life's restructuring was the center of a lot of publicity useful for Garamendi's political ambitions, illustrating the connection between politics and financial institution business risk.

In the United States, insurance guaranty funds resulted from adoption of model NAIC laws. Model laws were developed in 1972 and 1973 for life and health companies and property and casualty companies separately. Development of guaranty funds illustrates how NAIC works. The funds are creatures of individual states so each is somewhat different and covers only claims against companies operating within their jurisdictions. National associations for both life and casualty guaranty funds represent them in interstate liquidation issues. For example, the National Organization of Health and Life Guaranty Associations (NOHLGA) was a principal negotiator in the settlement negotiated by the California insurance commissioner to settle the Executive Life failure.

Regulation of Insurance Selling Activities

Sales practices of insurance brokers, agents, and companies are regulated in a number of ways. In the United States, most jurisdictions regulate pricing of insurance coverage. In order to avoid consumer confusion and possible fraud in sales of insurance coverage, most insurance regulators require use of standardized insurance forms or language. Finally, in order to qualify for the McCarron–Ferguson Act exemptions on federal regulation, states must regulate unfair sales practices.

Insurance brokers and agents must be licensed in most jurisdictions to sell, place, or underwrite insurance. In most states written examinations or coursework are required by insurance regulations. Since a license is required to conduct insurance business and most state commissioners can suspend or revoke an agent's or broker's license, licensing is an effective control on practices of selling insurance.

Pricing, also called rate making in property and casualty insurance, is regulated to varying degrees in different jurisdictions. The goal of rate regulation is to assure that insurance premiums are adequate, reasonable, and not unfairly discriminatory. Implementation of rate regulation or review can be according to one of five different rate review systems used by various regulators. The systems are listed here from most to least restrictive of insurance company pricing: (1) rates are set by the insurance regulator or a regulator-mandated rating bureau; (2) rates are submitted to the regulatory authority for approval before being used to charge customers (so-called *prior approval* rate regulation); (3) rates can be changed according to experience and used immediately but new coverage or changed classifications must be approved by regulators (so-called *modified prior approval* rate regulation); (4) regulator is simply notified of rates to be charged (or *file and use* regulation); and (5) finally, competitive rates or *open competition*.

All five rate making systems are used in the United States (Texas uses state-made rates, while California uses competition, etc.). The rationale for rate regulation is that consumers can be victims of price-fixing above competitive levels, or lack of sophistication prevents consumers from assessing the fairness of rates charged by insurance companies. The evidence on the necessity for rate regulation to prevent abuses is mixed. Casual observation in some insurance lines, for example title insurance, suggests that regulation can also be used by the insurance industry (as it is in other regulated industries) to hold rates above competitive levels.

California insurance rates have operated under open competition in many insurance lines since 1947. There is no persuasive evidence that rates are out of line with loss experience, but market increases in auto insurance rates caused a political revolt in the form of "Proposition 103," a ballot initiative to limit auto insurance rates and to force insurers to pay a rebate to compensate insurance customers for "excess profits." The outcome of this initiative is still being fought in the courts as insurance companies resist interference with rate-setting and argue that costs have risen more than rates. Some companies have withdrawn from the California market. The point is that insurance rate setting can become an important source of political risk, especially in vast and pervasive retail insurance markets like auto insurance.

Regulation of Insurance Selling Practices

Most insurance regulators have the authority to review and approve policy forms, or contracts, used by insurance companies. The regulatory goal is to make insurance, an inherently complex financial product, as easy to understand as possible and to ensure that policy coverage does not have loopholes or unfair provisions.

Insurance agents and brokers are prevented from using a variety of sales practices in many states. In life insurance, agents are prevented from a practice called *twisting,* which is pressuring the customer to switch life insurance carriers. New life insurance policies usually pay selling agents or brokers large sales commissions, with initial premiums covering sales expenses rather than providing coverage. Most jurisdictions require disclosures of the disadvantages to the insured of switching policies.

A number of insurance sales practices are prohibited by regulation: deceptive or false advertising, misrepresentation, or unfair claims settlement. *Rebating,* the return of premiums on a preferential basis to certain customers, is also prohibited in most jurisdictions. Violations of regulation of sales practices can lead to fines, injunctions, or revocation of the license to conduct an insurance business.

Although legislators and regulators are convinced that rebating discriminates against policy buyers not receiving rebates, limiting such sales practices as rebating may inhibit competition. It is the sellers of insurance who may benefit when rebates cannot be used to compete. Regulation of insurance sales practices may actually raise the cost of insurance to consumers by inhibiting competition.

Other aspects of the insurance business, like claims processing and policy terminations, are also subject to regulation. Most insurance commissions maintain complaint divisions sensitive to consumer dissatisfaction. Given the large cost of auto and health insurance, insurance regulation is becoming increasingly politicized. In California, the insurance commissioner has been an elected office since 1990. This normally unspectacular position has come to be viewed by some as a springboard to further political ambitions.

16.4 CURRENT ISSUES IN INSURANCE REGULATION

Risks to managers of insurance firms coming from changes in the legal and regulatory environment are large. Our review of insurance regulation in the preceding sections demonstrates that profitability of insurance operations can be changed by many aspects of regulation: changes in financial regulation, changes in rates or policy terms, and so forth. Changes in any of the areas discussed can impose costs, offer profitable opportunities, or change competitive conditions. This section reviews some broader, environmental sources of risk in the insurance business.

First, competition in the insurance business in the United States, Europe, and elsewhere has been reduced by the reluctance of legislatures to allow potential competitors like banks to underwrite or sell insurance except to a limited degree, for example in the United States credit insurance and in small towns. The separation of insurance and banking has no theoretical underpinning in economics. Despite enormous pressure from the banking industry, this separation has been maintained by a combination of large insurance companies and the powerful lobbying efforts of independent agents. Changes in laws separating insurance from other financial firms are discussed continuously. Expanding competition would dramatically alter the insurance business environment.

Competition elsewhere, such as Europe, has been influenced by the willingness of national governments to protect some segments of domestic insurance providers. European Economic Community rules have been changed in line with the "Europe 1992" initiative to make it possible for insurance companies to do business in all twelve countries. An attempt was made before the revisions in the General Agreement on Tariffs and Trade (GATT) in 1994 to improve trade in services, including insurance services, globally, but failed due to resistance by regulators and insurance companies fearing competition. Competitive developments from changes in international rules, or domestic rule changes in countries opening insurance markets to foreign competition, obviously present risks and opportunities to insurance companies in different jurisdictions.

A second risk to the insurance industry comes from the intrusion of politics into certain lines of insurance with wide consumer impact. One extremely important area of political discussion is health insurance. Health insurance is the focus of a national policy debate in the United States. Despite a major initiative by the Clinton Administration in 1994, major reform was not accomplished. The debate is not over, though, and the outcome of this political process could dramatically alter the balance between private and public health insurance in United States and abroad. As with any policy changes of this enormity, some segments of the insurance industry will be harmed and others will find large profit opportunities.

Another insurance business with wide consumer impact is auto insurance. Intervention in this market in the United States is largely at the state level. The rate setting and rules governing auto insurance coverage and liability have become political issues to some extent, expanding the risks of that insurance business to political risks. Some states have adopted auto liability rules, so-called "no fault" auto insurance, where damage claims are paid without establishing legal liability, reducing court costs and attorneys' fees. Liability rule and rate regulation can powerfully affect profitability of insurance lines.

A final area with the potential for pervasive change to the property and casualty insurance business is in legal treatment of damage claims. Often, liabilities for insurance, for example product liability, are determined by a court's assessment of direct damages and imposition of punitive damages. A widespread movement in the United States to revise tort laws to restrict large jury trial assessments of damages from accidents or other causes could have a dramatic effect on costs from insurance claims for insurance underwriters. Changes in laws or precedents in the courts altering liability under insurance contracts in many areas, such as product liability or pollution damage, would completely alter expected payouts under some insurance contracts.

The message of this section is clear: risks to the profitability of insurance services from changes in the competitive environment from regulation, legislation, and litigation are large. These risks occur at the international, national, and local levels. The fundamental demand for insurance is based on primal economic motives to manage and distribute risk. Changes in the legal environment of insurance services will not end the demand for insurance services, but can affect the costs and profits of offering those services. Regulatory changes will create challenges and opportunities for insurance service providers.

16.5 SUMMARY

The demand for insurance services is based on one of the most essential economic needs, control of risk. The supply of insurance services is conditioned by regulation of insurance: This regulation affects entry to the market through licensing and chartering requirements. The costs of providing insurance are influenced by regulation in the form of financial regulation and regulation of pricing, as well as by the determination of the liabilities of insurance carriers by the courts. Selling of insurance products is subject to product regulation and restrictions on sales practices. Microeconomic risks from regulatory changes must be included in the uncertainty associated with the hazards of concern to insurance customers: death and accidents. The competitive environment is conditioned around the world by regulatory structure. This environment is under pressure both because of the nature of the industry and because of political developments. Political risks are no less important to the future evolution of this industry than the elemental hazards that are its economic function to handle.

DISCUSSION QUESTIONS AND EXERCISES

1. The United States has no federal insurance regulation. Determine the name of your state regulator and its offices. Contact the office and determine the range of services provided to consumers. Assess the value of state versus national regulation of insurance in your state.
2. What are the pros and cons of federal flood insurance? Is this an uninsurable risk? Who gains and loses from the existence of flood insurance plans?
3. What are similarities and differences between consumers' cash demands on a casualty insurance company versus their cash demands from withdrawals from a checking account? What different probabilities affect these demands? What are problems in assessing these probabilities? What would be the implications on investment?
4. Review the Best's rating on an insurance company operating in your region. What mention is made of NAIC investment standards? How useful is this information and why is it useful?
5. Obtain prices for standard insurance coverage on some infrequent need, like title insurance or a performance bond. How much do these prices differ? Would you assess the market you examine to be competitively priced? What is the response of the insurance regulator in your region to the question of rate regulation for the insurance line you investigate?
6. What role do minimum capital requirements and licensing play to protect consumers and other insurance service demanders? How could they be circumvented? Are there examples of these rules working or not working in your region?
7. Obtain a "convention blank" for an insurance company doing business in your region. Assess the parts of this report in terms of their usefulness in assessing the risk of the company in question. Assess the value of the report to a securities analyst.
8. Point out the possible problems caused in the interpretation of a convention blank from different accounting standards (GAAP and SAP). Compare a convention blank to a 10-K or annual report for a publicly traded company. On which lines or tables do you find the major difference between these reports? What is the importance of these differences to an assessment of the company's future risk and performance?
9. Review your car or home insurance contract. Is this an easy contract to understand? What role does your regulator play in defining this language (check with the office of the regulator if not clear)? Is this contract misleading or incapable of being understood by the usual consumer? Assess the need for consumer protection and contract regulation based on this review.
10. Review the risk ratios (capital and surplus to liabilities and composition of assets) for a life insurance company. How can such calculations detect and fail to detect potential problems in paying claims?

REFERENCES

BLACK, KENNETH, JR., and HAROLD D. SKIPPER. 1994. *Life Insurance* (Twelfth Ed.). Englewood Cliffs, N.J.: Prentice Hall.

DOBBYN, JOHN B. 1989. *Insurance Law in a Nutshell* (Second Ed.). St. Paul, Minn.: West Publishing.

The Fact Book: Property/Casualty Insurance Facts. 1992. New York: Insurance Information Institute.

HILDER, DAVID B. 1988. "Hostile Offer by B.A.T. Hits State Regulatory Walls," *Wall Street Journal,* June 22, p. A6.

HUEBNER, S. S., KENNETH BLACK, JR., and ROBERT S. KLINE. 1982. *Property and Casualty Insurance* (Third Ed.). Englewood Cliffs, N.J.: Prentice Hall.

Life Insurance Fact Book. 1992. Washington, D.C.: American Council of Life Insurance.

PULLAM, SUSAN. 1991. "Regulators Drafting New Insurer Rules That Will Force Firms to Raise Capital," *Wall Street Journal,* June 10, p. B8.

PULLAM, SUSAN. 1992. "New York Calls its Department of Insurance Lax," *Wall Street Journal,* May 8, p. B5.

REJDA, GEORGE E. 1986. *Principles of Insurance*. Glenview, Ill.: Scott, Foresman and Company.

STEINMETZ, GREG. 1992. "Plan on Grading of Life Insurers Moves Forward," *Wall Street Journal,* November 13, p. A2.

STEINMETZ, GREG. 1994. "New Yardstick on Life Insurers Is Hard to Find, Tough to Use," *Wall Street Journal,* March 10, p. C1.

THOMAS, PAULETTE. 1992. "Dingell Unveils Insurance Industry Bill that Would Impose U.S. Rules on Firms," *Wall Street Journal,* April 10, p. A4.

Wall Street Journal 1992. "British Insurance for Bombings," December 22, p. A7.

C H A P T E R

17

The Tax Environment and Financial Services

Introduction

The objective of this chapter is to build an appreciation of the risks and opportunities presented to financial institution managers by changes in the tax code or regulations.

- How do taxes affect the demand for financial services?
- How are financial service firms taxed and how does this alter their activities?
- What are the forces at play to change the tax environment?

This chapter reviews the tax policy-making environment and recent history in the United States in an effort to provide answers to these questions and to prepare future managers for dealing with the realities and risks of changing markets for financial services due to changes in taxes.

No review can cover all the details of the changing global tax environment: Numerous tax services and technical publications accomplish this (at great expense to their subscribers). The goal here is to provide future managers with a perspective that will prepare them to anticipate future risks and opportunities offered by the tax codes around the world.

17.1 TAXES AND FINANCIAL SERVICES

Few industries are as influenced by the tax environment as financial service firms. Profitability of many financial service firms is affected not only by tax treatment of their income but even more by changes in the demand for financial products as influenced by taxation. Every change in the tax code hurts some financial institutions, and changes occur frequently. These changes force costly adjustments in products and marketing strategies, sometimes dealing death blows to a whole line of business. This happened to real estate syndication in the United States after the Tax Reform Act of 1986 altered taxation of income on real estate investments. Some tax law changes create new opportunities for profitable financial services. The leasing business boomed as a result of the Economic Recovery Tax Act of 1981.

Our discussion concentrates on the United States tax environment. Parallel analysis is appropriate to every sovereign country and region around the world. Tax changes, tax holidays, tax relief, tax surcharges, tax rebates, tax credits—governments around the world use these words or their translations and thousands more technical terms in the language of taxation. When tax language is spoken, written, and interpreted, it makes as much sense in democracies (like most developed countries) as in the most tyrannical autocracies or traumatized states (like Senegal or Iraq). To economists, tax talk often makes no economic sense at all.

The incoherence of a great deal of tax discussion makes understanding often irrational political and historical dynamics of tax policy essential to those who need to anticipate risks from changes in taxation. The basic problem facing both those who impose and those who pay taxes is that payment of taxes is not a voluntary surrendering of resources: voluntary surrendering of resources for nonpersonal use is charity. Taxation is part of fiscal policy, as described in Chapter 13—taxes are by their nature con*fisca*tory. Taxes take resources away from economic agents who have other preferred uses for their funds. In other words, taxes hurt, and taxpayers must be forced to pay.

Tax policy consists of distributing the pain of this involuntary taking of funds. Fiscal policy consists of deciding who will be hurt more, hurt less, or not hurt at all, and who will be made better off by changes in tax policy. These questions are weighed by policy makers under any governmental structure.

To begin our discussion, we describe in a general way the types of taxes that can be levied and collected. An overview of tax sources provides a guide to how attacks on the status quo can occur. Taxes must be directed at visible resources or at resources that can only be hidden by clever people at the risk of credible sanctions or penalties. This limits the types of taxes that can and have been imposed.

Taxes are levied on three basic ways economic value can be observed: as income, wealth, or exchanges of goods and services. Taxes can be collected on various forms these values take. Furthermore, income from wealth in the form of capital goods may be taxed at different rates than wealth in the form of real estate. Table 17.1 gives some examples of each of these different types of taxation using rudimentary breakdowns providing some illustrative examples from United States state and federal government tax treatment. The structure of Table 17.1 is globally valid. Particular entries in the table cells are always specific to a given tax authority.

To illustrate the risks from the political process in the form of changes in the tax environment, we review briefly here the last decade of federal tax policy in

TABLE 17.1 Examples of Tax Treatment of Economic Values in United States

	SOURCE OF ECONOMIC VALUE TAXED					
	INCOME			*WEALTH*		
ENTITY TAXED	*LABOR*	*CAPITAL*	*FINANCIAL INVESTMENTS*	*CAPITAL*	*FINANCIAL INVESTMENTS*	*EXCHANGES*
Individuals	Federal income tax, social security tax	Tax subsidy in nontaxation of housing services	Interest, dividends, capital gains taxes	Real estate taxes, auto licensing fees	Estate taxes, inflation on nominal assets	Sales taxes, user fees
Partnerships	Taxed like individuals: Limitations on passive income/losses by owners					
Corporations	Social security tax, workmen's compensation	Subsidy in depreciation deduction	Subsidy in interest deduction of debt and dividend exclusion	Investment tax credits, inventory taxes, development fees		Tax on recovery of depreciation
Foreigners						Import and export duties

the United States. As background, note that Article I, Section 7, of the U.S. Constitution reads as follows:

> All Bills for raising Revenue shall originate in the House of Representatives; but the Senate may propose or concur with Amendments as on other Bills.

The President of the United States may veto tax bills and return them to the House of Representatives as the originating branch of Congress, but as with other legislation, the veto may be overridden with a two-thirds votes of both houses of Congress. According to Section 8 of Article I, all taxes must be uniform throughout the United States.

This relatively simple political structure for the deliberation of federal taxes becomes more complicated in practice. The House of Representatives centers deliberation of tax bills in the House Ways and Means Committee, whose powerful chairman throughout the eighties was Dan Rostenkowski, a Democrat from Illinois. The chairmanship of the corresponding Senate Finance Committee alternated with the majority party in the Senate. The chairman of that committee was Republican Senator Robert Dole until 1984, when he became minority leader of the Senate and was succeeded by Robert Packwood of Oregon until the election of 1987 when the Republicans lost the Senate, at which time the senior Democrat on the committee, Lloyd Bentsen of Texas became chairman. Bentsen served until named Treasury Secretary by the newly elected Democrat president, Bill Clinton, in 1993. Bentsen was succeeded by the then senior Democrat on the committee, Senator Daniel Moynihan of New York. In the election of 1994, both houses obtained Republican majorities so both committees were then chaired by Republicans.

The various chairmen oversaw the deliberation of a sequence of major revenue bills in the Congress in the 1980s. This tax legislation continued a sequence of major legislative interventions in the federal tax code every few years in the past. Major tax acts before 1980 were the Revenue Acts of 1954, 1962, 1964, and 1969, and the Tax Reform Act of 1976. The Congress in the 1980s passed four major federal tax acts in a burst of tax writing activity: the Economic Recovery Tax Act of 1981 (ERTA), the Tax Equity and Fiscal Responsibility Act of 1982 (TEFRA), the Deficit Reduction Act of 1984 (DRA), and the monumentally important Tax Reform Act of 1986 (TRA 1986). We use these acts to illustrate the impact of changes on the tax law on the business environment facing financial service firms.

ERTA was passed as a major tax reduction measure in the early years of the Reagan Administration. The Republican Party had won a majority in the Senate with the Reagan electoral victory in 1980, a majority they kept until 1987. During the legislative deliberations preceding ERTA, Senator Robert Dole of Kansas was chairman of the Senate Finance Committee. The act had several major provisions, among them:

1. Reduction in maximum tax rates on personal income to a 50 percent marginal rate from a 70 percent rate
2. Reduction in the tax rate on capital gains to one half the income tax rate, or a maximum of 25 percent

3. Extension of Individual Retirement Accounts (IRAs) to all taxpayers, allowing $2000 to be deducted from taxable income
4. Removal of the corporate income tax surcharge imposed during the Lyndon Johnson presidency, effectively reducing the marginal corporate tax rate from 52 to 48 percent
5. Acceleration of tax benefits from depreciation expense deductions by reducing the depreciable life of assets, in the case of real estate to 10 from 20 years
6. Authorizing sale of leasing tax benefits from tax-exempt or unprofitable corporations to third parties who could use the tax benefits, so-called "safe harbor" leasing.

Each of these tax law changes provoked major adjustments in the behavior of individuals and corporations. Of special importance to us is the effect on the profitability and types of services offered by financial service firms. We discuss these briefly below to illustrate the risks involved in the tax environment for financial service firms.

The drop in the personal tax rate meant after-tax higher returns for private investors on taxable investments and reduced advantages for tax-exempt investments. However, the tax advantage of saving in the form of IRAs was easy to implement and spawned a boom in this form of tax shelter. Many financial service firms offered IRA deposit or other savings vehicles to exploit tax deductions for IRA contributions.

Offsetting the reduced incentive for individuals to shelter income because of lower marginal tax rates were increases in the after-tax return to investments in real estate. Real estate was attractive because of shorter depreciation write-offs in ERTA, an inflationary environment producing low-tax capital gains on real estate investments, and the tax deductibility of interest on funds borrowed to acquire real estate. Diversification and participation by smaller investors in these real estate tax advantages were possible by acquiring interests in real estate limited partnerships.

The changes to the corporate tax law in ERTA likewise reduced the incentives to shield corporate income. Nonetheless, the tax savings from safe-harbor leasing gained by taxable corporations from leasing capital equipment to untaxed corporations (with tax losses or heavy use of ITCs) provoked a boom in the leasing business. The investment tax credit and tax deductibility of interest for corporations combined to cause furious growth in leveraged leases and lease syndications placing leases in safe harbor nonleasing corporations with taxable income.

TEFRA was a Congressional response to the "unfair" advantage some individuals and corporations took of the lenient provisions of ERTA. TEFRA removed the safe-harbor provisions of ERTA (except in "hardship cases" like airlines), effectively killing the business of brokering tax advantages from nonfinancial firms with taxable incomes. The Deficit Reduction Act of 1984 overhauled the taxation of insurance companies. In the process, some of the tax advantages of mutual insurance companies relative to stock companies were removed and the overall tax rate of insurance companies in general was increased.

Despite the significance of ERTA, TEFRA, and DRA for the financial services industry, the big tax event of the 1980s was the Tax Reform Act of 1986 (TRA). This act was the most thorough reformulation of the federal Revenue Code since

1954, and although the Code was only amended, United States tax laws as codified now can be referred to as the Revenue Code of 1986. This act attempted to be "revenue neutral" in not changing the general level of federal tax receipts. The entire thrust of the act was to simplify the code and increase revenues through the elimination of tax breaks and offset those changes with a general reduction in tax rates. The act contained the following major provisions:

1. Simplification of the tax schedule to two tax rates for individuals with a maximum tax rate of 28 percent
2. Limitation of "passive losses" on individual investments in real estate (from interest and depreciation exceeding revenues) except for individuals earning less than $100,000 who participate in managing real estate who can deduct a maximum of $25,000 per year
3. Elimination of personal deductions for consumer debt interest (other than mortgage interest), dividend income, and state and local taxes
4. Elimination of tax deductions for contributions to IRAs for employees with company pension plans
5. Reduction of the maximum corporate tax rate from 48 to 34 percent
6. Elimination of the ITC
7. Standardized and slower depreciation deductions on investments, especially real estate, from 19 to 31.5 years
8. Elimination of a variety of industry-specific tax breaks.

The TRA was intended to be a permanent simplification of the tax code. As can be deduced by the above list of changes, many changes in individuals and corporations tax situations provoked a myriad of responses.

By 1991, tinkering with the TRA had begun: The individual tax rate was raised to 31 percent as part of the deal the Bush administration cut with Congress to reduce the federal deficit. In 1993, the Clinton Administration's Omnibus Budget Reconciliation Act (OBRA) of 1993, called the largest tax increase in United States history by critics, increased both individual and corporate maximum tax rates. The TRA was a monumental piece of legislation, but the tax code is too tempting to politicians. The simplified code of TRA is under siege and unlikely to last in its (relatively) simple form.

17.2 TAXES AND THE DEMAND FOR FINANCIAL SERVICES

The tax environment described above creates a demand for financial services in terms of the types of savings and credit vehicles offered to customers and services directly related to the management and payment of tax liabilities. Because of their different marketing problems and different tax treatment, these products are very different in the retail and wholesale markets. The discussion that follows illustrates some of the products that were offered in the recent past or are being offered as a result of tax policy. No discussion can completely describe the actual and potential supply of profitable financial products that are attractive in whole or in part due to taxation.

Retail Market

The retail market is differentiated by the wealth and income of individual clients. High income individuals and individuals with substantial wealth face higher marginal taxes. Financial service firms offer a number of services that provide tax advantages to these individuals. Several good examples are derived from asset management services, where tax-exempt municipal securities can yield higher after-tax returns to high tax rate individuals. For example, a municipal bond paying 6 percent interest is equivalent to a taxable bond paying 9 percent for taxpayers in the 31 percent marginal tax bracket.

Many asset management firms offer municipal bond funds that are exempt from federal and state and local taxes (e.g., Dreyfus California and Fidelity New York Funds). These financial services are marketed to residents of those states whose marginal tax rates make investment income in this form attractive. Often these funds are tied to other financial services, like transaction processing (check writing.)

During the period from ERTA to TRA, many extremely profitable financial services were offered to high income tax rate individuals to capture the favorable treatment of income from real estate. One very popular investment vehicle was real estate limited partnerships. Use of the partnership organization meant that individual shares of income and expenses from real estate ownership were added to investors' individual returns. Since the taxable incomes from real estate were computed using real estate revenues, like rental income, minus expenses including debt service and the accelerated depreciation possible for real estate under ERTA rules, many real estate partnerships had positive cash flows but negative income. These "passive losses" (as they were called) reduced taxable income for high income investors, even though many real estate limited partnerships were able to return cash to investors. In some of the best deals, investors got all or most of their investments back in a few years while saving on taxes and selling the properties at a profit after a short holding period.

The market for financial services based on forming, marketing, and servicing limited partnerships collapsed with the TRA, which reduced the rate of depreciation on real estate and more importantly eliminated passive losses for individuals earning more than $100,000 (individuals earning less could take losses from real estate up to $25,000 per year). As a result of the TRA, the demand for limited partnerships collapsed and some financial service firms (e.g., Integrated Resources) were unable to refocus their business on smaller partnerships (producing passive losses under the limits).

Financial service firms syndicating limited partnerships were often the general partners in the partnerships they sold. They earned management income for the properties and retained a share in the gains on sale. The collapse of real estate values in the period following TRA, which some observers feel was caused by TRA, caused firms selling limited partnerships serious problems or wiped them out due to reduced management fees and disappearance of capital gains. Risks from tax changes are dramatically illustrated by the fate of real estate limited partnership syndicators.

Other financial services based on tax treatment of savings for retirement are directed at individuals with smaller incomes or wealth. For example, certain individuals (those with no retirement plans at their jobs) may deduct contributions to Individual Retirement Accounts (IRAs) from taxable income. Income from retirement funds is not taxed until withdrawn at retirement, presumably at lower rates when retirees no longer have jobs. Savings in the form of IRA contributions in the United States grew to 30 percent of all savings from passage of ERTA until TRA reduced their attractiveness by limiting tax deductible contributions to those who had no retirement at work (Gravelle 1991).

Another tax advantage to self-employed workers are so-called Keogh retirement funds. These retirement savings can be deducted from taxable income for self-employed workers up to 20 percent of their income. IRA and Keogh funds can be packaged in a number of ways as financial services. Many deposit-taking institutions offer deposit accounts geared to IRAs. Brokers and asset managers offer a number of types of accounts to individual retirement accounts: For example, Merrill Lynch offers standardized retirement accounts that allow a complete range of investments, from stocks and bonds to mutual funds, and provides savers with necessary accounting services to report taxes on larger accounts.

Individual tax laws and a combination of corporate tax laws and litigation threats have created an explosive demand for retirement savings in the form of 401-K plans, named after the section in the tax code discussing them. These individual employee retirement funds replace corporate pension plans promising defined benefits with fixed contributions to an employee-managed or selected retirement fund (a defined contribution plan). The defined contribution reduces risks of underfunding pension liabilities to corporations in volatile financial markets. Many workers now manage their own retirement savings instead of relying on the traditional corporate pension fund. Increasing labor mobility may stimulate growth of 401-K plans in the future. Employers and individual workers are now seeking a variety of ways to acquire savings vehicles and asset management products in this fast-growing retail market.

Savings in the form of cash values on insurance policies are also a major factor affecting individual demand for financial services. The tax exemption of income earned on cash values of insurance policies, the so-called "inside buildup" (see the discussion in Chapter 11), makes insurance policies a desirable savings vehicle. The development and marketing of insurance products like universal life policies depends on this aspect of the tax treatment of individuals, which was preserved by TRA. The insurance industry hangs on every piece of tax legislation to preserve the important tax advantage of insurance.

A whole range of credit products are based on the tax treatment of individual interest expense. Since the TRA eliminated the tax deductibility of interest expense not related to purchases of housing or financial investments, many financial institutions have offered home equity loans (HELs) using equity in housing to secure loans. Many HELs function like lines of credit where maximum borrowing limits are based on equity in the borrower's home (value minus any mortgages), allowing borrowers to write checks to buy cars and vacations. Since these are home loans, the interest is tax deductible. However, changes in the tax law with the 1989 Tax Act limited how much could be borrowed and still qualify as a deduction from income.

TRA defined housing to include boats that could be used to sleep on as second homes. Since interest deductions used to finance purchases of these assets was deductible, many financial institutions specialized in marine loans and in financing vacation properties. On the other hand, demand for boat loans was sharply reduced when another change in the 1989 Tax Act imposed "luxury taxes" on boats costing over $100,000.

These examples are intended to illustrate how financial service firms must be alert to individual tax treatment in their specification of savings and credit vehicles for individuals. Changes in the tax code can be unexpected: The TRA impact on tax-advantaged real estate investments was barely anticipated weeks before the final version of the act passed. Tax law changes are clearly an element of risk facing financial institution managers.

Institutional Markets

The tax treatment of corporate income has had a particularly large impact on the financial services industry. Probably the most pervasive impact of specific United States tax law on financial services is the deductibility of interest expense from taxable income. Corporate interest can be deducted from taxable income in most countries. Debt is a tax-favored form of financing and influences the demand for credit by corporations. The burgeoning demand on debt instruments and credit has dramatically influenced the types of financial services offered to corporate users of funds.

The tax deductibility of interest favors debt instruments for longer term financing. Banks and other financial institutions are often faced with the risks of financing longer term credits with shorter term liabilities in economic environments where interest rates fluctuate with inflation expectations. Financial institutions providing credit services have sought ways to reduce these risks to their customers. Variable rate loans, hedging instruments, or participation in the appreciating value of real estate and other assets by including payments related to asset appreciation in debt instruments are examples of products developed. "Equity kickers," where lenders absorb interest rate risk in exchange for potential gains, must be carefully crafted so as to qualify as debt instruments with interest payments rather than as ownership participations.[1]

The rise of corporate debt–equity ratios in the United States to a peak in the late 1980s mirrored inflation, which reduced the real cost of debt, and high corporate tax rates. The reduction in the corporate tax rate with TRA and lower inflation has reduced the tax advantage of debt. Recently corporations have been reducing debt and raising proportionately more funds in the form of equity. Changes in desirable types of financing from changes in the tax code clearly affect

[1]Deposit-institution regulators are also concerned that credit instruments not be disguised equity investments. The Financial Accounting Standards Board and the IRS have established criteria for financial instruments to be treated like debt.

the types of services offered by investment banking firms and other financial service firms arranging for permanent funding of corporations.

Policy makers have used the tax treatment of corporate income in an effort to stimulate investment in capital. The Tax Act of 1954 introduced accelerated depreciation on equipment for corporations. Accelerated depreciation means that after-tax cash flows from equipment are greatest in the early years, implying higher rates of return. Depreciation schedules are often manipulated by Congress to affect capital costs relative to other corporate expenditures, as in ERTA and the TRA of 1986.

The investment tax credit (ITC) has been an on-again, off-again tax policy since first implemented in the Tax Act of 1964. The ITC reduces a capital-purchasing corporation's tax liability by a percentage of the costs of investments. The percentage has varied with different time periods and with the estimated life of the investment goods purchased. For example, until 1986, automobiles with estimated lives of 3 years had a 6 2/3 percent ITC, and equipment with more than five-year lives were eligible for a 10 percent ITC.

Because of their low investments in physical capital, financial services firms can rarely benefit directly from ITCs. Other corporations, like airlines, often do not have taxable incomes large enough to fully use available ITCs. Out of this disparity in tax liabilities between the direct usefulness of ITCs for financial and nonfinancial corporations was born one of the most important institutional credit products of the last three decades: leasing.

The leasing industry consists of banks, insurance companies, and other financial service firms, which either directly or through affiliates write lease contracts with operating corporations. The financing costs to the equipment users are transformed by a lease into tax-deductible-equipment leasing expenses. The leasing business is very competitive. In competitive markets, leasing fees reflect tax benefits to financial corporations (or other lessors, like partnerships) of accelerated depreciation and the ITC. Leasing was (and may be again) mainly a tax arbitrage.

Tax advantages from accelerated depreciation and the ITC produced even more elaborate financial transactions as financing from deposit-taking institutions was strained. For example, leveraged leases allowed financing of a large part of equipment purchased with debt supplied by third parties, who enjoy higher interest income possible because of tax reduction of the lessor through depreciation, ITC, and interest expense. Packaging and placing so-called leveraged leases generated substantial fees and servicing income for financial institutions like banks and brokerage firms.

The risks to financial service firms that had built businesses on leasing, like many money center banks and their leasing company affiliates, are demonstrated by the impact of changes in the tax law. ERTA allowed the tax benefits of leasing to be used by nonfinancial firms, so that leasing could be done in a "safe-harbor," protected from the tax man. These leases simply transferred the tax benefits of depreciation and the ITC to corporations that could use them. As a result of these so-called "tax benefit transfers," competition in the leasing business came from nonfinancial corporations. Some profitable United States corporations, like General Electric, paid no taxes in 1982 because of safe-harbor leasing.

Tax deductibility of payments to pension funds is part of the stimulus of the enormous growth in pension fund assets under management. Financial service firms employ vast resources managing the trillion dollar pool of private pension funds that has accumulated. Changes in the corporate tax rate can change the desired timing of contributions by corporations to pension funds. For example, in 1986, General Motors contributed $1.04 billion because corporate tax rates would be falling under the TRA, reducing the tax advantage (see Scholes and Wolfson 1992, p. 206).

A significant portion of financial services business is attributable to the tax-exemption of state and local government (called municipal) bond interest. We discussed previously the creation of retail-oriented investment vehicles packaging diversified investments in municipal bonds. The tax treatment of municipal bond income means that municipal bond before-tax interest rates are substantially below taxable rates. For example, in January 1993, taxable U.S. Treasury long-term bonds yielded 7.25 percent range and high-grade long-term municipals were yielding around 6 percent.

Two tax arbitrage possibilities based on municipal bonds have attracted institutional customers of financial service firms. First, state and local governments like to earn income by borrowing at tax-exempt rates and investing in taxable securities upon which they (as governments) do not pay a tax. The IRS recognizes this possibility and strictly limits how long and for what (stated) reasons governments can exploit this arbitrage possibility. Typically, governments raising funds for capital projects, like university dormitories, roads, public housing, and so on, are allowed to "temporarily" invest borrowed funds in taxable investments. A number of insurance companies sold municipalities guaranteed investment contracts (GICs) as a means to cash in on the temporary excess of funds over investment costs.

A second tax arbitrage opportunity exists if taxable corporations can borrow at the tax-exempt rate. Some tax treatment of investment, such as pollution control equipment, allows corporations to issue tax-exempt securities. A more aggressive strategy is when municipalities borrow in the tax-exempt market and build facilities leased or sold to corporations as incentives to locate in the community. Finally, many municipalities have legally issued tax exempt securities to finance housing for low income renters or buyers or favored constituents, like veterans.

All of these tax arbitrage opportunities have created a large demand for underwriting and placement of municipal securities. Since banks are allowed to underwrite municipal securities as long as they are general obligation (GO) bonds (secured by the general taxing power of the local government rather than just revenues from the investment projects), commercial banks compete with other financial service firms in the underwriting, distribution, and advising activities associated with these issues.

17.3 TAXATION OF FINANCIAL INSTITUTIONS

The foregoing discussion demonstrates risks to financial firms from changes in the tax code on the demand for financial services. Our attention now turns to the taxation of those firms themselves. Financial institutions are directly subject to many special tax treatments that affect after-tax profitability of many of their services. Special tax treatment is the basis for a substantial departure of financial service firm average tax rates from other corporations. The basis for differences lies in three areas: (1) tax treatment of expenses due to credit losses, most significant for banks and thrift institutions; (2) special treatment of interest earnings, capital gains, and interest deductions associated with financing activities, important for deposit-taking institutions and brokers; and (3) differences between treatment of corporations and other tax payers like mutuals and partnerships, having a major impact on insurance firms.

In principle, financial service corporations are taxed in the United States like all corporations under Section 11 of the federal corporate income tax code. They are not so treated at the state level. A detailed analysis of local taxation is not possible in this text but we note that special income and excise tax rules apply to financial institutions in many states and cities. For example, in California, banks are exempt from city taxes and pay a different state income tax than other corporations "in lieu" of local taxes. Insurance companies in California are exempt from income taxes but pay gross premium taxes, as in many states. Furthermore, California exempts insurance company income from taxes on their businesses owned as investments even though they are not related to insurance. Specialized state and local tax provisions affect the after-tax profitability of various financial institutions and lines of business.

Deposit-Taking Institution Taxes

The taxation of deposit-taking institutions has a long and tortured history in the United States. Savings and loan associations, traditionally mutual associations, were exempt from federal taxation until 1951. Credit unions are still exempt from federal taxation. The special tax treatment of classes of deposit-taking institutions often has no real foundation in economic theory or policy. A 1991 General Accounting Office (GAO) report, titled "Credit Unions," states:

> Credit unions, unlike other federally insured depository institutions, are exempt from federal income taxation. The legislative history does not give a clear rationale for the exemption. (p. 320)

The important lesson for financial institution managers is that the charter of an institution has tax implications and that these tax treatments are often arbitrary. In 1993, the House Banking Committee debated removal of the credit union federal tax exemption but credit unions are still not taxed.

The Federal tax code allows specialized treatment of deductions for actual and projected loan losses for banks and thrifts (Code Sections 585 and 593). The basic idea is that deposit-taking institutions can anticipate losses on credit activities in the future by establishing loan loss reserves rather than deducting actual losses as other corporations do. Until 1986, the tax law allowed banks to choose one of two methods for calculating deductions for loan loss provisions from taxable income: (1) the *experience method* where losses as a percent of loans are averaged over six years and the average is applied to tax-year ending loan amounts to calculate allowable reserves; or (2) the *percentage method* where deductions are allowed to bring loan loss reserves up to a percent of year-ending loans, .6 percent in 1986.

Banks naturally chose the method that minimized their tax liability. Table 17.2 illustrates how the loan loss provisions worked. It shows the effect of the two methods of calculations on the allowable provision for loan losses. In the example, the percentage method produces a higher tax deduction for loan loss provisions because the .6 percent is higher than average actual losses. Under either method, allowable provisions are higher than actual write-offs since total loans are growing. The tax law further allows a minimum provision equal to "base year" total reserves. If loans are declining, loss provisions resulting in the same percentage that base year reserves bear to base year loans are allowed.[2]

As long as bank loans grow, as they did in an inflationary period like the seventies and eighties, either method can produce loan loss deductions larger

TABLE 17.2 Example of Calculation of Loan Loss Provisions: Banks

ITEM	*AVERAGE PREVIOUS FIVE YEARS*	*CURRENT TAX YEAR*	*AVERAGE INCLUDING CURRENT TAX YEAR*
Loans	$140,000	$150,000	$141,667
Loan write-offs	350	375	354
Percent write-offs			.25%
	LAST YEAR	*CURRENT TAX YEAR*	
Allowable reserve:			
Year end			
(1) Experience method	$365	$375[a]	
(2) Percentage method	876	900[b]	
Provision for loan losses			
(1) Experience method		385[c]	
(2) Percentage method		399[d]	
Excess of provision over actual:		$10 – $24	

[a]$375 = .0025 times $150,000.
[b]$900 = .006 times $150,000.
[c]$385 = $375 – $365 + $375.
[d]$399 = $900 – $876 + $375.

[2]The tax law defines the base year as the last taxable year before 1988 or the year the experience method was first used.

than actual losses. This tax provision was a benefit to banks. The more advantageous method was the percentage method, because normally bank write-offs of bad loans were substantially less than .6 percent during most of that period. Larger loan losses in the 1980s reduced the benefit of the percentage method. TRA eliminated the percentage method, which could only benefit low loss banks not using the experience method in any case.

Section 593 of the tax code allows thrift institutions a third and very valuable method for the calculation of loan losses, the *percent of income* method. This wrinkle in the tax code is intended to favor home mortgage investments by savings institutions and historically has been a significant benefit to savings and loans. Qualified mortgage lenders, defined as savings and loans maintaining at least 60 percent of their assets in qualifying assets, specifically residential loans, are allowed to deduct up to 8 percent of before-tax *income* as a loan loss provision. Table 17.3 illustrates the increase in loan loss provisions and implied tax savings for a profitable thrift. There are restrictions on the total amount of reserves accumulated on the balance sheet and the total deduction relative to the amount of deposit financing, both illustrated on the table.

Loan loss provisions illustrate several major points about sources of risk to financial service firms from changes in tax laws: (1) tax rates and calculations change, as they did when the TRA removed the percentage method and changes in calculations available for thrifts and the changes meant changes in after-tax income; (2) tax laws are used to favor certain types of investments, such as residential mortgages, and favorable treatment can change for better or worse with policy changes; and (3) retention of tax breaks or creation of new breaks can sometimes be achieved with lobbying efforts coordinated with other powerful groups, such as homebuilders' associations, especially in crisis environments like the thrift crisis and recession of the late 1980s and early 1990s.

TABLE 17.3 Example of Calculation of Loan Loss Provisions: Thrifts

ITEM	*PREVIOUS YEAR*	*TAX YEAR*
Loans	\$140,000	\$150,000
Deposits	130,000	
Reserves	3,000	
Equity	30,000	
Taxable income		7,500
Allowable deduction		600
Limitations on deduction:		
(1) 12% of previous year's deposits minus equity and reserves		11,640
(2) Amount producing 6 percent reserves at year end		6,375[a]

[a]Assumes actual write-offs as in Table 17.2.

Interest Expense of Carrying Municipal Securities

Before ERTA of 1982, commercial banks were allowed another valuable tax provision that continues on certain "grandfathered" investment situations. Interest income from municipal bonds was and is not taxable to investors. For banks, the interest costs of carrying municipal securities was deductible from taxable income. Since banks can underwrite municipal bonds, and because of the tax advantages of investing in tax-exempt bonds while deducting interest paid to investors on bank deposits and other sources of funds at before-tax interest rates, banks were major investors in municipals. Municipal securities accounted for 10 percent of bank assets before TRA, about one-third of the outstanding amount of state and local debt. Other investors (nonfinancial corporations and such financial institutions as insurance companies) could not deduct interest expense related to the carrying costs of tax-exempt securities.

Banks' tax advantage from investing in municipals was reduced by ERTA to 85 percent of their interest revenue from state and local bonds bought after 1982 and by TEFRA to 80 percent for bonds bought after 1984, although interest on municipal bonds bought before 1982 was still completely exempt. The TRA completely removed the tax advantage on bonds bought after 1986 but the tax treatment on bonds bought before the act was preserved. Banks with historically high holdings of municipal bonds can still benefit from this tax treatment. For example, Banc One of Ohio had an average tax rate in 1991 of 25 percent, well below the 34 percent corporate rate, and 7 percent of the differential was due to its holding of municipals before 1986.

The strategic question for financial institution managers is how tax benefits come and go. In the case of the tax advantage in investing in municipals, why did the tax benefits persist so long? Why were Congress and the tax authorities so indulgent, since this advantaged treatment was long established in banking? The reason was Congressional fear of upsetting the market for municipal securities and the potential impact on state and local borrowing costs of removing the tax advantage. These reasons were argued persuasively to members of Congress and important committees by bank and local government lobbies over decades. This combination of political pressures together with the public's indifference to such a complicated wrinkle in the tax code allowed it to survive for decades.

Tax Losses and Troubled Institutions

The crisis in the thrift industry inspired a number of temporary tax law changes that provided tax advantages for the acquisition of failing institutions by profitable institutions. The discussion here is not an effort to update the current tax treatment of acquisitions but to illustrate how changes in the tax code can create value-producing opportunities (and take them away.)

Congress promoted the acquisition of failed thrifts as a means of saving money for the government deposit insurance agencies, primarily the Federal Savings and Loan Insurance Corporation (FSLIC). It favored these acquisitions in two ways. First, tax changes in the TRA that eliminated or reduced the tax treatment of operating losses through *tax loss carryforwards* of nonfinancial corporations were *not* applied to acquirers of failing thrifts. In other words, past losses of an acquired thrift could be carried forward to reduce the tax obligations of a profitable acquirer, making past thrift losses valuable whereas nonthrift losses were not so valuable. The value of a failed thrift to an acquirer was increased by the present value of the tax savings.

The second way Congress favored failing thrift acquisitions was by exempting from taxation the interest payments made by the deposit-insurer arranging the purchase of a failed institution. FSLIC and its successor, the Resolution Trust Corporation (RTC), promised payments structured either as interest on notes making up the difference between the value of assumed liabilities and the value of assets (which amounted to the amount of the insolvency of the failed institution), or so-called "yield maintenance" payments, which guaranteed returns on assets of unknown earning power. These income sources were valued higher than taxable sources of income by firms acquiring failing thrifts.

The availability of tax benefits to acquirers of failing thrift institutions and their expiration at the end of 1988 was the reason a large number of acquisitions of Texas thrifts were arranged by the Federal Savings and Loan Insurance Corporation (FSLIC) in 1988. During that year, 179 thrifts were placed with acquirers, including 75 thrifts in 35 transactions in the last month the tax treatment was available as the FSLIC rushed to take advantage of these tax breaks sweetening deals with failed thrifts. These last minute deals included many agreements by government insurance agencies which were criticized by the press and Congress. An effort later was made to revoke some of the terms retroactively.

Taxes and Insurance Companies

There are separate United States Tax Code sections covering life and casualty insurance companies income but the basic principle followed by Congress in taxing both types of insurance companies is similar. The taxation of insurance companies was simplified and updated by the Deficit Reduction Act of 1984. This act simplified the taxation of insurance companies by separating insurance company income and revenues into two types. The first type of income belongs to policyholders directly or indirectly because it supports the payment of their likely future claims. The other type of income belongs to the company, whether or not it is a stock company. Once the determination of the two types of income is made for an insurance company, the income to the company is taxed at the normal corporate tax rate, whereas the income to policyholders is not taxed at the federal level.

Life and Annuity Companies

For life insurance and annuity companies, the 1984 act defines *life insurance company taxable income* (LICTI), which consists of the difference between life insurance revenues and life insurance deductions. Revenues consist of the sum of all premium and investment income and decreases in reserves, where premiums include deposits or premiums left with the company.

Life insurance deductions from revenues to calculate LICTI include normal corporate expense deductions, such as operating expenses, and specialized life insurance business expenses for items like claims, benefits, and losses. Life insurance companies can also deduct additions to reserves for life and annuity contracts and dividends paid to policyholders. The method of calculating life insurance and annuity reserves is specified by the tax code. For stock life insurance companies, in addition to deductions for reserves, those portions of investment income required to fund future liabilities and credit policyholder participation in investment and underwriting experience are also deductible. In other words, life insurance companies can deduct from taxable income that portion of income used to fund future payments to policyholders. Finally, dividend income from other stock investments in other corporations is exempted from taxation.

A special tax benefit for life insurance companies with assets less than $500 million is provided in the form of the *small life insurance company* deduction. This deduction is 60 percent of LICTI up to $3 million, for a maximum deduction of $1.8 million. However, the small life insurance deduction is reduced for companies with LICTI over $3 million by 15 percent of the amount over $3 million. A company with LICTI of $5 million, for example, would have a small company deduction of only $1.5 million (which is $1.8 million minus 15 percent of $2 million, the amount by which $5 million exceeds $3 million) and the small company deduction would disappear completely at $15 million. A final deduction from LICTI is calculated as 20 percent of the excess of a company's LICTI over the small life insurance company deduction. For LICTI over $15 million, this deduction is simply 20 percent of LICTI; for smaller companies, it is 20 percent of the excess of LICTI over the small life insurance company deduction.

A final detail in the revised tax code applies to mutual life insurance companies. Since mutual companies are owned by their insured, 100 percent deduction of dividends to policyholders would shield this income completely from corporate taxation. The 1984 act determined that 55 percent of dividends counted as the standard policyholder participation in insurance company income and that the remainding 45 percent was income to policyholders as owners of the company. The law allows a deduction of 55 percent of dividends to policyholders of mutual companies. This percentage breakdown was determined by the facts before Congress in 1984 and will change with more recent experience of mutual companies.

The tax treatment of life insurance companies contains a number of implications for the organization of life insurance services. The tax law favors small size, dividend income, and participating policies. Use of these and similar tax treatments to advantage can create value for the owners of life insurance firms.

Other Insurance Companies

Non-life insurance companies, primarily property and casualty insurers, are treated under separate provisions of the Revenue Code (Section 831) but the basic idea is to make taxation of other insurance companies similar to that of life insurance companies. The special code sections focus on the different types of premium revenue and insurance expenses for non-life companies. Casualty insurance premium income can only be reduced by 80 percent of unearned premiums after 1986 and premium income is calculated to include 80 percent of reductions in unearned premiums after 1986. Loss expenses can be deducted as they occur, not necessarily as they are paid.

Two specialized aspects of the federal taxation of property and casualty companies are important examples of idiosyncracies of the tax treatment of these providers of financial services and are discussed here. First, as with life companies, there is a small insurance company benefit. Specifically, companies with less the $1.2 million in premium revenues are taxed only on their taxable investment income. This means that smaller companies are favored by the tax code.

A second provision of the federal tax code for non-life companies requires that deductions from taxable income from insurance losses for large companies be reduced by 15 percent of investment income from tax-exempt bonds and corporate dividends if acquired after August 8, 1986 (passage of the 1986 TRA). Since the investments of non-life insurance companies are primarily financed with prepaid premiums and unpaid claims, there are no interest expenses associated with these funds. Prior to 1986 casualty insurers were major investors in common and preferred stock (for dividend income) and municipal bonds. Possibly in response to the change in the tax treatment of dividend income, casualty insurance company investments in preferred and common stock have fallen from 23 to 19 percent of total investments between 1985 and 1990 (*1992 Property/Casualty Insurance Facts,* p. 21)

State and Local Taxation of Insurance Companies

State taxation of insurance companies in most states in the United States is not based on income. Most states levy a tax on premium revenues, the most common rate being 2 percent. In many states, premium taxes replace all other forms of state and local taxation except property taxes. Some states allow a deduction from taxable premiums for dividends paid to policyholders. Some states reduce premium taxes if assets are invested in that state. States have also adopted other tax preferences for domestic insurers, having the effect that out-of-state ("foreign" and "alien") insurance companies are tax disadvantaged. Some states have tax reciprocity, meaning that unfavorable treatment by other states will be reflected in the tax liabilities of companies from those states.

Tax Treatment of Securities Dealers

A special provision of the federal tax code (Section 851) allowed securities dealers to use unique accounting rules in calculating taxable income until OBRA in 1993. Specifically, securities dealers, unlike other corporations, were allowed to evaluate inventories of securities at their choice of cost, cost or market (whichever is lower), or market. The election of tax treatment could not be changed, but the cost or market method allowed a great deal of flexibility to securities dealers in booking taxable income and losses. Inventory losses could be deducted from taxable income *even if not realized*. This valuable tax treatment applied only to inventories of securities, not to securities carried for investment, and was removed by OBRA, which required assets to be valued at current market and immediate realization of taxable gains in securities investors. This is another example of risk from changes in the tax code.

Investment Companies and Mortgage Pools

An important aspect of United States tax law applies to regulated investment companies. The mutual fund business is built on Section 851 of the federal tax code, the provision that exempts income of regulated investment companies from income taxation if the income is paid to the beneficiaries as dividends.

The growth in privately sponsored mortgage-backed securities was inhibited by the inability of the underlying mortgages to be removed from the balance sheet without creating a taxable entity. This problem was addressed in the 1986 TRA by the creation of another tax exempt investment vehicle, namely the Real Estate Mortgage Investment Conduit (REMIC). These trusts, which hold mortgages and pass through interest and principal on the underlying assets, are a legal creature authorized by the change in the tax code to avoid creation of another level of tax between investors and issuers of mortgages.

17.4 TAXES AND VALUE PRODUCTION

This section outlines some generalities and some specifics of the United States tax treatment of users and providers of financial services. Tax codes in the various states of the United States and in other countries around the world differ. However, the importance of taxes to the formation of business and market strategies is universal: taxes paid are lost to individuals and firms. Tax avoidance can therefore create value. This tax avoidance can take the form of tax arbitrage (high tax payers swapping their tax liabilities to low tax payers) like leasing or real estate investments, or it can take the form of tax efficiency (paying minimum taxes by careful choice of investments) such as investing in municipal bond funds.

Taxes will never go away. The tax environment and changes in that environment provide financial institutions with opportunities to produce value in four basic ways: (1) careful planning of the provision of financial services to exploit tax treatment of financial institutions or their customers; (2) product development to serve tax-induced customer demands; (3) anticipation and quick response to changes in the tax code in terms of products and organization of activity; and (4) direct efforts to influence the tax environment through lobbying pressure on legislatures and tax authorities. We provide examples of each of these in the following discussion.

The first strategy for dealing with tax policy is to make sure that financial services are organized to minimize tax liabilities to financial firms or their customers. Taxes are partially responsible for the complex organizational structure and far-flung geographical operations of financial firms. For example, the low average tax rate paid by commercial banks in the early 1980s was attributed by a Congressional committee to three causes: tax exemption of municipal bond interest and exclusion of interest-carrying costs, the maximum use of the ITC in leasing activities, and finally, the foreign income tax credit. Since leasing activity was not allowed for some regulated banks, bank holding companies acquired leasing subsidiaries.

The foreign income tax credit allowed U.S. financial institutions credits for taxes paid abroad. Careful tax planning can minimize global taxes paid. For example, branches of U.S. operations are treated differently than subsidiaries, and losses and intercompany transfers or dividends have different tax implications in the international context (see Scholes and Wolfson 1992, Chap. 13, for further discussion). Furthermore, certain tax-free havens, such as the Bahamas and Cayman Islands, foster recording of business activity in these locations for the benefit of both financial firms and their customers. Most large multinational financial institutions hire staff and consultants to guide them in providing financial services in view of international taxation.

Income timing has also always been an aspect of financial institution strategy of dealing with the tax environment. By consolidating gains or losses in particular years, a financial institution may be able to lower its average tax rate over time. For example, if large gains are to be realized by asset sales, unavoidable losses are often taken to minimize the tax impact on the gains.

An example of the second strategy for value production in dealing with taxation, product development, comes from careful preparation for changes in the tax code. For example, Individual Retirement Accounts (IRAs) were developed to take advantage of provisions in the personal income tax code allowing individuals or married couples to deduct contributions to retirement accounts from taxable income and to shield income on those savings from income taxation. Although tax laws governing IRAs have changed several times, financial institutions have developed a number of products for savers taking advantage of these laws. IRA deposit accounts or brokerage accounts were developed by deposit-taking institutions and securities firms, respectively. HELs, discussed previously, are another example of a product developed in response to tax laws.

Financial institutions' reaction to the TRA illustrates the third strategy, which consists of responding quickly to changes in the tax environment. We have already reviewed the disaster unleashed on the market for real estate limited partnerships by the TRA. Such a disaster does contain the possibility of profits for some financial service providers seeking ways to minimize the impact of the disaster on the market. One method pursued by some brokers (like Shearson) was to try to convert the relatively illiquid limited partnership shares (each partnership was unique) into tradeable securities so that whatever value remained in partnerships could be realized.

Another example of exploiting tax changes is the response to the TRA by lenders to real estate developers, many of whom were wiped out with the TRA-induced collapse of commercial real estate values. Some lenders packaged and sold nonperforming real estate loans. Selling packages of loans produced write-downs on the value of assets which could be realized immediately, providing a tax deductable loss from current income. First National Bank of Chicago used this strategy, which requires many elements of value production: identification of markets for real estate loans (marketing and information), packaging assets resolving problems associated with continued loan servicing (transaction processing), and monitoring. First Chicago's strategy was a loss-minimizing response taking advantage of tax treatment of realized losses. These losses were due to changes in the market driven in part by changes in the tax law.

Financial institutions pursue the fourth strategy, use of political influence on tax legislation and regulation, as a persistent aspect of their daily operations. In most historical periods in most capitals, banks and bank organizations are the largest lobbyists, typically followed by insurance companies and securities firms. For example, while provisions of the TRA of 1986 were being discussed, financial institutions offering investments to the retail market were concerned about the possibility that withholding taxes would be imposed on income from a variety of retail investment vehicles. Withholding taxes would reduce immediate cash returns on these vehicles and limit possibilities for tax avoidance, plus cause enormous paperwork requirements for financial institutions. The withholding tax provisions did not survive in the final language of the TRA due to lobbying pressure brought by banks and others.

17.5 SUMMARY

Taxes are a basic fact of life for financial institutions. This chapter reviews the basic types of taxes that are imposed by taxing authorities. The important U.S. tax treatment of customers of financial institutions is reviewed to develop a framework within which to analyze the effect on the demand for financial products and services. The tax treatment of financial institutions in the United States is summarized to gain insights into how tax treatment can influence the activities of financial firms. Finally, basic strategies of dealing with the tax environment are enumerated for providers of financial services.

DISCUSSION QUESTIONS AND EXERCISES

1. What kind of tax treatment (as portrayed on Table 17.1) is each of the following taxes: sales taxes, estate taxes, taxes on dividend income, value-added taxes, stock transfer taxes?
2. Partnerships are taxed at the same rate as individuals. The TRA reduced the corporate income tax rate from 48 to 34 percent and the maximum individual rate from 50 to 31 percent but by 1993 marginal rates had been changed to 35 and 39.6 percent, respectively. What is the effect of having a corporate tax rate above the maximum rate on individuals on the attractiveness of the partnership form of organization? Show the tax impact using examples of different levels of income.
3. There is continual discussion of reimplementing the investment tax credit (ITC), which could affect the demand for products provided by financial services firms. Discuss which products and why.

4. Compare the accumulation after 10 years of $1,000 invested at 10 percent and fully taxable at 31 percent to an investment where the accumulation of interest is tax exempt. What makes this comparable to an insurance reserve? What is the percent impact of the tax treatment at different interest rates, say 5 percent?
5. What is the impact on the calculations in question 4 if the $1,000 can be augmented by the savings from a tax deduction for the amount, as would be the case with an IRA?
6. Retirement withdrawals from IRAs are taxed at the individuals's current income tax rate while life insurance benefits to beneficiaries are not taxed. What is the impact on the after-tax returns to the investments in questions 4 and 5?
7. Contrast the taxes of a bank and a savings and loan at a 35 percent corporate tax rate with $100 million in income and a loan portfolio of $60 million averaging .5 percent in loan losses.
8. Calculate the tax on five $5 million LICTI insurance companies versus one $25 million LICTI company. How could such a difference be exploited in a strategy?
9. Calculate the approximate federal tax liabilities of a bank, a savings and loan, and a credit union, all of whom have the same 5 percent margin on cost of funds over mortgage loans on 80 percent of their assets.
10. Identify financial services offered to the wholesale or retail market from marketing materials or advertisements of financial service firms. What aspects of the tax law drive these product offerings, and what risk is there to long-term existence from changes in the tax law?

REFERENCES

GRAVELLE, JANE G. 1991. "Do Individual Retirement Accounts Increase Savings?" *Economic Perspectives*. 5 (2), pp. 133–148.

Insurance Information Institute. *1992 Property/Casualty Insurance Facts*. New York.

SCHOLES, MYRON S. and MARK A. WOLFSON. 1992. *Taxes and Business Strategy: A Planning Approach*. Englewood Cliffs, N.J.: Prentice Hall.

C H A P T E R

18

Portfolio Management and Financial Services

Introduction

Most financial service firms invest in financial assets, often financed by liabilities specific to a financial service, such as insurance reserves. Most financial institutions present managers with portfolio management problems.

- What trade-offs face portfolio managers and financial institution executives when they acquire various assets or move into specific markets?
- What relations between assets and borrowing or issuance of financial service related liabilities are important in making the best portfolio choices?
- What are the similarities and differences between the concerns of a mutual fund manager and a bank executive?
- What types of risks concern managers of financial institutions?

This chapter addresses these issues within the framework of modern financial analysis.

The basic question addressed by this book is "How do financial institutions create value?" In introducing portfolio management and risk–return trade-offs, this question is particularly relevant. Value created by financial institutions comes mainly from performance of the six activities necessary to produce different financial services, the topics covered in Part II of the book. The managerial issues addressed in this and the following chapters are pervasive in the financial services industry but the focus here is less on *creating value* than on *efficient management.* Portfolio managers or executives managing financial institution balance sheets may have a competitive advantage in performing activities in their businesses but their ability to produce value for investors through portfolio management in efficient financial markets is limited by competitive forces.

18.1 PORTFOLIOS

Portfolio management is the most pervasive of all financial services. Portfolio management is one of the six basic financial services identified in Chapter 2 and discussed in Chapter 12 as a financial service offered to households and businesses by professional portfolio managers. In those discussions, we emphasize the services provided by mutual fund managers like the Dreyfus Corporation or Fidelity Investments, and pension fund managers, like Morgan Guaranty Trust Department or Merrill Lynch Retirement Funds.

In reality, all households and businesses manage portfolios. As described in Chapter 3, households and businesses hold a combination of real and financial assets financed by a combination of debt and equity which can be viewed as a portfolio. Portfolio management activities are central functions performed by financial service firms: For example, banks and insurance companies raise funds in part through the provision of such services as transaction processing and insurance underwriting. Funds raised by financial institutions are invested in earning assets like loans and privately placed corporate bonds. This means that many of the management problems facing traditional financial institutions can be viewed as problems associated with the management of leveraged portfolios.

Portfolio composition varies: Portfolios can be a simple collection of homogeneous assets owned by investors, such as corporate bonds in a bond mutual fund. On the other hand, portfolios can be complex holdings of a variety of assets financed by a variety of liabilities, some of which are related to the provision of financial services. One example of a complex portfolio is a property and casualty insurance company that uses funds from unearned premiums and unpaid claims and possibly from borrowing to finance investments in securities and credit instruments.

The issues addressed in this and the following three chapters are the same for all portfolios including all types of assets (and liabilities if relevant), whether those assets belong to beneficiaries or to owners of financial firms. The portfolio management principles discussed here are relevant to individual investors, institutional investors, and financial institution management. Our emphasis is on the role of portfolio management in the production of value in financial services.

The objective of portfolio management is the same as for all financial management activities: Maximize owners' wealth and returns at an acceptable level of risk. The desired level of risk may be determined by beneficiaries, as when mutual fund owners choose funds with particular classes of assets or declared purpose, or it may be primarily determined by the financial service offered, like life insurance. The assets and liabilities in the portfolio may be securities or they may represent other financial claims or sources of funds.

Problems facing different portfolio managers concerning allocations of assets and sources of funding can be very similar or can differ markedly by the specific requirements of the problem. Table 18.1 provides an overview of the defining characteristics of portfolio management problems in a variety of contexts. Bank executives manage a portfolio of bank assets and liabilities on behalf of shareholders; pension fund managers face problems of providing cash to pay future retirement claims by beneficiaries. The concerns of the bank executive and the pension fund manager are similar of different along a number of dimensions. Both worry about the risks and returns on their assets, but only bank executives worry about how much equity to use in financing activity, because pension funds do not issue debt. Other types of portfolios that must be managed are also shown in Table 18.1.

This chapter introduces the considerations modern portfolio theory introduces into the selection of assets, and liabilities where relevant. Basic types of risks and risk management techniques available to portfolio owners are presented next as a breakdown useful in subsequent analysis. Finally, the use of leverage in the portfolios of deposit-taking institutions, insurance companies, and other financial intermediaries is discussed. Subsequent chapters in Part IV deal with measurement and management of portfolio risks.

TABLE 18.1 Portfolio Management Characteristics and Restrictions

	TYPES OF ASSETS/LIABILITIES			
PORTFOLIO OWNER	*MARKETABLE*	*NONMARKETABLE*	*RELATED TO SERVICES*	*RESTRICTIONS ON LEVERAGE*
Investor in mutual fund	Stocks, bonds, money market instruments	None	No	Yes, no debt
Saver in credit union	Money market instruments	Savings shares, consumer loans	Yes: transaction and credit	Yes, no debt
Pension fund beneficiaries	Stocks, bonds, money market instruments	Real estate, private debt	Yes, but limited to insurance services	Yes, no debt
Owner of bank	Money market instruments, bonds	Consumer and institutional debt, deposits	Yes: transaction, credit, limited securities services	Some capital and reserve requirements, holding companies regulated
Owner of insurance company	Money market instruments, stocks, bonds	Real estate, private debt, insurance contracts	Yes: insurance and credit	Some capital requirements
Owner of securities firm	Stocks, bonds, money market instruments	Private debt, margin loans	Yes: securities services	Some

18.2 ASSET AND LEVERAGED PORTFOLIO MANAGEMENT

Values of all financial assets are determined by the expected future flows from owning the assets and by the risks associated with those cash flows. Chapters 4 and 13 discussed the determinants of common stock values and other assets as the present value of dividends and other cash flows to investors. Like all financial assets, common stocks are valued at the present value of their future cash flows. Maximizing the value of those expected future cash flows defines the objectives of managers of stock-owned financial firms.

We can write the value of any asset (or liability) V_{i0} as follows:

$$V_{i0} = \sum_{t=1}^{T_i} \frac{CF_{it}}{(1 + r_i)^t} \tag{18.1}$$

where V_{i0} is the current (t = 0) value of receiving future cash flows CF_{it}, discounted at the rate r_i over a total of T_i time periods into the future. Expected future cash flows can consist of contractual or promised payments, like interest and principal repayment for bonds. Cash flows could be the expected sale prices after some holding period, for example after holding precious metals. Asset and liability values may come from other cash payments, like fees or cash paid out as retirement benefits. In the case of common stocks discussed in Chapter 4, the cash flows each period are dividends D_t, or sale prices P_t, and the discount rate is the expected market rate of return (ROR) on stocks of the same risk.

In all finance, valuations consist of projecting expected future cash flows CF_{it}, and discounting them at an appropriate risk-adjusted discount rate or expected return r_i. The return on financial assets consists of cash flows from the assets and changes in their value. The expected return r_{i1} over the next period on any financial claim can be written:

$$r_{i1} = \frac{CF_{i1} + V_{i1} - V_{i0}}{V_{i0}} \tag{18.2}$$

where all next period's values are understood to be expected values. This equation is exactly analogous to equation (4.1) introduced in discussing the return on common stocks in Chapter 4. In the following, we refer to the current value of assets as A_{i0} and liabilities as L_{i0} and their returns as returns or yields, on the one hand, and yield costs, on the other.

Asset Management

The asset-portfolio management problem consists of choosing a set of financial assets. The value of a simple portfolio of I assets consists of the sum of individual asset values:

$$P_0 = \sum_{i=1}^{I} A_{i0} \tag{18.3}$$

where P_0 is the current value of a portfolio. The expected return on a portfolio is the change in value of the portfolio over time, which will be the weighted average return on the individual assets:

$$r_p = \sum_{1=i}^{I} \frac{A_{i0}}{P_0} r_{i0} = \sum_{i=1}^{I} w_{i0} r_{i0} \tag{18.4}$$

where w_{i0} represents the current weight of asset i in the portfolio, in other words asset i's value as a percent of total portfolio value.

Managing a portfolio of assets to achieve desired risk–return objectives is often called the asset-management problem. The important breakthroughs in asset-management in the last few decades have dealt with the risk attributes of diversified portfolios of assets. As discussed in Chapter 4 with respect to stocks, risks of an individual asset i or portfolios of assets P are typically measured by the standard deviation of returns, σ_i or σ_P, respectively.

The Nobel Prize winning insights of Harry Markowitz consisted of making concise mathematical statements of the relation between risks and returns of diversified portfolios of assets. The contribution was described in Chapter 4 as a rigorous statement of the advice to not put all your eggs in one basket. Markowitz emphasized that the risk of a portfolio is not just the weighted average of the standard deviation of returns of the assets in the portfolio. In fact, the standard deviation of a portfolio is *less* than the weighted average if the assets' returns are not perfectly correlated.

Markowitz showed (1952) that the risk of a portfolio of assets depends not only on the standard deviations but also on the correlations ρ_{ij} between individual asset returns. The dependency of σ_P on ρ_{ij} is shown rigorously in the following equation:

$$\sigma_P = \sqrt{\sum_{i=1}^{I} w_{i0}{}^2 \sigma_i^2 + \sum_{j=1}^{I} \sum_{i \neq j}^{I} w_i w_j \rho_{ij} \sigma_i \sigma_j}\,. \tag{18.5}$$

This complex expression has the simple implication that portfolio risk depends on asset weights, asset standard deviations, *and* on correlations between asset returns.

The significance of Markowitz's contribution can be seen most easily in a two-asset portfolio consisting of assets A_1 and A_2 and we drop time subscripts for convenience. In this case, using equation (18.5) above, the expected return can be written:

$$r_P = w_1 r_1 + w_2 r_2, \quad w_1 + w_2 = 1. \tag{18.6}$$

The weights sum to one because all the portfolio is invested in one of the two assets. The risk of this portfolio using equation (18.4) is written:

$$\sigma_P = \sqrt{w_1{}^2\, \sigma_1^2 + 2 w_1 w_2 \rho_{12} \sigma_1 \sigma_2 + w_2{}^2\, \sigma_2^2}\,. \tag{18.7}$$

The standard deviation or risk of the expected portfolio return is the square root of the expression in the radical.

Markowitz's insight can be seen by taking the largest possible value of ρ_{12}, namely positive one. A correlation coefficient of positive one means that the two asset returns are perfectly positively correlated: they always move together. Thus, the expression in the radical in equation (18.7) is a perfect square and the portfolio risk can be written:

$$\sigma_P = w_1\sigma_1 + w_2\sigma_2. \tag{18.8}$$

Perfect positive correlation between two risky assets is the worst case because no benefits from diversification can be expected. In that case, equation (18.8) shows rigorously that the portfolio risk is the weighted average of the asset risks, just as the return is the weighted average of the returns.

The easiest way to see the effect of correlations on the risk–return trade-off for two perfectly positively correlated assets is to graph them as in Figure 18.1. The risk–return trade-off for two perfectly correlated assets in various combinations in a portfolio, that is for different values of w_1 and w_2, lies along a straight line when return is graphed against risk. The straight line means that the worst case, perfect positive correlation between the two assets, implies that the possible risk–returns from investing in the two assets connects their individual risk–returns with a straight line.

A careful look at equation (18.7) shows that for any correlation between the two assets *less than positive one,* the portfolio standard deviation is less than the weighted average of the two standard deviations because the square root in the expression must be less that the weighted average of the two assets' standard

FIGURE 18.1 Risk return trade-offs: two assets

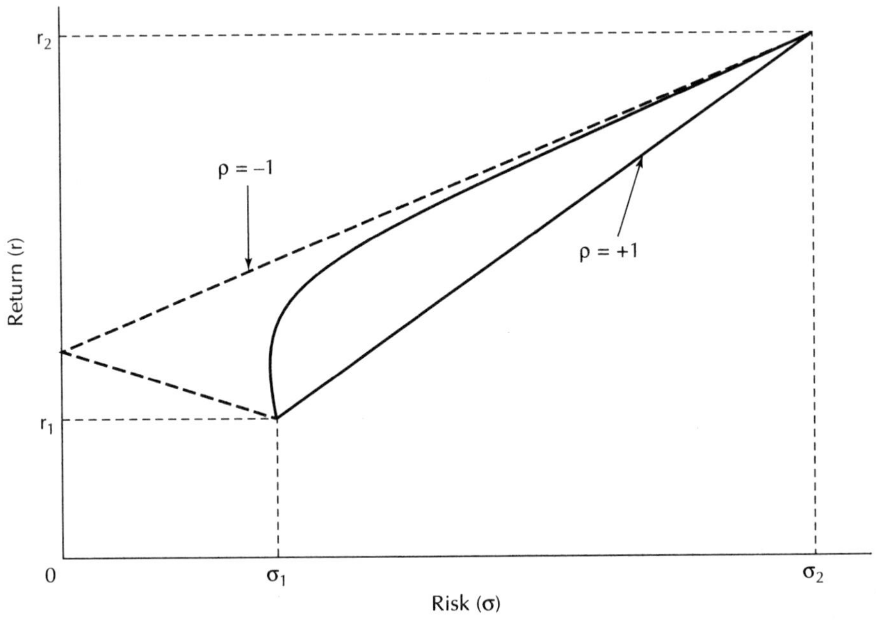

deviations when ρ_{12} is less than one. This means that the risk–return trade-offs from various investments in two assets that are less than perfectly correlated *lie inside the straight line connecting their respective risk–returns.*

The implication of equation (18.7) and Figure 18.1 is that diversification improves the risk–return trade-off: It pays not to put all your eggs in one basket/asset. Depending on the correlation, the combinations of risk and return possible from various combinations of assets, representing different weights w_1 and w_2, will lie more or less *inside* the straight line connecting the risk–return combinations for the two assets individually. The lower the correlation, the more the risk–return portfolio will lie inside the straight line. For each level of risk, a higher return than the simple weighted average of returns is available by combining assets A_1 and A_2 whenever their return correlation is less than one. Alternatively, for each level of expected return, a lower risk is available than the simple average of the two risks because the return correlation is less than one.

Depending on the expected returns and risks as represented by the standard deviations of returns and the correlation coefficient, more or less risk reduction may be possible with various combinations of two assets. In extreme cases, it may be possible to eliminate the risk of holding two assets. In particular, when the correlation between two asset returns is perfectly *negative,* shown as a dashed line in Figure 18.1, it may be possible to combine two assets such that there is very little or even no risk at all.[1]

The possibility that risk can be eliminated precisely can be shown easily by graphing the returns, which are perfectly negatively correlated against time. This is done in Figure 18.2, which shows that risk can be eliminated in the case of

FIGURE 18.2 Portfolio returns with two assets (perfectly negatively correlated returns)

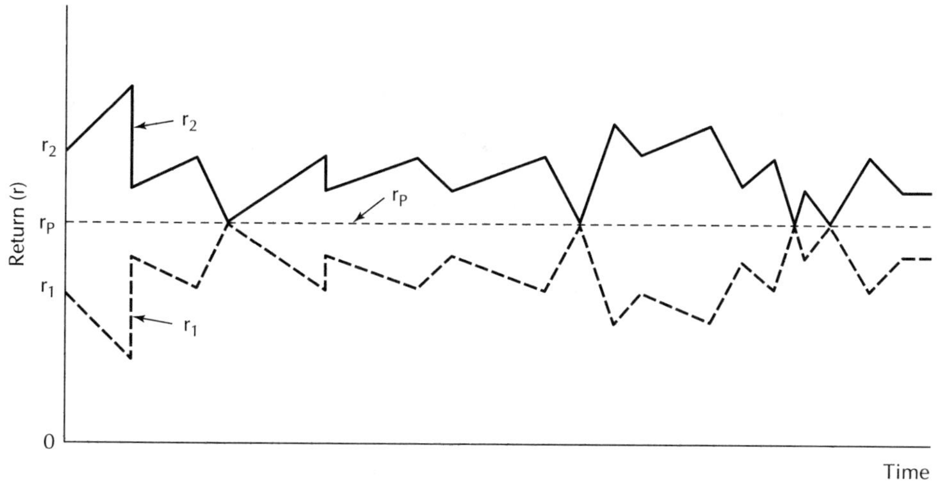

[1]In order to eliminate risk altogether in a portfolio completely invested in two perfectly negative correlated assets, w_1 must equal $\sigma_2/(\sigma_1 + \sigma_2)$.

perfectly negatively correlated assets because when one return is high, the other is low; in the case of perfect negative correlation between two assets, their returns move in opposite directions precisely. Managers of portfolios consisting of these two assets could utilize this relationship to cancel the low outcomes of one return with the high outcomes of the other returns.

The asset management story becomes mathematically more complicated when there are more than two assets, but graphically we can imagine that with any number of assets we can always consider them as portfolios of two at a time.[2] We have graphed the multiple asset problem in Figure 18.3 for three assets. For each pair of assets, A_1 and A_2, A_1 and A_3, and A_2 and A_3, given their pairwise correlations, a combination of risk–returns will be possible: These are shown as the arcs connecting the points corresponding to the risk–return trade-offs for the individual assets. Since the risk–return trade-offs from combinations of those assets lie inside the straight lines connecting those points whenever the correlations between these assets are less than one, the combinations have a scalloped appearance.

In a slightly more complicated extension of this analysis, then, we can think of each portfolio as an asset, and look at pairs of portfolios or a single asset and one portfolio as portfolios of two assets, even though they contain three or four assets. We have shown two such portfolio–asset combinations by the points P and Q. For example, the arc connecting P to asset A_3's risk–return represents combinations consisting of fixed proportions of assets A_1 and A_2 with varying amounts of asset A_3. By combining portfolios and assets, conceptually we can

FIGURE 18.3 Risk–return trade-offs: three assets

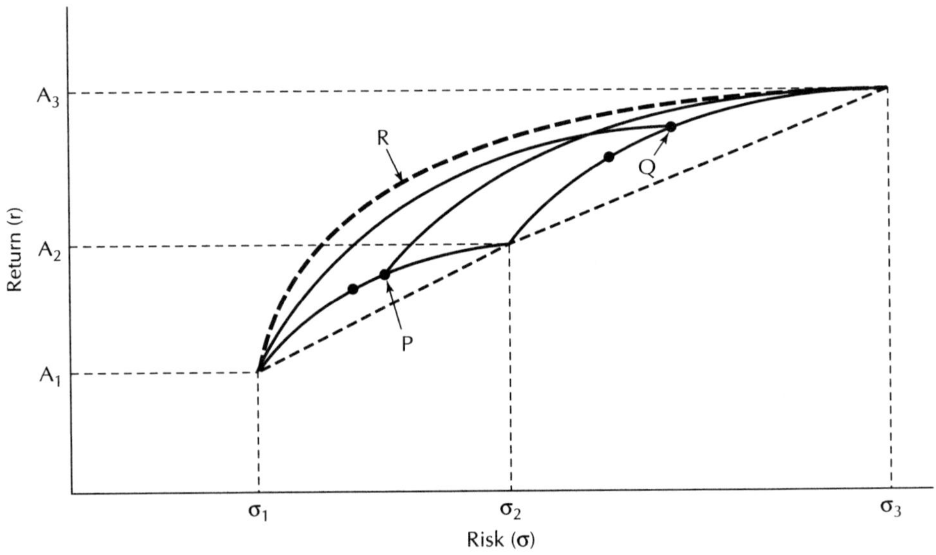

[2]For more detailed analysis of multiasset portfolio risks and returns see the classic treatments in Merton (1972) and Roll (1977).

think of all possible combinations of individual assets with each combination producing various possible risk–return possibilities. Figure 18.3 shows only a few of the many possible combinations of assets A_1, A_2, and A_3.

Markowitz's contribution was to show that for each level of expected return on a portfolio, there was a risk-minimizing combination of assets. For example, point R on the heavy dotted line in Figure 18.3 might contain 30 percent asset A, 20 percent asset B, and 50 percent asset C. There is one combination of risk-minimizing assets for each level of expected return. These combinations are shown in Figure 18.3 as the heavy dotted line: This line is called the *efficient frontier*. Each portfolio, or specific combination of A_1, A_2, and A_3 in our three-asset example, that minimizes risk for a given expected return is called an *efficient portfolio*.

The efficient frontier is an intuitively easy concept. Conceptually, we can think of determining the efficient frontier as a process of drawing the risk–return combinations for every conceivable portfolio and then drawing an outline or *envelope* of the best combinations. In practice, finding the envelope is more complicated: The problem of finding the maximum return for each level of risk can be solved using mathematical search techniques, namely quadratic programming. Markowitz worked for International Business Machines after his work on portfolios was first published. His research had the effect of stimulating a great deal of computer intensive research on how to solve large portfolio problems.

Leveraged Portfolios

Up to this point in the discussion, we have considered portfolios of assets. In other words, in all of the cases discussed above, the sum of the portfolio weights added up to unity and none of the weights were negative. Nonnegative portfolio weights are the mathematical counterpart to not having any liabilities.[3] If a portfolio owner can issue financial claims against the value of the portfolio, more assets can be acquired than the amount of equity or net worth of the portfolio. When this is the case, we say the portfolio is *leveraged*.

Some common portfolios associated with financial services are not leveraged. For example, mutual funds are composed of assets managed by fund managers using funds provided by investors in the form of mutual fund shares: Most mutual funds have no debt.[4] Similarly, pension funds have no debt, although in the case of pension funds the beneficiaries' claims on the cash flows from assets are more complicated than mutual funds shares' claims on the pro rata current value of the mutual fund assets. Mutual funds and pension funds are unleveraged portfolios.

Leveraged portfolios are extremely common. A simple example is an individual who buys assets like common stocks by borrowing money from his or her broker, that is, he or she buys stocks on margin. Households with financial assets

[3]Non-negative weights also mean no short sales which are sales of assets not owned and expose short sellers to profits opposite to those of an owner of the asset.

[4]Some "dual purpose" funds do issue debt or different classes of shares that may resemble liabilities.

and financing consumer durables and housing with loans and mortgages represent leveraged portfolios of real and financial assets. Corporations with debt likewise represent leveraged portfolios consisting of real and financial assets.

Most financial institution balance sheets represent leveraged portfolios. Simple examples are financial institutions that issue short-term financial instruments or longer term debt instruments to acquire assets like loans and securities. If a financial institution's liabilities are very liquid with many substitutes, they can be viewed by buyers in financial markets as very close or even perfect substitutes for traded assets having very similar risk–return characteristics. For example, a certificate of deposit issued by a bank is a very good substitute for a variety of money market instruments, like commercial paper or even U.S. Treasury bills.

More complex liabilities of financial institutions are sources of funds used to leverage holdings of assets in financial institution balance sheets. For example, banks finance assets partly with transaction deposits, and insurance companies do the same with insurance premiums or other contractual sources of funds. These liabilities are promises to pay customers cash in the future under the specific terms of their contracts, for example when they write checks in the case of deposits or file insurance claims under insurance policies. Despite the complexity of these expected future cash outflows, these liabilities can be evaluated in the same way as defined by equation (18.1).

To introduce the analytics of a leveraged portfolio, we can think of a simple single asset/single liability leveraged portfolio. One way to think of a leveraged portfolio is to think of one of the portfolio weights, say w_1, as negative, so that the portfolio manager is issuing a liability having the risk–return characteristics of asset 1 in the examples above. The other portfolio weight, w_2, representing purchases of the single asset with both equity and liabilities, is greater than one: the sum of the weights must still be equal to one.

In the case of a leveraged portfolio with one liability and one asset, equations (18.4) and (18.8) are still valid even though one portfolio weight is negative and the other is greater than one. Figure 18.4 shows the graphical relationship between risks and returns when asset 1 can be issued as a liability or claim on the total assets of the portfolio. The figure shows three possibilities: perfectly positive, perfectly negative, and an intermediate value of the correlation between the returns on the single asset and liability in the example.

In Figure 18.4, the risks and returns available from leveraging purchases of asset 2 with liabilities having the characteristic of asset 1 are shown to the right of the risk–return trade-off for asset 2. Of primary importance, of course, is that the expected yield cost of the liability is below the return on the asset. In this case, leverage increases the expected return on the leveraged portfolio. This is represented by the upward slope of the risk–return trade-offs for all three possibilities for the correlation coefficient shown in the figure.

Particularly important to the management of leveraged portfolios is the increase in risks associated with each level of return for leveraged portfolios. As in the two-asset case, the risk–return trade-offs are dramatically affected by the correlation between the asset and liability returns. However, the negative weight on the liability changes the sign in equation (18.7) for the standard deviation of

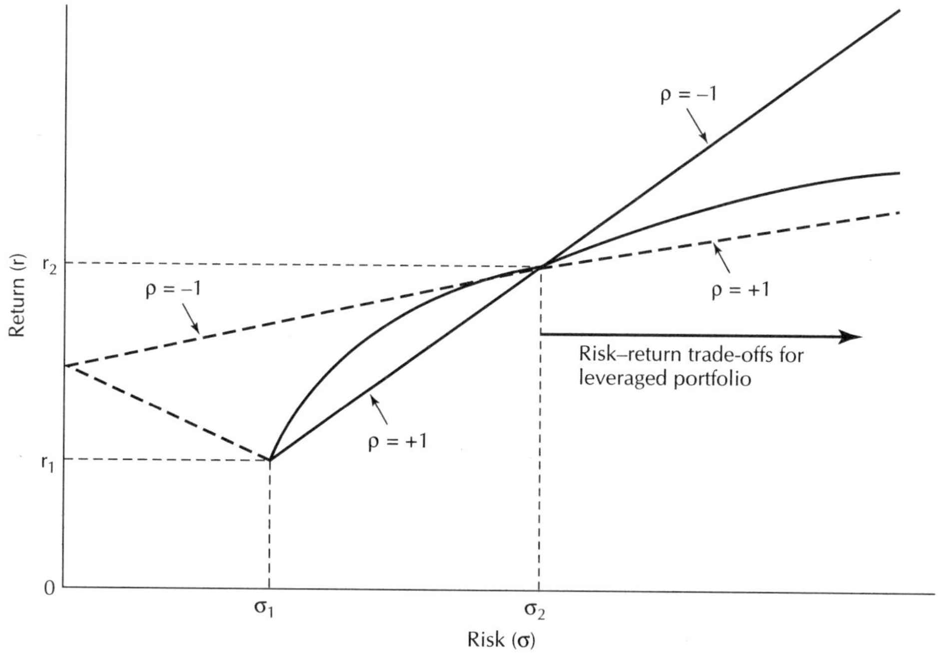

FIGURE 18.4 Risk return trade-offs: one asset and one liability

the portfolio. This means that in the case of the leveraged portfolio, the minimum possible risk for each return is associated with *perfectly positive* correlations. Conversely, the highest risks are associated with *perfectly negative* correlations. This is just the opposite of the risk–returns for the two-asset portfolio case.

In the single asset/single liability case we are discussing, the analysis of risks and returns bears out common sense: variation in the asset returns can be offset by equal variation in the liability yield costs or returns. We can visualize this relationship by plotting the returns of the two assets versus time as shown in Figure 18.5. We can see the offsetting variations in the asset and liability returns. The analytical framework is worthwhile because it provides us with logical structure to assess more complex situations.

The world is more complex because there is more than one asset and one liability. The analytical framework allows us to conceptually complicate our leveraged portfolio management by recognizing the existence of many assets and many liabilities. As with the multiple-asset management problem, the existence of many assets and many liabilities can be conceived as many different possible portfolios. Again, there will be an envelope of best possible risk–return combinations. In other words, there is an efficient frontier of assets and liabilities.

When considering the efficient frontier of the general asset–liability problem, it is not hard to believe that some liabilities with expected yield costs above some asset returns will be included in the efficient portfolios along the efficient frontier. The efficient portfolios will be the result not only of the returns of various assets

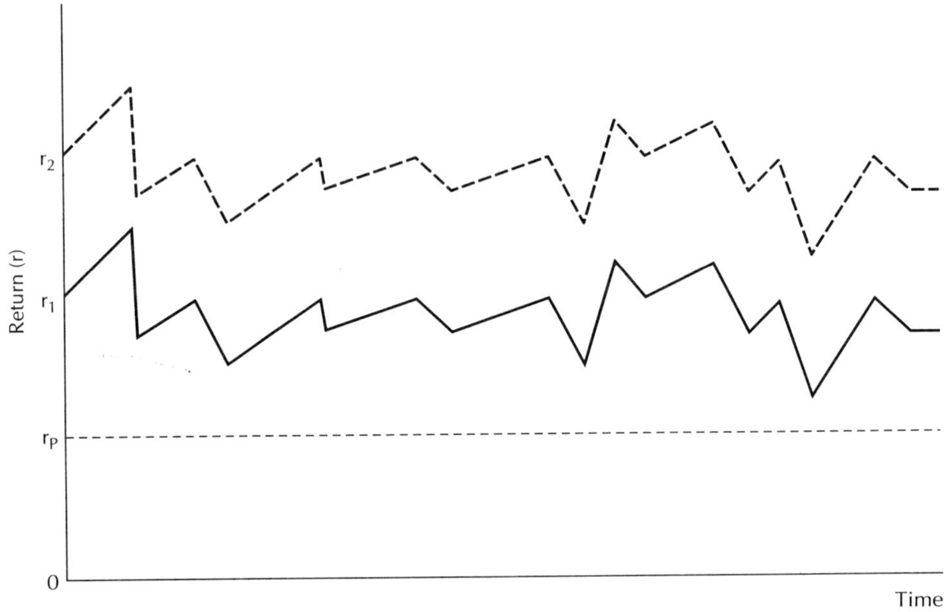

FIGURE 18.5 Portfolio returns on single asset/single liability portfolio (correlation perfectly positive)

and liabilities but also their correlations. For example, the fact that commercial banks invest in Treasury bills with returns below the cost of their certificates of deposit may be optimal from the point of view of minimizing risks for a given level of expected return because of the correlation of Treasury bill returns with other assets and liabilities in the bank portfolio.

Constrained Portfolios

Not all portfolio managers or financial institution managers can choose any possible point on the efficient frontier. Some portfolios are not possible either because of regulation, such as capital restrictions or asset restrictions as discussed in Part III of the text, or because of limitations imposed by the line of business and possibly by regulatory restrictions: Banks cannot finance asset purchases with funds derived from insurance and insurance companies do not issue much debt. The effect of these regulatory or business restrictions is to limit the efficient frontier to subsets of assets and liabilities. Solutions to the portfolio efficiency problems when the choices are limited are called *constrained portfolios.*

Obviously, any constrained portfolio represents an inferior risk–return combination than is available from the best risk–return combination possible when all assets and liabilities are available for inclusion in the portfolio with any weights. This is shown graphically in Figure 18.6, where the constrained efficient frontier lies *inside* the unconstrained efficient frontier. The constrained portfolio is inside because there are fewer assets and liabilities available to make up the portfolio

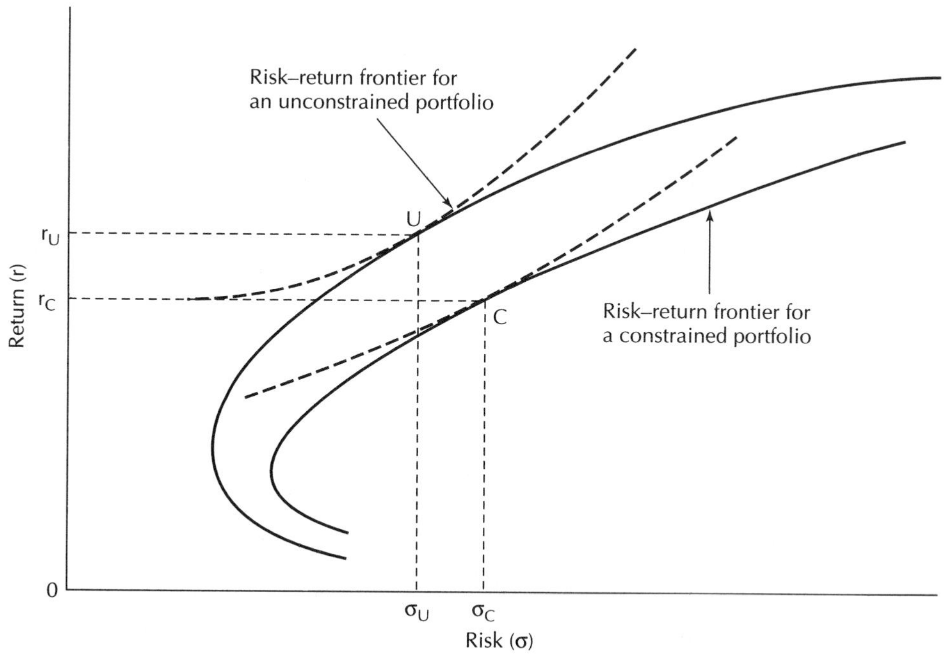

FIGURE 18.6 Constrained versus unconstrained portfolio risk-return tradeoffs

composition. Fewer assets and liabilities means that fewer different patterns of correlations between yield costs and returns can be included in the portfolio.

As an example of the effect of portfolio constraints, Koehn and Santomero (1980) examined the capital requirements of banks which limit their ability to leverage. Their analysis suggested that banks may assume more risk with capital restrictions than they would absent capital restrictions because the capital (leverage) restrictions tilt and flatten the efficient frontier: Investors with particular risk–return preferences, as discussed in Chapter 6, might choose banks with riskier portfolios. We have shown this effect in Figure 18.6 by indicating that investors with the indifference curve shown in Figure 18.6 would choose point U in the unconstrained case but must settle for point C with portfolio constraints. Point C has a lower expected return and higher risks than point U. Koehn and Santomero argue that minimum capital regulation may not necessarily reduce bank risk.

18.3 SINGLE-PERIOD VERSUS MULTIPERIOD PORTFOLIO MANAGEMENT

The preceding discussion introduced risk–return considerations governing the composition of efficient portfolios in a simple setting: Portfolio managers assess risks and returns of assets and liabilities and choose efficient combinations of them to achieve desired risk–return trade-offs. This discussion is based on a one-period analysis of portfolio management. Returns and standard deviations used in the analysis are defined over some definite time horizon. Actual portfolio returns will be realized at the end of that time period.

In reality, three factors change the conditions for portfolio management over many periods. First, changes in desired portfolio composition occur in response to changes in expectations of asset and liability risks and returns and changing constraints over time. Second, realized returns change portfolio weights and may require adjustment of asset and liability holdings. Finally, other changes occur due to factors outside the control of portfolio managers which increase or decrease the size of the portfolio or change asset and liability composition.

New information and economic events change expectations concerning risks and returns associated with individual assets and liabilities from period to period. In addition to changes in optimal portfolios due to changes in expectations, portfolio constraints may be changed by regulators or levels of business activity. For example, the Financial Institutions Reform, Recovery and Enhancement Act (FIRREA) of 1989 forced savings institutions to sell their corporate bonds. Multiperiod portfolio management must consider how to deal with changes in the optimum composition of the portfolio or how to add new assets and liabilities or delete investments or sources of funds from the portfolio due to changes in risks and returns or regulatory treatment.

Weights on individual assets change as returns on assets and liabilities are actually realized each period or through the passage of time. The composition of portfolios changes over multiple periods even in the absence of changes undertaken by the portfolio manager. For example, if a simple two-asset portfolio begins with 50 percent in each asset but one asset doubles in value and the other asset value falls by half, at the end of the period the portfolio weights are 80 percent for the gainer and 20 percent for the losing asset. If expectations for future returns for these assets have not changed with the actual realized returns, the portfolio weights on the assets are no longer the optimal 50 percent each.

Making adjustments to portfolio composition in response to changes in expectations or realized outcomes is called *portfolio rebalancing*. Portfolio rebalancing (discussed in Chapter 3 with respect to sectoral balance sheets or portfolios) can be an ongoing process, in which case the portfolio management rebalancing process is described as *continuous portfolio rebalancing*. Continuous portfolio rebalancing is useful as a conceptual benchmark but in practice is not feasible if only because portfolio managers must sleep.

In reality, portfolio rebalancing involves transactions costs and managerial time and attention, and contractual sources of funds like financial service firm liabilities take time to change levels. Rarely is it feasible to rebalance portfolios continuously. One of the problems to be addressed in dynamic portfolio management is the frequency of portfolio rebalancing, or how far from the efficient portfolio an actual portfolio is allowed to go before it is rebalanced. Alternatively, the question can be how frequently the portfolio must be monitored and how often rebalancing should occur. The answer to these questions determines the *rebalancing interval* in the case of portfolios that are not continuously rebalanced.

The third important change in portfolio management over time comes from changes in the size of the portfolio: Saving patterns or changes in economic values can dramatically alter the size of portfolios. For example, mutual funds grow or shrink as savers change their desired holdings of mutual funds. Banks and thrifts lose or gain deposits. Changes in the size of portfolios by selling or buying assets or paying cash on contractual liabilities can change portfolio composition temporarily, changing the weights of assets and liabilities. Changes in portfolio size were discussed in Chapter 3 as *portfolio growth,* interpreted as either positive or negative growth.

Portfolio growth can be due to macroeconomic factors or microeconomic factors such as an individual firm's performance on financial contracts. Deposit withdrawals or payments on insurance claims may require cash outflows and portfolio size reductions. Portfolio growth, either positive or negative, may force temporary changes in portfolio composition due to sudden receipts of cash with positive growth or asset sales or changes in liabilities to obtain cash with reductions in size. For example, a bank can finance unexpected deposit withdrawals by selling Treasury securities or by issuing large certificates of deposit. Portfolio growth may be associated with requirements for portfolio rebalancing.

Despite the complexities introduced into portfolio management problems by changes over time due to changes in risk–return assessments, actual asset and liability return realizations, and portfolio growth, the basic insights derived from the one-period model are valid in understanding the multiperiod portfolio management problem. Portfolio managers must still be concerned with maximizing the value of their portfolio subject to a desired level of risk in the multiperiod case. Correlations between asset and liability yields and costs are critical to multiperiod risks and returns of portfolios, just as in the single-period case. Decisions are based on assessments of the risks and returns associated with assets and liabilities given the information available at each moment of time.

The basic difference between single-period and multiperiod portfolio analysis is that portfolio decisions each period must be made realizing that changes will be required to the portfolio in future periods. Changes in optimal portfolio composition will result from changes in the future economic environment. In each subperiod of a longer portfolio management horizon, planning for the end-of-period portfolio must incorporate the flexibility to deal with new information and new circumstances that may face the portfolio manager.

Advanced theoretical analysis has been focused on the multiperiod portfolio management problem (see for example Hakanson 1971). The portfolio management problem involving continuous rebalancing is called *dynamic portfolio management,* a term suggesting that portfolio adjustments occur continuously through time as changes in the environment are incorporated into decisions (see, for example, Merton (1972) for a discussion of dynamic portfolio management problems and a list of references). The management science literature has focused some attention on asset–liability management over time where portfolio rebalancing is assumed to take place at discrete rebalancing intervals and economic changes are assumed to be limited to a finite set of scenarios.[5] All of these technical approaches to the portfolio management problem have as an objective the maximization of portfolio returns subject to an acceptable level of risk, just as in the single-period portfolio problem. The discussion in the next section expands the treatment of portfolio management to address portfolio balancing problems caused by external events over time informally but does not attempt to do so within the complex mathematical analyses that have been developed in the above-cited literature.

18.4 PORTFOLIO RISKS

Portfolio managers attempt to maximize returns given an acceptable level of risk. The risks they face are of two basic types: those concerned with future values or returns on the individual assets and liabilities that compose their portfolios, and those concerned with changes in the specific business environment confronting portfolio managers which affect their optimal portfolio size and composition. We review these two types of risk below.

The set of risks associated with expected asset returns is incorporated in the classification scheme introduced in Chapter 13 as macroeconomic risks and microeconomic risks. Macroeconomic risks are economy wide and microeconomic risks are firm-specific or industry-specific risks and are reflected in discount rates or expected returns used in discounting expected cash flows for individual assets and liabilities. The basic determinants of discount rates are: (1) the riskless short-term interest rate; (2) the short-term expected inflation premium; (3) the term-premium on long-term default-free bonds; and finally, (4) the risk premium for cash flows from risky assets, where risks include performance or default risk for risky bonds. For residual claims like common stock, the risk premium includes risks from other factors like future sales or costs. In addition, international transactions contain a foreign exchange risk premium. We list the five sources of risk as the rows in Table 18.2 to assist our discussion below. Changes in discount rates come from economic events producing changes in any of these components.

The second set of risks comes from changes affecting individual portfolios. When discussing portfolio problems, portfolio managers use terms to describe their portfolio management concerns which are commonly used by regulators, such as bank and insurance regulators, securities analysts, and other financial industry observers. Industry practitioners typically describe five different portfolio management risks as: (1) interest rate risk; (2) liquidity risk; (3) credit risk; (4) operating risk; and (5) currency risk. We list these terms as the columns in Table 18.2, and in

[5]For example, in a classic article that was very influential among bankers at the time, Cohen and Hammer (1967) applied linear programming techniques to the choice of assets and liabilities that could adjust at various time points in the future. See Cohen and Gibson (1978) for a variety of applications of management science to the asset–liability problem for banks.

TABLE 18.2 Macroeconomic Risk Factors and Portfolio Risks

	RISK TYPE				
MACROECONOMIC RISK FACTOR	*INTEREST RATE*	*LIQUIDITY*	*CREDIT*	*OPERATING*	*CURRENCY*
Riskless real short-term rate	X				
Inflation	X				
Term premium	X	X			
Default risk premium			X		X
Foreign exchange premium					X

the following discussion we define these risks and relate them to the more general classification scheme introduced in Chapter 13.

Interest Rate Risk

Interest rate risk is the effect of changes in interest rates on portfolio size and composition. We show the relation between the use by industry observers of the term interest rate risk and the broader conceptual determination of interest rates discussed in Chapter 13 in Table 18.2. The rows of that table list the basic components listed above, including foreign exchange premiums. The table indicates that interest rate risk is typically associated with real rate, inflation, and term premium risk, the first three components. In other words, interest rate risk is associated with the determinants of the general level of interest rates of different maturities and risks in an economy.

Interest rate risk is the focus of an enormous amount of attention by regulators and portfolio managers. For example, banks and other financial institutions are required to provide evidence of the degree to which their portfolios are subject to interest rate risk; in other words changes in portfolio values are associated with changes in the level of interest rates. We devote most of Chapter 19 to the measurement and management of interest rate risk.

Liquidity Risk

Liquidity risks are risks associated with meeting unexpected demands for cash. The importance of liquidity risk to the expected portfolio returns and variability of portfolios comes from the possible sudden requirement to liquidate (sell) assets to meet a cash need. Another less emphasized liquidity risk comes from an unexpected inflow of funds and inability to achieve optimal portfolios quickly because of the time required to acquire assets like carefully negotiated loans.

Liquidity risks come from the lower asset sale prices or lower asset returns associated with quick transactions relative to transactions implemented over longer time periods. For example, unexpected deposit withdrawals or deposit inflows in a deposit-taking institution like a bank cause liquidity problems because such assets as loans cannot be sold or made quickly at their intrinsic economic values.

Easily marketable assets typically have lower yields simply due to the convenience associated with being able to sell or buy them at predictable prices on short notice. Long-term asset prices often fluctuate more than short-term asset prices resulting in a *liquidity premium* on those assets, as discussed in Chapter 13. Table 18.2 associates liquidity problems of longer-term assets with the term premium on yields in the financial markets.

The risk of losses from sudden sales or purchases of assets can be reduced by holding easily marketable assets relative to more aggressive investing but only at the cost of lowering expected returns because liquid assets have lower returns. As an example, in 1991 Dreyfus Funds were holding large amounts of short-term assets to reduce the liquidity costs associated with unexpected redemption of mutual fund shares. Dreyfus holdings of short-term near-cash instruments relative to stocks or longer-term bonds hurt fund performance relative to other mutual funds. An opposite type of liquidity problem occurred in 1993 when mutual fund growth was so rapid that many managers could not invest the funds fast enough to maintain high yields.

Credit Risk

Credit risk consists of the failure of borrowers or securities issuers to pay interest and principal as scheduled. The usual significance of credit risk is to affect the expected future cash flows in the basic valuation equation (18.1). As discussed in Chapter 13, contractual cash flows on debt instruments are higher than the expected risk-adjusted cash flows with default or credit risk, therefore the discount rate associated with credit risk reflects a risk premium on the contractual cash flows. We have indicated the association of credit risk with default risk premiums on Table 18.2.

Credit risk causes two problems for portfolio managers. The first problem is due to changes in asset values from changes in default risk premiums economy wide and is associated with the risk premium on Table 18.2. A sudden increase in economy-wide credit risks, as occurred for example during the Stock Market Crash of 1987, will reduce the value of all financial claims that have default risk. This is clearly a risk affecting the risks and returns of portfolios of assets which have default or credit risk: this credit risk is due to the changes in credit risk premiums.

The second type of credit risk is associated with individual assets, such as specific loans or bonds, that fail to pay cash as scheduled. Credit risk arising from the possible failure to pay contractual payments on time may cause liquidity problems for the portfolio manager, due to unexpected changes in cash flows. For example, if a bank's portfolio lending is matched to deposits with the same maturity, loan failures mean that cash will not be available to pay off depositors as planned. The second type of credit risk is really a liquidity risk: Cash that was expected is not paid.

An equally important type of credit risk for financial institutions providing credit services (not usually emphasized in discussions of credit risk) is an increase in the demand for credit, for example, a long-term bank customer demanding credit unexpectedly. This demand for cash may come under the terms of a loan commitment in which the financial service firm is obligated to make the cash payment. Also likely is that the credit demand may not be a contractual obligation but the institution fears that failure to grant credit will damage or destroy a long-term customer relationship having economic value. This example of credit risk is again a liquidity problem: The financial firm must either raise funds on short notice, possibly at high costs, liquidate assets possibly at low prices, or lose the customer relationship.

Operating Risks

Operating risks result from the production and delivery of financial services. These problems are most often associated with portfolio management or transaction processing services. The former president of the Federal Reserve Bank of New York, E. Gerald Corrigan, made a major issue of risks associated with cash requirements coming from the payments system and securities clearing. Corrigan's concerns were connected to fears about breakdowns in the communications systems which on at least one occasion prevented delivery of $500 million of U.S. Treasury securities. Buyers of the securities were reluctant to advance cash when delivery was not made and there was a liquidity crisis for the clearing agent.

There are many examples of operating risks for financial service firms. For example, mutual fund managers were swamped with mutual fund share sell orders during the Stock Market Crash of October 1987. These managers could not accurately control liquidation of their stock portfolios due to late and inaccurate information on sale orders because phone lines were not able to physically handle the surge in telephone orders to buy or sell shares. Other examples of operating risks are the frequent problems facing banks or savings and loans experiencing a delay in payment through the check clearing system due to a snowstorm or power outage in some region.

Operating risks are also really liquidity problems: payments must be made suddenly to cover shortfalls in expected cash. In general, these operating risks are completely random and are not related to other macroeconomic factors. These risks are unsystematic and are generally not priced in terms of affecting the returns or yield costs of funds. There can be a credit component to the operating risk (failure of a counterparty to pay means an inadvertent loan to that counterparty) which may be reflected in some asset prices or contractual terms.

Operating risks are important to portfolio managers or financial service firm managers. Since operating risks typically mean a sudden and unexpected acceleration or delay in the delivery of assets or funds, they can be thought of as another specific example of liquidity risk. Methods of dealing with operating risk are similar to those associated with other types of liquidity risks. Since operating risks are not systematic, they should not be reflected in the discount rates for securities and are not related to macroeconomic risk factors in Table 18.2.

Currency Risks

Currency risks are associated with international investments not denominated in the home currency of the portfolio manager's beneficiaries. These risks are reflected in the foreign exchange premium in Table 18.2. These risks, involving the international payment of cash, are similar to credit risks and are not captured entirely in the forward exchange rate premium. For example, some currencies may be subject to political intervention, such as the inability to transfer earnings or profits out of the country due to exchange controls.

Currency risks on a global basis may be close to unsystematic, meaning that they are uncorrelated across economies and are not priced. Although currency risks may not be priced, they may be highly correlated to macroeconomic risk variables for a given country in question. These means that currency risks are like credit risks to whole classes of borrowers. Again, currency risks of this type are like the cash flow type of credit risk, that is, they are a specific type of liquidity risk.

Summary of Portfolio Risks

The five types of portfolio risks discussed by portfolio managers, regulators, and financial industry observers—interest rate risk, liquidity risk, credit risk, operating risk, and currency risk—are related to the macroeconomic and microeconomic risks we discussed in Chapter 13 as shown in Table 18.2. Interest rate risk is essentially an aggregate of three underlying economic risks: real rate, inflation, and term risks, as shown on the first three rows of that table. Credit risk and currency risks may be reflected in discount rates for assets based on market equilibrium prices for macroeconomic risks from those sources, as shown in the last two rows of the table. On the other hand, individual asset or liability credit risks and currency risks, as well as operating risks, can be seen to be specific cases of liquidity risk. These portfolio risks represent the dangers associated with the failure of cash flows to be received or paid as expected. Unexpected failures of cash inflows or outflows force sales or purchases of assets and liabilities on inconveniently (or disastrously) short notice.

18.5 PORTFOLIO RISK MANAGEMENT

The portfolio risks described in the preceding section—interest rate risk and the various sources of liquidity risk—can be managed in several ways. Although the only rational portfolio strategy is to maximize returns for a given level of risks in line with portfolio theory, one possible strategy is to do nothing about the portfolio risks of the previous section. Doing nothing about portfolio risks can be a rational portfolio management strategy, but unless the risks of the portfolio have been described and estimated, the decision to do nothing is made in ignorance—never an intelligent strategy. Understanding the amount and types of risks associated with a portfolio are the minimum a portfolio manager can do without being completely negligent, even if the ultimate decision is to do nothing about the risk exposure of the portfolio.

In this section we first review the evolution of portfolio management for deposit-taking institutions to introduce some common terminology and gain perspective on portfolio management issues. Focusing on banks and other deposit-taking institutions is not unreasonable, given the importance of those leveraged portfolios in the financial system. Next, we define the basic ways portfolio risks can be measured and managed as an introduction to the detailed discussion in the following three chapters. Finally, we assess the role of portfolio management in terms of the strategic objectives of financial service firms, typically to maximize shareholders' wealth.

Overview of Deposit-Taking Portfolio Management

The discussion among bank managers and officials of deposit-taking institutions has followed three distinct periods since the end of the Second World War. It is illuminating to review this discussion because it places in historical context the problems financial institutions and portfolio managers now face and will face in the future. One very real possibility is that future times may resemble periods in the past and that portfolio management strategies pursued then will be relevant again.

1945–1966

During the period from the end of the Second World War in 1945 to the "First Credit Crunch" of 1966, financial institutions had a pretty easy time. The flow of funds for 1945 show that private financial institutions ended the war with over 55 percent of their assets in U.S. Treasury securities. Purchases of Treasury securities were a major part in the financial sector's war effort. The dollar amount of private financial ownership of Treasuries declined rapidly between 1945 and 1950 and then held steady between $90 and $100 billion until 1965. In percentage terms, Treasuries fell gradually as a percent of total assets from 33 percent to 10 percent between 1950 and 1965.

During the period 1945 to 1965, bankers and other financial executives discussed their balance sheet or portfolio management problems as "asset management." The basic problem for these managers was to choose assets to maximize returns at their chosen level of risk. Their large holdings of Treasury securities made portfolio management pretty simple: Banks and other financial institutions used new funds to buy high return assets like loans. At worst, they had only to sell a bond to make a loan.

Sources of funds were not an area of concern to financial institution managers over this period either, at least relative to experience since 1965. Traditional sources of funds grew at stable rates, tracking closely the growth in the economy. Funds in the form of checking accounts were the exclusive preserve of banks prior to 1980. Savings accounts were the major private savings at both banks and thrift institutions. Both sources grew at steady rates after an initial drop in checking accounts at the end of the Second World War. Insurance reserves were another major savings vehicle that grew steadily. Low risk, profitable portfolio management was easy due to the simple task of shifting portfolio assets to higher yielding loans. Competition for funds was moderate given regulation.

Portfolio management over this period concentrated on asset management; diversification of risks and asset allocation were the primary focus of managers. Liquidity problems were not the major factor in portfolio choices as became true later. Gradual growth, protected markets, and relatively steady interest rates collectively meant that credit risk and operating risks were low priority concerns. Currency risks were not a major factor in portfolios of U.S. financial institutions before the massive international capital flows of recent times.

1966–1979

The "Great American Inflation," as we call in it Chapter 13, began in 1965 and produced its first dramatic impact on financial markets in the summer of 1966. The events of that period are an example of regulatory risk discussed in Chapter 13. As interest rates followed accelerating inflation upward in 1965 and early 1966, the Federal Reserve until August 1966 increased allowable Regulation Q maximum interest rates on both corporate and household time deposits so that banks could compete with other money market instruments like Treasury bills, which sold in $1,000 amounts in those days. In August 1966, interest rates surged again but the Fed did not raise interest rate ceilings, an example of regulatory risk.

The Fed stopped increasing the Regulation Q maximum in order to cool an "overheating" economy. As a result, banks suffered the worst losses of deposits they had experienced until that time. Thrift institutions were likewise pressed by the increased rates they had to pay to keep savings accounts. This was the "Credit Crunch" of 1966. Banks with foreign offices were able to replace outflows of funds from regulated deposits by borrowing in unregulated London and European deposit markets through their branches. The "Eurodollar" market was born! Banks that had formed holding companies issued commercial paper. The commercial paper market boomed!

After the Credit Crunch, banks and other financial institutions became adept at issuing nondeposit liabilities to solve liquidity problems caused by deposit withdrawals or surges in loan demand. This management focus on liability sources is called "liability management." Liability management meant that banks and thrifts and other financial institutions expanded the array of techniques available to raise funds on short notice. Prominent among these techniques, in addition to Eurodollar deposits and commercial paper, was more aggressive reliance on the Fed Funds market, which mushroomed in these years.

By the early 1970s, the Fed had ceased regulating interest rates on large certificate of deposits, a fund-raising vehicle pioneered by Citibank in the early 1960s. The use of money market instruments and alternative ways of meeting liquidity needs caused by the credit needs of customers of deposit-taking institutions caused financial institution managers to develop an array of alternatives to traditional sources of funds. Flexibility, avoidance of regulatory restrictions, and cost considerations all made reliance on global money markets an activity central to the liability management approach to managing portfolio liquidity needs.

1979 to the Present

On October 6, 1979, the historical change in Federal Reserve operating procedures discussed in Chapter 13 affected the nature of money markets in ways that are still being worked out. The interest rate variability tolerated by the Fed since that date has allowed changes in interest rates, at times up to 1000 basis points in weeks, that can result in enormous swings in highly leveraged financial institutions' profitability. The reaction of portfolio and financial institution managers has been to concentrate on the relation between earnings, costs, and cash flows from assets and liabilities simultaneously. Consideration of the liquidity and profit problems from managing highly leveraged portfolios or balance sheets of financial institutions came to be called "asset–liability" management, called ALM for short.

Asset–liability management covers a wide range of responses to the interactions of cash flows and yields on asset and liabilities. Portfolio managers forecast cash flows and earnings and costs. Consultants assist portfolio managers in using computers to simulate cash flows under a wide variety of economic and interest rate scenarios using ALM computer programs. Financial institution owners and regulators have insisted that many firms set up "asset–liability committees" (ALCOs) to consider problems caused by differences in cash flows and returns on assets and liabilities. Finally, a wide range of risk measurement and management tools discussed in the following chapters have developed or are applied with increased seriousness.

The major point to be gained from reviewing the evolution of portfolio and financial institution managers' focus from asset management, to liability management, and currently to ALM is that the problems of managers reflect macroeconomic events and regulatory and industry risk. Reduced variability in interest rates could reduce the attention paid to issues of hedging interest rate risks. Certainly new portfolio management issues will surface: It is only a matter of time before financial industry observers will have a new name to describe the problems facing portfolio managers.

Basic Approaches to Management of Portfolio Risks

If a portfolio or financial institution manager wishes to reduce or confront the portfolio risks rather than merely measuring and bearing those risks, there are two basic approaches: (1) use internal portfolio or balance sheet choices to reduce or control the impact coming from the risks; and (2) use off-balance sheet tools. An example of the first approach is to match cash flows from assets and liabilities, for example using 6-month deposits to finance 6-month loans. An example of the second approach would be lining up contingent sources of funds or using futures or options market to reduce or control the risks. We introduce internal portfolio risk management techniques in the next chapter. Chapters 20 and 21 discuss the use of off-balance-sheet methods, including futures and option markets, to manage portfolio risks.

The most important point for portfolio or financial institution managers to keep in mind is that risk is not avoidable. Furthermore, it is not economically rational to eliminate risk from a portfolio or balance sheet. In efficient markets, higher returns are earned by bearing risk. No portfolio or financial institution manager should be content with riskless rates of return: such returns are available more cheaply and reliably from direct investments in riskless assets like Treasury bills. The best financial managers estimate the risks they confront and bear those they believe they can deal with more effectively than competitors. Excess returns are possible for investors in financial institutions whose managers understand risks better than their competitors.

18.6 LEVERAGE POLICIES

For financial institutions like banks and insurance companies, the question of how much owners' capital to use to finance their value-producing activities is central to their business strategy. The leverage decision is made in terms of portfolio risk–return considerations discussed previously, in terms of regulation of financial institutions as discussed in Part III, and considering concerns of clients and customers of financial firms. This section places the leverage decision into the context of these often competing concerns.

Capital Structure in Efficient Markets

A starting point for any modern treatment of capital structure policy, including the amount of leverage used by financial service firms in financing their acquisition of assets, is the first analysis in the Nobel Prize winning stream of work of Franco Modigliani and Merton Miller (1958). The major result of this first work is often called the M–M capital structure irrelevancy theorem.

The initial M–M argument assumed no corporate or personal taxation, costless transactions, no reorganization or bankruptcy costs, and availability of information to all investors. Under these assumptions, any value to be derived from changing the packaging of total corporate income paid to investors as interest on debt or returns on equity can be captured simply by arbitrageurs. If unleveraged firms trade at high prices, arbitrageurs can buy both the debt and equity claims of leveraged companies in the same business, thereby creating financial claims that are equivalent in terms of risk–returns to all equity claims of unleveraged companies. Alternatively, if leveraged companies are worth more in the market, arbitrageurs can buy equity in unleveraged firms with borrowed funds, thereby creating the risk–return equivalent of leveraged company equity claims. In other words, investors can make or unmake leverage on their own. M–M's theorem is that management's choice of capital structure cannot produce value for investors in efficient markets and hence leverage does not matter.

M–M amended their argument to account for the existence of corporate tax deductibility of debt in a second study (1963). M–M recognized that deduction of interest from taxable income made debt financing attractive. In their second analysis of capital structure, the assumption of no corporate taxes was dropped. The implication of dropping that assumption but maintaining the others mentioned above is that corporations should use as much debt as possible. In other words, with corporate income taxation, firms should maximize leverage.

The line of argument opened by M–M occupies financial theorizing to this day. Far too many articles to summarize here have extended the analysis raised by M–M's original work.[6] Summarizing this discussion, we can say that modern financial theory argues that the choice of capital structure has to balance offsetting considerations. One consideration is that maximizing debt and leverage increases the value of tax savings from the deductibility of interest payments on debt. Offsetting this advantage of debt are possible costs from bankruptcy, business interruption, and legal fees coming with corporate failure. Bankruptcy is more likely when fixed interest payments to creditors are large relative to total corporate income since not paying interest and principal according to contractual terms causes bankruptcy.

Other considerations discussed in connection with debt concern the distorted incentives of equity owners who use funds from bond investors or other creditors. Since managers of a corporation's assets seek to maximize shareholders' value, they may not operate in the interest of bondholders. To analyze the principal–agent problem between stock and bondholders, financial economists point out that common stock in corporations can be viewed as analogous to a call option on the assets of a firm (see for example Smith and Warner (1979) and the discussion in Chapter 8 of this text). Call options (discussed in Chapter 20) are more valuable when the returns on underlying assets are riskier. Managers of corporations maximizing share values have an incentive to acquire riskier assets than desirable to bondholders. This principal–agent problem can only be resolved with costly negotiations, debt covenants, and monitoring of management, limiting the attractiveness of debt financing.

Corporate Financial Theory and Capital of Financial Institutions

The implication of corporate financial theory in efficient markets on the capital policy of financial institutions is that there are advantages to using leverage for all corporations, including financial institutions. In the absence of other considerations, there probably is a maximum amount of leverage that is optimal because the costs of borrowed funds or yield costs of other liabilities will increase to reflect risks associated with extreme leverage. If financial institutions were identical to other corporations, there would likely be limits to the value of using leverage.

[6]See, for example, the discussion in Ross, Westerfield, and Jaffe (1993), Chapters 13 to 16 and references, or other corporate finance textbooks.

Optimal capital structure for financial service firms cannot be considered like other corporations. One must look at some specifics of the financial services industry. First, many financial service firms raise funds in the form of deposits and insurance reserves that are the focus of public policy, such as the U.S. government policy of guaranteeing deposits up to $100,000. Second, the financial services industry is highly regulated; both the assets and capital structure of financial institutions are subject to regulatory review. Finally, the capital of financial institutions may be an important signal to their customers concerning their commitment to the quality of their products and services. Equity capital and reputational capital may be a significant performance bond on the part of the financial service providers. We discuss the effect of each of these three considerations on the capital policy of financial institutions.

Insured Liabilities of Financial Service Firms

Optimal capital structure for financial service firms has to consider the effects of government insurance on their liabilities. As discussed in Part III, some financial service firm liabilities, namely deposits, insurance policies, and securities held for customers, are insured by government insurance agencies. Government insurance of financial service firms' liabilities such as deposits means that holders of those financial claims are not much concerned about the issuing firms' assets. These clients are often primarily concerned with the soundness of the insurer of their claims, in the United States the Federal Deposit Insurance Corporation (FDIC), the state insurance guarantee funds, and the Securities Investors Protection Corporation (SIPC).

The M–M arguments discussed above assumed that claims on a firm's assets were priced based on the risk of the firm's assets. In the case of insured liabilities, the price (or cost of funds) for the financial firm's liabilities reflects the financial strength of the insurer. The insurance of deposits and other claims effectively means that the government offers to buy insured claims from holders at some prespecified price, equivalent to the government issuing a put option on those claims. SIPC insurance does not guarantee a value of the liabilities of securities firms to produce securities to clients but does guarantee the market value of securities "lent" to securities firms by customers. These government assurances reduce or eliminate investor concerns about financial firm assets and capital.

Insured liabilities of financial service firms may have a dramatic impact on the assessment of optimal leverage. If the insurance, such as the deposit insurance issued by the FDIC, is underpriced by the insurance agency, the government is effectively giving a subsidized put option to the shareholders in the financial firms issuing these liabilities (see Merton (1977) for the application of option pricing to deposit insurance). To maximize the value of the equity in a firm with subsidized liability insurance, the firm should maximize its use of insured liabilities. Maximizing use of leverage, according to this argument, maximizes the value of equity by maximizing the value of the liability put issued by the government insurer.

An equivalent but perhaps more intuitive statement of the value of the maximization of leverage with subsidized insurance of liabilities is that leverage maximizes the benefit of issuing liabilities where the prices and yields do not fully reflect assets risks as is assumed in M–M. In other words, liability insurance, which is pervasive in financial service firms, reduces the required rate of return to investors in the liabilities of financial firms. Liability insurance increases the spread between asset returns and the costs of funds, increasing the benefits of leverage.

The distortion in incentives for managers of financial institutions due to lack of market concern with the risk of financial service firms is at the center of the controversy concerning financial service firm regulation. For example, many observers of the financial services industry feel that expansion of deposit insurance in the 1980 Deregulation Act to $100,000 caused the problems in the banks and savings and loan segments of the financial services industry in the 1980s. Barth, for example, writes, "An assessment of available evidence indicates that federal deposit insurance itself is the unifying cause of the savings and loans' misfortunes" (1991, p. 48).

Regulation of Capital Structure

The regulation of financial service firms is discussed in Part III of this text. Capital structure and asset quality of many types of financial service firms, such as deposit-taking, insurance, and securities firms, are regulated. Optimal capital structure must be considered against the backdrop of regulation. It should be pointed out that most government regulation is only necessary because market forces do not limit financial institution management risk-taking because yield costs are held below market levels by government policies such as deposit insurance.

Asset and capital restrictions, as discussed above, mean that portfolio choices are constrained to a subset of possible asset and liability combinations. Constraints mean that expected risks and returns of assets and leverage may differ from the unregulated or unconstrained case. If regulation is effective, risks and returns of assets and liabilities and the degree of leverage of regulated financial service firms will achieve some carefully chosen public policy goal. Given the subtlety of the distortions and the complex effects on portfolio choice with constraints, it is likely that optimal constrained portfolios will be riskier or more leveraged than socially optimal. In other words, it is unlikely that regulation produces optimal results.

The presumption is that financial institution managers confronted with minimum capital restrictions will choose the maximum allowable leverage. This view supposes that optimal capital structure from the point of view of management attempting to maximize expected returns is minimum capital or maximum leverage. This policy maximizes returns to owners of regulated institutions through maximizing benefits of leverage such as favorable spreads. Legislatures provide regulators such as the Federal Reserve and the Office of Thrift Supervision with legal powers and sanctions, such as cease and desist orders or closure of institutions, to enforce leverage restrictions. Presumably, without threats regulators could not induce financial institutions to hold regulatory minimum capital.

The argument that regulated financial institutions will have minimum capital is defied by the statistics on capital of financial institutions. A review of the distribution of capital held by regulated institutions shows a wide range of capital asset ratios. Another important observation is that there is no correlation between capital ratios and rates of returns, measured either as market or accounting rates of return, for regulated institutions such as banks (see Dietrich (1992)). Simple leverage maximization using the minimum regulatory capital does not seem to be an optimal or even a good capital policy for many financial service firms.

Financial Service Firm Capital and Customer Relations

Equity capital invested in financial service firms may be important in ways that cannot be considered by viewing financial service firms simply as leveraged portfolios of assets and liabilities in a single-period context. Financial service firms produce services that are not completely captured in the concept of rates of return and yield costs of balance sheet items in short time frames. Many financial services, such as credit services, securities services, or asset-management services, are provided over longer time periods. The customer relationship over time depends on the reliability of the financial service firm's commitments to customers.

A financial firm's capital can represent a commitment to perform as expected on financial service contracts or make other commitments more credible to customers. Capital may resolve principal–agent problems for customers who could be damaged (as principals) from asymmetric information concerning the value of products or services offered by financial service firms or from moral hazard due to failure to perform as expected. For example, an investment banking firm taking a position using its own capital in a risky security while underwriting the issue is signaling to buyers of that security its conviction concerning the accurate pricing of the security. If the underwriting firm is wrong, it loses money too.

Financial institutions like brokers and asset managers rely on their reputations to increase their fees and other revenues. Loss of reputation through failure to perform as promised means more when the assets of the financial service firm, which will be damaged through loss of reputation, are financed with equity. Financial firms investing owners' funds to provide financial services signal the importance of providing good service to future customers and their reliance on a good reputation to recover their investment. Equity serves as a performance bond to customers.

Finally, capital can provide financial institutions with flexibility. For example, banks, which are subject to examination by regulators, can stick by credit customers having rough times without running into minimum capital problems when regulators force them to record credit losses (write down loans). Excess capital may assure customers of the commitment of financial institutions to serve customers in good times and bad. Capital may be associated with perceived quality of service and increased returns on assets through higher interest rates and fees which offset disadvantages of lower leverage. Many of the most profitable financial institutions, like Morgan Bank and Salomon Brothers, are well capitalized relative to industry peers.

18.7 SUMMARY

Portfolio management of a trust's assets or the complex structure of financial claims for a diversified financial institution like a bank or insurance company can be analyzed within the framework of modern developments in corporate finance: portfolio theory and efficient capital markets. The risks and returns of both leveraged and unleveraged portfolios can be analyzed using portfolio analysis. Portfolio risks are related to macroeconomic risks and these two views of risk integrated for assessing and choosing a portfolio strategy. Portfolio management strategies of financial institutions have evolved over time. In considering capital structure policy, financial institution managers must consider not only portfolio theory but the realities of liability insurance, regulation, and the role of capital in dealing with customers.

DISCUSSION QUESTIONS AND EXERCISES

1. Given expected returns of two assets of 10 and 20 percent and standard deviations of 20 and 30 percent, respectively, and a correlation coefficient of +1, what is the expected return of a portfolio consisting of 50 percent in each asset? 25 and 75 percent? 75 and 25 percent?
2. What are the answers to the above question if the correlation coefficient is –1?
3. What combination of the two assets will minimize returns if the correlation is +1? Negative 1?
4. Assume that the first asset in question 1 is a liability. What is the risk–return trade-off if 150 percent of net worth is invested in the asset and the correlation is +1? Negative 1? What are the risk–return trade-offs at 200 percent with the two values of the correlation coefficient?
5. Describe the assets and liabilities of traditional financial institutions like banks or thrifts in terms of the ranking of the rates of return on the assets and yield costs of liabilities and the likely correlations of the asset and liability returns. Can you use these relations to analyze the composition of typical balance sheets of these types of institutions?
6. What are the sources of liquidity risks for commercial banks? Savings institutions? Insurance companies? Relate the reasons why cash flows from both asset and liability activities of these institutions can force unexpected cash needs or excess cash.
7. Compare the capital to asset ratios from several financial institutions with similar charters. How do these ratios compare to national averages? Can you relate the difference to perceived differences in their relation to their customers? How does the capital policy correlate with the return on equity for these institutions? Are there departures from the assumed higher returns to equity with more leverage? If so, can you explain those departures?
8. What exactly is the risk from a loan default to a financial institution manager? Explain the negative impact of such an event on operating problems of the financial institution manager and the effect on the return and variability of returns for the institution.
9. How does investment in assets denominated in foreign currencies

affect the risk of future cash flows for portfolio managers? What is the exact nature of the risk and its impact on expected returns and their variability?

10. Provide examples of operating risk for financial institutions. How do these risks impact the return and variability of returns for the financial institution? How would investors in the institution adjust their expected returns to account for operating risks?

REFERENCES

BARTH, JAMES. 1991. *The Great Savings and Loan Debacle*. Washington, D.C.: The AEI Press.

COHEN, KALMAN and FREDERICK S. HAMMER. 1967. "Linear Programming and Optimal Bank Asset Management Decisions," *Journal of Finance* 22(2), pp. 147–165.

COHEN, KALMAN and STEPHEN E. GIBSON. 1978. *Management Science in Banking*. Boston and New York: Warren, Gorham and Lamont.

DIETRICH, J. KIMBALL. 1992. "Bank Capital and Risky Lending: Alternative Return Maximizing Strategies," Discussion paper, University of Southern California.

HAKANSON, NILS H. 1971. "Multi-Period Mean-Variance Analysis: Toward a General Theory of Portfolio Choice," *Journal of Finance,* 26(4), pp. 857–888.

KOEHN, MICHAEL and ANTHONY M. SANTOMERO. 1980. "Regulation of Bank Capital and Portfolio Risk," *Journal of Finance* XXXV (5), pp. 1235–1244.

MARKOWITZ, HARRY. 1952. "Portfolio Selection," *Journal of Finance* March 7(1), pp. 77–91.

MERTON, ROBERT C. 1972. "An Analytic Derivation of the Efficient Portfolio Frontier," *Journal of Financial and Quantitative Analysis,* 7(4), September, pp. 1851–1872.

MERTON, ROBERT C. 1977. "An Analytic Derivation of the Cost of Deposit Insurance and Loan Guarantees: An Application of Modern Option Pricing Theory," *Journal of Banking and Finance* 1(1), pp. 3–11.

MODIGLIANI, FRANCO and MERTON MILLER. 1958. "The Cost of Capital, Corporate Finance and the Theory of Investment," *American Economic Review* (June), 48(3), pp. 261–297.

MODIGLIANI, FRANCO and MERTON MILLER. 1963. "Corporate Income Taxes and the Cost of Capital: A Correction," *American Economic Review* (June), 53, pp. 433–443.

ROLL, RICHARD. 1977. "A Critique of the Asset Pricing Theory's Tests," *Journal of Financial Economics* 4, pp. 129–176.

ROSS, STEPHEN A., RANDOLPH W. WESTERFIELD, and JEFFREY F. JAFFE. 1993. *Corporate Finance* (3rd Ed.) Homewood, Ill.: Irwin.

SMITH, CLIFFORD and JERROD WARNER. 1979. "On Financial Contracting: An Analysis of Bond Covenants," *Journal of Financial Economics* 7 (June), pp. 117–161.

C H A P T E R

19

Portfolio Risks: Measurement and Management

Introduction

Portfolio managers or financial institution executives making balance sheet decisions are operating in a constantly changing economic environment.

- What happens to the value of a portfolio when interest rates change and how can the risk of value changes be measured?
- How can interest rate risk be managed with changes in portfolio or balance sheet composition?
- How can the other risks of portfolios, such as credit, liquidity, and currency risks, be assessed?
- What actions can be taken to control or plan for these risks and can value be produced through risk management activities?

Answers to these questions are at the heart of the modern financial institution manager's role and are of central concern to regulators and investors in financial service firms.

This chapter introduces risk measurement for a variety of portfolio risks, concentrating on the interest rate risk of fixed-income securities. Two basic approaches to risk management are presented in this chapter: adjustments in portfolio or balance sheet composition and swaps. These two techniques are similar in that they both deal with the composition of assets and liabilities, in the case of swaps or asset exchanges using third parties to exchange some asset or liability characteristics in a risk reducing fashion. The next two chapters focus on off-balance-sheet approaches to management using forward and futures contracts and options.

19.1 FIXED-INCOME SECURITIES AND INTEREST RATE RISK

We begin by discussing the interest rate risk of *fixed-income securities*. Fixed-income securities are those financial claims that promise to pay fixed cash amounts over some limited time period into the future. Fixed-income securities are contrasted to the cash payments on financial claims or obligations which are not fixed in nominal amounts, the two primary examples being *floating rate securities* and *residual claims*.

Typical fixed-income securities are bonds and self-amortizing loans. A corporate bond with a coupon interest payable until maturity when principal is redeemed is a standard example of a fixed-income security. A second common example is a home mortgage that has a level cash payment over its life, with the last payment completing the repayment of all interest and principal, a so-called *self-amortizing* loan. Within each of these types of fixed-income securities, of course, are a wide variety of financial instruments depending on the issuer and currency denomination: domestic and foreign corporate bonds and obligations of national, state, or local governments are some of the various types of bonds. Home and commercial mortgages and car loans represent standard examples of self-amortizing loans.

In contrast to fixed-income securities, many financial claims do not commit to fixed levels of future cash payments. Floating rate securities pay cash according to future interest rates or other indices that change unpredictably in the future, like floating rate corporate bonds or variable interest rate mortgages. Residual claims are primarily equity or ownership claims for corporations, most importantly common stock, but also include claims like limited partnership shares or participations in gains on real estate. These claims pay cash to owners out of the cash residual left to corporations or other business enterprises that have paid all cash obligations on their fixed claims.

Most discussions of interest rate risk focus on the most common fixed-income securities: bonds. Bonds pay cash based on a contractual interest rate times the amount borrowed or principal. The interest on most bonds is paid semi-annually until the bond matures, at which time the bond owner receives a last interest payment and the repayment of principal. The interest rate on most bonds is called the *coupon* rate because in earlier times bond certificates were issued to investors in bearer form, meaning whoever had possession of the bond certificate was presumed to own the bond. The bond certificate was printed with detachable coupons that were presented by the current owner (or bearer) to the paying agent for payment in cash. Now, most bonds are *registered,* meaning that ownership is recorded in computerized databases and changes in ownership and payment of interest are processed through a transaction processing system of the type described in Chapter 10.

The price of a bond reflects the present value at current market discount rates of the cash flows for the bond in line with the fundamental equation of value (18.1) discussed in the previous chapter. For bonds with a fixed coupon rate, c, the equation of value can be written as:

$$P_0 = \sum_{t=1}^{M} \frac{cF}{(1+i)^t} + \frac{F}{(1+i)^M} \tag{19.1}$$

where P is the price of the bond, F is the face value or the total repayment of principal due M periods in the future on the maturity date, and i is the discount rate or yield to maturity.

Most bonds are quoted not for a dollar or other currency price but as a percent p of face value, in other words, $p = P_0/F$. For example, a price quotation of 113 would be read as a bond costing 113 percent of the face value purchased. The pricing relation can be expressed as a variant of equation (19.1) as follows:

$$p_0 = \frac{P_o}{F} = \sum_{t=1}^{M} \frac{c}{(1+i)^t} + \frac{1}{(1+i)^M} = \frac{c}{i}\left(1 - \frac{1}{(1+i)^M}\right) + \frac{1}{(1+i)^M}. \quad (19.2)$$

The second expression in this variant of the bond price formula uses the simple expression for a limited period annuity and is easier to calculate than the sum of the present values shown as the middle expression in the equation.

The bond price formula, equation (19.1) or its variants, defines a relationship between yields to maturity and bond prices. We have graphed this relationship in Figure 19.1, which illustrates that the relationship between a bond price and its yield, given its coupon and maturity, is nonlinear. When yields change, prices change nonproportionately. The gain when yields decline or the loss when they increase relative to the purchase yield i* is read off the curve. The shape of the relation is determined by the coupon and maturity of the bond.

FIGURE 19.1 Bond prices and yields

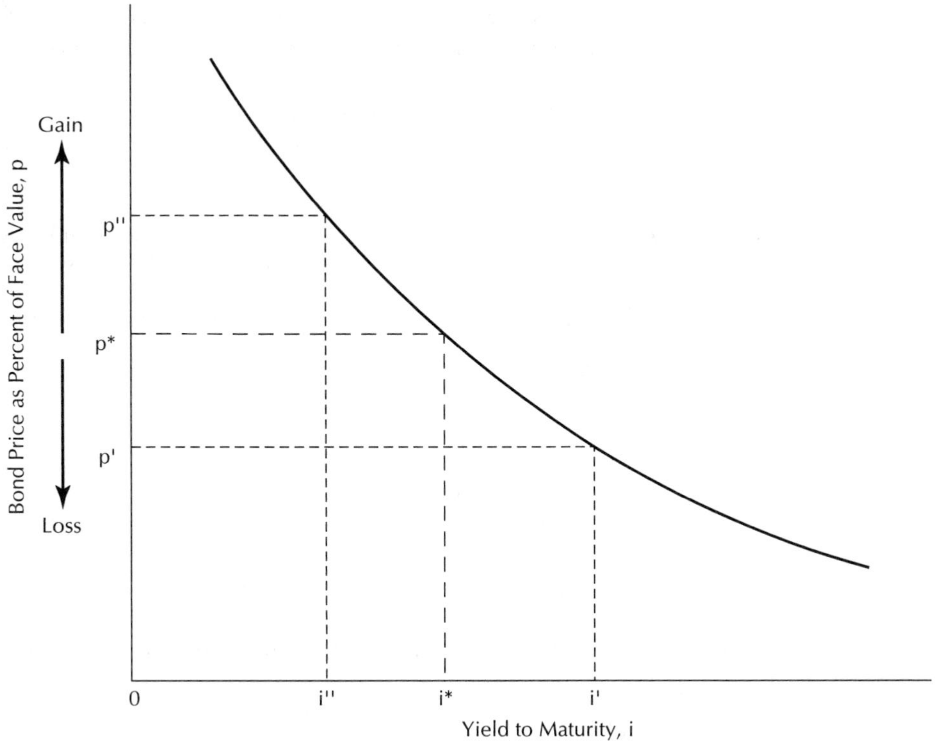

The market yield to maturity i, for the bond, is the market risk-adjusted return used to price the contractual cash flows of cF each period until maturity when the bond owner is supposed to receive cF + F. Default, renegotiation of the bond, or exercise of options included with the bond such as prepayment before maturity at the discretion of the issuer or conversion to other securities at the discretion of the bond owner will determine the actual cash flows in the future. Cash flows from all bonds contain additional risks due to the uncertain purchasing power of future cash flows.

Yields on bonds change daily, even minute by minute, as information reaches the market concerning future prospects for the economy or individual bond issuers. Price and yield information for actual traded bonds should be compared to formula (19.1). For example, the *Wall Street Journal* quotations for U.S. Treasury notes and bonds at 3:00 P.M. Eastern Standard Time on July 12, 1993, are provided in Table 19.1. As we see for that time and date, the 8.5 coupon issue maturing in July 1997, had an ask price of 113-22/32 percent of face value, and a yield to maturity of 4.71 percent. The convention of using percents and 32nds in pricing Treasury bonds requires a calculation to determine that the actual quotation is 1.136875 times the face value of the principal amount purchased. Thus in terms of the formula for that bond on that date, c = .085, p = 1.136875, i = .0471, and M is 4 years.

Bond Price Theorems

Interest rate risk for bonds represents the change in price that occurs when market yields change. The price behavior of coupon bonds has been thoroughly analyzed over the centuries, including a classic treatment of bond price determination and sensitivity by Homer and Leibowitz in 1972. The main results can be summarized in what are widely called the *bond price theorems* as follows:

1. Bond prices and yields move in opposite directions.
2. Bond prices are more sensitive to yield changes the longer their maturities.
3. The price sensitivity of bonds to yield changes increases at a decreasing rate with maturity.
4. High coupon bond prices are less sensitive to yield changes than low coupon bond prices.
5. With a change in yield of a given number of basis points, the associated percent gain is larger than the percent loss.

These bond price properties are completely familiar to active participants in the markets for fixed-income securities.

The "bond price theorems" simply represent mathematical properties of the bond price formula. To illustrate where these theorems come from, consider the first theorem and the most important thing for anyone to know about bonds: that bond prices and yields move in opposite directions. This is demonstrated by taking the derivative of the bond price formula (19.1) with respect to yields and obtaining:

$$\frac{\delta P_o}{\delta i} = \frac{-1cF}{(1+i)^2} + \frac{-2cF}{(1+i)^3} + \ldots + \frac{-McF}{(1+i)^{M+1}} + \frac{-MF}{(1+i)^{M+1}}. \qquad (19.3)$$

TABLE 19.1 Treasury Bonds, Notes, and Bills

Monday, July 12, 1993

Representative Over-the-Counter quotations based on transactions of $1 million or more.

Treasury bond, note and bill quotes are as of mid-afternoon. Colons in bid-and-asked quotes represent 32nds; 101:01 means 101 1/32. Net changes in 32nds. n-Treasury note. Treasury bill quotes in hundredths, quoted on terms of a rate of discount. Days to maturity calculated from settlement date. All yields are to maturity and based on the asked quote. Latest 13-week and 26-week bills are boldfaced. For bonds callable prior to maturity, yields are computed to the earliest call date for issues quoted above par and to the maturity date for issues below par. *-When issued.

Source: Federal Reserve Bank of New York.

U.S. Treasury strips as of 3 p.m. Eastern time, also based on transactions of $1 million or more. Colons in bid-and-asked quotes represent 32nds; 101:01 means 101 1/32. Net changes in 32nds. Yields calculated on the asked quotation. ci-stripped coupon interest. bp-Treasury bond, stripped principal. np-Treasury note, stripped principal. For bonds callable prior to maturity, yields are computed to the earliest call date for issues quoted above par and to the maturity date for issues below par.

Source: Bear, Stearns & Co. via Street Software Technology Inc.

GOVT. BONDS & NOTES

Rate	Maturity Mo/Yr	Bid	Asked	Chg.	Ask Yld.
7 1/4	Jul 93n	100:01	100:03	....	0.00
6 7/8	Jul 93n	100:05	100:07	− 1	2.15
8	Aug 93n	100:14	100:16	− 1	2.26
8 5/8	Aug 93	100:16	100:18	....	2.17
8 3/4	Aug 93n	100:15	100:17	− 2	2.63
11 7/8	Aug 93n	100:25	100:27	− 1	2.20
6 3/8	Aug 93n	100:13	100:15	− 1	2.70
6 1/8	Sep 93n	100:20	100:22	....	2.83
8 1/4	Sep 93n	101:03	101:05	− 1	2.73
7 1/8	Oct 93n	101:00	101:02	....	2.86
6	Oct 93n	100:26	100:28	....	2.98
7 3/4	Nov 93n	101:16	101:18	− 1	3.03
8 5/8	Nov 93	101:25	101:27	− 1	3.05
9	Nov 93n	101:29	101:31	− 1	3.05
11 3/4	Nov 93n	102:27	102:29	− 2	2.98
5 1/2	Nov 93n	100:27	100:29	− 1	3.07
5	Dec 93n	100:26	100:28	....	3.07
7 5/8	Dec 93n	102:00	102:02	− 1	3.09
7	Jan 94n	101:27	101:29	....	3.15
4 7/8	Jan 94n	100:27	100:29	− 1	3.19
6 7/8	Feb 94n	102:02	102:04	....	3.20
8 7/8	Feb 94n	103:07	103:09	....	3.21
9	Feb 94	103:09	103:11	− 1	3.22
5 3/8	Feb 94n	101:08	101:10	....	3.26
5 3/4	Mar 94n	101:21	101:23	....	3.29
8 1/2	Mar 94n	103:19	103:21	....	3.28
7	Apr 94n	102:21	102:23	− 1	3.32
5 3/8	Apr 94n	101:16	101:18	....	3.37
7	May 94n	102:29	102:31	....	3.38
9 1/2	May 94n	104:30	105:00	− 1	3.40
13 1/8	May 94n	108:02	108:04	− 1	3.22
5 1/8	May 94n	101:14	101:16	....	3.38
5	Jun 94n	101:13	101:15	....	3.44
8 1/2	Jun 94n	104:23	104:25	....	3.41
8	Jul 94n	104:13	104:15	....	3.43
4 1/4	Jul 94n	100:23	100:25	+ 1	3.48
6 7/8	Aug 94n	103:16	103:18	....	3.51
8 5/8	Aug 94n	105:11	105:13	....	3.52
8 3/4	Aug 94	105:15	105:19	....	3.47
12 5/8	Aug 94n	109:20	109:22	− 2	3.48
4 1/4	Aug 94n	100:23	100:25	....	3.54
4	Sep 94n	100:14	100:16	+ 1	3.58
8 1/2	Sep 94n	105:23	105:25	− 1	3.59
9 1/2	Oct 94n	107:02	107:04	− 1	3.64
4 1/4	Oct 94n	100:23	100:25	+ 1	3.63
6	Nov 94n	102:31	103:01	....	3.66
8 1/4	Nov 94n	105:28	105:30	....	3.66
10 1/8	Nov 94	108:11	108:13	....	3.63
11 5/8	Nov 94n	110:09	110:11		3.63
4 5/8	Nov 94n	101:07	101:09	....	3.66
4 5/8	Dec 94n	101:07	101:09	− 1	3.72
7 5/8	Dec 94n	105:15	105:17	....	3.70
8 5/8	Jan 95n	107:00	107:02	....	3.75
4 1/4	Jan 95n	100:21	100:23	....	3.77
3	Feb 95	99:26	100:26	+ 2	2.48
5 1/2	Feb 95n	102:18	102:20	+ 1	3.78
7 3/4	Feb 95n	106:00	106:02	....	3.78
0 1/2	Feb 95	110:07	110:09	− 1	3.77
1 1/4	Feb 95n	111:12	111:14	....	3.77
3 7/8	Feb 95n	100:02	100:04	+ 1	3.80
3 7/8	Mar 95n	100:00	100:02	....	3.84
8 3/8	Apr 95n	107:18	107:20	....	3.84
3 7/8	Apr 95n	99:30	100:00	+ 1	3.88
5 7/8	May 95n	103:13	103:15	....	3.90
8 1/2	May 95n	108:01	108:03	+ 1	3.89
10 3/8	May 95	111:10	111:12	− 1	3.90
11 1/4	May 95n	112:30	113:00	....	3.86
12 5/8	May 95	115:13	115:17	....	3.80
4 1/8	May 95n	100:10	100:12	....	3.92
4 1/8	Jun 95n	100:09	100:11	....	3.94
8 7/8	Jul 95n	109:12	109:14	....	3.93
4 5/8	Aug 95n	101:07	101:09	+ 1	3.98
8 1/2	Aug 95n	108:29	108:31	....	3.98
10 1/2	Aug 95n	112:31	113:01	....	3.94
8 5/8	Oct 95n	109:23	109:25	− 1	4.04
5 1/8	Nov 95n	102:07	102:09	....	4.09
8 1/2	Nov 95n	109:23	109:25	+ 1	4.07
9 1/2	Nov 95n	112:04	112:06	+ 4	3.99
11 1/2	Nov 95	116:14	116:18	− 2	4.01
9 1/4	Jan 96n	111:29	111:31	+ 1	4.16
7 1/2	Jan 96n	107:29	107:31	....	4.17
4 5/8	Feb 96n	101:02	101:04	+ 3	4.16
7 7/8	Feb 96n	108:28	108:30	....	4.20
8 7/8	Feb 96n	111:10	111:12	+ 1	4.19
7 1/2	Feb 96n	108:01	108:03	+ 1	4.22
7 3/4	Mar 96n	108:26	108:28	....	4.25
9 3/8	Apr 96n	113:01	113:03	....	4.29
7 5/8	Apr 96n	108:21	108:23	+ 1	4.28
4 1/4	May 96n	99:30	100:00	+ 1	4.25
7 3/8	May 96n	108:02	108:04	+ 1	4.30
7 5/8	May 96n	108:26	108:28	+ 1	4.32
7 7/8	Jun 96n	109:25	109:27	+ 1	4.30
7 7/8	Jul 96n	109:23	109:25	....	4.36
7 7/8	Jul 96n	109:25	109:27	− 1	4.39
7 1/4	Aug 96n	108:05	108:07	+ 1	4.41
7	Sep 96n	107:18	107:20	+ 2	4.43
8	Oct 96n	110:16	110:18	....	4.48
6 7/8	Oct 96n	107:07	107:09	+ 2	4.48
7 1/4	Nov 96n	108:11	108:13	+ 1	4.51
6 1/2	Nov 96n	106:03	106:05	+ 1	4.52
6 1/8	Dec 96n	105:03	105:05	+ 2	4.50
8	Jan 97n	110:30	111:00	+ 1	4.57
6 1/4	Jan 97n	105:12	105:14	+ 2	4.57
6 3/4	Feb 97n	107:01	107:03	+ 1	4.61
6 7/8	Mar 97n	107:16	107:18	....	4.64
8 1/2	Apr 97n	113:02	113:04	+ 1	4.65
6 7/8	Apr 97n	107:19	107:21	+ 2	4.65
8 1/2	May 97n	113:09	113:11	+ 2	4.66
6 3/4	May 97n	107:07	107:09	+ 1	4.68
6 3/8	Jun 97n	106:00	106:02	+ 1	4.68
8 1/2	Jul 97n	113:20	113:22	+ 1	4.71
5 1/2	Jul 97n	102:30	103:00	+ 2	4.68
8 5/8	Aug 97n	114:07	114:09	+ 1	4.74
5 5/8	Aug 97n	103:07	103:09	+ 2	4.74
5 1/2	Sep 97n	102:24	102:26	+ 2	4.76
8 3/4	Oct 97n	115:00	115:02	+ 2	4.80
5 3/4	Oct 97n	103:18	103:20	+ 2	4.81
8 7/8	Nov 97n	115:22	115:24	+ 2	4.81
6	Nov 97n	104:17	104:19	+ 2	4.82
6	Dec 97n	104:17	104:19	+ 2	4.84
7 7/8	Jan 98n	111:31	112:01	+ 1	4.87
5 5/8	Jan 98n	102:29	102:31	+ 1	4.89
8 1/8	Feb 98n	113:04	113:06	+ 2	4.88
5 1/8	Feb 98n	100:27	100:29	+ 2	4.90
5 1/8	Mar 98n	100:24	100:26	+ 2	4.93
7 7/8	Apr 98n	112:09	112:11	+ 2	4.93
5 1/8	Apr 98n	100:21	100:23	+ 2	4.95
9	May 98n	117:08	117:10	+ 1	4.93
5 3/8	May 98n	101:21	101:23	+ 2	4.97
5 1/8	Jun 98n	100:19	100:21	+ 1	4.97
8 1/4	Jul 98n	114:07	114:09	+ 2	4.99
9 1/4	Aug 98n	118:27	118:29	+ 2	5.00
7 1/8	Oct 98n	109:17	109:19	+ 3	5.03
3 1/2	Nov 98	99:06	100:06	+ 13	3.46
8 7/8	Nov 98n	117:21	117:23	+ 2	5.05
6 3/8	Jan 99n	106:01	106:03	+ 3	5.09
8 7/8	Feb 99n	118:02	118:04	+ 2	5.11
7	Apr 99n	109:01	109:03	+ 3	5.15
8 1/2	May 94-99	104:01	104:09	....	3.28
9 1/8	May 99n	119:23	119:25	+ 3	5.16
6 3/8	Jul 99n	105:31	106:01	+ 3	5.19
8	Aug 99n	114:10	114:12	+ 3	5.21
6	Oct 99n	103:28	103:30	+ 3	5.25
7 7/8	Nov 99n	113:28	113:30	+ 3	5.26
6 3/8	Jan 00n	105:24	105:26	+ 4	5.31
7 7/8	Feb 95-00	106:01	106:05	+ 3	3.84
8 1/2	Feb 00n	117:17	117:19	+ 3	5.30
5 1/2	Apr 00n	100:24	100:26	+ 2	5.36
8 7/8	May 00n	119:31	120:01	+ 5	5.34
8 3/8	Aug 95-00	108:07	108:11	− 5	4.16
8 3/4	Aug 00n	119:16	119:18	+ 4	5.39
8 1/2	Nov 00n	118:10	118:12	+ 4	5.43
7 3/4	Feb 01n	113:31	114:01	+ 4	5.47
11 3/4	Feb 01	138:27	138:31	+ 5	5.42
8	May 01n	115:22	115:24	+ 4	5.50
13 1/8	May 01	148:06	148:10	+ 6	5.46
7 7/8	Aug 01n	115:01	115:03	+ 4	5.54
8	Aug 96-01	109:30	110:02	− 1	4.48
13 3/8	Aug 01	150:24	150:28	+ 8	5.50
7 1/2	Nov 01n	112:20	112:22	+ 4	5.58
15 3/4	Nov 01	167:23	167:27	+ 4	5.50
14 1/4	Feb 02	158:17	158:21	+ 4	5.57
7 1/2	May 02n	112:24	112:26	+ 5	5.64
6 3/8	Aug 02n	104:24	104:26	+ 5	5.69
11 5/8	Nov 02	142:18	142:22	+ 8	5.67
6 1/4	Feb 03n	103:24	103:26	+ 2	5.73
10 3/4	Feb 03	136:21	136:25	+ 3	5.71
10 3/4	May 03	137:04	137:08	+ 3	5.74
11 1/8	Aug 03	140:16	140:20	+ 3	5.76
11 7/8	Nov 03	146:27	146:31	+ 6	5.78
12 3/8	May 04	152:13	152:17	+ 7	5.78
13 3/4	Aug 04	164:15	164:19	+ 6	5.78
11 5/8	Nov 04	147:04	147:08	+ 5	5.86
8 1/4	May 00-05	114:11	114:15	+ 2	5.67
12	May 05	151:13	151:17	+ 5	5.89
10 3/4	Aug 05	141:01	141:05	+ 4	5.93
9 3/8	Feb 06	129:25	129:29	+ 5	5.96
7 5/8	Feb 02-07	111:10	111:14	+ 3	5.91
7 7/8	Nov 02-07	113:15	113:19	+ 4	5.96
8 3/8	Aug 03-08	117:25	117:29	+ 4	5.99
8 3/4	Nov 03-08	120:29	121:01	+ 3	5.99
9 1/8	May 04-09	124:14	124:18	+ 3	6.01
10 3/8	Nov 04-09	135:13	135:17	+ 4	6.01
11 3/4	Feb 05-10	147:14	147:18	+ 4	6.00
10	May 05-10	133:10	133:14	+ 5	6.01
12 3/4	Nov 05-10	158:00	158:04	+ 6	6.01
13 7/8	May 06-11	169:08	169:12	+ 5	6.03
14	Nov 06-11	172:03	172:07	+ 7	6.04
10 3/8	Nov 07-12	138:27	138:31	+ 5	6.23
12	Aug 08-13	155:23	155:27	+ 8	6.24
13 1/4	May 09-14	170:00	170:04	+ 13	6.22
12 1/2	Aug 09-14	162:15	162:19	+ 10	6.27
11 3/4	Nov 09-14	155:04	155:08	+ 10	6.29
11 1/4	Feb 15	154:02	154:04	+ 13	6.54
10 5/8	Aug 15	147:03	147:05	+ 13	6.55
9 7/8	Nov 15	138:10	138:12	+ 11	6.57
9 1/4	Feb 16	130:30	131:00	+ 12	6.59
7 1/4	May 16	107:08	107:10	+ 9	6.62
7 1/2	Nov 16	110:06	110:08	+ 10	6.63
8 3/4	May 17	125:08	125:10	+ 10	6.62
8 7/8	Aug 17	126:26	126:28	+ 11	6.63
9 1/8	May 18	130:05	130:07	+ 11	6.63
9	Nov 18	128:23	128:25	+ 11	6.64
8 7/8	Feb 19	127:05	127:07	+ 11	6.65
8 1/8	Aug 19	117:29	117:31	+ 9	6.66
8 1/2	Feb 20	122:26	122:28	+ 11	6.65
8 3/4	May 20	126:03	126:05	+ 11	6.65
8 3/4	Aug 20	126:05	126:07	+ 11	6.65
7 7/8	Feb 21	115:03	115:05	+ 10	6.67
8 1/8	May 21	118:13	118:15	+ 10	6.66
8 1/8	Aug 21	118:13	118:15	+ 10	6.66
8	Nov 21	117:00	117:02	+ 10	6.65
7 1/4	Aug 22	107:21	107:23	+ 9	6.65
7 5/8	Nov 22	112:18	112:20	+ 11	6.64
7 1/8	Feb 23	106:15	106:17	+ 8	6.62

TABLE 19.1 (*continued*)

U.S. TREASURY STRIPS

Mat.	Type	Bid	Asked	Chg.	Ask Yld.
Aug 93	ci	99:23	99:23	....	3.17
Nov 93	ci	98:30	98:30	....	3.20
Feb 94	ci	98:03	98:04	....	3.27
May 94	ci	97:07	97:07	+ 1	3.39
Aug 94	ci	96:09	96:10	+ 1	3.48
Nov 94	ci	95:10	95:11	+ 1	3.61
Nov 94	np	95:08	95:09	+ 1	3.65
Feb 95	ci	94:03	94:05	+ 1	3.84
Feb 95	np	94:05	94:07	+ 1	3.79
May 95	ci	93:07	93:08	+ 1	3.84
May 95	np	93:03	93:05	+ 1	3.90
Aug 95	ci	92:05	92:07	+ 1	3.92
Aug 95	np	92:04	92:06	+ 1	3.94
Nov 95	ci	90:29	90:31	+ 1	4.09
Nov 95	np	91:01	91:03	+ 1	4.03
Feb 96	ci	89:21	89:23	+ 1	4.24
Feb 96	np	89:21	89:23	+ 1	4.24
May 96	ci	88:13	88:16	+ 1	4.36
May 96	np	88:12	88:15	+ 1	4.37
Aug 96	ci	87:03	87:05	+ 1	4.50
Nov 96	ci	85:28	85:30	+ 1	4.59
Nov 96	np	85:30	86:00	+ 1	4.57
Feb 97	ci	84:24	84:27	+ 1	4.64
May 97	ci	83:15	83:18	+ 1	4.74
May 97	np	83:15	83:18	+ 1	4.74
Aug 97	ci	82:12	82:15	+ 1	4.77
Aug 97	np	82:10	82:13	+ 1	4.79
Nov 97	ci	81:00	81:03	+ 1	4.89
Nov 97	np	81:01	81:04	+ 1	4.88
Feb 98	ci	80:02	80:05	+ 1	4.88
Feb 98	np	79:23	79:27	+ 1	4.97
May 98	ci	78:18	78:22	+ 1	5.02
May 98	np	78:18	78:22	+ 1	5.02
Aug 98	ci	77:09	77:13	+ 1	5.10
Aug 98	np	77:04	77:08	+ 1	5.14
Nov 98	ci	76:04	76:08	+ 1	5.15
Nov 98	np	76:04	76:08	+ 1	5.15
Feb 99	ci	74:24	74:28	+ 2	5.24
Feb 99	np	74:28	75:00	+ 2	5.21
May 99	ci	73:22	73:26	+ 2	5.27
May 99	np	73:22	73:26	+ 2	5.27
Aug 99	ci	72:15	72:19	+ 2	5.33
Aug 99	np	72:13	72:17	+ 2	5.34
Nov 99	ci	71:08	71:12	+ 2	5.39
Nov 99	np	71:20	71:25	+ 2	5.30
Feb 00	ci	70:02	70:06	+ 2	5.44
Feb 00	np	69:31	70:04	+ 2	5.46
May 00	ci	68:24	68:29	+ 2	5.52
May 00	np	68:23	68:27	+ 2	5.53
Aug 00	ci	67:23	67:28	+ 2	5.54
Aug 00	np	67:17	67:22	+ 2	5.58
Nov 00	ci	66:21	66:26	+ 2	5.57
Nov 00	np	66:15	66:20	+ 2	5.61
Feb 01	ci	65:15	65:19	+ 10	5.63
Feb 01	np	65:13	65:18	+ 2	5.64
May 01	ci	64:11	64:16	+ 15	5.67
May 01	np	64:04	64:08	+ 2	5.72
Aug 01	ci	63:10	63:15	+ 18	5.70
Aug 01	np	63:00	63:05	+ 2	5.76
Nov 01	ci	62:10	62:15	+ 17	5.72
Nov 01	np	62:01	62:05	+ 2	5.78
Feb 02	ci	60:25	60:30	+ 20	5.85
May 02	ci	59:21	59:26	+ 17	5.90
May 02	np	60:04	60:09	+ 2	5.81
Aug 02	ci	58:22	58:27	+ 17	5.9
Aug 02	np	59:06	59:11	+ 2	5.8
Nov 02	ci	57:25	57:30	+ 16	5.9
Feb 03	ci	56:11	56:16	+ 2	6.0
Feb 03	np	57:06	57:11	+ 3	5.8
May 03	ci	55:05	55:10	+ 2	6.1
Aug 03	ci	54:07	54:12	+ 2	6.1
Nov 03	ci	53:09	53:14	+ 2	6.1
Feb 04	ci	52:15	52:21	+ 6	6.1
May 04	ci	51:19	51:24	+ 6	6.1
Aug 04	ci	50:24	50:29	+ 6	6.1
Nov 04	ci	49:22	49:28	+ 6	6.2
Nov 04	bp	49:28	50:01	+ 3	6.2
Feb 05	ci	48:26	49:00	+ 6	6.2
May 05	ci	47:24	47:29	+ 6	6.3
May 05	bp	48:01	48:06	+ 3	6.2
Aug 05	ci	46:27	47:00	+ 6	6.3
Aug 05	bp	47:06	47:11	+ 3	6.2
Nov 05	ci	46:04	46:09	+ 6	6.3
Feb 06	ci	44:13	44:18	+ 3	6.5
Feb 06	bp	46:04	46:09	+ 3	6.2
May 06	ci	43:16	43:21	+ 3	6.5
Aug 06	ci	42:18	42:23	+ 3	6.6
Nov 06	ci	41:23	41:28	+ 3	6.6
Feb 07	ci	41:08	41:13	+ 3	6.5
May 07	ci	40:17	40:22	+ 3	6.6
Aug 07	ci	39:26	40:00	+ 3	6.61
Nov 07	ci	39:06	39:11	+ 3	6.61
Feb 08	ci	37:22	37:27	+ 1	6.77
May 08	ci	37:02	37:07	+ 3	6.77
Aug 08	ci	36:13	36:18	+ 3	6.78
Nov 08	ci	35:25	35:30	+ 3	6.78
Feb 09	ci	34:31	35:04	+ 3	6.82
May 09	ci	34:03	34:08	+ 3	6.88
Aug 09	ci	33:16	33:21	+ 3	6.88
Nov 09	ci	32:30	33:03	+ 9	6.88
Nov 09	bp	33:02	33:07	+ 3	6.86
Feb 10	ci	32:01	32:06	+ 3	6.95
May 10	ci	31:12	31:17	+ 3	6.97
Aug 10	ci	30:25	30:30	+ 3	6.98
Nov 10	ci	30:07	30:12	+ 3	6.99
Feb 11	ci	29:30	30:03	+ 3	6.94
May 11	ci	29:14	29:19	+ 3	6.94
Aug 11	ci	28:19	28:24	+ 1	7.01
Nov 11	ci	27:27	28:00	− 2	7.06
Feb 12	ci	27:10	27:15	+ 1	7.07
May 12	ci	26:29	27:02	+ 3	7.06
Aug 12	ci	26:14	26:19	+ 3	7.06
Nov 12	ci	26:04	26:09	+ 3	7.03
Feb 13	ci	25:17	25:22	+ 3	7.06
May 13	ci	25:03	25:08	+ 3	7.06
Aug 13	ci	24:19	24:24	+ 3	7.07
Nov 13	ci	24:06	24:10	+ 3	7.07
Feb 14	ci	23:23	23:27	+ 6	7.08
May 14	ci	22:30	23:02	+ 2	7.16
Aug 14	ci	22:17	22:21	+ 2	7.16
Nov 14	ci	22:06	22:10	+ 2	7.15
Feb 15	ci	21:20	21:24	+ 2	7.19
Feb 15	bp	21:24	21:28	+ 2	7.16
May 15	ci	21:08	21:12	+ 2	7.19
Aug 15	ci	20:28	21:00	+ 2	7.19
Aug 15	bp	20:29	21:01	+ 2	7.18
Nov 15	ci	20:16	20:20	+ 2	[illegible]
Nov 15	bp	20:19	20:23	+ 2	7.17
Feb 16	ci	20:11	20:16	+ 2	7.14
Feb 16	bp	20:10	20:14	+ 2	7.15
May 16	ci	19:31	20:03	+ 2	7.15
May 16	bp	20:11	20:16	+ 2	7.06
Aug 16	ci	19:19	19:24	+ 2	7.15
Nov 16	ci	19:10	19:14	+ 2	7.14
Nov 16	bp	19:14	19:18	+ 2	7.11
Feb 17	ci	18:27	18:31	+ 2	7.17
May 17	ci	18:16	18:20	+ 2	7.17
May 17	bp	18:16	18:20	+ 2	7.17
Aug 17	ci	18:06	18:10	+ 2	7.17
Aug 17	bp	18:05	18:09	+ 2	7.18
Nov 17	ci	17:28	18:00	+ 2	7.17
Feb 18	ci	17:20	17:24	+ 2	7.15
May 18	ci	17:11	17:15	+ 2	7.15
May 18	bp	17:09	17:13	+ 2	7.16
Aug 18	ci	17:01	17:05	+ 2	7.15
Nov 18	ci	16:23	16:27	+ 2	7.15
Nov 18	bp	16:22	16:26	+ 2	7.16
Feb 19	ci	16:15	16:19	+ 2	7.14
Feb 19	bp	16:15	16:19	+ 2	7.14
May 19	ci	16:07	16:11	+ 2	7.13
Aug 19	ci	16:00	16:03	+ 2	7.12
Aug 19	bp	15:29	16:01	+ 2	7.14
Nov 19	ci	15:23	15:27	+ 2	7.12
Feb 20	ci	15:13	15:16	+ 2	7.13
Feb 20	bp	15:13	15:16	+ 2	7.13
May 20	ci	15:04	15:08	+ 2	7.13
May 20	bp	14:30	15:02	+ 2	7.18
Aug 20	ci	14:28	14:31	+ 2	7.13
Aug 20	bp	14:23	14:26	+ 2	7.17
Nov 20	ci	14:22	14:26	+ 2	7.11
Feb 21	ci	14:14	14:17	+ 2	7.11
Feb 21	bp	14:21	14:25	+ 5	7.05
May 21	ci	14:06	14:09	+ 2	7.11
May 21	bp	14:15	14:19	+ 5	7.03
Aug 21	ci	13:30	14:01	+ 2	7.11
Aug 21	bp	14:07	14:11	+ 5	7.03
Nov 21	ci	13:22	13:26	+ 2	7.11
Nov 21	bp	13:30	14:02	+ 2	7.04
Feb 22	ci	13:30	14:02	+ 2	6.98
May 22	ci	13:24	13:27	+ 2	6.97
Aug 22	ci	13:17	13:21	+ 2	6.96
Aug 22	bp	13:28	14:00	+ 5	6.87
Nov 22	ci	13:11	13:15	+ 2	6.95
Nov 22	bp	13:22	13:26	+ 7	6.86
Feb 23	ci	13:31	14:03	+ 2	6.73
Feb 23	bp	13:17	13:21	+ 2	6.84

TREASURY BILLS

Maturity	Days to Mat.	Bid	Asked	Chg.	Ask Yld.
Jul 15 '93	1	2.49	2.39	+0.05	2.42
Jul 22 '93	8	2.67	2.57	−0.04	2.61
Jul 29 '93	15	2.76	2.66	....	2.70
Aug 05 '93	22	2.75	2.65	+0.01	2.69
Aug 12 '93	29	2.76	2.66	....	2.70
Aug 19 '93	36	2.87	2.83	−0.01	2.88
Aug 26 '93	43	2.92	2.88	....	2.93
Sep 02 '93	50	2.93	2.89	....	2.94
Sep 09 '93	57	2.94	2.90	−0.01	2.95
Sep 16 '93	64	2.98	2.96	−0.01	3.02
Sep 23 '93	71	3.01	2.99	....	3.05
Sep 30 '93	78	2.98	2.96	+0.01	3.02
Oct 07 '93	**85**	**3.01**	**2.99**	**−0.01**	**3.05**
Oct 14 '93	92	3.03	3.01	....	3.08
Oct 21 '93	99	3.03	3.01	....	3.08
Oct 28 '93	106	3.02	3.00	+0.01	3.07
Nov 04 '93	113	3.05	3.03	....	3.10
Nov 12 '93	121	3.06	3.04	....	3.11
Nov 18 '93	127	3.07	3.05	....	3.13
Nov 26 '93	135	3.07	3.05	−0.01	3.13
Dec 02 '93	141	3.08	3.06	−0.01	3.14
Dec 09 '93	148	3.09	3.07	....	3.15
Dec 16 '93	155	3.09	3.07	....	3.15
Dec 23 '93	162	3.10	3.08	....	3.17
Dec 30 '93	169	3.09	3.07	....	3.16
Jan 06 '94	**176**	**3.11**	**3.09**	....	**3.18**
Jan 13 '94	183	3.13	3.11	....	3.20
Feb 10 '94	211	3.16	3.14	−0.01	3.24
Mar 10 '94	239	3.18	3.16	....	3.26
Apr 07 '94	267	3.21	3.19	−0.02	3.30
May 05 '94	295	3.23	3.21	−0.01	3.32
Jun 02 '94	323	3.25	3.23	−0.01	3.35
Jun 30 '94	351	3.26	3.24	−0.01	3.36

SOURCE: The *Wall Street Journal*, July 13, 1993. Copyright © 1993 Dow Jones & Company. Reprinted by permission.

This derivative consists exclusively of negative terms, which simply means that $\delta P_0/\delta i < 0$; in other words prices and yields move in opposite directions.

All of the bond price theorems can be shown in the same way as the first theorem, if you have the required interest, patience, and skill to derive them. The point to make clear here is that the bond price theorems are *mathematically* true, they are not based on experiences or hunches. That is why they are called theorems and why they are so important to bond traders.

A more intuitive way of remembering these bond properties or theorems is to graph them. Figure 19.2 shows the price gains (above the horizontal axis) or losses (below) for two different coupons of different maturities with respect to yield changes (Δi). The first theorem is shown by the fact that decreases in yields associated with the upper curve marked $\Delta i < 0$ are in gain territory above the horizontal axis in the figure; increases in yields associated with the curve below the horizontal axis marked $\Delta i > 0$ produce losses.

The second bond price theorem is shown in Figure 19.2 by the fact that the prices changes are larger the longer the maturity (M). The third theorem is shown by the concavity of the gain/loss curves in the figure. The fourth theorem is seen in the fact that the gain/loss curves for the lower coupon bonds are outside the higher coupon bond gain/loss curves. Finally, theorem five can be seen in the fact that the gain curve is farther above the horizontal axis than the loss curve is below the axis. Students are advised to study the figure and use it as a way of remembering the effects of maturity, coupon rates, and yield changes on bond price sensitivity captured in the five bond price theorems.

Measurement of Interest Rate Risk of Bonds

The measurement of the price sensitivity of a given bond or fixed-income security to changes in yields uses a familiar concept from economics, namely elasticity. An elasticity in economics typically represents a ratio of two percentage changes. For example, the price elasticity of demand is the percent change in the amount demanded as a ratio of the percent change in price. A bond price elasticity is defined as the percent change in the price of the bond relative to a percent change

FIGURE 19.2 Bond price theorems

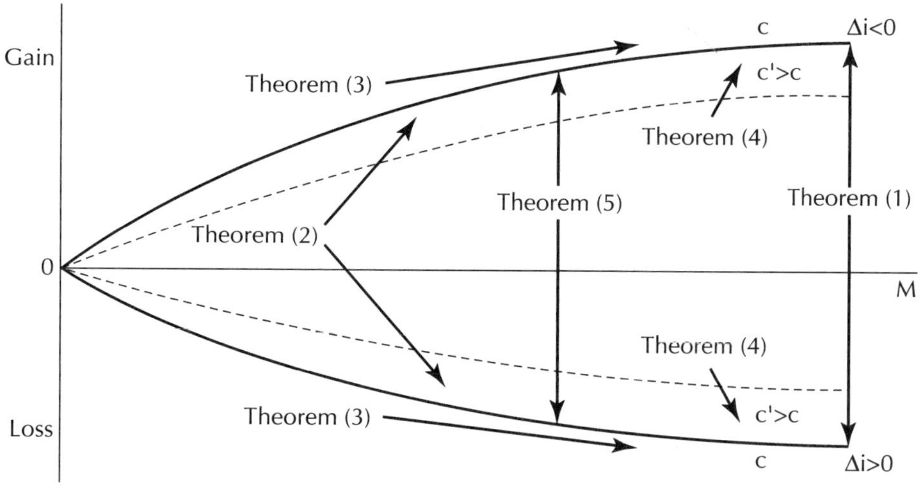

in *gross yields,* where gross yields are the yield to maturity plus one (to account for recovery of the investment). For the bond quote above, the price was 1.136875 (in decimal) and the gross yield was 1.0471.

Bond price elasticity with respect to gross yields is a widely used measure of interest rate risk of bonds and some other fixed-income instruments like mortgages. Before exploring the calculation of bond price elasticities, let us make clear how the elasticity number is used. Let us say, for example, that the bond price elasticity of the 8.5 percent 4-year Treasury from the above example had an elasticity of 3.5. This would mean that if gross yields changed 1 percent, the price would change 3.5 percent.

To continue the above example, a 1 percent change in gross yields corresponds to a 105 basis point change in yields in the above example (.01 times 1.0471). That is, a 1 percent change in gross yield corresponds to a change from the original yield of 4.71 percent to 5.76 or 3.66 (4.71 plus or minus 105 basis points). Using the elasticity, the price change would be 3.5 percent from 1.136875 or approximately .0397 or 3.97 percent, which translates into a 3-31/32 (3 plus .97 times 32) percent move in price in either direction. Alternatively, the price would move up to 1.1766 decimal price (1.035 times 1.136875) or down to 1.0984 decimal percent of face value (1.035 divided into 1.136875).[1]

19.2 DURATION AS INTEREST RATE RISK MEASURE: THEORY AND PRACTICE

In discussing and analyzing bond price and other fixed-income price elasticities, experts use the concept of duration. In fact, bond elasticity as defined above, the ratio of the percent change in price to be expected with a percent change in gross yields, is called *duration* or *Macaulay's duration* from Macaulay's use of the duration concept in his 1938 paper. Duration is a complex topic and deserves extensive discussion. While considering duration and its various uses and interpretations, and its limitations and misuses, keep in mind that duration is always a number, such as 3.5, that is associated with fixed-income securities, and it measures various attributes of those securities, including their price sensitivity to yield changes.

The first thing to know and keep in mind as we discuss duration is that duration for a given fixed-income security is a single number. This number has two apparently completely different interpretations of the same mathematical expression. The first interpretation is a *weighted average payment date* associated with the cash payments from the security. The second interpretation of the same number is as a *bond price elasticity* with respect to changes in gross yields. Many students are confused with these two different interpretations of a bond's duration, so we explain each interpretation carefully.

To appreciate the duration measure as an average time of cash payment, we begin with the usual textbook definition of Macaulay's duration. Macaulay used

[1]Since the ratio of the two percent changes is the elasticity, to find the percent change in price multiply the percent change in gross yield times the elasticity number: 3.5 times 1 = 3.5 percent, 1.035 times 1.136875 is 1.176666.

the duration concept to emphasize that use of a bond's maturity date grossly overstates the length of time that bond investments are tied up. The frequency of payment of interest (usually semiannually) means that a substantial portion of a bond's value is composed of cash payments (usually coupon interest) received well before maturity. Macaulay defined duration:

$$\text{Duration}_1 = d_1 = \frac{1}{P_o}\left(\frac{1cF}{(1+i)} + \frac{2cF}{(1+i)^2} + \ldots + \frac{McF}{(1+i)^M} + \frac{MF}{(1+i)^M}\right). \tag{19.4}$$

In this form, Macaulay's duration can readily be seen as the weighted average payment date of the cash flows from the bonds, where the weights are the present value of the cash payments at the yield to maturity as a percent of the total value of the bond. These weights are multiplied by the payment dates, 1, 2, . . . up to M. Following usual practice, we will note Macaulay's measure d_1 to distinguish this measure from other more complex but closely related duration measures.[2]

The calculation and interpretation of duration as a weighted average payment date makes clear the distortion of the maturity of a bond as a measure of the time dimension of bonds investments. The longest bonds, like U.S. Treasury bonds with 30-year maturities, have durations well under 20 at recent yields. Moreover, the higher the yield, the lower the duration relative to maturities: this can been seen by looking at equation (19.3). In periods of high interest rates like the late 1970s and early 1980s, use of final maturity dates as a measure of investment horizon substantially distorted the time value of the payments from fixed-income securities.

The second interpretation of duration is as an elasticity of bond prices with respect to changes in gross yields. This is the elasticity measure we discussed above. This elasticity can be defined as:

$$d_1 = \frac{dp}{di}\frac{(1+i)}{p} = \frac{\dfrac{dp}{p}}{\dfrac{di}{(1+i)}} = \frac{\text{percent change } p}{\text{percent change } (1+i)}. \tag{19.5}$$

This use of a given duration number measures the interest rate sensitivity of the bond. The relation between the two interpretations of duration can be seen by noting in the derivative of the bond price equation given in equation (19.2). Dividing that derivative by the initial bond value and multiplying by (1+i) gives the Macaulay duration formula in equation (19.3) and is the same as the definition of the elasticity measure in equation (19.4).

Calculation of Duration

Most textbooks provide two methods of actually calculating the number associated with a given bond's duration. This text provides three methods: (1) using Macaulay's definition equation (19.4); (2) calculating two bond prices at two different yields, and dividing the percent bond price changes by the percent gross

[2]Other duration measures use the term structure or other refinements in calculating the weighted average payment date and are not as widely used as d_1.

yield changes; and (3) using a closed form solution such as the one developed by the author and used in classes for many years.[3] We illustrate each in turn.

Macaulay's formula is the hardest to use in practice. Since each coupon payment date must be multiplied by the present value of the associated coupon payment and/or payment of principal, this formula is very time consuming if calculated by hand. Given the formula's wide use, it is worthwhile to present an example here in Table 19.2. To keep things simple, a four-year U.S. Treasury is used, the 8.5 percent coupon maturing in July 1997, evaluated as of July 1993. Panel A of the table shows that the calculation of the weighted average payment date using Macaulay's definition is 3.51. Again note that 3.51 represents both a time measure and the elasticity of this bond with respect to changes in gross yields.

The second method of calculating the bond price elasticity requires fewer calculations that the first. This method simply takes the bond data and reprices the bond at a second yield substantially different from the current yield. Panel B of Table 19.2 takes the same bond used in the previous examples and calculates the price of the bond if the yield were 5.71 instead of 4.71. Of course the bond price is lower, in fact it would fall 3.539 percent. Since a 1 percent yield change (.01) represents .955 percent change in the original gross yield 1.0471, the ratio of the percent change in price to the percent change in gross yield is 3.539/.955, which is 3.706. Thus, the bond elasticity using the second method is 3.706, substantially different than the estimate obtained using the Macaulay formula.

The second method of calculating fixed income elasticities is a very different approach from the first. The first method, Macaulay's definition, is related to the slope of the tangent line of the bond price line as shown in Figure 19.1 for the bond in question. The second method computes the average change over two distant points on that curve representing an arc between those two points. These two approaches are illustrated in Figure 19.3. The first method is similar to a "point elasticity" because it uses the slope of the curve at a point, whereas the second method is similar to an "arc elasticity" because it uses two points on the bond value curve. These terms are used with demand curves in microeconomics.

The third method of calculating duration uses the closed form of the bond price formula given in equation (19.2). Mathematically this method is identical to Macaulay's definition but uses the derivative to determine the slope. This formula requires fewer calculations than either of the other two methods but is not particularly pretty. The formula is:

$$d_1 = \left| -\frac{1+i}{i} - M + \frac{1}{pi}\left(cM + \frac{1}{(1+i)^{M-1}} \right) \right|. \tag{19.6}$$

Although it appears complicated, this formula can easily be programmed for computers or calculators, and because there is only one exponentiation in the formula, it requires less calculation time. Use of the closed form is illustrated in Panel C of Table 19.2 using i, c, and M adjusted for half-year payment periods. Converting to years by dividing by two is seen to produce an answer identical to the result from Macaulay's formula in Panel A.

[3] I have used the formula given here since 1981. Other closed form formulas have been published, for example by Chua (1984).

TABLE 19.2 Calculation of Duration

Example: 8.5 percent U.S. Treasury Note maturing July 1997 priced at 113 22/32 percent of face value on July 12, 1993, to yield 4.71 percent to maturity.

Panel A: Macaulay's Formula

DATE OF PAYMENT	*PAYMENT PERIOD*	*CASH AMOUNT*	*PRESENT VALUE*	*PRESENT VALUE TIMES PAYMENT PERIOD*
1/1994	0.5	42.5	41.53	20.77
7/1994	1	42.5	40.59	40.59
1/1995	1.5	42.5	39.67	59.50
7/1995	2	42.5	38.77	77.53
1/1996	2.5	42.5	37.88	94.71
7/1996	3	42.5	37.02	111.07
1/1997	3.5	42.5	36.18	126.64
7/1997	4	1042.5	867.34	3,469.37
Column Total			1,138.99*	4,000.17

Macaulay's Duration = 3.51 = 4000.17/1138.99

*Differs slightly from quoted price due to rounding.

Panel B: Ratio of Percent Changes in Prices

Price at 4.71 percent yield to maturity = \$1,138.99

Price at 5.71 percent yield to maturity = \$1,098.68

$$d_1 = \frac{\dfrac{(\$1,138.99 - \$1,098.68)}{\$1,138.99}}{\dfrac{.01}{1.0471}} = \frac{.03539}{.00955} = 3.706.$$

Panel C: Use of Closed Form Solution

Using semiannual c = .085/2 = .0425, i = .0471/2 = .02355, p = 113.6875 and M = 4 × 2 = 8 (half years):

$$d_1 = \left| -\frac{1+i}{i} - M + \frac{1}{pi}\left(cM + \frac{1}{(1+i)^{M-1}} \right) \right|$$

$$d_1 = \frac{\left| -\dfrac{1.02355}{.02355} - 8 + \dfrac{1}{1.136875 \times .02355}\left(.0425 \times 8 + \dfrac{1}{1.02355^7} \right) \right|}{2} = 3.51896.$$

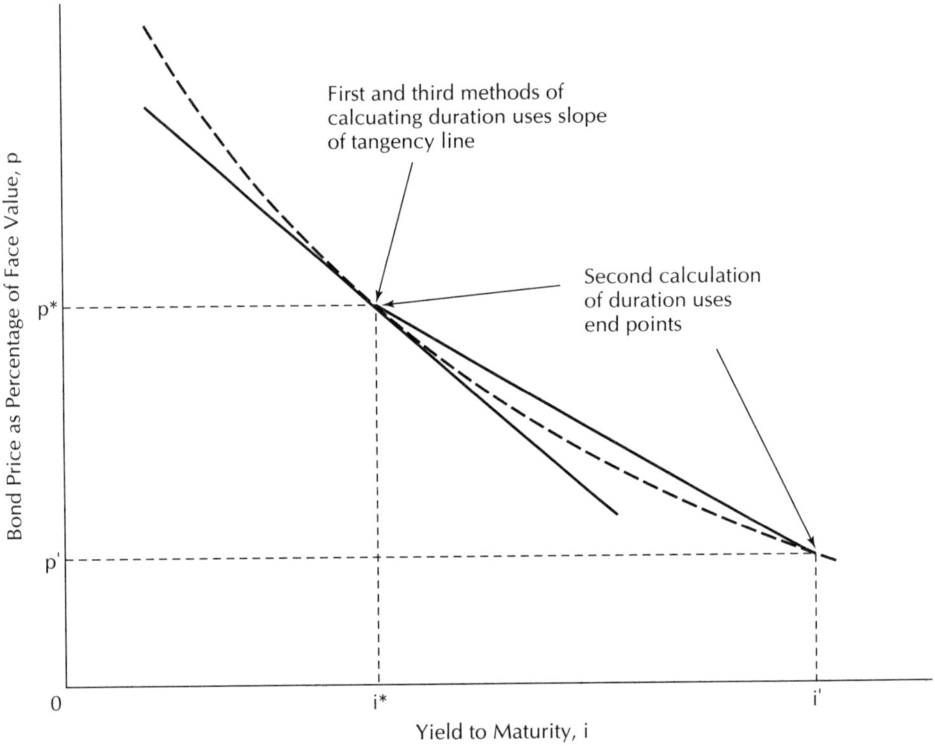

FIGURE 19.3 Three different calculations of duration compared

The second method of calculating the price sensitivity of a bond is often more accurate in predicting price changes with large changes in yields than the two methods based on the slope of the bond value curve. All three methods can only *approximate* price changes for given yield changes. For this reason, many bond analysts are concerned with how sharply curved the bond price and yield relation is, or how *convex* the curve is. A glance at Figure 19.3 shows that the more convex the curve, the more inexact will be the estimated price response to yield changes using the slope of the curve or the arc elasticity.

Price convexity of bonds is measured by bond professionals by looking at the second derivative of the bond value formula, which mathematically measures how much the slope of the bond price curve is changing. Convexity measures can improve but cannot eliminate the approximation in estimating price changes for given yield changes. Although it is important for students to be aware that duration is only an approximate assessment of bond price sensitivity to yield changes and that convexity measures based on second derivatives of the bond price theorem can improve those approximations, we concentrate our discussion in this chapter on the basic duration measure.[4]

[4]The second derivative is used because in a Taylor series expansion of the bond price change using the bond price formula higher order derivatives appear. For a complete treatment, see for example Fabozzi and Fabozzi (1989), pp. 69–79.

Duration of Self-Amortizing Loans

Self-amortizing loans, such as mortgages and car loans, have durations that are measured exactly as with bonds. The basic difference is that the cash flows for self-amortizing loans are fixed differently and there is no lump-sum repayment of principal. The level cash payment of X that pays off a loan of principal F with M equal payments to yield i is calculated:

$$X = \frac{iF}{\left(1 - \frac{1}{(1+i)^M}\right)}.$$

Most self-amortizing loans have monthly payments, so care must be taken to use a monthly yield and M measured in months and to reconvert to annual numbers. For example, a 4-year car loan of $20,000 yielding 12 percent has a monthly payment calculated as follows:

$$X = \frac{20,000 \times .01}{\left(1 - \left[1 \big/ (1.01)^{48}\right]\right)} = \$526.68.$$

The monthly payment of $526.68 is the expected cash flow for 48 months if the loan does not default or prepay.

Duration of fixed-income securities can be calculated using all three of the methods discussed with bonds. The closed form solution for duration uses a different formula than the one used for bonds, namely:

$$d_1 = \left| -\frac{1+i}{i} + \frac{M}{(1+i)^M - 1} \right|.$$

Using the above loan as an example, the duration calculated using this formula is:

$$d_1 = \frac{\left| -\frac{1.01}{.01} + \frac{48}{\left((1.01)^{48} - 1\right)} \right|}{12} = 1.88.$$

Note that the duration of this four-year self-amortizing loan with monthly payments has been annualized in this example by dividing by twelve and the duration is under two years. This is because the high cash flows begin immediately.

Durations of fixed-income securities are often unattractive for originating institutions or other investors for portfolio risk reasons. Asset-backed securities, like *collateralized mortgage obligations* (CMOs) or *real estate mortgage investment conduits* (REMICs), are ways of pooling mortgages and dividing cash flows into securities with different durations, as discussed in Chapter 9. The expected cash flows of CMOs, for example, can be divided into short and long duration claims on the pool, but of course the weighted average duration of the CMO has to be equal to the aggregate duration of the pool.

Properties of Duration with Bonds

As is clear from Macaulay's definition, one property of the duration of any fixed-income security is that it must be between zero and the security's maturity date since duration is a weighted average payment date. The closed-form duration formula used above can be used to demonstrate some other properties of duration that may help students use this concept to measure the price risk of fixed-income securities and to apply the concept in portfolio management as we discuss below.

A second property of duration can be demonstrated by calculating the duration of a bond with infinite maturity. This number represents the maximum duration or price sensitivity any bond can have at a given yield. Using the duration equation with M equal to infinity, it can be seen that:

$$d_1 = \left| -\frac{1+i}{i} \right|$$

since the last term in the duration formula becomes zero with M infinite and c/i equals p for a perpetuity. The M's in the equation cancel out, leaving the above equation. Using this equation we see that the maximum duration for a bond is the gross yield divided by the yield. For example, at 8 percent the maximum price sensitivity of any bond with any coupon and maturity date is 13.5. This number can therefore be used to check other estimates of duration or as a quick reference when thinking of the price sensitivity of bonds.

A third property of duration can be seen by examining zero coupon bonds, that is by evaluating the formula using c equal to 0. Then it can be seen that:

$$d_1 = |M|$$

since cM equals 0 and for a zero coupon $p = 1/(1+i)^M$, the (1+i)/i terms cancel leaving the expression. As must be true for a zero coupon bond, the duration is equal to the maturity (since that is the only payment date). This defines the upper bound of duration for any security: any bond with coupons will have a lower duration than its maturity date. This feature of coupon bonds limits their ability to manage certain types of interest rate risk, as we discuss below.

How Duration Works

One of the two main applications of duration advocated by users of the concept is to manage *holding period yield* risk. The second major use of duration, *immunization,* is a portfolio concept discussed below. Holding period yield risk is defined as the risk that the future realized yields from investments will have actual returns over the asset holding period which depart from levels expected when the investments were made. In other words, holding period yield risk is the risk that the value of an investment at the end of the asset holding period will not equal the compounded future value of the initial investment at original yields.

For example, assume a fixed income security will produce cash flows of \$1,000 at the end of each year for the next two years. To illustrate how duration works, we show two such cash flows in Figure 19.4, designated as CF(1) and CF(2). The fixed-income security is priced at \$1,735 to yield 10 percent, shown as PV in the figure; the present value consists of the sum of the present value of the two cash flows, \$909 and \$826, the designated PV(1) and PV(2) in the figure. Finally, assume the planned holding period or investment horizon is eight days short of one and one-half years, or 1.48 years. The end of the holding period is shown as H on the horizontal axis in Figure 19.4 and the total future value of the two cash flows at the original yield shown as FV of \$1998.

FIGURE 19.4 How duration works

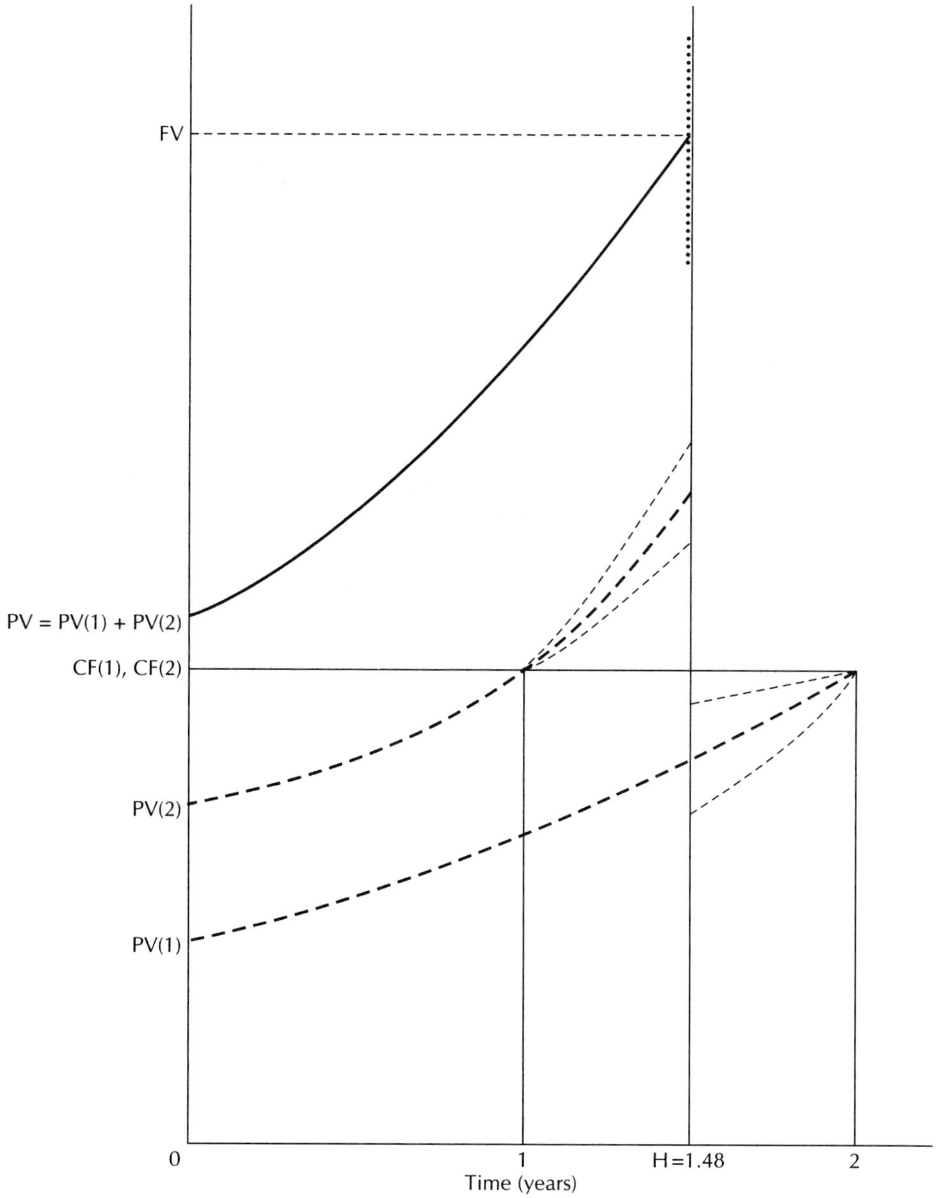

In principle, duration works to reduce holding period interest rate risk by balancing two different effects of interest rate changes on the returns of investments in fixed assets. The two basic sources of holding period interest rate risk are *reinvestment risk* and *capital gain risk*. Reinvestment risk is the risk or uncertainty concerning the future value of investments due to changes in interest earned on reinvested cash flows like coupon income. Capital gains risk is the risk associated with liquidation or sale of assets held at the end of the investment horizon.

Figure 19.4 depicts both reinvestment and capital gains risk from our example. The future value of $1,735 in 1.48 years at 10 percent is $1,998. Reinvestment risk comes from any change in interest rates from the current level of 10 percent which occurs before the first cash flow is received. If rates go down, for example, the first cash flow will produce less future value because it will be reinvested at a lower rate: this is shown by the lower dotted line from the first cash flow. These reduced reinvestment earnings would tend to reduce the future value to the lower end of the heavy dotted line shown at the end of the investment holding period.

Capital gains risk comes from the sale of the asset at the end of the holding period. If rates have gone down relative to initial yield levels as assumed above, the value of the remaining cash flows will increase. This is shown by the upper dotted line that depicts the discounted value at the end of the holding period of remaining fixed income cash flows at the lower yields which would determine the sale or liquidation value of the asset at that time. The higher sale value at lower yields tends to increase future value to the high end of the heavy dotted line.

Duration balances reinvestment and capital gains risk. If rates go down, as discussed in the above example, reinvested cash flows have a lower future value but sales of remaining claims on cash flows have higher values. If the duration of the asset is equal to the holding period, these two value changes will offset each other and the expected future value will be realized even though interest rates have changed. Obviously the opposite balancing will occur if yields rise: at the end of the holding period, higher reinvestment income will offset lower liquidation values. If the duration of the asset equals the holding period, reinvestment risk and capital gains risk are balanced to hedge against changes in expected future values at initial yields.

In the example, the duration of the fixed-income security at the time of purchase is 1.48.[5] We use this simple example of how duration works to observe several important properties of duration when it is used to hedge holding period yield risk. The first important thing to note is that there can only be parallel shifts in the term structure of interest rates if the balancing of future reinvestment income and capital gains changes is to be achieved precisely. If the shift in inter-

[5]This can be calculated using the Macaulay definition

$$1.48 = \frac{.909}{1.735} \times 1 + \frac{.826}{1.735} \times 2$$

from the present value factors and payment periods.

est rates is not parallel, the balancing of changes in holding period return from reinvestment and capital gains will not offset each other exactly or at all.

A second observation in our example is that a precise hedge is very simply achieved by buying discount securities with maturities equal to the holding period, since the duration of discounted securities equals their maturities. In the case where the duration and maturity of a riskless discount bond equals the holding period, there is no reinvestment or capital gains risk at all.

Finally, duration assumes that there is only one interest rate shift: after any interest rate shifts have occurred, the duration will not equal the holding period any more because the duration of assets changes with changes in yields, as can be seen from equation (19.6). The holding period hedge will not be effective after yields change, requiring portfolio rebalancing.

Duration Summary

Interest rate risk for individual fixed-income securities can be assessed with duration. The duration measure is widely used by bond and other fixed income traders. Students of financial institution management must be familiar with the properties of fixed-income securities, including duration. Nonetheless, there are some severe limitations with the use of duration in managing portfolios. We discuss a number of these problems in the next section.

19.3 CRITIQUE OF DURATION AND ALTERNATIVE RISK MEASURES

Duration measures the price sensitivity of fixed-income securities to changes in yields. The first limitation of duration is that it only assesses the risk of a *parallel* movement in interest rates. In other words, the price changes implied by the duration measure only apply if interest rates at all maturities change the same amount. As was discussed extensively in Chapter 13, the term structure of interest rates is constantly shifting, and usually not in a parallel fashion. This means that duration cannot capture one of the essential elements in interest rate risk: changes in term premiums.

A second problem is that duration assesses price sensitivity to the level of interest rates and not to the components of the interest rate level for particular interest rates for securities. Interest rates can change due to changes in any of the components of rates. It is even possible that the default risk component of interest rates could increase at the same time as term premiums decrease such that interest rate levels would not change much but the component parts of interest rates would shift. This in fact is exactly what happened during the Stock Market Crash in 1987 when U.S. Treasury securities increased in value and junk bonds followed the stock market downward.

A theoretical attack on the concept of duration as a risk measure has been made by Roll (1987), who argues that the risk measured by duration cannot be the risk expected by the market in pricing fixed-income securities. Roll shows that in market equilibrium parallel shifts in the term structure cannot be characteristic of expectations by transactors in the market because if parallel shifts were expected, all transactors could plan on making money risklessly by taking advantage of the different convexities (discussed above) of fixed incomes available in the market and setting up riskless hedges. A set of expectations clearing the market according to this arbitrage pricing argument cannot include expectations of the shifts in interest rates that duration measures are intended to protect against.

A major problem with duration, cited by Roll and others, is that it attempts to measure risk with a single number. Since duration is a single risk measure, it cannot capture the shifts in relative prices between bonds and other fixed incomes with different inflation, term, default, and exchange rate risk characteristics. Measuring the sensitivity of fixed-income securities to the total level of yields may not be useful in comparing the riskiness of different fixed-income securities for purposes of portfolio management. In different business environments it may be more likely for one component of interest rates, such as default risk premiums, to change than other components of the level of interest rates. Two bonds that have the same duration may not be equally sensitive to changes in components of the level of interest rates.

Alternative risk measures used with other securities can be estimated and used to measure fixed-income security risks from some of these components of yields if the securities are actively traded and frequent price observations are available. For example, beta coefficients as discussed in Chapter 4 can be estimated for bonds to assess their sensitivity to risks associated with general market conditions, including credit risk. The beta for fixed-income securities could be interpreted as representing uncertainty concerning future cash flows from all sources including default risk.

Arbitrage pricing theory (APT) risk measures (discussed in Chapter 4) can be estimated with fixed income securities as well. For example, this is what Roll (1987) recommends for the management of risks in thrift institutions. Roll suggests estimation of thrift institution share price exposure to APT risk measures to assess their net portfolio exposure to those risks. APT-estimated risk factors have the advantage of being multidimensional, assessing the risk of securities to all the components of yield levels, not just rate levels and market risk premiums. Both CAPM and APT approaches to risk assessment are limited to estimated fixed-income security price risks to general market or economy wide factors.

It may be desirable to look at specific attributes of firms or governments issuing financial claims and relate them to market yield differentials due to default risk or other characteristics of the issuer, like possible calls of convertible securities, which affect fixed-income yields. Many academic studies have assessed the sources of yield differentials on risky bonds from financial data or operating statistics. Fixed-income yield differentials due to financial or other issuer specific characteristics can be estimated using historical data on a sample of yields and financial data for issuers. The resulting statistical relations between financial and other factors can be used to assess the sensitivity of fixed-income yields to changes in those factors and consequently to assess the risk of fixed-income values to changes in firms or governments issuing securities.

Value Adjustments Based on Options

Price sensitivity of fixed-income securities to interest rate changes is only one dimension of the risk-determining values of fixed-income securities acquired by investors or issued by firms raising funds. Other risks are due to default, prepayment, callability of fixed incomes, and other possible influences on future cash flows. These aspects of risk can be analyzed as options. For example, the borrower has the option not to pay a mortgage payment, in effect forcing the lender to buy the house collateral for the amount of the loan balance. Risks like this can be priced with the option pricing techniques discussed in Chapter 21. The value of options important to a given fixed-income security is added or subtracted from the present value of contractual cash flows at riskless rates.

When yields to maturity on fixed-income securities are calculated using option-adjusted values for a fixed-income security, the yields are higher or lower reflecting the risk of decreased or increased value due to the options. For example, the callability feature of bonds represents an option held by the issuer of the bond to buy back at a fixed price (a call option) and hence reduces the value of the fixed income to the owner relative to noncallable issues: callable bond yields are higher than noncallable bonds. The spread between the total yield to maturity and default riskless rate for the same maturity (the Treasury rate) is called the *option-adjusted spread* by fixed income analysts. (See Chapter 2 in Ho (1993) for an application of this analysis to collateralized mortgage obligations.)

Option values affecting fixed-income prices and yields are determined by variables like the value of a bond when converted into stock for a convertible bond or the value of housing used as collateral for mortgages with default risk. Option values are determined not only by the level but the variance of relevant asset prices like the common stock of an issuing firm or housing prices for mortgages. Variables that influence the value of options associated with fixed-income securities are risk factors that cannot be captured in a single interest rate risk measure like duration.

Summary of Duration as an Interest Rate Risk Measure

Duration as a single risk measure for fixed-income securities is flawed. We have discussed how risk may not be single dimensional and duration cannot be a valid risk measure in market equilibrium. Despite these flaws, duration has achieved wide use by fixed-income securities specialists. The application of duration to portfolio management problems represents an improvement over unstructured and atheoretical risk analyses such as the maturity gaps discussed below. Furthermore, careful delineation of how duration works to measure and manage interest rate risk of portfolios makes clear how those risks affect the returns to portfolios and suggests possible alternative ways of measuring and managing those risks. We take up the use of duration in portfolio management in the following section.

19.4 MEASURING THE INTEREST RATE RISK OF A PORTFOLIO

The discussion to this point has concerned measurement of the risk of individual securities. We turn now to measurement of the risk of a portfolio of fixed-income securities. The crudest measure is introduced first: maturity classification and maturity gaps. This method of assessing risk is not very useful but is widely used by management and regulators. For example, maturity gaps for portfolios of banks and savings and loans are parts of mandatory regulatory reports.

Maturity classification of fixed-income securities hardly needs explanation. All assets and liabilities (in a leveraged portfolio) are classified by their maturity. The maturity concept is straightforward: this is when the fixed income principal is finally repaid. In the usual application, a bank or insurance company simply classifies fixed incomes into maturity intervals, such as under three months, three to six months, six months to a year, one to five years, and over five years. The total principal amount in each maturity classification is then computed. Tables of such maturity classifications of assets (and liabilities) are a standard fixture of annual reports and appendixes to regulatory filings for deposit-taking institutions and insurance companies.

Some securities have interest rates that are fixed over some time interval and then are adjusted partially or completely to current levels at what is called the *repricing interval*. The repricing interval can be applied to variable rate financial instruments, like adjustable rate mortgages tied to government interest rates or commercial loans indexed to the prime rate. Maturity gap analysis classifies these assets and liabilities by their repricing interval. Classification of assets (and liabilities) by repricing intervals is more complex than maturity classification because many adjustable rate securities adjust only periodically, and often only partially, to current levels.

An example of a maturity classification is given as Table 19.3 where Panel A lists the assets and liabilities. The amounts of the assets and liabilities in each maturity classification are totaled and shown in Panel B of the table. Maturity gaps are calculated for leveraged portfolios like bank balance sheets as is shown in the line "Maturity Gap" of Panel B of Table 19.3. The maturity gap represents the difference between the principal amounts of assets and liabilities of a given maturity group. The cumulative maturity gap accumulates the maturity gap totals. For example, the table shows positive gaps for under three months and three to six months but a negative gap for six to twelve months. The cumulative gap increases up to six months and is zero for under a year.

The maturity gap schedule as shown does very little to assess the interest rate risk of the portfolio in question. There are several problems with maturity gaps as a risk measurement tool. First, the schedule provides no summary or overall assessment of risk. How much interest rate risk is there in this portfolio and where does the variability in portfolio income come from? Maturity gap schedules do not provide any guide as to how we should interpret the information they contain. Second, the schedule uses principal amounts rather than market values of securities. This distorts the economic significance of changes in current values of assets and liabilities relative to changes in current interest rates.

TABLE 19.3 Maturity Classification

Panel A: Assets and Liabilities on July 12, 1993

ISSUE	*MATURITY*	*PRINCIPAL AMOUNT*
Assets		
T-Bill	August 12, 1993	$2,000,000
T-Bill	November 12, 1993	5,000,000
8 1/2% Note	July, 1997	5,000,000
7 1/2%	November 2001	8,000,000
Liabilities		
3% CD	June 12, 1994	7,000,000
8% Bond	November 2001	8,000,000

Panel B: Maturity Gap of Above Portfolio

	MONTHS TO MATURITY			*YEARS TO MATURITY*	
	< 3	*3 TO 6*	*6 TO 12*	*1 TO 5*	*OVER 5*
Assets	2,000,000	5,000,000		5,000,000	8,000,000
Liabilities			7,000,000		8,000,000
Maturity Gap	2,000,000	5,000,000	(7,000,000)	5,000,000	0
Cumulative Maturity Gap	2,000,000	7,000,000	0	5,000,000	5,000,000

Finally, the schedule accounts for only fixed-income security risks associated with maturity and does not account for the effect of other risk characteristics of fixed-income assets and liabilities, such as the coupon levels of individual securities.

Fixed Income Portfolio Duration Measures

Several alternative portfolio interest rate risk measures are based on duration measures for individual assets as discussed in previous sections. The simplest concept and perhaps most useful measure is the weighted average duration of a portfolio. In forming the portfolio weights, it is important to use the *market* values of securities rather than principal values or book (purchase) values because interest rate sensitivity as measured by duration is relative to current prices, represented by the p term in equation (19.6). The weights used to calculated the weighted-average duration are the percents of total current market value accounted for by individual assets.

The calculation of the weighted average duration for the portfolio shown in Table 19.3 is given in Table 19.4. Panel A of Table 19.4 shows the market values and the durations of each asset and liability in Table 19.3 as calculated using the formula in equation (19.6). Panel A shows the result of calculating the weights of

TABLE 19.4 Calculation of Weighted Average Duration

Panel A: Assets and Liabilities on July 12, 1993

ISSUE	*MATURITY*	*PRINCIPAL AMOUNT*	*MARKET VALUE*	*DURATION*	*PORTFOLIO WEIGHT*
Assets					
T-Bill	Aug 12, 1993	$2,000,000	$1,995,312	.083	.092
T-Bill	Nov 12, 1993	5,000,000	4,949,000	.333	.229
8 1/2% Note	Jul 15, 1997	5,000,000	5,681,250	3.519	.263
7 1/2%	Nov 15, 2001	8,000,000	9,010,000	6.459	.416
Total Assets		$20,000,000	$21,635,562		1.000
Liabilities					
3% CD	June 12, 1994	7,000,000	7,000,000[a]	.917	.452
8% Bond	Nov 15, 2001	8,000,000	8,497,514[a]	6.294	.548
Total Liabilities		$15,000,000	$15,497,574		1.000

[a]The CD is priced at par (current yield 3 percent) and the 8 percent coupon bond at a current yield of 7 percent.

Panel B: Duration Measures of Above Portfolio

Weighted Average Duration for the Above Portfolio of Assets

$$d^A_1 = .092 \times .083 + .229 \times .333 + .263 \times 3.519 + .416 \times 6.459 = 3.696$$

Weighted Average Duration for Above Liabilities

$$d^L_1 = .452 \times .917 + .548 \times 6.294 = 3.864$$

each asset and liability as a percent of the total market value of the portfolio assets and liabilities, respectively. Panel B shows the calculations necessary to compute the weighted average asset and liability durations for the portfolio. The weighted average duration of the assets in the portfolio is 3.696.

Several characteristics of the portfolio duration measures are immediately evident from the example presented in Tables 19.3 and 19.4 and earlier examples illustrating how duration works. First, the sensitivity of the market value of the assets in the portfolio with respect to parallel shifts in term structure has ready interpretation as an interest rate risk measure. If gross yields increase 1 percent, for example, the market value of the assets will fall 4.801 percent. Lower duration portfolios would be less sensitive, and higher duration portfolios more sensitive, to changes in gross yields. Second, if the portfolio is to be liquidated in 4.801 years, the future value of the portfolio is hedged against a one-time parallel shift in interest rates since changes in future value due to reinvestment of coupons and maturing securities and capital gains risk of liquidating securities still in the portfolio will cancel each other.

The weighted average duration risk measure can be readily used to compare portfolio interest rate risks or to assess the impact of changes in portfolio composition. For example, moving 10 percent of the 8-year bonds into the 1-month bills would reduce the weighted average duration by (.1 × .083 – .1 × 6.459) or – .638, reducing the asset portfolio duration to 3.058. The impact of other portfolio changes, including additions and deletions of assets, can be precisely measured in terms of the effect of the strategy on the weighted average duration.

A second characteristic of duration is also apparent from the example. Since duration measures sensitivity to *parallel* changes in the term structure, it will not capture completely changes in the term premium of the Treasury securities listed in the tables unless the interest rates of all maturities change the same percent amount of original gross yields. Parallel shifts in the level of interest rates with term premiums constant has been unusual in most financial markets. More often, short-term and long-term interest rates change in different amounts. Therefore, portfolio duration measures must be considered approximate interest rate risk measures.

A third observation on portfolio duration is that the impact of convexity as discussed in previous sections could materially affect the actual relative change in the value of assets and liabilities with large changes in interest rates, even if the change in gross yields is a constant percentage across the maturity spectrum. Longer duration (and maturity) bonds will have varying convexity depending on coupons and yield levels. The portfolio interest rate risk assessment using weighted average duration may be more misleading the higher the percentage of coupon bonds with varying convexities.

Finally, portfolio duration concepts can be applied to liabilities as well. The portfolio of assets shown in Tables 19.3 and 19.4 can be compared to the interest rate risk of the financial liabilities shown on those tables by computing the weighted average duration of the liabilities. It is clear from Panel B of Table 19.4 that the liabilities are much more interest rate sensitive than the assets. This means that if interest rates changed, the liquidation value of the assets minus the cost of repurchasing liabilities at current values would fall: in other words, the equity of the portfolio would decline.

Immunization of Interest Rate Risk in Leveraged Portfolios

The interest rate risk of assets relative to that of liabilities in leveraged portfolios is a critical risk to most financial institution executives considered as portfolio managers. This is the risk sensitivity of the value of invested equity to changes in interest rates. A bank executive or insurance company official is worried about the value of the equity of the firm—the difference in the value of assets and liabilities. Other portfolio managers, such as private pension funds managers, are also concerned about the interest rate sensitivity of their funded (or unfunded) pension fund liabilities relative to fund assets.

Duration can be used to manage the interest rate risk of equity in leveraged portfolios using the concept of *immunization*. The immunization concept is simply to reduce or eliminate the risk to the equity investment in a portfolio by balancing asset and liability interest rate risks. We illustrate the concepts of measuring relative interest rate risk of assets and liabilities and using duration to immunize a portfolio with the example in Tables 19.3 and 19.4. The example portfolio has a net worth at book value of \$5 million (the book value of assets minus the book value of liabilities, assuming all were purchased or issued at par). The market value of this equity is higher, namely \$6,138,048, representing the current liquidation value of the portfolio. These equity values are used to illustrate the sensitivity of this net investment to interest rate risk.

A commonly used measure of the equity interest rate risk is the *capital* or *equity duration,* which is the weighted average duration using equity (rather than the value of assets or liabilities) as the weights. In the example presented in Table 19.4, we can convert the weighted average asset and liability durations to an equity base by multiplying the weighted average asset duration by 3.525 (total assets \$21,635,562 divided by equity of \$6,138,048) and liabilities by 2.525 (the market value of liabilities divided by equity.) The resulting equity duration is 3.272 ($3.525 \times 3.696 - 2.525 \times 3.864$).

The positive equity duration of 3.272 measures the interest rate sensitivity of the net equity position in the leveraged portfolio. The measure can be interpreted as indicating that if gross interest yields increased (in a parallel fashion) by 1 percent, equity would decline in value 3.272 percent. Use of the equity duration measure is of course subject to all of the qualifications and concerns we previously raised about duration.

The equity duration measure is also used to illustrate how duration in leveraged portfolio management can be used to immunize or balance leveraged portfolios' interest rate risk. The term immunize suggests the protection of the value of equity in a leveraged portfolio from changes in interest rates. This is accomplished by finding a combination of assets and liabilities with durations such that the equity duration is zero.

In the above example, any number of portfolio strategies can be employed to immunize the leveraged portfolio by achieving a capital duration equal to zero. For example, if the liability structure is changed by shifting .241 from the CDs to the bonds, the weighted average liability increases by 3.272 and the capital duration would then be zero.[6] This portfolio shift is only one of many that can be used to "immunize" this portfolio: the asset duration could be lowered by shifting to lower duration assets or the leverage ratios could be changed. The advantage of the immunization concept is that the precise impact of various portfolio strategies can be assessed on the interest rate risk measure.

The effectiveness of duration as an interest rate risk management tool depends on the *level* of interest rates being the single source of systematic risk for both assets and liabilities. If there is only one source of risk, fixed-income asset and liability values and returns are perfectly positively correlated because they all move inversely to the level of interest rates. Given this correlation, perfect matching of

[6]This is calculated by solving the equation $y \times .917 - y \times 6.294 = 1.295$ for y, where y is the percent of shift *to* CDs to accomplish the necessary 1.295 (equals 3.272 capital duration with the old liability structure divided by the 2.525 liability to equity ratio) required increase in the liability duration weighted by equity. Since the answer is – .241, funds should be shifted to the bonds by this amount.

asset and liability variation is possible as discussed in Chapter 18. Immunization is a technique to make sure that the variance or standard deviations of assets and liabilities are matched to immunize interest rate risk. Note, however, that for immunization to work, there must only be one source of risk: the level of interest rates.

Since there are many sources of portfolio risk, the limitations with respect to duration also limit its usefulness in managing or eliminating interest rate risk. In real-life applications, leveraged portfolios have other risks than risk due to parallel shifts in the term structure. In most portfolios, there are risk premium differentials between assets and liabilities as well as term premium differentials. These risk premiums introduce additional sources of risk to the capital in a leveraged portfolio. For example, if a deposit-taking institution assets' default risks increased, their value could fall with a less than complete offsetting increase in liability risks due to deposit insurance. In other words, duration cannot be used to completely immunize capital in leveraged fixed-income portfolios where asset and liability yield spreads include variable term and risk premiums.

Duration Gaps

Another application of the concept of duration is to assess the sensitivity of net interest income to changes in interest rates over some time horizon, typically a year. Toevs (1983) has discussed the measurement and management of interest rate risk to net interest earnings using the concept of *duration gap*. We illustrate the concept of duration gap by assessing the risk of net interest income over a one-year time horizon, as in Toev. We illustrate the application of the duration gap analysis with the same portfolio discussed above.

The portfolio given in Table 19.3 can be projected to produce $384,000 in net interest income over the next year: the calculation is given in Panel A of Table 19.5. Duration gap analysis assumes that all long-term assets and liabilities, those with durations longer than one year, receive or require interest payments that will not change over the one-year "gap period." Duration gap analysis focuses on only those assets and liabilities that mature or reprice within the time period of interest, one year in our example, such that changes in interest rates will produce significant departures from the projected net interest income.

Duration gap analysis as presented by Toevs is applied to deposit-taking institutions. Deposit institutions can be viewed as levered portfolios that contain substantial noninterest earning assets and liabilities. In applying duration gap analysis to deposit-taking institutions to assess the sensitivity of net interest income over a one-year horizon, Toevs' analysis classifies all assets and liabilities into one of three basic types: (1) *not rate sensitive* assets and liabilities, such as fixed and cash assets and demand deposit liabilities; (2) *long-term* assets like fixed-rate mortgages and bonds that have durations longer than one year; and (3) *rate sensitive* assets and liabilities with durations of less than one year.

The duration gap is computed by multiplying the dollar amounts of *rate sensitive* assets and liabilities times the difference in their associated weighted average durations from one and then subtracting the resulting calculation for liabilities from the corresponding asset calculation. The difference between the durations

TABLE 19.5 Calculation

Panel A: Projected Net Interest Income for Portfolio from Table 19.2

PRO FORMA NET INTEREST INCOME	*EARNINGS PROJECTION CALCULATION*	*PROJECTED EARNINGS*
Asset with Duration Under One Year		
T-Bills[a]	.027*$2,000,000	
	+ .031*$5,000,000	+ $209,000
Liabilities with Duration Under One Year		
CD	.03*$7,000,000	– 210,000
Long-Term Assets (duration over one year)		
Note and Bond	.085*$5,000,000	
	+.07*$8,000,000	+ 1,025,000
Long-Term Liabilities (duration over one year)		
Bond	.08*$8,000,000	– 640,000
Projected Net Interest Income		$384,000

[a]Bill yields are based on quoted yields in Table 19.1.

Panel B: Calculation and Use of Duration Gap

ISSUE	*MATURITY*	*MARKET VALUE*	*DURATION*	*WEIGHT*
Assets				
T-Bill	Aug 12, 1993	$1,995,312	.083	.287
T-Bill	Nov 12, 1993	4,949,000	.333	.713
Rate Sensitive Assets		$6,944,312	.261[a]	
Liabilities				
3% CD	June 12, 1994	7,000,000[a]	.917	1.000
Rate Sensitive Liabilities		$7,000,000		

[a].287*.083 + .713*.333

Calculation

DURATION GAP = $6,944,312 × (1 – .261) – $7,000,000 × (1 – .917)

DURATION GAP = $4,548,920.

and unity is used since the focus is on the one-year interest rate sensitivity. An example of the calculation is provided in Panel B of Table 19.5 using the example portfolio and ignoring nonearning assets and liabilities. The duration gap is shown to be $4,548,920.

The duration gap estimates how sensitive net interest income is to changes in interest rates. Using our example from Table 19.5, if all interest rate levels increased by 1 percent or 100 basis points, the duration gap of $4,548,920 indicates that net interest revenue would increase $45,489 (.01 times $4,548,920) and a decrease in interest rate levels would produce a similar decrease. Since estimated net interest income was estimated to be $384,000, a 1 percent change in the level of interest rates would cause an 11.8 change in net interest income ($45,489 divided by $384,000).

A little reflection will reveal how the duration gap measurement assesses the sensitivity of net interest income to interest rate changes. If durations of assets or liabilities are equal to one (using one year as the gap period), changes in interest rates on those items will not affect net interest income. If duration is a little less than one, the difference from unity will be small, as in the CD duration of .917 in the example. Only a short time period at the changed interest rates will affect net interest income. If duration is substantially smaller, as with the rate sensitive asset duration of .261 in the example, the security will have to be rolled over many times in the course of the year and consequently net interest revenue will be greatly affected.

The duration gap calculation measures interest rate sensitivity in a way directly related to reported income. Reported income may be an important focus for financial institution managers. The calculation of duration gap suggests many ways to fine-tune the interest rate sensitivity of short-term net income. For example, by adjusting the amounts and durations of various rate-sensitive assets and liabilities, the duration gap could be set equal to zero. In this case, given the underlying assumptions made when using duration, there is no risk of departures of net interest income from projected values over the planning horizon.

While the duration gap analysis provides a reasonable short-term measure of interest rate sensitivity, concentration on short-term income is not optimal. As we have often discussed, the correct objective function is to maximize the value of the activity. There are two important shortcomings to duration gap, beyond the problems already identified with duration analysis. First, it ignores long-term assets and liabilities. The market values of these are much more sensitive to changes in interest rates and may be a much larger factor influencing the market value of the net worth of a portfolio and should not be ignored even in the short run. Second, there is no analysis of the optimal or efficient amount of interest rate risk exposure in duration gap analysis. As we discuss below, in efficient financial markets there are rewards for bearing interest rate risk. The efficient market return for bearing no risk is the riskless rate.

Managing Interest Rate Risk with Interest Rate Swaps

A hugely important development in the management of interest rate risk has been the development of the so-called *interest rate swap* market. Interest rate swaps are simply the exchanges of interest payment obligations on debt instruments of two financial transactors. A swap can occur, for example, if one corporation has borrowed on a fixed-rate basis by issuing corporate bonds with a fixed coupon rate and a second corporation borrows in the money market by rolling over short-term instruments like commercial paper. The two corporations could "swap" their interest payment obligations: the second corporation would borrow in the short-term market and pay the first corporation the coupon rate on the bond minus the current rate on short-term instruments, or receive the difference from the first corporation if the short-term rate is below the coupon rate, effectively paying the coupon rate for its funds. The first corporation is effectively paying the short-term interest rate since it pays its coupon interest and receives or pays the difference from the short-term rate.

Interest rate swaps represent a simple exchange of interest paying obligations between two borrowers. Why does this make sense? The question has a simple answer and a more complex answer. The simple answer is that interest rate swaps can be used to match asset and liability interest rate variability and reduce risk from variance in earnings. For example, if the corporation with the bond had short-term assets and the corporation borrowing short had long-term assets, the swap would assist each in reducing net interest or return variability. Interest rate swaps are a widely used interest rate risk management technique.

A more profound question asks why there should be any increase in economic efficiency from reductions in interest rate risk through the use of interest rate swaps. Borrowers can simply issue fixed or variable interest rate liabilities directly. Moreover, economy wide financial assets and liability values cancel each other so there is no net gain to the economy from interest risk management. The total supply of long-term and short-term interest rate instruments is not changed by the swap. Where does the value in swaps come from? The answer to this question is elusive but must be that value produced by swaps comes from removing inefficiencies in the market. Analysts argue that the risk premiums on difference classes of borrowers may depart from equilibrium levels such that the long and short borrowers in the above example may face relative risk premiums on their short- and long-term borrowings which create an advantage to the swap.

19.5 MEASUREMENT AND MANAGEMENT OF NONINTEREST PORTFOLIO RISK

The discussion to this point has concerned interest rate risk viewed as a single source of portfolio risk. As we have stressed many times, discount rates used to price securities have many components and thinking of discount rates, including yields to maturity used to price fixed-income securities, as a single factor of risk is too simple. This section explores ways to measure multifactor interest rate risk and ways to manage the portfolio risks discussed in Chapter 18, such as credit and currency risks.

A common and important first step to assess exposure to portfolio risks other than interest rate risks is simply to assess the degree of concentration of assets (and liabilities) with exposure to those types of risks. Classification and calculating the degree of concentration to portfolio risks are used by many portfolio managers and are required, for example by deposit-institution regulators for commercial banks and the securities laws for mutual funds. The goal of measuring asset concentration to specific risks is to ensure efficient levels of diversification in the sense of obtaining the maximum return given market expectations and evaluations of risk premiums associated with exposure to risk factors.

Reports measuring diversification require classification of assets (and, if relevant, liabilities) by the sources or types of risk of concern to managers and/or priced by the market. For example, credit risk is assumed to be highly correlated among firms in the same industry. Political risk, consisting of seizure of property or limitations on payments of income to owners or lenders, is supposed to be associated with specific regions or sovereign governments. Many countries and firms in those countries or regions may be subject to risks associated with specific products or commodities, such as oil. Currency risk is clearly highly related to the currency denomination and region originating assets. For that reason, many financial institutions calculate industry, country, and other breakdowns of loans and other assets.

As an example of types of risk, Table 19.6 reproduces tables from Bank of America's 1992 annual report. Panel A gives the breakdown of Bank of America's loans by type of borrower, such as consumer real estate or commercial and industrial loans. These data allow analysts to assess the exposure to credit risk associated with businesses and government versus consumers. Panel B provides the geographical breakdown of real estate construction loans, reflecting the credit risk associated with regional variations in real estate values and demand for residential and commercial space. Panel C shows the distribution of Bank of America's international assets, allowing the assessment of Bank of America's exposure to risks associated with economic and political risks in those regions. Panel D gives highly leverage transactions (HLT) loans by industry. The report contains other breakdowns of assets as well.

Diversification is an extremely important risk control measure, fundamental to modern financial analysis of the measurement and management of portfolio risks and returns. Tables such as those discussed above can measure the degree of diversification against a variety of risks. Effective diversification minimizes returns for given level of risk or return variability. The effects of diversification depend on not only the variability of returns but on correlations between returns on individual and classes assets. We have discussed common or systematic sources of risk, representing high correlation between asset returns and risk factors, and unsystematic, or uncorrelated, sources of return risks. The appearance of diversification by low concentration in many assets may in fact disguise underdiversification to some systematic portfolio risks.

A clear example of the misleading appearance of diversification in asset distribution tables is the experience of banks in the 1980s when loan losses drove many banks, including Bank of America, to the brink of extinction. In the early 1980s Bank of America showed broad loan diversification into at least four areas: less developed country (LDC) loans, commercial real estate loans, agricultural loans, and energy related loans (oil shipping and exploration). Declining inflation and reduced money supply growth around the world hit energy and other commodity markets hard. Reduced growth or reduction in prices of energy and commodities increased the risk to LDC commodity exporters, agricultural producers, and energy producers and shippers. These events influenced commercial real estate values in many regions, including Texas, through reductions in demand affected by those industries. The broad exposure to a common risk factor, global

TABLE 19.6 Breakdown of Assets reported by Bank of America, December 31, 1992

Panel A: Loans

(IN MILLIONS)	*DECEMBER 31* *1992*	*1991*
Domestic		
Consumer:		
Secured by first mortgages on residential properties	**$28,390**	$18,897
Installment[a]	**16,663**	10,961
Credit card	**8,306**	7,712
Individual lines of credit[a]	**8,347**	5,546
Other[a]	**354**	181
	62,060	43,297
Commercial:		
Commercial and industrial	**21,632**	13,831
Loans secured by real estate	**9,912**	5,309
Construction and development loans secured by real estate	**5,837**	3,793
Financial institutions	**2,017**	1,427
Agricultural	**1,704**	1,124
Lease financing	**1,889**	779
Loans for purchasing or carrying securities	**987**	216
Other	**1,360**	497
	45,338	26,976
	107,398	70,273
Foreign		
Commercial and industrial	**10,338**	9,538
Governments and official institutions	**3,513**	3,557
Banks and other financial institutions	**1,855**	2,080
Other	**1,419**	920
	17,125	16,095
	$124,523	$86,368

[a]Installment loans, individual lines of credit, and other consumer loans included the following aggregate amounts which were collateralized by residential real estate: $13,870 million and $9,281 million at December 31, 1992 and 1991, respectively.

Panel B: Domestic Construction and Development Loans
by Geographic Area and Project Type

DECEMBER 31, 1992 (IN MILLIONS)

	SUBDIVISION	*OFFICE*	*RETAIL*	*APARTMENT & CONDOMINIUM*	*LIGHT INDUSTRY*	*HOTEL*	*OTHER*	*TOTAL*
California	$1,111	$810	$452	$259	$229	$167	$317	$3,345[a]
Washington	221	203	237	136	65	39	88	989
Nevada	55	41	31	39	12	—	10	188
Arizona	86	3	82	19	2	31	—	223
Oregon	51	38	23	14	8	2	20	156
Pennsylvania	—	189	—	3	—	—	—	192
Other[b]	96	83	130	59	29	24	323	744
	$1,620	$1,367	$955	$529	$345	$263	$758	$5,837

DECEMBER 31, 1991 (IN MILLIONS)

	SUBDIVISION	*OFFICE*	*RETAIL*	*APARTMENT & CONDOMINIUM*	*LIGHT INDUSTRY*	*HOTEL*	*OTHER*	*TOTAL*
California	$1,001	$743	$217	$110	$139	$64	$354	$2,628[a]
Washington	212	112	84	128	17	10	53	616
Nevada	2	—	12	—	—	—	—	14
Arizona	17	4	—	—	—	—	—	21
Oregon	1	29	16	50	—	4	13	113
Pennsylvania	—	133	—	—	—	—	—	133
Massachusetts	—	80	—	—	—	—	—	80
Other[b]	—	95	22	10	39	22	—	188
	$1,233	$1,196	$351	$298	$195	$100	$420	$3,793

[a]Approximately 60 percent and 75 percent of Construction and Development loans in California at December 31, 1992 and 1991, respectively, were secured by properties in the following Southern California counties: Los Angeles, Orange, San Bernardino, San Diego, Riverside, and Ventura.

[b]No other state individually exceeded 2 percent of total construction and development loans.

TABLE 19.6 (*continued*)

Panel C: Distribution of International Assets

(IN MILLIONS)	YEAR	TOTAL ASSETS AT DECEMBER 31	GROSS INCOME	INCOME (LOSS) BEFORE INCOME TAXES	NET INCOME (LOSS)
		YEAR ENDED DECEMBER 31			
Domestic	1992	$154,667	$12,613	$2,101	$1,204
	1991	93,874	9,710	1,233	714
	1990	88,351	9,429	1,495	1,228
Europe, Middle East, and Africa	1992	8,517	1,160	75	71
	1991	6,920	1,088	129	95
	1990	7,702	1,243	47	9
Asia	1992	10,780	931	208	151
	1991	8,499	920	133	87
	1990	8,243	962	40	(2)
Latin America and the Caribbean	1992	5,373	474	313	75
	1991	4,935	422	406	246
	1990	5,007	529	(190)	(126)
Canada	1992	1,309	84	(15)	(9)
	1991	1,281	128	(28)	(18)
	1990	1,425	160	7	6
Total Foreign	1992	25,979	2,649	581	288
	1991	21,635	2,558	640	410
	1990	22,377	2,894	(96)	(113)
BankAmerica Corporation	1992	180,646	15,262	2,682	1,492
	1991	115,509	12,268	1,873	1,124
	1990	110,728	12,323	1,399	1,115

Panel D: HLT Loan Oustanding by Industry

(DOLLAR AMOUNTS IN MILLIONS)	DECEMBER 31, 1992 OUTSTANDINGS	DECEMBER 31, 1992 % OF HLT PORTFOLIO	DECEMBER 31, 1991 OUTSTANDINGS	DECEMBER 31, 1991 % OF HLT PORTFOLIO
Entertainment/media	$221	9%	$299	17%
Retail/wholesale-drug/grocery	220	9	135	8
Primary metals	219	9	13	—
Cable television	190	7	145	8
Textiles	175	7	144	8
Construction	152	6	49	3
Forest products	148	5	154	9
Truck and rail transportation	128	5	103	6
Other[a]	1,119	43	742	41
	$2,572[b]	100%	$1,784	100%

[a]No industry concentrations greater than 5 percent, except for consumer products totaling $88 million at December 31, 1991.

[b]Excludes HLT loan outstandings that had an aggregate carrying value prior to reclassification to assets pending disposition of $227 million. These HLT loan outstandings, which were primarily acquired in the Merger and identified for accelerated disposition, are recorded in assets pending disposition at their estimated NRVs.

SOURCE: Annual Report 1992, Bank America Corp.

reduction in inflation rates, was obscured by the apparent differences in these classifications.

Diversification by lending institutions can be achieved in the selection of loans made, but often industry specialization or geographical concentration makes diversification difficult for some credit institutions to capitalize on a comparative advantage in specific markets. The effect of inadequate diversification can be most severe for smaller, highly focused, credit-granting institutions. A number of means are available to diversify under these circumstances as discussed in Chapter 8. A primary means is to *participate* loans or credits or by *selling* parts of loans or dividing interest in credits. Financial institutions can originate underdiversified credits but achieve effective diversification by entering into participations for loans originated by and loans made by other financial institution portfolios.

Alternative Portfolio Risk Measures

Classification of portfolio assets and liabilities according to region or industry runs the danger of overlooking market-wide sources of risk to apparently different classes of assets, as in the preceding example: exposure to the risks of deflation. For assets and liabilities with active markets and consequently frequent price quotations, risk exposure to common factors in terms of correlations can be estimated statistically. We have discussed two such risk assessment methods based on correlations of returns to systematic risks factors.

Market risk for individual securities can be evaluated by statistically correlating historical asset returns with measures of the market return, producing the well-known *beta* coefficient. Individual asset measures are weighted to produce portfolio betas. Similarly, *arbitrage pricing theory* (APT) risk factors discussed in Chapter 4 can be estimated by estimating the correlations of asset returns to several risk factors. Estimated beta coefficients, APT, or other risk exposures can be used by portfolio managers to classify assets by risk exposure. Portfolio sensitivities to the risk factor or factors can be computed as the weighted average of the risk measures of the individual assets in the portfolio.

Significant obstacles to assessing the risks of assets and portfolios can exist when the assets and liabilities in the portfolio do not trade in active markets. Many financial institutions like banks viewed as leveraged portfolios have substantial investments and raise substantial funds in nontraded or thinly traded financial instruments. Risk assessment in terms of a portfolio's exposure to risk factors can often proceed but risk assessment can be difficult and imprecise. Two basic methods of risk assessment using risk factor models can be employed to assess the risk of portfolios of nontraded assets: (1) identifying comparables of nontraded assets among traded assets; and (2) allocating risks of traded equity in leveraged portfolios, like financial institutions, to balance sheet composition. We discuss both methods below.

The first method identifies correspondences between risk sensitivities between assets that trade actively in financial markets and the nontraded or thinly traded assets or liabilities in a portfolio. For example, the risk characteristics of thrift institutions' holdings of nonmarketable mortgages can be reasonably compared to General National Mortgage Association (GNMA or Ginnie Mae) securities of similar characteristics such as average coupon interest rate and maturity. APT risk factor weights estimated for Ginnie Maes could be used to assess the exposure to those risks in nontraded mortgages in a thrift portfolio.

A second method of assessing risks of portfolios containing nontraded or thinly traded assets and liabilities focuses on the net impact of the asset–liability mix on the risk of the traded equity in a financial institution like a bank or thrift. This method allocates those risks, for example the APT risks associated with a bank stock returns, to book measures of asset allocation using similar institutions over time or very long time series for an institution with frequent reporting of financial characteristics. For example, Dietrich (1989) allocates bank market risk to the APT risk factors and asset and liability composition of banks by statistically estimating the relation of monthly stock returns of many banks to the interaction of bank balance sheet items with APT risk factors. These results can be used to derive the effect individual assets and liabilities contribute to risk and the estimates then applied to individual bank balance sheets to estimate the sources of their net exposure to the APT risk factors.

Given estimated risk exposure of portfolios, managers can assess the impact of changes in portfolio composition on overall portfolio risk. For example, if an unacceptable exposure to the term premium portion of APT risk is found, portfolio adjustments to assets with less term structure risk, or matching liabilities with similar amounts of the same risk, can reduce the net risk exposure to that factor. Beta and APT risk measures, and other risk factors that may be relevant for financial institutions with specific risk concerns, such as specific industry risk or regional risk, allow financial institution managers to assess the impact of changes in portfolio composition on net exposure to risks.

As an example of the use of risk factors to adjust risk exposure, assume that a bank has net term structure risk of 1.5, average bank short-term assets have a risk factor of .1, and commercial and industrial loans have a risk factor estimated at 3. Shifting 10 percent of the banks portfolio from loans to short-term bonds would reduce its exposure to term structure risk by .29 to 1.21 (1.5 minus the effect of the change, $+ .1 \times .1 - .1 \times 3$). An alternative strategy could increase the amount of liabilities with more term structure risk offsetting the asset exposure to this risk, thereby reducing the net exposure to this type of risk.

The advantage of a multiple risk factor approach over a single risk measure like beta coefficients or duration is the increased realism of the risk environment that exists in the economy. A complexity is that with multiple risk factors many portfolio adjustments may be necessary to fine tune overall portfolio exposure to risks. For example, in the above case, if short-term bonds, commercial and industrial loans, and other assets have varying exposure to other risk factors of interest, changes in the portfolio to manage one risk, such as term structure risk, will affect exposure to other risks, like default risk premiums.

Liquidity Risk

The presence of liquidity risk in a portfolio, the risk from the inability to easily buy or sell assets or issue or redeem liabilities quickly to raise unexpected cash needs, is usually easy to identify. There is liquidity risk in a portfolio that contains assets and liabilities for which there is no market or the markets are thin and hence can only be sold at substantial discounts in short time frames. Most portfolios can be easily be classified by the proportion or amounts of assets and liabilities that are readily marketable in the case of unexpected cash needs.

It is more difficult to assess the effect of liquidity risk on the economic value of a portfolio. For thinly traded assets for which there are dealers, the economic impact of liquidity risk can be estimated by using bid and ask spreads available for transactions in the thinly traded assets. In this case, the estimated impact on portfolio value is the difference between the value of assets at the bid and the ask. This differential will be the effect of liquidity risk.

Many financial institutions and investment portfolios contain contractual assets and liabilities between two parties for which there is no market at all, for examples specific loans, demand deposits, and insurance policies. All of these contracts can produce unexpected demands for cash in the form of defaults on loans, deposit outflows, and policy claims. Liquidity risk is the cost of meeting these cash needs. To the extent that cash needs must be met from liquidation of nonmarketable contracts, the cost of liquidity can be estimated as the potential discounts from contract value that it would take to induce another (legally authorized) financial institution to take over these contractual business assets, such as loans, loan servicing, or asset management contracts, or the premiums over book amounts paid to financial institutions like insurance companies to assume responsibility for liabilities like insurance policies.

The potential costs of liquidating thinly traded and nonmarketable assets and liabilities is one way to assess liquidity risk. Another approach to liquidity risk is to assess the probabilities that cash needs will reach levels where liquidation costs become significant. This approach requires estimating probabilities of various levels of future cash needs under a variety of asset and liability valuation circumstances: for example, the probability that loan failures could require liquidation of nonmarketable assets to meet expected deposit withdrawals. Computer simulation of cash flow needs is used by many financial institutions to assess the probability of various levels of future cash needs. We discuss the simulation approach in the next section.

Tools available to manage liquidity risk are limited to several basic methods. Increasingly important, especially in the mortgage market, are asset exchanges, whereby illiquid assets (e.g., mortgages) are exchanged for marketable assets (e.g., mortgage-backed securities). Many thrift institutions originate many more mortgages than they hold in their portfolios, placing their mortgages with securities originators such as the Federal National Mortgage Association (FNMA or Fannie Mae) who issue mortgage-backed securities. For tax or portfolio balance reasons, many institutions then turn around and buy mortgage-backed securities, which are liquid, when of course they could have held their mortgages in their portfolios in the first place. What they have achieved with this asset exchange is liquidity. Thrifts and other mortgage originators are also interested in the mortgage servicing rights associated with the mortgages they originate, rights that are a valuable (and somewhat liquid) asset that does not show up on the balance sheet.

Asset exchanges have become particularly widespread among certain classes of consumer lenders. Not all credit originations are for portfolio investment.

Finance companies and banks use illiquid credit-card and automobile loan receivables to create asset-backed securities which are very marketable. To the extent that these institutions buy back asset-backed securities, the costs of securities origination and fees are the costs of removing the illiquidity from the originated assets.

Currency Risks

Currency risks are present whenever there are assets or liabilities that are denominated in foreign currencies. Since short-term currency risk in major currencies exposure can be readily hedged, as discussed in the next chapter, the economic effect of that risk can be assessed as the cost of hedging. For longer term currency risk or currency risk from small country currencies for which no markets exist, currency risk again can only be roughly estimated. It is possible, using currency swaps or related contracts, to exchange currency risk with other financial transactors exposed to the opposite risks. For example, one portfolio manager may need South African rands to pay contractual cash flows while another is earning rands on asset investments and does not need them. These two parties can *swap* their exchange needs, just as with interest rate swaps. The cost of currency exposure then becomes the cost of arranging the swap contract and the currency risks reduced to those of nonperformance on the contract. As with interest rate swaps, currency swaps do not appear on the balance sheet but are footnoted in the financial statements.

19.6 SIMULATION AS AN ASSET–LIABILITY MANAGEMENT ASSESSMENT TOOL

Duration and alternative risk measures discussed to this point attempt to quantify the effect of portfolio risks on the sensitivity of risk factors. As examples, portfolio duration measures sensitivity to interest rate risk and beta coefficients to market risk. An alternative technique, widely used by deposit-taking institutions (partially at the insistence of regulators), is computer simulation of the effect of alternative scenarios on the performance and value of portfolios or balance sheets.

We illustrate the use of *asset–liability models* based on computer simulations with the data from the example in Table 19.3. Simulation models can be more or less detailed. We attempt only to illustrate the use of the technique here with a simple example employing three scenarios: (1) generally falling yields, (2) generally increasing yields, and (3) increasing long-term yields with short rates constant (that is, a widening spread between long and short rates). The results of the simulation are provided in Table 19.7.

The format and results reported in asset–liability simulations will depend on the complexity of the computer model and the questions of interest to management. The example in Table 19.7 illustrates the effect of the three interest rate scenarios on net interest income for the next twelve months and the value of the period ending portfolio. The projected income added to ending portfolio value is

TABLE 19.7 Asset–Liability Simulation

	SCENARIOS AND MARKET VALUE AT END OF ONE YEAR					
	(1)	*MARKET VALUE*	*(2)*	*MARKET VALUE*	*(3)*	*MARKET VALUE*
Assets						
1-month T-Bill	1.70%	2,000,000	3.70%	1,993,609	2.70%	1,995,311
4-month T-Bill	2.11%	4,965,173	4.11%	4,933,037	3.61%	4,940,994
8.5 U.S. Treasury 1997	3.71%	5,670,867	5.71%	5,377,923	5.71%	5,377,923
7.5 U.S. Treasury 2001	4.58%	9,436,760	6.58%	8,421,560	6.58%	8,421,560
Liabilities						
1-Year CD	2.00%	7,068,627	4.00%	6,932,692	2.00%	7,068,627
8% Bond	6.00%	8,893,181	8.00%	8,000,000	8.00%	8,000,000
Market Value		6,110,992		5,793,436		5,667,160

	PRO FORMA INCOME STATEMENT FOR SCENARIOS		
	(1)	*(2)*	*(3)*
Income from bills	157,817	261,183	226,175
Cost of CDs	(204,190)	(215,810)	(204,190)
Interest on bonds	1,046,958	1,069,716	1,061,525
Interest on debt	(640,000)	(640,000)	(640,000)
Net interest income	360,585	475,089	443,510
Income + Net Market Value	6,471,576	6,268,525	6,110,669
Portfolio Return	10.064%	6.611%	3.926%

used to compute a one-year rate of return shown in the last line of the table. The potential return varies from 3.926 percent to 10.064 percent.

Projections in the simulation summarized in Table 19.7 assume that the short-term assets and liabilities are rolled over and that coupon interest is invested at the assumed short-term interest rates. Only three scenarios are evaluated. The complexity of an asset–liability computer simulation model, in terms of assumptions made concerning the application of cash flows, reinvestment policy, the number of scenarios, and the number of time periods used, can be more or less complex depending on how management intends to use the analysis.

Our example uses a small number of possible interest rate scenarios to illustrate asset–liability simulation models clearly. A widely used alternative simulation approach is to use hundreds of interest rate scenarios derived from statistical distributions of different interest rate developments. The interest rate scenarios in these large simulations, so-called *Monte Carlo* simulations because the computer simulates taking many interest rate scenarios selected as if they were where the ball landed with multiple turnings of a roulette wheel, can produce statistical distribution on the outcomes of concern to asset–liability managers. Statistical results like the mean return on period-ending equity, as in our example, as well as the variance of that return can be calculated. Simulation results can be more complex, for example calculating return variability over a number of time periods and keeping track of the incidence of insolvency (equity return is minus 100 percent).

Possible interest rate developments considered in a simulation can be based on analysis of likely future long- and short-term interest rate relationships and risk premiums, or they can be based on historical analysis of those relationships. Analysts have used many different models for assessing possible future interest rates in Monte Carlo simulations. At different points in the business cycle, simulation models model the effects of current management concerns about future interest rates. For example, when short-term interest rates appear to be low by historical standards, management may be most concerned with the impact of different patterns of increasing rates in the future.

Applying asset–liability models to deposit-taking institutions is a consulting service offered widely by specialists as regulators have stressed interest rate risk in their examinations. Complex models can capture the risk of portfolio performance to more than just interest rate risk. Customer behavior, as in deposit withdrawals and loan defaults, can also be modeled in computer simulations. These analyses are widely used by financial institution managers.

19.7 CRITIQUE OF VALUE PRODUCTION IN HEDGING INTEREST RATE RISK

Measurement of portfolio risks for a wide range of risks introduced in the previous chapter have been reviewed above. We discussed management of portfolio risks using changes in portfolio composition to accomplish risk reduction within the balance sheet. We described interest-rate and currency swaps as a way for two (or more) financial market participants to use each others' balance sheets as a means for reducing portfolio risk. We now address important questions about value production possibilities from portfolio risk reducing strategies.

The first point to note is that in completely efficient financial markets, portfolio risk management activities should produce no value. As persuasively argued by Black (1975), asset and liability prices and yields will reflect risk adjustments in an efficient market. Since managers are simply producing portfolios of financial instruments, in efficient markets no value can be produced by particular combinations of these assets. Sophisticated investors can always combine these same instruments or perfect substitutes in the same combinations themselves.

Black's discussion has major implications for the way financial institution managers should spend their time. Efficiency of the market and the fact that asset prices and yields reflect all information available to the market imply that management cannot add value by forecasting activity or managing liquidity—they cannot beat the market. The best estimates of future values are impounded in current market prices: forecasting is a waste of time. Liquidity can always be purchased in the overnight market at rates reflecting the best information about future short- and long-term interest rates and the evolution of the economy. Liquidity management produces no excess return either.

No manager of a financial institution or a portfolio accepts the implications of Black's discussion of funds management in efficient markets at face value. This book clearly cannot advocate Black's position either, since reading it would also be a waste of time by his reasoning. The importance of Black's analysis and efficient market analysis in general is to force decision makers to determine what market inefficiencies produce the value they identify as the basis for strategies. Managers must show rigorously why there is persistence in value-producing opportunities over the time frame needed to profit from them. Efficient market analysis is a benchmark against which to assess the value of a business strategy or plan.

The essence of efficient market analysis is that no returns above the riskless rate can be earned without bearing risk. This chapter has introduced a number of risk management techniques. It is clear that financial institution and portfolio managers should be aware of how much risk they expose their portfolios or balance sheets to. It is not the case that management's objective should be to minimize or eliminate risk. Management's objective is to maximize owners' wealth, which means taking advantage of those investment opportunities that have higher expected returns than are justified by their risk (and borrowing with lower costs than the liabilities' risks suggest).

Risk measurement and management are common in managing financial institutions. One market inefficiency possibly justifying risk management in the face of the efficient market critiques discussed above is that insolvency and bankruptcy costs are not priced in the market. For example, in the case of deposit-taking institutions, the franchise value from customer relationships and other valuable assets of the firm cannot be readily transferred in competitive markets due to regulation and other factors. Value may be produced by managing risks of insolvency to preserve franchise value.

A related argument explaining risk management activities of financial institutions and portfolio managers is that owners of financial institutions do not exercise control or are worried about their managers' job effectiveness. Managers take actions to protect their jobs as portfolio managers and manage risks to reduce the probability of insolvency causing them to lose their jobs. Managers may be more productive if their fear of losing their jobs is reduced, allowing them to concentrate on value-producing activities in offering financial services. Hedging activities can reduce risks from offering financial services like credit creating balance sheet risk exposure as a byproduct.

We cannot resolve the issue of the importance of risk-reducing strategies in value creation but we can summarize what we know for sure. First, risk bearing is the only way to earn excess returns over longer time horizons. Second, intelligent management must be aware of the risks created by their portfolio decisions, even if they take no action to reduce those risks. Finally, risk measurement and analysis of projected returns is necessary in order to identify value-producing opportunities stemming from market inefficiencies or imperfections.

19.8 SUMMARY

Financial institution managers are often managers of portfolios, either directly or indirectly, through the effect of their decisions on the balance sheets of financial institutions. We present ways of measuring interest rate risk of fixed-income securities and discuss methods used to manage exposure of portfolios to interest rate risk. We discuss other economic risk measures and portfolio risks like credit risk, liquidity risk, and currency risk. Asset–liability management models based on computer simulation are reviewed as an alternative portfolio risk assessment tool. The chapter ends by discussing the value-producing potential of risk management in efficient markets and concludes that value production comes from market inefficiencies. To identify market imperfections and value creation opportunities, as well as avoid insolvency, risk measurement and management is an essential management activity.

DISCUSSION QUESTIONS AND EXERCISES

1. Assume that three fixed-income securities have elasticities with respect to gross yield changes of .5, 3, and 10 and that yields are currently 10 percent. How much would each price change given a 50 basis point change in yields?
2. What is the duration of the current longest term U.S. Treasury? How much should its price change with a 50 basis point move in yields?
3. Calculate the monthly payment of a four-year car loan (with monthly payments) at 5 percent. What is its duration? Compare this duration to that of similar loans of three years and loans at 3 percent. Explain the differences you find.
4. Describe the cash flows associated with a pension fund liability for a worker scheduled to retire in fifteen years and to live fifteen years in retirement. What are the interest rate risks associated with funding this liability? How could they be hedged or managed?
5. Using the data in Table 19.3 and following tables, how could you eliminate the interest rate risk to the equity in the portfolio? Described several strategies.
6. Calculate the duration of a five-year Treasury note using all three methods discussed in the text. Contrast the answers and attempt to explain any differences.
7. What sources of liquidity risk does a casualty insurance company face? How could this risk be measured? How could they be managed?
8. Using Federal Reserve *Bulletins* or other sources of historical interest rate data for U.S. Treasuries, examine the term structure of interest rates at six-month intervals over several years in the past. How does the term structure shift over that period? How unreasonable is the assumption of parallel shifts in the term structure implicit in duration analysis?
9. Savings and loans are said to have more interest rate risk than commercial banks. Explain whether this is true using the interest rate risk concepts presented in this chapter.
10. Estimate the duration gap using the tables in the annual report for a bank or thrift, assuming average durations

for classes of securities and simple assignments of assets and liabilities into non–interest rate sensitive, rate sensitive, and long-term. What does this quantity measure? What does it mean for 100 basis moves in interest rates? Why might it not be an accurate forecaster of these effects?

REFERENCES

BIERWAG, GERALD O. 1987. *Duration Analysis*. Cambridge, Mass.: Ballinger Publishing.

BLACK, FISCHER. 1975. "Bank Funds Management in an Efficient Market," *Journal of Financial Economics,* 2 (4), pp. 323–339.

CHUA, JESS H. 1984. "A Closed-Form Formula for Calculating Bond Duration," *Financial Analysts Journal,* 40 (3), pp. 76–78.

DIETRICH, J. KIMBALL. 1989. "Bank Balance Sheet Composition and Stock Market Return Sensitivity to Macroeconomic Risk Factors," Discussion paper, University of Southern California.

FABOZZI, FRANK J. and T. DESSA FABOZZI. 1989. *Bond Markets, Analysis, and Strategies*. Englewood Cliffs, N.J.: Prentice Hall.

HO, THOMAS S. Y. (editor) 1993. *Fixed-Income Portfolio Management: Issues and Solutions,* Homewood, Ill.: Business One Irwin.

HOMER, SIDNEY and MARTIN L. LEIBOWITZ. 1972. *Inside the Yield Book*. Englewood Cliffs, N.J.: Prentice Hall.

MACAULAY, FREDERICK. 1938. *Some Theoretical Problems Suggested by the Movement of Interest Rates, Bond Yields, and Stock Prices in the U.S. Since 1856*. New York: National Bureau of Economic Research.

ROLL, RICHARD. 1987. "Managing Risk in Thrift Institutions: Beyond Duration Gap," October, John E. Anderson Graduate School of Management at the University of California–Los Angeles, Discussion Paper #13-88.

TOEVS, A. L. 1983. "Gap Management: Managing Interest Rate Risk in Banks and Thrifts," Federal Reserve Bank of San Francisco *Economic Review,* Spring, pp. 20–35.

CHAPTER

20

Forward and Futures Contracts and Portfolio Risks

Introduction

Portfolio risks result from asset and liability composition. Managers who can answer the following questions may hedge these risks in financial markets.

- How can the risks introduced in the previous chapters be managed by using forward and futures markets?
- What terminology and language are spoken in discussing the world of risk reducing products?
- How can value be created for investors by managing risk?
- What instruments and techniques exist to deal with the large variations in interest rate, exchange, and other risks?

This chapter provides answers to these questions by introducing forward and futures contracts as a means of managing asset value risks off the balance sheet. This contrasts with the approach taken in the previous chapter of managing portfolio or balance sheet risks by adjusting the composition of assets and/or liabilities.

The chapter begins by introducing terminology and concepts essential to describing forward and futures contracts. The basic economics of hedging is explained next, followed by the factors determining the relationships between current and future expected prices and the prices of futures and forward contracts. Finally, questions of the value produced by these instruments are raised. In today's markets, managers of financial institutions must be solidly grounded in the basics of these important instruments.

20.1 DESCRIPTION OF FORWARD AND FUTURES CONTRACTS

A forward contract is an agreement to buy or sell something at a future date for a price agreed upon now. These contracts differ from *cash* or *spot* purchases or sales for immediate delivery or delivery within a brief settlement period. Futures contracts are essentially the same but differ in ways we will discuss later. Futures and forward contracts have existed throughout recorded history. Recently, however, financial futures and forward contracts have mushroomed in importance so that the most heavily traded contract on the Chicago Board of Trade (CBOT), where historically agricultural contracts like wheat and soybeans dominated trading, is the long-term U.S. government bond futures contract. This section introduces terminology and price quotations on futures and forward contracts for financial instruments.

As we discuss in detail in subsequent sections, the economic value in futures and forward contracts is that they may allow holders of assets or issuers of liabilities to manage the risks to changes in their value. These contracts can be used to offset some or all of the changes in financial instruments' values due to their sensitivity to prices, interest rates, or the value of foreign currencies, thereby reducing the variability in the value of portfolios.

Reduction or elimination of the risk to the value of assets and/or liabilities of interest to financial decision makers is called *hedging*. The previous chapter discussed risk hedging strategies based on portfolio or balance sheet composition. Hedging strategies discussed in this chapter take place off the balance sheet and involve financial contracts with other firms or individuals.

Futures and forward contracts obligate one party to buy or take delivery of financial instruments or commodities at some time point in the future and the other party to sell or deliver those items according to very specific contract provisions. The basic difference between forward and futures contracts is that forward contracts are bilateral contracts between two firms or individuals, so-called counterparties to the contract. Futures contracts are standardized contracts that trade on futures exchanges, and the exchange or clearinghouse is the counterparty for both buyers and sellers and guarantees performance on the contract.

Financial institutions such as banks or securities firms act as counterparties in many forward contracts, offering these contracts as part of their risk management services to customers. These institutions' financial strength and reputations promise performance on the contracts. On futures contracts traded on organized exchanges, such as the U.S. Treasury bond futures contract trading on the CBOT mentioned above, each party has a contract with the CBOT Clearing Corporation. The exchange and the clearing corporation require cash, called margins, to be put up or posted by traders to guarantee performance on futures contracts. Futures and forward contracts are very similar in the role they play in hedging risk, but the differences between them, like the role of clearinghouses with futures, are significant. These differences affect their pricing and their ability to hedge: we discuss these differences in detail below.

Prices and Terms of Futures and Forward Contracts

The financial press contains daily quotations on many futures contracts and some newspapers provide typical terms on forward contracts for currencies. We concentrate here on interpretation of the futures quotations readily available in financial newspapers to illustrate the typical terms and conditions for futures and forward contracts. Terms on forward contracts are usually obtained by contacting financial firms acting as counterparties, like banks. We look at the U.S. Treasury bond futures traded on the CBOT and the Eurodollar futures contracts traded on the Chicago Mercantile Exchange (CME) as examples of typical futures and forward contract terms. Table 20.1 contains recent tables from futures trading for these contracts.

The top of each contract entry in the newspaper futures table presents a short summary of the standardized contracts. Table 20.2 contains detailed conditions of several representative financial futures contracts. The U.S. Treasury bond contracts are for $100,000 face value of principal. Detailed contract specifications (as seen on Table 20.2 and obtainable from the exchange or a commodities broker for other contracts) call for delivery of an 8 percent coupon 15-year maturity bond but allow delivery of any actual U.S. Treasury bonds with any coupon and more than 15 years to maturity (or closest call date). The detailed contract also specifies dollar adjustments in delivery prices when delivering bonds with different coupons and maturity dates. The contracts (like bonds in general) are quoted in percent of face value of the contract and the minimum contract price change or trading unit is 1/32 percent.

The first column in Table 20.1 presents contract delivery dates: December, March, and so on to the most distant delivery date, March 1995. Complete contract specifications summarized in Table 20.2 tell precisely how sellers (shorts) in futures markets deliver or settle in cash for each of these contracts. In the case of long-term bonds, delivery must be made before the last business day of the contract month. The last column in the Table 20.1 provides the *open interest* or the total number of contracts at the end of the day. Each contract represents both a buyer and a seller. Heavy trading in Treasury bond futures is evident in 293,003 December open interest, representing a principal value of $29.3 billion (number of contracts times $100,000).

The column headings indicate information on the day's trading in each contract. The *open* (for the December contract 119-09 or 119-9/32 percent or 1.1928125 times $100,000) is the contract price arrived at in trading at the beginning of the session. Buyers at that price promise to accept delivery of $100,000 of 8 percent U.S. Treasuries for a price of $119,281.25. The *high* (120-25) and *low* (119-03) prices for the contract over the course of the trading day are listed next. Prices at the *settle* (120-21), a formal price setting process at the end of the trading day closing out all unresolved transactions, are provided next. Finally, the table shows the change from the previous day's settle both in terms of the price and the yield to maturity under the column *change*.

Table 20.1 contains futures market data for $1,000,000 90-day Eurodollar futures trading on both the Chicago Mercantile Exchange (CME) and the London

FUTURES PRICES

Friday, October 8, 1993

Open Interest Reflects Previous Trading Day

GRAINS AND OILSEEDS

CORN (CBT) 5,000 bu.; cents per bu.

	Open	High	Low	Settle	Change	Lifetime High	Lifetime Low	Open Interest
Dec	242¼	243	240½	241¾	+ ¼	268½	225¼	160,496
Mr94	250	250¾	248¾	250¼	+ ¾	266½	232¾	50,097
May	254½	255¼	253½	255	+ 1	270½	238½	17,649
July	257½	258¼	256½	258	+ 1¼	270½	241	13,749
Sept	252	253	252	252¾	+ 1¼	259	240½	1,891
Dec	246	247½	246	247	+ 1½	255	236½	8,810

Est vol 35,000; vol Thur 36,933; open int 252,702, +1,599.

OATS (CBT) 5,000 bu.; cents per bu.

	Open	High	Low	Settle	Change	Lifetime High	Lifetime Low	Open Interest
Dec	136½	137¾	136½	136¾	− ¼	161	134	10,168
Mr94	141½	142	141	141¼	− ¾	163½	138¾	1,208
May	144	144	144	144	− ¼	164	141	583

Est vol 800; vol Thur 1,025; open int 11,986, −6.

SOYBEANS (CBT) 5,000 bu.; cents per bu.

	Open	High	Low	Settle	Change	Lifetime High	Lifetime Low	Open Interest
Nov	611	613	607½	608¾	− 1¾	757½	555½	85,552
Ja94	618	619¾	614½	615¼	− 2	756	576½	22,589
Mar	625	626	620¾	621½	− 2	754	589¾	14,094
May	628½	629¼	624½	625¼	− 2¾	751	592½	13,434
July	632	633½	628	629½	− 1¾	750	594½	11,746
Aug	631	631	628	628½	− 2¼	735	637	1,459
Sept	622½	622½	619	619	− 1½	676	623½	1,534
Nov	613	614	610½	611½	− 1¼	650	581½	6,856

Est vol 35,000; vol Thur 34,297; open int 157,283, −693.

SOYBEAN MEAL (CBT) 100 tons; $ per ton.

	Open	High	Low	Settle	Change	Lifetime High	Lifetime Low	Open Interest
Oct	191.00	191.40	189.50	190.10	− .20	239.20	181.70	4,377
Dec	190.50	190.70	188.90	189.70	+ .20	240.00	183.40	39,475
Ja94	191.20	191.20	189.40	189.70	− .60	239.50	184.60	10,665
Mar	192.20	192.50	190.20	190.70	− .70	237.50	185.20	9,493
May	193.60	193.60	191.30	191.50	− 1.10	232.00	185.50	6,028
July	195.50	195.50	193.20	193.30	− 1.20	230.00	193.20	4,527
Aug	195.50	195.50	193.50	193.50	− 1.00	225.00	191.50	1,366
Sept	195.50	195.50	194.10	193.60	− .90	210.00	194.10	780
Oct		....	....	193.30	− 2.20	202.00	195.00	692
Dec	195.50	195.50	193.50	193.70	− 1.80	209.00	193.50	299

Est vol 13,000; vol Thur 15,384; open int 77,702, +2,090.

SOYBEAN OIL (CBT) 60,000 lbs.; cents per lb.

	Open	High	Low	Settle	Change	Lifetime High	Lifetime Low	Open Interest
Oct	22.60	22.60	22.25	22.30	− .20	26.05	19.55	1,096
Dec	22.61	22.69	22.43	22.47	− .14	26.20	19.76	28,852
Ja94	22.73	22.75	22.55	22.59	− .11	25.95	20.90	7,278
Mar	22.84	22.89	22.70	22.76	− .07	26.10	21.13	9,379
May	22.85	22.95	22.78	22.82	− .03	26.00	21.30	4,717
July	22.85	22.97	22.75	22.83	+ .03	25.95	21.55	3,368
Aug	22.85	22.85	22.65	22.65	....	25.25	21.65	980
Sept	22.70	22.70	22.70	22.60	+ .05	25.15	22.70	643
Oct	22.35	22.40	22.35	22.37	+ .22	24.10	22.20	528
Dec	22.05	22.40	22.05	22.40	+ .35	23.75	22.00	691

Est vol 16,000; vol Thur 13,028; open int 57,532, −705.

WHEAT (CBT) 5,000 bu.; cents per bu.

	Open	High	Low	Settle	Change	Lifetime High	Lifetime Low	Open Interest
Dec	321½	323	321	322	− ½	360	294	35,000
Mr94	325½	327¼	325	326¼	....	353	300	18,515
May	321	323¼	321	321¾	+ ¾	333	300	1,875
July	309½	311¾	309½	311¼	+ 1¼	327	296	4,846

Est vol 7,500; vol Thur 18,149; open int 60,296, +1,485.

WHEAT (KC) 5,000 bu.; cents per bu.

	Open	High	Low	Settle	Change	Lifetime High	Lifetime Low	Open Interest
Dec	326	326½	324½	325¼	− ½	341½	293¼	20,438
Mr94	327	327	325½	326	− ½	329½	298	10,250
May	317	318	317	317¼	+ ¼	325	298	1,564
July	308½	309½	308½	309½	+ ¾	316	297	2,068
Sept	312	312¾	312	312¾	+ ¼	314	302½	169
Dec	....	....	....	318	− ¼	321	312½	529

Est vol 3,802; vol Thur 6,612; open int 35,018, +201.

WHEAT (MPLS) 5,000 bu.; cents per bu.

	Open	High	Low	Settle	Change	Lifetime High	Lifetime Low	Open Interest
Dec	327½	329½	327	328¼	+ ¾	342	290	8,928
Mr94	324¾	325¼	323¼	324¼	− ¼	343	297½	1,982
May	....	....	....	321	− 1	326½	299	139

Est vol 2,439; vol Thur 2,791; open int 11,108, +114.

BARLEY (WPG) 20 metric tons; Can. $ per ton

	Open	High	Low	Settle	Change	Lifetime High	Lifetime Low	Open Interest
Oct	79.10	79.10	79.10	79.10	− .70	102.80	75.50	155
Dec	80.50	80.70	80.00	80.00	− .80	96.20	78.20	1,117
Mr94		....	....	83.80	− .60	100.20	82.00	1,373
May		....	....	85.10	− .90	89.10	83.00	127

Est vol 180; vol Thur 236; open int 2,772, −5.

FLAXSEED (WPG) 20 metric tons; Can. $ per ton

	Open	High	Low	Settle	Change	Lifetime High	Lifetime Low	Open Interest
Oct	254.00	255.50	254.00	254.00	+ 4.00	301.80	243.40	812
Dec	256.00	257.00	253.00	254.30	+ 4.00	300.50	247.00	2,998
Mr94	264.50	264.50	263.50	263.50	+ 1.80	283.60	255.00	333

Est vol 165; vol Thur 115; open int 4,182, −4.

CANOLA (WPG) 20 metric tons; Can. $ per ton

	Open	High	Low	Settle	Change	Lifetime High	Lifetime Low	Open Interest
Nov	311.50	311.50	309.60	310.80	+ .10	354.60	281.00	21,155
Ja94	314.50	314.50	313.40	313.60	− .30	358.50	303.00	12,325
Mar	317.00	317.50	316.40	317.00	+ .40	362.90	307.50	10,686
June	321.20	321.30	321.00	321.00	− .50	367.80	319.00	5,320
Aug		....	....	322.80	....	371.90	323.50	2,286
Sept	316.90	316.90	316.00	316.00	− .90	358.50	316.00	1,267
Nov	317.00	317.00	316.00	316.50	− 1.50	342.20	316.00	5,019

Est vol 2,900; vol Thur 1,711; open int 57,535, −248.

WHEAT (WPG) 20 metric tons; Can. $ per ton

	Open	High	Low	Settle	Change	Lifetime High	Lifetime Low	Open Interest
Oct	91.20	91.80	91.20	91.80	− .20	108.80	88.00	1,425
Dec	93.00	93.00	91.20	91.30	− 1.60	108.30	90.00	4,401
Mr94	96.00	96.00	94.80	94.90	− 1.50	111.00	93.60	5,949
May	97.70	97.70	97.10	97.10	− 1.20	113.30	95.80	590
July	99.70	99.70	99.20	99.20	− .90	100.80	98.10	233

Est vol 1,415; vol Thur 1,052; open int 12,598, −179.

LIVESTOCK AND MEAT

CATTLE–FEEDER (CME) 50,000 lbs.; cents per lb.

	Open	High	Low	Settle	Change	Lifetime High	Lifetime Low	Open Interest
Oct	85.10	85.10	84.10	84.15	− .97	87.75	75.90	1,524
Nov	84.85	84.90	83.67	83.72	− 1.15	88.00	77.45	4,352
Ja94	84.00	84.05	82.95	83.05	− 1.00	86.90	79.90	1,635
Mar	82.40	82.40	81.50	81.55	− 1.02	85.35	81.20	817
Apr	81.85	81.85	80.90	80.90	− .90	85.00	80.90	232
May	80.80	80.80	80.10	80.10	− .87	84.40	80.10	236

Est vol 1,818; vol Thur 762; open int 8,837, −27.

CATTLE–LIVE (CME) 40,000 lbs.; cents per lb.

	Open	High	Low	Settle	Change	Lifetime High	Lifetime Low	Open Interest
Oct	71.95	72.05	70.90	70.92	− 1.12	76.70	67.55	5,937
Dec	73.77	73.97	72.70	72.72	− 1.20	76.65	68.10	28,916
Fb94	74.65	74.90	73.95	73.97	− .75	76.52	70.90	14,377
Apr	75.82	75.95	75.10	75.12	− .75	77.55	73.20	9,891
June	72.30	72.50	71.80	71.82	− .57	74.27	71.25	6,539
Aug	71.30	71.30	70.50	70.52	− .62	73.25	70.05	3,663
Oct	71.50	71.50	71.07	71.07	− .57	73.30	71.07	1,001

Est vol 15,026; vol Thur 12,535; open int 70,324, −532.

HOGS (CME) 40,000 lbs.; cents per lb.

	Open	High	Low	Settle	Change	Lifetime High	Lifetime Low	Open Interest
Oct	49.55	49.90	49.30	49.80	− .05	50.15	39.70	2,031
Dec	50.25	50.90	50.10	50.80	+ .32	50.90	40.07	11,620
Fb94	49.85	50.50	49.70	50.40	+ .45	50.50	40.20	3,255
Apr	47.50	48.10	47.40	47.95	+ .45	48.15	39.57	1,569
June	51.75	52.30	51.70	52.15	+ .30	52.85	45.27	820
July	50.82	51.10	50.40	51.05	+ .55	51.50	45.30	197
Aug	49.17	49.65	49.05	49.60	+ .42	49.85	46.35	143

Est vol 4,365; vol Thur 3,174; open int 19,666, +109.

PORK BELLIES (CME) 40,000 lbs.; cents per lb.

	Open	High	Low	Settle	Change	Lifetime High	Lifetime Low	Open Interest
Feb	57.70	58.50	57.70	58.15	+ .25	58.50	39.10	5,063
Mar	57.50	58.20	57.45	58.05	+ .35	58.20	38.60	614
May	57.75	58.20	57.70	57.70	+ .55	58.20	39.50	166
Jly	57.40	57.90	57.40	57.77	+ .57	57.90	39.30	565

Est vol 1,691; vol Thur 1,495; open int 6,505, +185.

FOOD AND FIBER

COCOA (CSCE) – 10 metric tons; $ per ton.

	Open	High	Low	Settle	Change	Lifetime High	Lifetime Low	Open Interest
Dec	1,112	1,137	1,112	1,124	+ 6	1,506	919	31,932
Mr94	1,158	1,175	1,152	1,160	+ 2	1,345	953	23,480
May	1,175	1,195	1,174	1,178	+ 4	1,368	978	9,204
July	1,195	1,203	1,192	1,194	+ 2	1,290	999	2,968
Sept	1,215	1,226	1,215	1,215	+ 6	1,308	1,020	4,271
Dec	1,227	1,231	1,227	1,227	+ 6	1,330	1,045	5,388
Mr95		....	....	1,237	+ 6	1,346	1,077	6,782
May	1,244	1,245	1,244	1,252	+ 6	1,360	1,111	6,263
July		....	....	1,265	+ 6	1,358	1,285	345

Est vol 9,968; vol Thurs 24,211; open int 90,633, −1,665.

COFFEE (CSCE) – 37,500 lbs.; cents per lb.

	Open	High	Low	Settle	Change	Lifetime High	Lifetime Low	Open Interest
Dec	72.30	74.20	72.30	74.10	+ 2.05	91.00	59.00	34,381
Mr94	75.30	76.70	75.10	76.60	+ 2.05	90.75	61.50	11,681
May	76.50	77.90	76.60	77.90	+ 2.10	90.50	63.25	3,056
July	77.90	78.85	78.85	79.20	+ 2.10	87.50	64.90	948
Sept	79.40	80.00	79.40	80.50	+ 2.10	88.50	68.50	162

Est vol 8,891; vol Thurs 6,153; open int 50,260, +248.

SUGAR–WORLD (CSCE) – 112,000 lbs.; cents per lb.

	Open	High	Low	Settle	Change	Lifetime High	Lifetime Low	Open Interest
Mar	10.65	10.64	10.61	10.73	+ .13	11.84	8.50	61,860
May	10.76	10.84	10.74	10.84	+ .09	11.68	8.65	14,552
July	10.81	10.90	10.79	10.90	+ .08	11.55	9.15	11,053
Oct	10.82	10.86	10.82	10.92	+ .10	10.90	9.42	6,721

Est vol 6,692; vol Thurs 16,399; open int 94,188, −1,104.

SUGAR–DOMESTIC (CSCE) – 112,000 lbs.; cents per lb.

	Open	High	Low	Settle	Change	Lifetime High	Lifetime Low	Open Interest
Nov	21.95	22.05	21.90	21.97	+ .01	22.07	21.25	547
Ja94	21.77	21.80	21.77	21.78	+ .01	21.92	21.35	2,901
Mar	21.70	21.72	21.72	21.73	+ .02	21.89	21.35	2,784
May	21.70	21.81	21.80	21.81	+ .05	22.00	21.35	2,300
July	21.79	21.96	21.96	21.97	+ .02	22.06	21.55	1,734
Sept	21.80	21.97	21.96	21.97	+ .01	22.07	21.80	1,489
Nov	....	....	....	21.97	....	22.03	21.82	285

Est vol 553; vol Thurs 1,472; open int 12,040, +281.

COTTON (CTN) – 50,000 lbs.; cents per lb.

	Open	High	Low	Settle	Change	Lifetime High	Lifetime Low	Open Interest
Dec	58.62	60.05	58.62	59.85	+ 1.17	64.25	54.60	18
Mr94	60.25	61.40	60.25	61.37	+ 1.10	64.20	55.62	18,552
May	60.90	61.95	61.50	61.95	+ 1.05	64.85	57.47	7,512
July	62.36	62.60	62.25	62.60	+ 1.04	65.00	58.30	4,051
Oct		....	....	62.80	+ 1.05	64.00	59.81	2,167
Dec	61.60	62.80	62.00	62.80	+ 1.05	62.90	59.48	2,967

Est vol 12,000; vol Thur 2,169; open int 35,497, −327.

ORANGE JUICE (CTN) – 15,000 lbs.; cents per lb.

	Open	High	Low	Settle	Change	Lifetime High	Lifetime Low	Open Interest
Nov	129.60	129.75	127.25	128.30	− .30	134.00	78.50	10,864
Ja94	130.50	131.00	128.75	129.55	− .30	133.70	82.15	5,025
Mar	131.80	131.80	130.00	130.00	− 1.35	134.25	84.50	2,194
May	132.50	133.25	131.50	132.15	− .20	134.50	89.00	1,498
July	133.15	133.15	133.15	133.15	− .20	135.00	110.00	333
Sept	133.65	133.65	133.65	133.65	− .20	133.65	119.00	326

Est vol 2,200; vol Thur 1,856; open int 20,230, −112.

METALS AND PETROLEUM

COPPER-HIGH (CMX) – 25,000 lbs.; cents per lb.

	Open	High	Low	Settle	Change	Lifetime High	Lifetime Low	Open Interest
Oct	75.10	75.10	74.80	74.80	+ .30	104.30	74.10	500
Nov	75.30	75.30	75.30	75.25	+ .40	104.35	74.45	713
Dec	75.55	75.95	75.40	75.60	+ .40	109.20	74.30	35,162
Ja94	75.75	76.05	75.75	75.85	+ .40	104.40	74.90	795
Feb		....	....	76.15	+ .40	99.20	75.30	515
Mar	76.55	76.75	76.30	76.40	+ .40	107.50	75.30	8,215
Apr		....	....	76.65	+ .40	89.20	76.00	212
May	77.05	77.20	76.85	76.90	+ .40	102.20	75.90	3,655
June		....	....	77.15	+ .40	89.50	76.50	257
July	77.70	77.70	77.40	77.40	+ .40	102.95	76.50	2,354
Aug		....	....	77.65	+ .40	86.80	77.80	259
Sept	78.00	78.00	78.00	77.90	+ .40	103.30	77.00	2,376
Dec	78.80	78.80	78.80	78.85	+ .40	101.90	78.00	2,090
Mr95		....	....	79.35	+ .40	88.50	80.00	118

Est vol 4,000; vol Thur 4,306; open int 57,353, +184.

GOLD (CMX) – 100 troy oz.; $ per troy oz.

	Open	High	Low	Settle	Change	Lifetime High	Lifetime Low	Open Interest
Oct	360.50	360.50	360.50	359.90	+ 3.10	411.50	330.80	117
Dec	360.00	362.20	358.50	361.50	+ 3.00	414.00	331.70	90,775
Fb94	362.30	363.50	361.40	363.20	+ 3.00	415.70	333.80	16,007
Apr	363.50	364.40	363.40	364.90	+ 3.00	418.50	335.20	7,875
June	365.50	366.00	363.60	366.60	+ 3.00	417.20	339.40	9,289
Aug		....	....	368.30	+ 2.90	415.00	341.50	4,065
Oct		....	....	370.10	+ 2.90	417.00	344.00	2,653
Dec	371.20	372.30	371.20	371.90	+ 2.90	426.50	343.00	10,054
Fb95		....	....	373.80	+ 2.90	411.00	363.50	2,252
Apr		....	....	375.80	+ 2.90	425.00	386.20	1,967
June		....	....	377.80	+ 2.90	430.00	351.00	2,473
Dec		....	....	384.20	+ 2.90	439.50	358.00	1,524
Ju96		....	....	391.30	+ 2.90	447.00	370.90	770
Dec		....	....	399.60	+ 2.90	443.00	379.60	574
De97		....	....	417.80	+ 2.90	477.00	402.00	451

Est vol 27,000; vol Thur 20,064; open int 150,901, −776.

PLATINUM (NYM) – 50 troy oz.; $ per troy oz.

	Open	High	Low	Settle	Change	Lifetime High	Lifetime Low	Open Interest
Oct				362.40	+ .70	427.50	336.00	122
Ja94	na	365.80	361.10	364.10	+ .70	427.00	335.50	11,190
Apr	364.50	367.00	364.50	365.90	+ .70	428.50	335.00	2,604
July	369.00	369.00	366.50	366.90	+ .50	428.00	357.00	1,198

Est vol 812; vol Thur 1,976; open int 15,116, −177.

PALLADIUM (NYM) 100 troy oz.; $ per troy oz.

	Open	High	Low	Settle	Change	Lifetime High	Lifetime Low	Open Interest
Dec	127.75	129.00	126.75	127.75	+ .45	142.50	91.85	3,127
Mr94	127.00	127.00	125.75	126.50	+ .45	139.50	99.00	638
June		....	....	125.00	+ .45	134.00	111.75	395

Est vol 232; vol Thur 300; open int 4,166, +7.

SILVER (CMX) – 5,000 troy oz.; cents per troy oz.

	Open	High	Low	Settle	Change	Lifetime High	Lifetime Low	Open Interest
Oct		....	....	433.9	− 2.3	547.0	401.0	1
Dec	437.0	440.0	430.0	436.0	− 2.3	553.0	362.0	57,531
Mr94	441.0	442.5	434.5	440.2	− 2.4	556.5	366.0	14,304
May	441.0	443.0	441.0	443.1	− 2.5	555.5	371.0	7,097
July	445.0	448.0	443.0	445.9	− 2.6	565.0	372.5	4,011
Sept	446.0	446.0	446.0	448.6	− 2.7	561.5	376.5	1,423
Dec	450.0	451.0	446.0	453.0	− 2.8	572.0	380.0	4,000
Mr95		....	....	457.9	− 2.9	572.0	416.5	1,139
May		....	....	461.3	− 2.9	584.0	418.0	112
Dec		....	....	471.7	− 3.2	600.0	434.0	480
De96		....	....	487.7	− 3.9	560.0	454.0	415
Jl97		....	....	500.2	− 3.9	....	....	100
De97		....	....	509.2	− 3.9	....	....	150

Est vol 16,000; vol Thur 19,485; open int 90,864, −1,136.

SILVER (CBT) – 1,000 troy oz.; cents per troy oz.

	Open	High	Low	Settle	Change	Lifetime High	Lifetime Low	Open Interest
Oct		....	....	434.5	− 0.5	547.0	358.5	7
Dec	435.0	439.0	428.0	434.5	− 2.0	551.0	361.0	4,145
Fb94	440.0	440.0	434.0	437.5	− 2.0	555.0	364.5	135
Apr		....	....	440.5	− 2.0	554.0	372.0	117
June	446.0	446.0	441.0	443.5	− 2.5	562.0	375.0	684

Est vol 100; vol TThur 509; open int 5,181, −156.

CRUDE OIL, Light Sweet (NYM) 1,000 bbls.; $ per bbl.

	Open	High	Low	Settle	Change	Lifetime High	Lifetime Low	Open Interest
Nov	18.45	18.57	18.38	18.55	+ .06	21.15	16.79	84,326
Dec	na	18.75	18.58	18.74	+ .06	23.00	17.14	83,786
Ja94	na	18.86	18.71	18.86	+ .06	21.15	17.40	42,312
Feb	na	18.94	18.82	18.97	+ .05	20.81	17.64	22,373
Mar	na	19.02	18.92	19.07	+ .05	21.10	17.86	17,093
Apr	19.00	19.10	19.00	19.15	+ .05	20.88	18.05	13,684
May	19.17	19.17	19.08	19.23	+ .05	21.07	18.20	11,840
June	19.20	19.22	19.18	19.30	+ .05	21.35	18.31	23,381
July	19.25	19.25	19.23	19.35	+ .05	20.78	18.50	11,684
Aug	19.28	19.28	19.28	19.40	+ .05	20.78	18.60	7,117
Sept	na	19.35	19.32	19.45	+ .05	20.78	18.72	9,703
Oct	19.37	19.37	19.37	19.49	+ .05	20.73	18.79	4,947
Nov	19.39	19.39	19.39	19.51	+ .05	20.69	18.80	6,691
Dec	19.41	19.41	19.41	19.53	+ .05	21.25	18.74	16,159
Ja95		....	....	19.57	+ .05	20.78	18.95	2,606
Feb		....	....	19.61	+ .05	19.21	19.00	829
Mar		....	....	19.65	+ .05	20.66	18.99	5,896
June	19.68	19.68	19.68	19.77	+ .05	21.21	18.99	16,241
Sept	19.70	19.70	19.70	19.83	+ .05	19.70	19.70	1,475
Dec	19.80	19.80	19.80	19.89	+ .05	20.80	19.00	11,509
Ju96	19.96	19.96	19.92	20.01	+ .05	20.26	19.00	13,284

Est vol 48,167; vol Thur 56,681; open int 406,936, −1,923.

HEATING OIL NO. 2 (NYM) 42,000 gal.; $ per gal.

	Open	High	Low	Settle	Change	Lifetime High	Lifetime Low	Open Interest
Nov	.5585	.5620	.5545	.5599	+ .0014	.6125	.5085	53,501
Dec	.5675	.5700	.5635	.5691	+ .0015	.6200	.5190	47,728
Ja94	.5690	.5745	.5680	.5731	+ .0015	.6225	.5280	25,608
Feb	na	.5730	.5675	.5720	+ .0014	.6200	.5325	10,974
Mar	.5700	.5700	.5580	.5616	+ .0015	.6050	.5285	11,005
Apr		....	....	.5491	+ .0015	.5875	.5220	6,462
May	.5370	.5370	.5370	.5381	+ .0015	.5750	.5160	2,462
June		....	....	.5326	+ .0015	.5800	.5120	4,275
July		....	....	.5338	+ .0015	.5710	.5145	6,638
Aug		....	....	.5398	+ .0015	.5617	.5245	781
Sept		....	....	.5493	+ .0015	.5717	.5340	529
Oct		....	....	.5650	....	.5730	.5455	548
Nov		....	....	.5683	+ .0015	.5830	.5550	309
Dec		....	....	.5783	+ .0015	.5900	.5650	1,584
Ja95		....	....	.5808	+ .0015	.5790	.5675	197

Est vol 25,794; vol Thur 22,570; open int 172,602, +1,398.

GASOLINE-NY Unleaded (NYM) 42,000 gal.; $ per gal.

	Open	High	Low	Settle	Change	Lifetime High	Lifetime Low	Open Interest
Nov	na	.5170	.5100	.5165	+ .0045	.5770	.4755	40,115
Dec	na	.5200	.5145	.5199	+ .0041	.5690	.4775	30,654
Ja94	na	.5215	.5185	.5222	+ .0033	.5670	.4795	15,132
Feb	na	.5260	.5225	.5280	+ .0031	.5705	.4890	5,493
Mar	.5335	.5355	.5335	.5379	+ .0025	.5800	.5020	4,162
Apr	.5675	.5675	.5675	.5719	+ .0025	.6250	.5365	3,248
May		....	....	.5789	+ .0025	.6130	.5450	1,679
June		....	....	.5819	+ .0025	.6100	.5530	241
Aug		....	....	.5714	+ .0025	.6000	.5870	556

Est vol 21,822; vol Thur 22,080; open int 101,363, +2,014.

NATURAL GAS, (NYM) 10,000 MMBtu.; $ per MMBtu's

	Open	High	Low	Settle	Change	Lifetime High	Lifetime Low	Open Interest
Nov	2.115	2.150	2.110	2.141	+ .019	2.582	1.765	17,058
Dec	2.290	2.320	2.280	2.309	+ .019	2.710	2.000	21,760
Ja94	2.325	2.350	2.325	2.348	+ .018	2.685	1.857	15,073
Feb	2.205	2.230	2.205	2.228	+ .018	2.465	1.800	9,995
Mar	2.130	2.160	2.130	2.153	+ .023	2.335	1.627	10,069
Apr	2.105	2.140	2.105	2.128	+ .023	2.285	1.565	7,057
May	2.110	2.140	2.110	2.128	+ .018	2.300	1.540	5,171
June	2.110	2.140	2.110	2.128	+ .018	2.300	1.560	5,699
July	2.110	2.140	2.110	2.128	+ .018	2.315	1.590	5,899
Aug	na	2.160	2.135	2.148	+ .018	2.335	1.715	5,476
Sept	2.155	2.175	2.153	2.168	+ .015	2.465	1.850	4,473
Oct	2.250	2.260	2.245	2.260	+ .015	2.470	1.995	3,668
Nov	2.340	2.360	2.330	2.355	+ .018	2.580	2.285	6,393
Dec	2.480	2.490	2.460	2.495	+ .020	2.730	2.410	7,625
Ja95	2.470	2.475	2.460	2.490	+ .020	2.720	2.500	3,526
Feb	2.360	2.360	2.360	2.370	+ .020	2.460	2.360	1,071
Mar	2.290	2.290	2.290	2.300	+ .020	2.360	2.280	1,859
Apr	2.240	2.240	2.240	2.265	+ .025	2.305	2.275	1,421

Est vol 19,568; vol Thur 23,991; open int 133,293, +1,390.

EXCHANGE ABBREVIATIONS
(for commodity futures and futures options)

CBT-Chicago Board of Trade; CME-Chicago Mercantile Exchange; CSCE-Coffee, Sugar & Cocoa Exchange, New York; CMX-Commodity Exchange, New York; IPE-International Petroleum Exchange; KC-Kansas City Board of Trade; LIFFE-London International Financial Futures Exchange; MCE-MidAmerica Commodity Exchange; MPLS-Minneapolis Grain Exchange; CTN-New York Cotton Exchange; NYM-New York Mercantile Exchange; PBOT-Philadelphia Board of Trade; WPG-Winnipeg Commodity Exchange.

BRENT CRUDE (IPE) 1,000 net bbls.; $ per bbl.

	Open	High	Low	Settle	Change	Lifetime High	Lifetime Low	Open Interest
Nov	17.20	17.23	17.09	17.19	+ .03	19.44	15.88	64,922
Dec	17.41	17.41	17.28	17.38	+ .02	19.38	16.10	51,058
Ja94	17.51	17.55	17.43	17.54	+ .03	13.35	16.32	21,131
Feb	17.65	17.68	17.56	17.68	+ .06	19.30	16.62	7,298
Mar	17.74	17.77	17.68	17.77	+ .09	18.97	16.85	5,791
Apr	17.71	17.78	17.71	17.76	+ .02	18.04	16.98	1,978
May	17.85	17.85	17.85	17.84	+ .01	18.10	17.10	1,408
June	17.90	17.90	17.90	17.90	....	18.03	17.23	1,772
July	17.94	17.94	17.92	17.92	− .02	18.08	17.48	3,228

Est vol 25,780; vol Thur 25,352; open int 158,856, −5,518.

GAS OIL (IPE) 100 metric tons; $ per ton

	Open	High	Low	Settle	Change	Lifetime High	Lifetime Low	Open Interest
Oct	173.25	173.50	172.00	172.25	− 1.25	184.00	155.75	15,602
Nov	174.25	174.25	172.25	173.00	− 1.00	186.00	155.50	29,408
Dec	174.50	174.75	173.00	173.50	− 1.00	186.00	159.50	27,485
Ja94	174.25	174.25	172.75	173.25	− 1.25	182.00	161.50	19,137
Feb	173.00	173.00	172.00	172.50	− .75	181.50	162.00	4,640
Mar	171.00	171.25	170.50	170.75	− .75	182.00	161.00	4,776
Apr		....	....	168.50	− 1.25	176.50	159.75	1,793
May	167.50	167.50	167.00	167.00	− 1.25	172.75	159.50	654
June	165.50	165.50	165.50	165.50	− 1.25	174.55	158.00	5,959
July	167.00	167.00	167.00	167.00	− .75	169.50	158.75	774
Sept	169.00	169.00	169.00	169.00	− 1.50	178.25	162.25	944

Est vol 14,164; vol Thur 13,149; open int 111,221, −3,436.

INTEREST RATE

TREASURY BONDS (CBT) – $100,000; pts. 32nds of 100%

	Open	High	Low	Settle	Chg	Yield Settle	Yield Chg	Open Interest
Dec	119-09	120-25	119-03	120-21	+ 44	6.186	− .106	293,003
Mr94	118-02	119-18	117-30	119-14	+ 43	6.280	− .105	16,331
June	117-14	118-13	117-14	118-11	+ 42	6.366	− .104	9,625
Sept	115-27	117-12	115-27	117-11	+ 42	6.445	− .106	15,681
Dec	115-11	116-25	115-11	116-25	+ 42	6.490	− .106	10,564
Mr95	....	....	....	116-00	+ 42	6.553	− .107	41

Est vol 400,000; vol Thur 140,251; op int 345,312, −1,935.

TREASURY BONDS (MCE) – $50,000; pts. 32nds of 100%

	Open	High	Low	Settle	Chg	Yield Settle	Yield Chg	Open Interest
Dec	119-04	120-25	119-04	120-16	+ 38	6.198	− .092	11,124

Est vol 3,900; vol Thur 1,826; open int 11,142, −196.

TREASURY NOTES (CBT) – $100,000; pts. 32nds of 100%

	Open	High	Low	Settle	Chg	Yield Settle	Yield Chg	Open Interest
Dec	115-26	116-19	115-21	116-18	+ 24	5.795	− .091	218,093
Mr94	114-24	115-22	114-24	115-21	+ 24	5.905	− .091	13,038
June	115-00	115-01	115-00	115-01	+ 24	5.981	− .093	531

Est vol 73,000; vol Thur 33,060; open int 231,665, −250.

5 YR TREAS NOTES (CBT) – $100,000; pts. 32nds of 100%

	Open	High	Low	Settle	Chg	Yield Settle	Yield Chg	Open Interest
Dec	113-07	113-22	13-045	13-205	+ 13.0	4.892	− .086	145,035
Mr94	12-125	12-295	12-125	12-285	+ 13.0	5.051	− .086	1,909

Est vol 38,500; vol Thur 22,044; open int 146,944, −2,527.

2 YR TREAS NOTES (CBT) – $200,000, pts. 32nds of 100%

	Open	High	Low	Settle	Chg	Yield Settle	Yield Chg	Open Interest
Dec	06-307	07-045	06-307	07-035	+ 4	4.254	− .063	28,961

Est vol 1,200; vol Thur 582; open int 28,961, +126.

30-DAY FEDERAL FUNDS (CBT)-$5 million; pts. of 100%

	Open	High	Low	Settle	Chg	Yield Settle	Yield Chg	Open Interest
Oct	96.95	96.96	96.95	96.96	+ .02	3.04	− .02	1,970
Nov	96.96	96.96	96.96	96.96	....	3.04	....	2,505
Dec	96.87	96.87	96.87	96.87	+ .02	3.13	− .02	1,194
Ja94	96.81	96.82	96.81	96.81	+ .02	3.19	− .02	1,074
Feb	96.88	96.88	96.87	96.88	+ .03	3.12	− .03	841
Mar	96.81	96.83	96.81	96.83	+ .04	3.17	− .04	873
Apr	96.80	96.80	96.79	96.79	+ .04	3.21	− .04	101

Est vol 555; vol Thur 187; open int 8,573, +63.

TREASURY BILLS (CME) – $1 mil.; pts. of 100%

	Open	High	Low	Settle	Chg	Discount Settle	Discount Chg	Open Interest
Dec	96.89	96.94	96.89	96.92	+ .02	3.08	− .02	19,161
Mr94	96.81	96.85	96.81	96.82	+ .03	3.18	− .03	9,433
June	96.68	96.69	96.68	96.68	+ .05	3.32	− .05	1,610

Est vol 3,693; vol Thur 2,505; open int 30,204, +180.

LIBOR-1 MO. (CME) – $3,000,000; points of 100%

	Open	High	Low	Settle	Chg	Yield Settle	Yield Chg	Open Interest
Oct	96.83	96.84	96.82	96.83	....	3.17	....	14,308
Nov	96.83	96.85	96.81	96.84	+ .01	3.16	− .01	11,691
Dec	96.32	96.39	96.32	96.38	+ .06	3.62	− .06	6,033
Ja94	96.73	96.79	96.73	96.79	+ .05	3.21	− .05	4,767
Feb	96.74	96.75	96.74	96.75	+ .05	3.25	− .05	1,645
Mar	96.67	96.68	96.67	96.67	+ .05	3.33	− .05	872
Jun	96.47	96.52	96.47	96.51	+ .05	3.49	− .05	566

Est vol 6,353; vol Thur 4,843; open int 39,882, +1,216.

MUNI BOND INDEX (CBT)-$1,000; times Bond Buyer MBI

	Open	High	Low	Settle	Chg	High	Low	Open Interest
Dec	104-10	105-08	104-09	105-05	+ 24	105-23	97-18	27,471
Mr94	103-16	104-14	103-16	104-11	+ 25	104-25	99-22	208

Est vol 6,500; vol Thur 1,037; open int 27,679, −2.
The index: Close 105-18; Yield 5.44.

EURODOLLAR (CME) – $1 million; pts of 100%

	Open	High	Low	Settle	Chg	Yield Settle	Yield Chg	Open Interest
Dec	96.55	96.61	96.54	96.58	+ .03	3.42	− .03	394,216
Mr94	96.53	96.62	96.52	96.58	+ .05	3.42	− .05	339,721
June	96.33	96.41	96.32	96.39	+ .06	3.61	− .06	217,105
Sept	96.10	96.21	96.10	96.10	+ .08	3.90	− .08	171,938
Dec	95.73	95.85	95.73	95.83	+ .09	4.17	− .09	128,993
Mr95	95.66	95.76	95.65	95.75	+ .09	4.25	− .09	137,986
June	95.45	95.56	95.45	95.55	+ .09	4.45	− .09	93,509
Sept	95.28	95.39	95.28	95.37	+ .08	4.63	− .08	79,294
Dec	94.99	95.09	94.99	95.08	+ .08	4.92	− .08	71,231
Mr96	94.95	95.05	94.95	95.04	+ .08	4.96	− .08	65,989
June	94.78	94.88	94.78	94.87	+ .08	5.13	− .08	49,030
Sept	94.63	94.74	94.63	94.74	+ .09	5.26	− .09	45,179
Dec	94.38	94.50	94.38	94.49	+ .10	5.51	− .10	39,070
Mr97	94.37	94.49	94.37	94.48	+ .10	5.52	− .10	35,944
June	94.30	94.36	94.24	94.35	+ .10	5.65	− .10	27,327
Sept	94.14	94.26	94.14	94.26	+ .10	5.74	− .10	24,313
Dec	93.93	94.04	93.91	94.04	+ .10	5.96	− .10	18,777
Mr98	93.94	94.06	93.94	94.06	+ .09	5.94	− .09	18,531
June	93.84	93.96	93.84	93.96	+ .09	6.04	− .09	15,067
Sept	93.80	93.90	93.78	93.90	+ .09	6.10	− .09	4,660
Dec	93.63	93.72	93.62	93.72	+ .08	6.28	− .08	1,004
Mr99	93.68	93.77	93.67	93.67	+ .08	6.33	− .08	817
June	93.63	93.72	93.62	93.72	+ .08	6.28	− .08	1,238
Sept	93.59	93.68	93.58	93.68	+ .08	3.32	− .08	1,205
Dec	93.44	93.49	93.39	93.49	+ .09	3.51	− .09	807
Mr00	93.48	93.52	93.43	93.53	+ .09	3.47	− .09	683
June	93.42	93.46	93.37	93.47	+ .09	3.53	− .09	598
Sept	93.38	93.42	93.33	93.43	+ .09	3.57	− .09	552

Est vol 347,021; vol Thur 168,819; open int 1,984,784, +2,067.

EURODOLLAR (LIFFE) – $1 million; pts of 100%

	Open	High	Low	Settle	Change	Lifetime High	Lifetime Low	Open Interest
Dec	96.54	96.60	96.54	96.60	+ .04	96.60	92.24	5,292
Mr94	96.53	96.59	96.53	96.60	+ .06	96.61	92.30	3,125
June	....	....	....	96.40	+ .06	96.35	93.36	1,302
Sept	....	....	....	96.20	+ .08	96.17	93.76	407
June	....	....	....	95.54	+ .06	95.34	94.68	129

Est vol 572; vol Thur 565; open int 10,353, +247.

STERLING (LIFFE) – £500,000; pts of 100%

	Open	High	Low	Settle	Change	Lifetime High	Lifetime Low	Open Interest
Dec	94.37	94.38	94.35	94.38	+ .02	94.85	88.95	126,711
Mr94	94.57	94.58	94.55	94.56	....	94.82	89.87	75,806
June	94.56	94.58	94.55	94.55	− .01	94.86	89.78	53,918
Sept	94.41	94.44	94.41	94.41	− .01	95.01	90.10	29,401
Dec	94.22	94.25	94.21	94.21	− .02	95.01	90.10	20,908
Mr95	94.00	94.02	93.98	93.99	− .01	95.03	90.70	15,445
June	93.78	93.80	93.78	93.78	....	94.93	91.73	10,173
Sept	93.57	93.59	93.57	93.58	+ .01	94.81	91.65	7,967
Dec	93.36	93.45	93.36	93.38	+ .02	94.66	92.25	6,767
Mr96	93.18	93.25	93.18	93.19	+ .01	94.61	92.82	4,751

Est vol 21,407; vol Thur 33,033; open int 351,907, +537.

LONG GILT (LIFFE) – £50,000; 32nds of 100%

	Open	High	Low	Settle	Change	Lifetime High	Lifetime Low	Open Interest
Dec	113-24	114-17	113-21	114-14	+ 0-20	114-18	103-05	102,669
Mr94	113-20	113-20	113-20	113-25	+ 0-20	113-20	111-26	714

Est vol 55,004; vol Thur 41,392; open int 103,383, +6,255.

EUROMARK (LIFFE) – DM 1,000,000; pts of 100%

	Open	High	Low	Settle	Change	Lifetime High	Lifetime Low	Open Interest
Dec	93.75	93.76	93.72	93.73	− .03	94.62	91.31	237,981
Mr94	94.37	94.41	94.35	94.36	− .01	94.77	91.53	113,665
June	94.76	94.80	94.74	94.76	− .01	94.88	91.71	86,236
Sept	94.98	95.03	94.97	94.99	....	95.03	91.81	66,641
Dec	95.05	95.09	95.05	95.06	+ .01	95.10	91.83	48,450
Mr95	95.10	95.15	95.10	95.12	+ .03	95.15	92.45	49,553
June	95.04	95.11	95.03	95.08	+ .03	95.11	93.15	19,391
Sept	94.91	94.98	94.90	94.96	+ .04	94.98	93.62	9,506
Dec	94.77	94.82	94.76	94.80	+ .02	94.82	93.72	5,014
Mr96	94.70	94.75	94.70	94.75	+ .03	94.76	94.47	2,509

Est vol 74,625; vol Thur 79,109; open int 638,946, +6,184.

EUROSWISS (LIFFE) – SFr 1,000,000; pts of 100%

	Open	High	Low	Settle	Change	Lifetime High	Lifetime Low	Open Interest
Dec	95.66	95.70	95.64	95.67	+ .02	96.11	94.83	30,987
Mr94	96.09	96.11	96.09	96.10	....	96.19	95.49	11,476
June	96.30	96.30	96.30	96.30	+ .01	96.34	95.79	5,251
Sept	....	....	....	96.40	+ .01	96.44	96.06	971

Est vol 2,155; vol Thur 9,261; open int 48,685, −1,373.

GERMAN GOV'T. BOND (LIFFE)
250,000 marks; pts of 100%

	Open	High	Low	Settle	Change	Lifetime High	Lifetime Low	Open Interest
Dec	99.55	99.97	99.48	99.85	+ .25	103.75	94.93	159,5[illegible]
Mr94	99.87	100.09	99.87	99.97	+ .26	99.86	98.30	2,5[illegible]

Est vol 111,773; vol Thur 87,844; open int 162,190, +2,863.

ITALIAN GOVT. BOND (LIFFE)
ITL 200,000,000; pts of 100%

	Open	High	Low	Settle	Change	Lifetime High	Lifetime Low	Open Interest
Dec	117.17	117.71	116.75	117.40	+ .10	118.16	102.05	77,43[illegible]
Mr94	116.75	117.37	116.70	117.18	+ .10	117.82	112.10	1,30[illegible]

Est vol 41,452; vol Thur 37,916; open int 78,731, +3,944.

FT–SE 100 INDEX (LIFFE) – £25 per index point

	Open	High	Low	Settle	Change	Lifetime High	Lifetime Low	Open Interest
Dec	3115.	3144.	3109.	3143.	+ 21.0	3149.	2804.	56,782
Mr94	3145.	3155.	3145.	3160.	+ 21.0	3155.	2873.	1,364

Est vol 7,635; vol Thur 5,793; open int 58,206, −361.

CURRENCY

JAPAN YEN (CME) – 12.5 million yen; $ per yen (.00)

	Open	High	Low	Settle	Change	Lifetime High	Lifetime Low	Open Interest
Dec	.9533	.9547	.9421	.9442	− .0099	.9950	.7970	55,377
Mr94	.9533	.9560	.9450	.9465	− .0099	.9930	.8700	2,715

Est vol 32,908; vol Thur 28,366; open int 58,159, −2,863.

DEUTSCHEMARK (CME) – 125,000 marks; $ per mark

	Open	High	Low	Settle	Change	Lifetime High	Lifetime Low	Open Interest
Dec	.6123	.6215	.6120	.6198	+ .0075	.6650	.5657	79,521
Mr94	.6105	.6166	.6105	.6154	+ .0074	.6205	.5646	2,827
June	....	....	....	.6120	+ .0074	.6160	.5607	210

Est vol 64,183; vol Thur 27,325; open int 82,558, −702.

CANADIAN DOLLAR (CME) – 100,000 dlrs.; $ per Can $

	Open	High	Low	Settle	Change	Lifetime High	Lifetime Low	Open Interest
Dec	.7460	.7503	.7460	.7493	+ .0026	.8310	.7425	48,019
Mr94	.7454	.7474	.7454	.7463	+ .0026	.7860	.7394	1,063
June	....	....	....	.7433	+ .0026	.7805	.7363	751
Sept	....	....	....	.7401	+ .0026	.7740	.7345	298

Est vol 5,032; vol Thur 3,664; open int 50,215, +157.

BRITISH POUND (CME) – 62,500 pds.; $ per pound

	Open	High	Low	Settle	Change	Lifetime High	Lifetime Low	Open Interest
Dec	1.5170	1.5314	1.5144	1.5302	+ .0132	1.5670	1.3930	24,946
Mr94	1.5140	1.5220	1.5070	1.5222	+ .0130	1.5550	1.3950	371

Est vol 13,587; vol Thur 7,457; open int 25,332, −701.

SWISS FRANC (CME) – 125,000 francs; $ per franc

	Open	High	Low	Settle	Change	Lifetime High	Lifetime Low	Open Interest
Dec	.6990	.7127	.6990	.7102	+ .0108	.7212	.6400	52,034
Mr94	.6990	.7110	.6990	.7087	+ .0109	.7195	.6470	825

Est vol 27,162; vol Thur 13,175; open int 52,881, +262.

AUSTRALIAN DOLLAR (CME) – 100,000 dlrs.; $ per A.$

	Open	High	Low	Settle	Change	Lifetime High	Lifetime Low	Open Interest
Dec	.6540	.6588	.6535	.6572	+ .0042	.7117	.6392	5,631

Est vol 561; vol Thur 734; open int 5,649, −205.

U.S. DOLLAR INDEX (FINEX) – 1,000 times USDX

	Open	High	Low	Settle	Change	Lifetime High	Lifetime Low	Open Interest
Dec	93.05	93.10	92.04	92.24	− .81	97.30	91.34	5,273
Mr94	93.85	93.85	93.15	93.05	− .82	98.00	91.78	2,013

Est vol 5,650; vol Thur 288; open int 7,325, −77.
The index: High 92.43; Low 91.48; Close 91.65 −1.29

INDEX

S&P 500 INDEX (CME)

	Open	High	Low	Settle	Chg	High	Low	Open Interest
Dec	461.60	462.20	456.90	461.35	+ 1.55	464.85	429.70	183,985
Mr94	462.50	463.00	457.90	462.25	+ 1.55	466.00	434.00	3,337
June		....	....	463.15	+ 1.55	467.00	444.50	1,585

Est vol 57,090; vol Thur 33,324; open int 188,940, −2,339.
Indx prelim High 460.99; Low 456.40; Close 460.30 +1.12

S&P MIDCAP 400 (CME) $500 times index

	Open	High	Low	Settle	Chg	High	Low	Open Interest
Dec	175.30	175.90	173.35	174.90	....	177.20	157.25	13,089

Est vol 620; vol Thur 1,616; open int 13,146, +1,559.
The index: High 174.65; Low 173.14; Close 174.01 −.20

NIKKEI 225 Stock Average (CME) – $5 times index

	Open	High	Low	Settle	Chg	High	Low	Open Interest
Dec	20450.	20500.	20400.	20405.	+ 15.0	21455.	16600.	18,041

Est vol 1,045; vol Thur 632; open int 18,096, +77.
The index: High 20405.04; Low 20180.02; Close 20578.64 +113.01

NYSE COMPOSITE INDEX (NYFE) 500 times index

	Open	High	Low	Settle	Chg	High	Low	Open Interest
Dec	256.60	256.75	253.50	256.30	+ .90	257.75	241.10	3,914
Mr94	256.20	256.70	254.95	256.70	+ .90	257.70	246.60	298

Est vol 4,353; vol Thur 2,022; open int 4,283, −56.
The index: High 256.24; Low 254.10; Close 255.81 +.37

OTHER FUTURES

Settlement prices of selected contracts. Actual volume (from previous session) and open interest of all contract months.

	Vol.	High	Low	Close	Net Change	Lifetime High	Lifetime Low	Open Interest
ANHYDROUS AMMONIA (CBT) 100 tons; $ per ton								
Dec	5	113.00	112.30	113.00	+ 1.50	113.50	99.00	383
BRITISH POUND (MCE) 12,500 pounds; $ per pound								
Dec	112	1.5310	1.5152	1.5302	+ .0132	1.5460	1.4270	621
CANADIAN DOLLAR (MCE) 50,000 Can. $; $ per Can. $								
Dec	22	.7503	.5483	.5493	+ .0027	.7820	.6818	79
CATTLE-LIVE (MCE) 20,000 lb.; ¢ per lb.								
Dec	72	73.97	72.70	72.72	1.20	76.65	68.10	143
CORN (MCE) 1,000 bu.; cents per bu.								
Dec	558	243	240½	241¾	+ ¼	268½	225½	6,251
COTTON-WORLD (CTN) 50,000 lbs.; cents per lbs.								
Dec	0	56.75	56.50	56.85	+ .45	63.30	53.85	313
CRB INDEX (NYFE) – 500 times index								
Dec	121	218.90	217.90	218.60	+ .50	225.70	207.00	2,417
The index: High 218.44; Low 217.45; Close 218.44 +1.07								
DEUTSCHEMARK (MCE) 62,500 marks; $ per mark								
Dec	71	.6216	.6124	.6202	+ .0079	.6243	.5664	287
DEUTSCHEMARK (PBOT) 125,000 marks; ¢ per mark								
Dec	0	.6190	.6190	.6190	....	.6269	.6144	72
DIAMMONIUM PHOSPHATE (CBT 100 tons; $ per ton								
Dec	154	127.20	126.50	126.70	− .10	127.30	110.50	1,185
DM ROLLING SPOT (CME) $250,000; DM per U.S. $								
Dec	494	1.6221	1.5995	1.6031	− .0196	1.6565	1.5888	299
EURODOLLAR (MCE) $500,000; pts. of 100%								
Dec	19	96.60	96.58	96.58	+ .03	96.60	94.48	122
EUROMARK (CME) DM 1,000,000; pts. of 100%								
Dec	65	93.74	93.74	93.74	− .03	94.22	93.76	957
EUROTOP 100 INDEX (CMX) – $100 times index								
Dec	180	1153.5	1146.3	1152.5	+ 2.10	1163.5	1012.5	1,000
The index: High 1135.00; Low 1127.50; Close 1133.20 +2.30								
FRENCH FRANC (CME) 500,000 FF; $ per franc								
Dec	120	1.7680	1.7450	1.7646	+ .0148	1.7676	1.7186	1,053
GSCI (CME) $250 X GSCI nearby index;								
Dec	174	179.90	179.10	179.90	....	182.20	172.20	2,314
The index: High 177.72; Low 176.79; Close 177.88 +.53								
GOLD-NY (MCE) 33.2 fine troy oz.; cents per troy oz.								
Dec	41	362.20	358.50	361.50	+ 3.00	414.00	331.70	724
GOLD-KILO (CBT) 32.15 troy oz.; $ per troy oz.								
Dec	48	362.00	359.00	362.00	+ 3.50	413.70	331.00	551
HOGS (MCE) 20,000 lb.; ¢ per lb.								
Dec	45	50.90	50.10	50.80	+ .32	51.05	40.07	499
JAPANESE YEN (MCE) 6.25 million yen; $ per yen (.00)								
Dec	327	.9535	.9421	.9442	− .0099	.9917	.8075	335
KC MINI VALUE LINE (KC) – 100 times index								
Dec	97	441.60	436.00	441.00	+ 1.65	442.20	405.25	318
KC VALUE LINE INDEX (KC) – 500 times index								
Dec	73	441.30	436.00	440.90	+ 1.35	442.20	404.30	940
The index: High 440.22; Low 438.17; Close 439.72 +.33								
LUMBER (CME) 160,000 bd .ft., $ per 1,000 bd.ft.								
Nov	876	308.30	296.00	307.50	+ 9.20	428.90	220.00	2,096
MILK-NONFAT DRY (CSCE) 44,000 lbs.; ¢ per lb.								
Nov	2	....	....	104.35	− .05	428.90	220.00	125
MAJOR MARKET INDEX (CME) $500 times index								
Nov	103	....	....	362.10	+ 1.05	369.90	356.60	1,933
The index: High 362.96; Low 358.89; Close 361.87 +.28								
OATS (MCE) 1,000 bu.; ¢ per bu.								
Dec	2	136½	136¼	136¾	− ¼	158½	135	135
OATS (MPLS) 5,000 bu.; ¢ per bu.								
Dec	0	....	....	131	....	155	127¼	21
PLATINUM (MCE) 25 troy oz.; cents per troy oz.								
Jan	8	365.70	363.20	364.10	+ .70	427.00	351.50	252
PROPANE (NYM) 42,000 gal.; ¢ per gal.								
Nov	71	30.90	30.85	30.90	− .10	36.75	30.00	2,325
RICE-ROUGH (MCE) 2000 cwt; $ per cwt								
Nov	1,463	7.930	7.710	7.740	− .030	8.700	5.300	3,843
RUSSELL 2000 INDEX (CME) $500 times index								
Dec	3	255.50	253.60	255.00	− .10	255.70	243.55	832
SHRIMP (MPLS) 5,000 lbs.; ¢ per lb.								
Dec	1	383	383	384	+ 4	390	326	88
SILVER (MCE) 1,000 troy oz.; cents per troy oz.								
Dec	56	4.400	4.300	436.0	− 2.3	553.0	362.0	2,097
SILVER (CBT) 5,000 troy oz.; cents per troy oz.								
Dec	509	436.5	432.0	436.5	+ 9.0	551.0	385.0	518
SOYBEANS (MCE) 1,000 bu.; cents per bu.								
Nov	3,632	613	607½	608¾	− 1¾	757½	555½	16,962
SOYBEAN MEAL (MCE) 20 tons; cents per ton								
Dec	17	190.70	188.90	189.70	+ .20	240.00	183.40	305
SWISS FRANC (MCE) 62,500 francs; $ per franc								
Dec	142	.7127	.6995	.7103	+ .0109	.7212	.6479	2,126
10 – YEAR T.NOTES (MCE) 50,000; pts. 32nds of 100%								
Dec	66	116-15	116-11	116-15	+ 21	116-07	111-24	389
WHEAT (MCE) 1,000 bu.; cents per bu.								
Dec	208	323	321	322	− ½	360	294	1,810
WHITE WHEAT (MPLS) 5,000 bu.; cents per bu.								
Dec	61	355	354	354	− 1	395	334	575
WILSHIRE SMALL CAP INDEX (CBT) $500 times index								
Dec	10	na	na	na	na	na	na	na
The index: High 328.02; Low 325.53; Close 326.96 −.48								

CURRENCY TRADING

EXCHANGE RATES

Friday, October 8, 1993

The New York foreign exchange selling rates below apply to trading among banks in amounts of $1 million and more, as quoted at 3 p.m. Eastern time by Bankers Trust Co., Telerate and other sources. Retail transactions provide fewer units of foreign currency per dollar.

Country	U.S. $ equiv. Fri.	U.S. $ equiv. Thurs.	Currency per U.S. $ Fri.	Currency per U.S. $ Thurs.
Argentina (Peso)	1.01	1.01	.99	.99
Australia (Dollar)	.6588	.6566	1.5179	1.5232
Austria (Schilling)	.08863	.08757	11.28	11.42
Bahrain (Dinar)	2.6518	2.6518	.3771	.3771
Belgium (Franc)	.02871	.02840	34.84	35.21
Brazil (Cruzeiro real)	.0075717	.0075717	132.07	132.07
Britain (Pound)	1.5265	[illegible]	.6558	.6564
30-Day Forward	1.5229	[illegible]	.6534	.6579
90-Day Forward	1.5270	1.5141	.6549	.6605
180-Day Forward	1.5189	1.5060	.6584	.6640
Canada (Dollar)	.7511	.7488	1.3313	1.3355
30-Day Forward	.7502	.7479	1.3329	1.3371
90-Day Forward	.7486	.7462	1.3359	1.3402
180-Day Forward	.7455	.7429	1.3413	1.3461
Czech. Rep. (Koruna)				
Commercial rate	.0347705	.0353482	28.7600	28.2900
Chile (Peso)	.002505	.002505	399.16	399.16
China (Renminbi)	.174856	.174856	5.7190	5.7190
Colombia (Peso)	.001448	.001448	690.84	690.84
Denmark (Krone)	.1538	.1521	6.5014	6.5756
Ecuador (Sucre)				
Floating rate	.000527	.000527	1897.03	1897.03
Finland (Markka)	.17503	.17337	5.7133	5.7681
France (Franc)	.17782	.17618	5.6238	5.6760
30-Day Forward	.17717	.17555	5.6443	5.6964
90-Day Forward	.17605	.17447	5.6801	5.7317
180-Day Forward	.17467	.17315	5.7252	5.7755
Germany (Mark)	.6236	.6161	1.6035	1.6230
30-Day Forward	.6217	.6141	1.6086	1.6283
90-Day Forward	.6182	.6108	1.6175	1.6371
180-Day Forward	.6141	.6068	1.6284	1.6480
Greece (Drachma)	.004287	.004256	233.25	234.95
Hong Kong (Dollar)	.12944	.12943	7.7255	7.7261
Hungary (Forint)	.0102997	.0104351	97.0900	95.8300
India (Rupee)	.03212	.03212	31.13	31.13
Indonesia (Rupiah)	.0004753	.0004753	2103.93	2103.93
Ireland (Punt)	1.4671	1.4547	.6816	.6874
Israel (Shekel)	.3559	.3567	2.8108	2.8032
Italy (Lira)	.0006309	.0006225	1585.06	1606.37
Japan (Yen)	.009434	.009528	106.00	104.95
30-Day Forward	.009439	.009534	105.94	104.89
90-Day Forward	.009455	.009550	105.77	104.72
180-Day Forward	.009475	.009571	105.55	104.48
Jordan (Dinar)	1.4789	1.4789	.6762	.6762
Kuwait (Dinar)	3.3455	3.3455	.2989	.2989
Lebanon (Pound)	.000580	.000580	1723.50	1723.50
Malaysia (Ringgit)	.3936	.3934	2.5405	2.5420
Malta (Lira)	2.6316	2.6316	.3800	.3800
Mexico (Peso)				
Floating rate	.3210273	.3210273	3.1150	3.1150
Netherland (Guilder)	.5547	.5482	1.8029	1.8243
New Zealand (Dollar)	.5516	.5499	1.8129	1.8185
Norway (Krone)	.1424	.1408	7.0233	7.1006
Pakistan (Rupee)	.0336	.0336	29.78	29.78
Peru (New Sol)	.4861	.4861	2.06	2.06
Philippines (Peso)	.03584	.03584	27.90	27.90
Poland (Zloty)	.00005030	.00005271	19882.00	18971.00
Portugal (Escudo)	.006029	.005967	165.87	167.57
Saudi Arabia (Riyal)	.26659	.26659	3.7511	3.7511
Singapore (Dollar)	.6388	.6351	1.5655	1.5745
Slovak Rep. (Koruna)	.0310270	.0310270	32.2300	32.2300
South Africa (Rand)				
Commercial rate	.2905	.2898	3.4425	3.4510
Financial rate	.2385	.2443	4.1925	4.0925
South Korea (Won)	.0012324	.0012314	811.40	812.10
Spain (Peseta)	.007665	.007578	130.46	131.97
Sweden (Krona)	.1254	.1240	7.9758	8.0623
Switzerland (Franc)	.7120	.7013	1.4045	1.4260
30-Day Forward	.7109	.7002	1.4066	1.4281
90-Day Forward	.7095	.6990	1.4094	1.4307
180-Day Forward	.7081	.6974	1.4123	1.4338
Taiwan (Dollar)	.037244	.037651	26.85	26.56
Thailand (Baht)	.03957	.03957	25.27	25.27
Turkey (Lira)	.0000804	.0000822	12440.00	12170.00
United Arab (Dirham)	.2723	.2723	3.6725	3.6725
Uruguay (New Peso)				
Financial	.237247	.237247	4.22	4.22
Venezuela (Bolivar)				
Floating rate	.01013	.01031	98.70	96.97
SDR	1.41825	1.41824	.70509	.70510
ECU	1.17800	1.16400	....	....

Special Drawing Rights (SDR) are based on exchange rates for the U.S., German, British, French and Japanese currencies. Source: International Monetary Fund.

European Currency Unit (ECU) is based on a basket of community currencies.

SOURCE: *The Wall Street Journal,* October 2, 1993.

TABLE 20.2 Contract Specifications for Futures Contracts

	Panel A: U.S. Government Bonds	
ITEM	*CONTRACT SPECIFICATIONS*	
Exchange	Chicago Board of Trade	Mid-America Commodity Exchange
Introduced	August 22, 1977	September 18, 1981
Specification/ basis	U.S. bonds which, if callable, are not callable for at least 15 years from the first day of the delivery month or, if not callable, have a maturity of at least 15 years from the first business day of the delivery month. Coupon based on 8% standard.	U.S. bonds with a nominal 8% coupon maturing at least 15 years from delivery date if not callable; if callable, not so for at least 15 years from delivery date.
Contract Unit	$100,000 face value.	$50,000 face value.
Quotation	Points	Points
Tick size	1/32 point	1/32 point
Tick Value	$31.25	$15.62
Delivery Months	March, June, September, December	March, June, September, December
Trading Hours	7:20 A.M.–2:00 P.M. (Monday to Friday) Central Standard Time plus evening hours 5:20 P.M. to 8:05 P.M. (Sunday to Thursday). GLOBEX trading 10:30 A.M. to 6:00 A.M. (Sunday to Thursday)	7:20 A.M. to 3:15 P.M. Central Standard Time.

Maximum Daily Limit	3 points, expandable to 4-1/2 points in certain circumstances. Limits are lifted the second business day preceding the first day of the delivery month.	3 points.
Last day of trading	Seven business days prior to the last business day of the delivery month. Trading ceases in expiring contract at 12:00 noon.	The business day prior to the last seven business days of the delivery month. Trading in an expiring contract ceases at noon.
Position limits		$100,000,000 face value net on the same side of the market in any one month or all months combined.
Delivery	Physical by Federal Reserve book-entry wire transfer system. Last delivery day is the last business day of the delivery month. The invoice price equals the futures settlement price times a conversion factor plus accrued interest. The conversion factor is the price of the delivered bond ($1 par value) to yield 8 percent.	Physical by Federal Reserve book-entry wire transfer system, invoice price on delivery is adjusted for coupon rates and term to maturity or call.

TABLE 20.2 (*continued*)

Panel B: Three-Month Eurodollar Futures

ITEM	*CONTRACT SPECIFICATIONS*	
Exchange	International Monetary Market (IMM) Division, Chicago Mercantile Exchange	London International Financial Futures and Options Exchange
Introduced	December 9, 1981	September 30, 1982
Specification/ basis	Eurodollar time deposit having a principal value of $1,000,000 with a three-month maturity	Cash settlement based on the interest rates for three-month Eurodollar deposits.
Contract Unit	$1,000,000.	$1,000,000.
Quotation	IMM Eurodollar Index points (100 minus yield on an annual basis for a 360-day year)	100 minus rate of interest.
Tick size	.01 point	.01
Tick Value	$25.00	$25.00
Delivery Months	Sixteen months in the March, June, September, December cycle plus the spot month	March, June, September, December
Trading Hours	7:20 A.M.–2:00 P.M. (Monday–Friday) Central Standard TimeST plus evening hours 2:20 P.M. to 4:00 P.M. and 6:00 P.M. to 6:00 A.M. (Sunday to Thursday) on GLOBEX.	8:30 A.M. to 4:00 P.M. London time.

Maximum Daily Limit	None on exchange; GLOBEX limit 2 points.	None.
Last day of trading	The second London bank business day preceding the third Wednesday of the contract month. Trading in expiring ceases at 9:16 A.M.	Two business days prior to the third Wednesday of the delivery month. Trading in an expiring contract ceases at 11:00 A.M.
Position limits	Position accountability for persons owning or controlling more that 10,000 contracts net long or short in all months combined.	None.
Delivery	Cash settlement on last day of trading.	Cash settlement takes place on the first business day after the last day of trading. Settlement is against the Exchange Delivery Settlement Prices which is based on the British Bankers' Association Interest Settlement Rate (BBAISR) for three-month Eurodollar deposits at 11:00 A.M. on the last day of trading. The settlement price is 100 minus the BBAISR (rounded accordingly)

Note: Also traded on Singapore International Monetary Exchange Limited ($1,000,000 contract unit) since September 7, 1984 and MidAmerica Commodity Exchange ($500,000 contract unit) since August 21, 1992.

TABLE 20.2 (*continued*)

Panel C: German Mark Futures

ITEM	*CONTRACT SPECIFICATIONS*	
Exchange	International Monetary Market Division, Chicago Mercantile Exchange	Singapore International Monetary Exchange Limited
Introduced	May 16, 1972	September 7, 1984
Specification/ basis	Physical delivery of Deutschmark currency	Physical delivery of Deutschmark currency.
Contract Unit	Deutschmark 125,000	Deutschmark 125,000
Quotation	U.S. dollars per Deutschmark	U.S. dollars per Deutschmark
Tick size	$.0001 (one point)	$.0001 (one point)
Tick Value	$12.50	$12.50
Delivery Months	Spot plus January, March, April, June, July, September, October, December cycle	Spot plus March, June, September, December
Trading Hours	7:20 A.M.–2:00 P.M. (Monday–Friday) Central Standard Time plus evening hours 2:30 P.M. to 6:00 A.M. (Sunday to Thursday) on GLOBEX.	8:20 A.M. to 5:10 P.M. local time.

Maximum Daily Limit	Opening limit (between 7:20 and 7:35 A.M.) of 200 points during regular hours; GLOBEX limit 400 points.	None.
Last day of trading	The second business day immediately preceding the third Wednesday of the contract month. Trading in expiring month ceases at 9:30 A.M.	Second business day preceding the third Wednesday of the contract month.
Position limits	Position accountability for persons owning or controlling more that 10,000 contracts net long or short in all months combined.	1000 contract net long or short in all contract moneths combined. Higher position limits may be granted for bona fide hedging transactions upon written application to the exchange.
Delivery	Physical on third Wednesday of the delivery month in the country of issuance at a bank designated by the clearing house.	Physical on the third Wednesday of the contract month.

Note: Also traded on Philadelphia Board of Trade (Deutschmark 125,000 contract unit) since August 8, 1986 and MidAmerica Commodity Exchange (Deutschmark 62,500 contract unit) since September 15, 1983.

SOURCE: Nick Battley, *The World's Futures and Options Markets* (Burr Ridge, IL: Irwin Professional Publishing, 1993).

International Financial Futures Exchange (LIFFE). Instead of delivering financial instruments, Eurodollar contracts settle in cash at maturity as seen in Table 20.2, an example of *cash settlement* contracts. Students should practice interpreting the terms introduced above by using these quotes (based on 360-day discount basis), which we use in examples throughout this discussion.

Futures and forward contracts can be used to hedge asset risks when values of these contacts move in the opposite direction to the changes in value of the assets or liabilities of interest in the portfolio. When the combined total of the change in the value of an asset or liability added to the change in the value of the futures or forward contract varies less than the asset or liability alone, some of the price, interest rate, or foreign exchange risk has been hedged. Hedging using futures or forward contracts is said to be *perfect* or *complete* when there is no variation in the sum of asset and futures or forward contract values despite changes in risk factors. In practice, no hedges are perfect. Hedges are said to be *imperfect, incomplete,* or *partial* if risks are not completely eliminated. We discuss factors determining why hedging can rarely be perfect below.

Hedging can be directed at individual asset risk exposure or net portfolio risk exposure. Hedging directed at individual asset risk exposure is called *microhedging* because it relies on price variations between futures or forward contracts and a narrow class of assets. Hedging can also be directed at the risk of an entire portfolio of assets or the net worth in a portfolio of assets and liabilities: this strategy is called *macrohedging*. An example of microhedging would be a bank that hedges its Treasury bill holdings with futures contracts. Macrohedging is more complicated, with financial managers attempting to hedge the net or aggregate risk of a number of assets and liabilities hedged with one or more futures or forward contracts.

Risk Exposure and Futures and Forward Positions: Terminology

The first order of business is to introduce standard terminology used by decision makers seeking to hedge risks in the futures or forward markets. Readers must keep in mind that in the recent historical past, trading in futures and forward contracts was dominated by trading in contracts for agricultural commodities and such other commodities as copper and gold. Terminology for financial forward and futures contracts is often borrowed from usage in traditional commodity trading. For example, financial futures contracts are traded on commodity futures exchanges by commodities brokers. Sometimes the terms used with respect to financial futures make less sense than when used with respect to commodities contracts.

We have collected some common terms used in discussing forward and futures in Table 20.3. The columns in that table describe the time frames: the present is of course *now,* when decisions must be made, denoted t_0. We know or determine through an analysis of our business plans now whether we currently have assets or will produce assets (which can mean that we plan to issue liabilities) at some future time point, t_F. Alternatively, we may establish now that we will need to buy assets now or at some point t_F in the future. Our business plans

TABLE 20.3 Standard Terms Used in Futures and Forward Markets

	TERM USED IN TIME PERIOD	
CONDITION DEFINED	*PRESENT TIME PERIOD (t_0)*	*FUTURE TIME PERIOD (t_F)*
Market where delivery price of asset determined	*Spot* or *cash* market	*Future* or *forward* market
Delivery price determined at t_0	*Spot* or *cash* price	*Forward* or *futures* price
Delivery price for asset at t_F	Expected *future spot* or *cash price*	*Spot* or *cash* price
Need asset for business purposes Have promised to deliver asset Sold asset	*Short*	*Short*
Hold asset or will produce asset Have promised to buy asset Bought asset	*Long*	*Long*

or commitments determine now our asset purchases or sales for business purposes in the future.

The assets emphasized in this discussion are financial assets or liabilities. We focus primarily on fixed income securities and foreign exchange in our discussion below, but the assets at risk can be any economic quantities of value, like gold, cattle, grain, or housing assets. Table 20.3 introduces the usual terminology to describe our position with respect to assets: if we have or will produce assets, we are *long*. Alternatively, if we need, will need, or have sold assets, we are *short*. The fundamental point here is that we have identified now, t_0, our long or short position now or at a future time, t_F.

The two columns show when asset transactions will take place. If we have immediate needs, we can acquire or sell assets in the spot or cash markets. For example, if an insurance company has received premiums at time t_0 and needs to fund future pension liabilities, the company has a *short* position in bonds (or other earning assets) because it needs assets. If a mortgage banker has an inventory of mortgages on hand from financing new home sales, the mortgage banker is *long* mortgages. As another example, an American exporter who has just received payment for goods in German marks is *long* marks.

The insurance company, the mortgage banker, and the exporter above are exposed to asset price or interest rate risk as long as they do nothing about their long or short positions in financial assets. The insurance company may lose interest earnings, the mortgage banker may experience capital losses, and the exporter may lose dollar profits if interest rates or exchange rates change before they act. Their risk exposure from changes in interest rates or exchange rates can be eliminated immediately in the cash market for the relevant asset in each case: by buying bonds in the case of the insurance company, selling mortgages in the case of the mortgage banker, and trading marks for dollars by the exporter. Each can eliminate the present long or short position in the cash market immediately.

20.2 HEDGING AND SPECULATING USING FUTURES AND FORWARD MARKETS

The problem we focus on now is more interesting than asset price risk which can be removed by purchase or sale immediately in cash markets. We consider future needs and the risks of fulfilling those needs. For example, if an insurance company expects a premium payment at some time t_F in the future, this means that the insurance company currently has a *short* position in its future holdings of income producing assets, using the terminology in Table 20.3. Mortgage bankers expecting to originate mortgages in the future according to business plans or commitments have a future *long* position in interest bearing securities. The corporation selling goods for German marks in the future under current contracts expects to be *long* in German marks in the future.

Future long or short positions resulting from plans or commitments expose financial institutions and their customers to asset price, interest rate, or exchange rate risk in the future. The concept of long and short positions determined by current plans and commitments introduced in Table 20.3 is important. Practice with applications of these concepts and familiarity with relevant terminology are critical for managers of financial institutions and portfolio managers.

In this section, we discuss and illustrate how futures and forward contracts can be used to manage financial risks. Futures and forward markets allow financial market transactors to enter into contracts at the present time which commit them to buying or selling assets for delivery and payment in the future at a price agreed upon now. These contract values will change in response to the same factors changing asset values. The total exposure to changes in portfolio asset value risks may be reduced or eliminated when contracts can be found that offset the changes in values of concern to decision makers.

Figure 20.1 illustrates the relation between changes in yields and the profits and losses from a long position in a fixed-income asset in the spot or futures market. If yields increase from purchase date levels, denoted i^*, or equivalently the price of assets falls relative to the price at which the forward or futures contract was made, the holder will sustain losses. Gains occur if yields fall below i^* and prices of underlying assets rise.

In the forward market, the loss or gain associated with the long position will not be realized until delivery of the asset is received at the contract delivery date, t_F. At time t_F the long contract holder in the forward of futures market accepts an asset that is worth less if yields rise or more if yields fall than would be the case

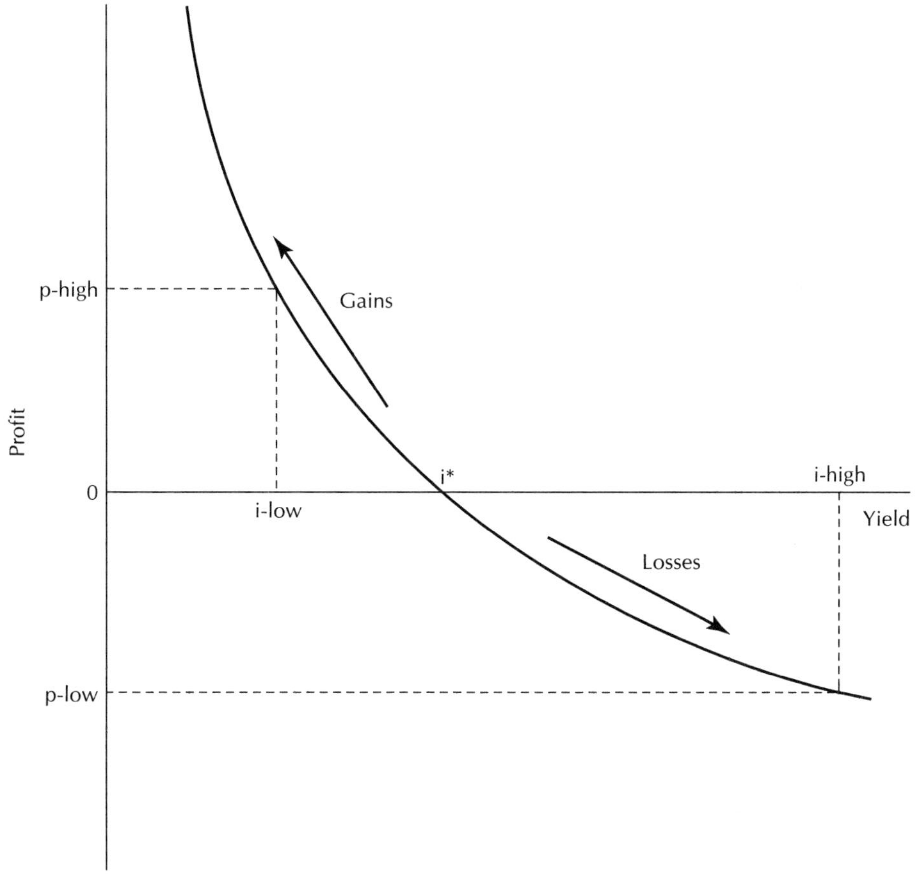

FIGURE 20.1 Yield and profits with long position in spot or futures

if yields were unchanged at i*. (In the futures market, as we discuss below, profits or losses from the futures position will be paid as realized.)

The opposite interest rate exposure faces the financial manager who is short a contract in the futures market, as shown in Figure 20.2. If rates rise above the initial yield i*, fixed income security prices will fall. The short can now buy assets cheaper either to fill the business need identified at time t_F or to make delivery to the futures contract maturing then at a price higher than the cash market cost of the asset. On the other hand, should yields fall, the short will have to pay higher prices to fill its asset needs or to cover a short position in the futures or forward markets. The profits and losses from short and long positions in the same asset move in precisely the opposite directions.

The opposite movement in the gains and losses from long and short positions can be used to hedge asset risk stemming from exposure to risk from an unhedged short or long position. We have shown the way these transactions eliminate exposure to interest rate or asset price risk in Figure 20.3 using diagonal arrows. For example, if you currently hold bonds, that is you have a long

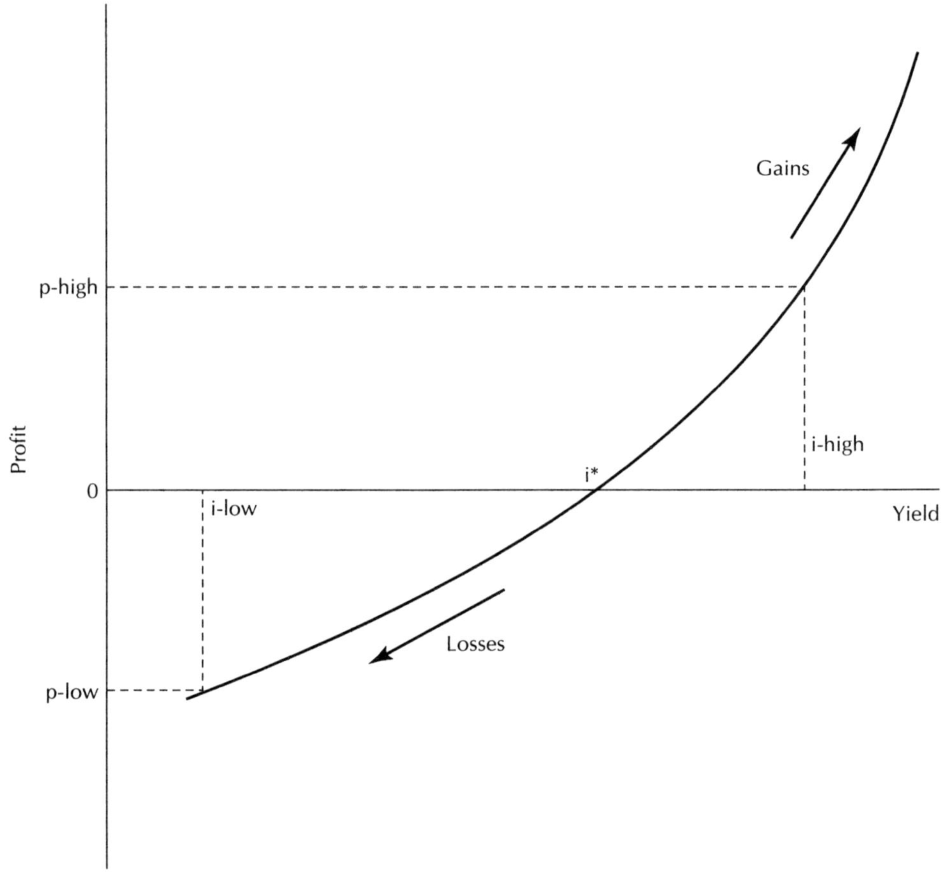

FIGURE 20.2 Yield and profits with short position in spot or futures

position in bonds, interest rate increases reduce your bonds' value: you lose money. On the other hand, if you have promised to deliver bonds at some future date in the futures market, that is you sell or *short* bonds, increases in interest rates mean you will be able to buy bonds to deliver to the contract at reduced prices: you will make money on the future position. If interest rates fall, you gain on the long position and lose on the short position. The values of long and short positions in bonds move in opposite directions. Gains on one position tend to offset losses on the other.

Figure 20.3 illustrate ways in which long and short positions can be used to offset changes to reduce or eliminate risk. To interpret the figure we use some examples: the insurance company above expecting premium income is *short* income producing assets because it knows it will need assets. It can eliminate its asset price risk by going *long* in the futures or forward markets, committing to buy in the future. This position is shown in Figure 20.3 by the light arrow: the insurance company purchases bonds for future delivery at prices agreed upon now.

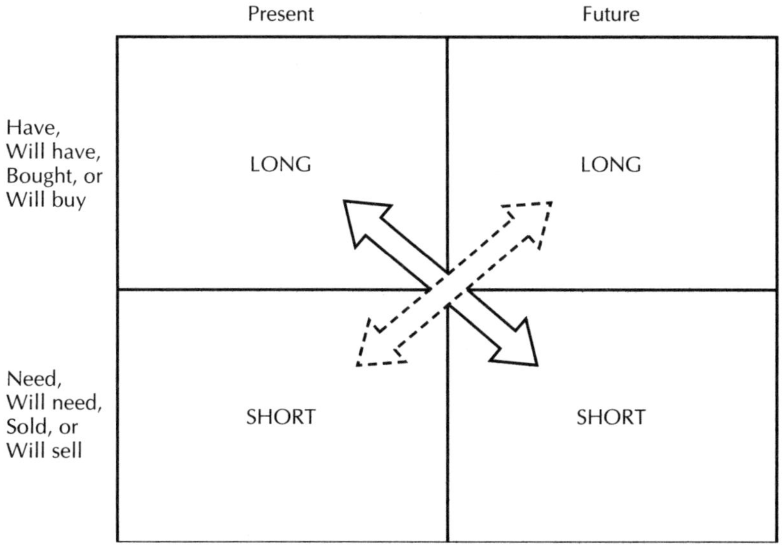

FIGURE 20.3 Hedging risk with futures or forward contracts

As a second example of the use of futures and forward markets, the mortgage banker who will be issuing mortgages according to a plan is long mortgages. The mortgage banker may reduce sensitivity to interest rates by going *short* in the futures market, promising to deliver interest bearing securities in the future at prices agreed upon today. The mortgage banker hedges by following the dark arrow. Finally, the exporter who with a long position in German marks can take an offsetting *short* position in marks by selling marks in the futures or forward markets, also using the dark arrow in Figure 20.3. Hedging transactions can be visualized in the figure by arrows crossing short and long positions in assets with the opposite position in futures or forward markets.

Example of Hedging Activity

For a detailed example of hedging with futures, we consider the case of a commercial bank on October 8, 1993, which anticipates a surge in short-term loan takedowns under fixed rate agreements in March 1994. These conditions are given in Table 20.4. The bank expects that this loan demand will require issuance of 90-day certificates of deposit (CDs) in the amount of $10 million in March. The current rate on the bank's CDs is 3.4 percent. The bank does not want to be exposed to the uncertainty of future interest rates on the deposits it issues since that would expose the spread over the loan rates to interest rate risk.

First, we determine the bank's position. Since it now plans to issue assets, namely CDs, the bank's exposure in the terminology of Figure 20.3 is *long* assets in March. The bank's financial risk managers seek an appropriate forward or future contract to hedge this risk. They determine that the Eurodollar rates follow their CD rates pretty closely so they select the 90-day Eurodollar futures market

TABLE 20.4 Example of Hedging CD Costs Using Futures

Panel A: Actions in Spot and Futures Markets

ACTIONS NOW (t_0)

PRESENT PLAN	*FUTURES MARKET*
Will need to issue $10 million in CDs in March 1994, current rate is 3.42 percent bankers' discount	Sell 10 March contracts in Eurodollar futures market at 3.42 percent bankers' discount

ACTIONS LATER (t_F)

FUTURE CONDITIONS	*RATES HIGHER (4 PERCENT)*	*RATES LOWER (3 PERCENT)*
Pay interest on CDs at current market[a]	($100,000)	($75,000)
Profit (loss) from covering short position in futures market[b]	14,500	(10,500)
Net Interest Cost of CD	($85,500)	($85,500)
Annualized Yield Cost on $10 million (4 times amount divided by amount borrowed)	3.42%	3.42%

[a]Interest on CDs paid on 360-day basis maturity. Example assumes prepayment of interest.

[b]Most contracts are not delivered but are settled at maturity with simple closing of contract and loss side paying profits to gain side. See text discussion.

Panel B: Income Statement Impact of Futures Transactions

PRO FORMA INCOME STATEMENT	*RATES HIGHER (4 PERCENT)*	*RATES LOWER (3 PERCENT)*
Interest Expense	($100,000)	($75,000)
Profit (loss) in futures	14,500	(10,500)
Impact on Net Income	($85,500)	($85,500)

to hedge the risk. They *short* 10 March 1994 contracts at the (annualized 360-day year) price 96.58 for a discount yield of 3.42, where we use the quotations in Table 20.1 for our example. Panel A of Table 20.4 presents the hedging strategy planned by the bank.

The example in Table 20.4 illustrates how futures markets work to hedge risk. In this example, two future possible interest rate scenarios in March 1994 are explored in Panel A of the table. In one, rates on both Eurodollars and the bank CDs rise to 4 percent (annualized) and in the other rates fall to 3 percent. The bank's borrowing costs increase or decrease exactly with the change in market rates for CDs. The profit or loss from the long futures market position in Eurodollars offsets the change in interest costs, so that when the net interest costs including gains or losses are included, the borrowing costs are fixed relative to the expected level of 3.42 percent.

Panel B of Table 20.4 provides the impact on the financial statements of a financial institutions using futures or forward to hedge interest rate risk. These changes in pro forma income statements illustrate an important aspect of hedging with futures or forward contracts. Although the management's strategy had locked into a level of net interest expense, the accounting for the hedge shows up in two places: interest expense and futures profits or losses.

Isolation of futures transactions gains and losses in financial statements may lead users of those statements to overlook the economic role of hedging activities. In some legal cases where management was cautious by hedging interest rate risk, it was accused by uninformed users of the financial statements of speculating in futures markets because of the reported losses in futures market trading. This problem can be even more important in the case of macrohedging discussed below where futures contracts hedging interest rate exposure are not tied down to specific financial instruments but are aimed at overall or net interest rate risk.

Speculation

Speculators take long or short positions in assets in order to profit from price or rate moves the speculator predicts are likely to happen. For example, taking a long position in bonds by buying bonds in the cash market is speculation. This makes sense if the speculator expects interest rates to go down since bond prices will then rise. Forward and futures markets are also used for speculation. Long positions in the futures market make money if yields fall before contracts expire because holders of the contracts can take delivery of bonds at a lower price than they can immediately resell them for in the cash market. Losers who are short in the futures contract typically buy their contract back from the holder of a long position guaranteeing the long position profits without the transactions costs and trouble of delivering bonds. Because the cash requirements for futures and forward markets are less than for buying bonds in the cash market, futures and forward markets are attractive to speculators.

Figure 20.3 is useful in distinguishing speculative and hedging activity by financial decision makers. In terms of Figure 20.3, a hedger offsets a long or short risk exposure by *crossing in the box*. Speculators simply take an uncrossed position, taking a long or short position depending on whether prices of assets are expected to go up or down, respectively. Speculators are completely exposed to the price movements of the assets or futures or forward contracts they have taken positions in. Hedgers have an offsetting position.

A great deal of regulatory and investor attention has been attracted to the question of whether financial managers are speculating or hedging. For example, regulators prohibit speculation on the part of insured institutions. Financial managers can explain their hedging strategies easily when they can show specific asset price risk offset by specific forward or futures contracts. On the other hand, when using complex cross hedges as discussed below, disputes by regulators and investors have occurred as to whether the use of futures and forward contracts was for speculation or hedging.

The above discussion highlights an essential but underappreciated aspect of futures and forward markets. If financial managers identify current or future asset risk exposure *and* there exist futures or forward markets where those risks can be hedged *and* they do not hedge, they are speculating. In other words, not using futures or forward markets is a speculative strategy for some financial institutions or their customers. Several examples illustrate this: The bank with future funding needs that does not hedge that risk is knowingly or unknowingly speculating on future interest rates. An insurance company expecting premium income which does not hedge its insurance liability funding requirements is speculating. Exporters receiving foreign currency without hedging are speculating. The key point is that futures and forward markets are not intrinsically speculative and failure to use them may in fact represent speculation. Regulators and investors often fail to understand this point.

20.3 PRACTICAL CONCERNS IN HEDGING WITH FORWARDS AND FUTURES

The example presented in Table 20.4 is idealized in order to simplify the discussion of how futures and forward contracts work to hedge interest rate risk. In practice, many issues make hedging with these contracts more difficult. We discuss several of these issues below. There are three important considerations for forward or futures markets to be useful in hedging these risks: (1) a market exists; (2) the prices, interest rates, exchange rates, or other risk factor on the contracts traded on the futures or forward market are highly correlated to the asset risks of concern; and (3) other factors, such as the total amount of price, interest rate, or exchange risk, are considered and can be incorporated into risk management strategies. We discuss each of these considerations.

Availability of Futures and Forward Markets

First, a forward or futures market must exist for forward or futures contracts to be useful in hedging. An obvious condition for forwards or futures to work is that a financial manager with risk exposure is able to find a counterparty to take the other side of the contract. Active markets, with many participants, exist for many financial instruments. Look at the *Wall Street Journal* or the *Financial Times* futures markets tables to gain an idea of the range of financial instruments and volume of trading in futures and forward markets. Summarizing available contracts, a variety of futures and forward contracts for fixed-income securities of both U.S. and foreign government issuers of different maturities, common currencies used in international trade, contracts on stock market indices, and commodities and precious metals, are all actively traded contracts. Published tables substantially underrepresent the forward contracts for which counterparties can be found readily. Commercial and investment banks specialize in identifying financial risks that financial managers wish to hedge and then earn fees by entering into forward contracts as counterparties.

Banks and others offering forward contracts for risky assets often find offsetting contract risk exposure with other participants in the market or hedge their risk in the futures markets. For example, large international commercial banks quote forward rates for foreign currencies and fixed-income securities, acting as counterparties for both the long and short positions in these contracts. Usually financial firms dealing in foreign exchange do not have large net exposure to the currency risks because they have entered contracts on both sides of the transaction. Banks and other financial institutions stake their reputations and capital as contract guarantees to their counterparties, assuring their customers acceptable levels of performance risk.

The availability of futures or forward contracts to hedge risks faced by portfolio managers is a dynamic area. Banks and other financial service firms are constantly looking for new forward contracts to offer clients to generate fees from risk management activities. New contracts are introduced on the organized exchanges each year. Depending on demand by portfolio managers and speculators, some contracts survive as successful products and others die.

Correlation of Contract Risks Must Be High

The price movements that are the basis of a portfolio's risk exposure and the offsetting price movements of futures or forward contracts must be close or the hedge will not work. In the example of hedging presented in Table 20.4, the Eurodollar futures market was assumed to be perfectly correlated with the bank's CD rates. In the case of most financial instruments, like mortgages or an individual firm's commercial paper, there is no trading in identical contracts.

Table 20.5 expands our previous example to demonstrate the impact if the movement in futures market rates is not perfectly correlated with the asset risk. The revised and more realistic example assumes that the spread between CDs and Eurodollars changes from zero to 10 basis points if rates fall and to five basis points if rates rise. In this case, the net interest cost of the CD is not perfectly offset by the loss or gain on the Eurodollar futures contact. The less than perfect correlation of contract rates with assets at risk is one source of an imperfect hedge.

The expanded example also includes the effect of brokerage costs on futures contracts. While futures traded on exchanges have negotiated and usually low commissions for institutional traders like financial institutions, the costs must be explicitly considered to assess the effectiveness of a hedge. Since brokerage costs are inevitable, they are not correlated with changes in asset values and hence are not a source of increased basis risk. These costs do however reduce the value of a hedge relative to an unhedged position.

In cases of mortgages or other more narrowly defined fixed-income securities, such as debt instruments of particular corporations, hedging can only be

TABLE 20.5 Expanded Example of Hedging CD Costs Using Futures

	ACTIONS NOW (t_0)	
PRESENT PLAN	*FUTURES MARKET*	
Will need to issue $10 million in CDs in March 1994; current rate is 3.42 percent bankers' discount	Sell 10 March contracts in Eurodollar futures market at 3.42	
	ACTIONS LATER (t_F)	
FUTURE CONDITIONS	*RATES HIGHER: EURODOLLARS 4 PERCENT, CDS 4.10 PERCENT*	*RATES LOWER: EURODOLLARS 3 PERCENT, CDS 3.05 PERCENT*
Pay interest on CDs at current market[a]	($102,500)	($76,250)
Futures commissions ($10 to open and close each contract)	($200)	($200)
Interest earned (lost) on maintenance margin[b]	$145	($79)
Profit (loss) from covering short position in futures market[c]	14,500	(10,500)
Net Interest Cost of CD	($88,055)	($87,029)
Annualized yield cost on $10 million (4 times amount divided by amount borrowed)	3.52 %	3.48 %

[a]Interest on CDs paid on 360-day basis maturity. Example assumes prepayment of interest.

[b]Assume interest on Eurodollars average midway between beginning and ending levels and opportunity rate equals Eurodollar rate.

[c]Most contracts are not delivered but are settled at maturity with simple closing of contract and loss side paying profits to gain side. See text discussion.

done using contracts for similar but not identical financial instruments. These contract prices may move closely but not exactly with the underlying risks. Use of contracts that are for similar but not identical assets is called *cross hedging*. Perfect hedges are not possible with cross hedging.

Financial advisors like brokers often provide advice on how to hedge using the best cross hedges. This advice consists of finding futures or forward market instruments or combinations of them that are highly correlated with the risk of importance. In providing this advice, financial analysts rely on the techniques discussed in the following paragraphs. Financial institutions providing this advice typically are attempting to generate futures or forward trading business.

In order to identify the best hedging strategy, regression analysis can be used. If a historical series of the financial instrument exposed to risk is regressed on the prices or rates for a security for which there is a futures contract, the regression results tell how closely the prices or returns of the security at risk and the futures contract move together. For example the R^2 of the regression tells how much of the variation of the security risk is correlated to the futures contract. Furthermore, the regression coefficient relating the futures contract to the security risk can be used to determine the best way to hedge the risks.

An example will illustrate the use of regression analysis for hedging risk to the value or returns on financial securities for which there is no exact counterpart in futures or forward market contracts. The mortgage banker committed to making mortgages in the above example is exposed to the risk of selling those mortgages in the future. Sales of the mortgages will be determined by mortgage rates at the time the mortgages are sold. Assume the mortgage banker wants to hedge his long position in mortgages with U.S. Treasury bond futures. Panel A of Table 20.6 presents monthly data for interest rates on 10-year Treasury bonds and new mortgages.

Panel B of Table 20.6 demonstrates that there is a strong statistical relation between long-term Treasury bond rates and new mortgage rates. The regression reported in the table has a coefficient of determination (R^2) of .760, meaning roughly that 76 percent of the variation in new mortgage rates is accounted for by variations in the Treasury rate. The coefficient relating bond rates to mortgage

TABLE 20.6 Example of Regression in Hedging with Futures

Panel A: Interest Rates (1991)

	10-YEAR U.S. TREASURY	*NEW MORTGAGES*
Jan	8.09	9.65
Feb	7.85	9.57
Mar	8.11	9.43
Apr	8.04	9.60
May	8.07	9.52
Jun	8.28	9.46
Jul	8.27	9.43
Aug	7.90	9.48
Sep	7.65	9.30
Oct	7.53	9.04
Nov	7.42	8.64
Dec	7.09	8.53

SOURCE: *Economic Report of the President.*

Panel B: Regression Estimation

$$\text{New mortgage rate} = 2.35 + .885 * \text{10-year Treasury}$$
$$(5.64)$$
$$R^2 = .760$$

rates is .885 (and very significant), suggesting that mortgage rates move less than bond rates. The interpretation of Table 20.6 is that Treasury rates and mortgage rates are closely but not exactly related.

Another problem associated with using Treasury securities to hedge mortgage asset risk is that the interest rate sensitivity or the durations (discussed in Chapter 19) of mortgages and Treasury bonds are not the same. For example, a 15-year Treasury yielding 8 percent deliverable in a Treasury bond futures contract would have a duration of around 9.2. Eight percent 30-year fixed-rate mortgages have durations of approximately 10.2 years (not adjusted for prepayment risk). Using these durations, the mortgage is about 1.11 times as interest rate sensitive as the bond (10.2 divided by 9.2).

The preceding calculations illustrate an important concept when perfect hedges are not available and asset managers must resort to cross hedges to manage risk. It may not be efficient to match the total asset amount with futures or forward contracts. The ratio of the futures or forward contract values to the amount of asset value of risk is called the *hedge ratio.* Hedging the mortgage banker's interest rate exposure with Treasury bond futures offers an imperfect hedge because mortgage rates move less but mortgages are more rate sensitive. To improve the hedge, a risk manager could use a hedge ratio of .98 since mortgage rates change .885 as much long-term Treasuries, which are are 1.11 times as rate sensitive as mortgages (.98 equals .885 times 1.11). A good cross hedge accounts for imperfect correlations of risk factors and differing risk sensitivity of assets.[1]

The mortgage banker (and his financial advisors) might well seek alternative futures or forward market instruments or contracts to hedge his asset price risk exposure better. The aim would be to find another contract or combination of contracts that maximizes the comovement of the futures or forward positions with the mortgage values. The measure of comovement is the R^2 from regressions like those discussed above. The contracts and their hedge ratios define the best relation between the asset value exposure by the hedges and the offsetting exposure obtained through the use of futures or forward contracts. Only when perfect hedge instruments are available, for example a financial manager is short Treasury bills and can eliminate that exposure in the futures market, is the hedge ratio one.

When the forward or futures contracts used in cross hedges do not have exactly the same price sensitivity as the underlying asset price risk, hedgers are said to be exposed to *basis risk.* There is basis risk with all cross hedges by definition. We illustrated the effect of basis risk with our bank CD example in Table 20.4. Many examples of basis risk can be presented: The mortgage rate and Treasury bond interest rate relation in the above example has a coefficient of determination of only .76, meaning that the two rates are not perfectly correlated. Another hedge with basis risk is hedging issuance of commercial paper planned by a corporation with Treasury bills since risk spreads of commercial paper over Treasuries change, as we discussed in Chapter 13. Furthermore, a particular company's risk spread over the average for commercial paper can change before the

[1]The mathematical statement of the correct hedge ratio is $D_i / D_j \bullet ß_{ij}$, where D's are durations, the subscript i represents the asset risk to be hedged, subscript j the asset deliverable in the futures or forward market, and $ß_{ij}$ is the regression coefficient on their two interest rates.

position is closed. Both these sources of spread changes mean that the interest rates at risk and futures or forward contract rates are not perfectly correlated. There is nearly always basis risk.

Another source of basis risk is that futures contract maturity dates may not be synchronous with the asset risk exposure facing the financial manager even if the assets are similar or identical. For example, in the case of the bank issuing CDs above, it was assumed that it needed the money in March. If the bank was hedging a borrowing need in February or April, there are no futures contract in Eurodollars available. The bank has basis risk because the rates in February or April will not be exactly what they are in March. The bank can still uses March contracts to hedge but will now be exposed to basis risk. One advantage of forward markets over futures markets is that maturity dates on contracts can be negotiated, reducing basis risk.

The above discussion can be summarized briefly. Basis risk is a factor whenever there is no futures or forward market in the same asset at risk for the financial manager. There are three main sources of basis risk: (1) use of cross hedges when the similar instruments do not have a futures or forward market; (2) maturities on contracts differ from the timing of the asset risk of concern; and (3) characteristics such as maturity or coupon in the forward or futures contracts cause differences in sensitivity to the underlying asset risk. In each of these cases, hedge ratios may have to be adjusted to achieve efficient hedging strategies.

Finding ways to help their customers avoid basis risk can be a source of value to financial service firms from advisory fees or trading activity. Clever research may identify unusual hedging instruments since some risks appear to be uncorrelated to any available contracts in the forward or futures markets. For example, asset price risks associated with political events in some countries might appear to be uncorrelated to any futures markets contracts. Astute risk managers may be able to identify correlations to hedge these risks. For example, risks concerning Middle East political events are highly correlated to oil prices. When problems occur in the Middle East, oil prices in futures markets typically increase. This relation might be used to hedge the price risk of securities issued by governments or firms based in the Middle East.

In order to assess the correlations between portfolio risk exposure and futures or forward market contract values, statistical analysis of historical data on prices, interest rates, or exchange rates are used as shown in our example. These statistical analyses can be used to establish how much basis risk exists and whether a risk can be hedged, or to fine tune a hedge ratio. In using the statistical results for any of these purposes, the assumption is made that the future will behave like the past. This assumption may not be valid as events unfold. Basis risk is nearly unavoidable. Financial managers must be alert and cautious when establishing hedges.

Production Risk

A final concern in evaluating futures and forward contracts as risk hedging tools is assessing the extent of asset risk exposure. For example, the bank in our example anticipated a $10 million funding need in March. This $10 million need is forecasted based on expectations concerning the range of alternative borrowing costs for the corporate customers in the example. If interest rates rise substantially in the future, borrowers may rely on the bank's fixed rate contract to replace other sources of funds like trade payables and take down (that is borrow as discussed in Chapter 7) more than expected under the fixed rate lines. If interest rates fall, borrowers may turn to alternative sources and not take down as much under the line. These changes in the amount of borrowing could change the amount of interest rate risk the bank faces.

Other examples of risks associated with the total amount of asset risk exposure can be derived from our other examples above. The insurance company plans to invest future premium payments in fixed-income securities and estimates the payment of premiums from current policies and new policies written under current marketing plans. However, changes in the economy in the future could change the demand for insurance, resulting in policy cancellations or more policy sales. The same type of uncertainty concerning the amount of asset value risk is true for the mortgages written by a mortgage banking firm or the foreign currency earnings of an exporter since their business activities could be affected by future economic developments.

The examples above suggest that not only the value of assets but the *amount* of risk exposure from future asset value exposure should be a concern to risk managers. Financial managers wishing to hedge a future exposure should account for the correlation between the amount of asset risk and the risk factor, such as interest rates or exchange rates. The importance of this correlation may be easiest to understand in the context of agricultural commodities like crops. The amount of risk exposure is called *production* risk in agricultural contexts.

Production risk comes from the fact that if a farmer's total production is down, it is likely that a common factor such as weather is responsible and that all farmers' production is down. If that is the case, commodity prices will be higher because of the tight supplies. If production is up due to a bumper crop, prices will be lower in the market. In order to guarantee a level of farm revenues, farmers with production risk may not need to hedge 100 percent of their expected crops. In order to guarantee their expected revenues, they should hedge less than 100 percent because if their production is down, prices will probably be higher; if prices are lower, their production will be higher. Their hedge ratio should be less than one.

Production risk is also a concern in the cases of loan takedowns, premium revenue, mortgage production, and foreign exchange earnings. If interest rates suddenly become very high, reflecting inflation or an overheated economy, some insurance contracts will be less attractive or useful to insurance customers: they will buy less insurance and pay fewer premiums. The lower premium revenue can be invested at higher interest rates. The insurance investment manager planning on hedging investment risk from premium revenues must consider any correlations between the asset risks of concern and the amount of risk. Similar concerns are relevant for the mortgage banker and exporter. Optimal hedge ratios should consider production risk and may be more or less than one due to correlations between the amount of risk and the underlying risk factors. Financial managers with these risks must assess production risks as well as basis risk.

Production risks may be assessed using statistical analysis of past relations between the amount of risk and underlying risks. For example, loan takedowns under various interest rate developments could be estimated using historical data on interest rates and loan takedowns. Premium revenues could be related to economic conditions including interest rate changes. Whenever historical relationships are used to assess future risks, managers should be cautious in using the implicit assumption that these relationships will hold in the future. This may not be the case due to structural shifts in the business analyzed.

The astute financial institution manager is aware of all the dimensions of managing exposure to asset price or interest rate risk. Judgment concerning changes in the economic effects on cash flows and revenues must augment statistical analysis of past conditions. Monitoring developments once hedging strategies have been implemented must be constant. Changes in historical or assumed correlations between asset risks and the risk variables due to changes in business conditions or structure must be incorporated in the analysis.

20.4 FORWARD AND FUTURES CONTRACT PRICES

We analyze the determinants of the prices of futures and forward contracts on financial instruments in this section. The main element driving the pricing of forward and futures contracts is the price of the asset or commodity to be delivered. At t_0 or now participants in the market know the current spot or cash price p_0 for the asset or commodity. Participants also have expectations concerning spot rates in the future, $E_0(p_F)$, when the futures contracts expire, t_F. By entering into a forward contract, participants plan to reduce or eliminate risk associated with buying or selling the asset at uncertain future spot prices. The current forward market price $F_{0,F}$ is determined by the supply and demand for contracts in the forward market. The current futures price, denoted as $G_{0,F}$, is similarly determined in the futures market. Our discussion of the relations between these various prices follows the arrows shown in Figure 20.4 relating these four prices.

We concentrate first on the relation between prices of forward contracts $F_{0,F}$ and the current spot market or cash price p_0. Forward contracts are bilateral contracts and entail no cash payments until the maturity date when delivery of the assets is made in exchange for cash. The promised performance on these contracts is expected without significant risk because of the trust and mutual knowledge of the counterparties. For example, an exporter selling forward foreign exchange to a bank bases his or her confidence in the contract performance on knowledge of the bank and its reputation. The bank bases its confidence in contractual performance on its knowledge of the customer.

Forward contract prices are determined by the fact that any seller in the forward market can buy the commodity or asset now and deliver it in the future, covering the short position. Using an agricultural example, the seller could buy wheat and sell it for forward delivery. The seller would have to store, insure, and borrow money to buy the wheat: these are the *costs of carry*. The forward contract price is then simply the current spot price of the wheat minus the costs of carry, or alternatively the costs of carry = $F_{0,F} - p_0$.

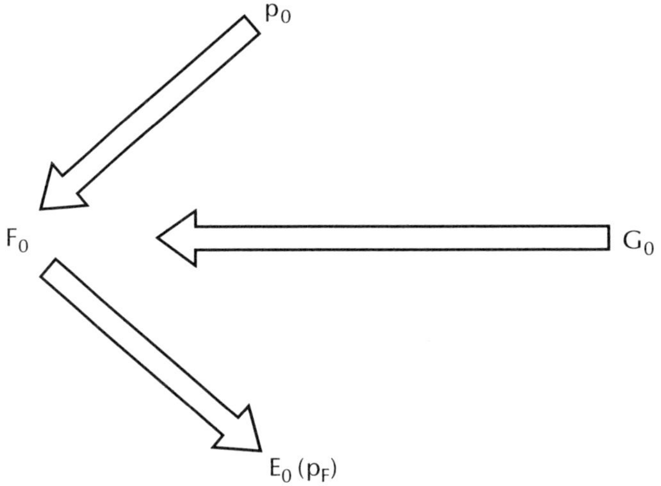

FIGURE 20.4 Relation between spot, forward, and futures prices

If the forward price were not simply the current spot price adjusted for the costs of carry to delivery date of forward contracts, an arbitrageur could make money. For example if the futures contract prices were greater than the adjusted current spot, riskless profits would be available by buying wheat with borrowed money and storing it for future delivery under a forward contract at the price higher than borrowing and storage costs. If forward prices were below the current spot plus adjustments for the costs of carry, grain elevator operators or other holders of grain inventories not needed immediately could sell wheat now and replace it later with wheat purchased in the forward market, profiting by the savings in storage costs and reduction in financing costs.

The economic force enforcing the equality between the current spot price plus the costs of carry and the forward rate is arbitrage. Similar exploitation of arbitrage profit opportunities enforce the relation between spot prices, cost of carry, and forward prices in financial forward contracts. Unlike commodities such as wheat and gold, instruments in financial forward and futures contracts have fixed maturity dates so that a financial instrument purchased in the spot market will have a shorter maturity in the future. Financial futures and forward contracts require different arbitrage strategies but arbitrage is still possible and still a potent force in the pricing of those contracts.

To illustrate how arbitrage works with financial assets, Table 20.7 gives hypothetical cash market prices for 3- and 6-month Treasury bills and shows how arbitrageurs profit if the forward interest rate quoted for delivery of a 3-month T-bill in three months is too low (the price is too high) relative to the spot rate and cost of carry. An arbitrageur could sell a 3-month T-bill forward now and borrow enough to buy a 6-month T-bill, requiring no net cash investment now. In three months, the 6-month bill will be 3-month bill and can be used to deliver to the

TABLE 20.7 Example of Arbitrage and Spot and Forward Prices

	SPOT (CASH) MARKET		FORWARD MARKET	
ASSET	*PRICE*[a]	*RATE (ANNUAL)*	*PRICE*[a]	*RATE (ANNUAL)*
3-month T-bill	99.0	4 %		
6-month T-bill	97.0	6 %		
Forward price higher than Spot Price and Cost of Carry				
3-month T-bill delivery three months			99.0	4 %
Action now	Sell 3-month T-bill for delivery in three months.			0
	Borrow to buy 6-month T-bill at T-bill rate.			+9,700
	Buy 6-month T-bill.			–9,700
Action in three months	Deliver 3-month T-bill to forward contract.			+9,900
	Pay off loan.			–9,780
Profit				+120
Forward price lower than Spot Price and Cost of Carry				
3-month T-bill delivery three months			98.0	8%
Action Now	Buy 3-month T-bill for delivery in three months.			0
	Sell 6-month T-bill short.			+9,850
	Buy ($9,850/.99) 3-month T-bills.			–9,850
Action in three months	3-Month bills mature.			+9,946
	Take delivery of 3-month T-bill and return to cover short.			–9,800
Profit				+146

[a]actual discount price (not 360-day discount basis)

maturing forward contract. The cash received from delivery of the bills in three months is more than enough to cover the borrowing costs (cost of carry) and consequently the arbitrageur makes a profit.

Table 20.7 illustrates arbitrage opportunities when the forward interest rate on Treasury bills is too high (their prices too low). In this case, an arbitrageur could buy T-bills for forward delivery and sell 6-month T-bills short, using the proceeds of the short sale to buy 3-month bills in the cash market. In three months, the maturing the 3-month bills provides more than enough cash to cover the forward contract and the bills received are returned to the short, again earning a profit.[2]

Careful reflection on the supply–demand impact of the arbitrage profit opportunities described in Table 20.7 indicates that the price discrepancies must disappear in market equilibrium. When forward prices are too high, arbitrageurs sell forward contracts, bringing their prices down. When forward prices are too low, arbitrageurs increase their demand for these contracts, raising their prices. Arbitrage affects spot market prices as well. The price differentials will respond to shifts in supply and demand until the spot price and cost of carry equivalence to the forward rate is established.

Another illustration of the relation of cost of carry and the forward contract price is provided by the forward market in foreign currency. Again consider the case of an exporter who has a long position in German marks 30 days in the future. Assume that a bank quotes a competitive forward rate of 60 cents for each mark delivered in 30 days and that the spot rate for marks is 60.2 cents. The exporter probably has checked out other foreign exchange dealers and knows that 60 cents is competitive: why is the rate 60 cents in the forward market and not 60.2 cents as in the spot market? In other words, what is the cost of carry for foreign exchange?

In the case of foreign exchange, the cost of carry must consider the returns on short-term assets in both currencies. This is because a long position in foreign currency, like our exporter receiving German marks in 30 days, has an alternative to hedging currency by a forward sale of marks. The exporter can negotiate a loan in marks now (or sell them short) and buy dollars in the spot market, using them to acquire dollar denominated short-term assets such as 30-day Treasury bills. In thirty days, the exporter would have dollars as the bills matured and could use the export earnings in marks to pay off the German mark loan.

The forward rate on currency must be related to spot exchange rates and short-term spot interest rates in both countries by the cost of carry or arbitrage is possible. The cost of carry in foreign exchange is the net differential interest cost in short-term assets in the two currencies. The relation between forward and spot exchange rates and interest rates in two economies is called *interest rate parity* in international financial management courses.

Forward Prices and Expected Future Spot Prices

Another important relationship between the prices shown in Figure 20.4 is between forward prices and expected future spot prices. An important issue to financial managers is whether the forward market price is an unbiased expecta-

[2]Capozza and Cornell (1979) discuss possible problems with implementing this strategy due to limitations on short sales and tax issues.

tion of the future spot price—that is, if $F_{0,F} = E_0(p_F)$. If the equality holds, the forward rate is an unbiased forecast of future spot rates. If not, the forward market trades at a *premium* (above) or a *discount* (below) to the expected future spot price. The relation between the forward price and the expected future spot price is related to the supply and demand of hedging transactions and the role of speculators in forward markets.

A few relationships between forward and future spot prices are obvious. For example, the spot price and the forward price must be the same on the day the forward contract expires, $p_F = F_{F,F}$, since market participants know what the spot price is at t_F and arbitrage will drive the two rates together. The important question is: What determines the relationship between forward and future spot prices before maturity of the contract?

The answer to this question lies in the relation between supply and demand for hedging in futures markets. This question has been extensively analyzed in past research. Again using the example of the exporter earning German marks in the future, if the demand for dollars in exchange for marks in the forward market exceeds the supply of dollars in exchange for marks because hedgers long in marks outnumber short hedgers and they are willing to pay a premium over the expected future spot rate to obtain a certain dollar price now, the forward market price could be above the expected future spot price. In this case, dollars trade at a *premium* relative to the expected future spot exchange rate for the mark. Since the spot rate and the forward rate must be equal at maturity, the forward price must gradually approach the expected future spot prices from above. The theory that forward prices approach spot prices from above is called *contango* by foreign exchange analysts.

Some economists (including John Maynard Keynes) argue that hedgers with current long positions who expect to sell in the future dominate forward markets in commodities. To eliminate commodity price risks they may be willing to receive lower prices than expected future spot prices in forward markets when they establish short futures positions to hedge their risks. Forward prices will be pushed below the expectation of future spot prices because hedgers will be willing to accept a discount to eliminate risk. In contrast to the above case, the forward rate is below the expected future spot and forward prices should move upward to the spot rate at maturity. Keynes called this condition *normal backwardization*.

Contango and normal backwardization have exactly opposite implications for the relation of forward prices and expected future spot prices. With contango, the forward price is an upward biased estimate of the expected future spot price. With normal backwardization, the forward price is a downward biased estimate of the expected future spot price. These two theories have opposite implications for the costs of short and long hedging but both imply that forward rates are not unbiased estimates of future spot rates. (See Telser (1958) for a review of the theories of contango and normal backwardization.)

Financial forward and futures contracts deal with future delivery of financial assets like fixed-income securities and currencies. There is no net supply of these financial instruments because for every holder of a financial claim there is an issuer. As emphasized in Chapter 3, no net wealth is represented by financial liabilities. This is different from commodity supplies where there are real assets. Price risk of real assets may be asymmetric for longs and shorts as is required with contango or normal backwardization and could bias forward rates above or below expected future spot rates. The absence of a net asset with financial claims means that bias of forwards relative to expected future spot rates, if it exists, must have another basis such as differences in risk preferences.

If speculators are active in forward markets, differences between forward rates and expected future spot rates should be less than if only hedgers enter those markets. Differences between forward and expected future prices would provide expected profit opportunities for them. If speculators are risk neutral, they will supply long or short positions whenever there is a premium or discount in the futures market for the expected future spot rate until the forward rate equals the expected future spot rate. If there is a premium or discount, it is because of a supply imbalance stemming from risk aversion by hedgers willing to pay more than the expected amounts to secure a fixed commitment or requiring compensation for risk aversion or a shortage of speculators willing to assume risk in order to earn expected profits.

The question of whether forward rates equal expected future spot rates can only be answered by looking at the evidence contained in historical series of those prices. Market equilibrium prices as discussed above depend on the relative supply of short and long hedgers and the presence of speculation. The evidence concerning whether forward rates are unbiased forecasts of expected future spot rates is not entirely conclusive. Most of the analysis of this issue has been conducted within the context of the term structure as discussed in Chapter 13 because forward rates used in transactions are not as readily available in the financial press as spot rates.

Korajczyk (1985) tested whether the forward rates are unbiased predictors of expected future spot rates for foreign exchange. He notes in his analysis that the interest rate parity theorem discussed above implies a relation between liquidity premium in the term structure of interest rates in the assets denominated in each foreign currency and the relation between forward and expected future spot rates. Specifically, if risk premiums in two countries differ such that expected real interest rates in those countries differ, the forward rate could be a biased estimate of the expected future spot rate. His carefully obtained results suggest that forward rates are biased but that the bias can be explained statistically by the difference in countries' expected real interest rates.

Relation Between Forward Prices and Futures Prices

The relationship between forward prices or rates and futures prices is the last price relationship pictured in Figure 20.4 with an arrow. As discussed above, forward contracts involve no exchange of cash until maturity and confidence in performance on contracts is based on transactors' reputations and financial strength. Futures contracts include the market clearing organization on both sides of the contract. In order to guarantee contract performance, exchange rules require cash margin or a pledge of valuable assets to settle contracts on a daily basis. Margin requirements set by exchanges are enforced by clearinghouses and brokers. In addition to contract standardization, the important difference between forward and futures contracts is the required posting of margin on futures contracts on a daily or even more frequent intervals.

Margin requirements on futures contracts are imposed upon initiation of the contract. These *initial margins* would be required of traders as soon as they enter a futures contract buying or selling assets for future delivery. For example, U.S. Treasury bond futures contracts trades opening a long or short position require depositing $2,000 per contract which can be in the form of U.S. Treasury bills. Further cash margin is required when losses are incurred in a futures position. These margin requirements are called *maintenance margins*. Profits on contracts produce *excess margin* that can be withdrawn in cash by the contract holder. Maintenance margins almost always result in daily cash inflows or outflows by holders of futures contracts as contract values change. Inability to meet additional margin requirements, called *margin calls,* results in the losing position being closed and the loss realized.

Using the quotations contained in Table 20.1, if we open a long position in U.S. Treasury bonds at 120-21, the initial margin of $2,000 can be met with Treasury bills and no cash margin will be required until the futures contracts price change, which it will almost certainly do the next day. As an example, assume the price in the futures market falls to 119-29 for a change of 24/32nds or .75 percent. The contract value has fallen by $750 (.0075 times $100,000, the contract amount). This $750 loss must be added in cash to the margin account with the brokerage or the contract will be closed by the clearinghouse. The short position has gained $750 and that amount is available to the short to be withdrawn in cash from his or her account at the broker's.

The process of paying cash into the margin account of position holders in futures contracts each day according to changes in the market value of the contract is called *marking to market*. Marking to market is the key difference between forward markets and futures markets. The paying or receiving of cash according to daily or more frequent movements in the value of futures prices means that the value of a futures position at the time of the maturity of the contract will be affected by the requirement of borrowing (or selling interest-bearing assets) to meet margin requirements if the holder has lost money or the interest earned on the investment of cash withdrawals if the holder has made money on the contract.

The effect of marking to market on the use of futures contracts can be illustrated with our bank example of Tables 20.4 and 20.5. The basic example in Table 20.4 ignored margin costs, but Table 20.5 includes the opportunity cost (or profit) from changing interest rates, assumed to average midway between their initial and terminal levels. These interest costs or earnings are unpredictable if short-term interest rate opportunities are changing unpredictably. Future short-term interest rates may have some relation to the risks being hedged.

The impact of the margin requirements requiring cash inflows or outflows before maturity of the futures contracts has been analyzed by Black (1976) and

Cox, Ingersoll, and Ross (1981). The cash inflows and outflows with futures contracts means that the futures contract price must be different that the forward contract price to account for expected interest costs or earnings on cash flows associated with margin calls. The two contract prices will only be the same if the short-term interest rate does not vary (this is the case analyzed by Black (1976)). Otherwise, the difference between forward and futures rates will be determined by the correlation of the contract value and changes in short-term interest rates (see the case analyzed by Cox, Ingersoll, and Ross (1981)).

The differences between forward and futures market prices for contracts of the same maturity in the case of nonzero interest rate correlation with the underlying asset or commodity values can be quickly characterized. The forward price will be higher than the futures price if the correlation between the forward contract price and short-term interest rates is negative. Conversely, the forward price will be lower than the futures price if short-term interest rates and forward contract prices are positively correlated.

The common sense explaining the relation between forward and futures prices is based on the observation that long positions in futures will pay more interest expense as their margins increase with losses. If the futures contract losses occurring with forward contract price declines are negatively correlated with short-term interest rates, the long futures contract will have higher interest costs meeting required margin calls as interest rates increase. Conversely, profits from the same position will earn less interest when withdrawn due to the negative correlation between forward contract prices and short-term interest rates. The hedger or speculator would be willing to pay less for the futures contract than the forward contract.

The above relationship between forward and futures price differentials and interest rates or bond prices does not refer to the underlying asset price. Cox, Ingersoll, and Ross develop the relation between the underlying asset and the forward–futures price differential and determine that if the *covariance* between the underlying asset price and short-term yields is greater than the *variance* of short-term yields, the forward price for the asset is higher than the futures price.[3] Equivalently, the forward price will also be larger than the futures price when the correlation of the asset price with short-term yields times the asset price standard deviation is greater than the short-term yield standard deviation.[4]

The propositions concerning the relation between forward and futures prices were carefully worked out in a theoretical model by Cox, Ingersoll, and Ross (1981). This analysis did not require risk aversion or any other assumptions concerning investor behavior other than efficient markets. The predictions of this model have held up in an empirical analysis of foreign exchange forward and futures contract prices by Meulbroek (1992).

[3]For example, the covariance between the Treasury bond price and the short-term Treasury bill yield could be expressed in terms of their correlation ($\rho_{\text{Bond,Bill}}$) and standard deviations (σ_{Bond}, σ_{Bill}) as covariance (Bonds, Bills) = $\rho_{\text{Bond,Bill}}\sigma_{\text{Bond}}\sigma_{\text{Bill}}$).

[4]Since the variance is the standard deviation squared, divide both the covariance and the variance with the standard deviation of short-term yields.

Choice of Futures or Forward Contracts

Differences in forward and futures prices do not mean that there are cheaper and more expensive ways to hedge. These differences represent the efficient market costs of the daily settling up required by futures contracts. In efficient markets, either forward or futures contracts are equally effective in hedging asset risks. To choose between forward and futures markets in hedging or speculating asset prices, there are three considerations. We discuss each next.

The first consideration is the existence of relevant markets. There may be a forward market and no futures market or vice versa. There are many forward markets for specific commodities and delivery of specific financial instruments such as mortgage-backed securities and no organized futures market trading in these assets. On the other hand, futures market exist in smaller contract sizes than may be relevant for some financial transactors. Forward foreign currency contracts are typically for a minimum of $1 million whereas futures contracts are approximately $100 thousand.

A second consideration is liquidity. If futures exist they can be very liquid because of the low costs of trading. The hedger or speculator can easily unwind a position in futures markets where forward markets represent bilateral contracts and may be difficult to cancel before maturity. Offsetting the issue of liquidity, of course, is the element of initial margins required of futures contracts and the marking to market that may require future cash payments.

The final consideration is the problem of using standardized contracts traded on the futures exchanges as opposed to using a specified contract available from writers of forward contracts. To the extent that standardized contracts have delivery periods or other delivery conditions that depart from the asset risk in question, a futures market may entail more basis risk than a forward market.

20.5 FUTURES AND FORWARDS AND VALUE IN PORTFOLIO MANAGEMENT

How can futures and forward contracts be used to produce value in managing portfolios? This section takes up three related aspects of the previous discussion on the use and valuation of futures and forward contracts in order to determine how these contracts or the concepts they represent may be used to create value for financial institutions.

Micro Hedging

Financial institution managers and portfolio managers can use futures and forward contracts to hedge the risk of specific assets within their balance sheets or portfolios. The economic question is: What value can be created by eliminating risk of holding or issuing specific assets or liabilities? The market equilibrium return to riskless investments is the riskless rate. Since management time and attention is not free and there are transactions costs associated with hedging, the return from riskless positions in risky assets and futures contracts must be below the return associated with investing directly in riskless assets like Treasury bills. What rationale is there for hedging specific asset and liability risk with futures or forward contracts?

Microhedging may make sense if it allows management or a firm to produce value in ways not possible if the underlying financial instruments were unhedged and risky. Three sources of value are possible: (1) a level of activity generating income above that attainable if risks were unhedged is possible; (2) profit opportunities from highly profitable activities or extremely undervalued assets that are not normally appropriate or desirable because of their risk characteristics can be exploited; and (3) management and employee attention can be focused on income-producing activities without having to carefully monitor the value of assets or liabilities at risk. We discuss each of these three sources of value below.

The first source of value of hedging activity in futures or forwards is that activity is higher than could be attempted absent hedging activity. Typically this means that a firm must take positions in assets the risk of which could endanger the solvency of the firm if not hedged. A good example of this is mortgage banks who originate mortgage portfolios with little capital and lots of short-term credit. Given an acceptable risk of insolvency, it may pay for the firm to hedge the resale value of its mortgage portfolio through forward or futures contract to increase its volume of business. The real source of value is the mortgage origination and servicing fees produced by originating mortgages because of the firm's strengths and competitive advantages. Mortgage portfolio risk only inhibits exploration of its competitive advantage unless the risk is hedged. Similar examples for microhedging could be derived from investment banking and market making activities and other financial services. The key point is that hedging activity allows *other* sources of value to be exploited.

A second source of value is the possibility of exploiting very profitable opportunities that are otherwise inappropriate for a given firm because of its expertise or business strategy. While markets are in general efficient, randomly available excess return opportunities should not be unexploited just because they should not be there and do not fit in with a broader set of portfolio or firm goals. For example, if a portfolio manager running a very low risk bond portfolio discovers an incredibly undervalued junk bond and can convert the risk into acceptable levels by hedging the risk with futures or forward contracts, the portfolio manager should do so. A microhedge if effective has locked in a profit and reduced risk to an acceptable level.

The third reason for hedging is to free management time and attention from risk in order to allocate energy to what they are good at. For example, bankers constantly worrying about the cost of their funds may not be able to aggressively market loans to businesses in an uncertain economic environment. No one can predict future interest rates, but eliminating concerns about their level may make management and employees marketing credit-related products more efficient. They can concentrate on non-interest related aspects of the demand for credit and not fret about changes in the interest rate environment. Of course, in order to hedge the microrisks of costs of funding credit-related services, the firm must be able to estimate the total exposure under its plans.

The general point is that when economic risks distract an organization from its primarily value-producing activities, such as negotiating and delivering credit services, eliminating risks through microhedging may create value by increasing the efficiency of the basic value-generating functions of the firm.

Macrohedging

Macrohedging focuses on the overall risk of a portfolio or balance sheet. We first define and discuss how to implement macrohedging and conclude by evaluating the use of macrohedging strategies as a means of creating value for owners of firms or beneficiaries of portfolios. A *macrohedge* is achieved when the value of a portfolio or the net worth of a balance sheet varies less with changes of risk variables through the use of a *smaller number* of financial futures or forward contracts than types of financial instruments contained in the portfolio or balance sheet. For example, if the return on a complex bond portfolio consisting of bonds from hundreds of issuers and maturities was less variable because of a few futures contracts, the portfolio would be macrohedged. Another example of a macrohedge would be a commercial bank that has hedged the future value of equity through the use of one or a small number of futures contracts. Defining a macrohedge does not of course mean that good macrohedge exists. Most macrohedging strategies will result in only *partial macrohedges*.

To implement a macrohedge strategy, the first requirement is a measure of portfolio or balance sheet sensitivity to risk. The aggregate portfolio duration risk measure described in Chapter 19 would be an example of an interest rate risk measure for a portfolio or balance sheet. The risk coefficients estimated using the capital asset pricing model (CAPM) or an implementation of arbitrage pricing theory model (APT) to the stock in a traded financial institution, as discussed in Chapters 4 and 19, are other examples of balance sheet risk assessment for financial service firms. These different measures provide the portfolio or balance sheet manager with an estimate of net risk to interest rates or other factors.

The macrohedge next assesses the value of various financial forward and futures instruments to hedge against the risk. It may be that a combination of contracts as discussed in the preceding sections will provide offsetting value changes to those risks of concern. Based on risk assessments and a choice of contracts to use as hedging instruments, the final task is to assess the amount of exposure. Depending on production risk and the accuracy of projections of the balance sheet composition, the hedge ratio may be set at more or less than 100 percent of the portfolio value or net equity. The usefulness of the hedge is measured by how closely values in the futures or forward positions offset changes in the value of the aggregate portfolio or net worth due to asset price risk in the portfolio. Perfect macrohedges are unlikely and changes in the economic environment will require constant monitoring of the hedge position.

To illustrate of the application of macrohedging techniques we use the portfolio in Table 19.4 from the previous chapter. As discussed in the text of that chapter, the equity value of $6.1 million had a sensitivity to interest rate risk as measured by its equity duration of 3.272. To hedge this risk, any combination of futures or forward contracts that has a duration of 3.272 would be a candidate hedging strategy. For example, shorting 13.09 Treasury bill futures contracts (3.272 divided by .25, the duration of a 90-day discounted Treasury bill) for delivery at the end of the portfolio holding period would provide offsetting value movements to the equity value in the portfolio. This strategy would require 80 contracts (13.09 contracts times 6.1 million where $1 million is the Treasury bill delivery amount) to macrohedge the value of the portfolio.

Other contracts or combinations of contracts producing the same interest rate sensitivity would also be candidates for the hedge strategy. The choice of contracts will depend on expected changes in term premiums and other factors and changes in portfolio composition requiring adjustments in the hedge. Depending on the assessment of the importance of adjustments in portfolio hedges, transaction costs, market liquidity, and even trading hours of exchanges could be considerations in choosing appropriate hedging strategy. If production risk or other portfolio adjustments alter the risk exposure, periodic changes in the hedge ratio would be required. Most realistically, the hedge would have to be monitored constantly and adjusted dynamically as interest rates moved and portfolio composition changed.

Portfolio risk exposure to other than interest rate risk would similarly identify futures or forward contracts that can replicate the net exposure of a portfolio to risk factors. Currency risks and equity market risks are straightforward examples of risks that could be summed and netted for a portfolio allowing macrohedging strategies. As discussed above, innovative risk measurement approaches to specific portfolios may identify commodity or other futures contracts that can be used to partially or perfectly hedge the risk of portfolio values.

Managerial Controls on Use of Futures and Forward Contracts

Regulators recognize and may even encourage macrohedging against the most feared risk of the day. Use of many futures and forward contracts are permitted but must be reported to regulators as "off-balance sheet activities." Tax authorities accept hedging losses as costs in tax calculations of current income rather than requiring contract losses to be recognized as long-term (Wartzman and Jereski 1993). The accounting profession through its Financial Accounting Standards Board (FASB) Statement Number 80 recognizes macrohedging in reporting income from financing activities, although there are carefully defined conditions to report the income net of futures and forward trading profits and losses. The existence of these official sanctions lends support to the use of hedging at both the micro and macro levels but requires that financial institution or portfolio managers demonstrate linkages between portfolio risks and the hedging strategy or suffer criticism or censure from regulators or investors.

Regulators, brokerage houses, and the Commodity Futures Trading Commission (CFTC) require firms trading futures contracts to have a policy adopted by their boards of directors concerning the use of futures. The policy must outline when the use of futures is appropriate, for example for hedging a specific type of risk exposure. The policy should authorize activity levels, for example specifying limits to trading activity or numbers of outstanding contracts allowed. An effective policy must control implementation of policy by requiring top management approvals and implementing reporting and monitoring systems.

Misunderstood or unauthorized trading activity in futures contracts has caused two spectacular recent losses: Mettallgesellschaft's loss of $1.33 billion in 1993 and the bankruptcy of the 200 year-old Barings Bank of England in 1995. In the first case, top management may not have understood the hedge placed by operating personnel and called for a disastrously premature liquidation of a position in oil future contracts (Culp and Miller (1994)). In the case of Barings, management was apparently unwilling—until it was too late—to control speculative activity by a single trader in Singapore because his profits were increasing top management's bonuses.

Financial institution managers advocating the use of futures in trading strategies (and other risk management tools discussed in the previous and following chapters) should explain their strategies clearly, seek explicit approval for them, and submit them to monitoring and control. The value-creation potential of the strategies, as well as the risks and controls, must be understandable by top management and investors using concepts discussed in this book if they have any merit. In efficient markets, riskless strategies earn the riskless rate. Risk management or speculative strategies must be justified in terms of value creation. If the strategies cannot be explained rigorously, they probably do not make any sense.

Value Creation from Macroledging

It is assumed in efficient markets that owners of portfolios or financial service firms can control risks through their own portfolio hedging strategies. Black (1975) argues that no value is added by such hedging strategies in discussing commercial banks. How can value be created from macrohedging? Two answers for the value of hedging activities by managers have been advanced by analysts.

The first answer is similar to that discussed in the previous chapter with respect to forecasting and liquidity planning. Financial service firms have charter or franchise value not reflected in balance sheet accounts. Protection of this value warrants hedging strategies that reduce the probability of insolvency of the firm. Charter value is lost if the firm disappears when the market for franchises is not competitive due to regulation. Protection of franchise value is a rationale to protect the value of the firm from risk by the implementing of macrohedges using futures or forward contracts.

A second answer explaining use of off-balance sheet or macrohedging strategies has been advanced by Campbell and Kracaw (1987). Their argument is that the management of a firm may be more efficient if executives are not concerned about losing their jobs. This argument is different from the argument concerning management efficiency in the microhedging discussion. Value creation in their analysis depends on the value of equity in the entire balance sheet or portfolio, not just the risk of particular assets or liabilities.

Campbell and Kracaw argue that a firm's management has a great deal of human capital tied up in the firms they work for and human capital cannot be readily diversified. Managers will shy away from exploiting risky investments or business strategies unless they can hedge themselves against risks of firm failure. Value is produced by protecting management from job losses and making them free to undertake positive net present value projects even though they are risky. The risk reduction is not necessary for owners of the firm who can diversify the risk but is necessary to induce managers to undertake valuable risky strategies.

In conclusion we note that many financial firms and portfolio managers use futures and forward contracts to hedge overall portfolio or balance sheet risk. The question of whether macrohedging activities create value for owners of financial service firms or beneficiaries of portfolios does not have a simple answer. Financial markets in general are efficient and excess returns are only available by taking risk. Good managers must be aware of risk exposure and the effect of risk management strategies on these risks. Whether the policy is to bear risks or to use futures and forward markets to shift or share those risks, good management should be able to justify its strategy in the analytical terms introduced in the above discussion.

20.6 VALUE PRODUCTION IN RISK MANAGEMENT SERVICES

Apart from management of balance sheet or portfolio risk, managers of financial service firms may be able to create value by offering risk management services or products to customers. As discussed in Chapter 6, differences in risk preferences or tolerances are a source of value when providers of financial services can make their customers better off by improving their risk–return trade-offs. There are three ways services provided by financial service firms can be based on futures and forward contracts and build on our previous discussion. First, financial products can contain features of futures or forward contracts useful for customers. Second, financial service firms may have a comparative advantage in issuing, trading, or brokering these contracts. And finally, financial risk management instruments is a fertile area to innovate and earn short-term excess returns because of the lack of competition for new products. We discuss each in turn.

Many financial services offered by banks, investment banks, insurance companies, and others contain elements that are similar to forward or futures contracts. Several examples will make the point: commercial banks make irrevocable loan commitments, insurance companies contract for "take-out financing" which provides long-term mortgage financing following construction loans, and investment banks underwrite security issues. All of these services are forms of forward contracts. These arrangements commit financial service firms to deliver money in the future in exchange for financial assets in the form of credit instruments at terms including prices or rates negotiated up front.

Value can be created whenever financial service firms can improve the risk–return trade-offs facing their customers. If forward contracts or financial instruments containing elements of forward contracts are desirable to these customers, they may be willing to pay a premium for them. It may be that expertise and experience make it possible for financial service firms to provide or design risk-reducing contracts for customers that customers would not think of or could not implement themselves at low costs. Financial institutions with many customers may be able to create portfolios of forward contracts that are less risky in the aggregate than individual contracts. The risk reduction could come from diversification or from the ability of financial institution managers to manage their aggregate exposure to risks through their own macrohedging strategies. An example of this source of value would be currency trading by banks, who offer forward contracts but typically have little net exposure from their entire book of forward exchange business.

A second source of value is in offering trading services in forward and futures contracts that are synergistic with other financial services offered by financial service firms. For example, commercial banks have access to information and clearing systems for cash movement as well as specialized credit departments dealing with international trade financing. All these other services might make foreign exchange dealing with banks more efficient than use of futures markets. Banks may have valuable experience with the customer's needs and could provide advice. The hedging transaction could be combined with other dimensions of international business like letters of credit and funds transfer, thereby economizing on the bank customer's management time. Forward market activity could generate other fees for the bank and economies of scope may allow the bank to compete aggressively to provide customers all these financial services with a cost advantage.

Another example of synergy in offering forward contracts with other services is in investment banking. The market information and distribution network available to investment banks gives them an advantage in offering forward commitments on securities which can make them compete aggressively for this business. The individual risks of not being able to sell a specific financial instrument delivered under commitments can be reduced by diversification coming from making many such deals. Risks of losses on positions purchased under commitments are lower given their access to institutional investors and retail networks who demand the types of securities in question.

The last and most important source of value associated with futures and forward contracts is product innovation. Financial service firms alert to customers' needs can design new contracts and services that will be valuable to customers by improving their risk–return trade-offs. Forward contracts often begin this process as financial institutions identify new risks of concern to customers which can be reduced or eliminated by the use of forward contracts or commitments. For example, guaranteed investment contracts (GICs) offered by insurance companies have become an important risk management tool for portfolio managers. Alert financial institution management and their product development and research staffs should be on the lookout for new demands by their customers for risk-management tools. A financial service firm first offering new contracts or risk-reducing services or making markets in them is often able to earn large fees due to its temporary monopoly in the product and limited competition in the future.

20.7 SUMMARY

Financial forward and futures are enormously important tools to manage asset, portfolio, or balance sheet risk. The terminology and conceptual framework to analyze exposure to risk and the interpretation of futures and forward contracts must be mastered in order to assess their economic usefulness. The prices of these contracts result from their relation to spot prices and costs of carrying assets into the future. Futures and forward contracts are similar in how they work but there are differences in them, meaning that forward and futures contract prices differ. Hedging strategies can be based on individual asset risks (microhedging) or the net portfolio or balance sheet risk (macrohedging). Managers must question carefully the value of risk-reducing strategies since the efficient market return to low risk portfolio strategies is low returns. Examination of the sources of value in hedging shows that financial service firms can have a comparative advantage in assisting customers in their risk management strategies but that innovation is the key to value creation.

DISCUSSION QUESTIONS AND EXERCISES

1. A bank expects to issue certificates of deposit in 45 days to fund loans. Is the bank in a long or short position with respect to interest bearing assets? What markets are available for the bank to hedge its interest rate risks?
2. Rank the dollar or other currency value of the open interest in the futures markets quotations in the *Wall Street Journal*. Which are the largest contracts? Contrast the open interest and trading volume in the various contract maturities for different futures instruments.
3. What would be the advantages and disadvantages of using Treasury bill futures or Eurodollar futures for hedging the risk of an issue of six-month CDs in April 1994? How could a financial manager determine what is the best instrument to use?
4. Using the quotations in Table 20.1, what is the dollar commitment to buy 10 contracts in December 1994, at the settle price in the table? How much money would the holder of such a contract make or lose if the futures price went to 120? to 110?
5. Using the contract in the above question, how much cash or margin would be available each day if following the opening of a short position on October 8 (at the settle price) the sequence of prices the following days was: 117-0, 116-24, 116-0, 115-24, 116-18, 118-5?
6. Calculate the duration for the Treasury bond contract at its current price and estimate how many contracts would be needed to macrohedge the equity in the portfolio from Table 19.4 if bond contracts were used instead of Treasury bill futures.
7. The Federal National Mortgage Association quotes qualifying mortgage lenders terms on their purchases of mortgages up to 90 days in the future. What type of contract is this and what exposure would these contracts serve to hedge?
8. Examine the tables accompanying the 10-K of a large commercial bank or

thrift institution and determine whether or not it is using financial forwards or futures. Discuss the extent of the use of these instruments and of any management discussion of these instruments.

9. As a corporate treasurer you are exposed to exchange risk. What are the advantages and disadvantages of using forwards and futures contracts? Where can you get each of these types of contracts? What other credit or financial services make dealing with a financial institution desirable?

10. Given bank equity of $4 million in a balance sheet with a net duration of 3, which futures instruments in what amounts could be used to hedge the risk? How would production risk matter?

REFERENCES

BATTLEY, NICK (ed). 1993. *The World's Futures and Options Markets.* Chicago: Probus Publishing Company.

BLACK, FISCHER. 1975. "Bank Funds Management in an Efficient Market," *Journal of Financial Economics* 2 (4), pp. 323–339.

BLACK, FISCHER. 1976. "The Pricing of Commodity Contracts," *Journal of Financial Economics* 3 (1/2), pp. 167–179. Also in R. E. Whaley, ed. 1992. *Selected Writings on Futures Markets: Interrelations Among Futures, Option and Futures Option Markets,* Book VI of *Readings in Futures Markets,* Chicago Board of Trade.

CAMPBELL, TIM S. and WILLIAM A. KRACAW. 1987. "Optimal Managerial Incentive Contracts and the Value of Corporate Insurance," *Journal of Financial and Quantitative Analysis* 22, pp. 315–328.

CAPOZZA, DENNIS R. and BRADFORD CORNELL. 1979. "Treasury Bill Pricing in the Spot and Futures Market," *Review of Economics and Statistics* 61, pp. 513–520.

COX, JOHN C., JONATHAN E. INGERSOLL, JR., and STEPHEN A. ROSS. 1981. "The Relation Between Forward Prices and Futures Prices," *Journal of Financial Economics* 9 (4), pp. 321–346. Also in R. E. Whaley, ed. 1992. *Selected Writings on Futures Markets: Interrelations Among Futures, Option and Futures Option Markets,* Book VI of *Readings in Futures Markets,* Chicago Board of Trade.

CULP, CHRISTOPHER L. and MERTON H. MILLER. 1994. "Hedging a Flow of Commodity Deliveries: Lessons from Metallgesellschaft," *Derivatives Quarterly* (Fall), pp. 7–15.

KORAJCZYK, ROBERT A. 1985. "The Pricing of Forward Contracts for Foreign Exchange," *Journal of Political Economy* 93 (2), pp. 346–368.

MEULBROEK, LISA. 1992. "A Comparison of Forward and Futures Prices of an Interest Rate-Sensitive Financial Asset," *Journal of Finance* XLVII (1), pp. 381–396.

TELSER, LESTER G. 1958. "Futures Trading and the Storage of Cotton and Wheat," *Journal of Political Economy* 66 (June), pp. 233–255.

WARTZMAN, RICK and LAURA JERESKI. 1993. "IRS, in Big Victory for Business, Shifts its Position on Losses Linked to Hedging." *Wall Street Journal,* October 19, p. A2.

CHAPTER

21

Options, Portfolio Risk, and Pricing Financial Services

Introduction

Recently, growth in the trading of option contracts on organized exchanges and over-the-counter has mushroomed to service a global demand for these instruments.

- What is the reason for explosive growth in option trading and option-like features of financial instruments?
- How can these instruments be used to hedge portfolio risks and what is their relevance to customer services?
- Why are the research departments of commercial and investment banks and insurance companies hiring experts in mathematics and computer programming to solve option pricing problems?
- Where is the value to the economy and financial service firms from all these option-related activities?

These questions are addressed in this chapter. This chapter cannot create expertise sufficient to solve all the option related problems found in financial markets but should place the extraordinary theoretical and market developments associated with options into perspective.

The chapter begins by defining options and interpreting option terminology as used in financial markets. Use of options to hedge risk and comparisons with futures and forwards is described. An extensive discussion illustrates the approaches and problems associated with option pricing. The relevance of option pricing and research departments devoted to solving option problems is presented in the final sections of the chapter.

21.1 OPTION CONTRACT CHARACTERISTICS

In difficult situations we all desire options. Financial options provide portfolio managers in risky environments with choices on how much risk to bear. Options are more flexible than futures contracts as their name would imply. This flexibility comes with costs. The flexibility of options is clearly worth more than they cost to financial markets as demonstrated by the phenomenal growth in the types of options and volume of trading in financial markets.

Options, like futures, have been around for a long time. Option contracts on assets like real estate have been common for millenia. Over-the-counter markets in common stock options were active prior to the 1970s. The dramatic increase in financial market variability beginning with the 1960s as discussed in Chapter 13 increased the demand for methods of managing asset price risk exposure. Securities firms and exchanges responded by increasing the supply of available options and initiating trading in standardized options on organized exchanges. Exchange traded options have mushroomed in importance since trading in stock options was initiated on the Chicago Board Options Exchange (CBOE) in 1973.[1] Active markets in over-the-counter options, such as interest and foreign exchange options offered by banks, have continued to grow in importance.

Option Contracts

An option is the *right,* not the obligation, to buy (a *call* option) or sell (a *put* option) an asset at an agreed-upon price (*strike price* or *conversion value*) before a given date (*maturity date*). The emphasized words represent the common vocabulary used to describe options. Since options represent the potential to make money by buying or selling assets at favorable prices, they have value. Because options represent contractual agreements between parties to buy or sell assets under specified terms, there must be someone willing to *write* (or sell) options for an option to exist in the market. Option writers are the shorts in call option transactions. As with futures and forwards in the last chapter, one can be long or short options.

Users and analysts of options distinguish basic types of options: *American, Bermuda,* and *European* options. American options can be exercised at any time before they expire and Bermuda options can be exercised at particular time points, but European options can only be exercised at maturity. American options allow owners more timing flexibility than either Bermuda or European options, thus making them worth more the other options. We return to differences between values of different types of options in our discussion of option pricing below.

The terms above can be illustrated by use of quotations for traded options printed in the financial press. Table 21.1 contains quotations for U.S. Treasury bond options on October 8, 1993. These options are standardized options on the futures contract for U.S. Treasury bonds traded on the Chicago Board of Trade (CBOT). Details concerning selected traded option contracts are provided in

[1]See Bernstein (1992) for a fascinating history of traded options and the development of modern option pricing theory.

TABLE 21.1 Options on Futures Quotations

FUTURES OPTIONS PRICES

Friday, October 8, 1993.

AGRICULTURAL

CORN (CBT)
5,000 bu.; cents per bu.

Strike	Calls–Settle			Puts–Settle		
Price	Dec	Mar	May	Dec	Mar	May
220	21¾	30¼	35	⅛	⅛	¼
230	12¾	21	26½	1⅛	1¼	1¾
240	6¾	13¼	18	4¾	4	4
250	3⅛	8¼	12½	11½	8¾	8¼
260	1⅜	4¾	8½	19¼	15	13½
270	⅝	2¾	5½	28⅝	....	....

Est vol 5,000 Thur 5,075 calls 1,098 puts
Op int Thur 122,503 calls 63,485 puts

SOYBEANS (CBT)
5,000 bu.; cents per bu.

Strike	Calls–Settle			Puts–Settle		
Price	Nov	Jan	Mar	Nov	Jan	Mar
550	58¾	....	72½	⅛	½	1¼
575	34½	42¼	49½	⅝	2	2⅞
600	13½	23¼	30½	4½	7⅝	9
625	3⅛	11¾	18	19¾	21¼	21½
650	1	6	11	42	39¾	38
675	½	3¼	6½	66½	62	59

Est vol 10,000 Thur 7,539 calls 2,626 puts
Op int Thur 157,364 calls 54,511 puts

SOYBEAN MEAL (CBT)
100 tons; $ per ton

Strike	Calls–Settle			Puts–Settle		
Price	Dec	Jan	Mar	Dec	Jan	Mar
180	10.10	....	....	.50	1.00	1.25
185	6.00	6.75	8.25	1.40	1.90	2.50
190	3.40	4.25	5.85	4.00	4.75	5.40
195	1.50	2.50	4.00	7.10	7.75	8.20
200	1.10	1.60	3.00	11.50	11.75	12.00
210	.50	.70	1.90	20.70	20.80	20.65

Est vol 1,500 Thur 465 calls 261 puts
Op int Thur 19,459 calls 15,346 puts

SOYBEAN OIL (CBT)
60,000 lbs.; cents per lb.

Strike	Calls–Settle			Puts–Settle		
Price	Dec	Jan	Mar	Dec	Jan	Mar
2150	1.070	....	....	.110	....	....
2200	.750	....	....	.250	.270	.330
2250	.500	.600	....	.500	.500	.580
2300	.300	....	....	.800	.820	.900
2350	.220	....	....	1.200	1.190	1.220
2400	.130	.230	.370	1.560	....	1.600

Est vol 250 Thur 25 calls 48 puts
Op int Thur 8,612 calls 10,375 puts

WHEAT (CBT)
5,000 bu.; cents per bu.

Strike	Calls–Settle			Puts–Settle		
Price	Dec	Mar	May	Dec	Mar	May
300	22¾	29¼	28½	1⅛	4¼	....
310	14¾	21⅝	22	3	6¼	....
320	8⅞	15¾	16½	6¾	9½	....
330	5	11⅛	9¾	13	14¾	....
340	2⅞	8¼	3½	20¾	....	....
350	1⅝	5⅞	2½	29½	....	....

Est vol 2,500 Thur 1,753 calls 2,480 puts
Op int Thur 34,585 calls 17,329 puts

WHEAT (KC)
5,000 bu.; cents per bu.

Strike	Calls–Settle			Puts–Settle		
Price	Dec	Mar	May	Dec	Mar	May
310	17	21⅞	17⅞	1¼	5¼	....
320	9½	15¾	14⅛	4½	9	....
330	4⅝	10½	10¼	9	13½	....
340	2	7⅜	7½	....	21⅛	....
350	¾	4½	....	25½	....	....
360	⅜	2¾	....	....	....	....

Est vol 456 Thur 250 calls 241 puts
Op int Thur 4,371 calls 3,365 puts

COTTON (CTN)
50,000 lbs.; cents per lb.

Strike	Calls–Settle			Puts–Settle		
Price	Dec	Mar	May	Dec	Mar	May
58	2.38	4.40	....	.58	1.08	1.35
59	1.79	3.75	....	.82	1.42	1.75
60	1.20	3.15	....	1.30	1.81	....
61	.90	2.58	3.50	1.97	2.27	2.55
62	.50	2.15	3.05	2.67	2.85	....
63	.32	1.78	2.60	3.45	3.35	....

Est vol 1,500 Thur 814 calls 347 puts
Op int Thur 18,702 calls 23,705 puts

ORANGE JUICE (CTN)
15,000 lbs.; cents per lb.

Strike	Calls–Settle			Puts–Settle		
Price	Dec	Jan	Feb	Dec	Jan	Feb
120	13.10	14.80	....	3.55	5.25	....
125	9.05	11.50	....	4.50	6.95	....
130	6.00	8.55	....	7.15	9.20	....
135	3.75	6.25	....	9.65	....	....
140	2.70	4.35	....	....	....	....
145	....	3.50	5.50	....	....	....

Est vol 90 Thur 126 calls 67 puts
Op int Thur 2,607 calls 2,745 puts

COFFEE (CSCE)
37,500 lbs.; cents per lb.

Strike	Calls–Settle			Puts–Settle		
Price	Dec	Mar	May	Dec	Mar	May
70.00	5.40	9.50	11.10	1.30	2.90	3.20
72.50	4.15	8.05	10.05	2.55	3.95	4.65
75.00	2.75	6.80	9.20	3.55	5.20	6.30
77.50	1.95	5.65	7.45	5.23	6.45	7.05
80.00	1.19	4.60	6.20	7.09	8.00	8.30
82.50	0.72	3.75	5.20	9.12	9.65	9.80

Est vol 3,957 Thur 1,307 calls 648 puts
Op int Thur 36,518 calls 21,388 puts

SUGAR–WORLD (CSCE)
112,000 lbs.; cents per lb.

Strike	Calls–Settle			Puts–Settle		
Price	Nov	Dec	Jan	Nov	Dec	Jan
9.50	1.23	1.28	1.31	0.00	0.05	0.08
10.00	0.73	0.88	0.92	0.00	0.11	0.19
10.50	0.23	0.51	0.60	0.00	0.28	0.37
11.00	0.00	0.28	0.39	0.27	0.55	0.66
11.50	0.00	0.14	0.22	0.77	0.91	0.99
12.00	0.00	0.08	0.15	1.27	1.35	1.42

Est vol 967 Thur 1,504 calls 1,468 puts
Op int Thur 38,519 calls 19,916 puts

COCOA (CSCE)
10 metric tons; $ per ton

Strike	Calls–Settle			Puts–Settle		
Price	Dec	Mar	May	Dec	Mar	May
1000	127	182	204	3	22	26
1050	83	144	170	9	34	42
1100	50	113	138	26	50	60
1150	32	97	109	58	87	81
1200	16	65	85	92	105	107
1250	7	53	68	133	143	140

Est vol 2,451 Thur 3,693 calls 3,698 puts
Op int Thur 26,133 calls 18,061 puts

OIL

CRUDE OIL (NYM)
1,000 bbls.; $ per bbl.

Strike	Calls–Settle			Puts–Settle		
Price	Nov	Dec	Jan	Nov	Dec	Jan
1750	1.07	1.34	1.53	.02	.10	.18
1800	.59	.93	1.17	.04	.19	.32
1850	.19	.57	.85	.14	.33	.49
1900	.07	.34	.56	.52	.60	.70
1950	.02	.16	.36	.97	.92	....
2000	.01	.07	.22	1.46	1.33	1.35

Est vol 20,319 Thur 8,435 calls 11,-801 puts
Op int Thur 214,637 calls 212,539 puts

HEATING OIL No.2 (NYM)
42,000 gal.; $ per gal.

Strike	Calls–Settle			Puts–Settle		
Price	Nov	Dec	Jan	Nov	Dec	Jan
52	.0405	.0509	.0562	.0007	.0020	.0034
54	.0224	.0338	.0404	.0024	.0048	.0075
56	.0075	.0191	.0266	.0076	.0100	.0136
58	.0020	.0105	.0173	.0221	.0214	.0242
60	.0006	.0050	.0110	.0406	.0358	....
62	.0003	.0025	.0062	....	.0532	....

Est vol 2,041 Thur 4,065 calls 2,848 puts
Op int Thur 56,696 calls 32,013 puts

GASOLINE–Unlead (NYM)
42,000 gal.; $ per gal.

Strike	Calls–Settle			Puts–Settle		
Price	Nov	Dec	Jan	Nov	Dec	Jan
48	.0370	.0417	.0448	.0005	.0020	.0029
50	.0185	.0253	.0291	.0020	.0055	.0070
52	.0050	.0130	.0172	.0093	.0131	.0150
54	.0011	.0060	.0090	.0246	.0260	.0267
56	.0003	.0025	.0042	.0437	.0424	.0416
58	.0001	.0011	.0020	.0635	.0610	.0595

Est vol 311 Thur 434 calls 863 puts
Op int Thur 12,684 calls 16,364 puts

NATURAL GAS (NYM)
10,000 MMBtu.; $ per MMBtu.

Strike	Calls–Settle			Puts–Settle		
Price	Nov	Dec	Jan	Nov	Dec	Jan
205	.107	....	....	.016	....	....
210	.068	....	....	.032	.035	.058
215	.042	....	....	.051	.045	.072
220	.022	.166	....	.081	.057	.087
225	.009	.142	.201	.118	.083	.104
230	.004	.103	.173	.163	.093	.125

Est vol 4,090 Thur 732 calls 886 puts
Op int Thur 22,442 calls 28,505 puts

BRENT CRUDE (IPE)
1,000 net bbls.; $ per bbl.

Strike	Calls–Settle			Puts–Settle		
Price	Nov	Dec	Jan	Nov	Dec	Jan
1600	1.19	1.45	1.68	0.00	0.07	0.14
1650	0.69	1.01	1.26	0.00	0.13	0.22
1700	0.02	0.64	0.90	0.03	0.26	0.36
1750	0.01	0.35	0.59	0.32	0.47	0.55
1800	0.00	0.17	0.38	0.81	0.79	0.84
1850	0.00	0.08	0.24	1.31	1.20	1.20

Est vol 1,398 Mon 150 calls 610 puts
Op int Mon 30,051 calls 30,185 puts

GAS OIL (IPE)
100 metric tons; $ per ton

Strike	Calls–Settle			Puts–Settle		
Price	Nov	Dec	Jan	Nov	Dec	Jan
1600	13.20	14.30	14.50	0.20	0.80	1.25
1650	8.80	10.18	10.70	0.80	1.65	2.45
1700	5.10	6.70	7.50	2.10	3.20	4.25
1750	2.55	4.05	5.00	4.55	5.55	6.75
1800	1.15	2.35	3.35	8.15	8.85	10.10
1850	0.40	1.30	2.10	2.40	12.80	13.85

Est vol 1,055 Thur 445 calls 215 puts
Op int Thur 11,788 calls 9,218 puts

LIVESTOCK

CATTLE-FEEDER (CME)
55,000 lbs.; cents per lb.

Strike	Calls–Settle			Puts–Settle		
Price	Oct	Nov	Jan	Oct	Nov	Jan
80	....	....	....	0.05	0.15	0.70
82	2.25	....	....	0.10	0.40	1.05
84	0.65	0.82	0.85	0.50	1.10	1.80
86	0.10	0.20	0.40	1.95	2.47	3.35
88	0.02	0.05	0.30	....	4.32	....
90	0.02	0.02	0.07	....	6.30	....

Est vol 251 Thur 61 calls 100 puts
Op int Thur 1,312 calls 4,887 puts

CATTLE-LIVE (CME)
40,000 lbs.; cents per lb.

Strike	Calls–Settle			Puts–Settle		
Price	Dec	Feb	Apr	Dec	Feb	Apr
70	....	....	....	0.40	0.57	0.52
72	1.72	....	....	1.00	1.05	0.95
74	0.75	1.82	....	2.02	1.85	1.60
76	0.27	1.00	1.67	3.52	....	2.55
78	0.07	0.50	0.90	....	....	....
80	0.00	0.20	0.45	....	....	....

Est vol 1,824 Thur 393 calls 773 puts
Op int Thur 10,656 calls 19,424 puts

HOGS–LIVE (CME)
40,000 lbs.; cents per lb.

Strike	Calls–Settle			Puts–Settle		
Price	Dec	Feb	Apr	Dec	Feb	Apr
46	4.95	4.85	3.00	0.17	0.50	1.10
48	3.22	3.35	1.85	0.45	0.97	1.90
50	1.80	2.15	1.10	1.10	1.75	3.10
52	0.90	1.25	....	2.10	2.82	....
54	0.35	0.65	....	....	....	....
56	0.10	....	....	....	....	....

Est vol 278 Thur 60 calls 118 puts
Op int Thur 1,970 calls 2,918 puts

METALS

COPPER (CMX)
25,000 lbs.; cents per lb.

Strike	Calls–Settle			Puts–Settle		
Price	Nov	Dec	Mar	Nov	Dec	Mar
72	3.90	4.35	6.10	0.30	0.85	1.70
74	2.35	3.05	4.75	0.75	1.45	2.35
76	1.20	1.90	3.70	1.60	2.30	3.30
78	0.55	1.25	2.80	2.95	3.65	4.40
80	0.20	0.80	2.20	4.60	5.20	5.80
82	0.15	0.40	1.65	6.55	6.80	7.25

TABLE 21.1 (*continued*)

Est vol 500 Thur 152 calls 171 puts
Op int Thur 7,901 calls 5,629 puts

GOLD (CMX)
100 troy ounces; $ per troy ounce

Strike	Calls–Settle			Puts–Settle		
Price	Nov	Dec	Feb	Nov	Dec	Feb
340	21.50	22.70	25.80	0.00	1.20	3.50
350	11.50	14.50	18.70	0.00	3.00	5.80
360	1.50	7.80	13.40	0.00	6.30	10.10
370	0.00	4.00	9.40	8.50	12.50	16.00
380	0.00	2.00	6.70	18.50	20.20	23.10
390	0.00	1.30	4.90	28.50	29.70	31.40

Est vol 6,500 Thur 2,832 calls 1,117 puts
Op int Thur 128,419 calls 43,144 puts

SILVER (CMX)
5,000 troy ounces; cts per troy ounce

Strike	Calls–Settle			Puts–Settle		
Price	Nov	Dec	Mar	Nov	Dec	Mar
375	61.0	62.7	72.0	0.0	1.7	7.7
400	36.0	41.0	54.7	0.0	5.0	15.0
425	11.0	24.5	40.8	0.0	13.5	25.7
450	0.0	13.3	30.0	14.0	27.3	39.8
475	0.0	8.0	23.5	39.0	47.0	58.5
500	0.0	5.0	17.7	64.0	69.0	77.0

Est vol 5,400 Thur 4,713 calls 1,230 puts
Op int Thur 69,204 calls 24,536 puts

INDEX

S&P 500 STOCK INDEX (CME)
$500 times premium

Strike	Calls–Settle			Puts–Settle		
Price	Oct	Nov	Dec	Oct	Nov	Dec
450	11.80	14.30	16.30	.45	3.00	5.05
455	7.20	10.35	12.65	.85	4.05	6.35
460	3.30	6.95	9.40	1.95	5.60	8.05
465	.90	4.20	6.60	4.55	7.85	10.20
470	.15	2.25	4.30	8.80	10.85	12.90
475	.05	1.05	2.55	....	....	16.10

Est vol 9,299 Thur 2,621 calls 9,006 puts
Op int Thur 48,022 calls 158,136 puts

GSCI (CME)
$250 times GSCI nearby Index

Strike	Calls–Settle			Puts–Settle		
Price	Nov	Dec	Jan	Nov	Dec	Jan
178	....	4.00	....	....	2.10	....
179	....	....	....	....	....	....
180	2.00	2.80	....	2.10	2.90	....
181	....	....	....	....	....	....
182	1.20	....	....	3.30	....	....
183	....	....	....	....	....	....

Est vol 0 Thur 90 calls 0 puts
Op int Thur 2,297 calls 2,297 puts

CURRENCY

JAPANESE YEN (CME)
12,500,000 yen; cents per 100 yen

Strike	Calls–Settle			Puts–Settle		
Price	Oct	Nov	Dec	Oct	Nov	Dec
9350	0.92	1.86	2.11	0.00	0.73	1.20
9400	0.43	1.36	1.83	0.01	0.94	1.41
9450	0.02	1.09	1.58	0.10	1.17	1.66
9500	0.00	0.88	1.35	0.58	1.46	1.93
9550	0.00	0.70	1.15	1.08	1.78	2.22
9600	0.00	0.54	0.97	1.58	2.11	2.54

Est vol 13,905 Thur 11,144 calls 11,604 puts
Op int Thur 54,066 calls 81,271 puts

DEUTSCHEMARK (CME)
125,000 marks; cents per mark

Strike	Calls–Settle			Puts–Settle		
Price	Oct	Nov	Dec	Oct	Nov	Dec
6100	0.98	1.43	1.75	.0008	0.45	0.77
6150	0.49	1.12	1.45	0.01	0.64	0.97
6200	0.05	0.84	1.19	0.07	0.86	1.21
6250	0.01	0.62	0.97	0.53	1.14	1.49
6300	.0008	0.45	0.78	1.02	1.47	1.79
6350	.0008	0.32	0.63	1.52	1.83	2.14

Est vol 48,005 Thur 7,615 calls 6,787 puts
Op int Thur 161,871 calls 145,706 puts

CANADIAN DOLLAR (CME)
100,000 Can.$, cents per Can.$

Strike	Calls–Settle			Puts–Settle		
Price	Oct	Nov	Dec	Oct	Nov	Dec
7400	0.93	1.17	1.34	.0000	0.24	0.42
7450	0.43	0.83	1.02	.0000	0.40	0.59
7500	.0000	0.54	0.75	0.07	0.61	0.82
7550	.0000	0.33	0.54	0.57	0.90	1.11
7600	.0000	0.19	0.37	1.07	1.26	1.43
7650	.0000	0.10	0.25	1.57	1.66	1.81

Est vol 1,093 Thur 801 calls 244 puts
Op int Thur 7,491 calls 6,511 puts

BRITISH POUND (CME)
62,500 pounds; cents per pound

Strike	Calls–Settle			Puts–Settle		
Price	Oct	Nov	Dec	Oct	Nov	Dec
1475	5.52	5.94	6.54	0.00	0.44	1.06
1500	3.02	3.96	4.80	0.00	0.96	1.80
1525	0.52	2.44	3.36	0.00	1.92	2.84
1550	0.00	1.34	2.20	1.98	3.32	4.16
1575	0.00	0.68	1.38	4.48	....	....
1600	0.00	0.34	0.82	....	7.30	7.76

Est vol 1,767 Thur 591 calls 745 puts
Op int Thur 15,026 calls 10,220 puts

SWISS FRANC (CME)
125,000 francs; cents per franc

Strike	Calls–Settle			Puts–Settle		
Price	Oct	Nov	Dec	Oct	Nov	Dec
7000	1.02	1.64	2.02	.0008	0.62	1.01
7050	0.52	1.33	1.74	.0008	0.81	1.22
7100	0.02	1.06	1.48	.0008	1.04	1.46
7150	.0008	0.83	1.25	0.48	1.31	1.73
7200	.0008	0.65	1.05	0.98	1.64	2.02
7250	.0008	0.49	0.87	....	....	....

Est vol 4,482 Thur 365 calls 717 puts
Op int Thur 12,799 calls 12,012 puts

U.S. DOLLAR INDEX (FINEX)
1,000 times index

Strike	Calls–Settle			Puts–Settle		
Price	Oct	Nov	Dec	Oct	Nov	Dec
90	2.24	....	....	.01	.56	.25
91	1.24	2.11	....	.01	.88	.50
92	.24	1.54	1.13	.01	1.30	.89
93	.01	1.08	.68	.76	1.83	1.43
94	.01	.73	.37	1.76	2.47	2.12
95	.01	.47	.18	2.76	3.20	2.93

Est vol 374 Thur 122 calls 86 puts
Op int Thur 1,841 calls 1,536 puts

INTEREST RATE

T-BONDS (CBT)
$100,000; points and 64ths of 100%

Strike	Calls–Settle			Puts–Settle		
Price	Nov	Dec	Mar	Nov	Dec	Mar
119	1-55	....	....	0-13	....	....
120	1-10	1-47	2-16	0-32	1-05	2-50
121	0-37	....	....	0-59	....	....
122	0-17	0-52	1-28	1-39	2-10	....
123	0-06	....	....	2-28	....	....
124	0-02	0-19	0-57	....	3-40	5-24

Est. vol. 200,000;
Thur vol. 43,843 calls; 57,946 puts
Op. int. Thur 445,878 calls; 410,241 puts

T-NOTES (CBT)
$100,000; points and 64ths of 100%

Strike	Calls–Settle			Puts–Settle		
Price	Nov	Dec	Mar	Nov	Dec	Mar
115	1-41	1-56	1-62	0-05	0-21	1-21
116	0-53	1-11	1-28	0-17	0-40	1-50
117	0-19	0-42	1-01	0-48	1-06	2-23
118	0-05	0-21	....	....	....	....
119	0-01	0-09	....	....	....	....
120	....	0-04	....	....	....	....

Est vol 22,000 Thur 13,665 calls 5,941 puts
Op int Thur 105,401 calls 121,493 puts

MUNICIPAL BOND INDEX (CBT)
$100,000; pts. & 64ths of 100%

Strike	Calls–Settle			Puts–Settle		
Price	Dec	Mar	Jun	Dec	Mar	Jun
103	2-34	....	....	0-23	....	....
104	1-51	....	....	0-40	....	....
105	....	....	....	....	....	....
106	0-46	....	....	....	....	....
107	....	....	....	....	....	....
108	....	....	....	....	....	....

Est vol 0 Thur 0 calls 60 puts
Op int Thur 4,376 calls 4,823 puts

5 YR TREAS NOTES (CBT)
$100,000; points and 64ths of 100%

Strike	Calls–Settle			Puts–Settle		
Price	Nov	Dec	Mar	Nov	Dec	Mar
11200	....	1-46	....	0-02	0-05	....
11250	1-12	1-19	1-14	0-03	0-09	0-53
11300	0-47	0-58	0-60	0-06	0-17	1-04
11350	0-25	0-38	0-46	0-16	0-29	1-20
11400	0-10	0-22	....	....	0-45	....
11450	0-04	0-12	0-25	....	....	....

Est vol 14,500 Thur 3,031 calls 4,376 puts
Op int Thur 45,028 calls 99,179 puts

EURODOLLAR (CME)
$ million; pts. of 100%

Strike	Calls–Settle			Puts–Settle		
Price	Dec	Mar	June	Dec	Mar	June
9600	0.59	0.61	0.51	0.01	0.03	0.12
9625	0.35	0.39	0.33	0.02	0.06	0.19
9650	0.14	0.21	0.19	0.06	0.12	0.30
9675	0.03	0.08	0.10	0.20	0.25	0.45
9700	.0004	0.02	0.04	0.42	0.44	....
9725	.0004	0.01	0.01	0.67	0.67	....

Est. vol. 104,086;
Thur vol. 25,065 calls; 35,735 puts
Op. int. Thur 632,397 calls; 801,113 puts

LIBOR – 1 Mo. (CME)
$3 million; pts. of 100%

Strike	Calls–Settle			Puts–Settle		
Price	Oct	Nov	Dec	Oct	Nov	Dec
9625	....	0.59	0.21	....	.0004	0.08
9650	0.33	0.34	0.08	.0004	.0004	0.20
9675	0.09	0.10	0.02	0.01	0.01	....
9700	0.18	0.01	0.01	0.18	0.17	....
9725	.0004	....	.0004	0.42	....	....
9750	....	....	....	....	....	....

Est vol 635 Thur 80 calls 200 puts
Op int Thur 4,208 calls 3,610 puts

TREASURY BILLS (CME)
$1 million; pts. of 100%

Strike	Calls–Settle			Puts–Settle		
Price	Dec	Mar	June	Dec	Mar	June
9650	0.43	0.37	0.35	0.01	0.06	0.17
9675	0.19	0.20	0.20	0.02	0.13	0.27
9700	0.03	0.09	0.10	0.11	0.27	0.42
9725	....	....	....	....	....	....
9750	....	....	....	....	....	....
9775	....	....	....	....	....	....

Est vol 201 Thur 0 calls 5 puts
Op int Thur 227 calls 1,120 puts

EURODOLLAR (LIFFE)
$1 million; pts. of 100%

Strike	Calls–Settle			Puts–Settle		
Price	Dec	Mar	Jun	Dec	Mar	Jun
9600	0.61	0.64	0.52	0.01	0.04	0.12
9625	0.36	0.41	0.34	0.01	0.06	0.19
9650	0.15	0.23	0.20	0.05	0.13	0.30
9675	0.04	0.10	0.12	0.19	0.25	0.47
9700	0.01	0.04	0.05	0.41	0.44	0.65
9725	0.00	0.01	0.02	0.65	0.66	0.87

Est vol Fri 0 calls 0 puts
Op int Thur 3,050 calls 2,240 puts

LONG GILT (LIFFE)
£50,000; 64ths of 100%

Strike	Calls–Settle			Puts–Settle		
Price	Dec	Mar	....	Dec	Mar	....
112	2-52	3-10	....	0-24	1-24	....
113	2-05	2-36	....	0-41	1-50	....
114	1-28	2-04	....	1-00	2-18	....
115	0-61	1-40	....	1-33	2-54	....
116	0-38	1-16	....	2-10	3-30	....
117	0-22	0-61	....	2-58	4-11	....
	....	....	....	....	....	....

Est vol Fri 2,393 calls [illegible],381 puts
Op int Thur 50,490 calls 39,770 puts

OTHER OPTIONS

Final or settlement prices of selected contracts. Volume and open interest are totals in all contract months.

CORN (MCE)
1,000 bu.; cents per bu.

Strike	Calls–Settle			Puts–Settle		
Price	Dec	Mar	May	Dec	Mar	May
240	6¾	13¼	18	4¾	4	4

Est vol 5 Thur 113 calls 4 puts
Op int Thur 841 calls 334 puts

DM ROLLING SPOT (CME)
$250,000; DM per U.S. $

Strike	Calls–Settle			Puts–Settle		
Price	Oct	Nov	Dec	Oct	Nov	Dec
6000	....	....	....	....	....	....

Est vol 4 Thur 0 calls 4 puts
Op int Thur 200 calls 5 puts

EASTERN CATASROPHE INS. (CBT)
$25,000 times ratio of losses/prem.

Strike	Calls–Settle			Puts–Settle		
Price	Sep	Dec	Mar	Sep	Dec	Mar
1200	0-01	0-11	....	....	....	....

Est vol 1,200 Thur 34 calls 0 puts
Op int Thur 640 calls 0 puts

TABLE 21.1 (*continued*)

EUROMARK (CME)						
DM 1,000,000; pts. of 100%						
Strike	Calls–Settle			Puts–Settle		
Price	Oct	Nov	Dec	Oct	Nov	Dec
9375	....	....	....	....	....	....
Est vol 0	Thur 0 calls 0 puts					
Op int Thur	500 calls 10 puts					
FRENCH FRANC (CME)						
500,000 FF; $ per franc						
Strike	Calls–Settle			Puts–Settle		
Price	Oct	Nov	Dec	Oct	Nov	Dec
7750	....	....	2.82	....	....	....
Est vol 0	Thur 3 calls 3,510 puts					
Op int Thur	501 calls 3,012 puts					
LUMBER (CME)						
160,000 bd .ft., $ per 1,000 bd.ft.						
Strike	Calls–Settle			Puts–Settle		
Price	Nov	Jan	Mar	Nov	Jan	Mar
310	12.10	35.00	....	....	....	....
Est vol 54	Thur 13 calls 55 puts					
Op int Thur	406 calls 779 puts					
NYSE COMPOSITE INDEX (NYFE)						
$500 times premium						
Strike	Calls–Settle			Puts–Settle		
Price	Oct	Nov	Dec	Oct	Nov	Dec
256	1.60	3.70	4.95	1.30	3.40	4.65
Est vol 177	Thur 16 calls 16 puts					
Op int Thur	830 calls 904 puts					
NIKKEI 225 STOCK AVG. (CME)						
$5 times Prem.						
Strike	Calls–Settle			Puts–Settle		
Price	Oct	Nov	Dec	Oct	Nov	Dec
20500	140	....	465	235	....	560
Est vol 11	Thur 19 calls 0 puts					
Op int Thur	638 calls 597 puts					
OATS (CBT)						
5,000 bu.; cents per bu.						
Strike	Calls–Settle			Puts–Settle		
Price	Dec	Mar	May	Dec	Mar	May
140	2¾	8¼	....	5½	6¼	7¼
Est vol 20	Thur 18 calls 7 puts					
Op int Thur	1,208 calls 918 puts					
PLATINUM (NYM)						
50 troy oz.; $ per troy oz.						
Strike	Calls–Settle			Puts–Settle		
Price	Nov	Dec	Jan	Nov	Dec	Jan
360	....	....	12.80	....	....	8.70
Est vol 192	Thur 341 calls 0 puts					
Op int Thur	2,380 calls 549 puts					
PORK BELLIES (CME)						
40,000 lbs.; cents per lb.						
Strike	Calls–Settle			Puts–Settle		
Price	Nov	Feb	Mar	Nov	Feb	Mar
58	2.50	11.02	11.22	....	0.97	1.30
Est vol 61	Thur 38 calls 20 puts					
Op int Thur	1,197 calls 1,233 puts					
RICE-ROUGH (MCE)						
2,000 cwt.; $ per cwt.						
Strike	Calls–Settle			Puts–Settle		
Price	Nov	Jan	Mar	Nov	Jan	Mar
7800	....	.540	....	....	....	....
Est vol 65	Thur 52 calls 76 puts					
Op int Thur	225 calls 1,047 puts					
SILVER (CBT)						
1,000 troy oz.; cents per troy oz.						
Strike	Calls–Settle			Puts–Settle		
Price	Dec	Feb	Apr	Dec	Feb	Apr
425	22.0	....	....	....	....	....
Est vol 100	Thur 66 calls 0 puts					
Op int Thur	1,002 calls 30 puts					
SOYBEANS (MCE)						
1,000 bu.; cents per bu.						
Strike	Calls–Settle			Puts–Settle		
Price	Nov	Jan	Mar	Nov	Jan	Mar
600	13½	23¼	30½	4½	7⅝	9
Est vol 75	Thur 66 calls 9 puts					
Op int Thur	2,173 calls 641 puts					
2 YR TREAS NOTE (CBT)						
$200,000; pts. 32nds of 100%						
Strike	Calls–Settle			Puts–Settle		
Price	Nov	Dec	Mar	Nov	Dec	Mar
10700	....	....	....	....	....	....
Est vol 0	Thur 0 calls 0 puts					
Op int Thur	176 calls 250 puts					
WHEAT (MCE)						
1,000 bu.; cents per bu.						
Strike	Calls–Settle			Puts–Settle		
Price	Dec	Mar	May	Dec	Mar	May
320	8⅞	15¾	16½	6¾	9½	....
Est vol 5	Thur 10 calls 0 puts					
Op int Thur	665 calls 8 puts					
WHEAT (MPLS)						
5,000 bu.; cents per bu.						
Strike	Calls–Settle			Puts–Settle		
Price	Dec	Mar	May	Dec	Mar	May
330	6	10	14	8½	16	21½
Est vol 23	Thur 12 calls 0 puts					
Op int Thur	772 calls 901 puts					

SOURCE: *The Wall Street Journal*, October 9, 1993.

Table 21.2. Quotations for the many interest rate over-the-counter options are not normally published and must be obtained from dealers. Treasury bond options can be exercised at any time prior to maturity, so they are American options in the sense defined above.

A call option on an asset that is selling for less than the exercise price is said to be *out of the money*. A call option on an asset selling for more than the exercise price is said to be *in the money*. Conversely, put options on assets selling below conversion prices are in the money whereas if asset prices are above put option strike prices, they are said to be out of the money. When asset prices are equal to conversion prices, options are said to be *at the money*.

To illustrate an option, consider the buyer of a December 1993, call option (the maturity month is shown in the columns of the table) at a strike price of 120 percent of the contract face value at prices quoted in Table 21.1. The call buyer acquires the right to buy a futures contract requiring delivery of long-term U.S. Treasury bonds in December in exchange for $120,000 in cash, 120 percent of the $100,000 contract face value. The maturity dates of options on interest rate sensitive futures contracts are usually a few weeks before the futures contract matures. Table 21.2 shows that the option on Treasury bond futures ceases trading on the Friday at least five business days before the beginning of the futures contract month and expires the following Saturday. As shown in Table 20.2 in the previous chapter, Treasury bond futures contracts cease trading seven business days before the end of the contract month and delivery takes place before the last business day. Prices of options on futures contracts at expiration will closely reflect the yields on long-term Treasuries in the spot market at expiration since they can be used to take delivery of actual Treasury bonds in about four weeks.

TABLE 21.2 Contract Specifications for Options Contracts

Panel A: Options on U.S. Government Bonds Futures

ITEM	*CONTRACT SPECIFICATIONS*	
Exchange	Chicago Board of Trade	Mid-America Commodity Exchange
Introduced	October 1, 1982	September 18, 1981
Specification/ basis	Chicago Board of Trade U.S. Treasury bond futures contract.	Mid-America U.S. Treasury bond futures contract.
Contract unit	One futures contract.	One futures contract.
Quotation	Points	Points
Tick size	1/64 point	1/32 point
Tick value	$15.625	$15.625
Expiration months	The front month of the current quarter plus the next three from the March, June, September, December cycle. If the front month is the contract month, no monthly contract is listed. Monthly options exercise into the nearest quarterly futures contract (e.g., November options exercise into December futures).	The front month of the current quarter plus the next three from the March, June, September, December cycle. If the front month is the contract month, no monthly contract is listed. Monthly options exercise into the nearest quarterly futures contract (e.g., November options exercise into December futures).
Strike prices	Integral multiples of two points.	Integral multiples of two points.
Trading hours	7:20 A.M. to 2:00 P.M. (Monday–Friday) Central Standard Time plus evening hours 5:20 P.M. to 8:05 P.M. (Sunday to Thursday). GLOBEX trading 10:30 A.M. to 6:00 A.M. (Sunday to Thursday).	7:20 A.M. to 3:15 P.M. Central Standard Time.
Maximum daily limit	3 points, expandable to 4—1/2 points in certain circumstances. Limits are lifted last trading day.	3 points.
Exercise	American (on any business day to expiry). Automatic exercise of options that are at least 2 points in the money on the last day of trading.	American (on any business day to expiry). Automatic exercise of options that are at least 2 points in the money on the last day of trading.
Expiry	10:00 A.M. on the first Saturday following the last day of trading.	10:00 A.M. on the first Saturday following the last day of trading.
Last day of trading	Noon on the last Friday preceding, by at least five business days, the last business day of the month preceding the option contract month.	Noon on the last Friday preceding, by at least five business days, the last business day of the month preceding the option contract month.
Position limits	None.	2000 futures-equivalent contracts net on the same side of the market in all months combined; 5000 option contracts in all months in each option category (long call, long put, short call, short put). No position limits for bona fide hedging positions.

Panel B: Options on Three-Month Eurodollar Futures Contracts

ITEM	*CONTRACT SPECIFICATIONS*	
Exchange	Index and Option Market Division, Chicago Mercantile Exchange (CME)	London International Financial Futures and Options Exchange (LIFFE)
Introduced	March 20, 1985	June 27, 1985
Specification/ basis	CME Eurodollar futures contract.	LIFFE Eurodollar futures contract.
Contract unit	One futures contract.	One Eurodollar futures contract.
Quotation	IMM Eurodollar Index points (100 minus yield on an annual basis for a 360-day year).	Multiples of .01 (i.e., .01%).
Tick size	.01 point (basis point). A trade may occur at a price of .005 index point whether or not it results in the liquidation of positions for both parties to the trade.	.01
Tick value	$25.00	$25.00
Strike price	At increments of .25 index points.	At .25 (i.e., .25%) intervals. Thirteen exercise prices are listed for new series. Additional prices are introduced on the business day after the Eurodollar futures contract settlement price is within .12 of the sixth highest or lowest existing strike price.
Expiration months	Six months in the March, June, September, December quarterly cycle plus two months not in the quarterly cycle.	March, June, September, December.
Trading hours	7:20 A.M. to 2:00 P.M. (Monday–Friday) Central Standard Time plus evening hours 2:30 P.M. to 4:00 P.M. and 6:00 P.M. to 6:00 A.M. (Sunday to Thursday) on GLOBEX.	8:30 A.M. to 4:00 P.M. London time.
Maximum daily limit	None on exchange; no GLOBEX trading is permitted in any option when primary futures contract is limit bid or offered.	None.
Exercise	American (on any business day to expiry). Automatic exercise of all in-the-money options following termination of trading.	American (on any business day to expiry). Automatic exercise of all in-the-money options following termination of trading.
Expiry		12:30 P.M. on the last trading day.
Last day of trading	Options in the quarterly cycle on the same day as the underlying futures contract. Trading in an expiring contract ceases at 9:30 A.M. Other options on the close of trading on the Friday preceding the third Wednesday of the contract month.	The last day of trading of the Eurodollar futures contract. Trading in an expiring contract ceases at 11:00 A.M.
Position limits	Position accountability for persons owning or controlling a combination of options and underlying futures of more than 10,000 futures-equivalent contracts net on the same side of the market in all months combined.	None.

Note: Options also traded on Singapore International Monetary Exchange Limited since September 25, 1987.

TABLE 21.2 (*continued*)

Panel C: Options on German Mark Futures Contracts

ITEM	*CONTRACT SPECIFICATIONS*	
Exchange	Index and Option Market Division, Chicago Mercantile Exchange	Singapore International Monetary Exchange Limited (SIMEX)
Introduced	January 24, 1984	November 27, 1987
Specification/basis	Chicago Mercantile Exchange German mark futures contract.	SIMEX German mark futures contract.
Contract Unit	One futures contract.	One futures contract.
Quotation	U.S. dollars per Deutschmark.	U.S. dollars per Deutschmark.
Tick size	\$.0001 (one point) A trade may occur at a price of \$.00005 whether or not it results in the liquidation of positions for both parties to the trade. If listed for volatility-quoted trading on GLOBEX, quotes possible at .05 per cent.	\$.0001 (one point).
Tick Value	\$12.50	\$12.50
Strike Price	At increments of \$.01. For the first four listed options expirations only, there are additional strike prices listed at increments of \$.005.	At increments of \$.01.
Expiration Months	Serial month listings include three options in the quarterly cycle (March, June, September, December) and two not in the cycle (January, February, April, May, July, August, October, November) plus one option exercible in next quarterly contract (e.g., March option on June contract)	Spot month plus the next two months plus months from the March, June, September, December cycle. For options that expire in months other than those in the March cycle, the underlying futures contract in the next month in the March cycle.
Trading hours	7:20 A.M. to 2:00 P.M. (Monday–Friday) Central Standard Time plus evening hours 2:30 P.M. to 6:00 A.M. (Sunday to Thursday) on GLOBEX.	8:20 A.M. to 5:10 P.M. local time.
Maximum daily limit	Option ceases trading when primary futures contract locks limit. The primary futures contract is the futures contract in the lead month configuration in the pit	None.
Exercise	American (on any business day to expiry). Automatic exercise of all in-the-money options following termination of trading	American (on any business day to expiry)
Expiry		7:30 P.M. on last day of trading.

ITEM	*CONTRACT SPECIFICATIONS*	
Last day of trading	Long-dated: Second Friday immediately preceding the third Wednesday of the contract month. Short-dated: First Friday immediately succeeding the third Wednesday of the contract month. In each case, if this date is an exchange holiday, trading ceases on the immediately preceding business day. Trading in an expiring contract ceases at 9:16 A.M.	Two Fridays before the third Wednesday of the contract month. If that Friday is an exchange holiday, the last day of trading is the business day immediately preceding.
Position limits	Position accountability for persons owning or controlling a combination of options and underlying futures contracts of more than 10,000 futures-equivalent contracts net on the same side of the market in all months combined.	1000 futures-equivalent contracts.

Note: Options on spot currency also traded on the Philadelphia Board of Trade for contract size German mark 62,500 since February 4, 1983.
SOURCE: Nick Battley, *The World's Futures and Options Markets* (Chicago: Probus Publishing, 1993).

The U.S. Treasury bond option described above was priced at 1-47 on October 8, meaning the call option can be bought for 1-47/64 or 1.734375 percent of the futures contract value. Since bond futures contracts are for $100,000, the Treasury bond futures December call in the table sells for $1,734.38. Upon writing the contract, the call writer receives $1,734.38. Checking Table 20.1 for futures contracts on the same date, we can see that the bond futures contract settled at 120-21 or 120.65625 percent of face value, or $120,656.25.

The futures contract value of $120,656.25 minus the exercise price of $120,000 means the option has an *exercise value* of $656.25 if the call option is immediately exercised. This option is "in the money." Of course it would not make sense to exercise the option immediately since the option costs $1,734.38 and is only worth $656.25, meaning an immediate loss. The option has value above immediate exercise value because bond prices may increase at some time before the option expires.

The difference between the exercise value of the option and its current market price is the *option premium*. In our example, the option premium over exercise value is $1,089.12 ($1,734.38 – $656.25). The factors determining option premiums has been extensively studied and option pricing has become a major tool in pricing financial contracts and securities. We discuss the theory and applications of option pricing below.

Put options work in a similar way. Using Table 21.1 again, a December 120 put on futures contract on U.S. Treasury bonds on October 8, 1993, was quoted for 1-05, read as 1-5/64 percent or .01078125 of contract value, that is, $1,078.13. The put option owner profits when yields rise (meaning prices fall). This is because the put option owner can buy the underlying asset at reduced prices and force the put writer to buy the asset at the strike price. In our above example of long-term U.S. Treasury bond options, if yields went up to 6.5 percent, the futures contract value would fall to 116-17 or 1.1653125 times the face value of the contract, $116,531.25. The put option owner can sell the futures contract for 120 percent of face value if yields rise to 6.5 percent, making a gross profit of $3,468.75 ($120,000 minus $116,531.25) or netting $2,390.63 after subtracting the cost of the put. If yields fall, the put option owner loses the premium to the put writer.

Options versus Futures and Forward Contracts

Our first objective is to compare option contracts and futures and forward contracts in terms of their payoffs in the future as underlying asset prices change. Option contracts can be analyzed using the same types of graphical presentations for futures contracts as used in Figure 20.2 and 20.3 in the preceding chapter. Figure 21.1 shows the profit from yield changes from owning a yield sensitive call option and holding it until maturity. The option premium paid by the call buyer is shown in the figure by the payoff line being below the horizontal axis, repre-

FIGURE 21.1 Yield and profits with call options

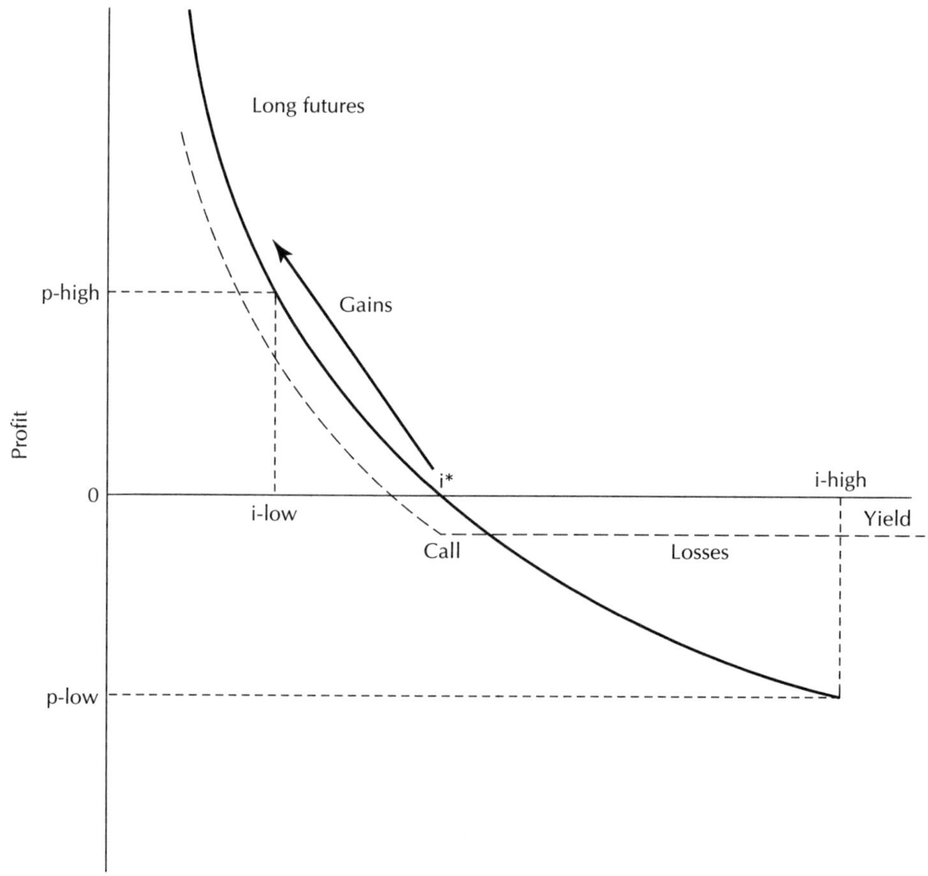

senting payment of the premium. If the call matures out of the money, the option is worthless and the call buyer loses the premium paid for the call. If the yields fall and the call finishes in the money, the call buyer makes a profit because the strike price is less than the market value of the assets. Figure 21.2 shows the same relations for a put option.

Figure 21.1 also shows the profit/loss from a long futures position in the same asset established at the strike price of the option and the call option. The major difference between the option and the long position is that the losses are limited to the option premium when asset values go down (yields increase) whereas profits from both go up with increases in asset values. When yields are down and prices up relative to the futures delivery price or the option strike price, both options and futures contracts make money. The owner can take delivery of the assets at the lower futures contract delivery yield (higher price) or exercise the option at the strike price and immediately sell the asset in the cash market at the lower yields (higher prices).

FIGURE 21.2 Yield and profits with put options

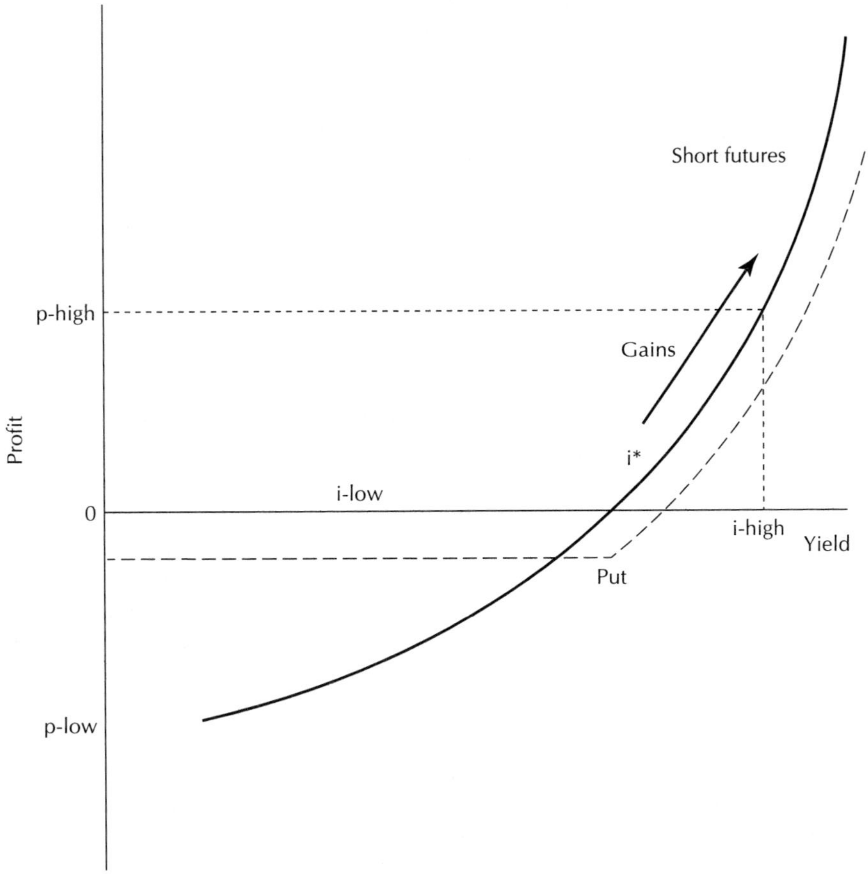

The important difference between options and futures can be seen by contrasting the maturity value of the call option to a futures contract when yields on the underlying assets go up and prices down. Futures contracts require taking delivery at maturity according to the contract terms no matter what happens to prices. Most commonly, the futures contract holder will repurchase the contract at current value meaning that *losses* on the long position in that contract will be realized when asset prices fall. In contrast, the call option owner's losses are limited to the premium paid at the time the option was purchased if asset prices fall.

The reason for the asymmetric profit/loss sensitivity of the option relative to the futures contract is that the holder has an *option* to purchase at the strike price, not an obligation to take delivery at the contract price as is the case with the long position in the futures contract. No one will choose to exercise an option that produces losses. On the other hand, the option holder has paid for this profit/loss asymmetry by paying the option premium, which is lost whenever the asset yield or price makes the option worthless at maturity.

Traded option strike prices are set at standardized increments by the exchange and these strike prices will rarely be exactly equal to the underlying asset price on any given day. In our example above, the strike price for the call option was 120, meaning that on the December expiration date we could pay $120,000 and receive a futures contract for long-term U.S. Treasury bonds maturing a few days later. The futures price on the day we bought the option (October 8, 1993) was 120-21, corresponding to a commitment to buy U.S. Treasury bonds according to the contract specifications for the equivalent of $120,656.25. As discussed above, we would pay $1,734.38 for the option.

If at the maturity of the option contract the futures contract price was below 120 percent of face value or $120,000, meaning that yields had gone up, we would not exercise the option. If on the other hand yields dropped to 5.5 percent by the expiration date of the option, the futures contract value would be approximately 129-28 or $129,875 (1.29875 times the face value of the contract). In this case, the option would now be worth $9,875 (contract value of $129,875 minus the exercise price of $120,000). In this case we can exercise the option and collect our profit. More likely, we would sell the option back to the option writer for $9,875 and not be troubled to exercise the option and sell the futures contract.

The put or call option writer's profits or losses are the mirror image of the option buyer's costs or gains. This is identical to the case of short and long positions in futures contracts. The difference is that the option writer's gain is limited at the maximum to the price received when the option was sold or written. Of course the option buyer's losses are limited to the identical amount. Gains for option buyer and losses for the option writer are limited only by the maximum possible price for the underlying asset.

Short and long positions in both options and futures and forward markets are opposites: One side's gain is the other side's losses. This is often described as a *zero sum game*. The sum of gains and losses to all participants in these markets is zero. This does not mean that value is not created by these contracts because it ignores their use in hedging. Hedging allows market participants to reduce uncertainty about future outcomes. Risk sharing by hedgers can increase expected utility of market participants following the discussion in Chapter 6. In addition, managers and decision makers who are more productive when not distracted or constrained by future uncertainties can concentrate more effectively on value-producing activities they are good at as we discussed with futures. Options markets like futures markets may increase expected utility and/or productivity and activity providing net positive value to the economy even though they are a zero-sum game.

21.2 HEDGING ASSET VALUE RISKS WITH OPTIONS

Option buyers earn profits at the maturity of their option contracts only if the underlying asset values change enough relative to their exercise values. Option writers have net gains only if prices do not move too much. Calls have positive value to call buyers (and negative value to call writers) if asset values are above their exercise values, that is, they are in the money. Puts are in the money if asset values are below exercise prices. Options with no exercise value expire worthless at maturity, allowing option writer to keep their premiums.

Since the value of options is asymmetric with respect to future asset value outcomes, they can used to hedge asset value risk against some outcomes and not others. Options can be used to hedge against *adverse* outcomes in terms of future asset values. Risk in financial theory is defined as uncertain outcomes, whether good or bad outcomes. For example, owners of assets (current long position) are hurt if prices of the asset go down and they profit if asset values increase. Financial theory treats both outcomes as risks associated with uncertain future values. Using options to hedge the future value risk of assets allows favorable movements in asset values to benefit hedgers and at the same time shields hedgers from the effects of bad outcomes. Options allow hedgers to participate in gains and limit losses.

Hedging with options requires choosing the right option position to offset adverse outcomes. An owner of assets wishing to hedge downside risk should buy put options that increase in value with downward movement of underlying asset prices but are worthless at maturity if asset prices increase. The put option owner's profit can offset the loss in asset value with adverse outcomes but increases in asset values can be kept. The future buyer of assets can hedge future purchase prices by buying calls, thereby limiting maximum prices in the future but allowing the hedger to benefit from lower asset values if they should occur.

Options are a means to *partially* hedge by protecting against only "bad" risks. In contrast, futures contracts *hedge* both "good" and "bad" risks. This desirable feature of hedging against only bad risks with options has a cost. Option buyers pay a premium for options which is lost if the option does not have value at maturity. The lost option premium reduces any profits from the favorable asset value changes. Option premiums are analogous to insurance against bad outcomes: the premium is lost if no bad outcomes occur.

We can illustrate the use of options for hedging using our examples from Chapter 20. For example, a bank wishing to hedge the cost of issuing certificates of deposit (CDs) could use options on Eurodollars rather than futures as discussed in the previous chapter. This way the bank could benefit from decreases in interest rates and be protected from increases in interest rates. Since the bank is selling CDs, it has a long position long in an asset. The correct hedge would be to buy a put option guaranteeing the bank a minimum sale price for its CDs if interest rates should go up. The profits from the put are added to the proceeds of the CD issue. The combination of option profits and asset sales hedge interest costs.

Table 21.3 shows how the hedge works using the quotes in Table 21.1. The bank buys a put option on the 90-day Eurodollar futures contract at a strike price of 9650, the closest strike price to the current price of the March futures contract,

TABLE 21.3 Example of Hedging CD Costs Using Options

Panel A: Actions in Spot and Options Market

ACTIONS NOW (t_0)

PRESENT PLAN	*OPTIONS MARKET*
Will need to issue $10 million in CDs in March 1994	Buy 10 March put options on Eurodollar futures at strike price of 96.50 for $3,000

ACTIONS LATER (t_F)

FUTURE CONDITIONS	*RATES HIGHER (5 PERCENT)*	*RATES LOWER (2 PERCENT)*
Pay interest on CDs at current market[a]	($125,000)	($50,000)
Net profit (loss) from put option[b]	34,500	(3,000)
Net interest cost of CD	($90,500)	($53,000)
Annualized yield cost on $10 million (4 times amount divided by amount borrowed)	3.62%	2.12%

Panel B: Income Statement Impact of Futures Transactions

PRO FORMA INCOME STATEMENT	*RATES HIGHER (5 PERCENT)*	*RATES LOWER (2 PERCENT)*
Interest expense	($125,000)	($50,000)
Profit (loss) in futures	34,500	(3,000)
Impact on net income	($90,500)	($53,000)

[a]Interest on CDs paid on 360-day basis maturity. Example assumes prepayment of interest.

[b]Futures value 95 or $9,875,000 minus the exercise price of 9,912,500 is put value of $37,500 minus the option premium of $3,000. Most contracts are not exercised but are offset at maturity with simple repurchase of the option. See the text discussion.

instead of shorting Eurodollars as in Chapter 20. The price of the 9650 put is quoted at .12 percent of the face value of the contract, corresponding to a put premium of $3,000 on 10 contracts of $1 million each (.0012 times 90/360 times $10,000,000). If interest rates rose to 5 percent, the option would be worth $37,500, reducing net interest costs to $90,500 as shown in Table 21.3. If rates fell to 2 percent, the $3,000 premium is lost since you would not exercise the put, but the cost of funds declines to $53,000 (including the option premium).

The example in Table 21.3 illustrates the similarity between options and insurance. The cost of funds is increased by 12 basis points, the option premium, with either an increase or decrease in interest rates. The cost of funds is either the maximum of 3.62 percent annual if rates go up or the lower rate plus .12 percent if rates go down. The 12 basis point (annualized) premium can be considered the cost of the insurance.

Other examples using options rather than futures or forward contracts to hedge risks from our discussion in Chapter 20 are readily provided. For example, an exporter long in German marks could buy a put on a German mark futures contract guaranteeing a minimum conversion price into dollars. If marks fall in dollar value, the exporter can exercise the put to make dollar profits offsetting the decline in the value of the mark. On the other hand, if marks increase in value, the exporter benefits from the better exchange rate after paying the put premium. An insurance company expecting to invest premium dollars in the future (a short asset position) can buy calls to guarantee maximum dollar costs (and minimum yields) while benefiting if interest rates go up and the dollar cost of assets falls, losing only the call premium.

Synthesizing Futures Contracts with Options

A look at the graphs in Figures 21.1 and 21.2 clearly reveals the contrasts between profit sensitivity to asset value changes of using futures as opposed to options. Options can be considered a way of decomposing the price sensitivity of long and short asset or futures positions into their four constituent components. The first two components correspond to a long asset or futures market position: (1) value increases when asset value increases relative to the contract or strike price (buy call); (2) value decreases when asset value falls (write put). The last two components correspond to a short position: (3) value increases when underlying asset value falls (buy put); and (4) value falls when underlying asset value increases (write call). Option contracts can be seen as a means of separately pricing each type of asset value risk.

The relation between option and futures price sensitivity means that arbitrage enforces price relationships between these contracts. For example, a long futures position is equivalent to option exposures (1) and (2) above, since the increase in futures market value will be mirrored in the call and the decline in value will be mirrored in the experience of the put writer. In other words, the combined call buyer and put writer have the same price risk as a long futures contract holder.

To illustrate the necessary price relationship between these contracts with an example, again use the data from Tables 20.1 and 21.1 for long-term U.S.

Treasury bonds. The long futures position on October 8, 1993, for March 1994, delivery has a contract value of 119-14. The March 1994 call with a strike price of 120 is 2-16 and the put 2-50. To buy a call and write a put would net 34/64 percent of face value (2-50 premium from writing put minus 2-16 from buying call). The net profit from options is \$531.25 (.0053125 times contract value of \$100,000). Since the strike price is 120, this means that the option holder can plan on receiving a bond in March for \$119,468.75 (\$120,000 paid to exercise the call or to receive the bond from the put buyer minus the net option premium of \$531.25). This is almost exactly equivalent to the futures delivery price of \$119,437.50, differing by only \$31.25.[2]

Hedging Portfolio Risks with Options

The previous discussion makes clear that the main difference between hedging with options and hedging with futures or forward contracts is that (1) hedging can be tailored to hedge against only adverse outcomes and (2) hedging with options is costly because favorable outcomes mean loss of option premiums paid. Options are similar to insurance: a premium is paid to avoid a large loss. In other respects, hedging with options can be compared directly to the analysis in the previous section. We review the practical concerns with portfolio hedging using options in light of that discussion.

Hedging asset risk with options requires matching option contracts with asset or portfolio risk exposure. The discussion of the previous chapter concerning futures contracts applies nearly completely to hedging with options. A *perfect hedge* with options completely shields portfolio returns from adverse movements in risk variables: the portfolio return in the face of adverse price changes is fixed by the option contracts. Absent a perfect hedge, the *best hedge* available using options minimizes risk to adverse movements over other possible option positions. The number of option contracts per unit of asset which accomplishes the best or perfect hedge is again the *optimal hedge ratio.*

The best hedge ratio matches the percent change in the total value of a number of option contracts to the portfolio risk being hedged. For a single asset hedge, the hedge ratio is calculated using an option price sensitivity measure called an *option delta* by specialists and defined as:

$$\delta = \left(\frac{\Delta \text{Option Value}}{\Delta \text{Asset Value}} \right).$$

Given the option delta, the hedge ratio for a single asset can be calculated as:

$$\text{Hedge Ratio} = \frac{1}{\left(\dfrac{\Delta \text{Option Value}}{\Delta \text{Asset Value}} \right)} = \frac{1}{\delta}$$

[2]The difference could be explained by transaction costs or different time the last transactions occurred in the day. The difference does not present any profit opportunity from arbitrage after commissions and other costs.

or one over the option delta. In our Eurodollar example, a hedge ratio of unity was used because of the high correlation assumed between CD rates and Eurodollars and because the contract was held until maturity. For the more complex portfolio situations described in the following, optimal hedge ratios must consider other factors.

As with futures and forward contracts, options are subject to basis risk. Even the partial hedges employed with options are exposed to basis risk. Basis risk consists of two cases with options as well as with futures and forwards: (1) the use of contracts on classes of assets that are not identical to the asset risk being hedged; and (2) the asset risk of a specific issuer differing from the risks of the average of a class of assets.

The problem of identifying the highest correlation with individual asset or net portfolio risk are the same as with futures and forward contracts. Regression analysis can use historical data to estimate the correlation of risks with available hedging instruments. Use of regression results presumes that the future correlation structure will be the same as in the past. These assumptions must be monitored constantly and they open management to criticism if subsequent events make such an assumption appear unfounded.

Options as well as futures face production risk but the risk is asymmetric. Production risk with adverse movements in asset prices are exactly the same with options as with futures or forward contracts. Since options do not hedge favorable movements in asset prices, hedges using options cannot protect against production risk with favorable outcomes. As an example, production risk might result in a borrowing institution increasing its hedge ratios because its demand for funds may be higher if the upward movement of interest rates is associated with an increased demand for credit. On the other hand, a downward movement of rates would result in decreased demand for credit in the economy. Net income at the lower loan demand levels would be reduced proportionately more by the unexercised option premiums because of the increase in the hedge ratio.

Partial hedging against adverse outcomes with options can be part of micro- or macro-hedging strategies as with futures and forward contracts. The problem with options as with futures or forward contracts with either micro- or macro-hedges is choosing the appropriate contract or set of contracts to hedge the risk. Identification of the best combination of options to be used by management in micro- or macro-hedges may be difficult technically, relying on regression or other techniques as with futures or forwards discussed in the previous chapter. Advisors or consultants may be useful in defining optimal hedging strategies but they may be hard to find later if trouble develops. Use of complicated techniques open management to criticism by regulators or investors who are not trained in financial hedging and do not understand them. Explaining complex hedging strategies to critics or courts of law may be difficult or impossible.

Portfolio Insurance

In principle, options can be used to limit the downside risk of a portfolio. For example, a manager required to limit the risk of a portfolio could buy risky assets and buy puts on the assets in the portfolio to limit losses to a predetermined level with the hope of earning a higher return than by investing in low risk assets. For example, a pension fund manager might want to guarantee pension fund asset values above levels considered underfunded by regulators, requiring the sponsor to inject cash. Use of options or other trading techniques to limit portfolio losses to predetermined limits is called *portfolio insurance*.

Put options theoretically could work to limit losses but they may not be practical. Traded option markets are often too thin to handle the volume of contracts necessary to hedge downside risks for large, complex portfolios. Option contract maturities may be too short to hedge downside risk over time horizons relevant for portfolio managers. A number of alternative portfolio management strategies that attempt to replicate the use of put options have been developed to limit losses of portfolios to tolerable levels. For example, portfolio allocations of investments in riskless and risky assets that change dynamically with changes in market conditions can produce the same results as using put options. These strategies are called *dynamic hedging*. Consultants and advisors are available to advise portfolio managers desiring portfolio insurance on strategies replicating put options (see Black and Jones 1986).

Portfolio managers often trade financial futures, such as stock index or long-term bond futures, rather than actual stocks for the risky portion of dynamic hedging strategies because of the liquidity and low transactions costs in futures markets. The ability of these strategies to replicate the put option required for effective portfolio insurance depends on whether portfolios are rebalanced frequently enough to maintain hedges and market values of futures and other contracts markets track underlying asset prices. Portfolio insurance earned a bad reputation during the 1987 Stock Market Crash when dynamic hedges failed due to price disparities between cash and futures markets and the inability to trade contracts in overwhelmed markets.

Practical Issues in Implementing Portfolio Hedges

Options, like futures, can be used to speculate as well as hedge. Top management responsible for the performance of portfolios must monitor and control the use of option contracts to avoid rogue behavior producing speculative losses when hedging was the goal. The discussion in the previous chapter concerning adoption of explicit policies is applicable to the use of option and option-related contracts. Relatively harmless strategies often used in low risk portfolios, for example the common strategy of insurance companies of writing calls against long positions in assets to increase portfolio income with call premiums, can produce sizable forfeiture of gains if markets move upward quickly and positions are not monitored.

Many over-the-counter option contracts are written or purchased by aggressive financial institutions to hedge risks specific to individual firms. For example, options relating to commodity prices and interest rates are valuable to firms having borrowing needs linked to material input prices. Over-the-counter options, as opposed to traded options, open counterparties to performance or default risk. The rapid growth in the over-the-counter market in very specific options means that extra care in evaluating the financial strength or resources of counterparties must be exercised by users of options to ensure the effectiveness of hedges.

21.3 OPTION PRICING THEORY

Arbitrage between futures and options prices enforces relationships between their values as discussed above. The pricing of call options can be explained in terms of the requirement in efficient markets that it not be possible to make profits with no investment and no risk. As discussed in Chapter 4, this is the basis of arbitrage pricing theory (APT). The application by Black and Scholes (1973) of this fundamental implication of efficient markets to option pricing has had a revolutionary impact on financial theory and analysis.

We illustrate the arbitrage pricing approach to option pricing in the simplest possible way by following Cox, Ross, and Rubinstein (1979). The simplest case for option pricing is when asset values (or other risk variables of interest) can have one of two possible values with equal probability at a single time point in the future. This pricing of options is called the *binomial* option pricing. We present two examples of binomial option pricing, the first very simple and the second slightly more realistic based on our Eurodollar example above.

The simple example of binomial option pricing is to value a call option on an asset currently worth \$9 which will be worth either \$4 or \$14 in one year. The current asset price and future outcomes for this case are provided in Panel A of Table 21.4. The implications for call option pricing of no profits from no net investment at no risk can be reviewed in Panel B of Table 21.4. The asset can be bought for \$9 now and will be worth \$4 or \$14 in one year. Borrow the present value of \$4 at the riskless rate of 10 percent now to reduce the purchase cost of the asset (the loan is completely collateralized). Write \$5 call options at \$5.40 now

TABLE 21.4 Simple Example of Binomial Option Pricing

Panel A: Two Outcomes: Current Asset Value \$9

OUTCOME	*VALUE OF ASSET*
High	\$14
Low	\$4

Panel B: Equilibrium Call Price at Strike \$5

		FUTURE OUTCOMES	
	NOW	*LOW*	*HIGH*
Sell 1.11[a] \$5 calls @ 4.86[b]	5.40	0	(10.00)
Buy asset	(9.00)	4.00	14.00
Borrow one year at 10%	3.60		
Repay loan		(4.00)	(4.00)
Profit	0.00	0.00	0.00

[a]1.11 = [\$10 (total call value with high outcome) divided by \$9 (conversion value per contract)].

[b]4.863 = [5.40 (call premium making column one total zero) divided by 1.11].

(making net investment now zero). At the low outcome, the option is worthless but the asset value is enough to pay off the $4 loan. With the high outcome, a $5 strike price implies the call option is worth $9 and $10 must be paid to produce no net profit, hence 1.11 call options must be written to ensure no net income with a high outcome. This means that each option must be worth $4.86 ($5.40 divided by 1.11). Any other value would produce profits with no risk and no net investment.

The number of options necessary to offset price movements of the asset in the future, 1.11, represents the optimal call option hedge ratio for the portfolio of options, assets, and debt in the simple example. In other words, precisely 1.11 call options written balances the risks of the complete portfolio. In the binomial case, the number is fixed because the initial cash flows are zero and in the future this number of options ensures that cash flows are zero for both the high and the low outcomes. In other, more complex option pricing models we will discuss, perfect hedges will require adjustment in hedge ratios as asset prices change through time.

Our second illustration of two-outcome option pricing is more complicated and is based on the March 1994, 90-day Eurodollar futures contract currently priced at 3.42 percent annualized discount, as shown in Table 20.1. Assume that annualized 90-day interest rates in March will either be 3.02 or 3.82 percent, a 40 basis point swing in six months. Panel A of Table 21.5 provides the value in March of the futures contract at each of these two possible outcomes. Panel B of Table 21.5 illustrates the cash flows from a no-cash investment position consisting of borrowing to buy Eurodollar deposits and writing call options exactly as in our previous simple example. The difference is that all asset prices are quoted using discounted interest rates and must be adjusted for 90-day maturity.

If we borrow an amount equal to the lower of the two possible futures contract values in March at current riskless interest rates, as in our earlier example, and buy Eurodollar deposits maturing in June 1994, we have cash flows as shown in the second and third lines of Panel B of the table. These deposits will be deliverable against a futures contract as 90-day Eurodollars in March. The loan repayment is shown in the fourth line of Panel B. Finally, writing call options that will be exercised only in the case of the higher valued outcome produces cash flows as shown in the first line of the table.

Table 21.5 illustrates the fact that unless the call option is priced at .03 percent of face value (corresponding to .12 annualized), it would be possible to earn profits on the position described above. See how this is true: If the lower outcome occurs, the call option is not exercised and the value of the Eurodollar deposit is enough to pay off the loan. If interest rates fall, the option will be exercised but the Eurodollar deposit will be worth more than enough to pay off the loan because it has increased in value with lower interest rates. Money will be left over after paying off the loan to repurchase the maturity value of options. At different exercise prices, a different number of options would be written to use up any funds left over. Only if the option price is equal to the amount shown in the table will each column sum to zero meaning no profits are earned. With no risk and no net investment, arbitrage pricing requires the zero profit at the bottom of the three columns.

TABLE 21.5 Example of Option Pricing for Eurodollars

Panel A: Two Outcomes: Current Rate 3.42 Percent

OUTCOME	*INTEREST RATE*	*90-DAY RATE*	*PRICE*	*ANNUALIZED DISCOUNT PRICE*
High rates	3.82%	.96%	99.05	96.18
Low rates	3.02%	.76%	99.25	96.98
Standard deviation of 90-day rate .2%				

Panel B: Equilibrium Call Price at Strike 99.1875
(Corresponds to Annualized Discount Strike of 96.75)

		FUTURE OUTCOMES	
	NOW	*LOW*	*HIGH*
Sell 3.11[a] 99.1875 calls @ 0.03[b]	0.09	0.00	(0.20)
Buy Eurodollar June deposit (3.42%)	(98.31)	99.05	99.25
Borrow until March (3.42%)	98.22		
Repay loan		(99.05)	(99.05)
Profit	0.00	0.00	0.00

Note: All calculations use 90-day prices actually used in delivery.
[a]3.11 = [.20 (total call value with high outcome) divided by .0625 (conversion value per contract)].
[b].03 = [.09 (call premium making column one total zero) divided by 3.11].

If call options are overvalued relative to the values shown in Tables 21.4 and 21.5, options can be written and earn riskless profits. The increased supply of calls issued by arbitrageurs would tend to reduce the call prices. If options are undervalued, the positions in the tables could be reversed and options purchased, producing riskless profits with no investment. The increased demand would tend to increase option prices. Arbitrage forces drive call options into line with these relationships. These forces are powerful in efficient markets.

Relation Between Put and Call Prices

The fact that puts and calls can be used to synthesize the same cash payoffs as underlying assets means that a pricing relationship between the asset and options exists. We illustrated that relationship by showing how close buying a call and writing a put was to the futures contract price for long-term U.S. Treasury bonds. The relationship enforced by arbitrage between asset prices and put and call option prices is called the *put–call parity* relation. We can write the relation as follows:

$$\text{Asset Value} = \text{Write Put} + \text{Buy Call} + \text{Present Value of Strike Price}.$$

An analogous relation can be written involving shorting the asset and reversing the option positions.

The put–call parity relation can be used to price European puts when there are no intermediate cash flows associated with the assets upon which the options are written. Pricing involves forming a zero investment, no risk, no profit portfolio as before. For example, the value of a European put option for our simple binomial example could be calculated using:

Buy Put + Buy Asset – Borrow Present Value of Strike Price – Sell Call = 0.

Using the values above:

Value of Put = –$9 + $4.50 + $4.86 = .36.

Table 21.6 illustrates how the put option price, combined with the call value calculated above, can be used with the asset and a loan to create a riskless portfolio with no net investment and no profits. This portfolio involves buying the asset with the proceeds of selling a call and a riskless loan and buying a put.

Complicating Factors in Option Pricing

In the simple option pricing examples illustrating arbitrage pricing of options, we have assumed only one period and owners of assets do not receive any cash flows before the options expire. The existence in reality of intermediate cash flows like cash dividends on stocks or coupon interest on bonds means that arbitrage pricing without accounting for cash flow effects may not be accurate. The reason is that the cash flows from ownership of assets are not paid to owners of options in replicating portfolios, reducing the value of options relative to the pricing model predictions. Departures observed in financial markets from theoretical option pricing values are often associated with dividends or other cash payments on underlying assets.

American call options on assets without intermediate cash flows have the same value as European call options because the call option always has more value if left unexercised before maturity if the call owner does not miss any cash payments to the owners of the asset. This fact is usually described as a call option

TABLE 21.6 Simple Example of European Put Price Using Put–Call Parity and Strike $5

		FUTURE OUTCOMES	
	NOW	*LOW*	*HIGH*
Sell $5 call @ 4.86	4.86	0	(9.00)
Buy asset	(9.00)	4.00	14.00
Borrow one year at 10%	4.50	(5.00)	(5.00)
Buy put	(.36)	1.00	
Profit	0.00	0.00	0.00

being "worth more alive than dead." The relation between European and American put options is not so clear. In the simple put pricing presented using Table 21.6, we assumed a European put option. Most traded put options are in fact American options, meaning that they have greater flexibility than European options. This greater flexibility is important for put options even in the absence of intermediate cash flows on the underlying asset. The reason is that the profits from the put option if the asset value falls can be invested if the option is exercised prior to maturity. The American put option pricing problem is more difficult than the American call option problem.

Properties of Simple Two-Outcome Option Pricing Model

The simple option pricing examples shown in Tables 21.4 and 21.5 have important properties that prove to be characteristic of all call option prices. Some of these properties are easily illustrated by looking carefully at the columns in the two tables which show the relationship between the total call option premiums and the amount borrowed, $5.40 and $3.60 in the simple example (Table 21.4) and .09 and 98.22 percent in the Eurodollar futures option example (Table 21.5). If the amount borrowed falls because interest rates are higher, the call premiums must increase to make the cash flows sum to zero. This means that the higher the interest rate on riskless loans, the higher are call prices. Note that if the maturity of the contract is longer, the proceeds of the discounted loan go down due to more interest paid, which also increases the necessary amount of call premium necessary to make cash flows sum to zero. Restating these results, the higher the level of riskless interest rates and the longer the time to expiration, the more valuable are call options.

Additional properties can also be dug out of the examples with a little more work. For example, increasing the strike price will reduce the value of the call since the amount of the conversion value with the high outcome in the future declines, requiring more options to use up the excess cash inflows. Furthermore, increasing the variability of the future price variations will increase the call premium, since the lower amount borrowed (with lower values at the low outcome) increases current premium income needed to make cash flows zero. The high outcome will produce higher profits per exercised call option, using up the excess of the value of the long position over the strike price. Both of these factors contribute to the option price result that the more variability in future values, the higher the value of the call option.

One last result is that higher values of underlying assets increase call values. In terms of the Eurodollar example in Table 21.5, this means that the purchase of the long position is more expensive, raising the required call premium income to the call writer to ensure a zero net investment. This proves that an increase in asset values increases call premiums.

The above discussion demonstrates five general properties of call option values:

1. Higher riskless interest rates increase call option values.
2. Greater variability in asset values raises call option values.
3. A longer time to maturity raises call option values.

4. A higher underlying asset value raises a call option's value.
5. A higher strike price lowers a call option's value.

These characteristics are true for more complex option pricing models and are worth remembering.

21.4 BLACK–SCHOLES AND OTHER OPTION PRICING MODELS

Arbitrage forces work to bring option prices into line with values like those shown in Tables 21.4 and 21.5 and occur even if time extends over more than a one-period horizon. Cox, Ross, and Rubinstein (1979) show that with two periods it may be necessary to change the call writer's portfolio balance of loans, options written, and long positions in assets from the initial period levels at the beginning of the second period in response to asset value changes to ensure no net cash flows. Nonetheless, with periodic rebalancing of the portfolio the hedge can be maintained such that no risk is borne by the option writer. Arbitrage will still enforces a unique price for the call option in each period if there are no profits to be made with no cash investment and no risk.

Cox, Ross, and Rubinstein also show that arbitrage works even if the future interest rate could have more than two possible outcomes and if time is sliced into finer subperiods. In fact, the characteristics of multiperiod multioutcome option pricing models when expanded to an infinite number of possible subperiods and a continuous range of future asset value outcomes are the characteristics of the famous Black–Scholes model mentioned earlier. Before introducing the Black–Scholes option pricing model, the complexities introduced by more realistic future values of important variables should be mentioned.

With more periods and more possible outcomes, establishing the hedges used in Tables 21.4 and 21.5 is still possible but more complex. With continuous changes in key variables, the portfolio including options must be adjusted constantly in order to keep the perfect hedge. Changing the hedge ratios in line with this continuous portfolio rebalancing to maintain hedges is impossible in reality. In addition to intermediate asset cash flows, another main issue with option pricing is how far the realities of transaction costs and other cash flows drive actual option prices from those suggested by option pricing models assuming continuous portfolio rebalancing. We return to this issue below.

Black–Scholes Option Pricing Formula

The Black–Scholes Option Pricing Formula was first published in 1973 and quickly led to a revolution in thinking not only about contingent claims pricing but corporate financial theory in general. Formulas very similar to the Black–Scholes formula had previously been published but did not have its impact because the earlier versions did not incorporate the critical breakthrough of arbitrage pricing theory (see Black (1989) for a history of the option pricing formula). Arbitrage pricing theory meant that an exact closed-form solution to the call option problem was possible and relied almost completely on observable variables like strike price, time to expiration, riskless interest rates, and asset values. Black and Scholes' particular contribution was that the formula used the readily observable riskless interest rate rather than the return on the asset. Only future asset variability has to be estimated to evaluate the formula. The formula quickly became the basis of trading in the newly opened Chicago Board Options Exchange.

The Black–Scholes option pricing formula is given as follows:

$$\text{Value of Call Option} = PN(D_1) - Ee^{-RT}N(D_2) \tag{21.6}$$

where P is the price of the asset, E is the exercise price of the call option, T is the time to expiration of the option, R is the riskless rate, and N is a function representing the cumulative normal probability of the quantities D_1 and D_2. To gain some intuition into option pricing formula, first note that since N stands for a cumulative normal probability function of a standardized normal variable it must have a value between zero and one. The call value option is therefore the difference between two values. The first value is P times $N(D_1)$ where the N function "adjusts" the asset price to less than P (since P multiplied by the function N must be less than P). The second value is Ee^{-RT} times $N(D_2)$ where Ee^{-RT} is the discounted value of the exercise price option continuously compounded at the riskless rate R to maturity T. Multiplying Ee^{-RT} times $N(D_2)$ "adjusts" the present value of the exercise price at expiration downward since again N is always less than one. We can think of the call value in the Black–Scholes option pricing formula as the difference between the adjusted asset price and the adjusted present value of the strike price.

A standardized normal variable has a mean zero and a standard deviation of one.[3] To appreciate the adjustments in the asset price and the strike price in the Black–Scholes model, first consider the cumulative probability distribution of a standardized normal variable. At zero the cumulative probability is .5, since half the standardized values are above and half below the mean. Look at the definitions of D_1 and D_2 given by Black and Scholes:

$$D_1 = \frac{\log\left(\frac{P}{E}\right)}{\sigma\sqrt{T}} + \frac{RT}{\sigma\sqrt{T}} + \frac{\sigma\sqrt{T}}{2} \tag{21.7}$$

$$D_2 = \frac{\log\left(\frac{P}{E}\right)}{\sigma\sqrt{T}} + \frac{RT}{\sigma\sqrt{T}} - \frac{\sigma\sqrt{T}}{2}. \tag{21.8}$$

These formidable expressions can be made somewhat more comprehensible by some concentrated review.

To understand D_1 and D_2 in the above expression first note that they are composed of three terms that are identical except for the minus sign on the last

[3]Any normally distributed variable is standardized by substracting the average from all possible values (making the mean zero) and dividing by the standard deviation of the variable (making the standard deviation of the standardized variable one).

term. The first two terms are divided by the numerator of the last term. The last term is half the standard deviation of the expected future return on the asset multiplied by the square root of the time to maturity. Thus D_1 and D_2 contain three terms, the first two of which are divided by or scaled by the time-adjusted standard deviation of the asset return and the last term consists of half the standard deviation of the expected return on the asset value.

The asset variability measure, the standard deviation of expected asset return multiplied by the square root of time, is a very important term in the two D expressions. Since risk in financial theory is symmetric, the standard deviation, σ, of the annual asset return was assumed by Black and Scholes to be the appropriate risk measure. The standard deviation of the expected annual rate of return is larger than the variability of the return over shorter time periods. Multiplying the standard deviation by the square root of the time to expiration reduces the standard deviation whenever T is less than one year. Use of the square root of time is due to the technical assumption of asset prices being log-normally distributed.

The standard deviation of asset returns is the only value in the Black–Scholes option pricing formula which must be estimated. Typically, historical data on asset returns are used to estimate this value. Some analysts have taken market values of options and solved the Black–Scholes formula for the standard deviation rather than using the formula to evaluate a call option. Solving for the standard deviation of the asset return given option and asset prices is useful in assessing market uncertainty concerning an asset or in pricing other options.

Our objective is to provide an intuitive explanation of the Black–Scholes option pricing formula. We noted that the standard deviation in the denominator of D_1 and D_2 has the effect of scaling all the terms in the numerator. Looking at the first term, the logarithm of (P/E) is approximately the percent the option is in or out of the money since the logarithm of a ratio is approximately a percent differential between the numerator and the denominator. For example, if P/E is .90 (the option is out of the money), log(P/E) is –.105; if P/E is 1.1 (the option is in the money), log(P/E) is +.095. If P and E are equal (the option is at the money), log(P/E) is zero.

To illustrate in an oversimplified fashion how the Black–Scholes formula works, look at the first term in D_1 and D_2 at an at-the-money option, implying logarithm (P/E) = 0. The cumulative normal distribution at its mean of zero has the value .5. If the time to maturity is 6 months (one-half year) and the riskless interest rate is 5 percent (continuously compounded) and P and E are equal at \$50, ignoring the last two term in D_1 and D_2 produces an option value of:

$$\$.617 = .5 \times \$50 \times (1 - .97531).$$

To complete our understanding of the Black–Scholes formula, we must assess the effect of the remaining terms in D_1 and D_2.

The second term in D_1 and D_2 is the ratio of the time-adjusted riskless rate to the time-adjusted standard deviation of the asset return. This value is typically small but will adjust the cumulative normal number upward since it is added to the first term. If we assume an annual standard deviation of the asset return of .20

multiplied by the square root of one half, the time-adjusted standard deviation is .141. In the example above we add to the assumed zero value of the first term .176 (the riskless rate .05 times one-half year or .025 divided by .141). This produces a cumulative normal probability of .57 instead of .50 as above, increasing the value of the formula by about 14 percent (7 over 50). A higher ratio of the time-adjusted riskless interest rate to the standard deviation of return would increase the option value even more.

The final terms in D_1 and D_2 have opposite signs. The negative term in D_2 tends to make the cumulative normal distribution term smaller in the second term of the Black–Scholes formula than the first. To illustrate this effect with the simple example above, if the time-adjusted standard deviation is .141, dividing that by 2 (as required in the formula), we can examine the effect on the cumulative normal distribution at its midpoint. The cumulative normal probability for D_1 at zero plus .071 is .528 and for D_2 zero minus the same amount is .472. The effect on the cumulative normal distributions at its midpoint is as large as it can be because of the bell shape of that distribution. The difference will be smaller everywhere away from the mean of zero. The difference between adjustments to the first and second terms in the Black–Scholes formula due to the last terms in D_1 and D_2 in our numerical example would be 5.6 percent at the maximum (.528 – .472).

The above relations are shown in Figure 21.3 for an at-the-money option (P/E = 1). The standard normal curve is centered at zero. D_1 is above RT to the

FIGURE 21.3 Probabilities in Black-Scholes option pricing formula

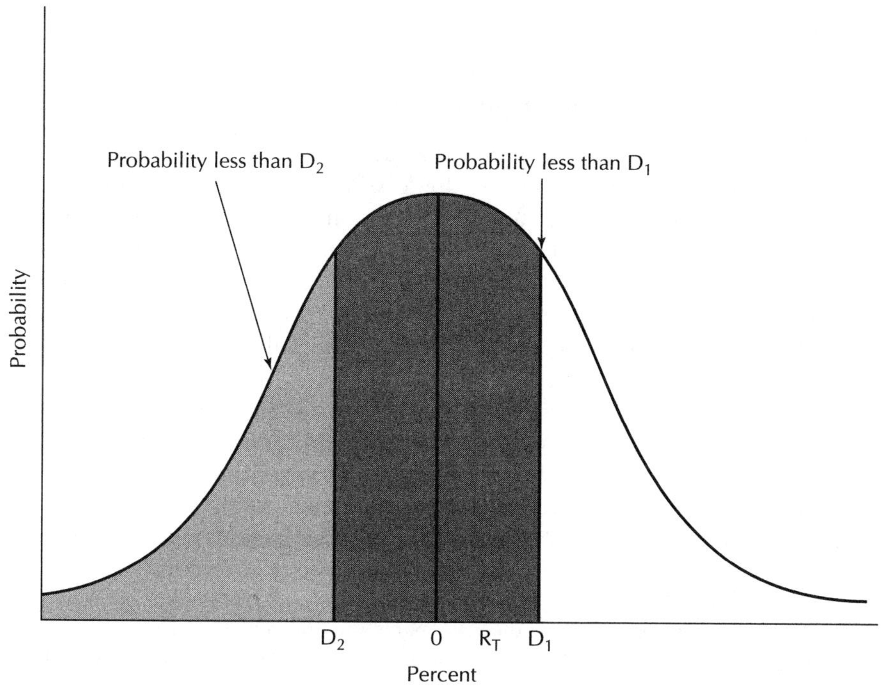

right of zero in the figure. D_2 is below RT and the cumulative probabilities are the shaded areas to the left of those two points. If the option is in the money ($P/E > 1$), D_1 and D_2 shift to the right, increasing cumulative probabilities and option values because the difference decreases between the probabilities with the move away from zero as noted above. Moving to the left decreases option values for out-of-the-money options, but the difference in cumulative probabilities still decreases.

One last observation on the Black–Scholes option pricing formula. The value $N(D_1)$ in the formula is equal to the price sensitivity of the call option with respect to changes in the value of the asset. The riskless hedge ratio of calls in a riskless portfolio consisting of one share of the asset, call options, and riskless loans, which is used in deriving the formula,[4] is the option price sensitivity divided into one. This hedge ratio in our simple formula above would be approximately two (one over .5), meaning two calls for each share of the asset. As noted above, sophisticated option market participants refer to $N(D_1)$ as the call option's δ.

The Black–Scholes option pricing formula is a complicated mathematical expression. We have reviewed this formula term by term in order to reduce it to comprehensible pieces. The effect of key variables on the value of call options using the Black–Scholes formula is exactly the same as with the simple binomial option pricing formulas discussed previously. The technical assumption of a log-normal distribution of future asset values with a standard deviation of returns increasing with the square root of time has introduced the mathematical complexities we have attacked in the discussion. Element by element, the formula is relatively easy to relate to common sense. Its power in finance is due to the fact that it utilizes arbitrage pricing with continuous trading and a continuous range of future asset values.

Closed-Form versus Other Option Pricing Models

The Black–Scholes option pricing formula is described as a *closed-form* formula because the expression can be evaluated directly for specific values of strike price, riskless interest rate, asset value, variability measure, and time to maturity easily. In fact, hand-held calculators can be programmed to solve the Black–Scholes option pricing formula. Robert Geske wrote such a program reproduced in Cox and Rubinstein (1985, *Options Markets* p. 343). Because of the relative simplicity of the Black–Scholes formula and its accurate evaluation for specific variable values, the formula is described an an *exact* option pricing formula.

Some option pricing problems are too complicated to solve for option values exactly. Closed-form solutions or formulas for more complex options simply cannot be derived, but mathematical conditions that the option price must obey may perhaps be stated precisely. A simple example of mathematical conditions that option values must obey is that the option cannot be worth less than zero or

[4]$N(D_1)$ is the derivative of the value of the call option with respect to the price of the asset. One over that amount is the number of calls necessary to offset a change in the value of the asset in a portfolio consisting of the asset and call options, one of which is short and the other long.

conversion value, whichever is higher. These conditions may be stated with enough precision that an evaluation of the option can be sought. These mathematical problems are typically solved using sophisticated mathematical approaches to solving problems, such as computer-based *numerical methods* that search for values that obey the mathematical conditions imposed by the option pricing problem.

Other option pricing problems may be solved by using *approximation techniques*. For example, the binomial option pricing approaches equivalence to the Black–Scholes formula as the number of outcomes and time periods expand. Evaluation of even simple approximations to option pricing problems can become complicated and time consuming to solve, even using computers. Mathematical sophistication may be necessary to prove that a given approximation method provides an appropriate answer to an option pricing at hand.

In many option pricing applications there are two levels of sophisticated mathematical analysis. They involve stating the option pricing problem and choosing the best ways to evaluate the answers to specific option pricing problems. In other words, there are two steps: (1) solving for the option pricing formula or stating the mathematical conditions on the option price and (2) evaluating the option by implementing approximation or numerical methods. The necessary training and skills to solve option pricing problems in practice can be seen to be very high.

21.5 THE PERVASIVENESS OF OPTIONS

The enormous impact of option pricing theory on the pricing of financial services is a result of the flexibility of options in replicating an unlimited variety of cash flow patterns associated with assets traded in financial markets. Using options to mimic the cash flows from investments or securities is possible by combining options into portfolios or combinations of options. If the cash flows can be replicated with options and the options reasonably priced, the value of the basic cash flows can be calculated as equal to the value of the replicating portfolio of options. We first illustrate the flexibility of options in replicating cash flows. We then review the assumptions necessary to employ option pricing theory since the assumptions underlying option pricing theory must be valid to use option pricing; hence we next discuss reasons why these assumptions may or may not be appropriate for some specific evaluation problems.

Figure 21.4 reviews and summarizes the payoffs at expiration for buyers and writers of puts and calls discussed at the beginning of this chapter. Panel A shows the payoffs in terms of asset values at expiration and Panel B in terms of interest rates at expiration. Each of the four quadrants relative to the exercise values in the diagrams is covered by a position in options. Payoffs occurring in each of the four quadrants relative to the exercise price can be used to replicate an asset cash flows in terms of combinations of options.

Replication of cash flow patterns associated with specific assets may require combinations of assets and liabilities and options at different exercise values. Such portfolios can produce expiration period payoffs with virtually any imaginable pattern. We illustrate how asset payoffs can be replicated by showing asset payoffs at the end of some time period graphically and then create the same payoffs from combinations of options and assets. The payoffs for each individual option and or asset can be added vertically in the graphs and the resulting total or net payoff to the portfolio are shown with heavy lines. In order to illustrate replication of assets, we use a number of basic examples widely used in the financial economics literature (Cox and Rubinstein (1985) provide an exhaustive and readable treatment of these issues).

The first example is the ability of combinations of options at different strike prices to replicate the claims on the assets of a corporation in terms of debt and equity. This use of options was first noted in Black and Scholes (1973) and has been extremely influential in shaping financial analysts' approach to pricing corporate liabilities. The example assumes that the value to the equity owners of a corporation is the uncertain future value of the corporation's assets after repaying debt obligations at maturity.

The numerical example follows our earlier simple binomial option pricing example presented in Table 21.4 where assets have a current value of $9 (now assumed to be millions). The firm has debt with a face value of $5 million. The

FIGURE 21.4 Profits and losses from options

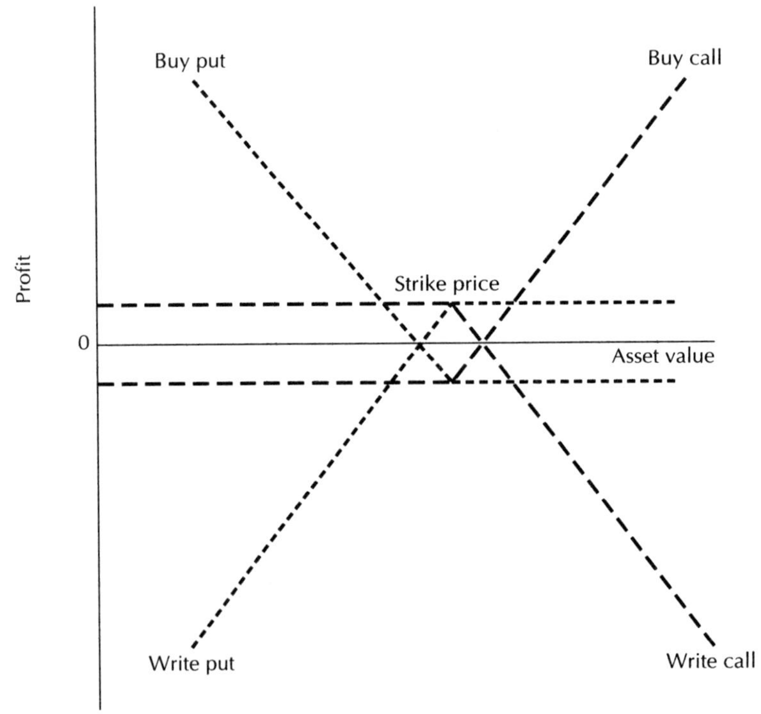

PANEL A: OPTIONS ON ASSET VALUES

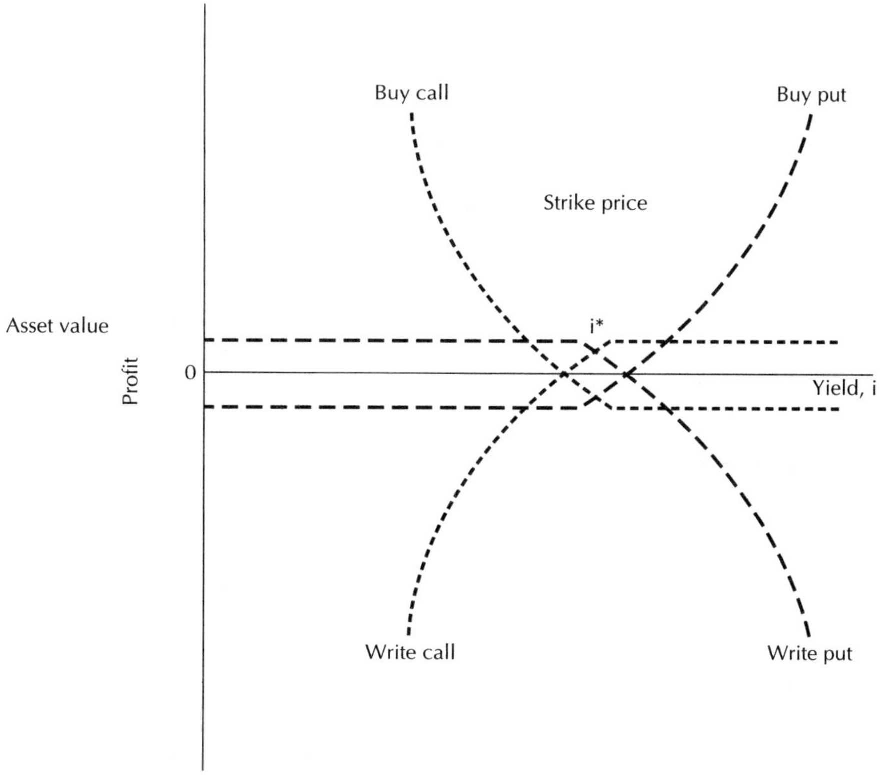

PANEL B: OPTIONS ON INTEREST RATES

payoffs to debt and equity for the firm are shown in Figure 21.5 utilizing the option payoffs at maturity of the puts and calls provided in Figure 21.4. Debt owners receive either the full payment of $5 million or the value of the assets of the firm if the future value is not enough to retire debt and bondholders foreclose, receiving the assets of the firm. Equity owners as described above receive either the assets of the firm minus the $5 million repayment of debt or nothing. The payoff to equity is identical to the payoff to a call option on the assets of the firm with a strike price equal to the $5 million maturity value of the debt. Using the results developed above in connection with Table 21.4, the equity is worth $4.86 million.

The example can also be used to price the debt in the simple case. Since the assets of the firm are worth $9 million total, the debt is worth the value of the assets minus the call held by the equity owners, or $4.14 million. Since the debt in the example pays $5 million when there is no default, the contract rate of (discounted) interest on the debt for one year is 20.8 percent ($5/$4.14 minus 1 in percent). This simple example illustrates how option theory can be used to price risky debt. The 20.8 percent risk-adjusted interest rate implied by the debt value contrasts with the 10 percent riskless rate assumed in the example given in Table 21.4.

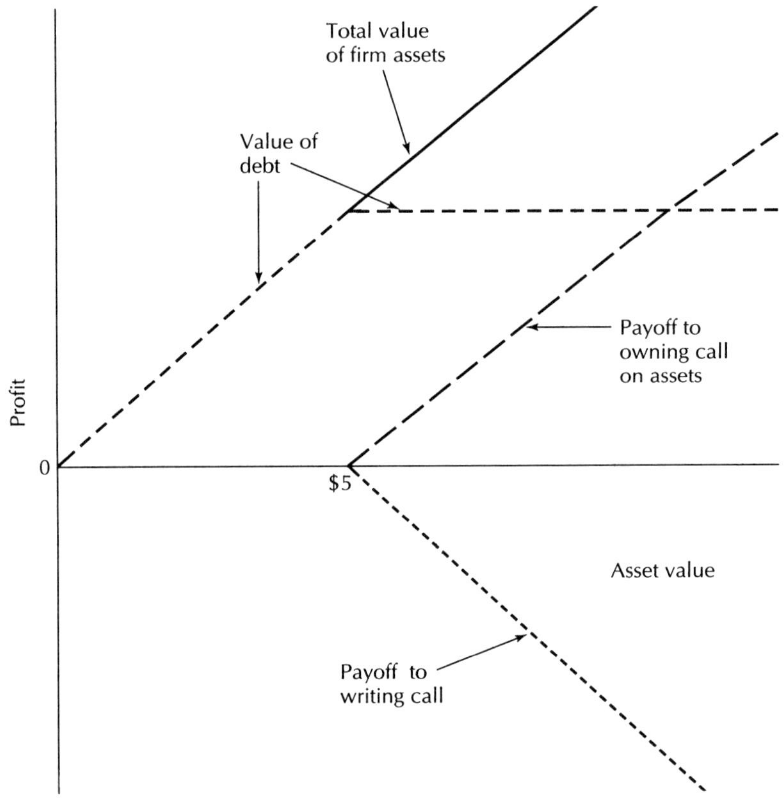

FIGURE 21.5 Equity and debt as options

The debt in this problem can also be seen as equivalent to another asset and option position. The debt payoff is equivalent to a $5 million riskless payment minus the value of writing a put on the assets of the firm with a strike price equal to the same $5 million face value of the debt. Since the put option cannot be exercised until the maturity of the debt, it is a European put option. Riskless debt is worth $4.5 million ($5 million divided by 1.10 to discount at 10 percent). The put option must be worth $.36 million ($4.5 – $4.14 million) in line with our earlier discussion of Table 21.6.

The example demonstrates that the payoff to owners of debt can be interpreted in different ways: (1) the payoff from ownership of the firm's assets and from writing a call on the firm's assets to owners of equity; or (2) holding a riskless bond and writing a put on the assets of the firm at the face value of debt. The total payoff shown in Figure 21.5 for debt is equivalent to either of these two ways of decomposing the debt cash flows. The fact that payoffs can be replicated with different combinations of assets and options allows analysts flexibility in pricing corporate liabilities using option pricing theory.

The relation between corporate liabilities and options makes clear how options can be used to price securities. In more complex cases, more complex option pricing models would be used. The equity in the firm of the example can be evaluated using the Black–Scholes option pricing formula if the uncertain future value of total firm assets is log-normally distributed. The risky debt of the firm can be evaluated as the value of the assets of the firm *minus* the value of a call option on the assets of the firm with a strike price of $5 million. Alternatively, the debt can be valued as the riskless bond equivalent minus the value of the put option implicitly held by equity owners of the firm.

A second example will illustrate a slightly more sophisticated use of options to price corporate liabilities. Instead of a single issue of discounted debt, assume the corporation in the above example has two issues of discounted debt, one subordinated to the other and each having a maturity value of $5 million for a total debt value of $10 million. In this case, the junior or subordinated debt will have maturity payoffs like those shown in Figure 21.6 while the senior debt is as before. The payoffs for the junior debt can be replicated with a position consisting of owning a call with strike price of $5 million and writing a call with strike price of $10 million. The payoff to subordinated debt shown in Figure 21.6 is the vertical addition of the payoffs from owning and writing these two calls. The subordinated debt in the form of junior discounted notes can be valued using the difference between the first and second call values.

FIGURE 21.6 Subordinated debt as options

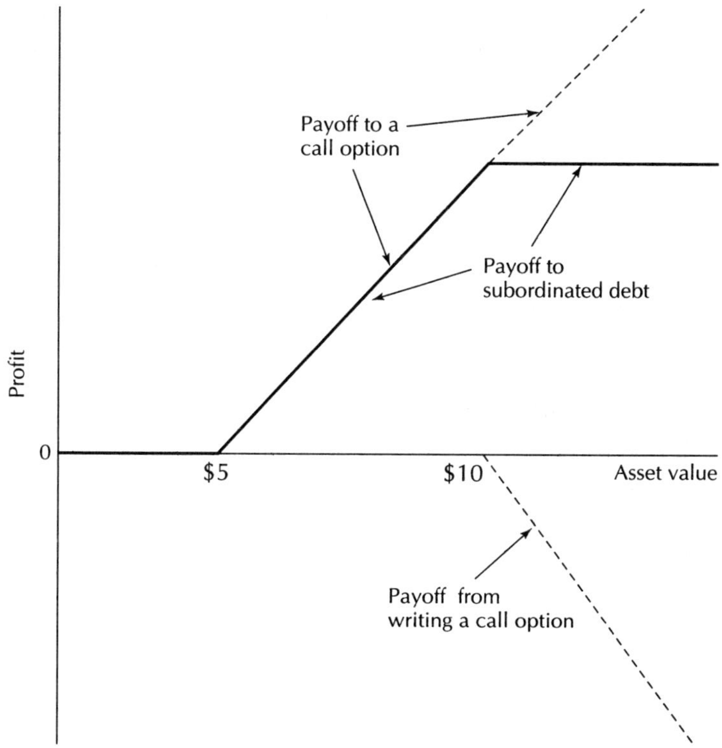

We can use the binomial pricing framework in Table 21.4 to price the subordinated debt (readers are encouraged to price the option at the higher strike price). The difference between the two calls is $2.7 million ($4.86 million for the call at $5 million minus $2.16 million for the $10 million call). The subordinated debt can be seen to yield 86 percent ($5 million divided by $2.7 million as net percent discount). Under our simple assumptions, option pricing has been used to evaluate and price the yields on senior (20.9 percent) and junior (86 percent) debt relative to the riskless rate of 10 percent and as well as to price the equity of the firm ($2.14 million) given the two issues of debt.

As a last example, we use more general assumptions concerning future outcomes and illustrate a very specific cash flow payoff. Assume that shares of an asset can take any future value between zero and infinity and that a market participant wants or needs a cash payoff only if shares in the asset are between $9 and $10 dollars at some future time period. This payoff can be constructed with an option position consisting of four call options: buying two calls on the asset, one at $9 and one at $10, and writing two calls at $9.50. The payoffs with these options are illustrated in Figure 21.7.

The basic option position consisting of four calls pays zero at values of the underlying shares below $9 and above $10. Between $9 and $10 the options produce payoffs increasing from zero to a maximum of fifty cents at $9.50 and back to zero at $10. If the market participant wanted a larger cash flow at $9.50 and if sufficient market depth in the options were available, multiples of the position could increase the cash flows. For example, 2,000 times the position, requiring buying or writing a total of 8,000 option contracts, would produce a $1,000 payoff if the asset shares were at $9.50 at expiration.

It is important to note again that the same payoff is possible using other combinations of options. For example, buying puts at $10 and $9 and writing two puts at $9.50 is only one of many alternative option positions producing payoffs as shown in Figure 21.7. The important point of this example is that options are extremely flexible and can be used to replicate to a close approximation virtually any imaginable cash flow. Since many options can be priced using simple or complex option pricing models, virtually any asset payoffs can be priced using prices for the options replicating those asset payoffs.

21.6 PRICING FINANCIAL PRODUCTS USING FUTURES AND OPTIONS

The ability of options to replicate specific cash flow patterns or hedge specific ranges of value of assets and the development of techniques to price options has made option pricing a major innovation for financial service firms. Many financial service firms, like large commercial banks, portfolio management firms, portfolio advisors and consultants, and investment banking firms, have staffs of mathematically sophisticated personnel. These technical staff people, though sometimes referred to as "rocket scientists" or "quantoids," are invaluable for applying option pricing to many financial asset pricing problems. These technical people are

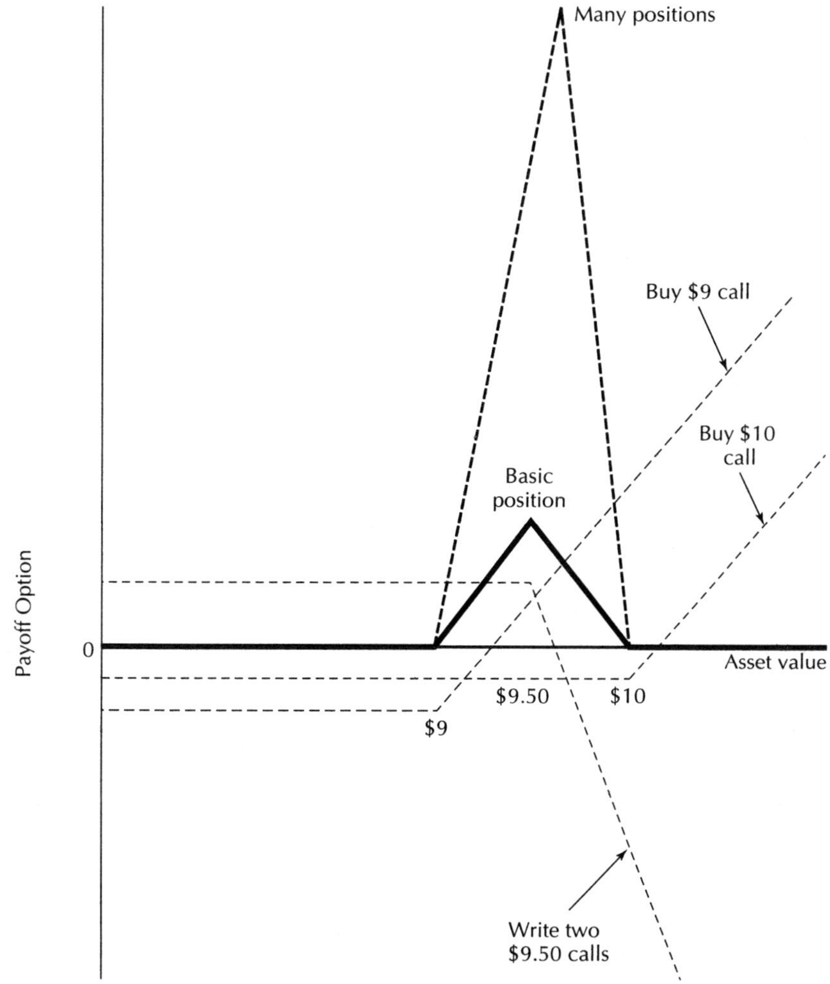

FIGURE 21.7 Payoff on shares between $9 and $10

expensive and difficult to manage effectively and may enjoy the last laugh despite the derogatory descriptions.

In this section we discuss various uses of option pricing in evaluating prices of financial products or services. We begin by reviewing the assumptions used in pricing options and the potential problems faced in applying option pricing in practice. Innovative solutions to option evaluation problems in some instances have allowed financial services to price and offer services at tolerable levels of risk that might not have been possible before the breakthroughs in option pricing discussed above. The application of option pricing in financial markets has required substantial imagination and technical skill, and the benefit of these applications has created the high compensation so-called rocket scientists command on Wall Street.

Assumptions for Pricing Options

The essential economic force allowing the pricing of options is arbitrage. The assumptions necessary to price options primarily have to do with the possibility of arbitrage. The barriers distorting the arbitrage pricing relation of no profits with no risk and no net investment must be inconsequential. Under some circumstances, not all the conditions necessary to use option pricing theory are exactly met but conditions in the market are close enough to use option pricing as a first approximation. We review the standard requirements necessary for arbitrage pricing of options and typical ways of getting around those requirements which option-pricing analysts have developed.

First, transactions costs must be low enough to make formation of portfolios exploiting arbitrage opportunities easy enough to drive the option prices into line with arbitrage pricing theory. Second, rebalancing portfolios frequently enough to maintain riskless hedges must be feasible. In addition to low transactions costs, markets must be liquid enough to make transactions possible without changing asset price relationships. In developed economies, transactions costs in actively traded securities are very low. This means that many financial options can be priced accurately assuming low transaction costs and market liquidity.

Theoretically all possible asset and option positions should be feasible at low transaction costs to ensure arbitrage pricing. Lack of liquidity or relatively high transaction costs may mean that the strict application of the option pricing is not warranted. For example, options on real estate assets often violate liquidity conditions. However, if close substitutes for nontraded assets are available, using arbitrage pricing to price options may not lead to serious pricing errors. For example, in pricing specific commercial real estate options in a given city like Paris, an analyst might assume that actively traded equity in real estate trusts on similar real estate are similar to the specific property at hand. As in all pricing models, specific risk can be reduced to tolerable levels if diversification reduces specific risk in portfolios of options and other assets to neglible (unpriced) levels.

Second, factors influencing option payoffs must be incorporated into the model. The Black–Scholes' formula assumes only one risk factor, the future value of the asset. Other option pricing problems may require more than one source of risk. Some two-factor option pricing models have been solved using complex computer solutions. For example, Kau *et al.* (1992) solve a two-factor risk option pricing model of the value of options implicit on home mortgages. Borrowers of typical home mortgages have two options: they can prepay the mortgage (exercising an implicit call option on the value of the mortgage) or default (exercising an implicit put option on the value of the home relative to the loan balance). The two risk factors in this option pricing problem are the level of interest rates and the value of residential real estate. The complication for option pricing is that the two risk factors interact with each other and this interaction must be incorporated in the option valuations. This problem had to be solved using numerical methods as discussed above. Some option pricing problems may be too difficult to solve.

Finally, hedged portfolios must account for all cash flows associated with assets. Distortions to the asset cash flow payoffs in the replicating portfolio using options and other assets must be small enough to be a negligible factor in the pricing relations. Major distortions in practice come from two sources: taxes and uncertain cash flows associated with underlying assets occurring before expiration of the options, such as dividends.

All the factors discussed limiting the ability to trade assets and options easily tend to create ranges of asset and option values within which arbitrage might not affect asset pricing. These ranges may be narrow and allow the use of option pricing with an adequate level of precision. The range may be too wide to allow sufficient precision in pricing the options or create factors too complex to incorporate in standard option pricing models. Analysts must carefully review the specific option pricing application at hand to ensure that the option values, if they can be calculated using assumptions that are not exactly true in reality, are indeed relevant to the real world problems they are meant to address.

Black–Scholes Assumptions and Interest Rate Options

When the assumptions of the Black–Scholes option pricing are not valid, alternative option pricing approaches must be used if available. The Black–Scholes assumptions concerning the expected distribution of future asset values are not valid in the case of interest sensitive assets. For this reason, interest rate options cannot be evaluated using the Black–Scholes option pricing methods. The enormous importance of these options has stimulated alternative approaches to pricing interest rate options. Alternative approaches used to evaluate options on interest-rate sensitive assets are typically one of two types: (1) multiperiod binomial option pricing or (2) simulation models. Both use expected present value analysis of future payoffs. We discuss each in turn.

The economic assumptions of any pricing model must be consistent. As discussed in Chapter 13, the term structure of interest rates implicit in current bond prices reflects expectations of future short-term rates. The distribution of future interest-rate sensitive asset values cannot be simply unrestricted log-normal distribution as assumed in Black–Scholes. The evolution of expected future asset values for bonds and other interest rate sensitive assets must be consistent with the term structure of interest rates observed at any point in time and the expected evolution of future interest rates.

Black, Derman, and Toy (1990) present a simple multiperiod binomial approach to pricing interest rate sensitive assets and options. This approach has been very influential and their presentation is fairly easy to follow. Their technique involves computing all possible future values of interest rate sensitive assets and options using a binomial evolution of interest rates. Short-term interest rates are assumed to go either up or down in each future period by specific amounts with specific probabilities. Their model calculates a term structure and future asset values that are consistent with the expected future changes in short-term interest rates. Values of assets and options are simply the present value of future asset or option payoffs which are nonzero multiplied by the assumed probability of those payoffs. Even binomial outcomes produce many payoffs after several periods, thus even binomial models can become computationally difficult with longer time horizons.

Simulation methods can be used for more generalized future economic scenarios. Using simulation, probabilities of key economic variables are used to generate many future asset and option values. Computers can generate these scenarios and keep track of the present value of nonzero outcomes. The frequency distribution of future values is used to weigh outcomes by their estimated probability of occurrence. Simulation methods are similar in theory to binomial methods but can be much more general in the assumptions concerning future evolution of the risk variables of interest.

Option Pricing Application to Financial Instruments

Several examples of financial products that can be priced and offered to customers without exposing financial service firms to intolerable levels of risk follow in this section. We have drawn some of the option-like payoffs for some common financial products based on interest rates in Figure 21.8. Some examples of financial services may seem easy after our discussion in the preceding two chapters.

FIGURE 21.8 Interest rate based financial services using options: Payoffs for credit-granting firm

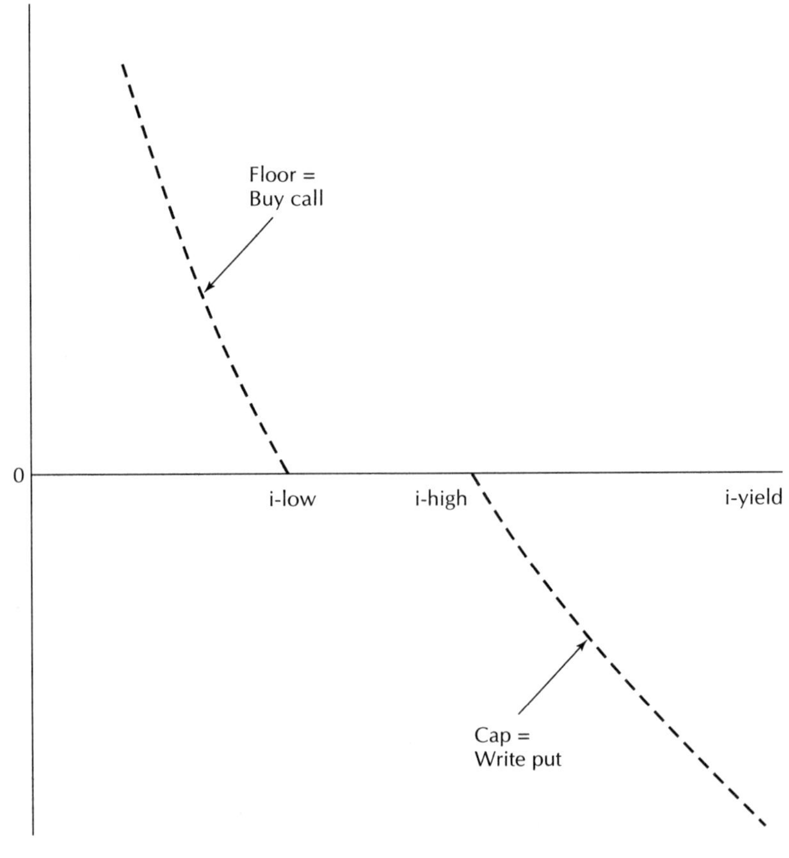

Some credit institutions are willing to offer fixed loan commitments or *note facilities* institutional customers can use at their discretion depending on interest rate developments. These services could well be recognizable to readers as a credit granting firm effectively writing put options on loans to customers. Relatively accurate pricing of interest rate puts for firms of different risk classes can be used in pricing these services in order to produce acceptable value for the service.

Other services, such as *interest rate caps,* may require more thought. An interest rate cap promises a borrowing customer a maximum interest rate on a loan no matter what happens in the credit markets. Again, the interest rate cap can be seen as guaranteeing the customer a minimum price on his or her security or loan issues and can be viewed as writing put options on credit instruments. An interest rate cap and a note facility are essentially the same and consequently expose the financial service firms offering them the same exposure to interest rate risk.

Some credit customers may be willing to reduce their costs of credit by promising a financial institution a minimum rate of interest on a loan, a so-called *interest rate floor.* Since the interest floor commits the customer to accepting a maximum value to its credit instruments, the interest rate floor corresponds to the credit granting firm receiving a call option from the customer. Since the customer has granted value to the credit-granting firm by committing to an interest rate floor, other price concessions may be in order for the customer.

An interesting financial service is to combine caps and floors into an *interest rate collar.* The collar confines the customer's loan or security interest to a minimum and a maximum percent, limiting the risk. The collar is clearly a combination of options, the cap representing value granted to the customer and the floor a concession by the customer having value to financial service firm. The collar can reduce the cost to the customer of insuring against upward movements in interest rates by promising to pay a minimum interest rate. Within a range covered by the collar, the customer will be able to benefit from interest rates below the cap.

An endless variety of features or attributes of financial instruments may be priced using option theory. For example, standard bond features such as callability or convertibility can be evaluated by treating these features as options. We have mentioned prepayment of mortgages and borrowers' ability to default as other financial features that can be priced using options. Many insurance products, such as casualty insurance, can be viewed as options. For example, auto accident insurance provides the owner of the automobile a put option if the auto asset becomes valueless. Many of the options observed in financial services have existed with traditional products and option pricing can refine evaluation of them. Other options can be developed as customer services and priced accurately enough to sell in the market.

21.7 VALUE PRODUCTION AND HEDGING WITH OPTIONS AND FUTURES

Option theory has revolutionized the theory of corporate finance and made practical evaluation of financial liabilities and assets unimaginable before 1973. How do these developments produce value for financial institutions? Three main uses of option theory are most important: (1) offering traditional and new financial products and services at better prices providing customers with desirable improvements in risk management; (2) more accurate pricing and management of traditional credit and risk management products; and (3) innovation in product offerings. We discuss each in turn but note that the lines between these three categories are not always clear. A common theme runs through these uses of option pricing theory as a source of value: the greatest payoff in terms of value created is innovation. New products and services have no competition and can be priced higher that competitive products and services.

Options break up the risk exposure into smaller segments, as we have discussed extensively above. By breaking risk into smaller pieces, options tend to "complete the market" as we discussed in a Chapter 6. Fine-tuning risk exposure can improve expected utility or risk–return trade-offs of financial market participants. They are willing to pay for these improvements in their economic environment. Fine tuning the valuation of these risk-shifting or risk-sharing financial options may increase the profitability of financial instruments containing option features or make it possible to offer them at tolerable levels of risk.

Option pricing has allowed financial service firms to price and absorb or hedge the risks associated with a variety of risk-shifting financial products, as we have discussed above. For example, consumers appear to prefer fixed-rate loans or loans with interest rate collars. These financial products can be evaluated more accurately using option pricing theory than was possible before. Financial institutions can hedge their risks more precisely using options and choose more precisely the nature of their exposure to risk factors, hence they may be able to offer customers risk management products not available before. The greater precision in measurement and management of risks due to options and option theory can be a source of value to financial service firms in terms of reduced losses or increased profits from offering financial services improving customers' risk exposure.

Financial service firms that rely on asset valuation have been able to use option pricing to evaluate complex assets better or with lower analytical costs than before these techniques were available. Increased accuracy and precision in asset valuation allows financial service firms to bargain or negotiate with a better assessment of the trade-offs and risks. Financial assets with complicated cash payoff features, such as collateralized mortgage obligations (CMOs) or assets convertible into other currencies or assets, can be priced accurately using options. Value is produced for financial service firms by being able to improve the terms they receive and offer customers. They can design and price financial products that improve customers' risk–return trade-offs and for which they are willing to pay. Because of the ability to price and hedge complex risks, financial service firms may be able to do deals that were regarded as too risky or complex in the past.

The major payoff to financial service firms is the profits to be made from product innovation. Options have been an enormous source of ideas for new products for customers. Business customers actively use a commercial bank over-the-counter market in variety of foreign currency and interest rate risk related option instruments. Citibank and others have begun offering retail customers deposit accounts that pay a minimum interest rate or a rate that depends on the stock market, clearly an option-related financial service. Option products and option pricing have been central to new product development to serve businesses, governments, and households risk management needs in the last few decades and will presumably continue to be in the future.

21.8 SUMMARY

Options have had a revolutionary impact on the financial services industry. Options represent a decomposition of risk exposure relative to other assets or futures and forward contracts. Pricing of options can be complex but option prices are extremely useful in pricing the risk of insurance against bad financial outcomes and pricing complex cash flows associated with a variety of financial instruments. All option pricing is based on arbitrage and requires conditions in financial markets which may not be met in fact. Options and option pricing have had and will continue to have vast potential to provide financial service firms with value-producing products and services.

DISCUSSION QUESTIONS AND EXERCISES

1. Interpret carefully the terms for several put and call options quoted in the financial press in terms of the text discussion. Analyze the types of risks these options can protect against and who the likely demanders of this protection would be in the economy.
2. Demonstrate the equivalance (or lack thereof) of put and call options on a futures contract for different delivery dates and the underlying futures contract. Discuss departures from the equivalence in terms of potential arbitrage possibilities.
3. Determine acceptable hedge strategies using options for the following risk exposures: (1) a mortgage banker with inventory of mortgages; (2) a seller of consumer products in England; (3) an insurance underwriter receiving premium revenues; and (4) an issuer of a long-term corporate bond in six months.
4. Calculate the change in a futures option price and the underlying futures contract over several days. What is the option's δ each day. Does the δ change? If so, what reasons can you advance to explain these changes?
5. Develop a binomial option pricing model for an option on an asset currently selling for \$20 which will be worth \$15 or \$25 in three months with equal probability. Assume the riskless rate is 4 percent and value the option for several strike prices. Do the general rules on option pricing given in the text hold true for your option values?
6. Discuss the construction of zero investment arbitrage portfolios of options and assets on the following: (1) building materials; (2) foreign currency bonds; (3) livestock; and (4) residential housing. Which of these have related options traded on financial markets? What assumptions have to be made to employ option pricing approaches to these examples?
7. Price an interest rate collar for Eurodollar borrowing issued in six months using quotes from the finan-

cial tables. Specify the cap and floor and which options you use to price this item.

8. Using our discussion of the Black–Scholes option pricing model, evaluate the elements of D_1 for a six-month option on an asset selling for half the exercise price with a riskless interest rate of 6 percent annually and a standard deviation of 40 percent. Using a cumulative normal probability table, price the option if the asset price is $100.
9. Use quoted options to replicate the following cash payoffs: (1) cash if General Motors stock sells for $50 or above within three months; (2) cash if Treasury bill rates are between 3 and 4 percent within four months; and (3) cash if long-term U.S. Treasury bonds fall below 6 percent yields in three months.
10. Assume IBM wants to issue 8 percent 10-year bonds that are callable and convertible into IBM stock. Use U.S. Treasury bond futures options and IBM stock options to adjust the price of these bonds. What is the implicit yield to maturity?

REFERENCES

BERNSTEIN, PETER L. 1992. *Capital Ideas.* New York: The Free Press.

BLACK, FISCHER. 1987. "How We Came Up with the Option Formula," *Journal of Portfolio Management* (Winter), pp. 4–8. Also in R. E. Whaley, ed. 1992. *Selected Writings on Futures Markets: Interrelations Among Futures, Option and Futures Option Markets,* Book VI, *Readings in Futures Markets,* Chicago Board of Trade.

BLACK, FISCHER, EMANUEL DERMAN, and WILLIAM TOY. 1990. "A One-Factor Model of Interest Rates and its Application to Treasury Bond Options," *Financial Analysts Journal,* January/February, pp. 33–39.

BLACK, FISCHER and ROBERT JONES. 1986. "Simplifying Portfolio Insurance," Portfolio Strategy paper series, Goldman Sachs, New York (August).

BLACK, FISCHER and MYRON SCHOLES. 1973. "The Pricing of Options and Corporate Liabilities," *Journal of Political Economy* 81 (3), pp. 637–654. Also in R. E. Whaley, ed. 1992. *Selected Writings on Futures Markets: Interrelations Among Futures, Option and Futures Option Markets,* Book VI, *Readings in Futures Markets,* Chicago Board of Trade.

COX, JOHN C., STEPHEN A. ROSS, and MARK RUBINSTEIN. 1979. "Option Pricing: A Simplified Approach," *Journal of Financial Economics* 7, pp. 229–263. Also in R. E. Whaley, ed. 1992. *Selected Writings on Futures Markets: Interrelations Among Futures, Option and Futures Option Markets,* Book VI, *Readings in Futures Markets,* Chicago Board of Trade.

COX, JOHN C. and MARK RUBINSTEIN. 1985. *Options Markets.* Englewood Cliffs, N.J.: Prentice Hall.

KAU, JAMES B., D. C. KEENAN, W. J. MULLER III, and J. F. EPPERSON. 1992. "A Generalized Valuation Model for Fixed-Rate Residential Mortgages," *Journal of Money, Credit, and Banking* 24, pp. 279–299.

MERTON, ROBERT C. 1973. "Theory of Rational Option Pricing," *Bell Journal of Economics* 4 (1), pp. 141–183. Also in R. E. Whaley, ed. 1992. *Selected Writings on Futures Markets: Interrelations Among Futures, Option and Futures Option Markets,* Book VI, *Readings in Futures Markets,* Chicago Board of Trade.

C H A P T E R

22

Projecting Financial Institution Performance

Introduction

No one knows what the future holds but the outcome of every management action depends on how those actions affect future business developments. Projecting future performance does not require clairvoyance but it does require a coherent approach and benefits greatly from some advanced techniques.

- What approaches can managers take to projecting the future under a variety of circumstances?
- How are important variables treated in making projections?
- What methods are there for projecting important variables and bringing the results of the projection effort together in meaningful ways?

This chapter describes basic approaches to projecting future performance of financial institutions. We begin by discussing the role of projections in financial institutions. Next, the types of variables and projection techniques are introduced. An introductory review of technical projection methods follows. Finally the use of financial projections is reviewed.

22.1 USE OF FINANCIAL FORECASTS AND PROJECTIONS

Forecasts and projections are important tools in financial decision making. The distinction between forecasts and projections is important. Forecasts are unqualified predictions about the most likely values for economic or financial variables of importance to decision makers. For example, a forecaster might predict that given current information there is a 90 percent probability that long-term interest rates will be between 7 and 9 percent within one year. Projections are conditional on other outcomes occurring in the future. For example, a projection might show that profits of Fifth Third Bancorp will increase $50 million *if* long-term interest rates increase to 9 percent but will be unchanged if interest rates turn out to be 7 percent. Since we are focusing on management of financial institutions, we concentrate most of our discussion on projections that assess the impact of a range of actions now and developments in the future.

Any discussion of projections or forecasts of financial institution performance must begin with an analysis of reasons to perform this activity. Fischer Black (1975) argues that there is no reason to project financial institution performance because in efficient markets all assets and liabilities are fairly valued. These values reflect rational expectations and all current information about future values of variables such as interest rates and economic activity. Black argues that forecasting and planning are a waste of time because in efficient markets managers cannot earn excess returns by buying and selling assets and liabilities using expensive forecasting and planning activities. Financial institution managers should focus on making money by performing the activities they do best, in the case of banking, by making loans and processing transactions.

Black is probably right that forecasting and planning cannot be used to beat the market in terms of earning higher than risk-adjusted returns on the investments in these activities. But most managers do not use financial projections to beat the market, and virtually all financial institutions use financial projections, suggesting that there are other reasons to engage in this activity. Three justifications for financial projections are: (1) communication, education, and coordination of members of complex organizations, in our case financial service firms; (2) assessment of the implication of possible courses of action and the impact of future events in order to avoid disasters and exploit opportunities; (3) valuation of financial service firms. We discuss each briefly in turn.

Financial institution projections are often a group effort. In many institutions, *bottom-up* projections are made by gathering projections from many different parts of the organization. Representatives of various units of a financial institution participate in the assumptions that go into a forecast or projection. For example, in a bank, consumer branch managers, wholesale loan divisions, and treasury officials can prepare estimates of future activity such as consumer and institutional loans, deposits, and trading activity.

Finance is a language, as we discussed in Part I. The process of communicating the results of assumptions and projections for many different aspects of a complex organization in a coherent format requires that a common understanding by all participants be reached about how the parts fit together. Forecasting or projecting future performance forces participants in different aspects of the organization to communicate in a form that can be summarized and incorporated into an organization-wide projection employing a common vernacular.

The best outcome of a bottom-up financial projection effort is that representatives of different parts of the organization appreciate more accurately how their actions impact other units and the institution as a whole. How different units interact on forecasted outcomes can only be assessed when agreement is reached about how the parts fit together. Financial projection is a useful communication and education tool for a financial institution and enables more effective coordination of disparate activities in complex organizations.

A second important role of projections is to pull together the implications of many different possible outcomes and alert management to potential problems or opportunities in the future. Projections that are internally consistent, as we discuss below, may highlight bottlenecks or implications of policies which are the result of interactions not easily foreseen without making financial projections. Often projections like this are *top-down* efforts, originating in the top management of the organization or in planning or strategy staff units.

Use of financial projections to avert disaster and to exploit opportunities to improve performance means that accuracy is not the key goal of the effort. The most important goals of financial projection for management in many cases are to identify problems and opportunities. If a projection implies disaster, the last thing a manager wants is for that projection to become reality. This is the reason a focus on the accuracy of projections misses the point: an excellent financial projection that forecasts disaster or the results of missed opportunities will hopefully never come true. Judging projections by their forecasting accuracy often misses the true purpose of the projection activity.

A final reason for making financial projections is to value financial institutions or activities. Decisions must be made now that can only be proven to be good or bad by developments in the future. Decisions to acquire or merge financial institutions or begin a new product promotion cannot wait until uncertainty about the future is resolved. Thus, projections are an essential tool for decision makers to determine whether an investment or business strategy can be a source of value. If there are no assumptions or future outcomes that can justify a decision to invest now, the investment should not be undertaken.

Financial projections for valuation of financial firms and marketing strategies must be internally consistent. Simple projections may be useful, as we discuss below, as benchmarks or plausibility checks. If the projections make use of information explicitly accounting for the activities of different units of complex organizations, the assumptions and projections must be incorporated in a coherent projection of possible future outcomes. All projections are for valuation in the sense that good projections are a means of maximizing the value of the institution.

22.2 MODELS USED IN FINANCIAL PROJECTIONS

Financial institution decision makers need many projections, from forecasts of a simple activity to results of the complex interactions of many units. For example, we may forecast the number of customers that will use a bank branch or project the net income of a major financial institution under a variety of environments. Projections of the simplest to the most complex problems utilize either *naive models, financial models,* or sophisticated analyses like *simulation or econometric models*. Each has a role to play in projecting financial institution performance and we discuss each in turn.

Naive projections are typically of two types: the future will be exactly like the past; or the future will extrapolate a past trend. Stated mathematically, we can project a variable X_{t+1} given its past value X_t as follows:

$$X_{t+1} = X_t \qquad (22.1)$$

or

$$X_{t+1} = X_t \times (1 + f), \qquad (22.2)$$

where f is a growth or some other factor like a seasonality or day of the week adjustment. The key attribute of naive projections or forecasts is that they use very little information other than the past value of the variable of concern and perhaps a growth rate or some other factor.

As an example of a naive forecast of the number of people in a bank lobby, managers could predict that tomorrow there will be the same number of people as today. Naive forecasts can be applied to simple problems or extremely complex problems. For example, in 1992 Fifth Third Bancorp's net income was $164 million. A naive projection of 1993 (or any future time period) would be $164 million. Still naive but slightly more complicated would be to assume that Fifth Third's income will grow in 1993 at the same rate as between 1992 and 1991, when net income was $138 million. This naive forecast of Fifth Third's net income is $195 million (calculated as $164 times ($164/$138)).

Naive projections or forecasts do not use detailed information available about changes in the economy or in the operations of specific financial institutions. They are easy to calculate and are an important benchmark against which to measure other financial projections. In some applications, naive forecasts may even be the most efficient. For example, in efficient markets the best forecast of future asset values is based on current values, perhaps adjusted for some trend, because values change only with new information that cannot be anticipated. Naive forecasts or projections are a place to begin and are an important reference point for more compex projections.

Most decision makers or planners incorporate several economic or financial variables to make projections. For example, to project Fifth Third's net income when long-term interest rates are 7 or 9 percent, the effect of interest rate differentials on the firm's earning assets and other costs and revenues must be accounted for. Many projections are developed within the framework of *financial models*. Financial models develop forecasts or projections using *pro forma* financial statements, where *pro forma* means in the form of but clearly not actual reported results. Because of the usefulness of financial models, our emphasis in this chapter will be on them.

When good financial models are used in projections, relationships between important variables are enforced. For example, balance sheets implicit in the projected activities balance. Net income in a consistent financial model is computed as revenues minus costs and taxes. Carefully implemented financial models impose reasonable relations between forecasted or projected economic and financial variables. Since financial models communicate results in financial statements, they can be readily interpreted and discussed by decision makers who use these statements in their business activity.

Sophisticated models, like simulation or econometric models, go beyond collecting a variety of projections or forecasts of economic and financial variables into familiar reporting formats. Simulation models attempt to replicate behavior of complex economic systems by incorporating feedback and the reactions of variables to various outcomes. Feedback relationships are often fixed by technical considerations or established by econometric estimates. Econometric models estimate the impact of economic behavior in reaction to changes in economic variables by utilizing data on historical experience covering a wide variety of situations.

The results of simulation models are often calculated many times with changing values for critical variables. Often the critical variables are specified into a set of *scenarios,* consisting of possible future outcomes of important exogenous variables in the projections, as discussed below. For example, net income for Fifth Third could be simulated assuming a high interest rate environment, a low interest rate outcome, and a base case or most-likely interest rate projection. Many firms project future performance with a wide range of scenarios.

Simulation models sometimes use computers to calculate hundreds of outcomes in order to estimate probability distributions of future values for important variables. These simulations, called *Monte Carlo* simulations and described in Chapter 18 as a tool for asset–liability management, use values for key variables generated randomly, as if determined by a roulette wheel (hence, their name). For example, a simulation model might estimate the probability distribution of net income for Fifth Third by mathematically modeling the reaction of borrowers, depositors, and users of payment services assuming different values for interest rates and economic activity determined by probabilities of future interest rates. Large numbers of outcomes are tabulated to estimate the probability of future values for key variables.

Econometric models estimate the relation between economic and financial variables from statistical analysis of historical relationships. Econometric models typically require long time periods of stable economic behavior to estimate relationships between variables of interest under a range of economic environments. Econometric models are based on theoretical models of economic behavior. The statistics from econometric analysis can be used to compute confidence intervals around future values of key variables. For example, an econometric model of loan demand could relate interest rates to loans and be used to create confidence intervals around loan demand at different future interest rate levels.

Econometric models often focus on a single economic or financial relation and ignore less important feedbacks and influences. These forecasting models are called *partial equilibrium* models because they only look at one aspect of economic behavior, such as the demand for loans. An ad hoc model relating interest rates and activity measures to loan demand for a financial institution as presented below is an example of a partial equilibrium model concentrating only on demand for loans.

More complete econometric analyses focus on entire interrelated economic systems of supplies and demands for real or financial variables. A *general equilibrium* econometric model accounts for the economic behavior affecting both the demand and the supply in relevant markets. For example, loan interest rates balance levels of loan demand and supply in equilibrium. Demand for loans is driven by activity variables such as inventory growth in the economy and other activity variables and interest rates, and supply is determined by financial savings in the form of deposits determined by personal income, changes in household wealth, and interest rates. Historical data on business and household activity and interest rates could be used to estimate the relation between loan market supply and demand and interest rates using more complete analysis of financial markets. Of course, no econometric model can be completely general, but models of loan demand or other variables can be embedded in more or less complex analyses.

Financial projections often mix different model approaches. Variables that are not of central significance may be projected using naive forecasts. Variables of critical importance may be modeled using different statistical or econometric results. Some variables, for example, may be projected as the results of simulations using relations estimated from econometric analyses. Results from various modeling techniques may be inputs into a financial model that enforces certain relations between variables of importance to management. We will illustrate modeling techniques later in the chapter.

22.3 SCOPE OF PROJECTIONS OR FORECASTS

Financial projections or forecasts can be more or less complex in two dimensions. The first dimension is in the level of detail for the variables analyzed. For example, an analyst can project total loans or subcategories of loans, such as credit card, mortgage, auto, and commercial and industrial loans. This dimension of complexity is described as the level of *aggregation*. Decision makers and analysts base the level of aggregation or disaggregation on several factors: (1) the use of the projection; (2) the availability of data and/or knowledge about disaggregated series; and (3) the time and resources available.

An important consideration in choosing the level of aggregation in projections is how important it is to look at disaggregated variables. In many cases, aggregated data can be projected more accurately than disaggregated data. A danger to be avoided in financial projections is introducing *false precision* by projecting disaggregations of variables which go beyond the ability of the analyst to analyze given data.

The second dimension of projections is the *time horizon* covered by the analysis. The horizon is sometimes called the *forecast or projection interval*, or other names. Several considerations enter into the choice of period for projections. One is the reliability of the projections beyond a certain time period. For example, it makes no sense to forecast loan demand one hundred years from now, but it is almost certainly possible to improve our estimates of loan demand next year over naive projections. The reliability of projections farther into the future declines as the likelihood of fundamental changes in the economy and the markets of interest increases.

Another consideration in choosing the time period for projections is the nature of the decision. If the decision is to staff tellers tomorrow, forecasting lobby traffic in ten years is not relevant. On the other hand, the impact of a decision over short projection horizons may extend beyond that horizon. For example, if we fire half the tellers because we will not need them tomorrow, we will incur great costs and inconvenience in two days when demand for teller services returns to previous days' levels. The choice of horizon for projections must consider the time relevant for the decision and the impact of the decision on future periods.

A final consideration in selecting a projection horizon is the economic significance of the variable in the distant future. Much of our focus in this chapter will be on financial projections for valuation. In valuation problems, important variables like cash flows from earnings are typically discounted using risk-adjusted discount rates. Any discount rate by definition reduces the effect of future outcomes of important variables on value. Discount rates typically encountered in risky valuation decisions normally reduce the importance of variables after a few years. For example, at a discount rate of 10 percent, one dollar in five years is valued at $.62, in ten years at $.38, and in twenty years at less than $.15. Financial analysts normally focus on the early years of a projection more carefully than on the later years and often account for all years after some time horizon with a *terminal value* that summarizes future values after an explicit projection period.

Specification of a financial projection and the types of models used depends on many factors. The projection can be tailored to meet specific needs or defined to do the most reasonable job given the information and resources at hand. The projection can include different levels of aggregation and time periods over different horizons. For example, a projection might use several loan categories over four quarters, followed by four annual time periods, aggregate loan categories beyond five years, then conclude explicit projections of all variables after a projection horizon of ten years, capturing activity after that time with terminal value projections.

22.4 TYPES OF VARIABLES IN PROJECTIONS

All projections or forecasts except naive models include several variables. In any forecast or projection, variables that are determined by economic forces external to the problem being analyzed are called *exogenous* variables. Variables that will be determined simultaneously with other variables in the analysis are called *endogenous* in terms of the projection. For analytical purposes, exogenous variables can be truly exogenous, as for example the number of hours in the day or the position of the North American continent on the earth's mantle. In other cases, analysts will assume that variables are exogenous because the feedback from model variables is too weak to matter or too hard to understand. For example, financial institutions may assume future interest rates to be exogenous, even though each institution's behavior contributes to the level of those rates.

Types of Exogenous and Endogenous Variables

Within the categories of exogenous and endogenous variables in projections, there are basic types of economic and financial variables. Types of variables are important in selecting the appropriate techniques or assumptions to use in projecting them. Variables can be classified into: (1) *state* variables; (2) *activity* variables; and (3) *relative price* variables. We present the types of variables and a brief description in Table 22.1 and discuss each in detail.

State variables define the status or nature of the economy or an economic unit, like a financial institution, at a point in time. An example of a state variable for an economy would be the population of a city or the number of residential homes in a country. Many state variables are determined by history and are not changeable, such as a financial institution's current equity capital. State variables at the beginning of a projection period are exogenous.

Although it is not necessary to forecast or project state variables that are determined by history, they are important because they define the economic environment or the state of an institution at the beginning of the forecast interval.

TABLE 22.1 Types of Variables Used in Financial or Economic Projections

TYPE OF VARIABLE	*CHARACTERISTICS*	*EXAMPLES*
Basic Variables		
State	Conditions determining the status of an *economy, region,* or *firm.*	*Economy:* Capital stock, population. *Region:* Housing stock, resources. *Firm:* Beginning shareholders equity, asset holdings.
Activity	Measures of economic activity representing supply and demand in markets.	*Economy:* GDP, consumption, retail sales. *Market:* Construction, car sales. *Firm:* Premium income, loans.
Relative price	Relative values of commodities or financial assets.	Gold, price of oil, interest rates, exchange rates.
Nonprojected Variables		
Policy	Chosen by decision makers or analyst.	*Economy:* Growth in money supply. *Firm:* Level of loans, insurance sales.
Restricted	Determined by law, regulation, or industry practice.	Reserve requirements, cash needs for liquidity, capital requirements.
Plug	Value required to satisfy balancing conditions.	*Economy:* Inventory investment balancing GDP with consumption, government expenditures, and fixed investment. *Firm:* Short-term borrowings to balance balance sheet.

Some state variables evolve in the future in ways that have nothing, or very little, to do with the economic variables considered by the user of the projections. For example, the age distribution of the population will not be influenced a great deal by whether long-term interest rates are 7 or 9 percent next year. Future values of some state values can be assumed to be exogenous for purposes of a projection.

Economic activity variables determine the level of demand and supply for goods and services in an economy. Examples of economic activity measures are gross domestic product (GDP) for a country, disposable income for a class of consumers, or construction activity in a region. Activity variables are critical determinants of the demand for financial services. The level of GDP for a country influences national and local demand for goods and services, for example the demand for housing and new construction of homes. Residential construction in a region affects the demand for construction loans from financial institutions offering credit services in that region.

For purposes of making projections for financial institutions, analysts must decide which variables will be determined within the projection and which will be taken as exogenous. In making projections, most firms assume that the future levels of GDP are exogenous. Since no economic activity exogenous variables can be forecasted with certainty, projections often use a range of values for exogenous variables in determining which are important for the projection. A set of assumptions concerning exogenous economic activity variables might define an *economic scenario,* as for example GDP will grow 2 percent in a base case scenario, 0 percent in a recession scenario, and 4 percent in a boom scenario.

When projecting activity for a firm, depending on its size and the use of the model, economic and financial variables may be considered endogenous or endogenous. Construction loans in a region might be determined by the construction lending policies of a financial institution making projections and therefore be determined endogenously in the projection model. Alternatively, the total construction loans in a region may be an activity variable that is considered exogenous but the firm's share of that market is determined by the firm's policies. In either case, the firm's construction loans will be an endogenous variable in the projection.

Historical data on economic or financial data are called *time series.* Times series data for economic activity are subject to both long term trends and short run disturbances, in line with our discussion of economic equilibrium in Chapter 13. Variables such as the GDP will increase over time with increasing population, wealth, improvements in productivity, and, in nominal terms, with inflation. Most regional variables (e.g., construction and other investments) will grow over time, influenced by a country's economic growth and inflation. Except in instances of regional decline or political disruption, it is assumed that most economic activity variables will grow with an economy as a whole.

Other economic variables represent *relative prices* or the ratio of the value (per unit) of two economic or financial variables. An example of one very important relative price is an *interest rate,* which represents the relative price of money or consumption now versus money or consumption in some time period in the future. Relative prices are determined by the interaction of supply and demand in goods and financial markets.

Relative prices like interest rates change over time, but in general they are not expected to continue to grow or decline over infinite time horizons like economic activity variables. For example, interest rates are not expected to go up or down forever, even though in most economic environments, they are expected to change. Relative prices, such as the price of oil in terms of gold, may change with wars in the Middle East or discoveries of gold or oil, but those relative price changes are not expected to continue to change in one direction forever. Relative prices and interest rates fluctuate with real and monetary shocks but do not trend in one direction for very long periods of time.

Statisticians and forecasters distinguish between time series of economic variables that tend to increase over long time periods, like a country's GDP, and variables that fluctuate within a range, like interest rates. Variables that can have long-term growth are called *nonstationary* because predictions of their long-term future values are always higher. Since these variables tend to increase, their historical average or *mean* value is generally increasing with the passage of time. Average GDP over time almost always goes up. GDP is a nonstationary economic variable.

Variables that fluctuate around values that do not change over time are called *stationary,* since their average values over long periods of time are relatively constant. For example, U.S. Treasury bill interest rates historically have been very low, in the range of 1 to 3 percent. In the period from the 1960s to the 1980s, Treasury bill rates increased to a range of 3 to 15 percent, but recently they have trended down toward historical levels. Even though Treasury bill interest rates fluctuate a great deal, they would be considered stationary by most economists because they cannot be expected to continue to increase or decrease over a very long time period.

Variables such as Treasury bill interest rates may display cyclical patterns. Many economic time series appear to be cyclical—for example, the unemployment rate or industrial production and capacity utilization measures. When economic variables tend to have cycles but return to longer term average values, they are said to be *mean reverting*. While at different points in the cycle average values change over long time periods they return to long-run average levels. Economists and financial market observers debate whether specific economic time series such as the Treasury bill interest rate are cyclical and mean reverting or are stationary and simply fluctuate within a range without apparent cycles. Implementation of financial projections using economic variables can be facilitated by assuming an economic time series is mean reverting or simply a random fluctuation.

Activity and relative price variables, either stationary or nonstationary, can be assumed to be exogenous or endogenous by analysts preparing projections or forecasts. The choices between one classification or another will be determined by the purpose of the projection and the extent of the modeling effort. Future values of these variables must all be provided before a projection effort can continue. Future values of other variables in projections are determined differently, as discussed next.

Nonprojected Variables

The last three kinds of variables we describe are different: these variables are not projected separately but are chosen by the analyst or determined by other variables. These variables are: (1) *policy* variables, (2) *restricted* variables, and (3) *residual* or *plug* variables. These are briefly defined in Table 22.1 and are each discussed here.

Variables chosen by the analyst are *policy* variables. Their values represent choices under the control of decision makers or values over a range of values that analysts wish to assess. An example would be a target level of an activity variable like construction loans or premium revenue which financial institution managers expect to achieve under a marketing plan or promotion. More complex models including economic behavior might use interest rates or prices as policy variables. For example, a construction loan interest rate might be the policy variable that determines construction loan volume or a level of life insurance premiums might be a policy variable determining insurance demand and premium revenue endogenously.

Policy variables are the focus of most projections. In using projections for communication, education, and coordination, varying policies for various units are valuable in assessing the effects of interactions of the units of the organization on outcomes of importance, such as income. In using projections to anticipate problems or opportunities, the effect of changes in policy variables may suggest possible solutions or strategies to management. Policy variables are extremely important for valuation when a merger or acquisition is a possible result of analysis. When a firm is acquired, all of its operations can be changed with new policies, such as the level of its costs and the mix of its activities. Changing policies are a potential source of value to the acquiring firm.

Another set of variables is determined by regulation or practice. Relations between different parts of a model or variables imposed by regulation or practice are called *restricted variables*. For example, deposit-taking institutions must keep reserves at central banks according to regulations—in the United States 10 percent of transaction accounts is required. Projected transaction accounts must be consistent with holdings of 10 percent reserves for complete projections of banks and thrifts. Insurance companies are often limited in the amount of premium revenue they can generate relative to capital and surplus. A complete projection must account for these relations.

Restrictions can be important in determining the relation between variables and the focus of the projection (e.g., net income). Holding deposit reserves, for example, means holding nonearning assets, thereby reducing income from investments for deposit-taking institutions. Some restrictions come from management policies, as when an insurance company holds 40 percent of earning assets as debt securities. Analysts must carefully consider restrictions between variables included in a projection.

The last type of variable in projections is the *residual* or *plug* variable. These variable values are not projected explicitly but are determined by all the other values. They assume their values in order to make projections or forecasts consistent—for example, balance sheets must balance. Some variable, such as short-term borrowings for a bank, has to be allowed to adjust in order to absorb imbalances remaining after policy variables and other variables have been projected. If assets, deposits, and other variables are determined by the model, short-term liabilities may be chosen as the residual variable to balance assets and liabilities.

Plug variables are important. Since the values of plug variables are unknown, the range of outcomes they may take must be possible. Continuing the above example, if short-term borrowings are the plug variable, it must be assumed that the market for these funds is sufficiently elastic to accommodate the projected needs at the interest rates likely to exist in the future. Values for plug or residual variables making a projection consistent must be plausible.

Sometimes the value for residual variables may be an important focus of the projection. The bank making projections in the above example may wish to use values for the residual values to plan short-term borrowing requirements. In this case, all the other variable inputs into projection can be viewed as determining the residual value. The plug variable under this interpretation is projected from a financial simulation and is an important variable rather than just a balancing variable.

Often analysts will arbitrarily choose a balancing variable, such as other assets, without careful consideration. This is dangerous. As we will see in examples below, the balancing quantities can have a major impact on projections of income or other important financial or economic values. In macroeconomic models, for example, inventory investment is often a residual variable balancing total production with demand for consumer goods, government spending, and fixed investment. Inventory is an important economic determinant of the demand for financing and source of business costs. Plug variables are not unimportant variables and choosing the plug variable should be done with caution.

Example: Specifying a Projection for Fifth Third Bancorp

To illustrate the different kinds of variables discussed above, we will specify a model for projecting earnings for Fifth Third Bancorp. The projection uses a financial model. As background, we reproduce the "Analysis of Fifth Third Bancorp" from Chapter 5 as Panel A of Table 22.2. At this point, we discuss the variables to be included in the model and will complete our presentation of the model after discussing projection methods later in the chapter. Panel B of Table 22.2 presents the variables in the financial model, illustrating the types of variables used in projections.

The financial model shown in Table 22.2 consists of projecting simplified income statement and balance sheet information. The projection is a *pro forma* model, as discussed above. The advantage of this model is that it follows the analysis already performed in Chapter 5 and presents projections within a familiar financial framework. The disadvantage of this version of the model is that it is highly aggregated, as we will discuss.

A financial model requires explicit projection of many or only a few variables depending on its exact specification. As shown in Table 22.2, only six variables are explicitly projected in the Fifth Third example: (1) noninterest revenue; (2) noninterest expense; (3) total assets; (5) rate of return on earning assets; (6) yield cost of liabilities; (7) and loss rates on earning assets. Other variables are policy variables or restricted variables determined by assumptions chosen by the analyst to

TABLE 22.2 Example of Financial Projection Model

Panel A: Analysis of Fifth Third Bancorporation

BASIC FINANCIAL DATA		*1991*	*1992*	*% CHANGE*
Income Statement				
Interest revenue (IR)		713,501	694,460	–2.67%
Interest expense (IE)		381,280	300,266	–21.25%
Provision for loan losses (PLL)		55,744	65,315	17.17%
Non-Interest revenue (NIR)		171,911	200,053	16.37%
Non-Interest expense (NIE)		249,792	289,276	15.81%
Earnings before tax (EBT)		198,596	239,656	20.68%
Earnings available for common (EAC)		138,150	164,092	18.78%
Number of common shares outstanding		59,200	59,632	
Earnings per share		$2.33	$2.75	
Balance Sheet (Partial)				
Cash and reserves (R)		501,188	565,948	12.92%
Fixed and other assets (FA)		352,677	353,466	0.22%
Total assets (TA)		8,826,130	10,213,320	15.72%
Book value of equity (BVE)		879,450	1,005,165	14.29%
Ratio Analysis				
Book rate of return (BROR)		15.71%	16.32%	3.92%
Composed of:				
Pullthrough (U) ×		69.56%	68.47%	–1.57%
Leverage (LEV) ×		10.04	10.16	1.24%
Return on total assets (ROTA)		2.25%	2.35%	4.28%
EBT/TA composed of:				
Net interest margin	((IR – IE)/EA	4.17%	4.24%	1.78%
– Loan losses	– (PLL/EA)) ×	0.70%	0.70%	0.51%
Earning asset ratio	(EA/TA)	90.33%	91.00%	0.74%
+ Burden	+ ((NIR – NIE)/TA)	–0.88%	–0.87%	–1.00%
(IR – IE)/EA composed of:				
Return on earning assets	IR/EA –	8.95%	7.47%	–16.51%
Cost of liabilities	(IE/L) ×	4.80%	3.26%	–32.04%
Liabilities to earning assets	(L/EA)	0.9968	0.9908	–0.60%

TABLE 22.2 (*continued*)

Panel B: Financial Model Fifth Third Bancorp

DESCRIPTION OF MODEL VARIABLES	*TYPES OF VARIABLES*
Pro Forma Income Statement	
+ Interest revenue	Endogenous
– Interest expense	Endogenous
– Provision for loan losses	Endogenous
+ Non-interest revenue	Projected activity
– Non-interest expense	Projected activity
Earnings before tax	Endogenous
– Taxes and preferred dividends	Restricted
Earnings available for common	Endogenous
number of shares outstanding	Policy
Earnings per share	Endogenous
Pro Forma Balance Sheet	
Cash and reserves	Restricted
Earning assets	Policy
Fixed and other assets	Exogenous policy
Total assets	Projected activity
Liabilities	Plug
Book value of equity	Beginning value state Ending value endogenous
Other Variables	
Economic Variables	
Rate on earning assets	Projected relative price
Cost of liabilities	Projected relative price
Loss rate on earning assets	Projected activity
Other variables	
Reserve requirements	Exogenous restricted
Liquidity needs	Policy restricted
Leverage ratio	Exogenous restricted

describe regulatory or practical limitations. The remaining variables are calculated in the model as endogenous variables or plug variables.

The classification of variables can change with model specification. For example, we assume in the model described in Table 22.2 that “Fixed and other assets” are a policy variable, chosen by the analyst to reflect Fifth Third’s strategy on fixed investments as a percent of total assets. Fixed assets could be a restricted variable, perhaps computed as a percent of earning assets or liabilities if the model were more disaggregated. For example, if liabilities were disaggregated into consumer and wholesale deposits and other liabilities, fixed assets could be a restricted variable related to consumer deposits to capture the relation between investments in branches to consumer services. Model specification is flexible.

Estimates of future values of projected variables can be derived in a number of ways, as described in the next section. Estimated most likely or mean values for projected variable will not be the only interesting values for projected variables, since no one can project the future with certainty. For example, in projecting total assets for Fifth Third, a number of factors will result in the future value being greater than or less than most likely values or mean estimates. In choosing a technique to project variables, methods providing information concerning the future range of values or statistical distributions of values is an important consideration.

In choosing projection methods, whether variables are activity or relative price variables is important. The statistical properties of these values, including whether they are stationary or nonstationary variables, may suggest the best estimation techniques to use. Knowledge about the economic determination of the values is also important in choosing the projection method. For example, loan volume is an activity variable representing supply and demand in the loan market which is probably nonstationary. This value will grow (or shrink) with underlying determinants of economic activity like the GDP or local activity measures. Projections of loan volume should account for developments in the overall economy.

Interest rates, as discussed in Chapter 13, represent a relative price reflecting a real rate, expected inflation, and term and risk premiums. These variables do not trend upward or downward forever, so are usually assumed to be stationary random variables. To capture expectations, making explicit projections with models may not be as efficient as looking at financial markets. For example, the term structure of interest rates or futures markets contains information on expectations concerning future values of interest rates and inflation. Projections of relative prices such as interest rates may best be derived from analysis of relevant markets.

Policy variables and restrictions also have many possible values in the future. The difference between projected variables and other variables is that values for projected values are explicitly analyzed to provide estimates of future values. Policy variables and restrictions on variables are assumed by analysts, chosen by model users, or imposed by regulations or model structure. Model users will decide which variable values are most important and make projections using a variety of values for them.

22.5 METHODS FOR PROJECTING VALUES OF VARIABLES

Management, statistics, and econometric textbooks describe many techniques to produce estimates for future values of variables like loans, GDP, or inventories. Most discussions of forecasting focus on techniques appropriate for projecting economic activity variables. In many cases, analysts assume that patterns contained in historical time series are useful in projecting the future. We will review the more common techniques used to make projections and provide examples of them here. Detailed technical discussions are beyond the coverage of this book. Our purpose is to help users and makers of projections to specify and implement models.

Internal Projections

Bottom-up projections for activity variables for an individual firm which rely on estimates prepared by personnel involved in the firms operations are called *internal projections*. To project loan volume, for example, lending officers and regional managers are asked to project future volume. Managers of insurance companies, securities firms, and other financial institutions likewise are asked to produce projections of key activity measures, such as premiums written, commission revenues, or assets under management. Bringing projections from parts of an organization together are a useful part of the education, communication, and coordination role of making the projections discussed above.

The advantage of internally generated projections is that information possessed by line managers concerning developments in the markets they know best are incorporated into projections. Higher level management can assess how various parts of the organization view opportunities for activity in their areas. The procedure of requiring that projections be prepared, gathering and reporting the projections, and finally using them in a model is both valuable for all participants in the process and fairly low cost. Most of the information required in internal projections is either available or readily made available by the people involved in the activities.

The disadvantage of internal projections is bias. Managers responsible for specific activities want to look their best for their superiors. These managers are inclined to either inflate the projections with optimistic activity levels to make their units look good or to reduce their projections in order to look good when actual results are reported. Bias in internal projections is a serious problem and has led more than one top management to overlook impending problems in their business. Good management practice compares internal projections to alternative estimates.

External Projections

Projections derived from historical data on the projected activity and related variables are called *external projections*. Preparation of external projections is important for top management involved in bottom-up projection efforts wanting outside validation or a plausibility check on internal forecasts. In evaluation problems, often no internal data are available. In these cases, external projections are the only means of producing possible future values for activity variables of interest.

There are several basic techniques of projecting activity variables using statistical or mathematical analysis: (1) *trend analysis* or *curve-fitting* techniques; (2) *time series* methods; (3) *econometric* methods; and (4) *simulation*. The choice of method depends on the situation, and often several methods may be used to provide additional validation of the values used in projections. All of these basic types can be more or less complex. In this section, we introduce each approach with some simple examples, as well as some nonstatistical methods.

Trend Analysis or Curve-Fitting. Trend analysis is a simple way of extrapolating past growth in economic time series. Trend analysis can be done by eyeballing graphed data, but statistical methods are almost as easy. A critical advantage of statistical methods, both with simple trend analysis and the more complex techniques discussed below, is that they provide diagnostic tools for the analyst to use to assess the reliability of the projections based on them.

To illustrate trend analysis for our example of Fifth Third Bancorp, Panel A of Table 22.3 provides a time series of Fifth Third's total assets, one of the seven variables requiring a projection according to our model specification above. Total assets are graphed in Figure 22.1. Inspection of the graph suggests a steady growth in Fifth Third's total assets. Trend analysis confirms this.

TABLE 22.3 Projecting Total Assets for Fifth Third Bancorp

Panel A: Historical Data on Total Assets

YEAR	*TOTAL ASSETS*	*NATURAL LOG OF TOTAL ASSETS*	*PROJECTED TOTAL ASSETS*
1980	1,184.152	7.07678216	1,145.04
1981	1,428.237	7.26419613	1,381.61
1982	1,720.874	7.45058759	1,667.06
1983	1,854.643	7.52544747	2,011.49
1984	2,363.109	7.76773335	2,427.09
1985	2,761.462	7.92351549	2,928.55
1986	3,492.051	8.15824452	3,533.61
1987	4,051.475	8.30683631	4,263.69
1988	5,245.800	8.56518299	5,144.61
1989	7,142.968	8.87388362	6,207.53
1990	7,955.804	8.98165702	7,490.06
1991	8,826.128	9.08547168	9,037.58
1992	10,213.296	9.23144566	10,904.82
1993			13,157.86
1994			15,876.39

Panel B: Regression of Total Assets on Years

Constant		−1512566.5
Standard error of Y estimates		884.069604
R squared		0.92510610
Number of observations		13
Degrees of freedom		11
Year Coefficient(s)	763.870374	
Standard error of coefficient	65.5315990	

Panel C: Regression of Logarithm of Total Assets on Years

Constant		−364.82871
Standard error of Y estimates		0.06418386
R squared		0.99299090
Number of observations		13
Degrees of freedom		11
Year Coefficient(s)	0.18781409	
Standard error of coefficient	0.00475762	

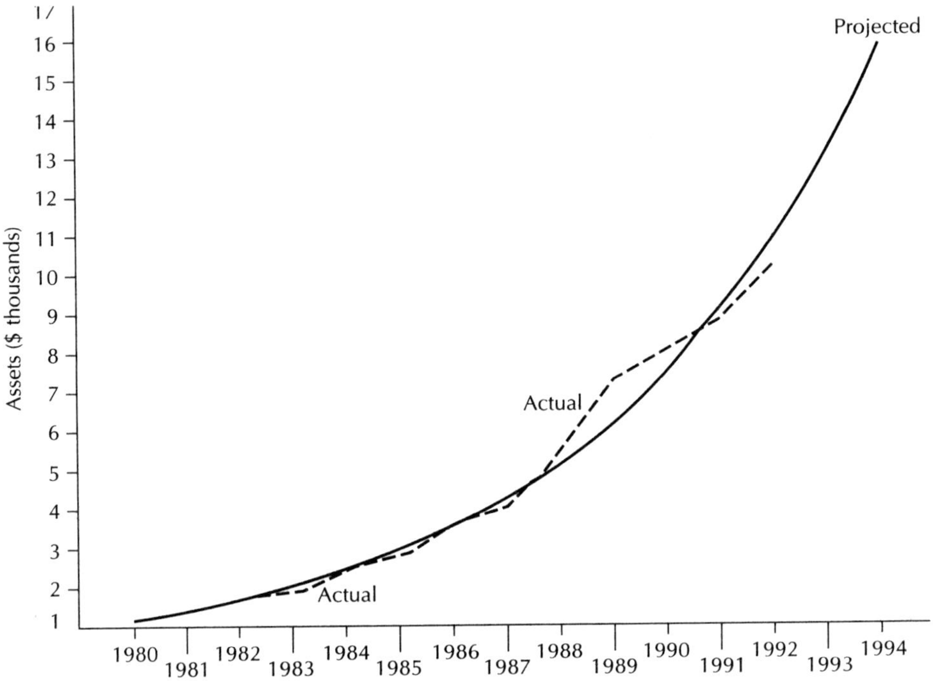

FIGURE 22.1 Actual and projected total assets for Fifth Third Bancorp

A trend analysis consists of fitting a line using least-squares regression through the time series. A line fit through total assets in currency units would project future increases (or decreases) in total assets in the same units. Panel B of Table 22.3 shows the results of regressing total assets in dollars on time stated as years.[1] These results show that over the period 1980 to 1992, Fifth Third's were estimated to increase $764 million per year. Total assets could be projected using this an annual increase.

Use of an annual currency increase in an economic value like total assets means that growth is slowing. To see this, the first year of the projection, 1993, would be 1992 total assets plus $764 million, or $10,977 million. This represents an increase of 6.9 percent ($764/$10,213). In 1994, total assets would be projected to be $11,741, representing a 6.5 percent increase. With constant currency unit increases, growth rates are declining. With many economic variables, a constant growth rate is a more reasonable assumption.

To estimate a constant growth rate using all the data in the time series, a regression of the *natural logarithm* of the variable to be projected against a time variable is calculated. Panel C of Table 22.3 provides the result of this analysis.

[1]Results were derived in Lotus 1-2-3. Any statistical package can compute these results. Years were used as time variable but the only important thing is that time measures increase in the unit time of concern. We are analyzing one year changes. If quarterly data were used, time could be measured in units of .25 years.

The regression shows that the average trend growth in Fifth Third's total assets from 1980 to 1992 is 18.8 percent, the coefficient on the year variable.[2] Projected values of variable are computed as the antilog of the regression estimates using future year values. For example, the 1993 forecast is the exponentiation or antilog of (−364.82871 + .188*1993), and correspondingly for 1994. Figure 22.1 shows the constant growth projections for Fifth Third's total assets.

Trend lines and other curve fitting techniques are very simple—they simply extrapolate patterns in historical data. Nonetheless, the statistical analysis provides us with some indicators of past trends. For example, both regressions for Fifth Third have R^2s well above .95 and the growth rates (time coefficients) are several times their standard errors implying statistical significance at high confidence levels.[3] Statistics from estimation give us information about the explanatory power of simple trends in the time series. If we believe trends will continue, we can use these statistics to calculate confidence intervals for our projections. Roughly, we estimate that our projections have a 95 percent chance of being within 2 standard errors of our coefficient estimates in the next year, or within $131 million (2 times $65.5 million) using the dollar estimates, if the future continues like the past.[4]

Time Series (Box–Jenkins) Methods. Time series methods use a historical database on the activity variable in question, as with simple trend or curve fitting techniques. Times series techniques are also called Box–Jenkins analysis after the researchers who developed techniques to estimate more generalized patterns in time series. Time series methods have advantages over simple trend or other models: (1) they allow more complicated patterns in the historical series, for example cycles or seasonality; (2) despite their flexibility, these methods given enough data are easy and inexpensive to estimate although they require some expertise; and (3) Box–Jenkins analyses are often justified in terms of economic theory. Forecasts of many activities in financial institutions are amenable to time-series analysis. Any data series with enough observations can be analyzed. Box–Jenkins forecasting of activity can assist management in more routine staffing and resource allocation problems than those requiring financial forecasts. For example, the flow of wire transfer activity or check volume in a deposit-taking institution, claims or sales activity for insurance, trading volume for brokers, or telephone inquiries for mutual fund managers can all be projected using these techniques. Given the advantages of time series analysis, it should be more widely used in the operations of financial institutions than it is.

[2]The coefficient on the year variable represents the derivative of the fitted function with respect to time. Since the dependent variable is in natural logarithms, the derivative is Δlog(Total Assets)/ΔTime = ΔTotal Assets/ΔTime) × 1/Total Assets = ΔTotal Assets/Total Assets, since the change in time is one unit. The last expression is a growth rate.

[3]The t-statistic, computed by dividing the standard error into the coefficient, is well over two, a rough cut-off for statistical significance at normal confidence levels.

[4]See a statistics or econometrics textbook (for example, Pyndyck and Rubenfeld (1976)) for details of interpreting and computing confidence intervals. Confidence intervals widen the farther outside the estimation period projections are made.

Time series analysis also has disadvantages. It requires keeping long histories of relevant data. It does not explicitly model supply and demand behavior, meaning that projections from time series methods cannot account for changes in the economic environment or policies changing the pattern of future values for critical variables. Another disadvantage is that the choice of a particular time series projection model is an art or matter of taste in many circumstances. In order to assess the advantages and disadvantages of using time series analysis, we develop an example. Readers should consult more complete texts for in-depth treatments of this projection method (for example, Pindyck and Rubinfeld (1991), Part III).

Time series analysis is used to project values for *stationary* time series, as the term was used previously. In other words, the estimated projection equation consists of parameters such as average growth and factors that determine how random shocks affect future values of the variables that are not changing over time. The fact that the forecasting equation does not change is the basis for the term *stationary*. Most economic activity measures (e.g., total assets for Fifth Third) are not stationary, because their means or averages increase each period with growth. The trick is to transform nonstationary variables like total assets into variables that can be predicted with a stationary projection equation.

Transforming nonstationary variables into stationary variables is usually not difficult. One simple method is to look at *changes*, called *first differences* by technicians, in activity variables. If we are projecting variable Y, first differences are defined:

$$Z_t = \Delta Y_t = Y_t - Y_{t-1} \tag{22.3}$$

where t are subscripts identifying the time period. For example, the first difference for Fifth Third's total assets in 1981, calculated from Table 22.3, Panel A, is:

$$\Delta\text{Total Assets}_{1981} = \$1{,}428.237 - \$1{,}184.152 = \$244.085.$$

Although the mean of a nonstationary variable is increasing due to growth, changes through time may be stationary. For example, changes each year in Fifth Third's total assets might have a constant mean. Changes in logarithms of an activity variable are growth rates. First differences in logarithms may be better than simple first differences, suggesting a constant growth rate, as discussed above in our trend analysis. In some cases, *changes in changes*, called *second differences*, are stationary when simple changes are not. When the second differences are stationary, the rate of change in changes has a constant mean each period, meaning that the changes are not accelerating.

Analysts determine whether an economic or financial data series is stationary by using the *autocorrelation* function of the data or its transformation into changes or changes in changes. The autocorrelation is simply the correlation of a time series on past values of itself. For example, if we correlate total assets for Fifth Third with assets in the previous year, we calculate a *first-order* autocorrelation of total assets. Another way of describing the autocorrelation is the correlation of a variable with a *lagged* value of itself. Of course, we lose one year of observation when we lag once, because the first observation in any sample has no previous period's value by definition. If we calculate the correlation of any time series variable with its value two periods before or lagged two periods, a *second-order* autocorrelation is the result. Time series analysts begin by calculating as many autocorrelations as are meaningful given the data they have. With annual data (e.g., total assets for Fifth Third) only four or five autocorrelations can be computed. With daily or hourly data available for some activity variables, such as teller transactions, shares of stock traded, or bank wire transfers, dozens of autocorrelations could be computed.

Analysts using time-series methods have many options in transforming data to find a stationary variable to project with time series analysis. They can compute first or second or more differences in levels or logarithms. They choose the best transformation using the *autocorrelation function,* namely the calculated autocorrelations for the time series for a number of periods. Usually the autocorrelations are shown in graphical or table form where rows or the axis represents the number of lags used in calculating each correlation. In stationary data, the autocorrelations become small and insignificant after a few lags in the transformed data. Usually first- or second-differences of economic data or their logarithms suffice to create autocorrelation functions that tail off rapidly.

We illustrate this process for a time series of quarterly total assets for Fifth Third Bancorp. Table 22.4 provides the autocorrelation function for this series.[5] Panel A of the table is the autocorrelation function for the level of total assets, Panel B for changes in total assets, and Panel C for changes in the logarithms of total assets for Fifth Third, estimated over the time period from the first quarter of 1982 to the second quarter of 1993. Note that when differences are calculated, the first observation, 1982-I, is lost in Panels B and C.

The first-order autocorrelation of quarter-ending total assets for Fifth Third is .931, very close to positive one. Each successive order of autocorrelation is slightly smaller: the second and third order autocorrelations are .862 and .794, and so on out to 16 lags. The autocorrelation function, the graph of the autocorrelation at each lag, starts high and gradually falls as the lags become larger. Time series analysts describe this type of autocorrelation function as *tailing off,* a clear symptom of nonstationarity in a series. As we suspected, the dollar level of total assets for Fifth Third, and for most financial institutions, is nonstationary since it is always growing.

Panels B and C of Table 22.4 portray the autocorrelation functions for the change in total assets and the change in the logarithm of total assets for Fifth Third. These autocorrelation functions display no pattern in the autocorrelations, which are pretty small at all lags. The statistics at the bottom of each panel, for example the Box–Pierce Q statistic, are statistical tests of the hypothesis that all the autocorrelations are inconsequentially different from zero, the so-called *null hypothesis.* In Panel A, the Q statistic has a probability of practically zero of being insignificant, suggesting that at least one, probably several, of the autocorrelations are different from zero. The Q statistic in Panel A confirms our visual rejection of the

[5]The output was produced by Micro TSP from Quantitative Micro Software, Irvine, California, one of many software packages available for personal computers to calculate these results.

TABLE 22.4 Autocorrelation Functions for Fifth Third Bancorp

Panel A: Total Assets Quarterly from 1982-I to 1993-II

AUTOCORRELATIONS	*PARTIAL AUTOCORRELATIONS*		*AC*	*PAC*
. ************	. ************	1	0.931	0.931
. ***********	. .	2	0.862	–0.029
. **********	. .	3	0.794	–0.033
. *********	. * .	4	0.726	–0.041
. *********	. .	5	0.658	–0.036
. ********	. .	6	0.592	–0.027
. *******	. .	7	0.526	–0.038
. ******	. * .	8	0.458	–0.061
. *****	. .	9	0.393	–0.019
. ****	. .	10	0.331	–0.032
. *** .	. * .	11	0.266	–0.061
. *** .	. * .	12	0.201	–0.056
. ** .	. .	13	0.140	–0.029
. * .	. .	14	0.081	–0.034
. .	. * .	15	0.015	–0.100
. * .	. * .	16	–0.048	–0.056

Box–Pierce	Q-Stat	186.47	Prob	0.0000	SE of Correlations 0.154
Ljung–Box	Q-Stat	218.02	Prob	0.0000	

Panel B: Change in Total Assets Quarterly from 1982-II to 1993-II

AUTOCORRELATIONS	*PARTIAL AUTOCORRELATIONS*		*AC*	*PAC*
. * .	. * .	1	0.051	0.051
. ** .	. ** .	2	–0.119	–0.122
. * .	. ** .	3	0.115	0.130
. * .	. * .	4	0.083	0.054
. ** .	. ** .	5	–0.152	–0.136
. * .	. * .	6	–0.059	–0.039
. ***.	. ***.	7	0.246	0.217
. ** .	. ** .	8	0.155	0.156
. ** .	. * .	9	–0.144	–0.104
. .	. * .	10	–0.017	–0.051
. ** .	. * .	11	0.168	0.098
.*** .	. ** .	12	–0.193	–0.161
. * .	. .	13	–0.082	0.034
. * .	. * .	14	0.065	–0.046
. * .	. .	15	0.089	0.034
. ** .	. ***.	16	0.151	0.260

Box–Pierce	Q-Stat	11.33	Prob	0.7890	SE of Correlations 0.156
Ljung–Box	Q-Stat	15.36	Prob	0.4985	

Panel C: Change in Logarithm of Total Assets Quarterly from 1982-II to 1993-II

AUTOCORRELATIONS	*PARTIAL AUTOCORRELATIONS*		*AC*	*PAC*
. *.	. *.	1	0.043	0.043
.** .	.** .	2	−0.178	−0.180
. .	. .	3	0.005	0.023
. .	.* .	4	−0.018	−0.053
.** .	.** .	5	−0.125	−0.121
.* .	.** .	6	−0.114	−0.120
. **.	. **.	7	0.165	0.139
. **.	. **.	8	0.169	0.123
.* .	.* .	9	−0.082	−0.053
. .	. .	10	−0.025	0.006
. *.	. .	11	0.064	0.032
.*** .	.*** .	12	−0.208	−0.201
.* .	. .	13	−0.063	0.029
. .	.* .	14	−0.012	−0.089
. .	. .	15	0.036	−0.018
. ****	. ****	16	0.305	0.324

Box–Pierce	Q-Stat	11.12	Prob	0.8023	SE of Correlations 0.156
Ljung–Box	Q-Stat	16.05	Prob	0.4495	

null hypothesis of no significant autocorrelations at a very high level. In Panels B and C, on the other hand, we cannot reject the hypothesis of zero correlations at the .7890 or .8023 levels, respectively, with substantial confidence. It is not likely that any of the autocorrelations of changes in total assets or the change in logarithms of total assets for Fifth Third are statistically significantly different from zero over the time period the autocorrelation function is estimated.

Once the decision is made that a given transformation of a time series of economic variables is stationary, we can estimate a time series model for the transformed variable. We focus on the change in logarithms for Fifth Third Bancorp, a constant growth formulation since stationarity implies the mean value of the change in logarithms of total assets is constant. To project total assets, we will exponentiate the logarithm produced by adding the changes in logarithms over the projection interval, technically *integrating* the changes in logarithm of total assets to compute the logarithm of projected total assets.

Time-series analysts distinguish two basic time series models: *moving average* and *autoregression* models. These two basic types can be mixed in a final projection equation. We describe each in turn. A moving average (MA) model assumes random shocks to mean values influence the variable for one or more periods into the future. For example, if we are projecting a variable Z, which can be first or second differences in the activity variable of interest, its value could be determined as follows:

$$Z_t = \mu + \epsilon_t - \theta_1 \epsilon_{t-1} \tag{22.5}$$

where μ is the mean of the stationary process, ϵ are the random shocks each period, and θ_1 is the moving average factor.

In moving average models, Z would change μ each period if there were no shocks. In the above specification, the effect of a shock lasts one period after it occurs. For example, if $\mu = .058$ and $\theta_1 = .56$ and the random shocks of this and the previous period are .01 and –.02, respectively, the variable Z this period is computed as .058 + .01 – .56 (–.02) or .0792. The random error this period would persist into next period multiplied by the moving average factor .56.

More complicated moving average models have many lagged random shock terms, each with its multiplicative factor. Analysts describe moving average projection equations as being of order Q, where Q is the number of past shocks assumed to influence the value of the variable of interest. In the preceding equation, we showed a moving average with Q = 1, often noted as MA(1) by time series analysts. The choice of Q defines a moving average model.

Autoregression models assign a predictive role to past values of the variable being projected. The simplest autoregression model can be written:

$$Z_t = \phi_1 Z_{t-1} + \epsilon_t \tag{22.6}$$

where ϕ_1 denotes a factor multiplied times the previous period's value for the variable to be projected and ϵ_t is the current random shock. For example, if $\phi_1 = -.34$, the previous period's value for Z was .04, and the current shock is .02, the current value of Z would be computed as –.34 (.04) + .02 or .0064. More complicated models can have many past values of the variable to be projected in the autocorrelation specification. Time series statisticians describe autoregressive equations by the number of lagged values or P. As with moving average models, the choice of P defines the autoregressive relation. The simple equation above is an AR(1) model.

Forecasting models can combine both autoregressive and moving average parts, becoming ARMA models. Variables that are differenced to make them stationary must be added together or integrated to produce projections according to how many times that have been differenced. Times series analysts use the term ARIMA models for autoregressive-integrated-moving average models. They describe the models in terms of P and Q and the number of differences to achieve stationarity. For example, ARIMA models for two variables could be (1,1,1) or (2,3,0), where the first variable must be differenced once to become stationary and the second three times. The first model contains one moving average and one autoregression term, and the second contains two autoregressive terms and no moving average terms.

Table 22.5 contains estimates of time series models for the logarithm of total assets required for the financial model for Fifth Third Bancorp. The table shows estimations of four ARIMA models for this series, namely (0,1,0), (1,1,0), (0,1,1), and (1,1,1), respectively, representing a pure random shock model (a random walk), a pure autoregression model, a pure moving average model, and a mixed model. According to the statistical analysis, the random walk does as well as the more complicated models. The R^2 is lower but the standard error is about the same as the more complicated autoregression and moving average models. The coefficients for the autoregression and moving average terms (the ϕ and θ factors) are not significant as demonstrated in the calculated t-tests below two (a standard cut-off for significance) and the low confidence to reject the null hypothesis.

TABLE 22.5 Time Series Model for Fifth Third Bancorp Logarithm of Total Assets

VARIABLE	*COEFFICIENT*	*STANDARD ERROR*	*T-STATISTIC*	*2-TAIL SIGNIFICANCE*
Random Walk (0,1,0) Model				
C	0.0578995	0.0076243	7.5940356	0.0000
R-squared	0.000000	Mean of dependent var		0.057899
Adjusted R-squared	0.000000	S.D. of dependent var		0.048820
Standard error of regression	0.048820	Sum of squared resid		0.095334
Log likelihood	66.13431	Durbin–Watson stat		1.617936
Pure Autogression (1,1,0) Model				
C	0.0577240	0.0096036	6.0106659	0.0000
AR(1)	0.1906842	0.1592321	1.1975235	0.2385
R-squared	0.036366	Mean of dependent var		0.057731
Adjusted R-squared	0.011007	S.D. of dependent var		0.049429
Standard error of regression	0.049157	Sum of squared resid		0.091822
Log likelihood	64.77808	F-statistic		1.434063
Durbin–Watson statistic	1.961873	Prob(F-statistic)		0.238519
Pure Moving Average (0,1,1) Model				
C	0.0579665	0.0075487	7.6790154	0.0000
MA(1)	0.2340429	0.1563148	1.4972539	0.1424
R-squared	0.044309	Mean of dependent var		0.057899
Adjusted R-squared	0.019804	S.D. of dependent var		0.048820
Standard error of regression	0.048334	Sum of squared resid		0.091110
Log likelihood	67.06338	F-statistic		1.808173
Durbin–Watson statistic	2.032835	Prob(F-statistic)		0.186496
Mixed Autoregression/Moving Average (1,1,1) Model				
C	0.0579679	0.0058394	9.9270143	0.0000
MA(1)	0.5643616	0.1836929	3.0723096	0.0040
AR(1)	–0.3425083	0.2165693	–1.5815186	0.1223
R-squared	0.052260	Mean of dependent var		0.057731
Adjusted R-squared	0.001031	S.D. of dependent var		0.049429
Standard error of regression	0.049404	Sum of squared resid		0.090308
Log likelihood	65.11071	F-statistic		1.020124
Durbin–Watson stat	1.991580	Prob(F-statistic)		0.370467

Quarterly time series models could be chosen to project other variables in the Fifth Third Bancorp financial model. Some variables, for example, wages, might use moving average or autocorrelation models. The important point to be understood here is that time series analysis is straightforward when data are

TABLE 22.6 Econometric Model for Fifth Third Bancorp for Total Assets

VARIABLE[a]	*COEFFICIENT*	*STANDARD ERROR*	*T-STATISTIC*	*2-TAIL SIGNIFICANCE*
C	−13349.237	2256.0008	−5.9172127	0.0000
QFYGM3	−493.56523	111.22281	−4.4376258	0.0001
GIN	61.332821	6.0537419	10.131390	0.0000
GV(−1)	−26.488412	6.5022615	−4.0737229	0.0003
GCDAU(−1)	−79.827457	17.812206	−4.4816155	0.0001
R-squared	0.882425	Mean of dependent var		5223.044
Adjusted R-squared	0.868593	S.D. of dependent var		2717.559
Standard error of regression	985.1194	Sum of squared resid		32995648
Log likelihood	−321.4809	F-statistic		63.79424
Durbin–Watson statistic	0.742690	Prob(F-statistic)		0.000000

[a] *Variable Definitions:*
GV Change in business inventories
GCDAU Auto output final sales personal consumption expenditures
GIN Gross private domestic investment, fixed investment, nonresidential
QFYGM3 3-month Treasury bill rate, quarterly average.

DATA SOURCES: *Compustat Bank Quarterly* and *Citibase.*

available. The statistics concerning goodness of fit and significance of factors are useful diagnostics. The techniques can be readily learned from standard textbooks and good computer programs are available to estimate these models. Financial institution managers should be familiar with time series techniques.

Econometric Models. Econometric analyses use statistical techniques to relate activity or other variables to a number of economic determinants. Good econometricians start with financial economics to determine the supply–demand relations between exogenous and endogenous variables in the analysis in the form of the so-called *structural equations*. From these equations, the analyst solves for the endogenous variables, usually in *reduced-form* equations where coefficients of exogenous variables contain a variety of supply and demand response elements. In practice, financial projections are often based on *ad hoc* equation models.

We present an informal model of total assets for Fifth Third Bancorp in Table 22.6. Projections of total assets are driven by economic activity variables determining loan demand which are assumed to be exogenous, namely total investment in inventories, business fixed investment, lagged consumption of automobiles. Total assets are also assumed to be related to the level of interest rates as measured by the average 3-month Treasury bill rate each quarter. The estimation equation can be used to project total assets given assumptions about future values for business fixed investment, inventory investment, consumption of automobiles, and the future Treasury bill rate.

Our econometric model finds a strong statistical relation between the exogenous variables and total assets. The R^2 and t-tests on individual coefficients are all significant. However, absent a structural model, the results cannot be interpreted as supply and demand responses. The equation does not have as much statistical power as the simpler time-series models previously discussed. It does have the advantage of relating Fifth Third's total assets to economic variables that are important to the bank's operations, such as inventory investments by business. Future values derived using this equation require projections of all the exogenous variables in the estimated relation.

Simulation. Simulation methods relate variables of interest to other variables using relations derived from statistical, econometric, or engineering analysis. A simulation model projects financial quantities, for example insurance claims, using an analysis of the system producing values for the variable of interest. Insurance claims are a delayed reaction to total policies in force, which in turn consists of continued policies and new policies sold each period in the past. Claims losses can be simulated by relating the insurance in force and insurance sales each period to the incidence and severity of claims based on statistical analysis or actuarial estimates. Another example of simulation would be to consider our model of Fifth Third as a simulation model for projecting total liabilities, which in that model are determined by everything else since total liabilities is the plug variable.

Nonstatistical Projections

Many variables can be projected using nonstatistical methods. For example, relative price variables such as interest rates can often be deduced from market data like the term structure of interest rates or futures market data. In efficient markets, predictions of future values implicit in market data are assumed to use all available information and may be more current and reliable than projections based on historical data. In interpreting market data, biases inherent in these numbers should be considered. For example, as discussed in Chapter 13, the term structure may contain term premiums, which means that forward rates are not unbiased predictions of future spot rates.

We will use futures market projections of interest rates in our discussion of Fifth Third Bancorp. Specifically, we use the futures market price for 3-month Treasury bills as a projection of the level of future interest rates. For example, Table 20.1 in Chapter 20 provides futures prices from October 8, 1993, suggesting that Treasury bill rates will be approximately 3.2 percent in the first half of 1994. Even if other projections for variables like interest rates are used, for example from econometric models or forecasting services, future markets and other financial markets provide a useful check on those projections.

22.6 USING PROJECTIONS

Individual variables are part of complete projections. For example, in our Fifth Third Bancorp financial model, projections for the exogenous variables derived using internal or external methods are used to complete the financial projection. To illustrate this process, we used the time trend estimates for the activity variables: noninterest revenue, noninterest expense, and total assets. We used a spread over the projected Treasury bill rate for return on earning assets and yield cost of liabilities and a historical average for loss rates on earning assets. These variables are shown in Table 22.7.

TABLE 22.7 Financial Projections for Fifth Third Bancorp

1992		*1993*		*1993*	
BASIC FINANCIAL DATA		*ASSUMPTIONS*	*MOST LIKELY*	*ASSUMPTIONS*	*LOW SPREAD, LOW ASSET*
INCOME STATEMENT					
IR	694,460	E	900,944	E	693,414
IE	300,266	E	382,493	E	318,008
PLL	65,315	E	60,063	E	46,228
NIR	200,053	Trend	217,000	Trend	217,000
NIE	289,276	Trend	249,100	Trend	249,100
EBT	239,656	E	426,288	E	297,079
EAC	164,092	E	298,401	E	183,329
No. of shares (MM)	59,632		60,000		60,000
EPS	$2.75		$4.97		$3.06
Balance Sheet (PARTIAL)					
R	565,948	Restr. 6.0%	789,420	Restr. 6.0%	612,799
FA	353,466	Policy	355,000	Policy	355,000
TA	10,213,320	Trend	13,157,000	Low trend	10,213,320
BVE	1,005,165	EA, p = 33.3%	1,204,099	EA, p = 33.3%	1,127,384
Ratio Analysis					
BROR	16.32%	E 24.8%		C 16.3%	
Composed of:					
PULLTHRU ×	68.47%	Restr. 70.0%		Restr. 70.0%	
LEVERAGE ×	10.16	E 10.9		E 9.1	
EBT/TA	2.35%	E 3.2%		E 2.9%	
EBT/TA composed of:					
((IR–IE)/EA –	4.24%	E 4.3%		E 4.1%	
PLL/EA) ×	0.70%	Proj. 0.5%		Proj. 0.5%	
EA/TA +	91.00%	E = 91.3%		E = 90.5%	
(NIR–NIE)/TA	–0.87%	E –0.2%		E –0.3%	
(IR–IE)/EA composed of:					
IR/EA –	7.47%	Proj. 7.50%		Proj. 7.50%	
IE/L ×	3.26%	Proj. 3.20%		Proj. 3.50%	
L/EA	0.9908	E 1.00		E 0.98	

A = assumed value, E = endogenous value, g = growth rate, p = payout.

The financial model for Fifth Third makes clear the advantages of a coherent model for projections. First, the results are easy to read. Two projections are presented in Table 22.7: a "most likely" base case and a "low spread, low asset growth" case. The impact on earnings per share, given other assumptions, of the projections is clear. In the base case, earnings per share are up sharply from \$2.75 in 1992 to nearly \$5 in 1993, whereas with a lower spread between earning assets and liabilities and no asset growth, earnings increase to only a little over \$3.00.

The model invites calculation of many different projections. The analyst using these projections could focus on the key sources of earnings or other important variables and their sensitivity to changes in exogenous or policy variable assumptions. With no asset growth and a slightly reduced net interest margin (from 4.24 percent to 4.1 percent in the no-growth case), earnings still increase. This increase in net income, approximately \$19 million (\$183,329 – \$164,092), comes from projected reductions in the provision for loan losses and a slight improvement in burden.

Analysts use financial models to identify critical variables in projections. No model results should be taken seriously until users understand how they work and where the results are coming from. Users of models should always do the following *plausibility checks:*

1. Compare results of projections from previous periods to assure that no large or unrealistic jumps or drops take place
2. Compute and compare activity ratios to assure that projected performance does not fall outside a reasonable range of performance
3. Assure that projections are internally consistent. For example, equity will increase by retained earnings. The model in Table 22.7 uses balance sheet constraints to make total liabilities balance total assets and shareholders' equity. Since interest expense is computed in this aggregated model on total liabilities, net income and liabilities must be determined simultaneously
4. Assure that endogenous variables are reasonable.

The Fifth Third model, although not complex, appears to satisfy these checks. Analysts must always be careful when examining model results to make sure that they make sense.

The financial model can be extremely useful in valuation. For example, using the rough range of earnings per share for Fifth Third of \$3 to \$5 in 1993 and with a price–earnings multiple of around 15 for this bank, the share value could be in the range of \$45 to \$75. The sensitivity of this valuation is easy for the analyst to determine. Disaggregation and refinement of the valuation model could be accomplished with more data and focus on specific issues.

Interpreting our Fifth Third model as a simulation model as discussed above, the two projections viewed as simulations imply total liabilities (total assets minus book value of equity) of \$11,952,901 (\$13,157,000 – \$1,204,099) to \$9,085,936 (\$10,213,320 – \$1,127,384). Management could use these estimates, as well as others, to plan funding for different asset growth rates for Fifth Third. This interpretation of the model also emphasizes the many uses to which good modeling efforts can be put.

22.7 SUMMARY

Projections and the process of making projections have many uses in financial institutions. The choice and mix of models between naive, financial, econometric, or simulation models, the determination of the scope of models in terms of projection horizon and level of disaggregation, and assignment of different types of exogenous and endogenous variables allows the analyst wide flexibility in model specification, so that models can match resources available and purposes for the projections. In specifying a projection model, analysts must determine the best techniques available to project required future value, choosing among internal and external projection methods. Many techniques are available to make projections and good models have many uses in financial planning and evaluation.

DISCUSSION QUESTIONS AND EXERCISES

1. Discuss and describe the classification of the following variables into activity or relative price variables: loan demand, securities investments, loan interest rates, checking deposits, deposit interest rates, deposit fees, deposit processing costs, new policies written, mortality costs, incidence of claims, investments, return on investments, trading volume, brokerage commissions, underwriting fees, assets under management, asset management fees.
2. Assume a 5 percent growth rate in the number of two-year residential fire insurance policies written, a claims frequency of 10 percent of policies in the first year and 5 percent the second year, a growth rate of 5 percent in severity (value) of claims starting in the first year at $50,000. Assuming average premiums of $1,000 per year for two years for policies written in the first year and growth of 5 percent in new policies after that, and 5,000 policies written in the first year with 10 percent growth in policies written, project premium revenue, claims losses, and underwriting profits for years two to five. What type of projection is this and how could these values be estimated in practice?
3. What kind of a model is discussed in question 2? How could the projection be improved? What are the various variables in the analysis?
4. What additional variables would be needed to complete a simple financial model of an insurance company. What kind of variables are these?
5. Assume the following moving average and autoregression factors: $\phi_1 = .75$, $\mu = .4$, $\theta_1 = .25$. If the initial value of $X = 5$ and random shocks in three periods are 4, –3, and 2, calculate the change in variable X (ΔX) for three time periods with a (1, 1, 0) and (0, 1, 1) and (1, 1, 1) models.
6. Using the answers in question 5, calculate the projected values for the *level* of the variable X in the next three periods.
7. What value could econometric forecasting services like Wharton EFS, Data Resources Incorporated (DRI), etc., have to managers responsible for producing projections?
8. What factors determine the demand for annuities for retirement? Which of these factors are state variables, economic activity variables, relative price variables, and policy variables?

9. Discuss the appropriate projection horizon used for staffing and facilities capacity for wire transfers, loan application processing, mortgage servicing, securities trading.
10. What time series patterns would appear in charges to credit cards, credit card interest rates, merchant deposits of credit card drafts, demand for card readers, and point-of-sale terminals for credit card charges? Which types of projection methods would be relevant for each?

REFERENCES

BLACK, FISCHER. 1975. "Bank Funds Management in an Efficient Market," *Journal of Financial Economics,* 4(2), pp. 323–339.

PINDYCK, ROBERT S. and DANIEL L. RUBINFELD. 1991. *Econometric Models and Economic Forecasts* (3rd Ed.). New York: McGraw Hill Book Company.

C H A P T E R

23

Financial Institution Operating Costs

Introduction

Cost efficiency is an obvious source of value for financial institutions as with any firms. Financial institution managers must be particularly conscious of costs in today's competitive environment. Some questions good managers must address are:

- What characteristics of costs and service production are relevant to value maximizing strategies?
- How can costs be estimated?
- What does the reported evidence concerning financial institution costs suggest about cost efficiency and what issues are unresolved?

This chapter opens with a general discussion of the economics of cost functions as relevant to financial institutions. We discuss problems in cost measurement unique to financial service firms. We review standard methods of estimating costs and particular problems experienced in applying these methods to financial firms. Finally, we review the voluminous research on financial service firm costs and find that it leaves many critical questions unanswered.

23.1 COSTS AND ACTIVITIES

Costs are central to value production in all businesses. Costs determine return on investment (ROI) as shown in the simple ROI formula introduced in Chapter 2:

$$\text{Return on Investment} = \frac{(\text{Price} - \text{Cost}) \times \text{Quantity}}{\text{Investment}}. \qquad (23.1)$$

Despite the importance of costs to financial service performance, a lack of knowledge and many disagreements surround financial institution costs. Many financial service firms came relatively late—following deregulation and increased competition in the 1970s—to a sense of urgency concerning knowing and controlling their costs. The lack of urgency was partly the result of operating in protected markets with limited competition where profitability was guaranteed.

A basic disagreement among observers of the financial services industry is whether large firms are more efficient. Efficiency means lower costs. One issue is whether financial institutions, like commercial banks, have *economies of scale*. Another issue is whether there are synergies between various financial services offered by one firm or *economies of scope*. To appreciate these issues, we must review some technical details from microeconomics.

Single Product or Activity Production

With a single product or activity, economies of scale are well defined. Firms experience economies of scale when increases in their single level of activity does not raise costs proportionately. For example, if activity triples and total costs double, there are economies of scale. Diseconomies of scale occur when increases in activity levels increase costs more than proportionately, as when activity doubles and total costs triple. We show total costs for various levels of output using four different production methods in Table 23.1A.

The relation between total costs and output is called a *cost function*. Cost functions can be seen as graphs of total costs on one axis and output on the other. We show the four cost functions from Table 23.1 labeled as production methods (1) to (4) in Figure 23.1, Panel A.

Total costs can be divided into fixed and variable costs. Fixed costs do not change with activity levels. Variable costs change with changes in output or activity. Fixed costs are defined with respect to a range of activity levels and over a given period of time. For example, the leasing cost of a facility like a bank branch or teller machine does not change over the lease period whether or not the branch or machine is used a little or a lot. Over time, fixed costs can change and are not fixed if new facilities are added to handle higher volumes of activity or if leases on facilities lapse or facilities are worn out (fully depreciated) or sold. The key defining characteristic of fixed costs is that up to a point in time and level of production, facilities cost the same no matter how much activity there is. These costs are considered fixed.

Variable costs change with the level of activity. Economists call variable costs *marginal* or *incremental* costs. Marginal costs are defined:

$$\text{Marginal Cost} = \Delta TC = TC(\text{Output } X + 1) - TC(\text{Output } X), \qquad (23.2)$$

where TC(X) is total costs at output X and ΔTC is the change in total cost. Marginal costs for the four production methods are shown in Table 23.1B.

Marginal costs increase or decrease with increases in activity levels according to the underlying technology or process involved in providing the service activity. When variable costs per unit of service decrease at high activity levels,

TABLE 23.1 Costs of Four Methods of Providing Financial Activity

	METHOD			
ACTIVITY LEVEL	*(1)*	*(2)*	*(3)*	*(4)*
A. Total Costs				
0	0.00	30.00	10.00	10.00
10	10.00	34.00	11.00	20.45
20	20.00	38.00	14.00	29.80
30	30.00	42.00	19.00	38.05
40	40.00	46.00	26.00	45.20
50	50.00	50.00	35.00	51.25
60	60.00	54.00	46.00	56.20
70	70.00	58.00	59.00	60.05
80	80.00	62.00	74.00	62.80
90	90.00	66.00	91.00	64.45
100	100.00	70.00	110.00	65.00
B. Marginal Costs				
10	1.00	0.40	0.10	1.05
20	1.00	0.40	0.30	0.94
30	1.00	0.40	0.50	0.83
40	1.00	0.40	0.70	0.72
50	1.00	0.40	0.90	0.61
60	1.00	0.40	1.10	0.50
70	1.00	0.40	1.30	0.38
80	1.00	0.40	1.50	0.28
90	1.00	0.40	1.70	0.17
100	1.00	0.40	1.90	0.05
C. Average Costs				
10	1.00	3.40	1.10	2.05
20	1.00	1.90	0.70	1.49
30	1.00	1.40	0.63	1.27
40	1.00	1.15	0.65	1.13
50	1.00	1.00	0.70	1.03
60	1.00	0.90	0.77	0.94
70	1.00	0.83	0.84	0.86
80	1.00	0.78	0.93	0.79
90	1.00	0.73	1.01	0.72
100	1.00	0.70	1.10	0.65

marginal costs are said to be declining. Declining marginal costs occur as production reaches efficient levels. When variable costs increase with activity levels, marginal costs are increasing. Marginal costs might occur as facilities or personnel are strained and become inefficient. Marginal or variable costs can be constant if output levels do not affect productivity.

Average costs are total costs divided by the level of output, specifically:

$$\text{Average Cost} = \frac{\text{Total Costs}}{\text{Level of Output}} = \frac{TC}{X} \qquad (23.3)$$

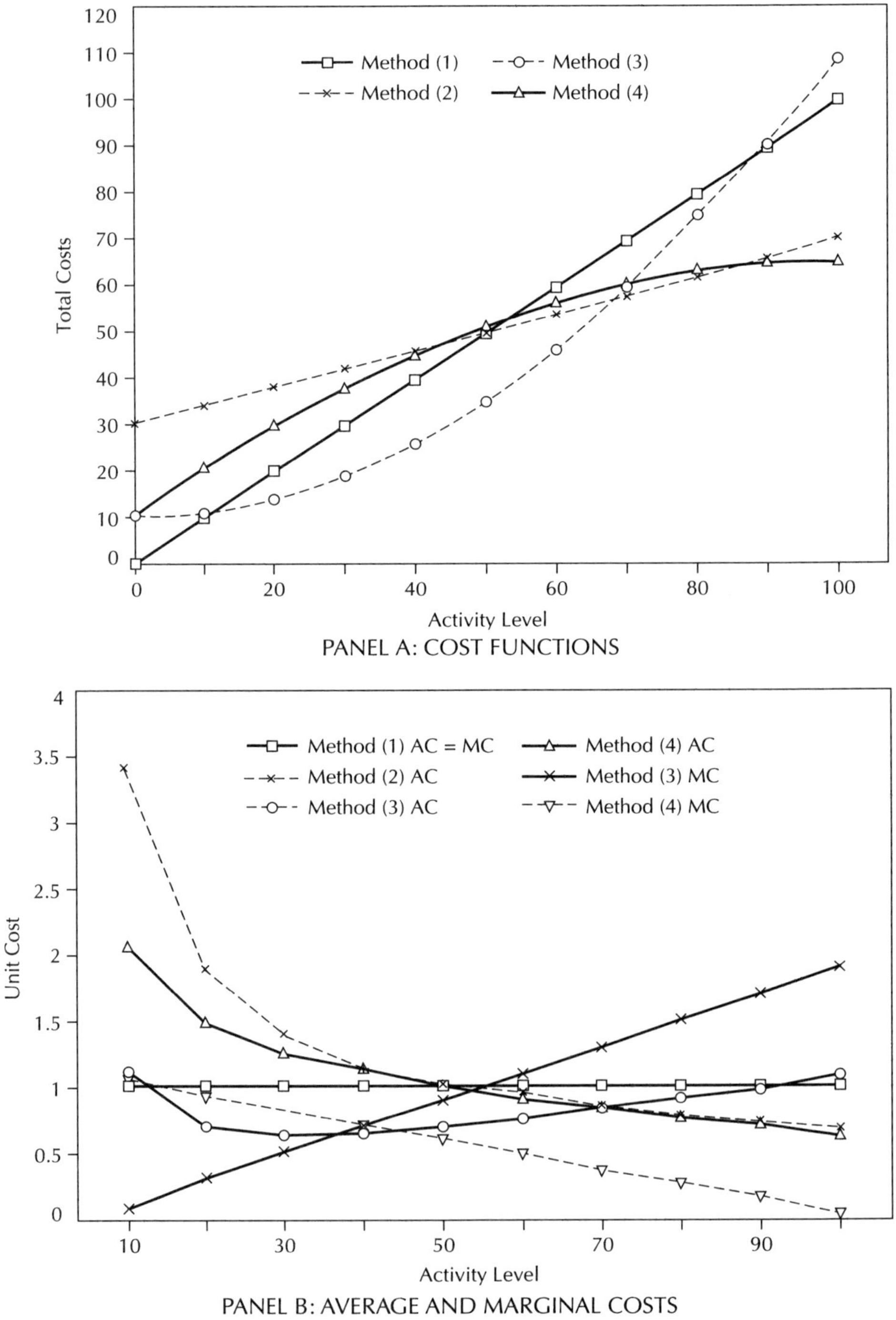

FIGURE 23.1 Cost functions and average and marginal costs

using the above abbreviations. Average costs are shown in Table 23.1C for the four production methods. Plotting average costs for different levels of output produces the average cost curve. The shape of the average cost curve relative to activity determines whether there are economies or diseconomies of scale.

Economies of scale over a range of activity levels mean that average costs per unit of activity are falling as output levels increase in that range. When average costs are falling, marginal costs per unit of activity must be below average costs. Average costs increase at higher activity levels when there are diseconomies of scale and marginal costs are above average costs. When costs and activity levels are proportional, average costs and marginal are constant. For many products and services, there may be both decreasing and increasing average costs over ranges of activity.

Figure 23.1, Panel B, shows average and marginal cost curves for activities produced with the four production methods from Panel A. Method (1) has constant marginal cost and no fixed costs so average costs and is equal to marginal cost and appears as a straight line in Panel B of Figure 23.1. Methods (2) and (3) display economies of scale since average costs are falling. Marginal costs (2) and (3) are below average costs in line with the preceding discussion. Method (3) has a so-called U-shaped cost function where average costs fall over a range of activity and then increase. Marginal costs for process (3) are below average cost over the range where average costs are falling and is above average costs when they start to rise.

If fixed costs are a large element in performing an activity and variable costs are not increasing, average costs will fall with larger outputs. In Figure 23.1, cost function (1) is a process having no fixed costs and constant variable costs. Method (2) has positive fixed costs but lower variable costs than process (1). Method (1) has constant average cost ($1 per unit). Panel B of Figure 23.1 shows that method (2) has declining average costs because fixed costs are averaged over more and more units. Average cost curves for processes (3) and (4) show different combinations of fixed and variable costs that change with the level of output.

A labor intensive operation with no equipment would be an example of a production activity with no fixed costs. A computer or machine intensive way of performing the same activity would have fixed costs. Over some levels of output, the no-fixed-cost method might have lower average costs. At higher levels, the method with fixed costs could be cheaper. We can see this with the average cost curve for cost function (2), which starts out higher than the $1 average for process (1), but falls below that average after approximately 50 units. All the processes have relatively higher or lower average costs depending on their mixture of fixed and variable costs and the level of activity.

Some observers believe that large fixed costs relative to other costs cause economies of scale in many financial services. Branch systems, clearing facilities, securities trading organizations, and so forth, require extensive data processing equipment and communications gear representing fixed costs. Personnel operating these systems require expensive training, also representing large fixed costs needed to provide these and other financial services. These services may operate at high or low activity levels with little change in costs. Many analysts assume that economies of scale are widespread in financial services, an important assumption and one we examine carefully in this chapter.

Multiple Outputs

The discussion of costs to this point considers only one output or activity. Multiple products or activities introduce a number of complications into the discussion of costs. Financial service firms typically provide a number of services representing a number of outputs or activities. We provide an example of a two-activity cost function in Table 23.2. Panel A of the table shows the costs of producing two activities A and B separately; Panels B and C show total costs of producing the two activities in different fixed ratios, 50:1 and 25:1.

TABLE 23.2 Costs of Providing Two Financial Activities

Panel A: Activities A and B Produced Independently

ACTIVITY A		*ACTIVITY B*	
ACTIVITY LEVEL	*TOTAL COST*	*ACTIVITY LEVEL*	*TOTAL COST*
0	$10.00	0	$50.00
1	11.10	50	50.08
2	12.20	100	50.20
3	13.29	150	50.38
4	14.38	200	50.60
5	15.48	250	50.88
6	16.56	300	51.20
7	17.65	350	51.58
8	18.74	400	52.00
9	19.82	450	52.48
10	20.90	500	53.00
20	31.60	1000	61.00
30	42.10	1500	74.00
40	52.40	2000	92.00
50	62.50	2500	115.00
60	72.40	3000	143.00
70	82.10	3500	176.00
80	91.60	4000	214.00
90	100.90	4500	257.00
100	110.00	5000	305.00
110	118.90	5500	358.00
120	127.60	6000	416.00
130	136.10	6500	479.00
140	144.40	7000	547.00
150	152.50	7500	620.00
160	160.40	8000	698.00
170	168.10	8500	781.00
180	175.60	9000	869.00
190	182.90	9500	962.00
200	190.00	10000	1060.00

With many outputs, total costs are the same as with one activity but average and marginal cost concepts require additional definition. With multiple activity levels, one activity number cannot be divided into total costs to obtain average costs. Discussion of costs for multiactivity firms must also account for the interrelationships between costs of different activities. A total cost graph like Figure 23.1 is not adequate to capture costs of performing two activities (For a technical discussion of multiple product cost concepts, see Baumol *et al.* 1982, especially Chapters 3 and 4).

Figure 23.2 is a three-dimensional drawing showing the total costs of producing the two activities A and B provided in Table 23.2. Figure 23.2 shows total costs as the vertical distance from the horizontal plane. Levels of two activities are shown on the two axes on the horizontal plane. If A and B are produced independently, total cost curves are defined as in Figure 23.1 as the graph above the

Panel B: B and A Produced in Proportion 50 to 1 (Ray X)

LEVEL OF ACTIVITY			
A	*B*	*TOTAL COST*	*RAY AVERAGE COST*
0	0	$60.00	—
1	50	61.17	$61.17
2	100	62.39	31.19
3	150	63.64	21.21
4	200	64.94	16.24
5	250	66.29	13.26
6	300	67.67	11.28
7	350	69.10	9.87
8	400	70.58	8.82
9	450	72.09	8.01
10	500	73.65	7.37
20	1000	91.60	4.58
30	1500	113.85	3.80
40	2000	140.40	3.51
50	2500	171.25	3.43
60	3000	206.40	3.44
70	3500	245.85	3.51
80	4000	289.60	3.62
90	4500	337.65	3.75
100	5000	390.00	3.90
110	5500	446.65	4.06
120	6000	507.60	4.23
130	6500	572.85	4.41
140	7000	642.40	4.59
150	7500	716.25	4.78
160	8000	794.40	4.97
170	8500	876.85	5.16
180	9000	963.60	5.35
190	9500	1054.65	5.55
200	10000	1150.00	5.75

TABLE 23.2 (*continued*)

Panel C: B and A Produced in Proportion 25 to 1 (Ray Y)

LEVEL OF ACTIVITY			
A	*B*	*TOTAL COST*	*RAY AVERAGE COST*
0	0	60.00	—
1	25	61.13	61.13
2	50	62.27	31.13
3	75	63.41	21.14
4	100	64.56	16.14
5	125	65.73	13.15
6	150	66.89	11.15
7	175	68.07	9.72
8	200	69.26	8.66
9	225	70.45	7.83
10	250	71.65	7.17
20	500	84.10	4.21
30	750	97.35	3.25
40	1000	111.40	2.79
50	1250	126.25	2.53
60	1500	141.90	2.37
70	1750	158.35	2.26
80	2000	175.60	2.20
90	2250	193.65	2.15
100	2500	212.50	2.13
110	2750	232.15	2.11
120	3000	252.60	2.11
130	3250	273.85	2.11
140	3500	295.90	2.11
150	3750	318.75	2.13
160	4000	342.40	2.14
170	4250	366.85	2.16
180	4500	392.10	2.18
190	4750	418.15	2.20
200	5000	445.00	2.23

horizontal A and B axes. If produced jointly, total costs represent the vertical distance of a point on the *cost surface* from the horizontal plane. Cost functions with multiple products become cost surfaces in three-dimensional or higher dimension space. Many activities conceptually could be drawn in multidimensional space where total costs are associated with combinations of outputs.

The A and B activities in Table 23.2 shown in Figure 23.2 could be two financial services, like balance accounting and check clearing. Line X from the origin represents combinations of B and A in fixed proportions 50 to 1 given in Panel B of Table 23.2, for example 1000 checks cleared and 20 customer accounts or 2000 checks and 40 accounts, and so on. Line Y represents a different proportion, 25 to 1, given in Panel C of Table 23.2, for example 1000 checks and 40

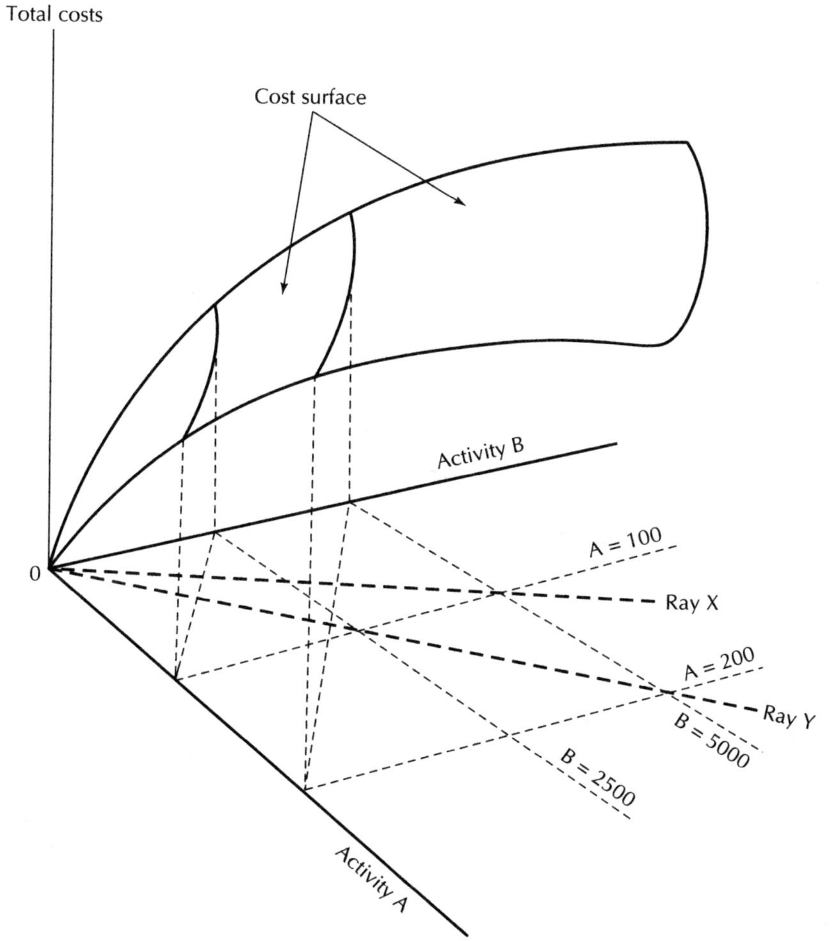

FIGURE 23.2 Multiple activity cost functions and cost surface

accounts or 1500 checks and 60 accounts. Straight lines from the origin like X and Y in Figure 23.2 are *rays* from the origin representing different proportions of two activities.

Although many activities are possible, two activities are sufficient to define terms and illustrate important cost concepts with multiple outputs in a graph. The total costs of producing A and B can be looked at from a number of angles, as illustrated in Panels A through E of Figure 23.3. Panels A and B show the total cost curves for output combinations along rays X and Y. Each combination of A and B along rays X and Y is an output *bundle* of A and B in fixed proportions. A bundle consists of customer accounts and checks processed. In the figure, bundles on ray X have twice as much B activity as bundles along ray Y. If we count each bundle by how many units of A are included (account balances), we can see that total costs are higher along ray X because of the higher B activity levels in those bundles.

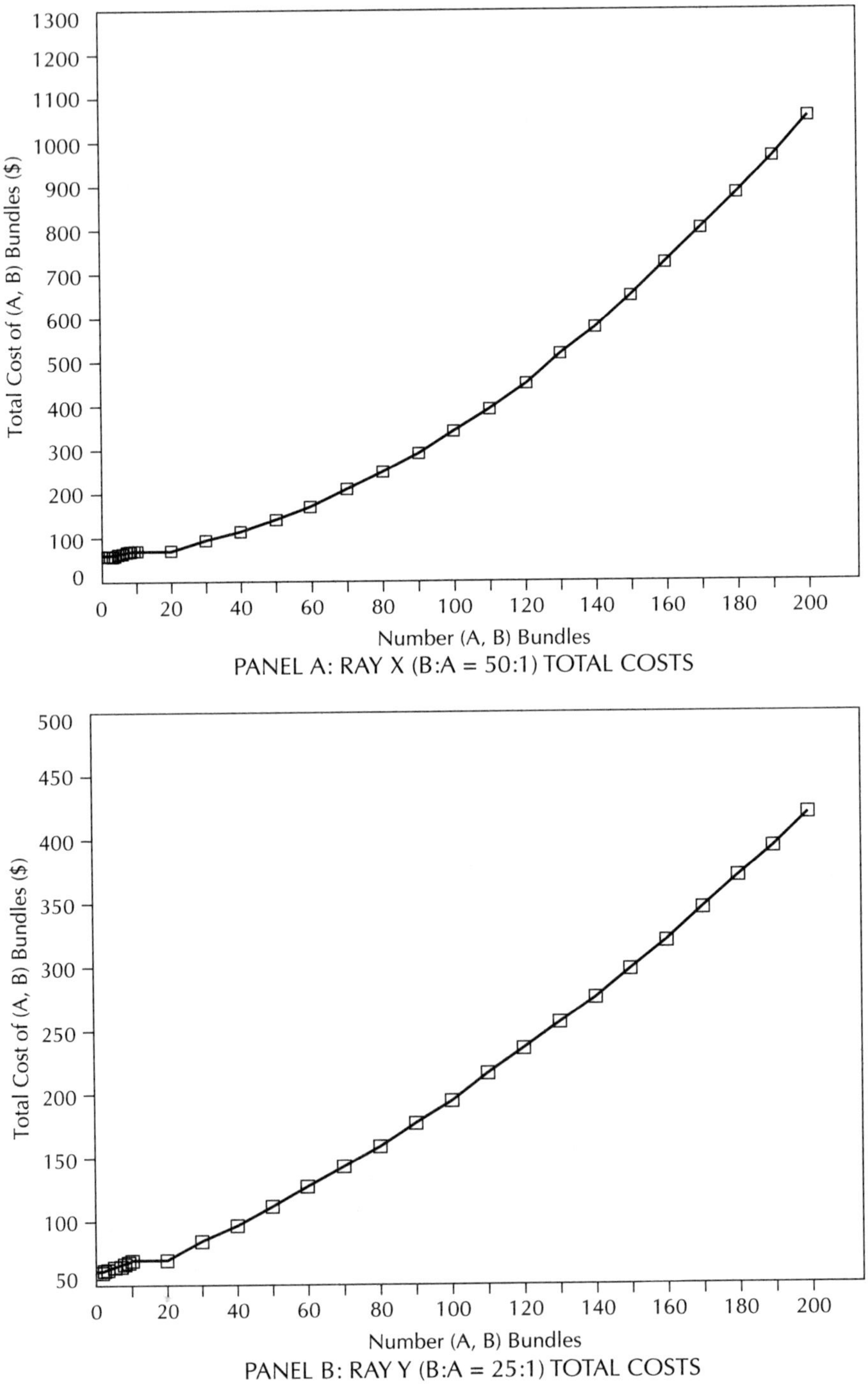

FIGURE 23.3 Multiple activity cost functions

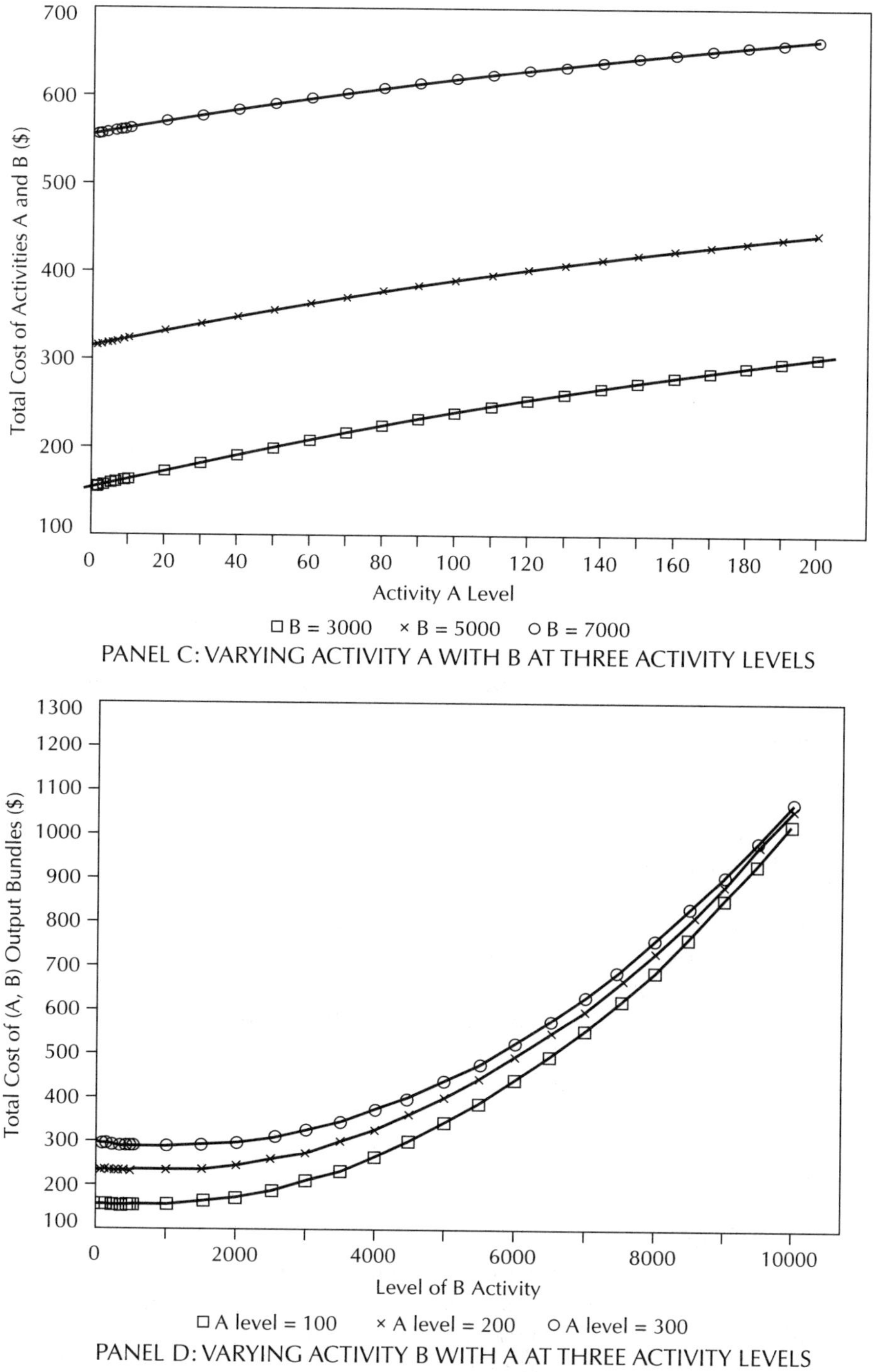

FIGURE 23.3 *(continued)*

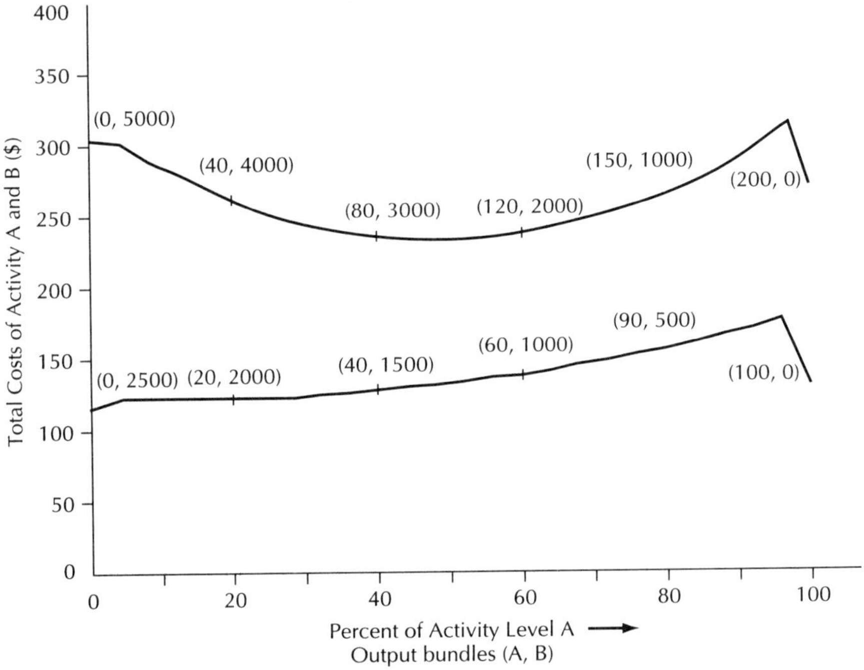

PANEL E: VARYING PROPORTIONS OF ACTIVITIES A AND B

FIGURE 23.3 *(continued)*

Another way to look at costs of producing two activities is to hold one activity level fixed while varying the other activity. One example is to hold account balances fixed while varying checks processed or vice versa. Total costs in this case are the intersection of the cost surface in Figure 23.2 with lines representing fixed amounts of one activity. For example, the middle line in Panel C shows total costs when fixing activity B at 5000 units and varying activity A from 0 to 200 units, corresponding to the line marked (B = 5000) in Figure 23.2. Panels C and D in Figure 23.3 show total costs of several bundles of producing activities A and B holding B constant in Panel C and A constant in Panel D.

Another way to look at the cost surface in Figure 23.2 is to change the proportions of activities. We can look at total costs from 100 percent concentration in one output to 100 percent in another and varying proportions in between. For example, the lower cost curve in Panel E of Figure 23.3 provides total costs of moving from 100 percent concentration in activity A (an (A,B) bundle of (100,0)) to 100 percent concentration in B (an (A,B) bundle of (0,5000)) and intermediate points in between, for example (50,2500). The left end of the lower total curve represents 100 accounts and no check processing and the right end 5000 checks and no accounts. The second and higher total cost curve represents doubling the outputs of A and B. Since the upper curve dips in the middle, it is described as *concave* with respect to joint production. The shapes of these curves are very different, with the lower scale operations displaying a *convex* shape (bulging upward).

If activities or outputs are in fixed combination, they can be considered a *composite good* and their average costs can be computed along a ray. *Ray average costs* represent average costs for fixed combinations of outputs over a range of output levels. The last column of Panels B and C of Table 23.2 show ray average costs computed for the X and Y combinations of A and B. These average cost curves are shown in Figure 23.4, Panel A for ray X and Panel B for ray Y. Ray X shows a U-shaped average cost curve, reaching a minimum at 50 (A,B) bundles (produced at a ratio of 50:1), whereas for ray Y the average costs decrease to 110 to 140 bundles.

Economies of scale are defined for ray average costs in the same way average costs are defined for a single activity except that the level of output is a combination of activities. If average costs decline for a fixed combination of goods along a ray over some range of output, then producing more of the activity will reduce average costs and result in economies of scale. Ray Y combinations of (A,B) show economies of scale over nearly the entire output range shown, thus favoring larger size activity levels. But when average costs increase over a range of outputs or activity levels, there are diseconomies of scale over that range of activity. Ray X shows diseconomies of scale after 50 bundles.

The concept of ray average costs and economies of scale for combinations of activities is valid for specified combinations of goods. In Figure 23.3, minimum average costs for combination X and Y are achieved at different levels of the single activities A and B. If X and Y represent different production methods—one capital intensive and one labor intensive—cost minimization must consider the combination of outputs in determining the lowest cost method of production.

When producing multiple outputs, the interrelationship of joint production become important. When changing the proportions or scope of activities produced, proportions of inputs and even the technology used for efficient production may change. An important concept in considering the effect of joint production of two or more activities is termed *economies of scope,* which in the case of two activities is technically defined as:

$$\text{Cost}(A,0) + \text{Cost}(0,B) - \text{Cost}(A,B) > 0, \qquad (23.4)$$

meaning that A and B can be produced jointly at lower total cost than independently. For example, using data from Table 23.2, producing 100 units of A and 5,000 units of B independently has a total cost of $415 ($110 and $305 from Panel A of the table) but they can be produced jointly for $390 (Panel B) at a point on ray X. Cost of joint production of activities A and B show economies of scope.

Economies of scope may not be true everywhere on a total cost surface for multiple outputs. In our example, producing 10 units of A and 250 units of B on ray Y can be done at lower cost independently than jointly, that is for $71.78 as opposed to $71.65. Economies of scope cannot be simply taken for granted as characteristic of joint production of two or more outputs with any combination of activities (along any ray) at any scale of production (distance from the origin).

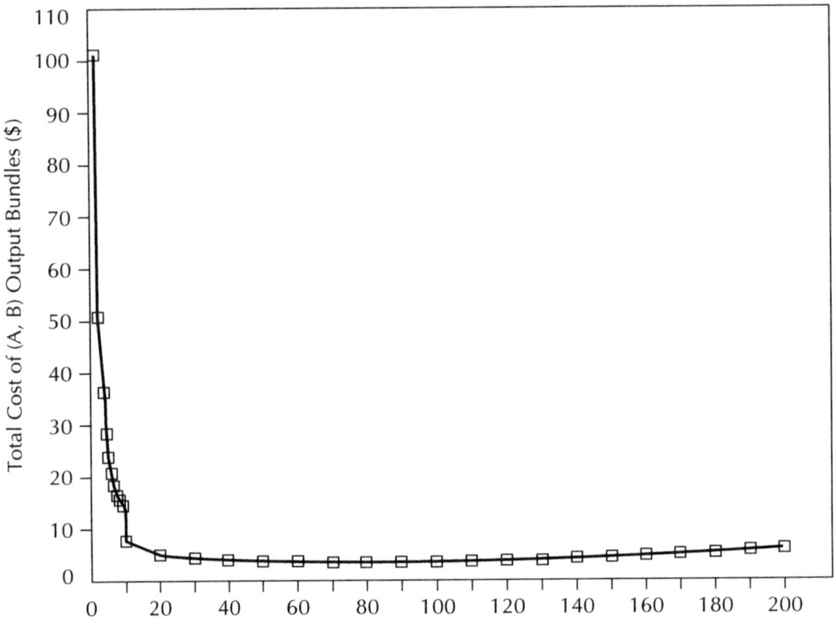

PANEL A: (B,A) AT 50:1

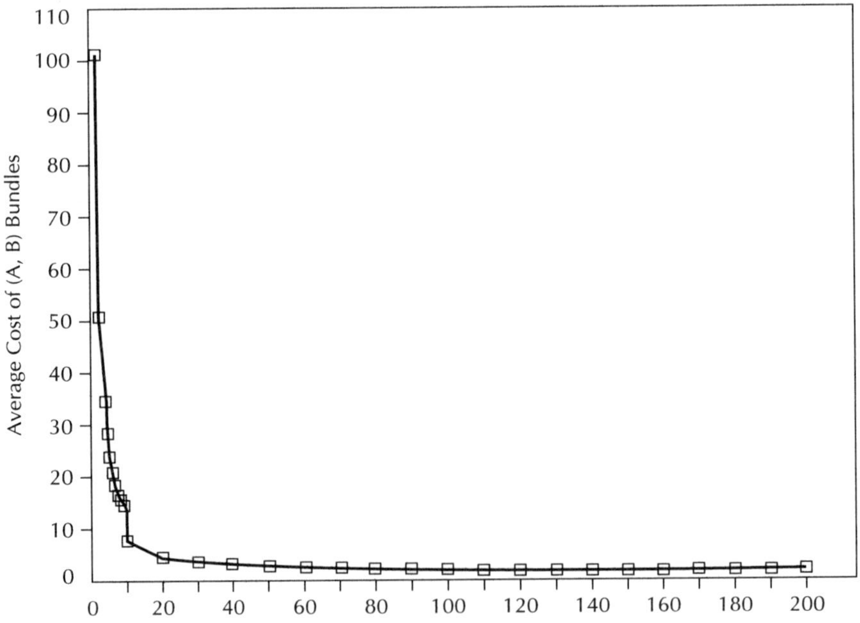

PANEL B: (B,A) AT 25:1

FIGURE 23.4 Ray average costs

Minimizing costs depends on the proportion of outputs and the scale of operations.

One important aspect of the analysis of total costs not considered to this point is *efficiency*. In our discussion, we have assumed that the total costs at each point of the cost surface for each combination of multiple outputs (A and B in our example) are the *minimum total costs,* the result of efficient production. But note that points along the total cost surface can represent different efficient—cost minimizing—technologies. For example, efficient production methods to produce combinations of goods in the proportions represented by rays X and Y in our example may represent two ways of producing activities A and B. The cost efficient method used for production combinations along ray X might use a mainframe computer with low skill clerical employees and the method for combinations along ray Y might use more highly trained employees using microcomputers.

Thus we can identify two kinds of inefficiency. The first type of inefficiency is using the wrong technology for a given output combination, for example a mainframe and low-cost clerical employees to produce an output combination along ray Y. Economists refer to this type of inefficiency as *allocative inefficiency* because inputs into production are not cost minimizing. The other type of inefficiency is simply not minimizing costs or producing maximum output with a technology. This type of inefficiency is sometimes called *X-inefficiency,* especially when unnecessary costs benefit management at the expense of investors and customers of the firm. X inefficiencies are presumed to be more prevalent in noncompetitive or regulated markets where price competition does not enforce discipline on managers. We will return to these concepts below.

The total cost surface in Figure 23.2 represents the lowest total costs management can achieve, thus assuming that management is aware of and knows how to implement the best technological solutions to producing each output bundle. Implicitly, management must understand the technology and have the incentive to minimize costs. In practice, there are many reasons why total costs could be higher than those implied by the efficient cost surface for producing multiple outputs. Poor incentives or uninformed management may mean that theoretically available economies of scale and scope will not be realized.

We emphasize two important attributes of costs with multiple outputs in financial services using Figures 23.2 to 23.4. First, the low cost technology depends on both the proportions of outputs needed and the scale of operations. This is true in all financial services with multiple outputs. Using our customer accounts and check processing example from above, a low volume of check users in small deposit-taking firms, perhaps serving a special market niche, may require a different technology from a large scale operation with high activity in accounts. With multiple outputs, simple discussions of economies of scale are not meaningful. Managers must consider the composition of output and the scale of output.

Second, an important characteristic of the cost functions shown in the figures is that economies of scale do not have a simple interpretation and vary along different combinations of output or rays in the total cost diagrams. Ray average costs can reflect economies of scale in producing combinations of activities but the relevance of these combinations cannot be determined independently of customer demand or marketing plans. Economies and diseconomies of scale do not simply occur with large size when there is more than one activity.

Although this discussion is general for any business or economic activity, the analysis of cost curves for financial services is particularly critical for the managerial and policy issues confronting this industry in the future because of the pervasiveness of joint production. Managers wish to create value for investors by producing services at low costs and policymakers strive for economic efficiency through laws and regulation. Application of these cost concepts and implementation of cost measurement to achieve these objectives are difficult in financial services for many reasons. We deal with conceptual problems first and then analyze problems in cost measurement in subsequent sections of this chapter.

23.2 INPUTS INTO PRODUCTION OF FINANCIAL SERVICES

A conceptual framework to assess the nature of costs in financial services is essential to understanding cost factors determining profitability. Our discussion of costs in financial services begins with a brief review of the six activities in the value chain for financial services as introduced in Chapter 2. This classification of activities is useful in a commonsense consideration of what inputs go into producing financial services. The goal is to develop fresh insights into cost efficiency and the nature of inputs required to provide financial services.

Pricing/Term Setting

The activity of setting prices and terms, as analyzed at length in Part II, is an important source of value. When performed effectively, this activity is based on research, negotiation, or application of advanced analytical techniques. In all cases, labor and human capital are important inputs. Training, experience, and careful evaluation of complex technical, market, and customer-specific information are required in most financial service pricing problems.

In retail markets, pricing and other terms are intrinsic to product design. In wholesale markets, more complicated and specific problems must be analyzed and negotiated. In all financial services, from new credit vehicles to sophisticated risk management products, innovation is an important source of short-term excess returns and value. Competitive advantage requires offering products for which there is little competition at the terms and prices demanded.

What are the cost elements in this activity? Product pricing and negotiations are labor intensive activities requiring skilled, creative, entrepreneurial people. Although some computer and communications experience may be required, the predominant costs in pricing and term setting are labor and human capital.

Marketing/Information

Developing information about demand and competition for financial services and telling potential customers about useful services at reasonable terms requires communication. In most wholesale financial services, communication is between institutional customers, usually represented by officials, and financial service firms, often represented by calling officers or other officials. This communication is a labor intensive activity. In order to communicate effectively about complex financial needs requiring sophisticated products or services, experienced and educated people are required.

Marketing and information gathering for retail markets also rely on personal customer contacts. In retail financial services that require data input or routine communication, modes of communication that save on labor costs through minimization of labor time, level of worker training, or substitution of labor by other means, can be used. Labor may be minimized by using automated response systems or by employing telephones and computers to program marketing calls in telemarketing. Training for workers may be reduced by relying on computerized artificial intelligence or other analytical devices, such as credit scoring. Capital in the form of computers and communication equipment may substitute for branches with high labor costs to reduce labor expenses.

Labor, skilled or unskilled, cannot be eliminated from the marketing and information activities required to produce retail financial services using capital intensive methods. Systems minimizing or substituting for labor must be designed and tested by skilled professionals. Systems relying on lower trained and less expensive labor must be supervised by motivated management staffs. Labor costs are large in marketing and information activities in both the wholesale and retail markets and hence are a major cost item for financial services.

Monitoring/Controlling

Keeping track of contract provisions as is required by monitoring can use computers or labor intensive systems. When contracts are violated, control procedures such as special collection efforts or legal actions can be triggered automatically by computer systems or introduced after careful analysis and judgment of the best strategies for dealing with unwanted outcomes of financial relationships. In all cases, monitoring and control activities require managerial review and motivated personnel to be an effective source of value. Retail and wholesale markets may require different approaches, given differences in the number and homogeneity of contracts or relationships in that market. Both require substantial labor inputs.

In keeping track of timeliness of loan or insurance premium payments in retail services, computerized accounting systems can flag late or missing payments and produce exception reports. Well-designed systems ensuring a high level of contract performance must be created by programmers and systems analysts with a complete understanding of both the financial products and their customers. Systems must be updated and changed to respond to changes in the economic environment, the market, and regulation. At some point, the functioning of the system must be assured by motivated management. Often computerized systems require substantial clerical and customer-contact staff to input results and ensure compliance.

Although computerized and otherwise automated monitoring and control systems may reduce labor inputs or replace expensive professional staff time with less skilled labor, the design and management of these systems typically require management of sophisticated system development and maintenance personnel and management of large clerical staffs. To be cost effective, systems substituting capital for lower cost labor do not avoid problems of management of large and expensive support personnel and managerial talent.

In wholesale markets, contract enforcement through monitoring and control activities is more likely part of a complex customer relationship. Specific contract language and complex specific business circumstances determine the most appropriate course of action for management and officials involved. For example, should a loan for which interest is late and covenants violated be called and a firm liquidated and work-out specialists be brought in or should the loan be renegotiated? These decisions are as important as the original credit decision and may involve accountants, attornies, and other professionals. Legal action as part of controls can be extremely expensive and cause greater losses than nonenforcement of contract terms. Clearly these actions require trained, experienced personnel. Monitoring and controlling specific institutional contracts, such as credit instruments, insurance policies, and underwriting services, are labor intensive activities.

Production/Delivery

Activities associated with production and delivery of financial services include staffing branches, back offices, computer centers, distribution systems, communication facilities, and all the other required support for officials of financial firms generating credit instruments, securities exchanges and issues, insurance policies, transaction processing, asset management services, or information and advice. Modern communications and computing technology have probably had a greater impact on the production and delivery of financial services than on any other link in the value chain.

All of the production and delivery systems associated with financial services have been heavy users of low-skilled clerical and secretarial workers. The back offices of many banks and securities firms are staffed with part-time workers and students. Many of these production systems, like loan or check processing or securities delivery, rely on large-scale computer systems. Many of the production and delivery systems for financial services consist of data entry, document preparation, information retrieval, and report generation, based on large integrated databases.

Despite the heavy investment in computers and often other physical assets such as branches, telecommunications equipment, trading floors, trucks and airplanes, labor is an important input into production and delivery activities. As with monitoring and control systems, talented system design and management personnel are required to manage the many people involved in operating and maintaining large-scale systems, despite the heavy use of capital-intensive technology. Nearly all financial institutions report salaries and wages as the largest noninterest expense, followed by equipment, communications, and space expenses.

Funding/Investing

Finding the cheapest funds or highest return investments to perform financial services requires personnel trained and experienced in evaluation and use of financial market technical, market, and customer-specific information. The communications and data processing revolution has only increased the range of alternatives available to managers responsible for the financing activities of financial institutions. Management of funding and investing activities is extremely labor intensive. Salaries and responsibilities of chief financial officers of financial institutions are evidence of both the importance of this activity and the high labor cost of efficient operations.

Funds or investments can be made more cheaply in large lots. Some believe that economies of funding and investing may lower costs from large-scale operations. Management time and transactions costs are definitely reduced for large financial transaction amounts. These considerations argue for economies of scale for large-scale funding or investing operations. Offsetting these cost-reducing aspects of large-scale funding and investing activities are the management control problems associated with large numbers of sophisticated financial personnel handling large sums of money. Costs from errors in judgment or losses from uncontrolled activity by officials increase with transaction size as well.

Professional labor costs are important in the costs of funding and investing activities of treasury and trading areas of financial institutions. Aside from financial costs determined by market conditions (interest expense and so on), portfolio management, transactions, and safekeeping are the large costs. The question is whether economies in these costs extend to very large amounts of funds associated with larger financial institutions. Given that management of professional organizations characteristic of the treasury and investment divisions of financial firms is complex, it is likely that economies of scale are exhausted at a smaller asset size than the largest banks and other financial institutions, perhaps $500 million (see McAllister and McManus (1993) for an economies of scale discussion focusing on bank portfolio (total assets) size). In competitive financial markets with active asset management available for small amounts of funds and competition for trading and safekeeping services, lower labor costs in funding and investing are probably not a source of economies of scale for financial firms with billions of dollars in assets.

Risk Bearing/Sharing

Risk management activities have become an important aspect of financial service firm operations. In managing financial market risks, new markets (e.g., the swap market) and risk management instruments (e.g., options and futures) have increased the necessary training and experience of personnel assigned to supervise and implement financial risk strategies. Most of the preceding discussion of labor costs with funding and investing activities applies to the management of financial risk.

Financial risks are large but are not the only risks confronting financial institution managers, as discussed in Part IV of this book. For example, liquidity and operating risks may be shifted or shared but may not be reduced through large size. These risks may or may not be reduced from diversification or redundancy with large scale operations if those operations are highly focused on providing services to narrowly defined markets, such as mortgage lending. In other cases, as discussed in Part II of this book, benefits of diversification can be achieved without large size, for example by diversifying credit risk with loan sales and participations or use of reinsurance. The benefits from diversification can be achieved by the effective use of new risk management instruments. In any case, all risk management activities require trained and experienced personnel who must be motivated, managed, and monitored.

Summary of the Costs in Value Chain Activities for Financial Firms

The above discussion is intended to highlight the inputs into performance of the activities in the value chain for financial services. Aside from such financial costs as interest or market value losses, inputs into these activities tend to be dominated by labor expenses. The labor is either professional labor or management and low-skilled labor. Computers and modern technology in communications have not reduced labor expenses so much as they have increased the services possible to financial service firm customers. We noted in Chapter 1 that employment in financial services is increasing.

Managing production of services in labor intensive operations limits the possibility of economies of scale. Identifying talent, motivating people, and monitoring performance are not economic functions that increase in efficiency with the size of operations. Large financial corporations must be broken down into specialized divisions and functional areas, and coordination and communication between parts of the organization then become more difficult. Flexibility to exploit opportunities or avoid problems is limited if layers of corporate structure must be penetrated to gain approval for decisions. Furthermore, rogue or dissident management groups can often underperform or create problems that go undetected in large bureaucratic organizations dealing in complex transactions and information. The importance of primarily variable labor costs in financial institutions offsets the likely importance of the fixed costs of facilities which some argue are the source of economies of scale.

23.3 FINANCIAL SERVICE FIRM OUTPUTS

Output measurement in any industry is difficult. For example, auto manufacturers produce sedans, sports cars, light trucks, and other vehicles. Output can be measured simply as the number of vehicles produced, but such a simple output measure misses wide differences in the attributes of individual units. Quality of output is another difficult to measure aspect of production. Recalls or future repair records are not reflected in a unit count of production although they reflect the quality of units produced. Crude as they are, though, manufacturing output measurements are precise relative to financial service output measurement.

Despite the dominance of service industry output in advanced economies and the growth in service sectors discussed in Chapter 1, controversy surrounds measurement of service sector output.[1] Estimates of productivity growth prepared by government agencies—in the United States, the Commerce and Labor Departments—can show opposite results. For example, for the period 1979 to 1989, the Bureau of Economic Analysis (Commerce Department) found no change in productivity in banking in the United States, but the Bureau of Labor Statistics (Labor Department) saw an important annual 2.3 percent increase.

The cost functions discussed previously relate total costs to output. In the case of multiple outputs, a cost surface relates the cost of efficient input combinations to levels of activity or outputs. Measurement of costs requires a clear definition of output. Definition of output for financial services, as with many service industries, is not only *not* well-defined, as we have discussed, but whatever measures are used are determined by data availability rather than carefully designed output measurement proxies.

Most analysis of financial institution costs has been directed at commercial banking, but much of this literature is relevant to other financial service firms as well. Berger and Humphrey (1992) distinguish three general approaches to output measurement in banking: (1) the asset approach, (2) the user cost approach, and (3) the value added approach. We discuss each of these in the following, noting that all are inadequate but that some are better proxies of true output than others.

The asset approach in the context of banking argues that banks produce bank assets, primarily loans, using labor and capital inputs, which cause operating costs, and financial inputs in the form of deposits and borrowed money, which cause interest costs. Many studies use loans as a measure of outputs and include deposits as well as other physical inputs as inputs (for example, Kolari and Zardkoohi (1987) and references). The limitations of measuring output in terms of asset amounts, or even number of assets (like loans) are obvious. Financial services can be provided to a greater or lesser degree with different assets and of course financial services are provided with liabilities, like transaction accounts.

A more flexible approach is the user cost approach, which does not prespecify whether assets or liabilities are inputs or outputs but rather determines whether they make a net contribution or reduction to revenues or returns (see Hancock (1985), a seminal contribution to this approach). User costs for a given period are defined as:

$$u_{x_i} = \rho - h_{x_i} \tag{23.5}$$

where user cost u for an asset or liability x_i is the firm's opportunity cost ρ minus the holding cost h for that asset or liability (see Fixler and Zieschang (1992) for a

[1]This discussion draws heavily on the "Introduction" and financial service chapters in Griliches (1992), which are recommended for an advanced level summary and review of the issues in financial service firm output measurement.

detailed discussion). The holding cost includes interest and gains received minus loan losses. If user costs are negative, products such as loans, are outputs because negative costs are positive returns. If user costs are positive, the products such as deposits are inputs. Assignment of inputs and outputs is a function of whether user costs are positive or negative as determined by the factors shown in the formula. Categorization of inputs and outputs is determined by the data but can change through time. Although the user cost approach is flexible, it emphasizes financial quantities such as balance sheet items and interest costs and does not focus on financial institution operations resulting in services not reflected on the balance sheet.

The value-added approach considers all financial activities to have the potential of providing outputs in terms of services and it concentrates on the operating costs of financial institutions. For example, using Federal Reserve Bank cost statistics discussed in the next section, capital and labor costs are allocated to financial data. According to one study, demand deposits in 1988 accounted for 36 percent of bank value added and commercial and industrial loans for 14 percent. These value-added figures are identified with output of services (This classification draws on a discussion by Berger and Humphrey (1992).)

Although all three approaches to output measurement have been widely used, they are all problematic from the managerial decision point of view emphasized in this book. The question of relevance to management is: "What are we good at?", which can mean "What can we produce at low cost relative to competitors?" Answers to these questions are used to organize activities in the value chain to create the most value in financial services.

In most financial service firms, operating costs incurred by financial service firms are due to hiring resources necessary to produce activities, like negotiating or monitoring, which are the source of competitive advantage. Many of these activities do have measurable outputs, as when successful negotiations produce a deal, the number of loan deals could be counted as output. But the negotiated terms in a deal can also be a source of value, as we discussed in Part II. Counting the pages of loan contracts or the number of covenants does not seem adequate to capture this value creation. Moreover, credit arrangements take place over time, with monitoring, controlling, and other activities that affect value creation occurring during this time. Some of these activities can also be counted, such as number of inventory counts or loan file reviews. All financial service activities could be scrutinized for measurable activities, but item counts seem an inadequate output measure for many of these activities.[2]

For some financial service activities, such as transaction processing, item counts may serve effectively as an output measure: checks cleared is a reasonable measure of output from a check clearing system. But narrow output definitions do not do justice to complex financial services. A transaction account, to

[2]See Bresnahan *et al.* (1992), Fixler and Zieschang (1992), and Mester (1992) for innovative attempts to measure financial service output in terms of the information value and monitoring services produced in securities trading and banking segments.

continue the example, includes many other services, such as check cashing, balance maintenance, balance inquiries, noncheck transfers, automatic payment, and so on.

Strategic Importance of Operating Costs for Financial Services

Enumeration of activities to relate outputs to costs of providing financial services is conceptually feasible, but given the inadequacy of some enumerations as output measures and the expense of making enumerations, the focus on output measurement may not always be justified by the refinement of costs estimates they provide. Despite the importance of cost control as a source of value, a pragmatic approach may be all that management can take to the problem of identifying efficient production of financial services.

The critical issue for management is whether a firm has a competitive advantage in some activities required for financial service production. If the firm does not have a cost advantage as determined from estimates of cost functions, market competition, or common sense, management must decide whether to have other suppliers perform the activity, to jointly provide the service with contractors, or to drop the service from the financial institution's marketing strategy. These questions may not have clear answers, but intelligent managers must be aware of the relevance of the questions and the implications of crude measures of costs, and must be alert to confirming or denying evidence in any form which suggests answers, such as an inability to match competitors' terms.

Two issues related to costs have dominated much of the strategy question for financial service firms: economies of scale and economies of scope. If there are economies of scale, large size provides a competitive advantage. If there are economies of scope, cost-minimizing output combinations can define a profitable strategy. In the next section we review approaches to estimating cost functions for financial institutions. Estimates of these function have been used to evaluate scale and scope economies in financial institutions. We warn readers that the answers are not clear and the evidence is clouded by the problems of input and output definition and measurement we have discussed.

23.4 ESTIMATING COSTS

Three approaches are used to estimate the costs of business activity and have been applied to financial service firms. These approaches are: (1) *cost accounting,* (2) *statistical cost analysis,* and (3) *process analysis.* None of these approaches has satisfactorily answered the strategic questions raised in the previous section. Creative managers will want to improve on the standard approaches in future cost analyses. Most of the published work using these approaches has analyzed costs of commercial banking. We discuss each cost estimation approach using banking as examples in the following discussion, but emphasize that these approaches are equally relevant to nonbanking financial services.

Cost Accounting

Cost accounting uses information generated by firms' accounting systems. The objective of cost accounting is to measure costs associated with some business unit, product, or project, called a *cost object* (see Horngren and Foster (1991) for an extended treatment). Costs incurred during the accounting period are allocated to the cost object. Incurred costs are either direct costs, which can be associated with the cost unit, or indirect costs, which can be allocated to the unit on some pro rata basis.

The best widely available example of cost accounting for financial service firms is the *Functional Cost Analysis* (FCA) study by Federal Reserve System. The FCA is a voluntary effort in which participating banks complete surveys of their activities, financial data, and cost allocations to fifteen cost objects grouped into three overall functions: (1) fund-providing functions, composed of demand deposit, time deposit, and nondeposit funds; (2) fund-using functions, composed of investments, and real estate, installment, credit card, commercial, agricultural, and construction loans; and (3) non–fund using functions, including international, safe deposit, trust, and data services for banking and nonbanking and customer use.

As an illustration of cost accounting, Table 23.3 provides selected tables from the "National Average Report: Commercial Banks" for 1989 from the FCA banks for demand deposits and installment loans. The tables illustrate several requirements for cost accounting of narrowly defined functions. For example, officer and employee salary costs are allocated to functions according to time allocations of personnel collected or made by accountants in participating banks.[3] Indirect costs such as publicity and "other operating expenses" are assigned to each function based on sharing rules (based on historical data). Finally, in order to compute item costs, compound output measures are calculated. For demand deposits, a "weight unit" of transactions (on-us debits, deposits, transit checks, and account maintenance) is used to compute average costs. For installment loans, costs are assigned to acquisition and maintenance of loans.

The FCA is valuable to participating banks, for each bank receives an individual report in which it is compared to similar banks, thus providing management with a means of comparing average costs. Similar cost analysis is possible for all financial institutions. Total allocated expenses to functions can be compared and the estimated average costs for some outputs, like loan acquisitions, can be calculated.

Cost accounting like the FCA has several shortcomings as a basis for strategic decision making where costs are an important factor. First, the costs are historical accounting costs, not current economic costs. Second, costs are average costs and not marginal costs useful in making incremental pricing or product design decisions. Third, average costs such as those calculated in the FCA are based on arbitrary weighted output measures and overhead allocations based on

[3]This discussion is based on the *Instruction Manual* for the FCA from the Federal Reserve Bank (1988).

TABLE 23.3 Federal Reserve Bank Functional Cost Analysis, 1989

Panel A: Demand Deposit Function

	49 BANKS		120 BANKS		37 BANKS	
	DEPOSITS UP TO $50M		*DEPOSITS $50M–$200M*		*DEPOSITS OVER $200M*	
1 Weight-units	3,539,499		10,529,939		40,948,354	
Volume						
2 Cash and due from banks	$1,263,681	12.45%	$3,285,409	11.38%	$16,267,761	12.78%
3 Cash items in process of collection	217,714	2.14	1,138,001	3.94	11,799,355	9.27
4 Funds invested in portfolio	8,669,219	85.41	24,455,204	84.68	99,175,685	77.94
5 Total demand deposits	$10,150,614	100.00%	$28,878,615	100.00%	$127,242,801	100.00%
Income						
6 Service and handling charges	$182,224	1.80%	$401,437	1.39%	$1,501,107	1.18%
7 Other income	14,571	.14	56,961	.20	310,211	.24
8 Total income	$196,796	1.94%	$458,398	1.59%	$1,811,319	1.42%
Expense						
9 Officer salaries	$41,578	.41%	$120,936	.42%	$467,918	.37%
10 Employee salaries	124,550	1.23	380,709	1.32	1,598,317	1.26
11 Fringe benefits	42,735	.42	131,444	.46	545,770	.43
12 Salaries and fringe, subtotal	$208,863	2.06%	$633,089	2.19%	$2,612,005	2.05%
13 Data services	37,660	.37	143,439	.50	765,859	.60
14 Furniture and equipment	32,338	.32	98,396	.34	354,658	.28
15 Occupancy	32,358	.32	114,025	.39	481,963	.38
16 Publicity and advertising	9,010	.09	26,358	.09	93,797	.07
17 Printing, stationery and supplies	22,846	.23	50,311	.17	173,089	.14
18 Postage, freight and deliveries	16,887	.17	49,763	.17	191,980	.15
19 Other operating expenses	62,882	.62	173,689	.60	769,569	.60
20 Total operating expense	$422,844	4.17%	$1,289,069	4.46%	$5,442,919	4.28%

TABLE 23.3 (*continued*)

	49 BANKS		*120 BANKS*		*37 BANKS*	
	DEPOSITS UP TO $50M		*DEPOSITS $50M–$200M*		*DEPOSITS OVER $200M*	
Earnings						
21 Net earnings before interest	–$226,048	–2.23%	–$830,671	–2.88%	–$3,631,600	–2.85%
22 Interest expense	235,288	2.32	696,243	2.41	2,349,498	1.85
23 Net earnings	–$461,336	–4.54%	–$1,526,914	–5.29%	–$5,981,098	–4.70%
Memoranda						
24 Portfolio income credit	772,482	7.61	2,228,734	7.72	9,442,603	7.41
25 Net earnings after portfolio credit	$311,146	3.07%	$701,820	2.43%	$3,441,505	2.70%
Number of demand deposit personnel						
26 Officers		1.37		3.88		13.24
27 Employees		9.52		29.12		105.62
28 Total personnel		10.89		33.00		118.87
29 Memo—tellers (included in employees)		5.38		15.09		52.63
30 Number of banking offices		2.20		4.41		14.89
31 Checking exp recovery from service chgs		46.54%		35.56%		33.28%
Composition						
32 Checking accounts	$9,834,348	96.88%	$28,040,625	97.10%	$123,773,758	97.27%
33 TT&L and official checks	316,265	3.12	837,989	2.90	3,469,042	2.73
34 Total demand deposits	$10,150,614	100.00%	$28,878,615	100.00%	$127,242,801	100.00%

Panel B: Demand Deposits—Special Checking Account Analysis

	9 BANKS		29 BANKS		6 BANKS	
	DEPOSITS UP TO $50M		DEPOSITS $50M–$200M		DEPOSITS OVER $200M	
1 Special checking weight-units						
Account data						
2 Number of accounts	807		1,360		3,567	
3 Average size of account	$606		$805		692	
4 Cost per weight-unit (cents)		10.88		12.50		9.70
Volume						
5 Cash and due from banks and cipc	$64,819	13.25%	$139,075	12.70%	$415,656	16.85%
6 Funds invested in portfolio	424,249	86.75	956,098	87.30	2,051,063	83.15
7 Total special checking volume	$489,068	100.00%	$1,095,173	100.00%	$2,466,718	100.00%
Income						
8 Service and handling charges	$47,033	9.62%	$87,444	7.98%	$193,468	7.84%
Expense						
9 On-us debits	$36,428	7.45%	$56,866	5.19%	$88,255	3.58%
10 Deposits	18,362	3.75	24,011	2.19	46,588	1.89
11 Transit checks	$4,132	.84	6,962	.64	8,333	.34
12 Account maintenance	22,094	4.52	97,496	8.90	204,441	8.29
13 Total operating expense	$81,016	16.57%	$185,336	16.92%	$347,617	14.09%
Earnings						
14 Net earnings	$33,983-	6.95-%	$97,892-	8.94-%	$154,148-	6.25-%
Memoranda						
15 Portfolio income credit	37,383	7.64	83,984	7.67	195,544	7.93
16 Net earnings after portfolio	$3,399	.70%	–$13,908	–1.27%	$41,396	1.68%

TABLE 23.3 (*continued*)

	9 BANKS		*29 BANKS*		*6 BANKS*	
	DEPOSITS UP TO $50M		*DEPOSITS $50M–$200M*		*DEPOSITS OVER $200M*	
	Earnings per account per month					
Income						
17 Service and handling charges		$4.85		$5.36		$4.52
Expense						
18 On-us debits		$3.76		$3.48		$2.06
19 Deposits		1.90		1.47		1.09
20 Transit checks		$.43		.43		.19
21 Account maintenance		2.28		5.97		4.78
22 Total expense		$8.36		$11.36		$8.12
Earnings						
23 Net earnings		–$3.51		–$6.00		–$3.60
Memoranda						
24 Portfolio income credit		3.86		5.15		4.57
25 Net earnings after portfolio credit		$.35		–$.85		$.97
Activity	Activity per account per month					
26 On-us debits	177,077	18.28	252,775	15.49	497,808	11.63
27 Deposits	41,126	4.24	52,069	3.19	128,222	3.00
28 Transit checks	36,637	3.78	60,585	3.71	80,180	1.87

Panel C: Installment Loan Function

	48 BANKS		*119 BANKS*		*37 BANKS*	
	DEPOSITS UP TO $50M		*DEPOSITS $50M–$200M*		*DEPOSITS OVER $200M*	
1 Number of loans outstanding	869		3,038		13,050	
Volume						
2 Consumer installment loans	$3,550,653	83.44%	$11,157,062	79.85%	$51,889,858	64.26%
3 Check credit loans	55,218	1.30	605,979	4.34	5,071,276	6.28
4 Consumer loans, subtotal	$3,605,871	84.74%	$11,763,041	84.19%	$56,961,133	70.54%
5 Commercial, equipment and other loans	620,751	14.59	1,744,080	12.48	20,624,978	25.54
6 Floor plan	28,685	.67	465,003	3.33	3,166,879	3.92
7 Commercial loans, subtotal	649,435	15.26%	$2,209,083	15.81%	$23,791,857	29.46%
8 Total installment loans	$4,255,307	100.00%	$13,972,124	100.00%	$80,752,991	100.00%
Income						
9 Consumer installment loans	$416,792	11.74%*	$1,318,405	11.82%*	$5,948,698	11.46%*
10 Check credit loans	4,125	7.47 *	84,774	13.99 *	668,948	13.19 *
11 Commercial, equipment and other loans	65,000	10.47 *	237,755	13.63 *	2,501,021	12.13 *
12 Floor plan	2,404	8.38	57,369	12.34	383,857	12.12
13 Interest and discount, subtotal	$488,320	11.48%	$1,698,304	12.15%	$9,502,525	11.77%
14 Other income	27,368	.64	65,677	.47	223,188	.28
15 Total income	$515,688	12.12%	$1,763,981	12.62%	$9,725,713	12.04%
Expense						
16 Officer salaries	$49,056	1.15%	$119,584	.86%	$412,838	.51%
17 Employee salaries	21,559	.51	74,581	.53	376,083	.47
18 Fringe benefits	15,834	.37	46,067	.33	205,780	.25
19 Salaries and fringe, subtotal	$86,449	2.03%	$240,232	1.72%	$994,702	1.23%
20 Data services	14,806	.35	35,347	.25	191,333	.24
21 Furniture and equipment	8,774	.21	20,730	.15	71,917	.09
22 Occupancy	11,436	.27	30,803	.22	137,774	.17
23 Publicity and advertising	5,541	.13	16,258	.12	62,113	.08
24 Other operating expenses	36,470	.86	98,783	.71	399,910	.50
25 Total operating expense	$163,477	3.84%	$442,153	3.16%	$1,857,750	2.30%

TABLE 23.3 (*continued*)

	48 BANKS		*119 BANKS*		*37 BANKS*	
	DEPOSITS UP TO $50M		*DEPOSITS $50M–$200M*		*DEPOSITS OVER $200M*	
Earnings						
26 Net earnings before losses	$352,211	8.28%	$1,321,828	9.46%	$7,867,963	9.74%
27 Net losses	19,616	.46	84,560	.61	334,301	.41
28 Net earnings	$332,595	7.82%	$1,237,268	8.86%	$7,533,662	9.33%
Memoranda						
29 Cost of money	313,213	7.36	971,200	6.95	5,627,915	6.97
30 Net earnings after cost of money	$19,383	.46%	$266,068	1.90%	$1,905,747	2.36%
Miscellaneous data						
Number of installment loan personnel						
31 Officers		1.42		3.41		11.52
32 Employees		1.53		5.34		22.41
33 Total personnel		2.95		8.75		33.93
34 Number of tellers (included in employees)		.47		1.02		3.10
35 Number of banking offices		2.21		4.43		14.89
36 3-year average loan losses	$28,048	.66%	$74,720	.53%	$262,340	.32%

*Gross yield

Panel D: Installment Loan Data

	48 BANKS	*119 BANKS*	*37 BANKS*
	DEPOSITS UP TO $50M	*DEPOSITS $50M–$200M*	*DEPOSITS OVER $200M*
Number of loans outstanding			
1 Consumer installment	752	2,405	9,002
2 Check credit	61	369	2,511
3 Commercial, equipment and other	53	242	1,227
4 Floor plan	4	22	309
5 Total	869	3,038	13,050
Average size loan			
6 Consumer installment	$4,724	$4,638	5,764
7 Check credit	900	1,644	2,020
8 Commercial, equipment and other	11,824	7,212	16,804
9 Floor plan	7,735	21,242	10,238
10 Total	$4,895	$4,600	6,188
Number of applications processed			
11 Consumer installment	691	1,944	7,129
12 Check credit	10	160	630
13 Commercial, equipment and other	64	147	634
14 Floor plan	11	100	824
15 Total	776	2,351	9,218
Loans made percent of applicants			
16 Consumer installment	76.20	72.03%	60.44%
17 Check credit	85.60	97.41	69.26
18 Commercial, equipment and other	73.92	94.65	80.94
19 Floor plan	175.62	104.23	87.15
20 Total	77.53	76.54%	64.84%
Number of loans made			

TABLE 23.3 (*continued*)

	48 BANKS	*119 BANKS*	*37 BANKS*
	DEPOSITS UP TO $50M	*DEPOSITS $50M–$200M*	*DEPOSITS OVER $200M*
Number of loans made			
21 Consumer installment	527	1,400	4,309
22 Check credit	9	156	437
23 Commercial, equipment and other	47	139	513
24 Floor plan	19	105	718
25 Total	602	1,800	5,977
Number of loan payments collected			
26 Consumer installment	7,857	27,745	103,731
27 Check credit	509	4,153	26,118
28 Commercial, equipment and other	504	2,180	13,407
29 Floor plan	32	207	1,999
30 Total	8,902	34,284	145,254
Production data			
31 Volume of loans per officer ($000)	$3,000	$4,095	$7,010
32 Loans made per officer	424	528	519
33 Loans outstanding per person	295	347	385
34 Applications processed per person	263	269	272
35 Loans made per person	204	206	176
36 Payments per employee	5,820	6,419	6,481

Panel E: Installment Loans—Unit Cost

	48 BANKS	*37 BANKS*
	DEPOSITS UP TO $50M	*DEPOSITS OVER $200M*
Allocation of installment loan expense		
1 Acquisition expense	$74,928	$926,686
2 Maintenance and liquidation expense	88,549	931,064
3 Total	$163,477	$1,857,750
Unit cost calculations		
4 Acquisition expense	$74,928	$926,686
5 Number of loans made	602	5,977
6 Cost to make a loan	124.49	$155.04
7 Maintenance and liquidation expense	$88,549	$931,064
8 Number of payments collected	8,902	145,254
9 Cost to collect a payment	$9.95	$6.41
Factors used in calculation of breakeven points		
10 Cost to make a loan	$124.49	$155.04
11 Cost to collect a payment	$9.95	$6.41
12 Loan loss rate: 3-year average	.66%	.32%
13 Cost of money rate	7.36%	6.97%
14 Annual percentage rate on amount loaned		
15 Number of payment periods		

SOURCE: Selected data from Federal Reserve Board of Governors, "National Average Report: Commercial Banks," for FCA banks, 1989.

comparables or experience not relevant to new initiatives. Finally, in reflecting reported accounting performance of financial firms, costs derived from cost accounting may not reflect efficient production or costs associated with a changed market environment or mix in outputs.

Statistical Cost Estimation

Statistical cost analysis estimates the relation between total costs and output using econometric techniques. For example, in many studies least squares regression analysis is used to estimate the best functional relationship between total costs and output. Multivariate regression analysis allows incorporating many variables into the relations to adjust for output mix and input amounts and prices.

Ad hoc Cost Functions. In statistical cost estimation, the choice of the functional form is very important. In some practical applications, functions relating costs to output are simply chosen for convenience. For example, a simple linear regression estimates an intercept a and slope term b for costs as a function of output:

$$TC = a + bX \tag{23.6}$$

where TC is total costs, X is output, and a and b are estimated. A linear cost function has constant marginal costs (the slope or b). A linear cost function implies decreasing average costs over all output ranges whenever the intercept term (fixed costs captured in the intercept a) is positive.

Other cost functions can be used. Common cost functions are the quadratic and cubic, written as follows:

$$TC = a + bX + cX^2 \tag{23.7}$$

$$TC = a + bX + cX^2 + dX^3. \tag{23.8}$$

A quadratic cost function can be concave or convex, implying falling or increasing average costs and economies or diseconomies of scale. At some output range, quadratics become dominated by the square term and can become negative if c is negative or very large if c is positive in equation (23.7). Cubic cost functions can be U-shaped over some range, demonstrating both economies and diseconomies of scale, but at some output will also be dominated by the highest power term. These functions are not satisfactory for many purposes because they may have extreme values when evaluated outside the estimation sample. They are also atheoretical in relating costs to outputs.

Production Functions and Cost Functions. Often cost functions are derived from production functions linking output to inputs. An example of a common production function is the Cobb–Douglas production function, which relates output to inputs as follows:

$$Y = AL^{\alpha}K^{\beta} \tag{23.9}$$

where L and K are inputs (labor and capital are often used) and α and β are parameters. If $\alpha + \beta = 1$, output is characterized by the constant returns to scale. If

$\alpha + \beta > 1$, there are economies of scale in that output increases more than proportionally to inputs, and the opposite is the case if the parameters sum to less than one.

Cost functions can be derived from production functions if the firm is assumed to maximize efficiency. Total costs in the two input case can be written:

$$TC = wL + rK, \tag{23.10}$$

where w and r are the costs associated with using different levels of L and K. By optimizing the production function with respect to inputs and substituting optimal input combinations into the cost function, a cost function can be derived. In the case of Cobb–Douglas, the logarithmic form of the cost function becomes:[4]

$$\ln TC = a' + b'\ln Y + c'\ln w + d'\ln r. \tag{23.11}$$

In this form, output and factor prices are used to explain costs of different firms or the same firm at different points in time if the firm is economically efficient. This function can be statistically estimated from data on input prices, output, and total costs. Statistical tests can be constructed to test whether $\alpha + \beta > 1$, that is, whether there are economies of scale.

Translog Production and Cost Functions. Cobb–Douglas production functions are limited because they imply diseconomies or economies of scale at all output levels. Cobb–Douglas functions can also only have one output. Many cost studies use other forms for the cost function. More general production functions and cost functions that allow multiple outputs and U-shaped costs curves have wider application. The most common function in studies of banking and other financial institution costs is the "transcendental logarithmic" or *translog* function.[5] This cost function in a two output case, where Y_1 and Y_2 are the outputs, can be written:

$$\begin{aligned}\ln TC = {} & a + bY_1 + c\ln Y_2 + d\ln w + e\ln r + f\ln Y^2{}_1 \\ & + g\ln Y^2{}_2 + h\ln w^2 + i\ln r^2 + j\ln w\ln Y_1 + + k\ln w\ln Y_2 \\ & + l\ln r\ln Y_1 + m\ln r\ln Y_2 + n\ln Y_1\ln Y_2 + o\ln w\ln r.\end{aligned} \tag{23.12}$$

In the simple two output, two input case shown in equation (23.12), the parameters a, b, c, and so forth, fifteen in all, must be estimated in regression analysis. Such an estimation uses logarithms of output measures, input prices, their squares, and all possible cross products. A fairly large sample must be available to estimate this many parameters.

More complex translog cost equations can and have been used to estimate cost surfaces with more than two outputs and with more than two inputs, but they obviously get much more complicated in terms of the number of parameters (a, b, c, etc.) to be estimated. All versions of the translog cost function include levels, squares, and cross products of the output and input price variables. The

[4]See Kolari and Zardkoohi (1987), Chapter 2, or Pindyck and Rubinfeld (1989), Chapter 7 and Appendix, for derivations.

[5]The translog cannot be derived directly from a production function except as an approximation. See Kolari and Zardkoohi (1987), p. 45.

advantage of the translog cost function is that it is U-shaped. This more general shape allows ray economies and diseconomies of scale over different output ranges. It is also used by many analysts to calculate economies of scope for financial service firms when total cost comparisons include positive levels of all outputs.[6]

The translog cost function has been criticized by McAllister and McManus (1993) because it imposes a U shape on total costs. When the cost function is estimated for banks of different size classifications, the low point of the U is reached at different levels. These authors argue that U-shaped total cost functions estimated in studies using smaller banks, such as those participating in the FCA study having less the $1 billion in assets, cannot be compared to those studies using banks having more than $1 billion in assets. Different samples with different low points in U-shaped cost functions yield contradictory evidence on the relevance of economies of scale in banking.

Process Analysis

Process analysis consists of the careful measurement and analysis of narrowly defined processes necessary to perform an activity, such as demand deposit processing. Process analysis focuses on the physical inputs such as capital and labor required to produce carefully specified activities. Time and motion studies, which analyze the amount of labor and the time taken to accomplish tasks, is an input into process analysis. This approach is closer to industrial engineering than accounting and takes a much more microeconomic look at the costs of particular functions.

Process analysis has the advantage of not being distorted by overhead allocations, required for cost accounting, or assumptions about error terms or efficiency, required for statistical cost analysis. Managers benefit from the close analysis of production technology and cost estimates can be varied over a wide variety of operating environments to assess costs and resource needs. The importance of resource availability to production capacity is highlighted by process analysis.

Process analysis can also be used to evaluate *shadow costs,* defined as the costs of resource limitations in terms of lost profits. If values can be attached to outputs, given the relation of output to inputs provided by process analysis, the change on the value of output by incremental relaxation of input restrictions can be calculated. Incremental profits are identified as the opportunity costs of resource limitations. By comparing input costs to shadow costs of resource limitations, managers may be able to identify costly bottlenecks in service production.

Process analysis is limited to narrow applications of well-defined production of outputs. Usually, the production technology is linear, meaning the outputs are proportional to variable inputs. The relation between inputs and outputs may be difficult and expensive to establish clearly. These relations, as we shall see, are critical to the accuracy of cost estimates derived from process analysis.

[6]Specialized firm costs cannot be used in the translog cost function because it is multiplicative in outputs (see Berger *et al* (1993)), p. 225.

Osborne (1982) provides an example of process analysis applied to demand deposit processing. The process analysis he uses is readily applicable to other routine transaction processing financial services, for example claims processing or securities clearing. More complex financial activities such as price and term negotiations or monitoring activities could be analyzed in a similar form but since labor costs in these activities vary so much and there are many variables determining measures of output, such as how many covenants in a loan agreement, the best use of process analysis would seem to be in routine operating activities.

In Osborne's analysis, demand deposit processing occurs within five cost areas: (1) the depositor, (2) the teller, (3) the check processing contractor, (4) the back room, and (5) everything else—in this case the clearing system. There are two transaction items: teller items and nonteller items. Costs are analyzed and estimated for contractor's services, teller handling, back-room handling, statement mailing, and shipping. Outputs (cost objects) are account balance services and account activity (teller and nonteller items).

Process analysis requires minimum labor, capital, and space requirements for each activity. For example, Osborne assumes teller handling requires t_T minutes of teller employee time costing e_T cents per minute for each teller transaction. In addition, a teller window capital cost is computed as the rental value of the space and capital improvements required for a teller to perform teller transactions kK_T. Tellers can perform a maximum number of transactions per time period M at a teller window. The total teller items requiring handling per month is H_T.

Osborne's example assumes tellers take 2.2 minutes per transaction, labor time at prevailing teller wage rates costing \$.068 per minute. Teller windows have a maximum capacity of 5000 items per month. A teller window occupies space worth \$400, estimated as the value of safe-deposit boxes that could occupy the same space as a teller's window. In this analysis, the cost of teller items is:

$$C = .15H_T + 400u\left(\frac{H_T}{5000}\right), \qquad (23.13)$$

where u is the minimum number of windows required to handle teller item volume. For example, a volume of 5,000 items has teller costs of \$1,150 per month, while 8,000 items costs \$2,000, requiring two teller windows.

The total cost in Osborne's process analysis of demand deposit processing is the sum of the five separate cost areas. Because of capacity restrictions, such as teller maximum or machine maximums in other processes, the average cost function for each activity in terms of output will have spikes where additional resources, like teller windows, are needed to handle higher volumes. The total cost function will include spikes coming from restrictions in all activities analyzed. For example, spikes at 5001, 10001, 15001, and so on, teller items will occur because a new teller window is needed at each of those levels of teller item handling.

Since outputs are typically proportional to inputs in process analysis except for capacity constraints producing spikes in cost functions, economies of scale will be determined by the relation of costs of expanding capacity, such as leasing a new teller window, and variable costs, such as teller time. Economies of scope will only exist if facilities can be shared to produce more than one output. Process analysis may be instructive for management in understanding determinants of costs in precisely defined areas, but the assumed cost, time, and capacity numbers will determine the importance of scale and scope economies.

Cost Analysis in Practice

In many real applications, some or all of the three approaches to estimating costs are used together. For example, many statistical cost estimations have been based on the FCA data, which are derived from accounting data. The FCA data, as we have discussed, depend on time allocations similar to those required for process analysis. For managers, the importance of knowing costs requires that creative use of all potential sources of information be made to assess marginal and average costs of providing financial services.

23.5 EMPIRICAL ESTIMATION OF COSTS AND IMPLICATIONS

The research on financial institutions is voluminous and is reviewed in several places.[7] In this section we review and critique briefly the published literature estimating financial institution cost functions. The summary conclusion is that managers of financial service firms have a lot to learn about the costs of providing financial services. Not only are marginal costs estimated crudely, but the question of existence or nonexistence of economies of scale and scope is open. Because of the labor intensivity of financial services, presumptions of scale economies must be tested rigorously. Managers assuming the existence of scope economies must be careful to incorporate the influence of output mix, as discussed with our example cost functions.

All cost studies use cost and output data for many financial institutions, usually several banks. Most studies assume that banks are efficient by using the cost functions derived explicitly from production functions, as in the Cobb–Douglas case discussed previously, or implicitly, as in the translog case. In estimating regression equations, an error term is added to the equations. A least squares estimation program minimizes the sum of the least squares. Other estimation techniques optimize estimation by alternative criteria, such as maximizing the likelihood function or probability of the parameters correctly producing the sample. Most regression techniques fit cost curves with roughly equal positive (higher cost) and negative (lower cost) departures from the line. Several authors reviewed in Berger *et al* (1993) have pointed out a shortcoming of this approach when financial institutions are inefficient.

Inefficiency means financial institutions do not combine inputs to minimize cost for given output levels. Since efficiency means minimum costs, departures

[7]See Kolari and Zardkoohi (1987) for banks and, more recently, see the *Journal of Banking and Finance,* "Special Issue on the Efficiency of Financial Institutions," edited by Berger *et al* (1993) for all financial institutions, including banks.

from the minimum costs should all be positive. Several analysts have dealt with this problem using regression analysis not assuming symmetric error terms or using nonparametric techniques, for example assuming that the lowest cost firms are efficient and comparing their costs and activities with others.

Berger *et al* (1993) reviewed these studies. They found that this research has produced estimates of bank efficiency in the range of 68 percent (Grabowski 1993) to 88 percent (Pi and Timme (1993)), meaning that efficient firms' costs are somewhere between two-thirds and 88 percent less costly than average banks. The most efficient credit unions are about 20 percent less costly than average inefficient credit unions. Efficient life insurance firms appear on average to be half as costly as average insurance firms. These results are controversial but suggest widespread inefficiency in the financial services industry.

Results on scale and scope economies are also controversial. Most financial institution cost research until recently has concentrated on banking. In banking, recent work has extensively employed the translog cost function discussed earlier. Economies of scale disappear at fairly low size for studies using smaller banks, typically relying on FCA data. For example, Berger *et al* (1993) report that average costs are minimized for banks with assets in the range of $75 to $300 million in assets, very small by international standards. When analyzing banks over $1 billion in assets, McAllister and McManus (1993) found constant average costs after $10 billion in assets, again small in terms of multinational banks. Berger *et al* (1993) found limited evidence for economies of scale in other financial services. Finally, other studies of insurance industry (e.g., Geehan (1977)) and securities industry (e.g., Goldberg *et al* (1991)) costs suggest little evidence of economies of scale or scope.

Additional evidence on the relation of size and cost efficiency can be obtained from analysis of mergers. Again, most of the published research deals with banks. For example, Cornett and Tehranian (1992) and Berger and Humphrey (1992) both examined post merger performance of commercial banks, using large samples of bank combinations. Both studies report that based on many operating characteristics (such as cash flow) or operating ratios (such as return on assets), only modest (if any) improvements in bank performance are detected after mergers. The implication of this is that larger size is not a source of cost efficiency and may be considered further evidence supporting the absence of economies of scale in banking.

Finally, market performance of financial service firms belies the hypothesis that large firms are more efficient as investments than smaller firms. Analysis of financial firms in the *Fortune Service 500* through 1993 reveals that the three largest U.S. bank holding companies—Citicorp, Bank America, and Chemical—ranked 80, 73, and 75 respectively out of 100 based on their ten-year total return to investors (dividends plus gains). Smaller banks, like Fifth Third (fifty-fifth in size) and State Street (fortieth) ranked first and second based on ten-year total returns. These top performing banks had assets between $10 and $16 billion, and the largest banks had assets between $140 to $214 billion. The best total returns of the seven largest thrifts reporting ten-year total returns was Washington Federal, with total assets of $2.7 billion compared to the largest thrift, H. F. Ahmanson, which ranked sixth out seven, and had total assets of $48 billion. The top ranked firm on the basis of total return from the largest diversified financial firms in the *Fortune 500* was Old Republic of Chicago with assets of $4 billion. The three largest diversified financials aside from Federal National Mortgage Association, a quasi-private firm, ranked 29, 32, and 26 out of 35.

Financial services are labor intensive organizations as stressed above. Large scale organizations are not necessary more efficient. Motivating and controlling people in large organizations is difficult. The probability of rogue operations or shirking is increased as the depth and breadth of a firm's operations increase. There may be economies of scale and scope in financial services, but managers building strategies on the assumption of cost efficiencies from large size coming either from growth or acquisition should analyze the evidence carefully.

23.6 SUMMARY

Improved knowledge of operating costs is critical for financial institution managers. Management's objective is to understand a firm's cost curve or cost surface to exploit economies of scale and scope. Managers can approach cost estimation using several techniques, including cost accounting, statistical cost estimation, and process analysis. Reported research results leave many cost-related questions open to managers of financial institutions. The evidence suggests that many firms are inefficient and that economies of scale and scope are minor or at least elusive sources of value. The reported evidence on financial institution costs is not persuasive for many reasons. Financial firm managers must be creative in estimating and assessing their costs in the future.

DISCUSSION QUESTIONS AND EXERCISES

1. Compute total costs for the following cost functions for output X at levels of 10, 20, 30, and so forth to 100:

   1. $TC_1 = 150 + .75*X$
   2. $TC_2 = 50 + .10*X + .05*X^2$
   3. $TC_3 = 200 + .5*X - .01*X^2$.

   What kind of cost functions are these? Which function is low cost over what range of output? How do these cost functions perform at higher levels of output, such as 200 or 1000?
2. Calculate the marginal costs from the three cost functions in question 1. Characterize these as constant, declining, or increasing cost functions.
3. Calculate average costs for the three cost functions in question 1. Do the marginal costs in question 2 conform to the average cost curves as discussed in the text? Do any of the cost functions display economies or diseconomies of scale? Over what range of outputs?
4. Economies of scope are sometimes referred to as cost synergies. Discuss two (or more) financial services offered by a single financial firm like a bank, broker, or insurance company in terms of the cost determinants of these services and the likelihood of cost synergies in providing these services.

5. If two financial service firms of equal size with different output mixes of two services C and D (output bundles of 10:1 (C:D) and 20:1 merge, what can you say about the merged firm output mix (assuming no change in their business from the merger)? Assuming each firm produced 10,000 C, draw their pre- and post-merger outputs on a diagram in terms of rays.
6. How could the cost surface over the rays in question 5 explain how the merged firm had reduced or increased costs? Show the implications for the cost surface of economies of scope.
7. If mainframe computers in one method of producing a financial service are a fixed cost of $100,000 per year and need operators costing $25,000 per year for each 100 units of output, and another method uses personal computers costing $2,000 per year and uses professionals costing $75,000 per year for each 100 units of output, at what output levels is one method better than another? Can you cite examples where these two methods might capture different financial services?
8. Assume a process analysis reveals that a facility costing $300 per month (30 days) can handle 500 transactions priced at $1 per transaction a day with operators who can process 200 transactions in an eight-hour day and make $10 per hour. Draw the total cost function for production levels up to 2000 transactions assuming operators can use more than one machine and can work part time. What is the marginal cost at 100, 500, 800, and 1000 transactions? If you have only one facility, what revenues are lost if demand over 500 transactions must be turned away? How does the analysis change if operators can only use one machine during a day or cannot work part time?
9. The user cost of loans is –10 percent and deposits +5 percent. Which is an input and which an output? Explain what this concept of inputs and outputs means. Could it be possible for a low-cost provider of deposits to have a user cost of –2 percent? What would be the outputs of this firm?
10. Why might cost efficiencies not be reflect in stock market performance? What other sources of value can offset cost inefficiencies? Can you use these arguments to explain mergers in financial institutions or the performance of the largest financial firms discussed in the text?

REFERENCES

Baumol, William J., John C. Panzer, and Robert D. Willig. 1982. *Contestable Markets and the Theory of Industry Structure*. New York: Harcourt Brace Jovanovich, Inc.

Bresnahan, Timothy F., Paul Milgrom, and Jonathan Paul. 1992. "The Real Output of the Stock Exchange," Chapter 5 in Griliches (1992), pp. 195–216.

Berger, Allen N. and David B. Humphrey. 1992. "Measurement and Efficiency Issues in Commercial Banking," Chapter 7 in Griliches (1992), pp. 245–300.

Berger, A. N., W. C. Hunter and S. G. Timme (eds.). 1993. "The efficiency of financial institutions: A review and preview of research past, present, and future," *Journal of Banking and Finance* 17, Nos. 2-3 (April), pp. 219–220.

Cornett, M. M. and H. Tehranian. 1992. "Changes in Corporate Performance

Associated with Bank Mergers," *Journal of Financial Economies,* 31, pp. 211–234.

FEDERAL RESERVE BANK. 1988. *Instruction Manual for Uniform Preparation of Schedules and Assembly of Required Data: Functional Cost Analysis.*

FIXLER, DENNIS J. and KIMBERLY D. ZIESCHANG. 1992. "User Costs, Shadow Prices, and the Real Output of Banks," Chapter 6 in Griliches (1992), pp. 219–243.

GEEHAN, RANDALL. 1977. "Returns to Scale in the Life Insurance Industry," *Bell Journal of Economics* 8, pp. 497–514.

GOLDBERG, LAWRENCE G., GERALD A. HANWECK, MICHAEL KEENAN, and ALLAN YOUNG. 1991. "Economies of Scale and Scope in the Securities Industry," *Journal of Banking and Finance* 13, pp. 91–107.

GRILICHES, ZVI (ed.). 1992. *Output Measurement in the Service Sectors.* Chicago: The University of Chicago Press.

HANCOCK, DIANA. 1985. "The Financial Firm: Production with Monetary and Nonmonetary Goods," *Journal of Political Economy* 93 (5), pp. 859–880.

HORNGREN, CHARLES T. and GEORGE FOSTER. 1991. *Cost Accounting* (7th Ed.). Englewood Cliffs, N.J.: Prentice Hall.

KOLARI, JAMES and ASGHAR ZARDKOOHI. 1987. *Bank Costs, Structure, and Performance.* Lexington Mass.: Lexington Books.

MCALLISTER, PATRICK H. and DOUGLAS MCMANUS. 1993. "Resolving the Scale Efficiency Puzzle in Banking," *Journal of Banking and Finance* 17 (2-3), pp. 389–405.

MESTER, LORETTA J. 1992. "Traditional and nontraditional banking: An information-theoretic approach," *Journal of Banking and Finance* 16, pp. 545–566.

OSBORNE, DALE K. 1982. "The Cost of Servicing Demand Deposits," *Journal of Money, Credit, and Banking* 14 (4) (Part I), pp. 479–493.

PINDYCK, ROBERT S. and DANIEL L. RUBINFELD. 1989. *Microeconomics.* New York: Macmillan.

CHAPTER

24

Optimizing Financial Institution Performance

Introduction

Optimizing financial institution performance consists of getting financial service employees to work efficiently with each other and with the economic and financial resources with which they are entrusted. The topics in this chapter are broadly concerned with organizing and paying financial institution employees and specifically consider the following questions:

- What approaches and issues are associated with compensation in the financial services industry?
- What considerations enter into how financial service firms organize their activities and what are the connections between organizational form and value production?
- How do multidivisional financial firms allocate costs and profits?
- What concerns should management of financial firms focus on as these firms grow and adapt to environmental changes?

These topics have been addressed by economists as discussed below but are usually not central to economic analysis. These subjects are less susceptible to rigorous analysis than other topics we have addressed in this book but their overwhelming importance mandates that these issues be highlighted in this book for future managers of financial service firms.

24.1 EMPLOYEE COMPENSATION

The core of value creation in financial service firms is good people—workers who can communicate with customers, process and analyze complex information, negotiate deals, and deliver quality products and services. Financial institutions are usually complex organizations, multidivisional firms like Fifth Third Bancorporation or Country Wide Financial or often large holding companies like BancOne or Travelers with many separate corporate entities offering different financial services in different markets. How can workers' personal interests be brought into line with those of their employers in large organizations?

The problem of motivating workers can be viewed as a principal–agent problem as introduced in Chapter 6 and explored extensively in Part II which analyzed sources of value in providing financial services. In that discussion, principals and agents were typically financial service firms and their customers involved in some relationship such as a credit arrangement or insurance policy. In discussing financial service firm workers, the financial service firm as employer is the principal and the worker is the agent whose actions can harm or help the firm. An extensive literature has evolved examining workers' relations to employers. See Sappington (1991) for a survey of compensation schemes or Milgrom and Roberts (1992) for a complete development of many of the issues in this chapter.

Problems between financial service firm employers and their workers are similar in many ways to manufacturing firms and very different in others. In all firms, workers' interests are to have high pay and make a low level of effort. Employers desire to pay workers little and extract maximum effort. Employers cannot tell how much effort workers put out relative to their capacity. Economic analysis of employment contracts examines compensation schemes that minimize the cost to employers of their inability to control or perfectly monitor workers' efforts because of information asymmetries.

In analysis of the simplest case, workers are characterized as being like tenant farmers who can vary their effort in working the land and their resulting output is observable (this treatment loosely follows Sappington (1991)). The question addressed is how the employer or landlord owning the land and the worker or tenant-farmer can enter an efficient compensation scheme in the sense that workers put out maximum effort. Analysis of this simple case demonstrates that the optimal compensation arrangement is for the landlord to charge the farmer a fixed rent and allow the farmer to keep all the production from the land. Since the worker or tenant farmer claims all output above a fixed amount, the worker is a residual claimant on production. Workers have the incentive to maximize effort and expected income equal to expected production minus the rent. In this simple case, employers pay workers the value of their output above a fixed amount.

Incentive contracts between principals and agents in the employment context must be altered to accommodate variations from the simplest case. One important potential difference between workers and employers is risk preferences reflected in differing tolerance to variations in income. Workers supporting families and depending exclusively on labor income to live may be more risk averse than employers who are wealthy owners or managers of corporations owned by diversified investors not concerned about firm-specific risk. Efficient compensation contracts when employees are risk averse typically include risk sharing by the employer in exchange for increased income security for workers. When a landlord shares output variations with a tenant farmer, he or she becomes a residual claimant to output just as the farmer is. In such arrangements, workers do not receive all the value of their output above a fixed amount. This compensation arrangement causes an efficiency loss because the farmer shares the benefits of effort with the landlord and will be less willing to put maximum effort into production.

Other complications arise when the worker (or tenant farmer) cannot be perfectly monitored or when there are information asymmetries. Imperfect monitoring occurs when output or factors such as weather cannot be observed and related to production, becoming confused with the effect of the worker's efforts. Information asymmetries occur when workers know more about production conditions, as when farmers know more than landlords about growing conditions and the productivity of land. As in the case of risk aversion, in these departures from the simplest case optimal compensation arrangements for workers involve sharing output and distributing the risk of output variations between workers and employers.

This discussion demonstrates that in departures from the assumptions of the simplest case, optimal compensation requires sharing output or profits and distributing risks of output variation between workers and employers. Although sharing output reduces workers' incentives to put out maximum effort because they gain only part of the payoff, these contracts are the most efficient arrangements and align the interests of employers and workers as much as possible. In view of apparent risk aversion among workers in financial services and the likelihood of imperfect monitoring and output measurement by employers, it is surprising how few compensation arrangements at lower levels of financial service firms are characterized by sharing the value of production or profits. Most financial service workers are paid by the hour or on an annual salary.

Given the labor intensivity and the value of human capital in financial services, compensation arrangements are vitally important to induce optimal performance of workers in financial service firms. Optimal employee compensation is at the heart of value production in this industry. Nonetheless, compensation arrangements of financial service firms differ widely among industry segments. Some firms are creative and innovative in paying workers, others cling to standard employer–employee arrangements. Compensation specialists are in great demand in the financial service industry.

To place employee compensation into a framework, we list and define standard compensation schemes observed in the financial services and other industries. We then characterize some distinguishing characteristics of financial service employment and assess the importance of the uniqueness of value creation in this industry in determining optimal employee compensation arrangements.

Workers' pay can be determined seven different ways: (1) *straight time* (typically hourly), (2) *salary* (usually annual), (3) *piece work,* (4) *participation contracts,* (5) *bonus systems,* (6) *tournaments,* and (7) *equity participation*. These compensation schemes are briefly defined and illustrated in Table 24.1. We will use this breakdown in analyzing compensation in financial services in the following discussion.

Each of the payment schemes shown in Table 24.1 is used in some segments of the financial services industry for some jobs. Often hybrid payment systems are used, for example combining salary and bonus systems. However, straight time and salary compensation schemes dominate worker pay in most

TABLE 24.1 Compensation Arrangements

TYPE OF COMPENSATION	*DESCRIPTION*	*EXAMPLES OF WHERE OBSERVED*
Straight time	Hourly or day payments when on the job	Part-time clerical workers, many back office functions
Salary and review	Compensation fixed at all levels of output	Most full time jobs in financial service firms except sales and trading
Piece work, commissions	Fixed payment per unit of production	Securities brokers, mortgage lenders, new accounts personnel in banks, insurance agents
Performance participation	Formula relating compensation to a performance measure such as divisional profits	Trading departments of investment banking firms
Bonus system	Bonus based on achieving specified targets of performance	Managers of branch banks
Tournament	Several employees compete for promotion and raise	Managers and executives in all areas of financial firms
Equity participation	Stock or stock options part of compensation	Top executives of most financial service firms

financial service firms. In view of the simple standard analysis discussed above, straight time and salary compensation methods may be the least desirable compensation schemes from the viewpoint of economic efficiency in financial services. These pay methods do not address principal–agent problems associated with employees of financial service firms.

Straight time pay means simply punching a clock and being paid for the time spent at the place of employment. This form of compensation is common for part-time workers and other clerical personnel important in back-office operations of financial institutions. Most hourly workers are not highly paid and workers and employers share the benefits of flexibility in staffing size and hours worked. Straight time workers rarely develop a sense of commitment to their employers and often quit as their skills reach desirable levels, especially in the operation of equipment such as check-encoding (proof) machines.

Salaried workers earn a set amount of money over a fixed time period, say a week or a year. They are expected to show up on time and do pretty much as told in the organization. Straight salaried workers have a larger fixed commitment from their employers in terms of length of time and they have more to lose in terms of future income committed by the employer by quitting.

Although the effort levels demanded of salaried workers fluctuate with demand for their services, the fixed commitment from the employer has the benefit of reducing uncertainty about future income. Most salaried jobs involve periodic (often annual) evaluation and reviews by management. Salaried jobs offer workers some incentive to improve skills to order to maximize their chances of retention and salary increases.

Piece work is the simplest pay scheme—workers are paid per unit of output. A few financial institutions use piece work compensation to pay workers for simple jobs like opening new accounts or completing money changing transactions. The problem with piece work is that if quality is a factor, workers will sacrifice quality for quantity of output. For example, if tellers are not responsible for cash errors, piece work encourages sloppy cash controls.

Piece work compensation schemes are probably underutilized in the more routine and less quality sensitive areas of financial service firms, such as back offices. In many cases financial service firms are reluctant to offer such payment schemes because of uncertainty about costs or revenues with output upon which piece work schemes could be based. We discussed cost and output measurement problems in the previous chapter. The danger of production-based incentive schemes is that workers will go to extremes to earn money, producing unprofitable goods or services. The need to optimize employee performance is yet another motivation for studying costs and measuring output better, as discussed in the previous chapter.

In sales activities, as when loan agents obtain mortgage loan applications, insurance agents sell policies, or securities brokers sell stocks and bonds, workers tend to minimize work effort unless compensation is related to production. Simple output-sharing compensation arrangements discussed above are reflected in worker pay in selling of financial services like mortgage loans, insurance policies, or trading activity. Many mortgage lenders pay sales agents commissions based on loan production. Insurance agents often keep a major portion of the first year's insurance premium. Most securities firms compensate brokers by splitting commissions on trades. In many cases, these employees are guaranteed a minimum salary or "draw" over some time period. These arrangements are similar to the tenant farmer sharing risk with the landlord because of the minimum pay and commissions related to loan volume, insurance sales, or stock trading.

When commissions or other pay schemes similar to piece work are used, most evidence suggests that workers respond energetically, but this in turn may cause financial firms problems. Insurance agents are accused of being "replacement artists," persuading insurance customers to unnecessarily replace economically valuable existing policies with new policies. Mortgage sale agents are accused of helping unqualified borrowers obtain mortgages. Brokers are accused of generating excessive trading activity by "churning" their customers' accounts to inflate commission income, potentially harming their employers' reputations and making them liable to lawsuits. This is the danger of piece work compensation when quality of service matters to the employer. More sophisticated compensation arrangements might improve on these pay methods, as discussed below.

Participation contracts make employee pay a function of some unit or division profits or other performance measures. For example, employees of securities trading firms are often compensated based on the profits of their specialized unit, such as a Treasury trading department. Managers of branches of banks and other financial service firms are often paid on the basis of their branch "profits." Paying workers based on performance aligns their interest with the performance of the division of the firm where they work. This can produce employee performance in line with the firm's goals if maximum profit center earnings are in line with maximization of the firm's overall value.

Participation pay based on unit profits introduces problems in calculating profit center earnings, a point we discuss below in conjunction with transfer pricing. Profit participation in units where profitability is hard to assess because of difficulty in setting transfer prices or because of poor control systems can lead to unchecked employee performance harming the firm. For example, Joseph Jett was a Kidder Peabody bond trader who falsely inflated trading profits to $350 million (while covering losses of $100 million) to obtain multimillion pay in 1992 (Siconolfi (1994)).

Bonus systems are usually combined with low salaries and compensate employees on the basis of exceeding some target levels of production or performance. For example, a life insurance district sales manager might be paid a $5,000 bonus for every 10 percent increase in policy sales over the preceding year's sales. Bonus systems can be thought of as modified piece work pay with bonuses determined by bracketed amount of production. Bonus systems are common with managers responsible for groups or teams of workers and provide managers with incentives to urge increased productivity of subordinates.

Targets or quotas used in paying bonuses are often negotiated by the employee and the manager. Although information asymmetries may make target setting subject to principal–agent problems, well-designed bonus systems may develop information concerning expected future activity levels useful in organization planning efforts. Bonus systems based purely on volume, like piece work pay, can distort the quality of products sold.

Employee compensation and job responsibilities based on a contest with other workers is known as a "tournament." A worker's performance that is evaluated as superior to other workers wins the promotion or job assignment or large pay increase. The evaluation scheme may be clearly based on quantitative objectives, such as producing the highest profits or sales, or it may be based on less well-defined qualitative criteria, for example demonstrating superior management skills by turning around a failing division rather than simply managing an untroubled division acceptably. Tournaments have the benefit of inducing competition and high levels of effort if the prize is big enough. Losing the tournament may reduce morale for other workers who may leave or shirk after the contest even though they performed nearly as well as the winner.

Finally, many executives receive pay in the form of stock or stock options. Stock ownership aligns top management's interest with those of shareholders and the same is true for stock options at conversion prices reasonably expected to be surpassed by market values under good management. The highest-paid executive in a *Fortune* executive compensation survey of 200 companies in 1993 was Sanford Weill of Travelers, Incorporated, the insurance and brokerage (Smith Barney Shearson) firm. His total pay was $45.6 million, of which $41.4 million was in the form of long-term incentives and stock grants. Other bankers and financial service executives in the survey also received generous stock option plans, often valued at more than salaries.

Typical compensation schemes described above can be used in combinations to solve some principal–agent problems between financial firm employers and their workers. Other problems may require more complicated or nonstandard compensation schemes. Economists have studied a wide range of problems involving information asymmetries and imperfect monitoring of workers' activity and found that solutions can involve complex compensation contracts based on a number of indicators in addition to production or time, for example the average performance of other workers or production of similar products.

Some principal–agent problems can be resolved by workers choosing among a menu of compensation agreements that induces them to reveal information about themselves or signal assessments of important market information or information concerning production conditions. Offering workers a choice of compensation schemes is rare in financial service firms. Financial service firms in general have not been sophisticated in developing compensation schemes.

Several dimensions of financial services discussed in Part II of this book differentiate production of financial services from manufacturing or other service production. The many activities in the value chain required to produce financial services mean the value produced by employees may not be effectively measured by a single output measure. The difference between financial services and other production or sales environments is undoubtedly relevant to the design of optimal compensation schemes for workers in the financial services industry. Optimal compensation of financial service employees may not be easily captured by a relation to a single measure, for example the number of loans, insurance policies, or trades sold per period.

Analyses of compensation in production contexts focus on production over short time intervals, such as the growing season in our simple tenant farmer example. But credit services, asset management services, and other financial services take place over long periods of time. They are part of a long-term relationship, possibly involving a number of products or services not fixed at the outset of the relationship. Financial firms' reputations are often important to their success in attracting new business.

Because of long-term commitments, variable level of demand for services by customers, and the importance of reputation, officials of financial service firms must sustain a level of customer satisfaction and trust sufficient to optimize the value of customer relationships. Piece work or commission-based pay tends to shorten the viewpoint to the number of transactions and can result in workers overlooking the benefits of long-term relations where future business may be infrequent but profitable. Many firms consider their employees' relations to their customers to be among their most important assets, a source of value in view of future business from financial service demands in the future and from referrals.

The time horizon over which financial services take place also means that future performance under financial service agreements impacts the value of the relationship. Employees must monitor customers to ensure that the relationship works as expected, for example in credit arrangements or insurance contracts. One way to induce employee engagement in long term performance of customer relationships is to have workers take a quasi-equity position in the profits from customers, as in a portfolio of customer loans. If the worker's pay depends not only on making the loan but also on the future performance of the loan, as it would if the worker "owned" a share of the profits from customers, incentives of employees and financial firms could be more effectively aligned.

Another complexity of financial relationships is that there is often more than one service or product. Bank calling officers are concerned primarily with their business customers' deposits and credit needs, but other products, like trust services and securities trading services, are also available. Compensation schemes must be tailored to induce financial service firm representatives to sell the whole range of products available or to induce referrals to other parts of the financial firm organization. For example, home mortgage sales people paid on a commission will neglect selling automatic checking deposit deductions for loan payments or other services unless explicitly motivated to do so. Cross-selling may take time and effort by workers to communicate complex information remote from their main sales activity. Unless rewarded, these employees find their time used more profitably to sell familiar products.

Sometimes financial service products are so different that the same compensation scheme for sales cannot be applied to them. For example, brokers expect immediate income from securities trades of their customers and will make as many trades as they can, praying for period of heavy trading volume. Insurance salesman take a long time to explain and sell insurance policies to their customers, usually receiving a large commission upon sale of the policy, often the first year's premium. For life insurance agents, a few sales can be a year's income. The differing sales problems for brokerage and insurance means optimal compensation schemes and sales culture must differ. The difference in insurance and securities sales is one explanation offered for Merrill Lynch's lack of success in selling insurance through brokerage offices.

Many financial services require a team effort. Motivating workers to function effectively in teams may require compensation contracts that include not only an individual worker's performance but also assessment by team members or a participation contract based on team performance. For example, investment banking fees generated by a team presentation to a corporate client could the basis for individuals' pay. The total compensation could be linked to the number of relevant investment banking services sold so that teams would be motivated to sell a wider range of products than just those of interest to the team members.

Finally, employees of financial service firms must be creative and innovative. New financial products and services are where the highest profitability will be found in the future. Pay schemes that encourage innovation and risk taking in product development or new customer services are essential in the financial services industry of the future. Compensation arrangements for employees expected to innovate must tolerate some unsuccessful efforts at innovation if a large number of ideas are required to identify valuable new products. Financial service firm workers must be willing to take the risks of experimentation and failed ideas at the same time as they are motivated to innovate. For example, employees could receive time off with pay to develop new ideas and could be given participation in new product profits or other inducements to come up with new ideas. Compensation arrangements like these are rare in financial service firms today.

24.2 FINANCIAL SERVICE FIRM ORGANIZATIONS

Human resources are a critical input into the provision of financial services. How can these resources best be organized in order to motivate workers to provide these services effectively and responsibly? Given the complexity of many tasks in this industry, how can worker performance be monitored? The legal form of business organization—corporation, partnership, sole proprietorship, or mutual—has a role in assigning responsibility and allocating rewards in complex organizations of individuals. Grouping workers into divisions or other firm units with reporting relationships and performance responsibilities influences how efficiently workers interact to achieve the firms' objectives. We discuss the legal structure and forms of organizations in turn.

Legal Form of Financial Firms

Regulation and taxation explain many legal aspects of organizational forms and the complexity of financial service firms. For example, until 1994 a bank in the United States had to have a separately incorporated bank subsidiary in every state where it wished to take deposits. Insurance companies often have many subsidiaries to do business in different states. Credit unions must be mutually owned. Holding company structures are widely used to evade restrictions on activities of regulated financial service firms, such as banks, thrifts, and insurance companies. Legal and regulatory considerations explain some, but not all, of the legal structure of financial service firms.

Business firms of all types can be considered as a system of agreements and contracts binding a variety of parties together in producing goods or services—suppliers, workers, managers, customers, creditors, and investors. All these parties have differing interests and desires and each party works naturally enough to maximize his or her own welfare, leading to conflicts of interest. Resolution of these conflicts is studied using principal–agent analysis as in the previous section.

A solution to conflicts affecting the efficiency and reliability of an organization may depend on which is the best legal structure for the tasks performed by the organization. According to the analysis of Fama and Jensen (1983a, 1983b) which we presented in Chapter 3, the corporate form of organization developed historically in order to undertake large, complex investments, spread risks, and limit liability to initial investments. Their argument is that corporate structure is favored by firms such as commercial banks that require skilled professional management to work with complex nonmarketable assets (e.g., commercial loans). Owners of corporations elect a board of directors with the power to fire management to oversee their interests. After paying all other parties with claims on the firm, such as workers and creditors, owners of corporations claim the income left over.

Fama and Jensen note that in contrast to corporations the partnership form of organization requires that partners share liability and income with professional colleagues. They contend that partnerships can be effective organizations when firms provide professional services like investment banking. Shared liability bonds partners to the highest level of performance because each partner's performance places the firm and its reputation and its future business at risk. Investment banks and brokers are frequently organized as partnerships.

In the Fama–Jensen argument, mutual organizations are efficient when assets are simply evaluated or readily marketable. Mutual organizations can be efficient ways of organizing activity when agency problems are not caused by asset or service complexity. Mutual fund shares sold to investors and deposit-taking institutions organized as mutuals (e.g., thrifts and credit unions) survive because their assets are marketable or relatively simple and mutual shareholders or members can enforce management discipline by threatening to withdraw funds.

Other arguments have been made for the mutual form of organization relative to stock companies. Rasmussen (1988) uses an agency argument to show that investors may trust mutual organizations to invest in safer assets than stock companies. The reason for the trust is that mutual company managers lose their jobs if the firm goes bankrupt from risky investments they have made. Because there are no shareholders in a mutual who could benefit from risky investments with potentially large payoffs (and only limited losses due to limited liability), managers have no incentive to take risks. Mutuals thus are a safe and efficient way of saving for risk averse individuals.

Another explanation for the existence of mutuals, made in this case in the context of the insurance industry, has been advanced by Mayers and Smith (1986). These authors argue that in insurance it may be more costly to resolve conflicts between creditors and owners than between customers and managers of firms. They argue that it may be more efficient to have only customer as owners, that is, a mutual form of organization. If policyholders are simultaneously owners of the corporation, the need for costly monitoring of stockholders to prevent expropriations of wealth from customer/creditors is eliminated. Customer owners may concentrate on overcoming conflicts between customer needs and management interests.

Another argument explaining the existence of mutual firms, more popular than academic, is that these organizations are run for the benefit of management. According to this view, managers take control of mutual firms and pay themselves large salaries and provide themselves with desirable perquisites. For example, the *Wall Street Journal* reported on large pay raises at mutual insurance companies in 1982 as follows:

> The widespread increases, disclosed in reports filed with state insurance regulators, add to the questions about who really controls mutual insurers. The companies are owned by their millions of policyholders rather than by stockholders. But critics say they are often run for the benefit of entrenched managements, which leads to inefficiency and cronyism. (May 14, 1982, p. 27)

Rasmussen, cited above, provides evidence of the low participation of mutual deposit-taking institution depositors at annual meetings, and suggests that management really does control most mutuals.

An argument that mutual firms exist because of management greed and demands for perquisites does not explain why mutuals developed in the first place. Management exploitation arguments do not explain how inefficient, high-cost mutuals survive competition from corporate organizations in the same business that can underprice and defeat inefficient competitors in the market for financial services.

Another argument for the existence of mutual organizations in financial services is first in many observers' minds: the tax treatment of mutuals. Many mutuals are tax exempt or tax advantaged. Credit unions do not pay taxes. Mutual funds do not pay taxes if they pass their income through to owners. Other mutuals are taxed, but usually income is only taxed to the extent that it is attributable to owners. The partnership form is also tax advantaged in that partners pay taxes as individuals only once on their share of the partnership's income. Corporations pay corporate income taxes and owners pay taxes on salaries from the corporation and dividends.

Tax rules discussed in Chapter 17 make mutual versus corporate or partnership organization important economically in terms of tax treatment. Nonetheless, economic arguments based on agency and management issues are probably more important in explaining the long history of the joint existence of many forms of organizations providing financial services. Mutual and corporate forms have coexisted in periods predating the corporate and personal income taxes and have survived innumerable changes in the tax code.

Organizational Structure

A wide variety of organizational structures are observed among financial service firms. Sizable organizations must be broken down into coherent units—units that may be the basis of profit centers used in motivating workers and monitoring performance. Organizational structure can be a means of lowering costs through improved coordination and communication or focusing effort and increasing revenues as part of a firm's strategy. The underlying idea of designing organizations is coordinating the efforts of many workers to foster efficiency and smooth flows of information and resources within the organization to accomplish goals of the firm.

An important aspect of an organization is the degree of centralization desired by managers or investors. Centralized organizations use organizational structure to control and monitor implementation of policies. Decision making in centralized organizations tends to be top down, with business initiatives generated by top management and performance at lower levels reviewed and approved in terms of organization objectives.

Decentralized organization structures encourage initiatives at lower levels of the organization. Decentralized management emphasizes coordination rather than control of individual units. Decentralized structure fosters flexible responses to local situations. Performance of decentralized units is in terms of broad organizational targets rather than implementation of specified business plans developed by the firm.

The trade-off between tightly centralized organizations that monitor and control performance versus decentralized business units with the ability to respond quickly to local business opportunities will be the crux of financial institutions' organizational development in the future. Advances in communications and computing technology and competition are dramatically changing the economics of coordinating, monitoring, reporting, and controlling diverse business units in both centralized and decentralized systems. Centralized and decentralized organizations may be best under differing competitive and technological circumstances.

Examples of centralized and decentralized organizations can currently be observed in two United States banking corporations. NationsBank, an outgrowth of North Carolina National Bank (NCNB) is highly centralized under its chairman High L. McColl, Jr., and controls its subordinate divisions tightly. A merger of a banking unit into NationsBank is followed by installation of managers from headquarters and standardization of systems. BancOne of Ohio, on the other hand, is highly decentralized under its chairman John B. McCoy. BancOne keeps local management in place following mergers and encourages local initiatives. Both organizations install financial control systems after mergers but NationsBank integrates subordinate units into a tightly controlled system while BankOne standardizes reporting to enable local managers to compare and evaluate their performance.

Three ways of organizing business organization are commonly observed in financial services: (1) customer or regional groupings, (2) product divisions, and (3) functional areas. The value creation matrix of Chapter 2, repeated here as Table 24.2, can be useful in understanding these organizing principles for workers and resources within either centralized or decentralized financial institutions. Product divisions in financial service firms can be visualized in Table 24.2 as grouping employees participating vertically into business units, for example transaction-based services. Functional organization corresponds to organization of workers horizontally in the table according to the activity they perform in the value chain, for example grouping employees with responsibility for communication and marketing in several product lines into business units. Most organizations use combinations of the three organizational principles to group resources and workers.

TABLE 24.2 Financial Services and Value Producing Activities

SERVICES/ ACTIVITIES	*CREDIT SERVICES*	*SECURITIES SERVICES*	*INSURANCE SERVICES*	*TRANSACTION PROCESSING*	*INFORMATION SERVICES*	*ADVISING/ MANAGEMENT*
Pricing/ Term setting						
Information/ Marketing			FUNCTIONAL GROUPING			
Monitoring/ Controlling						
Production/ Delivery				PRODUCT GROUPING		
Funding/ Investing						
Risk bearing/ Sharing						

Customer groups are used by many financial firms to organize activities. The goal is to be more effective in dealing with market segments, for example retail customers, by grouping experienced and trained personnel with similar market focus together. Many firms rely on geographical breakdowns of organizations to maximize efficiency in gathering local area market information and communicating effectively with financial services customers with similar needs. Financial institution branches in different geographical regions can be focused on particular market segments, such as retiree household depositors in Florida and mortgage borrowers in Utah and Arizona or middle market commercial borrowers in the Silicon Valley. Commercial banks and thrifts often use branches or groups of branches as business units. Many financial institutions have representative offices in large cities or different regions.

Product divisions are another common organizational form. For example, employees responsible for specific casualty insurance lines may be grouped together in a unit of a diversified insurance company. Trust services and corporate lending, representing asset management and wholesale credit services on Table 24.2, are separated into organizational units in many banks. The advantage of product organization is improved communication and shared experience of workers specializing in performing all activities in the value chain for similar products. The disadvantage of product organization is a narrow focus possibly insulating employees from developments in other markets. For example, an organization focused on deposit taking and transaction processing may not see asset management services such as mutual funds as a possible substitute product and competitive threat. Product organization can also obscure potential synergies from joint production of activities in the value chain for several financial services, for example by cross-selling products as part of marketing and communication with customers.

Organizations can also be grouped by functions, where employees might be organized into functional areas like funding and investing or communications and marketing in terms of the rows of Table 24.2. An advantage of functional organization is that it pools employees with special expertise and experience, as in marketing research. Functional organization may focus effort effectively, but it runs the danger of separating activities that are produced jointly in offering financial services, like production and delivery and marketing and communication of retail services through branches. Functional organization often works best in centralized organizations with a narrow product line where controls between organizational units can be imposed from above without obscuring important product or market relationships.

In setting up or changing organizational structure, the major focus of financial service firms should be to maximize the productivity of employees. The organization must reflect the most important information flows and cost synergies from shared efforts in performing the activities in the value chain necessary to offer financial products and services. The structure should induce desired levels of communication and teamwork, whether in servicing customers, developing new products, or implementing new procedures. Factors such as team identification and esprit de corps are important considerations in organizing activity.

24.3 TRANSFER PRICING

Multidivisional financial organizations are linked by a shared interest in many resources and personnel working in related areas. For example, commercial banks and thrifts lend money raised from depositors. If the depositors are household customers serviced by a retail banking division and lending is to the wholesale market in the corporate lending division, resources must flow between organizational entities. The prices or rates used to account for resource transfers within organizations are called *transfer prices.* These prices may be important in determining the reported profitability in different divisions of complex organizations.

The importance of transfer pricing can be demonstrated with a simple example based on real problems facing many banks and thrifts. There are two profit centers in the example, retail deposits and corporate lending. Balance sheets and income statements for the two divisions are presented in Table 24.3. The retail division has more deposits than it can lend to borrowers so it makes funds available to the corporate division which can lend more money than it can raise in deposits. For convenience, the interest rate or service cost of deposits is assumed to be 3 percent, the interest rate on loans is 6 percent, and the transfer price on the funds between divisions is 5 percent. Clearly the profitability of the two divisions depends on the transfer price. At 5 percent, the retail division is more profitable. At a transfer price of 4 percent, the corporate division would be more profitable.

The importance of transfer prices is based on several factors: (1) the effect of transfer prices on the allocation of resources in the firm and maximization of value for the entire firm; (2) the effect of transfer prices on the incentives and compensation of managers based on division profits; and (3) the production of information concerning the relative efficiency of divisions and internal sources of

TABLE 24.3 Transfer Pricing Example

RETAIL DIVISION			*CORPORATE DIVISION*		
Income Statement			**Income Statement**		
Interest on loans (6%)		$60	Interest on loans (6%)		$300
Earnings credit (5%)		$200	Interest cost (3%)		$30
Interest cost (3%)		$150	Earnings charge (5%)		$200
Profit		$110	Profit		$70
Balance Sheet			**Balance Sheet**		
Loans	$1,000	Deposits $5,000	Loans $5,000	Deposits	$1,000
Claims on wholesale division	$4,000			Liability to retail division	$4,000

the organization's competitive advantage relative to market competitors. We discuss each in turn.

Firms are formed to reduce transaction costs of doing business.[1] More efficient information flows and efficiency from better coordination of activities and economies of scope can be realized within organizations, thereby reducing the costs of transacting business having different components or stages in production. In large, multidivisional organizations, specialization by customers, products, or functions, as discussed in the previous section, results in resource transfers between divisions.

If transfer prices are not correct, division managers may overproduce products or services using undervalued inputs. They may produce the wrong products by responding to transfer prices that are too high, increasing profit center performance but reducing the firm's overall profits. If transfer prices for activities produced within the firm are set too high, profits may be lower than those possible using external suppliers in producing products or services. If transfer prices are set too low, the firm may not realize maximum profits from demand or technological dependencies linking production of products or services.

Current discussion of transfer pricing in the United States concerns the role of transfer prices in shifting income tax liabilities across international borders. Transfer prices for goods shipped internationally can be used to shift profits of multinational corporations. In the United States, section 482 of the Internal Revenue Service (IRS) regulations outlines acceptable methods for transfer prices used in filing company taxes when resources are shipped across international tax boundaries. In our preceding example, assume that retail deposits are from a United States subsidiary and loans are in a low-income-tax foreign country subsidiary of a multinational bank. Lowering the credit on deposits would move profits to the foreign subsidiary.

IRS rules provide methods to benchmark acceptable transfer prices. These methods are difficult to apply and lead to a great deal of conflict and litigation.[2] In 1987, for example, Nissan and Toyota automobile companies from Japan paid the IRS $604 million in taxes on income reduced by high transfer prices on autos shipped to the United States (the Japanese tax agency refunded the $604 million to the auto companies.).

The focus in this chapter is on the economic incentive effects of transfer prices although many of the issues are the same as in international tax disputes. The example of the deposit-taking firm reveals the importance of transfer pricing to the assignment of taxable profits earned in multidivisional corporations. When management compensation or performance evaluation is based on divisional profits, managers' pay or promotions in some divisions will be increased and others decreased by changes in transfer prices, just as tax liabilities are changed across international borders with transfer price adjustments. In many financial institutions, the fixing of transfer prices, like the cost of funds in our

[1]These ideas stem from Coase (1937) and have been elaborated by Williamson (1975).

[2]See Granfield and Weston (1990) for an analysis of IRS methods for reviewing transfer pricing.

example, is a serious political problem because of repercussions on management compensation.

Hirschleifer (1956) presents an economic analysis of the effects of transfer pricing within multidivisional firms where there are no important management incentive effects. The emphasis of Hirschleifer's analysis is multidivisional firm managers who maximize profits of their divisions and make decisions based on transfer prices for intermediate goods. Our discussion assumes that a central management sets transfer prices to maximize profits of a firm facing external markets and internal production conditions. Hirschleifer stresses that either final or intermediate goods division managers motivated to maximize firm (rather than divisional) profits would make the same transfer price decisions. Table 24.4 summarizes the results of Hirschleifer's analysis we discuss in the following.

According to Hirschleifer's analysis, intermediate goods transfer prices in general should be set equal to marginal costs of the intermediate goods at the firm's profit maximizing production level. Considering retail deposits to be an intermediate good from our example, transfer prices should be set at the marginal cost of funds that maximizes the deposit-taking firm's total profits. The third column of Table 24.4 provides interpretations of Hirschleifer's analysis in terms of our deposit-taking financial firm example. In case (1), loan deposit ratios are fixed and in case (3) the market for deposits is upward sloping, meaning the deposit-taking firm has market power in its deposit market. In both these cases, the optimal transfer price for the deposit division is where the marginal cost of deposits equals the marginal revenue from loans. In case (2), the deposit market is competitive and the optimal transfer price is the market rate on deposits. Since interest rates are fixed by competitive conditions in case (2), marginal deposit costs for the firm are equal to market rates. Therefore for cases (1) through (3), marginal cost transfer prices are optimal.

In cases where there is dependence between the intermediate good and final good demand, for example when deposit taking is not independent of loan demand, transfer pricing is more complicated. This is case (4) in Table 24.4. The effect of the deposit division's actions on the profitability of lending must be considered in the setting of transfer prices. If deposit taking tends to increase the demand for loans, perhaps by expanding customer contacts, optimal transfer prices will be between market rates and the marginal cost of funds. In the deposit-taking firm example, the credit rate on deposits should be above the marginal cost of funds to induce managers to increase the supply of deposits to levels maximizing joint profits from deposits and lending.

Hirschleifer's analysis stresses the importance of using marginal or incremental costs in setting transfer prices under competitive conditions where intermediate and final products are independent technologically and have no market dependencies, as in cases (1) to (3) in the table. Hirschleifer raises an important point concerning long-run effects of transfer prices when fixed costs are considered in addition to variable costs. Divisional profits including allocations for fixed costs may be negative using transfer prices based on marginal costs that maximize total firm profits. A determination as to whether to close divisions reporting losses when fixed costs are included cannot be made without looking at the total

TABLE 24.4 Transfer Pricing Rules from Hirshleifer (1956)

SUPPLY AND DEMAND CONDITIONS	*OPTIMAL TRANSFER PRICE RULE*	*EXAMPLE FOR DEPOSIT-TAKING FIRM*
(1) Single joint level of output for intermediate and final goods	Marginal cost of intermediate goods	Determine where marginal revenue from loans equals marginal costs of deposits and use transfer price for deposit funds equal to that marginal cost.
(2) Intermediate and final goods produced and marketed independently and intermediate goods market is competitive	Market price for intermediate goods which is equal to marginal cost of intermediate goods	Price deposits at prevailing market rates.
(3) Downward sloping demand curve for intermediate goods	Transfer price is set where sum of *net* marginal revenue from final goods and marginal revenue from intermediate market are equal to marginal cost of intermediate goods	Add marginal revenue from loans to marginal revenues from other uses of deposits and set transfer price equal to marginal cost of deposits at that rate.
(4) Demand dependence in that external intermediate goods sales reduce demand for final goods	Transfer price between marginal cost and market price	Use of deposit to purchase securities reduces loan demand: set transfer price to optimal rate for aggregate profits somewhere between market rates and marginal deposit costs.

firm profit picture including fixed costs for other divisions. Losses from one division may subsidize larger profits in other divisions. This could mean that divisions reporting losses when fixed costs are counted contribute to overall firm profitability in the long-run. Optimal transfer pricing may not produce division income statements useful in identifying firm-wide competitive advantages.

In cases (1) to (3) in Table 24.4 analyzed by Hirschleifer, marginal cost transfer pricing is a robust approach for optimizing short-run decisions (ignoring costs) with transfer prices. Technological and demand interdependencies complicate analysis of optimal transfer pricing. Hirschleifer's analysis also ignores incentive effects on divisional managers who must expend costly effort to produce in response to transfer pricing signals from central decision makers in the organization. Marginal cost or market pricing may not be optimal when accounting for these effects, as in case (4) of the table.

In an economic analysis of divisional managers responding to transfer pricing in producing intermediate inputs to a final output for a firm, Besanko and Sibley (1991) show why division profits should be calculated using transfer prices departing from market prices or marginal costs. Their analysis focuses on the principal–agent problem caused by managers compensated by profit-sharing within the firm who are buying inputs from the external market and producing outputs for the firm. The analysis is interesting because it shows the effects of technological dependencies between intermediate and final goods and management incentives on optimal transfer prices. Differences in transfer prices from market prices are necessary to make the incentives of the manager responsible for producing the intermediate input align with those of the organization as a whole.

The Besanko and Sibley analysis demonstrates how transfer prices induce managers of divisions to expend optimal effort while accounting for technological interdependencies between outputs for various divisions. For example, in our deposit-taking firm example, assume that managers of deposit-taking divisions stimulate loan demand for the lending division in the process of gathering deposits. By providing good service and calling on deposit customers, loan demand from the institution is increased. This causes a technological or market dependence between deposit and lending divisions. In this case, the deposit-taking division should receive a transfer rate higher than market rates or marginal costs to reflect the positive effect of deposit services on loan profitability. By paying higher rates on deposits, managers in the deposit division have greater incentives to increase their efforts. This is similar to case (4) in Table 24.4.

Transfer pricing is clearly important in all financial services. We can consider interdivisional transfers between, for example, deposit services and credit services as transfer prices between columns of the value creation matrix in Table 24.2. Additional examples are transfer prices on funds provided by insurance reserves used by credit service or asset management service divisions of insurance companies and transfer prices assigned to transaction processing costs associated with securities trading services offered by brokerage firms. Many other financial service firm examples of transfers between columns or rows of Table 24.2 are possible.

The importance of transfer pricing in financial services will continue to increase as financial services respond to competitive and technological developments. If we view separating the performance of activities listed in the rows of Table 24.2 by different firms or divisions as unbundling financial services, costs and transfer prices between rows of the table become important in determining competitive advantages in value chain. For example, decisions about whether to produce internally or outsource activities require knowledge of optimal transfer prices for activities produced within a firm and market prices for activities produced by external suppliers. Reasons for departures of internal transfer prices from marginal costs, for example demand or technological dependencies, must be understood.

Compensation of workers efficiently providing activities in the value chain necessary to offer financial services will depend on profit centers using optimal transfer prices. Synergies or technological and demand interdependencies can be the basis of value-creating strategies if they can be identified, if costs can measured adequately, and if workers can be motivated to perform as required. Use of optimal or at least good transfer prices are central to accomplishment of value creation in strategies based on transfers or resources between the rows or columns of the value matrix.

Transfer Prices in Practice

How are transfer prices set in multidivisional organizations? There are three practical ways to arrive at prices or rates between divisions of large organizations:[3] (1) market benchmarks, (2) political negotiations, and (3) cost estimates. We discuss the advantages and disadvantages of each of these methods in financial service firms. These three methods may be compared to criteria applied by the IRS to transfer prices used by multinational firms. The IRS guidelines are attempts to determine whether transfer prices used in international transactions are legitimate results of one of the three methods listed or are set arbitrarily to minimize global tax liabilities. In assessing transfer prices reported on tax returns, the IRS also looks at return on asset and return on equity calculations and market prices and markups for other firms (Granfield and Weston 1990 detail IRS acceptable methods). The IRS is not concerned about optimal or efficient organization of activity.

The advantage of market-based transfer prices is that they represent objective measures of alternatives to internal production of intermediate resources. Even if market measures are not used in transfer pricing problems, managers at all levels of organizations should be aware of the prices of substitutes available from the market. Knowledge of market alternatives can prevent negotiated prices from distorting allocation of resources too much and provide a useful benchmark for cost-based estimates. Managers can effectively use market prices in negotiations by simply using the argument that they could obtain resources, such as funds or computer power, from outside vendors at quoted values.

Market benchmarks have two disadvantages. First, in line with the discussion above, market-based transfer prices may not induce optimal effort and production in multidivisional organizations. Second, many transfers between divisions do not have perfect substitutes in the market. Many firms adjust transfer prices to account for market phenomena, for example by adjusting internal deposit transfers for differences in maturity using adjustments from the term structure of interest rates. Comparisons of internal transfers and adjustments to

[3]See for example Horngren and Foster (1991), Chapter 27.

market quotations may not adequately capture the economics of internal resources. For example, retail transaction deposits may be cheap because core deposits have low turnover despite their availability on demand.

Negotiated transfer prices have the advantage of accounting for special situations in the organization. Negotiations can in fact replicate internal markets where the unique economic trade-offs of the organization are explicitly reflected in transfer prices. In many instances, for example in pricing computer services or technical advice, transfer prices may effectively signal development of corporate strategy, say by computerizing diverse operations. To the extent that internal users are competing for divisional resources and transfer prices reflect internal demand, management can determine the efficiency of relying on internal units to perform activities instead of using market substitutes available externally.

The biggest problem with negotiated transfer prices is that they are subject to political manipulation. Most retail bankers complain that their operating units are not given sufficient credit for resources because transfer prices are fixed to benefit more powerful and entrenched management in areas such as corporate lending or investment banking services. Political transfer prices can blunt management incentives to provide intermediate resources efficiently.

Cost-based transfer prices are subject to all the problems of cost measurement discussed in the previous chapter. The rule for cost-based transfer prices is (see Horngren and Foster (1991), p. 863):

$$\text{Transfer Price} = \text{Variable Cost} + \text{Opportunity Cost.} \tag{24.1}$$

In terms of our cost measurement discussion, both elements of this equation are difficult. The rule includes as a first element *variable costs*. Variable costs avoid the problems of overhead allocations included in average cost methods, but are still difficult to measure, as discussed in the previous chapter. The *opportunity cost* component of transfer prices is the most difficult problem. Opportunity costs are defined as what the organization as a whole gives up or gains by using internal resources. This component will include the incentive and demand and technological interdependencies discussed above. Estimates of this component will be very difficult for financial service firms but are essential in setting optimal transfer prices.

Transfer pricing is at the core of efficient operation of multidivisional financial firms. None of the three methods of establishing transfer prices can be relied on to produce efficient allocation of effort in all instances. Pragmatic managers aware of the effect of transfer prices on decision making and compensation will derive estimates from all three methods. Transfer prices will be reviewed and evaluated constantly as the changing market environment and competition affect the competitive advantage of financial firms.

24.4 GROWTH AND CHANGE

This book began by discussing the many changes taking place in financial services. It must end by emphasizing the importance of flexibility and adaptability of firms and their managers and employees in the dynamic environment of the future. *Financial firms must be organized to change.* Change can mean growth, shrinkage, or broadening or narrowing focus. The importance of organization is that information concerning competitive advantages or ephemeral market opportunities must be communicated and acted upon quickly. Experimentation, failure, and false starts will all be necessary to find the most effective strategies.

How can firms organize effectively to achieve the agility necessary to respond to rapid market developments? There is no single answer. Decentralized organizations can be responsive to local market developments but foster rogue behavior and inefficiencies from poor coordination or monitoring. Centralized organizations can be unresponsive and slow to process developments into market responses. There is no single best answer. Intelligent managers must be constantly weigh these trade-offs as they organize effort.

Three basic characteristics of successful organizations appear to be important in the future: (1) employee incentives and compensation based on developments they can control in their markets or product areas; (2) good systems review identifying poor or disastrous performance relative to winning efforts; and (3) an atmosphere encouraging experimentation and risk-taking. New products must be encouraged both in operating divisions and research divisions. Communication between parts of the organization must be free and candid.

Most observers of the financial services industry believe the future will be characterized by the consolidation of many small financial firms. These consolidations are economically justified by synergies gained from larger organizations. Many financial institutions identify strategic planning with acquisitions. Acquisitions within markets and across international boundaries will be an even more common phenomenon in the future.

The underlying issue is growth. The presumption is that growth is good—despite this book's emphasis on return on investment. Growth is only good when it increases return on investments or maintains excessive returns. Growth can be realized internally and externally. In any case, growth should be built on a strategy of building on strengths and shedding areas of weakness where the criterion of performance is return on owner's investments.

Mergers and acquisitions have been common in financial services in recent decades. We began the book with some of the more notorious examples. *Mergers and Acquisitions* magazine has ranked commercial banking in the top three industries in the United States by number of mergers in each of the last ten years. What has been the result of these mergers? As discussed in the final section of the previous chapter, there is little evidence to support the argument that investors gain by mergers producing larger banking institutions. Problems from integrating management and workers into new organizations such that incentives and skills of merged firm employees maximize efficiency of the organization are enormous.

We conclude our analysis of the financial services industry with a challenge to future managers. Survival and success in the future can only be based on management decisions creating value through increased revenues or reduced costs. All decisions by good managers must identify and justify gains from consolidations. Managers proposing growth strategies must show explicitly the synergies to be obtained by mergers or internally funded growth. Not only must these synergies not be left as vague assurances of the benefits of size or diversification but the synergies must be explicitly related to reasonable revenue increases or cost reductions. Future managers are challenged to demonstrate convincingly the impact of their decisions on return on investment. Simple arguments based on economies of scale and scope are not a sufficient justification for internal or external growth.

This book is intended to provide future managers with a framework for developing arguments providing economic justification for financial service strategies in the future. Managers must be able to argue persuasively the value of growth or diversification from potential demand or production interdependencies between and within the rows and columns of the value matrix in Table 24.2. With labor-intensive and human-capital-intensive activities dominating the value chain in financial services, with the role of information distribution and analysis in the face of the technological developments favoring inexpensive information distribution and powerful local information processing power, managers must show the advantages of larger scale operations concretely. The best managers can and will be able to use the value matrix and the analytical tools provided in this book to show the gains from growth and/or change policies they advocate in terms of return on investment.

24.5 SUMMARY

Value produced by financial service firms comes largely from the skills and coordinated activities of workers. Motivating workers with incentive-based pay can be very important even though creative compensation schemes are currently infrequent in financial services. Organizational structures affect the ability of good people to work and communicate in firms. Organization is important to foster a spirit of innovation and experimentation required by the further evolution of the financial services industry. Transfer pricing within large scale organizations is a way to communicate top management objectives, to provide incentives to workers, and to identify competitive advantages of financial service firms. Given the importance of pay, organizations, and performance accounting in financial firms, strategies for growth and change must be carefully formulated in terms of synergies in the value matrix to be successful. The most successful firms, those with the highest return on investment, will not be built on hunches and hopes.

DISCUSSION QUESTIONS AND EXERCISES

1. Brokers are paid a commission for selling mutual funds with loads. How would you evaluate your broker's advice concerning purchase of load versus no-load mutual funds? How would you as a customer react to learning that a new account person at a deposit-taking institution received a commission for certain types of accounts? How would you feel if your

teller was paid on the basis of number of transactions completed? What are the overriding issues on incentive pay and customer reaction to financial services?

2. Assume the following pay schedules for workers in different institutions performing the same work in transaction processing where average employee effort produces 100 transactions per hour and where wrong processing occurs on average 5 percent of the time:

   a. $5.00 per hour.
   b. $.05 per item processed.
   c. $.06 per item processed minus $.10 for all wrongly process items identified later.
   d. $4.00 per hour plus bonus of $1.00 for each 20 items exceeding 80 per hour processed net of wrong items.

   How would you expect workers to perform under each pay scheme? Which is best and worse? Do you know part-time workers in financial services transaction processing? How are they paid?

3. How should the combination of salary and valuable stock options to top executives of financial service firms change depending on years to retirement? Would stock options offered upon retirement be beneficial to the firm? Why or why not?

4. A divisional manager in one firm receives 5 percent of divisional profits (revenues minus attributed costs); a corresponding manager in another firm receives a salary and a bonus equal to half of one year's profits above a 10 percent increase from the previous year. What are the incentive effects of the two compensation schemes? What are the advantages and disadvantages of each scheme?

5. Choose two or three financial institutions and attempt to draw their organizational charts from information obtained from annual reports and employees. What types of organizational principles are used and what advantages and disadvantages are associated with each organizational scheme?

6. An insurance-selling division receives a credit for providing funds from insurance reserves which is charged to two investment divisions: government securities and real estate investments. What considerations should be incorporated into setting these transfer prices? Should the transfer price to the two investing divisions be the same and the credit from the insurance sales division be the same? How could management encourage riskier investment strategies for the firm?

7. A loan officer makes loans with an average three-year maturity. Most defaults occur in the first two years. How could the loan officer be compensated to encourage monitoring of loans in the first two years?

8. When loans become bad, many lenders assign these loans to "work-out" loan specialists and call these credits "special assets." Lending officers often resist assignment of their loans to special asset groups until valuable time has passed. How could transfer pricing of loan assets be used to encourage value-maximizing strategies for loans in trouble?

9. What technological and demand dependencies could be relevant to transfer pricing between transaction processing and asset management divisions of a bank trust department? How could transfer prices be adjusted to maximize the profitability of the firm?

10. How can managers with technical expertise or specific information be motivated to maximize the value they create by forming joint ventures (shared equity between employees and financial service firms)? What are the different incentives for managers and financial institutions in (a) a franchise arrangement where a franchisee pays a percent of revenues and (b) a joint venture where profits are shared by a manager owner and a financial institution investor?

REFERENCES

BESANKO, DAVID and DAVID S. SIBLEY. 1991. "Compensation and Transfer Pricing in a Principal–Agent Model," *International Economic Review* 32 (1), pp. 55–68.

COASE, RONALD. 1937. "The Nature of the Firm," *Economica* 4, pp. 386–405.

FAMA, EUGENE F. 1980. "Banking in the Theory of Finance," *Journal of Monetary Economics* 6, pp. 39–57.

FAMA, EUGENE F. and MICHAEL C. JENSEN. 1983a. "Separation of Ownership and Control," *Journal of Law and Economics* (June), 26, pp. 301–325.

FAMA, EUGENE F. and MICHAEL C. JENSEN. 1983b. "Agency Problems and Residual Claims", *Journal of Law and Economics* (June), 26, pp. 327–349.

GRANFIELD, MICHAEL E. and J. FRED WESTON. 1990. "Effective Section 482 Enforcement and the Japanese Auto Cases," *Tax Notes,* March 5, pp. 1187–1197.

HIRSHLEIFER, JACK. 1956. "On the Economics of Transfer Pricing," *Journal of Business* 29, pp. 172–174.

HORNGREN, CHARLES T. and GEORGE FOSTER. 1991. *Cost Accounting: A Managerial Emphasis* (7th edition). Prentice Hall. Englewood Cliffs, New Jersey.

MAYERS, DAVID and CLIFFORD SMITH. 1986. "Ownership Structure and Control: The Mutualization of Stock Life Insurance Companies," *Journal of Financial Economics* 16, pp. 73–98.

MILGROM, PAUL and JOHN ROBERTS. 1992. *Economics, Organizations, and Management.* Englewood Cliffs, N.J.: Prentice Hall.

RASMUSSEN, ERIC. 1988. "Mutual Banks and Stock Banks," *Journal of Law and Economics* (October), pp. 395–421.

SAPPINGTON, DAVID E. M. 1991. "Incentives in Principal–Agent Relationships," *Journal of Economic Perspectives* 5, (2), pp. 45–66.

SICONOLFI, MICHAEL. 1994. "Kidder Trader in Bond Options Dismissed," *Wall Street Journal,* July 12, p. A3.

WILLIAMSON, OLIVER E. 1975. *Markets and Hierarchies.* New York: The Free Press.

Fortune. 1993. "What CEOs Make" (June 14, 1993) pp. 103–110.

Author Index

Subject Index